SELECTED ENVIRONMENTAL LAW STATUTES

1987–88 EDUCATIONAL EDITION

Marcia
289-~~4462~~ 3661
725-4920
23 Sparwell La.
Brunswick 04011

WEST PUBLISHING CO.
ST. PAUL, MINN., 1987

50 West Kellogg Boulevard
P.O. Box 64526
St. Paul, Minnesota 55164–0526

ISBN 0–314–60975–X

Sel.Env.Law Stats. '87 Ed.

Publisher's Explanation

The study and practice of environmental law is almost wholly shaded by federal legislation, the most prevasive of which are compiled in this pamphlet of Selected Environmental Law Statutes.

Statutes enacted by Congress are current through Public Law 99–664, the final law of the Second Session of the 99th Congress which adjourned on October 18, 1986.

The statutes contained in this pamphlet bear the title and section classifications of the United States Code. The popular names of the corresponding Acts are identified in the Margin Index on the back cover.

To reach all of the judicial constructions, historical notes and additional annotative material pertaining to any given statutory provision, the reader should review that provision in the United States Code Annotated or consult the other special research aids noted in this pamphlet following each section. The latter include references to the decisions of the Supreme Court of the United States; citations to United States Code Annotated provisions; the Code of Federal Regulations; the Key Number Digest System; Corpus Juris Secundum; West's Federal Forms; Federal Jury Practice and Instructions; West's Federal Practice Manual; Federal Practice and Procedure; and Administrative Law and Practice. WESTLAW supplements the United States Code Annotated electronically and provides many useful materials for additional research. (See the WESTLAW guide following this EXPLANATION.)

THE PUBLISHER

July, 1987

*

WESTLAW® ELECTRONIC RESEARCH GUIDE

1. Coordinating Legal Research With WESTLAW

This pamphlet provides federal statutory materials relating to environmental law. WESTLAW contains a Federal Environmental Law database which provides additional resources. This guide is to materials in WESTLAW.

2. Databases

A database is an aggregation of documents with one or more features in common. A database may contain statutes, court decisions, administrative materials, or commentaries. Every database has its own identifier. Database identifiers are used to identify the database to be searched. The WESTLAW Directory is a comprehensive listing of databases, with information about each database, and the types of documents each contains.

3. Updating Statutes

A WESTLAW search may be used to ascertain whether a particular section of the United States Code dealing with the environment has been amended after a bound volume or pocket part of the statutes was printed. Sign on to FENV–USC database and using the desired title number and section number, a query is entered in the following form:

CI(42 +3 7401)

This will retrieve section 7401 of Title 42 of the United Stated Code.

4. Retrieving Cases Citing A Statute

To find cases citing a particular statute, sign on to FENV–CS database and using the desired title number and section number, a query is entered in the following form:

"15 U.S.C.*" +4 2601

This will retrieve cases citing section 2601 of Title 15 of the United States Code.

5. Keynumber Search

WESTLAW may be used to search any topic and keynumber. Headnotes classified to the various subsections of the topic Health and Environment ⚷25.6 can be examined by signing on to FENV–CS database and entering

topic(Health and Environment) /p K25.6

or

199K25.6

6. Retrieving A Regulation In The Code of Federal Regulations

To find the text of a federal regulation, sign on to FENV–CFR database. Using the desired citation, a query is entered in the following form:

CI(30 +3 717.17)

This will retrieve section 717.17 of Title 30 of the Code of Federal Regulations.

7. Retrieving A Federal Register Document

To find the text of a Federal Register document, sign on to FENV–FR database. Using the desired citation, enter a query in the following form:

CI(52 +2 8225)

This will retrieve 52 FR 8225.

8. Insta-Cite™ For Retrieving Case History and Parallel Citations

Insta-Cite may be used to find parallel citations and the history of a case by entering a command in the following form:

IC 100 S.Ct. 2636

All parallel cites will be displayed together with the history of the case reported at 100 S.Ct. 2636.

9. Shepardizing™ A Case With WESTLAW

Sign on to the Shepard's® database. Enter a case citation in the following form:

SH 106 S.Ct. 755

The Shepard's information for the case reported at 106 S.Ct. 755 will be displayed.

10. General Information

The sample queries illustrate general methods of using WESTLAW to supplement statutory research. All WESTLAW techniques may be used for expanding or narrowing a search. Please see the WESTLAW Reference Manual.

TABLE OF CONTENTS

*

ENVIRONMENTAL PESTICIDE CONTROL

(7 U.S.C.A. §§ 136 to 136y.)

Related Provisions

See, also, Toxic Substances Control, 15 U.S.C.A. § 2601 et seq., post.

West's Federal Forms

Enforcement and review of decisions and orders of administrative agencies, see § 851 et seq.

Jurisdiction and venue in district courts, see § 1003 et seq.

Code of Federal Regulations

Arbitration of pesticide data disputes, see 29 CFR 1440.1.

Assistance for continuing environmental programs, etc., see 40 CFR 35.001 et seq.

Special classes of merchandise, see 19 CFR 12.110 et seq.

WESTLAW Electronic Research

See WESTLAW guide following the Explanation pages of this pamphlet.

§ 136. Definitions

For purposes of this subchapter—

(a) Active ingredient.—The term "active ingredient" means—

(1) in the case of a pesticide other than a plant regulator, defoliant, or desiccant, an ingredient which will prevent, destroy, repel, or mitigate any pest;

(2) in the case of a plant regulator, an ingredient which, through physiological action, will accelerate or retard the rate of growth or rate of maturation or otherwise alter the behavior of ornamental or crop plants or the product thereof;

(3) in the case of a defoliant, an ingredient which will cause the leaves or foliage to drop from a plant; and

(4) in the case of a desiccant, an ingredient which will artificially accelerate the drying of plant tissue.

(b) Administrator.—The term "Administrator" means the Administrator of the Environmental Protection Agency.

(c) Adulterated.—The term "adulterated" applies to any pesticide if:

(1) its strength or purity falls below the professed standard of quality as expressed on its labeling under which it is sold;

(2) any substance has been substituted wholly or in part for the pesticide; or

(3) any valuable constituent of the pesticide has been wholly or in part abstracted.

(d) Animal.—The term "animal" means all vertebrate and invertebrate species, including but not limited to man and other mammals, birds, fish, and shellfish.

(e) Certified applicator, etc.—

(1) Certified applicator.—The term "certified applicator" means any individual who is certified under section 136b of this title as authorized to use or supervise the use of any pesticide which is classified for restricted use. Any applicator who holds or applies registered pesticides, or use[1] dilutions of registered pesticides consistent with subsection (ee) of this section, only to provide a service of controlling pests without delivering any unapplied pesticide to any person so served is not deemed to be a seller or distributor of pesticides under this subchapter.

(2) **Private applicator.**—The term "private applicator" means a certified applicator who uses or supervises the use of any pesticide which is classified for restricted use for purposes of producing any agricultural commodity on property owned or rented by him or his employer or (if applied without compensation other than trading of personal services between producers of agricultural commodities) on the property of another person.

(3) **Commercial applicator.**—The term "commercial applicator" means an applicator (whether or not he is a private applicator with respect to some uses) who uses or supervises the use of any pesticide which is classified for restricted use for any purpose or on any property other than as provided by paragraph (2).

(4) **Under the direct supervision of a certified applicator.**—Unless otherwise prescribed by its labeling, a pesticide shall be considered to be applied under the direct supervision of a certified applicator if it is applied by a competent person acting under the instructions and control of a certified applicator who is available if and when needed, even though such certified applicator is not physically present at the time and place the pesticide is applied.

(f) **Defoliant.**—The term "defoliant" means any substance or mixture of substances intended for causing the leaves or foliage to drop from a plant, with or without causing abscission.

(g) **Desiccant.**—The term "desiccant" means any substance or mixture of substances intended for artificially accelerating the drying of plant tissue.

(h) **Device.**—The term "device" means any instrument or contrivance (other than a firearm) which is intended for trapping, destroying, repelling, or mitigating any pest or any other form of plant or animal life (other than man and other than bacteria, virus, or other microorganism on or in living man or other living animals); but not including equipment used for the application of pesticides when sold separately therefrom.

(i) **District court.**—The term "district court" means a United States district court, the District Court of Guam, the District Court of the Virgin Islands, and the highest court of American Samoa.

(j) **Environment.**—The term "environment" includes water, air, land, and all plants and man and other animals living therein, and the interrelationships which exist among these.

(k) **Fungus.**—The term "fungus" means any non-chlorophyll-bearing thallophyte (that is, any non-chlorophyll-bearing plant of a lower order than mosses and liverworts), as for example, rust, smut, mildew, mold, yeast, and bacteria, except those on or in living man or other animals and those on or in processed food, beverages, or pharmaceuticals.

(*l*) **Imminent hazard.**—The term "imminent hazard" means a situation which exists when the continued use of a pesticide during the time required for cancellation proceeding would be likely to result in unreasonable adverse effects on the environment or will involve unreasonable hazard to the survival of a species declared endangered or threatened by the Secretary pursuant to the Endangered Species Act of 1973.

(m) **Inert ingredient.**—The term "inert ingredient" means an ingredient which is not active.

(n) **Ingredient statement.**—The term "ingredient statement" means a statement which contains—

(1) the name and percentage of each active ingredient, and the total percentage of all inert ingredients, in the pesticide; and

(2) if the pesticide contains arsenic in any form, a statement of the percentages of total and water soluble arsenic, calculated as elementary arsenic.

(*o*) **Insect.**—The term "insect" means any of the numerous small invertebrate animals generally having the body more or less obviously segmented, for the most part belonging to the class insecta, comprising six-legged, usually winged forms, as for example, beetles, bugs, bees, flies, and to other allied classes of anthropods whose members are wingless and usually have more than six legs, as for example, spiders, mites, ticks, centipedes, and wood lice.

(p) **Label and labeling.—**

(1) **Label.**—The term "label" means the written, printed, or graphic matter on, or attached to, the pesticide or device or any of its containers or wrappers.

(2) **Labeling.**—The term "labeling" means all labels and all other written, printed, or graphic matter—

(A) accompanying the pesticide or device at any time; or

(B) to which reference is made on the label or in literature accompanying the pesticide or device, except to current official publications of the Environmental Protection Agency, the United States Departments of Agriculture and Interior, the Department of Health and Human Services, State experiment stations, State agricultural colleges, and other similar Federal or State institutions or agencies authorized by law to conduct research in the field of pesticides.

(q) **Misbranded.—**

(1) A pesticide is misbranded if—

(A) its labeling bears any statement, design, or graphic representation relative thereto or to its ingredients which is false or misleading in any particular;

(B) it is contained in a package or other container or wrapping which does not conform to the standards established by the Administrator pursuant to section 136w(c)(3) of this title;

(C) it is an imitation of, or is offered for sale under the name of, another pesticide;

(D) its label does not bear the registration number assigned under section 136e of this title to each establishment in which it was produced;

(E) any word, statement, or other information required by or under authority of this subchapter to appear on the label or labeling is not prominently placed thereon with such conspicuousness (as compared with other words, statements, designs, or graphic matter in the labeling) and in such terms as to render it likely to be read and understood by the ordinary individual under customary conditions of purchase and use;

(F) the labeling accompanying it does not contain directions for use which are necessary for effecting the purpose for which the product is intended and if complied with, together with any requirements imposed under section 136a(d) of this title, are adequate to protect health and the environment;

(G) the label does not contain a warning or caution statement which may be necessary and if complied with, together with any requirements imposed under section 136a(d) of this title, is adequate to protect health and the environment; or

(H) in the case of a pesticide not registered in accordance with section 136a of this title and intended for export, the label does not contain, in words prominently placed thereon with such conspicuousness (as compared with other words, statements, designs, or graphic matter in the labeling) as to render it likely to be noted by the ordinary individual under customary conditions of purchase and use, the following: "Not Registered for Use in the United States of America".

(2) A pesticide is misbranded if—

(A) the label does not bear an ingredient statement on that part of the immediate container (and on the outside container or wrapper of the retail package, if there be one, through which the ingredient statement on the immediate container cannot be clearly read) which is presented or displayed under customary conditions or purchase, except that a pesticide is not misbranded under this subparagraph if:

(i) The size of[2] form of the immediate container, or the outside container or wrapper of the retail package, makes it impracticable to place the ingredient statement on the part which is presented or displayed under customary conditions of purchase; and

(ii) the ingredient statement appears prominently on another part of the immediate container, or outside container or wrapper, permitted by the Administrator;

(B) the labeling does not contain a statement of the use classification under which the product is registered;

(C) there is not affixed to its container, and to the outside container or wrapper of the retail package, if there be one, through which the required information on the immediate container cannot be clearly read, a label bearing—

(i) the name and address of the producer, registrant, or person for whom produced;

(ii) the name, brand, or trademark under which the pesticide is sold;

(iii) the net weight or measure of the content: *Provided,* That the Administrator may permit reasonable variations; and

(iv) when required by regulation of the Administrator to effectuate the purposes of this subchapter, the registration number assigned to the pesticide under this subchapter, and the use classification; and

(D) the pesticide contains any substance or substances in quantities highly toxic to man, unless the label shall bear, in addition to any other matter required by this subchapter—

(i) the skull and crossbones;

(ii) the word "poison" prominently in red on a background of distinctly contrasting color; and

(iii) a statement of a practical treatment (first aid or otherwise) in case of poisoning by the pesticide.

(r) Nematode.—The term "nematode" means invertebrate animals of the phylum nemathelminthes and class nematoda, that is, unsegmented round worms with elongated, fusiform, or saclike bodies covered with cuticle, and inhabiting soil, water, plants, or plant parts; may also be called nemas or eelworms.

(s) Person.—The term "person" means any individual, partnership, association, corporation, or any organized group of persons whether incorporated or not.

(t) Pest.—The term "pest" means (1) any insect, rodent, nematode, fungus, weed, or (2) any other form of terrestrial or aquatic plant or animal life or virus, bacteria, or other micro-organism (except viruses, bacteria, or other micro-organisms on or in living man or other living animals) which the Administrator declares to be a pest under section 136w(c)(1) of this title.

(u) Pesticide.—The term "pesticide" means (1) any substance or mixture of substances intended for preventing, destroying, repelling, or mitigating any pest, and (2) any substance or mixture of substances intended for use as a plant regulator, defoliant, or desiccant: *Provided,* That the term "pesticide" shall not include any article (1)(a) that is a "new animal drug" within the meaning of section 321(w) of title 21, or (b) that has been determined by the Secretary of Health and Human Services not to be a new animal drug by a regulation establishing conditions of use for the article, or (2) that is an animal feed within the meaning of section 321(x) of title 21 bearing or containing an article covered by clause (1) of this proviso.

(v) Plant regulator.—The term "plant regulator" means any substance or mixture of substances intended, through physiological action, for accelerating or retarding the rate of growth or rate of maturation, or for otherwise altering the behavior of plants or the produce thereof, but shall not include substances to the extent that they are intended as plant nutrients, trace elements, nutritional chemicals, plant inoculants, and soil amendments. Also, the term "plant regulator" shall not be required to include any of such of those nutrient mixtures or soil amendments as are commonly known as vitamin-hormone horticultural products, intended for improvement, maintenance, survival, health, and propagation of plants, and as are not for pest destruction and are nontoxic, nonpoisonous in the undiluted packaged concentration.

(w) Producer and produce.—The term "producer" means the person who manufactures, prepares, compounds, propagates, or processes any pesticide or device or active ingredient used in producing a pesticide. The term "produce" means to manufacture, prepare, compound, propagate, or process any pesticide or device or active ingredient used in producing a pesticide. The dilution by individuals of formulated pesticides for their own use and according to the directions on registered labels shall not of itself result in such individuals being included in the definition of "producer" for the purposes of this subchapter.

(x) Protect health and the environment.—The terms "protect health and the environment" and "protection of health and the environment" mean protection against any unreasonable adverse effects on the environment.

(y) Registrant.—The term "registrant" means a person who has registered any pesticide pursuant to the provisions of this subchapter.

(z) Registration.—The term "registration" includes reregistration.

(aa) State.—The term "State" means a State, the District of Columbia, the Commonwealth of Puerto Rico, the Virgin Islands, Guam, the Trust Territory of the Pacific Islands, and American Samoa.

(bb) Unreasonable adverse effects on the environment.—The term "unreasonable adverse effects on the environment" means any unreasonable risk to man or the environment, taking into account the economic, social, and environmental costs and benefits of the use of any pesticide.

(cc) Weed.—The term "weed" means any plant which grows where not wanted.

(dd) Establishment.—The term "establishment" means any place where a pesticide or device or active ingredient used in producing a pesticide is produced, or held, for distribution or sale.

(ee) To use any registered pesticide in a manner inconsistent with its labeling.—The term "to use any registered pesticide in a manner inconsistent with its labeling" means to use any registered pesticide in a manner not permitted by the labeling: *Provided,* That the term shall not include (1) applying a pesticide at any dosage, concentration, or frequency less than that specified on the labeling, (2) applying a pesticide against any target pest not specified on the labeling if the application is to the crop, animal, or site specified on the labeling, unless the Administrator has required that the labeling specifically state that the pesticide may be used only for the pests specified on the labeling after the Administrator has determined that the use of the pesticide against other pests would cause an unreasonable adverse effect on the environment, (3) employing any method of application not prohibited by the labeling, or (4) mixing a pesticide or pesticides with a fertilizer when such mixture is not prohibited by the labeling: *Provided further,* That the term also shall not include any use of a pesticide in conformance with section 136c, 136p, or 136v of this title, or any use of a pesticide in a manner that the Administrator determines to be consistent with the purposes of this subchapter: *And provided further,* That after March 31, 1979, the term shall not include the use of a pesticide for agricultural or forestry purposes at a dilution less than label dosage unless before or after that date the Administrator issues a regulation or advisory opinion consistent with the study provided for in section 27(b) of the Federal Pesticide Act of 1978, which regulation or advisory opinion specifically requires the use of definite amounts of dilution.

(June 25, 1947, ch. 125, § 2, as added Oct. 21, 1972, Pub.L. 92–516, § 2, 86 Stat. 975, and amended Dec. 28, 1973, Pub.L. 93–205, § 13(f), 87 Stat. 903; Nov. 28, 1975, Pub.L. 94–140, § 9, 89 Stat. 754; Sept. 30, 1978, Pub.L. 95–396, § 1, 92 Stat. 819; Oct. 17, 1979, Pub.L. 96–88, title V, § 509(b), 93 Stat. 695.)

1 So in original. Probably should be "uses".

2 So in original. Probably should be "or".

Code of Federal Regulations

Arbitration of pesticide data disputes, see 29 CFR 1440.1.
Debarment and suspension under EPA assistance programs, see 40 CFR 32.100 et seq.
Tolerances and exemptions for pesticide chemicals in or on raw agricultural commodities, see 40 CFR 180.1 et seq.

Library References

Agriculture ⚷9.
Health and Environment ⚷25.5(1).
C.J.S. Agriculture § 83 et seq.
C.J.S. Health and Environment § 61 et seq.

United States Supreme Court

Appellate review, pesticide manufacturer's action challenging constitutionality of binding arbitration provisions of 1978 amendments of Act, see Thomas v. Union Carbide Agr. Products Co., 1985, 105 S.Ct. 3325, 87 L.Ed.2d 409.

§ 136a. Registration of pesticides

(a) Requirement.—Except as otherwise provided by this subchapter, no person in any State may distribute, sell, offer for sale, hold for sale, ship, deliver for shipment, or receive and (having so received) deliver or offer to deliver, to any person any pesticide which is not registered with the Administrator.

(b) Exemptions.—A pesticide which is not registered with the Administrator may be transferred if—

(1) the transfer is from one registered establishment to another registered establishment operated by the same producer solely for packaging at the second establishment or for use as a constituent part of another pesticide produced at the second establishment; or

(2) the transfer is pursuant to and in accordance with the requirements of an experimental use permit.

(c) Procedure for registration.—

(1) Statement required.—Each applicant for registration of a pesticide shall file with the Administrator a statement which includes—

(A) the name and address of the applicant and of any other person whose name will appear on the labeling;

(B) the name of the pesticide;

(C) a complete copy of the labeling of the pesticide, a statement of all claims to be made for it, and any directions for its use;

(D) except as otherwise provided in subsection (c)(2)(D) of this section, if requested by the Administrator, a full description of the tests made and the results thereof upon which the claims are based, or alternatively a citation to data that appear in the public literature or that previously had been submitted to the Administrator and that the Administrator may consider in accordance with the following provisions:

(i) With respect to pesticides containing active ingredients that are initially registered under this subchapter after September 30, 1978, data submitted to support the application for the original registration of the pesticide, or an application for an amendment adding any new use to the registration and that pertains solely to such new use, shall not, without the written permission of the original data submitted, be considered by the Administrator to support an application by another person during a period of ten years following the date the Administrator first registers the pesticide: *Provided,* That such permission shall not be required in the case of defensive data;

(ii) except as otherwise provided in subparagraph (D)(i) of this paragraph, with respect to data submitted after December 31, 1969, by an applicant or registrant to support an application for registration, experimental use permit, or amendment adding a new use to an existing registration, to support or maintain in effect an existing registration, or for reregistration, the Administrator may, without the permission of the original data submitter, consider any such item of data in support of an application by any other person (hereinafter in this subparagraph referred to as the "applicant") within the fifteen-year period following the date the data were originally submitted only if the applicant has made an offer to compensate the original data submitter and submitted such offer to the Administrator accompanied by evidence of delivery to the original data submitter of the offer. The terms and amount of compensation may be fixed by agreement between the original data submitter and the applicant, or, failing such agreement, binding arbitration under this subparagraph. If, at the end of ninety days after the date of delivery to the original data submitter of the offer to compensate, the original data submitter and the applicant have neither agreed on the amount and terms of compensation nor on a procedure for reaching an agreement on the amount and terms of compensation, either person may initiate binding arbitration proceedings by requesting the Federal Mediation and Conciliation Service to appoint an arbitrator from the roster of arbitrators maintained by such Service. The procedure and rules of the Service shall be applicable to the selection of such arbitrator and to such arbitration proceedings, and the findings and determination of the arbitrator shall be final and conclusive, and no official or court of the United States shall have power or jurisdiction to review any such findings and determination, except for fraud, misrepresentation, or other misconduct by one of the parties to the arbitration or the arbitrator where there is a verified complaint with supporting affidavits attesting to specific instances of such fraud, misrepresentation, or other misconduct. The parties to the arbitration shall share equally in the payment of the fee and expenses of the arbitrator. If the Administrator determines that an original data submitter has failed to participate in a procedure for reaching an agreement or in an arbitration proceeding as required by this subparagraph, or failed to comply with the terms of an agreement or arbitration decision concerning compensation under this subparagraph, the original data submitter shall forfeit the right to compensation for the use of the data in support of the application. Notwithstanding any other provision of this subchapter, if the Administrator determines that an applicant has failed to participate in a procedure for reaching an agreement or in an arbitration proceeding as required by this subparagraph, or failed to comply with the terms of an agreement or arbitration decision concerning compensation under this subparagraph, the Administrator shall deny the application or cancel the registration of the pesticide in support of which the data were used without further hearing. Before the Administrator takes action under either of the preceding two sentences, the Administrator shall furnish to the affected person, by certified mail, notice of intent to take action and allow fifteen days from the date of delivery of the notice for the affected person to respond. If a registration is denied or canceled under this subparagraph, the Administrator may make such order as the Administrator deems appropriate concerning the continued sale and use of existing stocks of such pesticide. Registration action by the Administrator shall not be delayed pending the fixing of compensation;

(iii) after expiration of any period of exclusive use and any period for which compensation is required for the use of an item of data under subparagraphs (D)(i) and (D)(ii) of this paragraph, the Administrator may consider such item of data in support of an application by any other applicant without the permission of the original data submitter and without an offer having been received to compensate the original data submitter for the use of such item of data;

(E) the complete formula of the pesticide; and

(F) a request that the pesticide be classified for general use, for restricted use, or for both.

(2)(A) Data in support of registration.—The Administrator shall publish guidelines specifying the kinds of information which will be required to support the registration of a pesticide and shall revise such guidelines from time to time. If thereafter he requires any additional kind of information under subparagraph (B) of this paragraph, he shall permit sufficient time for applicants to obtain such additional information. The Administrator, in establishing standards for data requirements for the registration of pesticides with respect to minor uses, shall make such standards commensurate with the anticipated extent of use, pattern of use, and the level and degree of potential exposure of man and the environment to the pesticide. In the development of these standards, the Administrator shall consider the economic factors of potential national volume of use, extent of distribution, and the impact of the cost of meeting the requirements on the incentives for any potential registrant to undertake the development of the required data. Except as provided by section 136h of this title, within 30 days after the Administrator registers a pesticide under this subchapter he shall make available to the public the data called for in the registration statement together with such other scientific information as he deems relevant to his decision.

(B) Additional data to support existing registration.—

(i) If the Administrator determines that additional data are required to maintain in effect an existing registration of a pesticide, the Administrator shall notify all existing registrants of the pesticide to which the determination relates and provide a list of such registrants to any interested person.

(ii) Each registrant of such pesticide shall provide evidence within ninety days after receipt of notification that it is taking appropriate steps to secure the additional data that are required. Two or more registrants may agree to develop jointly, or to share in the cost of developing, such data if they agree and advise the Administrator of their intent within ninety days after notification. Any registrant who agrees to share in the cost of producing the data shall be entitled to examine and rely upon such data in support of maintenance of such registration.

(iii) If, at the end of sixty days after advising the Administrator of their agreement to develop jointly, or share in the cost of developing, data, the registrants have not further agreed on the terms of the data development arrangement or on a procedure for reaching such agreement, any of such registrants may initiate binding arbitration proceedings by requesting the Federal Mediation and Conciliation Service to appoint an arbitrator from the roster of arbitrators maintained by such Service. The procedure and rules of the Service shall be applicable to the selection of such arbitrator and to such arbitration proceedings, and the findings and determination of the arbitrator shall be final and conclusive, and no official or court of the United States shall have power or jurisdiction to review any such findings and determination, except for fraud, misrepresentation, or other misconduct by one of the parties to the arbitration or the arbitrator where there is a verified complaint with supporting affidavits attesting to specific instances of such fraud, misrepresentation, or other misconduct. All parties to the arbitration shall share equally in the payment of the fee and expenses of the arbitrator.

(iv) Notwithstanding any other provision of this subchapter, if the Administrator determines that a registrant, within the time required by the Administrator, has failed to take appropriate steps to secure the data required under this subparagraph, to participate in a procedure for reaching agreement concerning a joint data development arrangement under this subparagraph or in an arbitration proceeding as required by this subparagraph, or to comply with the terms of an agreement or arbitration decision concerning a joint data development arrangement under this subparagraph, the Administrator may issue a notice of intent to suspend such registrant's registration of the pesticide for which additional data is required. The Administrator may include in the notice of intent to suspend such provisions as the Administrator deems appropriate concerning the continued sale and use of existing stocks of such pesticide. Any suspension proposed under this subparagraph shall become final and effective at the end of thirty days from receipt by the registrant of the notice of intent to suspend, unless during that time a request for hearing is made by a person adversely affected by the notice or the registrant has satisfied the Administrator that the registrant has complied fully with the requirements that served as a basis for the notice of intent to suspend. If a hearing is requested, a hearing shall be conducted under section 136d(d) of this title: *Provided,* That the only matters for resolution at that hearing shall be whether the registrant has failed to take the action that served as the basis for the notice of intent to suspend the registration of the pesticide for which additional data is required, and whether the Administrator's determination with respect to the disposition of existing stocks is consistent with this subchapter. If a hearing is held, a decision after completion of such hearing shall be final. Notwithstanding any other provision of this subchapter, a hearing shall be held and a determination made within seventy-five days after receipt of a request for such hearing. Any registration suspended under this subparagraph shall be reinstated by the Administrator if the Administrator determines that the registrant has complied fully with the requirements that served as a basis for the suspension of the registration.

(v) Any data submitted under this subparagraph shall be subject to the provisions of subsection (c)(1)(D) of this section. Whenever such data are submitted jointly by two or more registrants, an agent shall be agreed on at the time of the joint submission to handle any subsequent data compensation matters for the joint submitters of such data.

(C) Simplified procedures.—Within nine months after September 30, 1978, the Administrator shall, by regulation, prescribe simplified procedures for the registration of pesticides, which shall include the provisions of subparagraph (D) of this paragraph.

(D) Exemption.—No applicant for registration of a pesticide who proposes to purchase a registered pesticide from another producer in order to formulate such purchased pesticide into an end-use product shall be required to—

(i) submit or cite data pertaining to the safety of such purchased product; or

(ii) offer to pay reasonable compensation otherwise required by paragraph (1)(D) of this subsection for the use of any such data.

(3) Time for acting with respect to application.—The Administrator shall review the data after receipt of the application and shall, as expeditiously as possible, either register the pesticide in accordance with paragraph (5), or notify the applicant of his determination that it does not comply with the provisions of the subchapter in accordance with paragraph (6).

(4) Notice of application.—The Administrator shall publish in the Federal Register, promptly after receipt of the statement and other data required pursuant to paragraphs (1) and (2), a notice of each application for registration of any pesticide if it contains any new active ingredient or if it would entail a changed use pattern. The notice shall provide for a period of 30 days in which any Federal agency or any other interested person may comment.

(5) Approval of registration.—The Administrator shall register a pesticide if he determines that, when considered with any restrictions imposed under subsection (d) of this section—

(A) its composition is such as to warrant the proposed claims for it;

(B) its labeling and other material required to be submitted comply with the requirements of this subchapter;

(C) it will perform its intended function without unreasonable adverse effects on the environment; and

(D) when used in accordance with widespread and commonly recognized practice it will not generally cause unreasonable adverse effects on the environment.

The Administrator shall not make any lack of essentiality a criterion for denying registration of any pesticide. Where two pesticides meet the requirements of this paragraph, one should not be registered in preference to the other. In considering an application for the registration of a pesticide, the Administrator may waive data requirements pertaining to efficacy, in which event the Administrator may register the pesticide without determining that the pesticide's composition is such as to warrant proposed claims of efficacy. If a pesticide is found to be efficacious by any State under section 136v(c) of this title, a presumption is established that the Administrator shall waive data requirements pertaining to efficacy for use of the pesticide in such State.

(6) Denial of registration.—If the Administrator determines that the requirements of paragraph (5) for registration are not satisfied, he shall notify the applicant for registration of his determination and of his reasons (including the factual basis) therefor, and that, unless the applicant corrects the conditions and notifies the Administrator thereof during the 30-day period beginning with the day after the date on which the applicant receives the notice, the Administrator may refuse to register the pesticide. Whenever the Administrator refuses to register a pesticide, he shall notify the applicant of his decision and of his reasons (including the factual basis) therefor. The Administrator shall promptly publish in the Federal Register notice of such denial of registration and the reasons therefor. Upon such notification, the applicant for registration or other interested person with the concurrence of the applicant shall have the same remedies as provided for in section 136d of this title.

(7) Registration under special circumstances.—Notwithstanding the provisions of subsection (c)(5) of this section—

(A) The Administrator may conditionally register or amend the registration of a pesticide if the Administrator determines that (i) the pesticide and proposed use are identical or substantially similar to any currently registered pesticide and use thereof, or differ only in ways that would not significantly increase the risk of unreasonable adverse effects on the environment, and (ii) approving the registration or amendment in the manner proposed by the applicant would not significantly increase the risk of any unreasonable adverse effect on the environment. An applicant seeking conditional registration or amended registration under this subparagraph shall submit such data as would be required to obtain registration of a similar pesticide under subsection (c)(5) of this section: *Provided,* That, if the applicant is unable to submit an item of data because it has not yet been generated, the Administrator may register or amend the registration of the pesticide under such conditions as will require the submission of such data not later than the time such data are required to be submitted with respect to similar pesticides already registered under this subchapter.

(B) The Administrator may conditionally amend the registration of a pesticide to permit additional uses of such pesticide notwithstanding that data concerning the pesticide may be insufficient to support an unconditional amendment, if the Administrator determines that (i) the applicant has submitted satisfactory data pertaining to the proposed additional use, and (ii) amending the registration in the manner proposed by the applicant would not significantly increase the risk of any unreasonable adverse effect on the environment. Notwithstanding the foregoing provisions of this subparagraph, no registration of a pesticide may be amended to permit an additional use of such pesticide if the Administrator has issued a notice stating that such pesticide, or any ingredient thereof, meets or exceeds risk criteria associated in whole or in part with human dietary exposure enumerated in regulations issued under this subchapter, and during the pendency of any risk-benefit evaluation initiated by such notice, if (I) the additional use of such pesticide involves a major food or feed crop, or (II) the additional use of such pesticide involves a minor food or feed crop and the Administrator determines, with the concurrence of the Secretary of Agriculture, there is available an effective alternative pesticide that does not meet or exceed such risk criteria. An applicant seeking amended registration under this subparagraph shall submit such data as would be required to obtain registration of a similar pesticide under subsection (c)(5) of this section: *Provided,* That, if the applicant is unable to submit an item of data (other than data pertaining to the proposed additional use) because it has not yet been generated, the Administrator may amend the registration under such conditions as will require the submission of such data not later than the time such data are required to be submitted with respect to similar pesticides already registered under this subchapter.

(C) The Administrator may conditionally register a pesticide containing an active ingredient not contained in any currently registered pesticide for a period reasonably sufficient for the generation and submission of required data (which are lacking because a period reasonably sufficient for generation of the data has not elapsed since the Administrator first imposed the data requirement) on the condition that by the end of such period the Administrator receives such data and the data do not meet or exceed risk criteria enumerated in regulations issued under this subchapter, and on such other conditions as the Administrator may prescribe: *Provided,* That a conditional registration under this subparagraph shall be granted only if the Administrator determines that use of the pesticide during such period will not cause any unreasonable adverse effect on the environment, and that use of the pesticide is in the public interest.

(8) Interim administrative review.—Notwithstanding any other provision of this subchapter, the Administrator may not initiate a public interim administrative review process to develop a risk-benefit evaluation of the ingredients of a pesticide or any of its uses prior to initiating a formal action to cancel, suspend, or deny registration of such pesticide, required under this subchapter, unless such interim administrative process is based on a validated test or other significant evidence raising prudent concerns of unreasonable adverse risk to man or to the environment. Notice of the definition of the terms "validated test" and "other significant evidence" as used herein shall be published by the Administrator in the Federal Register.

(d) Classification of pesticides.—

(1) Classification for general use, restricted use, or both.—

(A) As a part of the registration of a pesticide the Administrator shall classify it as being for general use or for restricted use, provided that if the Administrator determines that some of the uses for which the pesticide is registered should be for general use and that other uses for which it is registered should be for restricted use, he shall classify it for both general use and restricted use. Pesticide uses may be classified by regulation on the initial classification, and registered pesticides may be classified prior to reregistration. If some of the uses of the pesticide are classified for general use, and other uses are classified for restricted use, the directions relating to its general uses shall be clearly separated and distinguished from those directions relating to its restricted uses: *Provided, however,* That the Administrator may require that its packaging and labeling for restricted uses shall be clearly distinguishable from its packaging and labeling for general uses.

(B) If the Administrator determines that the pesticide, when applied in accordance with its directions for use, warnings and cautions and for the uses for which it is registered, or for one or more of such uses, or in accordance with a widespread and commonly recognized practice, will not generally cause unreasonable adverse effects on the environment, he will classify the pesticide, or the particular use or uses of the pesticide to which the determination applies, for general use.

(C) If the Administrator determines that the pesticide, when applied in accordance with its directions for use, warnings and cautions and for the uses for which it is registered, or for one or more of such uses, or in accordance with a widespread and commonly recognized practice, may generally cause, without additional regulatory restrictions, unreasonable adverse effects on the environment, including injury to the applicator, he shall classify the pesticide, or the particular use or uses to which the determination applies, for restricted use:

(i) If the Administrator classifies a pesticide, or one or more uses of such pesticide, for restricted use because of a determination that the acute dermal or inhalation toxicity of the pesticide presents a hazard to the applicator or other persons, the pesticide shall be applied for any use to which the restricted classification applies only by or under the direct supervision of a certified applicator.

(ii) If the Administrator classifies a pesticide, or one or more uses of such pesticide, for restricted use because of a determination that its use without additional regulatory restriction may cause unreasonable adverse effects on the environment, the pesticide shall be applied for any use to which the determination applies only by or under the direct supervision of a certified applicator, or subject to such other restrictions as the Administrator may provide by regulation. Any such regulation shall be reviewable in the appropriate court of appeals upon petition of a person adversely affected filed within 60 days of the publication of the regulation in final form.

(2) **Change in classification.**—If the Administrator determines that a change in the classification of any use of a pesticide from general use to restricted use is necessary to prevent unreasonable adverse effects on the environment, he shall notify the registrant of such pesticide of such determination at least forty-five days before making the change and shall publish the proposed change in the Federal Register. The registrant, or other interested person with the concurrence of the registrant, may seek relief from such determination under section 136d(b) of this title.

(3) **Change in classification from restricted use to general use.**—The registrant of any pesticide with one or more uses classified for restricted use may petition the Administrator to change any such classification from restricted to general use. Such petition shall set out the basis for the registrant's position that restricted use classification is unnecessary because classification of the pesticide for general use would not cause unreasonable adverse effects on the environment. The Administrator, within sixty days after receiving such petition, shall notify the registrant whether the petition has been granted or denied. Any denial shall contain an explanation therefor and any such denial shall be subject to judicial review under section 136n of this title.

(e) **Products with same formulation and claims.**—Products which have the same formulation, are manufactured by the same person, the labeling of which contains the same claims, and the labels of which bear a designation identifying the product as the same pesticide may be registered as a single pesticide; and additional names and labels shall be added to the registration by supplemental statements.

(f) **Miscellaneous.**—

(1) **Effect of change of labeling or formulation.**—If the labeling or formulation for a pesticide is changed, the registration shall be amended to reflect such change if the Administrator determines that the change will not violate any provision of this subchapter.

(2) **Registration not a defense.**—In no event shall registration of an article be construed as a defense for the commission of any offense under this subchapter: *Provided,* That as long as no cancellation proceedings are in effect registration of a pesticide shall be prima facie evidence that the pesticide, its labeling and packaging comply with the registration provisions of the subchapter.

(3) **Authority to consult other federal agencies.**—In connection with consideration of any registration or application for registration under this section, the Administrator may consult with any other Federal agency.

(g) **Reregistration of pesticides.**—The Administrator shall accomplish the reregistration of all pesticides in the most expeditious manner practicable: *Provided,* That, to the extent appropriate, any pesticide that results in a postharvest residue in or on food or feed crops shall be given priority in the reregistration process.

(June 25, 1947, ch. 125, § 3, as added Oct. 21, 1972, Pub.L. 92–516, § 2, 86 Stat. 979, and amended Nov. 28, 1975, Pub.L. 94–140, § 12, 89 Stat. 755; Sept. 30, 1978, Pub.L. 95–396, §§ 2(a), 3–8, 92 Stat. 820, 824–827.)

Code of Federal Regulations

Arbitration of pesticide data disputes, see 29 CFR 1440.1.
Debarment and suspension under EPA assistance programs, see 40 CFR 32.100 et seq.
Registration, reregistration, and classification, see 40 CFR 162.1 et seq.

Library References

Agriculture ⚷9.
C.J.S. Agriculture § 83 et seq.

§ 136b. Use of restricted use pesticides; certified applicators

(a) **Certification procedure.**—

(1) **Federal certification.**—In any State for which a State plan for applicator certification has

not been approved by the Administrator, the Administrator, in consultation with the Governor of such State, shall conduct a program for the certification of applicators of pesticides: *Provided,* That such program shall conform to the requirements imposed upon the States under the provisions of subsection (a)(2) of this section and shall not require private applicators to take any examination to establish competency in the use of pesticides. Prior to the implementation of the program, the Administrator shall publish in the Federal Register for review and comment a summary of the Federal plan for applicator certification and shall make generally available within the State copies of the plan. The Administrator shall hold public hearings at one or more locations within the State if so requested by the Governor of such State during the thirty days following publication of the Federal Register notice inviting comment on the Federal plan. The hearings shall be held within thirty days following receipt of the request from the Governor. In any State in which the Administrator conducts a certification program, the Administrator may require any person engaging in the commercial application, sale, offering for sale, holding for sale, or distribution of any pesticide one or more uses of which have been classified for restricted use to maintain such records and submit such reports concerning the commercial application, sale, or distribution of such pesticide as the Administrator may by regulation prescribe. Subject to paragraph (2), the Administrator shall prescribe standards for the certification of applicators of pesticides. Such standards shall provide that to be certified, an individual must be determined to be competent with respect to the use and handling of the pesticides, or to the use and handling of the pesticide or class of pesticides covered by such individual's certification: *Provided, however,* That the certification standard for a private applicator shall, under a State plan submitted for approval, be deemed fulfilled by his completing a certification form. The Administrator shall further assure that such form contains adequate information and affirmations to carry out the intent of this subchapter, and may include in the form an affirmation that the private applicator has completed a training program approved by the Administrator so long as the program does not require the private applicator to take, pursuant to a requirement prescribed by the Administrator, any examination to establish competency in the use of the pesticide. The Administrator may require any pesticide dealer participating in a certification program to be licensed under a State licensing program approved by him.

(2) State certification.—If any State, at any time, desires to certify applicators of pesticides, the Governor of such State shall submit a State plan for such purpose. The Administrator shall approve the plan submitted by any State, or any modification thereof, if such plan in his judgment—

(A) designates a State agency as the agency responsible for administering the plan throughout the State;

(B) contains satisfactory assurances that such agency has or will have the legal authority and qualified personnel necessary to carry out the plan;

(C) gives satisfactory assurances that the State will devote adequate funds to the administration of the plan;

(D) provides that the State agency will make such reports to the Administrator in such form and containing such information as the Administrator may from time to time require; and

(E) contains satisfactory assurances that State standards for the certification of applicators of pesticides conform with those standards prescribed by the Administrator under paragraph (1).

Any State certification program under this section shall be maintained in accordance with the State plan approved under this section.

(b) State plans.—If the Administrator rejects a plan submitted under this paragraph, he shall afford the State submitting the plan due notice and opportunity for hearing before so doing. If the Administrator approves a plan submitted under this paragraph, then such State shall certify applicators of pesticides with respect to such State. Whenever the Administrator determines that a State is not administering the certification program in accordance with the plan approved under this section, he shall so notify the State and provide for a hearing at the request of the State, and, if appropriate corrective action is not taken within a reasonable time, not to exceed ninety days, the Administrator shall withdraw approval of such plan.

(c) Instruction in integrated pest management techniques.—Standards prescribed by the Administrator for the certification of applicators of pesticides under subsection (a) of this section, and State plans submitted to the Administrator under subsections (a) and (b) of this section, shall include provisions for making instructional materials concerning integrated pest management techniques available to individuals at their request in accordance with the provisions of section 136u(c) of this title, but such plans may not require that any individual receive instruction concerning such techniques or to be shown to be competent with respect to the use of such techniques. The Administrator and States implementing such plans shall provide that all interested individuals are notified on the availability of such instructional materials.

(June 25, 1947, ch. 125, § 4, as added Oct. 21, 1972, Pub.L. 92–516, § 2, 86 Stat. 983, and amended Nov. 28, 1975, Pub.L. 94–140, §§ 5, 11, 89 Stat. 753, 754; Sept. 30, 1978, Pub.L. 95–396, § 9, 92 Stat. 827.)

Code of Federal Regulations

Certification standards, etc., see 40 CFR 171.1 et seq.
Debarment and suspension under EPA assistance programs, see 40 CFR 32.100 et seq.

Library References

Agriculture ⚷9.
C.J.S. Agriculture § 83 et seq.

§ 136c. Experimental use permits

(a) Issuance.—Any person may apply to the Administrator for an experimental use permit for a pesticide. The Administrator shall review the application. After completion of the review, but not later than one hundred and twenty days after receipt of the application and all required supporting data, the Administrator shall either issue the permit or notify the applicant of the Administrator's determination not to issue the permit and the reasons therefor. The applicant may correct the application or request a waiver of the conditions for such permit within thirty days of receipt by the applicant of such notification. The Administrator may issue an experimental use permit only if the Administrator determines that the applicant needs such permit in order to accumulate information necessary to register a pesticide under section 136a of this title. An application for an experimental use permit may be filed at any time.

(b) Temporary tolerance level.—If the Administrator determines that the use of a pesticide may reasonably be expected to result in any residue on or in food or feed, he may establish a temporary tolerance level for the residue of the pesticide before issuing the experimental use permit.

(c) Use under permit.—Use of a pesticide under an experimental use permit shall be under the supervision of the Administrator, and shall be subject to such terms and conditions and be for such period of time as the Administrator may prescribe in the permit.

(d) Studies.—When any experimental use permit is issued for a pesticide containing any chemical or combination of chemicals which has not been included in any previously registered pesticide, the Administrator may specify that studies be conducted to detect whether the use of the pesticide under the permit may cause unreasonable adverse effects on the environment. All results of such studies shall be reported to the Administrator before such pesticide may be registered under section 136a of this title.

(e) Revocation.—The Administrator may revoke any experimental use permit, at any time, if he finds that its terms or conditions are being violated, or that its terms and conditions are inadequate to avoid unreasonable adverse effects on the environment.

(f) State issuance of permits.—Notwithstanding the foregoing provisions of this section, the Administrator shall, under such terms and conditions as he may by regulations prescribe, authorize any State to issue an experimental use permit for a pesticide. All provisions of section 136b of this title relating to State plans shall apply with equal force to a State plan for the issuance of experimental use permits under this section.

(g) Exemption for agricultural research agencies.—Notwithstanding the foregoing provisions of this section, the Administrator may issue an experimental use permit for a pesticide to any public or private agricultural research agency or educational institution which applies for such permit. Each permit shall not exceed more than a one-year period or such other specific time as the Administrator may prescribe. Such permit shall be issued under such terms and conditions restricting the use of the pesticide as the Administrator may require: *Provided*, That such pesticide may be used only by such research agency or educational institution for purposes of experimentation.

(June 25, 1947, ch. 125, § 5, as added Oct. 21, 1972, Pub.L. 92–516, § 2, 86 Stat. 983, and amended Nov. 28, 1975, Pub.L. 94–140, § 10, 89 Stat. 754; Sept. 30, 1978, Pub.L. 95–396, § 10, 92 Stat. 828.)

Code of Federal Regulations

Policies and procedures, see 40 CFR 172.1 et seq.
Debarment and suspension under EPA assistance programs, see 40 CFR 32.100 et seq.

Library References

Agriculture ⚷9.
C.J.S. Agriculture § 83 et seq.

§ 136d. Administrative review; suspension

(a) Cancellation after five years.—

(1) Procedure.—The Administrator shall cancel the registration of any pesticide at the end of the five-year period which begins on the date of its registration (or at the end of any five year period thereafter) unless the registrant, or other interested person with the concurrence of the registrant, before the end of such period, requests in accordance with regulations prescribed by the Administrator that the registration be continued in effect: *Provided,* That the Administrator may permit the continued sale and use of existing stocks of a pesticide whose registration is canceled under this subsection or subsection (b) of this section to such extent, under such conditions, and for such uses as he may specify if he determines that such sale or use is not inconsistent with the purposes of this subchapter and will not have unreasonable adverse effects on the environment. The Administrator shall publish in the Federal Register, at least 30 days prior to the expiration of such five-year period, notice that the registration will be canceled if the registrant or other interested person with the concurrence of the registrant does not request that the registration be continued in effect.

(2) **Information.**—If at any time after the registration of a pesticide the registrant has additional factual information regarding unreasonable adverse effects on the environment of the pesticide, he shall submit such information to the Administrator.

(b) Cancellation and change in classification.—If it appears to the Administrator that a pesticide or its labeling or other material required to be submitted does not comply with the provisions of this subchapter or, when used in accordance with widespread and commonly recognized practice, generally causes unreasonable adverse effects on the environment, the Administrator may issue a notice of his intent either—

(1) to cancel its registration or to change its classification together with the reasons (including the factual basis) for his action, or

(2) to hold a hearing to determine whether or not its registration should be canceled or its classification changed.

Such notice shall be sent to the registrant and made public. In determining whether to issue any such notice, the Administrator shall include among those factors to be taken into account the impact of the action proposed in such notice on production and prices of agricultural commodities, retail food prices, and otherwise on the agricultural economy. At least 60 days prior to sending such notice to the registrant or making public such notice, whichever occurs first, the Administrator shall provide the Secretary of Agriculture with a copy of such notice and an analysis of such impact on the agricultural economy. If the Secretary comments in writing to the Administrator regarding the notice and analysis within 30 days after receiving them, the Administrator shall publish in the Federal Register (with the notice) the comments of the Secretary and the response of the Administrator with regard to the Secretary's comments. If the Secretary does not comment in writing to the Administrator regarding the notice and analysis within 30 days after receiving them, the Administrator may notify the registrant and make public the notice at any time after such 30-day period notwithstanding the foregoing 60-day time requirement. The time requirements imposed by the preceding 3 sentences may be waived or modified to the extent agreed upon by the Administrator and the Secretary. Notwithstanding any other provision of this subsection and section 136w(d) of this title, in the event that the Administrator determines that suspension of a pesticide registration is necessary to prevent an imminent hazard to human health, then upon such a finding the Administrator may waive the requirement of notice to and consultation with the Secretary of Agriculture pursuant to this subsection and of submission to the Scientific Advisory Panel pursuant to section 136w(d) of this title and proceed in accordance with subsection (c) of this section. The proposed action shall become final and effective at the end of 30 days from receipt by the registrant, or publication, of a notice issued under paragraph (1), whichever occurs later, unless within that time either (i) the registrant makes the necessary corrections, if possible, or (ii) a request for a hearing is made by a person adversely affected by the notice. In the event a hearing is held pursuant to such a request or to the Administrator's determination under paragraph (2), a decision pertaining to registration or classification issued after completion of such hearing shall be final. In taking any final action under this subsection, the Administrator shall consider restricting a pesticide's use or uses as an alternative to cancellation and shall fully explain the reasons for these restrictions, and shall include among those factors to be taken into account the impact of such final action on production and prices of agricultural commodities, retail food prices, and otherwise on the agricultural economy, and he shall publish in the Federal Register an analysis of such impact.

(c) Suspension.—

(1) **Order.**—If the Administrator determines that action is necessary to prevent an imminent hazard during the time required for cancellation or change in classification proceedings, he may, by order, suspend the registration of the pesticide immediately. No order of suspension may be issued unless the Administrator has issued or at the same time issues notice of his intention to cancel the registration or change the classification of the pesticide.

Except as provided in paragraph (3), the Administrator shall notify the registrant prior to issuing any suspension order. Such notice shall include findings pertaining to the question of "imminent hazard". The registrant shall then have an opportunity, in accordance with the provisions of paragraph (2), for an expedited hearing before the Agency on the question of whether an imminent hazard exists.

(2) Expedite hearing.—If no request for a hearing is submitted to the Agency within five days of the registrant's receipt of the notification provided for by paragraph (1), the suspension order may be issued and shall take effect and shall not be reviewable by a court. If a hearing is requested, it shall commence within five days of the receipt of the request for such hearing unless the registrant and the Agency agree that it shall commence at a later time. The hearing shall be held in accordance with the provisions of subchapter II of chapter 5 of title 5, except that the presiding officer need not be a certified administrative law judge. The presiding officer shall have ten days from the conclusion of the presentation of evidence to submit recommended findings and conclusions to the Administrator, who shall then have seven days to render a final order on the issue of suspension.

(3) Emergency order.—Whenever the Administrator determines that an emergency exists that does not permit him to hold a hearing before suspending, he may issue a suspension order in advance of notification to the registrant. In that case, paragraph (2) shall apply except that (i) the order of suspension shall be in effect pending the expeditious completion of the remedies provided by that paragraph and the issuance of a final order on suspension, and (ii) no party other than the registrant and the Agency shall participate except that any person adversely affected may file briefs within the time allotted by the Agency's rules. Any person so filing briefs shall be considered a party to such proceeding for the purposes of section 136n(b) of this title.

(4) Judicial review.—A final order on the question of suspension following a hearing shall be reviewable in accordance with section 136n of this title, notwithstanding the fact that any related cancellation proceedings have not been completed. Any order of suspension entered prior to a hearing before the Administrator shall be subject to immediate review in an action by the registrant or other interested person with the concurrence of the registrant in an appropriate district court, solely to determine whether the order of suspension was arbitrary, capricious or an abuse of discretion, or whether the order was issued in accordance with the procedures established by law. The effect of any order of the court will be only to stay the effectiveness of the suspension order, pending the Administrator's final decision with respect to cancellation or change in classification. This action may be maintained simultaneously with any administrative review proceeding under this section. The commencement of proceedings under this paragraph shall not operate as a stay of order, unless ordered by the court.

(d) Public hearings and scientific review.—In the event a hearing is requested pursuant to subsection (b) of this section or determined upon by the Administrator pursuant to subsection (b) of this section, such hearing shall be held after due notice for the purpose of receiving evidence relevant and material to the issues raised by the objections filed by the applicant or other interested parties, or to the issues stated by the Administrator, if the hearing is called by the Administrator rather than by the filing of objections. Upon a showing of relevance and reasonable scope of evidence sought by any party to a public hearing, the Hearing Examiner shall issue a subpena to compel testimony or production of documents from any person. The Hearing Examiner shall be guided by the principles of the Federal Rules of Civil Procedure in making any order for the protection of the witness or the content of documents produced and shall order the payment of reasonable fees and expenses as a condition to requiring testimony of the witness. On contest, the subpena may be enforced by an appropriate United States district court in accordance with the principles stated herein. Upon the request of any party to a public hearing and when in the Hearing Examiner's judgment it is necessary or desirable, the Hearing Examiner shall at any time before the hearing record is closed refer to a Committee of the National Academy of Sciences the relevant questions of scientific fact involved in the public hearing. No member of any committee of the National Academy of Sciences established to carry out the functions of this section shall have a financial or other conflict of interest with respect to any matter considered by such committee. The Committee of the National Academy of Sciences shall report in writing to the Hearing Examiner within 60 days after such referral on these questions of scientific fact. The report shall be made public and shall be considered as part of the hearing record. The Administrator shall enter into appropriate arrangements with the National Academy of Sciences to assure an objective and competent scientific review of the questions presented to Committees of the Academy and to provide such other scientific advisory services as may be required by the Administrator for carrying out the purposes of this subchapter. As soon as practicable after completion of the hearing (including the report of the Academy) but not later than 90 days thereafter, the Administrator shall evaluate the data and reports before him and issue an order either revoking his notice of intention issued pursuant to this section, or shall issue an order either canceling the registration, changing the classification, denying the registration, or requiring modification of the labeling or packaging of the article. Such order shall be based only on substantial evidence of record of such hearing and shall set forth detailed findings of fact upon which the order is based.

(e) Conditional registration.—

(1) The Administrator shall issue a notice of intent to cancel a registration issued under section 136a(c)(7) of this title if (A) the Administrator, at any time during the period provided for satisfaction of any condition imposed, determines that the registrant has failed to initiate and pursue appropriate action toward fulfilling any condition imposed, or (B) at the end of the period provided for satisfaction of any condition imposed, that condition has not been met: *Provided,* That the Administrator may permit the continued sale and use of existing stocks of a pesticide whose conditional registration has been canceled under this subsection to such extent, under such conditions, and for such uses as the Administrator may specify if the Administrator determines that such sale or use is not inconsistent with the purposes of this subchapter and will not have unreasonable adverse effects on the environment.

(2) A cancellation proposed under this subsection shall become final and effective at the end of thirty days from receipt by the registrant of the notice of intent to cancel unless during that time a request for hearing is made by a person adversely affected by the notice. If a hearing is requested, a hearing shall be conducted under subsection (d) of this section: *Provided,* That the only matters for resolution at that hearing shall be whether the registrant has initiated and pursued appropriate action to comply with the condition or conditions within the time provided or whether the condition or conditions have been satisfied within the time provided, and whether the Administrator's determination with respect to the disposition of existing stocks is consistent with this subchapter. A decision after completion of such hearing shall be final. Notwithstanding any other provision of this section, a hearing shall be held and a determination made within seventy-five days after receipt of a request for such hearing.

(f) Judicial review.—Final orders of the Administrator under this section shall be subject to judicial review pursuant to section 136n of this title.

(June 25, 1947, ch. 125, § 6, as added Oct. 21, 1972, Pub.L. 92–516, § 2, 86 Stat. 984, and amended Nov. 28, 1975, Pub.L. 94–140, § 1, 89 Stat. 751; Mar. 27, 1978, Pub.L. 95–251, § 2(a)(2), 92 Stat. 183; Sept. 30, 1978, Pub.L. 95–396, §§ 11, 12, 92 Stat. 828; Nov. 8, 1984, Pub.L. 98–620, Title IV, § 402(4)(A), 98 Stat. 3357.)

Code of Federal Regulations

Debarment and suspension under EPA assistance programs, see 40 CFR 32.100 et seq.
Registration, reregistration, and classification, see 40 CFR 162.1 et seq.
Rules of practice, see 40 CFR 164.1 et seq.

Library References

Agriculture ⚷9.
Health and Environment ⚷25.15(1).
C.J.S. Agriculture § 83 et seq.
C.J.S. Health and Environment § 82 et seq.

§ 136e. Registration of establishments

(a) Requirement.—No person shall produce any pesticide subject to this subchapter or active ingredient used in producing a pesticide subject to this subchapter in any State unless the establishment in which it is produced is registered with the Administrator. The application for registration of any establishment shall include the name and address of the establishment and of the producer who operates such establishment.

(b) Registration.—Whenever the Administrator receives an application under subsection (a) of this section, he shall register the establishment and assign it an establishment number.

(c) Information required.—

(1) Any producer operating an establishment registered under this section shall inform the Administrator within 30 days after it is registered of the types and amounts of pesticides and, if applicable, active ingredients used in producing pesticides—

(A) which he is currently producing;

(B) which he has produced during the past year; and

(C) which he has sold or distributed during the past year.

The information required by this paragraph shall be kept current and submitted to the Administrator annually as required under such regulations as the Administrator may prescribe.

(2) Any such producer shall, upon the request of the Administrator for the purpose of issuing a stop sale order pursuant to section 136k of this

title, inform him of the name and address of any recipient of any pesticide produced in any registered establishment which he operates.

(d) Confidential records and information.—Any information submitted to the Administrator pursuant to subsection (c) of this section other than the names of the pesticides or active ingredients used in producing pesticides produced, sold, or distributed at an establishment shall be considered confidential and shall be subject to the provisions of section 136h of this title.

(June 25, 1947, ch. 125, § 7, as added Oct. 21, 1972, Pub.L. 92–516, § 2, 86 Stat. 987, and amended Sept. 30, 1978, Pub.L. 95–396, § 13, 92 Stat. 829.)

Code of Federal Regulations

Debarment and suspension under EPA assistance programs, see 40 CFR 32.100 et seq.
Procedures and reporting, requirements, see 40 CFR 167.1 et seq.

Library References

Agriculture ⇐9.
C.J.S. Agriculture § 83 et seq.

§ 136f. Books and records

(a) Requirements.—The Administrator may prescribe regulations requiring producers to maintain such records with respect to their operations and the pesticides and devices produced as he determines are necessary for the effective enforcement of this subchapter. No records required under this subsection shall extend to financial data, sales data other than shipment data, pricing data, personnel data, and research data (other than data relating to registered pesticides or to a pesticide for which an application for registration has been filed).

(b) Inspection.—For the purposes of enforcing the provisions of this subchapter, any producer, distributor, carrier, dealer, or any other person who sells or offers for sale, delivers or offers for delivery any pesticide or device subject to this subchapter, shall, upon request of any officer or employee of the Environmental Protection Agency or of any State or political subdivision, duly designated by the Administrator, furnish or permit such person at all reasonable times to have access to, and to copy: (1) all records showing the delivery, movement, or holding of such pesticide or device, including the quantity, the date of shipment and receipt, and the name of the consignor and consignee; or (2) in the event of the inability of any person to produce records containing such information, all other records and information relating to such delivery, movement, or holding of the pesticide or device. Any inspection with respect to any records and information referred to in this subsection shall not extend to financial data, sales data other than shipment data, pricing data, personnel data; and research data (other than data relating to registered pesticides or to a pesticide for which an application for registration has been filed). Before undertaking an inspection under this subsection, the officer or employee must present to the owner, operator, or agent in charge of the establishment or other place where pesticides or devices are held for distribution or sale, appropriate credentials and a written statement as to the reason for the inspection, including a statement as to whether a violation of the law is suspected. If no violation is suspected, an alternate and sufficient reason shall be given in writing. Each such inspection shall be commenced and completed with reasonable promptness.

(June 25, 1947, ch. 125, § 8, as added Oct. 21, 1972, Pub.L. 92–516, § 2, 86 Stat. 987, and amended Sept. 30, 1978, Pub.L. 95–396, § 14, 92 Stat. 829.)

Code of Federal Regulations

Debarment and suspension under EPA assistance programs, see 40 CFR 32.100 et seq.
Maintenance, etc., requirements, see 40 CFR 169.1 et seq.

Library References

Agriculture ⇐9.
C.J.S. Agriculture § 83 et seq.

§ 136g. Inspection of establishments, etc.

(a) In general.—For purposes of enforcing the provisions of this subchapter, officers or employees duly designated by the Administrator are authorized to enter at reasonable times, any establishment or other place where pesticides or devices are held for distribution or sale for the purpose of inspecting and obtaining samples of any pesticides or devices, packaged, labeled, and released for shipment, and samples of any containers or labeling for such pesticides or devices.

Before undertaking such inspection, the officers or employees must present to the owner, operator, or agent in charge of the establishment or other place where pesticides or devices are held for distribution or sale, appropriate credentials and a written statement as to the reason for the inspection, including a statement as to whether a violation of the law is suspected. If no violation is suspected, an alternate and sufficient reason shall be given in writing. Each such inspection shall be commenced and completed with reasonable promptness. If the officer or employee obtains any samples, prior to leaving the premises, he shall give to the owner, operator, or agent in charge a receipt describing the samples obtained and, if requested, a portion of each such sample equal in volume or weight to the portion retained. If an analysis is made of such samples, a copy of the results of such analysis shall be furnished promptly to the owner, operator, or agent in charge.

(b) Warrants.—For purposes of enforcing the provisions of this subchapter and upon a showing to an officer or court of competent jurisdiction that there is reason to believe that the provisions of this subchapter have been violated, officers or employees duly designated by the Administrator are empowered to obtain and to execute warrants authorizing—

(1) entry for the purpose of this section;

(2) inspection and reproduction of all records showing the quantity, date of shipment, and the name of consignor and consignee of any pesticide or device found in the establishment which is adulterated, misbranded, not registered (in the case of a pesticide) or otherwise in violation of this subchapter and in the event of the inability of any person to produce records containing such information, all other records and information relating to such delivery, movement, or holding of the pesticide or device; and

(3) the seizure of any pesticide or device which is in violation of this subchapter.

(c) Enforcement.—

(1) Certification of facts to Attorney General.—The examination of pesticides or devices shall be made in the Environmental Protection Agency or elsewhere as the Administrator may designate for the purpose of determining from such examinations whether they comply with the requirements of this subchapter. If it shall appear from any such examination that they fail to comply with the requirements of this subchapter, the Administrator shall cause notice to be given to the person against whom criminal or civil proceedings are contemplated. Any person so notified shall be given an opportunity to present his views, either orally or in writing, with regard to such contemplated proceedings, and if in the opinion of the Administrator it appears that the provisions of this subchapter have been violated by such person, then the Administrator shall certify the facts to the Attorney General, with a copy of the results of the analysis or the examination of such pesticide for the institution of a criminal proceeding pursuant to section 136*l*(b) of this title or a civil proceeding under section 136*l*(a) of this title, when the Administrator determines that such action will be sufficient to effectuate the purposes of this subchapter.

(2) Notice not required.—The notice of contemplated proceedings and opportunity to present views set forth in this subsection are not prerequisites to the institution of any proceeding by the Attorney General.

(3) Warning notices.—Nothing in this subchapter shall be construed as requiring the Administrator to institute proceedings for prosecution of minor violations of this subchapter whenever he believes that the public interest will be adequately served by a suitable written notice of warning.

(June 25, 1947, ch. 125, § 9, as added Oct. 21, 1972, Pub.L. 92–516, § 2, 86 Stat. 988.)

Code of Federal Regulations

Debarment and suspension under EPA assistance programs, see 40 CFR 32.100 et seq.

Library References

Agriculture ⚩9.
C.J.S. Agriculture § 83 et seq.

§ 136h. Protection of trade secrets and other information

(a) In general.—In submitting data required by this subchapter, the applicant may (1) clearly mark any portions thereof which in his opinion are trade secrets or commercial or financial information and (2) submit such market material separately from other material required to be submitted under this subchapter.

(b) Disclosure.—Notwithstanding any other provision of this subchapter and subject to the limitations in subsections (d) and (e) of this section, the Administrator shall not make public information which in his judgment contains or relates to trade secrets or commercial or financial information obtained from a person and privileged or confidential, except that, when necessary to carry out the provisions of this subchapter, information relating to formulas of products acquired by authorization of this subchapter may be revealed to any Federal agency consulted and may be revealed at a public hearing or in findings of fact issued by the Administrator.

(c) Disputes.—If the Administrator proposes to release for inspection information which the applicant or registrant believes to be protected from disclosure under subsection (b) of this section, he shall notify the applicant or registrant, in writing, by certified mail. The Administrator shall not thereafter make available for inspection such data until thirty days after receipt of the notice by the applicant or registrant. During this period, the applicant or registrant may institute an action in an appropriate district court for a declaratory judgment as to whether such information is subject to protection under subsection (b) of this section.

(d) Limitations.—

(1) All information concerning the objectives, methodology, results, or significance of any test or experiment performed on or with a registered or previously registered pesticide or its separate ingredients, impurities, or degradation products, and any information concerning the effects of such pesticide on any organism or the behavior of such pesticide in the environment, including, but not limited to, data on safety to fish and wildlife, humans and other mammals, plants, animals, and soil, and studies on persistence, translocation and fate in the environment, and metabolism, shall be available for disclosure to the public: *Provided,* That the use of such data for any registration purpose shall be governed by section 136a of this title: *Provided further,* That this paragraph does not authorize the disclosure of any information that—

(A) discloses manufacturing or quality control processes,

(B) discloses the details of any methods for testing, detecting, or measuring the quantity of any deliberately added inert ingredient of a pesticide, or

(C) discloses the identity or percentage quantity of any deliberately added inert ingredient of a pesticide,

unless the Administrator has first determined that disclosure is necessary to protect against an unreasonable risk of injury to health or the environment.

(2) Information concerning production, distribution, sale, or inventories of a pesticide that is otherwise entitled to confidential treatment under subsection (b) of this section may be publicly disclosed in connection with a public proceeding to determine whether a pesticide, or any ingredient of a pesticide, causes unreasonable adverse effects on health or the environment, if the Administrator determines that such disclosure is necessary in the public interest.

(3) If the Administrator proposes to disclose information described in clause (A), (B), or (C) of paragraph (1) or in paragraph (2) of this subsection, the Administrator shall notify by certified mail the submitter of such information of the intent to release such information. The Administrator may not release such information, without the submitter's consent, until thirty days after the submitter has been furnished such notice: *Provided,* That where the Administrator finds that disclosure of information described in clause (A), (B), or (C) of paragraph (1) of this subsection is necessary to avoid or lessen an imminent and substantial risk of injury to the public health, the Administrator may set such shorter period of notice (but not less than ten days) and such method of notice as the Administrator finds appropriate. During such period the data submitter may institute an action in an appropriate district court to enjoin or limit the proposed disclosure. The court may enjoin disclosure, or limit the disclosure or the parties to whom disclosure shall be made, to the extent that—

(A) in the case of information described in clause (A), (B), or (C) of paragraph (1) of this subsection, the proposed disclosure is not required to protect against an unreasonable risk of injury to health or the environment; or

(B) in the case of information described in paragraph (2) of this subsection, the public interest in availability of the information in the public proceeding does not outweigh the interests in preserving the confidentiality of the information.

(e) Disclosure to contractors.—Information otherwise protected from disclosure to the public under subsection (b) of this section may be disclosed to contractors with the United States and employees of such contractors if, in the opinion of the Administrator, such disclosure is necessary for the satisfactory performance by the contractor of a contract with the United States for the performance of work in connection with this subchapter and under such conditions as the Administrator may specify. The Administrator shall require as a condition to the disclosure of information under this subsection that the person receiving it take such security precautions respecting the information as the Administrator shall by regulation prescribe.

(f) Penalty for disclosure by federal employees.—(1) Any officer or employee of the United States or former officer or employee of the United States who, by virtue of such employment or official position, has obtained possession of, or has access to, material the disclosure of which is prohibited by subsection (b) of this section, and who, knowing that disclosure of such material is prohibited by such subsection, willfully discloses the material in any manner to any person not entitled to receive it, shall be fined not more than $10,000 or imprisoned for not more than one year, or both. Section 1905 of title 18 shall not apply with respect to the publishing, divulging, disclosure, or making known of, or making available, information reported or otherwise obtained under this subchapter. Nothing in this subchapter shall preempt any civil remedy under State or Federal law for wrongful disclosure of trade secrets.

(2) For the purposes of this section, any contractor with the United States who is furnished information as authorized by subsection (e) of this section, or any employee of any such contractor, shall be considered to be an employee of the United States.

(g) Disclosure to foreign and multinational pesticide producers.—(1) The Administrator shall not knowingly disclose information submitted by an applicant or registrant under this subchapter to any employee or agent of any business or other entity engaged in the production, sale, or distribution of pesticides in countries other than the United States or in addition to the United States or to any other person who intends to deliver such data to such foreign or multinational business or entity unless the applicant or registrant has consented to such disclosure. The Administrator shall require an affirmation from any person who intends to inspect data that such person does not seek access to the data for purposes of delivering it or offering it for sale to any such business or entity or its agents or employees and will not purposefully deliver or negligently cause the data to be delivered to such business or entity or its agents or employees. Notwithstanding any other provision of this subsection, the Administrator may disclose information to any person in connection with a public proceeding under law or regulation, subject to restrictions on the availability of information contained elsewhere in this subchapter, which information is relevant to a determination by the Administrator with respect to whether a pesticide, or any ingredient of a pesticide, causes unreasonable adverse effects on health or the environment.

(2) The Administrator shall maintain records of the names of persons to whom data are disclosed under this subsection and the persons or organizations they represent and shall inform the applicant or registrant of the names and affiliations of such persons.

(3) Section 1001 of title 18 shall apply to any affirmation made under paragraph (1) of this subsection.

(June 25, 1947, ch. 125, § 10, as added Oct. 21, 1972, Pub.L. 92–516, § 2, 86 Stat. 989, and amended Sept. 30, 1978, Pub.L. 95–396, § 15, 92 Stat. 829; Nov. 8, 1984, Pub.L. 98–620, Title IV, § 402(4)(B), 98 Stat. 3357.)

Code of Federal Regulations

Availability of information, see 40 CFR 2.100 et seq.
Debarment and suspension under EPA assistance programs, see 40 CFR 32.100 et seq.

Library References

Agriculture ⚷9.
Trade Regulations ⚷861.
C.J.S. Agriculture § 83 et seq.
C.J.S. Trade-Marks, Trade-Names, and Unfair Competition § 237.

§ 136i. Standards applicable to pesticide applicators

(a) In general.—No regulations prescribed by the Administrator for carrying out the provisions of this subchapter shall require any private applicator to maintain any records or file any reports or other documents.

(b) Separate standards.—When establishing or approving standards for licensing or certification, the Administrator shall establish separate standards for commercial and private applicators.

(June 25, 1947, ch. 125, § 11, as added Oct. 21, 1972, Pub.L. 92–516, § 2, 86 Stat. 989.)

Code of Federal Regulations

Debarment and suspension under EPA assistance programs, see 40 CFR 32.100 et seq.

Library References

Agriculture ⚷9.
C.J.S. Agriculture § 83 et seq.

§ 136j. Unlawful acts

(a) In general.—

(1) Except as provided by subsection (b) of this section, it shall be unlawful for any person in any State to distribute, sell, offer for sale, hold for sale, ship, deliver for shipment, or receive and (having so received) deliver or offer to deliver, to any person—

(A) any pesticide which is not registered under section 136a of this title, except as provided by section 136d(a)(1) of this title;

(B) any registered pesticide if any claims made for it as a part of its distribution or sale substantially differ from any claims made for it as a part of the statement required in connection with its registration under section 136a of this title;

(C) any registered pesticide the composition of which differs at the time of its distribution or sale from its composition as described in the statement required in connection with its registration under section 136a of this title;

(D) any pesticide which has not been colored or discolored pursuant to the provisions of section 136w(c)(5) of this title;

(E) any pesticide which is adulterated or misbranded; or

(F) any device which is misbranded.

(2) It shall be unlawful for any person—

(A) to detach, alter, deface, or destroy, in whole or in part, any labeling required under this subchapter;

(B) to refuse to keep any records required pursuant to section 136f of this title, or to refuse to allow inspection of any records or establishment pursuant to section 136f or 136g of this title, or to refuse to allow an officer or employee of the Environmental Protection

Agency to take a sample of any pesticide pursuant to section 136g of this title;

(C) to give a guaranty or undertaking provided for in subsection (b) of this section which is false in any particular, except that a person who receives and relies upon a guaranty authorized under subsection (b) of this section may give a guaranty to the same effect, which guaranty shall contain, in addition to his own name and address, the name and address of the person residing in the United States from whom he received the guaranty or undertaking;

(D) to use for his own advantage or to reveal, other than to the Administrator, or officials or employees of the Environmental Protection Agency or other Federal executive agencies, or to the courts, or to physicians, pharmacists, and other qualified persons, needing such information for the performance of their duties, in accordance with such directions as the Administrator may prescribe, any information acquired by authority of this subchapter which is confidential under this subchapter;

(E) who is a registrant, wholesaler, dealer, retailer, or other distributor to advertise a product registered under this subchapter for restricted use without giving the classification of the product assigned to it under section 136a of this title;

(F) to make available for use, or to use, any registered pesticide classified for restricted use for some or all purposes other than in accordance with section 136a(d) of this title and any regulations thereunder: *Provided,* That it shall not be unlawful to sell, under regulations issued by the Administrator, a restricted use pesticide to a person who is not a certified applicator for application by a certified applicator;

(G) to use any registered pesticide in a manner inconsistent with its labeling;

(H) to use any pesticide which is under an experimental use permit contrary to the provisions of such permit;

(I) to violate any order issued under section 136k of this title;

(J) to violate any suspension order issued under section 136d of this title;

(K) to violate any cancellation of registration of a pesticide under section 136d of this title, except as provided by section 136d(a)(1) of this title;

(L) who is a producer to violate any of the provisions of section 136e of this title;

(M) to knowingly falsify all or part of any application for registration, application for experimental use permit, any information submitted to the Administrator pursuant to section 136e of this title, any records required to be maintained pursuant to section 136f of this title, any report filed under this subchapter, or any information marked as confidential and submitted to the Administrator under any provision of this subchapter;

(N) who is a registrant, wholesaler, dealer, retailer, or other distributor to fail to file reports required by this subchapter;

(O) to add any substance to, or take any substance from, any pesticide in a manner that may defeat the purpose of this subchapter; or

(P) to use any pesticide in tests on human beings unless such human beings (i) are fully informed of the nature and purposes of the test and of any physical and mental health consequences which are reasonably foreseeable therefrom, and (ii) freely volunteer to participate in the test.

(b) Exemptions.—The penalties provided for a violation of paragraph (1) of subsection (a) of this section shall not apply to—

(1) any person who establishes a guaranty signed by, and containing the name and address of, the registrant or person residing in the United States from whom he purchased or received in good faith the pesticide in the same unbroken package, to the effect that the pesticide was lawfully registered at the time of sale and delivery to him, and that it complies with the other requirements of this subchapter, and in such case the guarantor shall be subject to the penalties which would otherwise attach to the person holding the guaranty under the provisions of this subchapter;

(2) any carrier while lawfully shipping, transporting, or delivering for shipment any pesticide or device, if such carrier upon request of any officer or employee duly designated by the Administrator shall permit such officer or employee to copy all of its records concerning such pesticide or device;

(3) any public official while engaged in the performance of his official duties;

(4) any person using or possessing any pesticide as provided by an experimental use permit in effect with respect to such pesticide and such use or possession; or

(5) any person who ships a substance or mixture of substances being put through tests in which the purpose is only to determine its value for pesticide purposes or to determine its toxicity or other properties and from which the user does not expect to receive any benefit in pest control from its use.

(June 25, 1947, ch. 125, § 12, as added Oct. 21, 1972, Pub.L. 92–516, § 2, 86 Stat. 989, and amended Sept. 30, 1978, Pub.L. 95–396, § 16, 92 Stat. 832.)

Code of Federal Regulations

Arbitration of pesticide data disputes, see 29 CFR 1440.1.
Availability of information, see 40 CFR 2.100 et seq.
Debarment and suspension under EPA, assistance programs, see 40 CFR 32.100 et seq.

Library References

Agriculture ⚷9, 16.
C.J.S. Agriculture §§ 30 et seq., 83 et seq.

§ 136k. Stop sale, use, removal, and seizure

(a) Stop sale, etc., orders.—Whenever any pesticide or device is found by the Administrator in any State and there is reason to believe on the basis of inspection or tests that such pesticide or device is in violation of any of the provisions of this subchapter, or that such pesticide or device has been or is intended to be distributed or sold in violation of any such provisions, or when the registration of the pesticide has been canceled by a final order or has been suspended, the Administrator may issue a written or printed "stop sale, use, or removal" order to any person who owns, controls, or has custody of such pesticide or device, and after receipt of such order no person shall sell, use, or remove the pesticide or device described in the order except in accordance with the provisions of the order.

(b) Seizure.—Any pesticide or device that is being transported or, having been transported, remains unsold or in original unbroken packages, or that is sold or offered for sale in any State, or that is imported from a foreign country, shall be liable to be proceeded against in any district court in the district where it is found and seized for confiscation by a process in rem for condemnation if—

(1) in the case of a pesticide—

(A) it is adulterated or misbranded;

(B) it is not registered pursuant to the provisions of section 136a of this title;

(C) its labeling fails to bear the information required by this subchapter;

(D) it is not colored or discolored and such coloring or discoloring is required under this subchapter; or

(E) any of the claims made for it or any of the directions for its use differ in substance from the representations made in connection with its registration;

(2) in the case of a device, it is misbranded; or

(3) in the case of a pesticide or device, when used in accordance with the requirements imposed under this subchapter and as directed by the labeling, it nevertheless causes unreasonable adverse effects on the environment. In the case of a plant regulator, defoliant, or desiccant, used in accordance with the label claims and recommendations, physical or physiological effects on plants or parts thereof shall not be deemed to be injury, when such effects are the purpose for which the plant regulator, defoliant, or desiccant was applied.

(c) Disposition after condemnation.—If the pesticide or device is condemned it shall, after entry of the decree, be disposed of by destruction or sale as the court may direct and the proceeds, if sold, less the court costs, shall be paid into the Treasury of the United States, but the pesticide or device shall not be sold contrary to the provisions of this subchapter or the laws of the jurisdiction in which it is sold: *Provided,* That upon payment of the costs of the condemnation proceedings and the execution and delivery of a good and sufficient bond conditioned that the pesticide or device shall not be sold or otherwise disposed of contrary to the provisions of the subchapter or the laws of any jurisdiction in which sold, the court may direct that such pesticide or device be delivered to the owner thereof. The proceedings of such condemnation cases shall conform, as near as may be to the proceedings in admiralty, except that either party may demand trial by jury of any issue of fact joined in any case, and all such proceedings shall be at the suit of and in the name of the United States.

(d) Court costs, etc.—When a decree of condemnation is entered against the pesticide or device, court costs and fees, storage, and other proper expenses shall be awarded against the person, if any, intervening as claimant of the pesticide or device.

(June 25, 1947, ch. 125, § 13, as added Oct. 21, 1972, Pub.L. 92–516, § 2, 86 Stat. 991.)

Code of Federal Regulations

Debarment and suspension under EPA assistance programs, see 40 CFR 32.100 et seq.

Library References

Agriculture ⚷9.
C.J.S. Agriculture § 83 et seq.

§ 136*l*. Penalties

(a) Civil penalties.—

(1) In general.—Any registrant, commercial applicator, wholesaler, dealer, retailer, or other distributor who violates any provision of this subchapter may be assessed a civil penalty by the Administrator of not more than $5,000 for each offense.

(2) Private applicator.—Any private applicator or other person not included in paragraph (1) who violates any provision of this subchapter subsequent to receiving a written warning from the Administrator or following a citation for a prior violation, may be assessed a civil penalty by the Administrator of not more than $1,000 for each offense: *Provided,* That any applicator not included under paragraph (1) of this subsection who holds or applies registered pesticides, or uses dilutions of registered pesticides, only to provide a service of controlling pests without delivering any unapplied pesticide to any person so served, and who violates any provision of this subchapter may be assessed a civil penalty by the Administrator of not more than $500 for the first offense nor more than $1,000 for each subsequent offense.

(3) Hearing.—No civil penalty shall be assessed unless the person charged shall have been given notice and opportunity for a hearing on such charge in the county, parish, or incorporated city of the residence of the person charged.

(4) Determination of penalty.—In determining the amount of the penalty, the Administrator shall consider the appropriateness of such penalty to the size of the business of the person charged, the effect on the person's ability to continue in business, and the gravity of the violation. Whenever the Administrator finds that the violation occurred despite the exercise of due care or did not cause significant harm to health or the environment, the Administrator may issue a warning in lieu of assessing a penalty.

(5) References to Attorney General.—In case of inability to collect such civil penalty or failure of any person to pay all, or such portion of such civil penalty as the Administrator may determine, the Administrator shall refer the matter to the Attorney General, who shall recover such amount by action in the appropriate United States district court.

(b) Criminal penalties.—

(1) In general.—Any registrant, commercial applicator, wholesaler, dealer, retailer, or other distributor who knowingly violates any provision of this subchapter shall be guilty of a misdemeanor and shall on conviction be fined not more than $25,000, or imprisoned for not more than one year, or both.

(2) Private applicator.—Any private applicator or other person not included in paragraph (1) who knowingly violates any provision of this subchapter shall be guilty of a misdemeanor and shall on conviction be fined not more than $1,000, or imprisoned for not more than 30 days, or both.

(3) Disclosure of information.—Any person, who, with intent to defraud, uses or reveals information relative to formulas of products acquired under the authority of section 136a of this title, shall be fined not more than $10,000, or imprisoned for not more than three years, or both.

(4) Acts of officers, agents, etc.—When construing and enforcing the provisions of this subchapter, the act, omission, or failure of any officer, agent, or other person acting for or employed by any person shall in every case be also deemed to be the act, omission, or failure of such person as well as that of the person employed.

(June 25, 1947, ch. 125, § 14, as added Oct. 21, 1972, Pub.L. 92–516, § 2, 86 Stat. 992, and amended Sept. 30, 1978, Pub.L. 95–396, § 17, 92 Stat. 832.)

Code of Federal Regulations

Debarment and suspension under EPA assistance programs, see 40 CFR 32.100 et seq.
Rules of practice, see 40 CFR 168.01 et seq.

Library References

Agriculture ⚷9, 16.
C.J.S. Agriculture §§ 30 et seq., 83 et seq.

§ 136m. Indemnities

(a) Requirement.—If—

(1) the Administrator notifies a registrant that he has suspended the registration of a pesticide because such action is necessary to prevent an imminent hazard;

(2) the registration of the pesticide is canceled as a result of a final determination that the use of such pesticide will create an imminent hazard; and

(3) any person who owned any quantity of such pesticide immediately before the notice to the registrant under paragraph (1) suffered losses by reason of suspension or cancellation of the registration,

the Administrator shall make an indemnity payment to such person, unless the Administrator finds that such person (i) had knowledge of facts which, in themselves, would have shown that such pesticide did not meet the requirements of section 136a(c)(5) of this title for registration, and (ii) continued thereafter to produce such pesticide without giving timely notice of such facts to the Administrator.

(b) Amount of payment.—

(1) In general.—The amount of the indemnity payment under subsection (a) of this section to any person shall be determined on the basis of the cost of the pesticide owned by such person immediately before the notice to the registrant referred to in subsection (a)(1) of this section; except that in no event shall an indemnity payment to any person exceed the fair market value of the pesticide owned by such person immediately before the notice referred to in subsection (a)(1) of this section.

(2) Special rule.—Notwithstanding any other provision of this subchapter the Administrator may provide a reasonable time for use or other disposal of such pesticide. In determining the quantity of any pesticide for which indemnity shall be paid under this subsection, proper adjustment shall be made for any pesticide used or otherwise disposed of by such owner.

(June 25, 1947, ch. 125, § 15, as added Oct. 21, 1972, Pub.L. 92–516, § 2, 86 Stat. 993.)

Code of Federal Regulations

Debarment and suspension under EPA assistance programs, see 40 CFR 32.100 et seq.

Library References

Agriculture ⚷9.
C.J.S. Agriculture § 83 et seq.

§ 136n. Administrative procedure; judicial review

(a) District court review.—Except as is otherwise provided in this subchapter, Agency refusals to cancel or suspend registrations or change classifications not following a hearing and other final Agency actions not committed to Agency discretion by law are judicially reviewable in the district courts.

(b) Review by court of appeals.—In the case of actual controversy as to the validity of any order issued by the Administrator following a public hearing, any person who will be adversely affected by such order and who had been a party to the proceedings may obtain judicial review by filing in the United States court of appeals for the circuit wherein such person resides or has a place of business, within 60 days after the entry of such order, a petition praying that the order be set aside in whole or in part. A copy of the petition shall be forthwith transmitted by the clerk of the court to the Administrator or any officer designated by him for that purpose, and thereupon the Administrator shall file in the court the record of the proceedings on which he based his order, as provided in section 2112 of Title 28. Upon the filing of such petition the court shall have exclusive jurisdiction to affirm or set aside the order complained of in whole or in part. The court shall consider all evidence of record. The order of the Administrator shall be sustained if it is supported by substantial evidence when considered on the record as a whole. The judgment of the court affirming or setting aside, in whole or in part, any order under this section shall be final, subject to review by the Supreme Court of the United States upon certiorari or certification as provided in section 1254 of Title 28. The commencement of proceedings under this section shall not, unless specifically ordered by the court to the contrary, operate as a stay of an order.

(c) Jurisdiction of district courts.—The district courts of the United States are vested with jurisdiction specifically to enforce, and to prevent and restrain violations of, this subchapter.

(d) Notice of judgments.—The Administrator shall, by publication in such manner as he may prescribe, give notice of all judgments entered in actions instituted under the authority of this subchapter.

(June 25, 1947, ch. 125, § 16, as added Oct. 21, 1972, Pub.L. 92–516, § 2, 86 Stat. 994, as amended Nov. 8, 1984, Pub.L. 98–620, Title IV, § 402(4)(C), 98 Stat. 3357.)

Federal Practice and Procedure

Review of administrative decisions in courts of appeals, see Wright, Miller, Cooper & Gressman: Jurisdiction § 3941.

Code of Federal Regulations

Debarment and suspension under EPA assistance programs, see 40 CFR 32.100 et seq.

Library References

Agriculture ⚷9.
Health and Environment ⚷25.15(1).
C.J.S. Agriculture § 83 et seq.
C.J.S. Health and Environment § 82 et seq.

§ 136*o*. Imports and exports

(a) Pesticides and devices intended for export.—Notwithstanding any other provision of this subchapter, no pesticide or device or active ingredient used in producing a pesticide intended solely for export to any foreign country shall be deemed in violation of this subchapter—

(1) when prepared or packed according to the specifications or directions of the foreign purchaser, except that producers of such pesticides and devices and active ingredients used in producing pesticides shall be subject to sections 136(p), (q)(1)(A), (C), (D), (E), (G), and (H), 136(q)(2)(A), (B), (C)(i) and (iii), and (D), 136e, and 136f of this title; and

(2) in the case of any pesticide other than a pesticide registered under section 136a or sold

under section 136d(a)(1) of this title, if, prior to export, the foreign purchaser has signed a statement acknowledging that the purchaser understands that such pesticide is not registered for use in the United States and cannot be sold in the United States under this subchapter. A copy of that statement shall be transmitted to an appropriate official of the government of the importing country.

(b) Cancellation notices furnished to foreign governments.—Whenever a registration, or a cancellation or suspension of the registration of a pesticide becomes effective, or ceases to be effective, the Administrator shall transmit through the State Department notification thereof to the governments of other countries and to appropriate international agencies. Such notification shall, upon request, include all information related to the cancellation or suspension of the registration of the pesticide and information concerning other pesticides that are registered under section 136a of this title and that could be used in lieu of such pesticide.

(c) Importation of pesticides and devices.—The Secretary of the Treasury shall notify the Administrator of the arrival of pesticides and devices and shall deliver to the Administrator, upon his request, samples of pesticides or devices which are being imported into the United States, giving notice to the owner or consignee, who may appear before the Administrator and have the right to introduce testimony. If it appears from the examination of a sample that it is adulterated, or misbranded or otherwise violated the provisions set forth in this subchapter, or is otherwise injurious to health or the environment, the pesticide or device may be refused admission, and the Secretary of the Treasury shall refuse delivery to the consignee and shall cause the destruction of any pesticide or device refused delivery which shall not be exported by the consignee within 90 days from the date of notice of such refusal under such regulations as the Secretary of the Treasury may prescribe: *Provided,* That the Secretary of the Treasury may deliver to the consignee such pesticide or device pending examination and decision in the matter on execution of bond for the amount of the full invoice value of such pesticide or device, together with the duty thereon, and on refusal to return such pesticide or device for any cause to the custody of the Secretary of the Treasury, when demanded, for the purpose of excluding them from the country, or for any other purpose, said consignee shall forfeit the full amount of said bond: *And provided further,* That all charges for storage, cartage, and labor on pesticides or devices which are refused admission or delivery shall be paid by the owner or consignee, and in default of such payment shall constitute a lien against any future importation made by such owner or consignee.

(d) Cooperation in international efforts.—The Administrator shall, in cooperation with the Department of State and any other appropriate Federal agency, participate and cooperate in any international efforts to develop improved pesticide research and regulations.

(e) Regulations.—The Secretary of the Treasury, in consultation with the Administrator, shall prescribe regulations for the enforcement of subsection (c) of this section.

(June 25, 1947, ch. 125, § 17, as added Oct. 21, 1972, Pub.L. 92–516, § 2, 86 Stat. 995, and amended Sept. 30, 1978, Pub.L. 95–396, § 18(a), 92 Stat. 833.)

Code of Federal Regulations

Debarment and suspension under EPA assistance programs, see 40 CFR 32.100 et seq.
Special classes of merchandise, see 19 CFR 12.110 to 12.117.

Library References

Agriculture ⚷9.
C.J.S. Agriculture § 83 et seq.

§ 136p. Exemption of Federal or State agencies

The Administrator may, at his discretion, exempt any Federal or State agency from any provision of this subchapter if he determines that emergency conditions exist which require such exemption. The Administrator, in determining whether or not such emergency conditions exist, shall consult with the Secretary of Agriculture and the Governor of any State concerned if they request such determination.

(June 25, 1947, ch. 125, § 18, as added Oct. 21, 1972, Pub.L. 92–516, § 2, 86 Stat. 995, and amended Nov. 28, 1975, Pub.L. 94–140, § 8, 89 Stat. 754.)

Code of Federal Regulations

Debarment and suspension under EPA assistance programs, see 40 CFR 32.100 et seq.
Policies and procedures, see 40 CFR 166.1 et seq.

Library References

Agriculture ⚷9.
C.J.S. Agriculture § 83 et seq.

§ 136q. Disposal and transportation

(a) Procedures.—The Administrator shall, after consultation with other interested Federal agencies, establish procedures and regulations for the disposal or storage of packages and containers of pesticides and for disposal or storage of excess amounts of such pesticides, and accept at convenient locations for safe disposal a pesticide the registration of which is canceled under section 136d(c) of this title if requested by the owner of the pesticide.

(b) Advice to Secretary of Transportation.—The Administrator shall provide advice and assistance to the Secretary of Transportation with respect to his functions relating to the transportation of hazardous materials under the Department of Transportation Act (49 U.S.C. 1657[1]), the Transportation of Explosives Act (18 U.S.C. 831–835), the Federal Aviation Act of 1958 (49 U.S.C. 1421–1430, 1472(h)), and the Hazardous Cargo Act (46 U.S.C. 2104, 2106, 3306.)

(c) Provisions for unused quantities.—Notification of cancellation of any pesticide shall include specific provisions for the disposal of the unused quantities of such pesticide.

(June 25, 1947, ch. 125, § 19, as added Oct. 21, 1972, Pub.L. 92–516, § 2, 86 Stat. 995, and amended Sept. 30, 1978, Pub.L. 95–396, § 19, 92 Stat. 833.)

[1] So in original. Probably should be "1655".

Code of Federal Regulations

Debarment and suspension under EPA assistance programs, see 40 CFR 32.100 et seq.
Procedures applicable, see 40 CFR 165.1 et seq.
Registration, reregistration, and classification, see 40 CFR 162.1 et seq.

Library References

Agriculture ⚷9.
C.J.S. Agriculture § 83 et seq.

§ 136r. Research and monitoring

(a) Research.—The Administrator shall undertake research including research by grant or contract with other Federal agencies, universities, or others as may be necessary to carry out the purposes of this subchapter, and he shall conduct research into integrated pest management in coordination with the Secretary of Agriculture. The Administrator shall also take care to insure that such research does not duplicate research being undertaken by any other Federal agency.

(b) National monitoring plan.—The Administrator shall formulate and periodically revise, in cooperation with other Federal, State, or local agencies, a national plan for monitoring pesticides.

(c) Monitoring.—The Administrator shall undertake such monitoring activities, including, but not limited to monitoring in air, soil, water, man, plants, and animals, as may be necessary for the implementation of this subchapter and of the national pesticide monitoring plan. The Administrator shall establish procedures for the monitoring of man and animals and their environment for incidential[1] pesticide exposure, including, but not limited to, the quantification of incidental human and environmental pesticide pollution and the secular trends thereof, and identification of the sources of contamination and their relationship to human and environmental effects. Such activities shall be carried out in cooperation with other Federal, State, and local agencies.

(June 25, 1947, ch. 125, § 20, as added Oct. 21, 1972, Pub.L. 92–516, § 2, 86 Stat. 996, and amended Sept. 30, 1978, Pub.L. 95–396, § 20, 92 Stat. 834.)

[1] So in original. Probably should be "incidental".

Code of Federal Regulations

Debarment and suspension under EPA assistance programs, see 40 CFR 32.100 et seq.
Granting policies and procedures, see 40 CFR 30.100 et seq.
Subagreements, see 40 CFR 33.001 et seq.

Library References

Agriculture ⚷9.
Health and Environment ⚷25.5(9).

C.J.S. Agriculture § 83 et seq.
C.J.S. Health and Environment § 65 et seq.

§ 136s. Solicitation of comments; notice of public hearings

(a) The Administrator, before publishing regulations under this subchapter, shall solicit the views of the Secretary of Agriculture in accordance with the procedure described in section 136w(a) of this title.

(b) In addition to any other authority relating to public hearings and solicitation of views, in connection with the suspension or cancellation of a pesticide registration or any other actions authorized under this subchapter, the Administrator may, at his discretion, solicit the views of all interested persons, either orally or in writing, and seek such advice from scientists, farmers, farm organizations, and other qualified persons as he deems proper.

(c) In connection with all public hearings under this subchapter the Administrator shall publish timely notice of such hearings in the Federal Register.

(June 25, 1947, ch. 125, § 21, as added Oct. 21, 1972, Pub.L. 92–516, § 2, 86 Stat. 996, and amended Nov. 28, 1975, Pub.L. 94–140, § 2(b), 89 Stat. 752.)

Code of Federal Regulations

Debarment and suspension under EPA assistance programs, see 40 CFR 32.100 et seq.
Registration, reregistration and classification, see 40 CFR 162.1 et seq.

Library References

Agriculture ⚷9.
C.J.S. Agriculture § 83 et seq.

§ 136t. Delegation and cooperation

(a) Delegation.—All authority vested in the Administrator by virtue of the provisions of this subchapter may with like force and effect be executed by such employees of the Environmental Protection Agency as the Administrator may designate for the purpose.

(b) Cooperation.—The Administrator shall cooperate with Department of Agriculture, any other Federal agency, and any appropriate agency of any State or any political subdivision thereof, in carrying out the provisions of this subchapter, and in securing uniformity of regulations.

(June 25, 1947, ch. 125, § 22, as added Oct. 21, 1972, Pub.L. 92–516, § 2, 86 Stat. 996.)

Code of Federal Regulations

Debarment and suspension under EPA assistance programs, see 40 CFR 32.100 et seq.

Library References

Agriculture ⚷9.
Health and Environment ⚷25.5(9).
C.J.S. Agriculture § 83 et seq.
C.J.S. Health and Environment § 65 et seq.

§ 136u. State cooperation, aid, and training

(a) Cooperative agreements.—The Administrator may enter into cooperative agreements with States and Indian tribes—

(1) to delegate to any State or Indian tribe the authority to cooperate in the enforcement of this subchapter through the use of its personnel or facilities, to train personnel of the State or Indian tribe to cooperate in the enforcement of this subchapter, and to assist States and Indian tribes in implementing cooperative enforcement programs through grants-in-aid; and

(2) to assist States in developing and administering State programs, and Indian tribes that enter into cooperative agreements, to train and certify applicators consistent with the standards the Administrator prescribes.

Effective with the fiscal year beginning October 1, 1978, there are authorized to be appropriated annually such funds as may be necessary for the Administrator to provide through cooperative agreements an amount equal to 50 percent of the anticipated cost to each State or Indian tribe, as agreed to under such cooperative agreements, of conducting training and certification programs during such fiscal year. If funds sufficient to pay 50 percent of the costs for any year are not appropriated, the share of each State and Indian tribe shall be reduced in a like proportion in allocating available funds.

(b) Contracts for training.—In addition, the Administrator may enter into contracts with Federal, State, or Indian tribal agencies for the purpose of encouraging the training of certified applicators.

(c) Information and education.—The Administrator shall, in cooperation with the Secretary of Agriculture, use the services of the cooperative State extension services to inform and educate pesticide users about accepted uses and other regulations made under this subchapter.

(June 25, 1947, ch. 125, § 23, as added Oct. 21, 1972, Pub.L. 92–516, § 2, 86 Stat. 996, and amended Sept. 30, 1978, Pub.L. 95–396, § 21, 92 Stat. 834.)

Code of Federal Regulations

Assistance for continuing environmental programs, etc., see 40 CFR 35.001 et seq.
Grant policies and procedures, see 40 CFR 30.100 et seq.
Subagreements, see 40 CFR 33.001 et seq.
Training grants, etc., see 40 CFR 45.100 et seq.

Library References

Agriculture ⚷9.
C.J.S. Agriculture § 83 et seq.

§ 136v. Authority of States

(a) A State may regulate the sale or use of any federally registered pesticide or device in the State, but only if and to the extent the regulation does not permit any sale or use prohibited by this subchapter.

(b) Such State shall not impose or continue in effect any requirements for labeling or packaging in addition to or different from those required under this subchapter.

(c)(1) A State may provide registration for additional uses of federally registered pesticides formulated for distribution and use within that State to meet special local needs in accord with the purposes of this subchapter and if registration for such use has not previously been denied, disapproved, or canceled by the Administrator. Such registration shall be deemed registration under section 136a of this title for all purposes of this subchapter, but shall authorize distribution and use only within such State.

(2) A registration issued by a State under this subsection shall not be effective for more than ninety days if disapproved by the Administrator within that period. Prior to disapproval, the Administrator shall, except as provided in paragraph (3) of this subsection, advise the State of the Administrator's intention to disapprove and the reasons therefor, and provide the State time to respond. The Administrator shall not prohibit or disapprove a registration issued by a State under this subsection (A) on the basis of lack of essentiality of a pesticide or (B) except as provided in paragraph (3) of this subsection, if its composition and use patterns are similar to those of a federally registered pesticide.

(3) In no instance may a State issue a registration for a food or feed use unless there exists a tolerance or exemption under the Federal Food, Drug, and Cosmetic Act [21 U.S.C. 301 et seq.] that permits the residues of the pesticides on the food or feed. If the Administrator determines that a registration issued by a State is inconsistent with the Federal Food, Drug, and Cosmetic Act, or the use of, a pesticide under a registration issued by a State constitutes an imminent hazard, the Administrator may immediately disapprove the registration.

(4) If the Administrator finds, in accordance with standards set forth in regulations issued under section 136w of this title, that a State is not capable of exercising adequate controls to assure that State registration under this section will be in accord with the purposes of this subchapter or has failed to exercise adequate controls, the Administrator may suspend the authority of the State to register pesticides until such time as the Administrator is satisfied that the State can and will exercise adequate controls. Prior to any such suspension, the Administrator shall advise the State of the Administrator's intention to suspend and the reasons therefor and provide the State time to respond.

(June 25, 1947, ch. 125, § 24, as added Oct. 21, 1972, Pub.L. 92–516, § 2, 86 Stat. 997, and amended Sept. 30, 1978, Pub.L. 95–396, § 22, 92 Stat. 835.)

Code of Federal Regulations

Availability of information, see 40 CFR 2.100 et seq.
Debarment and suspension under EPA assistance programs, see 40 CFR 32.100 et seq.
State issuance of experimental use permits, see 40 CFR 170.20 et seq.

Library References

Agriculture ⚷9.
C.J.S. Agriculture § 83 et seq.

§ 136w. Authority of Administrator

(a) Regulations.

(1) Authorization.—The Administrator is authorized, in accordance with the procedure described in paragraph (2), to prescribe regulations to carry out the provisions of this subchapter. Such regulations shall take into account the difference in concept and usage between various classes of pesticides and differences in environmental risk and the appropriate data for evaluating such risk between agricultural and nonagricultural pesticides.

(2) Procedure.—

(A) Proposed regulations.—At least 60 days prior to signing any proposed regulation for publication in the Federal Register, the Administrator shall provide the Secretary of Agriculture with a copy of such regulation. If the Secretary comments in writing to the Administrator regarding any such regulation within 30 days after receiving it, the Administrator shall publish in the Federal Register (with the proposed regulation) the comments of the Secretary and the response of the Administrator with regard to the Secretary's comments. If the Secretary does not comment in writing to the Administrator regarding the regulation within 30 days after receiving it, the Administrator may sign such regulation for publication in the Federal Register any time after such 30-day period notwithstanding the foregoing 60-day time requirement.

(B) Final regulations.—At least 30 days prior to signing any regulation in final form for publication in the Federal Register, the Administrator shall provide the Secretary of Agriculture with a copy of such regulation. If the Secretary comments in writing to the Administrator regarding any such final regulation within 15 days after receiving it, the Administrator shall publish in the Federal Register (with the final regulation) the comments of the Secretary, if requested by the Secretary, and the response of the Administrator concerning the Secretary's comments. If the Secretary does not comment in writing to the Administrator regarding the regulation within 15 days after receiving it, the Administrator may sign such regulation for publication in the Federal Register at any time after such 15-day period notwithstanding the foregoing 30-day time requirement. In taking any final action under this subsection, the Administrator shall include among those factors to be taken into account the effect of the regulation on production and prices of agricultural commodities, retail food prices, and otherwise on the agricultural economy, and the Administrator shall publish in the Federal Register an analysis of such effect.

(C) Time requirements.—The time requirements imposed by subparagraphs (A) and (B) may be waived or modified to the extent agreed upon by the Administrator and the Secretary.

(D) Publication in the Federal Register.—The Administrator shall, simultaneously with any notification to the Secretary of Agriculture under this paragraph prior to the issuance of any proposed or final regulation, publish such notification in the Federal Register.

(3) Congressional committees.—At such time as the Administrator is required under paragraph (2) of this subsection to provide the Secretary of Agriculture with a copy of proposed regulations and a copy of the final form of regulations, he shall also furnish a copy of such regulations to the Committee on Agriculture of the House of Representatives and the Committee on Agriculture, Nutrition, and Forestry of the Senate.

(4) Rule and regulation review.—

(A) Congressional review.—Notwithstanding any other provision of this subchapter, simultaneously with promulgation of any rule or regulation under this subchapter, the Administrator shall transmit a copy thereof to the Secretary of the Senate and the Clerk of the House of Representatives. Except as provided in subparagraph (B), the rule or regulation shall not become effective, if within 90 calendar days of continuous session of Congress after the date of promulgation, both Houses of Congress adopt a concurrent resolution, the matter after the resolving clause of which is as follows: "That Congress disapproves the rule or regulation promulgated by the Administrator of the Environmental Protection Agency dealing with the matter of , which rule or regulation was transmitted to Congress on ", the blank spaces therein being appropriately filled.

(B) Effective date.—If at the end of 60 calendar days of continuous session of Congress after the date of promulgation of a rule or regulation, no committee of either House of Congress has reported or been discharged from further consideration of a concurrent resolution disapproving the rule or regulation, and neither House has adopted such a resolution, the rule or regulation may go into effect immediately. If, within such 60 calendar days, such a committee has reported or been discharged from further consideration of such a resolution, or either House has adopted such a resolution, the rule or regulation may go into effect not sooner than 90 calendar days of continuous session of Congress after its promulgation unless disapproved as provided in subparagraph (A).

(C) Computation of review period.—

For the purposes of subparagraphs (A) and (B) of this paragraph—

(i) continuity of session is broken only by an adjournment of Congress sine die; and

(ii) the days on which either House is not in session because of an adjournment of more than 3 days to a day certain are excluded in the computation of 60 and 90 calendar days of continuous session of Congress.

(D) Effect of Congressional inaction.—Congressional inaction on or rejection of a resolution of disapproval shall not be deemed an expression of approval of such rule.

(E) Judicial review.—

(i) Any interested party, including any person who participated in the rulemaking involved, may institute such actions in the appropriate district court of the United States, including actions for declaratory judgment, as may be appropriate to construe the constitutionality of any provision of this paragraph. The district court immediately shall certify all questions of the constitutionality of this paragraph to the United States court of appeals for the circuit involved, which shall hear the matter sitting en banc.

(ii) Notwithstanding any other provision of law, any decision on a matter certified under clause (i) of this subparagraph shall be reviewable by appeal directly to the Supreme Court of the United States. Such appeal shall be brought not later than 20 days after the decision of the court of appeals.

(b) Exemption of pesticides.—The Administrator may exempt from the requirements of this subchapter by regulation any pesticide which he determines either (1) to be adequately regulated by another Federal agency, or (2) to be of a character which is unnecessary to be subject to this subchapter in order to carry out the purposes of this subchapter.

(c) Other authority.—The Administrator, after notice and opportunity for hearing, is authorized—

(1) to declare a pest any form of plant or animal life (other than man and other than bacteria, virus, and other micro-organisms on or in living man or other living animals) which is injurious to health or the environment;

(2) to determine any pesticide which contains any substance or substances in quantities highly toxic to man;

(3) to establish standards (which shall be consistent with those established under the authority of the Poison Prevention Packaging Act (Public Law 91–601) [15 U.S.C. 1471 et seq.]) with respect to the package, container, or wrapping in which a pesticide or device is enclosed for use or consumption, in order to protect children and adults from serious injury or illness resulting from accidental ingestion or contact with pesticides or devices regulated by this subchapter as well as to accomplish the other purposes of this subchapter;

(4) to specify those classes of devices which shall be subject to any provision of section 136(q)(1) or section 136e of this title upon his determination that application of such provision is necessary to effectuate the purposes of this subchapter;

(5) to prescribe regulations requiring any pesticide to be colored or discolored if he determines that such requirement is feasible and is necessary for the protection of health and the environment; and

(6) to determine and establish suitable names to be used in the ingredient statement.

(d) Scientific advisory panel.—The Administrator shall submit to an advisory panel for comment as to the impact on health and the environment of the action proposed in notices of intent issued under section 136d(b) of this title and of the proposed and final form of regulations issued under subsection (a) of this section within the same time periods as provided for the comments of the Secretary of Agriculture under such section 136d(b) and subsection (a) of this section. The time requirements for notices of intent and proposed and final forms of regulation may not be modified or waived unless in addition to meeting the requirements of section 136d(b) of this title or subsection (a) of this section, as applicable, the advisory panel has failed to comment on the proposed action within the prescribed time period or has agreed to the modification or waiver. The Administrator shall also solicit from the advisory panel comments, evaluations, and recommendations for operating guidelines to improve the effectiveness and quality of scientific analyses made by personnel of the Environmental Protection Agency that lead to decisions by the Administrator in carrying out the provisions of this subchapter. The comments, evaluations, and recommendations of the advisory panel submitted under this subsection and the response of the Administrator shall be published in the Federal Register in the same manner as provided for publication of the comments of the Secretary of Agriculture under such sections. The chairman of the advisory panel, after consultation with the Administrator, may create temporary subpanels on specific projects to assist the full advisory panel in expediting and preparing its evaluations, comments, and recommendations. The subpanels may be composed of scientists other than members of the advisory panel, as deemed necessary for the purpose of evaluating scientific studies relied upon by the Administrator with respect to proposed action. Such additional scientists shall be selected by the advisory panel. The panel referred to in this subsection shall consist of 7 members appointed by the Administrator from a list of 12 nominees, 6 nominated by the National Institutes of Health and 6 by the National Science Foundation utilizing a system of staggered terms of appointment. Members of the panel shall be selected on the basis of their professional qualifications to assess the effects of the impact of pesticides on health and the environment. To the extent feasible to insure multidisciplinary representation, the panel membership shall include representation for the disciplines of toxicology, pathology, environmental biology, and related sciences. If a vacancy occurs on the panel due to expiration of a term, resignation, or any other reason, each replacement shall be selected by the Administrator from a group of 4 nominees, 2 submitted by each of the nominating entities named in this subsection. The Administrator may extend the term of a panel member until the new member is appointed to fill the vacancy. If a vacancy occurs due to resignation, or reason other than expiration of a term, the Administrator shall appoint a member to serve during the unexpired term utilizing the nomination process set forth in this subsection. Should the list of nominees provided under this subsection be unsatisfactory, the Administrator may request an additional set of nominees from the nominating entities. The Administrator may require such information from the nominees to the advisory panel as he deems necessary, and he shall publish in the Federal Register the name, address, and professional affiliations of each nominee. Each member of the panel shall receive per diem compensation at a rate not in excess of that fixed for GS–18 of the General Schedule as may be determined by the Administrator, except that any such member who holds another office or position under the Federal Government the compensation for which exceeds such rate may elect to receive compensation at the rate provided for such other office or position in lieu of the compensation provided by this subsection. In order to assure the objectivity of the advisory panel, the Administrator shall promulgate regulations regarding conflicts of interest with respect to the members of the panel. The advisory panel established under this subsection shall terminate September 30, 1987. In performing the functions assigned by this subchapter, the panel shall consult and coordinate its activities with the Science Advisory Board established under the Environmental Research, Development, and Demonstration Authorization Act of 1978 [42 U.S.C.A. § 4365]. Whenever the Administrator exercises authority under section 136d(c) of this title to immediately suspend the registration of any pesticide to prevent an imminent hazard, the Administrator shall promptly submit to the advisory panel for comment, as to the impact on health and the environment, the action taken to suspend the registration of such pesticide.

(e) Peer review.—The Administrator shall, by written procedures, provide for peer review with respect to the design, protocols, and conduct of major scientific studies conducted under this subchapter by the Environmental Protection Agency or by any other Federal agency, any State or political subdivision thereof, or any institution or individual under grant, contract, or cooperative agreement from or with the Environmental Protection Agency. In such procedures, the Administrator shall also provide for peer review, using the advisory panel established under subsection (d) of this section or appropriate experts appointed by the Administrator from a current list of nominees maintained by such panel, with respect to the results of any such scientific studies relied upon by the Administrator with respect to actions the Administrator may take relating to the change in classification, suspension, or cancellation of a pesticide: *Provided,* That whenever the Administrator determines that circumstances do not permit the peer review of the results of any such scientific study prior to the Administrator's exercising authority under section 136d(c) of this title to immediately suspend the registration of any pesticide to prevent an imminent hazard, the Administrator shall promptly thereafter provide for the conduct of peer review as provided in this sentence. The evaluations and relevant documentation constituting the peer review that relate to the proposed scientific studies and the results of the completed scientific studies shall be included in the submission for comment forwarded by the Administrator to the advisory panel as provided in subsection (d) of this section. As used in this subsection, the term "peer review" shall mean an independent evaluation by scientific experts, either within or outside the Environmental Protection Agency, in the appropriate disciplines.

(June 25, 1947, ch. 125, § 25, as added Oct. 21, 1972, Pub.L. 92–516, § 2, 86 Stat. 997, and amended Nov. 28, 1975, Pub.L. 94–140, §§ 2(a), 6, 7, 89 Stat. 751, 753; S.Res. 4, Feb. 4, 1977; Sept. 30, 1978, Pub.L. 95–396, § 23, 92 Stat. 836; Dec. 17, 1980, Pub.L. 96–539, §§ 1, 2(a), 4, 94 Stat. 3194, 3195; Dec. 2, 1983, Pub.L. 98–201, § 1, 97 Stat. 1379; Nov. 8, 1984, Pub.L. 98–620, Title IV, § 402(4)(D), 98 Stat. 3357.)

Code of Federal Regulations

Acceptance of certain pesticides and disposal and storage of pesticides and containers, see 40 CFR 165.1 et seq.
Books and records of production and distribution, see 40 CFR 169.1 et seq.
Certification of applicators, see 40 CFR 171.1 et seq.
Debarment and suspension under EPA assistance programs, see 40 CFR 32.100 et seq.
Enforcement, see 40 CFR 162.1 et seq.
Exemption of Federal and State agencies under emergency conditions, see 40 CFR 166.1 et seq.
Experimental use permits, see 40 CFR 172.1 et seq.
Policies and procedures for State and local assistance, see 40 CFR 35.001 et seq.
Procurement of supplies, services, and construction under assistance agreements of Environmental Protection Agency, see 40 CFR 33.001 et seq.
Registration of pesticide-producing establishments, submission of reports, and labeling, see 40 CFR 167.1.
Rescission of State primary enforcement responsibility for pesticide use violations, see 40 CFR 173.1 et seq.
Worker protection standards, see 40 CFR 170.1 et seq.

Library References

Agriculture ⚷9.
Health and Environment ⚷25.5(9).
C.J.S. Agriculture § 83 et seq.
C.J.S. Health and Environment § 65 et seq.

§ 136w–1. State primary enforcement responsibility

(a) For the purposes of this subchapter, a State shall have primary enforcement responsibility for pesticide use violations during any period for which the Administrator determines that such State—

(1) has adopted adequate pesticide use laws and regulations; *Provided,* That the Administrator may not require a State to have pesticide use laws that are more stringent than this subchapter;

(2) has adopted and is implementing adequate procedures for the enforcement of such State laws and regulations; and

(3) will keep such records and make such reports showing compliance with paragraphs (1) and (2) of this subsection as the Administrator may require by regulation.

(b) Notwithstanding the provisions of subsection (a) of this section, any State that enters into a cooperative agreement with the Administrator under section 136u of this title for the enforcement of pesticide use restrictions shall have the primary enforcement responsibility for pesticide use violations. Any State that has a plan approved by the Administrator in accordance with the requirements of section 136b of this title that the Administrator determines meets the criteria set out in subsection (a) of this section shall have the primary enforcement responsibility for pesticide use violations. The Administrator shall make such determinations with respect to State plans under section 136b of this title in effect on September 30, 1978, not later than six months after that date.

(c) The Administrator shall have primary enforcement responsibility for those States that do not have primary enforcement responsibility under this subchapter. Notwithstanding the provisions of section 136(e)(1) of this title, during any period when the Administrator has such enforcement responsibility, section 136f(b) of this title shall apply to the books and records of commercial applicators and to any applicator who holds or applies pesticides, or use[1] dilutions of pesticides, only to provide a service of controlling pests without delivering any unapplied pesticide to any person so served, and section 136g(a) of this title shall apply to the establishment or other place where pesticides or devices are held for application by such persons with respect to pesticides or devices held for such application.

(June 25, 1947, ch. 125, § 26, as added Sept. 30, 1978, Pub.L. 95–396, § 24(2), 92 Stat. 836.)

[1] So in original. Probably should be "uses".

Library References

Agriculture ⚿9.
C.J.S. Agriculture § 83 et seq.

§ 136w–2. Failure by the State to assure enforcement of State pesticide use regulations

(a) Upon receipt of any complaint or other information alleging or indicating a significant violation of the pesticide use provisions of this subchapter, the Administrator shall refer the matter to the appropriate State officials for their investigation of the matter consistent with the requirements of this subchapter. If, within thirty days, the State has not commenced appropriate enforcement action, the Administrator may act upon the complaint or information to the extent authorized under this subchapter.

(b) Whenever the Administrator determines that a State having primary enforcement responsibility for pesticide use violations is not carrying out (or cannot carry out due to the lack of adequate legal authority) such responsibility, the Administrator shall notify the State. Such notice shall specify those aspects of the administration of the State program that are determined to be inadequate. The State shall have ninety days after receipt of the notice to correct any deficiencies. If after that time the Administrator determines that the State program remains inadequate, the Administrator may rescind, in whole or in part, the State's primary enforcement responsibility for pesticide use violations.

(c) Neither section 136w–1 of this title nor this section shall limit the authority of the Administrator to enforce this subchapter, where the Administrator determines that emergency conditions exist that require immediate action on the part of the Administrator and the State authority is unwilling or unable adequately to respond to the emergency.

(June 25, 1947, ch. 125, § 27, as added Sept. 30, 1978, Pub.L. 95–396, § 24(2), 92 Stat. 837.)

Code of Federal Regulations

Rescission of State primary enforcement responsibility for pesticide use violations, see 40 CFR 173.1 et seq.

Library References

Agriculture ⚿9.
C.J.S. Agriculture § 83 et seq.

§ 136w–3. Identification of pests; cooperation with Department of Agriculture's program

The Administrator, in coordination with the Secretary of Agriculture, shall identify those pests that must be brought under control. The Administrator shall also coordinate and cooperate with the Secretary of Agriculture's research and implementation programs to develop and improve the safe use and effectiveness of chemical, biological, and alternative methods to combat and control pests that reduce the quality and economical production and distribution of agricultural products to domestic and foreign consumers.

(June 25, 1947, ch. 125, § 28, as added Sept. 30, 1978, Pub.L. 95–396, § 24(2), 92 Stat. 838.)

Library References

Agriculture ⚿9.
C.J.S. Agriculture § 83 et seq.

§ 136w–4. Annual report

The Administrator shall submit an annual report to Congress before February 16 of each year and the first report shall be due February 15, 1979. The report shall include the total number of applications for conditional registration under sections 136a(c)(7)(B) and 136a(c)(7)(C) of this title that were filed during the immediately preceding fiscal year, and, with respect to those applications approved, the Administrator shall report the Administrator's findings in each case, the conditions imposed and any modification of such conditions in each case, and the quantities produced of such pesticides.

(June 25, 1947, ch. 125, § 29, as added Sept. 30, 1978, Pub.L. 95–396, § 24(2), 92 Stat. 838.)

§ 136x. Severability

If any provision of this subchapter or the application thereof to any person or circumstance is held invalid, the invalidity shall not affect other provisions or applications of this subchapter which can be given effect without regard to the invalid provision or application, and to this end the provisions of this subchapter are severable.

(June 25, 1947, ch. 125, § 30, formerly § 26, as added Oct. 21, 1972, Pub.L. 92–516, § 2, 86 Stat. 998, and renumbered Sept. 30, 1978, Pub.L. 95–396, § 24(1), 92 Stat. 836.)

Library References

Statutes ⚿64(2).
C.J.S. Statutes § 96 et seq.

§ 136y. Authorization of appropriations

There is authorized to be appropriated to carry out this subchapter for the period beginning October 1, 1985, and ending September 30, 1986, $68,604,200 of which not more than $11,993,100 shall be available for research under this subchapter.

(June 25, 1947, ch. 125, § 31, formerly § 27, as added Oct. 21, 1972, Pub.L. 92–516, § 2, 86 Stat. 998, amended July 2, 1975, Pub.L. 94–51, 89 Stat. 257; Oct. 10, 1975, Pub.L. 94–109, 89 Stat. 571; Nov. 28, 1975, Pub.L. 94–140, § 3, 89 Stat. 752, and renumbered and amended Sept. 30, 1978, Pub.L. 95–396, §§ 24(1), 25, 92 Stat. 836, 838; Dec. 17, 1980, Pub.L. 96–539, § 3, 94 Stat. 3195; Dec. 2, 1983, Pub.L. 98–201, § 2, 97 Stat. 1380; Dec. 23, 1985, Pub.L. 99–198, Title XVII, § 1768, 99 Stat. 1656.)

Library References

United States ⚷85.
C.J.S. United States § 123.

TOXIC SUBSTANCES CONTROL

(15 U.S.C.A. §§ 2601 to 2629)

Related Provisions

See, also, Environmental Pesticide Control, 7 U.S.C.A. § 136 et seq., ante.

West's Federal Forms

Claim to article arrested, see § 11227.
Judgment of condemnation, forfeiture and destruction, see § 4543.
Jurisdiction and venue in district courts, see § 1003 et seq.
Service of process, see § 1201 et seq.
Subpoenas, see § 3981 et seq.

Code of Federal Regulations

Asbestos, see 40 CFR 763.100.
Asbestos—
Recordkeeping, see 40 CFR 763.114.
Chemical imports and exports, see 40 CFR 707.60 et seq.
Premanufacture notification, exemptions, see 40 CFR 723.175.
Rulemaking procedures, see 40 CFR 750.1 et seq.

WESTLAW Electronic Research

See WESTLAW guide following the Explanation pages of this pamphlet.

§ 2601. Findings, policy, and intent

(a) Findings

The Congress finds that—

(1) human beings and the environment are being exposed each year to a large number of chemical substances and mixtures;

(2) among the many chemical substances and mixtures which are constantly being developed and produced, there are some whose manufacture, processing, distribution in commerce, use, or disposal may present an unreasonable risk of injury to health or the environment; and

(3) the effective regulation of interstate commerce in such chemical substances and mixtures also necessitates the regulation of intrastate commerce in such chemical substances and mixtures.

(b) Policy

It is the policy of the United States that—

(1) adequate data should be developed with respect to the effect of chemical substances and mixtures on health and the environment and that the development of such data should be the responsibility of those who manufacture and those who process such chemical substances and mixtures;

(2) adequate authority should exist to regulate chemical substances and mixtures which present an unreasonable risk of injury to health or the environment, and to take action with respect to chemical substances and mixtures which are imminent hazards; and

(3) authority over chemical substances and mixtures should be exercised in such a manner as not to impede unduly or create unnecessary economic barriers to technological innovation while fulfilling the primary purpose of this chapter to assure that such innovation and commerce in such chemical substances and mixtures do not present an unreasonable risk of injury to health or the environment.

(c) Intent of Congress

It is the intent of Congress that the Administrator shall carry out this chapter in a reasonable and prudent manner, and that the Administrator shall consider the environmental, economic, and social impact of any action the Administrator takes or proposes to take under this chapter.

(Oct. 11, 1976, Pub.L. 94–469, Title I, § 2, 90 Stat. 2003, redesignated Oct. 22, 1986, Pub.L. 99–519, § 3(c)(1), 100 Stat. 2989.)

Code of Federal Regulations

Policies and procedures for the awarding of grants, see 40 CFR 30.100 et seq.

Library References

Health and Environment ⚷25.5(3).
C.J.S. Health and Environment § 91 et seq.

§ 2602. Definitions

As used in this chapter:

(1) The term "Administrator" means the Administrator of the Environmental Protection Agency.

(2)(A) Except as provided in subparagraph (B), the term "chemical substance" means any organic or inorganic substance of a particular molecular identity, including—

(i) any combination of such substances occurring in whole or in part as a result of a chemical reaction or occurring in nature and

(ii) any element or uncombined radical.

(B) Such term does not include—

(i) any mixture,

(ii) any pesticide (as defined in the Federal Insecticide, Fungicide, and Rodenticide Act [7 U.S.C. 136 et seq.]) when manufactured, processed, or distributed in commerce for use as a pesticide,

(iii) tobacco or any tobacco product,

(iv) any source material, special nuclear material, or byproduct material (as such terms are defined in the Atomic Energy Act of 1954 [42 U.S.C. 2011 et seq.] and regulations issued under such Act),

(v) any article the sale of which is subject to the tax imposed by section 4181 of the Internal Revenue Code of 1954 [26 U.S.C. 4181] (determined without regard to any exemptions from such tax provided by section 4182 or 4221 or any other provision of such Code), and

(vi) any food, food additive, drug, cosmetic, or device (as such terms are defined in section 201 of the Federal Food, Drug, and Cosmetic Act [21 U.S.C. 321]) when manufactured, processed, or distributed in commerce for use as a food, food additive, drug, cosmetic, or device.

The term "food" as used in clause (vi) of this subparagraph includes poultry and poultry products (as defined in sections 4(e) and 4(f) of the Poultry Products Inspection Act [21 U.S.C. 453(e) and (f)]), meat and meat food products (as defined in section 1(j) of the Federal Meat Inspection Act [21 U.S.C. 601(j)]), and eggs and egg products (as defined in section 4 of the Egg Products Inspection Act [21 U.S.C. 1033]).

(3) The term "commerce" means trade, traffic, transportation, or other commerce (A) between a place in a State and any place outside of such State, or (B) which affects trade, traffic, transportation, or commerce described in clause (A).

(4) The terms "distribute in commerce" and "distribution in commerce" when used to describe an action taken with respect to a chemical substance or mixture or article containing a substance or mixture mean to sell, or the sale of, the substance, mixture, or article in commerce; to introduce or deliver for introduction into commerce, or the introduction or delivery for introduction into commerce of, the substance, mixture, or article; or to hold, or the holding of, the substance, mixture, or article after its introduction into commerce.

(5) The term "environment" includes water, air, and land and the interrelationship which exists among and between water, air, and land and all living things.

(6) The term "health and safety study" means any study of any effect of a chemical substance or mixture on health or the environment or on both, including underlying data and epidemiological studies, studies of occupational exposure to a chemical substance or mixture, toxicological, clinical, and ecological studies of a chemical substance or mixture, and any test performed pursuant to this chapter.

(7) The term "manufacture" means to import into the customs territory of the United States (as defined in general headnote 2 of the Tariff Schedules of the United States), produce, or manufacture.

(8) The term "mixture" means any combination of two or more chemical substances if the combination does not occur in nature and is not, in whole or in part, the result of a chemical reaction; except that such term does include any combination which occurs, in whole or in part, as a result of a chemical reaction if none of the chemical substances comprising the combination is a new chemical substance and if the combination could have been manufactured for commercial purposes without a chemical reaction at the time the chemical substances comprising the combination were combined.

(9) The term "new chemical substance" means any chemical substance which is not included in the chemical substance list compiled and published under section 2607(b) of this title.

(10) The term "process" means the preparation of a chemical substance or mixture, after its manufacture, for distribution in commerce—

(A) in the same form or physical state as, or in a different form or physical state from, that in which it was received by the person so preparing such substance or mixture, or

(B) as part of an article containing the chemical substance or mixture.

(11) The term "processor" means any person who processes a chemical substance or mixture.

(12) The term "standards for the development of test data" means a prescription of—

(A) the—

(i) health and environmental effects, and

(ii) information relating to toxicity, persistence, and other characteristics which affect health and the environment, for which test data for a chemical substance or mixture are to be developed and any analysis that is to be performed on such data, and

(B) to the extent necessary to assure that data respecting such effects and characteristics are reliable and adequate—

(i) the manner in which such data are to be developed,

(ii) the specification of any test protocol or methodology to be employed in the development of such data, and

(iii) such other requirements as are necessary to provide such assurance.

(13) The term "State" means any State of the United States, the District of Columbia, the Commonwealth of Puerto Rico, the Virgin Islands, Guam, the Canal Zone, American Samoa, the Northern Mariana Islands, or any other territory or possession of the United States.

(14) The term "United States", when used in the geographic sense, means all of the States.

(Oct. 11, 1976, Pub.L. 94–469, Title I, § 3, 90 Stat. 2004, redesignated Oct. 22, 1986, Pub.L. 99–519, § 3(c)(1), 100 Stat. 2989.)

Library References

Health and Environment ⚷25.5(9).
C.J.S. Health and Environment § 65 et seq.

§ 2603. Testing of chemical substances and mixtures

(a) Testing requirements

If the Administrator finds that—

(1)(A)(i) the manufacture, distribution in commerce, processing, use, or disposal of a chemical substance or mixture, or that any combination of such activities, may present an unreasonable risk of injury to health or the environment,

(ii) there are insufficient data and experience upon which the effects of such manufacture, distribution in commerce, processing, use, or disposal of such substance or mixture or of any combination of such activities on health or the environment can reasonably be determined or predicted, and

(iii) testing of such substance or mixture with respect to such effects is necessary to develop such data; or

(B)(i) a chemical substance or mixture is or will be produced in substantial quantities, and (I) it enters or may reasonably be anticipated to enter the environment in substantial quantities or (II) there is or may be significant or substantial human exposure to such substance or mixture,

(ii) there are insufficient data and experience upon which the effects of the manufacture, distribution in commerce, processing, use, or disposal of such substance or mixture or of any combination of such activities on health or the environment can reasonably be determined or predicted, and

(iii) testing of such substance or mixture with respect to such effects is necessary to develop such data; and

(2) in the case of a mixture, the effects which the mixture's manufacture, distribution in commerce, processing, use, or disposal or any combination of such activities may have on health or the environment may not be reasonably and more efficiently determined or predicted by testing the chemical substances which comprise the mixture;

the Administrator shall by rule require that testing be conducted on such substance or mixture to develop data with respect to the health and environmental effects for which there is an insufficiency of data and experience and which are relevant to a determination that the manufacture, distribution in commerce, processing, use, or disposal of such substance or mixture, or that any combination of such activities, does or does not present an unreasonable risk of injury to health or the environment.

(b) Testing requirement rule

(1) A rule under subsection (a) of this section shall include—

(A) identification of the chemical substance or mixture for which testing is required under the rule,

(B) standards for the development of test data for such substance or mixture, and

(C) with respect to chemical substances which are not new chemical substances and to mixtures, a specification of the period (which period may not be of unreasonable duration) within which the persons required to conduct the testing shall submit to the Administrator data developed in accordance with the standards referred to in subparagraph (B).

In determining the standards and period to be included, pursuant to subparagraphs (B) and (C), in a rule under subsection (a) of this section, the Administrator's considerations shall include the relative costs of the various test protocols and methodologies which may be required under the rule and the reasonably foreseeable availability of the facilities and personnel needed to perform the testing required under the rule. Any such rule may require the submission to the Administrator of preliminary data during the period prescribed under subparagraph (C).

(2)(A) The health and environmental effects for which standards for the development of test data may be prescribed include carcinogenesis, mutagenesis, teratogenesis, behavioral disorders, cumulative or synergistic effects, and any other effect which may present an unreasonable risk of injury to health or the environment. The characteristics of chemical substances and mixtures for which such standards may be prescribed include persistence, acute toxicity, subacute toxicity, chronic toxicity, and any other characteristic which may present such a risk. The methodologies that may be prescribed in such standards include epidemiologic studies, serial or hierarchical tests, in vitro tests, and whole animal tests, except that before prescribing epidemiologic studies of employees, the Administrator shall consult with the Director of the National Institute for Occupational Safety and Health.

(B) From time to time, but not less than once each 12 months, the Administrator shall review the adequacy of the standards for development of data prescribed in rules under subsection (a) of this section and shall, if necessary, institute proceedings to make appropriate revisions of such standards.

(3)(A) A rule under subsection (a) of this section respecting a chemical substance or mixture shall require the persons described in subparagraph (B) to conduct tests and submit data to the Administrator on such substance or mixture, except that the Administrator may permit two or more of such persons to designate one such person or a qualified third party to conduct such tests and submit such data on behalf of the persons making the designation.

(B) The following persons shall be required to conduct tests and submit data on a chemical substance or mixture subject to a rule under subsection (a) of this section:

(i) Each person who manufactures or intends to manufacture such substance or mixture if the Administrator makes a finding described in subsection (a)(1)(A)(ii) or (a)(1)(B)(ii) of this section with respect to the manufacture of such substance or mixture.

(ii) Each person who processes or intends to process such substance or mixture if the Administrator makes a finding described in subsection (a)(1)(A)(ii) or (a)(1)(B)(ii) of this section with respect to the processing of such substance or mixture.

(iii) Each person who manufactures or processes or intends to manufacture or process such substance or mixture if the Administrator makes a finding described in subsection (a)(1)(A)(ii) or (a)(1)(B)(ii) of this section with respect to the distribution in commerce, use, or disposal of such substance or mixture.

(4) Any rule under subsection (a) of this section requiring the testing of and submission of data for a particular chemical substance or mixture shall expire at the end of the reimbursement period (as defined in subsection (c)(3)(B) of this section) which is applicable to test data for such substance or mixture unless the Administrator repeals the rule before such date; and a rule under subsection (a) of this section requiring the testing of and submission of data for a category of chemical substances or mixtures shall expire with respect to a chemical substance or mixture included in the category at the end of the reimbursement period (as so defined) which is applicable to test data for such substance or mixture unless the Administrator before such date repeals the application of the rule to such substance or mixture or repeals the rule.

(5) Rules issued under subsection (a) of this section (and any substantive amendment thereto or repeal thereof) shall be promulgated pursuant to section 553 of title 5 except that (A) the Administrator shall give interested persons an opportunity for the oral presentation of data, views, or arguments, in addition to an opportunity to make written submissions; (B) a transcript shall be made of any oral presentation; and (C) the Administrator shall make and publish with the rule the findings described in paragraph (1)(A) or (1)(B) of subsection (a) of this section and, in the case of a rule respecting a mixture, the finding described in paragraph (2) of such subsection.

(c) Exemption

(1) Any person required by a rule under subsection (a) of this section to conduct tests and submit data on a chemical substance or mixture may apply to the Administrator (in such form and manner as the Administrator shall prescribe) for an exemption from such requirement.

(2) If, upon receipt of an application under paragraph (1), the Administrator determines that—

(A) the chemical substance or mixture with respect to which such application was submitted is equivalent to a chemical substance or mixture for which data has been submitted to the Administrator in accordance with a rule under subsection (a) of this section or for which data is being developed pursuant to such a rule, and

(B) submission of data by the applicant on such substance or mixture would be duplicative of data which has been submitted to the Administrator in accordance with such rule or which is being developed pursuant to such rule, the Administrator shall exempt, in accordance with paragraph (3) or (4), the applicant from conducting tests and submitting data on such substance or mixture under the rule with respect to which such application was submitted.

(3)(A) If the exemption under paragraph (2) of any person from the requirement to conduct tests and submit test data on a chemical substance or mixture is granted on the basis of the existence of previously submitted test data and if such exemption is granted during the reimbursement period for such test data (as prescribed by subparagraph (B)), then (unless such person and the persons referred to in clauses (i) and (ii) agree on the amount and method of reimbursement) the Administrator shall order the person granted the exemption to provide fair and equitable reimbursement (in an amount determined under rules of the Administrator)—

(i) to the person who previously submitted such test data, for a portion of the costs incurred by such person in complying with the requirement to submit such data, and

(ii) to any other person who has been required under this subparagraph to contribute with respect to such costs, for a portion of the amount such person was required to contribute.

In promulgating rules for the determination of fair and equitable reimbursement to the persons described in clauses (i) and (ii) for costs incurred with respect to a chemical substance or mixture, the Administrator shall, after consultation with the Attorney General and the Federal Trade Commission, consider all relevant factors, including the effect on the competitive position of the person required to provide reimbursement in relation to the person to be reimbursed and the share of the market for such substance or mixture of the person required to provide reimbursement in relation to the share of such market of the persons to be reimbursed. An order under this subparagraph shall, for purposes of judicial review, be considered final agency action.

(B) For purposes of subparagraph (A), the reimbursement period for any test data for a chemical substance or mixture is a period—

(i) beginning on the date such data is submitted in accordance with a rule promulgated under subsection (a) of this section, and

(ii) ending—

(I) five years after the date referred to in clause (i), or

(II) at the expiration of a period which begins on the date referred to in clause (i) and which is equal to the period which the Administrator determines was necessary to develop such data,

whichever is later.

(4)(A) If the exemption under paragraph (2) of any person from the requirement to conduct tests and submit test data on a chemical substance or mixture is granted on the basis of the fact that test data is being developed by one or more persons pursuant to a rule promulgated under subsection (a) of this section, then (unless such person and the persons referred to in clauses (i) and (ii) agree on the amount and method of reimbursement) the Administrator shall order the person granted the exemption to provide fair and equitable reimbursement (in an amount determined under rules of the Administrator)—

(i) to each such person who is developing such test data, for a portion of the costs incurred by each such person in complying with such rule, and

(ii) to any other person who has been required under this subparagraph to contribute with respect to the costs of complying with such rule, for a portion of the amount such person was required to contribute.

In promulgating rules for the determination of fair and equitable reimbursement to the persons described in clauses (i) and (ii) for costs incurred with respect to a chemical substance or mixture, the Administrator shall, after consultation with the Attorney General and the Federal Trade Commission, consider the factors described in the second sentence of paragraph (3)(A). An order under this subparagraph shall, for purposes of judicial review, be considered final agency action.

(B) If any exemption is granted under paragraph (2) on the basis of the fact that one or more persons are developing test data pursuant to a rule promulgated under subsection (a) of this section and if after such exemption is granted the Administrator determines that no such person has complied with such rule, the Administrator shall (i) after providing written notice to the person who holds such exemption and an opportunity for a hearing, by order terminate such exemption, and (ii) notify in writing such person of the requirements of the rule with respect to which such exemption was granted.

(d) Notice

Upon the receipt of any test data pursuant to a rule under subsection (a) of this section, the Administrator shall publish a notice of the receipt of such data in the Federal Register within 15 days of its receipt. Subject to section 2613 of this title, each such notice shall (1) identify the chemical substance or mixture for which data have been received; (2) list the uses or intended uses of such substance or mixture and the information required by the applicable standards for the development of test data; and (3) describe the nature of the test data developed. Except as otherwise provided in section 2613 of this title, such data shall be made available by the Administrator for examination by any person.

(e) Priority list

(1)(A) There is established a committee to make recommendations to the Administrator respecting the chemical substances and mixtures to which the Administrator should give priority consideration for the promulgation of a rule under subsection (a) of this section. In making such a recommendation with respect to any chemical substance or mixture, the committee shall consider all relevant factors, including—

(i) the quantities in which the substance or mixture is or will be manufactured,

(ii) the quantities in which the substance or mixture enters or will enter the environment,

(iii) the number of individuals who are or will be exposed to the substance or mixture in their places of employment and the duration of such exposure,

(iv) the extent to which human beings are or will be exposed to the substance or mixture,

(v) the extent to which the substance or mixture is closely related to a chemical substance or mixture which is known to present an unreasonable risk of injury to health or the environment,

(vi) the existence of data concerning the effects of the substance or mixture on health or the environment,

(vii) the extent to which testing of the substance or mixture may result in the development of data upon which the effects of the substance or mixture on health or the environment can reasonably be determined or predicted, and

(viii) the reasonably foreseeable availability of facilities and personnel for performing testing on the substance or mixture.

The recommendations of the committee shall be in the form of a list of chemical substances and mixtures which shall be set forth, either by individual substance or mixture or by groups of substances or mixtures, in the order in which the committee determines the Administrator should take action under subsection (a) of this section with respect to the substances and mixtures. In establishing such list, the committee shall give priority attention to those chemical substances and mixtures which are known to cause or contribute to or which are suspected of causing or contributing to cancer, gene mutations, or birth defects. The committee shall designate chemical substances and mixtures on the list with respect to which the committee determines the Administrator should, within 12 months of the date on which such substances and mixtures are first designated, initiate a proceeding under subsection (a) of this section. The total number of chemical substances and mixtures on the list which are designated under the preceding sentence may not, at any time, exceed 50.

(B) As soon as practicable but not later than nine months after January 1, 1977, the committee shall publish in the Federal Register and transmit to the Administrator the list and designations required by subparagraph (A) together with the reasons for the committee's inclusion of each chemical substance or mixture on the list. At least every six months after the date of the transmission to the Administrator of the list pursuant to the preceeding[1] sentence, the committee shall make such revisions in the list as it determines to be necessary and shall transmit them to the Administrator together with the committee's reasons for the revisions. Upon receipt of any such revision, the Administrator shall publish in the Federal Register the list with such revision, the reasons for such revision, and the designations made under subparagraph (A). The Administrator shall provide reasonable opportunity to any interested person to file with the Administrator written comments on the committee's list, any revision of such list by the committee, and designations made by the committee, and shall make such comments available to the public. Within the 12-month period beginning on the date of the first inclusion on the list of a chemical substance or mixture designated by the committee under subparagraph (A) the Administrator shall with respect to such chemical substance or mixture either initiate a rulemaking proceeding under subsection (a) of this section or if such a proceeding is not initiated within such period, publish in the Federal Register the Administrator's reason for not initiating such a proceeding.

(2)(A) The committee established by paragraph (1)(A) shall consist of eight members as follows:

(i) One member appointed by the Administrator from the Environmental Protection Agency.

(ii) One member appointed by the Secretary of Labor from officers or employees of the Department of Labor engaged in the Secretary's activities under the Occupational Safety and Health Act of 1970 [29 U.S.C. 651 et seq.].

(iii) One member appointed by the Chairman of the Council on Environmental Quality from the Council or its officers or employees.

(iv) One member appointed by the Director of the National Institute for Occupational Safety and Health from officers or employees of the Institute.

(v) One member appointed by the Director of the National Institute of Environmental Health

Sciences from officers or employees of the Institute.

(vi) One member appointed by the Director of the National Cancer Institute from officers or employees of the Institute.

(vii) One member appointed by the Director of the National Science Foundation from officers or employees of the Foundation.

(viii) One member appointed by the Secretary of Commerce from officers or employees of the Department of Commerce.

(B)(i) An appointed member may designate an individual to serve on the committee on the member's behalf. Such a designation may be made only with the approval of the applicable appointing authority and only if the individual is from the entity from which the member was appointed.

(ii) No individual may serve as a member of the committee for more than four years in the aggregate. If any member of the committee leaves the entity from which the member was appointed, such member may not continue as a member of the committee, and the member's position shall be considered to be vacant. A vacancy in the committee shall be filled in the same manner in which the original appointment was made.

(iii) Initial appointments to the committee shall be made not later than the 60th day after January 1, 1977. Not later than the 90th day after such date the members of the committee shall hold a meeting for the selection of a chairperson from among their number.

(C)(i) No member of the committee, or designee of such member, shall accept employment or compensation from any person subject to any requirement of this chapter or of any rule promulgated or order issued thereunder, for a period of at least 12 months after termination of service on the committee.

(ii) No person, while serving as a member of the committee, or designee of such member, may own any stocks or bonds, or have any pecuniary interest, of substantial value in any person engaged in the manufacture, processing, or distribution in commerce of any chemical substance or mixture subject to any requirement of this chapter or of any rule promulgated or order issued thereunder.

(iii) The Administrator, acting through attorneys of the Environmental Protection Agency, or the Attorney General may bring an action in the appropriate district court of the United States to restrain any violation of this subparagraph.

(D) The Administrator shall provide the committee such administrative support services as may be necessary to enable the committee to carry out its function under this subsection.

(f) Required actions

Upon the receipt of—

(1) any test data required to be submitted under this chapter, or

(2) any other information available to the Administrator,

which indicates to the Administrator that there may be a reasonable basis to conclude that a chemical substance or mixture presents or will present a significant risk of serious or widespread harm to human beings from cancer, gene mutations, or birth defects, the Administrator shall, within the 180-day period beginning on the date of the receipt of such data or information, initiate appropriate action under section 2604, 2605, or 2606 of this title to prevent or reduce to a sufficient extent such risk or publish in the Federal Register a finding that such risk is not unreasonable. For good cause shown the Administrator may extend such period for an additional period of not more than 90 days. The Administrator shall publish in the Federal Register notice of any such extension and the reasons therefor. A finding by the Administrator that a risk is not unreasonable shall be considered agency action for purposes of judicial review under chapter 7 of title 5. This subsection shall not take effect until two years after January 1, 1977.

(g) Petition for standards for the development of test data

A person intending to manufacture or process a chemical substance for which notice is required under section 2604(a) of this title and who is not required under a rule under subsection (a) of this section to conduct tests and submit data on such substance may petition the Administrator to prescribe standards for the development of test data for such substance. The Administrator shall by order either grant or deny any such petition within 60 days of its receipt. If the petition is granted, the Administrator shall prescribe such standards for such substance within 75 days of the date the petition is granted. If the petition is denied, the Administrator shall publish, subject to section 2613 of this title, in the Federal Register the reasons for such denial.

(Oct. 11, 1976, Pub.L. 94–469, Title I, § 4, 90 Stat. 2006, redesignated Oct. 22, 1986, Pub.L. 99–519, § 3(c)(1), 100 Stat. 2989.)

[1] So in original. Probably should be "preceding".

Library References

Health and Environment ⇐25.5(3).
C.J.S. Health and Environment § 91 et seq.

§ 2604. Manufacturing and processing notices

(a) In general

(1) Except as provided in subsection (h) of this section, no person may—

(A) manufacture a new chemical substance on or after the 30th day after the date on which the Administrator first publishes the list required by section 2607(b) of this title, or

(B) manufacture or process any chemical substance for a use which the Administrator has determined, in accordance with paragraph (2), is a significant new use,

unless such person submits to the Administrator, at least 90 days before such manufacture or processing, a notice, in accordance with subsection (d) of this section, of such person's intention to manufacture or process such substance and such person complies with any applicable requirement of subsection (b) of this section.

(2) A determination by the Administrator that a use of a chemical substance is a significant new use with respect to which notification is required under paragraph (1) shall be made by a rule promulgated after a consideration of all relevant factors, including—

(A) the projected volume of manufacturing and processing of a chemical substance,

(B) the extent to which a use changes the type or form of exposure of human beings or the environment to a chemical substance,

(C) the extent to which a use increases the magnitude and duration of exposure of human beings or the environment to a chemical substance, and

(D) the reasonably anticipated manner and methods of manufacturing, processing, distribution in commerce, and disposal of a chemical substance.

(b) Submission of test data

(1)(A) If (i) a person is required by subsection (a)(1) of this section to submit a notice to the Administrator before beginning the manufacture or processing of a chemical substance, and (ii) such person is required to submit test data for such substance pursuant to a rule promulgated under section 2603 of this title before the submission of such notice, such person shall submit to the Administrator such data in accordance with such rule at the time notice is submitted in accordance with subsection (a)(1) of this section.

(B) If—

(i) a person is required by subsection (a)(1) of this section to submit a notice to the Administrator, and

(ii) such person has been granted an exemption under section 2603(c) of this title from the requirements of a rule promulgated under section 2603 of this title before the submission of such notice,

such person may not, before the expiration of the 90 day period which begins on the date of the submission in accordance with such rule of the test data the submission or development of which was the basis for the exemption, manufacture such substance if such person is subject to subsection (a)(1)(A) of this section or manufacture or process such substance for a significant new use if the person is subject to subsection (a)(1)(B) of this section.

(2)(A) If a person—

(i) is required by subsection (a)(1) of this section to submit a notice to the Administrator before beginning the manufacture or processing of a chemical substance listed under paragraph (4), and

(ii) is not required by a rule promulgated under section 2603 of this title before the submission of such notice to submit test data for such substance,

such person shall submit to the Administrator data prescribed by subparagraph (B) at the time notice is submitted in accordance with subsection (a)(1) of this section.

(B) Data submitted pursuant to subparagraph (A) shall be data which the person submitting the data believes show that—

(i) in the case of a substance with respect to which notice is required under subsection (a)(1)(A) of this section, the manufacture, processing, distribution in commerce, use, and disposal of the chemical substance or any combination of such activities will not present an unreasonable risk of injury to health or the environment, or

(ii) in the case of a chemical substance with respect to which notice is required under subsection (a)(1)(B) of this section, the intended significant new use of the chemical substance will not present an unreasonable risk of injury to health or the environment.

(3) Data submitted under paragraph (1) or (2) shall be made available, subject to section 2613 of this title, for examination by interested persons.

(4)(A)(i) The Administrator may, by rule, compile and keep current a list of chemical substances with respect to which the Administrator finds that the manufacture, processing, distribution in commerce, use, or disposal, or any combination of such activities, presents or may present an unreasonable risk of injury to health or the environment.

(ii) In making a finding under clause (i) that the manufacture, processing, distribution in commerce, use, or disposal of a chemical substance or any combination of such activities presents or may present an unreasonable risk of injury to health or the environment, the Administrator shall consider all relevant factors, including—

(I) the effects of the chemical substance on health and the magnitude of human exposure to such substance; and

(II) the effects of the chemical substance on the environment and the magnitude of environmental exposure to such substance.

(B) The Administrator shall, in prescribing a rule under subparagraph (A) which lists any chemical substance, identify those uses, if any, which the Administrator determines, by rule under subsection (a)(2) of this section, would constitute a significant new use of such substance.

(C) Any rule under subparagraph (A), and any substantive amendment or repeal of such a rule, shall be promulgated pursuant to the procedures specified in section 553 of title 5, except that (i) the Administrator shall give interested persons an opportunity for the oral presentation of data, views, or arguments, in addition to an opportunity to make written submissions, (ii) a transcript shall be kept of any oral presentation, and (iii) the Administrator shall make and publish with the rule the finding described in subparagraph (A).

(c) Extension of notice period

The Administrator may for good cause extend for additional periods (not to exceed in the aggregate 90 days) the period, prescribed by subsection (a) or (b) of this section before which the manufacturing or processing of a chemical substance subject to such subsection may begin. Subject to section 2613 of this title, such an extension and the reasons therefor shall be published in the Federal Register and shall constitute a final agency action subject to judicial review.

(d) Content of notice; publications in the Federal Register

(1) The notice required by subsection (a) of this section shall include—

(A) insofar as known to the person submitting the notice or insofar as reasonably ascertainable, the information described in subparagraphs (A), (B), (C), (D), (F), and (G) of section 2607(a)(2) of this title, and

(B) in such form and manner as the Administrator may prescribe, any test data in the possession or control of the person giving such notice which are related to the effect of any manufacture, processing, distribution in commerce, use, or disposal of such substance or any article containing such substance, or of any combination of such activities, on health or the environment, and

(C) a description of any other data concerning the environmental and health effects of such substance, insofar as known to the person making the notice or insofar as reasonably ascertainable.

Such a notice shall be made available, subject to section 2613 of this title, for examination by interested persons.

(2) Subject to section 2613 of this title, not later than five days (excluding Saturdays, Sundays and legal holidays) after the date of the receipt of a notice under subsection (a) of this section or of data under subsection (b) of this section, the Administrator shall publish in the Federal Register a notice which—

(A) identifies the chemical substance for which notice or data has been received;

(B) lists the uses or intended uses of such substance; and

(C) in the case of the receipt of data under subsection (b) of this section, describes the nature of the tests performed on such substance and any data which was developed pursuant to subsection (b) of this section or a rule under section 2603 of this title.

A notice under this paragraph respecting a chemical substance shall identify the chemical substance by generic class unless the Administrator determines that more specific identification is required in the public interest.

(3) At the beginning of each month the Administrator shall publish a list in the Federal Register of (A) each chemical substance for which notice has been received under subsection (a) of this section and for which the notification period prescribed by subsection (a), (b), or (c) of this section has not expired, and (B) each chemical substance for which such notification period has expired since the last publication in the Federal Register of such list.

(e) Regulation pending development of information

(1)(A) If the Administrator determines that—

(i) the information available to the Administrator is insufficient to permit a reasoned evaluation of the health and environmental effects of a chemical substance with respect to which notice is required by subsection (a) of this section; and

(ii)(I) in the absence of sufficient information to permit the Administrator to make such an evaluation, the manufacture, processing, distribution in commerce, use, or disposal of such substance, or any combination of such activities, may present an unreasonable risk of injury to health or the environment, or

(II) such substance is or will be produced in substantial quantities, and such substance either enters or may reasonably be anticipated to enter the environment in substantial quantities or there is or may be significant or substantial human exposure to the substance,

the Administrator may issue a proposed order, to take effect on the expiration of the notification period applicable to the manufacturing or processing of such substance under subsection (a), (b), or (c) of this section, to prohibit or limit the manufacture, processing, distribution in commerce, use, or disposal of such substance or to prohibit or limit any combination of such activities.

(B) A proposed order may not be issued under subparagraph (A) respecting a chemical substance (i) later than 45 days before the expiration of the notification period applicable to the manufacture or processing of such substance under subsection (a), (b), or (c) of this section, and (ii) unless the Administrator has, on or before the issuance of the proposed order, notified, in writing, each manufacturer or processor, as the case may be, of such substance of the determination which underlies such order.

(C) If a manufacturer or processor of a chemical substance to be subject to a proposed order issued under subparagraph (A) files with the Administrator (within the 30-day period beginning on the date such manufacturer or processor received the notice required by subparagraph (B)(ii)) objections specifying with particularity the provisions of the order deemed objectionable and stating the grounds therefor, the proposed order shall not take effect.

(2)(A)(i) Except as provided in clause (ii), if with respect to a chemical substance with respect to which notice is required by subsection (a) of this section, the Administrator makes the determination described in paragraph (1)(A) and if—

(I) the Administrator does not issue a proposed order under paragraph (1) respecting such substance, or

(II) the Administrator issues such an order respecting such substance but such order does not take effect because objections were filed under paragraph (1)(C) with respect to it,

the Administrator, through attorneys of the Environmental Protection Agency, shall apply to the United States District Court for the District of Columbia or the United States district court for the judicial district in which the manufacturer or processor, as the case may be, of such substance is found, resides, or transacts business for an injunction to prohibit or limit the manufacture, processing, distribution in commerce, use, or disposal of such substance (or to prohibit or limit any combination of such activities).

(ii) If the Administrator issues a proposed order under paragraph (1)(A) respecting a chemical substance but such order does not take effect because objections have been filed under paragraph (1)(C) with respect to it, the Administrator is not required to apply for an injunction under clause (i) respecting such substance if the Administrator determines, on the basis of such objections, that the determinations under paragraph (1)(A) may not be made.

(B) A district court of the United States which receives an application under subparagraph (A)(i) for an injunction respecting a chemical substance shall issue such injunction if the court finds that—

(i) the information available to the Administrator is insufficient to permit a reasoned evaluation of the health and environmental effects of a chemical substance with respect to which notice is required by subsection (a) of this section; and

(ii)(I) in the absence of sufficient information to permit the Administrator to make such an evaluation, the manufacture, processing, distribution in commerce, use, or disposal of such substance, or any combination of such activities, may present an unreasonable risk of injury to health or the environment, or

(II) such substance is or will be produced in substantial quantities, and such substance either enters or may reasonably be anticipated to enter the environment in substantial quantities or there is or may be significant or substantial human exposure to the substance.

(C) Pending the completion of a proceeding for the issuance of an injunction under subparagraph (B) respecting a chemical substance, the court may, upon application of the Administrator made through attorneys of the Environmental Protection Agency, issue a temporary restraining order or a preliminary injunction to prohibit the manufacture, processing, distribution in commerce, use, or disposal of such a substance (or any combination of such activities) if the court finds that the notification period applicable under subsection (a), (b), or (c) of this section to the manufacturing or processing of such substance may expire before such proceeding can be completed.

(D) After the submission to the Administrator of test data sufficient to evaluate the health and environmental effects of a chemical substance subject to an injunction issued under subparagraph (B) and the evaluation of such data by the Administrator, the district court of the United States which issued such injunction shall, upon petition, dissolve the injunction unless the Administrator has initiated a proceeding for the issuance of a rule under section 2605(a) of this title respecting the substance. If such a proceeding has been initiated, such court shall continue the injunction in effect until the effective date of the rule promulgated in such proceeding or, if such proceeding is terminated without the promulgation of a rule, upon the termination of the proceeding, whichever occurs first.

(f) Protection against unreasonable risks

(1) If the Administrator finds that there is a reasonable basis to conclude that the manufacture, processing, distribution in commerce, use, or disposal of a chemical substance with respect to which notice is required by subsection (a) of this section, or that any combination of such activities, presents or will present an unreasonable risk of injury to health or environment before a rule promulgated under section 2605 of this title can protect against such risk, the Administrator shall, before the expiration of the notification period applicable under subsection (a), (b), or (c) of this section to the manufacturing or processing of such substance, take the action authorized by paragraph (2) or (3) to the extent necessary to protect against such risk.

(2) The Administrator may issue a proposed rule under section 2605(a) of this title to apply to a chemical substance with respect to which a finding was made under paragraph (1)—

(A) a requirement limiting the amount of such substance which may be manufactured, processed, or distributed in commerce,

(B) a requirement described in paragraph (2), (3), (4), (5), (6), or (7) of section 2605(a) of this title, or

(C) any combination of the requirements referred to in subparagraph (B).

Such a proposed rule shall be effective upon its publication in the Federal Register. Section 2605(d)(2)(B) of this title shall apply with respect to such rule.

(3)(A) The Administrator may—

(i) issue a proposed order to prohibit the manufacture, processing, or distribution in commerce of a substance with respect to which a finding was made under paragraph (1), or

(ii) apply, through attorneys of the Environmental Protection Agency, to the United States District Court for the District of Columbia or the United States district court for the judicial district in which the manufacturer, or processor, as the case may be, of such substance, is found, resides, or transacts business for an injunction to prohibit the manufacture, processing, or distribution in commerce of such substance.

A proposed order issued under clause (i) respecting a chemical substance shall take effect on the expiration of the notification period applicable under subsection (a), (b), or (c) of this section to the manufacture or processing of such substance.

(B) If the district court of the United States to which an application has been made under subparagraph (A)(ii) finds that there is a reasonable basis to conclude that the manufacture, processing, distribution in commerce, use, or disposal of the chemical substance with respect to which such application was made, or that any combination of such activities, presents or will present an unreasonable risk of injury to health or the environment before a rule promulgated under section 2605 of this title can protect against such risk, the court shall issue an injunction to prohibit the manufacture, processing, or distribution in commerce of such substance or to prohibit any combination of such activities.

(C) The provisions of subparagraphs (B) and (C) of subsection (e)(1) of this section shall apply with respect to an order issued under clause (i) of subparagraph (A); and the provisions of subparagraph (C) of subsection (e)(2) of this section shall apply with respect to an injunction issued under subparagraph (B).

(D) If the Administrator issues an order pursuant to subparagraph (A)(i) respecting a chemical substance and objections are filed in accordance with subsection (e)(1)(C) of this section, the Administrator shall seek an injunction under subparagraph (A)(ii) respecting such substance unless the Administrator determines, on the basis of such objections, that such substance does not or will not present an unreasonable risk of injury to health or the environment.

(g) Statement of reasons for not taking action

If the Administrator has not initiated any action under this section or section 2605 or 2606 of this title to prohibit or limit the manufacture, processing, distribution in commerce, use, or disposal of a chemical substance, with respect to which notification or data is required by subsection (a)(1)(B) or (b) of this section, before the expiration of the notification period applicable to the manufacturing or processing of such substance, the Administrator shall publish a statement of the Administrator's reasons for not initiating such action. Such a statement shall be published in the Federal Register before the expiration of such period. Publication of such statement in accordance with the preceding sentence is not a prerequisite to the manufacturing or processing of the substance with respect to which the statement is to be published.

(h) Exemptions

(1) The Administrator may, upon application, exempt any person from any requirement of subsection (a) or (b) of this section to permit such person to manufacture or process a chemical substance for test marketing purposes—

(A) upon a showing by such person satisfactory to the Administrator that the manufacture, processing, distribution in commerce, use, and disposal of such substance, and that any combination of such activities, for such purposes will not present any unreasonable risk of injury to health or the environment, and

(B) under such restrictions as the Administrator considers appropriate.

(2)(A) The Administrator may, upon application, exempt any person from the requirement of subsection (b)(2) of this section to submit data for a chemical substance. If, upon receipt of an application under the preceding sentence, the Administrator determines that—

(i) the chemical substance with respect to which such application was submitted is equivalent to a chemical substance for which data has been submitted to the Administrator as required by subsection (b)(2) of this section, and

(ii) submission of data by the applicant on such substance would be duplicative of data which has been submitted to the Administrator in accordance with such subsection,

the Administrator shall exempt the applicant from the requirement to submit such data on such substance. No exemption which is granted under this subparagraph with respect to the submission of data for a chemical substance may take effect before the beginning of the reimbursement period applicable to such data.

(B) If the Administrator exempts any person, under subparagraph (A), from submitting data required under subsection (b)(2) of this section for a chemical substance because of the existence of previously submitted data and if such exemption is granted during the reimbursement period for such data, then (unless such person and the persons referred to in clauses (i) and (ii) agree on the amount and method of reimbursement) the Administrator shall order the person granted the exemption to provide fair and equitable reimbursement (in an amount determined under rules of the Administrator)—

(i) to the person who previously submitted the data on which the exemption was based, for a portion of the costs incurred by such person in complying with the requirement under subsection (b)(2) of this section to submit such data, and

(ii) to any other person who has been required under this subparagraph to contribute with respect to such costs, for a portion of the amount such person was required to contribute.

In promulgating rules for the determination of fair and equitable reimbursement to the persons described in clauses (i) and (ii) for costs incurred with respect to a chemical substance, the Administrator shall, after consultation with the Attorney General and the Federal Trade Commission, consider all relevant factors, including the effect on the competitive position of the person required to provide reimbursement in relation to the persons to be reimbursed and the share of the market for such substance of the person required to provide reimbursement in relation to the share of such market of the persons to be reimbursed. For purposes of judicial review, an order under this subparagraph shall be considered final agency action.

(C) For purposes of this paragraph, the reimbursement period for any previously submitted data for a chemical substance is a period—

(i) beginning on the date of the termination of the prohibition, imposed under this section, on the manufacture or processing of such substance by the person who submitted such data to the Administrator, and

(ii) ending—

(I) five years after the date referred to in clause (i), or

(II) at the expiration of a period which begins on the date referred to in clause (i) and is equal to the period which the Administrator determines was necessary to develop such data,

whichever is later.

(3) The requirements of subsections (a) and (b) of this section do not apply with respect to the manufacturing or processing of any chemical substance which is manufactured or processed, or proposed to be manufactured or processed, only in small quantities (as defined by the Administrator by rule) solely for purposes of—

(A) scientific experimentation or analysis, or

(B) chemical research on, or analysis of such substance or another substance, including such research or analysis for the development of a product,

if all persons engaged in such experimentation, research, or analysis for a manufacturer or processor are notified (in such form and manner as the Administrator may prescribe) of any risk to health which the manufacturer, processor, or the Administrator has reason to believe may be associated with such chemical substance.

(4) The Administrator may, upon application and by rule, exempt the manufacturer of any new chemical substance from all or part of the requirements of this section if the Administrator determines that the manufacture, processing, distribution in commerce, use, or disposal of such chemical substance, or that any combination of such activities, will not present an unreasonable risk of injury to health or the environment. A rule promulgated under this paragraph (and any substantive amendment to, or repeal of, such a rule) shall be promulgated in accordance with paragraphs (2) and (3) of section 2605(c) of this title.

(5) The Administrator may, upon application, make the requirements of subsections (a) and (b) of this section inapplicable with respect to the manufacturing or processing of any chemical substance (A) which exists temporarily as a result of a chemical reaction in the manufacturing or processing of a mixture or another chemical substance, and (B) to which there is no, and will not be, human or environmental exposure.

(6) Immediately upon receipt of an application under paragraph (1) or (5) the Administrator shall publish in the Federal Register notice of the receipt of such application. The Administrator shall give interested persons an opportunity to comment upon any such application and shall, within 45 days of its receipt, either approve or deny the application. The Administrator shall publish in the Federal Register notice of the approval or denial of such an application.

(i) Definitions

For purposes of this section, the terms "manufacture" and "process" mean manufacturing or processing for commercial purposes.

(Oct. 11, 1976, Pub.L. 94-469, Title I, § 5, 90 Stat. 2012, redesignated Oct. 22, 1986, Pub.L. 99-519, § 3(c)(1), 100 Stat. 2989.)

Code of Federal Regulations

Premanufacture notification exemptions, see 40 CFR 723.175.

Library References

Health and Environment ⚖25.5(3).
C.J.S. Health and Environment § 91 et seq.

§ 2605. Regulation of hazardous chemical substances and mixtures

(a) Scope of regulation

If the Administrator finds that there is a reasonable basis to conclude that the manufacture, processing, distribution in commerce, use, or disposal of a chemical substance or mixture, or that any combination of such activities, presents or will present an unreasonable risk of injury to health or the environment, the Administrator shall by rule apply one or more of the following requirements to such substance or mixture to the extent necessary to protect adequately against such risk using the least burdensome requirements:

(1) A requirement (A) prohibiting the manufacturing, processing, or distribution in commerce of such substance or mixture, or (B) limiting the amount of such substance or mixture which may be manufactured, processed, or distributed in commerce.

(2) A requirement—

(A) prohibiting the manufacture, processing, or distribution in commerce of such substance or mixture for (i) a particular use or (ii) a particular use in a concentration in excess of a level specified by the Administrator in the rule imposing the requirement, or

(B) limiting the amount of such substance or mixture which may be manufactured, processed, or distributed in commerce for (i) a particular use or (ii) a particular use in a concentration in excess of a level specified by the Administrator in the rule imposing the requirement.

(3) A requirement that such substance or mixture or any article containing such substance or mixture be marked with or accompanied by clear and adequate warnings and instructions with respect to its use, distribution in commerce, or disposal or with respect to any combination of such activities. The form and content of such warnings and instructions shall be prescribed by the Administrator.

(4) A requirement that manufacturers and processors of such substance or mixture make and retain records of the processes used to manufacture or process such substance or mixture and monitor or conduct tests which are reasonable and necessary to assure compliance with the requirements of any rule applicable under this subsection.

(5) A requirement prohibiting or otherwise regulating any manner or method of commercial use of such substance or mixture.

(6)(A) A requirement prohibiting or otherwise regulating any manner or method of disposal of such substance or mixture, or of any article containing such substance or mixture, by its manufacturer or processor or by any other person who uses, or disposes of, it for commercial purposes.

(B) A requirement under subparagraph (A) may not require any person to take any action which would be in violation of any law or requirement of, or in effect for, a State or political subdivision, and shall require each person subject to it to notify each State and political subdivision in which a required disposal may occur of such disposal.

(7) A requirement directing manufacturers or processors of such substance or mixture (A) to give notice of such unreasonable risk of injury to distributors in commerce of such substance or mixture and, to the extent reasonably ascertainable, to other persons in possession of such substance or mixture or exposed to such substance or mixture, (B) to give public notice of such risk of injury, and (C) to replace or repurchase such substance or mixture as elected by the person to which the requirement is directed.

Any requirement (or combination of requirements) imposed under this subsection may be limited in application to specified geographic areas.

(b) Quality control

If the Administrator has a reasonable basis to conclude that a particular manufacturer or processor is manufacturing or processing a chemical substance or mixture in a manner which unintentionally causes the chemical substance or mixture to present or which will cause it to present an unreasonable risk of injury to health or the environment—

(1) the Administrator may by order require such manufacturer or processor to submit a description of the relevant quality control procedures followed in the manufacturing or processing of such chemical substance or mixture; and

(2) if the Administrator determines—

(A) that such quality control procedures are inadequate to prevent the chemical substance or mixture from presenting such risk of injury, the Administrator may order the manufacturer or processor to revise such quality control procedures to the extent necessary to remedy such inadequacy; or

(B) that the use of such quality control procedures has resulted in the distribution in commerce of chemical substances or mixtures which present an unreasonable risk of injury to health or the environment, the Administrator may order the manufacturer or processor to (i) give notice of such risk to processors or distributors in commerce of any such substance or mixture, or to both, and, to the extent reasonably ascertainable, to any other person in possession of or exposed to any such substance, (ii) to give public notice of such risk, and (iii) to provide such replacement or repurchase of any such substance or mixture as is necessary to adequately protect health or the environment.

A determination under subparagraph (A) or (B) of paragraph (2) shall be made on the record after opportunity for hearing in accordance with section 554 of title 5. Any manufacturer or processor subject to a requirement to replace or repurchase a chemical substance or mixture may elect either to replace or repurchase the substance or mixture and shall take either such action in the manner prescribed by the Administrator.

(c) Promulgation of subsection (a) rules

(1) In promulgating any rule under subsection (a) of this section with respect to a chemical substance or mixture, the Administrator shall consider and publish a statement with respect to—

(A) the effects of such substance or mixture on health and the magnitude of the exposure of human beings to such substance or mixture,

(B) the effects of such substance or mixture on the environment and the magnitude of the exposure of the environment to such substance or mixture,

(C) the benefits of such substance or mixture for various uses and the availability of substitutes for such uses, and

(D) the reasonably ascertainable economic consequences of the rule, after consideration of the effect on the national economy, small business, technological innovation, the environment, and public health.

If the Administrator determines that a risk of injury to health or the environment could be eliminated or reduced to a sufficient extent by actions taken under another Federal law (or laws) administered in whole or in part by the Administrator, the Administrator may not promulgate a rule under subsection (a) of this section to protect against such risk of injury unless the Administrator finds, in the Administrator's discretion, that it is in the public interest to protect against such risk under this chapter. In making such a finding the Administrator shall consider (i) all relevant aspects of the risk, as determined by the Administrator in the Administrator's discretion, (ii) a comparison of the estimated costs of complying with actions taken under this chapter and under such law (or laws), and (iii) the relative efficiency of actions under this chapter and under such law (or laws) to protect against such risk of injury.

(2) When prescribing a rule under subsection (a) of this section the Administrator shall proceed in accordance with section 553 of title 5 (without regard to any reference in such section to sections 556 and 557 of such title), and shall also (A) publish a notice of proposed rulemaking stating with particularity the reason for the proposed rule; (B) allow interested persons to submit written data, views, and arguments, and make all such submissions publicly available; (C) provide an opportunity for an informal hearing in accordance with paragraph (3); (D) promulgate, if appropriate, a final rule based on the matter in the rulemaking record (as defined in section 2618(a) of this title), and (E) make and publish with the rule the finding described in subsection (a) of this section.

(3) Informal hearings required by paragraph (2)(C) shall be conducted by the Administrator in accordance with the following requirements:

(A) Subject to subparagraph (B), an interested person is entitled—

(i) to present such person's position orally or by documentary submissions (or both), and

(ii) if the Administrator determines that there are disputed issues of material fact it is necessary to resolve, to present such rebuttal submissions and to conduct (or have conducted under subparagraph (B)(ii)) such cross-examination of persons as the Administrator determines (I) to be appropriate, and (II) to be required for a full and true disclosure with respect to such issues.

(B) The Administrator may prescribe such rules and make such rulings concerning procedures in such hearings to avoid unnecessary costs or delay. Such rules or rulings may include (i) the imposition of reasonable time limits on each interested person's oral presentations, and (ii) requirements that any cross-examination to which a person may be entitled under subparagraph (A) be conducted by the Administrator on behalf of that person in such manner as the Administrator determines (I) to be appropriate, and (II) to be required for a full and true disclosure with respect to disputed issues of material fact.

(C)(i) Except as provided in clause (ii), if a group of persons each of whom under subparagraphs (A) and (B) would be entitled to conduct (or have conducted) cross-examination and who are determined by the Administrator to have the same or similar interests in the proceeding cannot agree upon a single representative of such interests for purposes of cross-examination, the Administrator may make rules and rulings (I) limiting the representation of such interest for such purposes, and (II) governing the manner in which such cross-examination shall be limited.

(ii) When any person who is a member of a group with respect to which the Administrator has made a determination under clause (i) is unable to agree upon group representation with the other members of the group, then such person shall not be denied under the authority of clause (i) the opportunity to conduct (or have conducted) cross-examination as to issues affecting the person's particular interests if (I) the person satisfies the Administrator that the person has made a reasonable and good faith effort to reach agreement upon group representation with the other members of the group and (II) the Administrator determines that there are substantial and relevant issues which are not adequately presented by the group representative.

(D) A verbatim transcript shall be taken of any oral presentation made, and cross-examination conducted in any informal hearing under this subsection. Such transcript shall be available to the public.

(4)(A) The Administrator may, pursuant to rules prescribed by the Administrator, provide compensation for reasonable attorneys' fees, expert witness fees, and other costs of participating in a rulemaking proceeding for the promulgation of a rule under subsection (a) of this section to any person—

(i) who represents an interest which would substantially contribute to a fair determination of the issues to be resolved in the proceeding, and

(ii) if—

(I) the economic interest of such person is small in comparison to the costs of effective participation in the proceeding by such person, or

(II) such person demonstrates to the satisfaction of the Administrator that such person does not have sufficient resources adequately to participate in the proceeding without compensation under this subparagraph.

In determining for purposes of clause (i) if an interest will substantially contribute to a fair determination of the issues to be resolved in a proceeding, the Administrator shall take into account the number and complexity of such issues and the extent to which representation of such interest will contribute to widespread public participation in the proceeding and representation of a fair balance of interests for the resolution of such issues.

(B) In determining whether compensation should be provided to a person under subparagraph (A) and the amount of such compensation, the Administrator shall take into account the financial burden which will be incurred by such person in participating in the rulemaking proceeding. The Administrator shall take such action as may be necessary to ensure that the aggregate amount of compensation paid under this paragraph in any fiscal year to all persons who, in rulemaking proceedings in which they receive compensation, are persons who either—

(i) would be regulated by the proposed rule, or

(ii) represent persons who would be so regulated,

may not exceed 25 per centum of the aggregate amount paid as compensation under this paragraph to all persons in such fiscal year.

(5) Paragraph (1), (2), (3), and (4) of this subsection apply to the promulgation of a rule repealing, or making a substantive amendment to, a rule promulgated under subsection (a) of this section.

(d) Effective date

(1) The Administrator shall specify in any rule under subsection (a) of this section the date on which it shall take effect, which date shall be as soon as feasible.

(2)(A) The Administrator may declare a proposed rule under subsection (a) of this section to be effective upon its publication in the Federal Register and until the effective date of final action taken, in accordance with subparagraph (B), respecting such rule if—

(i) the Administrator determines that—

(I) the manufacture, processing, distribution in commerce, use, or disposal of the chemical substance or mixture subject to such proposed rule or any combination of such activities is likely to result in an unreasonable risk of serious or widespread injury to health or the environment before such effective date; and

(II) making such proposed rule so effective is necessary to protect the public interest; and

(ii) in the case of a proposed rule to prohibit the manufacture, processing, or distribution of a chemical substance or mixture because of the risk determined under clause (i)(I), a court has in an action under section 2606 of this title granted relief with respect to such risk associated with such substance or mixture.

Such a proposed rule which is made so effective shall not, for purposes of judicial review, be considered final agency action.

(B) If the Administrator makes a proposed rule effective upon its publication in the Federal Register, the Administrator shall, as expeditiously as possible, give interested persons prompt notice of such action, provide reasonable opportunity, in accordance with paragraphs (2) and (3) of subsection (c) of this section, for a hearing on such rule, and either promulgate such rule (as proposed or with modifications) or revoke it; and if such a hearing is requested, the Administrator shall commence the hearing within five days from the date such request is made unless the Administrator and the person making the request agree upon a later date for the hearing to begin, and after the hearing is concluded the Administrator shall, within ten days of the conclusion of the hearing, either promulgate such rule (as proposed or with modifications) or revoke it.

(e) Polychlorinated biphenyls

(1) Within six months after January 1, 1977, the Administrator shall promulgate rules to—

(A) prescribe methods for the disposal of polychlorinated biphenyls, and

(B) require polychlorinated biphenyls to be marked with clear and adequate warnings, and instructions with respect to their processing, distribution in commerce, use, or disposal or with respect to any combination of such activities.

Requirements prescribed by rules under this paragraph shall be consistent with the requirements of paragraphs (2) and (3).

(2)(A) Except as provided under subparagraph (B), effective one year after January 1, 1977, no person may manufacture, process, or distribute in commerce or use any polychlorinated biphenyl in any manner other than in a totally enclosed manner.

(B) The Administrator may by rule authorize the manufacture, processing, distribution in commerce or use (or any combination of such activities) of any polychlorinated biphenyl in a manner other than in a totally enclosed manner if the Administrator finds that such manufacture, processing, distribution in commerce, or use (or combination of such activities) will not present an unreasonable risk of injury to health or the environment.

(C) For the purposes of this paragraph, the term "totally enclosed manner" means any manner which will ensure that any exposure of human beings or the environment to a polychlorinated biphenyl will be insignificant as determined by the Administrator by rule.

(3)(A) Except as provided in subparagraphs (B) and (C)—

(i) no person may manufacture any polychlorinated biphenyl after two years after January 1, 1977, and

(ii) no person may process or distribute in commerce any polychlorinated biphenyl after two and one-half years after such date.

(B) Any person may petition the Administrator for an exemption from the requirements of subparagraph (A), and the Administrator may grant by rule such an exemption if the Administrator finds that—

(i) an unreasonable risk of injury to health or environment would not result, and

(ii) good faith efforts have been made to develop a chemical substance which does not present an unreasonable risk of injury to health or the environment and which may be substituted for such polychlorinated biphenyl.

An exemption granted under this subparagraph shall be subject to such terms and conditions as the Administrator may prescribe and shall be in effect for such period (but not more than one year from the date it is granted) as the Administrator may prescribe.

(C) Subparagraph (A) shall not apply to the distribution in commerce of any polychlorinated biphenyl if such polychlorinated biphenyl was sold for purposes other than resale before two and one half years after October 11, 1976.

(4) Any rule under paragraph (1), (2)(B), or (3)(B) shall be promulgated in accordance with paragraphs (2), (3), and (4) of subsection (c) of this section.

(5) This subsection does not limit the authority of the Administrator, under any other provision of this chapter or any other Federal law, to take action respecting any polychlorinated biphenyl.

(Oct. 11, 1976, Pub.L. 94–469, Title I, § 6, 90 Stat. 2020, redesignated Oct. 22, 1986, Pub.L. 99–519, § 3(c)(1), 100 Stat. 2989.)

Code of Federal Regulations

Asbestos, see 40 CFR 763.100.
Fully halogenated chlorofluoroalkanes, see 40 CFR 762.1 et seq.
Manufacturing, processing, distribution in commerce, and use prohibitions respecting polychlorinated biphenyls, see 40 CFR 761.1 et seq.
Rulemaking procedures, see 40 CFR 750.1 et seq.
Storage and disposal of waste material, see 40 CFR 775.180 et seq.

Library References

Health and Environment ⚷25.5(3).
C.J.S. Health and Environment § 91 et seq.

§ 2606. Imminent hazards

(a) Actions authorized and required

(1) The Administrator may commence a civil action in an appropriate district court of the United States—

(A) for seizure of an imminently hazardous chemical substance or mixture or any article containing such a substance or mixture,

(B) for relief (as authorized by subsection (b) of this section) against any person who manufactures, processes, distributes in commerce, or uses, or disposes of, an imminently hazardous chemical substance or mixture or any article containing such a substance or mixture, or

(C) for both such seizure and relief.

A civil action may be commenced under this paragraph notwithstanding the existence of a rule under section 2603, 2604, or 2605 of this title or an order under section 2604 of this title, and notwithstanding the pendency of any administrative or judicial proceeding under any provision of this chapter.

(2) If the Administrator has not made a rule under section 2605(a) of this title immediately effective (as authorized by section 2605(d)(2)(A)(i) of this title) with respect to an imminently hazardous chemical substance or mixture, the Administrator shall commence in a district court of the United States with respect to such substance or mixture or article containing such substance or mixture a civil action described in subparagraph (A), (B), or (C) of paragraph (1).

(b) Relief authorized

(1) The district court of the United States in which an action under subsection (a) of this section is brought shall have jurisdiction to grant such temporary or permanent relief as may be necessary to protect health or the environment from the unreasonable risk associated with the chemical substance, mixture, or article involved in such action.

(2) In the case of an action under subsection (a) of this section brought against a person who manufactures, processes, or distributes in commerce a chemical substance or mixture or an article containing a chemical substance or mixture, the relief authorized by paragraph (1) may include the issuance of a mandatory order requiring (A) in the case of purchasers of such substance, mixture, or article known to the defendant, notification to such purchasers of the risk associated with it; (B) public notice of such risk; (C) recall; (D) the replacement or repurchase of such substance, mixture, or article; or (E) any combination of the actions described in the preceding clauses.

(3) In the case of an action under subsection (a) of this section against a chemical substance, mixture, or article, such substance, mixture, or article may be proceeded against by process of libel for its seizure and condemnation. Proceedings in such an action shall conform as nearly as possible to proceedings in rem in admiralty.

(c) Venue and consolidation

(1)(A) An action under subsection (a) of this section against a person who manufactures, processes, or distributes a chemical substance or mixture or an article containing a chemical substance or mixture may be brought in the United States District Court for the District of Columbia, or for any judicial district in which any of the defendants is found, resides, or transacts business; and process in such an action may be served on a defendant in any other district in which such defendant resides or may be found. An action under subsection (a) of this section against a chemical substance, mixture, or article may be brought in any United States district court within the jurisdiction of which the substance, mixture, or article is found.

(B) In determining the judicial district in which an action may be brought under subsection (a) of this section in instances in which such action may be brought in more than one judicial district, the Administrator shall take into account the convenience of the parties.

(C) Subpoenas requiring attendance of witnesses in an action brought under subsection (a) of this section may be served in any judicial district.

(2) Whenever proceedings under subsection (a) of this section involving identical chemical substances, mixtures, or articles are pending in courts in two or more judicial districts, they shall be consolidated for trial by order of any such court upon application reasonably made by any party in interest, upon notice to all parties in interest.

(d) Action under section 2605 of this title

Where appropriate, concurrently with the filing of an action under subsection (a) of this section or as soon thereafter as may be practicable, the Administrator shall initiate a proceeding for the promulgation of a rule under section 2605(a) of this title.

(e) Representation

Notwithstanding any other provision of law, in any action under subsection (a) of this section, the Administrator may direct attorneys of the Environmental Protection Agency to appear and represent the Administrator in such an action.

(f) Definition

For the purposes of subsection (a) of this section, the term "imminently hazardous chemical substance or mixture" means a chemical substance or mixture which presents an imminent and unreasonable risk of serious or widespread injury to health or the environment. Such a risk to health or the environment shall be considered imminent if it is shown that the manufacture, processing, distribution in commerce, use, or disposal of the chemical substance or mixture, or that any combination of such activities, is likely to result in such injury to health or the environment before a final rule under section 2605 of this title can protect against such risk.

(Oct. 11, 1976, Pub.L. 94–469, Title I, § 7, 90 Stat. 2026, redesignated Oct. 22, 1986, Pub.L. 99–591, § 3(c)(1), 99 Stat. 2989.)

Library References

Health and Environment ⚬25.5(3).
C.J.S. Health and Environment § 91 et seq.

§ 2607. Reporting and retention of information

(a) Reports

(1) The Administrator shall promulgate rules under which—

(A) each person (other than a small manufacturer or processor) who manufactures or processes or proposes to manufacture or process a chemical substance (other than a chemical substance described in subparagraph (B)(ii)) shall maintain such records, and shall submit to the Administrator such reports, as the Administrator may reasonably require, and

(B) each person (other than a small manufacturer or processor) who manufactures or processes or proposes to manufacture or process—

(i) a mixture, or

(ii) a chemical substance in small quantities (as defined by the Administrator by rule) solely for purposes of scientific experimentation or analysis or chemical research on, or analysis of, such substance or another substance, including any such research or analysis for the development of a product,

shall maintain records and submit to the Administrator reports but only to the extent the Administrator determines the maintenance of records or submission of reports, or both, is necessary for the effective enforcement of this chapter.

The Administrator may not require in a rule promulgated under this paragraph the maintenance of records or the submission of reports with respect to changes in the proportions of the components of a mixture unless the Administrator finds that the maintenance of such records or the submission of such reports, or both, is necessary for the effective enforcement of this chapter. For purposes of the compilation of the list of chemical substances required under subsection (b) of this section, the Administrator shall promulgate rules pursuant to this subsection not later than 180 days after January 1, 1977.

(2) The Administrator may require under paragraph (1) maintenance of records and reporting with respect to the following insofar as known to the person making the report or insofar as reasonably ascertainable:

(A) The common or trade name, the chemical identity, and the molecular structure of each chemical substance or mixture for which such a report is required.

(B) The categories or proposed categories of use of each such substance or mixture.

(C) The total amount of each such substance and mixture manufactured or processed, reasonable estimates of the total amount to be manufactured or processed, the amount manufactured or processed for each of its categories of use, and reasonable estimates of the amount to be manufactured or processed for each of its categories of use or proposed categories of use.

(D) A description of the byproducts resulting from the manufacture, processing, use, or disposal of each such substance or mixture.

(E) All existing data concerning the environmental and health effects of such substance or mixture.

(F) The number of individuals exposed, and reasonable estimates of the number who will be exposed, to such substance or mixture in their places of employment and the duration of such exposure.

(G) In the initial report under paragraph (1) on such substance or mixture, the manner or method of its disposal, and in any subsequent report on such substance or mixture, any change in such manner or method.

To the extent feasible, the Administrator shall not require under paragraph (1), any reporting which is unnecessary or duplicative.

(3)(A)(i) The Administrator may by rule require a small manufacturer or processor of a chemical substance to submit to the Administrator such information respecting the chemical substance as the Administrator may require for publication of the first list of chemical substances required by subsection (b) of this section.

(ii) The Administrator may by rule require a small manufacturer or processor of a chemical substance or mixture—

(I) subject to a rule proposed or promulgated under section 2603, 2604(b)(4), or 2605 of this title, or an order in effect under section 2604(e) of this title, or

(II) with respect to which relief has been granted pursuant to a civil action brought under section 2604 or 2606 of this title,

to maintain such records on such substance or mixture, and to submit to the Administrator such reports on such substance or mixture, as the Administrator may reasonably require. A rule under this clause requiring reporting may require reporting with respect to the matters referred to in paragraph (2).

(B) The Administrator, after consultation with the Administrator of the Small Business Administration, shall by rule prescribe standards for determining the manufacturers and processors which qualify as small manufacturers and processors for purposes of this paragraph and paragraph (1).

(b) Inventory

(1) The Administrator shall compile, keep current, and publish a list of each chemical substance which is manufactured or processed in the United States. Such list shall at least include each chemical substance which any person reports, under section 2604 of this title or subsection (a) of this section, is manufactured or processed in the United States. Such list may not include any chemical substance which was not manufactured or processed in the United States within three years before the effective date of the rules promulgated pursuant to the last sentence of subsection (a)(1) of this section. In the case of a chemical substance for which a notice is submitted in accordance with section 2604 of this title, such chemical substance shall be included in such list as of the earliest date (as determined by the Administrator) on which such substance was manufactured or processed in the United States. The Administrator shall first publish such a list not later than 315 days after January 1, 1977. The Administrator shall not include in such list any chemical substance which is manufactured or processed only in small quantities (as defined by the Administrator by rule) solely for purposes of scientific experimentation or analysis or chemical research on, or analysis of, such substance or another substance, including such research or analysis for the development of a product.

(2) To the extent consistent with the purposes of this chapter, the Administrator may, in lieu of listing, pursuant to paragraph (1), a chemical substance individually, list a category of chemical substances in which such substance is included.

(c) Records

Any person who manufactures, processes, or distributes in commerce any chemical substance or mixture shall maintain records of significant adverse reactions to health or the environment, as determined by the Administrator by rule, alleged to have been caused by the substance or mixture. Records of such adverse reactions to the health of employees shall be retained for a period of 30 years from the date such reactions were first reported to or known by the person maintaining such records. Any other record of such adverse reactions shall be retained for a period of five years from the date the information contained in the record was first reported to or known by the person maintaining the record. Records required to be maintained under this subsection shall include records of consumer allegations of personal injury or harm to health, reports of occupational disease or injury, and reports or complaints of injury to the environment submitted to the manufacturer, processor, or distributor in commerce from any source. Upon request of any duly designated representative of the Administrator, each person who is required to maintain records under this subsection shall permit the inspection of such records and shall submit copies of such records.

(d) Health and safety studies

The Administrator shall promulgate rules under which the Administrator shall require any person who manufactures, processes, or distributes in commerce or who proposes to manufacture, process, or distribute in commerce any chemical substance or mixture (or with respect to paragraph (2), any person who has possession of a study) to submit to the Administrator—

(1) lists of health and safety studies (A) conducted or initiated by or for such person with respect to such substance or mixture at any time, (B) known to such person, or (C) reasonably ascertainable by such person, except that the Administrator may exclude certain types or categories of studies from the requirements of this subsection if the Administrator finds that submission of lists of such studies are unnecessary to carry out the purposes of this chapter; and

(2) copies of any study contained on a list submitted pursuant to paragraph (1) or otherwise known by such person.

(e) Notice to Administrator of substantial risks

Any person who manufactures, processes, or distributes in commerce a chemical substance or mixture and who obtains information which reasonably supports the conclusion that such substance or mixture presents a substantial risk of injury to health or the environment shall immediately inform the Administrator of such information unless such person has actual knowledge that the Administrator has been adequately informed of such information.

(f) Definitions

For purposes of this section, the terms "manufacture" and "process" mean manufacture or process for commercial purposes.

(Oct. 11, 1976, Pub.L. 94–469, Title I, § 8, 90 Stat. 2027, redesignated Oct. 22, 1986, Pub.L. 99–519, § 3(c)(1), 100 Stat. 2989.)

Code of Federal Regulations

Inventory reporting regulations, see 40 CFR 710.1 et seq.
Reporting and recordkeeping requirements for specific chemicals, see 40 CFR 704.95, 761.45.

Library References

Health and Environment ⇐25.5(9).
C.J.S. Health and Environment § 65 et seq.

§ 2608. Relationship to other Federal laws

(a) Laws not administered by the Administrator

(1) If the Administrator has reasonable basis to conclude that the manufacture, processing, distribution in commerce, use, or disposal of a chemical substance or mixture, or that any combination of such activities, presents or will present an unreasonable risk of injury to health or the environment and determines, in the Administrator's discretion, that such risk may be prevented or reduced to a sufficient extent by action taken under a Federal law not administered by the Administrator, the Administrator shall submit to the agency which administers such law a report which describes such risk and includes in such description a specification of the activity or combination of activities which the Administrator has reason to believe so presents such risk. Such report shall also request such agency—

(A)(i) to determine if the risk described in such report may be prevented or reduced to a sufficient extent by action taken under such law, and

(ii) if the agency determines that such risk may be so prevented or reduced, to issue an order declaring whether or not the activity or combination of activities specified in the description of such risk presents such risk; and

(B) to respond to the Administrator with respect to the matters described in subparagraph (A).

Any report of the Administrator shall include a detailed statement of the information on which it is based and shall be published in the Federal Register. The agency receiving a request under such a report shall make the requested determination, issue the requested order, and make the requested response within such time as the Administrator specifies in the request, but such time specified may not be less than 90 days from the date the request was made. The response of an agency shall be accompanied by a detailed statement of the findings and conclusions of the agency and shall be published in the Federal Register.

(2) If the Administrator makes a report under paragraph (1) with respect to a chemical substance or mixture and the agency to which such report was made either—

(A) issues an order declaring that the activity or combination of activities specified in the description of the risk described in the report does not present the risk described in the report, or

(B) initiates, within 90 days of the publication in the Federal Register of the response of the agency under paragraph (1), action under the law (or laws) administered by such agency to protect against such risk associated with such activity or combination of activities,

the Administrator may not take any action under section 2605 or 2606 of this title with respect to such risk.

(3) If the Administrator has initiated action under section 2605 or 2606 of this title with respect to a risk associated with a chemical substance or mixture which was the subject of a report made to an agency under paragraph (1), such agency shall before taking action under the law (or laws) administered by it to protect against such risk consult with the Administrator for the purpose of avoiding duplication of Federal action against such risk.

(b) Laws administered by the Administrator

The Administrator shall coordinate actions taken under this chapter with actions taken under other Federal laws administered in whole or in part by the Administrator. If the Administrator determines that a risk to health or the environment associated with a chemical substance or mixture could be eliminated or reduced to a sufficient extent by actions taken under the authorities contained in such other Federal laws, the Administrator shall use such authorities to protect against such risk unless the Administrator determines, in the Administrator's discretion, that it is in the public interest to protect against such risk by actions taken under this chapter. This subsection shall not be construed to relieve the Administrator of any requirement imposed on the Administrator by such other Federal laws.

(c) Occupational safety and health

In exercising any authority under this chapter, the Administrator shall not, for purposes of section 653(b)(1) of title 29, be deemed to be exercising statutory authority to prescribe or enforce standards or regulations affecting occupational safety and health.

(d) Coordination

In administering this chapter, the Administrator shall consult and coordinate with the Secretary of Health and Human Services and the heads of any other appropriate Federal executive department or agency, any relevant independent regulatory agency, and any other appropriate instrumentality of the Federal Government for the purpose of achieving the maximum enforcement of this chapter while imposing the least burdens of duplicative requirements on those subject to the chapter and for other purposes. The Administrator shall, in the report required by section 2629 of this title, report annually to the Congress on actions taken to coordinate with such other Federal departments, agencies, or instrumentalities, and on actions taken to coordinate the authority under this chapter with the authority granted under other Acts referred to in subsection (b) of this section.

(Oct. 11, 1976, Pub.L. 94–469, Title I, § 9, 90 Stat. 2030, redesignated Oct. 22, 1986, Pub.L. 99–519, § 3(c)(1), 100 Stat. 2989, and amended Oct. 17, 1979, Pub.L. 96–88, Title V, § 509(b), 93 Stat. 695.)

Code of Federal Regulations

Asbestos recordkeeping, see 40 CFR 763.114.
Ineligibility after violations, see 40 CFR 32.100.
Procurement under assistance programs, see 40 CFR 33.001.

Library References

Health and Environment ⚷25.5(2).
C.J.S. Health and Environment § 61 et seq.

§ 2609. Research, development, collection, dissemination, and utilization of data

(a) Authority

The Administrator shall, in consultation and cooperation with the Secretary of Health and Human Services and with other heads of appropriate departments and agencies, conduct such research, development, and monitoring as is necessary to carry out the purposes of this chapter. The Administrator may enter into contracts and may make grants for research, development, and monitoring under this subsection. Contracts may be entered into under this subsection without regard to section 3324(a) and (b) of Title 31 and section 5 of Title 41.

(b) Data systems

(1) The Administrator shall establish, administer, and be responsible for the continuing activities of an interagency committee which shall design, establish, and coordinate an efficient and effective system, within the Environmental Protection Agency, for the collection, dissemination to other Federal departments and agencies, and use of data submitted to the Administrator under this chapter.

(2)(A) The Administrator shall, in consultation and cooperation with the Secretary of Health and Human Services and other heads of appropriate departments and agencies design, establish, and coordinate an efficient and effective system for the retrieval of toxicological and other scientific data which could be useful to the Administrator in carrying out the purposes of this chapter. Systematized retrieval shall be developed for use by all Federal and other departments and agencies with responsibilities in the area of regulation or study of chemical substances and mixtures and their effect on health or the environment.

(B) The Administrator, in consultation and cooperation with the Secretary of Health and Human Services, may make grants and enter into contracts for the development of a data retrieval system described in subparagraph (A). Contracts may be entered into under this subparagraph without regard to section 3324(a) and (b) of Title 31 and section 5 of Title 41.

(c) Screening techniques

The Administrator shall coordinate, with the Assistant Secretary for Health of the Department of Health and Human Services, research undertaken by the Administrator and directed toward the development of rapid, reliable, and economical screening techniques for carcinogenic, mutagenic, teratogenic, and ecological effects of chemical substances and mixtures.

(d) Monitoring

The Administrator shall, in consultation and cooperation with the Secretary of Health and Human Services, establish and be responsible for research aimed at the development, in cooperation with local, State, and Federal agencies, of monitoring techniques and instruments which may be used in the detection of toxic chemical substances and mixtures and which are reliable, economical, and capable of being implemented under a wide variety of conditions.

(e) Basic research

The Administrator shall, in consultation and cooperation with the Secretary of Health and Human Services, establish research programs to develop the fundamental scientific basis of the screening and monitoring techniques described in subsections (c) and (d) of this section, the bounds of the reliability of such techniques, and the opportunities for their improvement.

(f) Training

The Administrator shall establish and promote programs and workshops to train or facilitate the training of Federal laboratory and technical personnel in existing or newly developed screening and monitoring techniques.

(g) Exchange of research and development results

The Administrator shall, in consultation with the Secretary of Health and Human Services and other heads of appropriate departments and agencies, establish and coordinate a system for exchange among Federal, State, and local authorities of research and development results respecting toxic chemical substances and mixtures, including a system to facilitate and promote the development of standard data format and analysis and consistent testing procedures.

(Oct. 11, 1976, Pub.L. 94–469, Title I, § 10, 90 Stat. 2031, redesignated Oct. 22, 1986, Pub.L. 99–519, § 3(c)(1), 100 Stat. 2989, and amended Oct. 17, 1979, Pub.L. 96–88, Title V, § 509(b), 93 Stat. 695; Sept. 13, 1982, Pub.L. 97–258, § 4(b), 96 Stat. 1067.)

Library References

Health and Environment ⚷25.5(9).
C.J.S. Health and Environment § 65 et seq.

§ 2610. Inspections and subpoenas

(a) In general

For purposes of administering this chapter, the Administrator, and any duly designated representative of the Administrator, may inspect any establishment, facility, or other premises in which chemical substances or mixtures are manufactured, processed, stored, or held before or after their distribution in commerce and any conveyance being used to transport chemical substances, mixtures, or such articles in connection with distribution in commerce. Such an inspection may only be made upon the presentation of appropriate credentials and of a written notice to the owner, operator, or agent in charge of the premises or conveyance to be inspected. A separate notice shall be given for each such inspection, but a notice shall not be required for each entry made during the period covered by the inspection. Each such inspection shall be commenced and completed with reasonable promptness and shall be conducted at reasonable times, within reasonable limits, and in a reasonable manner.

(b) Scope

(1) Except as provided in paragraph (2), an inspection conducted under subsection (a) of this section shall extend to all things within the premises or conveyance inspected (including records, files, papers, processes, controls, and facilities) bearing on whether the requirements of this chapter applicable to the chemical substances or mixtures within such premises or conveyance have been complied with.

(2) No inspection under subsection (a) of this section shall extend to—

(A) financial data,

(B) sales data (other than shipment data),

(C) pricing data,

(D) personnel data, or

(E) research data (other than data required by this chapter or under a rule promulgated thereunder),

unless the nature and extent of such data are described with reasonable specificity in the written notice required by subsection (a) of this section for such inspection.

(c) Subpoenas

In carrying out this chapter, the Administrator may by subpoena require the attendance and testimony of witnesses and the production of reports, papers, documents, answers to questions, and other information that the Administrator deems necessary. Witnesses shall be paid the same fees and mileage that are paid witnesses in the courts of the United States. In the event of contumacy, failure, or refusal of any person to obey any such subpoena, any district court of the United States in which venue is proper shall have jurisdiction to order any such person to comply with such subpoena. Any failure to obey such an order of the court is punishable by the court as a contempt thereof.

(Oct. 11, 1976, Pub.L. 94–469, Title I, § 11, 90 Stat. 2032, redesignated Oct. 22, 1986, Pub.L. 99–519, § 3(c)(1), 100 Stat. 2989.)

Library References

Health and Environment ⚷25.5(9).
C.J.S. Health and Environment § 65 et seq.

§ 2611. Exports

(a) In general

(1) Except as provided in paragraph (2) and subsection (b) of this section, this chapter (other than section 2607 of this title) shall not apply to any chemical substance, mixture, or to an article containing a chemical substance or mixture, if—

(A) it can be shown that such substance, mixture, or article is being manufactured, processed, or distributed in commerce for export from the United States, unless such substance, mixture, or article was, in fact, manufactured, processed, or distributed in commerce, for use in the United States, and

(B) such substance, mixture, or article (when distributed in commerce), or any container in which it is enclosed (when so distributed), bears a stamp or label stating that such substance, mixture, or article is intended for export.

(2) Paragraph (1) shall not apply to any chemical substance, mixture, or article if the Administrator finds that the substance, mixture, or article will present an unreasonable risk of injury to health within the United States or to the environment of the United States. The Administrator may require, under section 2603 of this title, testing of any chemical substance or mixture exempted from this chapter by paragraph (1) for the purpose of determining whether or not such substance or mixture presents an unreasonable risk of injury to health within the United States or to the environment of the United States.

(b) Notice

(1) If any person exports or intends to export to a foreign country a chemical substance or mixture for which the submission of data is required under section 2603 or 2604(b) of this title, such person shall notify the Administrator of such exportation or intent to export and the Administrator shall furnish to the government of such country notice of the availability of the data submitted to the Administrator under such section for such substance or mixture.

(2) If any person exports or intends to export to a foreign country a chemical substance or mixture for which an order has been issued under section 2604 of this title or a rule has been proposed or promulgated under section 2604 or 2605 of this title, or with respect to which an action is pending, or relief has been granted under section 2604 or 2606 of this title, such person shall notify the Administrator of such exportation or intent to export and the Administrator shall furnish to the government of such country notice of such rule, order, action, or relief.

(Oct. 11, 1976, Pub.L. 94–469, Title I, § 12, 90 Stat. 2033, redesignated Oct. 22, 1986, Pub.L. 99–519, § 3(c)(1), 100 Stat. 2989.)

Code of Federal Regulations

Chemical imports and exports, see 40 CFR 707.60 et seq.

Library References

Health and Environment ⚷25.5(3).
C.J.S. Health and Environment § 91 et seq.

§ 2612. Entry into customs territory of the United States

(a) In general

(1) The Secretary of the Treasury shall refuse entry into the customs territory of the United States (as defined in general headnote 2 to the Tariff Schedules of the United States) of any chemical substance, mixture, or article containing a chemical substance or mixture offered for such entry if—

(A) it fails to comply with any rule in effect under this chapter, or

(B) it is offered for entry in violation of section 2604 or 2605 of this title, a rule or order under section 2604 or 2605 of this title, or an order issued in a civil action brought under section 2604 or 2606 of this title.

(2) If a chemical substance, mixture, or article is refused entry under paragraph (1), the Secretary of the Treasury shall notify the consignee of such entry refusal, shall not release it to the consignee, and shall cause its disposal or storage (under such rules as the Secretary of the Treasury may prescribe) if it has not been exported by the consignee within 90 days from the date of receipt of notice of such refusal, except that the Secretary of the Treasury may, pending a review by the Administrator of the entry refusal, release to the consignee such substance, mixture, or article on execution of bond for the amount of the full invoice of such substance, mixture, or article (as such value is set forth in the customs entry), together with the duty thereon. On failure to return such substance, mixture, or article for any cause to the custody of the Secretary of the Treasury when demanded, such consignee shall be liable to the United States for liquidated damages equal to the full amount of such bond. All charges for storage, cartage, and labor on and for disposal of substances, mixtures, or articles which are refused entry or release under this section shall be paid by the owner or consignee, and in default of such payment shall constitute a lien against any future entry made by such owner or consignee.

(b) Rules

The Secretary of the Treasury, after consultation with the Administrator, shall issue rules for the administration of subsection (a) of this section.

(Oct. 11, 1976, Pub.L. 94–469, Title I, § 13, 90 Stat. 2034, redesignated Oct. 22, 1986, Pub.L. 99–519, § 3(c)(1), 100 Stat. 2989.)

Library References

Customs Duties ⚷63.
C.J.S. Customs Duties § 92 et seq.

§ 2613. Disclosure of data

(a) In general

Except as provided by subsection (b) of this section, any information reported to, or otherwise obtained by, the Administrator (or any representative of the Administrator) under this chapter, which is exempt from disclosure pursuant to subsection (a) of section 552 of title 5 by reason of subsection (b)(4) of such section, shall, notwithstanding the provisions of any other section of this chapter, not be disclosed by the Administrator or by any officer or employee of the United States, except that such information—

(1) shall be disclosed to any officer or employee of the United States—

(A) in connection with the official duties of such officer or employee under any law for the protection of health or the environment, or

(B) for specific law enforcement purposes;

(2) shall be disclosed to contractors with the United States and employees of such contractors if in the opinion of the Administrator such disclosure is necessary for the satisfactory performance by the contractor of a contract with the United States entered into on or after October 11, 1976, for the performance of work in connection with this chapter and under such conditions as the Administrator may specify;

(3) shall be disclosed if the Administrator determines it necessary to protect health or the environment against an unreasonable risk of injury to health or the environment; or

(4) may be disclosed when relevant in any proceeding under this chapter, except that disclosure in such a proceeding shall be made in such manner as to preserve confidentiality to the extent practicable without impairing the proceeding.

In any proceeding under section 552(a) of title 5 to obtain information the disclosure of which has been denied because of the provisions of this subsection, the Administrator may not rely on section 552(b)(3) of such title to sustain the Administrator's action.

(b) Data from health and safety studies

(1) Subsection (a) of this section does not prohibit the disclosure of—

(A) any health and safety study which is submitted under this chapter with respect to—

(i) any chemical substance or mixture which, on the date on which such study is to be disclosed has been offered for commercial distribution, or

(ii) any chemical substance or mixture for which testing is required under section 2603 of this title or for which notification is required under section 2604 of this title, and

(B) any data reported to, or otherwise obtained by, the Administrator from a health and safety study which relates to a chemical substance or mixture described in clause (i) or (ii) of subparagraph (A).

This paragraph does not authorize the release of any data which discloses processes used in the manufacturing or processing of a chemical substance or mixture or, in the case of a mixture, the release of data disclosing the portion of the mixture comprised by any of the chemical substances in the mixture.

(2) If a request is made to the Administrator under subsection (a) of section 552 of title 5 for information which is described in the first sentence of paragraph (1) and which is not information described in the second sentence of such paragraph, the Administrator may not deny such request on the basis of subsection (b)(4) of such section.

(c) Designation and release of confidential data

(1) In submitting data under this chapter, a manufacturer, processor, or distributor in commerce may (A) designate the data which such person believes is entitled to confidential treatment under subsection (a) of this section, and (B) submit such designated data separately from other data submitted under this chapter. A designation under this paragraph shall be made in writing and in such manner as the Administrator may prescribe.

(2)(A) Except as provided by subparagraph (B), if the Administrator proposes to release for inspection data which has been designated under paragraph (1)(A), the Administrator shall notify, in writing and by certified mail, the manufacturer, processor, or distributor in commerce who submitted such data of the intent to release such data. If the release of such data is to be made pursuant to a request made under section 552(a) of title 5, such notice shall be given immediately upon approval of such request by the Administrator. The Administrator may not release such data until the expiration of 30 days after the manufacturer, processor, or distributor in commerce submitting such data has received the notice required by this subparagraph.

(B)(i) Subparagraph (A) shall not apply to the release of information under paragraph (1), (2), (3), or (4) of subsection (a) of this section, except that the Administrator may not release data under paragraph (3) of subsection (a) of this section unless the Administrator has notified each manufacturer, processor, and distributor in commerce who submitted such data of such release. Such notice shall be made in writing by certified mail at least 15 days before the release of such data, except that if the Administrator determines that the release of such data is necessary to protect against an imminent, unreasonable risk of injury to health or the environment, such notice may be made by such means as the Administrator determines will provide notice at least 24 hours before such release is made.

(ii) Subparagraph (A) shall not apply to the release of information described in subsection (b)(1) of this section other than information described in the second sentence of such subsection.

(d) Criminal penalty for wrongful disclosure

(1) Any officer or employee of the United States or former officer or employee of the United States, who by virtue of such employment or official position has obtained possession of, or has access to, material the disclosure of which is prohibited by subsection (a) of this section, and who knowing that disclosure of such material is prohibited by such subsection, willfully discloses the material in any manner to any person not entitled to receive it, shall be guilty of a misdemeanor and fined not more than $5,000 or imprisoned for not more than one year, or both. Section 1905 of title 18 does not apply with respect to the publishing, divulging, disclosure, or making known of, or making available, information reported or otherwise obtained under this chapter.

(2) For the purposes of paragraph (1), any contractor with the United States who is furnished information as authorized by subsection (a)(2) of this section, and any employee of any such contractor, shall be considered to be an employee of the United States.

(e) Access by Congress

Notwithstanding any limitation contained in this section or any other provision of law, all information reported to or otherwise obtained by the Administrator (or any representative of the Administrator) under this chapter shall be made available, upon written request of any duly authorized committee of the Congress, to such committee.

(Oct. 11, 1976, Pub.L. 94–469, Title I, § 14, 90 Stat. 2034, redesignated Oct. 22, 1986, Pub.L. 99–519, § 3(c)(1), 100 Stat. 2989.)

Code of Federal Regulations

Confidentiality of business information, see 40 CFR 2.306.

Library References

Records ⚷54.
C.J.S. Records § 36.

§ 2614. Prohibited acts

It shall be unlawful for any person to—

(1) fail or refuse to comply with (A) any rule promulgated or order issued under section 2603 of this title, (B) any requirement prescribed by section 2604 or 2605 of this title, (C) any rule promulgated or order issued under section 2604 or 2605 of this title, or (D) any requirement of subchapter II of this chapter or any rule promulgated or order issued under subchapter II of this chapter;

(2) use for commercial purposes a chemical substance or mixture which such person knew or had reason to know was manufactured, processed, or distributed in commerce in violation of section 2604 or 2605 of this title, a rule or order under section 2604 or 2605 of this title, or an order issued in action brought under section 2604 or 2606 of this title;

(3) fail or refuse to (A) establish or maintain records, (B) submit reports, notices, or other information, or (C) permit access to or copying of records, as required by this chapter or a rule thereunder; or

(4) fail or refuse to permit entry or inspection as required by section 2610 of this title.

(Oct. 11, 1976, Pub.L. 94–469, Title I, § 15, 90 Stat. 2036, redesignated and amended Oct. 22, 1986, Pub.L. 99–519, §§ 3(b)(1), (c)(1), 100 Stat. 2988, 2989.)

Library References

Health and Environment ⚷37.
C.J.S. Health and Environment § 48 et seq.

§ 2615. Penalties

(a) Civil

(1) Any person who violates a provision of section 2614 of this title shall be liable to the United States for a civil penalty in an amount not to exceed $25,000 for each such violation. Each day such a violation continues shall, for purposes of this subsection, constitute a separate violation of section 2614 of this title.

(2)(A) A civil penalty for a violation of section 2614 of this title shall be assessed by the Administrator by an order made on the record after opportunity (provided in accordance with this subparagraph) for a hearing in accordance with section 554 of title 5. Before issuing such an order, the Administrator shall give written notice to the person to be assessed a civil penalty under such order of the Administrator's proposal to issue such order and provide such person an opportunity to request, within 15 days of the date the notice is received by such person, such a hearing on the order.

(B) In determining the amount of a civil penalty, the Administrator shall take into account the nature, circumstances, extent, and gravity of the violation or violations and, with respect to the violator, ability to pay, effect on ability to continue to do business, any history of prior such violations, the degree of culpability, and such other matters as justice may require.

(C) The Administrator may compromise, modify, or remit, with or without conditions, any civil penalty which may be imposed under this subsection. The amount of such penalty, when finally determined, or the amount agreed upon in compromise, may be deducted from any sums owing by the United States to the person charged.

(3) Any person who requested in accordance with paragraph (2)(A) a hearing respecting the assessment of a civil penalty and who is aggrieved by an order assessing a civil penalty may file a petition for judicial review of such order with the United States Court of Appeals for the District of Columbia Circuit or for any other circuit in which such person resides or transacts business. Such a petition may only be filed within the 30-day period beginning on the date the order making such assessment was issued.

(4) If any person fails to pay an assessment of a civil penalty—

(A) after the order making the assessment has become a final order and if such person does not file a petition for judicial review of the order in accordance with paragraph (3), or

(B) after a court in an action brought under paragraph (3) has entered a final judgment in favor of the Administrator,

the Attorney General shall recover the amount assessed (plus interest at currently prevailing rates from the date of the expiration of the 30-day period referred to in paragraph (3) or the date of such final judgment, as the case may be) in an action brought in any appropriate district court of the United States. In such an action, the validity, amount, and appropriateness of such penalty shall not be subject to review.

(b) Criminal

Any person who knowingly or willfully violates any provision of section 2614 of this title, shall, in addition to or in lieu of any civil penalty which may be imposed under subsection (a) of this section for such violation, be subject, upon conviction, to a fine of not more than $25,000 for each day of violation, or to imprisonment for not more than one year, or both.

(Oct. 11, 1976, Pub.L. 94–469, Title I, § 16, 90 Stat. 2037, redesignated Oct. 22, 1986, Pub.L. 99–519, § 3(c)(1), 100 Stat. 2989.)

Code of Federal Regulations

Rules of practice, see 40 CFR 22.01 et seq.

Library References

Health and Environment ⚷25.5(10), 38.
C.J.S. Health and Environment §§ 49, 103 et seq.

§ 2616. Specific enforcement and seizure

(a) Specific enforcement

(1) The district courts of the United States shall have jurisdiction over civil actions to—

(A) restrain any violation of section 2614 of this title,

(B) restrain any person from taking any action prohibited by section 2604 or 2605 of this title or by a rule or order under section 2604 or 2605 of this title,

(C) compel the taking of any action required by or under this chapter, or

(D) direct any manufacturer or processor of a chemical substance or mixture manufactured or processed in violation of section 2604 or 2605 of this title or a rule or order under section 2604 or 2605 of this title and distributed in commerce, (i) to give notice of such fact to distributors in commerce of such substance or mixture and, to the extent reasonably ascertainable, to other persons in possession of such substance or mixture or exposed to such substance or mixture, (ii) to give public notice of such risk of injury, and (iii) to either replace or repurchase such substance or mixture, whichever the person to which the requirement is directed elects.

(2) A civil action described in paragraph (1) may be brought—

(A) in the case of a civil action described in subparagraph (A) of such paragraph, in the United States district court for the judicial district wherein any act, omission, or transaction constituting a violation of section 2614 of this title occurred or wherein the defendant is found or transacts business, or

(B) in the case of any other civil action described in such paragraph, in the United States district court for the judicial district wherein the defendant is found or transacts business.

In any such civil action process may be served on a defendant in any judicial district in which a defendant resides or may be found. Subpoenas requiring attendance of witnesses in any such action may be served in any judicial district.

(b) Seizure

Any chemical substance or mixture which was manufactured, processed, or distributed in commerce in violation of this chapter or any rule promulgated or order issued under this chapter or any article containing such a substance or mixture shall be liable to be proceeded against, by process of libel, for the seizure and condemnation of such substance, mixture, or article, in any district court of the United States within the jurisdiction of which such substance, mixture, or article is found. Such proceedings shall conform as nearly as possible to proceedings in rem in admiralty.

(Oct. 11, 1976, Pub.L. 94–469, Title I, § 17, 90 Stat. 2037, redesignated Oct. 22, 1986, Pub.L. 99–519, § 3(c)(1), 100 Stat. 2989.)

Library References

Health and Environment ⚡25.5(10).
C.J.S. Health and Environment § 103 et seq.

§ 2617. Preemption

(a) Effect on State law

(1) Except as provided in paragraph (2), nothing in this chapter shall affect the authority of any State or political subdivision of a State to establish or continue in effect regulation of any chemical substance, mixture, or article containing a chemical substance or mixture.

(2) Except as provided in subsection (b) of this section—

(A) if the Administrator requires by a rule promulgated under section 2603 of this title the testing of a chemical substance or mixture, no State or political subdivision may, after the effective date of such rule, establish or continue in effect a requirement for the testing of such substance or mixture for purposes similar to those for which testing is required under such rule; and

(B) if the Administrator prescribes a rule or order under section 2604 or 2605 of this title (other than a rule imposing a requirement described in subsection (a)(6) of section 2605 of this title) which is applicable to a chemical substance or mixture, and which is designed to protect against a risk of injury to health or the environment associated with such substance or mixture, no State or political subdivision of a State may, after the effective date of such requirement, establish or continue in effect, any requirement which is applicable to such substance or mixture, or an article containing such substance or mixture, and which is designed to protect against such risk unless such requirement (i) is identical to the requirement prescribed by the Administrator, (ii) is adopted under the authority of the Clean Air Act [42 U.S.C. 7401 et seq.] or any other Federal law, or (iii) prohibits the use of such substance or mixture in such State or political subdivision (other than its use in the manufacture or processing of other substances or mixtures).

(b) Exemption

Upon application of a State or political subdivision of a State the Administrator may by rule exempt from subsection (a)(2) of this section, under such conditions as may be prescribed in such rule, a requirement of such State or political subdivision designed to protect against a risk of injury to health or the environment associated with a chemical substance, mixture, or article containing a chemical substance or mixture if—

(1) compliance with the requirement would not cause the manufacturing, processing, distribution in commerce, or use of the substance, mixture, or article to be in violation of the applicable requirement under this chapter described in subsection (a)(2) of this section, and

(2) the State or political subdivision requirement (A) provides a significantly higher degree of protection from such risk than the requirement under this chapter described in subsection (a)(2) of this section and (B) does not, through difficulties in marketing, distribution, or other factors, unduly burden interstate commerce.

(Oct. 11, 1976, Pub.L. 94–469, Title I, § 18, 90 Stat. 2038, redesignated Oct. 22, 1986, Pub.L. 99–519, § 3(c)(1), 100 Stat. 2989.)

Library References

States ⇐4.10.
C.J.S. States § 24.

§ 2618. Judicial review

(a) In general

(1)(A) Not later than 60 days after the date of the promulgation of a rule under section 2603(a), 2604(a)(2), 2604(b)(4), 2605(a), 2605(e), or 2607 or under subchapter II of this chapter, of this title, any person may file a petition for judicial review of such rule with the United States Court of Appeals for the District of Columbia Circuit or for the circuit in which such person resides or in which such person's principal place of business is located. Courts of appeals of the United States shall have exclusive jurisdiction of any action to obtain judicial review (other than in an enforcement proceeding) of such a rule if any district court of the United States would have had jurisdiction of such action but for this subparagraph.

(B) Courts of appeals of the United States shall have exclusive jurisdiction of any action to obtain judicial review (other than in an enforcement proceeding) of an order issued under subparagraph (A) or (B) of section 2605(b)(1) of this title if any district court of the United States would have had jurisdiction of such action but for this subparagraph.

(2) Copies of any petition filed under paragraph (1)(A) shall be transmitted forthwith to the Administrator and to the Attorney General by the clerk of the court with which such petition was filed. The provisions of section 2112 of title 28 shall apply to the filing of the rulemaking record of proceedings on which the Administrator based the rule being reviewed under this section and to the transfer of proceedings between United States courts of appeals.

(3) For purposes of this section, the term "rulemaking record" means—

(A) the rule being reviewed under this section;

(B) in the case of a rule under section 2603(a) of this title, the finding required by such section, in the case of a rule under section 2604(b)(4) of this title, the finding required by such section, in the case of a rule under section 2605(a) of this title, the finding required by section 2604(f) or 2605(a) of this title, as the case may be, in the case of a rule under section 2605(a) of this title, the statement required by section 2605(c)(1) of this title, and in the case of a rule under section 2605(e) of this title, the findings required by paragraph (2)(B) or (3)(B) of such section, as the case may be;

(C) any transcript required to be made of oral presentations made in proceedings for the promulgation of such rule;

(D) any written submission of interested parties respecting the promulgation of such rule; and

(E) any other information which the Administrator considers to be relevant to such rule and which the Administrator identified, on or before the date of the promulgation of such rule, in a notice published in the Federal Register.

(b) Additional submissions and presentations; modifications

If in an action under this section to review a rule the petitioner or the Administrator applies to the court for leave to make additional oral submissions or written presentations respecting such rule and shows to the satisfaction of the court that such submissions and presentations would be material and that there were reasonable grounds for the submissions and failure to make such submissions and presentations in the proceeding before the Administrator, the court may order the Administrator to provide additional opportunity to make such submissions and presentations. The Administrator may modify or set aside the rule being reviewed or make a new rule by reason of the additional submissions and presentations and shall file such modified or new rule with the return of such submissions and presentations. The court shall thereafter review such new or modified rule.

(c) Standard of review

(1)(A) Upon the filing of a petition under subsection (a)(1) of this section for judicial review of a rule, the court shall have jurisdiction (i) to grant appropriate relief, including interim relief, as provided in chapter 7 of title 5, and (ii) except as otherwise provided in subparagraph (B), to review such rule in accordance with chapter 7 of title 5.

(B) Section 706 of title 5 shall apply to review of a rule under this section, except that—

(i) in the case of review of a rule under section 2603(a), 2604(b)(4), 2605(a), or 2605(e) of this title, the standard for review prescribed by paragraph (2)(E) of such section 706 shall not apply and the court shall hold unlawful and set aside such rule if the court finds that the rule is not supported by substantial evidence in the rulemaking record (as defined in subsection (a)(3) of this section) taken as a whole;

(ii) in the case of review of a rule under section 2605(a) of this title, the court shall hold unlawful and set aside such rule if it finds that—

(I) a determination by the Administrator under section 2605(c)(3) of this title that the petitioner seeking review of such rule is not entitled to conduct (or have conducted) cross-examination or to present rebuttal submissions, or

(II) a rule of, or ruling by, the Administrator under section 2605(c)(3) of this title limiting such petitioner's cross-examination or oral presentations,

has precluded disclosure of disputed material facts which was necessary to a fair determination by the Administrator of the rulemaking proceeding taken as a whole; and section 706(2)(D) shall not apply with respect to a determination, rule, or ruling referred to in subclause (I) or (II); and

(iii) the court may not review the contents and adequacy of—

(I) any statement required to be made pursuant to section 2605(c)(1) of this title, or

(II) any statement of basis and purpose required by section 553(c) of title 5, to be incorporated in the rule

except as part of a review of the rulemaking record taken as a whole.

The term "evidence" as used in clause (i) means any matter in the rulemaking record.

(C) A determination, rule, or ruling of the Administrator described in subparagraph (B)(ii) may be reviewed only in an action under this section and only in accordance with such subparagraph.

(2) The judgment of the court affirming or setting aside, in whole or in part, any rule reviewed in accordance with this section shall be final, subject to review by the Supreme Court of the United States upon certiorari or certification, as provided in section 1254 of title 28.

(d) Fees and costs

The decision of the court in an action commenced under subsection (a) of this section, or of the Supreme Court of the United States on review of such a decision, may include an award of costs of suit and reasonable fees for attorneys and expert witnesses if the court determines that such an award is appropriate.

(e) Other remedies

The remedies as provided in this section shall be in addition to and not in lieu of any other remedies provided by law.

(Oct. 11, 1976, Pub.L. 94–469, Title I, § 19, 90 Stat. 2039, redesignated and amended Oct. 22, 1986, Pub.L. 99–519, § 3(b)(2), (c)(1), 100 Stat. 2989.)

Library References

Health and Environment ⚷25.15(6).
C.J.S. Health and Environment § 85 et seq.

§ 2619. Citizens' civil actions

(a) In general

Except as provided in subsection (b) of this section, any person may commence a civil action—

(1) against any person (including (A) the United States, and (B) any other governmental instrumentality or agency to the extent permitted by the eleventh amendment to the Constitution) who is alleged to be in violation of this chapter or any rule promulgated under section 2603, 2604, or 2605 of this title or order issued under section 2604 of this title to restrain such violation, or

(2) against the Administrator to compel the Administrator to perform any act or duty under this chapter which is not discretionary.

Any civil action under paragraph (1) shall be brought in the United States district court for the district in which the alleged violation occurred or in which the defendant resides or in which the defendant's principal place of business is located. Any action brought under paragraph (2) shall be brought in the United States District Court for the District of Columbia, or the United States district court for the judicial district in which the plaintiff is domiciled. The district courts of the United States shall have jurisdiction over suits brought under this section, without regard to the amount in controversy or the citizenship of the parties. In any civil action under this subsection process may be served on a defendant in any judicial district in which the defendant resides or may be found and subpoenas for witnesses may be served in any judicial district.

(b) Limitation

No civil action may be commenced—

(1) under subsection (a)(1) of this section to restrain a violation of this chapter or rule or order under this chapter—

(A) before the expiration of 60 days after the plaintiff has given notice of such violation (i) to the Administrator, and (ii) to the person who is alleged to have committed such violation, or

(B) if the Administrator has commenced and is diligently prosecuting a proceeding for the issuance of an order under section 2615(a)(2) of this title to require compliance with this chapter or with such rule or order or if the Attorney General has commenced and is diligently prosecuting a civil action in a court of the United States to require compliance with this chapter or with such rule or order, but if such proceeding or civil action is commenced after the giving of notice, any person giving such notice may intervene as a matter of right in such proceeding or action; or

(2) under subsection (a)(2) of this section before the expiration of 60 days after the plaintiff has given notice to the Administrator of the alleged failure of the Administrator to perform an act or duty which is the basis for such action or, in the case of an action under such subsection for the failure of the Administrator to file an action under section 2606 of this title, before the expiration of ten days after such notification.

Notice under this subsection shall be given in such manner as the Administrator shall prescribe by rule.

(c) General

(1) In any action under this section, the Administrator, if not a party, may intervene as a matter of right.

(2) The court, in issuing any final order in any action brought pursuant to subsection (a) of this section, may award costs of suit and reasonable fees for attorneys and expert witnesses if the court determines that such an award is appropriate. Any court, in issuing its decision in an action brought to review such an order, may award costs of suit and reasonable fees for attorneys if the court determines that such an award is appropriate.

(3) Nothing in this section shall restrict any right which any person (or class of persons) may have under any statute or common law to seek enforcement of this chapter or any rule or order under this chapter or to seek any other relief.

(d) Consolidation

When two or more civil actions brought under subsection (a) of this section involving the same defendant and the same issues or violations are pending in two or more judicial districts, such pending actions, upon application of such defendants to such actions which is made to a court in which any such action is brought, may, if such court in its discretion so decides, be consolidated for trial by order (issued after giving all parties reasonable notice and opportunity to be heard) of such court and tried in—

(1) any district which is selected by such defendant and in which one of such actions is pending.

(2) a district which is agreed upon by stipulation between all the parties to such actions and in which one of such actions is pending, or

(3) a district which is selected by the court and in which one of such actions is pending.

The court issuing such an order shall give prompt notification of the order to the other courts in which the civil actions consolidated under the order are pending.

(Oct. 11, 1976, Pub.L. 94–469, Title I, § 20, 90 Stat. 2041, redesignated and amended Oct. 22, 1986, Pub.L. 99–519, § 3(b)(3), (c)(1), 100 Stat. 2989.)

Code of Federal Regulations

Notice of intent to sue, see 40 CFR 702.60.

Library References

United States ⚖124.
C.J.S. United States § 175.

§ 2620. Citizens' petitions

(a) In general

Any person may petition the Administrator to initiate a proceeding for the issuance, amendment, or repeal of a rule under section 2603, 2605, or 2607 of this title or an order under section 2604(e) or 2605(b)(2) of this title.

(b) Procedures

(1) Such petition shall be filed in the principal office of the Administrator and shall set forth the facts which it is claimed establish that it is necessary to issue, amend, or repeal a rule under section 2603, 2605, or 2607 of this title or an order under section 2604(e), 2605(b)(1)(A), or 2605(b)(1)(B) of this title.

(2) The Administrator may hold a public hearing or may conduct such investigation or proceeding as the Administrator deems appropriate in order to determine whether or not such petition should be granted.

(3) Within 90 days after filing of a petition described in paragraph (1), the Administrator shall either grant or deny the petition. If the Administrator grants such petition, the Administrator shall promptly commence an appropriate proceeding in accordance with section 2603, 2604, 2605, or 2607 of this title. If the Administrator denies such petition, the Administrator shall publish in the Federal Register the Administrator's reasons for such denial.

(4)(A) If the Administrator denies a petition filed under this section (or if the Administrator fails to grant or deny such petition within the 90-day period) the petitioner may commence a civil action in a district court of the United States to compel the Administrator to initiate a rulemaking proceeding as requested in the petition. Any such action shall be filed within 60 days after the Administrator's denial of the petition or, if the Administrator fails to grant or deny the petition within 90 days after filing the petition, within 60 days after the expiration of the 90-day period.

(B) In an action under subparagraph (A) respecting a petition to initiate a proceeding to issue a rule under section 2603, 2605, or 2607 of this title or an order under section 2604(e) or 2605(b)(2) of this title, the petitioner shall be provided an opportunity to have such petition considered by the court in a de novo proceeding. If the petitioner demonstrates to the satisfaction of the court by a preponderance of the evidence that—

(i) in the case of a petition to initiate a proceeding for the issuance of a rule under section 2603 of this title or an order under section 2604(e) of this title—

(I) information available to the Administrator is insufficient to permit a reasoned evaluation of the health and environmental effects of the chemical substance to be subject to such rule or order; and

(II) in the absence of such information, the substance may present an unreasonable risk to health or the environment, or the substance is or will be produced in substantial quantities and it enters or may reasonably be anticipated to enter the environment in substantial quantities or there is or may be significant or substantial human exposure to it; or

(ii) in the case of a petition to initiate a proceeding for the issuance of a rule under section 2605 or 2607 of this title or an order under section 2605(b)(2) of this title, there is a reasonable basis to conclude that the issuance of such a rule or order is necessary to protect health or the environment against an unreasonable risk of injury to health or the environment.[1]

the court shall order the Administrator to initiate the action requested by the petitioner. If the court finds that the extent of the risk to health or the environment alleged by the petitioner is less than the extent of risks to health or the environment with respect to which the Administrator is taking action under this chapter and there are insufficient resources available to the Administrator to take the action requested by the petitioner, the court may permit the Administrator to defer initiating the action requested by the petitioner until such time as the court prescribes.

(C) The court in issuing any final order in any action brought pursuant to subparagraph (A) may award costs of suit and reasonable fees for attorneys and expert witnesses if the court determines that such an award is appropriate. Any court, in issuing its decision in an action brought to review such an order, may award costs of suit and reasonable fees for attorneys if the court determines that such an award is appropriate.

(5) The remedies under this section shall be in addition to, and not in lieu of, other remedies provided by law.

(Oct. 11, 1976, Pub.L. 94–469, Title I, § 21, 90 Stat. 2042, redesignated Oct. 22, 1986, Pub.L. 99–519, § 3(c)(1), 100 Stat. 2989.)

[1] So in original. The period should probably be a semicolon.

Library References

United States ⚷140.
C.J.S. United States § 198 et seq.

§ 2621. National defense waiver

The Administrator shall waive compliance with any provision of this chapter upon a request and determination by the President that the requested waiver is necessary in the interest of national defense. The Administrator shall maintain a written record of the basis upon which such waiver was granted and make such record available for in camera examination when relevant in a judicial proceeding under this chapter. Upon the issuance of such a waiver, the Administrator shall publish in the Federal Register a notice that the waiver was granted for national defense purposes, unless, upon the request of the President, the Administrator determines to omit such publication because the publication itself would be contrary to the interests of national defense, in which event the Administrator shall submit notice thereof to the Armed Services Committees of the Senate and the House of Representatives.

(Oct. 11, 1976, Pub.L. 94–469, Title I, § 22, 90 Stat. 2044, redesignated Oct. 22, 1986, Pub.L. 99–519, § 3(c)(1), 100 Stat. 2989.)

Library References

War and National Emergency ⚷38.
C.J.S. War and National Defense § 46.

§ 2622. Employee protection

(a) In general

No employer may discharge any employee or otherwise discriminate against any employee with respect to the employee's compensation, terms, conditions, or privileges of employment because the employee (or any person acting pursuant to a request of the employee) has—

(1) commenced, caused to be commenced, or is about to commence or cause to be commenced a proceeding under this chapter;

(2) testified or is about to testify in any such proceeding; or

(3) assisted or participated or is about to assist or participate in any manner in such a proceeding or in any other action to carry out the purposes of this chapter.

(b) Remedy

(1) Any employee who believes that the employee has been discharged or otherwise discriminated against by any person in violation of subsection (a) of this section may, within 30 days after such alleged violation occurs, file (or have any person file on the employee's behalf) a complaint with the Secretary of Labor (hereinafter in this section referred to as the "Secretary") alleging such discharge or discrimination. Upon receipt of such a complaint, the Secretary shall notify the person named in the complaint of the filing of the complaint.

(2)(A) Upon receipt of a complaint filed under paragraph (1), the Secretary shall conduct an investigation of the violation alleged in the complaint. Within 30 days of the receipt of such complaint, the Secretary shall complete such investigation and shall notify in writing the complainant (and any person acting on behalf of the complainant) and the person alleged to have committed such violation of the results of the investigation conducted pursuant to this paragraph. Within ninety days of the receipt of such complaint the Secretary shall, unless the proceeding on the complaint is terminated by the Secretary on the basis of a settlement entered into by the Secretary and the person alleged to have committed such violation, issue an order either providing the relief prescribed by subparagraph (B) or denying the complaint. An order of the Secretary shall be made on the record after notice and opportunity for agency hearing. The Secretary may not enter into a settlement terminating a proceeding on a complaint without the participation and consent of the complainant.

(B) If in response to a complaint filed under paragraph (1) the Secretary determines that a violation of subsection (a) of this section has occurred, the Secretary shall order (i) the person who committed such violation to take affirmative action to abate the violation, (ii) such person to reinstate the complainant to the complainant's former position together with the compensation (including back pay), terms, conditions, and privileges of the complainant's employment, (iii) compensatory damages, and (iv) where appropriate, exemplary damages. If such an order issued, the Secretary, at the request of the complainant, shall assess against the person against whom the order is issued a sum equal to the aggregate amount of all costs and expenses (including attorney's fees) reasonably incurred, as determined by the Secretary, by the complainant for, or in connection with, the bringing of the complaint upon which the order was issued.

(c) Review

(1) Any employee or employer adversely affected or aggrieved by an order issued under subsection (b) of this section may obtain review of the order in the United States Court of Appeals for the circuit in which the violation, with respect to which the order was issued, allegedly occurred. The petition for review must be filed within sixty days from the issuance of the Secretary's order. Review shall conform to chapter 7 of title 5.

(2) An order of the Secretary, with respect to which review could have been obtained under paragraph (1), shall not be subject to judicial review in any criminal or other civil proceeding.

(d) Enforcement

Whenever a person has failed to comply with an order issued under subsection (b)(2) of this section, the Secretary shall file a civil action in the United States district court for the district in which the violation was found to occur to enforce such order. In actions brought under this subsection, the district courts shall have jurisdiction to grant all appropriate relief, including injunctive relief and compensatory and exemplary damages.

(e) Exclusion

Subsection (a) of this section shall not apply with respect to any employee who, acting without direction from the employee's employer (or any agent of the employer), deliberately causes a violation of any requirement of this chapter.

(Oct. 11, 1976, Pub.L. 94–469, Title I, § 23, 90 Stat. 2044, redesignated Oct. 22, 1986, Pub.L. 99–519, § 3(c)(1), 100 Stat. 2989 and amended Nov. 8, 1984, Pub.L. 98–620, Title IV, § 402(19), 98 Stat. 3358.)

Code of Federal Regulations

Procedures for the handling of discrimination complaints, see 29 CFR 24.1 et seq.

Library References

Labor Relations ⚷9.5.
C.J.S. Labor Relations § 2.

§ 2623. Employment effects

(a) In general

The Administrator shall evaluate on a continuing basis the potential effects on employment (including reductions in employment or loss of employment from threatened plant closures) of—

(1) the issuance of a rule or order under section 2603, 2604, or 2605 of this title, or

(2) a requirement of section 2604 or 2605 of this title.

(b) Investigations

(1) Any employee (or any representative of an employee) may request the Administrator to make an investigation of—

(A) a discharge or layoff or threatened discharge or layoff of the employee, or

(B) adverse or threatened adverse effects on the employee's employment,

allegedly resulting from a rule or order under section 2603, 2604, or 2605 of this title or a requirement of section 2604 or 2605 of this title. Any such request shall be made in writing, shall set forth with reasonable particularity the grounds for the request, and shall be signed by the employee, or representative of such employee, making the request.

(2)(A) Upon receipt of a request made in accordance with paragraph (1) the Administrator shall (i) conduct the investigation requested, and (ii) if requested by any interested person, hold public hearings on any matter involved in the investigation unless the Administrator, by order issued within 45 days of the date such hearings are requested, denies the request for the hearings because the Administrator determines there are no reasonable grounds for holding such hearings. If the Administrator makes such a determination, the Administrator shall notify in writing the person requesting the hearing of the determination and the reasons therefor and shall publish the determination and the reasons therefor in the Federal Register.

(B) If public hearings are to be held on any matter involved in an investigation conducted under this subsection—

(i) at least five days' notice shall be provided the person making the request for the investigation and any person identified in such request,

(ii) such hearings shall be held in accordance with section 2605(c)(3) of this title, and

(iii) each employee who made or for whom was made a request for such hearings and the employer of such employee shall be required to present information respecting the applicable matter referred to in paragraph (1)(A) or (1)(B) together with the basis for such information.

(3) Upon completion of an investigation under paragraph (2), the Administrator shall make findings of fact, shall make such recommendations as the Administrator deems appropriate, and shall make available to the public such findings and recommendations.

(4) This section shall not be construed to require the Administrator to amend or repeal any rule or order in effect under this chapter.

(Oct. 11, 1976, Pub.L. 94–469, Title I, § 24, 90 Stat. 2045, redesignated Oct. 22, 1986, Pub.L. 99–519, § 3(c)(1), 100 Stat. 2989.)

§ 2624. Studies

(a) Indemnification study

The Administrator shall conduct a study of all Federal laws administered by the Administrator for the purpose of determining whether and under what conditions, if any, indemnification should be accorded any person as a result of any action taken by the Administrator under any such law. The study shall—

(1) include an estimate of the probable cost of any indemnification programs which may be recommended;

(2) include an examination of all viable means of financing the cost of any recommended indemnification; and

(3) be completed and submitted to Congress within two years from the effective date of enactment of this chapter.

The General Accounting Office shall review the adequacy of the study submitted to Congress pursuant to paragraph (3) and shall report the results of its review to the Congress within six months of the date such study is submitted to Congress.

(b) Classification, storage, and retrieval study

The Council on Environmental Quality, in consultation with the Administrator, the Secretary of Health and Human Services, the Secretary of Commerce, and the heads of other appropriate Federal departments or agencies, shall coordinate a study of the feasibility of establishing (1) a standard classification system for chemical substances and related substances, and (2) a standard means for storing and for obtaining rapid access to information respecting such substances. A report on such study shall be completed and submitted to Congress not later than 18 months after the effective date of enactment of this chapter.

(Oct. 11, 1976, Pub.L. 94–469, Title I, § 25, 90 Stat. 2046, redesignated Oct. 22, 1986, Pub.L. 99–519, § 3(c)(1), 100 Stat. 2989, and amended Oct. 17, 1979, Pub.L. 96–88, Title V, § 509(b), 93 Stat. 695.)

§ 2625. Administration of this chapter

(a) Cooperation of Federal agencies

Upon request by the Administrator, each Federal department and agency is authorized—

(1) to make its services, personnel, and facilities available (with or without reimbursement) to the Administrator to assist the Administrator in the administration of this chapter; and

(2) to furnish to the Administrator such information, data, estimates, and statistics, and to allow the Administrator access to all information in its possession as the Administrator may reasonably determine to be necessary for the administration of this chapter.

(b) Fees

(1) The Administrator may, by rule, require the payment of a reasonable fee from any person required to submit data under section 2603 or 2604 of this title to defray the cost of administering this chapter. Such rules shall not provide for any fee in excess of $2,500 or, in the case of a small business concern, any fee in excess of $100. In setting a fee under this paragraph, the Administrator shall take into account the ability to pay of the person required to submit the data and the cost to the Administrator of reviewing such data. Such rules may provide for sharing such a fee in any case in which the expenses of testing are shared under section 2603 or 2604 of this title.

(2) The Administrator, after consultation with the Administrator of the Small Business Administration, shall by rule prescribe standards for determining the persons which qualify as small business concerns for purposes of paragraph (1).

(c) Action with respect to categories

(1) Any action authorized or required to be taken by the Administrator under any provision of this chapter with respect to a chemical substance or mixture may be taken by the Administrator in accordance with that provision with respect to a category of chemical substances or mixtures. Whenever the Administrator takes action under a provision of this chapter with respect to a category of chemical substances or mixtures, any reference in this chapter to a chemical substance or mixture (insofar as it relates to such action) shall be deemed to be a reference to each chemical substance or mixture in such category.

(2) For purposes of paragraph (1):

(A) The term "category of chemical substances" means a group of chemical substances the members of which are similar in molecular structure, in physical, chemical, or biological properties, in use, or in mode of entrance into the human body or into the environment, or the members of which are in some other way suitable for classification as such for purposes of this chapter, except that such term does not mean a group of chemical substances which are grouped together solely on the basis of their being new chemical substances.

(B) The term "category of mixtures" means a group of mixtures the members of which are similar in molecular structure, in physical, chemical, or biological properties, in use, or in the mode of entrance into the human body or into the environment, or the members of which are in some other way suitable for classification as such for purposes of this chapter.

(d) Assistance office

The Administrator shall establish in the Environmental Protection Agency an identifiable office to provide technical and other nonfinancial assistance to manufacturers and processors of chemical substances and mixtures respecting the requirements of this chapter applicable to such manufacturers and processors, the policy of the Agency respecting the application of such requirements to such manufacturers and processors, and the means and methods by which such manufacturers and processors may comply with such requirements.

(e) Financial disclosures

(1) Except as provided under paragraph (3), each officer or employee of the Environmental Protection Agency and the Department of Health and Human Services who—

(A) performs any function or duty under this chapter, and

(B) has any known financial interest (i) in any person subject to this chapter or any rule or order in effect under this chapter, or (ii) in any person who applies for or receives any grant or contract under this chapter,

shall, on February 1, 1978, and on February 1 of each year thereafter, file with the Administrator or the Secretary of Health and Human Services (hereinafter in this subsection referred to as the "Secretary"), as appropriate, a written statement concerning all such interests held by such officer or employee during the preceding calendar year. Such statement shall be made available to the public.

(2) The Administrator and the Secretary shall—

(A) act within 90 days of January 1, 1977—

(i) to define the term "known financial interests" for purposes of paragraph (1), and

(ii) to establish the methods by which the requirement to file written statements specified in paragraph (1) will be monitored and enforced, including appropriate provisions for review by the Administrator and the Secretary of such statements; and

(B) report to the Congress on June 1, 1978, and on June 1 of each year thereafter with respect to such statements and the actions taken in regard thereto during the preceding calendar year.

(3) The Administrator may by rule identify specific positions with the Environmental Protection Agency, and the Secretary may by rule identify specific positions with the Department of Health and Human Services, which are of a nonregulatory or nonpolicymaking nature, and the Administrator and the Secretary may by rule provide that officers or employees occupying such positions shall be exempt from the requirements of paragraph (1).

(4) This subsection does not supersede any requirement of chapter 11 of title 18.

(5) Any officer or employee who is subject to, and knowingly violates, this subsection or any rule issued thereunder, shall be fined not more than $2,500 or imprisoned not more than one year, or both.

(f) Statement of basis and purpose

Any final order issued under this chapter shall be accompanied by a statement of its basis and purpose. The contents and adequacy of any such statement shall not be subject to judicial review in any respect.

(g) Assistant Administrator

(1) The President, by and with the advice and consent of the Senate, shall appoint an Assistant Administrator for Toxic Substances of the Environmental Protection Agency. Such Assistant Administrator shall be qualified individual who is, by reason of background and experience, especially qualified to direct a program concerning the effects of chemicals on human health and the environment. Such Assistant Administrator shall be responsible for (A) the collection of data, (B) the preparation of studies, (C) the making of recommendations to the Administrator for regulatory and other actions to carry out the purposes and to facilitate the administration of this chapter, and (D) such other functions as the Administrator may assign or delegate.

(2) The Assistant Administrator to be appointed under paragraph (1) shall be in addition to the Assistant Administrators of the Environmental Protection Agency authorized by section 1(d) of Reorganization Plan No. 3 of 1970.

(Oct. 11, 1976, Pub.L. 94–469, Title I, § 26, 90 Stat. 2046, redesignated Oct. 22, 1986, Pub.L. 99–519, § 3(c)(1), 100 Stat. 2989, and amended Oct. 17, 1979, Pub.L. 96–88, Title V, § 509(b), 93 Stat. 695; Sept. 13, 1982, Pub.L. 97–258, § 4(b), 96 Stat. 1067.)

Code of Federal Regulations

Requirements for reporting financial interests, see 40 CFR 3.300 to 3.305.

Library References

Health and Environment ⟹25.5(9).
C.J.S. Health and Environment § 65 et seq.

§ 2626. Development and evaluation of test methods

(a) In general

The Secretary of Health and Human Services, in consultation with the Administrator and acting through the Assistant Secretary for Health, may conduct, and make grants to public and nonprofit private entities and enter into contracts with public and private entities for, projects for the development and evaluation of inexpensive and efficient methods (1) for determining and evaluating the health and environmental effects of chemical substances and mixtures, and their toxicity, persistence, and other characteristics which affect health and the environment, and (2) which may be used for the development of test data to meet the requirements of rules promulgated under section 2603 of this title. The Administrator shall consider such methods in prescribing under section 2603 of this title standards for the development of test data.

(b) Approval by Secretary

No grant may be made or contract entered into under subsection (a) of this section unless an application therefor has been submitted to and approved by the Secretary. Such an application shall be submitted in such form and manner and contain such information as the Secretary may require. The Secretary may apply such conditions to grants and contracts under subsection (a) of this section as the Secretary determines are necessary to carry out the purposes of such subsection. Contracts may be entered into under such subsection without regard to section 3324(a) and (b) of Title 31 and section 5 of Title 41.

(c) Annual reports

(1) The Secretary shall prepare and submit to the President and the Congress on or before January 1 of each year a report of the number of grants made and contracts entered into under this section and the results of such grants and contracts.

(2) The Secretary shall periodically publish in the Federal Register reports describing the progress and results of any contract entered into or grant made under this section.

(Oct. 11, 1976, Pub.L. 94–469, Title I, § 27, 90 Stat. 2049, redesignated Oct. 22, 1986, Pub.L. 99–519, § 3(c)(1), 100 Stat. 2989, and amended Oct. 17, 1979, Pub.L. 96–88, Title V, § 509(b), 93 Stat. 695; Sept. 13, 1982, Pub.L. 97–258, § 4(b), 96 Stat. 1067.)

§ 2627. State programs

(a) In general

For the purpose of complementing (but not reducing) the authority of, or actions taken by, the Administrator under this chapter, the Administrator may make grants to States for the establishment and operation of programs to prevent or eliminate unreasonable risks within the States to health or the environment which are associated with a chemical substance or mixture and with respect to which the Administrator is unable or is not likely to take action under this chapter for their prevention or elimination. The amount of a grant under this subsection shall be determined by the Administrator, except that no grant for any State program may exceed 75 per centum of the establishment and operation costs (as determined by the Administrator) of such program during the period for which the grant is made.

(b) Approval by Administrator

(1) No grant may be made under subsection (a) of this section unless an application therefor is submitted to and approved by the Administrator. Such an application shall be submitted in such form and manner as the Administrator may require and shall—

(A) set forth the need of the applicant for a grant under subsection (a) of this section,

(B) identify the agency or agencies of the State which shall establish or operate, or both, the program for which the application is submitted,

(C) describe the actions proposed to be taken under such program,

(D) contain or be supported by assurances satisfactory to the Administrator that such program shall, to the extent feasible, be integrated with other programs of the applicant for environmental and public health protection,

(E) provide for the making of such reports and evaluations as the Administrator may require, and

(F) contain such other information as the Administrator may prescribe.

(2) The Administrator may approve an application submitted in accordance with paragraph (1) only if the applicant has established to the satisfaction of the Administrator a priority need, as determined under rules of the Administrator, for the grant for which the application has been submitted. Such rules shall take into consideration the seriousness of the health effects in a State which are associated with chemical substances or mixtures, including cancer, birth defects, and gene mutations, the extent of the exposure in a State of human beings and the environment to chemical substances and mixtures, and the extent to which chemical substances and mixtures are manufactured, processed, used, and disposed of in a State.

(c) Annual reports

Not later than six months after the end of each of the fiscal years 1979, 1980, and 1981, the Administrator shall submit to the Congress a report respecting the programs assisted by grants under subsection (a) of this section in the preceding fiscal year and the extent to which the Administrator has disseminated information respecting such programs.

(d) Authorization

For the purpose of making grants under subsection (a) of this section, there are authorized to be appropriated $1,500,000 for each of the fiscal years 1982 and 1983. Sums appropriated under this subsection shall remain available until expended.

(Oct. 11, 1976, Pub.L. 94–469, Title I, § 28, 90 Stat. 2049, redesignated Oct. 22, 1986, Pub.L. 99–519, § 3(c)(1), 100 Stat. 2989, and amended Dec. 29, 1981, Pub.L. 97–129, § 1(a), 95 Stat. 1686.)

§ 2628. Authorization of appropriations

There are authorized to be appropriated to the Administrator for purposes of carrying out this chapter (other than sections 2626 and 2627 of this title and subsections (a) and (c) through (g) of section 2609 of this title) $58,646,000 for the fiscal year 1982 and $62,000,000 for the fiscal year 1983. No part of the funds appropriated under this section may be used to construct any research laboratories.

(Oct. 11, 1976, Pub.L. 94–469, Title I, § 29, 90 Stat. 2050, redesignated Oct. 22, 1986, Pub.L. 99–519, § 3(c)(1), 100 Stat. 2989 and amended Dec. 29, 1981, Pub.L. 97–129, § 1(b), 95 Stat. 1686.)

§ 2629. Annual report

The Administrator shall prepare and submit to the President and the Congress on or before January 1, 1978, and on or before January 1 of each succeeding year a comprehensive report on the administration of this chapter during the preceding fiscal year. Such reports shall include—

(1) a list of the testing required under section 2603 of this title during the year for which the report is made and an estimate of the costs incurred during such year by the persons required to perform such tests;

(2) the number of notices received during such year under section 2604 of this title, the number of such notices received during such year under such section for chemical substances subject to a section 2603 rule, and a summary of any action

taken during such year under section 2604(g) of this title;

(**3**) a list of rules issued during such year under section 2605 of this title;

(**4**) a list, with a brief statement of the issues, of completed or pending judicial actions under this chapter and administrative actions under section 2615 of this title during such year;

(**5**) a summary of major problems encountered in the administration of this chapter; and

(**6**) such recommendations for additional legislation as the Administrator deems necessary to carry out the purposes of this chapter.

(Oct. 11, 1976, Pub.L. 94–469, Title I, § 30, 90 Stat. 2050, redesignated Oct. 22, 1986, Pub.L. 99–519, § 3(c)(1), 100 Stat. 2989.)

WATER POLLUTION PREVENTION AND CONTROL

(33 U.S.C.A. §§ 1251 to 1376)

CHAPTER 26—WATER POLLUTION PREVENTION AND CONTROL

SUBCHAPTER I—RESEARCH AND RELATED PROGRAMS

SUBCHAPTER II—GRANTS FOR CONSTRUCTION OF TREATMENT WORKS

Related Provisions

See, also, Safety of Public Water Systems, 42 U.S.C.A. § 300f et seq., post; Water Resources Research, 42 U.S.C.A. § 10301 et seq., post.

Cross References

Amortization of pollution control facilities, see section 169 of Title 26, Internal Revenue Code.

Appalachian regional development, grants for construction of sewage treatment works, see section 212 of the Appendix to Title 40, Public Buildings, Property, and Works.

Atomic energy, authority of Administrator under this chapter, see section 2022 of Title 42, The Public Health and Welfare.

Coal leases, provisions requiring compliance with this chapter, see section 201 of Title 30, Mineral Lands and Mining.

Colorado River Basin Project—
- Applicability of this chapter, see section 1577 of Title 43, Public Lands.
- Salinity control, see sections 1595 and 1597 of Title 43.

Conditions for issuance of license for ownership, etc., of deepwater port, see section 1503 of this title.

Construction of the Surface Mining Control and Reclamation Act of 1977 as not superseding, etc., this chapter, see section 1292 of Title 30, Mineral Lands and Mining.

Coordination of regulatory and inspection activities, see section 1303 of Title 30.

Deepwater port considered as "new source" for purposes of this chapter, see section 1502 of this title.

Definition of "dumping" for purposes of ocean dumping, see section 1402 of this title.

Demonstrations of energy-related pollution control technologies, see section 4363a of Title 42, The Public Health and Welfare.

Discharge of pollutants from vessels engaged in recovery or exploration of deep sea minerals subject to this chapter, see section 1419 of Title 30, Mineral Lands and Mining.

Establishment of contained spoil disposal facilities pursuant to requirements of this chapter, see section 1293a of this title.

Mine drainage, construction and operation of plants for control and treatment of water pollution, see section 1242 of Title 30, Mineral Lands and Mining.

Noise emission standards, consideration of standards under this chapter, see section 4905 of Title 42, The Public Health and Welfare.

Notification to National Response Center of any release of hazardous substance from vessel, see section 9603 of Title 42.

Pinelands National Reserve, plan for implementation of provisions of this chapter, see section 471i of Title 16, Conservation.

Power plant fuel use, applicable environmental requirements, see section 8302 of Title 42, The Public Health and Welfare.

Reclamation and irrigation projects, applicability of this chapter, see section 421h of Title 43, Public Lands.

Requirements of this chapter to be incorporated into requirements for coastal zone management, see section 1456 of Title 16, Conservation.
Rural communities assistance for solid waste disposal, see section 6949 of Title 42, The Public Health and Welfare.
Science Advisory Board, availability of proposed environmental criteria documents, standards, limitations or regulations, see section 4365 of Title 42.
Solid waste disposal—
Construction with this chapter, see section 6905 of Title 42.
Creation of greater amounts of waste by virtue of this chapter, see section 6901 of Title 42.
Solid waste management information and guidelines, see section 6907 of Title 42.
Supplements to Federal grant-in-aid programs for Appalachian regional development, see section 214 of the Appendix to Title 40, Public Buildings, Property, and Works.
Surface coal mining, regulations setting mining and reclamation performance standards, see section 1251 of Title 30, Mineral Lands and Mining.
Urban mass transportation, compliance with requirements of this chapter, see section 1604 of Title 49, Transportation.
Water research and development, cooperation with Federal agencies, State and local governments, etc., see section 10303 of Title 42, The Public Health and Welfare.

West's Federal Forms

Complaints in admiralty charging oil pollution, see §§ 11097, 11098, 11098.5.
Contempt proceedings, see § 5651 et seq.
Judgment for oil spill cleanup costs, penalty, see § 11755 and Comment thereunder.
Jurisdiction and venue in district courts, see 1003 et seq.
Preliminary injunctions and temporary restraining orders, see § 5271 et seq.
Production of documents, motions and orders, see § 3551 et seq.
Taxation of costs, see § 4612 et seq.

West's Federal Practice Manual

Concurrent Claims Court jurisdiction, see § 1834.

Code of Federal Regulations

Administration of federal contracts, grants or loans, see 40 CFR 15.1 et seq.
Civil penalties for violation of oil pollution prevention regulations, see 40 CFR 114.1 et seq.
Effluent guidelines and standards, see 40 CFR 401.10 et seq.
General regulatory policies, see 33 CFR 320.1 et seq.
Guidelines establishing test procedures for analysis of pollutants, see 40 CFR 136.1 et seq.
Oil pollution regulations, see 33 CFR Chap. I, Subchap. O.
Pollution removal damage claims, see 33 CFR 25.101 et seq.
Public participation in programs, see 40 CFR 25.1 et seq.
Research and demonstration grants, see 40 CFR 40.100 et seq.
Rural clean water program, see 7 CFR 634.1 et seq.
State and local assistance, see 40 CFR 35.001 et seq.
Water quality planning and management, see 40 CFR 130.0 et seq.

United States Supreme Court

Interstate water pollution, preemption of state nuisance law, see International Paper Co. v. Harmel Ouellette et al., 1987, 107 S.Ct. 805, 93 L.Ed.2d 883.

WESTLAW Electronic Research

See WESTLAW guide following the Explanation pages of this pamphlet.

SUBCHAPTER I—RESEARCH AND RELATED PROGRAMS

§ 1251. Congressional declaration of goals and policy

(a) Restoration and maintenance of chemical, physical and biological integrity of Nation's waters; national goals for achievement of objective

The objective of this chapter is to restore and maintain the chemical, physical, and biological integrity of the Nation's waters. In order to achieve this objective it is hereby declared that, consistent with the provisions of this chapter—

(1) it is the national goal that the discharge of pollutants into the navigable waters be eliminated by 1985;

(2) it is the national goal that wherever attainable, an interim goal of water quality which provides for the protection and propagation of fish, shellfish, and wildlife and provides for recreation in and on the water be achieved by July 1, 1983;

(3) it is the national policy that the discharge of toxic pollutants in toxic amounts be prohibited;

(4) it is the national policy that Federal financial assistance be provided to construct publicly owned waste treatment works;

(5) it is the national policy that areawide waste treatment management planning processes be developed and implemented to assure adequate control of sources of pollutants in each State; and

(6) it is the national policy that a major research and demonstration effort be made to develop technology necessary to eliminate the discharge of pollutants into the navigable waters, waters of the contiguous zone, and the oceans.

(b) Congressional recognition, preservation, and protection of primary responsibilities and rights of States

It is the policy of the Congress to recognize, preserve, and protect the primary responsibilities and rights of States to prevent, reduce, and eliminate pollution, to plan the development and use (including restoration, preservation, and enhancement) of land and water resources, and to consult with the Administrator in the exercise of his authority under this chapter. It is the policy of Congress that the States manage the construction grant program under this chapter and implement the permit programs under sections 1342 and 1344 of this title. It is further the policy of the Congress to support and aid research relating to the prevention, reduction, and elimination of pollution and to provide Federal technical services and financial aid to State and interstate agencies and municipalities in connection with the prevention, reduction, and elimination of pollution.

(c) Congressional policy toward Presidential activities with foreign countries

It is further the policy of Congress that the President, acting through the Secretary of State and such national and international organizations as he determines appropriate, shall take such action as may be necessary to insure that to the fullest extent possible all foreign countries shall take meaningful action for the prevention, reduction, and elimination of pollution in their waters and in international waters and for the achievement of goals regarding the elimination of discharge of pollutants and the improvement of water quality to at least the same extent as the United States does under its laws.

(d) Administrator of Environmental Protection Agency to administer chapter

Except as otherwise expressly provided in this chapter, the Administrator of the Environmental Protection Agency (hereinafter in this chapter called "Administrator") shall administer this chapter.

(e) Public participation in development, revision, and enforcement of any regulation, etc.

Public participation in the development, revision, and enforcement of any regulation, standard, effluent limitation, plan, or program established by the Administrator or any State under this chapter shall be provided for, encouraged, and assisted by the Administrator and the States. The Administrator, in cooperation with the States, shall develop and publish regulations specifying minimum guidelines for public participation in such processes.

(f) Procedures utilized for implementing chapter

It is the national policy that to the maximum extent possible the procedures utilized for implementing this chapter shall encourage the drastic minimization of paperwork and interagency decision procedures, and the best use of available manpower and funds, so as to prevent needless duplication and unnecessary delays at all levels of government.

(g) Authority of States over water

It is the policy of Congress that the authority of each State to allocate quantities of water within its jurisdiction shall not be superseded, abrogated or otherwise impaired by this chapter. It is the further policy of Congress that nothing in this chapter shall be construed to supersede or abrogate rights to quantities of water which have been established by any State. Federal agencies shall co-operate with State and local agencies to develop comprehensive solutions to prevent, reduce and eliminate pollution in concert with programs for managing water resources.

(June 30, 1948, ch. 758, title I, § 101, Oct. 18, 1972, as added Pub.L. 92–500, § 2, 86 Stat. 816, and amended Dec. 27, 1977, Pub.L. 95–217, §§ 5(a), 26(b), 91 Stat. 1567, 1575.)

Cross References

Modification of secondary treatment requirements, see section 1311 of this title.

Report to Congress to include recommendations concerning policy to reduce pollution, see section 1252 of this title.

Federal Practice and Procedure

Jurisdictional amount in controversy met in federal common-law nuisance action, see Wright, Miller & Cooper: Jurisdiction 2d § 3561.1.

Code of Federal Regulations

Procedures for decisionmaking, see 40 CFR 124.1 et seq.

Procurement under assistance agreements, see 40 CFR 33.001 et seq.

Public participation in programs, see 40 CFR 25.1 et seq.

Library References

Health and Environment ⚷25.7(3).

C.J.S. Health and Environment § 106.

United States Supreme Court

Interstate pollution, discharge of sewage into Lake Michigan, this chapter displacing federal common law of nuisance, see City of Milwaukee v. Illinois and Michigan, 1981, 101 S.Ct. 1784, 451 U.S. 304, 68 L.Ed.2d 114.

Preemption of federal common law of nuisance in area of water pollution, see Middlesex County Sewerage Authority v. National Sea Clammers Ass'n, 1981, 101 S.Ct. 2615, 453 U.S. 1, 69 L.Ed.2d 435.

Public nuisance in interstate or navigable waters, application of federal common law not inconsistent with this chapter, see Illinois v. City of Milwaukee, 1972, 92 S.Ct. 1385, 406 U.S. 91, 31 L.Ed.2d 712.

§ 1252. Comprehensive programs for water pollution control

(a) Preparation and development

The Administrator shall, after careful investigation, and in cooperation with other Federal agencies, State water pollution control agencies, interstate agencies, and the municipalities and industries involved, prepare or develop comprehensive programs for preventing, reducing, or eliminating the pollution of the navigable waters and ground waters and improving the sanitary condition of surface and underground waters. In the development of such comprehensive programs due regard shall be given to the improvements which are necessary to conserve such waters for the protection and propagation of fish and aquatic life and wildlife, recreational purposes, and the withdrawal of such waters for public water supply, agricultural, industrial, and other purposes. For the purpose of this section, the Administrator is authorized to make joint investigations with any such agencies of the condition of any waters in any State or States, and of the discharges of any sewage, industrial wastes, or substance which may adversely affect such waters.

(b) Planning for reservoirs; storage for regulation of streamflow

(1) In the survey or planning of any reservoir by the Corps of Engineers, Bureau of Reclamation, or other Federal agency, consideration shall be given to inclusion of storage for regulation of streamflow, except that any such storage and water releases shall not be provided as a substitute for adequate treatment or other methods of controlling waste at the source.

(2) The need for and the value of storage for regulation of streamflow (other than for water quality) including but not limited to navigation, salt water intrusion, recreation, esthetics, and fish and wildlife, shall be determined by the Corps of Engineers, Bureau of Reclamation, or other Federal agencies.

(3) The need for, the value of, and the impact of, storage for water quality control shall be determined by the Administrator, and his views on these matters shall be set forth in any report or presentation to Congress proposing authorization or construction of any reservoir including such storage.

(4) The value of such storage shall be taken into account in determining the economic value of the entire project of which it is a part, and costs shall be allocated to the purpose of regulation of streamflow in a manner which will insure that all project purposes, share equitably in the benefit of multiple-purpose construction.

(5) Costs of regulation of streamflow features incorporated in any Federal reservoir or other impoundment under the provisions of this chapter shall be determined and the beneficiaries identified and if the benefits are widespread or national in scope, the costs of such features shall be nonreimbursable.

(6) No license granted by the Federal Energy Regulatory Commission for a hydroelectric power project shall include storage for regulation of streamflow for the purpose of water quality control unless the Administrator shall recommend its inclusion and such reservoir storage capacity shall not exceed such proportion of the total storage required for the water quality control plan as the drainage area of such reservoir bears to the drainage area of the river basin or basins involved in such water quality control plan.

(c) Basins; grants to State agencies

(1) The Administrator shall, at the request of the Governor of a State, or a majority of the Governors when more than one State is involved, make a grant to pay not to exceed 50 per centum of the administrative expenses of a planning agency for a period not to exceed three years, which period shall begin after October 18, 1972, if such agency provides for adequate representation of appropriate State, interstate, local, or (when appropriate) international interests in the basin or portion thereof involved and is capable of developing an effective, comprehensive water quality control plan for a basin or portion thereof.

(2) Each planning agency receiving a grant under this subsection shall develop a comprehensive pollution control plan for the basin or portion thereof which—

(A) is consistent with any applicable water quality standards effluent and other limitations, and thermal discharge regulations established pursuant to current law within the basin;

(B) recommends such treatment works as will provide the most effective and economical means of collection, storage, treatment, and elimination of pollutants and recommends means to encourage both municipal and industrial use of such works;

(C) recommends maintenance and improvement of water quality within the basin or portion thereof and recommends methods of adequately financing those facilities as may be necessary to implement the plan; and

(D) as appropriate, is developed in cooperation with, and is consistent with any comprehensive plan prepared by the Water Resources Council, any areawide waste management plans developed pursuant to section 1288 of this title, and any State plan developed pursuant to section 1313(e) of this title.

(3) For the purposes of this subsection the term "basin" includes, but is not limited to, rivers and their tributaries, streams, coastal waters, sounds, estuaries, bays, lakes, and portions thereof as well as the lands drained thereby.

(d) Report to Congress

The Administrator, after consultation with the States, and River Basin Commissions established under the Water Resources Planning Act [42 U.S.C. 1962 et seq.], shall submit a report to Congress on or before July 1, 1978, which analyzes the relationship between programs under this chapter, and the programs by which State and Federal agencies allocate quantities of water. Such report shall include recommendations concerning the policy in section 1251(g) of this title to improve coordination of efforts to reduce and eliminate pollution in concert with programs for managing water resources.

(June 30, 1948, ch. 758, title I, § 102, as added Oct. 18, 1972, Pub.L. 92–500, § 2, 86 Stat. 817, and amended Aug. 4, 1977, Pub.L. 95–91, title IV, § 402(a)(i)(A), 91 Stat. 583; Dec. 27, 1977, Pub.L. 95–217, § 5(b), 91 Stat. 1567.)

Cross References

Modification of project for regulation of streamflow, see section 1252a of this title.

Report to Congress, progress and problems associated with developing comprehensive plans under this section, see section 1375 of this title.

West's Federal Forms

Sentence and fine, see § 7531 et seq.

Code of Federal Regulations

Administration of federal contracts, grants, or loans, see 40 CFR 15.1 et seq.

Library References

Health and Environment ⚷25.7(3).
C.J.S. Health and Environment § 106.

§ 1252a. Reservoir projects, water storage; modification; storage for other than for water quality, opinion of Federal agency, committee resolutions of approval; provisions inapplicable to projects with certain prescribed water quality benefits in relation to total project benefits

In the case of any reservoir project authorized for construction by the Corps of Engineers, Bureau of Reclamation, or other Federal agency when the Administrator of the Environmental Protection Agency determines pursuant to section 1252(b) of this title that any storage in such project for regulation of streamflow for water quality is not needed, or is needed in a different amount, such project may be modified accordingly by the head of the appropriate agency, and any storage no longer required for water quality may be utilized for other authorized purposes of the project when, in the opinion of the head of such agency, such use is justified. Any such modification of a project where the benefits attributable to water quality are 15 per centum or more but not greater than 25 per centum of the total project benefits shall take effect only upon the adoption of resolutions approving such modification by the appropriate committees of the Senate and House of Representatives. The provisions of the section shall not apply to any project where the benefits attributable to water quality exceed 25 per centum of the total project benefits.

(March 7, 1974, Pub.L. 93–251, title I, § 65, 88 Stat. 30.)

Library References

Health and Environment ⚷25.7(3).
Waters and Water Courses ⚷243.
C.J.S. Health and Environment § 106.
C.J.S. Waters § 350.

§ 1253. Interstate cooperation and uniform laws

(a) The Administrator shall encourage cooperative activities by the States for the prevention, reduction, and elimination of pollution, encourage the enactment of improved and, so far as practicable, uniform State laws relating to the prevention, reduction, and elimination of pollution; and encourage compacts between States for the prevention and control of pollution.

(b) The consent of the Congress is hereby given to two or more States to negotiate and enter into agreements or compacts, not in conflict with any law or treaty of the United States, for (1) cooperative effort and mutual assistance for the prevention and control of pollution and the enforcement of their respective laws relating thereto, and (2) the establishment of such agencies, joint or otherwise, as they may deem desirable for making effective such agreements and compacts. No such agreement or compact shall be binding or obligatory upon any State a party thereto unless and until it has been approved by the Congress.

(June 30, 1948, ch. 758, title I, § 103, as added Oct. 18, 1972, Pub.L. 92–500, § 2, 86 Stat. 818.)

Library References

States ⚷6.
C.J.S. States § 31 et seq.

§ 1254. Research, investigations, training, and information

(a) Establishment of national programs; cooperation; investigations; water quality surveillance system; reports

The Administrator shall establish national programs for the prevention, reduction, and elimination of pollution and as part of such programs shall—

(1) in cooperation with other Federal, State, and local agencies, conduct and promote the coordination and acceleration of, research, investigations, experiments, training, demonstrations, surveys, and studies relating to the causes, effects, extent, prevention, reduction, and elimination of pollution;

(2) encourage, cooperate with, and render technical services to pollution control agencies and other appropriate public or private agencies, institutions, and organizations, and individuals, including the general public, in the conduct of activities referred to in paragraph (1) of this subsection;

(3) conduct, in cooperation with State water pollution control agencies and other interested agencies, organizations and persons, public investigations concerning the pollution of any navigable waters, and report on the results of such investigations;

(4) establish advisory committees composed of recognized experts in various aspects of pollution and representatives of the public to assist in the examination and evaluation of research progress and proposals and to avoid duplication of research;

(5) in cooperation with the States, and their political subdivisions, and other Federal agencies establish, equip, and maintain a water quality surveillance system for the purpose of monitoring the quality of the navigable waters and ground waters and the contiguous zone and the oceans and the Administrator shall, to the extent practicable, conduct such surveillance by utilizing the resources of the National Aeronautics and Space Administration, the National Oceanic and Atmospheric Administration, the Geological Survey, and the Coast Guard, and shall report on such quality in the report required under subsection (a) of section 1375 of this title; and

(6) initiate and promote the coordination and acceleration of research designed to develop the most effective practicable tools and techniques for measuring the social and economic costs and benefits of activities which are subject to regulation under this chapter; and shall transmit a report on the results of such research to the Congress not later than January 1, 1974.

(b) Authorized activities of Administrator

In carrying out the provisions of subsection (a) of this section the Administrator is authorized to—

(1) collect and make available, through publications and other appropriate means, the results of and other information, including appropriate recommendations by him in connection therewith, pertaining to such research and other activities referred to in paragraph (1) of subsection (a) of this section;

(2) cooperate with other Federal departments and agencies, State water pollution control agencies, interstate agencies, other public and private agencies, institutions, organizations, industries involved, and individuals, in the preparation and conduct of such research and other activities referred to in paragraph (1) of subsection (a) of this section;

(3) make grants to State water pollution control agencies, interstate agencies, other public or nonprofit private agencies, institutions, organizations, and individuals, for purposes stated in paragraph (1) of subsection (a) of this section;

(4) contract with public or private agencies, institutions, organizations, and individuals, without regard to section 3324(a) and (b) of title 31 and section 5 of title 41, referred to in paragraph (1) of subsection (a) of this section;

(5) establish and maintain research fellowships at public or nonprofit private educational institutions or research organizations;

(6) collect and disseminate, in cooperation with other Federal departments and agencies, and with other public or private agencies, institutions, and organizations having related responsibilities, basic data on chemical, physical, and biological effects of varying water quality and other information pertaining to pollution and the prevention, reduction, and elimination thereof; and

(7) develop effective and practical processes, methods, and prototype devices for the prevention, reduction, and elimination of pollution.

(c) Research and studies on harmful effects of pollutants; cooperation with Secretary of Health and Human Services

In carrying out the provisions of subsection (a) of this section the Administrator shall conduct research on, and survey the results of other scientific studies on, the harmful effects on the health or welfare of persons caused by pollutants. In order to avoid duplication of effort, the Administrator shall, to the extent practicable, conduct such research in cooperation with and through the facilities of the Secretary of Health and Human Services.

(d) Sewage treatment; identification and measurement of effects of pollutants; augmented streamflow

In carrying out the provisions of this section the Administrator shall develop and demonstrate under varied conditions (including conducting such basic and applied research, studies, and experiments as may be necessary):

(1) Practicable means of treating municipal sewage, and other waterborne wastes to implement the requirements of section 1281 of this title;

(2) Improved methods and procedures to identify and measure the effects of pollutants, including those pollutants created by new technological developments; and

(3) Methods and procedures for evaluating the effects on water quality of augmented streamflows to control pollution not susceptible to other means of prevention, reduction, or elimination.

(e) Field laboratory and research facilities

The Administrator shall establish, equip, and maintain field laboratory and research facilities, including, but not limited to, one to be located in the northeastern area of the United States, one in the Middle Atlantic area, one in the southeastern area, one in the midwestern area, one in the southwestern area, one in the Pacific Northwest, and one in the State of Alaska, for the conduct of research, investigations, experiments, field demonstrations and studies, and training relating to the prevention, reduction and elimination of pollution. Insofar as practicable, each such facility shall be located near institutions of higher learning in which graduate training in such research might be carried out. In conjunction with the development of criteria under section 1343 of this title, the Administrator shall construct the facilities authorized for the National Marine Water Quality Laboratory established under this subsection.

(f) Great Lakes water quality research

The Administrator shall conduct research and technical development work, and make studies, with respect to the quality of the waters of the Great Lakes, including an analysis of the present and projected future water quality of the Great Lakes under varying conditions of waste treatment and disposal, an evaluation of the water quality needs of those to be served by such waters, an evaluation of municipal, industrial, and vessel waste treatment and disposal practices with respect to such waters, and a study of alternate means of solving pollution problems (including additional waste treatment measures) with respect to such waters.

(g) Treatment works pilot training programs; employment needs forecasting; training projects and grants; research fellowships; technical training; report to the President and transmittal to Congress

(1) For the purpose of providing an adequate supply of trained personnel to operate and maintain existing and future treatment works and related activities, and for the purpose of enhancing substantially the proficiency of those engaged in such activities, the Administrator shall finance pilot programs, in cooperation with State and interstate agencies, municipalities, educational institutions, and other organizations and individuals, of manpower development and training and retraining of persons in, on entering into, the field of operation and maintenance of treatment works and related activities. Such program and any funds expended for such a program shall supplement, not supplant, other manpower and training programs and funds available for the purposes of this paragraph. The Administrator is authorized, under such terms and conditions as he deems appropriate, to enter into agreements with one or more States, acting jointly or severally, or with other public or private agencies or institutions for the development and implementation of such a program.

(2) The Administrator is authorized to enter into agreements with public and private agencies and institutions, and individuals to develop and maintain an effective system for forecasting the supply of, and demand for, various professional and other occupational categories needed for the prevention, reduction, and elimination of pollution in each region, State, or area of the United States and, from time to time, to publish the results of such forecasts.

(3) In furtherance of the purposes of this chapter, the Administrator is authorized to—

(A) make grants to public or private agencies and institutions and to individuals for training projects, and provide for the conduct of training by contract with public or private agencies and institutions and with individuals without regard to section 3324(a) and (b) of title 31 and section 5 of title 41;

(B) establish and maintain research fellowships in the Environmental Protection Agency with such stipends and allowances, including traveling and subsistence expenses, as he may deem necessary to procure the assistance of the most promising research fellows; and

(C) provide, in addition to the program established under paragraph (1) of this subsection, training in technical matters relating to the causes, prevention, reduction, and elimination of pollution for personnel of public agencies and other persons with suitable qualifications.

(4) The Administrator shall submit, through the President, a report to the Congress not later than December 31, 1973, summarizing the actions taken under this subsection and the effectiveness of such actions, and setting forth the number of persons trained, the occupational categories for which training was provided, the effectiveness of other Federal, State, and local training programs in this field, together with estimates of future needs, recommendations on improving training programs, and such other information and recommendations, including legislative recommendations, as he deems appropriate.

(h) Lake pollution

The Administrator is authorized to enter into contracts with, or make grants to, public or private agencies and organizations and individuals for (A) the purpose of developing and demonstrating new or improved methods for the prevention, removal, reduction, and elimination of pollution in lakes, including the undesirable effects of nutrients and vegetation, and (B) the construction of publicly owned research facilities for such purpose.

(i) Oil pollution control studies

The Administrator, in cooperation with the Secretary of the Department in which the Coast Guard is operating, shall—

(1) engage in such research, studies, experiments, and demonstrations as he deems appropriate, relative to the removal of oil from any waters and to the prevention, control, and elimination of oil and hazardous substances pollution;

(2) publish from time to time the results of such activities; and

(3) from time to time, develop and publish in the Federal Register specifications and other technical information on the various chemical compounds used in the control of oil and hazardous substances spills.

In carrying out this subsection, the Administrator may enter into contracts with, or make grants to, public or private agencies and organizations and individuals.

(j) Solid waste disposal equipment for vessels

The Secretary of the department in which the Coast Guard is operating shall engage in such research, studies, experiments, and demonstrations as he deems appropriate relative to equipment which is to be installed on board a vessel and is designed to receive, retain, treat, or discharge human body wastes and the wastes from toilets and other receptacles intended to receive or retain body wastes with particular emphasis on equipment to be installed on small recreational vessels. The Secretary of the department in which the Coast Guard is operating shall report to Congress the results of such research, studies, experiments, and demonstrations prior to the effective date of any regulations established under section 1322 of this title. In carrying out this subsection the Secretary of the department in which the Coast Guard is operating may enter into contracts with, or make grants to, public or private organizations and individuals.

(k) Land acquisition

In carrying out the provisions of this section relating to the conduct by the Administrator of demonstration projects and the development of field laboratories and research facilities, the Administrator may acquire land and interests therein by purchase, with appropriated or donated funds, by donation, or by exchange for acquired or public lands under his jurisdiction which he classifies as suitable for disposition. The values of the properties so exchanged either shall be approximately equal, or if they are not approximately equal, the values shall be equalized by the payment of cash to the grantor or to the Administrator as the circumstances require.

(*l*) Collection and dissemination of scientific knowledge on effects and control of pesticides in water

(1) The Administrator shall, after consultation with appropriate local, State, and Federal agencies, public and private organizations, and interested individuals, as soon as practicable but not later than January 1, 1973, develop and issue to the States for the purpose of carrying out this chapter the latest scientific knowledge available in indicating the kind and extent of effects on health and welfare which may be expected from the presence of pesticides in the water in varying quantities. He shall revise and add to such information whenever necessary to reflect developing scientific knowledge.

(2) The President shall, in consultation with appropriate local, State, and Federal agencies, public and private organizations, and interested individuals, conduct studies and investigations of methods to control the release of pesticides into the environment which study shall include examination of the persistency of pesticides in the water environment and alternatives thereto. The President shall submit reports, from time to time, on such investigations to Congress together with his recommendations for any necessary legislation.

(m) Waste oil disposal study

(1) The Administrator shall, in an effort to prevent degradation of the environment from the disposal of waste oil, conduct a study of (A) the generation of used engine, machine, cooling, and similar waste oil, including quantities generated, the nature and quality of such oil, present collecting methods and disposal practices, and alternate uses of such oil; (B) the long-term, chronic biological effects of the disposal of such waste oil; and (C) the potential market for such oils, including the economic and legal factors relating to the sale of products made from such oils, the level of subsidy, if any, needed to encourage the purchase by public and private nonprofit agencies of products from such oil, and the practicability of Federal procurement, on a priority basis, of products made from such oil. In conducting such study, the Administrator shall consult with affected industries and other persons.

(2) The Administrator shall report the preliminary results of such study to Congress within six months after October 18, 1972, and shall submit a final report to Congress within 18 months after such date.

(n) Comprehensive studies of effects of pollution on estuaries and estuarine zones; reports

(1) The Administrator shall, in cooperation with the Secretary of the Army, the Secretary of Agriculture, the Water Resources Council, and with other appropriate Federal, State, interstate, or local public bodies and private organizations, institutions, and individuals, conduct and promote, and encourage contributions to, continuing comprehensive studies of the effects of pollution, including sedimentation, in the estuaries and estuarine zones of the United States on fish and wildlife, on sport and commercial fishing, on recreation, on water supply and water power, and on other beneficial purposes. Such studies shall also consider the effect of demographic trends, the exploitation of mineral resources and fossil fuels, land and industrial development, navigation, flood and erosion control, and other uses of estuaries and estuarine zones upon the pollution of the waters therein.

(2) In conducting such studies, the Administrator shall assemble, coordinate, and organize all existing pertinent information on the Nation's estuaries and estuarine zones; carry out a program of investigations and surveys to supplement existing information in representative estuaries and estuarine zones; and identify the problems and areas where further research and study are required.

(3) The Administrator shall submit to Congress, from time to time, reports of the studies authorized by this subsection but at least one such report during any six-year period. Copies of each such report shall be made available to all interested parties, public and private.

(4) For the purpose of this subsection, the term "estuarine zones" means an environmental system consisting of an estuary and those transitional areas which are consistently influenced or affected by water from an estuary such as, but not limited to, salt marshes, coastal and intertidal areas, bays, harbors, lagoons, inshore waters, and channels, and the term "estuary" means all or part of the mouth of a river or stream or other body of water having unimpaired natural connection with open sea and within which the sea water is measurably diluted with fresh water derived from land drainage.

(*o*) Methods of reducing total flow of sewage and unnecessary water consumption; reports

(1) The Administrator shall conduct research and investigations on devices, systems, incentives, pricing policy, and other methods of reducing the total flow of sewage, including, but not limited to, unnecessary water consumption in order to reduce the requirements for, and the costs of, sewage and waste treatment services. Such research and investigations shall be directed to develop devices, systems, policies, and methods capable of achieving the maximum reduction of unnecessary water consumption.

(2) The Administrator shall report the preliminary results of such studies and investigations to the Congress within one year after October 18, 1972, and annually thereafter in the report required under subsection (a) of section 1375 of this title. Such report shall include recommendations for any legislation that may be required to provide for the adoption and use of devices, systems, policies, or other methods of reducing water consumption and reducing the total flow of sewage. Such report shall include an estimate of the benefits to be derived from adoption and use of such devices, systems, policies, or other methods and also shall reflect estimates of any increase in private, public, or other cost that would be occasioned thereby.

(p) Agricultural pollution

In carrying out the provisions of subsection (a) of this section the Administrator shall, in cooperation with the Secretary of Agriculture, other Federal agencies, and the States, carry out a comprehensive study and research program to determine new and improved methods and the better application of existing methods of preventing, reducing, and eliminating pollution from agriculture, including the legal, economic, and other implications of the use of such methods.

(q) Sewage in rural areas; national clearinghouse for alternative treatment information

(1) The Administrator shall conduct a comprehensive program of research and investigation and pilot project implementation into new and improved methods of preventing, reducing, storing, collecting, treating, or otherwise eliminating pollution from sewage in rural and other areas where collection of sewage in conventional, communitywide sewage collection systems is impractical, uneconomical, or otherwise infeasible, or where soil conditions or other factors preclude the use of septic tank and drainage field systems.

(2) The Administrator shall conduct a comprehensive program of research and investigation and pilot project implementation into new and improved methods for the collection and treatment of sewage and other liquid wastes combined with the treatment and disposal of solid wastes.

(3) The Administrator shall establish, either within the Environmental Protection Agency, or through contract with an appropriate public or private non-

profit organization, a national clearinghouse which shall (A) receive reports and information resulting from research, demonstrations, and other projects funded under this chapter related to paragraph (1) of this subsection and to subsection (e)(2) of section 1255 of this title; (B) coordinate and disseminate such reports and information for use by Federal and State agencies, municipalities, institutions, and persons in developing new and improved methods pursuant to this subsection; and (C) provide for the collection and dissemination of reports and information relevant to this subsection from other Federal and State agencies, institutions, universities, and persons.

(r) Research grants to colleges and universities

The Administrator is authorized to make grants to colleges and universities to conduct basic research into the structure and function of freshwater aquatic ecosystems, and to improve understanding of the ecological characteristics necessary to the maintenance of the chemical, physical, and biological integrity of freshwater aquatic ecosystems.

(s) River Study Centers

The Administrator is authorized to make grants to one or more institutions of higher education (regionally located and to be designated as "River Study Centers") for the purpose of conducting and reporting on interdisciplinary studies on the nature of river systems, including hydrology, biology, ecology, economics, the relationship between river uses and land uses, and the effects of development within river basins on river systems and on the value of water resources and water related activities. No such grant in any fiscal year shall exceed $1,000,000.

(t) Thermal discharges

The Administrator shall, in cooperation with State and Federal agencies and public and private organizations, conduct continuing comprehensive studies of the effects and methods of control of thermal discharges. In evaluating alternative methods of control the studies shall consider (1) such data as are available on the latest available technology, economic feasibility including cost-effectiveness analysis, and (2) the total impact on the environment, considering not only water quality but also air quality, land use, and effective utilization and conservation of freshwater and other natural resources. Such studies shall consider methods of minimizing adverse effects and maximizing beneficial effects of thermal discharges. The results of these studies shall be reported by the Administrator as soon as practicable, but not later than 270 days after October 18, 1972, and shall be made available to the public and the States, and considered as they become available by the Administrator in carrying out section 1326 of this title and by the States in proposing thermal water quality standards.

(u) Authorization of appropriations

There is authorized to be appropriated (1) not to exceed $100,000,000 per fiscal year for the fiscal year ending June 30, 1973, the fiscal year ending June 30, 1974, and the fiscal year ending June 30, 1975, and not to exceed $14,039,000 for the fiscal year ending September 30, 1980, and not to exceed $20,697,000 for the fiscal year ending September 30, 1981, and not to exceed $22,770,000 for the fiscal year ending September 30, 1982, for carrying out the provisions of this section, other than subsections (g)(1) and (2), (p), (r), and (t) of this section, except that such authorizations are not for any research, development, or demonstration activity pursuant to such provisions; (2) not to exceed $7,500,000 for fiscal years 1973, 1974, and 1975, $2,000,000 for fiscal year 1977, $3,000,000 for fiscal year 1978, $3,000,000 for fiscal year 1979, $3,000,000 for fiscal year 1980, $3,000,000 for fiscal year 1981, and $3,000,000 for fiscal year 1982, for carrying out the provisions of subsection (g)(1) of this section; (3) not to exceed $2,500,000 for fiscal years 1973, 1974, and 1975, $1,000,000 for fiscal year 1977, $1,500,000 for fiscal year 1978, $1,500,000 for fiscal year 1979, $1,500,000 for fiscal year 1980, $1,500,000 for fiscal year 1981, and $1,500,000 for fiscal year 1982, for carrying out the provisions of subsection (g)(2) of this section; (4) not to exceed $10,000,000 for each of the fiscal years ending June 30, 1973, June 30, 1974, and June 30, 1975, for carrying out the provisions of subsection (p) of this section; (5) not to exceed $15,000,000 per fiscal year for the fiscal years ending June 30, 1973, June 30, 1974, and June 30, 1975, for carrying out the provisions of subsection (r) of this section; and (6) not to exceed $10,000,000 per fiscal year for the fiscal years ending June 30, 1973, June 30, 1974, and June 30, 1975, for carrying out the provisions of subsection (t) of this section.

(June 30, 1948, ch. 758, title I, § 104, as added Oct. 18, 1972, Pub.L. 92–500, § 2, 86 Stat. 819, and amended Dec. 28, 1973, Pub.L. 93–207, § 1(1), 87 Stat. 906; Jan. 2, 1975, Pub.L. 93–592, § 1, 88 Stat. 1924; Dec. 27, 1977, Pub.L. 95–217, §§ 4(a), (b), 6, 7, 91 Stat. 1566, 1567; Nov. 2, 1978, Pub.L. 95–576, § 1(a), 92 Stat. 2467; Oct. 17, 1979, Pub.L. 96–88, title V, § 509(b), 93 Stat. 695; Oct. 21, 1980, Pub.L. 96–483, § 1(a), 94 Stat. 2360.)

Cross References

Authorization of appropriations to carry out this chapter other than this section, see section 1376 of this title.

Coordination of programs under this section with study for achieving sanitation services in Alaskan villages, see section 1263 of this title.

Dissemination of information obtained under this section, see section 1255 of this title.
Federal standards for marine sanitation devices, see section 1322 of this title.
Grants to municipalities to assist in operation and maintenance of projects which received grants under this section, see section 1255 of this title.

Code of Federal Regulations

Fellowships, see 40 CFR 46.100 et seq.
Research and demonstration grants, see 40 CFR 40.100 et seq.
Training assistance, see 40 CFR 45.100 et seq.

Library References

Health and Environment ⚷25.7(3).
C.J.S. Health and Environment § 106.

§ 1255. Grants for research and development

(a) Demonstration projects covering storm waters, advanced waste treatment and water purification methods, and joint treatment systems for municipal and industrial wastes

The Administrator is authorized to conduct in the Environmental Protection Agency, and to make grants to any State, municipality, or intermunicipal or interstate agency for the purpose of assisting in the development of—

(1) any project which will demonstrate a new or improved method of preventing, reducing, and eliminating the discharge into any waters of pollutants from sewers which carry storm water or both storm water and pollutants; or

(2) any project which will demonstrate advanced waste treatment and water purification methods (including the temporary use of new or improved chemical additives which provide substantial immediate improvements to existing treatment processes), or new or improved methods of joint treatment systems for municipal and industrial wastes;

and to include in such grants such amounts as are necessary for the purpose of reports, plans, and specifications in connection therewith.

(b) Demonstration projects for advanced treatment and environmental enhancement techniques to control pollution in river basins

The Administrator is authorized to make grants to any State or States or interstate agency to demonstrate, in river basins or portions thereof, advanced treatment and environmental enhancement techniques to control pollution from all sources, within such basins or portions thereof, including nonpoint sources, together with in stream[1] water quality improvement techniques.

(c) Research and demonstration projects for prevention of water pollution by industry

In order to carry out the purposes of section 1311 of this title, the Administrator is authorized to (1) conduct in the Environmental Protection Agency, (2) make grants to persons, and (3) enter into contracts with persons, for research and demonstration projects for prevention of pollution of any waters by industry including, but not limited to, the prevention, reduction, and elimination of the discharge of pollutants. No grant shall be made for any project under this subsection unless the Administrator determines that such project will develop or demonstrate a new or improved method of treating industrial wastes or otherwise prevent pollution by industry, which method shall have industrywide application.

(d) Accelerated and priority development of waste management and waste treatment methods and identification and measurement methods

In carrying out the provisions of this section, the Administrator shall conduct, on a priority basis, an accelerated effort to develop, refine, and achieve practical application of:

(1) waste management methods applicable to point and nonpoint sources of pollutants to eliminate the discharge of pollutants, including, but not limited to, elimination of runoff of pollutants and the effects of pollutants from inplace or accumulated sources;

(2) advanced waste treatment methods applicable to point and nonpoint sources, including inplace or accumulated sources of pollutants, and methods for reclaiming and recycling water and confining pollutants so they will not migrate to cause water or other environmental pollution; and

(3) improved methods and procedures to identify and measure the effects of pollutants on the chemical, physical, and biological integrity of water, including those pollutants created by new technological developments.

(e) Research and demonstration projects covering agricultural pollution and pollution from sewage in rural areas; dissemination of information

(1) The Administrator is authorized to (A) make, in consultation with the Secretary of Agriculture, grants to persons for research and demonstration projects with respect to new and improved methods of preventing, reducing, and eliminating pollution from agriculture, and (B) disseminate, in cooperation with the Secretary of Agriculture, such information obtained under this subsection, section 1254(p) of this title, and section 1314 of this title as will encourage and enable the adoption of such methods in the agricultural industry.

(2) The Administrator is authorized, (A) in consultation with other interested Federal agencies, to make grants for demonstration projects with respect to new and improved methods of preventing, reducing, storing, collecting, treating, or otherwise eliminating pollution from sewage in rural and other areas where collection of sewage in conventional, community-wide sewage collection systems is impractical, uneconomical, or otherwise infeasible, or where soil conditions or other factors preclude the use of septic tank and drainage field systems, and (B) in cooperation with other interested Federal and State agencies, to disseminate such information obtained under this subsection as will encourage and enable the adoption of new and improved methods developed pursuant to this subsection.

(f) Limitations

Federal grants under subsection (a) of this section shall be subject to the following limitations:

(1) No grant shall be made for any project unless such project shall have been approved by the appropriate State water pollution control agency or agencies and by the Administrator;

(2) No grant shall be made for any project in an amount exceeding 75 per centum of cost thereof as determined by the Administrator; and

(3) No grant shall be made for any project unless the Administrator determines that such project will serve as a useful demonstration for the purpose set forth in clause (1) or (2) of subsection (a) of this section.

(g) Maximum grants

Federal grants under subsections (c) and (d) of this section shall not exceed 75 per centum of the cost of the project.

(h) Authorization of appropriations

For the purpose of this section there is authorized to be appropriated $75,000,000 per fiscal year for the fiscal year ending June 30, 1973, the fiscal year ending June 30, 1974, and the fiscal year ending June 30, 1975, and from such appropriations at least 10 per centum of the funds actually appropriated in each fiscal year shall be available only for the purposes of subsection (e) of this section.

(i) Assistance for research and demonstration projects

The Administrator is authorized to make grants to a municipality to assist in the costs of operating and maintaining a project which received a grant under this section, section 1254 of this title, or section 1263 of this title prior to December 27, 1977, so as to reduce the operation and maintenance costs borne by the recipients of services from such project to costs comparable to those for projects assisted under subchapter II of this chapter.

(j) Assistance for recycle, reuse, and land treatment projects

The Administrator is authorized to make a grant to any grantee who received an increased grant pursuant to section 1282(a)(2) of this title. Such grant may pay up to 100 per centum of the costs of technical evaluation of the operation of the treatment works, costs of training of persons (other than employees of the grantee), and costs of disseminating technical information on the operation of the treatment works.

(June 30, 1948, ch. 758, title I, § 105, as added Oct. 18, 1972, Pub.L. 92–500, § 2, 86 Stat. 825, and amended Jan. 2, 1975, Pub.L. 93–592, § 2, 88 Stat. 1925; Dec. 27, 1977, Pub.L. 95–217, §§ 8, 9, 91 Stat. 1568.)

[1] So in original.

Cross References

Alaska village demonstration projects, study to develop comprehensive program for achieving sanitation services to be coordinated with projects covering pollution from sewage in rural areas, see section 1263 of this title.

Authorization of appropriations to carry out the provisions of this chapter other than this section, see section 1376 of this title.

National clearinghouse to receive reports and information on projects covering pollution from sewage in rural areas, see section 1254 of this title.

Code of Federal Regulations

Administration of federal contracts, grants, or loans, see 40 CFR 15.1 et seq.

Debarment and suspension under Environmental Protection Agency assistance programs, see 40 CFR 32.100 et seq.

General regulation by Environmental Protection Agency of assistance programs, see 40 CFR 30.100 et seq.

Research and demonstration grants, see 40 CFR 40.100 et seq.

Library References

Health and Environment ⚷25.7(3).
C.J.S. Health and Environment § 106.

§ 1256. Grants for pollution control programs

(a) Authorization of appropriations for State and interstate programs

There are hereby authorized to be appropriated the following sums, to remain available until expended, to carry out the purpose of this section—

(1) $60,000,000 for the fiscal year ending June 30, 1973; and

(2) $75,000,000 for the fiscal year ending June 30, 1974, and the fiscal year ending June 30, 1975, $100,000,000 per fiscal year for the fiscal years 1977, 1978, 1979, and 1980, $75,000,000 per fiscal year for the fiscal years 1981 and 1982;

for grants to States and to interstate agencies to assist them in administering programs for the prevention, reduction, and elimination of pollution, including enforcement directly or through appropriate State law enforcement officers or agencies.

(b) Allotments

From the sums appropriated in any fiscal year, the Administrator shall make allotments to the several States and interstate agencies in accordance with regulations promulgated by him on the basis of the extent of the pollution problem in the respective States.

(c) Maximum annual payments

The Administrator is authorized to pay to each State and interstate agency each fiscal year either—

(1) the allotment of such State or agency for such fiscal year under subsection (b) of this section, or

(2) the reasonable costs as determined by the Administrator of developing and carrying out a pollution program by such State or agency during such fiscal year,

which ever amount is the lesser.

(d) Limitations

No grant shall be made under this section to any State or interstate agency for any fiscal year when the expenditure of non-Federal funds by such State or interstate agency during such fiscal year for the recurrent expenses of carrying out its pollution control program are less than the expenditure by such State or interstate agency of non-Federal funds for such recurrent program expenses during the fiscal year ending June 30, 1971.

(e) Grants prohibited to states not establishing water quality monitoring procedures or adequate emergency and contingency plans

Beginning in fiscal year 1974 the Administrator shall not make any grant under this section to any State which has not provided or is not carrying out as a part of its program—

(1) the establishment and operation of appropriate devices, methods, systems, and procedures necessary to monitor, and to compile and analyze data on (including classification according to eutrophic condition), the quality of navigable waters and to the extent practicable, ground waters including biological monitoring; and provision for annually updating such data and including it in the report required under section 1315 of this title;

(2) authority comparable to that in section 1364 of this title and adequate contingency plans to implement such authority.

(f) Conditions

Grants shall be made under this section on condition that—

(1) Such State (or interstate agency) files with the Administrator within one hundred and twenty days after October 18, 1972:

(A) a summary report of the current status of the State pollution control program, including the criteria used by the State in determining priority of treatment works; and

(B) such additional information, data, and reports as the Administrator may require.

(2) No federally assumed enforcement as defined in section 1319(a)(2) of this title is in effect with respect to such State or interstate agency.

(3) Such State (or interstate agency) submits within one hundred and twenty days after October 18, 1972, and before October 1 of each year thereafter for the Administrator's approval of its program for the prevention, reduction, and elimination of pollution in accordance with purposes and provisions of this chapter in such form and content as the Administrator may prescribe.

(g) Reallotment of unpaid allotments

Any sums allotted under subsection (b) of this section in any fiscal year which are not paid shall be reallotted by the Administrator in accordance with regulations promulgated by him.

(June 30, 1948, ch. 758, title I, § 106, as added Oct. 18, 1972, Pub.L. 92–500, § 2, 86 Stat. 827, and amended Jan. 2, 1975, Pub.L. 93–592, § 3, 88 Stat. 1925; April 21, 1976, Pub.L. 94–273, § 3(20), 90 Stat. 377; Dec. 27, 1977, Pub.L. 95–217, § 4(c), 91 Stat. 1566; Oct. 21, 1980, Pub.L. 96–483, § 1(b), 94 Stat. 2360.)

Code of Federal Regulations

Administration of federal contracts, grants, or loans, see 40 CFR 15.1 et seq.
State and local assistance, see 40 CFR 35.001 et seq.
Water quality planning and management, see 40 CFR 130.0 et seq.

Library References

Health and Environment ⇐25.7(3).
C.J.S. Health and Environment § 106.

§ 1257. Mine water pollution control demonstrations

(a) Comprehensive approaches to elimination or control of mine water pollution

The Administrator in cooperation with the Appalachian Regional Commission and other Federal agencies is authorized to conduct, to make grants for, or to contract for, projects to demonstrate comprehensive approaches to the elimination or control of acid or other mine water pollution resulting from active or abandoned mining operations and other environmental pollution affecting water quality within all or part of a watershed or river basin, including siltation from surface mining. Such projects shall demonstrate the engineering and economic feasibility and practicality of various abatement techniques which will contribute substantially to effective and practical methods of acid or other mine water pollution elimination or control, and other pollution affecting water quality, including techniques that demonstrate the engineering and economic feasibility and practicality of using sewage sludge materials and other municipal wastes to diminish or prevent pollution affecting water quality from acid, sedimentation, or other pollutants and in such projects to restore affected lands to usefulness for forestry, agriculture, recreation, or other beneficial purposes.

(b) Consistency of projects with objectives of Appalachian Regional Development Act of 1965

Prior to undertaking any demonstration project under this section in the Appalachian region (as defined in section 403 of the Appalachian Regional Development Act of 1965, as amended [40 App. U.S.C. 403]), the Appalachian Regional Commission shall determine that such demonstration project is consistent with the objectives of the Appalachian Regional Development Act of 1965, as amended [40 App. U.S.C. 1 et seq.].

(c) Watershed selection

The Administrator, in selecting watersheds for the purposes of this section, shall be satisfied that the project area will not be affected adversely by the influx of acid or other mine water pollution from nearby sources.

(d) Conditions upon Federal participation

Federal participation in such projects shall be subject to the conditions—

(1) that the State shall acquire any land or interests therein necessary for such project; and

(2) that the State shall provide legal and practical protection to the project area to insure against any activities which will cause future acid or other mine water pollution.

(e) Authorization of appropriations

There is authorized to be appropriated $30,000,000 to carry out the provisions of this section, which sum shall be available until expended.

(June 30, 1948, ch. 758, title I, § 107, as added Oct. 18, 1972, Pub.L. 92–500, § 2, 86 Stat. 828.)

Cross References

Authorization of appropriations to carry out the provisions of this chapter other than this section, see section 1376 of this title.

Code of Federal Regulations

Research and demonstration grants, see 40 CFR 40.100 et seq.

Library References

Health and Environment ⚷25.7(9).
C.J.S. Health and Environment § 108 et seq.

§ 1257a. State demonstration programs for cleanup of abandoned mines for use as waste disposal sites; authorization of appropriations

The Administrator of the Environmental Protection Agency is authorized to make grants to States to undertake a demonstration program for the cleanup of State-owned abandoned mines which can be used as hazardous waste disposal sites. The State shall pay 10 per centum of project costs. At a minimum, the Administrator shall undertake projects under such program in the States of Ohio, Illinois, and West Virginia. There are authorized to be appropriated $10,000,000 per fiscal year for each of the fiscal years ending September 30, 1982, September 30, 1983, and September 30, 1984, to carry out this section. Such projects shall be undertaken in accordance with all applicable laws and regulations.

(Oct. 21, 1980, Pub.L. 96–483, § 12, 94 Stat. 2363.)

Library References

Health and Environment ⚷25.7(9).
C.J.S. Health and Environment § 108 et seq.

§ 1258. Pollution control in the Great Lakes

(a) Demonstration projects

The Administrator, in cooperation with other Federal departments, agencies, and instrumentalities is authorized to enter into agreements with any State, political subdivision, interstate agency, or other public agency, or combination thereof, to carry out one or more projects to demonstrate new methods and techniques and to develop preliminary plans for the elimination or control of pollution, within all or any part of the watersheds of the Great Lakes. Such projects shall demonstrate the engineering and economic feasibility and practicality of removal of pollutants and prevention of any polluting matter from entering into the Great Lakes in the future and other reduction and remedial techniques which will contribute substantially to effective and practical methods of pollution prevention, reduction, or elimination.

(b) Conditions of Federal participation

Federal participation in such projects shall be subject to the condition that the State, political subdivision, interstate agency, or other public agency, or combination thereof, shall pay not less than 25 per centum of the actual project costs, which payment may be in any form, including, but not limited to, land or interests therein that is needed for the project, and personal property or services the value of which shall be determined by the Administrator.

(c) Authorization of appropriations

There is authorized to be appropriated $20,000,000 to carry out the provisions of subsections (a) and (b) of this section, which sum shall be available until expended.

(d) Lake Erie demonstration program

(1) In recognition of the serious conditions which exist in Lake Erie, the Secretary of the Army, acting through the Chief of Engineers, is directed to design and develop a demonstration waste water management program for the rehabilitation and environmental repair of Lake Erie. Prior to the initiation of detailed engineering and design, the program, along with the specific recommendations of the Chief of Engineers, and recommendations for its financing, shall be submitted to the Congress for statutory approval. This authority is in addition to, and not in lieu of, other waste water studies aimed at eliminating pollution emanating from select sources around Lake Erie.

(2) This program is to be developed in cooperation with the Environmental Protection Agency, other interested departments, agencies, and instrumentalities of the Federal Government, and the States and their political subdivisions. This program shall set forth alternative systems for managing waste water on a regional basis and shall provide local and State governments with a range of choice as to the type of system to be used for the treatment of waste water. These alternative systems shall include both advanced waste treatment technology and land disposal systems including aerated treatment-spray irrigation technology and will also include provisions for the disposal of solid wastes, including sludge. Such program should include measures to control point sources of pollution, area sources of pollution, including acid-mine drainage, urban runoff and rural runoff, and in place sources of pollution, including bottom loads, sludge banks, and polluted harbor dredgings.

(e) Authorization of appropriations for Lake Erie demonstration program

There is authorized to be appropriated $5,000,000 to carry out the provisions of subsection (d) of this section, which sum shall be available until expended.

(June 30, 1948, ch. 758, title I, § 108, as added Oct. 18, 1972, Pub.L. 92–500, § 2, 86 Stat. 828.)

Cross References

Authorization of appropriations to carry out the provisions of this chapter other than this section, see section 1376 of this title.

Code of Federal Regulations

Research and demonstration grants, see 40 CFR 40.100 et seq.

Library References

Health and Environment ⚷25.7(4).
C.J.S. Health and Environment § 108 et seq.

§ 1259. Training grants and contracts

(a) The Administrator is authorized to make grants to or contracts with institutions of higher education, or combinations of such institutions, to assist them in planning, developing, strengthening, improving, or carrying out programs or projects for the preparation of undergraduate students to enter an occupation which involves the design, operation, and maintenance of treatment works, and other facilities whose purpose is water quality control. Such grants or contracts may include payment of all or part of the cost of programs or projects such as—

(A) planning for the development or expansion of programs or projects for training persons in the operation and maintenance of treatment works;

(B) training and retraining of faculty members;

(C) conduct of short-term or regular session institutes for study by persons engaged in, or preparing to engage in, the preparation of students preparing to enter an occupation involving the operation and maintenance of treatment works;

(D) carrying out innovative and experimental programs of cooperative education involving alternate periods of full-time or part-time academic study at the institution and periods of full-time or part-time employment involving the operation and maintenance of treatment works; and

(E) research into, and development of, methods of training students or faculty, including the preparation of teaching materials and the planning of curriculum.

(b)(1) The Administrator may pay 100 per centum of any additional cost of construction of treatment works required for a facility to train and upgrade waste treatment works operation and maintenance personnel and for the costs of other State treatment works operator training programs, including mobile training units, classroom rental, specialized instructors, and instructional material.

(2) The Administrator shall make no more than one grant for such additional construction in any State (to serve a group of States, where, in his judgment, efficient training programs require multi-State programs), and shall make such grant after consultation with and approval by the State or States on the basis of (A) the suitability of such facility for training operation and maintenance personnel for treatment works throughout such State or States; and (B) a commitment by the State agency or agencies to carry out at such facility a program of training approved by the Administrator. In any case where a grant is made to serve two or more States, the Administrator is authorized to make an additional grant for a supplemental facility in each such State.

(3) The Administrator may make such grant out of the sums allocated to a State under section 1285 of this title, except that in no event shall the Federal cost of any such training facilities exceed $500,000.

(4) The Administrator may exempt a grant under this section from any requirement under section 1284(a)(3) of this title. Any grantee who received a grant under this section prior to enactment of the Clean Water Act of 1977 shall be eligible to have its grant increased by funds made available under such Act.

(June 30, 1948, ch. 758, title I, § 109, as added Oct. 18, 1972, Pub.L. 92–500, § 2, 86 Stat. 829, and amended Dec. 27, 1977, Pub.L. 95–217, § 10, 91 Stat. 1568.)

Cross References

Annual reports by Administrator of his activities under sections 1259 to 1261 of this title, including recommendations for revisions, see sections 1262 and 1375 of this title.
Application for grants, see section 1260 of this title.
Authorization of appropriations, see section 1262 of this title.
Definition of "institution of higher education" and "academic year", see section 1262 of this title.
Equitable distribution of grants throughout the United States, see section 1260 of this title.

Code of Federal Regulations

Training assistance, see 40 CFR 45.100 et seq.

Library References

Health and Environment ⚷25.7(21), (22).
C.J.S. Health and Environment § 106 et seq.

§ 1260. Applications; allocation

(1) A grant or contract authorized by section 1259 of this title may be made only upon application to the Administrator at such time or times and containing such information as he may prescribe, except that no such application shall be approved unless it—

(A) sets forth programs, activities, research, or development for which a grant is authorized under section 1259 of this title and describes the relation to any program set forth by the applicant in an application, if any, submitted pursuant to section 1261 of this title;

(B) provides such fiscal control and fund accounting procedures as may be necessary to assure proper disbursement of and accounting for Federal funds paid to the applicant under this section; and

(C) provides for making such reports, in such form and containing such information, as the Administrator may require to carry out his functions under this section, and for keeping such records and for affording such access thereto as the Administrator may find necessary to assure the correctness and verification of such reports.

(2) The Administrator shall allocate grants or contracts under section 1259 of this title in such manner as will most nearly provide an equitable distribution of the grants or contracts throughout the United States among institutions of higher education which show promise of being able to use funds effectively for the purpose of this section.

(3)(A) Payments under this section may be used in accordance with regulations of the Administrator, and subject to the terms and conditions set forth in an application approved under paragraph (1), to pay part of the compensation of students employed in connection with the operation and maintenance of treatment works, other than as an employee in connection with the operation and maintenance of treatment works or as an employee in any branch of the Government of the United States, as part of a program for which a grant has been approved pursuant to this section.

(B) Departments and agencies of the United States are encouraged, to the extent consistent with efficient administration, to enter into arrangements with institutions of higher education for the full-time, part-time, or temporary employment, whether in the competitive or excepted service, of students enrolled in programs set forth in applications approved under paragraph (1).

(June 30, 1948, ch. 758, title I, § 110, as added Oct. 18, 1972, Pub.L. 92–500, § 2, 86 Stat. 830.)

Cross References

Annual reports by Administrator of his activities under sections 1259 to 1261 of this title, including recommendations for revisions, see sections 1262 and 1375 of this title.
Approval of programs of institutions of higher education for purposes of scholarships, see section 1261 of this title.

Definition of "institution of higher education" and "academic year", see section 1262 of this title.

§ 1261. Scholarships

(1) The Administrator is authorized to award scholarships in accordance with the provisions of this section for undergraduate study by persons who plan to enter an occupation involving the operation and maintenance of treatment works. Such scholarships shall be awarded for such periods as the Administrator may determine but not to exceed four academic years.

(2) The Administrator shall allocate scholarships under this section among institutions of higher education with programs approved under the provisions of this section for the use of individuals accepted into such programs in such manner and according to such plan as will insofar as practicable—

(A) provide an equitable distribution of such scholarships throughout the United States; and

(B) attract recent graduates of secondary schools to enter an occupation involving the operation and maintenance of treatment works.

(3) The Administrator shall approve a program of any institution of higher education for the purposes of this section only upon application by the institution and only upon his finding—

(A) that such program has a principal objective the education and training of persons in the operation and maintenance of treatment works;

(B) that such program is in effect and of high quality, or can be readily put into effect and may reasonably be expected to be of high quality;

(C) that the application describes the relation of such program to any program, activity, research, or development set forth by the applicant in an application, if any, submitted pursuant to section 1260 of this title; and

(D) that the application contains satisfactory assurances that (i) the institution will recommend to the Administrator for the award of scholarships under this section, for study in such program, only persons who have demonstrated to the satisfaction of the institution a serious intent, upon completing the program, to enter an occupation involving the operation and maintenance of treatment works, and (ii) the institution will make reasonable continuing efforts to encourage recipients of scholarships under this section, enrolled in such program, to enter occupations involving the operation and maintenance of treatment works upon completing the program.

(4)(A) The Administrator shall pay to persons awarded scholarships under this section such stipends (including such allowances for subsistence and other expenses for such persons and their dependents) as he may determine to be consistent with prevailing practices under comparable supported programs.

(B) The Administrator shall (in addition to the stipends paid to persons under paragraph (1)) pay to the institution of higher education at which such person is pursuing his course of study such amount as he may determine to be consistent with prevailing practices under comparable federally supported programs.

(5) A person awarded a scholarship under the provisions of this section shall continue to receive the payments provided in this section only during such periods as the Administrator finds that he is maintaining satisfactory proficiency and devoting full time to study or research in the field in which such scholarship was awarded in an institution of higher education, and is not engaging in gainful employment other than employment approved by the Administrator by or pursuant to regulation.

(6) The Administrator shall by regulation provide that any person awarded a scholarship under this section shall agree in writing to enter and remain in an occupation involving the design, operation, or maintenance of treatment works for such period after completion of his course of studies as the Administrator determines appropriate.

(June 30, 1948, ch. 758, title I, § 111, as added Oct. 18, 1972, Pub.L. 92–500, § 2, 86 Stat. 831.)

Cross References

Annual reports by Administrator of his activities under sections 1259 to 1261 of this title, including recommendations for revisions, see sections 1262 and 1375 of this title.

Application for grants or contracts, see section 1260 of this title.

Definition of "institution of higher education" and "academic year", see section 1262 of this title.

Code of Federal Regulations

Training assistance, see 40 CFR 45.100 et seq.

Library References

Colleges and Universities ⚷9.

C.J.S. Colleges and Universities § 24 et seq.

§ 1262. Definitions and authorizations

(a) As used in sections 1259 through 1262 of this title—

(1) The term "institution of higher education" means an educational institution described in the first sentence of section 1141 of title 20 (other than an institution of any agency of the United States) which is accredited by a nationally recognized accrediting agency or association approved by the Administrator for this purpose. For purposes of this subsection, the Administrator shall

publish a list of nationally recognized accrediting agencies or associations which he determines to be reliable authority as to the quality of training offered.

(2) The term "academic year" means an academic year or its equivalent, as determined by the Administrator.

(b) The Administrator shall annually report his activities under sections 1259 through 1262 of this title, including recommendations for needed revisions in the provisions thereof.

(c) There are authorized to be appropriated $25,000,000 per fiscal year for the fiscal years ending June 30, 1973, June 30, 1974, and June 30, 1975, $6,000,000 for the fiscal year ending September 30, 1977, $7,000,000 for the fiscal year ending September 30, 1978, $7,000,000 for the fiscal year ending September 30, 1979, $7,000,000 for the fiscal year ending September 30, 1980, $7,000,000 for the fiscal year ending September 30, 1981, and $7,000,000 for the fiscal year ending September 30, 1982, to carry out sections 1259 through 1262 of this title.

(June 30, 1948, ch. 758, title I, § 112, as added Oct. 18, 1972, Pub.L. 92–500, § 2, 86 Stat. 832, and amended Jan. 2, 1975, Pub.L. 93–592, § 4, 88 Stat. 1925; Dec. 27, 1977, Pub.L. 95–217, § 4(d), 91 Stat. 1566; Oct. 21, 1980, Pub.L. 96–483, § 1(c), 94 Stat. 2360.)

Cross References

Authorization of appropriations to carry out the provisions of this chapter other than this section, see section 1376 of this title.

§ 1263. Alaska village demonstration projects

(a) Central community facilities for safe water; elimination or control of pollution

The Administrator is authorized to enter into agreements with the State of Alaska to carry out one or more projects to demonstrate methods to provide for central community facilities for safe water and eliminate or control of pollution in those native villages of Alaska without such facilities. Such project shall include provisions for community safe water supply systems, toilets, bathing and laundry facilities, sewage disposal facilities, and other similar facilities, and educational and informational facilities and programs relating to health and hygiene. Such demonstration projects shall be for the further purpose of developing preliminary plans for providing such safe water and such elimination or control of pollution for all native villages in such State.

(b) Utilization of personnel and facilities of Department of Health and Human Services

In carrying out this section the Administrator shall cooperate with the Secretary of Health and Human Services for the purpose of utilizing such of the personnel and facilities of that Department as may be appropriate.

(c) Omitted

(d) Authorization of appropriations

There is authorized to be appropriated not to exceed $2,000,000 to carry out this section. In addition, there is authorized to be appropriated to carry out this section not to exceed $200,000 for the fiscal year ending September 30, 1978, and $220,000 for the fiscal year ending September 30, 1979.

(e) Study to develop comprehensive program for achieving sanitation services; report to Congress

The Administrator is authorized to coordinate with the Secretary of the Department of Health and Human Services, the Secretary of the Department of Housing and Urban Development, the Secretary of the Department of the Interior, the Secretary of the Department of Agriculture, and the heads of any other departments or agencies he may deem appropriate to conduct a joint study with representatives of the State of Alaska and the appropriate Native organizations (as defined in Public Law 92–203) to develop a comprehensive program for achieving adequate sanitation services in Alaska villages. This study shall be coordinated with the programs and projects authorized by sections 1254(q) and 1255(e)(2) of this title. The Administrator shall submit a report of the results of the study, together with appropriate supporting data and such recommendations as he deems desirable, to the Committee on Environment and Public Works of the Senate and to the Committee on Public Works and Transportation of the House of Representatives not later than December 31, 1979. The Administrator shall also submit recommended administrative actions, procedures, and any proposed legislation necessary to implement the recommendations of the study no later than June 30, 1980.

(f) Technical, financial, and management assistance

The Administrator is authorized to provide technical, financial and management assistance for operation and maintenance of the demonstration projects constructed under this section, until such time as the recommendations of subsection (e) of this section are implemented.

(g) Definitions

For the purpose of this section, the term "village" shall mean an incorporated or unincorporated community with a population of ten to six hundred people living within a two-mile radius. The term "sanitation services" shall mean water supply, sewage disposal, solid waste disposal and other services necessary to maintain generally accepted standards of personal hygiene and public health.

(June 30, 1948, ch. 758, title I, § 113, as added Oct. 18, 1972, Pub.L. 92–500, § 2, 86 Stat. 832, and amended Dec. 27, 1977, Pub.L. 95–217, § 11, 91 Stat. 1568; Oct. 17, 1979, Pub.L. 96–88, title V, § 509(b), 93 Stat. 695.)

Cross References

Authorization of appropriations to carry out the provisions of this chapter other than this section, see section 1376 of this title.

Grants to municipalities to assist in costs of operating and maintaining projects which received grants under this section, see section 1255 of this title.

Code of Federal Regulations

Research and demonstration projects, see 40 CFR 40.100 et seq.

Library References

Health and Environment ⚷25.7(21).
C.J.S. Health and Environment § 106 et seq.

§ 1264. Omitted

§ 1265. In-place toxic pollutants

The Administrator is directed to identify the location of in-place pollutants with emphasis on toxic pollutants in harbors and navigable waterways and is authorized, acting through the Secretary of the Army, to make contracts for the removal and appropriate disposal of such materials from critical port and harbor areas. There is authorized to be appropriated $15,000,000 to carry out the provisions of this section, which sum shall be available until expended.

(June 30, 1948, c. 758, title I, § 115, as added Oct. 18, 1972, Pub.L. 92–500, § 2, 86 Stat. 833.)

Cross References

Authorization of appropriations to carry out the provisions of this chapter other than this section, see section 1376 of this title.

Hudson River reclamation demonstration project, funds available, see section 1266 of this title.

Library References

Health and Environment ⚷25.7(20), (22).
C.J.S. Health and Environment §§ 106 et seq., 113 et seq.

§ 1266. Hudson River reclamation demonstration project

(a) The Administrator is authorized to enter into contracts and other agreements with the State of New York to carry out a project to demonstrate methods for the selective removal of polychlorinated biphenyls contaminating bottom sediments of the Hudson River, treating such sediments as required, burying such sediments in secure landfills, and installing monitoring systems for such landfills. Such demonstration project shall be for the purpose of determining the feasibility of indefinite storage in secure landfills of toxic substances and of ascertaining the improvement of the rate of recovery of a toxic contaminated national waterway. No pollutants removed pursuant to this paragraph shall be placed in any landfill unless the Administrator first determines that disposal of the pollutants in such landfill would provide a higher standard of protection of the public health, safety, and welfare than disposal of such pollutants by any other method including, but not limited to, incineration or a chemical destruction process.

(b) The Administrator is authorized to make grants to the State of New York to carry out this section from funds allotted to such State under section 1285(a) of this title, except that the amount of any such grant shall be equal to 75 per centum of the cost of the project and such grant shall be made on condition that non-Federal sources provide the remainder of the cost of such project. The authority of this section shall be available until September 30, 1983. Funds allotted to the State of New York under section 1285(a) of this title shall be available under this subsection only to the extent that funds are not available, as determined by the Administrator, to the State of New York for the work authorized by this section under section 1265 or 1321 of this title or a comprehensive hazardous substance response and clean up fund. Any funds used under the authority of this subsection shall be deducted from any estimate of the needs of the State of New York prepared under section 1375(b) of this title. The Administrator may not obligate or expend more than $20,000,000 to carry out this section.

(June 30, 1948, ch. 758, title I, § 116, as added Oct. 21, 1980, Pub.L. 96–483, § 10, 94 Stat. 2363.)

Library References

Health and Environment ⚷25.7(21).
C.J.S. Health and Environment § 106 et seq.

SUBCHAPTER II—GRANTS FOR CONSTRUCTION OF TREATMENT WORKS

Cross References

Consideration of international water pollution control agreements in development of the ranking in order of priority of needs for construction of treatment works, see section 1371 of this title.

Grants to municipalities to reduce operation and maintenance costs to costs comparable to those for projects assisted under this subchapter, see section 1255 of this title.

Priority to applications from public bodies situated in areas affected by major disasters, see section 5153 of Title 42, The Public Health and Welfare.

Prohibition on making of grants until review and revision of water quality standards, see section 1313a of this title.

§ 1281. Congressional declaration of purpose

(a) Development and implementation of waste treatment management plans and practices

It is the purpose of this subchapter to require and to assist the development and implementation of waste treatment management plans and practices which will achieve the goals of this chapter.

(b) Application of technology: confined disposal of pollutants; consideration of advanced techniques

Waste treatment management plans and practices shall provide for the application of the best practicable waste treatment technology before any discharge into receiving waters, including reclaiming and recycling of water, and confined disposal of pollutants so they will not migrate to cause water or other environmental pollution and shall provide for consideration of advanced waste treatment techniques.

(c) Waste treatment management area and scope

To the extent practicable, waste treatment management shall be on an areawide basis and provide control or treatment of all point and nonpoint sources of pollution, including in place or accumulated pollution sources.

(d) Waste treatment management construction of revenue producing facilities

The Administrator shall encourage waste treatment management which results in the construction of revenue producing facilities providing for—

(1) the recycling of potential sewage pollutants through the production of agriculture, silviculture, or aquaculture products, or any combination thereof;

(2) the confined and contained disposal of pollutants not recycled;

(3) the reclamation of wastewater; and

(4) the ultimate disposal of sludge in a manner that will not result in environmental hazards.

(e) Waste treatment management integration of facilities

The Administrator shall encourage waste treatment management which results in integrating facilities for sewage treatment and recycling with facilities to treat, dispose of, or utilize other industrial and municipal wastes, including but not limited to solid waste and waste heat and thermal discharges. Such integrated facilities shall be designed and operated to produce revenues in excess of capital and operation and maintenance costs and such revenues shall be used by the designated regional management agency to aid in financing other environmental improvement programs.

(f) Waste treatment management "open space" and recreational considerations

The Administrator shall encourage waste treatment management which combines "open space" and recreational considerations with such management.

(g) Grants to construct publicly owned treatment works

(1) The Administrator is authorized to make grants to any State, municipality, or intermunicipal or interstate agency for the construction of publicly owned treatment works. On and after October 1, 1984, grants under this subchapter shall be made only for projects for secondary treatment or more stringent treatment, or any cost effective alternative thereto, new interceptors and appurtenances, and infiltration-in-flow correction. Notwithstanding the preceding sentence, the Administrator may make grants on and after October 1, 1984, for any project within the definition set forth in section 1292(2) of this title, other than for a project referred to in the preceding sentence, except that not more than 20 per centum (as determined by the Governor of the State) of the amount allotted to a State under section 1285 of this title for any fiscal year shall be obligated in such State under authority of this sentence.

(2) The Administrator shall not make grants from funds authorized for any fiscal year beginning after June 30, 1974, to any State, municipality, or intermunicipal or interstate agency for the erection, building, acquisition, alteration, remodeling, improvement, or extension of treatment works unless the grant applicant has satisfactorily demonstrated to the Administrator that—

(A) alternative waste management techniques have been studied and evaluated and the works proposed for grant assistance will provide for the application of the best practicable waste treatment technology over the life of the works consistent with the purposes of this subchapter; and

(B) as appropriate, the works proposed for grant assistance will take into account and allow to the extent practicable the application of technology at a later date which will provide for the reclaiming or recycling of water or otherwise eliminate the discharge of pollutants.

(3) The Administrator shall not approve any grant after July 1, 1973, for treatment works under this section unless the applicant shows to the satisfaction of the Administrator that each sewer collection system discharging into such treatment works is not subject to excessive infiltration.

(4) The Administrator is authorized to make grants to applicants for treatment works grants under this section for such sewer system evaluation studies as may be necessary to carry out the re-

quirements of paragraph (3) of this subsection. Such grants shall be made in accordance with rules and regulations promulgated by the Administrator. Initial rules and regulations shall be promulgated under this paragraph not later than 120 days after October 18, 1972.

(5) The Administrator shall not make grants from funds authorized for any fiscal year beginning after September 30, 1978, to any State, municipality, or intermunicipal or interstate agency for the erection, building, acquisition, alteration, remodeling, improvement, or extension of treatment works unless the grant applicant has satisfactorily demonstrated to the Administrator that innovative and alternative wastewater treatment processes and techniques which provide for the reclaiming and reuse of water, otherwise eliminate the discharge of pollutants, and utilize recycling techniques, land treatment, new or improved methods of waste treatment management for municipal and industrial waste (discharged into municipal systems) and the confined disposal of pollutants, so that pollutants will not migrate to cause water or other environmental pollution, have been fully studied and evaluated by the applicant taking into account subsection (d) of this section and taking into account and allowing to the extent practicable the more efficient use of energy and resources.

(6) The Administrator shall not make grants from funds authorized for any fiscal year beginning after September 30, 1978, to any State, municipality, or intermunicipal or interstate agency for the erection, building, acquisition, alteration, remodeling, improvement, or extension of treatment works unless the grant applicant has satisfactorily demonstrated to the Administrator that the applicant has analyzed the potential recreation and open space opportunities in the planning of the proposed treatment works.

(h) Grants to construct privately owned treatment works

A grant may be made under this section to construct a privately owned treatment works serving one or more principal residences or small commercial establishments constructed prior to, and inhabited on, December 27, 1977, where the Administrator finds that—

(1) a public body otherwise eligible for a grant under subsection (g) of this section has applied on behalf of a number of such units and certified that public ownership of such works is not feasible;

(2) such public body has entered into an agreement with the Administrator which guarantees that such treatment works will be properly operated and maintained and will comply with all other requirements of section 1284 of this title and includes a system of charges to assure that each recipient of waste treatment services under such a grant will pay its proportionate share of the cost of operation and maintenance (including replacement); and

(3) the total cost and environmental impact of providing waste treatment services to such residences or commercial establishments will be less than the cost of providing a system of collection and central treatment of such wastes.

(i) Waste treatment management methods, processes, and techniques to reduce energy requirements

The Administrator shall encourage waste treatment management methods, processes, and techniques which will reduce total energy requirements.

(j) Grants for treatment works utilizing processes and techniques of guidelines under section 1314(d)(3) of this title

The Administrator is authorized to make a grant for any treatment works utilizing processes and techniques meeting the guidelines promulgated under section 1314(d)(3) of this title, if the Administrator determines it is in the public interest and if in the cost effectiveness study made of the construction grant application for the purpose of evaluating alternative treatment works, the life cycle cost of the treatment works for which the grant is to be made does not exceed the life cycle cost of the most cost effective alternative by more than 15 per centum.

(k) Limitation on use of grants for publicly owned treatment works

No grant made after November 15, 1981, for a publicly owned treatment works, other than for facility planning and the preparation of construction plans and specifications, shall be used to treat, store, or convey the flow of any industrial user into such treatment works in excess of a flow per day equivalent to fifty thousand gallons per day of sanitary waste. This subsection shall not apply to any project proposed by a grantee which is carrying out an approved project to prepare construction plans and specifications for a facility to treat wastewater, which received its grant approval before May 15, 1980. This subsection shall not be in effect after November 15, 1981.

(*l*) Grants for facility plans, or plans, specifications, and estimates for proposed project for construction of treatment works; limitations, allotments, advances, etc.

(1) After December 29, 1981, Federal grants shall not be made for the purpose of providing assistance solely for facility plans, or plans, specifications, and estimates for any proposed project for the construction of treatment works. In the event that the proposed project receives a grant under this section for construction, the Administrator shall make an allowance in such grant for non-Federal funds expended during the facility planning and advanced engineering and design phase at the prevailing Federal share under section 1282(a) of this title, based on the percentage of total project costs which the Administrator determines is the general experience for such projects.

(2)(A) Each State shall use a portion of the funds allotted to such State each fiscal year, but not to exceed 10 per centum of such funds, to advance to potential grant applicants under this subchapter the costs of facility planning or the preparation of plans, specifications, and estimates.

(B) Such an advance shall be limited to the allowance for such costs which the Administrator establishes under paragraph (1) of this subsection, and shall be provided only to a potential grant applicant which is a small community and which in the judgment of the State would otherwise be unable to prepare a request for a grant for construction costs under this section.

(C) In the event a grant for construction costs is made under this section for a project for which an advance has been made under this paragraph, the Administrator shall reduce the amount of such grant by the allowance established under paragraph (1) of this subsection. In the event no such grant is made, the State is authorized to seek repayment of such advance on such terms and conditions as it may determine.

(m) Grants for State of California projects

(1) Notwithstanding any other provisions of this subchapter, the Administrator is authorized to make a grant from any funds otherwise allotted to the State of California under section 1285 of this title to the project (and in the amount) specified in Order WQG 81–1 of the California State Water Resources Control Board.

(2) Notwithstanding any other provision of this chapter, the Administrator shall make a grant from any funds otherwise allotted to the State of California to the city of Eureka, California, in connection with project numbered C–06–2772, for the purchase of one hundred and thirty-nine acres of property as environmental mitigation for siting of the proposed treatment plant.

(3) Notwithstanding any other provision of this chapter, the Administrator shall make a grant from any funds otherwise allotted to the State of California to the city of San Diego, California, in connection with that city's aquaculture sewage process (total resources recovery system) as an innovative and alternative waste treatment process.

(n) Water quality problems; funds, scope, etc.

(1) On and after October 1, 1984, upon the request of the Governor of an affected State, the Administrator is authorized to use funds available to such State under section 1285 of this title to address water quality problems due to the impacts of discharges from combined storm water and sanitary sewer overflows, which are not otherwise eligible under this subsection, where correction of such discharges is a major priority for such State.

(2) Beginning fiscal year 1983, the Administrator shall have available $200,000,000 per fiscal year in addition to those funds authorized in section 1287 of this title to be utilized to address water quality problems of marine bays and estuaries subject to lower levels of water quality due to the impacts of discharges from combined storm water and sanitary sewer overflows from adjacent urban complexes, not otherwise eligible under this subsection. Such sums may be used as deemed appropriate by the Administrator as provided in paragraphs (1) and (2) of this subsection, upon the request of and demonstration of water quality benefits by the Governor of an affected State.

(*o*) Capital financing plan

The Administrator shall encourage and assist applicants for grant assistance under this subchapter to develop and file with the Administrator a capital financing plan which, at a minimum—

(1) projects the future requirements for waste treatment services within the applicant's jurisdiction for a period of no less than ten years;

(2) projects the nature, extent, timing, and costs of future expansion and reconstruction of treatment works which will be necessary to satisfy the applicant's projected future requirements for waste treatment services; and

(3) sets forth with specificity the manner in which the applicant intends to finance such future expansion and reconstruction.

(June 30, 1948, ch. 758, title II, § 201, as added Oct. 18, 1972, Pub.L. 92–500, § 2, 86 Stat. 833, and amended Dec. 27, 1977, Pub.L. 95–217, §§ 12–16, 91 Stat. 1569, 1570; Oct. 21, 1980, Pub.L. 96–483, §§ 2(d), 3, 94 Stat. 2361; Dec. 29, 1981, Pub.L. 97–117, §§ 2(a), 3(a), 4–6, 10(c), 95 Stat. 1623–1626.)

Cross References

Action of Administrator deemed major Federal action for purposes of environmental policy, see section 1371 of this title.
Allotment of additional funds, see section 1286 of this title.
Amount of grants for treatment works, see section 1282 of this title.
Areawide waste treatment management planning process consistent with this section, see section 1288 of this title.
Cost-effectiveness, Congressional statement of policy, see section 1298 of this title.

Definition of "treatment works", see section 1292 of this title.
Grants for sewage collection systems, see section 1291 of this title.
Grants to designated regional operating agencies, see section 1288 of this title.
Grants to State for reasonable costs of administration of any aspects of this section, see section 1285 of this title.
Guidelines for cost-effectiveness analysis, see section 1297 of this title.
Matters determinable prior to approval of grant under this section, see section 1284 of this title.
Plans, specifications, and estimates for project for construction of treatment works plant, see section 1283 of this title.
Promulgation of guidelines for identifying innovative and alternative wastewater treatment processes referred to in this section, see section 1314 of this title.
Publication of information on alternative waste treatment management techniques available to implement this section, see section 1314 of this title.
Report of estimated costs to Congress, see section 1375 of this title.
Terms and conditions for extension of timetable for achievement of objectives, see section 1311 of this title.
Treatment of amount of grant under this section in excess of costs of construction of treatment works as grant of the Federal share of cost of construction of a sewage collection system, see section 1281a of this title.

Library References

Health and Environment ⚷25.7(21).
C.J.S. Health and Environment § 106 et seq.

§ 1281a. Total treatment system funding

Notwithstanding any other provision of law, in any case where the Administrator of the Environmental Protection Agency finds that the total of all grants made under section 1281 of this title for the same treatment works exceeds the actual construction costs for such treatment works (as defined in this chapter) such excess amount shall be a grant of the Federal share (as defined in this chapter) of the cost of construction of a sewage collection system if—

(1) such sewage collection system was constructed as part of the same total treatment system as the treatment works for which such grants under section 1281 of this title were approved, and

(2) an application for assistance for the construction of such sewage collection system was filed in accordance with section 3102 of title 42 before all such grants under section 1281 of this title were made and such grant under section 3102 of title 42 could not be approved due to lack of funding under such section 3102 of title 42.

The total of all grants for sewage collection systems made under this section shall not exceed $2,800,000.

(Dec. 27, 1977, Pub.L. 95–217, § 78, 91 Stat. 1611.)

Library References

Health and Environment ⚷25.7(21).
C.J.S. Health and Environment § 106 et seq.

§ 1282. Federal share

(a) Amount of grants for treatment works

(1) The amount of any grant for treatment works made under this chapter from funds authorized for any fiscal year beginning after June 30, 1971, and ending before October 1, 1984, shall be 75 per centum of the cost of construction thereof (as approved by the Administrator), and for any fiscal year beginning on or after October 1, 1984, shall be 55 per centum of the cost of construction thereof (as approved by the Administrator), unless modified to a lower percentage rate uniform throughout a State by the Governor of that State with the concurrence of the Administrator. Within ninety days after October 21, 1980, the Administrator shall issue guidelines for concurrence in any such modification, which shall provide for the consideration of the unobligated balance of sums allocated to the State under section 1285 of this title, the need for assistance under this subchapter in such State, and the availability of State grant assistance to replace the Federal share reduced by such modification. The payment of any such reduced Federal share shall not constitute an obligation on the part of the United States or a claim on the part of any State or grantee to reimbursement for the portion of the Federal share reduced in any such State. Any grant (other than for reimbursement) made prior to October 18, 1972, from any funds authorized for any fiscal year beginning after June 30, 1971, shall, upon the request of the applicant, be increased to the applicable percentage under this section. Notwithstanding the first sentence of this paragraph, in any case where a primary, secondary, or advanced waste treatment facility or its related interceptors or a project for infiltration-in-flow correction has received a grant for erection, building, acquisition, alteration, remodeling, improvement, extension, or correction before October 1, 1984, all segments and phases of such facility, interceptors, and project for infiltration-in-flow correction shall be eligible for grants at 75 per centum of the cost of construction thereof.

(2) The amount of any grant made after September 30, 1978, and before October 1, 1981, for any eligible treatment works or significant portion thereof utilizing innovative or alternative wastewater treatment processes and techniques referred to in section 1281(g)(5) of this title shall be 85 per centum of the cost of construction thereof, unless modified by the Governor of the State with the concurrence of the Administrator to a percentage rate no less than 15 per centum greater than the modified uniform percentage rate in which the Administrator has concurred pursuant to paragraph (1) of this subsection. The amount of any grant made after September 30, 1981, for any eligible treatment

works or unit processes and techniques thereof utilizing innovative or alternative wastewater treatment processes and techniques referred to in section 1281(g)(5) of this title shall be a percentage of the cost of construction thereof equal to 20 per centum greater than the percentage in effect under paragraph (1) of this subsection for such works or unit processes and techniques, but in no event greater that 85 per centum of the cost of construction thereof. No grant shall be made under this paragraph for construction of a treatment works in any State unless the proportion of the State contribution to the non-Federal share of construction costs for all treatment works in such State receiving a grant under this paragraph is the same as or greater than the proportion of the State contribution (if any) to the non-Federal share of construction costs for all treatment works receiving grants in such State under paragraph (1) of this subsection.

(3) In addition to any grant made pursuant to paragraph (2) of this subsection, the Administrator is authorized to make a grant to fund all of the costs of the modification or replacement of any facilities constructed with a grant made pursuant to paragraph (2) if the Administrator finds that such facilities have not met design performance specifications unless such failure is attributable to negligence on the part of any person and if such failure has significantly increased capital or operating and maintenance expenditures.

(4) For the purposes of this section, the term "eligible treatment works" means those treatment works in each State which meet the requirements of section 1281(g)(5) of this title and which can be fully funded from funds available for such purpose in such State.

(b) Amount of grants for construction of treatment works not commenced prior to July 1, 1971

The amount of the grant for any project approved by the Administrator after January 1, 1971, and before July 1, 1971, for the construction of treatment works, the actual erection, building or acquisition of which was not commenced prior to July 1, 1971, shall, upon the request of the applicant, be increased to the applicable percentage under subsection (a) of this section for grants for treatment works from funds for fiscal years beginning after June 30, 1971, with respect to the cost of such actual erection, building, or acquisition. Such increased amount shall be paid from any funds allocated to the State in which the treatment works is located without regard to the fiscal year for which such funds were authorized. Such increased amount shall be paid for such project only if—

(1) a sewage collection system that is a part of the same total waste treatment system as the treatment works for which such grant was approved is under construction or is to be constructed for use in conjunction with such treatment works, and if the cost of such sewage collection system exceeds the cost of such treatment works, and

(2) the State water pollution control agency or other appropriate State authority certifies that the quantity of available ground water will be insufficient, inadequate, or unsuitable for public use, including the ecological preservation and recreational use of surface water bodies, unless effluents from publicly-owned treatment works after adequate treatment are returned to the ground water consistent with acceptable technological standards.

(c) Availability of sums allotted to Puerto Rico

Notwithstanding any other provision of law, sums allotted to the Commonwealth of Puerto Rico under section 1285 of this title for fiscal year 1981 shall remain available for obligation for the fiscal year for which authorized and for the period of the next succeeding twenty-four months. Such sums and any unobligated funds available to Puerto Rico from allotments for fiscal years ending prior to October 1, 1981, shall be available for obligation by the Administrator of the Environmental Protection Agency only to fund the following systems: Aguadilla, Arecibo, Mayaguez, Carolina, and Camuy Hatillo. These funds may be used by the Commonwealth of Puerto Rico to fund the non-Federal share of the costs of such projects. To the extent that these funds are used to pay the non-Federal share, the Commonwealth of Puerto Rico shall repay to the Environmental Protection Agency such amounts on terms and conditions developed and approved by the Administrator in consultation with the Governor of the Commonwealth of Puerto Rico. Agreement on such terms and conditions, including the payment of interest to be determined by the Secretary of the Treasury, shall be reached prior to the use of these funds for the Commonwealth's non-Federal share. No Federal funds awarded under this provision shall be used to replace local governments funds previously expended on these projects.

(June 30, 1948, ch. 758, title II, § 202, as added Oct. 18, 1972, Pub.L. 92–500, § 2, 86 Stat. 834, and amended Dec. 27, 1977, Pub.L. 95–217, § 17, 91 Stat. 1571; Oct. 21, 1980, Pub.L. 96–483, § 9, 94 Stat. 2362; Dec. 29, 1981, Pub.L. 97–117, §§ 7, 8(a), (b), 95 Stat. 1625; Oct. 19, 1982, Pub.L. 97–357, Title V, § 501, 96 Stat. 1712.)

Cross References

Allowance in construction grants for non-Federal funds expended during facility planning, etc., stage, see section 1281 of this title.

Grants to grantees who received an increased grant under this section, see section 1255 of this title.
Increase in Federal share for construction of treatment works utilizing innovative processes pursuant to this section, see section 1285 of this title.

Library References

Health and Environment ⚩25.7(21).
C.J.S. Health and Environment § 106 et seq.

§ 1283. Plans, specifications, estimates, and payments

(a) Submission; contractual nature of approval by Administrator

Each applicant for a grant shall submit to the Administrator for his approval, plans, specifications, and estimates for each proposed project for the construction of treatment works for which a grant is applied for under section 1281(g)(1) of this title from funds allotted to the State under section 1285 of this title and which otherwise meets the requirements of this chapter. The Administrator shall act upon such plans, specifications, and estimates as soon as practicable after the same have been submitted, and his approval of any such plans, specifications, and estimates shall be deemed a contractual obligation of the United States for the payment of its proportional contribution to such project. In the case of a treatment works that has an estimated total cost of $8,000,000 or less (as determined by the Administrator), and the population of the applicant municipality is twenty-five thousand or less (according to the most recent United States census), upon completion of an approved facility plan, a single grant may be awarded for the combined Federal share of the cost of preparing construction plans and specifications, and the building and erection of the treatment works.

(b) Periodic payments

The Administrator shall, from time to time as the work progresses, make payments to the recipient of a grant for costs of construction incurred on a project. These payments shall at no time exceed the Federal share of the cost of construction incurred to the date of the voucher covering such payment plus the Federal share of the value of the materials which have been stockpiled in the vicinity of such construction in conformity to plans and specifications for the project.

(c) Final payments

After completion of a project and approval of the final voucher by the Administrator, he shall pay out of the appropriate sums the unpaid balance of the Federal share payable on account of such project.

(d) Projects eligible

Nothing in this chapter shall be construed to require, or to authorize the Administrator to require, that grants under this chapter for construction of treatment works be made only for projects which are operable units usable for sewage collection, transportation, storage, waste treatment, or for similar purposes without additional construction.

(e) Technical and legal assistance in administration and enforcement of contracts; intervention in civil actions

At the request of a grantee under this subchapter, the Administrator is authorized to provide technical and legal assistance in the administration and enforcement of any contract in connection with treatment works assisted under this subchapter, and to intervene in any civil action involving the enforcement of such a contract.

(June 30, 1948, ch. 758, title II, § 203, as added Oct. 18, 1972, Pub.L. 92–500, § 2, 86 Stat. 835, and amended Jan. 2, 1974, Pub.L. 93–243, § 2, 87 Stat. 1069; Dec. 27, 1977, Pub.L. 95–217, §§ 18, 19, 91 Stat. 1571, 1572; Oct. 21, 1980, Pub.L. 96–483, § 6, 94 Stat. 2362; Dec. 29, 1981, Pub.L. 97–117, § 9, 95 Stat. 1626.)

Cross References

Certification by State for priority of grant for construction of treatment works, see section 1284 of this title.
Sums obligated under this section to be credited to State to which last allotted, see section 1285 of this title.
Timetable for achievement of effluent limitations for publicly owned treatment works approved under this section, see section 1311 of this title.

Library References

Health and Environment ⚩25.7(21).
C.J.S. Health and Environment § 106 et seq.

§ 1284. Limitations and conditions

(a) Determinations by Administrator

Before approving grants for any project for any treatment works under section 1281(g)(1) of this title the Administrator shall determine—

(1) that such works are included in any applicable areawide waste treatment management plan developed under section 1288 of this title;

(2) that such works are in conformity with any applicable State plan under section 1313(e) of this title;

(3) that such works have been certified by the appropriate State water pollution control agency as entitled to priority over such other works in the State in accordance with any applicable State plan under section 1313(e) of this title, except that any priority list developed pursuant to section 1313(e)(3)(H) of this title may be modified by such State in accordance with regulations promulgated

by the Administrator to give higher priority for grants for the Federal share of the cost of preparing construction drawings and specifications for any treatment works utilizing processes and techniques meeting the guidelines promulgated under section 1314(d)(3) of this title and for grants for the combined Federal share of the cost of preparing construction drawings and specifications and the building and erection of any treatment works meeting the requirements of the next to the last sentence of section 1283(a) of this title which utilizes processes and techniques meeting the guidelines promulgated under section 1314(d)(3) of this title;.[1]

(4) that the applicant proposing to construct such works agrees to pay the non-Federal costs of such works and has made adequate provisions satisfactory to the Administrator for assuring proper and efficient operation, including the employment of trained management and operations personnel, and the maintenance of such works in accordance with a plan of operation approved by the State water pollution control agency or, as appropriate, the interstate agency, after construction thereof;

(5) that the size and capacity of such works relate directly to the needs to be served by such works, including sufficient reserve capacity. The amount of reserve capacity provided shall be approved by the Administrator on the basis of a comparison of the cost of constructing such reserves as a part of the works to be funded and the anticipated cost of providing expanded capacity at a date when such capacity will be required, after taking into account, in accordance with regulations promulgated by the Administrator, efforts to reduce total flow of sewage and unnecessary water consumption. The amount of reserve capacity eligible for a grant under this subchapter shall be determined by the Administrator taking into account the projected population and associated commercial and industrial establishments within the jurisdiction of the applicant to be served by such treatment works as identified in an approved facilities plan, an areawide plan under section 1288 of this title, or an applicable municipal master plan of development. For the purpose of this paragraph, section 1288 of this title, and any such plan, projected population shall be determined on the basis of the latest information available from the United States Department of Commerce or from the States as the Administrator, by regulation, determines appropriate. Beginning October 1, 1984, no grant shall be made under this subchapter to construct that portion of any treatment works providing reserve capacity in excess of existing needs (including existing needs of residential, commercial, industrial, and other users) on the date of approval of a grant for the erection, building, acquisition, alteration, remodeling, improvement, or extension of a project for secondary treatment or more stringent treatment or new interceptors and appurtenances, except that in no event shall reserve capacity of a facility and its related interceptors to which this subsection applies be in excess of existing needs on October 1, 1990. In any case in which an applicant proposes to provide reserve capacity greater than that eligible for Federal financial assistance under this subchapter, the incremental costs of the additional reserve capacity shall be paid by the applicant;

(6) that no specification for bids in connection with such works shall be written in such a manner as to contain proprietary, exclusionary, or discriminatory requirements other than those based upon performance, unless such requirements are necessary to test or demonstrate a specific thing or to provide for necessary interchangeability of parts and equipment. When in the judgment of the grantee, it is impractical or uneconomical to make a clear and accurate description of the technical requirements, a "brand name or equal" description may be used as a means to define the performance or other salient requirements of a procurement, and in doing so the grantee need not establish the existence of any source other than the brand or source so named.

(b) Additional determinations; issuance of guidelines; approval by Administrator; system of charges

(1) Notwithstanding any other provision of this subchapter, the Administrator shall not approve any grant for any treatment works under section 1281(g)(1) of this title after March 1, 1973, unless he shall first have determined that the applicant (A) has adopted or will adopt a system of charges to assure that each recipient of waste treatment services within the applicant's jurisdiction, as determined by the Administrator, will pay its proportionate share (except as otherwise provided in this paragraph) of the costs of operation and maintenance (including replacement) of any waste treatment services provided by the applicant; and (B) has legal, institutional, managerial, and financial capability to insure adequate construction, operation, and maintenance of treatment works throughout the applicant's jurisdiction, as determined by the Administrator. In any case where an applicant which, as of December 27, 1977, uses a system of dedicated ad valorem taxes and the Administrator determines that the applicant has a system of charges which results in the distribution of operation and maintenance costs for treatment works within the applicant's jurisdiction, to each user class, in proportion to the contribution to the total cost of operation and maintenance of such works by each user class (taking into account total waste water loading of such works, the constituent elements of the wastes, and other appropriate factors), and such applicant is otherwise in compliance with clause (A) of this paragraph with respect to each industrial user, then such dedicated ad valorem tax system shall be deemed to be the user charge system meeting the requirements of clause (A) of this paragraph for the residential user class and such small non-residential user classes as defined by the Administrator. In defining small non-residential users, the Administrator shall consider the volume of wastes discharged into the treatment works by such users and the constituent elements of such wastes as well as such other factors as he deems appropriate.

(2) The Administrator shall, within one hundred and eighty days after October 18, 1972, and after consultation with appropriate State, interstate, municipal, and intermunicipal agencies, issue guidelines applicable to payment of waste treatment costs by industrial and nonindustrial recipients of waste treatment services which shall establish (A) classes of users of such services, including categories of industrial users; (B) criteria against which to determine the adequacy of charges imposed on classes and categories of users reflecting all factors that influence the cost of waste treatment, including strength, volume, and delivery flow rate characteristics of waste; and (C) model systems and rates of user charges typical of various treatment works serving municipal-industrial communities.

(3) Approval by the Administrator of a grant to an interstate agency established by interstate compact for any treatment works shall satisfy any other requirement that such works be authorized by Act of Congress.

(4) A system of charges which meets the requirement of clause (A) of paragraph (1) of this subsection may be based on something other than metering the sewage or water supply flow of residential recipients of waste treatment services, including ad valorem taxes. If the system of charges is based on something other than metering the Administrator shall require (A) the applicant to establish a system by which the necessary funds will be available for the proper operation and maintenance of the treatment works; and (B) the applicant to establish a procedure under which the residential user will be notified as to that portion of his total payment which will be allocated to the cost of the waste treatment services.

(c) Applicability of reserve capacity restrictions to primary, secondary, or advanced waste treatment facilities or related interceptors

The next to the last sentence of paragraph (5) of subsection (a) of this section shall not apply in any case where a primary, secondary, or advanced waste treatment facility or its related interceptors has received a grant for erection, building, acquisition, alteration, remodeling, improvement, or extension before October 1, 1984, and all segments and phases of such facility and interceptors shall be funded based on a 20-year reserve capacity in the case of such facility and a 20-year reserve capacity in the case of such interceptors, except that, if a grant for such interceptors has been approved prior to December 29, 1981, such interceptors shall be funded based on the approved reserve capacity not to exceed 40 years.

(d) Engineering requirements; certification by owner and operator; contractual assurances, etc.

(1) A grant for the construction of treatment works under this subchapter shall provide that the engineer or engineering firm supervising construction or providing architect engineering services during construction shall continue its relationship to the grant applicant for a period of one year after the completion of construction and initial operation of such treatment works. During such period such engineer or engineering firm shall supervise operation of the treatment works, train operating personnel, and prepare curricula and training material for operating personnel. Costs associated with the implementation of this paragraph shall be eligible for Federal assistance in accordance with this subchapter.

(2) On the date one year after the completion of construction and initial operation of such treatment works, the owner and operator of such treatment works shall certify to the Administrator whether or not such treatment works meet the design specifications and effluent limitations contained in the grant agreement and permit pursuant to section 1342 of this title for such works. If the owner and operator of such treatment works cannot certify that such treatment works meet such design specifications and effluent limitations, any failure to meet such design specifications and effluent limitations shall be corrected in a timely manner, to allow such affirmative certification, at other than Federal expense.

(3) Nothing in this section shall be construed to prohibit a grantee under this subchapter from requiring more assurances, guarantees, or indemnity or other contractual requirements from any party to a contract pertaining to a project assisted under this

subchapter, than those provided under this subsection.

(June 30, 1948, ch. 758, title II, § 204, as added Oct. 18, 1972, Pub.L. 92–500, § 2, 86 Stat. 835, and amended Dec. 27, 1977, Pub.L. 95–217, §§ 20–24, 91 Stat. 1572, 1573; Oct. 21, 1980, Pub.L. 96–483, § 2(a), (b), 94 Stat. 2360, 2361; Dec. 29, 1981, Pub.L. 97–117, §§ 10(a), (b), 11, 12, 95 Stat. 1626, 1627.)

1 So in original. The par. ends with both a period and semicolon.

Cross References

Exemption of training grants from requirements of this section, see section 1259 of this title.
Grants for construction of privately owned treatment works, see section 1281 of this title.
Grants to any State from amount reserved to such State for the reasonable costs of administration, see section 1285 of this title.
State permit programs, compliance with this section, see section 1342 of this title.

Code of Federal Regulations

General pretreatment regulations for existing and new sources of pollution, see 40 CFR 403.1 et seq.

Library References

Health and Environment ⚷25.7(21).
C.J.S. Health and Environment § 106 et seq.

§ 1285. Allotment of grant funds

(a) Funds for fiscal years during period June 30, 1972, and September 30, 1977; determination of amount

Sums authorized to be appropriated pursuant to section 1287 of this title for each fiscal year beginning after June 30, 1972, and before September 30, 1977, shall be allotted by the Administrator not later than the January 1st immediately preceding the beginning of the fiscal year for which authorized, except that the allotment for fiscal year 1973 shall be made not later than 30 days after October 18, 1972. Such sums shall be allotted among the States by the Administrator in accordance with regulations promulgated by him, in the ratio that the estimated cost of constructing all needed publicly owned treatment works in each State bears to the estimated cost of construction of all needed publicly owned treatment works in all of the States. For the fiscal years ending June 30, 1973, and June 30, 1974, such ratio shall be determined on the basis of table III of House Public Works Committee Print No. 92–50. For the fiscal year ending June 30, 1975, such ratio shall be determined one-half on the basis of table I of House Public Works Committee Print Numbered 93–28 and one-half on the basis of table II of such print, except that no State shall receive an allotment less than that which it received for the fiscal year ending June 30, 1972, as set forth in table III of such print. Allotments for fiscal years which begin after the fiscal year ending June 30, 1975, shall be made only in accordance with a revised cost estimate made and submitted to Congress in accordance with section 1375(b) of this title and only after such revised cost estimate shall have been approved by law specifically enacted after October 18, 1972.

(b) Availability and use of funds allotted for fiscal years during period June 30, 1972, and September 30, 1977; reallotment

(1) Any sums allotted to a State under subsection (a) of this section shall be available for obligation under section 1283 of this title on and after the date of such allotment. Such sums shall continue available for obligation in such State for a period of one year after the close of the fiscal year for which such sums are authorized. Any amounts so allotted which are not obligated by the end of such one-year period shall be immediately reallotted by the Administrator, in accordance with regulations promulgated by him, generally on the basis of the ratio used in making the last allotment of sums under this section. Such reallotted sums shall be added to the last allotments made to the States. Any sum made available to a State by reallotment under this subsection shall be in addition to any funds otherwise allotted to such State for grants under this subchapter during any fiscal year.

(2) Any sums which have been obligated under section 1283 of this title and which are released by the payment of the final voucher for the project shall be immediately credited to the State to which such sums were last allotted. Such released sums shall be added to the amounts last allotted to such State and shall be immediately available for obligation in the same manner and to the same extent as such last allotment.

(c) Funds for fiscal years during period October 1, 1977, and September 30, 1981; funds for fiscal years 1982 to 1985; determination of amount

(1) Sums authorized to be appropriate pursuant to section 1287 of this title for the fiscal years during the period beginning October 1, 1977, and ending September 30, 1981, shall be allotted for each such year by the Administrator not later than the tenth day which begins after December 27, 1977. Notwithstanding any other provision of law, sums authorized for the fiscal years ending September 30, 1978, September 30, 1979, September 30, 1980, and September 30, 1981, shall be allotted in accordance with table 3 of Committee Print Numbered 95–30 of the Committee on Public Works and Transportation of the House of Representatives.

(2) Sums authorized to be appropriated pursuant to section 1287 of this title for the fiscal years 1982, 1983, 1984, and 1985 shall be allotted for each such year by the Administrator not later than the tenth

day which begins after December 29, 1981. Notwithstanding any other provision of law, sums authorized for the fiscal year ending September 30, 1982, shall be allotted in accordance with table 3 of Committee Print Numbered 95–30 of the Committee on Public Works and Transportation of the House of Representatives. Sums authorized for the fiscal years ending September 30, 1983, September 30, 1984, and September 30, 1985, shall be allotted in accordance with the following table:

States:	Fiscal years 1983 through 1985
Alabama	.011398
Alaska	.006101
Arizona	.006885
Arkansas	.006668
California	.072901
Colorado	.008154
Connecticut	.012487
Delaware	.004965
District of Columbia	.004965
Florida	.034407
Georgia	.017234
Hawaii	.007895
Idaho	.004965
Illinois	.046101
Indiana	.024566
Iowa	.013796
Kansas	.009201
Kentucky	.012973
Louisiana	.011205
Maine	.007788
Maryland	.024653
Massachusetts	.034608
Michigan	.043829
Minnesota	.018735
Mississippi	.009184
Missouri	.028257
Montana	.004965
Nebraska	.005214
Nevada	.004965
New Hampshire	.010186
New Jersey	.041654
New Mexico	.004965
New York	.113097
North Carolina	.018396
North Dakota	.004965
Ohio	.057383
Oklahoma	.008235
Oregon	.011515
Pennsylvania	.040377
Rhode Island	.006750
South Carolina	.010442
South Dakota	.004965
Tennessee	.014807
Texas	.038726
Utah	.005371
Vermont	.004965
Virginia	.020861
Washington	.017726
West Virginia	.015890
Wisconsin	.027557
Wyoming	.004965
Samoa	.000915
Guam	.000662
Northern Marianas	.000425
Puerto Rico	.013295
Pacific Trust Territories	.001305
Virgin Islands	.000531
United States totals	.999996

(d) Availability and use of funds; reallotment

Sums allotted to the States for a fiscal year shall remain available for obligation for the fiscal year for which authorized and for the period of the next succeeding twelve months. The amount of any allotment not obligated by the end of such twenty-four-month period shall be immediately reallotted by the Administrator on the basis of the same ratio as applicable to sums allotted for the then current fiscal year, except that none of the funds reallotted by the Administrator for fiscal year 1978 and for fiscal years thereafter shall be allotted to any State which failed to obligate any of the funds being reallotted. Any sum made available to a State by reallotment under this subsection shall be in addition to any funds otherwise allotted to such State for grants under this subchapter during any fiscal year.

(e) Minimum allotment; additional appropriations; ratio of amount available

For the fiscal years 1978, 1979, 1980, 1981, 1982, 1983, 1984, and 1985, no State shall receive less than one-half of 1 per centum of the total allotment under subsection (c) of this section, except that in the case of Guam, Virgin Islands, American Samoa, and the Trust Territories not more than thirty-three one-hundredths of 1 per centum in the aggregate shall be allotted to all four of these jurisdictions. For the purpose of carrying out this subsection there are authorized to be appropriated, subject to such amounts as are provided in appropriation Acts, not to exceed $75,000,000 for each of fiscal years 1978, 1979, 1980, 1981, 1982, 1983, 1984, and 1985. If for any fiscal year the amount appropriated under authority of this subsection is less than the amount necessary to carry out this subsection, the amount each State receives under this subsection for such year shall bear the same ratio to the amount such State would have received under this subsection in such year if the amount necessary to carry it out had been appropriated as the amount appropriated for such year bears to the amount necessary to carry out this subsection for such year.

(f) Omitted

(g) Reservation of funds; state management assistance

(1) The Administrator is authorized to reserve each fiscal year not to exceed 2 per centum of the amount authorized under section 1287 of this title for purposes of the allotment made to each State under this section on or after October 1, 1977, except in the case of any fiscal year beginning on or after October 1, 1981, and ending before October 1, 1985, in which case the percentage authorized to be reserved shall not exceed 4 per centum.[1] or $400,000 whichever amount is the greater. Sums so reserved shall be available for making grants to such State under paragraph (2) of this subsection for the same period as sums are available from such allotment under subsection (d) of this section, and any such grant shall be available for obligation only during such period. Any grant made from sums reserved under this subsection which has not been obligated by the end of the period for which available shall be added to the amount last allotted to such State under this section and shall be immediately available for obligation in the same manner and to the same extent as such last allotment. Sums authorized to be reserved by this paragraph shall be in addition to and not in lieu of any other funds which may be authorized to carry out this subsection.

(2) The Administrator is authorized to grant to any State from amounts reserved to such State under this subsection, the reasonable costs of administering any aspects of sections 1281, 1283, 1284, and 1292 of this title the responsibility for administration of which the Administrator has delegated to such State. The Administrator may increase such grant to take into account the reasonable costs of administering an approved program under section 1342 or 1344 of this title, administering a state-wide waste treatment management planning program under section 1288(b)(4) of this title, and managing waste treatment construction grants for small communities.

(h) Alternate systems for small communities

The Administrator shall set aside from funds authorized for each fiscal year beginning on or after October 1, 1978, four per centum of the sums allotted to any State with a rural population of 25 per centum or more of the total population of such State, as determined by the Bureau of the Census. The Administrator may set aside no more than four per centum of the sums allotted to any other State for which the Governor requests such action. Such sums shall be available only for alternatives to conventional sewage treatment works for municipalities having a population of three thousand five hundred or less, or for the highly dispersed sections of larger municipalities, as defined by the Administrator.

(i) Increase in Federal share for construction; projects utilizing innovative processes and techniques

Not less than one-half of one per centum of funds allotted to a State for each of the fiscal years ending September 30, 1979, September 30, 1980, September 30, 1981, September 30, 1982, September 30, 1983, September 30, 1984, and September 30, 1985, under subsection (a) of this section shall be expended only for increasing the Federal share of grants for construction of treatment works utilizing innovative processes and techniques pursuant to section 1282(a)(2) of this title. Including the expenditures authorized by the preceding sentence, a total or two per centum of the funds allotted to a State for each of the fiscal years ending September 30, 1979, and September 30, 1980, and 3 per centum of the funds allotted to a State for the fiscal year ending September 30, 1981, under subsection (a) of this section shall be expended only for increasing grants for construction of treatment works from 75 per centum to 85 per centum pursuant to section 1282(a)(2) of this title. Including the expenditures authorized by the first sentence of this subsection, a total (as determined by the Governor of the State) of not less than 4 per centum nor more than 7½ per centum of the funds allotted to such State for any fiscal year beginning after September 30, 1981, under subsection (c) of this section shall be expended only for increasing the Federal share of grants for construction of treatment works pursuant to section 1282(a)(2) of this title.

(j) Water quality management plan

(1) The Administrator shall reserve each fiscal year not to exceed 1 per centum of the sums allotted and available for obligation to each State under this section for each fiscal year beginning on or after October 1, 1981, or $100,000, whichever amount is the greater.

(2) Such sums shall be used by the Administrator to make grants to the States to carry out water quality management planning, including, but not limited to—

(A) identifying most cost effective and locally acceptable facility and non-point measures to meet and maintain water quality standards;

(B) developing an implementation plan to obtain State and local financial and regulatory commitments to implement measures developed under subparagraph (A);

(C) determining the nature, extent, and causes of water quality problems in various areas of the

State and interstate region, and reporting on these annually; and

(D) determining those publicly owned treatment works which should be constructed with assistance under this subchapter, in which areas and in what sequence, taking into account the relative degree of effluent reduction attained, the relative contributions to water quality of other point or nonpoint sources, and the consideration of alternatives to such construction, and implementing section 1313(e) of this title.

(3) In carrying out planning with grants made under paragraph (2) of this subsection, a State shall develop jointly with local, regional, and interstate entities, a plan for carrying out the program and give funding priority to such entities and designated or undesignated public comprehensive planning organizations to carry out the purposes of this subsection.

(4) All activities undertaken under this subsection shall be in coordination with other related provisions of this chapter.

(k) New York City Convention Center

The Administrator shall allot to the State of New York from sums authorized to be appropriated for the fiscal year ending September 30, 1982, an amount necessary to pay the entire cost of conveying sewage from the Convention Center of the city of New York to the Newtown sewage treatment plant, Brooklyn-Queens area, New York. The amount allotted under this subsection shall be in addition to and not in lieu of any other amounts authorized to be allotted to such State under this chapter.

(June 30, 1948, ch. 758, title II, § 205, as added Oct. 18, 1972, Pub.L. 92–500, § 2, 86 Stat. 837, and amended Jan. 2, 1974, Pub.L. 93–243, § 1, 87 Stat. 1069; Dec. 27, 1977, Pub.L. 95–217, §§ 25, 26(a), 27, 28, 91 Stat. 1574, 1575; Oct. 21, 1980, Pub.L. 96–483, § 11, 94 Stat. 2363; Dec. 29, 1981, Pub.L. 97–117, §§ 8(c), 13–16, 95 Stat. 1625, 1627–1629.)

1 So in original. Probably should be a comma.

Cross References

Amount of grants for treatment works, see section 1282 of this title.
Availability of sums allotted to Puerto Rico, see section 1282 of this title.
Hudson River reclamation project, grants from funds allotted to State of New York under this section, see section 1266 of this title.
Submission of plans, specifications, etc., for proposed project for construction of treatment works, see section 1283 of this title.
Training grants from sums allocated to a State under this section, see section 1259 of this title.
Water quality problems, use of funds available under this section, see section 1281 of this title.

Code of Federal Regulations

Administration of federal contracts, grants or loans, see 40 CFR 15.1 et seq.
State and local assistance, see 40 CFR 35.001 et seq.
Water quality planning and management, see 40 CFR 130.0 et seq.

Library References

Health and Environment ⚷25.7(21).
C.J.S. Health and Environment § 106 et seq.

United States Supreme Court

Construction of word "sums" with phrase "all sums" within provisions of this section, see Train v. City of New York, 1975, 95 S.Ct. 839, 420 U.S. 35, 43 L.Ed.2d 1.

§ 1286. Reimbursement and advanced construction

(a) Publicly owned treatment works construction initiated after June 30, 1966, but before July 1, 1973; reimbursement formula

Any publicly owned treatment works in a State on which construction was initiated after June 30, 1966, but before July 1, 1973, which was approved by the appropriate State water pollution control agency and which the Administrator finds meets the requirements of section 1158 of this title in effect at the time of the initiation of construction shall be reimbursed a total amount equal to the difference between the amount of Federal financial assistance, if any, received under such section 1158 of this title for such project and 50 per centum of the cost of such project, or 55 per centum of the project cost where the Administrator also determines that such treatment works was constructed in conformity with a comprehensive metropolitan treatment plan as described in section 1158(f) of this title as in effect immediately prior to October 18, 1972. Nothing in this subsection shall result in any such works receiving Federal grants from all sources in excess of 80 per centum of the cost of such project.

(b) Publicly owned treatment works construction initiated between June 30, 1956, and June 30, 1966; reimbursement formula

Any publicly owned treatment works constructed with or eligible for Federal financial assistance under this Act in a State between June 30, 1956, and June 30, 1966, which was approved by the State water pollution control agency and which the Administrator finds meets the requirements of section 1158 of this title prior to October 18, 1972 but which was constructed without assistance under such section 1158 of this title or which received such assistance in an amount less than 30 per centum of the cost of such project shall qualify for payments and reimbursement of State or local funds used for such project from sums allocated to such State under this section in an amount which shall not exceed the difference between the amount of such assistance, if any, received for such project and 30 per centum of the cost of such project.

(c) Application for reimbursement

No publicly owned treatment works shall receive any payment or reimbursement under subsection (a) or (b) of this section unless an application for such assistance is filed with the Administrator within the one year period which begins on October 18, 1972. Any application filed within such one year period may be revised from time to time, as may be necessary.

(d) Allocation of funds

The Administrator shall allocate to each qualified project under subsection (a) of this section each fiscal year for which funds are appropriated under subsection (e) of this section an amount which bears the same ratio to the unpaid balance of the reimbursement due such project as the total of such funds for such year bears to the total unpaid balance of reimbursement due all such approved projects on the date of enactment of such appropriation. The Administrator shall allocate to each qualified project under subsection (b) of this section each fiscal year for which funds are appropriated under subsection (e) of this section an amount which bears the same ratio to the unpaid balance of the reimbursement due such project as the total of such funds for such year bears to the total unpaid balance of reimbursement due all such approved projects on the date of enactment of such appropriation.

(e) Authorization of appropriations

There is authorized to be appropriated to carry out subsection (a) of this section not to exceed $2,600,000,000 and, to carry out subsection (b) of this section, not to exceed $750,000,000. The authorizations contained in this subsection shall be the sole source of funds for reimbursements authorized by this section.

(f) Additional funds

(1) In any case where a substantial portion of the funds allotted to a State for the current fiscal year under this subchapter have been obligated under section 1281(g) of this title, or will be so obligated in a timely manner (as determined by the Administrator), and there is construction of any treatment works project without the aid of Federal funds and in accordance with all procedures and all requirements applicable to treatment works projects, except those procedures and requirements which limit construction of projects to those constructed with the aid of previously allotted Federal funds, the Administrator, upon his approval of an application made under this subsection therefor, is authorized to pay the Federal share of the cost of construction of such project when additional funds are allotted to the State under this subchapter if prior to the construction of the project the Administrator approves plans, specifications, and estimates therefor in the same manner as other treatment works projects. The Administrator may not approve an application under this subsection unless an authorization is in effect for the first fiscal year in the period for which the application requests payment and such requested payment for that fiscal year does not exceed the State's expected allotment from such authorization. The Administrator shall not be required to make such requested payment for any fiscal year—

(A) to the extent that such payment would exceed such State's allotment of the amount appropriated for such fiscal year; and

(B) unless such payment is for a project which, on the basis of an approved funding priority list of such State, is eligible to receive such payment based on the allotment and appropriation for such fiscal year.

To the extent that sufficient funds are not appropriated to pay the full Federal share with respect to a project for which obligations under the provisions of this subsection have been made, the Administrator shall reduce the Federal share to such amount less than 75 per centum as such appropriations do provide.

(2) In determining the allotment for any fiscal year under this subchapter, any treatment works project constructed in accordance with this section and without the aid of Federal funds shall not be considered completed until an application under the provisions of this subsection with respect to such project has been approved by the Administrator, or the availability of funds from which this project is eligible for reimbursement has expired, whichever first occurs.

(June 30, 1948, ch. 758, title II, § 206, as added Oct. 18, 1972, Pub.L. 92–500, § 2, 86 Stat. 836, and amended Dec. 28, 1973, Pub.L. 93–207, § 1(2), 87 Stat. 906; Dec. 27, 1977, Pub.L. 95–217, § 29(a), 91 Stat. 1576; Oct. 21, 1980, Pub.L. 96–483, § 5, 94 Stat. 2361.)

Cross References

Authorization of appropriations to carry out this chapter other than this section, see section 1376 of this title.
Authorization of appropriations to carry out this subchapter other than subsec. (e) of this section, see section 1287 of this title.
Loan guarantees, see section 1293 of this title.

Library References

Health and Environment ⚷25.7(21).
C.J.S. Health and Environment § 106 et seq.

§ 1287. Authorization of appropriations

There is authorized to be appropriated to carry out this subchapter, other than sections 1286(e), 1288 and 1289 of this title, for the fiscal year ending June 30, 1973, not to exceed $5,000,000,000, for the fiscal year ending June 30, 1974, not to exceed $6,000,000,000, and for the fiscal year ending June 30, 1975, not to exceed $7,000,000,000, and subject to such amounts as are provided in appropriation Acts, for the fiscal year ending September 30, 1977, $1,000,000,000 for the fiscal year ending September 30, 1978, $4,500,000,000 and for the fiscal years ending September 30, 1979, September 30, 1980, not to exceed $5,000,000,000; for the fiscal year ending September 30, 1981, not to exceed $2,548,837,000; and for the fiscal years ending September 30, 1982, September 30, 1983, September 30, 1984, and September 30, 1985, not to exceed $2,400,000,000 per fiscal year.

(June 30, 1948, ch. 758, title II, § 207, as added Oct. 18, 1972, Pub.L. 92–500, § 2, 86 Stat. 839, and amended Dec. 28, 1973, Pub.L. 93–207, § 1(3), 87 Stat. 906; Dec. 27, 1977, Pub.L. 95–217, § 30, 91 Stat. 1576; Aug. 13, 1981, Pub.L. 97–35, Title XVIII, § 1801(a), 95 Stat. 764; Dec. 29, 1981, Pub.L. 97–117, § 17, 95 Stat. 1630.)

Cross References

Authorization of appropriations to carry out this chapter other than this section, see section 1376 of this title.

Time for allotment of sums authorized to be appropriated pursuant to this section for fiscal years during period beginning Oct. 1, 1977, and ending Sept. 30, 1981, see section 1285 of this title.

Water quality problems, funds available, see section 1281 of this title.

Library References

Health and Environment ⚷25.7(21).
C.J.S. Health and Environment § 106 et seq.

§ 1288. Areawide waste treatment management

(a) Identification and designation of areas having substantial water quality control problems

For the purpose of encouraging and facilitating the development and implementation of areawide waste treatment management plans—

(1) The Administrator, within ninety days after October 18, 1972, and after consultation with appropriate Federal, State, and local authorities, shall by regulation publish guidelines for the identification of those areas which, as a result of urban-industrial concentrations or other factors, have substantial water quality control problems.

(2) The Governor of each State, within sixty days after publication of the guidelines issued pursuant to paragraph (1) of this subsection, shall identify each area within the State which, as a result of urban-industrial concentrations or other factors, has substantial water quality control problems. Not later than one hundred and twenty days following such identification and after consultation with appropriate elected and other officials of local governments having jurisdiction in such areas, the Governor shall designate (A) the boundaries of each such area, and (B) a single representative organization, including elected officials from local governments or their designees, capable of developing effective areawide waste treatment management plans for such area. The Governor may in the same manner at any later time identify any additional area (or modify an existing area) for which he determines areawide waste treatment management to be appropriate, designate the boundaries of such area, and designate an organization capable of developing effective areawide waste treatment management plans for such area.

(3) With respect to any area which, pursuant to the guidelines published under paragraph (1) of this subsection, is located in two or more States, the Governors of the respective States shall consult and cooperate in carrying out the provisions of paragraph (2), with a view toward designating the boundaries of the interstate area having common water quality control problems and for which areawide waste treatment management plans would be most effective, and toward designating, within one hundred and eighty days after publication of guidelines issued pursuant to paragraph (1) of this subsection, of a single representative organization capable of developing effective areawide waste treatment management plans for such area.

(4) If a Governor does not act, either by designating or determining not to make a designation under paragraph (2) of this subsection, within the time required by such paragraph, or if, in the case of an interstate area, the Governors of the States involved do not designate a planning organization within the time required by paragraph (3) of this subsection, the chief elected officials of local governments within an area may by agreement designate (A) the boundaries for such an area, and (B) a single representative organization including elected officials from such local governments, or their designees, capable of developing an areawide waste treatment management plan for such area.

(5) Existing regional agencies may be designated under paragraphs (2), (3), and (4) of this subsection.

(6) The State shall act as a planning agency for all portions of such State which are not designated under paragraphs (2), (3), or (4) of this subsection.

(7) Designations under this subsection shall be subject to the approval of the Administrator.

(b) Planning process

(1)(A) Not later than one year after the date of designation of any organization under subsection (a) of this section such organization shall have in operation a continuing areawide waste treatment management planning process consistent with section 1281 of this title. Plans prepared in accordance with this process shall contain alternatives for waste treatment management, and be applicable to all wastes generated within the area involved. The initial plan prepared in accordance with such process shall be certified by the Governor and submitted to the Administrator not later than two years after the planning process is in operation.

(B) For any agency designated after 1975 under subsection (a) of this section and for all portions of a State for which the State is required to act as the planning agency in accordance with subsection (a)(6) of this section, the initial plan prepared in accordance with such process shall be certified by the Governor and submitted to the Administrator not later than three years after the receipt of the initial grant award authorized under subsection (f) of this section.

(2) Any plan prepared under such process shall include, but not be limited to—

(A) the identification of treatment works necessary to meet the anticipated municipal and industrial waste treatment needs of the area over a twenty-year period, annually updated (including an analysis of alternative waste treatment systems), including any requirements for the acquisition of land for treatment purposes; the necessary waste water collection and urban storm water runoff systems; and a program to provide the necessary financial arrangements for the development of such treatment works, and an identification of open space and recreation opportunities that can be expected to result from improved water quality, including consideration of potential use of lands associated with treatment works and increased access to water-based recreation;

(B) the establishment of construction priorities for such treatment works and time schedules for the initiation and completion of all treatment works;

(C) the establishment of a regulatory program to—

(i) implement the waste treatment management requirements of section 1281(c) of this title,

(ii) regulate the location, modification, and construction of any facilities within such area which may result in any discharge in such area, and

(iii) assure that any industrial or commercial wastes discharged into any treatment works in such area meet applicable pretreatment requirements;

(D) the identification of those agencies necessary to construct, operate, and maintain all facilities required by the plan and otherwise to carry out the plan;

(E) the identification of the measures necessary to carry out the plan (including financing), the period of time necessary to carry out the plan, the costs of carrying out the plan within such time, and the economic, social, and environmental impact of carrying out the plan within such time;

(F) a process to (i) identify, if appropriate, agriculturally and silviculturally related nonpoint sources of pollution, including return flows from irrigated agriculture, and their cumulative effects, runoff from manure disposal areas, and from land used for livestock and crop production, and (ii) set forth procedures and methods (including land use requirements) to control to the extent feasible such sources;

(G) a process to (i) identify, if appropriate, mine-related sources of pollution including new, current, and abandoned surface and underground mine runoff, and (ii) set forth procedures and methods (including land use requirements) to control to the extent feasible such sources;

(H) a process to (i) identify construction activity related sources of pollution, and (ii) set forth procedures and methods (including land use requirements) to control to the extent feasible such sources;

(I) a process to (i) identify, if appropriate, salt water intrusion into rivers, lakes, and estuaries resulting from reduction of fresh water flow from any cause, including irrigation, obstruction, ground water extraction, and diversion, and (ii) set forth procedures and methods to control such intrusion to the extent feasible where such procedures and methods are otherwise a part of the waste treatment management plan;

(J) a process to control the disposition of all residual waste generated in such area which could affect water quality; and

(K) a process to control the disposal of pollutants on land or in subsurface excavations within such area to protect ground and surface water quality.

(3) Areawide waste treatment management plans shall be certified annually by the Governor or his designee (or Governors or their designees, where more than one State is involved) as being consistent with applicable basin plans and such areawide waste treatment management plans shall be submitted to the Administrator for his approval.

(4)(A) Whenever the Governor of any State determines (and notifies the Administrator) that consistency with a statewide regulatory program under section 1313 of this title so requires, the requirements of clauses (F) through (K) of paragraph (2) of this subsection shall be developed and submitted by the Governor to the Administrator for approval for application to a class or category of activity throughout such State.

(B) Any program submitted under subparagraph (A) of this paragraph which, in whole or in part, is to control the discharge or other placement of dredged or fill material into the navigable waters shall include the following:

(i) A consultation process which includes the State agency with primary jurisdiction over fish and wildlife resources.

(ii) A process to identify and manage the discharge or other placement of dredged or fill material which adversely affects navigable waters, which shall complement and be coordinated with a State program under section 1344 of this title conducted pursuant to this chapter.

(iii) A process to assure that any activity conducted pursuant to a best management practice will comply with the guidelines established under section 1344(b)(1) of this title, and sections 1317 and 1343 of this title.

(iv) A process to assure that any activity conducted pursuant to a best management practice can be terminated or modified for cause including, but not limited to, the following:

(I) violation of any condition of the best management practice;

(II) change in any activity that requires either a temporary or permanent reduction or elimination of the discharge pursuant to the best management practice.

(v) A process to assure continued coordination with Federal and Federal-State water-related planning and reviewing processes, including the National Wetlands Inventory.

(C) If the Governor of a State obtains approval from the Administrator of a statewide regulatory program which meets the requirements of subparagraph (B) of this paragraph and if such State is administering a permit program under section 1344 of this title, no person shall be required to obtain an individual permit pursuant to such section, or to comply with a general permit issued pursuant to such section, with respect to any appropriate activity within such State for which a best management practice has been approved by the Administrator under the program approved by the Administrator pursuant to this paragraph.

(D)(i) Whenever the Administrator determines after public hearing that a State is not administering a program approved under this section in accordance with the requirements of this section, the Administrator shall so notify the State, and if appropriate corrective action is not taken within a reasonable time, not to exceed ninety days, the Administrator shall withdraw approval of such program. The Administrator shall not withdraw approval of any such program unless he shall first have notified the State, and made public, in writing, the reasons for such withdrawal.

(ii) In the case of a State with a program submitted and approved under this paragraph, the Administrator shall withdraw approval of such program under this subparagraph only for a substantial failure of the State to administer its program in accordance with the requirements of this paragraph.

(c) Regional operating agencies

(1) The Governor of each State, in consultation with the planning agency designated under subsection (a) of this section, at the time a plan is submitted to the Administrator, shall designate one or more waste treatment management agencies (which may be an existing or newly created local, regional, or State agency or political subdivision) for each area designated under subsection (a) of this section and submit such designations to the Administrator.

(2) The Administrator shall accept any such designation, unless, within 120 days of such designation, he finds that the designated management agency (or agencies) does not have adequate authority—

(A) to carry out appropriate portions of an areawide waste treatment management plan developed under subsection (b) of this section;

(B) to manage effectively waste treatment works and related facilities serving such area in conformance with any plan required by subsection (b) of this section;

(C) directly or by contract, to design and construct new works, and to operate and maintain new and existing works as required by any plan developed pursuant to subsection (b) of this section;

(D) to accept and utilize grants, or other funds from any source, for waste treatment management purposes;

(E) to raise revenues, including the assessment of waste treatment charges;

(F) to incur short- and long-term indebtedness;

(G) to assure in implementation of an areawide waste treatment management plan that each participating community pays its proportionate share of treatment costs;

(H) to refuse to receive any wastes from any municipality or subdivision thereof, which does not comply with any provisions of an approved plan under this section applicable to such area; and

(I) to accept for treatment industrial wastes.

(d) Conformity of works with area plan

After a waste treatment management agency having the authority required by subsection (c) of this section has been designated under such subsection for an area and a plan for such area has been approved under subsection (b) of this section, the Administrator shall not make any grant for construction of a publicly owned treatment works under section 1281(g)(1) of this title within such area except to such designated agency and for works in conformity with such plan.

(e) Permits not to conflict with approved plans

No permit under section 1342 of this title shall be issued for any point source which is in conflict with a plan approved pursuant to subsection (b) of this section.

(f) Grants

(1) The Administrator shall make grants to any agency designated under subsection (a) of this section for payment of the reasonable costs of developing and operating a continuing areawide waste treatment management planning process under subsection (b) of this section.

(2) For the two-year period beginning on the date the first grant is made under paragraph (1) of this subsection to an agency, if such first grant is made before October 1, 1977, the amount of each such grant to such agency shall be 100 per centum of the costs of developing and operating a continuing areawide waste treatment management planning process under subsection (b) of this section, and thereafter the amount granted to such agency shall not exceed 75 per centum of such costs in each succeeding one-year period. In the case of any other grant made to an agency under such paragraph (1) of this subsection, the amount of such grant shall not exceed 75 per centum of the costs of developing and operating a continuing areawide waste treatment management planning process in any year.

(3) Each applicant for a grant under this subsection shall submit to the Administrator for his approval each proposal for which a grant is applied for under this subsection. The Administrator shall act upon such proposal as soon as practicable after it has been submitted, and his approval of that proposal shall be deemed a contractual obligation of the United States for the payment of its contribution to such proposal, subject to such amounts as are provided in appropriation Acts. There is authorized to be appropriated to carry out this subsection not to exceed $50,000,000 for the fiscal year ending June 30, 1973, not to exceed $100,000,000 for the fiscal year ending June 30, 1974, and not to exceed $150,000,000 per fiscal year for the fiscal years ending June 30, 1975, September 30, 1977, September 30, 1978, September 30, 1979, and September 30, 1980, and not to exceed $100,000,000 per fiscal year for the fiscal years ending September 30, 1981, and September 30, 1982.

(g) Technical assistance by Administrator

The Administrator is authorized, upon request of the Governor or the designated planning agency, and without reimbursement, to consult with, and provide technical assistance to, any agency designated under subsection (a) of this section in the development of areawide waste treatment management plans under subsection (b) of this section.

(h) Technical assistance by Secretary of the Army

(1) The Secretary of the Army, acting through the Chief of Engineers, in cooperation with the Administrator is authorized and directed, upon request of the Governor or the designated planning organization, to consult with, and provide technical assistance to, any agency designed[1] under subsection (a) of this section in developing and operating a continuing areawide waste treatment management planning process under subsection (b) of this section.

(2) There is authorized to be appropriated to the Secretary of the Army, to carry out this subsection, not to exceed $50,000,000 per fiscal year for the fiscal years ending June 30, 1973, and June 30, 1974.

(i) State best management practices program

(1) The Secretary of the Interior, acting through the Director of the United States Fish and Wildlife Service, shall, upon request of the Governor of a State, and without reimbursement, provide technical assistance to such State in developing a statewide program for submission to the Administrator under subsection (b)(4)(B) of this section and in implementing such program after its approval.

(2) There is authorized to be appropriated to the Secretary of the Interior $6,000,000 to complete the National Wetlands Inventory of the United States, by December 31, 1981, and to provide information from such Inventory to States as it becomes avail-

able to assist such States in the development and operation of programs under this chapter.

(j) Agricultural cost sharing

(1) The Secretary of Agriculture, with the concurrence of the Administrator, and acting through the Soil Conservation Service and such other agencies of the Department of Agriculture as the Secretary may designate, is authorized and directed to establish and administer a program to enter into contracts, subject to such amounts as are provided in advance by appropriation acts, of not less than five years nor more than ten years with owners and operators having control of rural land for the purpose of installing and maintaining measures incorporating best management practices to control nonpoint source pollution for improved water quality in those States or areas for which the Administrator has approved a plan under subsection (b) of this section where the practices to which the contracts apply are certified by the management agency designated under subsection (c)(1) of this section to be consistent with such plans and will result in improved water quality. Such contracts may be entered into during the period ending not later than September 31, 1988. Under such contracts the land owner or operator shall agree—

(i) to effectuate a plan approved by a soil conservation district, where one exists, under this section for his farm, ranch, or other land substantially in accordance with the schedule outlined therein unless any requirement thereof is waived or modified by the Secretary;

(ii) to forfeit all rights to further payments or grants under the contract and refund to the United States all payments and grants received thereunder, with interest, upon his violation of the contract at any stage during the time he has control of the land if the Secretary, after considering the recommendations of the soil conservation district, where one exists, and the Administrator, determines that such violation is of such a nature as to warrant termination of the contract, or to make refunds or accept such payment adjustments as the Secretary may deem appropriate if he determines that the violation by the owner or operator does not warrant termination of the contract;

(iii) upon transfer of his right and interest in the farm, ranch, or other land during the contract period to forfeit all rights to further payments or grants under the contract and refund to the United States all payments or grants received thereunder, with interest, unless the transferee of any such land agrees with the Secretary to assume all obligations of the contract;

(iv) not to adopt any practice specified by the Secretary on the advice of the Administrator in the contract as a practice which would tend to defeat the purposes of the contract;

(v) to such additional provisions as the Secretary determines are desirable and includes in the contract to effectuate the purposes of the program or to facilitate the practical administration of the program.

(2) In return for such agreement by the landowner or operator the Secretary shall agree to provide technical assistance and share the cost of carrying out those conservation practices and measures set forth in the contract for which he determines that cost sharing is appropriate and in the public interest and which are approved for cost sharing by the agency designated to implement the plan developed under subsection (b) of this section. The portion of such cost (including labor) to be shared shall be that part which the Secretary determines is necessary and appropriate to effectuate the installation of the water quality management practices and measures under the contract, but not to exceed 50 per centum of the total cost of the measures set forth in the contract; except the Secretary may increase the matching cost share where he determines that (1) the main benefits to be derived from the measures are related to improving offsite water quality, and (2) the matching share requirement would place a burden on the landowner which would probably prevent him from participating in the program.

(3) The Secretary may terminate any contract with a landowner or operator by mutual agreement with the owner or operator if the Secretary determines that such termination would be in the public interest, and may agree to such modification of contracts previously entered into as he may determine to be desirable to carry out the purposes of the program or facilitate the practical administration thereof or to accomplish equitable treatment with respect to other conservation, land use, or water quality programs.

(4) In providing assistance under this subsection the Secretary will give priority to those areas and sources that have the most significant effect upon water quality. Additional investigations or plans may be made, where necessary, to supplement approved water quality management plans, in order to determine priorities.

(5) The Secretary shall, where practicable, enter into agreements with soil conservation districts, State soil and water conservation agencies, or State water quality agencies to administer all or part of the program established in this subsection under regulations developed by the Secretary. Such agreements shall provide for the submission of such reports as the Secretary deems necessary, and for payment by the United States of such portion of the costs incurred in the administration of the program as the Secretary may deem appropriate.

(6) The contracts under this subsection shall be entered into only in areas where the management agency designated under subsection (c)(1) of this section assures an adequate level of participation by owners and operators having control of rural land in such areas. Within such areas the local soil conservation district, where one exists, together with the Secretary of Agriculture, will determine the priority of assistance among individual land owners and operators to assure that the most critical water quality problems are addressed.

(7) The Secretary, in consultation with the Administrator and subject to section 1314(k) of this title, shall, not later than September 30, 1978, promulgate regulations for carrying out this subsection and for support and cooperation with other Federal and non-Federal agencies for implementation of this subsection.

(8) This program shall not be used to authorize or finance projects that would otherwise be eligible for assistance under the terms of Public Law 83–566 [16 U.S.C. 1001 et seq.].

(9) There are hereby authorized to be appropriated to the Secretary of Agriculture $200,000,000 for fiscal year 1979, $400,000,000 for fiscal year 1980, $100,000,000 for fiscal year 1981, and $100,000,000 for fiscal year 1982, to carry out this subsection. The program authorized under this subsection shall be in addition to, and not in substitution of, other programs in such area authorized by this or any other public law.

(June 30, 1948, ch. 758, title II, § 208, as added Oct. 18, 1972, Pub.L. 92–500, § 2, 86 Stat. 839, and amended Dec. 27, 1977, Pub.L. 95–217, §§ 4(e), 31, 32, 33(a), 34, 35, 91 Stat. 1566, 1576–1579; Oct. 21, 1980, Pub.L. 96–483, § 1(d), (e), 94 Stat. 2360.)

1 So in original probably should read "designated".

Cross References

Authorization of appropriations to carry out this chapter, other than subsec. (f) and (h), see section 1376 of this title.
Authorization of appropriations to carry out this subchapter other than this section, see section 1287 of this title.
Basin planning, see section 1289 of this title.
Continuing planning processes incorporating all elements of any areawide waste management plan under this section, see section 1313 of this title.
Designation of agency designated under this section for purposes of developing solid waste disposal plans, see section 6946 of Title 42. The Public Health and Welfare.
Exclusion from gross income of portion of payments received under this section, see section 126 of Title 26, Internal Revenue Code.
Grants to State agencies for development of pollution control plan for basin in conjunction with any areawide waste management plan developed pursuant to this section, see section 1252 of this title.
Grants to States for reasonable costs of administration of an approved program, see section 1285 of this title.
Identification and evaluation of nonpoint sources of pollution, see section 1314 of this title.
Limitations and conditions of grants, see section 1284 of this title.
"Municipality" defined for purposes of this chapter, see section 1362 of this title.
Non-prohibited discharge of dredged or fill material resulting from any activity with respect to which a State has an approved program under this section, see section 1344 of this title.
Reports to Congress on progress of plans developed under this section, see section 1375 of this title.

Code of Federal Regulations

General pretreatment regulations for existing and new sources of pollution, see 40 CFR 403.1 et seq.
Rural clean water program, see 7 CFR 634.1 et seq.
State and local assistance, see 40 CFR 35.001 et seq.
Water quality planning and management, see 40 CFR 130.0 et seq.

§ 1289. Basin planning

(a) Preparation of Level B plans

The President, acting through the Water Resources Council, shall, as soon as practicable, prepare a Level B plan under the Water Resources Planning Act [42 U.S.C. 1962 et seq.] for all basins in the United States. All such plans shall be completed not later than January 1, 1980, except that priority in the preparation of such plans shall be given to those basins and portions thereof which are within those areas designated under paragraphs (2), (3), and (4) of subsection (a) of section 1288 of this title.

(b) Reporting requirements

The President, acting through the Water Resources Council, shall report annually to Congress on progress being made in carrying out this section. The first such report shall be submitted not later than January 31, 1973.

(c) Authorization of appropriations

There is authorized to be appropriated to carry out this section not to exceed $200,000,000.

(June 30, 1948, ch. 758, title II, § 209, as added Oct. 18, 1972, Pub.L. 92–500, § 2, 86 Stat. 843.)

Library References

Health and Environment ⇐25.5(1).
C.J.S. Health and Environment § 61 et seq.

Cross References

Authorization of appropriations to carry out this chapter other than this section, see section 1376 of this title.
Authorization of appropriations to carry out this subchapter other than this section, see section 1287 of this title.
Continuing planning processes resulting in plans for all navigable waters incorporating plans under this section, see section 1313 of this title.
Reports to Congress on progress of plans developed under this section, see section 1375 of this title.

§ 1290. Annual survey

The Administrator shall annually make a survey to determine the efficiency of the operation and maintenance of treatment works constructed with grants made under this chapter, as compared to the efficiency planned at the time the grant was made. The results of such annual survey shall be included in the report required under section 1375(a) of this title.

(June 30, 1948, ch. 758, title II, § 210, as added Oct. 18, 1972, Pub.L. 92–500, § 2, 86 Stat. 843.)

Cross References

Reports to Congress containing a summary of the results of the survey taken under this section, see section 1375 of this title.

§ 1291. Sewage collection systems

(a) Existing and new systems

No grant shall be made for a sewage collection system under this subchapter unless such grant (1) is for replacement or major rehabilitation of an existing collection system and is necessary to the total integrity and performance of the waste treatment works servicing such community, or (2) is for a new collection system in an existing community with sufficient existing or planned capacity adequately to treat such collected sewage and is consistent with section 1281 of this title.

(b) Use of population density as test

If the Administrator uses population density as a test for determining the eligibility of a collector sewer for assistance it shall be only for the purpose of evaluating alternatives and determining the needs for such system in relation to ground or surface water quality impact.

(c) Pollutant discharges from separate storm sewer systems

No grant shall be made under this subchapter from funds authorized for any fiscal year during the period beginning October 1, 1977, and ending September 30, 1985, for treatment works for control of pollutant discharges from separate storm sewer systems.

(June 30, 1948, ch. 758, title II, § 211, as added Oct. 18, 1972, Pub.L. 92–500, § 2, 86 Stat. 843, and amended Dec. 27, 1977, Pub.L. 95–217, § 36, 91 Stat. 1581; Dec. 29, 1981, Pub.L. 97–117, § 2(b), 95 Stat. 1623.)

Library References

Health and Environment ⚷25.7(21).
C.J.S. Health and Environment § 106 et seq.

§ 1292. Definitions

As used in this subchapter—

(1) The term "construction" means any one or more of the following: preliminary planning to determine the feasibility of treatment works, engineering, architectural, legal, fiscal, or economic investigations or studies, surveys, designs, plans, working drawings, specifications, procedures, field testing of innovative or alternative waste water treatment processes and techniques meeting guidelines promulgated under section 1314(d)(3) of this title, or other necessary actions, erection, building, acquisition, alteration, remodeling, improvement, or extension of treatment works, or the inspection or supervision of any of the foregoing items.

(2)(A) The term "treatment works" means any devices and systems used in the storage, treatment, recycling, and reclamation of municipal sewage or industrial wastes of a liquid nature to implement section 1281 of this title, or necessary to recycle or reuse water at the most economical cost over the estimated life of the works, including intercepting sewers, outfall sewers, sewage collection systems, pumping, power, and other equipment, and their appurtenances; extensions, improvements, remodeling, additions, and alterations thereof; elements essential to provide a reliable recycled supply such as standby treatment units and clear well facilities; and any works, including site acquisition of the land that will be an integral part of the treatment process (including land used for the storage of treated wastewater in land treatment systems prior to land application) or is used for ultimate disposal of residues resulting from such treatment.

(B) In addition to the definition contained in subparagraph (A) of this paragraph, "treatment works" means any other method or system for preventing, abating, reducing, storing, treating, separating, or disposing of municipal waste, including storm water runoff, or industrial waste, including waste in combined storm water and sanitary sewer systems. Any application for construction grants which includes wholly or in part such methods or systems shall, in accordance with guidelines published by the Administrator pursuant to subparagraph (C) of this paragraph, contain adequate data and analysis demonstrating such proposal to be, over the life of such works, the most cost efficient alternative to comply with sections 1311 or 1312 of this title, or the requirements of section 1281 of this title.

(C) For the purposes of subparagraph (B) of this paragraph, the Administrator shall, within one hundred and eighty days after October 18, 1972, publish and thereafter revise no less often than annually, guidelines for the evaluation of methods, including cost-effective analysis, described in subparagraph (B) of this paragraph.

(3) The term "replacement" as used in this subchapter means those expenditures for obtaining and installing equipment, accessories, or appurtenances during the useful life of the treatment works necessary to maintain the capacity and performance for which such works are designed and constructed.

(June 30, 1948, ch. 758, title II, § 212, as added Oct. 18, 1972, Pub.L. 92–500, § 2, 86 Stat. 844, and amended Dec. 27, 1977, Pub.L. 95–217, § 37, 91 Stat. 1581; Dec. 29, 1981, Pub.L. 97–117, § 8(d), 95 Stat. 1626.)

Cross References

Estimate of costs of treatment works as defined in this section, see section 1375 of this title.
Grants for projects within definition set forth in this section, see section 1281 of this title.
Grants to States for reasonable cost of administering this section, see section 1285 of this title.
Permits for disposal or use of sewage sludge, see section 1345 of this title.
Pretreatment standards for prevention of discharge of pollutant through treatment works as defined in this section, see section 1317 of this title.
Violation of permit conditions, see section 1342 of this title.

§ 1293. Loan guarantees

(a) State or local obligations issued exclusively to Federal Financing Bank for publicly owned treatment works; determination of eligibility of project by Administrator

Subject to the conditions of this section and to such terms and conditions as the Administrator determines to be necessary to carry out the purposes of this subchapter, the Administrator is authorized to guarantee, and to make commitments to guarantee, the principal and interest (including interest accruing between the date of default and the date of the payment in full of the guarantee) of any loan, obligation, or participation therein of any State, municipality, or intermunicipal or interstate agency issued directly and exclusively to the Federal Financing Bank to finance that part of the cost of any grant-eligible project for the construction of publicly owned treatment works not paid for with Federal financial assistance under this subchapter (other than this section), which project the Administrator has determined to be eligible for such financial assistance under this subchapter, including, but not limited to, projects eligible for reimbursement under section 1286 of this title.

(b) Conditions for issuance

No guarantee, or commitment to make a guarantee, may be made pursuant to this section—

(1) unless the Administrator certifies that the issuing body is unable to obtain on reasonable terms sufficient credit to finance its actual needs without such guarantee; and

(2) unless the Administrator determines that there is a reasonable assurance of repayment of the loan, obligation, or participation therein.

A determination of whether financing is available at reasonable rates shall be made by the Secretary of the Treasury with relationship to the current average yield on outstanding marketable obligations of municipalities of comparable maturity.

(c) Fees for application investigation and issuance of commitment guarantee

The Administrator is authorized to charge reasonable fees for the investigation of an application for a guarantee and for the issuance of a commitment to make a guarantee.

(d) Commitment for repayment

The Administrator, in determining whether there is a reasonable assurance of repayment, may require a commitment which would apply to such repayment. Such commitment may include, but not be limited to, any funds received by such grantee from the amounts appropriated under section 1286 of this title.

(June 30, 1948, ch. 758, title II, § 213, as added Oct. 19, 1976, Pub.L. 94–558, 90 Stat. 2639, and amended Oct. 21, 1980, Pub.L. 96–483, § 2(e), 94 Stat. 2361.)

Code of Federal Regulations

Administration of federal contracts, grants, or loans, see 40 CFR 15.1 et seq.
Loan guarantees for construction of treatment works, see 40 CFR 39.100 et seq.

Library References

Health and Environment ⚷25.7(21).
C.J.S. Health and Environment § 106 et seq.

§ 1293a. Contained spoil disposal facilities

(a) Construction, operation, and maintenance; period; conditions; requirements

The Secretary of the Army, acting through the Chief of Engineers, is authorized to construct, operate, and maintain, subject to the provisions of subsection (c) of this section, contained spoil disposal facilities of sufficient capacity for a period not to exceed ten years, to meet the requirements of this section. Before establishing each such facility, the Secretary of the Army shall obtain the concurrence of appropriate local governments and shall consider the views and recommendations of the Administrator of the Environmental Protection Agency and shall comply with requirements of section 1171 of this title, and of the National Environmental Policy Act of 1969 [42 U.S.C. 4321 et seq.]. Section 401 of this title shall not apply to any facility authorized by this section.

(b) Time for establishment; consideration of area needs; requirements

The Secretary of the Army, acting through the Chief of Engineers, shall establish the contained spoil disposal facilities authorized in subsection (a) of this section at the earliest practicable date, taking into consideration the views and recommendations of the Administrator of the Environmental Protection Agency as to those areas which, in the Administrator's judgment, are most urgently in need of such facilities and pursuant to the requirements of the National Environmental Policy Act of 1969 [42 U.S.C. 4321 et seq.] and the Federal Water Pollution Control Act [33 U.S.C. 1251 et seq.].

(c) Written agreement requirement; terms of agreement

Prior to construction of any such facility, the appropriate State or States, interstate agency, municipality, or other appropriate political subdivision of the State shall agree in writing to (1) furnish all lands, easements, and rights-of-way necessary for the construction, operation, and maintenance of the facility; (2) contribute to the United States 25 per centum of the construction costs, such amount to be payable either in cash prior to construction, in installments during construction, or in installments, with interest at a rate to be determined by the Secretary of the Treasury, as of the beginning of the fiscal year in which construction is initiated, on the basis of the computed average interest rate payable by the Treasury upon its outstanding marketable public obligations, which are neither due or callable for redemption for fifteen years from date of issue; (3) hold and save the United States free from damages due to construction, operation, and maintenance of the facility; and (4) except as provided in subsection (f) of this section, maintain the facility after completion of its use for disposal purposes in a manner satisfactory to the Secretary of the Army.

(d) Waiver of construction costs contribution from non-Federal interests; findings of participation in waste treatment facilities for general geographical area and compliance with water quality standards; waiver of payments in event of written agreement before occurrence of findings

The requirement for appropriate non-Federal interest or interests to furnish an agreement to contribute 25 per centum of the construction costs as set forth in subsection (c) of this section shall be waived by the Secretary of the Army upon a finding by the Administrator of the Environmental Protection Agency that for the area to which such construction applies, the State or States involved, interstate agency, municipality, and other appropriate political subdivision of the State and industrial concerns are participating in and in compliance with an approved plan for the general geographical area of the dredging activity for construction, modification, expansion, or rehabilitation of waste treatment facilities and the Administrator has found that applicable water quality standards are not being violated. In the event such findings occur after the appropriate non-Federal interest or interests have entered into the agreement required by subsection (c) of this section, any payments due after the date of such findings as part of the required local contribution of 25 per centum of the construction costs shall be waived by the Secretary of the Army.

(e) Federal payment of costs for disposal of dredged spoil from project

Notwithstanding any other provision of law, all costs of disposal of dredged spoil from the project for the Great Lakes connecting channels, Michigan, shall be borne by the United States.

(f) Title to lands; easements, and rights-of-way; retention by non-Federal interests; conveyance of facilities; agreement of transferee

The participating non-Federal interest or interests shall retain title to all lands, easements, and rights-of-way furnished by it pursuant to subsection (c) of this section. A spoil disposal facility owned by a non-Federal interest or interests may be conveyed to another party only after completion of the facility's use for disposal purposes and after the transferee agrees in writing to use or maintain the facility in a manner which the Secretary of the Army determines to be satisfactory.

(g) Federal licenses or permits; charges; remission of charge

Any spoil disposal facilities constructed under the provisions of this section shall be made available to Federal licensees or permittees upon payment of an appropriate charge for such use. Twenty-five per centum of such charge shall be remitted to the participating non-Federal interest or interests except for those excused from contributing to the construction costs under subsections (d) and (e) of this section.

(h) Provisions applicable to Great Lakes and their connecting channels

This section, other than subsection (i), shall be applicable only to the Great Lakes and their connecting channels.

(i) Research, study, and experimentation program relating to dredged spoil extended to navigable waters, etc.; cooperative program; scope of program; utilization of facilities and personnel of Federal agency

The Chief of Engineers, under the direction of the Secretary of the Army, is hereby authorized to extend to all navigable waters, connecting channels, tributary streams, other waters of the United States and waters contiguous to the United States, a comprehensive program of research, study, and experimentation relating to dredged spoil. This program shall be carried out in cooperation with other Federal and State agencies, and shall include, but not be limited to, investigations on the characteristics of dredged spoil, and alternative methods of its disposal. To the extent that such study shall include the effects of such dredge spoil on water quality, the facilities and personnel of the Environmental Protection Agency shall be utilized.

(Dec. 31, 1970, Pub.L. 91–611, title I, § 123, 84 Stat. 1823, March 7, 1974, Pub.L. 93–251, title I, § 23, 88 Stat. 20.)

Library References

Health and Environment ⟹25.7(21).
C.J.S. Health and Environment § 106 et seq.

§ 1294. Public information and education on recycling and reuse of wastewater, use of land treatment, and reduction of wastewater volume

The Administrator shall develop and operate within one year of December 27, 1977, a continuing program of public information and education on recycling and reuse of wastewater (including sludge), the use of land treatment, and methods for the reduction of wastewater volume.

(June 30, 1948, ch. 758, title II, § 214, as added Dec. 27, 1977, Pub.L. 95–217, § 38, 91 Stat. 1581.)

§ 1295. Requirements for American materials

Notwithstanding any other provision of law, no grant for which application is made after February 1, 1978, shall be made under this subchapter for any treatment works unless only such unmanufactured articles, materials, and supplies as have been mined or produced in the United States, and only such manufactured articles, materials, and supplies as have been manufactured in the United States, substantially all from articles, materials, or supplies mined, produced, or manufactured, as the case may be, in the United States will be used in such treatment works. This section shall not apply in any case where the Administrator determines, based upon those factors the Administrator deems relevant, including the available resources of the agency, it to be inconsistent with the public interest (including multilateral government procurement agreements) or the cost to be unreasonable, or if articles, materials, or supplies of the class or kind to be used or the articles, materials, or supplies from which they are manufactured are not mined, produced, or manufactured, as the case may be, in the United States in sufficient and reasonably available commercial quantities and of a satisfactory quality.

(June 30, 1948, ch. 758, title II, § 215, as added Dec. 27, 1977, Pub.L. 95–217, § 39, 91 Stat. 1581.)

§ 1296. Determination of priority of projects

Notwithstanding any other provision of this chapter, the determination of the priority to be given each category of projects for construction of publicly owned treatment works within each State shall be made solely by that State, except that if the Administrator, after a public hearing, determines that a specific project will not result in compliance with the enforceable requirements of this chapter, such project shall be removed from the State's priority list and such State shall submit a revised priority list. These categories shall include, but not be limited to (A) secondary treatment, (B) more stringent treatment, (C) infiltration-in-flow correction, (D) major sewer system rehabilitation, (E) new collector sewers and appurtenances, (F) new interceptors and appurtenances, and (G) correction of combined sewer overflows. Not less than 25 per centum of funds allocated to a State in any fiscal year under this subchapter for construction of publicly owned treatment works in such State shall be obligated for those types of projects referred to in clauses (D), (E), (F), and (G) of this section, if such projects are on such State's priority list for that year and are otherwise eligible for funding in that fiscal year. It is the policy of Congress that projects for wastewater treatment and management undertaken with Federal financial assistance under this chapter by any State, municipality, or intermunicipal or interstate agency shall be projects which, in the estimation of the State, are designed to achieve optimum water quality management, consistent with the public health and water quality goals and requirements of this chapter.

(June 30, 1948, ch. 758, title II, § 216, as added Dec. 27, 1977, Pub.L. 95–217, § 40, 91 Stat. 1582, and amended Dec. 29, 1981, Pub.L. 97–117, § 18, 95 Stat. 1630.)

§ 1297. Guidelines for cost-effectiveness analysis

Any guidelines for cost-effectiveness analysis published by the Administrator under this subchapter shall provide for the identification and selection of cost effective alternatives to comply with the objectives and goals of this chapter and sections 1281(b), 1281(d), 1281(g)(2)(A), and 1311(b)(2)(B) of this title.

(June 30, 1948, ch. 758, title II, § 217, as added Dec. 27, 1977, Pub.L. 95–217, § 41, 91 Stat. 1582.)

§ 1298. Cost effectiveness

(a) Congressional statement of policy

It is the policy of Congress that a project for waste treatment and management undertaken with Federal financial assistance under this chapter by any State, municipality, or intermunicipal or interstate agency shall be considered as an overall waste treatment system for waste treatment and management, and shall be that system which constitutes the most economical and cost-effective combination of devices and systems used in the storage, treatment, recycling, and reclamation of municipal sewage or industrial wastes of a liquid nature to implement section 1281 of this title, or necessary to recycle or reuse water at the most economical cost over the estimated life of the works, including intercepting sewers, outfall sewers, sewage collection systems, pumping power, and other equipment, and their appurtenances; extension, improvements, remodeling, additions, and alterations thereof; elements essential to provide a reliable recycled supply such as standby treatment units and clear well facilities; and any works, including site acquisition of the land that will be an integral part of the treatment process (including land use for the storage of treated wastewater in land treatment systems prior to land application) or which is used for ultimate disposal of residues resulting from such treatment; water efficiency measures and devices; and any other method or system for preventing, abating, reducing, storing, treating, separating, or disposing of municipal waste, including storm water runoff, or industrial waste, including waste in combined storm water and sanitary sewer systems; to meet the requirements of this chapter.

(b) Determination by Administrator as prerequisite to approval of grant

In accordance with the policy set forth in subsection (a) of this section, before the Administrator approves any grant to any State, municipality, or intermunicipal or interstate agency for the erection, building, acquisition, alteration, remodeling, improvement, or extension of any treatment works the Administrator shall determine that the facilities plan of which such treatment works are a part constitutes the most economical and cost-effective combination of treatment works over the life of the project to meet the requirements of this chapter, including, but not limited to, consideration of construction costs, operation, maintenance, and replacement costs.

(c) Value engineering review

In furtherance of the policy set forth in subsection (a) of this section, the Administrator shall require value engineering review in connection with any treatment works, prior to approval of any grant for the erection, building, acquisition, alteration, remodeling, improvement, or extension of such treatment works, in any case in which the cost of such erection, building, acquisition, alteration, remodeling, improvement, or extension is projected to be in excess of $10,000,000. For purposes of this subsection, the term "value engineering review" means a specialized cost control technique which uses a systematic and creative approach to identify and to focus on unnecessarily high cost in a project in order to arrive at a cost saving without sacrificing the reliability or efficiency of the project.

(d) Projects affected

This section applies to projects for waste treatment and management for which no treatment works including a facilities plan for such project have received Federal financial assistance for the preparation of construction plans and specifications under this chapter before December 29, 1981.

(June 30, 1948, ch. 758, title II, § 218, as added Dec. 29, 1981, Pub.L. 97-117, § 19, 95 Stat. 1630.)

Library References

Health and Environment ⚷25.7(1).
C.J.S. Health and Environment § 106 et seq.

§ 1299. State certification of projects

Whenever the Governor of a State which has been delegated sufficient authority to administer the construction grant program under this subchapter in that State certifies to the Administrator that a grant application meets applicable requirements of Federal and State law for assistance under this subchapter, the Administrator shall approve or disapprove such application within 45 days of the date of receipt of such application. If the Administrator does not approve or disapprove such application within 45 days of receipt, the application shall be deemed approved. If the Administrator disapproves such application the Administrator shall state in writing the reasons for such disapproval. Any grant approved or deemed approved under this section shall be subject to amounts provided in appropriation Acts.

(June 30, 1948, ch. 758, title II, § 219, as added Dec. 29, 1981, Pub.L. 97-117, § 20, 95 Stat. 1630.)

Library References

Health and Environment ⚷25.7(10).
C.J.S. Health and Environment § 106 et seq.

SUBCHAPTER III—STANDARDS AND ENFORCEMENT

§ 1311. Effluent limitations

(a) Illegality of pollutant discharges except in compliance with law

Except as in compliance with this section and sections 1312, 1316, 1317, 1328, 1342, and 1344 of this title, the discharge of any pollutant by any person shall be unlawful.

(b) Timetable for achievement of objectives

In order to carry out the objective of this chapter there shall be achieved—

(1)(A) not later than July 1, 1977, effluent limitations for point sources, other than publicly owned treatment works, (i) which shall require the application of the best practicable control technology currently available as defined by the Administrator pursuant to section 1314(b) of this title, or (ii) in the case of a discharge into a publicly owned treatment works which meets the requirements of subparagraph (B) of this paragraph, which shall require compliance with any applicable pretreatment requirements and any requirements under section 1317 of this title; and

(B) for publicly owned treatment works in existence on July 1, 1977, or approved pursuant to section 1283 of this title prior to June 30, 1974 (for which construction must be completed within four years of approval), effluent limitations based upon secondary treatment as defined by the Administrator pursuant to section 1314(d)(1) of this title; or,

(C) not later than July 1, 1977, any more stringent limitation, including those necessary to meet water quality standards, treatment standards, or schedules of compliance, established pursuant to any State law or regulations (under authority preserved by section 1370 of this title) or any other Federal law or regulation, or required to implement any applicable water quality standard established pursuant to this chapter.

(2)(A) for pollutants identified in subparagraphs (C), (D), and (F) of this paragraph, effluent limitations for categories and classes of point sources, other than publicly owned treatment works, which (i) shall require application of the best available technology economically achievable for such category or class, which will result in reasonable further progress toward the national goal of eliminating the discharge of all pollutants, as determined in accordance with regulations issued by the Administrator pursuant to section 1314(b)(2) of this title, which such effluent limitations shall require the elimination of discharges of all pollutants if the Administrator finds, on the basis of information available to him (including information developed pursuant to section 1325 of this title), that such elimination is technologically and economically achievable for a category or class of point sources as determined in accordance with regulations issued by the Administrator pursuant to section 1314(b)(2) of this title, or (ii) in the case of the introduction of a pollutant into a publicly owned treatment works which meets the requirements of subparagraph (B) of this paragraph, shall require compliance with any applicable pretreatment requirements and any other requirement under section 1317 of this title;

(B) Repealed. Pub.L. 97–117, § 21(b), Dec. 29, 1981, 95 Stat. 1632.

(C) not later than July 1, 1984, with respect to all toxic pollutants referred to in table 1 of Committee Print Numbered 95–30 of the Committee on Public Works and Transportation of the House of Representatives compliance with effluent limitations in accordance with subparagraph (A) of this paragraph;

(D) for all toxic pollutants listed under paragraph (1) of subsection (a) of section 1317 of this title which are not referred to in subparagraph (C) of this paragraph compliance with effluent limitations in accordance with subparagraph (A) of this paragraph not later than three years after the date such limitations are established;

(E) not later than July 1, 1984, effluent limitations for categories and classes of point sources, other than publicly owned treatment works, which in the case of pollutants identified pursuant to section 1314(a)(4) of this title shall require application of the best conventional pollutant control technology as determined in accordance with regulations issued by the Administrator pursuant to section 1314(b)(4) of this title; and

(F) for all pollutants (other than those subject to subparagraphs (C), (D), or (E) of this paragraph) compliance with effluent limitations in accordance with subparagraph (A) of this paragraph not later than 3 years after the date such limitations are established, or not later than July 1, 1984, whichever is later, but in no case later than July 1, 1987.

(c) Modification of timetable

The Administrator may modify the requirements of subsection (b)(2)(A) of this section with respect to any point source for which a permit application is filed after July 1, 1977, upon a showing by the owner or operator of such point source satisfactory to the Administrator that such modified requirements (1) will represent the maximum use of technology within the economic capability of the owner or operator; and (2) will result in reasonable further progress toward the elimination of the discharge of pollutants.

(d) Review and revision of effluent limitations

Any effluent limitation required by paragraph (2) of subsection (b) of this section shall be reviewed at least every five years and, if appropriate, revised pursuant to the procedure established under such paragraph.

(e) All point discharge source application of effluent limitations

Effluent limitations established pursuant to this section or section 1312 of this title shall be applied to all point sources of discharge of pollutants in accordance with the provisions of this chapter.

(f) Illegality of discharge of radiological, chemical, or biological warfare agents or high-level radioactive waste

Notwithstanding any other provisions of this chapter it shall be unlawful to discharge any radiological, chemical, or biological warfare agent or high-level radioactive waste into the navigable waters.

(g) Waiver for certain pollutants

(1) The Administrator, with the concurrence of the State, shall modify the requirements of subsection (b)(2)(A) of this section with respect to the discharge of any pollutant (other than pollutants identified pursuant to section 1314(a)(4) of this title, toxic pollutants subject to section 1317(a) of this title, and the thermal component of discharges) from any point source upon a showing by the owner or operator of such point source satisfactory to the Administrator that—

(A) such modified requirements will result at a minimum in compliance with the requirements of subsection (b)(1)(A) or (C) of this section, whichever is applicable;

(B) such modified requirements will not result in any additional requirements on any other point or nonpoint source; and

(C) such modification will not interfere with the attainment or maintenance of that water quality which shall assure protection of public water supplies, and the protection and propagation of a balanced population of shellfish, fish, and wildlife, and allow recreational activities, in and on the water and such modification will not result in the discharge of pollutants in quantities which may reasonably be anticipated to pose an unacceptable risk to human health or the environment because of bioaccumulation, persistency in the environment, acute toxicity, chronic toxicity (including carcinogenicity, mutagenicity or teratogenicity), or synergistic propensities.

(2) If an owner or operator of a point source applies for a modification under this subsection with respect to the discharge of any pollutant, such owner or operator shall be eligible to apply for modification under subsection (c) of this section with respect to such pollutant only during the same time period as he is eligible to apply for a modification under this subsection.

(h) Modification of secondary treatment requirements

The Administrator, with the concurrence of the State, may issue a permit under section 1342 of this title which modifies the requirements of subsection (b)(1)(B) of this section with respect to the discharge of any pollutant from a publicly owned treatment works into marine waters, if the applicant demonstrates to the satisfaction of the Administrator that—

(1) there is an applicable water quality standard specific to the pollutant for which the modification is requested, which has been identified under section 1314(a)(6) of this title;

(2) such modified requirements will not interfere with the attainment or maintenance of that water quality which assures protection of public water supplies and the protection and propagation of a balanced, indigenous population of shellfish, fish, and wildlife, and allows recreational activities, in and on the water;

(3) the applicant has established a system for monitoring the impact of such discharge on a representative sample of aquatic biota, to the extent practicable;

(4) such modified requirements will not result in any additional requirements on any other point or nonpoint source;

(5) all applicable pretreatment requirements for sources introducing waste into such treatment works will be enforced;

(6) to the extent practicable, the applicant has established a schedule of activities designed to eliminate the entrance of toxic pollutants from nonindustrial sources into such treatment works;

(7) there will be no new or substantially increased discharges from the point source of the pollutant to which the modification applies above that volume of discharge specified in the permit.

For the purposes of this subsection the phrase "the discharge of any pollutant into marine waters" refers to a discharge into deep waters of the territorial sea or the waters of the contiguous zone, or into saline estuarine waters where there is strong tidal movement and other hydrological and geological characteristics which the Administrator determines necessary to allow compliance with paragraph (2) of this subsection, and section 1251(a)(2) of this title. A municipality which applies secondary treatment shall be eligible to receive a permit pursuant to this subsection which modifies the requirements of subsection (b)(1)(B) of this section with respect to the discharge of any pollutant from any treatment works owned by such municipality into marine waters. No permit issued under this subsection shall authorize the discharge of sewage sludge into marine waters.

(i) Municipal time extensions

(1) Where construction is required in order for a planned or existing publicly owned treatment works to achieve limitations under subsection (b)(1)(B) or (b)(1)(C) of this section, but (A) construction cannot be completed within the time required in such subsection, or (B) the United States has failed to make financial assistance under this chapter available in time to achieve such limitations by the time specified in such subsection, the owner or operator of such treatment works may request the Administrator (or if appropriate the State) to issue a permit pursuant to section 1342 of this title or to modify a permit issued pursuant to that section to extend such time for compliance. Any such request shall be filed with the Administrator (or if appropriate the State) within 180 days after December 27, 1977. The Administrator (or if appropriate the State) may grant such request and issue or modify such a permit, which shall contain a schedule of compliance for the publicly owned treatment works based on the earliest date by which such financial assistance will be available from the United States and construction can be completed, but in no event later than July 1, 1988, and shall contain such other terms and conditions, including those necessary to carry out subsections (b) through (g) of section 1281 of this title, section 1317 of this title, and such interim effluent limitations applicable to that treatment works as the Administrator determines are necessary to carry out the provisions of this chapter.

(2)(A) Where a point source (other than a publicly owned treatment works) will not achieve the requirements of subsections (b)(1)(A) and (b)(1)(C) of this section and—

(i) if a permit issued prior to July 1, 1977, to such point source is based upon a discharge into a publicly owned treatment works; or

(ii) if such point source (other than a publicly owned treatment works) had before July 1, 1977, a contract (enforceable against such point source) to discharge into a publicly owned treatment works; or

(iii) if either an application made before July 1, 1977, for a construction grant under this chapter for a publicly owned treatment works, or engineering or architectural plans or working drawings made before July 1, 1977, for a publicly owned treatment works, show that such point source was to discharge into such publicly owned treatment works,

and such publicly owned treatment works is presently unable to accept such discharge without construction, and in the case of a discharge to an existing publicly owned treatment works, such treatment works has an extension pursuant to paragraph (1) of this subsection, the owner or operator of such point source may request the Administrator (or if appropriate the State) to issue or modify such a permit pursuant to such section 1342 of this title to extend such time for compliance. Any such request shall be filed with the Administrator (or if appropriate the State) within 180 days after December 27, 1977, or the filing of a request by the appropriate publicly owned treatment works under paragraph (1) of this subsection, whichever is later. If the Administrator (or if appropriate the State) finds that the owner or operator of such point source has acted in good faith, he may grant such request and issue or modify such a permit, which shall contain a schedule of compliance for the point source to achieve the requirements of subsections (b)(1)(A) and (C) of this section and shall contain such other terms and conditions, including pretreatment and interim effluent limitations and water conservation requirements applicable to that point source, as the Administrator determines are necessary to carry out the provisions of this chapter.

(B) No time modification granted by the Administrator (or if appropriate the State) pursuant to paragraph (2)(A) of this subsection shall extend beyond the earliest date practicable for compliance or beyond the date of any extension granted to the appropriate publicly owned treatment works pursuant to paragraph (1) of this subsection, but in no event shall it extend beyond July 1, 1988; and no such time modification shall be granted unless (i) the publicly owned treatment works will be in operation and available to the point source before July 1, 1988, and will meet the requirements of subsections (b)(1)(B) and (C) of this section after receiving the discharge from that point source; and (ii) the point source and the publicly owned treatment works have entered into an enforceable contract requiring the point source to discharge into the publicly owned treatment works, the owner or operator of such point source to pay the costs required under section 1284 of this title, and the publicly owned treatment works to accept the discharge from the point source; and (iii) the permit for such point source requires that point source to meet all requirements under section 1317(a) and (b) of this title during the period of such time modification.

(j) Modification procedures

(1) Any application filed under this section for a modification of the provisions of—

(A) subsection (b)(1)(B) of this section under subsection (h) of this section shall be filed not later that[1] the 365th day which begins after December 29, 1981;

(B) subsection (b)(2)(A) of this section as it applies to pollutants identified in subsection (b)(2)(F) of this section shall be filed not later than 270 days after the date of promulgation of an applicable effluent guideline under section 1314 of this title or not later than 270 days after December 27, 1977, whichever is later.

(2) Any application for a modification filed under subsection (g) of this section shall not operate to stay any requirement under this chapter, unless in the judgment of the Administrator such a stay or the modification sought will not result in the discharge of pollutants in quantities which may reasonably be anticipated to pose an unacceptable risk to human health or the environment because of bioaccumulation, persistency in the environment, acute toxicity, chronic toxicity (including carcinogenicity, mutagenicity, or teratogenicity), or synergistic propensities, and that there is a substantial likelihood that the applicant will succeed on the merits of such application. In the case of an application filed under subsection (g) of this section, the Administrator may condition any stay granted under this paragraph on requiring the filing of a bond or other appropriate security to assure timely compliance with the requirements from which a modification is sought.

(k) Innovative technology

In the case of any facility subject to a permit under section 1342 of this title which proposes to comply with the requirements of subsection (b)(2)(A) of this section by replacing existing production capacity with an innovative production process which will result in an effluent reduction significantly greater than that required by the limitation otherwise applicable to such facility and moves toward the national goal of eliminating the discharge of all pollutants, or with the installation of an innovative control technique that has a substantial likelihood for enabling the facility to comply with the applicable effluent limitation by achieving a significantly greater effluent reduction than that required by the applicable effluent limitation and moves toward the national goal of eliminating the discharge of all pollutants, or by achieving the required reduction with an innovative system that has the potential for significantly lower costs than the systems which have been determined by the Administrator to be economically achievable, the Administrator (or the State with an approved program under section 1342 of this title, in consultation with the Administrator) may establish a date for compliance under subsection (b)(2)(A) of this section no later than July 1, 1987, if it is also determined that such innovative system has the potential for industrywide application.

(*l*) Toxic pollutants

The Administrator may not modify any requirement of this section as it applies to any specific pollutant which is on the toxic pollutant list under section 1317(a)(1) of this title.

(m) Modification of effluent limitation requirements for point sources

(1) The Administrator, with the concurrence of the State, may issue a permit under section 1342 of this title which modifies the requirements of subsections (b)(1)(A) and (b)(2)(E) of this section, and of section 1343 of this title, with respect to effluent limitations to the extent such limitations relate to biochemical oxygen demand and pH from discharges by an industrial discharger in such State into deep waters of the territorial seas, if the applicant demonstrates and the Administrator finds that—

(A) the facility for which modification is sought is covered at the time of the enactment of this subsection by National Pollutant Discharge Elimination System permit number CA0005894 or CA0005282;

(B) the energy and environmental costs of meeting such requirements of subsections (b)(1)(A) and (b)(2)(E) of this section and section 1343 of this title exceed by an unreasonable amount the benefits to be obtained, including the objectives of this chapter;

(C) the applicant has established a system for monitoring the impact of such discharges on a representative sample of aquatic biota;

(D) such modified requirements will not result in any additional requirements on any other point or nonpoint source;

(E) there will be no new or substantially increased discharges from the point source of the pollutant to which the modification applies above that volume of discharge specified in the permit;

(F) the discharge is into waters where there is strong tidal movement and other hydrological and geological characteristics which are necessary to allow compliance with this subsection and section 1251(a)(2) of this title;

(G) the applicant accepts as a condition to the permit a contractual obligation to use funds in the amount required (but not less than $250,000 per year for ten years) for research and development of water pollution control technology, including but not limited to closed cycle technology;

(H) the facts and circumstances present a unique situation which, if relief is granted, will not establish a precedent or the relaxation of the requirements of this chapter applicable to similarly situated discharges; and

(I) no owner or operator of a facility comparable to that of the applicant situated in the United States has demonstrated that it would be put at a competitive disadvantage to the applicant (or the parent company or any subsidiary thereof) as a result of the issuance of a permit under this subsection.

(2) The effluent limitations established under a permit issued under paragraph (1) shall be sufficient to implement the applicable State water quality standards, to assure the protection of public water supplies and protection and propagation of a balanced, indigenous population of shellfish, fish, fauna, wildlife, and other aquatic organisms, and to allow recreational activities in and on the water. In setting such limitations, the Administrator shall take into account any seasonal variations and the need for an adequate margin of safety, considering the lack of essential knowledge concerning the relationship between effluent limitations and water quality and the lack of essential knowledge of the effects of discharges on beneficial uses of the receiving waters.

(3) A permit under this subsection may be issued for a period not to exceed five years, and such a permit may be renewed for one additional period not to exceed five years upon a demonstration by the applicant and a finding by the Administrator at the time of application for any such renewal that the provisions of this subsection are met.

(4) The Administrator may terminate a permit issued under this subsection if the Administrator determines that there has been a decline in ambient water quality of the receiving waters during the period of the permit even if a direct cause and effect relationship cannot be shown: *Provided,* That if the effluent from a source with a permit issued under this subsection is contributing to a decline in ambient water quality of the receiving waters, the Administrator shall terminate such permit.

(June 30, 1948, ch. 758, title III, § 301, as added Oct. 18, 1972, Pub.L. 92–500, § 2, 86 Stat. 844, and amended Dec. 27, 1977, Pub.L. 95–217, §§ 42–47, 53(c), 91 Stat. 1582–1586, 1590; Dec. 29, 1981, Pub.L. 97–117, §§ 21, 22(a)–(d), 95 Stat. 1631, 1632; Jan. 8, 1983, Pub.L. 97–440, 96 Stat. 2289.)

1 So in original. Probably should be "than".

Cross References

Criminal penalties for violation of this section, see section 1319 of this title.

Definition of "effluent standard or limitation" for purposes of citizen suits, see section 1365 of this title.

Definition of "treatment works", see section 1292 of this title.

Development and publication of information on factors necessary for protection of public water supplies, see section 1314 of this title.

Employee protection, deliberate violations by employee acting without direction from employer, see section 1367 of this title.

Guidelines for cost-effectiveness analysis, see section 1297 of this title.

Identification of areas with insufficient effluent limitations, see section 1313 of this title.

National Study Commission, establishment, see section 1325 of this title.

Permits for discharge of pollutants, see section 1342 of this title.

Permits for dredged or fill material, see section 1344 of this title.

Research and demonstration projects to carry out the purposes of this section, see section 1255 of this title.

Review of Administrator's actions, see section 1369 of this title.

State certification of applicants for federal license, see section 1341 of this title.

Thermal discharges, effluent limitations for protection and propagation of shellfish, etc., see section 1326 of this title.

Toxic and pretreatment effluent standards, see section 1317 of this title.

Water quality related effluent limitations, see section 1312 of this title.

Federal Practice and Procedure

Intervention of right, see Wright & Miller: Civil § 1906 et seq.

Code of Federal Regulations

Criteria and standards for the National Pollutant Discharge Elimination System, see 40 CFR 125.1 et seq.

Effluent guidelines and standards, see 40 CFR Chap. I, Subchap. N.

Guidelines establishing test procedures for analysis of pollutants, see 40 CFR 136.1 et seq.

Secondary treatment regulation, see 40 CFR 133.100 et seq.

Library References

Health and Environment ⟹25.7(10).
C.J.S. Health and Environment § 106 et seq.

United States Supreme Court

Court's authority to impose more stringent effluent limitations under federal common law than those imposed by federal agency, City of Milwaukee v. Illinois and Michigan, 1981, 101 S.Ct. 1784, 451 U.S. 304, 68 L.Ed.2d 114.

Regulations setting effluent limitations, existing point sources, allowance for individual variations, see E.I. du Pont de Nemours & Co. v. Train, 1977, 97 S.Ct. 965, 430 U.S. 112, 51 L.Ed.2d 204.

§ 1312. Water quality related effluent limitations

(a) Establishment

Whenever, in the judgment of the Administrator, discharges of pollutants from a point source or group of point sources, with the application of effluent limitations required under section 1311(b)(2) of this title, would interfere with the attainment or maintenance of that water quality in a specific portion of the navigable waters which shall assure protection of public water supplies, agricultural and industrial uses, and the protection and propagation of a balanced population of shellfish, fish and wildlife, and allow recreational activities in and on the water, effluent limitations (including alternative effluent control strategies) for such point source or sources shall be established which can reasonably be expected to contribute to the attainment or maintenance of such water quality.

(b) Notice; hearing; adjustment of limitation by Administrator

(1) Prior to establishment of any effluent limitation pursuant to subsection (a) of this section, the Administrator shall issue notice of intent to establish such limitation and within ninety days of such notice hold a public hearing to determine the relationship of the economic and social costs of achieving any such limitation or limitations, including any economic or social dislocation in the affected community or communities, to the social and economic benefits to be obtained (including the attainment of the objective of this chapter) and to determine whether or not such effluent limitations can be implemented with available technology or other alternative control strategies.

(2) If a person affected by such limitation demonstrates at such hearing that (whether or not such technology or other alternative control strategies are available) there is no reasonable relationship between the economic and social costs and the benefits to be obtained (including attainment of the objective of this chapter), such limitation shall not become effective and the Administrator shall adjust such limitation as it applies to such person.

(c) Delay in application of other limitations

The establishment of effluent limitations under this section shall not operate to delay the application of any effluent limitation established under section 1311 of this title.

(June 30, 1948, ch. 758, title III, § 302, as added Oct. 18, 1972, Pub.L. 92–500, § 2, 86 Stat. 846.)

Cross References

Alternate methods for preventing, etc., municipal waste as within definition of "treatment works," see section 1292 of this title.
Approval of continuing planning process, see section 1313 of this title.
Best management practices for industry, see section 1314 of this title.
Certification from State of compliance with provisions of this section, see section 1341 of this title.
Discharge of pollutants as unlawful except as when in compliance with this section, see section 1311 of this title.
Effluent standards for purposes of citizen suits, see section 1365 of this title.
Enforcement of provisions of this section, see section 1319 of this title.
Permits for discharge of pollutants, see section 1342 of this title.
Review of Administrator's actions, see section 1369 of this title.
Violations by employees acting without direction from employer, see section 1367 of this title.

Library References

Health and Environment ⚷25.7(10).
C.J.S. Health and Environment § 106 et seq.

§ 1313. Water quality standards and implementation plans

(a) Existing water quality standards

(1) In order to carry out the purpose of this chapter, any water quality standard applicable to interstate waters which was adopted by any State and submitted to, and approved by, or is a waiting approval by, the Administrator pursuant to this Act as in effect immediately prior to October 18, 1972, shall remain in effect unless the Administrator determined that such standard is not consistent with the applicable requirements of this Act as in effect immediately prior to October 18, 1972. If the Administrator makes such a determination he shall, within three months after October 18, 1972, notify the State and specify the changes needed to meet such requirements. If such changes are not adopted by the State within ninety days after the date of such notification, the Administrator shall promulgate such changes in accordance with subsection (b) of this section.

(2) Any State which, before October 18, 1972, has adopted, pursuant to its own law, water quality standards applicable to intrastate waters shall submit such standards to the Administrator within thirty days after October 18, 1972. Each such standard shall remain in effect, in the same manner and to the same extent as any other water quality standard established under this chapter unless the Administrator determines that such standard is inconsistent with the applicable requirements of this Act as in effect immediately prior to October 18, 1972. If the Administrator makes such a determination he shall not later than the one hundred and twentieth day after the date of submission of such standards, notify the State and specify the changes needed to meet such requirements. If such changes are not adopted by the State within ninety days after such notification, the Administrator shall promulgate such changes in accordance with subsection (b) of this section.

(3)(A) Any State which prior to October 18, 1972, has not adopted pursuant to its own laws water quality standards applicable to intrastate waters shall, not later than one hundred and eighty days after October 18, 1972, adopt and submit such standards to the Administrator.

(B) If the Administrator determines that any such standards are consistent with the applicable requirements of this Act as in effect immediately prior to October 18, 1972, he shall approve such standards.

(C) If the Administrator determines that any such standards are not consistent with the applicable requirements of this Act as in effect immediately prior to October 18, 1972, he shall, not later than the ninetieth day after the date of submission of such standards, notify the State and specify the changes to meet such requirements. If such changes are not adopted by the State within ninety days after the date of notification, the Administrator shall promulgate such standards pursuant to subsection (b) of this section.

(b) Proposed regulations

(1) The Administrator shall promptly prepare and publish proposed regulations setting forth water quality standards for a State in accordance with the applicable requirements of this Act as in effect immediately prior to October 18, 1972, if—

(A) the State fails to submit water quality standards within the times prescribed in subsection (a) of this section.

(B) a water quality standard submitted by such State under subsection (a) of this section is determined by the Administrator not to be consistent with the applicable requirements of subsection (a) of this section.

(2) The Administrator shall promulgate any water quality standard published in a proposed regulation not later than one hundred and ninety days after the date he publishes any such proposed standard, unless prior to such promulgation, such State has adopted a water quality standard which the Administrator determines to be in accordance with subsection (a) of this section.

(c) Review; revised standards; publication

(1) The Governor of a State or the State water pollution control agency of such State shall from time to time (but at least once each three year period beginning with October 18, 1972) hold public hearings for the purpose of reviewing applicable water quality standards and, as appropriate, modifying and adopting standards. Results of such review shall be made available to the Administrator.

(2) Whenever the State revises or adopts a new standard, such revised or new standard shall be submitted to the Administrator. Such revised or new water quality standard shall consist of the designated uses of the navigable waters involved and the water quality criteria for such waters based upon such uses. Such standards shall be such as to protect the public health or welfare, enhance the quality of water and serve the purposes of this chapter. Such standards shall be established taking into consideration their use and value for public water supplies, propagation of fish and wildlife, recreational purposes, and agricultural, industrial, and other purposes, and also taking into consideration their use and value for navigation.

(3) If the Administrator, within sixty days after the date of submission of the revised or new standard, determines that such standard meets the requirements of this chapter, such standard shall thereafter be the water quality standard for the applicable waters of that State. If the Administrator determines that any such revised or new standard is not consistent with the applicable requirements of this chapter, he shall not later than the ninetieth day after the date of submission of such standard notify the State and specify the changes to meet such requirements. If such changes are not adopted by the State within ninety days after the date of notification, the Administrator shall promulgate such standard pursuant to paragraph (4) of this subsection.

(4) The Administrator shall promptly prepare and publish proposed regulations setting forth a revised or new water quality standard for the navigable waters involved—

(A) if a revised or new water quality standard submitted by such State under paragraph (3) of this subsection for such waters is determined by the Administrator not to be consistent with the applicable requirements of this chapter, or

(B) in any case where the Administrator determines that a revised or new standard is necessary to meet the requirements of this chapter.

The Administrator shall promulgate any revised or new standard under this paragraph not later than ninety days after he publishes such proposed standards, unless prior to such promulgation, such State has adopted a revised or new water quality standard which the Administrator determines to be in accordance with this chapter.

(d) Identification of areas with insufficient controls; maximum daily load

(1)(A) Each State shall identify those waters within its boundaries for which the effluent limitations required by section 1311(b)(1)(A) and section 1311(b)(1)(B) of this title are not stringent enough to implement any water quality standard applicable to such waters. The State shall establish a priority ranking for such waters, taking into account the severity of the pollution and the uses to be made of such waters.

(B) Each State shall identify those waters or parts thereof within its boundaries for which controls on thermal discharges under section 1311 of this title are not stringent enough to assure protection and propagation of a balanced indigenous population of shellfish, fish, and wildlife.

(C) Each State shall establish for the waters identified in paragraph (1)(A) of this subsection, and in accordance with the priority ranking, the total maximum daily load, for those pollutants which the Administrator identifies under section 1314(a)(2) of this title as suitable for such calculation. Such load shall be established at a level necessary to implement the applicable water quality standards with seasonal variations and a margin of safety which takes into account any lack of knowledge concerning the relationship between effluent limitations and water quality.

(D) Each State shall estimate for the waters identified in paragraph (1)(B) of this subsection the total maximum daily thermal load required to assure protection and propagation of a balanced, indigenous population of shellfish, fish, and wildlife. Such estimates shall take into account the normal water temperatures, flow rates, seasonal variations, existing sources of heat input, and the dissipative capacity of the identified waters or parts thereof. Such estimates shall include a calculation of the maximum heat input that can be made into each such part and shall include a margin of safety which takes into account any lack of knowledge concerning the development of thermal water quality criteria for such protection and propagation in the identified waters or parts thereof.

(2) Each State shall submit to the Administrator from time to time, with the first such submission not later than one hundred and eighty days after the date of publication of the first identification of pollutants under section 1314(a)(2)(D) of this title, for his approval the waters identified and the loads established under paragraphs (1)(A), (1)(B), (1)(C), and (1)(D) of this subsection. The Administrator shall either approve or disapprove such identification and load not later than thirty days after the date of submission. If the Administrator approves such identification and load, such State shall incorporate them into its current plan under subsection (e) of this section. If the Administrator disapproves such identification and load, he shall not later than thirty days after the date of such disapproval identify such waters in such State and establish such loads for such waters as he determines necessary to implement the water quality standards applicable to such waters and upon such identification and establishment the State shall incorporate them into its current plan under subsection (e) of this section.

(3) For the specific purpose of developing information, each State shall identify all waters within its boundaries which it has not identified under paragraph (1)(A) and (1)(B) of this subsection and estimate for such waters the total maximum daily load with seasonal variations and margins of safety, for those pollutants which the Administrator identifies under section 1314(a)(2) of this title as suitable for such calculation and for thermal discharges, at a level that would assure protection and propagation of a balanced indigenous population of fish, shellfish, and wildlife.

(e) Continuing planning process

(1) Each State shall have a continuing planning process approved under paragraph (2) of this subsection which is consistent with this chapter.

(2) Each State shall submit not later than 120 days after October 18, 1972, to the Administrator for his approval a proposed continuing planning process which is consistent with this chapter. Not later than thirty days after the date of submission of such a process the Administrator shall either approve or disapprove such process. The Administrator shall from time to time review each State's approved planning process for the purpose of insuring that such planning process is at all times consistent with this chapter. The Administrator shall not approve any State permit program under subchapter IV of this chapter for any State which does not have an approved continuing planning process under this section.

(3) The Administrator shall approve any continuing planning process submitted to him under this section which will result in plans for all navigable waters within such State, which include, but are not limited to, the following:

(A) effluent limitations and schedules of compliance at least as stringent as those required by section 1311(b)(1), section 1311(b)(2), section 1316, and section 1317 of this title, and at least as stringent as any requirements contained in any applicable water quality standard in effect under authority of this section;

(B) the incorporation of all elements of any applicable area-wide waste management plans under section 1288 of this title, and applicable basin plans under section 1289 of this title;

(C) total maximum daily load for pollutants in accordance with subsection (d) of this section;

(D) procedures for revision;

(E) adequate authority for intergovernmental cooperation;

(F) adequate implementation, including schedules of compliance, for revised or new water quality standards, under subsection (c) of this section;

(G) controls over the disposition of all residual waste from any water treatment processing;

(H) an inventory and ranking, in order of priority, of needs for construction of waste treatment works required to meet the applicable requirements of sections 1311 and 1312 of this title.

(f) Earlier compliance

Nothing in this section shall be construed to affect any effluent limitation, or schedule of compliance required by any State to be implemented prior to the dates set forth in sections 1311(b)(1) and 1311(b)(2) of this title nor to preclude any State from requiring compliance with any effluent limitation or schedule of compliance at dates earlier than such dates.

(g) Heat standards

Water quality standards relating to heat shall be consistent with the requirements of section 1326 of this title.

(h) Thermal water quality standards

For the purposes of this chapter the term "water quality standards" includes thermal water quality standards.

(June 30, 1948, ch. 758, title III, § 303, as added Oct. 18, 1972, Pub.L. 92–500, § 2, 86 Stat. 846.)

Cross References

Approval of grants for treatment works, certification for priority, see section 1284 of this title.

License or permit to conduct activities resulting in discharge into navigable waters, certification by State of compliance with this section, see section 1341 of this title.

Period of protection from more stringent effluent limitations following discharge point source modification, see section 1326 of this title.

Planning process, consistency with State wide regulatory program, see section 1288 of this title.

Pollution control plans for basins, development in cooperation with State plan developed pursuant to this section, see section 1252 of this title.

Publication of information on and the identification of pollutants suitable for maximum daily load measurement correlated with the achievement of water quality objectives, see section 1314 of this title.

Reports to Congress on progress and problems associated with plans under this section, see section 1375 of this title.

Time for completion of review, revision, and adoption or promulgation of revised or new water quality standards, see section 1313a of this title.

Water quality management plan, see section 1285 of this title.

Code of Federal Regulations

Water quality planning and management, see 40 CFR 130.0 et seq.
Water quality standards, see 40 CFR 131.1 et seq.

Library References

Health and Environment ⚷25.7(10).
C.J.S. Health and Environment § 106 et seq.

United States Supreme Court

Preemption of state requirements on sewage discharge, initial federal standards, see Lake Carriers' Ass'n v. MacMullan, 1972, 92 S.Ct. 1749, 406 U.S. 498, 32 L.Ed. 257.

§ 1313a. Revised water quality standards

The review, revision, and adoption or promulgation of revised or new water quality standards pursuant to section 303(c) of the Federal Water Pollution Control Act [33 U.S.C. 1313(c)] shall be completed by the date three years after December 29, 1981. No grant shall be made under title II of the Federal Water Pollution Control Act [33 U.S.C. 1281 et seq.] after such date until water quality standards are reviewed and revised pursuant to section 303(c), [33 U.S.C. 1313(c)] except where the State has in good faith submitted such revised water quality standards and the Administrator has not acted to approve or disapprove such submission within one hundred and twenty days of receipt.

(Dec. 29, 1981, Pub.L. 97–117, § 24, 95 Stat. 1632.)

Library References

Health and Environment ⚷25.7(10).
C.J.S. Health and Environment § 106 et seq.

§ 1314. Information and guidelines

(a) Criteria development and publication

(1) The Administrator, after consultation with appropriate Federal and State agencies and other interested persons, shall develop and publish, within one year after October 18, 1972 (and from time to time thereafter revise) criteria for water quality accurately reflecting the latest scientific knowledge (A) on the kind and extent of all identifiable effects on health and welfare including, but not limited to, plankton, fish, shellfish, wildlife, plant life, shorelines, beaches, esthetics, and recreation which may be expected from the presence of pollutants in any body of water, including ground water; (B) on the concentration and dispersal of pollutants, or their byproducts, through biological, physical, and chemical processes; and (C) on the effects of pollutants on biological community diversity, productivity, and stability, including information on the factors affecting rates of eutrophication and rates of organic and inorganic sedimentation for varying types of receiving waters.

(2) The Administrator, after consultation with appropriate Federal and State agencies and other interested persons, shall develop and publish, within one year after October 18, 1972 (and from time to time thereafter revise) information (A) on the factors necessary to restore and maintain the chemical, physical, and biological integrity of all navigable waters, ground waters, waters of the contiguous zone, and the oceans; (B) on the factors necessary for the protection and propagation of shellfish, fish, and wildlife for classes and categories of receiving waters and to allow recreational activities in and on the water; and (C) on the measurement and classification of water quality; and (D) for the purpose of

section 1313 of this title, on and the identification of pollutants suitable for maximum daily load measurement correlated with the achievement of water quality objectives.

(3) Such criteria and information and revisions thereof shall be issued to the States and shall be published in the Federal Register and otherwise made available to the public.

(4) The Administrator shall, within 90 days after December 27, 1977, and from time to time thereafter, publish and revise as appropriate information identifying conventional pollutants, including but not limited to, pollutants classified as biological oxygen demanding, suspended solids, fecal coliform, and pH. The thermal component of any discharge shall not be identified as a conventional pollutant under this paragraph.

(5)(A) The Administrator, to the extent practicable before consideration of any request under section 1311(g) of this title and within six months after December 27, 1977, shall develop and publish information on the factors necessary for the protection of public water supplies, and the protection and propagation of a balanced population of shellfish, fish and wildlife, and to allow recreational activities, in and on the water.

(B) The Administrator, to the extent practicable before consideration of any application under section 1311(h) of this title and within six months after December 27, 1977, shall develop and publish information on the factors necessary for the protection of public water supplies, and the protection and propagation of a balanced indigenous population of shellfish, fish and wildlife, and to allow recreational activities, in and on the water.

(6) The Administrator shall, within three months after December 27, 1977, and annually thereafter, for purposes of section 1311(h) of this title publish and revise as appropriate information identifying each water quality standard in effect under this chapter or State law, the specific pollutants associated with such water quality standard, and the particular waters to which such water quality standard applies.

(b) Effluent limitation guidelines

For the purpose of adopting or revising effluent limitations under this chapter the Administrator shall, after consultation with appropriate Federal and State agencies and other interested persons, publish within one year of October 18, 1972, regulations, providing guidelines for effluent limitations, and, at least annually thereafter, revise, if appropriate, such regulations. Such regulations shall—

(1)(A) identify, in terms of amounts of constituents and chemical, physical, and biological characteristics of pollutants, the degree of effluent reduction attainable through the application of the best practicable control technology currently available for classes and categories of point sources (other than publicly owned treatment works); and

(B) specify factors to be taken into account in determining the control measures and practices to be applicable to point sources (other than publicly owned treatment works) within such categories or classes. Factors relating to the assessment of best practicable control technology currently available to comply with subsection (b)(1) of section 1311 of this title shall include consideration of the total cost of application of technology in relation to the effluent reduction benefits to be achieved from such application, and shall also take into account the age of equipment and facilities involved, the process employed, the engineering aspects of the application of various types of control techniques, process changes, non-water quality environmental impact (including energy requirements), and such other factors as the Administrator deems appropriate;

(2)(A) identify, in terms of amounts of constituents and chemical, physical, and biological characteristics of pollutants, the degree of effluent reduction attainable through the application of the best control measures and practices achievable including treatment techniques, process and procedure innovations, operating methods, and other alternatives for classes and categories of point sources (other than publicly owned treatment works); and

(B) specify factors to be taken into account in determining the best measures and practices available to comply with subsection (b)(2) of section 1311 of this title to be applicable to any point source (other than publicly owned treatment works) within such categories or classes. Factors relating to the assessment of best available technology shall take into account the age of equipment and facilities involved, the process employed, the engineering aspects of the application of various types of control techniques, process changes, the cost of achieving such effluent reduction, non-water quality environmental impact (including energy requirements), and such other factors as the Administrator deems appropriate;

(3) identify control measures and practices available to eliminate the discharge of pollutants from categories and classes of point sources, taking into account the cost of achieving such elimination of the discharge of pollutants; and

(4)(A) identify, in terms of amounts of constituents and chemical, physical, and biological characteristics of pollutants, the degree of effluent reduction attainable through the application of the best conventional pollutant control technology (including measures and practices) for classes and categories of point sources (other than publicly owned treatment works); and

(B) specify factors to be taken into account in determining the best conventional pollutant control technology measures and practices to comply with section 1311(b)(2)(E) of this title to be applicable to any point source (other than publicly owned treatment works) within such categories or classes. Factors relating to the assessment of best conventional pollutant control technology (including measures and practices) shall include consideration of the reasonableness of the relationship between the costs of attaining a reduction in effluents and the effluent reduction benefits derived, and the comparison of the cost and level of reduction of such pollutants from the discharge from publicly owned treatment works to the cost and level of reduction of such pollutants from a class or category of industrial sources, and shall take into account the age of equipment and facilities involved, the process employed, the engineering aspects of the application of various types of control techniques, process changes, non-water quality environmental impact (including energy requirements), and such other factors as the Administrator deems appropriate.

(c) Pollution discharge elimination procedures

The Administrator, after consultation, with appropriate Federal and State agencies and other interested persons, shall issue to the States and appropriate water pollution control agencies within 270 days after October 18, 1972 (and from time to time thereafter) information on the processes, procedures, or operating methods which result in the elimination or reduction of the discharge of pollutants to implement standards of performance under section 1316 of this title. Such information shall include technical and other data, including costs, as are available on alternative methods of elimination or reduction of the discharge of pollutants. Such information, and revisions thereof, shall be published in the Federal Register and otherwise shall be made available to the public.

(d) Secondary treatment information; alternative waste treatment management techniques; innovative and alternative wastewater treatment processes; facilities deemed equivalent of secondary treatment

(1) The Administrator, after consultation with appropriate Federal and State agencies and other interested persons, shall publish within sixty days after October 18, 1972 (and from time to time thereafter) information, in terms of amounts of constituents and chemical, physical, and biological characteristics of pollutants, on the degree of effluent reduction attainable through the application of secondary treatment.

(2) The Administrator, after consultation with appropriate Federal and State agencies and other interested persons, shall publish within nine months after October 18, 1972 (and from time to time thereafter) information on alternative waste treatment management techniques and systems available to implement section 1281 of this title.

(3) The Administrator, after consultation with appropriate Federal and State agencies and other interested persons, shall promulgate within one hundred and eighty days after December 27, 1977, guidelines for identifying and evaluating innovative and alternative wastewater treatment processes and techniques referred to in section 1281(g)(5) of this title.

(4) For the purposes of this subsection, such biological treatment facilities as oxidation ponds, lagoons, and ditches and trickling filters shall be deemed the equivalent of secondary treatment. The Administrator shall provide guidance under paragraph (1) of this subsection on design criteria for such facilities, taking into account pollutant removal efficiencies and, consistent with the objectives of this chapter, assuring that water quality will not be adversely affected by deeming such facilities as the equivalent of secondary treatment.

(e) Best management practices for industry

The Administrator, after consultation with appropriate Federal and State agencies and other interested persons, may publish regulations, supplemental to any effluent limitations specified under subsections (b) and (c) of this section for a class or category of point sources, for any specific pollutant which the Administrator is charged with a duty to regulate as a toxic or hazardous pollutant under section 1317(a)(1) or 1321 of this title, to control plant site runoff, spillage or leaks, sludge or waste disposal, and drainage from raw material storage which the Administrator determines are associated with or ancillary to the industrial manufacturing or treatment process within such class or category of point sources and may contribute significant amounts of such pollutants to navigable waters. Any applicable controls established under this subsection shall be included as a requirement for the purposes of section 1311, 1312, 1316, 1317, or 1343 of this title, as the case may be, in any permit issued to a point source pursuant to section 1342 of this title.

(f) Identification and evaluation of nonpoint sources of pollution; processes, procedures, and methods to control pollution

The Administrator, after consultation with appropriate Federal and State agencies and other interested persons, shall issue to appropriate Federal agencies, the States, water pollution control agencies, and agencies designated under section 1288 of this title, within one year after October 18, 1972 (and from time to time thereafter) information including (1) guidelines for identifying and evaluating the nature and extent of nonpoint sources of pollutants, and (2) processes, procedures, and methods to control pollution resulting from—

(A) agricultural and silvicultural activities, including runoff from fields and crop and forest lands;

(B) mining activities, including runoff and siltation from new, currently operating, and abandoned surface and underground mines;

(C) all construction activity, including runoff from the facilities resulting from such construction;

(D) the disposal of pollutants in wells or in subsurface excavations;

(E) salt water intrusion resulting from reductions of fresh water flow from any cause, including extraction of ground water, irrigation, obstruction, and diversion; and

(F) changes in the movement, flow, or circulation of any navigable waters or ground waters, including changes caused by the construction of dams, levees, channels, causeways, or flow diversion facilities.

Such information and revisions thereof shall be published in the Federal Register and otherwise made available to the public.

(g) Guidelines for pretreatment of pollutants

(1) For the purpose of assisting States in carrying out programs under section 1342 of this title, the Administrator shall publish, within one hundred and twenty days after October 18, 1972, and review at least annually thereafter and, if appropriate, revise guidelines for pretreatment of pollutants which he determines are not susceptible to treatment by publicly owned treatment works. Guidelines under this subsection shall be established to control and prevent the discharge into the navigable waters, the contiguous zone, or the ocean (either directly or through publicly owned treatment works) of any pollutant which interferes with, passes through, or otherwise is incompatible with such works.

(2) When publishing guidelines under this subsection, the Administrator shall designate the category or categories of treatment works to which the guidelines shall apply.

(h) Test procedures guidelines

The Administrator shall, within one hundred and eighty days from October 18, 1972, promulgate guidelines establishing test procedures for the analysis of pollutants that shall include the factors which must be provided in any certification pursuant to section 1341 of this title or permit application pursuant to section 1342 of this title.

(i) Guidelines for monitoring, reporting, enforcement, funding, personnel, and manpower

The Administrator shall (1) within sixty days after October 18, 1972, promulgate guidelines for the purpose of establishing uniform application forms and other minimum requirements for the acquisition of information from owners and operators of point-sources of discharge subject to any State program under section 1342 of this title, and (2) within sixty days from October 18, 1972, promulgate guidelines establishing the minimum procedural and other elements of any State program under section 1342 of this title, which shall include:

(A) monitoring requirements;

(B) reporting requirements (including procedures to make information available to the public);

(C) enforcement provisions; and

(D) funding, personnel qualifications, and manpower requirements (including a requirement that no board or body which approves permit applications or portions thereof shall include, as a member, any person who receives, or has during the previous two years received, a significant portion of his income directly or indirectly from permit holders or applicants for a permit).

(j) Restoration and enhancement of publicly owned freshwater lakes

The Administrator shall issue information biennially on methods, procedures, and processes as may be appropriate to restore and enhance the quality of the Nation's publicly owned freshwater lakes.

(k) Agreements with Secretaries of Agriculture, Army, and Interior to provide maximum utilization of programs to achieve and maintain water quality; transfer of funds; authorization of appropriations

(1) The Administrator shall enter into agreements with the Secretary of Agriculture, the Secretary of the Army, and the Secretary of the Interior, and the heads of such other departments, agencies, and instrumentalities of the United States as the Administrator determines, to provide for the maximum utilization of other Federal laws and programs for the purpose of achieving and maintaining water quality through appropriate implementation of plans approved under section 1288 of this title.

(2) The Administrator is authorized to transfer to the Secretary of Agriculture, the Secretary of the Army, and the Secretary of the Interior and the heads of such other departments, agencies, and instrumentalities of the United States as the Administrator determines, any funds appropriated under paragraph (3) of this subsection to supplement funds otherwise appropriated to programs authorized pursuant to any agreement under paragraph (1).

(3) There is authorized to be appropriated to carry out the provisions of this subsection, $100,000,000 per fiscal year for the fiscal years 1979 through 1983.

(June 30, 1948, ch. 758, title III, § 304, as added Oct. 18, 1972, Pub.L. 92–500, § 2, 86 Stat. 850, and amended Dec. 27, 1977, Pub.L. 95–217, §§ 48–51, 62(b), 91 Stat. 1587, 1588, 1598; Dec. 29, 1981, Pub.L. 97–117, § 23, 95 Stat. 1632.)

Cross References

Authorization of appropriations to carry out this chapter other than this section, see section 1376 of this title.
Definition of "construction" as including field testing of innovative techniques meeting guidelines promulgated under this section, see section 1292 of this title.
Dissemination of information gained under this section, see section 1255 of this title.
Establishment of total maximum daily load for pollutants identified under this section, see section 1313 of this title.
Grants for treatment works utilizing guidelines under this section, see section 1281 of this title.
Higher priority for grants for cost of preparing construction drawings for treatment works utilizing processes meeting guidelines promulgated under this section, see section 1284 of this title.
Permits for discharge of pollutants, see section 1342 of this title.
Program of cooperation for utilizing wastewater control systems utilizing innovative treatment processes for which guidelines have been promulgated under this section, see section 1323 of this title.
Regulations for carrying out agricultural cost sharing, subject to this section, see section 1288 of this title.
Standards for commercial vessels on the Great Lakes requiring at minimum the equivalent of secondary treatment as defined under this section, see section 1322 of this title.
State reports on water quality, see section 1315 of this title.
Subpoena for obtaining information under this section, see section 1369 of this title.
Timetable for achievement of effluent limitations, see section 1311 of this title.
Toxic and pretreatment effluent standards, see section 1317 of this title.
Waiver of requirements for transmittal of State permit applications to Administrator, see section 1344 of this title.

Code of Federal Regulations

Criteria and standards for the National Pollutant Discharge Elimination System, see 40 CFR 125.1 et seq.
Effluent guidelines and standards, see 40 CFR Chap. I, Subchap. N.
Guidelines establishing test procedures for analysis of pollutants, see 40 CFR 136.1 et seq.
Secondary treatment regulation, see 40 CFR 133.100 et seq.

Library References

Health and Environment ⚷25.7(10).
C.J.S. Health and Environment § 106 et seq.

United States Supreme Court

Guidelines under this section, use in regulations establishing existing point source effluent limitations, see E.I. du Pont de Nemours & Co. v. Train, 1977, 97 S.Ct. 965, 430 U.S. 112, 51 L.Ed.2d 204.

§ 1315. State reports on water quality; transmittal to Congress

(a) Omitted.

(b)(1) Each State shall prepare and submit to the Administrator by April 1, 1975, and shall bring up to date by April 1, 1976, and biennially thereafter, a report which shall include—

(A) a description of the water quality of all navigable waters in such State during the preceding year, with appropriate supplemental descriptions as shall be required to take into account seasonal, tidal, and other variations, correlated with the quality of water required by the objective of this chapter (as identified by the Administrator pursuant to criteria published under section 1314(a) of this title) and the water quality described in subparagraph (B) of this paragraph;

(B) an analysis of the extent to which all navigable waters of such State provide for the protection and propagation of a balanced population of shellfish, fish, and wildlife, and allow recreational activities in and on the water;

(C) an analysis of the extent to which the elimination of the discharge of pollutants and a level of water quality which provides for the protection and propagation of a balanced population of shellfish, fish, and wildlife and allows recreational activities in and on the water, have been or will be achieved by the requirements of this chapter, together with recommendations as to additional action necessary to achieve such objectives and for what waters such additional action is necessary;

(D) an estimate of (i) the environmental impact, (ii) the economic and social costs necessary to achieve the objective of this chapter in such State, (iii) the economic and social benefits of such achievement, and (iv) an estimate of the date of such achievement; and

(E) a description of the nature and extent of nonpoint sources of pollutants, and recommendations as to the programs which must be undertaken to control each category of such sources, including an estimate of the costs of implementing such programs.

(2) The Administrator shall transmit such State reports, together with an analysis thereof, to Congress on or before October 1, 1975, and October 1, 1976, and biennially thereafter.

(June 30, 1948, ch. 758, title III, § 305, as added Oct. 18, 1972, Pub.L. 92–500, § 2, 86 Stat. 853, and amended Dec. 27, 1977, Pub.L. 95–217, § 52, 91 Stat. 1589.)

Cross References

Grants prohibited to States not complying with requirements of this section, see section 1256 of this title.

Records required to be kept for carrying out the requirements of this section, see section 1318 of this title.

Subpoenas for obtaining information under this section, see section 1369 of this title.

Code of Federal Regulations

Water quality planning and management, see 40 CFR 130.0 et seq.

§ 1316. National standards of performance

(a) Definitions

For purposes of this section:

(1) The term "standard of performance" means a standard for the control of the discharge of pollutants which reflect the greatest degree of effluent reduction which the Administrator determines to be achievable through application of the best available demonstrated control technology, processes, operating methods, or other alternatives, including, where practicable, a standard permitting no discharge of pollutants.

(2) The term "new source" means any source, the construction of which is commenced after the publication of proposed regulations prescribing a standard of performance under this section which will be applicable to such source, if such standard is thereafter promulgated in accordance with this section.

(3) The term "source" means any building, structure, facility, or installation from which there is or may be the discharge of pollutants.

(4) The term "owner or operator" means any person who owns, leases, operates, controls, or supervises a source.

(5) The term "construction" means any placement, assembly, or installation of facilities or equipment (including contractual obligations to purchase such facilities or equipment) at the premises where such equipment will be used, including preparation work at such premises.

(b) Categories of sources; Federal standards of performance for new sources

(1)(A) The Administrator shall, within ninety days after October 18, 1972, publish (and from time to time thereafter shall revise) a list of categories of sources, which shall, at the minimum, include:

pulp and paper mills;
paperboard, builders paper and board mills;
meat product and rendering processing;
dairy product processing;
grain mills;
canned and preserved fruits and vegetables processing;
canned and preserved seafood processing;
sugar processing;
textile mills;
cement manufacturing;
feedlots;
electroplating;
organic chemicals manufacturing;
inorganic chemicals manufacturing;
plastic and synthetic materials manufacturing;
soap and detergent manufacturing;
fertilizer manufacturing;
petroleum refining;
iron and steel manufacturing;
nonferrous metals manufacturing;
phosphate manufacturing;
steam electric powerplants;
ferroalloy manufacturing;
leather tanning and finishing;
glass and asbestos manufacturing;
rubber processing; and
timber products processing.

(B) As soon as practicable, but in no case more than one year, after a category of sources is included in a list under subparagraph (A) of this paragraph, the Administrator shall propose and publish regulations establishing Federal standards of performance for new sources within such category. The Administrator shall afford interested persons an opportunity for written comment on such proposed regulations. After considering such comments, he shall promulgate, within one hundred and twenty days after publication of such proposed regulations, such standards with such adjustments as he deems appropriate. The Administrator shall, from time to time, as technology and alternatives change, revise such standards following the procedure required by this subsection for promulgation of such standards. Standards of performance, or revisions thereof, shall become effective upon promulgation. In establishing or revising Federal standards of performance for new sources under this section, the Administrator shall take into consideration the cost of achieving such effluent reduction, and any non-water quality, environmental impact and energy requirements.

(2) The Administrator may distinguish among classes, types, and sizes within categories of new sources for the purpose of establishing such standards and shall consider the type of process employed (including whether batch or continuous).

(3) The provisions of this section shall apply to any new source owned or operated by the United States.

(c) State enforcement of standards of performance

Each State may develop and submit to the Administrator a procedure under State law for applying and enforcing standards of performance for new sources located in such State. If the Administrator finds that the procedure and the law of any State require the application and enforcement of standards of performance to at least the same extent as required by this section, such State is authorized to apply and enforce such standards of performance (except with respect to new sources owned or operated by the United States).

(d) Protection from more stringent standards

Notwithstanding any other provision of this chapter, any point source the construction of which is commenced after October 18, 1972, and which is so constructed as to meet all applicable standards of performance shall not be subject to any more stringent standard of performance during a ten-year period beginning on the date of completion of such construction or during the period of depreciation or amortization of such facility for the purposes of section 167 or 169 (or both) of title 26 whichever period ends first.

(e) Illegality of operation of new sources in violation of applicable standards of performance

After the effective date of standards of performance promulgated under this section, it shall be unlawful for any owner or operator of any new source to operate such source in violation of any standard of performance applicable to such source.

(June 30, 1948, ch. 758, title III, § 306, as added Oct. 18, 1972, Pub.L. 92–500, § 2, 86 Stat. 854.)

Cross References

Applicant for Federal license or permit, certification of compliance with provisions of this section, see section 1341 of this title.
Approval of continuing planning processes resulting in plans including effluent limitations and schedules of compliance as stringent as those required by this section, see section 1313 of this title.
Employee protection, employees in deliberate violation of this section, see section 1367 of this title.
Enforcement of conditions of this section, see section 1319 of this title.
Federal facilities, exemptions from requirements of this chapter other than this section, see section 1323 of this title.
Illegality of pollutant discharges except in compliance with this section, see section 1311 of this title.
Information on the processes and procedures resulting in reduction or elimination of pollutants to implement standards of performance under this section, see section 1314 of this title.
Judicial review of administrator's action in promulgating standards under this section, see section 1369 of this title.
Notice of citizen actions, see section 1365 of this title.
Notice of intent to propose standard of performance for new source required by this section, see section 1374 of this title.
Permit for discharge of any pollutant by new source as defined under this section deemed major Federal action, see section 1371 of this title.
Permits for discharge of pollutants meeting requirements of this section, see section 1342 of this title.
State permit program, see section 1342 of this title.
Thermal discharges, protection and propagation of fish and wildlife, see section 1326 of this title.

Code of Federal Regulations

Effluent guidelines and standards, see 40 CFR Chap. I, Subchap. N.

Library References

Health and Environment ⇔25.7(10).
C.J.S. Health and Environment § 106 et seq.

§ 1317. Toxic and pretreatment effluent standards

(a) Toxic pollutant list; revision; hearing; promulgation of standards; effective date; consultation

(1) On and after December 27, 1977, the list of toxic pollutants or combination of pollutants subject to this chapter shall consist of those toxic pollutants listed in table 1 of Committee Print Numbered 95–30 of the Committee on Public Works and Transportation of the House of Representatives, and the Administrator shall publish, not later than the thirtieth day after December 27, 1977, that list. From time to time thereafter, the Administrator may revise such list and the Administrator is authorized to add to or remove from such list any pollutant. The Administrator in publishing any revised list, including the addition or removal of any pollutant from such list, shall take into account toxicity of the pollutant, its persistence, degradability, the usual or potential presence of the affected organisms in any waters, the importance of the affected organisms, and the nature and extent of the effect of the toxic pollutant on such organisms. A determination of the Administrator under this paragraph shall be final except that if, on judicial review, such determination was based on arbitrary and capricious action of the Administrator, the Administrator shall make a redetermination.

(2) Each toxic pollutant listed in accordance with paragraph (1) of this subsection shall be subject to effluent limitations resulting from the application of

the best available technology economically achievable for the applicable category or class of point sources established in accordance with sections 1311(b)(2)(A) and 1314(b)(2) of this title. The Administrator, in his discretion, may publish in the Federal Register a proposed effluent standard (which may include a prohibition) establishing requirements for a toxic pollutant which, if an effluent limitation is applicable to a class or category of point sources, shall be applicable to such category or class only if such standard imposes more stringent requirements. Such published effluent standard (or prohibition) shall take into account the toxicity of the pollutant, its persistence, degradability, the usual or potential presence of the affected organisms in any waters, the importance of the affected organisms and the nature and extent of the effect of the toxic pollutant on such organisms, and the extent to which effective control is being or may be achieved under other regulatory authority. The Administrator shall allow a period of not less than sixty days following publication of any such proposed effluent standard (or prohibition) for written comment by interested persons on such proposed standard. In addition, if within thirty days of publication of any such proposed effluent standard (or prohibition) any interested person so requests, the Administrator shall hold a public hearing in connection therewith. Such a public hearing shall provide an opportunity for oral and written presentations, such cross-examination as the Administrator determines is appropriate on disputed issues of material fact, and the transcription of a verbatim record which shall be available to the public. After consideration of such comments and any information and material presented at any public hearing held on such proposed standard or prohibition, the Administrator shall promulgate such standard (or prohibition) with such modification as the Administrator finds are justified. Such promulgation by the Administrator shall be made within two hundred and seventy days after publication of proposed standard (or prohibition). Such standard (or prohibition) shall be final except that if, on judicial review, such standard was not based on substantial evidence, the Administrator shall promulgate a revised standard. Effluent limitations shall be established in accordance with sections 1311(b)(2)(A) and 1314(b)(2) of this title for every toxic pollutant referred to in table 1 of Committee Print Numbered 95–30 of the Committee on Public Works and Transportation of the House of Representatives as soon as practicable after December 27, 1977, but no later than July 1, 1980. Such effluent limitations or effluent standards (or prohibitions) shall be established for every other toxic pollutant listed under paragraph (1) of this subsection as soon as practicable after it is so listed.

(3) Each such effluent standard (or prohibition) shall be reviewed and, if appropriate, revised at least every three years.

(4) Any effluent standard promulgated under this section shall be at that level which the Administrator determines provides an ample margin of safety.

(5) When proposing or promulgating any effluent standard (or prohibition) under this section, the Administrator shall designate the category or categories of sources to which the effluent standard (or prohibition) shall apply. Any disposal of dredged material may be included in such a category of sources after consultation with the Secretary of the Army.

(6) Any effluent standard (or prohibition) established pursuant to this section shall take effect on such date or dates as specified in the order promulgating such standard, but in no case, more than one year from the date of such promulgation. If the Administrator determines that compliance within one year from the date of promulgation is technologically infeasible for a category of sources, the Administrator may establish the effective date of the effluent standard (or prohibition) for such category at the earliest date upon which compliance can be feasibly attained by sources within such category, but in no event more than three years after the date of such promulgation.

(7) Prior to publishing any regulations pursuant to this section the Administrator shall, to the maximum extent practicable within the time provided, consult with appropriate advisory committees, States, independent experts, and Federal departments and agencies.

(b) Pretreatment standards; hearing; promulgation; compliance period; revision; application to State and local laws

(1) The Administrator shall, within one hundred and eighty days after October 18, 1972, and from time to time thereafter, publish proposed regulations establishing pretreatment standards for introduction of pollutants into treatment works (as defined in section 1292 of this title) which are publicly owned for those pollutants which are determined not to be susceptible to treatment by such treatment works or which would interfere with the operation of such treatment works. Not later than ninety days after such publication, and after opportunity for public hearing, the Administrator shall promulgate such pretreatment standards. Pretreatment standards under this subsection shall specify a time for compliance not to exceed three years from the date of promulgation and shall be established to prevent the discharge of any pollutant through treatment works (as defined in section 1292 of this title) which are publicly owned, which pollutant in-

terferes with, passes through, or otherwise is incompatible with such works. If, in the case of any toxic pollutant under subsection (a) of this section introduced by a source into a publicly owned treatment works, the treatment by such works removes all or any part of such toxic pollutant and the discharge from such works does not violate that effluent limitation or standard which would be applicable to such toxic pollutant if it were discharged by such source other than through a publicly owned treatment works, and does not prevent sludge use or disposal by such works in accordance with section 1345 of this title, then the pretreatment requirements for the sources actually discharging such toxic pollutant into such publicly owned treatment works may be revised by the owner or operator of such works to reflect the removal of such toxic pollutant by such works.

(2) The Administrator shall, from time to time, as control technology, processes, operating methods, or other alternatives change, revise such standards following the procedure established by this subsection for promulgation of such standards.

(3) When proposing or promulgating any pretreatment standard under this section, the Administrator shall designate the category or categories of sources to which such standard shall apply.

(4) Nothing in this subsection shall affect any pretreatment requirement established by any State or local law not in conflict with any pretreatment standard established under this subsection.

(c) New sources of pollutants into publicly owned treatment works

In order to insure that any source introducing pollutants into a publicly owned treatment works, which source would be a new source subject to section 1316 of this title if it were to discharge pollutants, will not cause a violation of the effluent limitations established for any such treatment works, the Administrator shall promulgate pretreatment standards for the category of such sources simultaneously with the promulgation of standards of performance under section 1316 of this title for the equivalent category of new sources. Such pretreatment standards shall prevent the discharge of any pollutant into such treatment works, which pollutant may interfere with, pass through, or otherwise be incompatible with such works.

(d) Operation in violation of standards unlawful

After the effective date of any effluent standard or prohibition or pretreatment standard promulgated under this section, it shall be unlawful for any owner or operator of any source to operate any source in violation of any such effluent standard or prohibition or pretreatment standard.

(June 30, 1948, ch. 758, title III, § 307, as added Oct. 18, 1972, Pub.L. 92–500, § 2, 86 Stat. 856, and amended Dec. 27, 1977, Pub.L. 95–217, §§ 53(a), (b), 54(a), 91 Stat. 1589–1591.)

Cross References

Application for Federal license or permit, certificate of compliance with this section, see section 1341 of this title.
Approval of continuing planning process which includes effluent limitations as stringent as those in this section, see section 1313 of this title.
Areawide waste treatment management, see section 1288 of this title.
Best management practices for industry, see section 1314 of this title.
Definition of "hazardous substance" for purposes of liability and compensation for hazardous substances releases, see section 9601 of Title 42, The Public Health and Welfare.
Employee protection, deliberate violations by employee, see section 1367 of this title.
Enforcement of provisions of this chapter, see section 1319 of this title.
Federal facilities pollution control, exemption from provisions of this chapter other than this section, see section 1323 of this title.
Illegality of pollutant discharges except when in compliance with this section, see section 1311 of this title.
Judicial review of Administrator's actions, see section 1369 of this title.
Non-prohibited discharge of dredged or fill material, see section 1344 of this title.
Notice of action brought with respect to violation of this section, see section 1365 of this title.
Notice of action on proposed toxic effluent standard required by this section, see section 1374 of this title.
Permits for discharge of pollutants, see section 1342 of this title.
State permit programs, see section 1342 of this title.

Code of Federal Regulations

Effluent guidelines and standards, see 40 CFR Chap. I, Subchap. N.
Guidelines establishing test procedures for analysis of pollutants, see 40 CFR 136.1 et seq.
Public hearings on effluent standards for toxic pollutants, see 40 CFR 104.1 et seq.
Toxic pollutant effluent standards, see 40 CFR 129.1 et seq.

Library References

Health and Environment ⚷25.7(12).
C.J.S. Health and Environment § 107 et seq.

§ 1318. Records and reports; inspections

(a) Maintenance; monitoring equipment; entry; access to information

Whenever required to carry out the objective of this chapter, including but not limited to (1) developing or assisting in the development of any effluent limitation, or other limitation, prohibition, or effluent standard, pretreatment standard, or standard of performance under this chapter; (2) determining whether any person is in violation of any such effluent limitation, or other limitation, prohibition or effluent standard, pretreatment standard, or standard of performance; (3) any requirement established under this section; or (4) carrying out sections 1315, 1321, 1342, 1344 (relating to State permit programs), and 1364 of this title—

(A) the Administrator shall require the owner or operator of any point source to (i) establish and maintain such records, (ii) make such reports, (iii) install, use, and maintain such monitoring equipment or methods (including where appropriate, biological monitoring methods), (iv) sample such effluents (in accordance with such methods, at such locations, at such intervals, and in such manner as the Administrator shall prescribe), and (v) provide such other information as he may reasonably require; and

(B) the Administrator or his authorized representative, upon presentation of his credentials—

(i) shall have a right of entry to, upon, or through any premises in which an effluent source is located or in which any records required to be maintained under clause (A) of this subsection are located, and

(ii) may at reasonable times have access to and copy any records, inspect any monitoring equipment or method required under clause (A), and sample any effluents which the owner or operator of such source is required to sample under such clause.

(b) Availability to public; trade secrets exception

Any records, reports, or information obtained under this section (1) shall, in the case of effluent data, be related to any applicable effluent limitations, toxic, pretreatment, or new source performance standards, and (2) shall be available to the public, except that upon a showing satisfactory to the Administrator by any person that records, reports, or information, or particular part thereof (other than effluent data), to which the Administrator has access under this section, if made public would divulge methods or processes entitled to protection as trade secrets of such person, the Administrator shall consider such record, report, or information, or particular portion thereof confidential in accordance with the purposes of section 1905 of title 18, except that such record, report, or information may be disclosed to other officers, employees, or authorized representatives of the United States concerned with carrying out this chapter or when relevant in any proceeding under this chapter.

(c) Application of State law

Each State may develop and submit to the Administrator procedures under State law for inspection, monitoring, and entry with respect to point sources located in such State. If the Administrator finds that the procedures and the law of any State relating to inspection, monitoring, and entry are applicable to at least the same extent as those required by this section, such State is authorized to apply and enforce its procedures for inspection, monitoring, and entry with respect to point sources located in such State (except with respect to point sources owned or operated by the United States).

(June 30, 1948, ch. 758, title III, § 308, as added Oct. 18, 1972, Pub.L. 92–500, § 2, 86 Stat. 858, and amended Dec. 27, 1977, Pub.L. 95–217, § 67(c)(1), 91 Stat. 1606.)

Cross References

Enforcement action for violation of any condition which implements this section, see section 1319 of this title.

Guidelines for use of imminent hazard, enforcement, and emergency response authorities, see section 9606 of Title 42, The Public Health and Welfare.

Non-prohibited discharge of dredged or fill material, see section 1344 of this title.

Permits for discharge of pollutants, see section 1342 of this title.

Code of Federal Regulations

Electrical and electronic components point source category, see 40 CFR 469.10 et seq.

General pretreatment regulations for existing and new sources of pollution, see 40 CFR 403.1 et seq.

Iron and steel manufacturing point source category, see 40 CFR 420.01 et seq.

Metal finishing point source category, see 40 CFR 433.10 et seq.

Plastics molding and forming point source category, see 40 CFR 463.1 et seq.

Public information, see 40 CFR 2.100 et seq.

Secondary treatment regulation, see 40 CFR 133.100 et seq.

Toxic pollutant effluent standards, see 40 CFR 129.1 et seq.

Library References

Health and Environment ⟹25.7(18).

C.J.S. Health and Environment § 113 et seq.

§ 1319. Enforcement

(a) State enforcement; compliance orders

(1) Whenever, on the basis of any information available to him, the Administrator finds that any person is in violation of any condition or limitation which implements section 1311, 1312, 1316, 1317, 1318, 1328, or 1345 of this title in a permit issued by a State under an approved permit program under section 1342 or 1344 of this title he shall proceed under his authority in paragraph (3) of this subsection or he shall notify the person in alleged violation and such State of such finding. If beyond the thirtieth day after the Administrator's notification the State has not commenced appropriate enforcement action, the Administrator shall issue an order requiring such person to comply with such condition or limitation or shall bring a civil action in accordance with subsection (b) of this section.

(2) Whenever, on the basis of information available to him, the Administrator finds that violations of permit conditions or limitations as set forth in paragraph (1) of this subsection are so widespread that such violations appear to result from a failure of the State to enforce such permit conditions or limitations effectively, he shall so notify the State. If the Administrator finds such failure extends beyond the thirtieth day after such notice, he shall give public notice of such finding. During the period beginning with such public notice and ending when such State satisfies the Administrator that it will enforce such conditions and limitations (hereafter referred to in this section as the period of "federally assumed enforcement"), except where an extension has been granted under paragraph (5)(B) of this subsection, the Administrator shall enforce any permit condition or limitation with respect to any person—

(A) by issuing an order to comply with such condition or limitation, or

(B) by bringing a civil action under subsection (b) of this section.

(3) Whenever on the basis of any information available to him the Administrator finds that any person is in violation of section 1311, 1312, 1316, 1317, 1318, 1328, or 1345 of this title, or is in violation of any permit condition or limitation implementing any of such sections in a permit issued under section 1342 of this title by him or by a State or in a permit issued under section 1344 of this title by a State, he shall issue an order requiring such person to comply with such section or requirement, or he shall bring a civil action in accordance with subsection (b) of this section.

(4) A copy of any order issued under this subsection shall be sent immediately by the Administrator to the State in which the violation occurs and other affected States. In any case in which an order under this subsection (or notice to a violator under paragraph (1) of this subsection) is issued to a corporation, a copy of such order (or notice) shall be served on any appropriate corporate officers. An order issued under this subsection relating to a violation of section 1318 of this title shall not take effect until the person to whom it is issued has had an opportunity to confer with the Administrator concerning the alleged violation.

(5)(A) Any order issued under this subsection shall be by personal service, shall state with reasonable specificity the nature of the violation, and shall specify a time for compliance not to exceed thirty days in the case of a violation of an interim compliance schedule or operation and maintenance requirement and not to exceed a time the Administrator determines to be reasonable in the case of a violation of a final deadline, taking into account the seriousness of the violation and any good faith efforts to comply with applicable requirements.

(B) The Administrator may, if he determines (i) that any person who is a violator of, or any person who is otherwise not in compliance with, the time requirements under this chapter or in any permit issued under this chapter, has acted in good faith, and has made a commitment (in the form of contracts or other securities) of necessary resources to achieve compliance by the earliest possible date after July 1, 1977, but not later than April 1, 1979; (ii) that any extension under this provision will not result in the imposition of any additional controls on any other point or nonpoint source; (iii) that an application for a permit under section 1342 of this title was filed for such person prior to December 31, 1974; and (iv) that the facilities necessary for compliance with such requirements are under construction, grant an extension of the date referred to in section 1311(b)(1)(A) of this title to a date which will achieve compliance at the earliest time possible but not later than April 1, 1979.

(6) Whenever, on the basis of information available to him, the Administrator finds (A) that any person is in violation of section 1311(b)(1)(A) or (C) of this title, (B) that such person cannot meet the requirements for a time extension under section 1311(i)(2) of this title, and (C) that the most expeditious and appropriate means of compliance with this chapter by such person is to discharge into a publicly owned treatment works, then, upon request of such person, the Administrator may issue an order requiring such person to comply with this chapter at the earliest date practicable, but not later than July 1, 1983, by discharging into a publicly owned treatment works if such works concur with such order. Such order shall include a schedule of compliance.

(b) Civil actions

The Administrator is authorized to commence a civil action for appropriate relief, including a permanent or temporary injunction, for any violation for which he is authorized to issue a compliance order under subsection (a) of this section. Any action under this subsection may be brought in the district court of the United States for the district in which the defendant is located or resides or is doing business, and such court shall have jurisdiction to restrain such violation and to require compliance. Notice of the commencement of such action shall be given immediately to the appropriate State.

(c) Criminal penalties

(1) Any person who willfully or negligently violates section 1311, 1312, 1316, 1317, or 1318 of this title, or any permit condition or limitation implementing any of such sections in a permit issued under section 1342 of this title by the Administrator or by a State or in a permit issued under section 1344 of this title by a State, shall be punished by a fine of not less than $2,500 nor more than $25,000 per day of violation, or by imprisonment for not more than one year, or by both. If the conviction is for a violation committed after a first conviction of such person under this paragraph, punishment shall be by a fine of not more than $50,000 per day of violation, or by imprisonment for not more than two years, or by both.

(2) Any person who knowingly makes any false statement, representation, or certification in any application, record, report, plan, or other document filed or required to be maintained under this chapter or who falsifies, tampers with, or knowingly renders inaccurate any monitoring device or method required to be maintained under this chapter, shall upon conviction, be punished by a fine of not more than $10,000, or by imprisonment for not more than six months, or by both.

(3) For the purposes of this subsection, the term "person" shall mean, in addition to the definition contained in section 1362(5) of this title, any responsible corporate officer.

(d) Civil penalties

Any person who violates section 1311, 1312, 1316, 1317, 1318, 1328, or 1345 of this title, or any permit condition or limitation implementing any of such sections in a permit issued under section 1342 of this title by the Administrator, or by a State, or in a permit issued under section 1344 of this title by a State, and any person who violates any order issued by the Administrator under subsection (a) of this section, shall be subject to a civil penalty not to exceed $10,000 per day of such violation.

(e) State liability for judgments and expenses

Whenever a municipality is a party to a civil action brought by the United States under this section, the State in which such municipality is located shall be joined as a party. Such State shall be liable for payment of any judgment, or any expenses incurred as a result of complying with any judgment, entered against the municipality in such action to the extent that the laws of that State prevent the municipality from raising revenues needed to comply with such judgment.

(f) Wrongful introduction of pollutants into treatments works

Whenever, on the basis of any information available to him, the Administrator finds that an owner or operator of any source is introducing a pollutant into a treatment works in violation of subsection (d) of section 1317 of this title, the Administrator may notify the owner or operator of such treatment works and the State of such violation. If the owner or operator of the treatment works does not commence appropriate enforcement action within 30 days of the date of such notification, the Administrator may commence a civil action for appropriate relief, including but not limited to, a permanent or temporary injunction, against the owner or operator of such treatment works. In any such civil action the Administrator shall join the owner or operator of such source as a party to the action. Such action shall be brought in the district court of the United States in the district in which the treatment works is located. Such court shall have jurisdiction to restrain such violation and to require the owner or operator of the treatment works and the owner or operator of the source to take such action as may be necessary to come into compliance with this chapter. Notice of commencement of any such action shall be given to the State. Nothing in this subsection shall be construed to limit or prohibit any other authority the Administrator may have under this chapter.

(June 30, 1948, ch. 758, title III, § 309, as added Oct. 18, 1972, Pub.L. 92–500, § 2, 86 Stat. 859, and amended Dec. 27, 1977, Pub.L. 95–217, §§ 54(b), 55, 56, 67(c)(2), 91 Stat. 1591, 1592, 1606.)

Cross References

Condition of grant to State that no federally assumed enforcement as defined in this section is in effect, see section 1256 of this title.
Costs of response incurred by Federal Government in connection with discharge recoverable in action brought under this section, see section 9607 of Title 42, The Public Health and Welfare.
Guidelines for use of imminent hazard, enforcement, and emergency response authorities, see section 9606 of Title 42.
Jurisdiction of district courts to apply civil penalties under this section, see section 1365 of this title.
Liability of owner or operator for costs of removal incurred in connection with a discharge of oil or hazardous substance, see section 1321 of this title.
National pollutant discharge elimination system, authority of Administrator to take action under this section, see section 1342 of this title.
Permits for dredged or fill material, authority of Administrator to take action under this section, see section 1344 of this title.
Prohibition of Federal procurement contracts with persons convicted under this section, see section 1368 of this title.

Code of Federal Regulations

General pretreatment regulations for existing and new sources of pollution, see 40 CFR 403:1 et seq.

Library References

Health and Environment ⟹25.7(17).
C.J.S. Health and Environment § 113 et seq.

§ 1320. International pollution abatement

(a) Hearing; participation by foreign nations

Whenever the Administrator, upon receipts of reports, surveys, or studies from any duly constituted international agency, has reason to believe that pollution is occurring which endangers the health or welfare of persons in a foreign country, and the Secretary of State requests him to abate such pollution, he shall give formal notification thereof to the State water pollution control agency of the State or States in which such discharge or discharges originate and to the appropriate interstate agency, if any. He shall also promptly call such a hearing, if he believes that such pollution is occurring in sufficient quantity to warrant such action, and if such foreign country has given the United States essentially the same rights with respect to the prevention and control of pollution occurring in that country as is given that country by this subsection. The Administrator, through the Secretary of State, shall invite the foreign country which may be adversely affected by the pollution to attend and participate in the hearing, and the representative of such country shall, for the purpose of the hearing and any further proceeding resulting from such hearing, have all the rights of a State water pollution control agency. Nothing in this subsection shall be construed to modify, amend, repeal, or otherwise affect the provisions of the 1909 Boundary Waters Treaty between Canada and the United States or the Water Utilization Treaty of 1944 between Mexico and the United States (59 Stat. 1219), relative to the control and abatement of pollution in waters covered by those treaties.

(b) Functions and responsibilities of Administrator not affected

The calling of a hearing under this section shall not be construed by the courts, the Administrator, or any person as limiting, modifying, or otherwise affecting the functions and responsibilities of the Administrator under this section to establish and enforce water quality requirements under this chapter.

(c) Hearing board; composition; findings of fact; recommendations; implementation of board's decision

The Administrator shall publish in the Federal Register a notice of a public hearing before a hearing board of five or more persons appointed by the Administrator. A majority of the members of the board and the chairman who shall be designated by the Administrator shall not be officers or employees of Federal, State, or local governments. On the basis of the evidence presented at such hearing, the board shall within sixty days after completion of the hearing make findings of fact as to whether or not such pollution is occurring and shall thereupon by decision, incorporating its findings therein, make such recommendations to abate the pollution as may be appropriate and shall transmit such decision and the record of the hearings to the Administrator. All such decisions shall be public. Upon receipt of such decision, the Administrator shall promptly implement the board's decision in accordance with the provisions of this chapter.

(d) Report by alleged polluter

In connection with any hearing called under this subsection, the board is authorized to require any person whose alleged activities result in discharges causing or contributing to pollution to file with it in such forms as it may prescribe, a report based on existing data, furnishing such information as may reasonably be required as to the character, kind, and quantity of such discharges and the use of facilities or other means to prevent or reduce such discharges by the person filing such a report. Such report shall be made under oath or otherwise, as the board may prescribe, and shall be filed with the board within such reasonable period as it may prescribe, unless additional time is granted by it. Upon a showing satisfactory to the board by the person filing such report that such report or portion thereof (other than effluent data), to which the Administrator has access under this section, if made public would divulge trade secrets or secret processes of such person, the board shall consider such report or portion thereof confidential for the purposes of section 1905 of title 18. If any person required to file any report under this paragraph shall fail to do so within the time fixed by the board for filing the same, and such failure shall continue for thirty days after notice of such default, such person shall forfeit to the United States the sum of $1,000 for each and every day of the continuance of such failure, which forfeiture shall be payable into the Treasury of the United States, and shall be recoverable in a civil suit in the name of the United States in the district court of the United States where such person has his principal office or in any district in which he does business. The Administrator may upon application therefor remit or mitigate any forfeiture provided for under this subsection.

(e) Compensation of board members

Board members, other than officers or employees of Federal, State, or local governments, shall be for each day (including travel-time) during which they are performing board business, entitled to receive compensation at a rate fixed by the Administrator but not in excess of the maximum rate of pay for grade GS–18, as provided in the General Schedule under section 5332 of title 5, and shall, notwithstanding the limitations of sections 5703 and 5704 of title 5, be fully reimbursed for travel, subsistence and related expenses.

(f) Enforcement proceedings

When any such recommendation adopted by the Administrator involves the institution of enforcement proceedings against any person to obtain the abatement of pollution subject to such recommendation, the Administrator shall institute such proceedings if he believes that the evidence warrants such proceedings. The district court of the United States shall consider and determine de novo all relevant issues, but shall receive in evidence the record of the proceedings before the conference or hearing board. The court shall have jurisdiction to enter such judgment and orders enforcing such judgment as it deems appropriate or to remand such proceedings to the Administrator for such further action as it may direct.

(June 30, 1948, ch. 758, title III, § 310, as added Oct. 18, 1972, Pub.L. 92–500, § 2, 86 Stat. 860.)

Library References

International Law ⚷10.
C.J.S. International Law § 12.

§ 1321. Oil and hazardous substance liability

(a) Definitions

For the purpose of this section, the term—

(1) "oil" means oil of any kind or in any form, including, but not limited to, petroleum, fuel oil, sludge, oil refuse, and oil mixed with wastes other than dredged spoil;

(2) "discharge" includes, but is not limited to, any spilling, leaking, pumping, pouring, emitting, emptying or dumping, but excludes (A) discharges in compliance with a permit under section 1342 of this title, (B) discharges resulting from circumstances identified and reviewed and made a part of the public record with respect to a permit issued or modified under section 1342 of this title, and subject to a condition in such permit, and (C) continuous or anticipated intermittent discharges from a point source, identified in a permit or permit application under section 1342 of this title, which are caused by events occurring within the scope of relevant operating or treatment systems;

(3) "vessel" means every description of watercraft or other artificial contrivance used, or capable of being used, as a means of transportation on water other than a public vessel;

(4) "public vessel" means a vessel owned or bareboat-chartered and operated by the United States, or by a State or political subdivision thereof, or by a foreign nation, except when such vessel is engaged in commerce;

(5) "United States" means the States, the District of Columbia, the Commonwealth of Puerto Rico, the Canal Zone, Guam, American Samoa, the Virgin Islands, and the Trust Territory of the Pacific Islands;

(6) "owner or operator" means (A) in the case of a vessel, any person owning, operating, or chartering by demise, such vessel, and (B) in the case of an onshore facility, and an offshore facility, any person owning or operating such onshore facility or offshore facility, and (C) in the case of any abandoned offshore facility, the person who owned or operated such facility immediately prior to such abandonment;

(7) "person" includes an individual, firm, corporation, association, and a partnership.

(8) "remove" or "removal" refers to removal of the oil or hazardous substances from the water and shorelines or the taking of such other actions as may be necessary to minimize or mitigate damage to the public health or welfare, including, but not limited to, fish, shellfish, wildlife, and public and private property, shorelines, and beaches;

(9) "contiguous zone" means the entire zone established or to be established by the United States under article 24 of the Convention on the Territorial Sea and the Contiguous Zone;

(10) "onshore facility" means any facility (including, but not limited to, motor vehicles and rolling stock) of any kind located in, on, or under, any land within the United States other than submerged land;

(11) "offshore facility" means any facility of any kind located in, on, or under, any of the navigable waters of the United States, and any facility of any kind which is subject to the jurisdiction of the United States and is located in, on, or under any other waters, other than a vessel or a public vessel;

(12) "act of God" means an act occasioned by an unanticipated grave natural disaster;

(13) "barrel" means 42 United States gallons at 60 degrees Fahrenheit;

(14) "hazardous substance" means any substance designated pursuant to subsection (b)(2) of this section;

(15) "inland oil barge" means a non-self-propelled vessel carrying oil in bulk as cargo and certificated to operate only in the inland waters of the United States, while operating in such waters;

(16) "inland waters of the United States" means those waters of the United States lying inside the baseline from which the territorial sea is measured and those waters outside such baseline which are a part of the Gulf Intracoastal Waterway.[1]

(17) "Otherwise[2] subject to the jurisdiction of the United States" means subject to the jurisdiction of the United States by virtue of United

States citizenship, United States vessel documentation or numbering, or as provided for by international agreement to which the United States is a party.

(b) Congressional declaration of policy against discharges of oil or hazardous substances; designation of hazardous substances; study of higher standard of care incentives and report to Congress; liability; penalties; civil actions: penalty limitations, separate offenses, jurisdiction, mitigation of damages and costs, recovery of removal costs and alternative remedies

(1) The Congress hereby declares that it is the policy of the United States that there should be no discharges of oil or hazardous substances into or upon the navigable waters of the United States, adjoining shorelines, or into or upon the waters of the contiguous zone, or in connection with activities under the Outer Continental Shelf Lands Act [43 U.S.C.A. § 1331 et seq.] or the Deepwater Port Act of 1974 [33 U.S.C.A. § 1501 et seq.], or which may affect natural resources belonging to, appertaining to, or under the exclusive management authority of the United States (including resources under the Magnuson Fishery Conservation and Management Act [16 U.S.C. 1801 et seq.]).

(2)(A) The Administrator shall develop, promulgate, and revise as may be appropriate, regulations designating as hazardous substances, other than oil as defined in this section, such elements and compounds which, when discharged in any quantity into or upon the navigable waters of the United States or adjoining shorelines or the waters of the contiguous zone or in connection with activities under the Outer Continental Shelf Lands Act [43 U.S.C. 1331 et seq.] or the Deepwater Port Act of 1974 [33 U.S.C. 1501 et seq.], or which may affect natural resources belonging to, appertaining to, or under the exclusive management authority of the United States (including resources under the Magnuson Fishery Conservation and Management Act [16 U.S.C. 1801 et seq.]), present an imminent and substantial danger to the public health or welfare, including, but not limited to, fish, shellfish, wildlife, shorelines, and beaches.

(B) The Administrator shall within 18 months after November 2, 1978, conduct a study and report to the Congress on methods, mechanisms, and procedures to create incentives to achieve a higher standard of care in all aspects of the management and movement of hazardous substances on the part of owners, operators, or persons in charge of onshore facilities, offshore facilities, or vessels. The Administrator shall include in such study (1) limits of liability, (2) liability for third party damages, (3) penalties and fees, (4) spill prevention plans, (5) current practices in the insurance and banking industries, and (6) whether the penalty enacted in subclause (bb) of clause (iii) of subparagraph (B) of subsection (b)(2) of section 311 of Public Law 92–500 should be enacted.

(3) The discharge of oil or hazardous substances (i) into or upon the navigable waters of the United States, adjoining shorelines, or into or upon the waters of the contiguous zone, or (ii) in connection with activities under the Outer Continental Shelf Lands Act [43 U.S.C. 1331 et seq.] or the Deepwater Port Act of 1974 [33 U.S.C. 1501 et seq.], or which may affect natural resources belonging to, appertaining to, or under the exclusive management authority of the United States (including resources under the Magnuson Fishery Conservation and Management Act [16 U.S.C. 1801 et seq.]), in such quantities as may be harmful as determined by the President under paragraph (4) of this subsection, is prohibited, except (A) in the case of such discharges into the waters of the contiguous zone or which may affect natural resources belonging to, appertaining to, or under the exclusive management authority of the United States (including resources under the Magnuson Fishery Conservation and Management Act), where permitted under the Protocol of 1978 Relating to the International Convention for the Prevention of Pollution from Ships, 1973, and (B) where permitted in quantities and at times and locations or under such circumstances or conditions as the President may, by regulation, determine not to be harmful. Any regulations issued under this subsection shall be consistent with maritime safety and with marine and navigation laws and regulations and applicable water quality standards.

(4) The President shall by regulation determine for the purposes of this section those quantities of oil and any hazardous substances the discharge of which may be harmful to the public health or welfare of the United States, including but not limited to fish, shellfish, wildlife, and public and private property, shorelines, and beaches.

(5) Any person in charge of a vessel or of an onshore facility or an offshore facility shall, as soon as he has knowledge of any discharge of oil or a hazardous substance from such vessel or facility in violation of paragraph (3) of this subsection, immediately notify the appropriate agency of the United States Government of such discharge. Any such person (A) in charge of a vessel from which oil or a hazardous substance is discharged in violation of paragraph (3) (i) of this subsection, or (B) in charge of a vessel from which oil or a hazardous substance is discharged in violation of paragraph (3)(ii) of this subsection and who is otherwise subject to the jurisdiction of the United States at the time of the discharge, or (C) in charge of an onshore facility or an offshore facility, who fails to notify immediately such agency of such discharge shall, upon conviction, be fined not more than $10,000, or imprisoned for not more than one year, or both. Notification received pursuant to this paragraph or information obtained by the exploitation of such notification shall not be used against any such person in any criminal case, except a prosecution for perjury or for giving a false statement.

(6)(A) Any owner, operator, or person in charge of any onshore facility or offshore facility from which oil or a hazardous substance is discharged in violation of paragraph (3) of this subsection shall be assessed a civil penalty by the Secretary of the department in which the Coast Guard is operating of not more than $5,000 for each offense. Any owner, operator, or person in charge of any vessel from which oil or a hazardous substance is discharged in violation of paragraph (3)(i) of this subsection, and any owner, operator, or person in charge of a vessel from which oil or a hazardous substance is discharged in violation of paragraph (3)(ii) who is otherwise subject to the jurisdiction of the United States at the time of the discharge, shall be assessed a civil penalty by the Secretary of the department in which the Coast Guard is operating of not more than $5,000 for each offense. No penalty shall be assessed unless the owner or operator charged shall have been given notice and opportunity for a hearing on such charge. Each violation is a separate offense. Any such civil penalty may be compromised by such Secretary. In determining the amount of the penalty, or the amount agreed upon in compromise, the appropriateness of such penalty to the size of the business of the owner or operator charged, the effect on the owner or operator's ability to continue in business, and the gravity of the violation, shall be considered by such Secretary. The Secretary of the Treasury shall withhold at the request of such Secretary the clearance required by section 91 of Title 46, of any vessel the owner or operator of which is subject to the foregoing penalty. Clearance may be granted in such cases upon the filing of a bond or other surety satisfactory to such Secretary.

(B) The Administrator, taking into account the gravity of the offense, and the standard of care manifested by the owner, operator, or person in charge, may commence a civil action against any such person subject to the penalty under subparagraph (A) of this paragraph to impose a penalty based on consideration of the size of the business of the owner or operator, the effect on the ability of the owner or operator to continue in business, the gravity of the violation, and the nature, extent, and degree of success of any efforts made by the owner, operator, or person in charge to minimize or mitigate the effects of such discharge. The amount of such penalty shall not exceed $50,000, except that where the United States can show that such discharge was the result of willful negligence or willful misconduct within the privity and knowledge of the owner, operator, or person in charge, such penalty shall not exceed $250,000. Each violation is a separate offense. Any action under this subparagraph may be brought in the district court of the United States for the district in which the defendant is located or resides or is doing business, and such court shall have jurisdiction to assess such penalty. No action may be commenced under this clause where a penalty has been assessed under clause (A) of this paragraph.

(C) In addition to establishing a penalty for the discharge of a hazardous substance, the Administrator may act to mitigate the damage to the public health or welfare caused by such discharge. The cost of such mitigation shall be deemed a cost incurred under subsection (c) of this section for the removal of such substance by the United States Government.

(D) Any costs of removal incurred in connection with a discharge excluded by subsection (a)(2)(C) of this section shall be recoverable from the owner or operator of the source of the discharge in an action brought under section 1319(b) of this title.

(E) Civil penalties shall not be assessed under both this section and section 1319 of this title for the same discharge.

(c) Removal of discharged oil or hazardous substances; National Contingency Plan

(1) Whenever any oil or a hazardous substance is discharged, or there is a substantial threat of such discharge, into or upon the navigable waters of the United States, adjoining shorelines, or into or upon the waters of the contiguous zone, or in connection with activities under the Outer Continental Shelf Lands Act [43 U.S.C.A. § 1331 et seq.] or the Deepwater Port Act of 1974 [33 U.S.C.A. § 1501 et seq.], or which may affect natural resources belonging to, appertaining to, or under the exclusive management authority of the United States (including resources under the Magnuson Fishery Conservation and Management Act [16 U.S.C.A. § 1801 et seq.]) the President is authorized to act to remove or arrange for the removal of such oil or substance at any time, unless he determines such removal will be done properly by the owner or operator of the vessel, onshore facility, or offshore facility from which the discharge occurs.

(2) Within sixty days after October 18, 1972, the President shall prepare and publish a National Contingency Plan for removal of oil and hazardous substances, pursuant to this subsection. Such National Contingency Plan shall provide for efficient, coordinated, and effective action to minimize damage from oil and hazardous substance discharges, including containment, dispersal, and removal of oil and hazardous substances, and shall include, but not be limited to—

(A) assignment of duties and responsibilities among Federal departments and agencies in coordination with State and local agencies, including, but not limited to, water pollution control, conservation, and port authorities;

(B) identification, procurement, maintenance, and storage of equipment and supplies;

(C) establishment or designation of a strike force consisting of personnel who shall be trained, prepared, and available to provide necessary services to carry out the Plan, including the establishment at major ports, to be determined by the President, of emergency task forces of trained personnel, adequate oil and hazardous substance pollution control equipment and material, and a detailed oil and hazardous substance pollution prevention and removal plan;

(D) a system of surveillance and notice designed to insure earliest possible notice of discharges of oil and hazardous substances and imminent threats of such discharges to the appropriate State and Federal agencies;

(E) establishment of a national center to provide coordination and direction for operations in carrying out the Plan;

(F) procedures and techniques to be employed in identifying, containing, dispersing, and removing oil and hazardous substances;

(G) a schedule, prepared in cooperation with the States, identifying (i) dispersants and other chemicals, if any, that may be used in carrying out the Plan, (ii) the waters in which such dispersants and chemicals may be used, and (iii) the quantities of such dispersant or chemical which can be used safely in such waters, which schedule shall provide in the case of any dispersant, chemical, or waters not specifically identified in such schedule that the President, or his delegate, may, on a case-by-case basis, identify the dispersants and other chemicals which may be used, the waters in which they may be used, and the quantities which can be used safely in such waters; and

(H) a system whereby the State or States affected by a discharge of oil or hazardous substance may act where necessary to remove such discharge and such State or States may be reimbursed from the fund established under subsection (k) of this section for the reasonable costs incurred in such removal.

The President may, from time to time, as he deems advisable revise or otherwise amend the National Contingency Plan. After publication of the National Contingency Plan, the removal of oil and hazardous substances and actions to minimize damage from oil and hazardous substance discharges shall, to the greatest extent possible, be in accordance with the National Contingency Plan.

(d) Marine disaster discharges

Whenever a marine disaster in or upon the navigable waters of the United States has created a substantial threat of a pollution hazard to the public health or welfare of the United States, including, but not limited to, fish, shellfish, and wildlife and the public and private shorelines and beaches of the United States, because of a discharge, or an imminent discharge, of large quantities of oil, or of a hazardous substance from a vessel the United States may (A) coordinate and direct all public and private efforts directed at the removal or elimination of such threat; and (B) summarily remove, and, if necessary, destroy such vessel by whatever means are available without regard to any provisions of law governing the employment of personnel or the expenditure of appropriated funds. Any expense incurred under this subsection or under the Intervention on the High Seas Act [33 U.S.C. 1471 et seq.] (or the convention defined in section 2(3) thereof [33 U.S.C. 1471(3)]) shall be a cost incurred by the United States Government for the purposes of subsection (f) of this section in the removal of oil or hazardous substance.

(e) Judicial relief

In addition to any other action taken by a State or local government, when the President determines there is an imminent and substantial threat to the public health or welfare of the United States, including, but not limited to, fish, shellfish, and wildlife and public and private property, shorelines, and beaches within the United States, because of an actual or threatened discharge of oil or hazardous substance into or upon the navigable waters of the United States from an onshore or offshore facility, the President may require the United States attorney of the district in which the threat occurs to secure such relief as may be necessary to abate such threat, and the district courts of the United States shall have jurisdiction to grant such relief as the public interest and the equities of the case may require.

(f) Liability for actual costs of removal

(1) Except where an owner or operator can prove that a discharge was caused solely by (A) an act of God, (B) an act of war, (C) negligence on the part of the United States Government, or (D) an act or omission of a third party without regard to whether any such act or omission was or was not negligent, or any combination of the foregoing clauses, such owner or operator of any vessel from which oil or a hazardous substance is discharged in violation of subsection (b)(3) of this section shall, notwithstanding any other provision of law, be liable to the United States Government for the actual costs incurred under subsection (c) of this section for the removal of such oil or substance by the United States Government in an amount not to exceed, in the case of an inland oil barge $125 per gross ton of such barge, or $125,000, whichever is greater, and in the case of any other vessel, $150 per gross ton of such vessel (or, for a vessel carrying oil or hazardous substances as cargo, $250,000), whichever is greater, except that where the United States can show that such discharge was the result of willful negligence or willful misconduct within the privity and knowledge of the owner, such owner or operator shall be liable to the United States Government for the full amount of such costs. Such costs shall constitute a maritime lien on such vessel which may be recovered in an action in rem in the district court of the United States for any district within which any vessel may be found. The United States may also bring an action against the owner or operator of such vessel in any court of competent jurisdiction to recover such costs.

(2) Except where an owner or operator of an onshore facility can prove that a discharge was caused solely by (A) an act of God, (B) an act of war, (C) negligence on the part of the United States Government, or (D) an act or omission of a third party without regard to whether any such act or omission was or was not negligent, or any combination of the foregoing clauses, such owner or operator of any such facility from which oil or a hazardous substance is discharged in violation of subsection (b)(3) of this section shall be liable to the United States Government for the actual costs incurred under subsection (c) of this section for the removal of such oil or substance by the United States Government in an amount not to exceed $50,000,000, except that where the United States can show that such discharge was the result of willful negligence or willful misconduct within the privity and knowledge of the owner, such owner or operator shall be liable to the United States Government for the full amount of such costs. The United States may bring an action against the owner or operator of such facility in any court of competent jurisdiction to recover such costs. The Administrator is authorized, by regulation, after consultation with the Secretary of Commerce and the Small Business Administration, to establish reasonable and equitable classifications of those onshore facilities having a total fixed storage capacity of 1,000 barrels or less which he determines because of size, type, and location do not present a substantial risk of the discharge of oil or a hazardous substance in violation of subsection (b)(3) of this section, and apply with respect to such classifications differing limits of liability which may be less than the amount contained in this paragraph.

(3) Except where an owner or operator of an offshore facility can prove that a discharge was caused solely by (A) an act of God, (B) an act of war, (C) negligence on the part of the United States Government, or (D) an act or omission of a third party without regard to whether any such act or omission was or was not negligent, or any combination of the foregoing clauses, such owner or operator of any such facility from which oil or a hazardous substance is discharged in violation of subsection (b)(3) of this section shall, notwithstanding any other provision of law, be liable to the United States Government for the actual costs incurred under subsection (c) of this section for the removal of such oil or substance by the United States Government in an amount not to exceed $50,000,000, except that where the United States can show that such discharge was the result of willful negligence or willful misconduct within the privity and knowledge of the owner, such owner or operator shall be liable to the United States Government for the full amount of such costs. The United States may bring an action against the owner or operator of such a facility in any court of competent jurisdiction to recover such costs.

(4) The costs of removal of oil or a hazardous substance for which the owner or operator of a vessel or onshore or offshore facility is liable under subsection (f) of this section shall include any costs or expenses incurred by the Federal Government or any State government in the restoration or replacement of natural resources damaged or destroyed as a result of a discharge of oil or a hazardous substance in violation of subsection (b) of this section.

(5) The President, or the authorized representative of any State, shall act on behalf of the public as trustee of the natural resources to recover for the costs of replacing or restoring such resources. Sums recovered shall be used to restore, rehabilitate, or acquire the equivalent of such natural resources by the appropriate agencies of the Federal Government, or the State government.

(g) Third party liability

Where the owner or operator of a vessel (other than an inland oil barge) carrying oil or hazardous substances as cargo or an onshore or offshore facility which handles or stores oil or hazardous substances in bulk, from which oil or a hazardous substance is discharged in violation of subsection (b) of this section, alleges that such discharge was caused solely by an act or omission of a third party, such owner or operator shall pay to the United States Government the actual costs incurred under subsection (c) of this section for removal of such oil or substance and shall be entitled by subrogation to all rights of the United States Government to recover such costs from such third party under this subsection. In any case where an owner or operator of a vessel, of an onshore facility, or of an offshore facility, from which oil or a hazardous substance is discharged in violation of subsection (b)(3) of this section, proves that such discharge of oil or hazardous substance was caused solely by an act or omission of a third party, or was caused solely by such an act or omission in combination with an act of God, an act of war, or negligence on the part of the United States Government, such third party shall, notwithstanding any other provision of law, be liable to the United States Government for the actual costs incurred under subsection (c) of this section for removal of such oil or substance by the United States Government, except where such third party can prove that such discharge was caused solely by (A) an act of God, (B) an act of war, (C) negligence on the part of the United States Government, or (D) an act or omission of another party without regard to whether such act or omission was or was not negligent, or any combination of the foregoing clauses. If such third party was the owner or operator of a vessel which caused the discharge of oil or a hazardous substance in violation of subsection (b)(3) of this section, the liability of such third party under this subsection shall not exceed, in the case of an inland oil barge $125 per gross ton of such barge, or $125,000, whichever is greater, and in the case of any other vessel, $150 per gross ton of such vessel (or, for a vessel carrying oil or hazardous substances as cargo, $250,000), whichever is greater. In any other case the liability of such third party shall not exceed the limitation which would have been applicable to the owner or operator of the vessel or the onshore or offshore facility from which the discharge actually occurred if such owner or operator were liable. If the United States can show that the discharge of oil or a hazardous substance in violation of subsection (b)(3) of this section was the result of willful negligence or willful misconduct within the privity and knowledge of such third party, such third party shall be liable to the United States Government for the full amount of such removal costs. The United States may bring an action against the third party in any court of competent jurisdiction to recover such removal costs.

(h) Rights against third parties who caused or contributed to discharge

The liabilities established by this section shall in no way affect any rights which (1) the owner or operator of a vessel or of an onshore facility or an offshore facility may have against any third party whose acts may in any way have caused or contributed to such discharge, or (2) The [2] United States Government may have against any third party whose actions may in any way have caused or contributed to the discharge of oil or hazardous substance.

(i) Recovery of removal costs

(1) In any case where an owner or operator of a vessel or an onshore facility or an offshore facility from which oil or a hazardous substance is discharged in violation of subsection (b)(3) of this section acts to remove such oil or substance in accordance with regulations promulgated pursuant to this section, such owner or operator shall be entitled to recover the reasonable costs incurred in such removal upon establishing, in a suit which may be brought against the United States Government in the United States Claims Court, that such discharge was caused solely by (A) an act of God, (B) an act of war, (C) negligence on the part of the United States Government, or (D) an act or omission of a third party without regard to whether such act or omission was or was not negligent, or of any combination of the foregoing causes.

(2) The provisions of this subsection shall not apply in any case where liability is established pursuant to the Outer Continental Shelf Lands Act [43 U.S.C. 1331 et seq.], or the Deepwater Port Act of 1974 [33 U.S.C. 1501 et seq.].

(3) Any amount paid in accordance with a judgment of the United States Claims Court pursuant to this section shall be paid from the funds established pursuant to subsection (k) of this section.

(j) Regulations; penalty

(1) Consistent with the National Contingency Plan required by subsection (c)(2) of this section, as soon as practicable after October 18, 1972, and from time to time thereafter, the President shall issue regulations consistent with maritime safety and with marine and navigation laws (A) establishing methods and procedures for removal of discharged oil and hazardous substances, (B) establishing criteria for the development and implementation of local and regional oil and hazardous substance removal contingency plans, (C) establishing procedures, methods, and equipment and other requirements for equipment to prevent discharges of oil and hazardous substances from vessels and from onshore facilities and offshore facilities, and to contain such discharges, and (D) governing the inspection of vessels carrying cargoes of oil and hazardous substances and the inspection of such cargoes in order to reduce the likelihood of discharges of oil from vessels in violation of this section.

(2) Any owner or operator of a vessel or an onshore facility or an offshore facility and any other person subject to any regulation issued under paragraph (1) of this subsection who fails or refuses to comply with the provisions of any such regulations, shall be liable to a civil penalty of not more than $5,000 for each such violation. This paragraph shall not apply to any owner or operator of any vessel from which oil or a hazardous substance is discharged in violation of paragraph (3)(ii) of subsection (b) of this section unless such owner, operator, or person in charge is otherwise subject to the jurisdiction of the United States. Each violation shall be a separate offense. The President may assess and compromise such penalty. No penalty shall be assessed until the owner, operator, or other person charged shall have been given notice and an opportunity for a hearing on such charge. In determining the amount of the penalty, or the amount agreed upon in compromise, the gravity of the violation, and the demonstrated good faith of the owner, operator, or other person charged in attempting to achieve rapid compliance, after notification of a violation, shall be considered by the President.

(k) Authorization of appropriations; supplemental appropriations

(1) There is hereby authorized to be appropriated to a revolving fund to be established in the Treasury such sums as may be necessary to maintain such fund at a level of $35,000,000 to carry out the provisions of subsections (c), (d), (i), and (*l*) of this section. Any other funds received by the United States under this section shall also be deposited in said fund for such purposes. All sums appropriated to, or deposited in, said fund shall remain available until expended.

(2) The Secretary of Transportation shall notify the Congress whenever the unobligated balance of the fund is less than $12,000,000, and shall include in such notification a recommendation for a supplemental appropriation relating to the sums that are needed to maintain the fund at the level provided in paragraph (1).

(*l*) Administration

The President is authorized to delegate the administration of this section to the heads of those Federal departments, agencies, and instrumentalities which he determines to be appropriate. Any moneys in the fund established by subsection (k) of this section shall be available to such Federal departments, agencies, and instrumentalities to carry out the provisions of subsections (c) and (i) of this section. Each such department, agency, and instrumentality, in order to avoid duplication of effort, shall, whenever appropriate, utilize the personnel, services, and facilities of other Federal departments, agencies, and instrumentalities.

(m) Boarding and inspection of vessels; arrest; execution of warrants or other process

Anyone authorized by the President to enforce the provisions of this section may, except as to public vessels, (A) board and inspect any vessel upon the navigable waters of the United States or the waters of the contiguous zone, (B) with or without a warrant arrest any person who violates the provisions of this section or any regulation issued thereunder in his presence or view, and (C) execute any warrant or other process issued by an officer or court of competent jurisdiction.

(n) Jurisdiction

The several district courts of the United States are invested with jurisdiction for any actions, other than actions pursuant to subsection (i)(1) of this section, arising under this section. In the case of Guam and the Trust Territory of the Pacific Islands, such actions may be brought in the district court of Guam, and in the case of the Virgin Islands such actions may be brought in the district court of the Virgin Islands. In the case of American Samoa and the Trust Territory of the Pacific Islands, such actions may be brought in the District Court of the United States for the District of Hawaii and such court shall have jurisdiction of such actions. In the case of the Canal Zone, such actions may be brought in the United States District Court for the District of the Canal Zone.

(*o*) Obligation for damages unaffected; local authority not preempted; existing Federal authority not modified or affected

(1) Nothing in this section shall affect or modify in any way the obligations of any owner or operator of any vessel, or of any owner or operator of any onshore facility or offshore facility to any person or agency under any provision of law for damages to any publicly owned or privately owned property resulting from a discharge of any oil or hazardous substance or from the removal of any such oil or hazardous substance.

(2) Nothing in this section shall be construed as preempting any State or political subdivision thereof from imposing any requirement or liability with respect to the discharge of oil or hazardous substance into any waters within such State.

(3) Nothing in this section shall be construed as affecting or modifying any other existing authority of any Federal department, agency, or instrumentality, relative to onshore or offshore facilities under this chapter or any other provision of law, or to affect any State or local law not in conflict with this section.

(p) Financial responsibility

(1) Any vessel over three hundred gross tons, including any barge of equivalent size, but not including any barge that is not self-propelled and that does not carry oil or hazardous substances as cargo or fuel, using any port or place in the United States or the navigable waters of the United States for any purpose shall establish and maintain under regulations to be prescribed from time to time by the President, evidence of financial responsibility of, in the case of an inland oil barge $125 per gross ton of such barge, or $125,000, whichever is greater, and in the case of any other vessel, $150 per gross ton of such vessel (or, for a vessel carrying oil or hazardous substances as cargo, $250,000), whichever is greater, to meet the liability to the United States which such vessel could be subjected under this section. In cases where an owner or operator owns, operates, or charters more than one such vessel, financial responsibility need only be established to meet the maximum liability to which the largest of such vessels could be subjected. Financial responsibility may be established by any one of, or a combination of, the following methods acceptable to the President: (A) evidence of insurance, (B) surety bonds, (C) qualification as a self-insurer, or (D) other evidence of financial responsibility. Any bond filed shall be issued by a bonding company authorized to do business in the United States.

(2) The provisions of paragraph (1) of this subsection shall be effective April 3, 1971, with respect to oil and one year after October 18, 1972, with respect to hazardous substances. The President shall delegate the responsibility to carry out the provisions of this subsection to the appropriate agency head within sixty days after October 18, 1972. Regulations necessary to implement this subsection shall be issued within six months after October 18, 1972.

(3) Any claim for costs incurred by such vessel may be brought directly against the insurer or any other person providing evidence of financial responsibility as required under this subsection. In the case of any action pursuant to this subsection such insurer or other person shall be entitled to invoke all rights and defenses which would have been available to the owner or operator if an action had been brought against him by the claimant, and which would have been available to him if an action had been brought against him by the owner or operator.

(4) Any owner or operator of a vessel subject to this subsection, who fails to comply with the provisions of this subsection or any regulation issued thereunder, shall be subject to a fine of not more than $10,000.

(5) The Secretary of the Treasury may refuse the clearance required by section 91 of title 46 to any vessel subject to this subsection, which does not have evidence furnished by the President that the financial responsibility provisions of paragraph (1) of this subsection have been complied with.

(6) The Secretary of the Department in which the Coast Guard is operated may (A) deny entry to any port or place in the United States or the navigable waters of the United States, to, and (B) detain at the port or place in the United States from which it is about to depart for any other port or place in the United States, any vessel subject to this subsection, which upon request, does not produce evidence furnished by the President that the financial responsibility provisions of paragraph (1) of this subsection have been complied with.

(q) Establishment of maximum limit of liability with respect to onshore or offshore facilities

The President is authorized to establish, with respect to any class or category of onshore or offshore facilities, a maximum limit of liability under subsections (f)(2) and (3) of this section of less than $50,000,000, but not less than $8,000,000.

(r) Liability limitations not to limit liability under other legislation

Nothing in this section shall be construed to impose, or authorize the imposition of, any limitation on liability under the Outer Continental Shelf Lands Act [43 U.S.C. 1331 et seq.] or the Deepwater Port Act of 1974 [33 U.S.C. 1501 et seq.].

(June 30, 1948, ch. 758, title III, § 311, as added Oct. 18, 1972, Pub.L. 92–500, § 2, 86 Stat. 862, and amended Dec. 28, 1973, Pub.L. 93–207, § 1(4), 87 Stat. 906; Dec. 27, 1977, Pub.L. 95–217, §§ 57, 58(a)–(g), (i), (k)–(m), 91 Stat. 1593–1596; Nov. 2, 1978, Pub.L. 95–576, § 1(b), 92 Stat. 2467; Oct. 21, 1980, Pub.L. 96–478, § 13(b), 94 Stat. 2303; Oct. 21, 1980, Pub.L. 96–483, § 8, 94 Stat. 2362; Dec. 22, 1980, Pub.L. 96–561, title II, § 238(b), 94 Stat. 3300; April 2, 1982, Pub.L. 97–164, title I, § 161(5), 96 Stat. 49.)

1 So in original. The period should be a semicolon.

2 So in original. Probably should not be capitalized.

Cross References

Authorization of appropriations to carry out this chapter with certain exceptions, see section 1376 of this title.

Coordination of guidelines for use of imminent hazard, enforcement, and emergency response authorities with powers under this section, see section 9606 of Title 42, The Public Health and Welfare.

Definition of "hazardous substance" for purposes of comprehensive environmental response, compensation, and liability provisions, see section 9601 of Title 42.

Definition of "removal costs" for purposes of offshore oil spill pollution fund, see section 1811 of Title 43, Public Lands.

Demonstration of financial responsibility in accordance with this section, see section 1653 of Title 43.

Designation of hazardous substance under this section as constituting hazardous material in relation to vessels and seamen, see section 2101 of Title 46, Shipping.

Effective date of regulations issued pursuant to this section, see section 9652 of Title 42, The Public Health and Welfare.

Establishment and maintenance of records to carry out this section, see section 1318 of this title.
Establishment of reportable released quantities of hazardous substances, see section 9602 of Title 42, The Public Health and Welfare.
Federal oil pollution preventive measures on the high seas, availability of revolving fund monies, see section 1486 of this title.
Hazardous Substance Superfund, payment of claims incurred as result of carrying out national contingency plan established under this section, see section 9611 of Title 42, The Public Health and Welfare.
Hudson River reclamation demonstration project, see section 1266 of this title.
Oil within meaning of this section as included in definition of "material", see section 1402 of this title.
Prohibition of discharge of oil from any offshore facility or vessel, see section 1821 of Title 43, Public Lands.
Regulations respecting assessment of damages to natural resources, see section 9651 of Title 42, The Public Health and Welfare.
Regulations supplemental to effluent limitations for specific hazardous pollutants, see section 1314 of this title.
Removal of oil in accordance with National Contingency Plan established pursuant to this section, see section 1517 of this title.
Revision of National Contingency Plan, see section 9605 of Title 42, The Public Health and Welfare.
Transfer of unobligated funds under this section, see section 9654 of Title 42.

Federal Practice and Procedure

Exceptions to sovereign immunity, see Wright, Miller & Cooper: Jurisdiction 2d § 3656 et seq.

West's Federal Practice Manual

Concurrent Claims Court jurisdiction, see § 1834.

Code of Federal Regulations

Civil penalties for violation of oil pollution prevention regulations, see 40 CFR 114.1 et seq.
Designation of substances, reportable quantities, and notification requirements for release of substances, see 40 CFR 302.1 et seq.
Financial responsibility for oil pollution—Alaska pipeline, see 33 CFR 131.1 et seq.
Financial responsibility for water pollution, see 33 CFR 130.1 et seq.
Hazardous substances—
  Designation, see 40 CFR 116.1 et seq.
  Determination of reportable quantities, see 40 CFR 117.1 et seq.
Liability limits for small onshore storage facilities, see 40 CFR 113.1 et seq.
Limitations on discharge of oil, see 40 CFR 110.1 et seq., 112.1 et seq.
Oil pollution regulations, see 33 CFR Chap. I, Subchap. O.
Pollution contingency plan, see 40 CFR 300.1 et seq.
Pollution of coastal and navigable waters, reports by United States Customs Service officers, see 19 CFR 4.0 et seq.
Pollution removal damage claims, see 33 CFR 25.101 et seq.
Trans-Alaska pipeline liability fund, see 43 CFR 29.1 et seq.

United States Supreme Court

State regulation or control, oil spills, waiver of preemption, Askew v. American Waterways Operators Inc., 1973, 93 S.Ct. 1590, 411 U.S. 325, 36 L.Ed.2d 280.

§ 1322. Marine sanitation devices

(a) Definitions

For the purpose of this section, the term—

(1) "new vessel" includes every description of watercraft or other artificial contrivance used, or capable of being used, as a means of transportation on the navigable waters, the construction of which is initiated after promulgation of standards and regulations under this section;

(2) "existing vessel" includes every description of watercraft or other artificial contrivance used, or capable of being used, as a means of transportation on the navigable waters, the construction of which is initiated before promulgation of standards and regulations under this section;

(3) "public vessel" means a vessel owned or bareboat chartered and operated by the United States, by a State or political subdivision thereof, or by a foreign nation, except when such vessel is engaged in commerce;

(4) "United States" includes the States, the District of Columbia, the Commonwealth of Puerto Rico, the Virgin Islands, Guam, American Samoa, the Canal Zone, and the Trust Territory of the Pacific Islands;

(5) "marine sanitation device" includes any equipment for installation on board a vessel which is designed to receive, retain, treat, or discharge sewage, and any process to treat such sewage;

(6) "sewage" means human body wastes and the wastes from toilets and other receptacles intended to receive or retain body wastes except that, with respect to commercial vessels on the Great Lakes, such term shall include graywater;

(7) "manufacturer" means any person engaged in the manufacturing, assembling, or importation of marine sanitation devices or of vessels subject to standards and regulations promulgated under this section;

(8) "person" means an individual, partnership, firm, corporation, or association, but does not include an individual on board a public vessel;

(9) "discharge" includes, but is not limited to, any spilling, leaking, pumping, pouring, emitting, emptying or dumping;

(10) "commercial vessels" means those vessels used in the business of transporting property for compensation or hire, or in transporting property in the business of the owner, lessee, or operator of the vessel;

(11) "graywater" means galley, bath, and shower water.

(b) Federal standards of performance

(1) As soon as possible, after October 18, 1972, and subject to the provisions of section 1254(j) of this title, the Administrator, after consultation with the Secretary of the department in which the Coast Guard is operating, after giving appropriate consideration to the economic costs involved, and within the limits of available technology, shall promulgate Federal standards of performance for marine sanitation devices (hereafter in this section referred to as "standards") which shall be designed to prevent the discharge of untreated or inadequately treated sewage into or upon the navigable waters from new vessels and existing vessels, except vessels not equipped with installed toilet facilities. Such standards and standards established under subsection (c)(1)(B) of this section shall be consistent with maritime safety and the marine and navigation laws and regulations and shall be coordinated with the regulations issued under this subsection by the Secretary of the department in which the Coast Guard is operating. The Secretary of the department in which the Coast Guard is operating shall promulgate regulations, which are consistent with standards promulgated under this subsection and subsection (c) of this section and with maritime safety and the marine and navigation laws and regulations governing the design, construction, installation, and operation of any marine sanitation device on board such vessels.

(2) Any existing vessel equipped with a marine sanitation device on the date of promulgation of initial standards and regulations under this section, which device is in compliance with such initial standards and regulations, shall be deemed in compliance with this section until such time as the device is replaced or is found not to be in compliance with such initial standards and regulations.

(c) Initial standards; effective dates; revision; waiver

(1)(A) Initial standards and regulations under this section shall become effective for new vessels two years after promulgation; and for existing vessels five years after promulgation. Revisions of standards and regulations shall be effective upon promulgation, unless another effective date is specified, except that no revision shall take effect before the effective date of the standard or regulation being revised.

(B) The Administrator shall, with respect to commercial vessels on the Great Lakes, establish standards which require at a minimum the equivalent of secondary treatment as defined under section 1314(d) of this title. Such standards and regulations shall take effect for existing vessels after such time as the Administrator determines to be reasonable for the upgrading of marine sanitation devices to attain such standard.

(2) The Secretary of the department in which the Coast Guard is operating with regard to his regulatory authority established by this section, after consultation with the Administrator, may distinguish among classes, type, and sizes of vessels as well as between new and existing vessels, and may waive applicability of standards and regulations as necessary or appropriate for such classes, types, and sizes of vessels (including existing vessels equipped with marine sanitation devices on the date of promulgation of the initial standards required by this section), and, upon application, for individual vessels.

(d) Vessels owned and operated by the United States

The provisions of this section and the standards and regulations promulgated hereunder apply to vessels owned and operated by the United States unless the Secretary of Defense finds that compliance would not be in the interest of national security. With respect to vessels owned and operated by the Department of Defense, regulations under the last sentence of subsection (b)(1) of this section and certifications under subsection (g)(2) of this section shall be promulgated and issued by the Secretary of Defense.

(e) Pre-promulgation consultation

Before the standards and regulations under this section are promulgated, the Administrator and the Secretary of the department in which the Coast Guard is operating shall consult with the Secretary of State; the Secretary of Health and Human Services; the Secretary of Defense; the Secretary of the Treasury; the Secretary of Commerce; other interested Federal agencies; and the States and industries interested; and otherwise comply with the requirements of section 553 of title 5.

(f) Regulation by States or political subdivisions thereof; complete prohibition upon discharge of sewage

(1) After the effective date of the initial standards and regulations promulgated under this section, no State or political subdivision thereof shall adopt or enforce any statute or regulation of such State or political subdivision with respect to the design, manufacture, or installation or use of any marine sanitation device on any vessel subject to the provisions of this section.

(2) If, after promulgation of the initial standards and regulations and prior to their effective date, a vessel is equipped with a marine sanitation device in compliance with such standards and regulations and the installation and operation of such device is in accordance with such standards and regulations, such standards and regulations shall, for the pur-

poses of paragraph (1) of this subsection, become effective with respect to such vessel on the date of such compliance.

(3) After the effective date of the initial standards and regulations promulgated under this section, if any State determines that the protection and enhancement of the quality of some or all of the waters within such State require greater environmental protection, such State may completely prohibit the discharge from all vessels of any sewage, whether treated or not, into such waters, except that no such prohibition shall apply until the Administrator determines that adequate facilities for the safe and sanitary removal and treatment of sewage from all vessels are reasonably available for such water to which such prohibition would apply. Upon application of the State, the Administrator shall make such determination within 90 days of the date of such application.

(4)(A) If the Administrator determines upon application by a State that the protection and enhancement of the quality of specified waters within such State requires such a prohibition, he shall by regulation completely prohibit the discharge from a vessel of any sewage (whether treated or not) into such waters.

(B) Upon application by a State, the Administrator shall, by regulation, establish a drinking water intake zone in any waters within such State and prohibit the discharge of sewage from vessels within that zone.

(g) Sales limited to certified devices; certification of test device; recordkeeping; reports

(1) No manufacturer of a marine sanitation device shall sell, offer for sale, or introduce or deliver for introduction in interstate commerce, or import into the United States for sale or resale any marine sanitation device manufactured after the effective date of the standards and regulations promulgated under this section unless such device is in all material respects substantially the same as a test device certified under this subsection.

(2) Upon application of the manufacturer, the Secretary of the department in which the Coast Guard is operating shall so certify a marine sanitation device if he determines, in accordance with the provisions of this paragraph, that it meets the appropriate standards and regulations promulgated under this section. The Secretary of the department in which the Coast Guard is operating shall test or require such testing of the device in accordance with procedures set forth by the Administrator as to standards of performance and for such other purposes as may be appropriate. If the Secretary of the department in which the Coast Guard is operating determines that the device is satisfactory from the standpoint of safety and any other requirements of maritime law or regulation, and after consideration of the design, installation, operation, material, or other appropriate factors, he shall certify the device. Any device manufactured by such manufacturer which is in all material respects substantially the same as the certified test device shall be deemed to be in conformity with the appropriate standards and regulations established under this section.

(3) Every manufacturer shall establish and maintain such records, make such reports, and provide such information as the Administrator or the Secretary of the department in which the Coast Guard is operating may reasonably require to enable him to determine whether such manufacturer has acted or is acting in compliance with this section and regulations issued thereunder and shall, upon request of an officer or employee duly designated by the Administrator or the Secretary of the department in which the Coast Guard is operating, permit such officer or employee at reasonable times to have access to and copy such records. All information reported to or otherwise obtained by the Administrator or the Secretary of the Department in which the Coast Guard is operating or their representatives pursuant to this subsection which contains or relates to a trade secret or other matter referred to in section 1905 of title 18 shall be considered confidential for the purpose of that section, except that such information may be disclosed to other officers or employees concerned with carrying out this section. This paragraph shall not apply in the case of the construction of a vessel by an individual for his own use.

(h) Sale and resale of properly equipped vessels; operability of certified marine sanitation devices

After the effective date of standards and regulations promulgated under this section, it shall be unlawful—

(1) for the manufacturer of any vessel subject to such standards and regulations to manufacture for sale, to sell or offer for sale, or to distribute for sale or resale any such vessel unless it is equipped with a marine sanitation device which is in all material respects substantially the same as the appropriate test device certified pursuant to this section;

(2) for any person, prior to the sale or delivery of a vessel subject to such standards and regulations to the ultimate purchaser, wrongfully to remove or render inoperative any certified marine sanitation device or element of design of such device installed in such vessel;

(3) for any person to fail or refuse to permit access to or copying of records or to fail to make

reports or provide information required under this section; and

(4) for a vessel subject to such standards and regulations to operate on the navigable waters of the United States, if such vessel is not equipped with an operable marine sanitation device certified pursuant to this section.

(i) Jurisdiction to restrain violations; contempts

The district courts of the United States shall have jurisdictions to restrain violations of subsection (g)(1) of this section and subsections (h)(1) through (3) of this section. Actions to restrain such violations shall be brought by, and in, the name of the United States. In case of contumacy or refusal to obey a subpena served upon any person under this subsection, the district court of the United States for any district in which such person is found or resides or transacts business, upon application by the United States and after notice to such person, shall have jurisdiction to issue an order requiring such person to appear and give testimony or to appear and produce documents, and any failure to obey such order of the court may be punished by such court as a contempt thereof.

(j) Penalties

Any person who violates subsection (g)(1) of this section or clause (1) or (2) of subsection (h) of this section shall be liable to a civil penalty of not more than $5,000 for each violation. Any person who violates clause (4) of subsection (h) of this section or any regulation issued pursuant to this section shall be liable to a civil penalty of not more than $2,000 for each violation. Each violation shall be a separate offense. The Secretary of the department in which the Coast Guard is operating may assess and compromise any such penalty. No penalty shall be assessed until the person charged shall have been given notice and an opportunity for a hearing on such charge. In determining the amount of the penalty, or the amount agreed upon in compromise, the gravity of the violation, and the demonstrated good faith of the person charged in attempting to achieve rapid compliance, after notification of a violation, shall be considered by said Secretary.

(k) Enforcement authority

The provisions of this section shall be enforced by the Secretary of the department in which the Coast Guard is operating and he may utilize by agreement, with or without reimbursement, law enforcement officers or other personnel and facilities of the Administrator, other Federal agencies, or the States to carry out the provisions of this section.

(*l*) Boarding and inspection of vessels; execution of warrants and other process

Anyone authorized by the Secretary of the department in which the Coast Guard is operating to enforce the provisions of this section may, except as to public vessels, (1) board and inspect any vessel upon the navigable waters of the United States and (2) execute any warrant or other process issued by an officer or court of competent jurisdiction.

(m) Enforcement in United States possessions

In the case of Guam and the Trust Territory of the Pacific Islands, actions arising under this section may be brought in the district court of Guam, and in the case of the Virgin Islands such actions may be brought in the district court of the Virgin Islands. In the case of American Samoa and the Trust Territory of the Pacific Islands, such actions may be brought in the District Court of the United States for the District of Hawaii and such court shall have jurisdiction of such actions. In the case of the Canal Zone, such actions may be brought in the District Court for the District of the Canal Zone.

(June 30, 1948, ch. 758, title III, § 312, as added Oct. 18, 1972, Pub.L. 92–500, § 2, 86 Stat. 871, and amended Dec. 27, 1977, Pub.L. 95–217, § 59, 91 Stat. 1596; Oct. 17, 1979, Pub.L. 96–88, title V, § 509(b), 93 Stat. 695.)

Cross References

Definition of "material" for purposes of ocean dumping as not including sewage from vessels within the meaning of this section, see section 1402 of this title.

Definition of "pollutant" as not including sewage from vessels within the meaning of this section, see section 1362 of this title.

Solid waste disposal equipment for vessels, see section 1254 of this title.

Code of Federal Regulations

Standards for marine sanitation devices, see 33 CFR 159.1 et seq., 40 CFR 140.1 et seq.

§ 1323. Federal facilities pollution control

(a) Each department, agency, or instrumentality of the executive, legislative, and judicial branches of the Federal Government (1) having jurisdiction over any property or facility, or (2) engaged in any activity resulting, or which may result, in the discharge or runoff of pollutants, and each officer, agent, or employee thereof in the performance of his official duties, shall be subject to, and comply with, all Federal, State, interstate, and local requirements, administrative authority, and process and sanctions respecting the control and abatement of water pollution in the same manner, and to the same extent as any nongovernmental entity including the payment of reasonable service charges. The preceding sentence shall apply (A) to any requirement whether substantive or procedural (including any recordkeeping or reporting requirement, any requirement respecting permits and any other requirement, whatsoever), (B) to the exercise of any Federal, State, or local administrative authority, and (C) to any process and sanction, whether enforced in Federal, State, or local courts or in any other manner. This subsection shall apply notwithstanding any immunity of such agencies, officers, agents, or employees under any law or rule of law. Nothing in this section shall be construed to prevent any department, agency, or instrumentality of the Federal Government, or any officer, agent, or employee thereof in the performance of his official duties, from removing to the appropriate Federal district court any proceeding to which the department, agency, or instrumentality or officer, agent, or employee thereof is subject pursuant to this section, and any such proceeding may be removed in accordance with section 1441 et seq. of title 28. No officer, agent, or employee of the United States shall be personally liable for any civil penalty arising from the performance of his official duties, for which he is not otherwise liable, and the United States shall be liable only for those civil penalties arising under Federal law or imposed by a State or local court to enforce an order or the process of such court. The President may exempt any effluent source of any department, agency, or instrumentality in the executive branch from compliance with any such a requirement if he determines it to be in the paramount interest of the United States to do so; except that no exemption may be granted from the requirements of section 1316 or 1317 of this title. No such exemptions shall be granted due to lack of appropriation unless the President shall have specifically requested such appropriation as a part of the budgetary process and the Congress shall have failed to make available such requested appropriation. Any exemption shall be for a period not in excess of one year, but additional exemptions may be granted for periods of not to exceed one year upon the President's making a new determination. The President shall report each January to the Congress all exemptions from the requirements of this section granted during the preceding calendar year, together with his reason for granting such exemption. In addition to any such exemption of a particular effluent source, the President may, if he determines it to be in the paramount interest of the United States to do so, issue regulations exempting from compliance with the requirements of this section any weaponry, equipment, aircraft, vessels, vehicles, or other classes or categories of property, and access to such property, which are owned or operated by the Armed Forces of the United States (including the Coast Guard) or by the National Guard of any State and which are uniquely military in nature. The President shall reconsider the need for such regulations at three-year intervals.

(b)(1) The Administrator shall coordinate with the head of each department, agency, or instrumentality of the Federal Government having jurisdiction over any property or facility utilizing federally owned wastewater facilities to develop a program of cooperation for utilizing wastewater control systems utilizing those innovative treatment processes and techniques for which guidelines have been promulgated under section 1314(d)(3) of this title. Such program shall include an inventory of property and facilities which could utilize such processes and techniques.

(2) Construction shall not be initiated for facilities for treatment of wastewater at any Federal property or facility after September 30, 1979, if alternative methods for wastewater treatment at such property or facility utilizing innovative treatment processes and techniques, including but not limited to methods utilizing recycle and reuse techniques and land treatment are not utilized, unless the life cycle cost of the alternative treatment works exceeds the life cycle cost of the most cost effective alternative by more than 15 per centum. The Administrator may waive the application of this paragraph in any case where the Administrator determines it to be in the public interest, or that compliance with this paragraph would interfere with the orderly compliance with conditions of a permit issued pursuant to section 1342 of this title.

(June 30, 1948, ch. 758, title III, § 313), as added Oct. 18, 1972, Pub.L. 92–500, § 2, 86 Stat. 875, and amended Dec. 27, 1977, Pub.L. 95–217, §§ 60, 61(a), 91 Stat. 1597, 1598.)

Cross References

Citizen suits to enforce effluent standards, see section 1365 of this title.

Library References

Health and Environment ⚷25.7(3).
C.J.S. Health and Environment § 106.

United States Supreme Court

Federal installations, compliance with state requirements, necessity of state permit from state with federally approved program, see Environmental Protection Agency v. California, ex rel. State Water Resources Control Bd., 1976, 96 S.Ct. 2022, 426 U.S. 200, 48 L.Ed.2d 578.

§ 1324. Clean lakes

(a) Requirements imposed upon States

Each State shall prepare or establish, and submit to the Administrator for his approval—

(1) an identification and classification according to eutrophic condition of all publicly owned fresh water lakes in such State;

(2) procedures, processes, and methods (including land use requirements), to control sources of pollution of such lakes; and

(3) methods and procedures, in conjunction with appropriate Federal agencies, to restore the quality of such lakes.

(b) Financial assistance to States

The Administrator shall provide financial assistance to States in order to carry out methods and procedures approved by him under this section. The Administrator shall provide financial assistance to States to prepare the identification and classification surveys required in subsection (a)(1) of this section.

(c) Maximum amount of grant; authorization of appropriations

(1) The amount granted to any State for any fiscal year under this section shall not exceed 70 per centum of the funds expended by such State in such year for carrying out approved methods and procedures under this section.

(2) There is authorized to be appropriated $50,000,000 for the fiscal year ending June 30, 1973; $100,000,000 for the fiscal year 1974; $150,000,000 for the fiscal year 1975, $50,000,000 for fiscal year 1977, $60,000,000 for fiscal year 1978, $60,000,000 for fiscal year 1979, $60,000,000 for fiscal year 1980, $30,000,000 for fiscal year 1981, and $30,000,000 for fiscal year 1982 for grants to States under this section which such sums shall remain available until expended. The Administrator shall provide for an equitable distribution of such sums to the States with approved methods and procedures under this section.

(June 30, 1948, ch. 758, title III, § 314, as added Oct. 18, 1972, Pub.L. 92–500, § 2, 86 Stat. 875, and amended Dec. 27, 1977, Pub.L. 95–217, §§ 4(f), 62(a), 91 Stat. 1567, 1598; Oct. 21, 1980, Pub.L. 96–483, § 1(f), 94 Stat. 2360.)

Cross References

Authorization of appropriations to carry out this chapter other than this section, see section 1376 of this title.

Library References

Health and Environment ⚷25.7(4).
C.J.S. Health and Environment § 108 et seq.

§ 1325. National Study Commission

(a) Establishment

There is established a National Study Commission, which shall make a full and complete investigation and study of all of the technological aspects of achieving, and all aspects of the total economic, social, and environmental effects of achieving or not achieving, the effluent limitations and goals set forth for 1983 in section 1311(b)(2) of this title.

(b) Membership; chairman

Such Commission shall be composed of fifteen members, including five members of the Senate, who are members of the Environment and Public Works committee, appointed by the President of the Senate, five members of the House, who are members of the Public Works and Transportation committee, appointed by the Speaker of the House, and five members of the public appointed by the President. The Chairman of such Commission shall be elected from among its members.

(c) Contract authority

In the conduct of such study, the Commission is authorized to contract with the National Academy of Sciences and the National Academy of Engineering (acting through the National Research Council), the National Institute of Ecology, Brookings Institution, and other nongovernmental entities, for the investigation of matters within their competence.

(d) Cooperation of departments, agencies, and instrumentalities of executive branch

The heads of the departments, agencies and instrumentalities of the executive branch of the Federal Government shall cooperate with the Commission in carrying out the requirements of this section, and shall furnish to the Commission such information as the Commission deems necessary to carry out this section.

(e) Report to Congress

A report shall be submitted to the Congress of the results of such investigation and study, together with recommendations, not later than three years after October 18, 1972.

(f) Compensation and allowances

The members of the Commission who are not officers or employees of the United States, while attending conferences or meetings of the Commission or while otherwise serving at the request of the Chairman shall be entitled to receive compensation at a rate not in excess of the maximum rate of pay for Grade GS–18, as provided in the General Schedule under section 5332 of title 5, including traveltime and while away from their homes or regular places of business they may be allowed travel expenses, including per diem in lieu of subsistence as authorized by law for persons in the Government service employed intermittently.

(g) Appointment of personnel

In addition to authority to appoint personnel subject to the provisions of title 5 governing appointments in the competitive service, and to pay such personnel in accordance with the provisions of chapter 51 and subchapter III of chapter 53 of such title relating to classification and General Schedule pay rates, the Commission shall have authority to enter into contracts with private or public organizations who shall furnish the Commission with such administrative and technical personnel as may be necessary to carry out the purpose of this section. Personnel furnished by such organizations under this subsection are not, and shall not be considered to be, Federal employees for any purposes, but in the performance of their duties shall be guided by the standards which apply to employees of the legislative branches under rules 41 and 43 of the Senate and House of Representatives, respectively.

(h) Authorization of appropriation

There is authorized to be appropriated, for use in carrying out this section, not to exceed $17,250,000.

(June 30, 1948, ch. 758, title III, § 315, as added Oct. 18, 1972, Pub.L. 92–500, § 2, 86 Stat. 875, and amended Dec. 28, 1973, Pub.L. 93–207, § 1(5), 87 Stat. 906; Jan. 2, 1975, Pub.L. 93–592, § 5, 88 Stat. 1925; March 23, 1976, Pub.L. 94–238, 90 Stat. 250; H.Res. 988, Oct. 8, 1974; S.Res. 4, Feb. 4, 1977.)

Cross References

Authorization of appropriations to carry out this chapter other than this section, see section 1376 of this title.

Timetable for achievement of objectives, see section 1311 of this title.

§ 1326. Thermal discharges

(a) Effluent limitations that will assure protection and propagation of balanced, indigenous population of shellfish, fish, and wildlife

With respect to any point source otherwise subject to the provisions of section 1311 of this title or section 1316 of this title, whenever the owner or operator of any such source, after opportunity for public hearing, can demonstrate to the satisfaction of the Administrator (or, if appropriate, the State) that any effluent limitation proposed for the control of the thermal component of any discharge from such source will require effluent limitations more stringent than necessary to assure the projection[1] and propagation of a balanced, indigenous population of shellfish, fish, and wildlife in and on the body of water into which the discharge is to be made, the Administrator (or, if appropriate, the State) may impose an effluent limitation under such sections for such plant, with respect to the thermal component of such discharge (taking into account the interaction of such thermal component with other pollutants), that will assure the protection and propagation of a balanced, indigenous population of shellfish, fish, and wildlife in and on that body of water.

(b) Cooling water intake structures

Any standard established pursuant to section 1311 of this title or section 1316 of this title and applicable to a point source shall require that the location, design, construction, and capacity of cooling water intake structures reflect the best technology available for minimizing adverse environmental impact.

(c) Period of protection from more stringent effluent limitations following discharge point source modification commenced after October 18, 1972

Notwithstanding any other provision of this chapter, any point source of a discharge having a thermal component, the modification of which point source is commenced after October 18, 1972, and which, as modified, meets effluent limitations established under section 1311 of this title or, if more stringent, effluent limitations established under section 1313 of this title and which effluent limitations will assure protection and propagation of a balanced, indigenous population of shellfish, fish, and wildlife in or on the water into which the discharge is made, shall not be subject to any more stringent effluent limitation with respect to the thermal component of its discharge during a ten year period beginning on the date of completion of such modification or during the period of depreciation or amortization of such facility for the purpose of section 167 or 169 (or both) of title 26, whichever period ends first.

(June 30, 1948, ch. 758, title III, § 316, as added Oct. 18, 1972, Pub.L. 92–500, § 2, 86 Stat. 876.)

[1] So in original. Probably should be "protection".

Cross References

Water quality standards relating to heat to be consistent with requirements of this section, see section 1313 of this title.

Code of Federal Regulations

Effluent guidelines and standards, see 40 CFR 401.10 et seq.

Library References

Health and Environment ⚷25.7(12).
C.J.S. Health and Environment § 107 et seq.

§ 1327. Omitted

§ 1328. Aquaculture

(a) Authority to permit discharge of specific pollutants

The Administrator is authorized, after public hearings, to permit the discharge of a specific pollutant or pollutants under controlled conditions associated with an approved aquaculture project under Federal or State supervision pursuant to section 1342 of this title.

(b) Procedures and guidelines

The Administrator shall by regulation establish any procedures and guidelines which the Administrator deems necessary to carry out this section. Such regulations shall require the application to such discharge of each criterion, factor, procedure, and requirement applicable to a permit issued under section 1342 of this title, as the Administrator determines necessary to carry out the objective of this chapter.

(c) State administration

Each State desiring to administer its own permit program within its jurisdiction for discharge of a specific pollutant or pollutants under controlled conditions associated with an approved aquaculture project may do so if upon submission of such program the Administrator determines such program is adequate to carry out the objective of this chapter.

(June 30, 1948, ch. 758, title III, § 318, as added Oct. 18, 1972, Pub.L. 92–500, § 2, 86 Stat. 877, and amended Dec. 27, 1977, Pub.L. 95–217, § 63, 91 Stat. 1599.)

Cross References

Enforcement of provisions of this section, see section 1319 of this title.
Illegality of pollutant discharges except as in compliance with this section, see section 1311 of this title.
Permit for discharge of pollutants except as provided in this section, see section 1342 of this title.

Code of Federal Regulations

Environmental Protection Agency administered permit programs: the National Pollutant Discharge Elimination System, see 40 CFR 122.1 et seq.
State program requirements, see 40 CFR 123.1 et seq.

SUBCHAPTER IV—PERMITS AND LICENSES

Cross References

Continuing planning process, approval of State permit program, see section 1313 of this title.

§ 1341. Certification

(a) Compliance with applicable requirements; application; procedures; license suspension

(1) Any applicant for a Federal license or permit to conduct any activity including, but not limited to, the construction or operation of facilities, which may result in any discharge into the navigable waters, shall provide the licensing or permitting agency a certification from the State in which the discharge originates or will originate, or, if appropriate, from the interstate water pollution control agency having jurisdiction over the navigable waters at the point where the discharge originates or will originate, that any such discharge will comply with the applicable provisions of sections 1311, 1312, 1313, 1316, and 1317 of this title. In the case of any such activity for which there is not an applicable effluent limitation or other limitation under sections 1311(b) and 1312 of this title, and there is not an applicable standard under sections 1316 and 1317 of this title, the State shall so certify, except that any such certification shall not be deemed to satisfy section 1371(c) of this title. Such State or interstate agency shall establish procedures for public notice in the case of all applications for certification by it and, to the extent it deems appropriate, procedures for public hearings in connection with specific applications. In any case where a State or interstate agency has no authority to give such a certification, such certification shall be from the Administrator. If the State, interstate agency, or Administrator, as the case may be, fails or refuses to act on a request for certification, within a reasonable period of time (which shall not exceed one year) after receipt of such request, the certification requirements of this subsection shall be waived with respect to such Federal application. No license or permit shall be granted until the certification required by this section has been obtained or has been waived as provided in the preceding sentence. No license or permit shall be granted if certification has been denied by the State, interstate agency, or the Administrator, as the case may be.

(2) Upon receipt of such application and certification the licensing or permitting agency shall immediately notify the Administrator of such application and certification. Whenever such a discharge may affect, as determined by the Administrator, the quality of the waters of any other State, the Administrator within thirty days of the date of notice of application for such Federal license or permit shall so notify such other State, the licensing or permitting agency, and the applicant. If, within sixty days after receipt of such notification, such other State determines that such discharge will affect the quality of its waters so as to violate any water quality requirements in such State, and within such sixty-day period notifies the Administrator and the licensing or permitting agency in writing of its objection to the issuance of such license or permit and requests a public hearing on such objection, the licensing or permitting agency shall hold such a hearing. The Administrator shall at such hearing submit his evaluation and recommendations with respect to any such objection to the licensing or permitting agency. Such agency, based upon the recommendations of such State, the Administrator, and upon any additional evidence, if any, presented to the agency at the hearing, shall condition such license or permit in such manner as may be necessary to insure compliance with applicable water quality requirements. If the imposition of conditions cannot insure such compliance such agency shall not issue such license or permit.

(3) The certification obtained pursuant to paragraph (1) of this subsection with respect to the construction of any facility shall fulfill the requirements of this subsection with respect to certification in connection with any other Federal license or permit required for the operation of such facility unless, after notice to the certifying State, agency, or Administrator, as the case may be, which shall be given by the Federal agency to whom application is made for such operating license or permit, the State, or if appropriate, the interstate agency or the Administrator, notifies such agency within sixty days after receipt of such notice that there is no longer reasonable assurance that there will be compliance with the applicable provisions of sections 1311, 1312, 1313, 1316, and 1317 of this title because of changes since the construction license or permit certification was issued in (A) the construction or operation of the facility, (B) the characteristics of the waters into which such discharge is made, (C) the water quality criteria applicable to such waters or (D) applicable effluent limitations or other requirements. This paragraph shall be inapplicable in any case where the applicant for such operating license or permit has failed to provide the certifying State, or, if appropriate, the interstate agency or the Administrator, with notice of any proposed changes in the construction or operation of the facility with respect to which a construction license or permit has been granted, which changes may result in violation of section 1311, 1312, 1313, 1316, or 1317 of this title.

(4) Prior to the initial operation of any federally licensed or permitted facility or activity which may result in any discharge into the navigable waters and with respect to which a certification has been obtained pursuant to paragraph (1) of this subsection, which facility or activity is not subject to a Federal operating license or permit, the licensee or permittee shall provide an opportunity for such certifying State, or, if appropriate, the interstate agency or the Administrator to review the manner in which the facility or activity shall be operated or conducted for the purposes of assuring that applicable effluent limitations or other limitations or other applicable water quality requirements will not be violated. Upon notification by the certifying State, or if appropriate, the interstate agency or the Administrator that the operation of any such federally licensed or permitted facility or activity will violate applicable effluent limitations or other limitations or other water quality requirements such Federal agency may, after public hearing, suspend such license or permit. If such license or permit is suspended, it shall remain suspended until notification is received from the certifying State, agency, or Administrator, as the case may be, that there is reasonable assurance that such facility or activity will not violate the applicable provisions of section 1311, 1312, 1313, 1316, or 1317 of this title.

(5) Any Federal license or permit with respect to which a certification has been obtained under paragraph (1) of this subsection may be suspended or revoked by the Federal agency issuing such license or permit upon the entering of a judgment under this chapter that such facility or activity has been operated in violation of the applicable provisions of section 1311, 1312, 1313, 1316, or 1317 of this title.

(6) Except with respect to a permit issued under section 1342 of this title, in any case where actual construction of a facility has been lawfully commenced prior to April 3, 1970, no certification shall be required under this subsection for a license or permit issued after April 3, 1970, to operate such facility, except that any such license or permit issued without certification shall terminate April 3, 1973, unless prior to such termination date the person having such license or permit submits to the Federal agency which issued such license or permit a certification and otherwise meets the requirements of this section.

[(7) Redesignated (6)].

(b) Compliance with other provisions of law setting applicable water quality requirements

Nothing in this section shall be construed to limit the authority of any department or agency pursuant to any other provision of law to require compliance with any applicable water quality requirements. The Administrator shall, upon the request of any Federal department or agency, or State or interstate agency, or applicant, provide, for the purpose of this section, any relevant information on applicable effluent limitations, or other limitations, standards, regulations, or requirements, or water quality criteria, and shall, when requested by any such department or agency or State or interstate agency, or applicant, comment on any methods to comply with such limitations, standards, regulations, requirements, or criteria.

(c) Authority of Secretary of the Army to permit use of spoil disposal areas by Federal licensees or permittees

In order to implement the provisions of this section, the Secretary of the Army, acting through the Chief of Engineers, is authorized, if he deems it to be in the public interest, to permit the use of spoil disposal areas under his jurisdiction by Federal licensees or permittees, and to make an appropriate charge for such use. Moneys received from such licensees or permittees shall be deposited in the Treasury as miscellaneous receipts.

(d) Limitations and monitoring requirements of certification

Any certification provided under this section shall set forth any effluent limitations and other limitations, and monitoring requirements necessary to assure that any applicant for a Federal license or permit will comply with any applicable effluent limitations and other limitations, under section 1311 or 1312 of this title, standard of performance under section 1316 of this title, or prohibition, effluent standard, or pretreatment standard under section 1317 of this title, and with any other appropriate requirement of State law set forth in such certification, and shall become a condition on any Federal license or permit subject to the provisions of this section.

(June 30, 1948, ch. 758, title IV, § 401, as added Oct. 18, 1972, Pub.L. 92–500, § 2, 86 Stat. 877, and amended Dec. 27, 1977, Pub.L. 95–217, §§ 61(b), 64, 91 Stat. 1598, 1599.)

Cross References

Citizen suits for violation of effluent standards, see section 1365 of this title.

Licensing authority of any Federal agency under environmental policy provisions, see section 1371 of this title.

Test procedures for analysis of pollutants to include factors to be provided in any certification pursuant to this section, see section 1314 of this title.

Library References

Health and Environment ⇔25.7(13).
C.J.S. Health and Environment § 107 et seq.

§ 1342. National pollutant discharge elimination system

(a) Permits for discharge of pollutants

(1) Except as provided in sections 1328 and 1344 of this title, the Administrator may, after opportunity for public hearing issue a permit for the discharge of any pollutant, or combination of pollutants, notwithstanding section 1311(a) of this title, upon condition that such discharge will meet either all applicable requirements under sections 1311, 1312, 1316, 1317, 1318, and 1343 of this title, or prior to the taking of necessary implementing actions relating to all such requirements, such conditions as the Administrator determines are necessary to carry out the provisions of this chapter.

(2) The Administrator shall prescribe conditions for such permits to assure compliance with the requirements of paragraph (1) of this subsection, including conditions on data and information collection, reporting, and such other requirements as he deems appropriate.

(3) The permit program of the Administrator under paragraph (1) of this subsection, and permits issued thereunder, shall be subject to the same terms, conditions, and requirements as apply to a State permit program and permits issued thereunder under subsection (b) of this section.

(4) All permits for discharges into the navigable waters issued pursuant to section 407 of this title shall be deemed to be permits issued under this subchapter, and permits issued under this subchapter shall be deemed to be permits issued under section 407 of this title, and shall continue in force and effect for their term unless revoked, modified, or suspended in accordance with the provisions of this chapter.

(5) No permit for a discharge into the navigable waters shall be issued under section 407 of this title after October 18, 1972. Each application for a permit under section 407 of this title, pending on October 18, 1972, shall be deemed to be an application for a permit under this section. The Administrator shall authorize a State, which he determines has the capability of administering a permit program which will carry out the objectives of this chapter to issue permits for discharges into the navigable waters within the jurisdiction of such State. The Administrator may exercise the authority granted him by the preceding sentence only during the period which begins on October 18, 1972, and ends either on the ninetieth day after the date of the first promulgation of guidelines required by section 1314(i)(2) of this title, or the date of approval by the Administrator of a permit program for such State under subsection (b) of this section, whichever date first occurs, and no such authorization to a State shall extend beyond the last day of such period. Each such permit shall be subject to such conditions as the Administrator determines are necessary to carry out the provisions of this chapter. No such permit shall issue if the Administrator objects to such issuance.

(b) State permit programs

At any time after the promulgation of the guidelines required by subsection (i)(2) of section 1314 of this title, the Governor of each State desiring to administer its own permit program for discharges into navigable waters within its jurisdiction may submit to the Administrator a full and complete description of the program it proposes to establish and administer under State law or under an interstate compact. In addition, such State shall submit a statement from the attorney general (or the attorney for those State water pollution control agencies which have independent legal counsel), or from the chief legal officer in the case of an interstate agency, that the laws of such State, or the interstate compact, as the case may be, provide adequate authority to carry out the described program. The Administrator shall approve each submitted program unless he determines that adequate authority does not exist:

(1) To issue permits which—

(A) apply, and insure compliance with, any applicable requirements of sections 1311, 1312, 1316, 1317, and 1343 of this title;

(B) are for fixed terms not exceeding five years; and

(C) can be terminated or modified for cause including, but not limited to, the following:

(i) violation of any condition of the permit;

(ii) obtaining a permit by misrepresentation, or failure to disclose fully all relevant facts;

(iii) change in any condition that requires either a temporary or permanent reduction or elimination of the permitted discharge;

(D) control the disposal of pollutants into wells;

(2)(A) To issue permits which apply, and insure compliance with, all applicable requirements of section 1318 of this title; or

(B) To inspect, monitor, enter, and require reports to at least the same extent as required in section 1318 of this title;

(3) To insure that the public, and any other State the waters of which may be affected, receive notice of each application for a permit and to provide an opportunity for public hearing before a ruling on each such application;

(4) To insure that the Administrator receives notice of each application (including a copy thereof) for a permit;

(5) To insure that any State (other than the permitting State), whose waters may be affected by the issuance of a permit may submit written recommendations to the permitting State (and the Administrator) with respect to any permit application and, if any part of such written recommendations are not accepted by the permitting State, that the permitting State will notify such affected State (and the Administrator) in writing of its failure to so accept such recommendations together with its reasons for so doing;

(6) To insure that no permit will be issued if, in the judgment of the Secretary of the Army acting through the Chief of Engineers, after consultation with the Secretary of the department in which the Coast Guard is operating, anchorage and navigation of any of the navigable waters would be substantially impaired thereby;

(7) To abate violations of the permit or the permit program, including civil and criminal penalties and other ways and means of enforcement;

(8) To insure that any permit for a discharge from a publicly owned treatment works includes conditions to require the identification in terms of character and volume of pollutants of any significant source introducing pollutants subject to pretreatment standards under section 1317(b) of this title into such works and a program to assure compliance with such pretreatment standards by each such source, in addition to adequate notice to the permitting agency of (A) new introductions into such works of pollutants from any source which would be a new source as defined in section 1316 of this title if such source were discharging pollutants, (B) new introductions of pollutants into such works from a source which would be subject to section 1311 of this title if it were discharging such pollutants, or (C) a substantial change in volume or character of pollutants being introduced into such works by a source introducing pollutants into such works at the time of issuance of the permit. Such notice shall include information on the quality and quantity of effluent to be introduced into such treatment works and any anticipated impact of such change in the quantity or quality of effluent to be discharged from such publicly owned treatment works; and

(9) To insure that any industrial user of any publicly owned treatment works will comply with sections 1284(b), 1317, and 1318 of this title.

(c) Suspension of Federal program upon submission of State program; withdrawal of approval of State program

(1) Not later than ninety days after the date on which a State has submitted a program (or revision thereof) pursuant to subsection (b) of this section, the Administrator shall suspend the issuance of permits under subsection (a) of this section as to those navigable waters subject to such program unless he determines that the State permit program does not meet the requirements of subsection (b) of this section or does not conform to the guidelines issued under section 1314(i)(2) of this title. If the Administrator so determines, he shall notify the State of any revisions or modifications necessary to conform to such requirements or guidelines.

(2) Any State permit program under this section shall at all times be in accordance with this section and guidelines promulgated pursuant to section 1314(i)(2) of this title.

(3) Whenever the Administrator determines after public hearing that a State is not administering a program approved under this section in accordance with requirements of this section, he shall so notify the State and, if appropriate corrective action is not taken within a reasonable time, not to exceed ninety days, the Administrator shall withdraw approval of such program. The Administrator shall not withdraw approval of any such program unless he shall first have notified the State, and made public, in writing, the reasons for such withdrawal.

(d) Notification of Administrator

(1) Each State shall transmit to the Administrator a copy of each permit application received by such State and provide notice to the Administrator of every action related to the consideration of such permit application, including each permit proposed to be issued by such State.

(2) No permit shall issue (A) if the Administrator within ninety days of the date of his notification under subsection (b)(5) of this section objects in writing to the issuance of such permit, or (B) if the Administrator within ninety days of the date of transmittal of the proposed permit by the State objects in writing to the issuance of such permit as being outside the guidelines and requirements of this chapter. Whenever the Administrator objects to the issuance of a permit under this paragraph such written objection shall contain a statement of the reasons for such objection and the effluent limitations and conditions which such permit would include if it were issued by the Administrator.

(3) The Administrator may, as to any permit application, waive paragraph (2) of this subsection.

(4) In any case where, after December 27, 1977, the Administrator, pursuant to paragraph (2) of this subsection, objects to the issuance of a permit, on request of the State, a public hearing shall be held by the Administrator on such objection. If the State does not resubmit such permit revised to meet such objection within 30 days after completion of the hearing, or, if no hearing is requested within 90 days after the date of such objection, the Administrator may issue the permit pursuant to subsection (a) of this section for such source in accordance with the guidelines and requirements of this chapter.

(e) Waiver of notification requirement

In accordance with guidelines promulgated pursuant to subsection (i)(2) of section 1314 of this title, the Administrator is authorized to waive the requirements of subsection (d) of this section at the time he approves a program pursuant to subsection (b) of this section for any category (including any class, type, or size within such category) of point sources within the State submitting such program.

(f) Point source categories

The Administrator shall promulgate regulations establishing categories of point sources which he determines shall not be subject to the requirements of subsection (d) of this section in any State with a program approved pursuant to subsection (b) of this section. The Administrator may distinguish among classes, types, and sizes within any category of point sources.

(g) Other regulations for safe transportation, handling, carriage, storage, and stowage of pollutants

Any permit issued under this section for the discharge of pollutants into the navigable waters from a vessel or other floating craft shall be subject to any applicable regulations promulgated by the Secretary of the department in which the Coast Guard is operating, establishing specifications for safe transportation, handling, carriage, storage, and stowage of pollutants.

(h) Violation of permit conditions; restriction or prohibition upon introduction of pollutant by source not previously utilizing treatment works

In the event any condition of a permit for discharges from a treatment works (as defined in section 1292 of this title) which is publicly owned is violated, a State with a program approved under subsection (b) of this section or the Administrator, where no State program is approved or where the Administrator determines pursuant to section 1319(a) of this title that a State with an approved program has not commenced appropriate enforcement action with respect to such permit, may proceed in a court of competent jurisdiction to restrict or prohibit the introduction of any pollutant into such treatment works by a source not utilizing such treatment works prior to the finding that such condition was violated.

(i) Federal enforcement not limited

Nothing in this section shall be construed to limit the authority of the Administrator to take action pursuant to section 1319 of this title.

(j) Public information

A copy of each permit application and each permit issued under this section shall be available to the public. Such permit application or permit, or portion thereof, shall further be available on request for the purpose of reproduction.

(k) Compliance with permits

Compliance with a permit issued pursuant to this section shall be deemed compliance, for purposes of sections 1319 and 1365 of this title, with sections 1311, 1312, 1316, 1317, and 1343 of this title, except any standard imposed under section 1317 of this title for a toxic pollutant injurious to human health. Until December 31, 1974, in any case where a permit for discharge has been applied for pursuant to this section, but final administrative disposition of such application has not been made, such discharge shall not be a violation of (1) section 1311, 1316, or 1342 of this title, or (2) section 407 of this title, unless the Administrator or other plaintiff proves that final administrative disposition of such application has not been made because of the failure of the applicant to furnish information reasonably required or requested in order to process the application. For the 180-day period beginning on October 18, 1972, in the case of any point source discharging any pollutant or combination of pollutants immediately prior to such date which source is not subject to section 407 of this title, the discharge by such source shall not be a violation of this chapter if such a source applies for a permit for discharge pursuant to this section within such 180-day period.

(*l*) Irrigation return flows

The Administrator shall not require a permit under this section for discharges composed entirely of return flows from irrigated agriculture, nor shall the Administrator directly or indirectly, require any State to require such a permit.

(June 30, 1948, ch. 758, title IV, § 402, as added Oct. 18, 1972, Pub.L. 92–500, § 2, 86 Stat. 880, and amended Dec. 27, 1977, Pub.L. 95–217, §§ 33(c), 50, 54(c)(1), 65, 66, 91 Stat. 1577, 1588, 1591, 1599, 1600.)

Cross References

Aquaculture discharges of specific pollutants under controlled conditions, see section 1328 of this title.
Certification by owner of treatment works of compliance with permit specifications, see section 1284 of this title.
Citizen suits for violation of permit, see section 1365 of this title.
Control of specific pollutants as requirement for permit under this section, see section 1314 of this title.
Discharge of dredged or fill material not prohibited by this section, see section 1344 of this title.
Enforcement for violations of permits, see section 1319 of this title.
Establishment and maintenance of records, see section 1318 of this title.
Exclusion of discharge in compliance with permit from definition of "discharge", see section 1321 of this title.
Federal facilities pollution control, waiver of conditions, see section 1323 of this title.
Federally permitted release as meaning discharges in compliance with a permit under this section, see section 9601 of Title 42, The Public Health and Welfare.
Grants for reasonable costs of administering an approved program under this section, see section 1285 of this title.
Illegality of pollutant discharges except in compliance with this section, see section 1311 of this title.
Issuance of permits after promulgation of guidelines for determination of degradation of waters of territorial seas, see section 1343 of this title.
Necessity of permit for construction of facility lawfully commenced on certain date, see section 1341 of this title.
Permit for disposal or use of sewage sludge, see section 1345 of this title.
Permit under this section deemed major Federal action, see section 1371 of this title.
Permit under this section not to conflict with a plan approved pursuant to section 1288 of this title, see section 1288 of this title.
Public health agency coordination, see section 1373 of this title.
Review of Administrator's action in issuing or denying permit, see section 1369 of this title.
Solid or dissolved material in domestic sewage or solid or dissolved materials or industrial discharges which are point sources subject to permits under this section excluded from definition of "solid waste", see section 6903 of Title 42.
State implementation of permit programs under this section, see section 1251 of this title.

Code of Federal Regulations

Criteria and standards for National Pollutant Discharge Elimination System, see 40 CFR 125.1 et seq.
Environmental Protection Agency administered permit programs: the National Pollutant Discharge Elimination System, see 40 CFR 122.1 et seq.
General pretreatment regulations for existing and new sources of pollution, see 40 CFR 403.1 et seq.
State program requirements, see 40 CFR 123.1 et seq.

Library References

Health and Environment ⇐25.7(13).
C.J.S. Health and Environment § 107 et seq.

United States Supreme Court

Federal permits, necessity for public hearings, see Costle v. Pacific Legal Foundation, 1980, 100 S.Ct. 1095, 445 U.S. 198, 63 L.Ed.2d 329.

§ 1343. Ocean discharge criteria

(a) Issuance of permits

No permit under section 1342 of this title for a discharge into the territorial sea, the waters of the contiguous zone, or the oceans shall be issued, after promulgation of guidelines established under subsection (c) of this section, except in compliance with such guidelines. Prior to the promulgation of such guidelines, a permit may be issued under such section 1342 of this title if the Administrator determines it to be in the public interest.

(b) Waiver

The requirements of subsection (d) of section 1342 of this title may not be waived in the case of permits for discharges into the territorial sea.

(c) Guidelines for determining degradation of waters

(1) The Administrator shall, within one hundred and eighty days after October 18, 1972 (and from time to time thereafter), promulgate guidelines for determining the degradation of the waters of the territorial seas, the contiguous zone, and the oceans, which shall include:

(A) the effect of disposal of pollutants on human health or welfare, including but not limited to plankton, fish, shellfish, wildlife, shorelines, and beaches;

(B) the effect of disposal of pollutants on marine life including the transfer, concentration, and dispersal of pollutants or their byproducts through biological, physical, and chemical processes; changes in marine ecosystem diversity, productivity, and stability; and species and community population changes;

(C) the effect of disposal, of pollutants on esthetic, recreation, and economic values;

(D) the persistence and permanence of the effects of disposal of pollutants;

(E) the effect of the disposal of varying rates, of particular volumes and concentrations of pollutants;

(F) other possible locations and methods of disposal or recycling of pollutants including land-based alternatives; and

(G) the effect on alternate uses of the oceans, such as mineral exploitation and scientific study.

(2) In any event where insufficient information exists on any proposed discharge to make a reasonable judgment on any of the guidelines established pursuant to this subsection no permit shall be issued under section 1342 of this title.

(June 30, 1948, ch. 758, title IV, § 403, as added Oct. 18, 1972, Pub.L. 92–500, § 2, 86 Stat. 883.)

Cross References

Best management practices for industry, see section 1314 of this title.
Determination of State's authority to issue permits for dredged or fill material, see section 1344 of this title.
Field laboratory and research facilities, see section 1254 of this title.
Modification of effluent limitation requirements for point sources, see section 1311 of this title.
Permits for discharge of pollutants, see section 1342 of this title.
Planning process to assure compliance with this section, see section 1288 of this title.

§ 1344. Permits for dredged or fill material

(a) Discharge into navigable waters at specified disposal sites

The Secretary may issue permits, after notice and opportunity for public hearings for the discharge of dredged or fill material into the navigable waters at specified disposal sites. Not later than the fifteenth day after the date an applicant submits all the information required to complete an application for a permit under this subsection, the Secretary shall publish the notice required by this subsection.

(b) Specification for disposal sites

Subject to subsection (c) of this section, each such disposal site shall be specified for each such permit by the Secretary (1) through the application of guidelines developed by the Administrator, in conjunction with the Secretary, which guidelines shall be based upon criteria comparable to the criteria applicable to the territorial seas, the contiguous zone, and the ocean under section 1343(c) of this title, and (2) in any case where such guidelines under clause (1) alone would prohibit the specification of a site, through the application additionally of the economic impact of the site on navigation and anchorage.

(c) Denial or restriction of use of defined areas as disposal sites

The Administrator is authorized to prohibit the specification (including the withdrawal of specification) of any defined area as a disposal site, and he is authorized to deny or restrict the use of any defined area for specification (including the withdrawal of specification) as a disposal site, whenever he determines, after notice and opportunity for public hearings, that the discharge of such materials into such area will have an unacceptable adverse effect on municipal water supplies, shellfish beds and fishery areas (including spawning and breeding areas), wildlife, or recreational areas. Before making such determination, the Administrator shall consult with the Secretary. The Administrator shall set forth in writing and make public his findings and his reasons for making any determination under this subsection.

(d) "Secretary" defined

The term "Secretary" as used in this section means the Secretary of the Army, acting through the Chief of Engineers.

(e) General permits on State, regional, or nationwide basis

(1) In carrying out his functions relating to the discharge of dredged or fill material under this subsection, the Secretary may, after notice and opportunity for public hearing, issue general permits on a State, regional, or nationwide basis for any category of activities involving discharges of dredged or fill material if the Secretary determines that the activities in such category are similar in nature, will cause only minimal adverse environmental effects when performed separately, and will have only minimal cumulative adverse effect on the environment. Any general permit issued under this subsection shall (A) be based on the guidelines described in subsection (b)(1) of this section, and (B) set forth the requirements and standards which shall apply to any activity authorized by such general permit.

(2) No general permit issued under this subsection shall be for a period of more than five years after the date of its issuance and such general permit may be revoked or modified by the Secretary if, after opportunity for public hearing, the Secretary determines that the activities authorized by such general permit have an adverse impact on the environment or such activities are more appropriately authorized by individual permits.

(f) Non-prohibited discharge of dredged or fill material

(1) Except as provided in paragraph (2) of this subsection, the discharge of dredged or fill material—

(A) from normal farming, silviculture, and ranching activities such as plowing, seeding, cultivating, minor drainage, harvesting for the production of food, fiber, and forest products, or upland soil and water conservation practices;

(B) for the purpose of maintenance, including emergency reconstruction of recently damaged parts, of currently serviceable structures such as dikes, dams, levees, groins, riprap, breakwaters, causeways, and bridge abutments or approaches, and transportation structures;

(C) for the purpose of construction or maintenance of farm or stock ponds or irrigation ditches, or the maintenance of drainage ditches;

(D) for the purpose of construction of temporary sedimentation basins on a construction site which does not include placement of fill material into the navigable waters;

(E) for the purpose of construction or maintenance of farm roads or forest roads, or temporary roads for moving mining equipment, where such roads are constructed and maintained, in accordance with best management practices, to assure that flow and circulation patterns and chemical and biological characteristics of the navigable waters are not impaired, that the reach of the navigable waters is not reduced, and that any adverse effect on the aquatic environment will be otherwise minimized;

(F) resulting from any activity with respect to which a State has an approved program under section 1288(b)(4) of this title which meets the requirements of subparagraphs (B) and (C) of such section,

is not prohibited by or otherwise subject to regulation under this section or section 1311(a) oı 1342 of this title (except for effluent standards or prohibitions under section 1317 of this title).

(2) Any discharge of dredged or fill material into the navigable waters incidental to any activity having as its purpose bringing an area of the navigable waters into a use to which it was not previously subject, where the flow or circulation of navigable waters may be impaired or the reach of such waters be reduced, shall be required to have a permit under this section.

(g) State administration

(1) The Governor of any State desiring to administer its own individual and general permit program for the discharge of dredged or fill material into the navigable waters (other than those waters which are presently used, or are susceptible to use in their natural condition or by reasonable improvement as a means to transport interstate or foreign commerce shoreward to their ordinary high water mark, including all waters which are subject to the ebb and flow of the tide shoreward to their mean high water mark, or mean higher high water mark on the west coast, including wetlands adjacent thereto) within its jurisdiction may submit to the Administrator a full and complete description of the program it proposes to establish and administer under State law or under an interstate compact. In addition, such State shall submit a statement from the attorney general (or the attorney for those State agencies which have independent legal counsel), or from the chief legal officer in the case of an interstate agency, that the laws of such State, or the interstate compact, as the case may be, provide adequate authority to carry out the described program.

(2) Not later than the tenth day after the date of the receipt of the program and statement submitted by any State under paragraph (1) of this subsection, the Administrator shall provide copies of such program and statement to the Secretary and the Secretary of the Interior, acting through the Director of the United States Fish and Wildlife Service.

(3) Not later than the ninetieth day after the date of the receipt by the Administrator of the program and statement submitted by any State, under paragraph (1) of this subsection, the Secretary and the Secretary of the Interior, acting through the Director of the United States Fish and Wildlife Service, shall submit any comments with respect to such program and statement to the Administrator in writing.

(h) Determination of State's authority to issue permits under State program; approval; notification; transfers to State program

(1) Not later than the one-hundred-twentieth day after the date of the receipt by the Administrator of a program and statement submitted by any State under paragraph (1) of this subsection, the Administrator shall determine, taking into account any comments submitted by the Secretary and the Secretary of the Interior, acting through the Director of the United States Fish and Wildlife Service, pursuant to subsection (g) of this section, whether such State has the following authority with respect to the issuance of permits pursuant to such program:

(A) To issue permits which—

(i) apply, and assure compliance with, any applicable requirements of this section, including, but not limited to, the guidelines established under subsection (b)(1) of this section, and sections 1317 and 1343 of this title;

(ii) are for fixed terms not exceeding five years; and

(iii) can be terminated or modified for cause including, but not limited to, the following:

(I) violation of any condition of the permit;

(II) obtaining a permit by misrepresentation, or failure to disclose fully all relevant facts;

(III) change in any condition that requires either a temporary or permanent reduction or elimination of the permitted discharge.

(B) To issue permits which apply, and assure compliance with, all applicable requirements of section 1318 of this title, or to inspect, monitor, enter, and require reports to at least the same extent as required in section 1318 of this title.

(C) To assure that the public, and any other State the waters of which may be affected, receive notice of each application for a permit and to provide an opportunity for public hearing before a ruling on each such application.

(D) To assure that the Administrator receives notice of each application (including a copy thereof) for a permit.

(E) To assure that any State (other than the permitting State), whose waters may be affected by the issuance of a permit may submit written recommendations to the permitting State (and the Administrator) with respect to any permit application and, if any part of such written recommendations are not accepted by the permitting State, that the permitting State will notify such affected State (and the Administrator) in writing of its failure to so accept such recommendations together with its reasons for so doing.

(F) To assure that no permit will be issued if, in the judgment of the Secretary, after consultation with the Secretary of the department in which the Coast Guard is operating, anchorage and navigation of any of the navigable waters would be substantially impaired thereby.

(G) To abate violations of the permit or the permit program, including civil and criminal penalties and other ways and means of enforcement.

(H) To assure continued coordination with Federal and Federal-State water-related planning and review processes.

(2) If, with respect to a State program submitted under subsection (g)(1) of this section, the Administrator determines that such State—

(A) has the authority set forth in paragraph (1) of this subsection, the Administrator shall approve the program and so notify (i) such State and (ii) the Secretary, who upon subsequent notification from such State that it is administering such program, shall suspend the issuance of permits under subsections (a) and (e) of this section for activities with respect to which a permit may be issued pursuant to such State program; or

(B) does not have the authority set forth in paragraph (1) of this subsection, the Administrator shall so notify such State, which notification shall also describe the revisions or modifications necessary so that such State may resubmit such program for a determination by the Administrator under this subsection.

(3) If the Administrator fails to make a determination with respect to any program submitted by a State under subsection (g)(1) of this section within one-hundred-twenty days after the date of the receipt of such program, such program shall be deemed approved pursuant to paragraph (2)(A) of this subsection and the Administrator shall so notify such State and the Secretary who, upon subsequent notification from such State that it is administering such program, shall suspend the issuance of permits under subsection (a) and (e) of this section for activities with respect to which a permit may be issued by such State.

(4) After the Secretary receives notification from the Administrator under paragraph (2) or (3) of this subsection that a State permit program has been approved, the Secretary shall transfer any applications for permits pending before the Secretary for activities with respect to which a permit may be issued pursuant to such State program to such State for appropriate action.

(5) Upon notification from a State with a permit program approved under this subsection that such State intends to administer and enforce the terms and conditions of a general permit issued by the Secretary under subsection (e) of this section with respect to activities in such State to which such general permit applies, the Secretary shall suspend the administration and enforcement of such general permit with respect to such activities.

(i) Withdrawal of approval

Whenever the Administrator determines after public hearing that a State is not administering a program approved under subsection (h)(2)(A) of this section, in accordance with this section, including, but not limited to, the guidelines established under subsection (b)(1) of this section, the Administrator shall so notify the State, and, if appropriate corrective action is not taken within a reasonable time, not to exceed ninety days after the date of the receipt of such notification, the Administrator shall (1) withdraw approval of such program until the Administrator determines such corrective action has been taken, and (2) notify the Secretary that the Secretary shall resume the program for the issuance of permits under subsections (a) and (e) of this section for activities with respect to which the State was issuing permits and that such authority of the Secretary shall continue in effect until such time as the Administrator makes the determination described in clause (1) of this subsection and such State again has an approved program.

(j) Copies of applications for State permits and proposed general permits to be transmitted to Administrator

Each State which is administering a permit program pursuant to this section shall transmit to the Administrator (1) a copy of each permit application received by such State and provide notice to the Administrator of every action related to the consideration of such permit application, including each permit proposed to be issued by such State, and (2) a copy of each proposed general permit which such State intends to issue. Not later than the tenth day after the date of the receipt of such permit application or such proposed general permit, the Administrator shall provide copies of such permit application or such proposed general permit to the Secretary and the Secretary of the Interior, acting through the Director of the United States Fish and Wildlife Service. If the Administrator intends to provide written comments to such State with respect to such permit application or such proposed general permit, he shall so notify such State not later than the thirtieth day after the date of the receipt of such application or such proposed general permit and provide such written comments to such State, after consideration of any comments made in writing with respect to such application or such proposed general permit by the Secretary and the Secretary of the Interior, acting through the Director of the United States Fish and Wildlife Service, not later than the ninetieth day after the date of such receipt. If such State is so notified by the Administrator, it shall not issue the proposed permit until after the receipt of such comments from the Administrator, or after such ninetieth day, whichever first occurs. Such State shall not issue such proposed permit after such ninetieth day if it has received such written comments in which the Administrator objects (A) to the issuance of such proposed permit and such proposed permit is one that has been submitted to the Administrator pursuant to subsection (h)(1)(E) of this section, or (B) to the issuance of such proposed permit as being outside the requirements of this section, including, but not limited to, the guidelines developed under subsection (b)(1) of this section unless it modifies such proposed permit in accordance with such comments. Whenever the Administrator objects to the issuance of a permit under the preceding sentence such written objection shall contain a statement of the reasons for such objection and the conditions which such permit would include if it were issued by the Administrator. In any case where the Administrator objects to the issuance of a permit, on request of the State, a public hearing shall be held by the Administrator on such objection. If the State does not resubmit such permit revised to meet such objection within 30 days after completion of the hearing or, if no hearing is requested within 90 days after the date of such objection, the Secretary may issue the permit pursuant to subsection (a) or (e) of this section, as the case may be, for such source in accordance with the guidelines and requirements of this chapter.

(k) Waiver

In accordance with guidelines promulgated pursuant to subsection (i)(2) of section 1314 of this title, the Administrator is authorized to waive the requirements of subsection (j) of this section at the time of the approval of a program pursuant to subsection (h)(2)(A) of this section for any category (including any class, type, or size within such category) of discharge within the State submitting such program.

(*l*) Categories of discharges not subject to requirements

The Administrator shall promulgate regulations establishing categories of discharges which he determines shall not be subject to the requirements of subsection (j) of this section in any State with a program approved pursuant to subsection (h)(2)(A) of this section. The Administrator may distinguish among classes, types, and sizes within any category of discharges.

(m) Comments on permit applications or proposed general permits by Secretary of the Interior acting through Director of United States Fish and Wildlife Service

Not later than the ninetieth day after the date on which the Secretary notifies the Secretary of the Interior, acting through the Director of the United States Fish and Wildlife Service that (1) an application for a permit under subsection (a) of this section has been received by the Secretary, or (2) the Secretary proposes to issue a general permit under subsection (e) of this section, the Secretary of the Interior, acting through the Director of the United States Fish and Wildlife Service, shall submit any comments with respect to such application or such proposed general permit in writing to the Secretary.

(n) Enforcement authority not limited

Nothing in this section shall be construed to limit the authority of the Administrator to take action pursuant to section 1319 of this title.

(*o*) Public availability of permits and permit applications

A copy of each permit application and each permit issued under this section shall be available to the public. Such permit application or portion thereof, shall further be available on request for the purpose of reproduction.

(p) Compliance

Compliance with a permit issued pursuant to this section, including any activity carried out pursuant to a general permit issued under this section, shall be deemed compliance, for purposes of sections 1319 and 1365 of this title, with sections 1311, 1317, and 1343 of this title.

(q) Minimization of duplication, needless paperwork, and delays in issuance; agreements

Not later than the one-hundred-eightieth day after December 27, 1977, the Secretary shall enter into agreements with the Administrator, the Secretaries of the Departments of Agriculture, Commerce, Interior, and Transportation, and the heads of other appropriate Federal agencies to minimize, to the maximum extent practicable, duplication, needless paperwork, and delays in the issuance of permits under this section. Such agreements shall be developed to assure that, to the maximum extent practicable, a decision with respect to an application for a permit under subsection (a) of this section will be made not later than the ninetieth day after the date the notice for such application is published under subsection (a) of this section.

(r) Federal projects specifically authorized by Congress

The discharge of dredged or fill material as part of the construction of a Federal project specifically authorized by Congress, whether prior to or on or after December 27, 1977, is not prohibited by or otherwise subject to regulation under this section, or a State program approved under this section, or section 1311(a) or 1342 of this title (except for effluent standards or prohibitions under section 1317 of this title), if information on the effects of such discharge, including consideration of the guidelines developed under subsection (b)(1) of this section, is included in an environmental impact statement for such project pursuant to the National Environmental Policy Act of 1969 [42 U.S.C. 4321 et seq.] and such environmental impact statement has been submitted to Congress before the actual discharge of dredged or fill material in connection with the construction of such project and prior to either authorization of such project or an appropriation of funds for such construction.

(s) Violation of permits

(1) Whenever on the basis of any information available to him the Secretary finds that any person is in violation of any condition or limitation set forth in a permit issued by the Secretary under this section, the Secretary shall issue an order requiring such person to comply with such condition or limitation, or the Secretary shall bring a civil action in accordance with paragraph (3) of this subsection.

(2) A copy of any order issued under this subsection shall be sent immediately by the Secretary to the State in which the violation occurs and other affected States. Any order issued under this subsection shall be by personal service and shall state with reasonable specificity the nature of the violation, specify a time for compliance, not to exceed thirty days, which the Secretary determines is reasonable, taking into account the seriousness of the violation and any good faith efforts to comply with applicable requirements. In any case in which an order under this subsection is issued to a corporation, a copy of such order shall be served on any appropriate corporate officers.

(3) The Secretary is authorized to commence a civil action for appropriate relief, including a permanent or temporary injunction for any violation for which he is authorized to issue a compliance order under paragraph (1) of this subsection. Any action under this paragraph may be brought in the district court of the United States for the district in which the defendant is located or resides or is doing business, and such court shall have jurisdiction to restrain such violation and to require compliance. Notice of the commencement of such acton[1] shall be given immediately to the appropriate State.

(4)(A) Any person who willfully or negligently violates any condition or limitation in a permit issued by the Secretary under this section shall be punished by a fine of not less than $2,500 nor more than $25,000 per day of violation, or by imprisonment for not more than one year, or by both. If the conviction is for a violation committed after a first conviction of such person under this paragraph, punishment shall be by a fine of not more than $50,000 per day of violation, or by imprisonment for not more than two years, or by both.

(B) For the purposes of this paragraph, the term "person" shall mean, in addition to the definition contained in section 1362(5) of this title, any responsible corporate officer.

(5) Any person who violates any condition or limitation in a permit issued by the Secretary under this section, and any person who violates any order issued by the Secretary under paragraph (1) of this subsection, shall be subject to a civil penalty not to exceed $10,000 per day of such violation.

(t) Navigable waters within State jurisdiction

Nothing in this section shall preclude or deny the right of any State or interstate agency to control the discharge of dredged or fill material in any portion of the navigable waters within the jurisdiction of such State, including any activity of any Federal agency, and each such agency shall comply with such State or interstate requirements both substantive and procedural to control the discharge of dredged or fill material to the same extent that any person is subject to such requirements. This section shall not be construed as affecting or impairing the authority of the Secretary to maintain navigation.

(June 30, 1948, ch. 758, title IV, § 404, as added Oct. 18, 1972, Pub.L. 92–500, § 2, 86 Stat. 884, and amended Dec. 27, 1977, Pub.L. 95–217, § 67(a), (b), 91 Stat. 1600.)

1 So in original. Probably should read "action".

Cross References

Areawide waste treatment management, compliance with guidelines established under this section, see section 1288 of this title.
Definition of "federally permitted release", see section 9601 of Title 42, The Public Health and Welfare.
Enforcement of permit provisions, see section 1319 of this title.
Grant to State for reasonable cost of administering an approved program under this section, see section 1285 of this title.
Illegality of pollutant discharges except as in compliance with this section, see section 1311 of this title.
Permits for discharge of pollutants, see section 1342 of this title.
Records and reports, see section 1318 of this title.
State management of permit program, see section 1254 of this title.

Code of Federal Regulations

Enforcement, supervision and inspection, see 33 CFR 326.1 et seq.
General regulatory policies, see 33 CFR 320.1 et seq.
Nationwide permits, see 33 CFR 330.1 et seq.
Permits for discharges of dredged or fill material into waters of the United States, see 33 CFR 323.1 et seq.
Procedures applicable to dredged and fill material, see 40 CFR 230.1 et seq., 231.1 et seq.
Processing of Department of the Army permits, see 33 CFR 325.1 et seq.
Public hearings, see 33 CFR 327.1 et seq.
State program transfer regulations, see 40 CFR 233.1 et seq.

Library References

Health and Environment ⚷25.7(13).
C.J.S. Health and Environment § 107 et seq.

§ 1345. Disposal or use of sewage sludge

(a) Permit

Notwithstanding any other provision of this chapter or of any other law, in any case where the disposal of sewage sludge resulting from the operation of a treatment works as defined in section 1292 of this title (including the removal of in-place sewage sludge from one location and its deposit at another location) would result in any pollutant from such sewage sludge entering the navigable waters, such disposal is prohibited except in accordance with a permit issued by the Administrator under section 1342 of this title.

(b) Issuance of permit; regulations

The Administrator shall issue regulations governing the issuance of permits for the disposal of sewage sludge subject to subsection (a) of this section and section 1342 of this title. Such regulations shall require the application to such disposal of each criterion, factor, procedure, and requirement applicable to a permit issued under section 1342 of this title.

(c) State permit program

Each State desiring to administer its own permit program for disposal of sewage sludge subject to subsection (a) of this section within its jurisdiction may do so in accordance with section 1342 of this title.

(d) Regulations providing guidelines

The Administrator, after consultation with appropriate Federal and State agencies and other interested persons, shall develop and publish, within one year after December 27, 1977, and from time to time thereafter, regulations providing guidelines for the disposal of sludge and the utilization of sludge for various purposes. Such regulations shall—

(1) identify uses for sludge, including disposal;

(2) specify factors to be taken into account in determining the measures and practices applicable to each such use or disposal (including publication of information on costs);

(3) identify concentrations of pollutants which interfere with each such use or disposal.

The Administrator is authorized to revise any regulation issued under this subsection.

(e) Local determination; compliance with guidelines

The determination of the manner of disposal or use of sludge is a local determination except that it shall be unlawful for the owner or operator of any publicly owned treatment works to dispose of sludge from such works for any use for which guidelines have been established pursuant to subsection (d) of this section, except in accordance with such guidelines.

(June 30, 1948, ch. 758, title IV, § 405, as added Oct. 18, 1972, Pub.L. 92–500, § 2, 86 Stat. 884, and amended Dec. 27, 1977, Pub.L. 95–217, §§ 54(d), 68, 91 Stat. 1591, 1606.)

Cross References

Enforcement provisions, see section 1319 of this title.
Pretreatment standards, see section 1317 of this title.

Code of Federal Regulations

Classification of solid waste disposal facilities and practices, see 40 CFR 257.1 et seq.

Environmental Protection Agency administered permit programs: the National Pollutant Discharge Elimination System, see 40 CFR 122.1 et seq.
General pretreatment regulations for existing and new sources of pollution, see 40 CFR 403.1 et seq.
State program requirements, see 40 CFR 123.1 et seq.

Library References

Health and Environment ⇐25.7(13).
C.J.S. Health and Environment § 107 et seq.

SUBCHAPTER V—GENERAL PROVISIONS

§ 1361. Administration

(a) Authority of Administrator to prescribe regulations

The Administrator is authorized to prescribe such regulations as are necessary to carry out his functions under this chapter.

(b) Utilization of other agency officers and employees

The Administrator, with the consent of the head of any other agency of the United States, may utilize such officers and employees of such agency as may be found necessary to assist in carrying out the purposes of this chapter.

(c) Recordkeeping

Each recipient of financial assistance under this chapter shall keep such records as the Administrator shall prescribe, including records which fully disclose the amount and disposition by such recipient of the proceeds of such assistance, the total cost of the project or undertaking in connection with which such assistance is given or used, and the amount of that portion of the cost of the project or undertaking supplied by other sources, and such other records as will facilitate effective audit.

(d) Audit

The Administrator and the Comptroller General of the United States, or any of their duly authorized representatives, shall have access, for the purpose of audit and examination, to any books, documents, papers, and records of the recipients that are pertinent to the grants received under this chapter.

(e) Awards for outstanding technological achievement or innovative processes, methods, or devices in waste treatment and pollution abatement programs

(1) It is the purpose of this subsection to authorize a program which will provide official recognition by the United States Government to those industrial organizations and political subdivisions of States which during the preceding year demonstrated an outstanding technological achievement or an innovative process, method, or device in their waste treatment and pollution abatement programs. The Administrator shall, in consultation with the appropriate State water pollution control agencies, establish regulations under which such recognition may be applied for and granted, except that no applicant shall be eligible for an award under this subsection if such applicant is not in total compliance with all applicable water quality requirements under this chapter, or otherwise does not have a satisfactory record with respect to environmental quality.

(2) The Administrator shall award a certificate or plaque of suitable design to each industrial organization or political subdivision which qualifies for such recognition under regulations established under this subsection.

(3) The President of the United States, the Governor of the appropriate State, the Speaker of the House of Representatives, and the President pro tempore of the Senate shall be notified of the award by the Administrator and the awarding of such recognition shall be published in the Federal Register.

(f) Detail of Environmental Protection Agency personnel to State water pollution control agencies

Upon the request of a State water pollution control agency, personnel of the Environmental Protection Agency may be detailed to such agency for the purpose of carrying out the provisions of this chapter.

(June 30, 1948, ch. 758, title V, § 501, as added Oct. 18, 1972, Pub.L. 92–500, § 2, 86 Stat. 885.)

Code of Federal Regulations

Civil penalties for violation of oil pollution prevention regulations, see 40 CFR 114.1 et seq.
Criteria and standards for the National Pollutant Discharge Elimination System, see 40 CFR 125.1 et seq.
Designation of substances, reportable quantities, and notification requirements for release of substances, see 40 CFR 302.1 et seq.
Effluent guidelines and standards, see 40 CFR Chap. I, Subchap. N.
Guidelines establishing test procedures for analysis of pollutants, see 40 CFR 136.1 et seq.
Guidelines for specification of disposal sites for dredged or fill material, see 40 CFR 230.1 et seq.
Judicial review under Environmental Protection Agency administered statutes, see 40 CFR 23.1 et seq.
Oil pollution prevention, see 40 CFR 112.1 et seq.
Public information, see 40 CFR 2.100 et seq.
Secondary treatment regulation, see 40 CFR 133.100 et seq.
State and local assistance, see 40 CFR 35.001 et seq.
Toxic pollutant effluent standards, see 40 CFR 129.1 et seq.

Library References

Health and Environment ⇐25.7(3).
C.J.S. Health and Environment § 106.

§ 1362. Definitions

Except as otherwise specifically provided, when used in this chapter:

(1) The term "State water pollution control agency" means the State agency designated by the Gov-

ernor having responsibility for enforcing State laws relating to the abatement of pollution.

(2) The term "interstate agency" means an agency of two or more States established by or pursuant to an agreement or compact approved by the Congress, or any other agency of two or more States, having substantial powers or duties pertaining to the control of pollution as determined and approved by the Administrator.

(3) The term "State" means a State, the District of Columbia, the Commonwealth of Puerto Rico, the Virgin Islands, Guam, American Samoa, and the Trust Territory of the Pacific Islands.

(4) The term "municipality" means a city, town, borough, county, parish, district, association, or other public body created by or pursuant to State law and having jurisdiction over disposal of sewage, industrial wastes, or other wastes, or an Indian tribe or an authorized Indian tribal organization, or a designated and approved management agency under section 1288 of this title.

(5) The term "person" means an individual, corporation, partnership, association, State, municipality, commission, or political subdivision of a State, or any interstate body.

(6) The term "pollutant" means dredged spoil, solid waste, incinerator residue, sewage, garbage, sewage sludge, munitions, chemical wastes, biological materials, radioactive materials, heat, wrecked or discarded equipment, rock, sand, cellar dirt and industrial, municipal, and agricultural waste discharged into water. This term does not mean (A) "sewage from vessels" within the meaning of section 1322 of this title; or (B) water, gas, or other material which is injected into a well to facilitate production of oil or gas, or water derived in association with oil or gas production and disposed of in a well, if the well used either to facilitate production or for disposal purposes is approved by authority of the State in which the well is located, and if such State determines that such injection or disposal will not result in the degradation of ground or surface water resources.

(7) The term "navigable waters" means the waters of the United States, including the territorial seas.

(8) The term "territorial seas" means the belt of the seas measured from the line of ordinary low water along that portion of the coast which is in direct contact with the open sea and the line marking the seaward limit of inland waters, and extending seaward a distance of three miles.

(9) The term "contiguous zone" means the entire zone established or to be established by the United States under article 24 of the Convention of the Territorial Sea and the Contiguous Zone.

(10) The term "ocean" means any portion of the high seas beyond the contiguous zone.

(11) The term "effluent limitation" means any restriction established by a State or the Administrator on quantities, rates, and concentrations of chemical, physical, biological, and other constituents which are discharged from point sources into navigable waters, the waters of the contiguous zone, or the ocean, including schedules of compliance.

(12) The term "discharge of a pollutant" and the term "discharge of pollutants" each means (A) any addition of any pollutant to navigable waters from any point source, (B) any addition of any pollutant to the waters of the contiguous zone or the ocean from any point source other than a vessel or other floating craft.

(13) The term "toxic pollutant" means those pollutants, or combinations of pollutants, including disease-causing agents, which after discharge and upon exposure, ingestion, inhalation or assimilation into any organism, either directly from the environment or indirectly by ingestion through food chains, will, on the basis of information available to the Administrator, cause death, disease, behavioral abnormalities, cancer, genetic mutations, physiological malfunctions (including malfunctions in reproduction) or physical deformations, in such organisms or their offspring.

(14) The term "point source" means any discernible, confined and discrete conveyance, including but not limited to any pipe, ditch, channel, tunnel, conduit, well, discrete fissure, container, rolling stock, concentrated animal feeding operation, or vessel or other floating craft, from which pollutants are or may be discharged. This term does not include return flows from irrigated agriculture.

(15) The term "biological monitoring" shall mean the determination of the effects on aquatic life, including accumulation of pollutants in tissue, in receiving waters due to the discharge of pollutants (A) by techniques and procedures, including sampling of organisms representative of appropriate levels of the food chain appropriate to the volume and the physical, chemical, and biological characteristics of the effluent, and (B) at appropriate frequencies and locations.

(16) The term "discharge" when used without qualification includes a discharge of a pollutant, and a discharge of pollutants.

(17) The term "schedule of compliance" means a schedule of remedial measures including an enforceable sequence of actions or operations leading to compliance with an effluent limitation, other limitation, prohibition, or standard.

(18) The term "industrial user" means those industries identified in the Standard Industrial Classi-

fication Manual, Bureau of the Budget, 1967, as amended and supplemented, under the category of "Division D—Manufacturing" and such other classes of significant waste producers as, by regulation, the Administrator deems appropriate.

(19) The term "pollution" means the man-made or man-induced alteration of the chemical, physical, biological, and radiological integrity of water.

(June 30, 1948, ch. 758, title V, § 502, as added Oct. 18, 1972, Pub.L. 92–500, § 2, 86 Stat. 886, and amended Dec. 27, 1977, Pub.L. 95–217, § 33(b), 91 Stat. 1577.)

Cross References

Definition of "person" for purposes of—
Criminal penalties, see section 1319 of this title.
Violation of permits, see section 1344 of this title.
Definition of "territorial sea" and "contiguous zone" see section 9601 of Title 42, The Public Health and Welfare.
Ocean thermal energy conversion facility or plantship not deemed vessel for purposes of this section, see section 9117 of Title 42.
State certifying authority, amortization of pollution control facilities, see section 169 of Title 26, Internal Revenue Code.
Vessel or other floating craft engaged in commercial recovery or exploration as vessel under this section, see section 1419 of Title 30, Mineral Lands and Mining.

§ 1363. Water Pollution Control Advisory Board

(a) Establishment; composition; terms of office

(1) There is hereby established in the Environmental Protection Agency a Water Pollution Control Advisory Board, composed of the Administrator or his designee, who shall be Chairman, and nine members appointed by the President, none of whom shall be Federal officers or employees. The appointed members, having due regard for the purposes of this chapter, shall be selected from among representatives of various State, interstate, and local governmental agencies, of public or private interests contributing to, affected by, or concerned with pollution, and of other public and private agencies, organizations, or groups demonstrating an active interest in the field of pollution prevention and control, as well as other individuals who are expert in this field.

(2)(A) Each member appointed by the President shall hold office for a term of three years, except that (i) any member appointed to fill a vacancy occurring prior to the expiration of the term for which his predecessor was appointed shall be appointed for the remainder of such term, and (ii) the terms of office of the members first taking office after June 30, 1956, shall expire as follows: three at the end of one year after such date, three at the end of two years after such date, and three at the end of three years after such date, as designated by the President at the time of appointment, and (iii) the term of any member under the preceding provisions shall be extended until the date on which his successor's appointment is effective. None of the members appointed by the President shall be eligible for reappointment within one year after the end of his preceding term.

(B) The members of the Board who are not officers or employees of the United States, while attending conferences or meetings of the Board or while serving at the request of the Administrator, shall be entitled to receive compensation at a rate to be fixed by the Administrator, but not exceeding $100 per diem, including travel-time, and while away from their homes or regular places of business they may be allowed travel expenses, including per diem in lieu of subsistence, as authorized by law for persons in the Government service employed intermittently.

(b) Functions

The Board shall advise, consult with, and make recommendations to the Administrator on matters of policy relating to the activities and functions of the Administrator under this chapter.

(c) Clerical and technical assistance

Such clerical and technical assistance as may be necessary to discharge the duties of the Board shall be provided from the personnel of the Environmental Protection Agency.

(June 30, 1948, ch. 758, title V, § 503, as added Oct. 18, 1972, Pub.L. 92–500, § 2, 86 Stat. 887.)

Library References

Health and Environment ⚷25.7(3).
C.J.S. Health and Environment § 106.

§ 1364. Emergency powers

(a) Emergency powers

Notwithstanding any other provision of this chapter, the Administrator upon receipt of evidence that a pollution source or combination of sources is presenting an imminent and substantial endangerment to the health of persons or to the welfare of persons where such endangerment is to the livelihood of such persons, such as inability to market shellfish, may bring suit on behalf of the United States in the appropriate district court to immediately restrain any person causing or contributing to the alleged pollution to stop the discharge of pollutants causing or contributing to such pollution or to take such other action as may be necessary.

(b) Repealed. Pub.L. 96–510, title III, § 304(a), Dec. 11, 1980, 94 Stat. 2809

(June 30, 1948, ch. 758, title V, § 504, as added Oct. 18, 1972, Pub.L. 92–500, § 2, 86 Stat. 888, and amended Dec. 27, 1977, Pub.L. 95–217, § 69, 91 Stat. 1607; Dec. 11, 1980, Pub.L. 96–510, title III, § 304(a), 94 Stat. 2809.)

Cross References

Guidelines for using imminent hazard, enforcement, and emergency response authorities, see section 9606 of Title 42, The Public Health and Welfare.

Prohibition of grants to states not providing as part of their program authority comparable to that in this section, see section 1256 of this title.

Records and reports, see section 1318 of this title.

Transfer of funds appropriated under this section, see section 9654 of Title 42, The Public Health and Welfare.

§ 1365. Citizen suits

(a) Authorization; jurisdiction

Except as provided in subsection (b) of this section, any citizen may commence a civil action on his own behalf—

(1) against any person (including (i) the United States, and (ii) any other governmental instrumentality or agency to the extent permitted by the eleventh amendment to the Constitution) who is alleged to be in violation of (A) an effluent standard or limitation under this chapter or (B) an order issued by the Administrator or a State with respect to such a standard or limitation, or

(2) against the Administrator where there is alleged a failure of the Administrator to perform any act or duty under this chapter which is not discretionary with the Administrator.

The district courts shall have jurisdiction, without regard to the amount in controversy or the citizenship of the parties, to enforce such an effluent standard or limitation, or such an order, or to order the Administrator to perform such act or duty, as the case may be, and to apply any appropriate civil penalties under section 1319(d) of this title.

(b) Notice

No action may be commenced—

(1) under subsection (a)(1) of this section—

(A) prior to sixty days after the plaintiff has given notice of the alleged violation (i) to the Administrator, (ii) to the State in which the alleged violation occurs, and (iii) to any alleged violator of the standard, limitation, or order, or

(B) if the Administrator or State has commenced and is diligently prosecuting a civil or criminal action in a court of the United States, or a State to require compliance with the standard, limitation, or order, but in any such action in a court of the United States any citizen may intervene as a matter of right.

(2) under subsection (a)(2) of this section prior to sixty days after the plaintiff has given notice of such action to the Administrator,

except that such action may be brought immediately after such notification in the case of an action under this section respecting a violation of sections 1316 and 1317(a) of this title. Notice under this subsection shall be given in such manner as the Administrator shall prescribe by regulation.

(c) Venue; intervention by Administrator

(1) Any action respecting a violation by a discharge source of an effluent standard or limitation or an order respecting such standard or limitation may be brought under this section only in the judicial district in which such source is located.

(2) In such action under this section, the Administrator, if not a party, may intervene as a matter of right.

(d) Litigation costs

The court, in issuing any final order in any action brought pursuant to this section, may award costs of litigation (including reasonable attorney and expert witness fees) to any party, whenever the court determines such award is appropriate. The court may, if a temporary restraining order or preliminary injunction is sought, require the filing of a bond or equivalent security in accordance with the Federal Rules of Civil Procedure.

(e) Statutory or common law rights not restricted

Nothing in this section shall restrict any right which any person (or class of persons) may have under any statute or common law to seek enforcement of any effluent standard or limitation or to seek any other relief (including relief against the Administrator or a State agency).

(f) Effluent standard or limitation

For purposes of this section, the term "effluent standard or limitation under this chapter" means (1) effective July 1, 1973, an unlawful act under subsection (a) of section 1311 of this title, (2) an effluent limitation or other limitation under section 1311 or 1312 of this title; (3) standard of performance under section 1316 of this title; (4) prohibition, effluent standard or pretreatment standards under section 1317 of this title; (5) certification under section 1341 of this title; or (6) a permit or condition thereof issued under section 1342 of this title, which is in effect under this chapter (including a requirement applicable by reason of section 1323 of this title).

(g) Citizen

For the purposes of this section the term "citizen" means a person or persons having an interest which is or may be adversely affected.

(h) Civil action by State Governors

A Governor of a State may commence a civil action under subsection (a) of this section, without regard to the limitations of subsection (b) of this section, against the Administrator where there is alleged a failure of the Administrator to enforce an effluent standard or limitation under this chapter the violation of which is occurring in another State and is causing an adverse effect on the public health or welfare in his State, or is causing a violation of any water quality requirement in his State.

(June 30, 1948, ch. 758, title V, § 505, as added Oct. 18, 1972, Pub.L. 92–500, § 2, 86 Stat. 888.)

Cross References

Compliance with permit as compliance, for purposes of this section, with other provisions of this chapter, see sections 1342 and 1344 of this title.

Code of Federal Regulations

Notice prior to suit, see 40 CFR 135.1 et seq.

United States Supreme Court

Law governing, action by state in federal court alleging public nuisance by water pollution, see Illinois v. City of Milwaukee, 1972, 92 S.Ct. 1385, 406 U.S. 91, 31 L.Ed.2d 712.

§ 1366. Appearance

The Administrator shall request the Attorney General to appear and represent the United States in any civil or criminal action instituted under this chapter to which the Administrator is a party. Unless the Attorney General notifies the Administrator within a reasonable time, that he will appear in a civil action, attorneys who are officers or employees of the Environmental Protection Agency shall appear and represent the United States in such action.

(June 30, 1948, ch. 758, title V, § 506, as added Oct. 18, 1972, Pub.L. 92–500, § 2, 86 Stat. 889.)

Library References

Attorney General ⚷6.
C.J.S. Attorney General § 7 et seq.

§ 1367. Employee protection

(a) Discrimination against persons filing, instituting, or testifying in proceedings under this chapter prohibited

No person shall fire, or in any other way discriminate against, or cause to be fired or discriminated against, any employee or any authorized representative of employees by reason of the fact that such employee or representative has filed, instituted, or caused to be filed or instituted any proceeding under this chapter, or has testified or is about to testify in any proceeding resulting from the administration or enforcement of the provisions of this chapter.

(b) Application for review; investigation; hearing; review

Any employee or a representative of employees who believes that he has been fired or otherwise discriminated against by any person in violation of subsection (a) of this section may, within thirty days after such alleged violation occurs, apply to the Secretary of Labor for a review of such firing or alleged discrimination. A copy of the application shall be sent to such person who shall be the respondent. Upon receipt of such application, the Secretary of Labor shall cause such investigation to be made as he deems appropriate. Such investigation shall provide an opportunity for a public hearing at the request of any party to such review to enable the parties to present information relating to such alleged violation. The parties shall be given written notice of the time and place of the hearing at least five days prior to the hearing. Any such hearing shall be of record and shall be subject to section 554 of title 5. Upon receiving the report of such investigation, the Secretary of Labor shall make findings of fact. If he finds that such violation did occur, he shall issue a decision, incorporating an order therein and his findings, requiring the party committing such violation to take such affirmative action to abate the violation as the Secretary of Labor deems appropriate, including, but not limited to, the rehiring or reinstatement of the employee or representative of employees to his former position with compensation. If he finds that there was no such violation, he shall issue an order denying the application. Such order issued by the Secretary of Labor under this subparagraph shall be subject to judicial review in the same manner as orders and decisions of the Administrator are subject to judicial review under this chapter.

(c) Costs and expenses

Whenever an order is issued under this section to abate such violation, at the request of the applicant, a sum equal to the aggregate amount of all costs and expenses (including the attorney's fees), as determined by the Secretary of Labor, to have been reasonably incurred by the applicant for, or in connection with, the institution and prosecution of such proceedings, shall be assessed against the person committing such violation.

(d) Deliberate violations by employee acting without direction from his employer or his agent

This section shall have no application to any employee who, acting without direction from his employer (or his agent) deliberately violates any prohibition of effluent limitation or other limitation under section 1311 or 1312 of this title, standards of performance under section 1316 of this title, effluent standard, prohibition or pretreatment standard under section 1317 of this title, or any other prohibition or limitation established under this chapter.

(e) Investigations of employment reductions

The Administrator shall conduct continuing evaluations of potential loss or shifts of employment which may result from the issuance of any effluent limitation or order under this chapter, including, where appropriate, investigating threatened plant closures or reductions in employment allegedly resulting from such limitation or order. Any employee who is discharged or laid-off, threatened with discharge or lay-off, or otherwise discriminated against by any person because of the alleged results of any effluent limitation or order issued under this chapter, or any representative of such employee, may request the Administrator to conduct a full investigation of the matter. The Administrator shall thereupon investigate the matter and, at the request of any party, shall hold public hearings on not less than five days notice, and shall at such hearings require the parties, including the employer involved, to present information relating to the actual or potential effect of such limitation or order on employment and on any alleged discharge, lay-off, or other discrimination and the detailed reasons or justification therefor. Any such hearing shall be of record and shall be subject to section 554 of title 5. Upon receiving the report of such investigation, the Administrator shall make findings of fact as to the effect of such effluent limitation or order on employment and on the alleged discharge, lay-off, or discrimination and shall make such recommendations as he deems appropriate. Such report, findings, and recommendations shall be available to the public. Nothing in this subsection shall be construed to require or authorize the Administrator to modify or withdraw any effluent limitation or order issued under this chapter.

(June 30, 1948, ch. 758, title V, § 507, as added Oct. 18, 1972, Pub.L. 92–500, § 2, 86 Stat. 890.)

Cross References

Subpoena for carrying out this section, see section 1369 of this title.

Code of Federal Regulations

Complaint procedures, see 29 CFR 24.1 et seq.
Employee protection hearings, see 40 CFR 108.1 et seq.

Library References

Labor Relations ⟹372.
C.J.S. Labor Relations § 356 et seq.

§ 1368. Federal procurement

(a) Contracts with violators prohibited

No Federal agency may enter into any contract with any person, who has been convicted of any offense under section 1319(c) of this title, for the procurement of goods, materials, and services if such contract is to be performed at any facility at which the violation which gave rise to such conviction occurred, and if such facility is owned, leased, or supervised by such person. The prohibition in the preceding sentence shall continue until the Administrator certifies that the condition giving rise to such conviction has been corrected.

(b) Notification of agencies

The Administrator shall establish procedures to provide all Federal agencies with the notification necessary for the purposes of subsection (a) of this section.

(c) Omitted

(d) Exemptions

The President may exempt any contract, loan, or grant from all or part of the provisions of this section where he determines such exemption is necessary in the paramount interest of the United States and he shall notify the Congress of such exemption.

(e) Annual report to Congress

The President shall annually report to the Congress on measures taken in compliance with the purpose and intent of this section, including, but not limited to, the progress and problems associated with such compliance.

(June 30, 1948, ch. 758, title V, § 508, as added Oct. 18, 1972, Pub.L. 92–500, § 2, 86 Stat. 891.)

West's Federal Practice Manual

Debarment and suspension, see § 1562.

Code of Federal Regulations

Procurement under assistance agreements, see 40 CFR 33.001 et seq.

Library References

Health and Environment ⟹25.7(22).
C.J.S. Health and Environment § 106 et seq.

§ 1369. Administrative procedure and judicial review

(a) Subpenas

(1) For purposes of obtaining information under section 1315 of this title, or carrying out section 1367(e) of this title, the Administrator may issue subpenas for the attendance and testimony of witnesses and the production of relevant papers, books, and documents, and he may administer oaths. Except for effluent data, upon a showing satisfactory to the Administrator that such papers, books, documents, or information or particular part thereof, if made public, would divulge trade secrets or secret processes, the Administrator shall consider such record, report, or information or particular portion

thereof confidential in accordance with the purposes of section 1905 of title 18, except that such paper, book, document, or information may be disclosed to other officers, employees, or authorized representatives of the United States concerned with carrying out this chapter, or when relevant in any proceeding under this chapter. Witnesses summoned shall be paid the same fees and mileage that are paid witnesses in the courts of the United States. In case of contumacy or refusal to obey a subpena served upon any person under this subsection, the district court of the United States for any district in which such person is found or resides or transacts business, upon application by the United States and after notice to such person, shall have jurisdiction to issue an order requiring such person to appear and give testimony before the Administrator, to appear and produce papers, books, and documents before the Administrator, or both, and any failure to obey such order of the court may be punished by such court as a contempt thereof.

(2) The district courts of the United States are authorized, upon application by the Administrator, to issue subpenas for attendance and testimony of witnesses and the production of relevant papers, books, and documents, for purposes of obtaining information under sections 1314(b) and (c) of this title. Any papers, books, documents, or other information or part thereof, obtained by reason of such a subpena shall be subject to the same requirements as are provided in paragraph (1) of this subsection.

(b) Review of Administrator's actions

(1) Review of the Administrator's action (A) in promulgating any standard of performance under section 1316 of this title, (B) in making any determination pursuant to section 1316(b)(1)(C) of this title, (C) in promulgating any effluent standard, prohibition, or pretreatment standard under section 1317 of this title, (D) in making any determination as to a State permit program submitted under section 1342(b) of this title, (E) in approving or promulgating any effluent limitation or other limitation under section 1311, 1312, or 1316 of this title, and (F) in issuing or denying any permit under section 1342 of this title, may be had by any interested person in the Circuit Court of Appeals of the United States for the Federal judicial district in which such person resides or transacts such business upon application by such person. Any such application shall be made within ninety days from the date of such determination, approval, promulgation, issuance or denial, or after such date only if such application is based solely on grounds which arose after such ninetieth day.

(2) Action of the Administrator with respect to which review could have been obtained under paragraph (1) of this subsection shall not be subject to judicial review in any civil or criminal proceeding for enforcement.

(c) Additional evidence

In any judicial proceeding brought under subsection (b) of this section in which review is sought of a determination under this chapter required to be made on the record after notice and opportunity for hearing, if any party applies to the court for leave to adduce additional evidence, and shows to the satisfaction of the court that such additional evidence is material and that there were reasonable grounds for the failure to adduce such evidence in the proceeding before the Administrator, the court may order such additional evidence (and evidence in rebuttal thereof) to be taken before the Administrator, in such manner and upon such terms and conditions as the court may deem proper. The Administrator may modify his findings as to the facts, or make new findings, by reason of the additional evidence so taken and he shall file such modified or new findings, and his recommendation, if any, for the modification or setting aside of his original determination, with the return of such additional evidence.

(June 30, 1948, ch. 758, title V, § 509, as added Oct. 18, 1972, Pub.L. 92–500, § 2, 86 Stat. 891, and amended Dec. 28, 1973, Pub.L. 93–207, § 1(6), 87 Stat. 906.)

Federal Practice and Procedure

Review of administrative decisions in courts of appeals, see Wright, Miller, Cooper & Gressman: Jurisdiction §§ 3941, 3944.

Code of Federal Regulations

Judicial review under Environmental Protection Agency administered statutes, see 40 CFR 23.1 et seq.
Public information, see 40 CFR 2.100 et seq.

United States Supreme Court

Jurisdiction, court of appeals review of federal administrator's objection to state permit, see Crown Simpson Pulp Co. v. Costle, 1980, 100 S.Ct. 1093, 445 U.S. 193, 63 L.Ed.2d 312.

§ 1370. State authority

Except as expressly provided in this chapter, nothing in this chapter shall (1) preclude or deny the right of any State or political subdivision thereof or interstate agency to adopt or enforce (A) any standard or limitation respecting discharges of pollutants, or (B) any requirement respecting control or abatement of pollution; except that if an effluent limitation, or other limitation, effluent standard, prohibition, pretreatment standard, or standard of performance is in effect under this chapter, such State or political subdivision or interstate agency may not adopt or enforce any effluent limitation, or other limitation, effluent standard, prohibition, pretreatment standard, or standard of performance which is less stringent than the effluent limitation, or other limitation, effluent standard, prohibition, pretreatment standard, or standard of performance under this chapter; or (2) be construed as impairing or in any manner affecting any right or jurisdiction of the States with respect to the waters (including boundary waters) of such States.

(June 30, 1948, ch. 758, title V, § 510, as added Oct. 18, 1972, Pub.L. 92–500, § 2, 86 Stat. 893.)

Cross References

Timetable for achievement of effluent limitations, see section 1311 of this title.

Library References

Health and Environment ⇐25.7(10).
C.J.S. Health and Environment § 106 et seq.

§ 1371. Authority under other laws and regulations

(a) Impairment of authority or functions of officials and agencies; treaty provisions

This chapter shall not be construed as (1) limiting the authority or functions of any officer or agency of the United States under any other law or regulation not inconsistent with this chapter; (2) affecting or impairing the authority of the Secretary of the Army (A) to maintain navigation or (B) under the Act of March 3, 1899, (30 Stat. 1112); except that any permit issued under section 1344 of this title shall be conclusive as to the effect on water quality of any discharge resulting from any activity subject to section 403 of this title, or (3) affecting or impairing the provisions of any treaty of the United States.

(b) Discharges of pollutants into navigable waters

Discharges of pollutants into the navigable waters subject to the Rivers and Harbors Act of 1910 (36 Stat. 593; 33 U.S.C. 421) and the Supervisory Harbors Act of 1888 (25 Stat. 209; 33 U.S.C. 441–451b) shall be regulated pursuant to this chapter, and not subject to such Act of 1910 and the Act of 1888 except as to effect on navigation and anchorage.

(c) Action of the Administrator deemed major Federal action; construction of the National Environmental Policy Act of 1969

(1) Except for the provision of Federal financial assistance for the purpose of assisting the construction of publicly owned treatment works as authorized by section 1281 of this title, and the issuance of a permit under section 1342 of this title for the discharge of any pollutant by a new source as defined in section 1316 of this title, no action of the Administrator taken pursuant to this chapter shall be deemed a major Federal action significantly affecting the quality of the human environment within the meaning of the National Environmental Policy Act of 1969 (83 Stat. 852) [42 U.S.C. 4321 et seq.]; and

(2) Nothing in the National Environmental Policy Act of 1969 (83 Stat. 852) shall be deemed to—

(A) authorize any Federal agency authorized to license or permit the conduct of any activity which may result in the discharge of a pollutant into the navigable waters to review any effluent limitation or other requirement established pursuant to this chapter or the adequacy of any certification under section 1341 of this title; or

(B) authorize any such agency to impose, as a condition precedent to the issuance of any license or permit, any effluent limitation other than any such limitation established pursuant to this chapter.

(d) Consideration of international water pollution control agreements

Notwithstanding this chapter or any other provision of law, the Administrator (1) shall not require any State to consider in the development of the ranking in order of priority of needs for the construction of treatment works (as defined in subchapter II of this chapter), any water pollution control agreement which may have been entered into between the United States and any other nation, and (2) shall not consider any such agreement in the approval of any such priority ranking.

(June 30, 1948, ch. 758, title V, § 511, as added Oct. 18, 1972, Pub.L. 92–500, § 2, 86 Stat. 893, and amended Jan. 2, 1974, Pub.L. 93–243, § 3, 87 Stat. 1069.)

Cross References

Permits and licenses, compliance with requirements, see section 1341 of this title.

Library References

Health and Environment ⇐25.7(3).
C.J.S. Health and Environment § 106.

§ 1372. Labor standards

The Administrator shall take such action as may be necessary to insure that all laborers and mechanics employed by contractors or subcontractors on treatment works for which grants are made under this chapter shall be paid wages at rates not less than those prevailing for the same type of work on similar construction in the immediate locality, as determined by the Secretary of Labor, in accordance with the Davis-Bacon Act (46 Stat. 1494; 40 U.S.C., sec. 276a through 276a–5). The Secretary of Labor shall have, with respect to the labor standards specified in this subsection,[1] the authority and functions set forth in Reorganization Plan Numbered 14 of 1950 (15 F.R. 3176) and section 276c of title 40.

(June 30, 1948, ch. 758, title V, § 513, as added Oct. 18, 1972, Pub.L. 92–500, § 2, 86 Stat. 894.)

[1] So in original. Probably should be "section".

Code of Federal Regulations

Labor standards provisions applicable to contracts covering federally financed and assisted construction, see 29 CFR 5.1 et seq.

Procedures for predetermination of wage rates, see 29 CFR 1.1 et seq.

Library References

Labor Relations ⚷1128.
C.J.S. Labor Relations § 1038.

§ 1373. Public health agency coordination

The permitting agency under section 1342 of this title shall assist the applicant for a permit under such section in coordinating the requirements of this chapter with those of the appropriate public health agencies.

(June 30, 1948, ch. 758, title V, § 514, as added Oct. 18, 1972, Pub.L. 92–500, § 2, 86 Stat. 894.)

§ 1374. Effluent Standards and Water Quality Information Advisory Committee

(a) Establishment; membership; term

(1) There is established on[1] Effluent Standards and Water Quality Information Advisory Committee, which shall be composed of a Chairman and eight members who shall be appointed by the Administrator within sixty days after October 18, 1972.

(2) All members of the Committee shall be selected from the scientific community, qualified by education, training, and experience to provide, assess, and evaluate scientific and technical information on effluent standards and limitations.

(3) Members of the Committee shall serve for a term of four years, and may be reappointed.

(b) Action on proposed regulations

(1) No later than one hundred and eighty days prior to the date on which the Administrator is required to publish any proposed regulations required by section 1314(b) of this title, any proposed standard of performance for new sources required by section 1316 of this title, or any proposed toxic effluent standard required by section 1317 of this title, he shall transmit to the Committee a notice of intent to propose such regulations. The Chairman of the Committee within ten days after receipt of such notice may publish a notice of a public hearing by the Committee, to be held within thirty days.

(2) No later than one hundred and twenty days after receipt of such notice, the Committee shall transmit to the Administrator such scientific and technical information as is in its possession, including that presented at any public hearing, related to the subject matter contained in such notice.

(3) Information so transmitted to the Administrator shall constitute a part of the administrative record and comments on any proposed regulations or standards as information to be considered with other comments and information in making any final determinations.

(4) In preparing information for transmittal, the Committee shall avail itself of the technical and scientific services of any Federal agency, including the United States Geological Survey and any national environmental laboratories which may be established.

(c) Secretary; legal counsel; compensation

(1) The Committee shall appoint and prescribe the duties of a Secretary, and such legal counsel as it deems necessary. The Committee shall appoint such other employees as it deems necessary to exercise and fulfill its powers and responsibilities. The compensation of all employees appointed by the Committee shall be fixed in accordance with chapter 51 and subchapter III of chapter 53 of title 5.

(2) Members of the Committee shall be entitled to receive compensation at a rate to be fixed by the President but not in excess of the maximum rate of pay for grade GS–18, as provided in the General Schedule under section 5332 of title 5.

(d) Quorum; special panel

Five members of the Committee shall constitute a quorum, and official actions of the Committee shall be taken only on the affirmative vote of at least five members. A special panel composed of one or more members upon order of the Committee shall conduct any hearing authorized by this section and submit the transcript of such hearing to the entire Committee for its action thereon.

(e) Rules

The Committee is authorized to make such rules as are necessary for the orderly transaction of its business.

(June 30, 1948, ch. 758, title V, § 515, as added Oct. 18, 1972, Pub.L. 92–500, § 2, 86 Stat. 894.)

[1] So in original. Probably should be "an".

Library References

United States ⚷29.
C.J.S. United States § 34 et seq.

§ 1375. Reports to Congress

(a) Implementation of chapter objectives; status and progress of programs

Within ninety days following the convening of each session of Congress, the Administrator shall submit to the Congress a report, in addition to any other report required by this chapter, on measures taken toward implementing the objective of this chapter, including, but not limited to, (1) the progress and problems associated with developing comprehensive plans under section 1252 of this title, areawide plans under section 1288 of this title, basin plans under section 1289 of this title, and plans under section 1313(e) of this title; (2) a summary of actions taken and results achieved in the field of water pollution control research, experiments, studies, and related matters by the Administrator and other Federal agencies and by other persons and agencies under Federal grants or contracts; (3) the progress and problems associated with the development of effluent limitations and recommended control techniques; (4) the status of State programs, including a detailed summary of the progress obtained as compared to that planned under State program plans for development and enforcement of water quality requirements; (5) the identification and status of enforcement actions pending or completed under this chapter during the preceding year; (6) the status of State, interstate, and local pollution control programs established pursuant to, and assisted by, this chapter; (7) a summary of the results of the survey required to be taken under section 1290 of this title; (8) his activities including recommendations under sections 1259 through 1261 of this title; and (9) all reports and recommendations made by the Water Pollution Control Advisory Board.

(b) Detailed estimates and comprehensive study on costs; State estimates, survey form

(1) The Administrator, in cooperation with the States, including water pollution control agencies and other water pollution control planning agencies, shall make (A) a detailed estimate of the cost of carrying out the provisions of this chapter; (B) a detailed estimate, biennially revised, of the cost of construction of all needed publicly owned treatment works in all of the States and of the cost of construction of all needed publicly owned treatment works in each of the States; (C) a comprehensive study of the economic impact on affected units of government of the cost of installation of treatment facilities; and (D) a comprehensive analysis of the national requirements for and the cost of treating municipal, industrial, and other effluent to attain the water quality objectives as established by this chapter or applicable State law. The Administrator shall submit such detailed estimate and such comprehensive study of such cost to the Congress no later than February 10 of each odd-numbered year. Whenever the Administrator, pursuant to this subsection, requests and receives an estimate of cost from a State, he shall furnish copies of such estimate together with such detailed estimate to Congress.

(2) Notwithstanding the second sentence of paragraph (1) of this subsection, the Administrator shall make a preliminary detailed estimate called for by subparagraph (B) of such paragraph and shall submit such preliminary detailed estimate to the Congress no later than September 3, 1974. The Administrator shall require each State to prepare an estimate of cost for such State, and shall utilize the survey form EPA–1, O.M.B. No. 158–R0017, prepared for the 1973 detailed estimate, except that such estimate shall include all costs of compliance with section 1281(g)(2)(A) of this title and water quality standards established pursuant to section 1313 of this title, and all costs of treatment works as defined in section 1292(2) of this title, including all eligible costs of constructing sewage collection systems and correcting excessive infiltration or inflow and all eligible costs of correcting combined storm and sanitary sewer problems and treating storm water flows. The survey form shall be distributed by the Administrator to each State no later than January 31, 1974.

(c) Status of combined sewer overflows in municipal treatment works operations

The Administrator shall submit to the Congress by October 1, 1978, a report on the status of combined sewer overflows in municipal treatment works operations. The report shall include (1) the status of any projects funded under this chapter to address combined sewer overflows (2) a listing by State of combined sewer overflow needs identified in the 1977 State priority listings, (3) an estimate for each applicable municipality of the number of years necessary, assuming an annual authorization and appropriation for the construction grants program of $5,000,000,000, to correct combined sewer overflow problems, (4) an analysis using representative municipalities faced with major combined sewer overflow needs, of the annual discharges of pollutants from overflows in comparison to treated effluent discharges, (5) an analysis of the technological alternatives available to municipalities to correct major combined sewer overflow problems, and (6) any recommendations of the Administrator for legislation to address the problem of combined sewer overflows, including whether a separate authorization and grant program should be established by the Congress to address combined sewer overflows.

(d) Status on use of municipal secondary effluent and sludge for agricultural and other purposes that utilize nutrient value of treated wastewater effluent

The Administrator shall submit to the Congress by October 1, 1978, a report on the status of the use of municipal secondary effluent and sludge for agricultural and other purposes that utilize the nutrient value of treated wastewater effluent. The report shall include (1) a summary of results of research and development programs, grants, and contracts carried out by the Environmental Protection Agency pursuant to sections 1254 and 1255 of this title, regarding alternatives to disposal, landfill, or incineration of secondary effluent of sludge, (2) an estimate of the amount of sludge generated by public treatment works and its disposition, including an estimate of annual energy costs to incinerate sludge, (3) an analysis of current technologies for the utilization, reprocessing, and other uses of sludge to utilize the nutrient value of sludge, (4) legal, institutional, public health, economic, and other impediments to the greater utilization of treated sludge, and (5) any recommendations of the Administrator for legislation to encourage or require the expanded utilization of sludge for agricultural and other purposes. In carrying out this subsection, the Administrator shall consult with, and use the services of the Tennessee Valley Authority and other departments, agencies, and instrumentalities of the United States, to the extent it is appropriate to do so.

(e) Legislative recommendations on program requiring coordination between water supply and wastewater control plans as condition for construction grants; public hearing

The Administrator, in cooperation with the States, including water pollution control agencies, and other water pollution control planning agencies, and water supply and water resources agencies of the States and the United States shall submit to Congress, within two years of December 27, 1977, a report with recommendations for legislation on a program to require coordination between water supply and wastewater control plans as a condition to grants for construction of treatment works under this chapter. No such report shall be submitted except after opportunity for public hearings on such proposed report.

(June 30, 1948, ch. 758, title V, § 516, as added Oct. 18, 1972, Pub.L. 92–500, § 2, 86 Stat. 895, and amended Jan. 2, 1974, Pub.L. 93–243, § 4, 87 Stat. 1069; Dec. 27, 1977, Pub.L. 95–217, §§ 70–72, 91 Stat. 1608, 1609.)

Cross References

Allotment of grant funds for construction of treatment works, see section 1285 of this title.

Annual survey of efficiency of treatment works constructed with grants made under this chapter, see section 1290 of this title.

Deduction of funds for Hudson River reclamation demonstration project from estimates prepared pursuant to this section, see section 1266 of this title.

Report on quality of navigable waters, ground water, etc., see section 1254 of this title.

§ 1376. Authorization of appropriations

There are authorized to be appropriated to carry out this chapter, other than sections 1254, 1255, 1256(a), 1257, 1258, 1262, 1263, 1264, 1265, 1286, 1287, 1288(f) and (h), 1289, 1314, 1321(c), (d), (i), (*l*), and (k), 1324, 1325, and 1327 of this title, $250,000,000 for the fiscal year ending June 30, 1973, $300,000,000 for the fiscal year ending June 30, 1974, $350,000,000 for the fiscal year ending June 30, 1975, $100,000,000 for the fiscal year ending September 30, 1977, $150,000,000 for the fiscal year ending September 30, 1978, $150,000,000 for the fiscal year ending September 30, 1979, $150,000,000 for the fiscal year ending September 30, 1980, $150,000,000 for the fiscal year ending September 30, 1981, and $161,000,000 for the fiscal year ending September 30, 1982.

(June 30, 1948, ch. 758, title V, § 517, as added Oct. 18, 1972, Pub.L. 92–500, § 2, 86 Stat. 896, and amended Dec. 27, 1977, Pub.L. 95–217, § 4(g), 91 Stat. 1567; Oct. 21, 1980, Pub.L. 96–483, § 1(g), 94 Stat. 2360.)

OCEAN DUMPING

(33 U.S.C.A. §§ 1401 to 1445)

CHAPTER 27—OCEAN DUMPING

Related Provisions

See, also, Water Pollution Prevention and Control, 33 U.S.C.A. § 1251 et seq., ante; Ocean Pollution Research, 33 U.S.C.A. § 1701 et seq., post; Prevention of Pollution from Ships, 33 U.S.C.A. § 1901 et seq., post; and Water Resources Research, 42 U.S.C.A. § 10301 et seq., post.

Cross References

Application of solid waste disposal provisions, see section 6905 of Title 42, The Public Health and Welfare.
Deepwater port license, conditions for issuance, see section 1503 of this title.
Nuclear waste, ocean disposal of, see section 10104 of Title 42, The Public Health and Welfare.

West's Federal Forms

Jurisdiction and venue in district courts, matters pertaining to, see § 1003 et seq.
Preliminary injunctions and temporary restraining orders, see § 5271 et seq.
Sentence and fine, see § 7531 et seq.

Code of Federal Regulations

Enforcement, supervision, and inspection, see 33 CFR 326.1 et seq.
General regulatory policies, see 33 CFR 320.1 et seq.
Nationwide permits, see 33 CFR 330.1 et seq.
Ocean dumping, see 40 CFR Chap. I, Subchap. H.
Permits for discharges of dredged or fill material into water of the United States, see 33 CFR 323.1 et seq.
Processing of army department permits, see 33 CFR 325.1 et seq.
Public hearings, see 33 CFR 327.1 et seq.
Public information, see 40 CFR 2.100 et seq.

WESTLAW Electronic Research

See WESTLAW guide following the Explanation pages of this pamphlet.

§ 1401. Congressional finding, policy, and declaration of purpose

(a) Dangers of unregulated dumping

Unregulated dumping of material into ocean waters endangers human health, welfare, and amenities, and the marine environment, ecological systems, and economic potentialities.

(b) Policy of regulation and prevention or limitation

The Congress declares that it is the policy of the United States to regulate the dumping of all types of materials into ocean waters and to prevent or strictly limit the dumping into ocean waters of any material which would adversely affect human health, welfare, or amenities, or the marine environment, ecological systems, or economic potentialities.

(c) Regulation of dumping and transportation for dumping purposes

It is the purpose of this chapter to regulate (1) the transportation by any person of material from the United States and, in the case of United States vessels, aircraft, or agencies, the Transportation of material from a location outside the United States, when in either case the transportation is for the purpose of dumping the material into ocean waters, and (2) the dumping of material transported by any person from a location outside the United States, if the dumping occurs in the territorial sea or the contiguous zone of the United States.

(Oct. 23, 1972, Pub.L. 92–532, § 2, 86 Stat. 1052; March 22, 1974, Pub.L. 93–254, § 1(1), 88 Stat. 50.)

§ 1402. Definitions

For the purposes of this chapter the term—

(a) "Administrator" means the Administrator of the Environmental Protection Agency.

(b) "Ocean waters" means those waters of the open seas lying seaward of the base line from which the territorial sea is measured, as provided for in the Convention on the Territorial Sea and the Contiguous Zone (15 UST 1606; TIAS 5639).

(c) "Material" means matter of any kind or description, including, but not limited to, dredged material, solid waste, incinerator residue, garbage, sewage, sewage sludge, munitions, radiological, chemical, and biological warfare agents, radioactive materials, chemicals, biological and laboratory waste, wreck or discarded equipment, rock, sand, excavation debris, and industrial, municipal, agricultural, and other waste; but such term does not mean sewage from vessels within the meaning of section 1322 of this title. Oil within the meaning of section 1321 of this title shall be included only to the extent that such oil is taken on board a vessel or aircraft for the purpose of dumping.

(d) "United States" includes the several States, the District of Columbia, the Commonwealth of Puerto Rico, the Canal Zone, the territories and possessions of the United States, and the Trust Territory of the Pacific Islands.

(e) "Person" means any private person or entity, or any officer, employee, agent, department, agency, or instrumentality of the Federal Government, of any State or local unit of government, or of any foreign government.

(f) "Dumping" means a disposition of material: *Provided,* That it does not mean a disposition of any effluent from any outfall structure to the extent that such disposition is regulated under the provisions of the Federal Water Pollution Control Act, as amended [33 U.S.C. 1251 et seq.], under the provisions of section 407 of this title, or under the provisions of the Atomic Energy Act of

1954, as amended [42 U.S.C. 2011 et seq.], nor does it mean a routine discharge of effluent incidental to the propulsion of, or operation of motor-driven equipment on, vessels: *Provided, further,* That it does not mean the construction of any fixed structure or artificial island nor the intentional placement of any device in ocean waters or on or in the submerged land beneath such waters, for a purpose other than disposal, when such construction or such placement is otherwise regulated by Federal or State law or occurs pursuant to an authorized Federal or State program: *And Provided further,* That it does not include the deposit of oyster shells, or other materials when such deposit is made for the purpose of developing, maintaining, or harvesting fisheries resources and is otherwise regulated by Federal or State law or occurs pursuant to an authorized Federal or State program.

(g) "District court of the United States" includes the District Court of Guam, the District Court of the Virgin Islands, the District Court of Puerto Rico, the District Court of the Canal Zone, and in the case of American Samoa and the Trust Territory of the Pacific Islands, the District Court of the United States for the District of Hawaii, which court shall have jurisdiction over actions arising therein.

(h) "Secretary" means the Secretary of the Army.

(i) "Dredged material" means any material excavated or dredged from the navigable waters of the United States.

(j) "High-level radioactive waste" means the aqueous waste resulting from the operation of the first cycle solvent extraction system, or equivalent and the concentrated waste from subsequent extraction cycles, or equivalent, in a facility for reprocessing irradiated reactor fuels, or irradiated fuel from nuclear power reactors.

(k) "Transport" or "transportation" refers to the carriage and related handling of any material by a vessel, or by any other vehicle, including aircraft.

(*l*) "Convention" means the Convention on the Prevention of Marine Pollution by Dumping of Wastes and Other Matter.

(Oct. 23, 1972, Pub.L. 92–532, § 3, 86 Stat. 1052; March 22, 1974, Pub.L. 93–254, § 1(2), 88 Stat. 50.)

SUBCHAPTER I—REGULATION

Cross References

Criminal penalties for improper disposition of hazardous waste, federal enforcement of, see section 6928 of Title 42, The Public Health and Welfare.

Dumping of sewage sludge and industrial waste, see section 1412a of this title.

Generators of hazardous waste, standards applicable, see section 6922 of Title 42, The Public Health and Welfare.

Transporters of hazardous waste, standards applicable, see section 6923 of Title 42.

§ 1411. Prohibited acts

(a) Except as may be authorized by a permit issued pursuant to section 1412 or section 1413 of this title, and subject to regulations issued pursuant to section 1418 of this title,

(1) no person shall transport from the United States, and

(2) in the case of a vessel or aircraft registered in the United States or flying the United States flag or in the case of a United States department, agency, or instrumentality, no person shall transport from any location

any material for the purpose of dumping it into ocean waters.

(b) Except as may be authorized by a permit issued pursuant to section 1412 of this title, and subject to regulations issued pursuant to section 1418 of this title, no person shall dump any material transported from a location outside the United States (1) into the territorial sea of the United States, or (2) into a zone contiguous to the territorial sea of the United States, extending to a line twelve nautical miles seaward from the base line from which the breadth of the territorial sea is measured, to the extent that it may affect the territorial sea or the territory of the United States.

(Oct. 23, 1972, Pub.L. 92–532, title I, § 101, 86 Stat. 1053; March 22, 1974, Pub.L. 93–254, § 1(3), 88 Stat. 51.)

Cross References

Alternative disposal methods, duty of Administrator to develop, see section 1443 of this title.

Dumping of sewage sludge and industrial waste, see section 1412a of this title.

Environmental Protection Agency permits, see 1412 of this title.

Library References

Health and Environment ⚷25.7(3).
C.J.S. Health and Environment § 106.

§ 1412. Dumping permit program

(a) Environmental Protection Agency permits

Except in relation to dredged material, as provided for in section 1413 of this title, and in relation to radiological, chemical, and biological warfare agents and high-level radioactive waste, for which no permit may be issued, the Administrator may issue permits, after notice and opportunity for public hearings, for the transportation from the United States or, in the case of an agency or instrumentality of the United States, or in the case of a vessel or aircraft registered in the United States or flying the United States flag, for the transportation from a location outside the United States, of material for the purpose of dumping it into ocean waters, or for the dumping of material into the waters described in section 1411(b) of this title, where the Administrator determines that such dumping will not unreasonably degrade or endanger human health, welfare, or amenities, or the marine environment, ecological systems, or economic potentialities. The Administrator shall establish and apply criteria for reviewing and evaluating such permit applications, and, in establishing or revising such criteria, shall consider, but not be limited in his consideration to, the following:

(A) The need for the proposed dumping.

(B) The effect of such dumping on human health and welfare, including economic, esthetic, and recreational values.

(C) The effect of such dumping on fisheries resources, plankton, fish, shellfish, wildlife, shore lines and beaches.

(D) The effect of such dumping on marine ecosystems, particularly with respect to—

(i) the transfer, concentration, and dispersion of such material and its byproducts through biological, physical, and chemical processes.

(ii) potential changes in marine ecosystem diversity, productivity, and stability, and

(iii) species and community population dynamics.

(E) The persistence and permanence of the effects of the dumping.

(F) The effect of dumping particular volumes and concentrations of such materials.

(G) Appropriate locations and methods of disposal or recycling, including land-based alternatives and the probable impact of requiring use of such alternate locations or methods upon considerations affecting the public interest.

(H) The effect on alternate uses of oceans, such as scientific study, fishing, and other living resource exploitation, and nonliving resource exploitation.

(I) In designating recommended sites, the Administrator shall utilize wherever feasible locations beyond the edge of the Continental Shelf.

In establishing or revising such criteria, the Administrator shall consult with Federal, State, and local officials, and interested members of the general public, as may appear appropriate to the Administrator. With respect to such criteria as may affect the civil works program of the Department of the Army, the Administrator shall also consult with the Secretary. In reviewing applications for permits, the Administrator shall make such provision for consultation with interested Federal and State agencies as he deems useful or necessary. No permit shall be issued for a dumping of material which will violate applicable water quality standards. To the extent that he may do so without relaxing the requirements of this subchapter, the Administrator, in establishing or revising such criteria, shall apply the standards and criteria binding upon the United States under the Convention, including its Annexes.

(b) Permit categories

The Administrator may establish and issue various categories of permits, including the general permits described in section 1414(c) of this title.

(c) Sites and times for dumping

The Administrator may, considering the criteria established pursuant to subsection (a) of this section, designate recommended sites or times for dumping and, when he finds it necessary to protect critical areas, shall, after consultation with the Secretary, also designate sites or times within which certain materials may not be dumped.

(d) Fish wastes

No permit is required under this subchapter for the transportation for dumping or the dumping of fish wastes, except when deposited in harbors or other protected or enclosed coastal waters, or where the Administrator finds that such deposits could endanger health, the environment, or ecological systems in a specific location. Where the Administrator makes such a finding, such material may be deposited only as authorized by a permit issued by the Administrator under this section.

(e) Foreign State permits; acceptance

In the case of transportation of material, by an agency or instrumentality of the United States or by a vessel or aircraft registered in the United States or flying the United States flag, from a location in a foreign State Party to the Convention, a permit issued pursuant to the authority of that foreign State Party, in accordance with Convention requirements, and which otherwise could have been issued pursuant to subsection (a) of this section, shall be accepted, for the purposes of this subchapter, as if it were issued by the Administrator under the authority of this section: *Provided*, That in the case of an agency or instrumentality of the United States, no application shall be made for a permit to be issued pursuant to the authority of a foreign

State Party to the Convention unless the Administrator concurs in the filing of such application.

(Oct. 23, 1972, Pub.L. 92–532, title I, § 102, 86 Stat. 1054; March 22, 1974, Pub.L. 93–254, § 1(4), 88 Stat. 51; Dec. 22, 1980, Pub.L. 96–572, § 3, 94 Stat. 3345.)

Cross References

Appropriate locations for dumping dredged material, see section 1413 of this title.
Dumping of dredged material in Long Island Sound from any Federal, etc., project, see section 1416 of this title.
"Federally permitted release" defined, see section 9601 of Title 42, The Public Health and Welfare.
General permits, conditions for, see section 1414 of this title.
Prohibited acts, see section 1411 of this title.
Revocation and suspension of permits, see section 1415 of this title.

Code of Federal Regulations

Ocean dumping, see 40 CFR Chap. I, Subchap. H.

Library References

Health and Environment ⚷25.7(13).
C.J.S. Health and Environment § 107 et seq.

§ 1412a. Dumping of sewage sludge and industrial waste

(a) Cessation; exceptions

The Administrator of the Environmental Protection Agency (hereinafter referred to in this section as the "Administrator") shall end the dumping of sewage sludge and industrial waste into ocean waters, or into waters described in section 101(b) of the Marine Protection, Research, and Sanctuaries Act of 1972 [33 U.S.C. 1411(b)], as soon as possible after November 4, 1977, but, except as provided in subsections (b) and (c) of this section, in no case may the Administrator issue any permit, or any renewal thereof (under Title I of such Act of 1972 [33 U.S.C. 1411 et seq.]) which authorizes any such dumping after December 31, 1981.

(b) Permits for dumping of industrial waste; issuance, etc.

After December 31, 1981, the Administrator may issue permits under such Title I [33 U.S.C. 1411 et seq.] for the dumping of industrial waste into ocean waters, or into waters described in such section 101(b) [33 U.S.C. 1411(b)], if the Administrator determines—

(1) that the proposed dumping is necessary to conduct research—

(A) on new technology related to ocean dumping, or

(B) to determine whether the dumping of such substance will unreasonably degrade or endanger human health, welfare, or amenities, or the marine environment, ecological systems, or economic potentialities;

(2) that the scale of the proposed dumping is such that the dumping will have minimal adverse impact upon the human health, welfare, and amenities, and the marine environment, ecological systems, and economic potentialities; and

(3) after consultation with the Secretary of Commerce, that the potential benefits of such research will outweigh any such adverse impact.

Each permit issued pursuant to this subsection shall be subject to such conditions and restrictions as the Administrator determines to be necessary to minimize possible adverse impacts of such dumping. No permit issued by the Administrator pursuant to this subsection may have an effective period of more than six consecutive months.

(c) Emergency permits for dumping of industrial waste; issuance, etc.

After December 31, 1981, the Administrator may issue emergency permits under such Title I [33 U.S.C. 1411 et seq.] for the dumping of industrial waste into ocean waters, or into waters described in such section 101(b) [33 U.S.C. 1411(b)], if the Administrator determines that there has been demonstrated to exist an emergency, requiring the dumping of such waste, which poses an unacceptable risk relating to human health and admits of no other feasible solution. As used herein, "emergency" refers to situations requiring action with a marked degree of urgency.

(d) Definitions

For purposes of this section—

(1) the term "sewage sludge" means any solid, semisolid, or liquid waste generated by a municipal wastewater treatment plant the ocean dumping of which may unreasonably degrade or endanger human health, welfare, or amenities, or the marine environment, ecological systems, and economic potentialities; and

(2) the term "industrial waste" means any solid, semisolid, or liquid waste generated by a manufacturing or processing plant the ocean dumping of which may unreasonably degrade or endanger human health, welfare, or amenities, or the marine environment, ecological systems, and economic potentialities.

(Nov. 4, 1977, Pub.L. 95–153, § 4, 91 Stat. 1255; Dec. 22, 1980, Pub.L. 96–572, § 2, 94 Stat. 3344.)

Cross References

Cooperation with public authorities, agencies, and institutions, private agencies and institutions, and individuals, see section 1443 of this title.

Library References

Health and Environment ⚷25.7(13), (19).
C.J.S. Health and Environment §§ 107 et seq., 113 et seq.

§ 1413. Dumping permit program for dredged material

(a) Issuance by Secretary of the Army

Subject to the provisions of subsections (b), (c), and (d) of this section, the Secretary may issue permits, after notice and opportunity for public hearings, for the transportation of dredged material for the purpose of dumping it into ocean waters, where the Secretary determines that the dumping will not unreasonably degrade or endanger human health, welfare, or amenities, or the marine environment, ecological systems, or economic potentialities.

(b) Independent determination of need for dumping, other methods of disposal, and appropriate locations

In making the determination required by subsection (a) of this section, the Secretary shall apply those criteria, established pursuant to section 1412(a) of this title, relating to the effects of the dumping. Based upon an evaluation of the potential effect of a permit denial on navigation, economic and industrial development, and foreign and domestic commerce of the United States, the Secretary shall make an independent determination as to the need for the dumping. The Secretary shall also make an independent determination as to other possible methods of disposal and as to appropriate locations for the dumping. In considering appropriate locations, he shall, to the extent feasible, utilize the recommended sites designated by the Administrator pursuant to section 1412(c) of this title.

(c) Disagreement of Administrator with determination of Secretary of the Army

Prior to issuing any permit under this section, the Secretary shall first notify the Administrator of his intention to do so. In any case in which the Administrator disagrees with the determination of the Secretary as to compliance with the criteria established pursuant to section 1412(a) of this title relating to the effects of the dumping or with the restrictions established pursuant to section 1412(c) of this title relating to critical areas, the determination of the Administrator shall prevail. Unless the Administrator grants a waiver pursuant to subsection (d) of this section, the Secretary shall not issue a permit which does not comply with such criteria and with such restrictions.

(d) Waiver of requirements

If, in any case, the Secretary finds that, in the disposition of dredged material, there is no economically feasible method or site available other than a dumping site the utilization of which would result in non-compliance with the criteria established pursuant to section 1412(a) of this title relating to the effects of dumping or with the restrictions established pursuant to section 1412(c) of this title relating to critical areas, he shall so certify and request a waiver from the Administrator of the specific requirements involved. Within thirty days of the receipt of the waiver request, unless the Administrator finds that the dumping of the material will result in an unacceptably adverse impact on municipal water supplies, shell-fish beds, wildlife, fisheries (including spawning and breeding areas), or recreational areas, he shall grant the waiver.

(e) Federal projects involving dredged material

In connection with Federal projects involving dredged material, the Secretary may, in lieu of the permit procedure, issue regulations which will require the application to such projects of the same criteria, other factors to be evaluated, the same procedures, and the same requirements which apply to the issuance of permits under subsections (a), (b), (c), and (d) of this section.

(Oct. 23, 1972, Pub.L. 92–532, title I, § 103, 86 Stat. 1055.)

Cross References

Environmental Protection Agency permits, see section 1412 of this title.
"Federally permitted release" defined, see section 9601 of Title 42, The Public Health and Welfare.
General permits, see section 1414 of this title.
Prohibited acts, see section 1411 of this title.
Revocation and suspension of permits, see section 1415 of this title.

Code of Federal Regulations

Enforcement, supervision, and inspection, see 33 CFR 326.1 et seq.
General regulatory policies, see 33 CFR 320.1 et seq.
Nationwide permits, see 33 CFR 330.1 et seq.
Permits for discharges of dredged or fill material into waters of the United States, see 33 CFR 323.1 et seq.
Permits for ocean dumping of dredged material, see 33 CFR 324.1 et seq.
Processing of Department of the Army permits, see 33 CFR 325.1 et seq.
Public hearings, see 33 CFR 327.1 et seq.

Library References

Health and Environment ⚷25.7(13).
C.J.S. Health and Environment § 107 et seq.

§ 1414. Permit conditions

(a) Designated and included conditions

Permits issued under this subchapter shall designate and include (1) the type of material authorized to be transported for dumping or to be dumped; (2) the amount of material authorized to be transported for dumping or to be dumped; (3) the location where such transport for dumping will be terminated or where such dumping will occur; (4) the length of time for which the permits are valid and their expiration date; (5) any special provisions deemed necessary by the Administrator or the Secretary, as the case may be, after consultation with the Secretary of the Department in which the Coast Guard is operating, for the monitoring and surveillance of the transportation or dumping; and (6) such other matters as the Administrator or the Secretary, as the case may be, deems appropriate.

(b) Permit processing fees; reporting requirements

The Administrator or the Secretary, as the case may be, may prescribe such processing fees for permits and such reporting requirements for actions taken pursuant to permits issued by him under this subchapter as he deems appropriate.

(c) General permits

Consistent with the requirements of sections 1412 and 1413 of this title, but in lieu of a requirement for specific permits in such case, the Administrator or the Secretary, as the case may be, may issue general permits for the transportation for dumping, or dumping, or both, of specified materials or classes of materials for which he may issue permits, which he determines will have a minimal adverse environmental impact.

(d) Review

Any permit issued under this subchapter shall be reviewed periodically and, if appropriate, revised. The Administrator or the Secretary, as the case may be, may limit or deny the issuance of permits, or he may alter or revoke partially or entirely the terms of permits issued by him under this subchapter, for the transportation for dumping, or for the dumping, or both, of specified materials or classes of materials, where he finds that such materials cannot be dumped consistently with the criteria and other factors required to be applied in evaluating the permit application. No action shall be taken under this subsection unless the affected person or permittee shall have been given notice and opportunity for a hearing on such action as proposed.

(e) Information for review and evaluation of applications

The Administrator or the Secretary, as the case may be, shall require an applicant for a permit under this subchapter to provide such information as he may consider necessary to review and evaluate such application.

(f) Public information

Information received by the Administrator or the Secretary, as the case may be, as a part of any application or in connection with any permit granted under this subchapter shall be available to the public as a matter of public record, at every stage of the proceeding. The final determination of the Administrator or the Secretary, as the case may be, shall be likewise available.

(g) Display of issued permits

A copy of any permit issued under this subchapter shall be placed in a conspicuous place in the vessel which will be used for the transportation or dumping authorized by such permit, and an additional copy shall be furnished by the issuing official to the Secretary of the department in which the Coast Guard is operating, or its designee.

(h) Low-level radioactive waste; research purposes

Notwithstanding any provision of this subchapter to the contrary, during the two-year period beginning on January 6, 1983, no permit may be issued under this subchapter that authorizes the dumping of any low-level radioactive waste unless the Administrator of the Environmental Protection Agency determines—

(1) that the proposed dumping is necessary to conduct research—

(A) on new technology related to ocean dumping, or

(B) to determine the degree to which the dumping of such substance will degrade the marine environment;

(2) that the scale of the proposed dumping is limited to the smallest amount of such material and the shortest duration of time that is necessary to fulfill the purposes of the research, such that the dumping will have minimal adverse impact upon human health, welfare, and amenities, and the marine environment, ecological systems, economic potentialities, and other legitimate uses;

(3) after consultation with the Secretary of Commerce, that the potential benefits of such research will outweigh any such adverse impact; and

(4) that the proposed dumping will be preceded by appropriate baseline monitoring studies of the proposed dump site and its surrounding environment.

Each permit issued pursuant to this subsection shall be subject to such conditions and restrictions as the Administrator determines to be necessary to minimize possible adverse impacts of such dumping.

(i) Radioactive Material Disposal Impact Assessment; Congressional approval

(1) Two years after January 6, 1983, the Administrator may not issue a permit under this subchapter for the disposal of radioactive waste material until the applicant, in addition to complying with all other requirements of this subchapter, prepares, with respect to the site at which the disposal is proposed, a

Radioactive Material Disposal Impact Assessment which shall include—

(A) a listing of all radioactive materials in each container to be disposed, the number of containers to be dumped, the structural diagrams of each container, the number of curies of each material in each container, and the exposure levels in rems at the inside and outside of each container;

(B) an analysis of the environmental impact of the proposed action, at the site at which the applicant desires to dispose of the material, upon human health and welfare and marine life;

(C) any adverse environmental effects at the site which cannot be avoided should the proposal be implemented;

(D) an analysis of the resulting environmental and economic conditions if the containers fail to contain the radioactive waste material when initially deposited at the specific site;

(E) a plan for the removal or containment of the disposed nuclear material if the container leaks or decomposes;

(F) a determination by each affected State whether the proposed action is consistent with its approved Coastal Zone Management Program;

(G) an analysis of the economic impact upon other users of marine resources;

(H) alternatives to the proposed action;

(I) comments and results of consultation with State officials and public hearings held in the coastal States that are nearest to the affected areas;

(J) a comprehensive monitoring plan to be carried out by the applicant to determine the full effect of the disposal on the marine environment, living resources, or human health, which plan shall include, but not be limited to, the monitoring of exterior container radiation samples, the taking of water and sediment samples, and fish and benthic animal samples, adjacent to the containers, and the acquisition of such other information as the Administrator may require; and

(K) such other information which the Administrator may require in order to determine the full effects of such disposal.

(2) The Administrator shall include, in any permit to which paragraph (1) applies, such terms and conditions as may be necessary to ensure that the monitoring plan required under paragraph (1)(J) is fully implemented, including the analysis by the Administrator of the samples required to be taken under the plan.

(3) The Administrator shall submit a copy of the assessment prepared under paragraph (1) with respect to any permit to the Committee on Merchant Marine and Fisheries of the House of Representatives and the Committee on Environment and Public Works of the Senate.

(4)(A) Upon a determination by the Administrator that a permit to which this subsection applies should be issued, the Administrator shall transmit such a recommendation to the House of Representatives and the Senate.

(B) No permit may be issued by the Administrator under this chapter for the disposal of radioactive materials in the ocean unless the Congress, by approval of a resolution described in paragraph (D) within 90 days of continuous session of the Congress beginning on the date after the date of receipt by the Senate and the House of Representatives of such recommendation, authorizes the Administrator to grant a permit to dispose of radioactive material under this chapter.

(C) For purposes of this subsection—

(1) continuity of session of the Congress is broken only by an adjournment sine die;

(2) the days on which either House is not in session because of an adjournment of more than three days to a day certain are excluded in the computation of the 90 day calendar period.

(D) For the purposes of this subsection, the term "resolution" means a joint resolution, the resolving clause of which is as follows: "That the House of Representatives and the Senate approve and authorize the Administrator of the Environmental Protection Agency to grant a permit[1] under the Marine Protection, Research, and Sanctuaries Act of 1972 to dispose of radioactive materials in the ocean as recommended by the Administrator to the Congress on ______, 19—."; the first blank space therein to be filled with the appropriate applicant to dispose of nuclear material and the second blank therein to be filled with the date on which the Administrator submits the recommendation to the House of Representatives and the Senate.

(Oct. 23, 1972, Pub.L. 92–532, title I, § 104, 86 Stat. 1056; Jan. 6, 1983, Pub.L. 97–424, Title IV, § 424(a), 96 Stat. 2165.)

1 So in original. Probably should be followed by "to" and a blank space.

Cross References

Permit categories, see section 1412 of this title.

Code of Federal Regulations

Contents of permits; revision, revocation, or limitation of ocean dumping permits, see 40 CFR 223.1 et seq.
Public information, see 40 CFR 2.100 et seq.

Library References

Health and Environment ⚷25.7(13).
C.J.S. Health and Environment § 107 et seq.

§ 1414a. Special provisions regarding certain dumping sites

(a) New York Bight Apex.

(1) For purposes of this subsection—

(A) The term "Apex" means the New York Bight Apex consisting of the ocean waters of the Atlantic Ocean westward of 73 degrees 30 minutes west longitude and northward of 40 degrees 10 minutes north latitude.

(B) The term "Apex site" means that site within the Apex at which the dumping of municipal sludge occurred before October 1, 1983.

(C) The term "eligible authority" means any sewerage authority or other unit of State or local government that on November 2, 1983, was authorized under court order to dump municipal sludge at the Apex site.

(2) No person may apply for a permit under this subchapter in relation to the dumping of, or the transportation for purposes of dumping, municipal sludge within the Apex unless that person is an eligible authority.

(3) The Administrator may not issue, or renew, any permit under this subchapter that authorizes the dumping of, or the transportation for purposes of dumping, municipal sludge within the Apex after the earlier of—

(A) December 15, 1987; or

(B) the day determined by the Administrator to be the first day on which municipal sludge generated by eligible authorities can reasonably be dumped at a site designated under section 1412 of this title other than a site within the Apex.

(b) Restriction on Use of the 106–Mile Site.

The Administrator may not issue or renew any permit under this subchapter which authorizes any person, other than a person that is an eligible authority within the meaning of subsection (a)(1)(C) of this section, to dump, or to transport for the purposes of dumping, municipal sludge within the site designated under section 1412(c) of this title by the Administrator and known as the "106–Mile Ocean Waste Dump Site" (as described in 49 F.R. 19005).

(Pub.L. 92–532, Title I, § 104A, as added Nov. 17, 1986, Pub.L. 99–662, Title XI, § 1172(b), 100 Stat. 4259.)

§ 1415. Penalties

(a) Assessment of civil penalty by Administrator; remission or mitigation; court action for appropriate relief

Any person who violates any provision of this subchapter, or of the regulations promulgated under this subchapter, or a permit issued under this subchapter shall be liable to a civil penalty of not more than $50,000 for each violation to be assessed by the Administrator. No penalty shall be assessed until the person charged shall have been given notice and an opportunity for a hearing of such violation. In determining the amount of the penalty, the gravity of the violation, prior violations, and the demonstrated good faith of the person charged in attempting to achieve rapid compliance after notification of a violation shall be considered by said Administrator. For good cause shown, the Administrator may remit or mitigate such penalty. Upon failure of the offending party to pay the penalty, the Administrator may request the Attorney General to commence an action in the appropriate district court of the United States for such relief as may be appropriate.

(b) Criminal penalties

In addition to any action which may be brought under subsection (a) of this section, a person who knowingly violates this subchapter, regulations promulgated under this subchapter, or a permit issued under this subchapter shall be fined not more than $50,000, or imprisoned for not more than one year, or both.

(c) Separate offenses

For the purpose of imposing civil penalties and criminal fines under this section, each day of a continuing violation shall constitute a separate offense as shall the dumping from each of several vessels, or other sources.

(d) Injunctive relief

The Attorney General or his delegate may bring actions for equitable relief to enjoin an imminent or continuing violation of this subchapter, of regulations promulgated under this subchapter, or of permits issued under this subchapter, and the district courts of the United States shall have jurisdiction to grant such relief as the equities of the case may require.

(e) Liability of vessels in rem

A vessel, except a public vessel within the meaning of section 13 of the Federal Water Pollution Control Act, as amended, used in a violation, shall be liable in rem for any civil penalty assessed or criminal fine imposed and may be proceeded against in any district court of the United States having jurisdiction thereof; but no vessel shall be liable unless it shall appear that one or more of the owners, or bareboat charterers, was at the time of the violation a consenting party or privy to such violation.

(f) Revocation and suspension of permits

If the provisions of any permit issued under section 1412 or 1413 of this title are violated, the Administrator or the Secretary, as the case may be, may revoke the permit or may suspend the permit for a specified period of time. No permit shall be revoked or suspended unless the permittee shall have been given notice and opportunity for a hearing on such violation and proposed suspension or revocation.

(g) Civil suits by private persons

(1) Except as provided in paragraph (2) of this subsection any person may commence a civil suit on his own behalf to enjoin any person, including the United States and any other governmental instrumentality or agency (to the extent permitted by the eleventh amendment to the Constitution), who is alleged to be in violation of any prohibition, limitation, criterion, or permit established or issued by or under this subchapter. The district courts shall have jurisdiction, without regard to the amount in controversy or the citizenship of the parties, to enforce such prohibition, limitation, criterion, or permit, as the case may be.

(2) No action may be commenced—

(A) prior to sixty days after notice of the violation has been given to the Administrator or to the Secretary, and to any alleged violator of the prohibition, limitation, criterion, or permit; or

(B) if the Attorney General has commenced and is diligently prosecuting a civil action in a court of the United States to require compliance with the prohibition, limitation, criterion, or permit; or

(C) if the Administrator has commenced action to impose a penalty pursuant to subsection (a) of this section, or if the Administrator, or the Secretary, has initiated permit revocation or suspension proceedings under subsection (f) of this section; or

(D) if the United States has commenced and is diligently prosecuting a criminal action in a court of the United States or a State to redress a violation of this subchapter.

(3)(A) Any suit under this subsection may be brought in the judicial district in which the violation occurs.

(B) In any such suit under this subsection in which the United States is not a party, the Attorney General, at the request of the Administrator or Secretary, may intervene on behalf of the United States as a matter of right.

(4) The court, in issuing any final order in any suit brought pursuant to paragraph (1) of this subsection may award costs of litigation (including reasonable attorney and expert witness fees) to any party, whenever the court determines such award is appropriate.

(5) The injunctive relief provided by this subsection shall not restrict any right which any person (or class of persons) may have under any statute or common law to seek enforcement of any standard or limitation or to seek any other relief (including relief against the Administrator, the Secretary, or a State agency).

(h) Emergencies

No person shall be subject to a civil penalty or to a criminal fine or imprisonment for dumping materials from a vessel if such materials are dumped in an emergency to safeguard life at sea. Any such emergency dumping shall be reported to the Administrator under such conditions as he may prescribe.

(Oct. 23, 1972, Pub.L. 92–532, title I, § 105, 86 Stat. 1057.)

Code of Federal Regulations

Rules of practice, see 40 CFR 22.01 et seq.

Library References

Health and Environment ⚷25.7(23).
C.J.S. Health and Environment § 113 et seq.

§ 1416. Relationship to other laws

(a) Voiding of preexisting licenses

After the effective date of this subchapter, all licenses, permits, and authorizations other than those issued pursuant to this subchapter shall be void and of no legal effect, to the extent that they purport to authorize any activity regulated by this subchapter, and whether issued before or after the effective date of this subchapter.

(b) Actions under authority of Rivers and Harbors Act

The provisions of subsection (a) of this section shall not apply to actions taken before the effective date of this subchapter under the authority of the Rivers and Harbors Act of 1899 (30 Stat. 1151), as amended (33 U.S.C. 401 et seq.).

(c) Impairment of navigation

Prior to issuing any permit under this subchapter, if it appears to the Administrator that the disposition of material, other than dredged material, may adversely affect navigation in the territorial sea of the United States, or in the approaches to any harbor of the United States, or may create an artificial island on the Outer Continental Shelf, the Administrator shall consult with the Secretary and no permit shall be issued if the Secretary determines that navigation will be unreasonably impaired.

(d) Consistent State programs

After the effective date of this subchapter, no State shall adopt or enforce any rule or regulation relating to any activity regulated by this subchapter. Any State may, however, propose to the Administrator criteria relating to the dumping of materials into ocean waters within its jurisdiction, or into other ocean waters to the extent that such dumping may affect waters within the jurisdiction of such State, and if the Administrator determines, after notice and opportunity for hearing, that the proposed criteria are not inconsistent with the purposes of this subchapter, may adopt those criteria and may issue regulations to implement such criteria. Such determination shall be made by the Administrator within one hundred and twenty days of receipt of the proposed criteria. For the purposes of this subsection, the term "State" means any State, interstate or regional authority, Federal territory or Commonwealth or the District of Columbia.

(e) Existing conservation programs not affected

Nothing in this subchapter shall be deemed to affect in any manner or to any extent any provision of the Fish and Wildlife Coordination Act as amended (16 U.S.C. 661–666c).

(f) Dumping of dredged material in Long Island Sound from any Federal, etc., project

In addition to other provisions of law and notwithstanding the specific exclusion relating to dredged material in the first sentence in section 1412(a) of this title, the dumping of dredged material in Long Island Sound from any Federal project (or pursuant to Federal authorization) or from a dredging project by a non-Federal applicant exceeding 25,000 cubic yards shall comply with the criteria established pursuant to the second sentence of section 1412(a) of this title relating to the effects of dumping. Subsection (d) of this section shall not apply to this subsection.

(g) Savings clause

Nothing in this subchapter shall restrict, affect or modify the rights of any person (1) to seek damages or enforcement of any standard or limitation under State law, including State common law, or (2) to seek damages under other Federal law, including maritime tort law, resulting from noncompliance with any requirement of this subchapter or any permit under this subchapter.

(Oct. 23, 1972, Pub.L. 92–532, title I, § 106, 86 Stat. 1058; Dec. 22, 1980, Pub.L. 96–572, § 4, 94 Stat. 3345; Oct. 17, 1986, Pub.L. 99–499, Title I, § 127(d), 100 Stat. 1693.)

§ 1417. Enforcement

(a) Utilization of other departments, agencies, and instrumentalities

The Administrator or the Secretary, as the case may be, may, whenever appropriate, utilize by agreement, the personnel, services and facilities of other Federal departments, agencies, and instrumentalities, or State agencies or instrumentalities, whether on a reimbursable or a nonreimbursable basis, in carrying out his responsibilities under this subchapter.

(b) Delegation of review and evaluation authority

The Administrator or the Secretary may delegate responsibility and authority for reviewing and evaluating permit applications, including the decision as to whether a permit will be issued, to an officer of his agency, or he may delegate, by agreement, such responsibility and authority to the heads of other Federal departments or agencies, whether on a reimbursable or nonreimbursable basis.

(c) Surveillance and other enforcement activity

The Secretary of the department in which the Coast Guard is operating shall conduct surveillance and other appropriate enforcement activity to prevent unlawful transportation of material for dumping, or unlawful dumping. Such enforcement activity shall include, but not be limited to, enforcement of regulations issued by him pursuant to section 1418 of this title, relating to safe transportation, handling, carriage, storage, and stowage. The Secretary of the Department in which the Coast Guard is operating shall supply to the Administrator and to the Attorney General, as appropriate, such information of enforcement activities and such evidentiary material assembled as they may require in carrying out their duties relative to penalty assessments, criminal prosecutions, or other actions involving litigation pursuant to the provisions of this subchapter.

(Oct. 23, 1972, Pub.L. 92–532, title I, § 107, 86 Stat. 1059.)

Code of Federal Regulations

Contents of permits; revision, revocation or limitation of ocean dumping permits, see 40 CFR 223.1 et seq.

Library References

Health and Environment ⚷25.7(17).
C.J.S. Health and Environment § 113 et seq.

§ 1418. Regulations

In carrying out the responsibilities and authority conferred by this subchapter, the Administrator, the Secretary, and the Secretary of the department in which the Coast Guard is operating are authorized to issue such regulations as they may deem appropriate.

(Oct. 23, 1972, Pub.L. 92–532, title I, § 108, 86 Stat. 1059.)

Cross References

Prohibited acts, see section 1411 of this title.
Surveillance and other enforcement activity, see section 1417 of this title.

Code of Federal Regulations

Ocean dumping, see 40 CFR Chap. I, Subchap. H.
Public information, see 40 CFR 2.100 et seq.

§ 1419. International cooperation

The Secretary of State, in consultation with the Administrator, shall seek effective international action and cooperation to insure protection of the marine environment, and may, for this purpose, formulate, present, or support specific proposals in the United Nations and other component international organizations for the development of appropriate international rules and regulations in support of the policy of this chapter.

(Oct. 23, 1972, Pub.L. 92–532, title I, § 109, 86 Stat. 1060.)

Library References

International Law ⚷10.
C.J.S. International Law § 12.

§ 1420. Authorization of appropriations

There are hereby authorized to be appropriated not to exceed $3,600,000 for fiscal year 1973, not to exceed $5,500,000 for each of the fiscal years 1974 and 1975, not to exceed $5,300,000 for fiscal year 1976, not to exceed $1,325,000 for the transition period (July 1 through September 30, 1976), not to exceed $4,800,000 for fiscal year 1977, not to exceed $4,800,000 for fiscal year 1978, not to exceed $2,000,000 for each of fiscal year 1980, fiscal year 1981, and not to exceed $4,213,000 for fiscal year 1982, for the purposes and administration of this subchapter, and for succeeding fiscal years only such sums as the Congress may authorize by law.

(Oct. 23, 1972, Pub.L. 92–532, title I, § 111, 86 Stat. 1060; Oct. 26, 1974, Pub.L. 93–472, 88 Stat. 1430; July 25, 1975, Pub.L. 94–62, § 1, 89 Stat. 303; June 30, 1976, Pub.L. 94–326, § 1, 90 Stat. 725; Nov. 4, 1977, Pub.L. 95–153, § 1, 91 Stat. 1255; Dec. 22, 1980, Pub.L. 96–572, § 1, 94 Stat. 3344; June 23, 1981, Pub.L. 97–16, 95 Stat. 100.)

Library References

Health and Environment ⚷25.7(21).
C.J.S. Health and Environment § 106 et seq.

§ 1421. Annual report to Congress

The Administrator shall on or before February 1 of each year report to the Congress on the administration of this subchapter during the preceding fiscal year, including recommendations for additional legislation if deemed necessary.

(Oct. 23, 1972, Pub.L. 92–532, title I, § 112, 86 Stat. 1060; June 30, 1976, Pub.L. 94–326, § 2, 90 Stat. 725; Oct. 19, 1980, Pub.L. 96–470, Title II, § 209(f), 94 Stat. 2245.)

SUBCHAPTER II—RESEARCH

Cross References

Comprehensive ocean pollution program, contents of, see section 1704 of this title.

§ 1441. Monitoring and research program

The Secretary of Commerce, in coordination with the Secretary of the Department in which the Coast Guard is operating and with the Administrator shall, within six months of October 23, 1972, initiate a comprehensive and continuing program of monitoring and research regarding the effects of the dumping of material into ocean waters or other coastal waters where the tide ebbs and flows or into the Great Lakes or their connecting waters.

(Oct. 23, 1972, Pub.L. 92–532, title II, § 201, 86 Stat. 1060; April 7, 1986, Pub.L. 99–272, Title VI, § 6061, 100 Stat. 131.)

§ 1442. Research program respecting possible long-range effects of pollution, overfishing, and man-induced changes of ocean ecosystems

(a) Secretary of Commerce

(1) The Secretary of Commerce, in close consultation with other appropriate Federal departments, agencies, and instrumentalities shall, within six months of October 23, 1972, initiate a comprehensive and continuing program of research with respect to the possible long-range effects of pollution, overfishing, and man-induced changes of ocean ecosystems. These responsibilities shall include the scientific assessment of damages to the natural resources from spills of petroleum or petroleum products. In carrying out such research, the Secretary of Commerce shall take into account such factors as existing and proposed international policies affecting oceanic problems, economic considerations involved in both the protection and the use of the oceans, possible alternatives to existing programs, and ways in which the health of the oceans may best be preserved for the benefit of succeeding generations of mankind.

(2) The Secretary of Commerce shall ensure that the program under this section complements, when appropriate, the activities undertaken by other Federal agencies pursuant to subchapter I of this chap-

ter and section 1443 of this title. That program shall include but not be limited to—

(A) the development and assessment of scientific techniques to define and quantify the degradation of the marine environment;

(B) the assessment of the capacity of the marine environment to receive materials without degradation;

(C) continuing monitoring programs to assess the health of the marine environment, including but not limited to the monitoring of bottom oxygen concentrations, contaminant levels in biota, sediments, and the water column, diseases in fish and shellfish, and changes in types and abundance of indicator species;

(D) the development of methodologies, techniques, and equipment for disposal of waste materials to minimize degradation of the marine environment.

(b) Action with other nations

In carrying out his responsibilities under this section, the Secretary of Commerce, under the foreign policy guidance of the President and pursuant to international agreements and treaties made by the President with the advice and consent of the Senate, may act alone or in conjunction with any other nation or group of nations, and shall make known the results of his activities by such channels of communication as may appear appropriate.

(c) Cooperation of other departments, agencies, and independent instrumentalities

Each department, agency, and independent instrumentality of the Federal Government is authorized and directed to cooperate with the Secretary of Commerce in carrying out the purposes of this section and, to the extent permitted by law, to furnish such information as may be requested.

(d) Utilization of personnel, services, and facilities; inter-agency agreements

The Secretary of Commerce, is carrying out his responsibilities under this section, shall, to the extent feasible utilize the personnel, services, and facilities of other Federal departments, agencies, and instrumentalities (including those of the Coast Guard for monitoring purposes), and is authorized to enter into appropriate inter-agency agreements to accomplish this action.

(e) Redesignated (d)

(Oct. 23, 1972, Pub.L. 92–532, title II, § 202, 86 Stat. 1060; July 25, 1975, Pub.L. 94–62, § 2, 89 Stat. 303; Oct. 6, 1980, Pub.L. 96–381, § 3, 94 Stat. 1524; Oct. 19, 1980, Pub.L. 96–470, Title II, § 201(f), 94 Stat. 2242; April 7, 1986, Pub.L. 99–272, Title VI, § 6062, 100 Stat. 131.)

§ 1443. Cooperation with public authorities, agencies, and institutions, private agencies and institutions, and individuals; regional management plans for waste disposal; report on sewage disposal in New York metropolitan area

(a) The Administrator of the Environmental Protection Agency shall—

(1) conduct research, investigations, experiments, training, demonstrations, surveys, and studies for the purpose of—

(A) determining means of minimizing or ending, as soon as possible after October 6, 1980, the dumping into ocean waters, or waters described in section 1411(b) of this title, of material which may unreasonably degrade or endanger human health, welfare, or amenities, or the marine environment, ecological systems, or economic potentialities, and

(B) developing disposal methods as alternatives to the dumping described in subparagraph (A); and

(2) encourage, cooperate with, promote the coordination of, and render financial and other assistance to appropriate public authorities, agencies, and institutions (whether Federal, State, interstate, or local) and appropriate private agencies, institutions, and individuals in the conduct of research and other activities described in paragraph (1).

(b) Nothing in this section shall be construed to affect in any way the December 31, 1981, termination date, established in section 1412a of this title, for the ocean dumping of sewage sludge.

(c) The Administrator, in cooperation with the Secretary, the Secretary of Commerce, and other officials of appropriate Federal, State, and local agencies, shall assess the feasibility in coastal areas of regional management plans for the disposal of waste materials. Such plans should integrate where appropriate Federal, State, regional, and local waste disposal activities into a comprehensive regional disposal strategy. These plans should address, among other things—

(1) the sources, quantities, and types of materials that require and will require disposal;

(2) the environmental, economic, social, and human health factors (and the methods used to assess these factors) associated with disposal alternatives;

(3) the improvements in production processes, methods of disposal, and recycling to reduce the adverse effects associated with such disposal alternatives;

(4) the applicable laws and regulations governing waste disposal; and

(5) improvements in permitting processes to reduce administrative burdens.

(d) The Administrator, in cooperation with the Secretary of Commerce, shall submit to the Congress and the President, not later than one year after April 7, 1986, a report on sewage sludge disposal in the New York City metropolitan region. The report shall—

(1) consider the factors listed in subsection (c) of this section as they relate to landfilling, incineration, ocean dumping, or any other feasible disposal or reuse/recycling option;

(2) include an assessment of the cost of these alternatives; and

(3) recommend such regulatory or legislative changes as may be necessary to reduce the adverse impacts associated with sewage sludge disposal.

(Oct. 23, 1972, Pub.L. 92–532, title II, § 203, 86 Stat. 1061; Oct. 6, 1980, Pub.L. 96–381, § 1, 94 Stat. 1523; April 7, 1986, Pub.L. 99–272, Title VI, § 6063, 100 Stat. 131.)

§ 1444. Annual reports

(a) In March of each year, the Secretary of Commerce shall report to the Congress on his activities under this subchapter during the previous fiscal year. The report shall include—

(1) the Secretary's findings made under section 1441 of this title, including an evaluation of the short-term ecological effects and the social and economic factors involved with the dumping;

(2) the results of activities undertaken pursuant to section 1442 of this title;

(3) with the concurrence of the Administrator and after consulting with officials of other appropriate Federal agencies, an identification of the short- and long-term research requirements associated with activities under subchapter I of this chapter, and a description of how Federal research under this subchapter and subchapter I of this chapter will meet those requirements; and

(4) activities of the Department of Commerce under section 665 of Title 16.

(b) In March of each year, the Administrator shall report to the Congress on his activities during the previous fiscal year under section 1443 of this title.

(Oct. 23, 1972, Pub.L. 92–532, title II, § 204, formerly § 205, 86 Stat. 1061; as added Pub.L. 96–572, § 5, Dec. 22, 1980, 94 Stat. 3345, and renumbered and amended Pub.L. 99–272, Title VI, § 6065, April 7, 1986, 100 Stat. 132.

§ 1445. Authorization of appropriations

There are authorized to be appropriated for the first fiscal year after October 23, 1972, and for the next two fiscal years thereafter such sums as may be necessary to carry out this subchapter, but the sums appropriated for any such fiscal year may not exceed $6,000,000. There are authorized to be appropriated not to exceed $1,500,000 for the transition period (July 1 through September 30, 1976), not to exceed $5,600,000 for fiscal year 1977, not to exceed $6,500,000 for fiscal year 1978, not to exceed $11,396,000 for fiscal year 1981, not to exceed $12,000,000 for fiscal year 1982, not to exceed $10,635,000 for fiscal year 1986, and not to exceed $11,114,000 for fiscal year 1987.

(Oct. 23, 1972, Pub.L. 92–532, Title II, § 205, formerly § 204, 86 Stat. 1061; July 25, 1975, Pub.L. 94–62, § 3, 89 Stat. 303; June 30, 1976, Pub.L. 94–326, § 3, 90 Stat. 725; Nov. 4, 1977, Pub.L. 95–153, § 2, 91 Stat. 1255; Oct. 6, 1980, Pub.L. 96–381, § 2, 94 Stat. 1523, renumbered and amended Pub.L. 99–272, Title VI, § 6064, April 7, 1986, 100 Stat. 132.

Library References

Health and Environment ⚷25.7(20).
C.J.S. Health and Environment § 113 et seq.

SAFETY OF PUBLIC WATER SYSTEMS

(42 U.S.C.A. §§ 300f to 300j–11)

CHAPTER 6A—PUBLIC HEALTH SERVICE

SUBCHAPTER XII—SAFETY OF PUBLIC WATER SYSTEMS

Part A—Definitions

Related Provisions

See, also, Water Pollution Prevention and Control, 33 U.S.C.A. § 1251 et seq., ante; and Water Resources Research, 42 U.S.C.A. § 10301 et seq., post.

SUBCHAPTER XII—SAFETY OF PUBLIC WATER SYSTEMS

Cross References

Applicability of Solid Waste Disposal Act to activity or substance which is subject to this subchapter, see section 6905 of this title.
Comprehensive management plan for Pinelands National Reserve to include plan for implementation of this subchapter, see section 471i of Title 16, Conservation.
Proposed environmental criteria regulation under this subchapter, functions of Science Advisory Board respecting, see section 4365 of this title.
Responsiveness of research on wastewater treatment and treatment of water for potable use to needs in implementing this subchapter, see section 10303(b), (e) of this title.

West's Federal Forms

Intervention, see § 3111 et seq.
Jurisdiction and venue in district courts, see § 1000 et seq.
Preliminary injunctions and temporary restraining orders, see § 5271 et seq.
Taxation of costs, see § 46.12 et seq.

Code of Federal Regulations

Decisionmaking procedures applicable to permit programs, see 40 CFR 124.1 et seq.
Environmental impact and related procedures, see 23 CFR 771.101 et seq.
Environmental protection agency grants, policies and procedures, see 40 CFR 30.100 et seq.
Grant policies and procedures, see 40 CFR 35.400 et seq.
Implementation and enforcement of national primary drinking water regulations, see 40 CFR 142.1 et seq.
Primary and secondary drinking water provisions, see 40 CFR 141.1 et seq., 143.1 et seq.
Underground injection control programs, technical standards, see 40 CFR 146.1 et seq.

WESTLAW Electronic Research

See WESTLAW guide following the Explanation pages of this pamphlet.

PART A—DEFINITIONS

§ 300f. Definitions

For purposes of this subchapter:

(1) The term "primary drinking water regulation" means a regulation which—

(A) applies to public water systems;

(B) specifies contaminants which, in the judgment of the Administrator, may have any adverse effect on the health of persons;

(C) specifies for each such contaminant either—

(i) a maximum contaminant level, if, in the judgment of the Administrator, it is economically and technologically feasible to ascertain the level of such contaminant in water in public water systems, or

(ii) if, in the judgment of the Administrator, it is not economically or technologically feasible to so ascertain the level of such contaminant, each treatment technique known to the Administrator which leads to a reduction in the level of such contaminant sufficient to satisfy the requirements of section 300g–1 of this title; and

(D) contains criteria and procedures to assure a supply of drinking water which dependably complies with such maximum contaminant levels; including quality control and testing procedures to insure compliance with such levels and to insure proper operation and maintenance of the system, and requirements as to (i) the minimum quality of water which may be taken into the system and (ii) siting for new facilities for public water systems.

(2) The term "secondary drinking water regulation" means a regulation which applies to public water systems and which specifies the maximum contaminant levels which, in the judgment of the Administrator, are requisite to protect the public welfare. Such regulations may apply to any contaminant in drinking water (A) which may adversely affect the odor or appearance of such water and consequently may cause a substantial number of the persons served by the public water system providing such water to discontinue its use, or (B) which may otherwise adversely affect the public welfare. Such regulations may vary according to geographic and other circumstances.

(3) The term "maximum contaminant level" means the maximum permissible level of a contaminant in water which is delivered to any user of a public water system.

(4) The term "public water system" means a system for the provision to the public of piped water for human consumption, if such system has at least fifteen service connections or regularly serves at least twenty-five individuals. Such term includes (A) any collection, treatment, storage, and distribution facilities under control of the operator of such system and used primarily in connection with such system, and (B) any collection or pretreatment storage facilities not under such control which are used primarily in connection with such system.

(5) The term "supplier of water" means any person who owns or operates a public water system.

(6) The term "contaminant" means any physical, chemical, biological, or radiological substance or matter in water.

(7) The term "Administrator" means the Administrator of the Environmental Protection Agency.

(8) The term "Agency" means the Environmental Protection Agency.

(9) The term "Council" means the National Drinking Water Advisory Council established under section 300j–5 of this title.

(10) The term "municipality" means a city, town, or other public body created by or pursuant to State law, or an Indian Tribe.

(11) The term "Federal agency" means any department, agency, or instrumentality of the United States.

(12) The term "person" means an individual, corporation, company, association, partnership, State, municipality, or Federal agency (and includes officers, employees, and agents of any corporation, company, association, State, municipality, or Federal agency).

(13) The term "State" includes, in addition to the several States, only the District of Columbia, Guam, the Commonwealth of Puerto Rico, the Northern Mariana Islands, the Virgin Islands, American Samoa, and the Trust Territory of the Pacific Islands.

(14) The term "Indian Tribe" means any Indian tribe having a Federally recognized governing body carrying out substantial governmental duties and powers over any area.

(July 1, 1944, ch. 373, title XIV, § 1401, as added Dec. 16, 1974, Pub.L. 93–523, § 2(a), 88 Stat. 1661, and amended June 23, 1976, Pub.L. 94–317, title III, § 301(b)(2), 90 Stat. 707; Oct. 12, 1976, Pub.L. 94–484, title IX, § 905(b)(1), 90 Stat. 2325; Nov. 16, 1977, Pub.L. 95–190, § 8(b), 91 Stat. 1397; June 19, 1986, Pub.L. 99–339, Title III, § 302(b), 100 Stat. 666.)

PART B—PUBLIC WATER SYSTEMS

Library References

Waters and Water Courses ⚖196, 202.
C.J.S. Waters §§ 232 et seq., 280.

§ 300g. Coverage

Subject to sections 300g–4 and 300g–5 of this title, national primary drinking water regulations under this part shall apply to each public water system in each State; except that such regulations shall not apply to a public water system—

(1) which consists only of distribution and storage facilities (and does not have any collection and treatment facilities);

(2) which obtains all of its water from, but is not owned or operated by, a public water system to which such regulations apply;

(3) which does not sell water to any person; and

(4) which is not a carrier which conveys passengers in interstate commerce.

(July 1, 1944, ch. 373, title XIV, § 1411, as added Dec. 16, 1974, Pub.L. 93–523, § 2(a), 88 Stat. 1662.)

Library References

Waters and Water Courses ⚖64.
C.J.S. Waters § 43 et seq.

§ 300g–1. National drinking water regulations

(a) National primary drinking water regulations; maximum contaminant level goals; simultaneous publication of regulations and goals

(1) Effective on June 19, 1986, each national interim or revised primary drinking water regulation

promulgated under this section before June 19, 1986, shall be deemed to be a national primary drinking water regulation under subsection (b) of this section. No such regulation shall be required to comply with the standards set forth in subsection (b)(4) of this section unless such regulation is amended to establish a different maximum contaminant level after June 19, 1986.

(2) After June 19, 1986, each recommended maximum contaminant level published before June 19, 1986, shall be treated as a maximum contaminant level goal.

(3) Whenever a national primary drinking water regulation is proposed under paragraph (1), (2), or (3) of subsection (b) of this section for any contaminant, the maximum contaminant level goal for such contaminant shall be proposed simultaneously. Whenever a national primary drinking water regulation is promulgated under paragraph (1), (2), or (3) of subsection (b) of this section for any contaminant, the maximum contaminant level goal for such contaminant shall be published simultaneously.

(4) Paragraph (3) shall not apply to any recommended maximum contaminant level published before June 19, 1986.

(b) Standard setting schedules and deadlines; substitution of contaminants; additional contaminants; adequate safety margin in levels; "feasible" defined; technology, techniques, or other means to meet contaminant level; alternative treatment techniques; filtration and disinfection as required treatment techniques; amendment, review, effective date, and supersedure of regulations; addition of substances unrelated contamination

(1) In the case of those contaminants listed in the Advance Notice of Proposed Rulemaking published in volume 47, Federal Register, page 9352, and in volume 48, Federal Register, page 45502, the Administrator shall publish maximum contaminant level goals and promulgate national primary drinking water regulations—

(A) not later than 12 months after June 19, 1986, for not less than 9 of those listed contaminants;

(B) not later than 24 months after June 19, 1986, for not less than 40 of those listed contaminants; and

(C) not later than 36 months after June 19, 1986, for the remainder of such listed contaminants.

(2)(A) If the Administrator identifies a drinking water contaminant the regulation of which, in the judgment of the Administrator, is more likely to be protective of public health (taking into account the schedule for regulation under paragraph (1)) than a contaminant referred to in paragraph (1), the Administrator may publish a maximum contaminant level goal and promulgate a national primary drinking water regulation for such identified contaminant in lieu of regulating the contaminant referred to in such paragraph. There may be no more than 7 contaminants in paragraph (1) for which substitutions may be made. Regulation of a contaminant identified under this paragraph shall be in accordance with the schedule applicable to the contaminant for which the substitution is made.

(B) If the Administrator identifies one or more contaminants for substitution under this paragraph, the Administrator shall publish in the Federal Register not later than one year after June 19, 1986, a list of contaminants proposed for substitution, the contaminants referred to in paragraph (1) for which substitutions are to be made, and the basis for the judgment that regulation of such proposed substitute contaminants is more likely to be protective of public health (taking into account the schedule for regulation under such paragraph). Following a period of 60 days for public comment, the Administrator shall publish in the Federal Register a final list of contaminants to be substituted and contaminants referred to in paragraph (1) for which substitutions are to be made, together with responses to significant comments.

(C) Any contaminant referred to in paragraph (1) for which a substitution is made, pursuant to subparagraph (A) of this paragraph, shall be included on the priority list to be published by the Administrator not later than January 1, 1988, pursuant to paragraph (3)(A).

(D) The Administrator's decision to regulate a contaminant identified pursuant to this paragraph in lieu of a contaminant referred to in paragraph (1) shall not be subject to judicial review.

(3)(A) The Administrator shall publish maximum contaminant level goals and promulgate national primary drinking water regulations for each contaminant (other than a contaminant referred to in paragraph (1) or (2) for which a national primary drinking water regulation was promulgated) which, in the judgment of the Administrator, may have any adverse effect on the health of persons and which is known or anticipated to occur in public water systems. Not later than January 1, 1988, and at 3 year intervals thereafter, the Administrator shall publish a list of contaminants which are known or anticipated to occur in public water systems and which may require regulation under this chapter.

(B) For the purpose of establishing the list under subparagraph (A), the Administrator shall form an advisory working group including members from the National Toxicology Program and the Environmental Protection Agency's Offices of Drinking Water, Pesticides, Toxic Substances, Ground Water, Solid Waste and Emergency Response and any others the Administrator deems appropriate. The Administrator's consideration of priorities shall include, but not be limited to, substances referred to in section 9601(14) of this title, and substances registered as pesticides under the Federal Insecticide, Fungicide, and Rodenticide Act [7 U.S.C. 136 et seq.].

(C) Not later than 24 months after the listing of contaminants under subparagraph (A), the Administrator shall publish proposed maximum contaminant level goals and national primary drinking water regulations for not less than 25 contaminants from the list established under subparagraph (A).

(D) Not later than 36 months after the listing of contaminants under subparagraph (A), the Administrator shall publish a maximum contaminant goal and promulgate a national primary drinking water regulation for those contaminants for which proposed maximum contaminant level goals and proposed national primary drinking water regulations were published under subparagraph (C).

(4) Each maximum contaminant level goal established under this subsection shall be set at the level at which no known or anticipated adverse effects on the health of persons occur and which allows an adequate margin of safety. Each national primary drinking water regulation for a contaminant for which a maximum contaminant level goal is established under this subsection shall specify a maximum level for such contaminant which is as close to the maximum contaminant level goal as is feasible.

(5) For the purposes of this subsection, the term "feasible" means feasible with the use of the best technology, treatment techniques and other means which the Administrator finds, after examination for efficacy under field conditions and not solely under laboratory conditions, are available (taking cost into consideration). For the purpose of paragraph (4), granular activated carbon is feasible for the control of synthetic organic chemicals, and any technology, treatment technique, or other means found to be the best available for the control of synthetic organic chemicals must be at least as effective in controlling synthetic organic chemicals as granular activated carbon.

(6) Each national primary drinking water regulation which establishes a maximum contaminant level shall list the technology, treatment techniques, and other means which the Administrator finds to be feasible for purposes of meeting such maximum contaminant level, but a regulation under this paragraph shall not require that any specified technology, treatment technique, or other means be used for purposes of meeting such maximum contaminant level.

(7)(A) The Administrator is authorized to promulgate a national primary drinking water regulation that requires the use of a treatment technique in lieu of establishing a maximum contaminant level, if the Administrator makes a finding that it is not economically or technologically feasible to ascertain the level of the contaminant. In such case, the Administrator shall identify those treatment techniques which, in the Administrator's judgment, would prevent known or anticipated adverse effects on the health of persons to the extent feasible. Such regulations shall specify each treatment technique known to the Administrator which meets the requirements of this paragraph, but the Administrator may grant a variance from any specified treatment technique in accordance with section 300g–4(a)(3) of this title.

(B) Any schedule referred to in this subsection for the promulgation of a national primary drinking water regulation for any contaminant shall apply in the same manner if the regulation requires a treatment technique in lieu of establishing a maximum contaminant level.

(C)(i) Not later than 18 months after June 19, 1986, the Administrator shall propose and promulgate national primary drinking water regulations specifying criteria under which filtration (including coagulation and sedimentation, as appropriate) is required as a treatment technique for public water systems supplied by surface water sources. In promulgating such rules, the Administrator shall consider the quality of source waters, protection afforded by watershed management, treatment practices (such as disinfection and length of water storage) and other factors relevant to protection of health.

(ii) In lieu of the provisions of section 300g–4 of this title the Administrator shall specify procedures by which the State determines which public water systems within its jurisdiction shall adopt filtration under the criteria of clause (i). The State may require the public water system to provide studies or other information to assist in this determination. The procedures shall provide notice and opportunity for public hearing on this determination. If the State determines that filtration is required, the State shall prescribe a schedule for compliance by the public water system with the filtration requirement. A schedule shall require compliance within 18 months of a determination made under clause (iii).

(iii) Within 18 months from the time that the Administrator establishes the criteria and procedures under this subparagraph, a State with primary enforcement responsibility shall adopt any necessary regulations to implement this subparagraph. Within 12 months of adoption of such regulations the State shall make determinations regarding filtration for all the public water systems within its jurisdiction supplied by surface waters.

(iv) If a State does not have primary enforcement responsibility for public water systems, the Administrator shall have the same authority to make the determination in clause (ii) in such State as the State would have under that clause. Any filtration requirement or schedule under this subparagraph shall be treated as if it were a requirement of a national primary drinking water regulation.

(8) Not later than 36 months after June 19, 1986, the Administrator shall propose and promulgate national primary drinking water regulations requiring disinfection as a treatment technique for all public water systems. The Administrator shall simultaneously promulgate a rule specifying criteria that will be used by the Administrator (or delegated State authorities) to grant variances from this requirement according to the provisions of sections 300g-4(a)(1)(B) and 300g-4(a)(3) of this title. In implementing section 300j-1(g) of this title the Administrator or the delegated State authority shall, where appropriate, give special consideration to providing technical assistance to small public water systems in complying with the regulations promulgated under this paragraph.

(9) Revised national primary drinking water regulations shall be amended whenever changes in technology, treatment techniques, and other means permit greater protection of the health of persons, but in any event such regulations shall be reviewed at least once every 3 years. Such review shall include an analysis of innovations or changes in technology, treatment techniques or other activities that have occurred over the previous 3-year period and that may provide for greater protection of the health of persons. The findings of such review shall be published in the Federal Register. If, after opportunity for public comment, the Administrator concludes that the technology, treatment techniques, or other means resulting from such innovations or changes are not feasible within the meaning of paragraph (5), an explanation of such conclusion shall be published in the Federal Register.

(10) Revised national primary drinking water regulations promulgated under this subsection (and amendments thereto) shall take effect eighteen months after the date of their promulgation. Regulations under subsection (a) of this section shall be superseded by regulations under this subsection to the extent provided by the regulations under this subsection.

(11) No national primary drinking water regulation may require the addition of any substance for preventive health care purposes unrelated to contamination of drinking water.

(c) Secondary regulations; publication of proposed regulations; promulgation; amendments

The Administrator shall publish proposed national secondary drinking water regulations within 270 days after December 16, 1974. Within 90 days after publication of any such regulation, he shall promulgate such regulation with such modifications as he deems appropriate. Regulations under this subsection may be amended from time to time.

(d) Regulations; public hearings; administrative consultations

Regulations under this section shall be prescribed in accordance with section 553 of title 5 (relating to rulemaking), except that the Administrator shall provide opportunity for public hearing prior to promulgation of such regulations. In proposing and promulgating regulations under this section, the Administrator shall consult with the Secretary and the National Drinking Water Advisory Council.

(e) Science Advisory Board comments

The Administrator shall request comments from the Science Advisory Board (established under the Environmental Research, Development, and Demonstration Act of 1978) prior to proposal of a maximum contaminant level goal and national primary drinking water regulation. The Board shall respond, as it deems appropriate, within the time period applicable for promulgation of the national primary drinking water standard concerned. This subsection shall, under no circumstances, be used to delay final promulgation of any national primary drinking water standard.

(July 1, 1944, ch. 373, title XIV, § 1412, as added Dec. 16, 1974, Pub.L. 93-523, § 2(a), 88 Stat. 1662, and amended Nov. 16, 1977, Pub.L. 95-190, §§ 3(c), 12(a), 91 Stat. 1394, 1398; June 19, 1986, Pub.L. 99-339, Title I, § 101(a), (b), (c)(1), (d), (e), 100 Stat. 642-646.)

Cross References

Bottled drinking water standards, see section 349 of Title 21, Food and Drugs.

Code of Federal Regulations

Additional primary and secondary drinking water provisions, see 40 CFR 141.1 et seq., 143.1 et seq.

Environmental impact and related procedures, see 23 CFR 771.101 et seq.

Library References

Waters and Water Courses ⚷202.
C.J.S. Waters § 280.

§ 300g–2. State primary enforcement responsibility; regulations; notice and hearing; publication in Federal Register; applications

(a) For purposes of this subchapter, a State has primary enforcement responsibility for public water systems during any period for which the Administrator determines (pursuant to regulations prescribed under subsection (b) of this section) that such State—

(1) has adopted drinking water regulations which are no less stringent than the national primary drinking water regulations in effect under sections 300g–1(a) and 300g–1(b) of this title;

(2) has adopted and is implementing adequate procedures for the enforcement of such State regulations, including conducting such monitoring and making such inspections as the Administrator may require by regulation;

(3) will keep such records and make such reports with respect to its activities under paragraphs (1) and (2) as the Administrator may require by regulation;

(4) if it permits variances or exemptions, or both, from the requirements of its drinking water regulations which meet the requirements of paragraph (1), permits such variances and exemptions under conditions and in a manner which is not less stringent than the conditions under, and the manner in which variances and exemptions may be granted under sections 300g–4 and 300g–5 of this title;

(5) has adopted and can implement an adequate plan for the provision of safe drinking water under emergency circumstances.

(b)(1) The Administrator shall, by regulation (proposed within 180 days of December 16, 1974), prescribe the manner in which a State may apply to the Administrator for a determination that the requirements of paragraphs (1), (2), (3), and (4) of subsection (a) of this section are satisfied with respect to the State, the manner in which the determination is made, the period for which the determination will be effective, and the manner in which the Administrator may determine that such requirements are no longer met. Such regulations shall require that before a determination of the Administrator that such requirements are met or are no longer met with respect to a State may become effective, the Administrator shall notify such State of the determination and the reasons therefor and shall provide an opportunity for public hearing on the determination. Such regulations shall be promulgated (with such modifications as the Administrator deems appropriate) within 90 days of the publication of the proposed regulations in the Federal Register. The Administrator shall promptly notify in writing the chief executive officer of each State of the promulgation of regulations under this paragraph. Such notice shall contain a copy of the regulations and shall specify a State's authority under this subchapter when it is determined to have primary enforcement responsibility for public water systems.

(2) When an application is submitted in accordance with the Administrator's regulations under paragraph (1), the Administrator shall within 90 days of the date on which such application is submitted (A) make the determination applied for, or (B) deny the application and notify the applicant in writing of the reasons for his denial.

(July 1, 1944, ch. 373, title XIV, § 1413, as added Dec. 16, 1974, Pub.L. 93–523, § 2(a), 88 Stat. 1665, as amended June 19, 1986, Pub.L. 99–339, Title I, § 101(c)(2), 100 Stat. 646.)

Code of Federal Regulations

Implementation and enforcement of national primary drinking water regulations, see 40 CFR 142.1 et seq.

Library References

States ⇐4.10.
C.J.S. States § 24.

§ 300g–3. Enforcement of drinking water regulations

(a) Notice to State and public water system; issuance of administrative order; civil action

(1)(A) Whenever the Administrator finds during a period during which a State has primary enforcement responsibility for public water systems (within the meaning of section 300g–2(a) of this title) that any public water system—

(i) for which a variance under section 300g–4 or an exemption under section 300g–5 of this title is not in effect, does not comply with any national primary drinking water regulation in effect under section 300g–1 of this title, or

(ii) for which a variance under section 300g–4 or an exemption under section 300g–5 of this title is in effect, does not comply with any schedule or other requirement imposed pursuant thereto,

he shall so notify the State and such public water system and provide such advice and technical assistance to such State and public water system as may be appropriate to bring the system into compliance with such regulation or requirement by the earliest feasible time.

(B) If, beyond the thirtieth day after the Administrator's notification under subparagraph (A), the State has not commenced appropriate enforcement action, the Administrator shall issue an order under subsection (g) of this section requiring the public water system to comply with such regulation or requirement or the Administrator shall commence a civil action under subsection (b) of this section.

(2) Whenever, on the basis of information available to him, the Administrator finds during a period during which a State does not have primary enforcement responsibility for public water systems that a public water system in such State—

(A) for which a variance under section 300g-4(a)(2) or an exemption under section 300g-5(f) of this title is not in effect, does not comply with any national primary drinking water regulation in effect under section 300g-1 of this title, or

(B) for which a variance under section 300g-4(a)(2) or an exemption under section 300g-5(f) of this title is in effect, does not comply with any schedule or other requirement imposed pursuant thereto,

the Administrator shall issue an order under subsection (g) of this section requiring the public water system to comply with such regulation or requirement or the Administrator shall commence a civil action under subsection (b) of this section.

(b) Judicial determinations in appropriate Federal district courts; civil penalties; separate violations

The Administrator may bring a civil action in the appropriate United States district court to require compliance with a national primary drinking water regulation, with an order issued under subsection (g) of this section, or with any schedule or other requirement imposed pursuant to a variance or exemption granted under section 300g-4 or 300g-5 of this title if—

(1) authorized under paragraph (1) or (2) of subsection (a) of this section, or

(2) if requested by (A) the chief executive officer of the State in which is located the public water system which is not in compliance with such regulation or requirement, or (B) the agency of such State which has jurisdiction over compliance by public water systems in the State with national primary drinking water regulations or State drinking water regulations.

The court may enter, in an action brought under this subsection, such judgment as protection of public health may require, taking into consideration the time necessary to comply and the availability of alternative water supplies; and, if the court determines that there has been a violation of the regulation or schedule or other requirement with respect to which the action was brought, the court may, taking into account the seriousness of the violation, the population at risk, and other appropriate factors, impose on the violator a civil penalty of not to exceed $25,000 for each day in which such violation occurs.

(c) Notice of owner or operator of public water system to persons served; regulations for form, manner, and frequency of notice; amendment of regulations to provide different types and frequencies of notice; penalties

Each owner or operator of a public water system shall give notice to the persons served by it—

(1) of any failure on the part of the public water system to—

(A) comply with an applicable maximum contaminant level or treatment technique requirement of, or a testing procedure prescribed by, a national primary drinking water regulation, or

(B) perform monitoring required by section 300j-4(a) of this title, and

(2) if the public water system is subject to a variance granted under section 300g-4(a)(1)(A) or 300g-4(a)(2) of this title for an inability to meet a maximum contaminant level requirement or is subject to an exemption granted under section 300g-5 of this title, of—

(A) the existence of such variance or exemption, and

(B) any failure to comply with the requirements of any schedule prescribed pursuant to the variance or exemption.

The Administrator shall by regulation prescribe the form, manner, and frequency for giving notice under this subsection. Within 15 months after June 19, 1986, the Administrator shall amend such regulations to provide for different types and frequencies of notice based on the differences between violations which are intermittent or infrequent and violations which are continuous or frequent. Such regulations shall also take into account the seriousness of any potential adverse health effects which may be involved. Notice of any violation of a maximum contaminant level or any other violation designated by the Administrator as posing a serious potential adverse health effect shall be given as soon as possible, but in no case later than 14 days after the violation. Notice of a continuous violation of a regulation other than a maximum contaminant level shall be given no less frequently than every 3 months. Notice of violations judged to be less serious shall be given no less frequently than annually. The Administrator shall specify the types of notice to be used to provide information as promptly and effectively as possible taking into account both the seriousness of any potential adverse health effects and the likelihood of reaching all affected persons. Notification of violations shall include notice by general circulation newspaper serving the area and, whenever appropriate, shall also include a press release to electronic media and individual mailings. Notice under this subsection shall provide a clear and readily understandable explanation of the violation, any potential adverse health effects, the steps that the system is taking to correct such violation, and the necessity for seeking alternative water supplies, if any, until the violation is corrected. Until such amended regulations are promulgated, the regulations in effect on June 19, 1986, shall remain in effect. The Administrator may also require the owner or operator of a public water system to give notice to the persons served by it of contaminant levels of any unregulated contaminant required to be monitored under section 300j–4(a) of this title. Any person who violates this subsection or regulations issued under this subsection shall be subject to a civil penalty of not to exceed $25,000.

(d) Notice of noncompliance with secondary drinking water regulations

Whenever, on the basis of information available to him, the Administrator finds that within a reasonable time after national secondary drinking water regulations have been promulgated, one or more public water systems in a State do not comply with such secondary regulations, and that such noncompliance appears to result from a failure of such State to take reasonable action to assure that public water systems throughout such State meet such secondary regulations, he shall so notify the State.

(e) State authority to adopt or enforce laws or regulations respecting drinking water regulations or public water systems unaffected

Nothing in this subchapter shall diminish any authority of a State or political subdivision to adopt or enforce any law or regulation respecting drinking water regulations or public water systems, but no such law or regulation shall relieve any person of any requirement otherwise applicable under this subchapter.

(f) Notice and public hearing; availability of recommendations transmitted to State and public water system

If the Administrator makes a finding of noncompliance (described in subparagraph (A) or (B) of subsection (a)(1) of this section) with respect to a public water system in a State which has primary enforcement responsibility, the Administrator may, for the purpose of assisting that State in carrying out such responsibility and upon the petition of such State or public water system or persons served by such system, hold, after appropriate notice, public hearings for the purpose of gathering information from technical or other experts, Federal, State, or other public officials, representatives of such public water system, persons served by such system, and other interested persons on—

(1) the ways in which such system can within the earliest feasible time be brought into compliance with the regulation or requirement with respect to which such finding was made, and

(2) the means for the maximum feasible protection of the public health during any period in which such system is not in compliance with a national primary drinking water regulation or requirement applicable to a variance or exemption.

On the basis of such hearings the Administrator shall issue recommendations which shall be sent to such State and public water system and shall be made available to the public and communications media.

(g) Administrative order requiring compliance; notice and hearing; civil penalty; civil actions

(1) In any case in which the Administrator is authorized to bring a civil action under this section or under section 300j–4 of this title with respect to any regulation, schedule, or other requirement, the Administrator also may issue an order to require compliance with such regulation, schedule, or other requirement.

(2) An order issued under this subsection shall not take effect until after notice and opportunity for public hearing and, in the case of a State having primary enforcement responsibility for public water systems in that State, until after the Administrator has provided the State with an opportunity to confer with the Administrator regarding the proposed order. A copy of any order proposed to be issued under this subsection shall be sent to the appropriate State agency of the State involved if the State has primary enforcement responsibility for public water systems in that State. Any order issued under this subsection shall state with reasonable specificity the nature of the violation. In any case in which an order under this subsection is issued to a corporation, a copy of such order shall be issued to appropriate corporate officers.

(3)(A) Any person who violates, or fails or refuses to comply with, an order under this subsection shall be liable to the United States for a civil penalty of not more than $25,000 per day of violation.

(B) Whenever any civil penalty sought by the Administrator under this paragraph does not exceed a total of $5,000, the penalty shall be assessed by the Administrator after notice and opportunity for a hearing on the record in accordance with section 554 of Title 5.

(C) Whenever any civil penalty sought by the Administrator under this paragraph exceeds $5,000, the penalty shall be assessed by a civil action brought by the Administrator in the appropriate United States district court (as determined under the provisions of Title 28).

(D) If any person fails to pay an assessment of a civil penalty after it has become a final and unappealable order, or after the appropriate court of appeals has entered final judgment in favor of the Administrator, the Attorney General shall recover the amount for which such person is liable in any appropriate district court of the United States. In any such action, the validity and appropriateness of the final order imposing the civil penalty shall not be subject to review.

(July 1, 1944, ch. 373, title XIV, § 1414, as added Dec. 16, 1974, Pub.L. 93–523, § 2(a), 88 Stat. 1666, and amended Nov. 16, 1977, Pub.L. 95–190, § 12(b), 91 Stat. 1398; June 19, 1986, Pub.L. 99–339, Title I, §§ 102, 103, 100 Stat. 647, 648.)

Code of Federal Regulations

Implementation and enforcement of national primary drinking water regulations, see 40 CFR 142.1 et seq.

Library References

States ⟹4.10.
C.J.S. States § 24.

§ 300g–4. Variances

(a) Characteristics of raw water sources; specific treatment technique; notice to Administrator, reasons for variance; compliance, enforcement; approval or revision of schedules and revocation of variances; review of variances and schedules; publication in Federal Register, notice and results of review; notice to State; considerations respecting abuse of discretion in granting variances or failing to prescribe schedules; State corrective action; authority of Administrator in State without primary enforcement responsibility; alternative treatment techniques

Notwithstanding any other provision of this part, variances from national primary drinking water regulations may be granted as follows:

(1)(A) A State which has primary enforcement responsibility for public water systems may grant one or more variances from an applicable national primary drinking water regulation to one or more public water systems within its jurisdiction which, because of characteristics of the raw water sources which are reasonably available to the systems, cannot meet the requirements respecting the maximum contaminant levels of such drinking water regulation. A variance may only be issued to a system after the system's application of the best technology, treatment techniques, or other means, which the Administrator finds are available (taking costs into consideration). The Administrator shall propose and promulgate his finding of the best available technology, treatment techniques or other means available for each contaminant for purposes of this subsection at the time he proposes and promulgates a maximum contaminant level for each such contaminant. The Administrator's finding of best available technology, treatment techniques or other means for purposes of this subsection may vary depending on the number of persons served by the system or for other physical conditions related to engineering feasibility and costs of compliance with maximum contaminant levels as considered appropriate by the Administrator. Before a State may grant a variance under this subparagraph, the State must find that the variance will not result in an unreasonable risk to health. If a State grants a public water system a variance under this subparagraph, the State shall prescribe at the time the variance is granted, a schedule for—

(i) compliance (including increments of progress) by the public water system with each contaminant level requirement with respect to which the variance was granted, and

(ii) implementation by the public water system of such additional control measures as the State may require for each contaminant, subject to such contaminant level requirement, during the period ending on the date compliance with such a requirement is required.

Before a schedule prescribed by a State pursuant to this subparagraph may take effect, the State shall provide notice and opportunity for a public hearing on the schedule. A notice given pursuant to the preceding sentence may cover the prescribing of more than one such schedule and a hearing held pursuant to such notice shall include each of the schedules covered by the notice. A schedule prescribed pursuant to this subparagraph for a public water system granted a variance shall require compliance by the system with each contaminant level requirement with respect to which the variance was granted as expeditiously as practicable (as the State may reasonably determine).

(B) A State which has primary enforcement responsibility for public water systems may grant to one or more public water systems within its jurisdiction one or more variances from any provision of a national primary drinking water regulation which requires the use of a specified treatment technique with respect to a contaminant if the public water system applying for the variance demonstrates to the satisfaction of the State that such treatment technique is not necessary to protect the health of persons because of the nature of the raw water source of such system. A variance granted under this subparagraph shall be conditioned on such monitoring and other requirements as the Administrator may prescribe.

(C) Before a variance proposed to be granted by a State under subparagraph (A) or (B) may take effect, such State shall provide notice and opportunity for public hearing on the proposed variance. A notice given pursuant to the preceding sentence may cover the granting of more than one variance and a hearing held pursuant to such notice shall include each of the variances covered by the notice. The State shall promptly notify the Administrator of all variances granted by it. Such notification shall contain the reason for the variance (and in the case of a variance under subparagraph (A), the basis for the finding required by that subparagraph before the granting of the variance) and documentation of the need for the variance.

(D) Each public water system's variance granted by a State under subparagraph (A) shall be conditioned by the State upon compliance by the public water system with the schedule prescribed by the State pursuant to that subparagraph. The requirements of each schedule prescribed by a State pursuant to that subparagraph shall be enforceable by the State under its laws. Any requirement of a schedule on which a variance granted under that subparagraph is conditioned may be enforced under section 300g–3 of this title as if such requirement was part of a national primary drinking water regulation.

(E) Each schedule prescribed by a State pursuant to subparagraph (A) shall be deemed approved by the Administrator unless the variance for which it was prescribed is revoked by the Administrator under subparagraph (G) or the schedule is revised by the Administrator under such subparagraph.

(F) Not later than 18 months after the effective date of the interim national primary drinking water regulations the Administrator shall complete a comprehensive review of the variances granted under subparagraph (A) (and schedules prescribed pursuant thereto) and under subparagraph (B) by the States during the one-year period beginning on such effective date. The Administrator shall conduct such subsequent reviews of variances and schedules as he deems necessary to carry out the purposes of this subchapter, but each subsequent review shall be completed within each 3-year period following the completion of the first review under this subparagraph. Before conducting any review under this subparagraph, the Administrator shall publish notice of the proposed review in the Federal Register. Such notice shall (i) provide information respecting the location of data and other information respecting the variances to be reviewed (including data and other information concerning new scientific matters bearing on such variances), and (ii) advise of the opportunity to submit comments on the variances reviewed and on the need for continuing them. Upon completion of any such review, the Administrator shall publish in the Federal Register the results of his review together with findings responsive to comments submitted in connection with such review.

(G)(i) If the Administrator finds that a State has, in a substantial number of instances, abused its discretion in granting variances under subparagraph (A) or (B) or that in a substantial number of cases the State has failed to prescribe schedules in accordance with subparagraph (A), the Administrator shall notify the State of his findings. In determining if a State has abused its discretion in granting variances in a substantial number of instances, the Administrator shall consider the number of persons who are affected by the variances and if the requirements applicable to the granting of the variances were complied with. A notice under this clause shall—

(I) identify each public water system with respect to which the finding was made,

(II) specify the reasons for the finding, and

(III) as appropriate, propose revocations of specific variances or propose revised schedules or other requirements for specific public water systems granted variances, or both.

(ii) The Administrator shall provide reasonable notice and public hearing on the provisions of each notice given pursuant to clause (i) of this subparagraph. After a hearing on a notice pursuant to such clause, the Administrator shall (I) rescind the finding for which the notice was given and promptly notify the State of such rescission, or (II) promulgate (with such modifications as he deems appropriate) such variance revocations and revised schedules or other requirements proposed in such notice as he deems appropriate. Not later than 180 days after the date a notice is given pursuant to clause (i) of this subparagraph, the Administrator shall complete the hearing on the notice and take the action required by the preceding sentence.

(iii) If a State is notified under clause (i) of this subparagraph of a finding of the Administrator made with respect to a variance granted a public water system within that State or to a schedule or other requirement for a variance and if, before a revocation of such variance or a revision of such schedule or other requirement promulgated by the Administrator takes effect, the State takes corrective action with respect to such variance or schedule or other requirement which the Administrator determines makes his finding inapplicable to such variance or schedule or other requirement, the Administrator shall rescind the application of his finding to that variance or schedule or other requirement. No variance revocation or revised schedule or other requirement may take effect before the expiration of 90 days following the date of the notice in which the revocation or revised schedule or other requirement was proposed.

(2) If a State does not have primary enforcement responsibility for public water systems, the Administrator shall have the same authority to grant variances in such State as the State would have under paragraph (1) if it had primary enforcement responsibility.

(3) The Administrator may grant a variance from any treatment technique requirement of a national primary drinking water regulation upon a showing by any person that an alternative treatment technique not included in such requirement is at least as efficient in lowering the level of the contaminant with respect to which such requirement was prescribed. A variance under this paragraph shall be conditioned on the use of the alternative treatment technique which is the basis of the variance.

(b) Enforcement of schedule or other requirement

Any schedule or other requirement on which a variance granted under paragraph (1)(B) or (2) of subsection (a) of this section is conditioned may be enforced under section 300g–3 of this title as if such schedule or other requirement was part of a national primary drinking water regulation.

(c) Applications for variances; regulations: reasonable time for acting

If an application for a variance under subsection (a) of this section is made, the State receiving the application or the Administrator, as the case may be, shall act upon such application within a reasonable period (as determined under regulations prescribed by the Administrator) after the date of its submission.

(d) "Treatment technique requirement" defined

For purposes of this section, the term "treatment technique requirement" means a requirement in a national primary drinking water regulation which specifies for a contaminant (in accordance with section 300f(1)(C)(ii) of this title) each treatment technique known to the Administrator which leads to a reduction in the level of such contaminant sufficient to satisfy the requirements of section 300g–1(b)(3) of this title.

(July 1, 1944, ch. 373, title XIV, § 1415, as added Dec. 16, 1974, Pub.L. 93–523, § 2(a), 88 Stat. 1669, as amended June 19, 1986, Pub.L. 99–339, Title I, § 104, 100 Stat. 649.)

Code of Federal Regulations

Implementation and enforcement of national primary drinking water regulations, see 40 CFR 142.1 et seq.

Library References

Waters and Water Courses ⚷64.
C.J.S. Waters § 43 et seq.

§ 300g–5. Exemptions

(a) Requisite findings

A State which has primary enforcement responsibility may exempt any public water system within the State's jurisdiction from any requirement respecting a maximum contaminant level or any treatment technique requirement, or from both, of an applicable national primary drinking water regulation upon a finding that—

(1) due to compelling factors (which may include economic factors), the public water system is unable to comply with such contaminant level or treatment technique requirement,

(2) the public water system was in operation on the effective date of such contaminant level or treatment technique requirement, or, for a system that was not in operation by that date, only if no reasonable alternative source of drinking water is available to such new system, and,

(3) the granting of the exemption will not result in an unreasonable risk to health.

(b) Compliance schedule and implementation of control measures; notice and hearing; dates for compliance with schedule; extension of final date for compliance; compliance, enforcement; approval or revision of schedules and revocation of exemptions

(1) If a State grants a public water system an exemption under subsection (a) of this section, the State shall prescribe, at the time the exemption is granted, a schedule for—

(A) compliance (including increments of progress) by the public water system with each contaminant level requirement and treatment technique requirement with respect to which the exemption was granted, and

(B) implementation by the public water system of such control measures as the State may require for each contaminant, subject to such contaminant level requirement or treatment technique requirement, during the period ending on the date compliance with such requirement is required.

Before a schedule prescribed by a State pursuant to this subsection may take effect, the State shall provide notice and opportunity for a public hearing on the schedule. A notice given pursuant to the preceding sentence may cover the prescribing of more than one such schedule and a hearing held pursuant to such notice shall include each of the schedules covered by the notice.

(2)(A) A schedule prescribed pursuant to this subsection for a public water system granted an exemption under subsection (a) of this section shall require compliance by the system with each contaminant level and treatment technique requirement with respect to which the exemption was granted as expeditiously as practicable (as the State may reasonably determine) but (except as provided in subparagraph (B))—

(i) in the case of an exemption granted with respect to a contaminant level or treatment technique requirement prescribed by the national primary drinking water regulations promulgated under section 300g–1(a) of this title, not later than 12 months after June 19, 1986; and

(ii) in the case of an exemption granted with respect to a contaminant level or treatment technique requirement prescribed by national primary drinking water regulations, other than a regulation referred to in section 300g–1(a) of this title, 12 months after the date of the issuance of the exemption.

(B) The final date for compliance provided in any schedule in the case of any exemption may be extended by the State (in the case of a State which has primary enforcement responsibility) or by the Administrator (in any other case) for a period not to exceed 3 years after the date of the issuance of the exemption if the public water system establishes that—

(i) the system cannot meet the standard without capital improvements which cannot be completed within the period of such exemption;

(ii) in the case of a system which needs financial assistance for the necessary improvements, the system has entered into an agreement to obtain such financial assistance; or

(iii) the system has entered into an enforceable agreement to become a part of a regional public water system; and

the system is taking all practicable steps to meet the standard.

(C) In the case of a system which does not serve more than 500 service connections and which needs financial assistance for the necessary improvements, an exemption granted under clause (i) or (ii) of of subparagraph (B) may be renewed for one or more additional 2-year periods if the system establishes that it is taking all practicable steps to meet the requirements of subparagraph (B).

(3) Each public water system's exemption granted by a State under subsection (a) of this section shall be conditioned by the State upon compliance by the public water system with the schedule prescribed by the State pursuant to this subsection. The requirements of each schedule prescribed by a State pursuant to this subsection shall be enforceable by the State under its laws. Any requirement of a schedule on which an exemption granted under this section is conditioned may be enforced under section 300g–3 of this title as if such requirement was part of a national primary drinking water regulation.

(4) Each schedule prescribed by a State pursuant to this subsection shall be deemed approved by the Administrator unless the exemption for which it was prescribed is revoked by the Administrator under subsection (d)(2) of this section or the schedule is revised by the Administrator under such subsection.

(c) Notice to Administrator; reasons for exemption

Each State which grants an exemption under subsection (a) of this section shall promptly notify the Administrator of the granting of such exemption. Such notification shall contain the reasons for the exemption (including the basis for the finding required by subsection (a)(3) of this section before the exemption may be granted) and document the need for the exemption.

(d) Review of exemptions and schedules; publication in Federal Register, notice and results of review; notice to State; considerations respecting abuse of discretion in granting exemptions or failing to prescribe schedules; State corrective action

(1) Not later than 18 months after the effective date of the interim national primary drinking water regulations the Administrator shall complete a comprehensive review of the exemptions granted (and schedules prescribed pursuant thereto) by the States during the one-year period beginning on such effective date. The Administrator shall conduct such subsequent reviews of exemptions and schedules as he deems necessary to carry out the purposes of this subchapter, but each subsequent review shall be completed within each 3-year period following the completion of the first review under this subparagraph. Before conducting any review under this subparagraph, the Administrator shall publish notice of the proposed review in the Federal Register. Such notice shall (A) provide information respecting the location of data and other information respecting the exemptions to be reviewed (including data and other information concerning new scientific matters bearing on such exemptions), and (B) advise of the opportunity to submit comments on the exemptions reviewed and on the need for continuing them. Upon completion of any such review, the Administrator shall publish in the Federal Register the results of his review, together with findings responsive to comments submitted in connection with such review.

(2)(A) If the Administrator finds that a State has, in a substantial number of instances, abused its discretion in granting exemptions under subsection (a) of this section or failed to prescribe schedules in accordance with subsection (b) of this section, the Administrator shall notify the State of his findings. In determining if a State has abused its discretion in granting exemptions in a substantial number of instances, the Administrator shall consider the number of persons who are affected by the exemptions and if the requirements applicable to the granting of the exemptions were complied with. A notice under this subparagraph shall—

(i) identify each exempt public water system with respect to which the finding was made,

(ii) specify the reasons for the finding, and

(iii) as appropriate, propose revocations of specific exemptions or propose revised schedules for specific exempt public water systems, or both.

(B) The Administrator shall provide reasonable notice and public hearing on the provisions of each notice given pursuant to subparagraph (A). After a hearing on a notice pursuant to subparagraph (A), the Administrator shall (i) rescind the finding for which the notice was given and promptly notify the State of such rescission, or (ii) promulgate (with such modifications as he deems appropriate) such exemption revocations and revised schedules proposed in such notice as he deems appropriate. Not later than 180 days after the date a notice is given pursuant to subparagraph (A), the Administrator shall complete the hearing on the notice and take the action required by the preceding sentence.

(C) If a State is notified under subparagraph (A) of a finding of the Administrator made with respect to an exemption granted a public water system within that State or to a schedule prescribed pursuant to such an exemption and if before a revocation of such exemption or a revision of such schedule promulgated by the Administrator takes effect the State takes corrective action with respect to such exemption or schedule which the Administrator determines makes his finding inapplicable to such exemption or schedule, the Administrator shall rescind the application of his finding to that exemption or schedule. No exemption revocation or revised schedule may take effect before the expiration of 90 days following the date of the notice in which the revocation or revised schedule was proposed.

(e) "Treatment technique requirement" defined

For purposes of this section, the term "treatment technique requirement" means a requirement in a national primary drinking water regulation which specifies for a contaminant (in accordance with section 300f(1)(C)(ii) of this title) each treatment technique known to the Administrator which leads to a reduction in the level of such contaminant sufficient to satisfy the requirements of section 300g–1(b) of this title.

(f) Authority of Administrator in a State without primary enforcement responsibility

If a State does not have primary enforcement responsibility for public water systems, the Administrator shall have the same authority to exempt public water systems in such State from maximum contaminant level requirements and treatment technique requirements under the same conditions and in the same manner as the State would be authorized to grant exemptions under this section if it had primary enforcement responsibility.

(g) Applications for exemptions; regulations; reasonable time for acting

If an application for an exemption under this section is made, the State receiving the application or the Administrator, as the case may be, shall act upon such application within a reasonable period (as determined under regulations prescribed by the Administrator) after the date of its submission.

(July 1, 1944, ch. 373, title XIV, § 1416, as added Dec. 16, 1974, Pub.L. 93–523, § 2(a), 88 Stat. 1672, and amended Nov. 16, 1977, Pub.L. 95–190, § 10(a), 91 Stat. 1398; Dec. 5, 1980, Pub.L. 96–502, §§ 1, 4(b), 94 Stat. 2737, 2738; June 19, 1986, Pub.L. 99–339, Title I, §§ 101(c)(4), 105, 100 Stat. 646, 649.)

Code of Federal Regulations

Implementation and enforcement of national primary drinking water regulations, see 40 CFR 142.1 et seq.

Library References

Waters and Water Courses ⚷202.
C.J.S. Waters § 280.

§ 300g–6. Prohibition on use of lead pipes, solder, or flux

(a) In general

(1) Prohibition

Any pipe, solder, or flux, which is used after June 19, 1986, in the installation or repair of—

(A) any public water system, or

(B) any plumbing in a residential or nonresidential facility providing water for human consumption which is connected to a public water system,

shall be lead free (within the meaning of subsection (d) of this section). This paragraph shall not apply to leaded joints necessary for the repair of cast iron pipes.

(2) Public notice requirements

(A) In general

Each public water system shall identify and provide notice to persons that may be affected by lead contamination of their drinking water where such contamination results from either or both of the following:

(i) The lead content in the construction materials of the public water distribution system.

(ii) Corrosivity of the water supply sufficient to cause leaching of lead.

The notice shall be provided in such manner and form as may be reasonably required by the Administrator. Notice under this paragraph shall be provided notwithstanding the absence of a violation of any national drinking water standard.

(B) Contents of notice

Notice under this paragraph shall provide a clear and readily understandable explanation of—

(i) the potential sources of lead in the drinking water,

(ii) potential adverse health effects,

(iii) reasonably available methods of mitigating known or potential lead content in drinking water,

(iv) any steps the system is taking to mitigate lead content in drinking water, and

(v) the necessity for seeking alternative water supplies, if any.

(b) State enforcement

(1) Enforcement of prohibition

The requirements of subsection (a)(1) of this section shall be enforced in all States effective 24 months after June 19, 1986. States shall enforce such requirements through State or local plumbing codes, or such other means of enforcement as the State may determine to be appropriate.

(2) Enforcement of public notice requirements

The requirements of subsection (a)(2) of this section shall apply in all States effective 24 months after June 19, 1986.

(c) Penalties

If the Administrator determines that a State is not enforcing the requirements of subsection (a) of this section as required pursuant to subsection (b) of this section, the Administrator may withhold up to 5 percent of Federal funds available to that State for State program grants under section 300j–2(a) of this title.

(d) Definition of lead free

For purposes of this section, the term "lead free"—

(1) when used with respect to solders and flux refers to solders and flux containing not more than 0.2 percent lead, and

(2) when used with respect to pipes and pipe fittings refers to pipes and pipe fittings containing not more than 8.0 percent lead.

(July 1, 1944, c. 373, Title XIV, § 1417, as added June 19, 1986, Pub.L. 99–339, Title I, § 109(a)(1), 100 Stat. 651.)

PART C—PROTECTION OF UNDERGROUND SOURCES OF DRINKING WATER

Library References

Waters and Water Courses ⚷196, 202.
C.J.S. Waters §§ 232 et seq., 280.

§ 300h. Regulations for State programs

(a) Publication of proposed regulations; promulgation; amendments; public hearings; administrative consultations

(1) The Administrator shall publish proposed regulations for State underground injection control programs within 180 days after December 16, 1974. Within 180 days after publication of such proposed regulations, he shall promulgate such regulations with such modifications as he deems appropriate. Any regulation under this subsection may be amended from time to time.

(2) Any regulation under this section shall be proposed and promulgated in accordance with section 553 of title 5 (relating to rulemaking), except that the Administrator shall provide opportunity for public hearing prior to promulgation of such regulations. In proposing and promulgating regulations under this section, the Administrator shall consult with the Secretary, the National Drinking Water Advisory Council, and other appropriate Federal entities and with interested State entities.

(b) Minimum requirements; restrictions

(1) Regulations under subsection (a) of this section for State underground injection programs shall contain minimum requirements for effective programs to prevent underground injection which endangers drinking water sources within the meaning of subsection (d)(2) of this section. Such regulations shall require that a State program, in order to be approved under section 300h-1 of this title—

(A) shall prohibit, effective on the date on which the applicable underground injection control program takes effect, any underground injection in such State which is not authorized by a permit issued by the State (except that the regulations may permit a State to authorize underground injection by rule);

(B) shall require (i) in the case of a program which provides for authorization of underground injection by permit, that the applicant for the permit to inject must satisfy the State that the underground injection will not endanger drinking water sources, and (ii) in the case of a program which provides for such an authorization by rule, that no rule may be promulgated which authorizes any underground injection which endangers drinking water sources;

(C) shall include inspection, monitoring, recordkeeping, and reporting requirements; and

(D) shall apply (i) as prescribed by section 300j-6(b) of this title, to underground injections by Federal agencies, and (ii) to underground injections by any other person whether or not occurring on property owned or leased by the United States.

(2) Regulations of the Administrator under this section for State underground injection control programs may not prescribe requirements which interfere with or impede—

(A) the underground injection of brine or other fluids which are brought to the surface in connection with oil or natural gas production or natural gas storage operations, or

(B) any underground injection for the secondary or tertiary recovery of oil or natural gas,

unless such requirements are essential to assure that underground sources of drinking water will not be endangered by such injection.

(3)(A) The regulations of the Administrator under this section shall permit or provide for consideration of varying geologic, hydrological, or historical conditions in different States and in different areas within a State.

(B)(i) In prescribing regulations under this section the Administrator shall, to the extent feasible, avoid promulgation of requirements which would unnecessarily disrupt State underground injection control programs which are in effect and being enforced in a substantial number or[1] States.

(ii) For the purpose of this subparagraph, a regulation prescribed by the Administrator under this section shall be deemed to disrupt a State underground injection control program only if it would be infeasible to comply with both such regulation and the State underground injection control program.

(iii) For the purpose of this subparagraph, a regulation prescribed by the Administrator under this section shall be deemed unnecessary only if, without such regulation, underground sources of drinking water will not be endangered by an underground injection.

(C) Nothing in this section shall be construed to alter or affect the duty to assure that underground sources of drinking water will not be endangered by any underground injection.

(c) Temporary permits; notice and hearing

(1) The Administrator may, upon application of the Governor of a State which authorizes underground injection by means of permits, authorize such State to issue (without regard to subsection (b)(1)(B)(i) of this section) temporary permits for underground injection which may be effective until the expiration of four years after December 16, 1974, if—

(A) the Administrator finds that the State has demonstrated that it is unable and could not reasonably have been able to process all permit applications within the time available;

(B) the Administrator determines the adverse effect on the environment of such temporary permits is not unwarranted;

(C) such temporary permits will be issued only with respect to injection wells in operation on the date on which such State's permit program approved under this part first takes effect and for which there was inadequate time to process its permit application; and

(D) the Administrator determines the temporary permits require the use of adequate safeguards established by rules adopted by him.

(2) The Administrator may, upon application of the Governor of a State which authorizes underground injection by means of permits, authorize such State to issue (without regard to subsection (b)(1)(B)(i) of this section), but after reasonable notice and hearing, one or more temporary permits each of which is applicable to a particular injection well and to the underground injection of a particular fluid and which may be effective until the expiration of four years after December 16, 1974, if the State finds, on the record of such hearing—

(A) that technology (or other means) to permit safe injection of the fluid in accordance with the applicable underground injection control program is not generally available (taking costs into consideration);

(B) that injection of the fluid would be less harmful to health than the use of other available means of disposing of waste or producing the desired product; and

(C) that available technology or other means have been employed (and will be employed) to reduce the volume and toxicity of the fluid and to minimize the potentially adverse effect of the injection on the public health.

(d) "Underground injection" defined; underground injection endangerment of drinking water sources

For purposes of this part:

(1) The term "underground injection" means the subsurface emplacement of fluids by well injection. Such term does not include the underground injection of natural gas for purposes of storage.

(2) Underground injection endangers drinking water sources if such injection may result in the presence in underground water which supplies or can reasonably be expected to supply any public water system of any contaminant, and if the presence of such contaminant may result in such system's not complying with any national primary drinking water regulation or may otherwise adversely affect the health of persons.

1 So in original. Probably should read "of".

(July 1, 1944, ch. 373, title XIV, § 1421, as added Dec. 16, 1974, Pub.L. 93-523, § 2(a), 88 Stat. 1674, and amended Nov. 16, 1977, Pub.L. 95-190, § 6(b), 91 Stat. 1396; Dec. 5, 1980, Pub.L. 96-502, §§ 3, 4(c), 94 Stat. 2738; June 19, 1986, Pub.L. 99-339, Title II, § 201(a), 100 Stat. 653.)

Code of Federal Regulations

Environmental Protection Agency,
Administration of permit programs, see 40 CFR 122.1 et seq.
Decisionmaking procedures applicable to permit programs, see 40 CFR 124.1 et seq.
Underground injection control program, see 40 CFR 144.1.
Technical criteria and standards for, see 40 CFR 146.1 et seq.

Library References

Waters and Water Courses ⚷64.
C.J.S. Waters § 43 et seq.

§ 300h-1. State primary enforcement responsibility

(a) List of States in need of control program; amendment of list

Within 180 days after December 16, 1974, the Administrator shall list in the Federal Register each State for which in his judgment a State underground injection control program may be necessary to assure that underground injection will not endanger drinking water sources. Such list may be amended from time to time.

(b) State applications; notice to Administrator of compliance with revised or added requirements; approval or disapproval by Administrator; duration of State primary enforcement responsibility; public hearing

(1)(A) Each State listed under subsection (a) of this section shall within 270 days after the date of promulgation of any regulation under section 300h of this title (or, if later, within 270 days after such State is first listed under subsection (a) of this section) submit to the Administrator an application which contains a showing satisfactory to the Administrator that the State—

(i) has adopted after reasonable notice and public hearings, and will implement, an underground injection control program which meets the requirements of regulations in effect under section 300h of this title; and

(ii) will keep such records and make such reports with respect to its activities under its underground injection control program as the Administrator may require by regulation.

The Administrator may, for good cause, extend the date for submission of an application by any State under this subparagraph for a period not to exceed an additional 270 days.

(B) Within 270 days of any amendment of a regulation under section 300h of this title revising or adding any requirement respecting State underground injection control programs, each State listed under subsection (a) of this section shall submit (in such form and manner as the Administrator may require) a notice to the Administrator containing a showing satisfactory to him that the State underground injection control program meets the revised or added requirement.

(2) Within ninety days after the State's application under paragraph (1)(A) or notice under paragraph (1)(B) and after reasonable opportunity for presentation of views, the Administrator shall by rule either approve, disapprove, or approve in part and disapprove in part, the State's underground injection control program.

(3) If the Administrator approves the State's program under paragraph (2), the State shall have primary enforcement responsibility for underground water sources until such time as the Administrator determines, by rule, that such State no longer meets the requirements of clause (i) or (ii) of paragraph (1)(A) of this subsection.

(4) Before promulgating any rule under paragraph (2) or (3) of this subsection, the Administrator shall provide opportunity for public hearing respecting such rule.

(c) Program by Administrator for State without primary enforcement responsibility; restrictions

If the Administrator disapproves a State's program (or part thereof) under subsection (b)(2) of this section, if the Administrator determines under subsection (b)(3) of this section that a State no longer meets the requirements of clause (i) or (ii) of subsection (b)(1)(A) of this section, or if a State fails to submit an application or notice before the date of expiration of the period specified in subsection (b)(1) of this section, the Administrator shall by regulation within 90 days after the date of such disapproval, determination, or expiration (as the case may be) prescribe (and may from time to time by regulation revise) a program applicable to such State meeting the requirements of section 300h(b) of this title. Such program may not include requirements which interfere with or impede—

(1) the underground injection of brine or other fluids which are brought to the surface in connection with oil or natural gas production or natural gas storage operations, or

(2) any underground injection for the secondary or tertiary recovery of oil or natural gas,

unless such requirements are essential to assure that underground sources of drinking water will not be endangered by such injection. Such program shall apply in such State to the extent that a program adopted by such State which the Administrator determines meets such requirements is not in effect. Before promulgating any regulation under this section, the Administrator shall provide opportunity for public hearing respecting such regulation.

(d) "Applicable underground injection control program" defined

For purposes of this subchapter, the term "applicable underground injection control program" with respect to a State means the program (or most recent amendment thereof) (1) which has been adopted by the State and which has been approved under subsection (b) of this section, or (2) which has been prescribed by the Administrator under subsection (c) of this section.

(e) Primary enforcement responsibility by Indian tribe

An Indian Tribe may assume primary enforcement responsibility for underground injection control under this section consistent with such regulations as the Administrator has prescribed pursuant to this part and section 300j–11 of this title. The area over which such Indian Tribe exercises governmental jurisdiction need not have been listed under subsection (a) of this section, and such Tribe need not submit an application to assume primary enforcement responsibility within the 270-day deadline noted in subsection (b)(1)(A) of this section. Until an Indian Tribe assumes primary enforcement responsibility, the currently applicable underground injection control program shall continue to apply. If an applicable underground injection control program does not exist for an Indian Tribe, the Administrator shall prescribe such a program pursuant to subsection (c) of this section, and consistent with section 300h(b) of this title, within 270 days after June 19, 1986, unless an Indian Tribe first obtains approval to assume primary enforcement responsibility for underground injection control.

(July 1, 1944, ch. 373, title XIV, § 1422, as added Dec. 16, 1974, Pub.L. 93–523, § 2(a), 88 Stat. 1676, and amended Nov. 16, 1977, Pub.L. 95–190, § 6(a), 91 Stat. 1396; June 19, 1986, Pub.L. 99–339, Title II, § 201(a), Title III, § 302(c), 100 Stat. 653, 666.)

Code of Federal Regulations

Environmental Protection Agency,
  Administration of permit programs, see 40 CFR 122.1 et seq.
  Decisionmaking procedures applicable to permit programs, see 40 CFR 124.1 et seq.
Underground injection control programs,
  Additional requirements respecting, see 40 CFR 123.51 to 123.55.
  Technical criteria and standards for, see 40 CFR 146.1 et seq.

Library References

States ⚷4.10.
C.J.S. States § 24.

§ 300h–2. Enforcement of program

(a) Notice to State and violator; issuance of administrative order; civil action

(1) Whenever the Administrator finds during a period during which a State has primary enforcement responsibility for underground water sources (within the meaning of section 300h–1(b)(3) of this title or section 300h–4(c) of this title) that any person who is subject to a requirement of an applicable underground injection control program in such State is violating such requirement, he shall so notify the State and the person violating such requirement. If beyond the thirtieth day after the Administrator's notification the State has not commenced appropriate enforcement action, the Administrator shall issue an order under subsection (c) of this section requiring the person to comply with such requirement or the Administrator shall commence a civil action under subsection (b) of this section.

(2) Whenever the Administrator finds during a period during which a State does not have primary enforcement responsibility for underground water sources that any person subject to any requirement of any applicable underground injection control program in such State is violating such requirement, the Administrator shall issue an order under subsection (c) of this section requiring the person to comply with such requirement or the Administrator shall commence a civil action under subsection (b) of this section.

(b) Civil and criminal actions

Civil actions referred to in paragraphs (1) and (2) of subsection (a) of this section shall be brought in the appropriate United States district court. Such court shall have jurisdiction to require compliance with any requirement of an applicable underground injection program or with an order issued under subsection (c) of this section. The court may enter such judgment as protection of public health may require. Any person who violates any requirement of an applicable underground injection control program or an order requiring compliance under subsection (c) of this section—

(1) shall be subject to a civil penalty of not more than $25,000 for each day of such violation, and

(2) if such violation is willful, such person may, in addition to or in lieu of the civil penalty authorized by paragraph (1), be imprisoned for not more than 3 years, or fined in accordance with Title 18, or both.

(c) Administrative orders

(1) In any case in which the Administrator is authorized to bring a civil action under this section with respect to any regulation or other requirement of this part other than those relating to—

(A) the underground injection of brine or other fluids which are brought to the surface in connection with oil or natural gas production, or

(B) any underground injection for the secondary or tertiary recovery of oil or natural gas,

the Administrator may also issue an order under this subsection either assessing a civil penalty of not more than $10,000 for each day of violation for any past or current violation, up to a maximum administrative penalty of $125,000, or requiring compliance with such regulation or other requirement, or both.

(2) In any case in which the Administrator is authorized to bring a civil action under this section with respect to any regulation, or other requirement of this part relating to—

(A) the underground injection of brine or other fluids which are brought to the surface in connection with oil or natural gas production, or

(B) any underground injection for the secondary or tertiary recovery of oil or natural gas,

the Administrator may also issue an order under this subsection either assessing a civil penalty of not more than $5,000 for each day of violation for any past or current violation, up to a maximum administrative penalty of $125,000, or requiring compliance with such regulation or other requirement, or both.

(3)(A) An order under this subsection shall be issued by the Administrator after opportunity (provided in accordance with this subparagraph) for a hearing. Before issuing the order, the Administrator shall give to the person to whom it is directed written notice of the Administrator's proposal to issue such order and the opportunity to request, within 30 days of the date the notice is received by such person, a hearing on the order. Such hearing shall not be subject to section 554 or 556 of Title 5 but shall provide a reasonable opportunity to be heard and to present evidence.

(B) The Administrator shall provide public notice of, and reasonable opportunity to comment on, any proposed order.

(C) Any citizen who comments on any proposed order under subparagraph (B) shall be given notice of any hearing under this subsection and of any order. In any hearing held under subparagraph (A), such citizen shall have a reasonable opportunity to be heard and to present evidence.

(D) Any order issued under this subsection shall become effective 30 days following its issuance unless an appeal is taken pursuant to paragraph (6).

(4)(A) Any order issued under this subsection shall state with reasonable specificity the nature of the violation and may specify a reasonable time for compliance.

(B) In assessing any civil penalty under this subsection, the Administrator shall take into account appropriate factors, including (i) the seriousness of the violation; (ii) the economic benefit (if any) resulting from the violation; (iii) any history of such violations; (iv) any good-faith efforts to comply with the applicable requirements; (v) the economic impact of the penalty on the violator; and (vi) such other matters as justice may require.

(5) Any violation with respect to which the Administrator has commenced and is diligently prosecuting an action, or has issued an order under this subsection assessing a penalty, shall not be subject to an action under subsection (b) of this section or section 300h–3(c) or 300j–8 of this title, except that the foregoing limitation on civil actions under section 300j–8 of this title, shall not apply with respect to any violation for which—

(A) a civil action under section 300j–8(a)(1) of this title has been filed prior to commencement of an action under this subsection, or

(B) a notice of violation under section 300j–8(b)(1) of this title has been given before commencement of an action under this subsection and an action under section 300j–8(a)(1) of this title is filed before 120 days after such notice is given.

(6) Any person against whom an order is issued or who commented on a proposed order pursuant to paragraph (3) may file an appeal of such order with the United States District Court for the District of Columbia or the district in which the violation is alleged to have occurred. Such an appeal may only be filed within the 30-day period beginning on the date the order is issued. Appellant shall simultaneously send a copy of the appeal by certified mail to the Administrator and to the Attorney General. The Administrator shall promptly file in such court a certified copy of the record on which such order was imposed. The district court shall not set aside or remand such order unless there is not substantial evidence on the record, taken as a whole, to support the finding of a violation or, unless the Administrator's assessment of penalty or requirement for compliance constitutes an abuse of discretion. The district court shall not impose additional civil penalties for the same violation unless the Administrator's assessment of a penalty constitutes an abuse of discretion. Notwithstanding section 300j–7(a)(2) of this title, any order issued under paragraph (3) shall be subject to judicial review exclusively under this paragraph.

(7) If any person fails to pay an assessment of a civil penalty—

(A) after the order becomes effective under paragraph (3), or

(B) after a court, in an action brought under paragraph (6), has entered a final judgment in favor of the Administrator,

the Administrator may request the Attorney General to bring a civil action in an appropriate district court to recover the amount assessed (plus costs, attorneys' fees, and interest at currently prevailing rates from the date the order is effective or the date of such final judgment, as the case may be). In such an action, the validity, amount, and appropriateness of such penalty shall not be subject to review.

(8) The Administrator may, in connection with administrative proceedings under this subsection, issue subpoenas compelling the attendance and testimony of witnesses and subpoenas duces tecum, and may request the Attorney General to bring an action to enforce any subpoena under this section. The district courts shall have jurisdiction to enforce such subpoenas and impose sanction.

(d) State authority to adopt or enforce laws or regulations respecting underground injection unaffected

Nothing in this subchapter shall diminish any authority of a State or political subdivision to adopt or enforce any law or regulation respecting underground injection but no such law or regulation shall relieve any person of any requirement otherwise applicable under this subchapter.

(July 1, 1944, ch. 373, title XIV, § 1423, as added Dec. 16, 1974, Pub.L. 93–523, § 2(a), 88 Stat. 1677, and amended Dec. 5, 1980, Pub.L. 96–502, § 2(b), 94 Stat. 2738; June 19, 1986, Pub.L. 99–339, Title II, § 202, 100 Stat. 654.)

Code of Federal Regulations

Environmental Protection Agency,
Administration of permit programs, see 40 CFR 122.1 et seq.
Decisionmaking procedures applicable to permit programs, see 40 CFR 124.1 et seq.
Requirements, see 40 CFR 145.1.
Underground injection control programs, technical criteria and standards for, see 40 CFR 146.1 et seq.

§ 300h–3. Interim regulation of underground injections

(a) Necessity for well operation permit; designation of one aquifer areas

(1) Any person may petition the Administrator to have an area of a State (or States) designated as an area in which no new underground injection well may be operated during the period beginning on the date of the designation and ending on the date on which the applicable underground injection control program covering such area takes effect unless a permit for the operation of such well has been issued by the Administrator under subsection (b) of this section. The Administrator may so designate an area within a State if he finds that the area has one aquifer which is the sole or principal drinking water source for the area and which, if contaminated, would create a significant hazard to public health.

(2) Upon receipt of a petition under paragraph (1) of this subsection, the Administrator shall publish it in the Federal Register and shall provide an opportunity to interested persons to submit written data, views, or arguments thereon. Not later than the 30th day following the date of the publication of a petition under this paragraph in the Federal Register, the Administrator shall either make the designation for which the petition is submitted or deny the petition.

(b) Well operation permits; publication in Federal Register; notice and hearing; issuance or denial; conditions for issuance

(1) During the period beginning on the date an area is designated under subsection (a) of this sec-

tion and ending on the date the applicable underground injection control program covering such area takes effect, no new underground injection well may be operated in such area unless the Administrator has issued a permit for such operation.

(2) Any person may petition the Administrator for the issuance of a permit for the operation of such a well in such an area. A petition submitted under this paragraph shall be submitted in such manner and contain such information as the Administrator may require by regulation. Upon receipt of such a petition, the Administrator shall publish it in the Federal Register. The Administrator shall give notice of any proceeding on a petition and shall provide opportunity for agency hearing. The Administrator shall act upon such petition on the record of any hearing held pursuant to the preceding sentence respecting such petition. Within 120 days of the publication in the Federal Register of a petition submitted under this paragraph, the Administrator shall either issue the permit for which the petition was submitted or shall deny its issuance.

(3) The Administrator may issue a permit for the operation of a new underground injection well in an area designated under subsection (a) of this section only if he finds that the operation of such well will not cause contamination of the aquifer of such area so as to create a significant hazard to public health. The Administrator may condition the issuance of such a permit upon the use of such control measures in connection with the operation of such well, for which the permit is to be issued, as he deems necessary to assure that the operation of the well will not contaminate the aquifer of the designated area in which the well is located so as to create a significant hazard to public health.

(c) Civil penalties; separate violations; penalties for willful violations; temporary restraining order or injunction

Any person who operates a new underground injection well in violation of subsection (b) of this section, (1) shall be subject to a civil penalty of not more than $5,000 for each day in which such violation occurs, or (2) if such violation is willful, such person may, in lieu of the civil penalty authorized by clause (1), be fined not more than $10,000 for each day in which such violation occurs. If the Administrator has reason to believe that any person is violating or will violate subsection (b) of this section, he may petition the United States district court to issue a temporary restraining order or injunction (including a mandatory injunction) to enforce such subsection.

(d) "New underground injection well" defined

For purposes of this section, the term "new underground injection well" means an underground injection well whose operation was not approved by appropriate State and Federal agencies before December 16, 1974.

(e) Areas with one aquifer; publication in Federal Register; commitments for Federal financial assistance

If the Administrator determines, on his own initiative or upon petition, that an area has an aquifer which is the sole or principal drinking water source for the area and which, if contaminated, would create a significant hazard to public health, he shall publish notice of that determination in the Federal Register. After the publication of any such notice, no commitment for Federal financial assistance (through a grant, contract, loan guarantee, or otherwise) may be entered into for any project which the Administrator determines may contaminate such aquifer through a recharge zone so as to create a significant hazard to public health, but a commitment for Federal financial assistance may, if authorized under another provision of law, be entered into to plan or design the project to assure that it will not so contaminate the aquifer.

(July 1, 1944, ch. 373, title XIV, § 1424, as added Dec. 16, 1974, Pub. L. 93-523, § 2(a), 88 Stat. 1678.

Code of Federal Regulations

Review of projects affecting the Edwards Underground Reservoir, see 40 CFR 149.1 et seq.

Library References

Health and Environment ⚷25.7(13).
C.J.S. Health and Environment § 107 et seq.

§ 300h-4. Optional demonstration by States relating to oil or natural gas

(a) Approval of State underground injection control program; alternative showing of effectiveness of program by State

For purposes of the Administrator's approval or disapproval under section 300h-1 of this title of that portion of any State underground injection control program which relates to—

(1) the underground injection of brine or other fluids which are brought to the surface in connection with oil or natural gas production or natural gas storage operations, or

(2) any underground injection for the secondary or tertiary recovery of oil or natural gas,

in lieu of the showing required under subparagraph (A) of section 300h-1(b)(1) of this title the State may demonstrate that such portion of the State program meets the requirements of subparagraphs (A) through (D) of section 300h(b)(1) of this title and represents an effective program (including adequate recordkeeping and reporting) to prevent underground injection which endangers drinking water sources.

(b) Revision or amendment of requirements of regulation; showing of effectiveness of program by State

If the Administrator revises or amends any requirement of a regulation under section 300h of this title relating to any aspect of the underground injection referred to in subsection (a) of this section, in the case of that portion of a State underground injection control program for which the demonstration referred to in subsection (a) of this section has been made, in lieu of the showing required under section 300h–1(b)(1)(B) of this title the State may demonstrate that, with respect to that aspect of such underground injection, the State program meets the requirements of subparagraphs (A) through (D) of section 300h(b)(1) of this title and represents an effective program (including adequate recordkeeping and reporting) to prevent underground injection which endangers drinking water sources.

(c) Primary enforcement responsibility of State; voiding by Administrator under duly promulgated rule

(1) Section 300h–1(b)(3) of this title shall not apply to that portion of any State underground injection control program approved by the Administrator pursuant to a demonstration under subsection (a) of this section (and under subsection (b) of this section where applicable).

(2) If pursuant to such a demonstration, the Administrator approves such portion of the State program, the State shall have primary enforcement responsibility with respect to that portion until such time as the Administrator determines, by rule, that such demonstration is no longer valid. Following such a determination, the Administrator may exercise the authority of subsection (c) of section 300h–1 of this title in the same manner as provided in such subsection with respect to a determination described in such subsection.

(3) Before promulgating any rule under paragraph (2), the Administrator shall provide opportunity for public hearing respecting such rule.

(July 1, 1944, ch. 373, title XIV, § 1425, as added Dec. 5, 1980, Pub.L. 96–502, § 2(a), 94 Stat. 2737; as amended June 19, 1986, Pub.L. 99–339, Title II, § 201(a), 100 Stat. 653.)

Library References

Waters and Water Courses ⚷196, 202.
C.J.S. Waters §§ 232 et seq., 280.

§ 300h–5. Regulation of State programs

(a) Monitoring methods

Not later than 18 months after June 19, 1986, the Administrator shall modify regulations issued under this chapter for Class I injection wells to identify monitoring methods, in addition to those in effect on November 1, 1985, including groundwater monitoring. In accordance with such regulations, the Administrator, or delegated State authority, shall determine the applicability of such monitoring methods, wherever appropriate, at locations and in such a manner as to provide the earliest possible detection of fluid migration into, or in the direction of, underground sources of drinking water from such wells, based on its assessment of the potential for fluid migration from the injection zone that may be harmful to human health or the environment. For purposes of this subsection, a class I injection well is defined in accordance with 40 CFR 146.05 as in effect on November 1, 1985.

(b) Report

The Administrator shall submit a report to Congress, no later than September 1987, summarizing the results of State surveys required by the Administrator under this section. The report shall include each of the following items of information:

(1) The numbers and categories of class V wells which discharge nonhazardous waste into or above an underground source of drinking water.

(2) The primary contamination problems associated with different categories of these disposal wells.

(3) Recommendations for minimum design, construction, installation, and siting requirements that should be applied to protect underground sources of drinking water from such contamination wherever necessary.

(July 1, 1944, c. 373, Title XIV, § 1426, as added June 19, 1986, Pub.L. 99–339, Title II, § 201(b), 100 Stat. 653.)

§ 300h–6. Sole source aquifer demonstration program

(a) Purpose

The purpose of this section is to establish procedures for development, implementation, and assessment of demonstration programs designed to protect critical aquifer protection areas located within areas designated as sole or principal source aquifers under section 300h–3(e) of this title.

(b) Definition

For purposes of this section, the term "critical aquifer protection area" means either of the following:

(1) All or part of an area located within an area for which an application or designation as a sole or principal source aquifer pursuant to section 300h–3(e) of this title, has been submitted and approved by the Administrator not later than 24

months after June 19, 1986, and which satisfies the criteria established by the Administrator under subsection (d) of this section.

(2) All or part of an area which is within an aquifer designated as a sole source aquifer as of June 19, 1986, and for which an areawide ground water quality protection plan has been approved under section 208 of the Clean Water Act [33 U.S.C.A. § 1288] prior to June 19, 1986.

(c) Application

Any State, municipal or local government or political subdivision thereof or any planning entity (including any interstate regional planning entity) that identifies a critical aquifer protection area over which it has authority or jurisdiction may apply to the Administrator for the selection of such area for a demonstration program under this section. Any applicant shall consult with other government or planning entities with authority or jurisdiction in such area prior to application. Applicants, other than the Governor, shall submit the application for a demonstration program jointly with the Governor.

(d) Criteria

Not later than 1 year after June 19, 1986, the Administrator shall, by rule, establish criteria for identifying critical aquifer protection areas under this section. In establishing such criteria, the Administrator shall consider each of the following:

(1) The vulnerability of the aquifer to contamination due to hydrogeologic characteristics.

(2) The number of persons or the proportion of population using the ground water as a drinking water source.

(3) The economic, social and environmental benefits that would result to the area from maintenance of ground water of high quality.

(4) The economic, social and environmental costs that would result from degradation of the quality of the ground water.

(e) Contents of application

An application submitted to the Administrator by any applicant for a demonstration program under this section shall meet each of the following requirements:

(1) The application shall propose boundaries for the critical aquifer protection area within its jurisdiction.

(2) The application shall designate or, if necessary, establish a planning entity (which shall be a public agency and which shall include representation of elected local and State governmental officials) to develop a comprehensive management plan (hereinafter in this section referred to as the "plan") for the critical protection area. Where a local government planning agency exists with adequate authority to carry out this section with respect to any proposed critical protection area, such agency shall be designated as the planning entity.

(3) The application shall establish procedures for public participation in the development of the plan, for review, approval, and adoption of the plan, and for assistance to municipalities and other public agencies with authority under State law to implement the plan.

(4) The application shall include a hydrogeologic assessment of surface and ground water resources within the critical protection area.

(5) The application shall include a comprehensive management plan for the proposed protection area.

(6) The application shall include the measures and schedule proposed for implementation of such plan.

(f) Comprehensive plan

(1) The objective of a comprehensive management plan submitted by an applicant under this section shall be to maintain the quality of the ground water in the critical protection area in a manner reasonably expected to protect human health, the environment and ground water resources. In order to achieve such objective, the plan may be designed to maintain, to the maximum extent possible, the natural vegetative and hydrogeological conditions. Each of the following elements shall be included in such a protection plan:

(A) A map showing the detailed boundary of the critical protection area.

(B) An identification of existing and potential point and nonpoint sources of ground water degradation.

(C) An assessment of the relationship between activities on the land surface and ground water quality.

(D) Specific actions and management practices to be implemented in the critical protection area to prevent adverse impacts on ground water quality.

(E) Identification of authority adequate to implement the plan, estimates of program costs, and sources of State matching funds.

(2) Such plan may also include the following:

(A) A determination of the quality of the existing ground water recharged through the special protection area and the natural recharge capabilities of the special protection area watershed.

(B) Requirements designed to maintain existing underground drinking water quality or improve underground drinking water quality if prevailing conditions fail to meet drinking water standards, pursuant to this chapter and State law.

(C) Limits on Federal, State, and local government, financially assisted activities and projects which may contribute to degradation of such ground water or any loss of natural surface and subsurface infiltration of purification capability of the special protection watershed.

(D) A comprehensive statement of land use management including emergency contingency planning as it pertains to the maintenance of the quality of underground sources of drinking water or to the improvement of such sources if necessary to meet drinking water standards pursuant to this chapter and State law.

(E) Actions in the special protection area which would avoid adverse impacts on water quality, recharge capabilities, or both.

(F) Consideration of specific techniques, which may include clustering, transfer of development rights, and other innovative measures sufficient to achieve the objectives of this section.

(G) Consideration of the establishment of a State institution to facilitate and assist funding a development transfer credit system.

(H) A program for State and local implementation of the plan described in this subsection in a manner that will insure the continued, uniform, consistent protection of the critical protection area in accord with the purposes of this section.

(I) Pollution abatement measures, if appropriate.

(g) Plans under section 208 of the Clean Water Act

A plan approved before June 19, 1986, under section 208 of the Clean Water Act [33 U.S.C.A. § 1288] to protect a sole source aquifer designated under section 300h–3(e) of this title shall be considered a comprehensive management plan for the purposes of this section.

(h) Consultation and hearings

During the development of a comprehensive management plan under this section, the planning entity shall consult with, and consider the comments of, appropriate officials of any municipality and State or Federal agency which has jurisdiction over lands and waters within the special protection area, other concerned organizations and technical and citizen advisory committees. The planning entity shall conduct public hearings at places within the special protection area for the purpose of providing the opportunity to comment on any aspect of the plan.

(i) Approval or disapproval

Within 120 days after receipt of an application under this section, the Administrator shall approve or disapprove the application. The approval or disapproval shall be based on the determination that the critical protection area satisfies the criteria established under subsection (d) of this section and that a demonstration program for the area would provide protection for ground water quality consistent with the objectives stated in subsection (f) of this section. The Administrator shall provide to the Governor a written explanation of the reasons for the disapproval of any such application. Any petitioner may modify and resubmit any application which is not approved. Upon approval of an application, the Administrator may enter into a cooperative agreement with the applicant to establish a demonstration program under this section.

(j) Grants and reimbursement

Upon entering a cooperative agreement under subsection (i) of this section, the Administrator may provide to the applicant, on a matching basis, a grant of 50 per centum of the costs of implementing the plan established under this section. The Administrator may also reimburse the applicant of an approved plan up to 50 per centum of the costs of developing such plan, except for plans approved under section 208 of the Clean Water Act [33 U.S.C.A. § 1288]. The total amount of grants under this section for any one aquifer, designated under section 300h–3(e) of this title, shall not exceed $4,000,000 in any one fiscal year.

(k) Activities funded under other law

No funds authorized under this subsection [1] may be used to fund activities funded under other sections of this chapter or the Clean Water Act [33 U.S.C.A. § 1251 et seq.], the Solid Waste Disposal Act [42 U.S.C.A. § 6901 et seq.], the Comprehensive Environmental Response, Compensation, and Liability Act of 1980 [42 U.S.C.A. § 9601 et seq.] or other environmental laws.

(*l*) Report

Not later than December 31, 1989, each State shall submit to the Administrator a report assessing the impact of the program on ground water quality and identifying those measures found to be effective in protecting ground water resources. No later than September 30, 1990, the Administrator shall submit to Congress a report summarizing the State reports, and assessing the accomplishments of the sole source aquifer demonstration program including an identification of protection methods found to be most effective and recommendations for their application to protect ground water resources from contamination whenever necessary.

(m) Savings provision

Nothing under this section shall be construed to amend, supersede or abrogate rights to quantities of water which have been established by interstate water compacts, Supreme Court decrees, or State water laws; or any requirement imposed or right provided under any Federal or State environmental or public health statute.

(n) Authorization of appropriations

There are authorized to be appropriated to carry out this section not more than the following amounts:

Fiscal year[1]	*Amount*
1987	$10,000,000
1988	15,000,000
1989	17,500,000
1990	17,500,000
1991	17,500,000

Matching grants under this section may also be used to implement or update any water quality management plan for a sole or principal source aquifer approved (before June 19, 1986) by the Administrator under section 208 of the Federal Water Pollution Control Act [33 U.S.C. 1288].

[1] So in original. Probably should be "section".

(July 1, 1986, c. 373, Title XIV, § 1427, as added June 19, 1986, Pub.L. 99–339, Title II, § 203, 100 Stat. 657, and amended June 19, 1986, Pub.L. 99–339, Title III, § 301(f), 100 Stat. 664.)

§ 300h–7. State programs to establish wellhead protection areas

(a) State programs

The Governor or Governor's designee of each State shall, within 3 years of June 19, 1986, adopt and submit to the Administrator a State program to protect wellhead areas within their jurisdiction from contaminants which may have any adverse effect on the health of persons. Each State program under this section shall, at a minimum—

(1) specify the duties of State agencies, local governmental entities, and public water supply systems with respect to the development and implementation of programs required by this section;

(2) for each wellhead, determine the wellhead protection area as defined in subsection (e) of this section based on all reasonably available hydrogeologic information on ground water flow, recharge and discharge and other information the State deems necessary to adequately determine the wellhead protection area;

(3) identify within each wellhead protection area all potential anthropogenic sources of contaminants which may have any adverse effect on the health of persons;

(4) describe a program that contains, as appropriate, technical assistance, financial assistance, implementation of control measures, education, training, and demonstration projects to protect the water supply within wellhead protection areas from such contaminants;

(5) include contingency plans for the location and provision of alternate drinking water supplies for each public water system in the event of well or wellfield contamination by such contaminants; and

(6) include a requirement that consideration be given to all potential sources of such contaminants within the expected wellhead area of a new water well which serves a public water supply system.

(b) Public participation

To the maximum extent possible, each State shall establish procedures, including but not limited to the establishment of technical and citizens' advisory committees, to encourage the public to participate in developing the protection program for wellhead areas. Such procedures shall include notice and opportunity for public hearing on the State program before it is submitted to the Administrator.

(c) Disapproval

(1) In general

If, in the judgment of the Administrator, a State program (or portion thereof, including the definition of a wellhead protection area), is not adequate to protect public water systems as required by this section, the Administrator shall disapprove such program (or portion thereof). A State program developed pursuant to subsection (a) of this section shall be deemed to be adequate unless the Administrator determines, within 9 months of the receipt of a State program, that such program (or portion thereof) is inadequate for the purpose of protecting public water systems as required by this section from contaminants that may have any adverse effect on the health of persons. If the Administrator determines that a proposed State program (or any portion thereof) is inadequate, the Administrator shall submit a written statement of the reasons for such determination to the Governor of the State.

(2) Modification and resubmission

Within 6 months after receipt of the Administrator's written notice under paragraph (1) that any proposed State program (or portion thereof) is inadequate, the Governor or Governor's designee, shall modify the program based upon the recommendations of the Administrator and resubmit the modified program to the Administrator.

(d) Federal assistance

After the date 3 years after June 19, 1986, no State shall receive funds authorized to be appropriated under this section except for the purpose of implementing the program and requirements of paragraphs (4) and (6) of subsection (a) of this section.

(e) Definition of wellhead protection area

As used in this section, the term "wellhead protection area" means the surface and subsurface area surrounding a water well or wellfield, supplying a public water system, through which contaminants are reasonably likely to move toward and reach such water well or wellfield. The extent of a wellhead protection area, within a State, necessary to provide protection from contaminants which may have any adverse effect on the health of persons is to be determined by the State in the program submitted under subsection (a) of this section. Not later than one year after June 19, 1986, the Administrator shall issue technical guidance which States may use in making such determinations. Such guidance may reflect such factors as the radius of influence around a well or wellfield, the depth of drawdown of the water table by such well or wellfield at any given point, the time or rate of travel of various contaminants in various hydrologic conditions, distance from the well or wellfield, or other factors affecting the likelihood of contaminants reaching the well or wellfield, taking into account available engineering pump tests or comparable data, field reconnaissance, topographic information, and the geology of the formation in which the well or wellfield is located.

(f) Prohibitions

(1) Activities under other laws

No funds authorized to be appropriated under this section may be used to support activities authorized by the Federal Water Pollution Control Act [33 U.S.C. 1251 et seq.], the Solid Waste Disposal Act [42 U.S.C. 6901 et seq.], the Comprehensive Environmental Response, Compensation, and Liability Act of 1980 [42 U.S.C. 9601 et seq.], or other sections of this chapter.

(2) Individual sources

No funds authorized to be appropriated under this section may be used to bring individual sources of contamination into compliance.

(g) Implementation

Each State shall make every reasonable effort to implement the State wellhead area protection program under this section within 2 years of submitting the program to the Administrator. Each State shall submit to the Administrator a biennial status report describing the State's progress in implementing the program. Such report shall include amendments to the State program for water wells sited during the biennial period.

(h) Federal agencies

Each department, agency, and instrumentality of the executive, legislative, and judicial branches of the Federal Government having jurisdiction over any potential source of contaminants identified by a State program pursuant to the provisions of subsection (a)(3) of this section shall be subject to and comply with all requirements of the State program developed according to subsection (a)(4) of this section applicable to such potential source of contaminants, both substantive and procedural, in the same manner, and to the same extent, as any other person is subject to such requirements, including payment of reasonable charges and fees. The President may exempt any potential source under the jurisdiction of any department, agency, or instrumentality in the executive branch if the President determines it to be in the paramount interest of the United States to do so. No such exemption shall be granted due to the lack of an appropriation unless the President shall have specifically requested such appropriation as part of the budgetary process and the Congress shall have failed to make available such requested appropriations.

(i) Additional requirement

(1) In general

In addition to the provisions of subsection (a) of this section, States in which there are more than 2,500 active wells at which annular injection is used as of January 1, 1986, shall include in their State program a certification that a State program exists and is being adequately enforced that provides protection from contaminants which may have any adverse effect on the health of persons and which are associated with the annular injection or surface disposal of brines associated with oil and gas production.

(2) Definition

For purposes of this subsection, the term "annular injection" means the reinjection of brines associated with the production of oil or gas between the production and surface casings of a conventional oil or gas producing well.

(3) Review

The Administrator shall conduct a review of each program certified under this subsection.

(4) Disapproval

If a State fails to include the certification required by this subsection or if in the judgment of the Administrator the State program certified under this subsection is not being adequately enforced, the Administrator shall disapprove the State program submitted under subsection (a) of this section.

(j) Coordination with other laws

Nothing in this section shall authorize or require any department, agency, or other instrumentality of the Federal Government or State or local government to apportion, allocate or otherwise regulate the withdrawal or beneficial use of ground or surface waters, so as to abrogate or modify any existing rights to water established pursuant to State or Federal law, including interstate compacts.

(k) Authorization of appropriations

Unless the State program is disapproved under this section, the Administrator shall make grants to the State for not less than 50 or more than 90 percent of the costs incurred by a State (as determined by the Administrator) in developing and implementing each State program under this section. For purposes of making such grants there is authorized to be appropriated not more than the following amounts:

Fiscal year	*Amount*
1987	$20,000,000
1988	20,000,000
1989	35,000,000
1990	35,000,000
1991	35,000,000

(July 1, 1944, c. 373, Title XIV, § 1428, as added June 19, 1986, Pub.L. 99–339, Title II, § 205, 100 Stat. 660, amended June 19, 1986, Pub.L. 99–339, Title III, § 301(e), 100 Stat. 664.)

PART D—EMERGENCY POWERS

§ 300i. Emergency powers

(a) Actions authorized against imminent and substantial endangerment to health

Notwithstanding any other provision of this subchapter, the Administrator, upon receipt of information that a contaminant which is present in or is likely to enter a public water system or an underground source of drinking water may present an imminent and substantial endangerment to the health of persons, and that appropriate State and local authorities have not acted to protect the health of such persons, may take such actions as he may deem necessary in order to protect the health of such persons. To the extent he determines it to be practicable in light of such imminent endangerment, he shall consult with the State and local authorities in order to confirm the correctness of the information on which action proposed to be taken under this subsection is based and to ascertain the action which such authorities are or will be taking. The action which the Administrator may take may include (but shall not be limited to) (1) issuing such orders as may be necessary to protect the health of persons who are or may be users of such system (including travelers), including orders requiring the provision of alternative water supplies by persons who caused or contributed to the endangerment, and (2) commencing a civil action for appropriate relief, including a restraining order or permanent or temporary injunction.

(b) Penalties for violations; separate offenses

Any person who violates or fails or refuses to comply with any order issued by the Administrator under subsection (a)(1) of this section may, in an action brought in the appropriate United States district court to enforce such order, be subject to a civil penalty of not to exceed $5,000 for each day in which such violation occurs or failure to comply continues.

(July 1, 1944, ch. 373, title XIV, § 1431, as added Dec. 16, 1974, Pub.L. 93–523, § 2(a), 88 Stat. 1680, as amended June 19, 1986, Pub.L. 99–339, Title II, § 204, 100 Stat. 660.)

Cross References

Guidelines for using imminent hazard, enforcement, and emergency response authorities, see section 9606 of this title.

Code of Federal Regulations

Environmental Protection Agency,
- Administration of permit programs, see 40 CFR 122.1 et seq.
- Decisionmaking procedures applicable to permit programs, see 40 CFR 124.1 et seq.

Underground injection control programs, technical criteria and standards for, see 40 CFR 146.1 et seq.

Library References

Health and Environment ⚷38.
C.J.S. Health and Environment § 49 et seq.

§ 300i–1. Tampering with public water systems

(a) Tampering

Any person who tampers with a public water system shall be imprisoned for not more than 5 years, or fined in accordance with Title 18, or both.

(b) Attempt or threat

Any person who attempts to tamper, or makes a threat to tamper, with a public drinking water system be imprisoned for not more than 3 years, or fined in accordance with Title 18, or both.

(c) Civil penalty

The Administrator may bring a civil action in the appropriate United States district court (as determined under the provisions of Title 28) against any person who tampers, attempts to tamper, or makes a threat to tamper with a public water system. The court may impose on such person a civil penalty of not more than $50,000 for such tampering or not more than $20,000 for such attempt or threat.

(d) Definition of "tamper"

For purposes of this section, the term "tamper" means—

(1) to introduce a contaminant into a public water system with the intention of harming persons; or

(2) to otherwise interfere with the operation of a public water system with the intention of harming persons.

(July 1, 1944, c. 373, Title XIV, § 1432, as added June 19, 1986, Pub.L. 99–339, Title I, § 108, 100 Stat. 651.)

PART E—GENERAL PROVISIONS

§ 300j. Assurances of availability of adequate supplies of chemicals necessary for treatment of water

(a) Certification of need application

If any person who uses chlorine, activated carbon, lime, ammonia, soda ash, potassium permanganate, caustic soda, or other chemical or substance for the purpose of treating water in any public water system or in any public treatment works determines that the amount of such chemical or substance necessary to effectively treat such water is not reasonably available to him or will not be so available to him when required for the effective treatment of such water, such person may apply to the Administrator for a certification (hereinafter in this section referred to as a "certification of need") that the amount of such chemical or substance which such person requires to effectively treat such water is not reasonably available to him or will not be so available when required for the effective treatment of such water.

(b) Application requirements; publication in Federal Register; waiver; certification, issuance or denial

(1) An application for a certification of need shall be in such form and submitted in such manner as the Administrator may require and shall (A) specify the persons the applicant determines are able to provide the chemical or substance with respect to which the application is submitted, (B) specify the persons from whom the applicant has sought such chemical or substance, and (C) contain such other information as the Administrator may require.

(2) Upon receipt of an application under this section, the Administrator shall (A) publish in the Federal Register a notice of the receipt of the application and a brief summary of it, (B) notify in writing each person whom the President or his delegate (after consultation with the Administrator) determines could be made subject to an order required to be issued upon the issuance of the certification of need applied for in such application, and (C) provide an opportunity for the submission of written comments on such application. The requirements of the preceding sentence of this paragraph shall not apply when the Administrator for good cause finds (and incorporates the finding with a brief statement of reasons therefor in the order issued) that waiver of such requirements is necessary in order to protect the public health.

(3) Within 30 days after—

(A) the date a notice is published under paragraph (2) in the Federal Register with respect to an application submitted under this section for the issuance of a certification of need, or

(B) the date on which such application is received if as authorized by the second sentence of such paragraph no notice is published with respect to such application,

the Administrator shall take action either to issue or deny the issuance of a certification of need.

(c) Certification of need; issuance; executive orders; implementation of orders; equitable apportionment of orders; factors considered

(1) If the Administrator finds that the amount of a chemical or substance necessary for an applicant under an application submitted under this section to effectively treat water in a public water system or in a public treatment works is not reasonably available to the applicant or will not be so available to him when required for the effective treatment of such water, the Administrator shall issue a certification of need. Not later than seven days following the issuance of such certification, the President or his delegate shall issue an order requiring the provision to such person of such amounts of such chemical or substance as the Administrator deems necessary in the certification of need issued for such person. Such order shall apply to such manufacturers, producers, processors, distributors, and repackagers of such chemical or substance as the President or his delegate deems necessary and appropri-

ate, except that such order may not apply to any manufacturer, producer, or processor of such chemical or substance who manufactures, produces, or processes (as the case may be) such chemical or substance solely for its own use. Persons subject to an order issued under this section shall be given a reasonable opportunity to consult with the President or his delegate with respect to the implementation of the order.

(2) Orders which are to be issued under paragraph (1) to manufacturers, producers, and processors of a chemical or substance shall be equitably apportioned, as far as practicable, among all manufacturers, producers, and processors of such chemical or substance; and orders which are to be issued under paragraph (1) to distributors and repackagers of a chemical or substance shall be equitably apportioned, as far as practicable, among all distributors and repackagers of such chemical or substance. In apportioning orders issued under paragraph (1) to manufacturers, producers, processors, distributors, and repackagers of chlorine, the President or his delegate shall, in carrying out the requirements of the preceding sentence, consider—

(A) the geographical relationships and established commercial relationships between such manufacturers, producers, processors, distributors, and repackagers and the persons for whom the orders are issued;

(B) in the case of orders to be issued to producers of chlorine, the (i) amount of chlorine historically supplied by each such producer to treat water in public water systems and public treatment works, and (ii) share of each such producer of the total annual production of chlorine in the United States; and

(C) such other factors as the President or his delegate may determine are relevant to the apportionment of orders in accordance with the requirements of the preceding sentence.

(3) Subject to subsection (f) of this section, any person for whom a certification of need has been issued under this subsection may upon the expiration of the order issued under paragraph (1) upon such certification apply under this section for additional certifications.

(d) Breach of contracts; defense

There shall be available as a defense to any action brought for breach of contract in a Federal or State court arising out of delay or failure to provide, sell, or offer for sale or exchange a chemical or substance subject to an order issued pursuant to subsection (c)(1) of this section, that such delay or failure was caused solely by compliance with such order.

(e) Penalties for noncompliance with orders; temporary restraining orders and preliminary or permanent injunctions

(1) Whoever knowingly fails to comply with any order issued pursuant to subsection (c)(1) of this section shall be fined not more than $5,000 for each such failure to comply.

(2) Whoever fails to comply with any order issued pursuant to subsection (c)(1) of this section shall be subject to a civil penalty of not more than $2,500 for each such failure to comply.

(3) Whenever the Administrator or the President or his delegate has reason to believe that any person is violating or will violate any order issued pursuant to subsection (c)(1) of this section, he may petition a United States district court to issue a temporary restraining order or preliminary or permanent injunction (including a mandatory injunction) to enforce the provision of such order.

(f) Termination date

No certification of need or order issued under this section may remain in effect for more than one year.

(July 1, 1944, ch. 373, title XIV, § 1441, as added Dec. 16, 1974, Pub.L. 93–523, § 2(a), 88 Stat. 1680, as amended Nov. 16, 1977, Pub.L. 95–190, § 7, 91 Stat. 1396; Sept. 6, 1979, Pub.L. 96–63, § 3, 93 Stat. 411; June 19, 1986, Pub.L. 99–339, Title III, § 301(d), 100 Stat. 664.)

Library References

Waters and Water Courses ⚷64.
C.J.S. Waters § 43 et seq.

§ 300j–1. Research, technical assistance, information, training of personnel

(a) Specific powers and duties of Administrator

(1) The Administrator may conduct research, studies, and demonstrations relating to the causes, diagnosis, treatment, control, and prevention of physical and mental diseases and other impairments of man resulting directly or indirectly from contaminants in water, or to the provision of a dependably safe supply of drinking water, including—

(A) improved methods (i) to identify and measure the existence of contaminants in drinking water (including methods which may be used by State and local health and water officials), and (ii) to identify the source of such contaminants;

(B) improved methods to identify and measure the health effects of contaminants in drinking water;

(C) new methods of treating raw water to prepare it for drinking, so as to improve the efficiency of water treatment and to remove contaminants from water;

(D) improved methods for providing a dependably safe supply of drinking water, including improvements in water purification and distribution, and methods of assessing the health related hazards of drinking water; and

(E) improved methods of protecting underground water sources of public water systems from contamination.

(2)(A) The Administrator shall, to the maximum extent feasible, provide technical assistance to the States and municipalities in the establishment and administration of public water system supervision programs (as defined in section 300j–2(c)(1) of this title).

(B) The Administrator is authorized to provide technical assistance and to make grants to States, or publicly owned water systems to assist in responding to and alleviating any emergency situation affecting public water systems (including sources of water for such systems) which the Administrator determines to present substantial danger to the public health. Grants provided under this subparagraph shall be used only to support those actions which (i) are necessary for preventing, limiting or mitigating danger to the public health in such emergency situation and (ii) would not, in the judgment of the Administrator, be taken without such emergency assistance. The Administrator may carry out the program authorized under this subparagraph as part of, and in accordance with the terms and conditions of, any other program of assistance for environmental emergencies which the Administrator is authorized to carry out under any other provision of law. No limitation on appropriations for any such other program shall apply to amounts appropriated under this subparagraph.

(3)(A) The Administrator shall conduct studies, and make periodic reports to Congress, on the costs of carrying out regulations prescribed under section 300g–1 of this title.

(B) Not later than eighteen months after November 16, 1977, the Administrator shall submit a report to Congress which identifies and analyzes—

(i) the anticipated costs of compliance with interim and revised national primary drinking water regulations and the anticipated costs to States and units of local governments in implementing such regulations;

(ii) alternative methods of (including alternative treatment techniques for) compliance with such regulations;

(iii) methods of paying the costs of compliance by public water systems with national primary drinking water regulations, including user charges, State or local taxes or subsidies, Federal grants (including planning or construction grants, or both), loans, and loan guarantees, and other methods of assisting in paying the costs of such compliance;

(iv) the advantages and disadvantages of each of the methods referred to in clauses (ii) and (iii);

(v) the sources of revenue presently available (and projected to be available) to public water systems to meet current and future expenses; and

(vi) the costs of drinking water paid by residential and industrial consumers in a sample of large, medium, and small public water systems and of individually owned wells, and the reasons for any differences in such costs.

The report required by this subparagraph shall identify and analyze the items required in clauses (i) through (v) separately with respect to public water systems serving small communities. The report required by this subparagraph shall include such recommendations as the Administrator deems appropriate.

(4) Omitted

(5) The Administrator shall carry out a study of methods of underground injection which do not result in the degradation of underground drinking water sources.

(6) The Administrator shall carry out a study of methods of preventing, detecting, and dealing with surface spills of contaminants which may degrade underground water sources for public water systems.

(7) The Administrator shall carry out a study of virus contamination of drinking water sources and means of control of such contamination.

(8) The Administrator shall carry out a study of the nature and extent of the impact on underground water which supplies or can reasonably be expected to supply public water systems of (A) abandoned injection or extraction wells; (B) intensive application of pesticides and fertilizers in underground water recharge areas; and (C) ponds, pools, lagoons, pits, or other surface disposal of contaminants in underground water recharge areas.

(9) The Administrator shall conduct a comprehensive study of public water supplies and drinking water sources to determine the nature, extent, sources of and means of control of contamination by chemicals or other substances suspected of being carcinogenic. Not later than six months after December 16, 1974, he shall transmit to the Congress the initial results of such study, together with such recommendations for further review and corrective action as he deems appropriate.

(10) The Administrator shall carry out a study of the reaction of chlorine and humic acids and the effects of the contaminants which result from such reaction on public health and on the safety of drinking water, including any carcinogenic effect.

(11) The Administrator shall carry out a study of polychlorinated biphenyl contamination of actual or potential sources of drinking water, contamination of such sources by other substances known or suspected to be harmful to public health, the effects of such contamination, and means of removing, treating, or otherwise controlling such contamination. To assist in carrying out this paragraph, the Administrator is authorized to make grants to public agencies and private nonprofit institutions.

(b) Other powers and duties of Administrator

In carrying out this subchapter, the Administrator is authorized to—

(1) collect and make available information pertaining to research, investigations, and demonstrations with respect to providing a dependably safe supply of drinking water together with appropriate recommendations in connection therewith;

(2) make available research facilities of the Agency to appropriate public authorities, institutions, and individuals engaged in studies and research relating to the purposes of this subchapter;

(3) make grants to, and enter into contracts with, any public agency, educational institution, and any other organization, in accordance with procedures prescribed by the Administrator, under which he may pay all or part of the costs (as may be determined by the Administrator) of any project or activity which is designed—

(A) to develop, expand, or carry out a program (which may combine training education and employment) for training persons for occupations involving the public health aspects of providing safe drinking water;

(B) to train inspectors and supervisory personnel to train or supervise persons in occupations involving the public health aspects of providing safe drinking water; or

(C) to develop and expand the capability of programs of States and municipalities to carry out the purposes of this subchapter (other than by carrying out State programs of public water system supervision or underground water source protection (as defined in section 300j–2(c) of this title)).

(c) Report to Congress on present and projected future availability of safe drinking water; additional contents; utilization of information and data

Not later than eighteen months after November 16, 1977, the Administrator shall submit a report to Congress on the present and projected future availability of an adequate and dependable supply of safe drinking water to meet present and projected future need. Such report shall include an analysis of the future demand for drinking water and other competing uses of water, the availability and use of methods to conserve water or reduce demand, the adequacy of present measures to assure adequate and dependable supplies of safe drinking water, and the problems (financial, legal, or other) which need to be resolved in order to assure the availability of such supplies for the future. Existing information and data compiled by the National Water Commission and others shall be utilized to the extent possible.

(d) Establishment of training programs and grants for training; training fees

The Administrator shall—

(1) provide training for, and make grants for training (including postgraduate training) of (A) personnel of State agencies which have primary enforcement responsibility and of agencies or units of local government to which enforcement responsibilities have been delegated by the State, and (B) personnel who manage or operate public water systems, and

(2) make grants for postgraduate training of individuals (including grants to educational institutions for traineeships) for purposes of qualifying such individuals to work as personnel referred to in paragraph (1).

Reasonable fees may be charged for training provided under paragraph (1)(B) to persons other than personnel of State or local agencies but such training shall be provided to personnel of State or local agencies without charge.

(e) Repealed. Pub.L. 99–339, Title III, § 304(a), June 19, 1986, 100 Stat. 667

(f) Authorization of appropriations

There are authorized to be appropriated to carry out the provisions of this section other than subsection (a)(2)(B) of this section and provisions relating to research $15,000,000 for the fiscal year ending June 30, 1975; $25,000,000 for the fiscal year ending June 30, 1976; $35,000,000 for the fiscal year ending June 30, 1977; $17,000,000 for each of the fiscal years 1978 and 1979; $21,405,000 for the fiscal year ending September 30, 1980; $30,000,000 for the fiscal year ending September 30, 1981; and $35,000,000 for the fiscal year ending September 30,

1982. There are authorized to be appropriated to carry out subsection (a)(2)(B) of this section $8,000,000 for each of the fiscal years 1978 through 1982. There are authorized to be appropriated to carry out subsection (a)(2)(B) of this section not more than the following amounts:

Fiscal year:	*Amount*
1987	$7,650,000
1988	7,650,000
1989	8,050,000
1990	8,050,000
1991	8,050,000

There are authorized to be appropriated to carry out the provisions of this section (other than subsection (g) of this section, subsection (a)(2)(B) of this section, and provisions relating to research), not more than the following amounts:

Fiscal year:	*Amount*
1987	$35,600,000
1988	35,600,000
1989	38,020,000
1990	38,020,000
1991	38,020,000

(g) Technical assistance for small systems; authorization of appropriations; amount to be utilized for public water systems owned or operated by Indian tribes

The Administrator is authorized to provide technical assistance to small public water systems to enable such systems to achieve and maintain compliance with national drinking water regulations. Such assistance may include "circuit-rider" programs, training, and preliminary engineering studies. There are authorized to be appropriated to carry out this subsection $10,000,000 for each of the fiscal years 1987 through 1991. Not less than the greater of—

(1) 3 percent of the amounts appropriated under this subsection, or

(2) $280,000

shall be utilized for technical assistance to public water systems owned or operated by Indian tribes.

(July 1, 1944, ch. 373, title XIV, § 1442, as added Dec. 16, 1974, Pub.L. 93–523, § 2(a), 88 Stat. 1682, and amended Nov. 16, 1977, Pub.L. 95–190, §§ 2(a), 3(a), (b), (e)(1), 4, 9, 10(b), 13, 91 Stat. 1393–1395, 1397–1399; Sept. 6, 1979, Pub.L. 96–63, § 1, 93 Stat. 411; Dec. 5, 1980, Pub.L. 96–502, § 5, 94 Stat. 2738; June 19, 1986, Pub.L. 99–339, Title I, § 107, Title III, §§ 301(a), (g), 304(a), 100 Stat. 651, 663, 665, 667.)

Code of Federal Regulations

Environmental Protection Agency grants, policies and procedures respecting, see 40 CFR 30.100 et seq.
Subagreements, see 40 CFR 33.001 et seq.

Library References

Health and Environment ⟹20.
C.J.S. Health and Environment § 2 et seq.

§ 300j–2. Grants for State programs

(a) Public water systems supervision programs; applications for grants; allotment of sums; waiver of grant restrictions; notice of approval or disapproval of application; authorization of appropriations

(1) From allotments made pursuant to paragraph (4), the Administrator may make grants to States to carry out public water system supervision programs.

(2) No grant may be made under paragraph (1) unless an application therefor has been submitted to the Administrator in such form and manner as he may require. The Administrator may not approve an application of a State for its first grant under paragraph (1) unless he determines that the State—

(A) has established or will establish within one year from the date of such grant a public water system supervision program, and

(B) will, within that one year, assume primary enforcement responsibility for public water systems within the State.

No grant may be made to a State under paragraph (1) for any period beginning more than one year after the date of the State's first grant unless the State has assumed and maintains primary enforcement responsibility for public water systems within the State. The prohibitions contained in the preceding two sentences shall not apply to such grants when made to Indian Tribes.

(3) A grant under paragraph (1) shall be made to cover not more than 75 per centum of the grant recipient's costs (as determined under regulations of the Administrator) in carrying out, during the one-year period beginning on the date the grant is made, a public water system supervision program.

(4) In each fiscal year the Administrator shall, in accordance, with regulations, allot the sums appropriated for such year under paragraph (5) among the States on the basis of population, geographical area, number of public water systems, and other relevant factors. No State shall receive less than 1 per centum of the annual appropriation for grants under paragraph (1): *Provided,* That the Administrator may, by regulation, reduce such percentage in accordance with the criteria specified in this paragraph: *And provided further,* That such percentage shall not apply to grants allotted to Guam, American Samoa, or the Virgin Islands.

(5) The prohibition contained in the last sentence of paragraph (2) may be waived by the Administra-

tor with respect to a grant to a State through fiscal year 1979 but such prohibition may only be waived if, in the judgment of the Administrator—

(A) the State is making a diligent effort to assume and maintain primary enforcement responsibility for public water systems within the State;

(B) the State has made significant progress toward assuming and maintaining such primary enforcement responsibility; and

(C) there is reason to believe the State will assume such primary enforcement responsibility by October 1, 1979.

The amount of any grant awarded for the fiscal years 1978 and 1979 pursuant to a waiver under this paragraph may not exceed 75 per centum of the allotment which the State would have received for such fiscal year if it had assumed and maintained such primary enforcement responsibility. The remaining 25 per centum of the amount allotted to such State for such fiscal year shall be retained by the Administrator, and the Administrator may award such amount to such State at such time as the State assumes such responsibility before the beginning of fiscal year 1980. At the beginning of each fiscal years [1] 1979 and 1980 the amounts retained by the Administrator for any preceding fiscal year and not awarded by the beginning of fiscal year 1979 or 1980 to the States to which such amounts were originally allotted may be removed from the original allotment and reallotted for fiscal year 1979 or 1980 (as the case may be) to States which have assumed primary enforcement responsibility by the beginning of such fiscal year.

(6) The Administrator shall notify the State of the approval or disapproval of any application for a grant under this section—

(A) within ninety days after receipt of such application, or

(B) not later than the first day of the fiscal year for which the grant application is made,

whichever is later.

(7) For purposes of making grants under paragraph (1) there are authorized to be appropriated $15,000,000 for the fiscal year ending June 30, 1976, $25,000,000 for the fiscal year ending June 30, 1977, $35,000,000 for fiscal year 1978, $45,000,000 for fiscal year 1979, $29,450,000 for the fiscal year ending September 30, 1980, $32,000,000 for the fiscal year ending September 30, 1981, and $34,000,000 for the fiscal year ending September 30, 1982. For the purposes of making grants under paragraph (1) there are authorized to be appropriated not more than the following amounts:

Fiscal year:	*Amount*
1987	$37,200,000
1988	37,200,000
1989	40,150,000
1990	40,150,000
1991	40,150,000

(b) Underground water source protection programs; applications for grants; allotment of sums; authorization of appropriations

(1) From allotments made pursuant to paragraph (4), the Administrator may make grants to States to carry out underground water source protection programs.

(2) No grant may be made under paragraph (1) unless an application therefor has been submitted to the Administrator in such form and manner as he may require. No grant may be made to any State under paragraph (1) unless the State has assumed primary enforcement responsibility within two years after the date the Administrator promulgates regulations for State underground injection control programs under section 300h of this title. The prohibition contained in the preceding sentence shall not apply to such grants when made to Indian Tribes.

(3) A grant under paragraph (1) shall be made to cover not more than 75 per centum of the grant recipient's costs (as determined under regulations of the Administrator) in carrying out, during the one-year period beginning on the date the grant is made, and underground water source protection program.

(4) In each fiscal year the Administrator shall, in accordance with regulations, allot the sums appropriated for such year under paragraph (5) among the States on the basis of population, geographical area, and other relevant factors.

(5) For purposes of making grants under paragraph (1) there are authorized to be appropriated $5,000,000 for the fiscal year ending June 30, 1976, $7,500,000 for the fiscal year ending June 30, 1977, $10,000,000 for each of the fiscal years 1978 and 1979, $7,795,000 for the fiscal year ending September 30, 1980, $18,000,000 for the fiscal year ending September 30, 1981, and $21,000,000 for the fiscal year ending September 30, 1982. For the purpose of making grants under paragraph (1) there are authorized to be appropriated not more than the following amounts:

Fiscal year:	*Amount*
1987	$19,700,000
1988	19,700,000
1989	20,850,000
1990	20,850,000

Fiscal year:	*Amount*
1991	20,850,000

(c) Definitions

For purposes of this section:

(1) The term "public water system supervision program" means a program for the adoption and enforcement of drinking water regulations (with such variances and exemptions from such regulations under conditions and in a manner which is not less stringent than the conditions under, and the manner in, which variances and exemptions may be granted under sections 300g–4 and 300g–5 of this title) which are no less stringent than the national primary drinking water regulations under section 300g–1 of this title, and for keeping records and making reports required by section 300g–2(a)(3) of this title.

(2) The term "underground water source protection program" means a program for the adoption and enforcement of a program which meets the requirements of regulations under section 300h of this title and for keeping records and making reports required by section 300h–1(b)(1)(A)(ii) of this title. Such term includes, where applicable, a program which meets the requirements of section 300h–4 of this title.

(July 1, 1944, ch. 373, title XIV, § 1443, as added Dec. 16, 1974, Pub.L. 93–523, § 2(a), 88 Stat. 1684, and amended Nov. 16, 1977, Pub.L. 95–190, §§ 2(b), (c), 5(a), 91 Stat. 1393, 1395; Sept. 6, 1979, Pub.L. 96–63, § 2, 93 Stat. 411; Dec. 5, 1980, Pub.L. 96–502, §§ 2(c), 4(d), 94 Stat. 2738; June 19, 1986, Pub.L. 99–339, Title III, §§ 301(b), (c), 302(d), 100 Stat. 664, 666.)

1 So in original. Probably should be "year".

Code of Federal Regulations

Grants,
- Awarded by Environmental Protection Agency, see 40 CFR 30.100 et seq.
- For programs for air pollution control, public water system supervision, solid and hazardous waste management, pesticide enforcement and underground water source protection, see 40 CFR 35.400 to 35.786.

Subagreements, see 40 CFR 33.001 et seq.

Library References

United States ⚷82(2).
C.J.S. United States § 122.

§ 300j–3. Special project grants and guaranteed loans

(a) Special study and demonstration project grants

The Administrator may make grants to any person for the purposes of—

(1) assisting in the development and demonstration (including construction) of any project which will demonstrate a new or improved method, approach, or technology, for providing a dependably safe supply of drinking water to the public; and

(2) assisting in the development and demonstration (including construction) of any project which will investigate and demonstrate health implications involved in the reclamation, recycling, and reuse of waste waters for drinking and the processes and methods for the preparation of safe and acceptable drinking water.

(b) Limitations

Grants made by the Administrator under this section shall be subject to the following limitations:

(1) Grants under this section shall not exceed 66⅔ per centum of the total cost of construction of any facility and 75 per centum of any other costs, as determined by the Administrator.

(2) Grants under this section shall not be made for any project involving the construction or modification of any facilities for any public water system in a State unless such project has been approved by the State agency charged with the responsibility for safety of drinking water (or if there is no such agency in a State, by the State health authority).

(3) Grants under this section shall not be made for any project unless the Administrator determines, after consulting the National Drinking Water Advisory Council, that such project will serve a useful purpose relating to the development and demonstration of new or improved techniques, methods, or technologies for the provision of safe water to the public for drinking.

(4) Priority for grants under this section shall be given where there are known or potential public health hazards which require advanced technology for the removal of particles which are too small to be removed by ordinary treatment technology.

(c) Authorization of appropriations

For the purposes of making grants under subsections (a) and (b) of this section there are authorized to be appropriated $7,500,000 for the fiscal year ending June 30, 1975; and $7,500,000 for the fiscal year ending June 30, 1976; and $10,000,000 for the fiscal year ending June 30, 1977.

(d) Loan guarantees to public water systems; conditions; indebtedness limitation; regulations

The Administrator during the fiscal years ending June 30, 1975, and June 30, 1976, shall carry out a program of guaranteeing loans made by private lenders to small public water systems for the purpose of enabling such systems to meet national primary drinking water regulations prescribed under section 300g–1 of this title. No such guarantee may be made with respect to a system unless (1) such system cannot reasonably obtain financial assistance necessary to comply with such regulations from any other source, and (2) the Administrator determines that any facilities constructed with a loan guaranteed under this subsection is not likely to be made obsolete by subsequent changes in primary regulations. The aggregate amount of indebtedness guaranteed with respect to any system may not exceed $50,000. The aggregate amount of indebtedness guaranteed under this subsection may not exceed $50,000,000. The Administrator shall prescribe regulations to carry out this subsection.

(July 1, 1944, ch. 373, title XIV, § 1444, as added Dec. 16, 1974, Pub.L. 93–523, § 2(a), 88 Stat. 1685, as amended June 19, 1986, Pub.L. 99–339, Title I, § 101(c)(3), 100 Stat. 646.)

Code of Federal Regulations

Environmental Protection Agency grants, policies and procedures respecting, see 40 CFR 30.100 et seq.
Subagreements, see 40 CFR 33.001 et seq.

Library References

United States ⇐82(1).
C.J.S. United States § 122.

§ 300j–3a. Grants to public sector agencies

(a) Assistance for development and demonstration projects

The Administrator of the Environmental Protection Agency shall offer grants to public sector agencies for the purposes of—

(1) assisting in the development and demonstration (including construction) of any project which will demonstrate a new or improved method, approach, or technology for providing a dependably safe supply of drinking water to the public; and

(2) assisting in the development and demonstration (including construction) of any project which will investigate and demonstrate health and conservation implications involved in the reclamation, recycling, and reuse of wastewaters for drinking and agricultural use or the processes and methods for the preparation of safe and acceptable drinking water.

(b) Limitations

Grants made by the Administrator under this section shall be subject to the following limitations:

(1) Grants under this section shall not exceed 66⅔ per centum of the total cost of construction of any facility and 75 per centum of any other costs, as determined by the Administrator.

(2) Grants under this section shall not be made for any project involving the construction or modification of any facilities for any public water system in a State unless such project has been approved by the State agency charged with the responsibility for safety of drinking water (or if there is no such agency in a State, by the State health authority).

(3) Grants under this section shall not be made for any project unless the Administrator determines, after consultation, that such project will serve a useful purpose relating to the development and demonstration of new or improved techniques, methods, or technologies for the provision of safe water to the public for drinking.

(c) Authorization of appropriations

There are authorized to be appropriated for the purposes of this section $25,000,000 for fiscal year 1978.

(Nov. 8, 1977, Pub.L. 95–155, § 5, 91 Stat. 1258; Oct. 18, 1978, Pub.L. 95–477, § 7(a)(1), 92 Stat. 1511.)

§ 300j–3b. Contaminant standards or treatment technique guidelines

(1) Not later than nine months after October 18, 1978, the Administrator shall promulgate guidelines establishing supplemental standards or treatment technique requirements for microbiological, viral, radiological, organic, and inorganic contaminants, which guidelines shall be conditions, as provided in paragraph (2), of any grant for a demonstration project for water reclamation, recycling, and reuse funded under section 300j–3a of this title or under section 300j–3(a)(2) of this title, where such project involves direct human consumption of treated wastewater. Such guidelines shall provide for sufficient control of each such contaminant, such that in the Administrator's judgement, no adverse effects on the health of persons may reasonably be anticipated to occur, allowing an adequate margin of safety.

(2) A grant referred to in paragraph (1) for a project which involves direct human consumption of treated wastewater may be awarded on or after the date of promulgation of guidelines under this section only if the applicant demonstrates to the satisfaction of the Administrator that the project—

(A) will comply with all national primary drinking water regulations under section 300g–1 of this title;

(B) will comply with all guidelines under this section; and

(C) will in other respects provide safe drinking water.

Any such grant awarded before the date of promulgation of such guidelines shall be conditioned on the applicant's agreement to comply to the maximum feasible extent with such guidelines as expeditiously as practicable following the date of promulgation thereof.

(3) Guidelines under this section may, in the discretion of the Administrator—

(A) be nationally and uniformly applicable to all projects funded under section 300j–3a of this title or section 300j–1(a)(2) of this title;

(B) vary for different classes or categories of such projects (as determined by the Administrator);

(C) be established and applicable on a project-by-project basis; or

(D) any combination of the above.

(4) Nothing in this section shall be construed to prohibit or delay the award of any grant referred to in paragraph (1) prior to the date of promulgation of such guidelines.

(Oct. 18, 1978, Pub.L. 95–477, § 7(b), 92 Stat. 1511.)

§ 300j–4. Records and inspections

(a) Persons subject to requirements; size of system as consideration for monitoring; monitoring for unregulated contaminants; addition to or deletion from list; waiver of monitoring requirement; authorization of appropriations

(1) Every person who is a supplier of water, who is or may be otherwise subject to a primary drinking water regulation prescribed under section 300g–1 of this title or to an applicable underground injection control program (as defined in section 300h–1(c) of this title), who is or may be subject to the permit requirement of section 300h–3 of this title or to an order issued under section 300j of this title, or who is a grantee, shall establish and maintain such records, make such reports, conduct such monitoring, and provide such information as the Administrator may reasonably require by regulation to assist him in establishing regulations under this subchapter, in determining whether such person has acted or is acting in compliance with this subchapter, in administering any program of financial assistance under this subchapter, in evaluating the health risks of unregulated contaminants, or in advising the public of such risks. In requiring a public water system to monitor under this subsection, the Administrator may take into consideration the system size and the contaminants likely to be found in the system's drinking water.

(2) Not later than 18 months after June 19, 1986, the Administrator shall promulgate regulations requiring every public water system to conduct a monitoring program for unregulated contaminants. The regulations shall require monitoring of drinking water supplied by the system and shall vary the frequency and schedule of monitoring requirements for systems based on the number of persons served by the system, the source of supply, and the contaminants likely to be found. Each system shall be required to monitor at least once every 5 years after the effective date of the Administrator's regulations unless the Administrator requires more frequent monitoring.

(3) Regulations under paragraph (2) shall list unregulated contaminants for which systems may be required to monitor, and shall include criteria by which the primary enforcement authority in each State could show cause for addition or deletion of contaminants from the designated list. The primary State enforcement authority may delete contaminants for an individual system, in accordance with these criteria, after obtaining approval of assessment of the contaminants potentially to be found in the system. The Administrator shall approve or disapprove such an assessment submitted by a State within 60 days. A State may add contaminants, in accordance with these criteria, without making an assessment, but in no event shall such additions increase Federal expenditures authorized by this section.

(4) Public water systems conducting monitoring of unregulated contaminants pursuant to this section shall provide the results of such monitoring to the primary enforcement authority.

(5) Notification of the availability of the results of the monitoring programs required under paragraph (2), and notification of the availability of the results of the monitoring program referred to in paragraph (6), shall be given to the persons served by the system and the Administrator.

(6) The Administrator may waive the monitoring requirement under paragraph (2) for a system which has conducted a monitoring program after January 1, 1983, if the Administrator determines the program to have been consistent with the regulations promulgated under this section.

(7) Any system supplying less than 150 service connections shall be treated as complying with this subsection if such system provides water samples or the opportunity for sampling according to rules established by the Administrator.

(8) There are authorized to be appropriated $30,000,000 in the fiscal year ending September 30, 1987 to remain available until expended to carry out the provisions of this subsection.

(b) Entry of establishments, facilities, or other property; inspections; conduct of certain tests; audit and examination of records; entry restrictions; prohibition against informing of a proposed entry

(1) Except as provided in paragraph (2), the Administrator, or representatives of the Administrator duly designated by him, upon presenting appropriate credentials and a written notice to any supplier of water or other person subject to (A) a national primary drinking water regulation prescribed under section 300g–1 of this title, (B) an applicable underground injection control program, or (C) any requirement to monitor an unregulated contaminant pursuant to subsection (a) of this section, or person in charge of any of the property of such supplier or other person referred to in clause (A), (B), or (C), is authorized to enter any establishment, facility, or other property of such supplier or other person in order to determine whether such supplier or other person has acted or is acting in compliance with this subchapter, including for this purpose, inspection, at reasonable times, of records, files, papers, processes, controls, and facilities, or in order to test any feature of a public water system, including its raw water source. The Administrator or the Comptroller General (or any representative designated by either) shall have access for the purpose of audit and examination to any records, reports, or information of a grantee which are required to be maintained under subsection (a) of this section or which are pertinent to any financial assistance under this subchapter.

(2) No entry may be made under the first sentence of paragraph (1) in an establishment, facility, or other property of a supplier of water or other person subject to a national primary drinking water regulation if the establishment, facility, or other property is located in a State which has primary enforcement responsibility for public water systems unless, before written notice of such entry is made, the Administrator (or his representative) notifies the State agency charged with responsibility for safe drinking water of the reasons for such entry. The Administrator shall, upon a showing by the State agency that such an entry will be detrimental to the administration of the State's program of primary enforcement responsibility, take such showing into consideration in determining whether to make such entry. No State agency which receives notice under this paragraph of an entry proposed to be made under paragraph (1) may use the information contained in the notice to inform the person whose property is proposed to be entered of the proposed entry; and if a State agency so uses such information, notice to the agency under this paragraph is not required until such time as the Administrator determines the agency has provided him satisfactory assurances that it will no longer so use information contained in a notice under this paragraph.

(c) Penalty

Whoever fails or refuses to comply with any requirement of subsection (a) of this section or to allow the Administrator, the Comptroller General, or representatives of either, to enter and conduct any audit or inspection authorized by subsection (b) of this section shall be subject to a civil penalty of not to exceed $25,000.

(d) Confidential information; trade secrets and secret processes; information disclosure; "information required under this section" defined

(1) Subject to paragraph (2), upon a showing satisfactory to the Administrator by any person that any information required under this section from such person, if made public, would divulge trade secrets or secret processes of such person, the Administrator shall consider such information confidential in accordance with the purposes of section 1905 of title 18. If the applicant fails to make a showing satisfactory to the Administrator, the Administrator shall give such applicant thirty days' notice before releasing the information to which the application relates (unless the public health or safety requires an earlier release of such information).

(2) Any information required under this section (A) may be disclosed to other officers, employees, or authorized representatives of the United States concerned with carrying out this subchapter or to committees of the Congress, or when relevant in any proceeding under this subchapter, and (B) shall be disclosed to the extent it deals with the level of contaminants in drinking water. For purposes of this subsection the term "information required under this section" means any papers, books, documents, or information, or any particular part thereof, reported to or otherwise obtained by the Administrator under this section.

(e) "Grantee" and "person" defined

For purposes of this section, (1) the term "grantee" means any person who applies for or receives financial assistance, by grant, contract, or loan guarantee under this subchapter, and (2) the term "person" includes a Federal agency.

(July 1, 1944, ch. 373, title XIV, § 1445, as added Dec. 16, 1974, Pub.L. 93–523, § 2(a), 88 Stat. 1686, and amended Nov. 16, 1977, Pub.L. 95–190, § 12(c), (d), 91 Stat. 1398; June 19, 1986, Pub.L. 99–339, Title I, § 106, Title III, § 301(h), 100 Stat. 650, 665.)

Cross References

Guidelines for using imminent hazard, enforcement, and emergency response authorities, see section 9606 of this title.

Code of Federal Regulations

Environmental Protection Agency,
- Administration of permit programs, see 40 CFR 122.1 et seq.
- Decisionmaking procedures applicable to permit programs, see 40 CFR 124.1 et seq.

Implementation and enforcement of national primary drinking water regulations, see 40 CFR 142.1 et seq.

Policies and procedures governing requests for public information, see 40 CFR 2.100 et seq.

Underground injection control programs, technical criteria and standards for, see 40 CFR 146.1 et seq.

§ 300j–5. National Drinking Water Advisory Council

(a) Establishment; membership; representation of interests; term of office, vacancies; reappointment

There is established a National Drinking Water Advisory Council which shall consist of fifteen members appointed by the Administrator after consultation with the Secretary. Five members shall be appointed from the general public; five members shall be appointed from appropriate State and local agencies concerned with water hygiene and public water supply; and five members shall be appointed from representatives of private organizations or groups demonstrating an active interest in the field of water hygiene and public water supply. Each member of the Council shall hold office for a term of three years, except that—

(1) any member appointed to fill a vacancy occurring prior to the expiration of the term for which his predecessor was appointed shall be appointed for the remainder of such term; and

(2) the terms of the members first taking office shall expire as follows: Five shall expire three years after December 16, 1974, five shall expire two years after such date, and five shall expire one year after such date, as designated by the Administrator at the time of appointment.

The members of the Council shall be eligible for reappointment.

(b) Functions

The Council shall advise, consult with, and make recommendations to, the Administrator on matters relating to activities, functions, and policies of the Agency under this subchapter.

(c) Compensation and allowances; travel expenses

Members of the Council appointed under this section shall, while attending meetings or conferences of the Council or otherwise engaged in business of the Council, receive compensation and allowances at a rate to be fixed by the Administrator, but not exceeding the daily equivalent of the annual rate of basic pay in effect for grade GS–18 of the General Schedule for each day (including traveltime) during which they are engaged in the actual performance of duties vested in the Council. While away from their homes or regular places of business in the performance of services for the Council, members of the Council shall be allowed travel expenses, including per diem in lieu of subsistence, in the same manner as persons employed intermittently in the Government service are allowed expenses under section 5703(b) of title 5.

(d) Advisory committee termination provision inapplicable

Section 14(a) of the Federal Advisory Committee Act (relating to termination) shall not apply to the Council.

(July 1, 1944, ch. 373, title XIV, § 1446, as added Dec. 16, 1974, Pub.L. 93–523, § 2(a), 88 Stat. 1688.)

Library References

United States ⚷29.
C.J.S. United States § 34 et seq.

§ 300j–6. Federal agencies

(a) Compliance with Federal, State, and local requirements, etc.; scope of applicability of compliance requirements, etc.; liability for civil penalties

Each Federal agency (1) having jurisdiction over any federally owned or maintained public water system or (2) engaged in any activity resulting, or which may result in, underground injection which endangers drinking water (within the meaning of section 300h(d)(2) of this title) shall be subject to, and comply with, all Federal, State, and local requirements, administrative authorities, and process and sanctions respecting the provision of safe drinking water and respecting any underground injection program in the same manner, and to the same extent, as any nongovernmental entity. The preceding sentence shall apply (A) to any requirement whether substantive or procedural (including any recordkeeping or reporting requirement, any requirement respecting permits, and any other requirement whatsoever), (B) to the exercise of any Federal, State, or local administrative authority, and (C) to any process or sanction, whether enforced in Federal, State, or local courts or in any other manner. This subsection shall apply, notwithstanding any immunity of such agencies, under any law or rule of law. No officer, agent, or employee of the United States shall be personally liable for any civil penalty under this subchapter with respect to any act or omission within the scope of his official duties.

(b) Waiver; national security; records available in judicial proceedings; publication in Federal Register; notice to Congressional Committees

The Administrator shall waive compliance with subsection (a) of this section upon request of the

Secretary of Defense and upon a determination by the President that the requested waiver is necessary in the interest of national security. The Administrator shall maintain a written record of the basis upon which such waiver was granted and make such record available for in camera examination when relevant in a judicial proceeding under this subchapter. Upon the issuance of such a waiver, the Administrator shall publish in the Federal Register a notice that the waiver was granted for national security purposes, unless, upon the request of the Secretary of Defense, the Administrator determines to omit such publication because the publication itself would be contrary to the interests of national security, in which event the Administrator shall submit notice to the Armed Services Committee of the Senate and House of Representatives.

(c) Indian rights and sovereignty as unaffected

(1) Nothing in the Safe Drinking Water Amendments of 1977 shall be construed to alter or affect the status of American Indian lands or water rights nor to waive any sovereignty over Indian lands guaranteed by treaty or statute.

(2) For the purposes of this chapter, the term "Federal agency" shall not be construed to refer to or include any American Indian tribe, nor to the Secretary of the Interior in his capacity as trustee of Indian lands.

(July 1, 1944, ch. 373, title XIV, § 1447, as added Dec. 16, 1974, Pub.L. 93–523, § 2(a), 88 Stat. 1688, and amended Nov. 16, 1977, Pub.L. 95–190, § 8(a), (d), 91 Stat. 1396, 1397.)

Code of Federal Regulations

Underground injection control programs, technical criteria and standards for, see 40 CFR 146.1 et seq.

§ 300j–7. Judicial review

(a) Courts of appeals; petition for review; actions respecting regulations; filing period; grounds arising after expiration of filing period; exclusiveness of remedy

A petition for review of—

(1) actions pertaining to the establishment of national primary drinking water regulations (including maximum contaminant level goals) may be filed only in the United States Court of Appeals for the District of Columbia circuit; and

(2) any other action of the Administrator under this chapter may be filed in the circuit in which the petitioner resides or transacts business which is directly affected by the action.

Any such petition shall be filed within the 45-day period beginning on the date of the promulgation of the regulation or issuance of the order with respect to which review is sought or on the date of the determination with respect to which review is sought, and may be filed after the expiration of such 45-day period if the petition is based solely on grounds arising after the expiration of such period. Action of the Administrator with respect to which review could have been obtained under this subsection shall not be subject to judicial review in any civil or criminal proceeding for enforcement or in any civil action to enjoin enforcement.

(b) District courts; petition for review; actions respecting variances or exemptions; filing period; grounds arising after expiration of filing period; exclusiveness of remedy

The United States district courts shall have jurisdiction of actions brought to review (1) the granting of, or the refusing to grant, a variance or exemption under section 300g–4 or 300g–5 of this title or (2) the requirements of any schedule prescribed for a variance or exemption under such section or the failure to prescribe such a schedule. Such an action may only be brought upon a petition for review filed with the court within the 45-day period beginning on the date the action sought to be reviewed is taken or, in the case of a petition to review the refusal to grant a variance or exemption or the failure to prescribe a schedule, within the 45-day period beginning on the date action is required to be taken on the variance, exemption, or schedule, as the case may be. A petition for such review may be filed after the expiration of such period if the petition is based solely on grounds arising after the expiration of such period. Action with respect to which review could have been obtained under this subsection shall not be subject to judicial review in any civil or criminal proceeding for enforcement or in any civil action to enjoin enforcement.

(c) Judicial order for additional evidence before Administrator; modified or new findings; recommendation for modification or setting aside of original determination

In any judicial proceeding in which review is sought of a determination under this subchapter required to be made on the record after notice and opportunity for hearing, if any party applies to the court for leave to adduce additional evidence and shows to the satisfaction of the court that such additional evidence is material and that there were reasonable grounds for the failure to adduce such evidence in the proceeding before the Administrator, the court may order such additional evidence (and evidence in rebuttal thereof) to be taken before the Administrator, in such manner and upon such terms and conditions as the court may deem proper. The Administrator may modify his findings as to the facts, or make new findings, by reason of the additional evidence so taken, and he shall file such modified or new findings, and his recommendation, if any, for the modification or setting aside of his original determination, with the return of such additional evidence.

(July 1, 1944, ch. 373, title XIV, § 1448, as added Dec. 16, 1974, Pub.L. 93-523, § 2(a), 88 Stat. 1689, as amended June 19, 1986, Pub.L. 99-339, Title III, § 303, 100 Stat. 667.)

Library References

Health and Environment ⚖25.15(1).
C.J.S. Health and Environment § 82 et seq.

§ 300j-8. Citizen's civil action

(a) Persons subject to civil action; jurisdiction of enforcement proceedings

Except as provided in subsection (b) of this section, any person may commence a civil action on his own behalf—

(1) against any person (including (A) the United States, and (B) any other governmental instrumentality or agency to the extent permitted by the eleventh amendment to the Constitution) who is alleged to be in violation of any requirement prescribed by or under this subchapter, or

(2) against the Administrator where there is alleged a failure of the Administrator to perform any act or duty under this subchapter which is not discretionary with the Administrator.

No action may be brought under paragraph (1) against a public water system for a violation of a requirement prescribed by or under this subchapter which occurred within the 27-month period beginning on the first day of the month in which this subchapter is enacted. The United States district courts shall have jurisdiction, without regard to the amount in controversy or the citizenship of the parties, to enforce in an action brought under this subsection any requirement prescribed by or under this subchapter or to order the Administrator to perform an act or duty described in paragraph (2), as the case may be.

(b) Conditions for commencement of civil action; notice

No civil action may be commenced—

(1) under subsection (a)(1) of this section respecting violation of a requirement prescribed by or under this subchapter—

(A) prior to sixty days after the plaintiff has given notice of such violation (i) to the Administrator, (ii) to any alleged violator of such requirement and (iii) to the State in which the violation occurs, or

(B) if the Administrator, the Attorney General, or the State has commenced and is diligently prosecuting a civil action in a court of the United States to require compliance with such requirement, but in any such action in a court of the United States any person may intervene as a matter of right; or

(2) under subsection (a)(2) of this section prior to sixty days after the plaintiff has given notice of such action to the Administrator.

Notice required by this subsection shall be given in such manner as the Administrator shall prescribe by regulation. No person may commence a civil action under subsection (a) of this section to require a State to prescribe a schedule under section 300g-4 or 300g-5 of this title for a variance or exemption, unless such person shows to the satisfaction of the court that the State has in a substantial number of cases failed to prescribe such schedules.

(c) Intervention of right

In any action under this section, the Administrator or the Attorney General, if not a party, may intervene as a matter of right.

(d) Costs; attorney fees; expert witness fees; filing of bond

The court, in issuing any final order in any action brought under subsection (a) of this section, may award costs of litigation (including reasonable attorney and expert witness fees) to any party whenever the court determines such an award is appropriate. The court may, if a temporary restraining order or preliminary injunction is sought, require the filing of a bond or equivalent security in accordance with the Federal Rules of Civil Procedure.

(e) Availability of other relief

Nothing in this section shall restrict any right which any person (or class of persons) may have under any statute or common law to seek enforcement of any requirement prescribed by or under this subchapter or to seek any other relief. Nothing in this section or in any other law of the United States shall be construed to prohibit, exclude, or restrict any State or local government from—

(1) bringing any action or obtaining any remedy or sanction in any State or local court, or

(2) bringing any administrative action or obtaining any administrative remedy or sanction,

against any agency of the United States under State or local law to enforce any requirement respecting the provision of safe drinking water or respecting any underground injection control program. Nothing in this section shall be construed to authorize judicial review of regulations or orders of the Administrator under this subchapter, except as provided in section 300j-7 of this title. For provisions providing for application of certain requirements to such agencies in the same manner as to nongovernmental entities, see section 300j–6 of this title.

(July 1, 1944, ch. 373, title XIV, § 1449, as added Dec. 16, 1974, Pub.L. 93–523, § 2(a), 88 Stat. 1690, and amended Nov. 16, 1977, Pub.L. 95–190, § 8(c), 91 Stat. 1397.)

§ 300j–9. General provisions

(a) Regulations; delegation of functions

(1) The Administrator is authorized to prescribe such regulations as are necessary or appropriate to carry out his functions under this subchapter.

(2) The Administrator may delegate any of his functions under this subchapter (other than prescribing regulations) to any officer or employee of the Agency.

(b) Utilization of officers and employees of Federal agencies

The Administrator, with the consent of the head of any other agency of the United States, may utilize such officers and employees of such agency as he deems necessary to assist him in carrying out the purposes of this subchapter.

(c) Assignment of Agency personnel to State or interstate agencies

Upon the request of a State or interstate agency, the Administrator may assign personnel of the Agency to such State or interstate agency for the purposes of carrying out the provisions of this subchapter.

(d) Payments of grants; adjustments; advances; reimbursement; installments; conditions; eligibility for grants; "nonprofit agency or institution" defined

(1) The Administrator may make payments of grants under this subchapter (after necessary adjustment on account of previously made underpayments or overpayments) in advance or by way of reimbursement, and in such installments and on such conditions as he may determine.

(2) Financial assistance may be made available in the form of grants only to individuals and nonprofit agencies or institutions. For purposes of this paragraph, the term "nonprofit agency or institution" means an agency or institution no part of the net earnings of which inure, or may lawfully inure, to the benefit of any private shareholder or individual.

(e) Labor standards

The Administrator shall take such action as may be necessary to assure compliance with provisions of the Act of March 3, 1931 (known as the Davis-Bacon Act; 40 U.S.C. 276a—276a–5). The Secretary of Labor shall have, with respect to the labor standards specified in this subsection, the authority and functions set forth in Reorganization Plan Numbered 14 of 1950 (15 F.R. 3176; 64 Stat. 1267) and section 276c of title 40.

(f) Appearance and representation of Administrator through Attorney General or attorney appointees

The Administrator shall request the Attorney General to appear and represent him in any civil action instituted under this subchapter to which the Administrator is a party. Unless, within a reasonable time, the Attorney General notifies the Administrator that he will appear in such action, attorneys appointed by the Administrator shall appear and represent him.

(g) Authority of Administrator under other provisions unaffected

The provisions of this subchapter shall not be construed as affecting any authority of the Administrator under part G of subchapter II of this chapter.

(h) Reports to Congressional Committees; review by Office of Management and Budget: submittal of comments to Congressional Committees

Not later than April 1 of each year, the Administrator shall submit to the Committee on Commerce, Science, and Transportation of the Senate and the Committee on Energy and Commerce of the House of Representatives a report respecting the activities of the Agency under this subchapter and containing such recommendations for legislation as he considers necessary. The report of the Administrator under this subsection which is due not later than April 1, 1975, and each subsequent report of the Administrator under this subsection shall include a statement on the actual and anticipated cost to public water systems in each State of compliance with the requirements of this subchapter. The Office of Management and Budget may review any report required by this subsection before its submission to such committees of Congress, but the Office may not revise any such report, require any revision in any such report, or delay its submission beyond the day prescribed for its submission, and may submit to such committees of Congress its comments respecting any such report.

(i) Discrimination prohibition; procedural requirements; prohibition inapplicable to undirected but deliberate violations

(1) No employer may discharge any employee or otherwise discriminate against any employee with respect to his compensation, terms, conditions, or privileges of employment because the employee (or any person acting pursuant to a request of the employee) has—

(A) commenced, caused to be commenced, or is about to commence or cause to be commenced a proceeding under this subchapter or a proceeding for the administration or enforcement of drinking water regulations or underground injection control programs of a State,

(B) testified or is about to testify in any such proceeding, or

(C) assisted or participated or is about to assist or participate in any manner in such a proceeding or in any other action to carry out the purposes of this subchapter.

(2)(A) Any employee who believes that he has been discharged or otherwise discriminated against by any person in violation of paragraph (1) may, within 30 days after such violation occurs, file (or have any person file on his behalf) a complaint with the Secretary of Labor (hereinafter in this subsection referred to as the "Secretary") alleging such discharge or discrimination. Upon receipt of such a complaint, the Secretary shall notify the person named in the complaint of the filing of the complaint.

(B)(i) Upon receipt of a complaint filed under subparagraph (A), the Secretary shall conduct an investigation of the violation alleged in the complaint. Within 30 days of the receipt of such complaint, the Secretary shall complete such investigation and shall notify in writing the complainant (and any person acting in his behalf) and the person alleged to have committed such violation of the results of the investigation conducted pursuant to this subparagraph. Within 90 days of the receipt of such complaint the Secretary shall, unless the proceeding on the complaint is terminated by the Secretary on the basis of a settlement entered into by the Secretary and the person alleged to have committed such violation, issue an order either providing the relief prescribed by clause (ii) or denying the complaint. An order of the Secretary shall be made on the record after notice and opportunity for agency hearing. The Secretary may not enter into a settlement terminating a proceeding on a complaint without the participation and consent of the complainant.

(ii) If in response to a complaint filed under subparagraph (A) the Secretary determines that a violation of paragraph (1) has occurred, the Secretary shall order (I) the person who committed such violation to take affirmative action to abate the violation, (II) such person to reinstate the complainant to his former position together with the compensation (including back pay), terms, conditions, and privileges of his employment, (III) compensatory damages, and (IV) where appropriate, exemplary damages. If such an order is issued, the Secretary, at the request of the complainant, shall assess against the person against whom the order is issued a sum equal to the aggregate amount of all costs and expenses (including attorneys' fees) reasonably incurred, as determined by the Secretary, by the complainant for, or in connection with, the bringing of the complaint upon which the order was issued.

(3)(A) Any person adversely affected or aggrieved by an order issued under paragraph (2) may obtain review of the order in the United States Court of Appeals for the circuit in which the violation, with respect to which the order was issued, allegedly occurred. The petition for review must be filed within sixty days from the issuance of the Secretary's order. Review shall conform to chapter 7 of title 5. The commencement of proceedings under this subparagraph shall not, unless ordered by the court, operate as a stay of the Secretary's order.

(B) An order of the Secretary with respect to which review could have been obtained under subparagraph (A) shall not be subject to judicial review in any criminal or other civil proceeding.

(4) Whenever a person has failed to comply with an order issued under paragraph (2)(B), the Secretary shall file a civil action in the United States District Court for the district in which the violation was found to occur to enforce such order. In actions brought under this paragraph, the district courts shall have jurisdiction to grant all appropriate relief including, but not limited to, injunctive relief, compensatory, and exemplary damages.

(5) Any nondiscretionary duty imposed by this section is enforceable in mandamus proceeding brought under section 1361 of title 28.

(6) Paragraph (1) shall not apply with respect to any employee who, acting without direction from his employer (or the employer's agent), deliberately causes a violation of any requirement of this subchapter.

(July 1, 1944, ch. 373, title XIV, § 1450, as added Dec. 16, 1974, Pub.L. 93–523, § 2(a), 88 Stat. 1691, and amended S.Res. 4, Feb. 4, 1977; H.Res. 549, Mar. 25, 1980; Nov. 8, 1984, Pub.L. 98–620, Title IV, § 402(38), 98 Stat. 3360.)

Code of Federal Regulations

Environmental Protection Agency,
- Administration of permit programs, see 40 CFR 122.1 et seq.
- Decisionmaking procedures applicable to permit programs, see 40 CFR 124.1 et seq.

Grant policies and procedures, see 40 CFR 35.400 to 35.786.

Implementation and enforcement of national primary drinking water regulations, see 40 CFR 142.1 et seq.

Labor standards applicable to contracts covering federally financed and assisted construction, see 29 CFR 5.0 et seq.

Procedures for determination of prevailing wage rates for laborers and mechanics, see 29 CFR 1.1 et seq.

Procedures governing disposition of discrimination complaints, see 29 CFR 24.1 et seq.

Public participation in programs and activities, see 40 CFR 25.1 et seq.

Underground injection control programs, technical criteria and standards for, see 40 CFR 146.1 et seq.

Library References

Health and Environment ⚩25.7(3).
Labor Relations ⚩7.
C.J.S. Health and Environment § 106.
C.J.S. Labor Relations § 2 et seq.

§ 300j-10. Appointment of scientific, etc., personnel by Administrator of Environmental Protection Agency for implementation of responsibilities; compensation

To the extent that the Administrator of the Environmental Protection Agency deems such action necessary to the discharge of his functions under title XIV of the Public Health Service Act [42 U.S.C. 300f et seq.] (relating to safe drinking water) and under other provisions of law, he may appoint personnel to fill not more than thirty scientific, engineering, professional, legal, and administrative positions within the Environmental Protection Agency without regard to the civil service laws and may fix the compensation of such personnel not in excess of the maximum rate payable for GS-18 of the General Schedule under section 5332 of title 5.

(Nov. 16, 1977, Pub.L. 95-190, § 11(b), 91 Stat. 1398.)

Library References

Health and Environment ⚩25.5(9).
C.J.S. Health and Environment § 65 et seq.

§ 300j-11. Indian tribes

(a) In general

Subject to the provisions of subsection (b) of this section, the Administrator—

(1) is authorized to treat Indian Tribes as States under this subchapter,

(2) may delegate to such Tribes primary enforcement responsibility for public water systems and for underground injection control, and

(3) may provide such Tribes grant and contract assistance to carry out functions provided by this subchapter.

(b) EPA regulations

(1) Specific provisions

The Administrator shall, within 18 months after June 19, 1986, promulgate final regulations specifying those provisions of this subchapter for which it is appropriate to treat Indian Tribes as States. Such treatment shall be authorized only if:

(A) the Indian Tribe is recognized by the Secretary of the Interior and has a governing body carrying out substantial governmental duties and powers;

(B) the functions to be exercised by the Indian Tribe are within the area of the Tribal Government's jurisdiction; and

(C) the Indian Tribe is reasonably expected to be capable, in the Administrator's judgment, of carrying out the functions to be exercised in a manner consistent with the terms and purposes of this subchapter and of all applicable regulations.

(2) Provisions where treatment as State inappropriate

For any provision of this subchapter where treatment of Indian Tribes as identical to States is inappropriate, administratively infeasible or otherwise inconsistent with the purposes of this subchapter, the Administrator may include in the regulations promulgated under this section, other means for administering such provision in a manner that will achieve the purpose of the provision. Nothing in this section shall be construed to allow Indian Tribes to assume or maintain primary enforcement responsibility for public water systems or for underground injection control in a manner less protective of the health of persons than such responsibility may be assumed or maintained by a State. An Indian tribe shall not be required to exercise criminal enforcement jurisdiction for purposes of complying with the preceding sentence.

(July 1, 1944, ch. 373, title XIV, § 1451, as added June 19, 1986, Pub.L. 99-339, Title III, § 302(a), 100 Stat. 665.)

NATIONAL ENVIRONMENTAL POLICY

(42 U.S.C.A. §§ 4321 to 4370a)

CHAPTER 55—NATIONAL ENVIRONMENTAL POLICY

WESTLAW Electronic Research

See WESTLAW guide following the Explanation pages of this pamphlet.

§ 4321. Congressional declaration of purpose

The purposes of this chapter are: To declare a national policy which will encourage productive and enjoyable harmony between man and his environment; to promote efforts which will prevent or eliminate damage to the environment and biosphere and stimulate the health and welfare of man; to enrich the understanding of the ecological systems and natural resources important to the Nation; and to establish a Council on Environmental Quality.

(Jan. 1, 1970, Pub.L. 91–190, § 2, 83 Stat. 852.)

Cross References

Pacific Salmon Fishing, regulations of Secretary of Commerce under treaty not subject to this chapter, see section 3636 of Title 16, Conservation.

Federal Practice and Procedure

Environmental class actions, see Wright & Miller: Civil § 1782.
Jurisdiction of district courts over claims arising under Acts of Congress pertaining to commerce and monopolies, see Wright, Miller & Cooper: Jurisdiction § 3574.

West's Federal Practice Manual

Federal environmental law, see § 4381 et seq.

Library References

Health and Environment ⟹25.5.
C.J.S. Health and Environment § 61 et seq.

United States Supreme Court

Other statutes, not repealed by implication by this chapter, Aberdeen & Rockfish R. Co. v. Students Challenging Regulatory Agency Procedures, 1975, 95 S.Ct. 2336, 422 U.S. 289, 45 L.Ed.2d 191.

SUBCHAPTER I—POLICIES AND GOALS

§ 4331. Congressional declaration of national environmental policy

(a) Creation and maintenance of conditions under which man and nature can exist in productive harmony

The Congress, recognizing the profound impact of man's activity on the interrelations of all components of the natural environment, particularly the profound influences of population growth, high-density urbanization, industrial expansion, resource exploitation, and new and expanding technological advances and recognizing further the critical importance of restoring and maintaining environmental quality to the overall welfare and development of man, declares that it is the continuing policy of the Federal Government, in cooperation with State and local governments, and other concerned public and private organizations, to use all practicable means and measures, including financial and technical assistance, in a manner calculated to foster and promote the general welfare, to create and maintain conditions under which man and nature can exist in productive harmony, and fulfill the social, economic, and other requirements of present and future generations of Americans.

(b) Continuing responsibility of Federal Government to use all practicable means to improve and coordinate Federal plans, functions, programs, and resources

In order to carry out the policy set forth in this chapter, it is the continuing responsibility of the Federal Government to use all practicable means, consistent with other essential considerations of national policy, to improve and coordinate Federal plans, functions, programs, and resources to the end that the Nation may—

(1) fulfill the responsibilities of each generation as trustee of the environment for succeeding generations;

(2) assure for all Americans safe, healthful, productive, and esthetically and culturally pleasing surroundings;

(3) attain the widest range of beneficial uses of the environment without degradation, risk to health or safety, or other undesirable and unintended consequences;

(4) preserve important historic, cultural, and natural aspects of our national heritage, and maintain, wherever possible, an environment which supports diversity and variety of individual choice;

(5) achieve a balance between population and resource use which will permit high standards of living and a wide sharing of life's amenities; and

(6) enhance the quality of renewable resources and approach the maximum attainable recycling of depletable resources.

(c) Responsibility of each person to contribute to preservation and enhancement of environment

The Congress recognizes that each person should enjoy a healthful environment and that each person has a responsibility to contribute to the preservation and enhancement of the environment.

(Jan. 1, 1970, Pub. L. 91–190, title I, § 101, 83 Stat. 852.)

Federal Practice and Procedure

Environmental class actions, see Wright & Miller: Civil § 1782.
Mandatory right to blanket injunction under this chapter, see Wright & Miller: Civil § 2904.

Library References

Health and Environment ⚷25.5.
C.J.S. Health and Environment § 61 et seq.

United States Supreme Court

Environmental effect and environmental impact, terms defined, Metropolitan Edison Co. v. People Against Nuclear Energy, 1983, 103 S.Ct. 1556, 460 U.S. 766, 75 L.Ed.2d 534.

§ 4332. Cooperation of agencies; reports; availability of information; recommendations; international and national coordination of efforts

The Congress authorizes and directs that, to the fullest extent possible: (1) the policies, regulations, and public laws of the United States shall be interpreted and administered in accordance with the policies set forth in this chapter, and (2) all agencies of the Federal Government shall—

(A) utilize a systematic, interdisciplinary approach which will insure the integrated use of the natural and social sciences and the environmental design arts in planning and in decisonmaking which may have an impact on man's environment;

(B) identify and develop methods and procedures, in consultation with the Council on Environmental Quality established by subchapter II of this chapter, which will insure that presently unquantified environmental amenities and values may be given appropriate consideration in decisionmaking along with economic and technical considerations;

(C) include in every recommendation or report on proposals for legislation and other major Federal actions significantly affecting the quality of the human environment, a detailed statement by the responsible official on—

(i) the environmental impact of the proposed action,

(ii) any adverse environmental effects which cannot be avoided should the proposal be implemented,

(iii) alternatives to the proposed action,

(iv) the relationship between local short-term uses of man's environment and the maintenance and enhancement of long-term productivity, and

(v) any irreversible and irretrievable commitments of resources which would be involved in the proposed action should it be implemented.

Prior to making any detailed statement, the responsible Federal official shall consult with and obtain the comments of any Federal agency which has jurisdiction by law or special expertise with respect to any environmental impact involved. Copies of such statement and the comments and views of the appropriate Federal, State, and local agencies, which are authorized to develop and enforce environmental standards, shall be made available to the President, the Council on Environmental Quality and to the public as provided by section 552 of title 5, and shall accompany the proposal through the existing agency review processes;

(D) Any detailed statement required under subparagraph (C) after January 1, 1970, for any major Federal action funded under a program of grants to States shall not be deemed to be legally insufficient solely by reason of having been prepared by a State agency or official, if:

(i) the State agency or official has statewide jurisdiction and has the responsibility for such action,

(ii) the responsible Federal official furnishes guidance and participates in such preparation,

(iii) the responsible Federal official independently evaluates such statement prior to its approval and adoption, and

(iv) after January 1, 1976, the responsible Federal official provides early notification to, and solicits the views of, any other State or any Federal land management entity of any action or any alternative thereto which may have significant impacts upon such State or affected Federal land management entity and, if there is any disagreement on such impacts, prepares a written assessment of such impacts and views for incorporation into such detailed statement.

The procedures in this subparagraph shall not relieve the Federal official of his responsibilities for the scope, objectivity, and content of the entire statement or of any other responsibility under this chapter; and further, this subparagraph does not affect the legal sufficiency of statements prepared by State agencies with less than statewide jurisdiction.[1]

(E) study, develop, and describe appropriate alternatives to recommended courses of action in any proposal which involves unresolved conflicts concerning alternative uses of available resources;

(F) recognize the worldwide and long-range character of environmental problems and, where consistent with the foreign policy of the United States, lend appropriate support to initiatives, resolutions, and programs designed to maximize international cooperation in anticipating and preventing a decline in the quality of mankind's world environment;

(G) make available to States, counties, municipalities, institutions, and individuals, advice and information useful in restoring, maintaining, and enhancing the quality of the environment;

(H) initiate and utilize ecological information in the planning and development of resource-oriented projects; and

(I) assist the Council on Environmental Quality established by subchapter II of this chapter.

(Jan. 1, 1970, Pub.L. 91–190, title I, § 102, 83 Stat. 853; Aug. 9, 1975, Pub.L. 94–83, 89 Stat. 424.)

[1] So in original. The period probably should be a semicolon.

Cross References

National marine sanctuaries, procedures for designation, preparation of draft environmental impact statement by Secretary of Commerce, see section 1434 of Title 16, Conservation.

Federal Practice and Procedure

Discretion of court to issue declaratory judgment, see Wright, Miller & Kane: Civil 2d § 2759.
Environmental class actions, see Wright & Miller: Civil § 1782.
Requirement of environmental impact statement, see Wright, Miller & Cooper: Jurisdiction § 3531.
Standing to seek declaratory judgment, see Wright, Miller & Kane: Civil 2d § 2757.

West's Federal Practice Manual

Environmentally concerned departments and agencies, see § 4381.10 et seq.
Mineral leases, see §§ 5401.5, 5468.
Relation to energy policy, see § 4342.5.
Relation to government contracts, see § 1530.

Code of Federal Regulations

Requirements, standards, etc.,
- Agency for International Development, see 22 CFR 216.1 et seq.
- Agricultural Stabilization and Conservation Service, see 7 CFR 799.1 et seq.
- Bureau of Land Management, see 43 CFR 3040 et seq., 6290.0–2 et seq.
- Civil Aeronautics Board, see 14 CFR 201.1 et seq., 261.1 et seq., 312.1 et seq., 399.1 et seq.
- Coast Guard, see 46 CFR 10.01–1 et seq., 12.01 et seq., 31.01–1 et seq., 71.01–1 et seq., 91.01–1 et seq., 105.01–1 et seq., 176.01–1 et seq., 187.01–1 et seq., 189.01–1 et seq.
- Committee for Purchase from the Blind and Other Severely Handicapped, see 41 CFR 51–6.1 et seq.
- Consumer Products Safety Commission, review, see 16 CFR 1021.1 et seq.
- Council on Environmental Quality, see 40 CFR 1500.1 et seq., 1510.1 et seq.
- Defense Department, see 32 CFR 214.1 et seq.
- Energy Research and Development Administration, see 10 CFR 711.1 et seq.
- Environmental Protection Agency, see 40 CFR Ch. 1.
- Federal Aviation Administration, see 14 CFR 21.1 et seq., 36.1 et seq., 91.1 et seq.
- Federal Highway Administration, see 23 CFR 420.101 et seq., 712.101 et seq., 751.1 et seq., 770.200 et seq., 771.1 et seq., 772.1 et seq.
- Federal Maritime Commission, see 46 CFR 547.1 et seq.
- Federal Trade Commission, see 16 CFR 1.1 et seq.
- Food and Drug Administration, see 21 CFR 25.1 et seq.
- Housing and Urban Development, see 24 CFR 58.1 et seq.
- Interstate Commerce Commission, see 49 CFR 1108.1 et seq.
- Law Enforcement Assistance Administration, see 28 CFR 19.1 et seq.
- National Aeronautics and Space Administration, see 14 CFR 1204.200 et seq.

Requirements, standards, etc.—Cont'd
National Highway Traffic Safety Administration, see 49 CFR 520.1 et seq.
National Marine Fisheries Service, see 50 CFR 251.1 et seq.
Navy Department, see 32 CFR 775.1 et seq.
Nuclear Regulatory Commission, see 10 CFR 2.1 et seq., 51.1 et seq.
Occupational Safety and Health Administration, see 29 CFR 1999.1 et seq.
Office of Education, see 45 CFR 100a.185, 100b.185.
Soil Conservation Service, see 7 CFR 650.1 et seq.
Tennessee Valley Authority, see 18 CFR 305.1 et seq.
Urban Mass Transportation Administration, see 49 CFR 613.100 et seq.

United States Supreme Court

Agency decisions, review, see Strycker's Bay Neighborhood Council, Inc. v. Karlen, N.Y., 1980, 100 S.Ct. 497, 444 U.S. 223, 62 L.Ed.2d 433.

Construction with other laws, see Weinberger v. Catholic Action of Hawaii/Peace Ed. Project, 1981, 102 S.Ct. 197, 454 U.S. 139, 70 L.Ed.2d 298.

Judicial review of agency actions, duties and functions of court, see Aberdeen & Rockfish Ry. Co. v. Students Challenging Regulatory Agency Procedures, 1972, 93 S.Ct. 1, 409 U.S. 1207, 34 L.Ed.2d 21.

§ 4333. Conformity of administrative procedures to national environmental policy

All agencies of the Federal Government shall review their present statutory authority, administrative regulations, and current policies and procedures for the purpose of determining whether there are any deficiencies or inconsistencies therein which prohibit full compliance with the purposes and provisions of this chapter and shall propose to the President not later than July 1, 1971, such measures as may be necessary to bring their authority and policies into conformity with the intent, purposes, and procedures set forth in this chapter.

(Jan. 1, 1970, Pub.L. 91–190, title I, § 103, 83 Stat. 854.)

Federal Practice and Procedure

Environmental class actions, see Wright & Miller: Civil § 1782.

§ 4334. Other statutory obligations of agencies

Nothing in section 4332 or 4333 of this title shall in any way affect the specific statutory obligations of any Federal agency (1) to comply with criteria or standards of environmental quality, (2) to coordinate or consult with any other Federal or State agency, or (3) to act, or refrain from acting contingent upon the recommendations or certification of any other Federal or State agency.

(Jan. 1, 1970, Pub.L. 91–190, title I, § 104, 83 Stat. 854.)

Federal Practice and Procedure

Environmental class actions, see Wright & Miller: Civil § 1782.

West's Federal Practice Manual

Quotas for minority businesses, see § 16555.

Code of Federal Regulations

Department of Defense, environmental effects, see 32 CFR 214.1 et seq.

§ 4335. Efforts supplemental to existing authorizations

The policies and goals set forth in this chapter are supplementary to those set forth in existing authorizations of Federal agencies.

(Jan. 1, 1970, Pub.L. 91–190, title I, § 105, 83 Stat. 854.)

Federal Practice and Procedure

Environmental class actions, see Wright & Miller: Civil § 1782.

SUBCHAPTER II—COUNCIL ON ENVIRONMENTAL QUALITY

§ 4341. Reports to Congress; recommendations for legislation

The President shall transmit to the Congress annually beginning July 1, 1970, an Environmental Quality Report (hereinafter referred to as the "report") which shall set forth (1) the status and condition of the major natural, manmade, or altered environmental classes of the Nation, including, but not limited to, the air, the aquatic, including marine, estuarine, and fresh water, and the terrestrial environment, including, but not limited to, the forest, dryland, wetland, range, urban, suburban, and rural environment; (2) current and foreseeable trends in the quality, management and utilization of such environments and the effects of those trends on the social, economic, and other requirements of the Nation; (3) the adequacy of available natural resources for fulfilling human and economic requirements of the Nation in the light of expected population pressures; (4) a review of the programs and activities (including regulatory activities) of the Federal Government, the State and local governments, and nongovernmental entities or individuals, with particular reference to their effect on the environment and on the conservation, development and utilization of natural resources; and (5) a program for remedying the deficiencies of existing programs and activities, together with recommendations for legislation.

(Jan. 1, 1970, Pub.L. 91–190, title II, § 201, 83 Stat. 854.)

Federal Practice and Procedure

Environmental class actions, see Wright & Miller: Civil § 1782.

Library References

Health and Environment ⇐1, 25.5.
C.J.S. Health and Environment §§ 4 et seq., 61 et seq.

§ 4342. Establishment; membership; Chairman; appointments

There is created in the Executive Office of the President a Council on Environmental Quality (hereinafter referred to as the "Council"). The Council shall be composed of three members who shall be appointed by the President to serve at his pleasure, by and with the advice and consent of the Senate. The President shall designate one of the members of the Council to serve as Chairman. Each member shall be a person who, as a result of his training, experience, and attainments, is exceptionally well qualified to analyze and interpret environmental trends and information of all kinds; to appraise programs and activities of the Federal Government in the light of the policy set forth in subchapter I of this chapter; to be conscious of and responsive to the scientific, economic, social, esthetic, and cultural needs and interests of the Nation; and to formulate and recommend national policies to promote the improvement of the quality of the environment.

(Jan. 1, 1970, Pub.L. 91–190, title II, § 202, 83 Stat. 854.)

Federal Practice and Procedure

Environmental class actions, see Wright & Miller: Civil § 1782.

West's Federal Practice Manual

Council on Environmental Quality, see § 4382.5.

§ 4343. Employment of personnel, experts and consultants

(a) The Council may employ such officers and employees as may be necessary to carry out its functions under this chapter. In addition, the Council may employ and fix the compensation of such experts and consultants as may be necessary for the carrying out of its functions under this chapter, in accordance with section 3109 of title 5 (but without regard to the last sentence thereof).

(b) Notwithstanding section 1342 of title 31, the Council may accept and employ voluntary and uncompensated services in furtherance of the purposes of the Council.

(Jan. 1, 1970, Pub.L. 91–190, title II, § 203, 83 Stat. 855; July 3, 1975, Pub.L. 94–52, § 2, 89 Stat. 258; as amended Sept. 13, 1982, Pub.L. 97–258, § 4(b), 96 Stat. 1067.)

Federal Practice and Procedure

Environmental class actions, see Wright & Miller: Civil § 1782.

§ 4344. Duties and functions

It shall be the duty and function of the Council—

(1) to assist and advise the President in the preparation of the Environmental Quality Report required by section 4341 of this title;

(2) to gather timely and authoritative information concerning the conditions and trends in the quality of the environment both current and prospective, to analyze and interpret such information for the purpose of determining whether such conditions and trends are interfering, or are likely to interfere, with the achievement of the policy set forth in subchapter I of this chapter, and to compile and submit to the President studies relating to such conditions and trends;

(3) to review and appraise the various programs and activities of the Federal Government in the light of the policy set forth in subchapter I of this chapter for the purpose of determining the extent to which such programs and activities are contributing to the achievement of such policy, and to make recommendations to the President with respect thereto;

(4) to develop and recommend to the President national policies to foster and promote the improvement of environmental quality to meet the conservation, social, economic, health, and other requirements and goals of the Nation;

(5) to conduct investigations, studies, surveys, research, and analyses relating to ecological systems and environmental quality;

(6) to document and define changes in the natural environment, including the plant and animal systems, and to accumulate necessary data and other information for a continuing analysis of these changes or trends and an interpretation of their underlying causes;

(7) to report at least once each year to the President on the state and condition of the environment; and

(8) to make and furnish such studies, reports thereon, and recommendations with respect to matters of policy and legislation as the President may request.

(Jan. 1, 1970, Pub.L. 91–190, title II, § 204, 83 Stat. 855.)

Federal Practice and Procedure

Environmental class actions, see Wright & Miller: Civil § 1782.

West's Federal Practice Manual

Council on Environmental Quality, see § 4382.5.

§ 4345. Consultation with Citizens' Advisory Committee on Environmental Quality and other representatives

In exercising its powers, functions, and duties under this chapter, the Council shall—

(1) consult with the Citizens' Advisory Committee on Environmental Quality established by Executive Order numbered 11472, dated May 29, 1969, and with such representatives of science, industry, agriculture, labor, conservation organizations, State and local governments and other groups, as it deems advisable; and

(2) utilize, to the fullest extent possible, the services, facilities, and information (including statistical information) of public and private agencies and organizations, and individuals, in order that duplication of effort and expense may be avoided, thus assuring that the Council's activities will not unnecessarily overlap or conflict with similar activities authorized by law and performed by established agencies.

(Jan. 1, 1970, Pub.L. 91–190, title II, § 205, 83 Stat. 855.)

Federal Practice and Procedure

Environmental class actions, see Wright & Miller: Civil § 1782.

§ 4346. Tenure and compensation of members

Members of the Council shall serve full time and the Chairman of the Council shall be compensated at the rate provided for Level II of the Executive Schedule Pay Rates (5 U.S.C. 5313). The other members of the Council shall be compensated at the rate provided for Level IV or[1] the Executive Schedule Pay Rates (5 U.S.C. 5315).

(Jan. 1, 1970, Pub.L. 91–190, title II, § 206, 83 Stat. 856.)

[1] So in original. Probably should read "of".

§ 4346a. Travel reimbursement by private organizations and Federal, State, and local governments

The Council may accept reimbursements from any private nonprofit organization or from any department, agency, or instrumentality of the Federal Government, any State, or local government, for the reasonable travel expenses incurred by an officer or employee of the Council in connection with his attendance at any conference, seminar, or similar meeting conducted for the benefit of the Council.

(Pub.L. 91–190, title II, § 207, as added July 3, 1975, Pub.L. 94–52, § 3, 89 Stat. 258.)

§ 4346b. Expenditures in support of international activities

The Council may make expenditures in support of its international activities, including expenditures for: (1) international travel; (2) activities in implementation of international agreements; and (3) the support of international exchange programs in the United States and in foreign countries.

(Pub.L. 91–190, title II, § 208, as added July 3, 1975, Pub.L. 94–52, § 3, 89 Stat. 258.)

Federal Practice and Procedure

Environmental class actions, see Wright & Miller: Civil § 1782.

§ 4347. Authorization of appropriations

There are authorized to be appropriated to carry out the provisions of this chapter not to exceed $300,000 for fiscal year 1970, $700,000 for fiscal year 1971, and $1,000,000 for each fiscal year thereafter.

(Jan. 1, 1970, Pub.L. 91–190, title II, § 209, formerly § 207, 83 Stat. 856, renumbered July 3, 1975, Pub.L. 94–52, § 3, 89 Stat. 258.)

SUBCHAPTER III—MISCELLANEOUS PROVISIONS

§ 4361. Plan for research, development and demonstration

The Administrator of the Environmental Protection Agency shall transmit to the Congress, within 6 months after October 11, 1976, a comprehensive 5-year plan for environmental research, development, and demonstration. This plan shall be appropriately revised annually, and such revisions shall be transmitted to the Congress no later than two weeks after the President submits his annual budget to the Congress in such year.

(Oct. 11, 1976, Pub.L. 94–475, § 5, 90 Stat. 2071.)

Federal Practice and Procedure

Environmental class actions, see Wright & Miller: Civil § 1782.

§ 4361a. Budget projections in annual revisions of plan for research, development, and demonstration

The Administrator of the Environmental Protection Agency, in each annual revision of the five-year plan transmitted to the Congress under section 4361 of this title, shall include budget projections for a "no-growth" budget, for a "moderate-growth" budget, and for a "high-growth" budget. In addition, each such annual revision shall include a detailed explanation of the relationship of each budget projection to the existing laws which authorize the Administration's environmental research, development, and demonstration programs.

(Nov. 8, 1977, Pub.L. 95–155, § 4, 91 Stat. 1258.)

§ 4361b. Implementation by Administrator of Environmental Protection Agency of recommendations of "CHESS" Investigative Report; waiver; inclusion of status of implementation requirements in annual revisions of plan for research, development, and demonstration

The Administrator of the Environmental Protection Agency shall implement the recommendations of the report prepared for the House Committee on Science and Technology entitled "The Environmental Protection Agency Research Program with primary emphasis on the Community Health and Environmental Surveillance System (CHESS): An Investigative Report", unless for any specific recommendation he determines (1) that such recommendation has been implemented, (2) that implementation of such recommendation would not enhance the quality of the research, or (3) that implementation of such recommendation will require funding which is not available. Where such funding is not available, the Administrator shall request the required authorization or appropriation for such implementation. The Administrator shall report the status of such implementation in each annual revision of the five-year plan transmitted to the Congress under section 4361 of this title.

(Nov. 8, 1977, Pub.L. 95–155, § 10, 91 Stat. 1262.)

§ 4361c. Staff management

(a) Appointments for educational programs

(1) The Administrator is authorized to select and appoint up to 75 full-time permanent staff members in the Office of Research and Development to pursue full-time educational programs for the purpose of (A) securing an advanced degree or (B) securing academic training, for the purpose of making a career change in order to better carry out the Agency's research mission.

(2) The Administrator shall select and appoint staff members for these assignments according to rules and criteria promulgated by him. The Agency may continue to pay the salary and benefits of the appointees as well as reasonable and appropriate relocation expenses and tuition.

(3) The term of each appointment shall be for up to one year, with a single renewal of up to one year in appropriate cases at the discretion of the Administrator.

(4) Staff members appointed to this program shall not count against any Agency personnel ceiling during the term of their appointment.

(b) Post-doctoral research fellows

(1) The Administrator is authorized to appoint up to 25 Post-doctoral Research Fellows in accordance with the provisions of section 213.3102(aa) of title 5 of the Code of Federal Regulations.

(2) Persons holding these appointments shall not count against any personnel ceiling of the Agency.

(c) Non-government research associates

(1) The Administrator is authorized and encouraged to utilize research associates from outside the Federal Government in conducting the research, development, and demonstration programs of the Agency.

(2) These persons shall be selected and shall serve according to rules and criteria promulgated by the Administrator.

(d) Women and minority groups

For all programs in this section, the Administrator shall place special emphasis on providing opportunities for education and training of women and minority groups.

(Oct. 18, 1978, Pub.L. 95–477, § 6, 92 Stat. 1510.)

Federal Practice and Procedure

Environmental class actions, see Wright & Miller: Civil § 1782.

§ 4362. Interagency cooperation on prevention of environmental cancer and heart and lung disease

(a) Not later than three months after August 7, 1977, there shall be established a Task Force on Environmental Cancer and Heart and Lung Disease (hereinafter referred to as the "Task Force"). The Task Force shall include representatives of the Environmental Protection Agency, the National Cancer Institute, the National Heart, Lung, and Blood Institute, the National Institute of Occupational Safety and Health, and the National Institute on Environmental Health Sciences, and shall be chaired by the Administrator (or his delegate).

(b) The Task Force shall—

(1) recommend a comprehensive research program to determine and quantify the relationship between environmental pollution and human cancer and heart and lung disease;

(2) recommend comprehensive strategies to reduce or eliminate the risks of cancer or such other diseases associated with environmental pollution;

(3) recommend research and such other measures as may be appropriate to prevent or reduce the incidence of environmentally related cancer and heart and lung diseases;

(4) coordinate research by, and stimulate cooperation between, the Environmental Protection Agency, the Department of Health and Human Services, and such other agencies as may be appropriate to prevent environmentally related cancer and heart and lung diseases; and

(5) report to Congress, not later than one year after August 7, 1977, and annually thereafter, on the problems and progress in carrying out this section.

(Aug. 7, 1977, Pub.L. 95–95, title IV, § 402, 91 Stat. 791, 793; Oct. 17, 1979, Pub.L. 96–88, title V, § 509(b), 93 Stat. 695.)

Federal Practice and Procedure

Environmental class actions, see Wright & Miller: Civil § 1782.

§ 4362a. Task Force on Environmental Cancer and Heart and Lung Disease; membership of Director of National Center for Health Statistics and of head of Center for Disease Control

The Director of the National Center for Health Statistics and the head of the Center for Disease Control (or the successor to such entity) shall each serve as members of the Task Force on Environmental Cancer and Heart and Lung Disease established under section 4362 of this title.

(Nov. 9, 1978, Pub.L. 95–623, § 9, 92 Stat. 3455.)

Federal Practice and Procedure

Environmental class actions, see Wright & Miller: Civil § 1782.

§ 4363. Continuing and long-term environmental research and development

The Administrator of the Environmental Protection Agency shall establish a separately identified program of continuing, long-term environmental research and development for each activity listed in section 2(a) of this Act. Unless otherwise specified by law, at least 15 per centum of funds appropriated to the Administrator for environmental research and development for each activity listed in section 2(a) of this Act shall be obligated and expended for such long-term environmental research and development under this section.

(Nov. 8, 1977, Pub.L. 95–155, § 6, 91 Stat. 1259; Dec. 22, 1980, Pub.L. 96–569, § 2(f), 94 Stat. 3337.)

Federal Practice and Procedure

Environmental class actions, see Wright & Miller: Civil § 1782.

§ 4363a. Pollution control technologies demonstrations

(1) The Administrator shall continue to be responsible for conducting and shall continue to conduct full-scale demonstrations of energy-related pollution control technologies as necessary in his judgment to fulfill the provisions of the Clean Air Act as amended [42 U.S.C.A. § 7401 et seq.] the Federal Water Pollution Control Act as amended [33 U.S.C.A. § 1251 et seq.] and other pertinent pollution control statutes.

(2) Energy-related environmental protection projects authorized to be administered by the Environmental Protection Agency under this Act, shall not be transferred administratively to the Department of Energy or reduced through budget amendment. No action shall be taken through administrative or budgetary means to diminish the ability of the Environmental Protection Agency to initiate such projects.

(Oct. 18, 1978, Pub.L. 95–477, § 2(d), 92 Stat. 1508; April 7, 1980, Pub.L. 96–229, § 2(d), 94 Stat. 325, 327.)

Federal Practice and Procedure

Environmental class actions, see Wright & Miller: Civil § 1782.

§ 4364. Expenditure of funds for research and development related to regulatory program activities

(a) Coordination, etc., with research needs and priorities of program offices and Environmental Protection Agency

The Administrator of the Environmental Protection Agency shall assure that the expenditure of any funds appropriated pursuant to this Act or any other provision of law for environmental research and development related to regulatory program activities shall be coordinated with and reflect the research needs and priorities of the program offices, as well as the overall research needs and priorities of the Agency, including those defined in the five-year research plan.

(b) Program offices subject to coverage

For purposes of subsection (a) of this section, the appropriate program offices are—

(1) the Office of Air and Waste Management, for air quality activities;

(2) the Office of Water and Hazardous Materials, for water quality activities and water supply activities;

(3) the Office of Pesticides, for environmental effects of pesticides;

(4) the Office of Solid Waste, for solid waste activities;

(5) the Office of Toxic Substances, for toxic substance activities;

(6) the Office of Radiation Programs, for radiation activities; and

(7) the Office of Noise Abatement and Control, for noise activities.

(c) Report to Congress; contents

The Administrator shall submit to the President and the Congress a report concerning the most appropriate means of assuring, on a continuing basis, that the research efforts of the Agency reflect the needs and priorities of the regulatory program offices, while maintaining a high level of scientific quality. Such report shall be submitted on or before March 31, 1978.

(Nov. 8, 1977, Pub.L. 95–155, § 7, 91 Stat. 1259.)

§ 4365. Science Advisory Board

(a) Establishment; requests for advice by Administrator of Environmental Protection Agency and Congressional committees

The Administrator of the Environmental Protection Agency shall establish a Science Advisory Board which shall provide such scientific advice as may be requested by the Administrator, the Committee on Environment and Public Works of the United States Senate, or the Committees on Science and Technology, Energy and Commerce, or Public Works and Transportation of the House of Representatives.

(b) Membership; Chairman; meetings; qualifications of members

Such Board shall be composed of at least nine members, one of whom shall be designated Chairman, and shall meet at such times and places as may be designated by the Chairman of the Board in consultation with the Administrator. Each member of the Board shall be qualified by education, training, and experience to evaluate scientific and technical information on matters referred to the Board under this section.

(c) Review and comment on plan for research, development, and demonstration and annual revisions; transmission to Congress

In addition to providing scientific advice when requested by the Administrator under subsection (a) of this section, the Board shall review and comment on the Administration's five-year plan for environmental research, development, and demonstration provided for by section 4361 of this title and on each annual revision thereof. Such review and comment shall be transmitted to the Congress by the Administrator, together with his comments thereon, at the time of the transmission to the Congress of the annual revision involved.

(d) Review and report to Administrator, President, and Congress concerning authorized health effects research, etc.

The Board shall conduct a review of and submit a report to the Administrator, the President, and the Congress, not later than October 1, 1978, concerning—

(1) the health effects research authorized by this Act and other laws;

(2) the procedures generally used in the conduct of such research;

(3) the internal and external reporting of the results of such research;

(4) the review procedures for such research and results;

(5) the procedures by which such results are used in internal and external recommendations on policy, regulations, and legislation; and

(6) the findings and recommendations of the report to the House Committee on Science and Technology entitled "The Environmental Protection Agency's Research Program with primary emphasis on the Community Health and Environmental Surveillance System (CHESS): An Investigative Report".

The review shall focus special attention on the procedural safeguards required to preserve the scientific integrity of such research and to insure reporting and use of the results of such research in subsequent recommendations. The report shall include specific recommendations on the results of the review to ensure scientific integrity throughout the Agency's health effects research, review, reporting, and recommendation process.

(e) Proposed environmental criteria document, standard, limitation, or regulation; functions respecting in conjunction with Administrator

(1) The Administrator, at the time any proposed criteria document, standard, limitation, or regulation under the Clean Air Act [42 U.S.C. 7401 et seq.], the Federal Water Pollution Control Act [33 U.S.C. 1251 et seq.], the Resource Conservation and Recovery Act of 1976 [42 U.S.C. 6901 et seq.], the Noise Control Act [42 U.S.C. 4901 et seq.], the Toxic Substances Control Act [15 U.S.C. 2601 et seq.], or the Safe Drinking Water Act [42 U.S.C. 300f et seq.], or under any other authority of the Administrator, is provided to any other Federal agency for formal review and comment, shall make available to the Board such proposed criteria document, standard, limitation, or regulation, together with relevant scientific and technical information in the possession of the Environmental Protection Agency on which the proposed action is based.

(2) The Board may make available to the Administrator, within the time specified by the Administrator, its advice and comments on the adequacy of the scientific and technical basis of the proposed criteria document, standard, limitation, or regulation, together with any pertinent information in the Board's possession.

(f) Utilization of technical and scientific capabilities of Federal agencies and national environmental laboratories for determining adequacy of scientific and technical basis of proposed criteria document, etc.

In preparing such advice and comments, the Board shall avail itself of the technical and scientific capabilities of any Federal agency, including the Environmental Protection Agency and any national environmental laboratories.

(g) Member committees and investigative panels; establishment; chairmanship

The Board is authorized to constitute such member committees and investigative panels as the Administrator and the Board find necessary to carry out this section. Each such member committee or investigative panel shall be chaired by a member of the Board.

(h) Appointment and compensation of secretary and other personnel; compensation of members

(1) Upon the recommendation of the Board, the Administrator shall appoint a secretary, and such other employees as deemed necessary to exercise and fulfill the Board's powers and responsibilities. The compensation of all employees appointed under this paragraph shall be fixed in accordance with chapter 51 and subchapter III of chapter 53 of title 5.

(2) Members of the Board may be compensated at a rate to be fixed by the President but not in excess of the maximum rate of pay for grade GS–18, as provided in the General Schedule under section 5332 of title 5.

(i) Consultation and coordination with Scientific Advisory Panel

In carrying out the functions assigned by this section, the Board shall consult and coordinate its activities with the Scientific Advisory Panel established by the Administrator pursuant to section 136w(d) of title 7.

(Nov. 8, 1977, Pub.L. 95–155, § 8, 91 Stat. 1260, H.Res. 549, Mar. 25, 1980, amended Dec. 22, 1980, Pub.L. 96–569, § 3, 94 Stat. 3337.)

§ 4366. Identification and coordination of research, development, and demonstration activities

(a) Consultation and cooperation of Administrator of Environmental Protection Agency with heads of Federal agencies; inclusion of activities in annual revisions of plan for research, etc.

The Administrator of the Environmental Protection Agency, in consultation and cooperation with the heads of other Federal agencies, shall take such actions on a continuing basis as may be necessary or appropriate—

(1) to identify environmental research, development, and demonstration activities, within and outside the Federal Government, which may need to be more effectively coordinated in order to minimize unnecessary duplication of programs, projects, and research facilities;

(2) to determine the steps which might be taken under existing law, by him and by the heads of such other agencies, to accomplish or promote such coordination, and to provide for or encourage the taking of such steps; and

(3) to determine the additional legislative actions which would be needed to assure such coordination to the maximum extent possible.

The Administrator shall include in each annual revision of the five-year plan provided for by section 4361 of this title a full and complete report on the actions taken and determinations made during the preceding year under this subsection, and may submit interim reports on such actions and determinations at such other times as he deems appropriate.

(b) Coordination of programs by Administrator

The Administrator of the Environmental Protection Agency shall coordinate environmental research, development, and demonstration programs of such Agency with the heads of other Federal agencies in order to minimize unnecessary duplication of programs, projects, and research facilities.

(c) Joint study by Council on Environmental Quality in consultation with Office of Science and Technology Policy for coordination of activities; report to President and Congress; report by President to Congress on implementation of joint study and report

(1) In order to promote the coordination of environmental research and development activities, and to assure that the action taken and methods used (under subsection (a) of this section and otherwise) to bring about such coordination will be as effective as possible for that purpose, the Council on Environmental Quality in consultation with the Office of Science and Technology Policy shall promptly undertake and carry out a joint study of all aspects of the coordination of environmental research and development. The Chairman of the Council shall prepare a report on the results of such study, together with such recommendations (including legislative recommendations) as he deems appropriate, and shall submit such report to the President and the Congress not later than May 31, 1978.

(2) Not later than September 30, 1978, the President shall report to the Congress on steps he has taken to implement the recommendations included in the report under paragraph (1), including any recommendations he may have for legislation.

(Nov. 8, 1977, Pub.L. 95–155, § 9, 91 Stat. 1261.)

Federal Practice and Procedure

Environmental class actions, see Wright & Miller: Civil § 1782.

Library References

United States ⇐29, 31, 40, 41.

C.J.S. United States §§ 31, 34 et seq., 38 et seq.

§ 4367. Reporting requirements of financial interests of officers and employees of Environmental Protection Agency

(a) Covered officers and employees

Each officer or employee of the Environmental Protection Agency who—

(1) performs any function or duty under this Act; and

(2) has any known financial interest in any person who applies for or receives grants, contracts, or other forms of financial assistance under this Act,

shall, beginning on February 1, 1978, annually file with the Administrator a written statement concerning all such interests held by such officer or employee during the preceding calendar year. Such statement shall be available to the public.

(b) Implementation of requirements by Administrator

The Administrator shall—

(1) act within ninety days after November 8, 1977—

(A) to define the term "known financial interest" for purposes of subsection (a) of this section; and

(B) to establish the methods by which the requirement to file written statements specified in subsection (a) of this section will be monitored and enforced, including appropriate provision for the filing by such officers and employees of such statements and the review by the Administrator of such statements; and

(2) report to the Congress on June 1 of each calendar year with respect to such disclosures and the actions taken in regard thereto during the preceding calendar year.

(c) Exemption of positions by Administrator

In the rules prescribed under subsection (b) of this section, the Administrator may identify specific positions of a nonpolicymaking nature within the Administration and provide that officers or employees occupying such positions shall be exempt from the requirements of this section.

(d) Violations; penalties

Any officer or employee who is subject to, and knowingly violates, this section, shall be fined not more than $2,500 or imprisoned not more than one year, or both.

(Nov. 8, 1977, Pub.L. 95–155, § 12, 91 Stat. 1263.)

Federal Practice and Procedure

Environmental class actions, see Wright & Miller: Civil § 1782.

§ 4368. Grants to qualified citizens groups

(1) There is authorized to be appropriated to the Environmental Protection Agency, for grants to qualified citizens groups in States and regions, $3,000,000.

(2) Grants under this section may be made for the purpose of supporting and encouraging participation by qualified citizens groups in determining how scientific, technological, and social trends and changes affect the future environment and quality of life of an area, and for setting goals and identifying measures for improvement.

(3) The term "qualified citizens group" shall mean a nonprofit organization of citizens having an area based focus, which is not single-issue oriented and which can demonstrate a prior record of interest and involvement in goal-setting and research concerned with improving the quality of life, including plans to identify, protect and enhance significant natural and cultural resources and the environment.

(4) A citizens group shall be eligible for assistance only if certified by the Governor in consultation with the State legislature as a bona fide organization entitled to receive Federal assistance to pursue the aims of this program. The group shall further demonstrate its capacity to employ usefully the funds for the purposes of this program and its broad-based representative nature.

(5) After an initial application for assistance under this section has been approved, the Administrator may make grants on an annual basis, on condition that the Governor recertify the group and that the applicant submits to the Administrator annually—

(A) an evaluation of the progress made during the previous year in meeting the objectives for which the grant was made;

(B) a description of any changes in the objectives of the activities; and

(C) a description of the proposed activities for the succeeding one year period.

(6) A grant made under this program shall not exceed 75 per centum of the estimated cost of the project or program for which the grant is made, and no group shall receive more than $50,000 in any one year.

(7) No financial assistance provided under this section shall be used to support lobbying or litigation by any recipient group.

(Oct. 18, 1978, Pub.L. 95–477, § 3(d), 92 Stat. 1509.)

Federal Practice and Procedure

Environmental class actions, see Wright & Miller: Civil § 1782.

Library References

United States ⚖82(2).
C.J.S. United States § 122.

§ 4368a. Utilization of talents of older Americans in projects of pollution prevention, abatement, and control

(a) Technical assistance to environmental agencies

Notwithstanding any other provision of law relating to Federal grants and cooperative agreements, the Administrator of the Environmental Protection Agency is authorized to make grants to, or enter into cooperative agreements with, private nonprofit organizations designated by the Secretary of Labor under title V of the Older Americans Act of 1965 [42 U.S.C. 3056 et seq.] to utilize the talents of older Americans in programs authorized by other provisions of law administered by the Administrator (and consistent with such provisions of law) in providing technical assistance to Federal, State, and local environmental agencies for projects of pollution prevention, abatement, and control. Funding for such grants or agreements may be made available from such programs or through title V of the Older Americans Act of 1965 [42 U.S.C.A. 3056 et seq.] and title IV of the Job Training Partnership Act [29 U.S.C.A. 1671 et seq.].

(b) Pre-award certifications

Prior to awarding any grant or agreement under subsection (a) of this section, the applicable Federal, State, or local environmental agency shall certify to the Administrator that such grants or agreements will not—

(1) result in the displacement of individuals currently employed by the environmental agency concerned (including partial displacement through reduction of nonovertime hours, wages, or employment benefits);

(2) result in the employment of any individual when any other person is in a layoff status from the same or substantially equivalent job within the jurisdiction of the environmental agency concerned; or

(3) affect existing contracts for services.

(c) Prior appropriations Acts

Grants or agreements awarded under this section shall be subject to prior appropriation Acts.

(June 12, 1984, Pub.L. 98–313, § 2, 98 Stat. 235.)

§ 4369. Miscellaneous reports

(a) Availability to Congressional committees

All reports to or by the Administrator relevant to the Agency's program of research, development, and demonstration shall promptly be made available to the Committee on Science and Technology of the House of Representatives and the Committee on Environment and Public Works of the Senate, unless otherwise prohibited by law.

(b) Transmittal of jurisdictional information

The Administrator shall keep the Committee on Science and Technology of the House of Representatives and the Committee on Environment and Public Works of the Senate fully and currently informed with respect to matters falling within or related to the jurisdiction of the committees.

(c) Comment by Government agencies and the public

The reports provided for in section 5910 of this title shall be made available to the public for comment, and to the heads of affected agencies for comment and, in the case of recommendations for action, for response.

(d) Transmittal of research information to the Department of Energy

For the purpose of assisting the Department of Energy in planning and assigning priorities in research development and demonstration activities related to environmental control technologies, the Administrator shall actively make available to the Department all information on research activities and results of research programs of the Environmental Protection Agency.

(Oct. 18, 1978, Pub.L. 95–477, § 5, 92 Stat. 1510.)

§ 4369a. Reports on environmental research and development activities of the Agency

(a) Reports to keep Congressional committees fully and currently informed

The Administrator shall keep the appropriate committees of the House and the Senate fully and currently informed about all aspects of the environmental research and development activities of the Environmental Protection Agency.

(b) Annual reports relating requested funds to activities to be carried out with those funds

Each year, at the time of the submission of the President's annual budget request, the Administrator shall make available to the appropriate committees of Congress sufficient copies of a report fully describing funds requested and the environmental research and development activities to be carried out with these funds.

(April 7, 1980, Pub.L. 96–229, § 4, 94 Stat. 328.)

§ 4370. Reimbursement for use of facilities

(a) Authority to allow outside groups or individuals to use research and test facilities; reimbursement

The Administrator is authorized to allow appropriate use of special Environmental Protection Agency research and test facilities by outside groups or individuals and to receive reimbursement or fees for costs incurred thereby when he finds this to be in the public interest. Such reimbursement or fees are to be used by the Agency to defray the costs of use by outside groups or individuals.

(b) Rules and regulations

The Administrator may promulgate regulations to cover such use of Agency facilities in accordance with generally accepted accounting, safety, and laboratory practices.

(c) Waiver of reimbursement by Administrator

When he finds it is in the public interest the Administrator may waive reimbursement or fees for outside use of Agency facilities by nonprofit private or public entities.

(April 7, 1980, Pub.L. 96–229, § 5, 94 Stat. 328.)

Federal Practice and Procedure

Environmental class actions, see Wright & Miller: Civil § 1782.

§ 4370a. Assistant Administrators of Environmental Protection Agency; appointment; duties

(a) The President, by and with the advice and consent of the Senate, may appoint three Assistant Administrators of the Environmental Protection Agency in addition to—

(1) the five Assistant Administrators provided for in section 1(d) of Reorganization Plan Numbered 3 of 1970;

(2) the Assistant Administrator provided by section 2625(g) of Title 15; and

(3) the Assistant Administrator provided by section 6911a of this title.

(b) Each Assistant Administrator appointed under subsection (a) of this section shall perform such duties as the Administrator of the Environmental Protection Agency may prescribe.

(Aug. 23, 1983, Pub.L. 98–80, § 1, 97 Stat. 485.)

NOISE CONTROL

(42 U.S.C.A. §§ 4901 to 4918)

CHAPTER 65—NOISE CONTROL

Related Provisions

See, also, Abatement of Aviation Noise, 49 U.S.C.A. § 2101 et seq., post.

Cross References

Availability of proposed environmental criteria document, standard, limitation, or regulation under this chapter to Science Advisory Board, see section 4365 of this title.

Complaints, information, or recommendations for rules and regulations to protect public or environment from injury from aircraft operating within Grand Canyon National Park submitted under this chapter, see section 228g of Title 16, Conservation.

Test of automobile propulsion systems to determine compliance with exhaust emission standards or other promulgated requirements of this chapter, see section 2706 of Title 15, Commerce and Trade.

West's Federal Forms

Indictment and information, see § 7101 et seq.
Jurisdiction and venue in district courts, see § 1003 et seq.
Preliminary injunctions and temporary restraining orders, see § 5271 et seq.
Production of documents, motions and orders pertaining to, see § 3551 et seq.
Sentence and fine, see § 7531 et seq.
Taxation of costs, see § 4612 et seq.

United States Supreme Court

Preemption of state and local control over nighttime aircraft noise, see City of Burbank et al. v. Lockheed Air Terminal, Inc., 1973, 93 S.Ct. 1854, 411 U.S. 624, 36 L.Ed.2d 547.

WESTLAW Electronic Research

See WESTLAW guide following the Explanation pages of this pamphlet.

§ 4901. Congressional findings and statement of policy

(a) The Congress finds—

(1) that inadequately controlled noise presents a growing danger to the health and welfare of the Nation's population, particularly in urban areas;

(2) that the major sources of noise include transportation vehicles and equipment, machinery, appliances, and other products in commerce; and

(3) that, while primary responsibility for control of noise rests with State and local governments, Federal action is essential to deal with major noise sources in commerce control of which require national uniformity of treatment.

(b) The Congress declares that it is the policy of the United States to promote an environment for all Americans free from noise that jeopardizes their health or welfare. To that end, it is the purpose of this chapter to establish a means for effective coordination of Federal research and activities in noise control, to authorize the establishment of Federal noise emission standards for products distributed in commerce, and to provide information to the public respecting the noise emission and noise reduction characteristics of such products.

(Oct. 27, 1972, Pub.L. 92–574, § 2, 86 Stat. 1234.)

Library References

Health and Environment ⚷25.8.
C.J.S. Health and Environment § 61 et seq.

§ 4902. Definitions

For purposes of this chapter:

(1) The term "Administrator" means the Administrator of the Environmental Protection Agency.

(2) The term "person" means an individual, corporation, partnership, or association, and (except as provided in sections 4910(e) and 4911(a) of this title) includes any officer, employee, department, agency, or instrumentality of the United States, a State, or any political subdivision of a State.

(3) The term "product" means any manufactured article or goods or component thereof; except that such term does not include—

(A) any aircraft, aircraft engine, propeller, or appliance, as such terms are defined in section 1301 of title 49; or

(B)(i) any military weapons or equipment which are designed for combat use; (ii) any rockets or equipment which are designed for research, experimental, or developmental work to be performed by the National Aeronautics and Space Administration; or (iii) to the extent provided by regulations of the Administrator, any other machinery or equipment designed for use in experimental work done by or for the Federal Government.

(4) The term "ultimate purchaser" means the first person who in good faith purchases a product for purposes other than resale.

(5) The term "new product" means (A) a product the equitable or legal title of which has never been transferred to an ultimate purchaser, or (B) a product which is imported or offered for importation into the United States and which is manufactured after the effective date of a regulation under section 4905 or 4907 of this title which would have been applicable to such product had it been manufactured in the United States.

(6) The term "manufacturer" means any person engaged in the manufacturing or assembling of new products, or the importing of new products for resale, or who acts for, and is controlled by, any such person in connection with the distribution of such products.

(7) The term "commerce" means trade, traffic, commerce, or transportation—

(A) between a place in a State and any place outside thereof, or

(B) which affects trade, traffic, commerce, or transportation described in subparagraph (A).

(8) The term "distribute in commerce" means sell in, offer for sale in, or introduce or deliver for introduction into, commerce.

(9) The term "State" includes the District of Columbia, the Commonwealth of Puerto Rico, the Virgin Islands, American Samoa, Guam, and the Trust Territory of the Pacific Islands.

(10) The term "Federal agency" means an executive agency (as defined in section 105 of title 5) and includes the United States Postal Service.

(11) The term "environmental noise" means the intensity, duration, and the character of sounds from all sources.

(Oct. 27, 1972, Pub.L. 92–574, § 3, 86 Stat. 1234.)

§ 4903. Federal programs

(a) Furtherance of Congressional policy

The Congress authorizes and directs that Federal agencies shall, to the fullest extent consistent with their authority under Federal laws administered by them, carry out the programs within their control in such a manner as to further the policy declared in section 4901(b) of this title.

(b) Presidential authority to exempt activities or facilities from compliance requirements

Each department, agency, or instrumentality of the executive, legislative, and judicial branches of the Federal Government—

(1) having jurisdiction over any property or facility, or

(2) engaged in any activity resulting, or which may result, in the emission of noise,

shall comply with Federal, State, interstate, and local requirements respecting control and abatement of environmental noise to the same extent that any person is subject to such requirements. The President may exempt any single activity or facility, including noise emission sources or classes thereof, of any department, agency, or instrumentality in the executive branch from compliance with any such requirement if he determines it to be in the paramount interest of the United States to do so; except that no exemption, other than for those products referred to in section 4902(3)(B) of this title, may be granted from the requirements of sections 4905, 4916, and 4917 of this title. No such exemption shall be granted due to lack of appropriation unless the President shall have specifically requested such appropriation as a part of the budgetary process and the Congress shall have failed to make available such requested appropriation. Any exemption shall be for a period not in excess of one year, but additional exemptions may be granted for periods of not to exceed one year upon the President's making a new determination. The President shall report each January to the Congress all exemptions from the requirements of this section granted during the preceding calendar year, together with his reason for granting such exemption.

(c) Coordination of programs of Federal agencies; standards and regulations; status reports

(1) The Administrator shall coordinate the programs of all Federal agencies relating to noise research and noise control. Each Federal agency shall, upon request, furnish to the Administrator such information as he may reasonably require to determine the nature, scope, and results of the noise-research and noise-control programs of the agency.

(2) Each Federal agency shall consult with the Administrator in prescribing standards or regulations respecting noise. If at any time the Administrator has reason to believe that a standard or regulation, or any proposed standard or regulation, of any Federal agency respecting noise does not protect the public health and welfare to the extent he believes to be required and feasible, he may request such agency to review and report to him on the advisability of revising such standard or regulation to provide such protection. Any such request may be published in the Federal Register and shall be accompanied by a detailed statement of the information on which it is based. Such agency shall complete the requested review and report to the Administrator within such time as the Administrator specifies in the request, but such time specified may not be less than ninety days from the date the request was made. The report shall be published in the Federal Register and shall be accompanied by a detailed statement of the findings and conclusions of the agency respecting the revision of its standard or regulation. With respect to the Federal Aviation Administration, section 1431 of title 49 shall apply in lieu of this paragraph.

(3) On the basis of regular consultation with appropriate Federal agencies, the Administrator shall compile and publish, from time to time, a report on the status and progress of Federal activities relating to noise research and noise control. This report shall describe the noise-control programs of each Federal agency and assess the contributions of those programs to the Federal Government's overall efforts to control noise.

(Oct. 27, 1972, Pub.L. 92–574, § 4, 86 Stat. 1235.)

§ 4904. Identification of major noise sources

(a) Development and publication of criteria

(1) The Administrator shall, after consultation with appropriate Federal agencies and within nine months of October 27, 1972, develop and publish criteria with respect to noise. Such criteria shall reflect the scientific knowledge most useful in indi-

cating the kind and extent of all identifiable effects on the public health or welfare which may be expected from differing quantities and qualities of noise.

(2) The Administrator shall, after consultation with appropriate Federal agencies and within twelve months of October 27, 1972, publish information on the levels of environmental noise the attainment and maintenance of which in defined areas under various conditions are requisite to protect the public health and welfare with an adequate margin of safety.

(b) Compilation and publication of reports on noise sources and control technology

The Administrator shall, after consultation with appropriate Federal agencies, compile and publish a report or series of reports (1) identifying products (or classes of products) which in his judgment are major sources of noise, and (2) giving information on techniques for control of noise from such products, including available data on the technology, costs, and alternative methods of noise control. The first such report shall be published not later than eighteen months after October 27, 1972.

(c) Supplemental criteria and reports

The Administrator shall from time to time review and, as appropriate, revise or supplement any criteria or reports published under this section.

(d) Publication in Federal Register

Any report (or revision thereof) under subsection (b)(1) of this section identifying major noise sources shall be published in the Federal Register. The publication or revision under this section of any criteria or information on control techniques shall be announced in the Federal Register, and copies shall be made available to the general public.

(Oct. 27, 1972, Pub.L. 92–574, § 5, 86 Stat. 1236.)

§ 4905. Noise emission standards for products distributed in commerce

(a) Proposed regulations

(1) The Administrator shall publish proposed regulations, meeting the requirements of subsection (c) of this section, for each product—

(A) which is identified (or is part of a class identified) in any report published under section 4904(b)(1) of this title as a major source of noise,

(B) for which, in his judgment, noise emission standards are feasible, and

(C) which falls in one of the following categories:

(i) Construction equipment.

(ii) Transportation equipment (including recreational vehicles and related equipment).

(iii) Any motor or engine (including any equipment of which an engine or motor is an integral part).

(iv) Electrical or electronic equipment.

(2)(A) Initial proposed regulations under paragraph (1) shall be published not later than eighteen months after October 27, 1972, and shall apply to any product described in paragraph (1) which is identified (or is a part of a class identified) as a major source of noise in any report published under section 4904(b)(1) of this title on or before the date of publication of such initial proposed regulations.

(B) In the case of any product described in paragraph (1) which is identified (or is part of a class identified) as a major source of noise in a report published under section 4904(b)(1) of this title after publication of the initial proposed regulations under subparagraph (A) of this paragraph, regulations under paragraph (1) for such product shall be proposed and published by the Administrator not later than eighteen months after such report is published.

(3) After proposed regulations respecting a product have been published under paragraph (2), the Administrator shall, unless in his judgment noise emission standards are not feasible for such product, prescribe regulations, meeting the requirements of subsection (c) of this section, for such product—

(A) not earlier than six months after publication of such proposed regulations, and

(B) not later than—

(i) twenty-four months after October 27, 1972, in the case of a product subject to proposed regulations published under paragraph (2)(A), or

(ii) in the case of any other product, twenty-four months after the publication of the report under section 4904(b)(1) of this title identifying it (or a class of products of which it is a part) as a major source of noise.

(b) Authority to publish regulations not otherwise required

The Administrator may publish proposed regulations, meeting the requirements of subsection (c) of this section, for any product for which he is not required by subsection (a) of this section to prescribe regulations but for which, in his judgment, noise emission standards are feasible and are requisite to protect the public health and welfare. Not earlier than six months after the date of publication of such proposed regulations respecting such product, he may prescribe regulations, meeting the requirements of subsection (c) of this section, for such product.

(c) Contents of regulations; appropriate consideration of other standards; participation by interested persons; revision

(1) Any regulation prescribed under subsection (a) or (b) of this section (and any revision thereof) respecting a product shall include a noise emission standard which shall set limits on noise emissions from such product and shall be a standard which in the Administrator's judgment, based on criteria published under section 4904 of this title, is requisite to protect the public health and welfare, taking into account the magnitude and conditions of use of such product (alone or in combination with other noise sources), the degree of noise reduction achievable through the application of the best available technology, and the cost of compliance. In establishing such a standard for any product, the Administrator shall give appropriate consideration to standards under other laws designed to safeguard the health and welfare of persons, including any standards under the National Traffic and Motor Vehicle Safety Act of 1966 [15 U.S.C. 1381 et seq.], the Clean Air Act [42 U.S.C. 7401 et seq.], and the Federal Water Pollution Control Act [33 U.S.C. 1251 et seq.]. Any such noise emission standards shall be a performance standard. In addition, any regulation under subsection (a) or (b) of this section (and any revision thereof) may contain testing procedures necessary to assure compliance with the emission standard in such regulation, and may contain provisions respecting instructions of the manufacturer for the maintenance, use, or repair of the product.

(2) After publication of any proposed regulations under this section, the Administrator shall allow interested persons an opportunity to participate in rulemaking in accordance with the first sentence of section 553(c) of title 5.

(3) The Administrator may revise any regulation prescribed by him under this section by (A) publication of proposed revised regulations, and (B) the promulgation, not earlier than six months after the date of such publication, of regulations making the revision; except that a revision which makes only technical or clerical corrections in a regulation under this section may be promulgated earlier than six months after such date if the Administrator finds that such earlier promulgation is in the public interest.

(d) Warranty by manufacturer of conformity of product with regulations; transfer of cost obligation from manufacturer to dealer prohibited

(1) On and after the effective date of any regulation prescribed under subsection (a) or (b) of this section, the manufacturer of each new product to which such regulation applies shall warrant to the ultimate purchaser and each subsequent purchaser that such product is designed, built, and equipped so as to conform at the time of sale with such regulation.

(2) Any cost obligation of any dealer incurred as a result of any requirement imposed by paragraph (1) of this subsection shall be borne by the manufacturer. The transfer of any such cost obligation from a manufacturer to any dealer through franchise or other agreement is prohibited.

(3) If a manufacturer includes in any advertisement a statement respecting the cost or value of noise emission control devices or systems, such manufacturer shall set forth in such statement the cost or value attributed to such devices or systems by the Secretary of Labor (through the Bureau of Labor Statistics). The Secretary of Labor, and his representatives, shall have the same access for this purpose to the books, documents, papers, and records of a manufacturer as the Comptroller General has to those of a recipient of assistance for purposes of section 311 of the Clean Air Act [42 U.S.C. 7611].

(e) State and local regulations

(1) No State or political subdivision thereof may adopt or enforce—

(A) with respect to any new product for which a regulation has been prescribed by the Administrator under this section, any law or regulation which sets a limit on noise emissions from such new product and which is not identical to such regulation of the Administrator; or

(B) with respect to any component incorporated into such new product by the manufacturer of such product, any law or regulation setting a limit on noise emissions from such component when so incorporated.

(2) Subject to sections 4916 and 4917 of this title, nothing in this section precludes or denies the right of any State or political subdivision thereof to establish and enforce controls on environmental noise (or one or more sources thereof) through the licensing, regulation, or restriction of the use, operation, or movement of any product or combination of products.

(f) Publication of notice of receipt of revision petitions and proposed revised regulations

At any time after the promulgation of regulations respecting a product under this section, a State or political subdivision thereof may petition the Administrator to revise such standard on the grounds that a more stringent standard under subsection (c) of this section is necessary to protect the public health and welfare. The Administration shall publish notice of receipt of such petition in the Federal Register and shall within ninety days of receipt of such petition respond by (1) publication of proposed revised regulations in accordance with subsection (c)(3) of this section, or (2) publication in the Federal Register of a decision not to publish such proposed revised regulations at that time, together with a detailed explanation for such decision.

(Oct. 27, 1972, Pub.L. 92–574, § 6, 86 Stat. 1237; Nov. 8, 1978, Pub.L. 95–609, § 5, 92 Stat. 3081.)

Cross References

Noise emission standards under this section as federal standard under Automobile Fuel Efficiency Act of 1980, see section 2002 of Title 15, Commerce and Trade.

Code of Federal Regulations

Construction equipment standards, see 40 CFR 204.1 et seq.
Transportation equipment controls, see 40 CFR 205.1 et seq.

§ 4906. Omitted

§ 4907. Labeling

(a) Regulations

The Administrator shall by regulation designate any product (or class thereof)—

(1) which emits noise capable of adversely affecting the public health or welfare; or

(2) which is sold wholly or in part on the basis of its effectiveness in reducing noise.

(b) Manner of notice; form; methods and units of measurement

For each product (or class thereof) designated under subsection (a) of this section the Administrator shall by regulation require that notice be given to the prospective user of the level of the noise the product emits, or of its effectiveness in reducing noise, as the case may be. Such regulations shall specify (1) whether such notice shall be affixed to the product or to the outside of its container, or to both, at the time of its sale to the ultimate purchaser or whether such notice shall be given to the prospective user in some other manner, (2) the form of the notice, and (3) the methods and units of measurement to be used. Section 4905(c)(2) of this title shall apply to the prescribing of any regulation under this section.

(c) State regulation of product labeling

This section does not prevent any State or political subdivision thereof from regulating product labeling or information respecting products in any way not in conflict with regulations prescribed by the Administrator under this section.

(Oct. 27, 1972, Pub.L. 92–574, § 8, 86 Stat. 1241.)

Code of Federal Regulations

Product noise labeling requirements, see 40 CFR 211.101 et seq.

§ 4908. Imports

The Secretary of the Treasury shall, in consultation with the Administrator, issue regulations to carry out the provisions of this chapter with respect to new products imported or offered for importation.

(Oct. 27, 1972, Pub.L. 92–574, § 9, 86 Stat. 1242.)

§ 4909. Prohibited acts

(a) Except as otherwise provided in subsection (b) of this section, the following acts or the causing thereof are prohibited:

(1) In the case of a manufacturer, to distribute in commerce any new product manufactured after the effective date of a regulation prescribed under section 4905 of this title which is applicable to such product, except in conformity with such regulation.

(2)(A) The removal or rendering inoperative by any person, other than for purposes of maintenance, repair, or replacement, of any device or element of design incorporated into any product in compliance with regulations under section 4905 of this title, prior to its sale or delivery to the ultimate purchaser or while it is in use, or (B) the use of a product after such device or element of design has been removed or rendered inoperative by any person.

(3) In the case of a manufacturer, to distribute in commerce any new product manufactured after the effective date of a regulation prescribed under section 4907(b) of this title (requiring information respecting noise) which is applicable to such product, except in conformity with such regulation.

(4) The removal by any person of any notice affixed to a product or container pursuant to regulations prescribed under section 4907(b) of this title, prior to sale of the product to the ultimate purchaser.

(5) The importation into the United States by any person of any new product in violation of a regulation prescribed under section 4908 of this title which is applicable to such product.

(6) The failure or refusal by any person to comply with any requirement of section 4910(d) or 4912(a) of this title or regulations prescribed under section 4912(a), 4916, or 4917 of this title.

(b)(1) For the purpose of research, investigations, studies, demonstrations, or training, or for reasons of national security, the Administrator may exempt for a specified period of time any product, or class thereof, from paragraphs (1), (2), (3), and (5) of subsection (a) of this section, upon such terms and conditions as he may find necessary to protect the public health or welfare.

(2) Paragraphs (1), (2), (3), and (4) of subsection (a) of this section shall not apply with respect to any product which is manufactured solely for use outside any State and which (and the container of which) is labeled or otherwise marked to show that it is manufactured solely for use outside any State; except that such paragraphs shall apply to such product if it is in fact distributed in commerce for use in any State.

(Oct. 27, 1972, Pub.L. 92–574, § 10, 86 Stat. 1242.)

Code of Federal Regulations

Prohibitions attached to distribution of certain products, see 40 CFR 204.1 et seq., 205.1 et seq., 211.1 et seq.

§ 4910. Enforcement

(a) Criminal penalties

(1) Any person who willfully or knowingly violates paragraph (1), (3), (5), or (6) of subsection (a) of section 4909 of this title shall be punished by a fine of not more than $25,000 per day of violation, or by imprisonment for not more than one year, or by both. If the conviction is for a violation committed after a first conviction of such person under this subsection, punishment shall be by a fine of not more than $50,000 per day of violation, or by imprisonment for not more than two years, or by both.

(2) Any person who violates paragraph (1), (3), (5), or (6) of subsection (a) of section 4909 of this title shall be subject to a civil penalty not to exceed $10,000 per day of such violation.

(b) Separate violations

For the purpose of this section, each day of violation of any paragraph of section 4909(a) of this title shall constitute a separate violation of that section.

(c) Actions to restrain violations

The district courts of the United States shall have jurisdiction of actions brought by and in the name of the United States to restrain any violations of section 4909(a) of this title.

(d) Orders issued to protect the public health and welfare; notice; opportunity for hearing

(1) Whenever any person is in violation of section 4909(a) of this title, the Administrator may issue an order specifying such relief as he determines is necessary to protect the public health and welfare.

(2) Any order under this subsection shall be issued only after notice and opportunity for a hearing in accordance with section 554 of title 5.

(e) "Person" defined

The term "person," as used in this section, does not include a department, agency, or instrumentality of the United States.

(Oct. 27, 1972, Pub.L. 92–574, § 11, 86 Stat. 1242; Nov. 8, 1978, Pub.L. 95–609, § 4, 92 Stat. 3081.)

Code of Federal Regulations

Additional definitions and enforcement provisions, see 40 CFR 204.1 et seq., 205.1 et seq., 209.1 et seq., 211.101 et seq.

Library References

Health and Environment ⇐37.
C.J.S. Health and Environment § 48 et seq.

§ 4911. Citizen suits

(a) Authority to commence suits

Except as provided in subsection (b) of this section, any person (other than the United States) may commence a civil action on his own behalf—

(1) against any person (including (A) the United States, and (B) any other governmental instrumentality or agency to the extent permitted by the eleventh amendment to the Constitution) who is alleged to be in violation of any noise control requirement (as defined in subsection (e) of this section), or

(2) against—

(A) the Administrator of the Environmental Protection Agency where there is alleged a failure of such Administrator to perform any act or duty under this chapter which is not discretionary with such Administrator, or

(B) the Administrator of the Federal Aviation Administration where there is alleged a failure of such Administrator to perform any act or duty under section 1431 of title 49 which is not discretionary with such Administrator.

The district courts of the United States shall have jurisdiction, without regard to the amount in controversy, to restrain such person from violating such noise control requirement or to order such Administrator to perform such act or duty, as the case may be.

(b) Notice

No action may be commenced—

(1) under subsection (a)(1) of this section—

(A) prior to sixty days after the plaintiff has given notice of the violation (i) to the Administrator of the Environmental Protection Agency (and to the Federal Aviation Administrator in the case of a violation of a noise control requirement under such section 1431 of title 49) and (ii) to any alleged violator of such requirement, or

(B) if an Administrator has commenced and is diligently prosecuting a civil action to require compliance with the noise control requirement, but in any such action in a court of the United States any person may intervene as a matter of right, or

(2) under subsection (a)(2) of this section prior to sixty days after the plaintiff has given notice to the defendant that he will commence such action.

Notice under this subsection shall be given in such manner as the Administrator of the Environmental Protection Agency shall prescribe by regulation.

(c) Intervention

In an action under this section, the Administrator of the Environmental Protection Agency, if not a party, may intervene as a matter of right. In an action under this section respecting a noise control requirement under section 1431 of title 49, the Administrator of the Federal Aviation Administration, if not a party, may also intervene as a matter of right.

(d) Litigation costs

The court, in issuing any final order in any action brought pursuant to subsection (a) of this section, may award costs of litigation (including reasonable attorney and expert witness fees) to any party, whenever the court determines such an award is appropriate.

(e) Other common law or statutory rights of action

Nothing in this section shall restrict any right which any person (or class of persons) may have under any statute or common law to seek enforcement of any noise control requirement or to seek any other relief (including relief against an Administrator).

(f) "Noise control requirement" defined

For purposes of this section, the term "noise control requirement" means paragraph (1), (2), (3), (4), or (5) of section 4909(a) of this title, or a standard, rule, or regulation issued under section 4916 or 4917 of this title or under section 1431 of title 49.

(Oct. 27, 1972, Pub. L. 92–574, § 12, 86 Stat. 1243.)

Federal Practice and Procedure

Allowability of suit by any person, see Wright, Miller & Cooper: Jurisdiction § 3531.

West's Federal Practice Manual

Intervention of right, see § 8839.

Code of Federal Regulations

Debarment and suspension, see 40 CFR 32.100 et seq.
Notice requirements, see 40 CFR 210.1 et seq.

Library References

Nuisance ⇐82.
C.J.S. Nuisances § 76 et seq.

§ 4912. Records, reports, and information

(a) Duties of manufacturers of products

Each manufacturer of a product to which regulations under section 4905 or 4907 of this title apply shall—

(1) establish and maintain such records, make such reports, provide such information, and make such tests, as the Administrator may reasonably require to enable him to determine whether such manufacturer has acted or is acting in compliance with this chapter,

(2) upon request of an officer or employee duly designated by the Administrator, permit such officer or employee at reasonable times to have access to such information and the results of such tests and to copy such records, and

(3) to the extent required by regulations of the Administrator, make products coming off the assembly line or otherwise in the hands of the manufacturer available for testing by the Administrator.

(b) Confidential information; disclosure

(1) All information obtained by the Administrator or his representatives pursuant to subsection (a) of this section, which information contains or relates to a trade secret or other matter referred to in section 1905 of title 18, shall be considered confidential for the purpose of that section, except that such information may be disclosed to other Federal officers or employees, in whose possession it shall remain confidential, or when relevant to the matter in controversy in any proceeding under this chapter.

(2) Nothing in this subsection shall authorize the withholding of information by the Administrator, or by any officers or employees under his control, from the duly authorized committees of the Congress.

(c) Violations and penalties

Any person who knowingly makes any false statement, representation, or certification in any application, record, report, plan, or other document filed or required to be maintained under this chapter or who falsifies, tampers with, or knowingly renders inaccurate any monitoring device or method required to be maintained under this chapter, shall upon conviction be punished by a fine of not more than $10,000, or by imprisonment for not more than six months, or by both.

(Oct. 27, 1972, Pub.L. 92–574, § 13, 86 Stat. 1244.)

Code of Federal Regulations

Records, reports and information, see 40 CFR 2.100 et seq., 204.1 et seq., 205.1 et seq., 211.101 et seq.

§ 4913. Quiet communities, research, and public information

To promote the development of effective State and local noise control programs, to provide an adequate Federal noise control research program designed to meet the objectives of this chapter, and to otherwise carry out the policy of this chapter, the Administrator shall, in cooperation with other Federal agencies and through the use of grants, contracts, and direct Federal actions—

(a) develop and disseminate information and educational materials to all segments of the public on the public health and other effects of noise and the most effective means for noise control, through the use of materials for school curricula, volunteer organizations, radio and television programs, publication, and other means;

(b) conduct or finance research directly or with any public or private organization or any person on the effects, measurement, and control of noise, including but not limited to—

(1) investigation of the psychological and physiological effects of noise on humans and the effects of noise on domestic animals, wildlife, and property, and the determination of dose/response relationships suitable for use in decision-making, with special emphasis on the nonauditory effects of noise;

(2) investigation, development, and demonstration of noise control technology for products subject to possible regulation under sections 4905 and 4907 of this title and section 1431 of title 49;

(3) investigation, development, and demonstration of monitoring equipment and other technology especially suited for use by State and local noise control programs;

(4) investigation of the economic impact of noise on property and human activities; and

(5) investigation and demonstration of the use of economic incentives (including emission charges) in the control of noise;

(c) administer a nationwide Quiet Communities Program which shall include, but not be limited to—

(1) grants to States, local governments, and authorized regional planning agencies for the purpose of—

(A) identifying and determining the nature and extent of the noise problem within the subject jurisdiction;

(B) planning, developing, and establishing a noise control capacity in such jurisdiction, including purchasing initial equipment;

(C) developing abatement plans for areas around major transportation facilities (including airports, highways, and rail yards) and other major stationary sources of noise, and, where appropriate, for the facility or source itself; and,

(D) evaluating techniques for controlling noise (including institutional arrangements) and demonstrating the best available techniques in such jurisdiction;

(2) purchase of monitoring and other equipment for loan to State and local noise control programs to meet special needs or assist in the beginning implementation of a noise control program or project;

(3) development and implementation of a quality assurance program for equipment and monitoring procedures of State and local noise control programs to help communities assure that their data collection activities are accurate;

(4) conduct of studies and demonstrations to determine the resource and personnel needs of States and local governments required for the establishment and implementation of effective noise abatement and control programs; and

(5) development of educational and training materials and programs, including national and regional workshops, to support State and local noise abatement and control programs;

except that no actions, plans or programs hereunder shall be inconsistent with existing Federal authority under this chapter to regulate sources of noise in interstate commerce;

(d) develop and implement a national noise environmental assessment program to identify trends in noise exposure and response, ambient levels, and compliance data and to determine otherwise the effectiveness of noise abatement actions through the collection of physical, social, and human response data;

(e) establish regional technical assistance centers which use the capabilities of university and private organizations to assist State and local noise control programs;

(f) provide technical assistance to State and local governments to facilitate their development and enforcement of noise control, including direct onsite assistance of agency or other personnel with technical expertise, and preparation of model State or local legislation for noise control; and

(g) provide for the maximum use in programs assisted under this section of senior citizens and persons eligible for participation in programs under the Older Americans Act [42 U.S.C. 3001 et seq.].

(Oct. 27, 1972, Pub.L. 92–574, § 14, 86 Stat. 1244; Nov. 8, 1978, Pub.L. 95–609, § 2, 92 Stat. 3079.)

Library References

Health and Environment ⚷25.8.
United States ⚷82(2).
C.J.S. Health and Environment § 61 et seq.
C.J.S. United States § 122.

§ 4914. Development of low-noise-emission products

(a) Definitions

For the purpose of this section:

(1) The term "Committee" means the Low-Noise-Emission Product Advisory Committee.

(2) The term "Federal Government" includes the legislative, executive, and judicial branches of the Government of the United States, and the government of the District of Columbia.

(3) The term "low-noise-emission product" means any product which emits noise in amounts significantly below the levels specified in noise emission standards under regulations applicable under section 4905 of this title at the time of procurement to that type of product.

(4) The term "retail price" means (A) the maximum statutory price applicable to any type of product; or (B) in any case where there is no applicable maximum statutory price, the most recent procurement price paid for any type of product.

(b) Certification of products; Low-Noise-Emission Product Advisory Committee

(1) The Administrator shall determine which products qualify as low-noise-emission products in accordance with the provisions of this section.

(2) The Administrator shall certify any product—

(A) for which a certification application has been filed in accordance with paragraph (5)(A) of this subsection;

(B) which is a low-noise-emission product as determined by the Administrator; and

(C) which he determines is suitable for use as a substitute for a type of product at that time in use by agencies of the Federal Government.

(3) The Administrator may establish a Low-Noise-Emission Product Advisory Committee to assist him in determining which products qualify as low-noise-emission products for purposes of this section. The Committee shall include the Administrator or his designee, a representative of the National Bureau of Standards, and representatives of such other Federal agencies and private individuals as the Administrator may deem necessary from time to time. Any member of the Committee not employed on a full-time basis by the United States may receive the daily equivalent of the annual rate of basic pay in effect for Grade GS–18 of the General Schedule for each day such member is engaged upon work of the Committee. Each member of the Committee shall be reimbursed for travel expenses, including per diem in lieu of subsistence as authorized by section 5703 of title 5 for persons in the Government service employed intermittently.

(4) Certification under this section shall be effective for a period of one year from the date of issuance.

(5)(A) Any person seeking to have a class or model of product certified under this section shall file a certification application in accordance with regulations prescribed by the Administrator.

(B) The Administrator shall publish in the Federal Register a notice of each application received.

(C) The Administrator shall make determinations for the purpose of this section in accordance with procedures prescribed by him by regulation.

(D) The Administrator shall conduct whatever investigation is necessary, including actual inspection of the product at a place designated in regulations prescribed under subparagraph (A).

(E) The Administrator shall receive and evaluate written comments and documents from interested persons in support of, or in opposition to, certification of the class or model of product under consideration.

(F) Within ninety days after the receipt of a properly filed certification application the Administrator shall determine whether such product is a low-noise-emission product for purposes of this section. If the Administrator determines that such product is a low-noise-emission product, then within one hundred and eighty days of such determination the Administrator shall reach a decision as to whether such product is a suitable substitute for any class or classes of products presently being purchased by the Federal Government for use by its agencies.

(G) Immediately upon making any determination or decision under subparagraph (F), the Administrator shall publish in the Federal Register notice of such determination or decision, including reasons therefor.

(c) Federal procurement of low-noise-emission products

(1) Certified low-noise-emission products shall be acquired by purchase or lease by the Federal Government for use by the Federal Government in lieu of other products if the Administrator of General Services determines that such certified products have procurement costs which are no more than 125 per centum of the retail price of the least expensive type of product for which they are certified substitutes.

(2) Data relied upon by the Administrator in determining that a product is a certified low-noise-emission product shall be incorporated in any contract for the procurement of such product.

(d) Product selection

The procuring agency shall be required to purchase available certified low-noise-emission products which are eligible for purchase to the extent they are available before purchasing any other products for which any low-noise-emission product is a certified substitute. In making purchasing selections between competing eligible certified low-noise-emission products, the procuring agency shall give priority to any class or model which does not require extensive periodic maintenance to retain its low-noise-emission qualities or which does not involve operating costs significantly in excess of those products for which it is a certified substitute.

(e) Waiver of statutory price limitations

For the purpose of procuring certified low-noise-emission products any statutory price limitations shall be waived.

(f) Tests of noise emissions from products purchased by Federal government

The Administrator shall, from time to time as he deems appropriate, test the emissions of noise from certified low-noise-emission products purchased by the Federal Government. If at any time he finds that the noise-emission levels exceed the levels on which certification under this section was based, the Administrator shall give the supplier of such product written notice of this finding, issue public notice of it, and give the supplier an opportunity to make necessary repairs, adjustments, or replacements. If no such repairs, adjustments, or replacements are made within a period to be set by the Administrator, he may order the supplier to show cause why the product involved should be eligible for recertification.

(g) Authorization of appropriations

There are authorized to be appropriated for paying additional amounts for products pursuant to, and for carrying out the provisions of, this section, $1,000,000 for the fiscal year ending June 30, 1973, and $2,000,000 for each of the two succeeding fiscal years, $2,200,000 for the fiscal year ending June 30, 1976, $550,000 for the transition period of July 1, 1976, through September 30, 1976, and $2,420,000 for the fiscal year ending September 30, 1977.

(h) Promulgation of procedures

The Administrator shall promulgate the procedures required to implement this section within one hundred and eighty days after October 27, 1972.

(Oct. 27, 1972, Pub.L. 92–574, § 15, 86 Stat. 1245; May 31, 1976, Pub.L. 94–301, § 1, 90 Stat. 590.)

Code of Federal Regulations

Certification procedures, see 40 CFR 203.1 et seq.

Transportation equipment noise emission controls, see 40 CFR 205.1 et seq.

§ 4915. Judicial review

(a) Petition for review

A petition for review of action of the Administrator of the Environmental Protection Agency in promulgating any standard or regulation under sections 4905, 4916, or 4917 of this title or any labeling regulation under section 4907 of this title may be filed only in the United States Court of Appeals for the District of Columbia Circuit, and a petition for review of action of the Administrator of the Federal Aviation Administration in promulgating any standard or regulation under section 1431 of title 49 may be filed only in such court. Any such petition shall be filed within ninety days from the date of such promulgation, or after date if such petition is based solely on grounds arising after such ninetieth day. Action of either Administrator with respect to which review could have been obtained under this subsection shall not be subject to judicial review in civil or criminal proceedings for enforcement.

(b) Additional evidence

If a party seeking review under this chapter applies to the court for leave to adduce additional evidence, and shows to the satisfaction of the court that the information is material and was not available at the time of the proceeding before the Administrator of such Agency or Administration (as the case may be), the court may order such additional evidence (and evidence in rebuttal thereof) to be taken before such Administrator, and to be adduced upon the hearing, in such manner and upon such terms and conditions as the court may deem proper. Such Administrator may modify his findings as to the facts, or make new findings, by reason of the additional evidence so taken, and he shall file with the court such modified or new findings, and his recommendation, if any, for the modification or setting aside of his original order, with the return of such additional evidence.

(c) Stay of agency action

With respect to relief pending review of an action by either Administrator, no stay of an agency action may be granted unless the reviewing court determines that the party seeking such stay is (1) likely to prevail on the merits in the review proceeding and (2) will suffer irreparable harm pending such proceeding.

(d) Subpenas

For the purpose of obtaining information to carry out this chapter, the Administrator of the Environmental Protection Agency may issue subpenas for the attendance and testimony of witnesses and the production of relevant papers, books, and documents, and he may administer oaths. Witnesses summoned shall be paid the same fees and mileage that are paid witnesses in the courts of the United States. In cases of contumacy or refusal to obey a subpena served upon any person under this subsection, the district court of the United States for any district in which such person is found or resides or transacts business, upon application by the United States and after notice to such person, shall have jurisdiction to issue an order requiring such person to appear and give testimony before the Administrator, to appear and produce papers, books, and documents before the Administrator, or both, and any failure to obey such order of the court may be punished by such court as a contempt thereof.

(Oct. 27, 1972, Pub.L. 92–574, § 16, 86 Stat. 1247.)

Federal Practice and Procedure

Review of administrative decisions in courts of appeals, see Wright, Miller, Cooper & Gressman: Jurisdiction § 3941.

§ 4916. Railroad noise emission standards

(a) Regulations; standards; consultation with Secretary of Transportation

(1) Within nine months after October 27, 1972, the Administrator shall publish proposed noise emission regulations for surface carriers engaged in interstate commerce by railroad. Such proposed regulations shall include noise emission standards setting such limits on noise emissions resulting from operation of the equipment and facilities of surface carriers engaged in interstate commerce by railroad which reflect the degree of noise reduction achievable through the application of the best available technology, taking into account the cost of compliance. These regulations shall be in addition to any regulations that may be proposed under section 4905 of this title.

(2) Within ninety days after the publication of such regulations as may be proposed under paragraph (1) of this subsection, and subject to the provisions of section 4915 of this title, the Administrator shall promulgate final regulations. Such regulations may be revised, from time to time, in accordance with this subsection.

(3) Any standard or regulation, or revision thereof, proposed under this subsection shall be promulgated only after consultation with the Secretary of Transportation in order to assure appropriate consideration for safety and technological availability.

(4) Any regulation or revision thereof promulgated under this subsection shall take effect after such period as the Administrator finds necessary, after consultation with the Secretary of Transportation, to permit the development and application of the requisite technology, giving appropriate consideration to the cost of compliance within such period.

(b) Regulations to insure compliance with noise emission standards

The Secretary of Transportation, after consultation with the Administrator, shall promulgate regulations to insure compliance with all standards promulgated by the Administrator under this section. The Secretary of Transportation shall carry out such regulations through the use of his powers and duties of enforcement and inspection authorized by the Safety Appliance Acts [45 U.S.C. 1 et seq.], subtitle IV of Title 49, and the Department of Transportation Act [49 U.S.C. 1651 et seq.]. Regulations promulgated under this section shall be subject to the provisions of sections 4909, 4910, 4911, and 4915 of this title.

(c) State and local standards and controls

(1) Subject to paragraph (2) but notwithstanding any other provision of this chapter, after the effective date of a regulation under this section applicable to noise emissions resulting from the operation of any equipment or facility of a surface carrier engaged in interstate commerce by railroad, no State or political subdivision thereof may adopt or enforce any standard applicable to noise emissions resulting from the operation of the same equipment or facility of such carrier unless such standard is identical to a standard applicable to noise emissions resulting from such operation prescribed by any regulation under this section.

(2) Nothing in this section shall diminish or enhance the rights of any State or political subdivision thereof to establish and enforce standards or controls on levels of environmental noise, or to control, license, regulate, or restrict the use, operation, or

movement of any product if the Administrator, after consultation with the Secretary of Transportation, determines that such standard, control, license, regulation, or restriction is necessitated by special local conditions and is not in conflict with regulations promulgated under this section.

(d) Definitions

The terms "carrier" and "railroad" as used in this section shall have the same meaning as such terms have under section 22 of title 45.

(Oct. 27, 1972, Pub.L. 92–574, § 17, 86 Stat. 1248.)

Code of Federal Regulations

Railroad noise emission standards, see 49 CFR 210.1 et seq.
Standards applicable, see 40 CFR 201.1 et seq.

Library References

Health and Environment ⚿25.8.
C.J.S. Health and Environment § 61 et seq.

§ 4917. Motor carrier noise emission standards

(a) Regulations; standards; consultation with Secretary of Transportation

(1) Within nine months after October 27, 1972, the Administrator shall publish proposed noise emission regulations for motor carriers engaged in interstate commerce. Such proposed regulations shall include noise emission standards setting such limits on noise emissions resulting from operation of motor carriers engaged in interstate commerce which reflect the degree of noise reduction achievable through the application of the best available technology, taking into account the cost of compliance. These regulations shall be in addition to any regulations that may be proposed under section 4905 of this title.

(2) Within ninety days after the publication of such regulations as may be proposed under paragraph (1) of this subsection, and subject to the provisions of section 4915 of this title, the Administrator shall promulgate final regulations. Such regulations may be revised from time to time, in accordance with this subsection.

(3) Any standard or regulation, or revision thereof, proposed under this subsection shall be promulgated only after consultation with the Secretary of Transportation in order to assure appropriate consideration for safety and technological availability.

(4) Any regulation or revision thereof promulgated under this subsection shall take effect after such period as the Administrator finds necessary, after consultation with the Secretary of Transportation, to permit the development and application of the requisite technology, giving appropriate consideration to the cost of compliance within such period.

(b) Regulations to insure compliance with noise emission standards

The Secretary of Transportation, after consultation with the Administrator shall promulgate regulations to insure compliance with all standards promulgated by the Administrator under this section. The Secretary of Transportation shall carry out such regulations through the use of his powers and duties of enforcement and inspection authorized by subtitle IV of Title 49 and the Department of Transportation Act [49 U.S.C. 1651 et seq.]. Regulations promulgated under this section shall be subject to the provisions of sections 4909, 4910, 4911, and 4915 of this title.

(c) State and local standards and controls

(1) Subject to paragraph (2) of this subsection but notwithstanding any other provision of this chapter, after the effective date of a regulation under this section applicable to noise emissions resulting from the operation of any motor carrier engaged in interstate commerce, no State or political subdivision thereof may adopt or enforce any standard applicable to the same operation of such motor carrier, unless such standard is identical to a standard applicable to noise emissions resulting from such operation prescribed by any regulation under this section.

(2) Nothing in this section shall diminish or enhance the rights of any State or political subdivision thereof to establish and enforce standards or controls on levels of environmental noise, or to control, license, regulate, or restrict the use, operation, or movement of any product if the Administrator, after consultation with the Secretary of Transportation, determines that such standard, control, license, regulation, or restriction is necessitated by special local conditions and is not in conflict with regulations promulgated under this section.

(d) Definitions

For purposes of this section, the term "motor carrier" includes a common carrier by motor vehicle, a contract carrier by motor vehicle, and a private carrier of property by motor vehicle as those terms are defined by section 10102 of Title 49.

(Oct. 27, 1972, Pub.L. 92–574, § 18, 86 Stat. 1249.)

Code of Federal Regulations

Compliance requirements, see 49 CFR 325.1 et seq.
Standards applicable, see 40 CFR 202.10 et seq.

Library References

Health and Environment ⚿25.8.
C.J.S. Health and Environment § 61 et seq.

§ 4918. Authorization of appropriations

There are authorized to be appropriated to carry out this chapter (other than for research and development) $15,000,000 for the fiscal year ending September 30, 1979.

(Oct. 27, 1972, Pub.L. 92–574, § 19, 86 Stat. 1250; May 31, 1976, Pub.L. 94–301, § 2, 90 Stat. 590; Nov. 8, 1978, Pub.L. 95–609, § 6, 92 Stat. 3081.)

SOLID WASTE DISPOSAL

(42 U.S.C.A. §§ 6901 to 6991i)

CHAPTER 82—SOLID WASTE DISPOSAL

SUBCHAPTER I. GENERAL PROVISIONS

Sec.

6901. Congressional findings.
- (a) Solid waste.
- (b) Environment and health.
- (c) Materials.
- (d) Energy.

6901a. Congressional findings: used oil recycling.

6902. Objectives and national policy.
- (a) Objectives.
- (b) National policy.

6903. Definitions.

6904. Governmental cooperation.
- (a) Interstate cooperation.
- (b) Consent of Congress to compacts.

6905. Application of chapter and integration with other Acts.
- (a) Application of chapter.
- (b) Integration with other Acts.
- (c) Integration with the Surface Mining Control and Reclamation Act of 1977.

6906. Financial disclosure.
- (a) Statement.
- (b) Action by Administrator.
- (c) Exemption.
- (d) Penalty.

6907. Solid waste management information and guidelines.
- (a) Guidelines.
- (b) Notice.

SUBCHAPTER II. OFFICE OF SOLID WASTE: AUTHORITIES OF THE ADMINISTRATOR

6911. Office of Solid Waste and Interagency Coordinating Committee.
- (a) Office of Solid Waste.
- (b) Interagency Coordinating Committee.

6911a. Assistant Administrator of Environmental Protection Agency; appointment, etc.

6912. Authorities of Administrator.
- (a) Authorities.
- (b) Revision of regulations.
- (c) Criminal investigations.

6913. Resource Recovery and Conservation Panels.

6914. Grants for discarded tire disposal.
- (a) Grants.
- (b) Authorization of appropriations.

6914a. Labeling of lubricating oil.

6915. Annual report.

6916. General authorization.
- (a) General administration.
- (b) Resource Recovery and Conservation Panels.
- (c) Hazardous waste.
- (d) State and local support.
- (e) Criminal investigations.

Sec.

6916. General authorization—Cont'd
- (f) Underground storage tanks.

6917. Office of ombudsman.
- (a) Establishment; functions.
- (b) Authority to render assistance.
- (c) Effect on procedures for grievance, appeals, or administrative matters.
- (d) Termination.

SUBCHAPTER III. HAZARDOUS WASTE MANAGEMENT

6921. Identification and listing of hazardous waste.
- (a) Criteria for identification or listing.
- (b) Identification and listing.
- (c) Petition by State Governor.
- (d) Small quantity generator waste.
- (e) Specified wastes.
- (f) Delisting procedures.
- (g) EP toxicity.
- (h) Additional characteristics.
- (i) Clarification of household waste exclusion.

6922. Standards applicable to generators of hazardous waste.
- (a) In general.
- (b) Waste minimization.

6923. Standards applicable to transporters of hazardous waste.
- (a) Standards.
- (b) Coordination with regulations of Secretary of Transportation.
- (c) Fuel from hazardous waste.

6924. Standards applicable to owners and operators of hazardous waste treatment, storage, and disposal facilities.
- (a) In general.
- (b) Salt dome formations, salt bed formations, underground mines and caves.
- (c) Liquids in landfills.
- (d) Prohibitions on land disposal of specified wastes.
- (e) Solvents and dioxins.
- (f) Disposal into deep injection wells; specified subsection (d) wastes, solvents and dioxins.
- (g) Additional land disposal prohibition determination.
- (h) Variance from land disposal prohibitions.
- (i) Publication of determination.
- (j) Storage of hazardous waste prohibited from land disposal.
- (k) Definition of land disposal.
- (*l*) Ban on dust suppression.
- (m) Treatment standards for waste subject to land disposal prohibition.
- (n) Air emissions.
- (*o*) Minimum technological requirements.
- (p) Ground water monitoring.
- (q) Hazardous waste used as fuel.

SUBCHAPTER IV. STATE OR REGIONAL SOLID WASTE PLANS.

Sec.

6943. Requirements for approval of plans—Cont'd
- (b) Discretionary plan provisions relating to recycled oil.
- (c) Energy and materials conservation and recovery feasibility planning and assistance.
- (d) Size of waste-to-energy facilities.

6944. Criteria for sanitary landfills; sanitary landfills required for all disposal.
- (a) Criteria for sanitary landfills.
- (b) Disposal required to be in sanitary landfills, etc.
- (c) Effective date.

6945. Upgrading of open dumps.
- (a) Closing or upgrading of existing open dumps.
- (b) Inventory.
- (c) Control of hazardous disposal.

6946. Procedure for development and implementation of State plan.
- (a) Identification of regions.
- (b) Identification of State and local agencies and responsibilities.
- (c) Interstate regions.

6947. Approval of State plan; Federal assistance.
- (a) Plan approval.
- (b) Eligibility of States for Federal financial assistance.
- (c) Existing activities.

6948. Federal assistance.
- (a) Authorization of Federal financial assistance.
- (b) State allotment.
- (c) Distribution of Federal financial assistance within the State.
- (d) Technical assistance.
- (e) Special communities.
- (f) Assistance to States for discretionary program for recycled oil.
- (g) Assistance to municipalities for energy and materials conservation and recovery planning activities.

6949. Rural communities assistance.
- (a) In general.
- (b) Allotment.
- (c) Limit.
- (d) Authorization of appropriations.

6949a. Adequacy of certain guidelines and criteria.
- (a) Study.
- (b) Report.
- (c) Revisions of guidelines and criteria.

SUBCHAPTER V. DUTIES OF THE SECRETARY OF COMMERCE IN RESOURCE AND RECOVERY.

6951. Functions.

6952. Development of specifications for secondary materials.

6953. Development of markets for recovered materials.

6954. Technology promotion.

6955. Marketing policies, establishment; nondiscrimination requirement.

6956. Authorization of appropriations.

SUBCHAPTER VI. FEDERAL RESPONSIBILITIES

Sec.

6961. Application of Federal, State, and local law to Federal facilities.

6962. Federal procurement.
- (a) Application of section.
- (b) Procurement subject to other law.
- (c) Requirements.
- (d) Specifications.
- (e) Guidelines.
- (f) Procurement of services.
- (g) Executive Office.
- (h) Definitions.
- (i) Procurement program.

6963. Cooperation with Environmental Protection Agency.
- (a) General rule.
- (b) Information relating to energy and materials conservation and recovery.

6964. Applicability of solid waste disposal guidelines to Executive agencies.
- (a) Compliance.
- (b) Licenses and permits.

SUBCHAPTER VII—MISCELLANEOUS PROVISIONS

6971. Employee protection.
- (a) General.
- (b) Remedy.
- (c) Costs.
- (d) Exception.
- (e) Employment shifts and loss.
- (f) Occupational safety and health.

6972. Citizens' suits.
- (a) In general.
- (b) Actions prohibited.
- (c) Notice.
- (d) Intervention.
- (e) Costs.
- (f) Other rights preserved.
- (g) Transporters.

6973. Imminent hazard.
- (a) Authority of Administrator.
- (b) Violations.
- (c) Immediate notice.
- (d) Public participation in settlements.

6974. Petition for regulations; public participation.
- (a) Petition.
- (b) Public participation.

6975. Separability of provisions.

6976. Judicial review.
- (a) Review of final regulations and certain petitions.
- (b) Review of certain actions under sections 6925 and 6926 of this title.

6977. Grants or contracts for training projects.
- (a) General authority.
- (b) Purposes.
- (c) Study.

6978. Payments.
- (a) General rule.
- (b) Prohibition.

6979. Labor standards.

6979a. Transferred.

Cross References

Applicable environmental requirements defined as including standards, limitations, or other requirements established by this chapter, see section 8302 of this title.

By product material managed in conformity with general requirements of this chapter, see section 2114 of this title.

Definitions of this chapter applied to chapter on Comprehensive Environmental Response, Compensation, and Liability, see section 9601 of this title.

Duty of Administrator under this chapter to make available to Science Advisory Board proposed environmental criteria document, see section 4365 of this title.

Hazardous waste and qualified hazardous waste disposal facility as defined in this chapter subject to taxation, see section 4682 of Title 26, Internal Revenue Code.

Health and environmental standards for uranium mill tailings consistent with requirements of this chapter, see section 2022 of this title.

Persons subject to penalties for not complying with transportation of hazardous wastes as defined by this chapter, see section 11901 of Title 49, Transportation.

Responsibility of Environmental Protection Agency for environmental, economic, and institutional aspects of solid waste projects and that such projects are consistent with guidelines provided in this chapter, see section 5919 of this title.

Surface Mining Control and Reclamation Act as not superseding, amending, modifying or repealing this chapter, see section 1292 of Title 30, Mineral Lands and Mining.

West's Federal Forms

Enforcement and review of administrative agency decisions and orders, see § 851 et seq.

Jurisdiction and venue in district courts, see § 1003 et seq.

Preliminary injunctions and temporary restraining orders, see § 5271 et seq.

Sentence and fine, see § 7531 et seq.

Code of Federal Regulations

Classification of solid waste disposal facilities and practices, see 40 CFR 257.1 et seq.

Federal waste permit program, see 40 CFR 270.1 et seq.

Hazardous waste management generally, see 40 CFR 260.1 et seq.

Identification and listing of hazardous waste, see 40 CFR 261.1 et seq.

Solid waste generally, see 40 CFR Chap. I, Subchap. I.

Solid waste management guidelines and procedures, see 40 CFR 244.100 et seq., 245.100 et seq., 246.100 et seq.

State and local assistance, see 40 CFR 35.001 et seq.

State program transfer regulations, see 40 CFR 233.1 et seq.

WESTLAW Electronic Research

See WESTLAW guide following the Explanation pages of this pamphlet.

SUBCHAPTER I—GENERAL PROVISIONS

§ 6901. Congressional findings

(a) Solid waste

The Congress finds with respect to solid waste—

(1) that the continuing technological progress and improvement in methods of manufacture, packaging, and marketing of consumer products has resulted in an ever-mounting increase, and in a change in the characteristics, of the mass material discarded by the purchaser of such products;

(2) that the economic and population growth of our Nation, and the improvements in the standard of living enjoyed by our population, have required increased industrial production to meet our needs, and have made necessary the demolition of old buildings, the construction of new buildings, and the provision of highways and other avenues of transportation, which, together with related industrial, commercial, and agricultural operations, have resulted in a rising tide of scrap, discarded, and waste materials;

(3) that the continuing concentration of our population in expanding metropolitan and other urban areas has presented these communities with serious financial, management, intergovernmental, and technical problems in the disposal of solid wastes resulting from the industrial, commercial, domestic, and other activities carried on in such areas;

(4) that while the collection and disposal of solid wastes should continue to be primarily the function of State, regional, and local agencies, the problems of waste disposal as set forth above have become a matter national in scope and in concern and necessitate Federal action through financial and technical assistance and leadership in the development, demonstration, and application of new and improved methods and processes to reduce the amount of waste and unsalvageable materials and to provide for proper and economical solid waste disposal practices.

(b) Environment and health

The Congress finds with respect to the environment and health, that—

(1) although land is too valuable a national resource to be needlessly polluted by discarded materials, most solid waste is disposed of on land in open dumps and sanitary landfills;

(2) disposal of solid waste and hazardous waste in or on the land without careful planning and management can present a danger to human health and the environment;

(3) as a result of the Clean Air Act [42 U.S.C. 7401 et seq.], the Water Pollution Control Act [33 U.S.C. 1251 et seq.], and other Federal and State laws respecting public health and the environment, greater amounts of solid waste (in the form of sludge and other pollution treatment residues) have been created. Similarly, inadequate and environmentally unsound practices for the disposal or use of solid waste have created greater amounts of air and water pollution and other problems for the environment and for health;

(4) open dumping is particularly harmful to health, contaminates drinking water from underground and surface supplies, and pollutes the air and the land;

(5) the placement of inadequate controls on hazardous waste management will result in substantial risks to human health and the environment;

(6) if hazardous waste management is improperly performed in the first instance, corrective action is likely to be expensive, complex, and time consuming;

(7) certain classes of land disposal facilities are not capable of assuring long-term containment of certain hazardous wastes, and to avoid substantial risk to human health and the environment, reliance on land disposal should be minimized or eliminated, and land disposal, particularly landfill and surface impoundment, should be the least favored method for managing hazardous wastes; and

(8) alternatives to existing methods of land disposal must be developed since many of the cities in the United States will be running out of suitable solid waste disposal sites within five years unless immediate action is taken.

(c) Materials

The Congress finds with respect to materials, that—

(1) millions of tons of recoverable material which could be used are needlessly buried each year;

(2) methods are available to separate usable materials from solid waste; and

(3) the recovery and conservation of such materials can reduce the dependence of the United States on foreign resources and reduce the deficit in its balance of payments.

(d) Energy

The Congress finds with respect to energy, that—

(1) solid waste represents a potential source of solid fuel, oil, or gas that can be converted into energy;

(2) the need exists to develop alternative energy sources for public and private consumption in order to reduce our dependence on such sources as petroleum products, natural gas, nuclear and hydroelectric generation; and

(3) technology exists to produce usable energy from solid waste.

(Pub.L. 89–272, title II, § 1002, as added Oct. 21, 1976, Pub.L. 94–580, § 2, 90 Stat. 2796, and amended Nov. 8, 1978, Pub.L. 95–609, § 7(a), 92 Stat. 3081; Nov. 8, 1984, Pub.L. 98–616, title I, § 101(a), 98 Stat. 3224.)

Code of Federal Regulations

Grants, see 40 CFR 30.100 et seq., 40.100 et seq.
Hazardous waste treatment facilities, standards for owners of, see 40 CFR 264.1 et seq., 265.1 et seq.
Procurement under assistance agreements, see 40 CFR 33.001 et seq.

§ 6901a. Congressional findings: used oil recycling

The Congress finds and declares that—

(1) used oil is a valuable source of increasingly scarce energy and materials;

(2) technology exists to re-refine, reprocess, reclaim, and otherwise recycle used oil;

(3) used oil constitutes a threat to public health and the environment when reused or disposed of improperly; and

that, therefore, it is in the national interest to recycle used oil in a manner which does not constitute a threat to public health and the environment and which conserves energy and materials.

(Oct. 15, 1980, Pub.L. 96–463, § 2, 94 Stat. 2055.)

§ 6902. Objectives and national policy

(a) Objectives

The objectives of this chapter are to promote the protection of health and the environment and to conserve valuable material and energy resources by—

(1) providing technical and financial assistance to State and local governments and interstate agencies for the development of solid waste management plans (including resource recovery and resource conservation systems) which will promote improved solid waste management techniques (including more effective organizational arrangements), new and improved methods of collection, separation, and recovery of solid waste, and the environmentally safe disposal of nonrecoverable residues;

(2) providing training grants in occupations involving the design, operation, and maintenance of solid waste disposal systems;

(3) prohibiting future open dumping on the land and requiring the conversion of existing open dumps to facilities which do not pose a danger to the environment or to health;

(4) assuring that hazardous waste management practices are conducted in a manner which protects human health and the environment;

(5) requiring that hazardous waste be properly managed in the first instance thereby reducing the need for corrective action at a future date;

(6) minimizing the generation of hazardous waste and the land disposal of hazardous waste by encouraging process substitution, materials recovery, properly conducted recycling and reuse, and treatment;

(7) establishing a viable Federal-State partnership to carry out the purposes of this chapter and insuring that the Administrator will, in carrying out the provisions of subchapter III of this chapter give a high priority to assisting and cooperating with States in obtaining full authorization of State programs under subchapter III of this chapter;

(8) providing for the promulgation of guidelines for solid waste collection, transport, separation, recovery, and disposal practices and systems;

(9) promoting a national research and development program for improved solid waste management and resource conservation techniques, more effective organizational arrangements, and new and improved methods of collection, separation, and recovery, and recycling of solid wastes and environmentally safe disposal of nonrecoverable residues;

(10) promoting the demonstration, construction, and application of solid waste management, resource recovery, and resource conservation systems which preserve and enhance the quality of air, water, and land resources; and

(11) establishing a cooperative effort among the Federal, State, and local governments and private enterprise in order to recover valuable materials and energy from solid waste.

(b) National policy

The Congress hereby declares it to be the national policy of the United States that, wherever feasible, the generation of hazardous waste is to be reduced or eliminated as expeditiously as possible. Waste that is nevertheless generated should be treated, stored, or disposed of so as to minimize the present and future threat to human health and the environment.

(Pub.L. 89–272, title II, § 1003, as added Oct. 21, 1976, Pub.L. 94–580, § 2, 90 Stat. 2798, and amended Nov. 8, 1984, Pub.L. 98–616, title I, § 101(b), 98 Stat. 3224.)

§ 6903. Definitions

As used in this chapter:

(1) The term "Administrator" means the Administrator of the Environmental Protection Agency.

(2) The term "construction," with respect to any project of construction under this chapter, means (A) the erection or building of new structures and acquisition of lands or interests therein, or the acquisition, replacement, expansion, remodeling, alteration, modernization, or extension of existing structures, and (B) the acquisition and installation of initial equipment of, or required in connection with, new or newly acquired structures or the expanded, remodeled, altered, modernized or extended part of existing structures (including trucks and other motor vehicles, and tractors, cranes, and other machinery) necessary for the proper utilization and operation of the facility after completion of the project; and includes preliminary planning to determine the economic and engineering feasibility and the public health and safety aspects of the project, the engineering, architectural, legal, fiscal, and economic investigations and studies, and any surveys, designs, plans, working drawings, specifications, and other action necessary for the carrying out of the project, and (C) the inspection and supervision of the process of carrying out the project to completion.

(2A) The term "demonstration" means the initial exhibition of a new technology process or practice or a significantly new combination or use of technologies, processes or practices, subsequent to the development stage, for the purpose of proving technological feasibility and cost effectiveness.

(3) The term "disposal" means the discharge, deposit, injection, dumping, spilling, leaking, or placing of any solid waste or hazardous waste into or on any land or water so that such solid waste or hazardous waste or any constituent thereof may enter the environment or be emitted into the air or discharged into any waters, including ground waters.

(4) The term "Federal agency" means any department, agency, or other instrumentality of the Federal Government, any independent agency or establishment of the Federal Government includ-

ing any Government corporation, and the Government Printing Office.

(5) The term "hazardous waste" means a solid waste, or combination of solid wastes, which because of its quantity, concentration, or physical, chemical, or infectious characteristics may—

(A) cause, or significantly contribute to an increase in mortality or an increase in serious irreversible, or incapacitating reversible, illness; or

(B) pose a substantial present or potential hazard to human health or the environment when improperly treated, stored, transported, or disposed of, or otherwise managed.

(6) The term "hazardous waste generation" means the act or process of producing hazardous waste.

(7) The term "hazardous waste management" means the systematic control of the collection, source separation, storage, transportation, processing, treatment, recovery, and disposal of hazardous wastes.

(8) For purposes of Federal financial assistance (other than rural communities assistance), the term "implementation" does not include the acquisition, leasing, construction, or modification of facilities or equipment or the acquisition, leasing, or improvement of land.

(9) The term "intermunicipal agency" means an agency established by two or more municipalities with responsibility for planning or administration of solid waste.

(10) The term "interstate agency" means an agency of two or more municipalities in different States, or an agency established by two or more States, with authority to provide for the management of solid wastes and serving two or more municipalities located in different States.

(11) The term "long-term contract" means, when used in relation to solid waste supply, a contract of sufficient duration to assure the viability of a resource recovery facility (to the extent that such viability depends upon solid waste supply).

(12) The term "manifest" means the form used for identifying the quantity, composition, and the origin, routing, and destination of hazardous waste during its transportation from the point of generation to the point of disposal, treatment, or storage.

(13) The term "municipality" (A) means a city, town, borough, county, parish, district, or other public body created by or pursuant to State law, with responsibility for the planning or administration of solid waste management, or an Indian tribe or authorized tribal organization or Alaska Native village or organization, and (B) includes any rural community or unincorporated town or village or any other public entity for which an application for assistance is made by a State or political subdivision thereof.

(14) The term "open dump" means any facility or site where solid waste is disposed of which is not a sanitary landfill which meets the criteria promulgated under section 6944 of this title and which is not a facility for disposal of hazardous waste.

(15) The term "person" means an individual, trust, firm, joint stock company, corporation (including a government corporation), partnership, association, State, municipality, commission, political subdivision of a State, or any interstate body.

(16) The term "procurement item" means any device, good, substance, material, product, or other item whether real or personal property which is the subject of any purchase, barter, or other exchange made to procure such item.

(17) The term "procuring agency" means any Federal agency, or any State agency or agency of a political subdivision of a State which is using appropriated Federal funds for such procurement, or any person contracting with any such agency with respect to work performed under such contract.

(18) The term "recoverable" refers to the capability and likelihood of being recovered from solid waste for a commercial or industrial use.

(19) The term "recovered material" means waste material and byproducts which have been recovered or diverted from solid waste, but such term does not include those materials and byproducts generated from, and commonly reused within, an original manufacturing process.

(20) The term "recovered resources" means material or energy recovered from solid waste.

(21) The term "resource conservation" means reduction of the amounts of solid waste that are generated, reduction of overall resource consumption, and utilization of recovered resources.

(22) The term "resource recovery" means the recovery of material or energy from solid waste.

(23) The term "resource recovery system" means a solid waste management system which provides for collection, separation, recycling, and recovery of solid wastes, including disposal of nonrecoverable waste residues.

(24) The term "resource recovery facility" means any facility at which solid waste is processed for the purpose of extracting, converting

to energy, or otherwise separating and preparing solid waste for reuse.

(25) The term "regional authority" means the authority established or designated under section 6946 of this title.

(26) The term "sanitary landfill" means a facility for the disposal of solid waste which meets the criteria published under section 6944 of this title.

(26A) The term "sludge" means any solid, semisolid or liquid waste generated from a municipal, commercial, or industrial wastewater treatment plant, water supply treatment plant, or air pollution control facility or any other such waste having similar characteristics and effects.

(27) The term "solid waste" means any garbage, refuse, sludge from a waste treatment plant, water supply treatment plant, or air pollution control facility and other discarded material, including solid, liquid, semisolid, or contained gaseous material resulting from industrial, commercial, mining, and agricultural operations, and from community activities, but does not include solid or dissolved material in domestic sewage, or solid or dissolved materials in irrigation return flows or industrial discharges which are point sources subject to permits under section 1342 of title 33, or source, special nuclear, or byproduct material as defined by the Atomic Energy Act of 1954, as amended (68 Stat. 923) [42 U.S.C. 2011 et seq.].

(28) The term "solid waste management" means the systematic administration of activities which provide for the collection, source separation, storage, transportation, transfer, processing, treatment, and disposal of solid waste.

(29) The term "solid waste management facility" includes—

(A) any resource recovery system or component thereof,

(B) any system, program, or facility for resource conservation, and

(C) any facility for the collection, source separation, storage, transportation, transfer, processing, treatment or disposal of solid wastes, including hazardous wastes, whether such facility is associated with facilities generating such wastes or otherwise.

(30) The terms "solid waste planning", "solid waste management", and "comprehensive planning" include planning or management respecting resource recovery and resource conservation.

(31) The term "State" means any of the several States, the District of Columbia, the Commonwealth of Puerto Rico, the Virgin Islands, Guam, American Samoa, and the Commonwealth of the Northern Mariana Islands.

(32) The term "State authority" means the agency established or designated under section 6947 of this title.

(33) The term "storage", when used in connection with hazardous waste, means the containment of hazardous waste, either on a temporary basis or for a period of years, in such a manner as not to constitute disposal of such hazardous waste.

(34) The term "treatment", when used in connection with hazardous waste, means any method, technique, or process, including neutralization, designed to change the physical, chemical, or biological character or composition of any hazardous waste so as to neutralize such waste or so as to render such waste nonhazardous, safer for transport, amendable for recovery, amenable for storage, or reduced in volume. Such term includes any activity or processing designed to change the physical form or chemical composition of hazardous waste so as to render it nonhazardous.

(35) The term "virgin material" means a raw material, including previously unused copper, aluminum, lead, zinc, iron, or other metal or metal ore, any undeveloped resource that is, or with new technology will become, a source of raw materials.

(36) The term "used oil" means any oil which has been—

(A) refined from crude oil,

(B) used, and

(C) as a result of such use, contaminated by physical or chemical impurities.

(37) The term "recycled oil" means any used oil which is reused, following its original use, for any purpose (including the purpose for which the oil was originally used). Such term includes oil which is re-refined, reclaimed, burned, or reprocessed.

(38) The term "lubricating oil" means the fraction of crude oil which is sold for purposes of reducing friction in any industrial or mechanical device. Such term includes re-refined oil.

(39) The term "re-refined oil" means used oil from which the physical and chemical contaminants acquired through previous use have been removed through a refining process.

(Pub.L. 89–272, title II, § 1004, as added Oct. 21, 1976, Pub.L. 94–580, § 2, 90 Stat. 2798, and amended Nov. 8, 1978, Pub.L. 95–609, § 7(b), 92 Stat. 3081; Oct. 15, 1980, Pub.L. 96–463, § 3, 94 Stat. 2055; Oct. 21, 1980, Pub.L. 96–482, § 2, 94 Stat. 2334.)

Cross References

Disposal, hazardous waste, and treatment, as defined by this section as applied to hazardous substances releases, liability and compensation, see section 9601 of this title.

Solid waste as defined in this section as applied to synthetic fuel conversion facilities and municipal organic waste energy generation facilities, see section 5919 of this title.

§ 6904. Governmental cooperation

(a) Interstate cooperation

The provisions of this chapter to be carried out by States may be carried out by interstate agencies and provisions applicable to States may apply to interstate regions where such agencies and regions have been established by the respective States and approved by the Administrator. In any such case, action required to be taken by the Governor of a State, respecting regional designation shall be required to be taken by the Governor of each of the respective States with respect to so much of the interstate region as is within the jurisdiction of that State.

(b) Consent of Congress to compacts

The consent of the Congress is hereby given to two or more States to negotiate and enter into agreements or compacts, not in conflict with any law or treaty of the United States, for—

(1) cooperative effort and mutual assistance for the management of solid waste or hazardous waste (or both) and the enforcement of their respective laws relating thereto, and

(2) the establishment of such agencies, joint or otherwise, as they may deem desirable for making effective such agreements or compacts.

No such agreement or compact shall be binding or obligatory upon any State a party thereto unless it is agreed upon by all parties to the agreement and until it has been approved by the Administrator and the Congress.

(Pub.L. 89–272, title II, § 1005, as added Oct. 21, 1976, Pub.L. 94–580, § 2, 90 Stat. 2801.)

§ 6905. Application of chapter and integration with other Acts

(a) Application of chapter

Nothing in this chapter shall be construed to apply to (or to authorize any State, interstate, or local authority to regulate) any activity or substance which is subject to the Federal Water Pollution Control Act [33 U.S.C. 1251 et seq.], the Safe Drinking Water Act [42 U.S.C. 300f et seq.], the Marine Protection, Research and Sanctuaries Act of 1972 [33 U.S.C. 1401 et seq.], or the Atomic Energy Act of 1954 [42 U.S.C. 2011 et seq.] except to the extent that such application (or regulation) is not inconsistent with the requirements of such Acts.

(b) Integration with other Acts

(1) The Administrator shall integrate all provisions of this chapter for purposes of administration and enforcement and shall avoid duplication, to the maximum extent practicable, with the appropriate provisions of the Clean Air Act [42 U.S.C. 7401 et seq.], the Federal Water Pollution Control Act [33 U.S.C. 1251 et seq.], the Federal Insecticide, Fungicide, and Rodenticide Act [7 U.S.C. 136 et seq.], the Safe Drinking Water Act [42 U.S.C. 300f et seq.], the Marine Protection, Research and Sanctuaries Act of 1972 [33 U.S.C. 1401 et seq.], and such other Acts of Congress as grant regulatory authority to the Administrator. Such integration shall be effected only to the extent that it can be done in a manner consistent with the goals and policies expressed in this chapter and in the other acts referred to in this subsection.

(2)(A) As promptly as practicable after November 8, 1984, the Administrator shall submit a report describing—

(i) the current data and information available on emissions of polychlorinated dibenzo-p-dioxins from resource recovery facilities burning municipal solid waste;

(ii) any significant risks to human health posed by these emissions; and

(iii) operating practices appropriate for controlling these emissions.

(B) Based on the report under subparagraph (A) and on any future information on such emissions, the Administrator may publish advisories or guidelines regarding the control of dioxin emissions from such facilities. Nothing in this paragraph shall be construed to preempt or otherwise affect the authority of the Administrator to promulgate any regulations under the Clean Air Act [42 U.S.C. 7401 et seq.] regarding emissions of polychlorinated dibenzo-p-dioxins.

(3) Notwithstanding any other provisions of law, in developing solid waste plans, it is the intention of this chapter that in determining the size of a waste-to-energy facility, adequate provisions shall be given to the present and reasonably anticipated future needs, including those needs created by thorough implementation of section 6962(h) of this title, of the recycling and resource recovery interests within the area encompassed by the solid waste plan.

(c) Integration with the Surface Mining Control and Reclamation Act of 1977

(1) No later than 90 days after October 21, 1980, the Administrator shall review any regulations applicable to the treatment, storage, or disposal of any

coal mining wastes or overburden promulgated by the Secretary of the Interior under the Surface Mining and Reclamation Act of 1977 [30 U.S.C. 1201 et seq.]. If the Administrator determines that any requirement of final regulations promulgated under any section of subchapter III of this chapter relating to mining wastes or overburden is not adequately addressed in such regulations promulgated by the Secretary, the Administrator shall promptly transmit such determination, together with suggested revisions and supporting documentation, to the Secretary.

(2) The Secretary of the Interior shall have exclusive responsibility for carrying out any requirement of subchapter III of this chapter with respect to coal mining wastes or overburden for which a surface coal mining and reclamation permit is issued or approved under the Surface Mining Control and Reclamation Act of 1977 [30 U.S.C. 1201 et seq.]. The Secretary shall, with the concurrence of the Administrator, promulgate such regulations as may be necessary to carry out the purposes of this subsection and shall integrate such regulations with regulations promulgated under the Surface Mining Control and Reclamation Act of 1977.

(Pub.L. 89–272, title II, § 1006, as added Oct. 21, 1976, Pub.L. 94–580, § 2, 90 Stat. 2802, and amended Oct. 21, 1980, Pub.L. 96–482, § 3, 94 Stat. 2334; Nov. 8, 1984, Pub.L. 98–616, title I, § 102, title V, § 501(f)(2), 98 Stat. 3225, 3276.)

Code of Federal Regulations

Definitions and requirements, see 10 CFR 122.1 et seq., 123.1 et seq.
Hazardous waste standards, see 40 CFR 260.1 et seq. to 271.1 et seq.

§ 6906. Financial disclosure

(a) Statement

Each officer or employee of the Administrator who—

(1) performs any function or duty under this chapter; and

(2) has any known financial interest in any person who applies for or receives financial assistance under this chapter

shall, beginning on February 1, 1977, annually file with the Administrator a written statement concerning all such interests held by such officer or employee during the preceding calendar year. Such statement shall be available to the public.

(b) Action by Administrator

The Administrator shall—

(1) act within ninety days after October 21, 1976—

(A) to define the term "known financial interest" for purposes of subsection (a) of this section; and

(B) to establish the methods by which the requirement to file written statements specified in subsection (a) of this section will be monitored and enforced, including appropriate provision for the filing by such officers and employees of such statements and the review by the Administrator of such statements; and

(2) report to the Congress on June 1, 1978, and of each succeeding calendar year with respect to such disclosures and the actions taken in regard thereto during the preceding calendar year.

(c) Exemption

In the rules prescribed under subsection (b) of this section, the Administrator may identify specific positions within the Environmental Protection Agency which are of a nonpolicy-making nature and provide that officers or employees occupying such positions shall be exempt from the requirements of this section.

(d) Penalty

Any officer or employee who is subject to, and knowingly violates, this section shall be fined not more than $2,500 or imprisoned not more than one year, or both.

(Pub.L. 89–272, title II, § 1007, as added Oct. 21, 1976, Pub.L. 94–580, § 2, 90 Stat. 2802.)

Code of Federal Regulations

Responsibilities and conduct of EPA employees, generally, see 40 CFR 3.100 et seq.

§ 6907. Solid waste management information and guidelines

(a) Guidelines

Within one year of October 21, 1976, and from time to time thereafter, the Administrator shall, in cooperation with appropriate Federal, State, municipal, and intermunicipal agencies, and in consultation with other interested persons, and after public hearings, develop and publish suggested guidelines for solid waste management. Such suggested guidelines shall—

(1) provide a technical and economic description of the level of performance that can be attained by various available solid waste management practices (including operating practices) which provide for the protection of public health and the environment;

(2) not later than two years after October 21, 1976, describe levels of performance, including appropriate methods and degrees of control, that provide at a minimum for (A) protection of public health and welfare; (B) protection of the quality of ground waters and surface waters from leachates; (C) protection of the quality of surface waters from runoff through compliance with effluent limitations under the Federal Water Pollution Control Act, as amended [33 U.S.C. 1251 et seq.]; (D) protection of ambient air quality through compliance with new source performance standards or requirements of air quality implementation plans under the Clean Air Act, as amended [42 U.S.C. 7401 et seq.]; (E) disease and vector control; (F) safety; and (G) esthetics; and

(3) provide minimum criteria to be used by the States to define those solid waste management practices which constitute the open dumping of solid waste or hazardous waste and are to be prohibited under subchapter IV of this chapter.

Where appropriate, such suggested guidelines also shall include minimum information for use in deciding the adequate location, design, and construction of facilities associated with solid waste management practices, including the consideration of regional, geographic, demographic, and climatic factors.

(b) Notice

The Administrator shall notify the Committee on Environment and Public Works of the Senate and the Committee on Energy and Commerce of the House of Representatives a reasonable time before publishing any suggested guidelines or proposed regulations under this chapter of the content of such proposed suggested guidelines or proposed regulations under this chapter.

(Pub.L. 89–272, title II, § 1008, as added Oct. 21, 1976, Pub.L. 94–580, § 2, 90 Stat. 2803, and amended S.Res. 4, Feb. 4, 1977; Nov. 8, 1978, Pub.L. 95–609, § 7(c), (d), 92 Stat. 3081; H.Res. 549, Mar. 25, 1980.)

Cross References

Responsibility of Environmental Protection Agency for environmental, economic, and institutional aspects of municipal waste reprocessing projects and that such projects are consistent with guidelines provided in this section, see section 5920 of this title.

Responsibility of Environmental Protection Agency for environmental, economic, and institutional aspects of solid waste projects and that such projects are consistent with guidelines provided in this section, see section 5919 of this title.

Code of Federal Regulations

Classification of solid waste disposal facilities and practices, criteria, see 40 CFR 257.1 et seq.

Solid waste management guidelines and procedures, see 40 CFR 244.100 et seq., 245.100 et seq., 246.100 et seq.

Solid wastes generally, see 40 CFR Chap. 1, Subchap. I.

SUBCHAPTER II—OFFICE OF SOLID WASTE; AUTHORITIES OF THE ADMINISTRATOR

§ 6911. Office of Solid Waste and Interagency Coordinating Committee

(a) Office of Solid Waste

The Administrator shall establish within the Environmental Protection Agency an Office of Solid Waste (hereinafter referred to as the "Office") to be headed by an Assistant Administrator of the Environmental Protection Agency. The duties and responsibilities (other than duties and responsibilities relating to research and development) of the Administrator under this chapter (as modified by applicable reorganization plans) shall be carried out through the Office.

(b) Interagency Coordinating Committee

(1) There is hereby established an Interagency Coordinating Committee on Federal Resource Conservation and Recovery Activities which shall have the responsibility for coordinating all activities dealing with resource conservation and recovery from solid waste carried out by the Environmental Protection Agency, the Department of Energy, the Department of Commerce, and all other Federal agencies which conduct such activities pursuant to this chapter or any other Act. For purposes of this subsection, the term "resource conservation and recovery activities" shall include, but not be limited to, all research, development and demonstration projects on resource conservation or energy, or material, recovery from solid waste, and all technical or financial assistance for State or local planning for, or implementation of, projects related to resource conservation or energy or material, recovery from solid waste. The Committee shall be chaired by the Administrator of the Environmental Protection Agency or such person as the Administrator may designate. Members of the Committee shall include representatives of the Department of Energy, the Department of Commerce, the Department of the Treasury, and each other Federal agency which the Administrator determines to have programs or responsibilities affecting resource conservation or recovery.

(2) The Interagency Coordinating Committee shall include oversight of the implementation of

(A) the May 1979 Memorandum of Understanding on Energy Recovery from Municipal Solid Waste between the Environmental Protection Agency and the Department of Energy;

(B) the May 30, 1978, Interagency Agreement between the Department of Commerce and the Environmental Protection Agency on the Implementation of the Resource Conservation and Recovery Act; and

(C) any subsequent agreements between these agencies or other Federal agencies which address Federal resource recovery or conservation activities.

(3) The Interagency Coordinating Committee shall submit to the Congress by March 1, 1981, and on March 1 each year thereafter, a five-year action plan for Federal resource conservation or recovery activities which shall identify means and propose programs to encourage resource conservation or material and energy recovery and increase private and municipal investment in resource conservation or recovery systems, especially those which provide for material conservation or recovery as well as energy conservation or recovery. Such plan shall describe, at a minimum, a coordinated and nonduplicatory plan for resource recovery and conservation activities for the Environmental Protection Agency, the Department of Energy, the Department of Commerce, and all other Federal agencies which conduct such activities.

(Pub.L. 89–272, title II, § 2001, as added Oct. 21, 1976, Pub.L. 94–580, § 2, 90 Stat. 2804, and amended Oct. 21, 1980, Pub.L. 96–482, § 4(c), 94 Stat. 2335; Dec. 11, 1980, Pub.L. 96–510, Title III, § 307(a), 94 Stat. 2810.)

Library References

Health and Environment ⚷1.
C.J.S. Health and Environment § 4 et seq.

§ 6911a. Assistant Administrator of Environmental Protection Agency; appointment, etc.

The Assistant Administrator of the Environmental Protection Agency appointed to head the Office of Solid Waste shall be in addition to the five Assistant Administrators of the Environmental Protection Agency provided for in section 1(d) of Reorganization Plan Numbered 3 of 1970 and the additional Assistant Administrator provided by the Toxic Substances Control Act [15 U.S.C. 2601 et seq.], shall be appointed by the President by and with the advice and consent of the Senate.

(Dec. 11, 1980, Pub.L. 96–510, Title III, § 307(b), 94 Stat. 2810, as amended Aug. 23, 1983, Pub.L. 98–80, § 2(c)(2)(B), 97 Stat. 485.)

§ 6912. Authorities of Administrator

(a) Authorities

In carrying out this chapter, the Administrator is authorized to—

(1) prescribe, in consultation with Federal, State, and regional authorities, such regulations as are necessary to carry out his functions under this chapter;

(2) consult with or exchange information with other Federal agencies undertaking research, development, demonstration projects, studies, or investigations relating to solid waste;

(3) provide technical and financial assistance to States or regional agencies in the development and implementation of solid waste plans and hazardous waste management programs;

(4) consult with representatives of science, industry, agriculture, labor, environmental protection and consumer organizations, and other groups, as he deems advisable;

(5) utilize the information, facilities, personnel and other resources of Federal agencies, including the National Bureau of Standards and the National Bureau of the Census, on a reimbursable basis, to perform research and analyses and conduct studies and investigations related to resource recovery and conservation and to otherwise carry out the Administrator's functions under this chapter; and

(6) to delegate to the Secretary of Transportation the performance of any inspection or enforcement function under this chapter relating to the transportation of hazardous waste where such delegation would avoid unnecessary duplication of activity and would carry out the objectives of this chapter and of the Hazardous Materials Transportation Act [49 U.S.C. 1801 et seq.].

(b) Revision of regulations

Each regulation promulgated under this chapter shall be reviewed and, where necessary, revised not less frequently than every three years.

(c) Criminal investigations

In carrying out the provisions of this chapter, the Administrator, and duly-designated agents and employees of the Environmental Protection Agency, are authorized to initiate and conduct investigations under the criminal provisions of this chapter, and to refer the results of these investigations to the Attorney General for prosecution in appropriate cases.

(Pub.L. 89–272, title II, § 2002, as added Oct. 21, 1976, Pub.L. 94–580, § 2, 90 Stat. 2804, and amended Oct. 21, 1980, Pub.L. 96–482, § 5, 94 Stat. 2335; Nov. 8, 1984, Pub.L. 98–616, title IV, § 403(d)(4), 98 Stat. 3272.)

Code of Federal Regulations

Hazardous waste generally, see 40 CFR 260.1 et seq. to 271.1 et seq.
Identification of regions and agencies for solid waste management, see 40 CFR 255.1 et seq.

§ 6913. Resource Recovery and Conservation Panels

The Administrator shall provide teams of personnel, including Federal, State, and local employees or contractors (hereinafter referred to as "Resource Conservation and Recovery Panels") to provide Federal agencies, States and local governments upon request with technical assistance on solid waste management, resource recovery, and resource conservation. Such teams shall include technical, marketing, financial, and institutional specialists, and the services of such teams shall be provided without charge to States or local governments.

(Pub.L. 89–272, title II, § 2003, as added Oct. 21, 1976, Pub.L. 94–580, § 2, 90 Stat. 2804, and amended Nov. 8, 1978, Pub.L. 95–609, § 7(e), 92 Stat. 3081; Oct. 21, 1980, Pub.L. 96–482, § 5, 94 Stat. 2355.)

§ 6914. Grants for discarded tire disposal

(a) Grants

The Administrator shall make available grants equal to 5 percent of the purchase price of tire shredders (including portable shredders attached to tire collection trucks) to those eligible applicants best meeting criteria promulgated under this section. An eligible applicant may be any private purchaser, public body, or public-private joint venture. Criteria for receiving grants shall be promulgated under this section and shall include the policy to offer any private purchaser the first option to receive a grant, the policy to develop widespread geographic distribution of tire shredding facilities, the need for such facilities within a geographic area, and the projected risk and viability of any such venture. In the case of an application under this section from a public body, the Administrator shall first make a determination that there are no private purchasers interested in making an application before approving a grant to a public body.

(b) Authorization of appropriations

There is authorized to be appropriated $750,000 for each of the fiscal years 1978 and 1979 to carry out this section.

(Pub.L. 89–272, title II, § 2004, as added Oct. 21, 1976, Pub.L. 94–580, § 2, 90 Stat. 2805.)

§ 6914a. Labeling of lubricating oil

For purposes of any provision of law which requires the labeling of commodities, lubricating oil shall be treated as lawfully labeled only if it bears the following statement, prominently displayed:

"DON'T POLLUTE—CONSERVE RESOURCES; RETURN USED OIL TO COLLECTION CENTERS".

(Pub.L. 89–272, title II, § 2005, as added Oct. 15, 1980, Pub.L. 96–463, § 4(a), 94 Stat. 2056.)

§ 6915. Annual report

The Administrator shall transmit to the Congress and the President, not later than ninety days after the end of each fiscal year, a comprehensive and detailed report on all activities of the Office during the preceding fiscal year. Each such report shall include—

(1) a statement of specific and detailed objectives for the activities and programs conducted and assisted under this chapter;

(2) statements of the Administrator's conclusions as to the effectiveness of such activities and programs in meeting the stated objectives and the purposes of this chapter, measured through the end of such fiscal year;

(3) a summary of outstanding solid waste problems confronting the Administrator, in order of priority;

(4) recommendations with respect to such legislation which the Administrator deems necessary or desirable to assist in solving problems respecting solid waste;

(5) all other information required to be submitted to the Congress pursuant to any other provision of this chapter; and

(6) the Administrator's plans for activities and programs respecting solid waste during the next fiscal year.

(Pub.L. 89–272, title II, § 2006, formerly § 2005, as added Oct. 21, 1976, Pub.L. 94–580, § 2, 90 Stat. 2805, and renumbered Oct. 15, 1980, Pub.L. 96–463, § 4(a), 94 Stat. 2056, and amended Nov. 8, 1984, Pub.L. 98–616, title V, § 502(b), 98 Stat. 3276.)

§ 6916. General authorization

(a) General administration

There are authorized to be appropriated to the Administrator for the purpose of carrying out the provisions of this chapter, $35,000,000 for the fiscal year ending September 30, 1977, $38,000,000 for the fiscal year ending September 30, 1978, $42,000,000 for the fiscal year ending September 30, 1979, $70,000,000 for the fiscal year ending September 30, 1980, $80,000,000 for the fiscal year ending September 30, 1981, $80,000,000 for the fiscal year ending September 30, 1982, $70,000,000 for the fiscal year ending September 30, 1985, $80,000,000 for the fiscal year ending September 30, 1986, $80,000,000 for the fiscal year ending September 30, 1987, and $80,000,000 for the fiscal year 1988.

(b) Resource Recovery and Conservation Panels

Not less than 20 percent of the amount appropriated under subsection (a) of this section, or $5,000,000 per fiscal year, whichever is less, shall be used only for purposes of Resource Recovery and Conservation Panels established under section 6913 of this title (including travel expenses incurred by such panels in carrying out their functions under this chapter).

(c) Hazardous waste

Not less than 30 percent of the amount appropriated under subsection (a) of this section shall be used only for purposes of carrying out subchapter III of this chapter (relating to hazardous waste) other than section 6931 of this title.

(d) State and local support

Not less than 25 per centum of the total amount appropriated under this chapter, up to the amount authorized in section 6948(a)(1) of this title, shall be used only for purposes of support to State, regional, local, and interstate agencies in accordance with subchapter IV of this chapter other than section 6948(a)(2) or 6949 of this title.

(e) Criminal investigations

There is authorized to be appropriated to the Administrator $3,246,000 for the fiscal year 1985, $2,408,300 for the fiscal year 1986, $2,529,000 for the fiscal year 1987, and $2,529,000 for the fiscal year 1988 to be used—

(1) for additional officers or employees of the Environmental Protection Agency authorized by the Administrator to conduct criminal investigations (to investigate, or supervise the investigation of, any activity for which a criminal penalty is provided) under this chapter; and

(2) for support costs for such additional officers or employees.

(f) Underground storage tanks

(1) There are authorized to be appropriated to the Administrator for the purpose of carrying out the provisions of subchapter IX of this chapter (relating to regulation of underground storage tanks), $10,000,000 for each of the fiscal years 1985 through 1988.

(2) There is authorized to be appropriated $25,000,000 for each of the fiscal years 1985 through 1988 to be used to make grants to the States for purposes of assisting the States in the development and implementation of approved State underground storage tank release detection, prevention, and correction programs under subchapter IX of this chapter.

(Pub.L. 89–272, Title II, § 2007, formerly § 2006, as added Oct. 21, 1976, Pub.L. 94–580, § 2, 90 Stat. 2805, renumbered Oct. 15, 1980, Pub.L. 96–463, § 4(a), 94 Stat. 2055, and amended Oct. 21, 1980, Pub.L. 96–482, §§ 6, 31(a), 94 Stat. 2336, 2352; Nov. 8, 1984, Pub.L. 98–616, § 2(a), (i), 98 Stat. 3222, 3223.)

§ 6917. Office of ombudsman

(a) Establishment; functions

The Administrator shall establish an Office of Ombudsman, to be directed by an Ombudsman. It shall be the function of the Office of Ombudsman to receive individual complaints, grievances, requests for information submitted by any person with respect to any program or requirement under this chapter.

(b) Authority to render assistance

The Ombudsman shall render assistance with respect to the complaints, grievances, and requests submitted to the Office of Ombudsman, and shall make appropriate recommendations to the Administrator.

(c) Effect on procedures for grievance, appeals, or administrative matters

The establishment of the Office of Ombudsman shall not affect any procedures for grievances, appeals, or administrative matters in any other provision of this chapter, any other provision of law, or any Federal regulation.

(d) Termination

The Office of the Ombudsman shall cease to exist 4 years after November 8, 1984.

(Pub.L. 89–272, title II, § 2008, as added Nov. 8, 1984, Pub.L. 98–616, title I, § 103(a), 98 Stat. 3225.)

SUBCHAPTER III—HAZARDOUS WASTE MANAGEMENT

Cross References

Liability of owners or operators of hazardous waste disposal facilities receiving permit under this subchapter or after the period of monitoring required by this subchapter, see section 9607 of this title.

Notification requirements respecting released substances, see section 9603 of this title.

Remedial actions provided by the President upon condition that State assure availability of hazardous waste disposal facility in compliance with requirements of this subchapter, see section 9604 of this title.

Remedy or remedial action not including offsite transport of hazardous substances, or the storage, treatment, destruction, or secure disposition offsite of such substances unless such action will create new capacity to manage in compliance with this subchapter, see section 9604 of this title.

Reports and studies concerning additional hazardous wastes and construction and operation of hazardous waste facilities, see section 9651 of this title.

Requirements for facilities, including those under this subchapter, to establish and maintain evidence of financial responsibility, promulgated no earlier than five years after December 11, 1980, see section 9608 of this title.

Rules for protection from hazards at inactive or depository uranium mill tailings sites consistent with standards required by this subchapter, see section 2022 of this title.

§ 6921. Identification and listing of hazardous waste

(a) Criteria for identification or listing

Not later than eighteen months after October 21, 1976, the Administrator shall, after notice and opportunity for public hearing, and after consultation with appropriate Federal and State agencies, develop and promulgate criteria for identifying the characteristics of hazardous waste, and for listing hazardous waste, which should be subject to the provisions of this subchapter, taking into account toxicity, persistence, and degradability in nature, potential for accumulation in tissue, and other related factors such as flammability, corrosiveness, and other hazardous characteristics. Such criteria shall be revised from time to time as may be appropriate.

(b) Identification and listing

(1) Not later than eighteen months after October 21, 1976, and after notice and opportunity for public hearing, the Administrator shall promulgate regulations identifying the characteristics of hazardous waste, and listing particular hazardous wastes (within the meaning of section 6903(5) of this title), which shall be subject to the provisions of this subchapter. Such regulations shall be based on the criteria promulgated under subsection (a) of this section and shall be revised from time to time thereafter as may be appropriate. The Administrator, in cooperation with the Agency for Toxic Substances and Disease Registry and the National Toxicology Program, shall also identify or list those hazardous wastes which shall be subject to the provisions of this subchapter solely because of the presence in such wastes of certain constituents (such as identified carcinogens, mutagens, or teratagens) at levels in excess of levels which endanger human health.

(2)(A) Notwithstanding the provisions of paragraph (1) of this subsection, drilling fluids, produced waters, and other wastes associated with the exploration, development, or production of crude oil or natural gas or geothermal energy shall be subject only to existing State or Federal regulatory programs in lieu of this subchapter until at least 24 months after October 21, 1980, and after promulgation of the regulations in accordance with subparagraphs (B) and (C) of this paragraph. It is the sense of the Congress that such State or Federal programs should include, for waste disposal sites which are to be closed, provisions requiring at least the following:

(i) The identification through surveying, platting, or other measures, together with recordation of such information on the public record, so as to assure that the location where such wastes are disposed of can be located in the future; except however, that no such surveying, platting, or other measure identifying the location of a disposal site for drilling fluids and associated wastes shall be required if the distance from the disposal site to the surveyed or platted location to the associated well is less than two hundred lineal feet; and

(ii) A chemical and physical analysis of a produced water and a composition of a drilling fluid suspected to contain a hazardous material, with such information to be acquired prior to closure and to be placed on the public record.

(B) Not later than six months after completion and submission of the study required by section 6982(m) of this title, the Administrator shall, after public hearings and opportunity for comment, determine either to promulgate regulations under this subchapter for drilling fluids, produced waters, and other wastes associated with the exploration, development, or production of crude oil or natural gas or geothermal energy or that such regulations are unwarranted. The Administrator shall publish his decision in the Federal Register accompanied by an explanation and justification of the reasons for it. In making the decision under this paragraph, the Administrator shall utilize the information developed or accumulated pursuant to the study required under section 6982(m) of this title.

(C) The Administrator shall transmit his decision, along with any regulations, if necessary, to both Houses of Congress. Such regulations shall take effect only when authorized by Act of Congress.

(3)(A) Notwithstanding the provisions of paragraph (1) of this subsection, each waste listed below shall, except as provided in subparagraph (B) of this paragraph, be subject only to regulation under other applicable provisions of Federal or State law in lieu of this subchapter until at least six months after the date of submission of the applicable study required to be conducted under subsection (f), (n), *(o)*, or (p) of section 6982 of this title and after promulgation of regulations in accordance with subparagraph (C) of this paragraph:

(i) Fly ash waste, bottom ash waste, slag waste, and flue gas emission control waste generated primarily from the combustion of coal or other fossil fuels.

(ii) Solid waste from the extraction, beneficiation, and processing of ores and minerals, including phosphate rock and overburden from the mining of uranium ore.

(iii) Cement kiln dust waste.

(B)(i) Owners and operators of disposal sites for wastes listed in subparagraph (A) may be required by the Administrator, through regulations prescribed under authority of section 6912 of this title—

(I) as to disposal sites for such wastes which are to be closed, to identify the locations of such sites through surveying, platting, or other measures, together with recordation of such information on the public record, to assure that the locations where such wastes are disposed of are known and can be located in the future, and

(II) to provide chemical and physical analysis and composition of such wastes, based on available information, to be placed on the public record.

(ii)(I) In conducting any study under subsection (f), (n), *(o)*, or (p), of section 6982 of this title, any officer, employee, or authorized representative of the Environmental Protection Agency, duly designated by the Administrator, is authorized, at reasonable times and as reasonably necessary for the purposes of such study, to enter any establishment where any waste subject to such study is generated, stored, treated, disposed of, or transported from; to inspect, take samples, and conduct monitoring and testing; and to have access to and copy records relating to such waste. Each such inspection shall be commenced and completed with reasonable promptness. If the officer, employee, or authorized representative obtains any samples prior to leaving the premises, he shall give to the owner, operator, or agent in charge a receipt describing the sample obtained and if requested a portion of each such sample equal in volume or weight to the portion retained. If any analysis is made of such samples, or monitoring and testing performed, a copy of the results shall be furnished promptly to the owner, operator, or agent in charge.

(II) Any records, reports, or information obtained from any person under subclause (I) shall be available to the public, except that upon a showing satisfactory to the Administrator by any person that records, reports, or information, or particular part thereof, to which the Administrator has access under this subparagraph if made public, would divulge information entitled to protection under section 1905 of Title 18, the Administrator shall consider such information or particular portion thereof confidential in accordance with the purposes of that section, except that such record, report, document, or information may be disclosed to other officers, employees, or authorized representatives of the United States concerned with carrying out this chapter. Any person not subject to the provisions of section 1905 of Title 18 who knowingly and willfully divulges or discloses any information entitled to protection under this subparagraph shall, upon conviction, be subject to a fine of not more than $5,000 or to imprisonment not to exceed one year, or both.

(iii) The Administrator may prescribe regulations, under the authority of this chapter, to prevent radiation exposure which presents an unreasonable risk to human health from the use in construction or land reclamation (with or without revegetation) of (I) solid waste from the extraction, beneficiation, and processing of phosphate rock or (II) overburden from the mining of uranium ore.

(iv) Whenever on the basis of any information the Administrator determines that any person is in violation of any requirement of this subparagraph, the Administrator shall give notice to the violator of his failure to comply with such requirement. If such violation extends beyond the thirtieth day after the Administrator's notification, the Administrator may issue an order requiring compliance within a specified time period or the Administrator may commence a civil action in the United States district court in the district in which the violation occurred for appropriate relief, including a temporary or permanent injunction.

(C) Not later than six months after the date of submission of the applicable study required to be conducted under subsection (f), (n), *(o)*, or (p), of section 6982 of this title, the Administrator shall, after public hearings and opportunity for comment, either determine to promulgate regulations under this subchapter for each waste listed in subparagraph (A) of this paragraph or determine that such regulations are unwarranted. The Administrator shall publish his determination, which shall be based on information developed or accumulated pursuant to such study, public hearings, and comment, in the Federal Register accompanied by an explanation and justification of the reasons for it.

(c) Petition by State Governor

At any time after the date eighteen months after October 21, 1976, the Governor of any State may petition the Administrator to identify or list a material as a hazardous waste. The Administrator shall act upon such petition within ninety days following his receipt thereof and shall notify the Governor of such action. If the Administrator denies such petition because of financial considerations, in providing such notice to the Governor he shall include a statement concerning such considerations.

(d) Small quantity generator waste

(1) By March 31, 1986, the Administrator shall promulgate standards under sections 6922, 6923, and 6924 of this title for hazardous waste generated by a generator in a total quantity of hazardous waste greater than one hundred kilograms but less than one thousand kilograms during a calendar month.

(2) The standards referred to in paragraph (1), including standards applicable to the legitimate use, reuse, recycling, and reclamation of such wastes, may vary from the standards applicable to hazardous waste generated by larger quantity generators, but such standards shall be sufficient to protect human health and the environment.

(3) Not later than two hundred and seventy days after November 8, 1984, any hazardous waste which is part of a total quantity generated by a generator generating greater than one hundred kilograms but less than one thousand kilograms during one calendar month and which is shipped off the premises on which such waste is generated shall be accompanied by a copy of the Environmental Protection Agency Uniform Hazardous Waste Manifest form signed by the generator. This form shall contain the following information:

(A) the name and address of the generator of the waste;

(B) the United States Department of Transportation description of the waste, including the proper shipping name, hazard class, and identification number (UN/NA), if applicable;

(C) the number and type of containers;

(D) the quantity of waste being transported; and

(E) the name and address of the facility designated to receive the waste.

If subparagraph (B) is not applicable, in lieu of the description referred to in such subparagraph (B), the form shall contain the Environmental Protection Agency identification number, or a generic description of the waste, or a description of the waste by hazardous waste characteristic. Additional requirements related to the manifest form shall apply only if determined necessary by the Administrator to protect human health and the environment.

(4) The Administrator's responsibility under this subchapter to protect human health and the environment may require the promulgation of standards under this subchapter for hazardous wastes which are generated by any generator who does not generate more than one hundred kilograms of hazardous waste in a calendar month.

(5) Until the effective date of standards required to be promulgated under paragraph (1), any hazardous waste identified or listed under section 6921 of this title generated by any generator during any calendar month in a total quantity greater than one hundred kilograms but less than one thousand kilograms, which is not treated, stored, or disposed of at a hazardous waste treatment, storage or disposal facility with a permit under section 6925 of this title, shall be disposed of only in a facility which is permitted, licensed, or registered by a State to manage municipal or industrial solid waste.

(6) Standards promulgated as provided in paragraph (1) shall, at a minimum require that all treatment, storage, or disposal of hazardous wastes generated by generators referred to in paragraph (1) shall occur at a facility with interim status or a permit under this subchapter, except that onsite storage of hazardous waste generated by a generator generating a total quantity of hazardous waste greater than one hundred kilograms, but less than one thousand kilograms during a calendar month, may occur without the requirement of a permit for up to one hundred and eighty days. Such onsite storage may occur without the requirement of a permit for not more than six thousand kilograms for up to two hundred and seventy days if such generator must ship or haul such waste over two hundred miles.

(7)(A) Nothing in this subsection shall be construed to affect or impair the validity of regulations promulgated by the Secretary of Transportation pursuant to the Hazardous Materials Transportation Act [49 U.S.C. 1801 et seq.].

(B) Nothing in this subsection shall be construed to affect, modify, or render invalid any requirements in regulations promulgated prior to January 1, 1983 applicable to any acutely hazardous waste identified or listed under section 6921 of this title which is generated by any generator during any calendar month in a total quantity less than one thousand kilograms.

(8) Effective March 31, 1986, unless the Administrator promulgates standards as provided in paragraph (1) of this subsection prior to such date, hazardous waste generated by any generator in a total quantity greater than one hundred kilograms but less than one thousand kilograms during a calendar month shall be subject to the following requirements until the standards referred to in paragraph (1) of this subsection have become effective:

(A) the notice requirements of paragraph (3) of this subsection shall apply and in addition, the information provided in the form shall include the name of the waste transporters and the name and address of the facility designated to receive the waste;

(B) except in the case of the onsite storage referred to in paragraph (6) of this subsection, the treatment, storage, or disposal of such waste shall occur at a facility with interim status or a permit under this subchapter;

(C) generators of such waste shall file manifest exception reports as required of generators producing greater amounts of hazardous waste per month except that such reports shall be filed by January 31, for any waste shipment occurring in the last half of the preceding calendar year, and by July 31, for any waste shipment occurring in the first half of the calendar year; and

(D) generators of such waste shall retain for three years a copy of the manifest signed by the designated facility that has received the waste.

Nothing in this paragraph shall be construed as a determination of the standards appropriate under paragraph (1).

(9) The last sentence of section 6930(b) of this title shall not apply to regulations promulgated under this subsection.

(e) Specified wastes

(1) Not later than 6 months after November 8, 1984, the Administrator shall, where appropriate, list under subsection (b)(1) of this section, additional wastes containing chlorinated dioxins or chlorinated-dibenzofurans. Not later than one year after November 8, 1984, the Administrator shall, where appropriate, list under subsection (b)(1) of this section wastes containing remaining halogenated dioxins and halogenated-dibenzofurans.

(2) Not later than fifteen months after November 8, 1984, the Administrator shall make a determination of whether or not to list under subsection (b)(1) of this section the following wastes: Chlorinated Aliphatics, Dioxin, Dimethyl Hydrazine, TDI (toluene diisocyanate), Carbamates, Bromacil, Linuron, Organo-bromines, solvents, refining wastes, chlorinated aromatics, dyes and pigments, inorganic chemical industry wastes, lithium batteries, coke byproducts, paint production wastes, and coal slurry pipeline effluent.

(f) Delisting procedures

(1) When evaluating a petition to exclude a waste generated at a particular facility from listing under this section, the Administrator shall consider factors (including additional constituents) other than those for which the waste was listed if the Administrator has a reasonable basis to believe that such additional factors could cause the waste to be a hazardous waste. The Administrator shall provide notice and opportunity for comment on these additional factors before granting or denying such petition.

(2)(A) To the maximum extent practicable the Administrator shall publish in the Federal Register a proposal to grant or deny a petition referred to in paragraph (1) within twelve months after receiving a complete application to exclude a waste generated at a particular facility from being regulated as a hazardous waste and shall grant or deny such a petition within twenty-four months after receiving a complete application.

(B) The temporary granting of such a petition prior to November 8, 1984, without the opportunity for public comment and the full consideration of such comments shall not continue for more than twenty-four months after November 8, 1984. If a final decision to grant or deny such a petition has not been promulgated after notice and opportunity for public comment within the time limit prescribed by the preceding sentence, any such temporary granting of such petition shall cease to be in effect.

(g) EP toxicity

Not later than twenty-eight months after November 8, 1984, the Administrator shall examine the deficiencies of the extraction procedure toxicity characteristic as a predictor of the leaching potential of wastes and make changes in the extraction procedure toxicity characteristic, including changes in the leaching media, as are necessary to insure that it accurately predicts the leaching potential of wastes which pose a threat to human health and the environment when mismanaged.

(h) Additional characteristics

Not later than two years after November 8, 1984, the Administrator shall promulgate regulations under this section identifying additional characteristics of hazardous waste, including measures or indicators of toxicity.

(i) Clarification of household waste exclusion

A resource recovery facility recovering energy from the mass burning of municipal solid waste shall not be deemed to be treating, storing, disposing of, or otherwise managing hazardous wastes for the purposes of regulation under this subchapter, if—

(1) such facility—

(A) receives and burns only—

(i) household waste (from single and multiple dwellings, hotels, motels, and other residential sources), and

(ii) solid waste from commercial or industrial sources that does not contain hazardous waste identified or listed under this section, and

(B) does not accept hazardous wastes identified or listed under this section, and

(2) the owner or operator of such facility has established contractual requirements or other appropriate notification or inspection procedures to assure that hazardous wastes are not received at or burned in such facility.

(Pub.L. 89–272, title II, § 3001, as added Oct. 21, 1976, Pub.L. 94–580, § 2, 90 Stat. 2806, and amended Oct. 21, 1980, Pub.L. 96–482, § 7, 94 Stat. 2336; Nov. 8, 1984, Pub.L. 98–616, title II, §§ 221(a), 222, 223(a), 98 Stat. 3248, 3251, 3252.)

Code of Federal Regulations

Hazardous waste, identification and listing of, see 40 CFR 261.1 et seq.
Hazardous waste management, generally, see 40 CFR 260.1 et seq.
Standards, see 40 CFR 262.10 et seq.

§ 6922. Standards applicable to generators of hazardous waste

(a) In general

Not later than eighteen months after October 21, 1976, and after notice and opportunity for public hearings and after consultation with appropriate Federal and State agencies, the Administrator shall promulgate regulations establishing such standards, applicable to generators of hazardous waste identified or listed under this subchapter, as may be necessary to protect human health and the environment. Such standards shall establish requirements respecting—

(1) recordkeeping practices that accurately identify the quantities of such hazardous waste generated, the constituents thereof which are significant in quantity or in potential harm to human health or the environment, and the disposition of such wastes;

(2) labeling practices for any containers used for the storage, transport, or disposal of such hazardous waste such as will identify accurately such waste;

(3) use of appropriate containers for such hazardous waste;

(4) furnishing of information on the general chemical composition of such hazardous waste to persons transporting, treating, storing, or disposing of such wastes;

(5) use of a manifest system and any other reasonable means necessary to assure that all such hazardous waste generated is designated for treatment, storage, or disposal in, and arrives at, treatment, storage, or disposal facilities (other than facilities on the premises where the waste is generated) for which a permit has been issued as provided in this subchapter, or pursuant to title I of the Marine Protection, Research, and Sanctuaries Act (86 Stat. 1052) [33 U.S.C. 1411 et seq.]; and

(6) submission of reports to the Administrator (or the State agency in any case in which such agency carries out a permit program pursuant to this subchapter) at least once every two years, setting out—

(A) the quantities and nature of hazardous waste identified or listed under this subchapter that he has generated during the year;

(B) the disposition of all hazardous waste reported under subparagraph (A);

(C) the efforts undertaken during the year to reduce the volume and toxicity of waste generated; and

(D) the changes in volume and toxicity of waste actually achieved during the year in question in comparison with previous years, to the extent such information is available for years prior to November 8, 1984.

(b) Waste minimization

Effective September 1, 1985, the manifest required by subsection (a)(5) of this section shall contain a certification by the generator that—

(1) the generator of the hazardous waste has a program in place to reduce the volume or quantity and toxicity of such waste to the degree determined by the generator to be economically practicable; and

(2) the proposed method of treatment, storage, or disposal is that practicable method currently available to the generator which minimizes the present and future threat to human health and the environment.

(Pub.L. 89–272, title II, § 3002, as added Oct. 21, 1976, Pub.L. 94–580, § 2, 90 Stat. 2806, and amended Nov. 8, 1978, Pub.L. 95–609, § 7(f), 92 Stat. 3082; Oct. 21, 1980, Pub.L. 96–482, § 8, 94 Stat. 2338; Nov. 8, 1984, Pub.L. 98–616, title II, § 224(a), 98 Stat. 3252.)

Code of Federal Regulations

Generators of hazardous waste, standards applicable to, see 40 CFR 262.10 et seq.
Identification and listing of hazardous waste, see 40 CFR, 261.1 et seq.

§ 6923. Standards applicable to transporters of hazardous waste

(a) Standards

Not later than eighteen months after October 21, 1976, and after opportunity for public hearings, the Administrator, after consultation with the Secretary of Transportation and the States, shall promulgate regulations establishing such standards, applicable to transporters of hazardous waste identified or listed under this subchapter, as may be necessary to protect human health and the environment. Such standards shall include but need not be limited to requirements respecting—

(1) recordkeeping concerning such hazardous waste transported, and their source and delivery points;

(2) transportation of such waste only if properly labeled;

(3) compliance with the manifest system referred to in section 6922(5) of this title; and

(4) transportation of all such hazardous waste only to the hazardous waste treatment, storage, or disposal facilities which the shipper designates on the manifest form to be a facility holding a permit issued under this subchapter, or pursuant to title I of the Marine Protection, Research, and Sanctuaries Act (86 Stat. 1052) [33 U.S.C. 1411 et seq.].

(b) Coordination with regulations of Secretary of Transportation

In case of any hazardous waste identified or listed under this subchapter which is subject to the Hazardous Materials Transportation Act (88 Stat. 2156; 49 U.S.C. 1801 et seq.), the regulations promulgated by the Administrator under this section shall be consistent with the requirements of such Act and the regulations thereunder. The Administrator is authorized to make recommendations to the Secretary of Transportation respecting the regulations of such hazardous waste under the Hazardous Materials Transportation Act and for addition of materials to be covered by such Act.

(c) Fuel from hazardous waste

Not later than two years after November 8, 1984, and after opportunity for public hearing, the Administrator shall promulgate regulations establishing standards, applicable to transporters of fuel produced (1) from any hazardous waste identified or listed under section 6921 of this title, or (2) from any hazardous waste identified or listed under section 6921 of this title and any other material, as may be necessary to protect human health and the environment. Such standards may include any of the requirements set forth in paragraphs (1) through (4) of subsection (a) of this section as may be appropriate.

(Pub.L. 89–272, title II, § 3003, as added Oct. 21, 1976, Pub.L. 94–580, § 2, 90 Stat. 2807, and amended Nov. 8, 1978, Pub.L. 95–609, § 7(g), 92 Stat. 3082; Nov. 8, 1984, Pub.L. 98–616, title II, § 204(b)(2), 98 Stat. 3238.)

Code of Federal Regulations

Transporters of hazardous waste, standards applicable to, see 40 CFR 263.10 et seq.

§ 6924. Standards applicable to owners and operators of hazardous waste treatment, storage, and disposal facilities

(a) In general

Not later than eighteen months after October 21, 1976, and after opportunity for public hearings and after consultation with appropriate Federal and State agencies, the Administrator shall promulgate regulations establishing such performance standards, applicable to owners and operators of facilities for the treatment, storage, or disposal of hazardous waste identified or listed under this subchapter, as may be necessary to protect human health and the environment. In establishing such standards the Administrator shall, where appropriate, distinguish in such standards between requirements appropriate for new facilities and for facilities in existence on the date of promulgation of such regulations. Such standards shall include, but need not be limited to, requirements respecting—

(1) maintaining records of all hazardous wastes identified or listed under this chapter which is treated, stored, or disposed of, as the case may be, and the manner in which such wastes were treated, stored, or disposed of;

(2) satisfactory reporting, monitoring, and inspection and compliance with the manifest system referred to in section 6922(5) of this title;

(3) treatment, storage, or disposal of all such waste received by the facility pursuant to such operating methods, techniques, and practices as may be satisfactory to the Administrator;

(4) the location, design, and construction of such hazardous waste treatment, disposal, or storage facilities;

(5) contingency plans for effective action to minimize unanticipated damage from any treatment, storage, or disposal of any such hazardous waste;

(6) the maintenance of operation of such facilities and requiring such additional qualifications as to ownership, continuity of operation, training for personnel, and financial responsibility (including financial responsibility for corrective action) as may be necessary or desirable; and

(7) compliance with the requirements of section 6925 of this title respecting permits for treatment, storage, or disposal.

No private entity shall be precluded by reason of criteria established under paragraph (6) from the ownership or operation of facilities providing hazardous waste treatment, storage, or disposal services where such entity can provide assurances of financial responsibility and continuity of operation consistent with the degree and duration of risks associated with the treatment, storage, or disposal of specified hazardous waste.

(b) Salt dome formations, salt bed formations, underground mines and caves

(1) Effective on November 8, 1984, the placement of any noncontainerized or bulk liquid hazardous waste in any salt dome formation, salt bed formation, underground mine, or cave is prohibited until such time as—

(A) the Administrator has determined, after notice and opportunity for hearings on the record in the affected areas, that such placement is protective of human health and the environment;

(B) the Administrator has promulgated performance and permitting standards for such facilities under this subchapter, and;

(C) a permit has been issued under section 6925(c) of this title for the facility concerned.

(2) Effective on November 8, 1984, the placement of any hazardous waste other than a hazardous waste referred to in paragraph (1) in a salt dome formation, salt bed formation, underground mine, or cave is prohibited until such time as a permit has been issued under section 6925(c) of this title for the facility concerned.

(3) No determination made by the Administrator under subsection (d), (e), or (g) of this section regarding any hazardous waste to which such subsection (d), (e), or (g) applies shall affect the prohibition contained in paragraph (1) or (2) of this subsection.

(4) Nothing in this subsection shall apply to the Department of Energy Waste Isolation Pilot Project in New Mexico.

(c) Liquids in landfills

(1) Effective 6 months after November 8, 1984, the placement of bulk or noncontainerized liquid hazardous waste or free liquids contained in hazardous waste (whether or not absorbents have been added) in any landfill is prohibited. Prior to such date the requirements (as in effect on April 30, 1983) promulgated under this section by the Administrator regarding liquid hazardous waste shall remain in force and effect to the extent such requirements are applicable to the placement of bulk or noncontainerized liquid hazardous waste, or free liquids contained in hazardous waste, in landfills.

(2) Not later than fifteen months after November 8, 1984, the Administrator shall promulgate final regulations which—

(A) minimize the disposal of containerized liquid hazardous waste in landfills, and

(B) minimize the presence of free liquids in containerized hazardous waste to be disposed of in landfills.

Such regulations shall also prohibit the disposal in landfills of liquids that have been absorbed in materials that biodegrade or that release liquids when compressed as might occur during routine landfill operations. Prior to the date on which such final regulations take effect, the requirements (as in effect on April 30, 1983) promulgated under this section by the Administrator shall remain in force and effect to the extent such requirements are applicable to the disposal of containerized liquid hazardous waste, or free liquids contained in hazardous waste, in landfills.

(3) Effective twelve months after November 8, 1984, the placement of any liquid which is not a hazardous waste in a landfill for which a permit is required under section 6925(c) of this title or which is operating pursuant to interim status granted under section 6925(e) of this title is prohibited unless the owner or operator of such landfill demonstrates to the Administrator, or the Administrator determines, that—

(A) the only reasonably available alternative to the placement in such landfill is placement in a landfill or unlined surface impoundment, whether or not permitted under section 6925(c) of this title or operating pursuant to interim status under section 6925(e) of this title, which contains, or may reasonably be anticipated to contain, hazardous waste; and

(B) placement in such owner or operator's landfill will not present a risk of contamination of any underground source of drinking water.

As used in subparagraph (B), the term "underground source of drinking water" has the same meaning as provided in regulations under the Safe Drinking Water Act (title XIV of the Public Health Service Act) [42 U.S.C. 300f et seq.]

(4) No determination made by the Administrator under subsection (d), (e), or (g) of this section regarding any hazardous waste to which such subsection (d), (e), or (g) applies shall affect the prohibition contained in paragraph (1) of this subsection.

(d) Prohibitions on land disposal of specified wastes

(1) Effective 32 months after November 8, 1984 (except as provided in subsection (f) of this section with respect to underground injection into deep injection wells), the land disposal of the hazardous wastes referred to in paragraph (2) is prohibited unless the Administrator determines the prohibition on one or more methods of land disposal of such waste is not required in order to protect human health and the environment for as long as the waste remains hazardous, taking into account—

(A) the long-term uncertainties associated with land disposal,

(B) the goal of managing hazardous waste in an appropriate manner in the first instance, and

(C) the persistence, toxicity, mobility, and propensity to bioaccumulate of such hazardous wastes and their hazardous constituents.

For the purposes of this paragraph, a method of land disposal may not be determined to be protective of human health and the environment for a hazardous waste referred to in paragraph (2) (other than a hazardous waste which has complied with the pretreatment regulations promulgated under subsection (m) of this section), unless, upon application by an interested person, it has been demonstrated to the Administrator, to a reasonable degree of certainty, that there will be no migration of hazardous constituents from the disposal unit or injection zone for as long as the wastes remain hazardous.

(2) Paragraph (1) applies to the following hazardous wastes listed or identified under section 6921 of this title:

(A) Liquid hazardous wastes, including free liquids associated with any solid or sludge, containing free cyanides at concentrations greater than or equal to 1,000 mg/l.

(B) Liquid hazardous wastes, including free liquids associated with any solid or sludge, containing the following metals (or elements) or compounds of these metals (or elements) at concentrations greater than or equal to those specified below:

(i) arsenic and/or compounds (as As) 500 mg/l;

(ii) cadmium and/or compounds (as Cd) 100 mg/l;

(iii) chromium (VI and/or compounds (as Cr VI)) 500 mg/l;

(iv) lead and/or compounds (as Pb) 500 mg/l;

(v) mercury and/or compounds (as Hg) 20 mg/l;

(vi) nickel and/or compounds (as Ni) 134 mg/l;

(vii) selenium and/or compounds (as Se) 100 mg/l; and

(viii) thallium and/or compounds (as Th) 130 mg/l.

(C) Liquid hazardous waste having a pH less than or equal to two (2.0).

(D) Liquid hazardous wastes containing polychlorinated biphenyls at concentrations greater than or equal to 50 ppm.

(E) Hazardous wastes containing halogenated organic compounds in total concentration greater than or equal to 1,000 mg/kg.

When necessary to protect human health and the environment, the Administrator shall substitute more stringent concentration levels than the levels specified in subparagraphs (A) through (E).

(3) During the period ending forty-eight months after November 8, 1984, this subsection shall not apply to any disposal of contaminated soil or debris resulting from a response action taken under section 9604 or 9606 of this title or a corrective action required under this subchapter.

(e) Solvents and dioxins

(1) Effective twenty-four months after November 8, 1984 (except as provided in subsection (f) of this section with respect to underground injection into deep injection wells), the land disposal of the hazardous wastes referred to in paragraph (2) is prohibited unless the Administrator determines the prohibition of one or more methods of land disposal of such waste is not required in order to protect human health and the environment for as long as the waste remains hazardous, taking into account the factors referred to in subparagraphs (A) through (C) of subsection (d)(1) of this section. For the purposes of this paragraph, a method of land disposal may not be determined to be protective of human health and the environment for a hazardous waste referred to in paragraph (2) (other than a hazardous waste which has complied with the pretreatment regulations promulgated under subsection (m) of this section), unless upon application by an interested person it has been demonstrated to the Administrator, to a reasonable degree of certainty, that there will be no migration of hazardous constituents from the disposal unit or injection zone for as long as the wastes remain hazardous.

(2) The hazardous wastes to which the prohibition under paragraph (1) applies are as follows—

(A) dioxin-containing hazardous wastes numbered F020, F021, F022, and F023 (as referred to in the proposed rule published by the Administrator in the Federal Register for April 4, 1983), and

(B) those hazardous wastes numbered F001, F002, F003, F004, and F005 in regulations promulgated by the Administrator under section 3001 (40 C.F.R. 261.31 (July 1, 1983)), as those regulations are in effect on July 1, 1983.

(3) During the period ending forty-eight months after November 8, 1984, this subsection shall not apply to any disposal of contaminated soil or debris resulting from a response action taken under section 9604 or 9606 of this title or a corrective action required under this subchapter.

(f) Disposal into deep injection wells; specified subsection (d) wastes, solvents and dioxins

(1) Not later than forty-five months after November 8, 1984, the Administrator shall complete a review of the disposal of all hazardous wastes referred to in paragraph (2) of subsection (d) of this section and in paragraph (2) of subsection (e) of this section by underground injection into deep injection wells.

(2) Within forty-five months after November 8, 1984, the Administrator shall make a determination regarding the disposal by underground injection into deep injection wells of the hazardous wastes referred to in paragraph (2) of subsection (d) of this section and the hazardous wastes referred to in paragraph (2) of subsection (e) of this section. The Administrator shall promulgate final regulations prohibiting the disposal of such wastes into such wells if it may reasonably be determined that such disposal may not be protective of human health and the environment for as long as the waste remains hazardous, taking into account the factors referred to in subparagraphs (A) through (C) of subsection (d)(1) of this section. In promulgating such regulations, the Administrator shall consider each hazardous waste referred to in paragraph (2) of subsection (d) of this section or in paragraph (2) of subsection (e) of this section which is prohibited from disposal into such wells by any State.

(3) If the Administrator fails to make a determination under paragraph (2) for any hazardous waste referred to in paragraph (2) of subsection (d) of this section or in paragraph (2) of subsection (e) of this section within forty-five months after November 8, 1984, such hazardous waste shall be prohibited from disposal into any deep injection well.

(4) As used in this subsection, the term "deep injection well" means a well used for the underground injection of hazardous waste other than a well to which section 6979a(a) of this title applies.

(g) Additional land disposal prohibition determination

(1) Not later than twenty-four months after November 8, 1984, the Administrator shall submit a schedule to Congress for—

(A) reviewing all hazardous wastes listed (as of November 8, 1984) under section 6921 of this title other than those wastes which are referred to in subsection (d) or (e) of this section; and

(B) taking action under paragraph (5) of this subsection with respect to each such hazardous waste.

(2) The Administrator shall base the schedule on a ranking of such listed wastes considering their intrinsic hazard and their volume such that decisions regarding the land disposal of high volume hazardous wastes with high intrinsic hazard shall, to the maximum extent possible, be made by the date forty-five months after November 8, 1984. Decisions regarding low volume hazardous wastes with lower intrinsic hazard shall be made by the date sixty-six months after November 8, 1984.

(3) The preparation and submission of the schedule under this subsection shall not be subject to the Paperwork Reduction Act of 1980. No hearing on the record shall be required for purposes of preparation or submission of the schedule. The schedule shall not be subject to judicial review.

(4) The schedule under this subsection shall require that the Administrator shall promulgate regulations in accordance with paragraph (5) or make a determination under paragraph (5)—

(A) for at least one-third of all hazardous wastes referred to in paragraph (1) by the date forty-five months after November 8, 1984;

(B) for at least two-thirds of all such listed wastes by the date fifty-five months after November 8, 1984; and

(C) for all such listed wastes and for all hazardous wastes identified under section 6921 of this title by the date sixty-six months after November 8, 1984.

In the case of any hazardous waste identified or listed under section 6921 of this title after November 8, 1984, the Administrator shall determine whether such waste shall be prohibited from one or more methods of land disposal in accordance with paragraph (5) within six months after the date of such identification or listing.

(5) Not later than the date specified in the schedule published under this subsection, the Administrator shall promulgate final regulations prohibiting one or more methods of land disposal of the hazardous wastes listed on such schedule except for methods of land disposal which the Administrator determines will be protective of human health and the environment for as long as the waste remains hazardous, taking into account the factors referred to in subparagraphs (A) through (C) of subsection (d)(1) of this section. For the purposes of this paragraph, a method of land disposal may not be determined to be protective of human health and the environment (except with respect to a hazardous waste which has complied with the pretreatment regulations promulgated under subsection (m) of this section) unless, upon application by an interested person, it has been demonstrated to the Administrator, to a reasonable degree of certainty, that

there will be no migration of hazardous constituents from the disposal unit or injection zone for as long as the wastes remain hazardous.

(6)(A) If the Administrator fails (by the date forty-five months after November 8, 1984) to promulgate regulations or make a determination under paragraph (5) for any hazardous waste which is included in the first one-third of the schedule published under this subsection, such hazardous waste may be disposed of in a landfill or surface impoundment only if—

(i) such facility is in compliance with the requirements of subsection *(o)* of this section which are applicable to new facilities (relating to minimum technological requirements); and

(ii) prior to such disposal, the generator has certified to the Administrator that such generator has investigated the availability of treatment capacity and has determined that the use of such landfill or surface impoundment is the only practical alternative to treatment currently available to the generator.

The prohibition contained in this subparagraph shall continue to apply until the Administrator promulgates regulations or makes a determination under paragraph (5) for the waste concerned.

(B) If the Administrator fails (by the date 55 months after November 8, 1984) to promulgate regulations or make a determination under paragraph (5) for any hazardous waste which is included in the first two-thirds of the schedule published under this subsection, such hazardous waste may be disposed of in a landfill or surface impoundment only if—

(i) such facilities in compliance with the requirements of subsection *(o)* of this section which are applicable to new facilities (relating to minimum technological requirements); and

(ii) prior to such disposal, the generator has certified to the Administrator that such generator has investigated the availability of treatment capacity and has determined that the use of such landfill or surface impoundment is the only practical alternative to treatment currently available to the generator.

The prohibition contained in this subparagraph shall continue to apply until the Administrator promulgates regulations or makes a determination under paragraph (5) for the waste concerned.

(C) If the Administrator fails to promulgate regulations, or make a determination under paragraph (5) for any hazardous waste referred to in paragraph (1) within 66 months after November 8, 1984, such hazardous waste shall be prohibited from land disposal.

(h) Variance from land disposal prohibitions

(1) A prohibition in regulations under subsection (d), (e), (f), or (g) of this section shall be effective immediately upon promulgation.

(2) The Administrator may establish an effective date different from the effective date which would otherwise apply under subsection (d), (e), (f), or (g) of this section with respect to a specific hazardous waste which is subject to a prohibition under subsection (d), (e), (f), or (g) of this section or under regulations under subsection (d), (e), (f), or (g) of this section. Any such other effective date shall be established on the basis of the earliest date on which adequate alternative treatment, recovery, or disposal capacity which protects human health and the environment will be available. Any such other effective date shall in no event be later than 2 years after the effective date of the prohibition which would otherwise apply under subsection (d), (e), (f), or (g) of this section.

(3) The Administrator, after notice and opportunity for comment and after consultation with appropriate State agencies in all affected States, may on a case-by-case basis grant an extension of the effective date which would otherwise apply under subsection (d), (e), (f), or (g) of this section or under paragraph (2) for up to one year, where the applicant demonstrates that there is a binding contractual commitment to construct or otherwise provide such alternative capacity but due to circumstances beyond the control of such applicant such alternative capacity cannot reasonably be made available by such effective date. Such extension shall be renewable once for no more than one additional year.

(4) Whenever another effective date (hereinafter referred to as a "variance") is established under paragraph (2), or an extension is granted under paragraph (3), with respect to any hazardous waste, during the period for which such variance or extension is in effect, such hazardous waste may be disposed of in a landfill or surface impoundment only if such facility is in compliance with the requirements of subsection *(o)* of this section.

(i) Publication of determination

If the Administrator determines that a method of land disposal will be protective of human health and the environment, he shall promptly publish in the Federal Register notice of such determination, together with an explanation of the basis for such determination.

(j) Storage of hazardous waste prohibited from land disposal

In the case of any hazardous waste which is prohibited from one or more methods of land disposal under this section (or under regulations promulgated by the Administrator under any provision of this section) the storage of such hazardous waste is prohibited unless such storage is solely for the purpose of the accumulation of such quantities of hazardous waste as are necessary to facilitate proper recovery, treatment or disposal.

(k) Definition of land disposal

For the purposes of this section, the term "land disposal", when used with respect to a specified hazardous waste, shall be deemed to include, but not be limited to, any placement of such hazardous waste in a landfill, surface impoundment, waste pile, injection well, land treatment facility, salt dome formation, salt bed formation, or underground mine or cave.

(*l*) Ban on dust suppression

The use of waste or used oil or other material, which is contaminated or mixed with dioxin or any other hazardous waste identified or listed under section 6921 of this title (other than a waste identified solely on the basis of ignitability), for dust suppression or road treatment is prohibited.

(m) Treatment standards for waste subject to land disposal prohibition

(1) Simultaneously with the promulgation of regulations under subsection (d), (e), (f), or (g) of this section prohibiting one or more methods of land disposal of a particular hazardous waste, and as appropriate thereafter, the Administrator shall, after notice and an opportunity for hearings and after consultation with appropriate Federal and State agencies, promulgate regulations specifying those levels or methods of treatment, if any, which substantially diminish the toxicity of the waste or substantially reduce the likelihood of migration of hazardous constituents from the waste so that short-term and long-term threats to human health and the environment are minimized.

(2) If such hazardous waste has been treated to the level or by a method specified in regulations promulgated under this subsection, such waste or residue thereof shall not be subject to any prohibition promulgated under subsection (d), (e), (f), or (g) of this section and may be disposed of in a land disposal facility which meets the requirements of this subchapter. Any regulation promulgated under this subsection for a particular hazardous waste shall become effective on the same date as any applicable prohibition promulgated under subsection (d), (e), (f), or (g) of this section.

(n) Air emissions

Not later than thirty months after November 8, 1984, the Administrator shall promulgate such regulations for the monitoring and control of air emissions at hazardous waste treatment, storage, and disposal facilities, including but not limited to open tanks, surface impoundments, and landfills, as may be necessary to protect human health and the environment.

(*o*) Minimum technological requirements

(1) The regulations under subsection (a) of this section shall be revised from time to time to take into account improvements in the technology of control and measurement. At a minimum, such regulations shall require, and a permit issued pursuant to section 6925(c) of this title after November 8, 1984, by the Administrator or a State shall require—

(A) for each new landfill or surface impoundment, each new landfill or surface impoundment unit at an existing facility, each replacement of an existing landfill or surface impoundment unit, and each lateral expansion of an existing landfill or surface impoundment unit, for which an application for a final determination regarding issuance of a permit under section 6925(c) of this title is received after November 8, 1984—

(i) the installation of two or more liners and a leachate collection system above (in the case of a landfill) and between such liners; and

(ii) ground water monitoring; and

(B) for each incinerator which receives a permit under section 6925(c) of this title after November 8, 1984, the attainment of the minimum destruction and removal efficiency required by regulations in effect on June 24, 1982.

The requirements of this paragraph shall apply with respect to all waste received after the issuance of the permit.

(2) Paragraph (1)(A)(i) shall not apply if the owner or operator demonstrates to the Administrator, and the Administrator finds for such landfill or surface impoundment, that alternative design and operating practices, together with location characteristics, will prevent the migration of any hazardous constituents into the ground water or surface water at least as effectively as such liners and leachate collection systems.

(3) The double-liner requirement set forth in paragraph (1)(A)(i) may be waived by the Administrator for any monofill, if—

(A) such monofill contains only hazardous wastes from foundry furnace emission controls or metal casting molding sand,

(B) such wastes do not contain constituents which would render the wastes hazardous for reasons other than the Extraction Procedure

("EP") toxicity characteristics set forth in regulations under this subchapter, and

(C) such monofill meets the same requirements as are applicable in the case of a waiver under section 6925(j)(2) or (4) of this title.

(4)(A) Not later than thirty months after November 8, 1984, the Administrator shall promulgate standards requiring that new landfill units, surface impoundment units, waste piles, underground tanks and land treatment units for the storage, treatment, or disposal of hazardous waste identified or listed under section 6921 of this title shall be required to utilize approved leak detection systems.

(B) For the purposes of subparagraph (A)—

(i) the term "approved leak detection system" means a system or technology which the Administrator determines to be capable of detecting leaks of hazardous constituents at the earliest practicable time; and

(ii) the term "new units" means units on which construction commences after the date of promulgation of regulations under this paragraph.

(5)(A) The Administrator shall promulgate regulations or issue guidance documents implementing the requirements of paragraph (1)(A) within two years after November 8, 1984.

(B) Until the effective date of such regulations or guidance documents, the requirement for the installation of two or more liners may be satisfied by the installation of a top liner designed, operated, and constructed of materials to prevent the migration of any constituent into such liner during the period such facility remains in operation (including any post-closure monitoring period), and a lower liner designed, operated and constructed to prevent the migration of any constituent through such liner during such period. For the purpose of the preceding sentence, a lower liner shall be deemed to satisfy such requirement if it is constructed of at least a 3-foot thick layer of recompacted clay or other natural material with a permeability of no more than $1X10^{-7}$ centimeter per second.

(6) Any permit under section 6925 of this title which is issued for a landfill located within the State of Alabama shall require the installation of two or more liners and a leachate collection system above and between such liners, notwithstanding any other provision of this chapter.

(7) In addition to the requirements set forth in this subsection, the regulations referred to in paragraph (1) shall specify criteria for the acceptable location of new and existing treatment, storage, or disposal facilities as necessary to protect human health and the environment. Within 18 months after November 8, 1984, the Administrator shall publish guidance criteria identifying areas of vulnerable hydrogeology.

(p) Ground water monitoring

The standards under this section concerning ground water monitoring which are applicable to surface impoundments, waste piles, land treatment units, and landfills shall apply to such a facility whether or not—

(1) the facility is located above the seasonal high water table;

(2) two liners and a leachate collection system have been installed at the facility; or

(3) the owner or operator inspects the liner (or liners) which has been installed at the facility.

This subsection shall not be construed to affect other exemptions or waivers from such standards provided in regulations in effect on November 8, 1984, or as may be provided in revisions to those regulations, to the extent consistent with this subsection. The Administrator is authorized on a case-by-case basis to exempt from ground water monitoring requirements under this section (including subsection (*o*) of this section) any engineered structure which the Administrator finds does not receive or contain liquid waste (nor waste containing free liquids), is designed and operated to exclude liquid from precipitation or other runoff, utilizes multiple leak detection systems within the outer layer of containment, and provides for continuing operation and maintenance of these leak detection systems during the operating period, closure, and the period required for post-closure monitoring and for which the Administrator concludes on the basis of such findings that there is a reasonable certainty hazardous constituents will not migrate beyond the outer layer of containment prior to the end of the period required for post-closure monitoring.

(q) Hazardous waste used as fuel

(1) Not later than two years after November 8, 1984, and after notice and opportunity for public hearing, the Administrator shall promulgate regulations establishing such—

(A) standards applicable to the owners and operators of facilities which produce a fuel—

(i) from any hazardous waste identified or listed under section 6921 of this title, or

(ii) from any hazardous waste identified or listed under section 6921 of this title and any other material;

(B) standards applicable to the owners and operators of facilities which burn, for purposes of energy recovery, any fuel produced as provided in subparagraph (A) or any fuel which otherwise contains any hazardous waste identified or listed under section 6921 of this title; and

(C) standards applicable to any person who distributes or markets any fuel which is produced as provided in subparagraph (A) or any fuel which otherwise contains any hazardous waste identified or listed under section 6921 of this title

as may be necessary to protect human health and the environment. Such standards may include any of the requirements set forth in paragraphs (1) through (7) of subsection (a) of this section as may be appropriate. Nothing in this subsection shall be construed to affect or impair the provisions of section 6921(b)(3) of this title. For purposes of this subsection, the term "hazardous waste listed under section 6921 of this title" includes any commercial chemical product which is listed under section 6921 of this title and which, in lieu of its original intended use, is (i) produced for use as (or as a component of) a fuel, (ii) distributed for use as a fuel, or (iii) burned as a fuel.

(2)(A) This subsection, subsection (r) of this section, and subsection (s) of this section shall not apply to petroleum refinery wastes containing oil which are converted into petroleum coke at the same facility at which such wastes were generated, unless the resulting coke product would exceed one or more characteristics by which a substance would be identified as a hazardous waste under section 6921 of this title.

(B) The Administrator may exempt from the requirements of this subsection, subsection (r) of this section, or subsection (s) of this section facilities which burn de minimis quantities of hazardous waste as fuel, as defined by the Administrator, if the wastes are burned at the same facility at which such wastes are generated; the waste is burned to recover useful energy, as determined by the Administrator on the basis of the design and operating characteristics of the facility and the heating value and other characteristics of the waste; and the waste is burned in a type of device determined by the Administrator to be designed and operated at a destruction and removal efficiency sufficient such that protection of human health and environment is assured.

(C)(i) After the date of November 8, 1984, and until standards are promulgated and in effect under paragraph (2) of this subsection, no fuel which contains any hazardous waste may be burned in any cement kiln which is located within the boundaries of any incorporated municipality with a population greater than five hundred thousand (based on the most recent census statistics) unless such kiln fully complies with regulations (as in effect on November 8, 1984 under this subchapter which are applicable to incinerators.

(ii) Any person who knowingly violates the prohibition contained in clause (i) shall be deemed to have violated section 6928(d)(2) of this title.

(r) Labeling

(1) Notwithstanding any other provision of law, until such time as the Administrator promulgates standards under subsection (q) of this section specifically superceding this requirement, it shall be unlawful for any person who is required to file a notification in accordance with paragraph (1) or (3) of section 6930 of this title to distribute or market any fuel which is produced from any hazardous waste identified or listed under section 6921 of this title, or any fuel which otherwise contains any hazardous waste identified or listed under section 6921 of this title if the invoice or the bill of sale fails—

(A) to bear the following statement: "WARNING: THIS FUEL CONTAINS HAZARDOUS WASTES", and

(B) to list the hazardous wastes contained therein.

Beginning ninety days after November 8, 1984, such statement shall be located in a conspicuous place on every such invoice or bill of sale and shall appear in conspicuous and legible type in contrast by typography, layouts, or color with other printed matter on the invoice or bill of sale.

(2) Unless the Administrator determines otherwise as may be necessary to protect human health and the environment, this subsection shall not apply to fuels produced from petroleum refining waste containing oil if—

(A) such materials are generated and reinserted onsite into the refining process;

(B) contaminants are removed; and

(C) such refining waste containing oil is converted along with normal process streams into pertroleum-derived [1] fuel products at a facility at which crude oil is refined into petroleum products and which is classified as a number SIC 2911 facility under the Office of Management and Budget Standard Industrial Classification Manual.

(3) Unless the Administrator determines otherwise as may be necessary to protect human health and the environment, this subsection shall not apply to fuels produced from oily materials, resulting from normal petroleum refining, production and transportation practices, if (A) contaminants are removed; and (B) such oily materials are converted along with normal process streams into petroleum-derived fuel products at a facility at which crude oil is refined into petroleum products and which is classified as a number SIC 2911 facility under the Office of Management and Budget Standard[2] Classification Manual.

(s) Recordkeeping

Not later than fifteen months after November 8, 1984, the Administrator shall promulgate regulations requiring that any person who is required to file a notification in accordance with subparagraph (1), (2), or (3), of section 6930(a) of this title shall maintain such records regarding fuel blending, distribution, or use as may be necessary to protect human health and the environment.

(t) Financial responsibility provisions

(1) Financial responsibility required by subsection (a) of this section may be established in accordance with regulations promulgated by the Administrator by any one, or any combination, of the following: insurance, guarantee, surety bond, letter of credit, or qualification as a self-insurer. In promulgating requirements under this section, the Administrator is authorized to specify policy or other contractual terms, conditions, or defenses which are necessary or are unacceptable in establishing such evidence of financial responsibility in order to effectuate the purposes of this chapter.

(2) In any case where the owner or operator is in bankruptcy, reorganization, or arrangement pursuant to the Federal Bankruptcy Code or where (with reasonable diligence) jurisdiction in any State court or any Federal Court cannot be obtained over an owner or operator likely to be solvent at the time of judgment, any claim arising from conduct for which evidence of financial responsibility must be provided under this section may be asserted directly against the guarantor providing such evidence of financial responsibility. In the case of any action pursuant to this subsection, such guarantor shall be entitled to invoke all rights and defenses which would have been available to the owner or operator if any action had been brought against the owner or operator by the claimant and which would have been available to the guarantor if an action had been brought against the guarantor by the owner or operator.

(3) The total liability of any guarantor shall be limited to the aggregate amount which the guarantor has provided as evidence of financial responsibility to the owner or operator under this chapter. Nothing in this subsection shall be construed to limit any other State or Federal statutory, contractual or common law liability of a guarantor to its owner or operator including, but not limited to, the liability of such guarantor for bad faith either in negotiating or in failing to negotiate the settlement of any claim. Nothing in this subsection shall be construed to diminish the liability of any person under section 9607 or 9611 of this title or other applicable law.

(4) For the purpose of this subsection, the term "guarantor" means any person, other than the owner or operator, who provides evidence of financial responsibility for an owner or operator under this section.

(u) Continuing releases at permitted facilities

Standards promulgated under this section shall require, and a permit issued after November 8, 1984, by the Administrator or a State shall require, corrective action for all releases of hazardous waste or constituents from any solid waste management unit at a treatment, storage, or disposal facility seeking a permit under this subchapter, regardless of the time at which waste was placed in such unit. Permits issued under section 6925 of this title shall contain schedules of compliance for such corrective action (where such corrective action cannot be completed prior to issuance of the permit) and assurances of financial responsibility for completing such corrective action.

(v) Corrective action beyond facility boundary

As promptly as practicable after November 8, 1984, the Administrator shall amend the standards under this section regarding corrective action required at facilities for the treatment, storage, or disposal, of hazardous waste listed or identified under section 6921 of this title to require that corrective action be taken beyond the facility boundary where necessary to protect human health and the environment unless the owner or operator of the facility concerned demonstrates to the satisfaction of the Administrator that, despite the owner or operator's best efforts, the owner or operator was unable to obtain the necessary permission to undertake such action. Such regulations shall take effect immediately upon promulgation, notwithstanding section 6930(b) of this title, and shall apply to—

(1) all facilities operating under permits issued under subsection (c) of this section, and

(2) all landfills, surface impoundments, and waste pile units (including any new units, replacements of existing units, or lateral expansions of existing units) which receive hazardous waste after July 26, 1982.

Pending promulgation of such regulations, the Administrator shall issue corrective action orders for facilities referred to in paragraphs (1) and (2), on a case-by-case basis, consistent with the purposes of this subsection.

(w) Underground tanks

Not later than March 1, 1985, the Administrator shall promulgate final permitting standards under this section for underground tanks that cannot be entered for inspection. Within forty-eight months after November 8, 1984, such standards shall be modified, if necessary, to cover at a minimum all requirements and standards described in section 6991b of this title.

(x) Mining and other special wastes

If (1) solid waste from the extraction, beneficiation or processing of ores and minerals, including phosphate rock and overburden from the mining of uranium, (2) fly ash waste, bottom ash waste, slag waste, and flue gas emission control waste generated primarily from the combustion of coal or other fossil fuels, or (3) cement kiln dust waste, is subject to regulation under this subchapter, the Administrator is authorized to modify the requirements of subsections (c), (d), (e), (f), (g), (*o*), and (u) of this section and section 6925(j) of this title, in the case of landfills or surface impoundments receiving such solid waste, to take into account the special characteristics of such wastes, the practical difficulties associated with implementation of such requirements, and site-specific characteristics, including but not limited to the climate, geology, hydrology and soil chemistry at the site, so long as such modified requirements assure protection of human health and the environment.

(Pub.L. 89–272, title II, § 3004, as added Oct. 21, 1976, Pub.L. 94–580, § 2, 90 Stat. 2807, and amended Oct. 21, 1980, Pub.L. 96–482, § 9, 94 Stat. 2338; Nov. 8, 1984, Pub.L. 98–616, title II, §§ 201(a), 202(a), 203, 204(b)(1), 205–209, 98 Stat. 3226, 3233, 3234, 3236, 3238–3240.)

[1] So in original. Probably should be petroleum-derived.

[2] So in original. Probably should be Standard Industrial Classification.

Code of Federal Regulations

Definitions and requirements, see 40 CFR 122.1 et seq.

Owners and operations of hazardous waste facilities, standards applicable to, see 40 CFR 264.1 et seq., 265.1 et seq., 267.1 et seq.

§ 6925. Permits for treatment, storage, or disposal of hazardous waste

(a) Permit requirements

Not later than eighteen months after October 21, 1976, the Administrator shall promulgate regulations requiring each person owning or operating an existing facility or planning to construct a new facility for the treatment, storage, or disposal of hazardous waste identified or listed under this subchapter to have a permit issued pursuant to this section. Such regulations shall take effect on the date provided in section 6930 of this title and upon and after such date the treatment, storage, or disposal of any such hazardous waste and the construction of any new facility for the treatment, storage, or disposal of any such hazardous waste is prohibited except in accordance with such a permit. No permit shall be required under this section in order to construct a facility if such facility is constructed pursuant to an approval issued by the Administrator under section 2605(e) of Title 15 for the incineration of polycholorinated[1] biphenyls and any person owning or operating such a facility may, at any time after operation or construction of such facility has begun, file an application for a permit pursuant to this section authorizing such facility to incinerate hazardous waste identified or listed under this subchapter.

(b) Requirements of permit application

Each application for a permit under this section shall contain such information as may be required under regulations promulgated by the Administrator, including information respecting—

(1) estimates with respect to the composition, quantities, and concentrations of any hazardous waste identified or listed under this subchapter, or combinations of any such hazardous waste and any other solid waste, proposed to be disposed of, treated, transported, or stored, and the time, frequency, or rate of which such waste is proposed to be disposed of, treated, transported, or stored; and

(2) the site at which such hazardous waste or the products of treatment of such hazardous waste will be disposed of, treated, transported to, or stored.

(c) Permit issuance

(1) Upon a determination by the Administrator (or a State, if applicable), of compliance by a facility for which a permit is applied for under this section with the requirements of this section and section 6924 of this title, the Administrator (or the State) shall issue a permit for such facilities. In the event permit applicants propose modification of their facilities, or in the event the Administrator (or the State) determines that modifications are necessary to conform to the requirements under this section and section 6924 of this title, the permit shall specify the time allowed to complete the modifications.

(2)(A)(i) Not later than the date four years after November 8, 1984, in the case of each application under this subsection for a permit for a land disposal facility which was submitted before such date, the Administrator shall issue a final permit pursuant to such application or issue a final denial of such application.

(ii) Not later than the date five years after November 8, 1984, in the case of each application for a permit under this subsection for an incinerator facility which was submitted before such date, the Administrator shall issue a final permit pursuant to such application or issue a final denial of such application.

(B) Not later than the date eight years after November 8, 1984, in the case of each application for a permit under this subsection for any facility (other than a facility referred to in subparagraph (A)) which was submitted before such date, the Administrator shall issue a final permit pursuant to such application or issue a final denial of such application.

(C) The time periods specified in this paragraph shall also apply in the case of any State which is administering an authorized hazardous waste program under section 6926 of this title. Interim status under subsection (e) of this section shall terminate for each facility referred to in subparagraph (A)(ii) or (B) on the expiration of the five- or eight-year period referred to in subparagraph (A) or (B), whichever is applicable, unless the owner or operator of the facility applies for a final determination regarding the issuance of a permit under this subsection within—

(i) two years after November 8, 1984 (in the case of a facility referred to in subparagraph (A)(ii)), or

(ii) four years after November 8, 1984 (in the case of a facility referred to in subparagraph (B)).

(3) Any permit under this section shall be for a fixed term, not to exceed 10 years in the case of any land disposal facility, storage facility, or incinerator or other treatment facility. Each permit for a land disposal facility shall be reviewed five years after date of issuance or reissuance and shall be modified as necessary to assure that the facility continues to comply with the currently applicable requirements of this section and section 6924 of this title. Nothing in this subsection shall preclude the Administrator from reviewing and modifying a permit at any time during its term. Review of any application for a permit renewal shall consider improvements in the state of control and measurement technology as well as changes in applicable regulations. Each permit issued under this section shall contain such terms and conditions as the Administrator (or the State) determines necessary to protect human health and the environment.

(d) Permit revocation

Upon a determination by the Administrator (or by a State, in the case of a State having an authorized hazardous waste program under section 6926 of this title) of noncompliance by a facility having a permit under this chapter with the requirements of this section or section 6924 of this title, the Administrator (or State, in the case of a State having an authorized hazardous waste program under section 6926 of this title) shall revoke such permit.

(e) Interim status

(1) Any person who—

(A) owns or operates a facility required to have a permit under this section which facility—

(i) was in existence on November 19, 1980, or

(ii) is in existence on the effective date of statutory or regulatory changes under this chapter that render the facility subject to the requirement to have a permit under this section,

(B) has complied with the requirements of section 6930(a) of this title, and

(C) has made an application for a permit under this section

shall be treated as having been issued such permit until such time as final administrative disposition of such application is made, unless the Administrator or other plaintiff proves that final administrative disposition of such application has not been made because of the failure of the applicant to furnish information reasonably required or requested in order to process the application. This paragraph shall not apply to any facility which has been previously denied a permit under this section or if authority to operate the facility under this section has been previously terminated.

(2) In the case of each land disposal facility which has been granted interim status under this subsection before November 8, 1984, interim status shall terminate on the date twelve months after November 8, 1984, unless the owner or operator of such facility—

(A) applies for a final determination regarding the issuance of a permit under subsection (c) of this section for such facility before the date twelve months after November 8, 1984; and

(B) certifies that such facility is in compliance with all applicable groundwater monitoring and financial responsibility requirements.

(3) In the case of each land disposal facility which is in existence on November 8, 1984 that render the facility subject to the requirement to have a permit under this section and which is granted interim status under this subsection, interim status shall terminate on the date twelve months after the date on which the facility first becomes subject to such permit requirement unless the owner or operator of such facility—

(A) applies for a final determination regarding the issuance of a permit under subsection (c) of this section for such facility before the date twelve months after the date on which the facility first becomes subject to such permit requirement; and

(B) certifies that such facility is in compliance with all applicable groundwater monitoring and financial responsibility requirements.

(f) Coal mining wastes and reclamation permits

Notwithstanding subsection (a) through (e) of this section, any surface coal mining and reclamation permit covering any coal mining wastes or overburden which has been issued or approved under the Surface Mining Control and Reclamation Act of 1977 [30 U.S.C. 1201 et seq.] shall be deemed to be a permit issued pursuant to this section with respect to the treatment, storage, or disposal of such wastes or overburden. Regulations promulgated by the Administrator under this subchapter shall not be applicable to treatment, storage, or disposal of coal mining wastes and overburden which are covered by such a permit.

(g) Research, development and demonstration permits

(1) The Administrator may issue a research, development, and demonstration permit for any hazardous waste treatment facility which proposes to utilize an innovative and experimental hazardous waste treatment technology or process for which permit standards for such experimental activity have not been promulgated under this subchapter. Any such permit shall include such terms and conditions as will assure protection of human health and the environment. Such permits—

(A) shall provide for the construction of such facilities, as necessary, and for operation of the facility for not longer than one year (unless renewed as provided in paragraph (4)), and

(B) shall provide for the receipt and treatment by the facility of only those types and quantities of hazardous waste which the Administrator deems necessary for purposes of determining the efficacy and performance capabilities of the technology or process and the effects of such technology or process on human health and the environment, and

(C) shall include such requirements as the Administrator deems necessary to protect human health and the environment (including, but not limited to, requirements regarding monitoring, operation, insurance or bonding, financial responsibility, closure, and remedial action), and such requirements as the Administrator deems necessary regarding testing and providing of information to the Administrator with respect to the operation of the facility.

The Administrator may apply the criteria set forth in this paragraph in establishing the conditions of each permit without separate establishment of regulations implementing such criteria.

(2) For the purpose of expediting review and issuance of permits under this subsection, the Administrator may, consistent with the protection of human health and the environment, modify or waive permit application and permit issuance requirements established in the Administrator's general permit regulations except that there may be no modification or waiver of regulations regarding financial responsibility (including insurance) or of procedures established under section 6974(b)(2) of this title regarding public participation.

(3) The Administrator may order an immediate termination of all operations at the facility at any time he determines that termination is necessary to protect human health and the environment.

(4) Any permit issued under this subsection may be renewed not more than three times. Each such renewal shall be for a period of not more than 1 year.

(h) Waste minimization

Effective September 1, 1985, it shall be a condition of any permit issued under this section for the treatment, storage, or disposal of hazardous waste on the premises where such waste was generated that the permittee certify, no less often than annually, that—

(1) the generator of the hazardous waste has a program in place to reduce the volume or quantity and toxicity of such waste to the degree determined by the generator to be economically practicable; and

(2) the proposed method of treatment, storage, or disposal is that practicable method currently available to the generator which minimizes the present and future threat to human health and the environment.

(i) Interim status facilities receiving wastes after July 26, 1982

The standards concerning ground water monitoring, unsaturated zone monitoring, and corrective action, which are applicable under section 6924 of this title to new landfills, surface impoundments, land treatment units, and waste-pile units required to be permitted under subsection (c) of this section shall also apply to any landfill, surface impoundment, land treatment unit, or waste-pile unit qualifying for the authorization to operate under subsection (e) of this section which receives hazardous waste after July 26, 1982.

(j) Interim status surface impoundments

(1) Except as provided in paragraph (2), (3), or (4), each surface impoundment in existence on No-

vember 8, 1984, and qualifying for the authorization to operate under subsection (e) of this section shall not receive, store, or treat hazardous waste after the date four years after November 8, 1984, unless such surface impoundment is in compliance with the requirements of section 6924(*o*)(1)(A) of this title which would apply to such impoundment if it were new.

(2) Paragraph (1) of this subsection shall not apply to any surface impoundment which (A) has at least one liner, for which there is no evidence that such liner is leaking; (B) is located more than one-quarter mile from an underground source of drinking water; and (C) is in compliance with generally applicable ground water monitoring requirements for facilities with permits under subsection (c) of this section.

(3) Paragraph (1) of this subsection shall not apply to any surface impoundment which (A) contains treated waste water during the secondary or subsequent phases of an aggressive biological treatment facility subject to a permit issued under section 1342 of Title 33 (or which holds such treated waste water after treatment and prior to discharge); (B) is in compliance with generally applicable ground water monitoring requirements for facilities with permits under subsection (c) of this section; and (C)(i) is part of a facility in compliance with section 1311(b)(2) of Title 33, or (ii) in the case of a facility for which no effluent guidelines required under section 1314(b)(2) of Title 33 are in effect and no permit under section 1342(a)(1) of Title 33 implementing section 1311(b)(2) of Title 33 has been issued, is part of a facility in compliance with a permit under section 1342 of Title 33, which is achieving significant degradation of toxic pollutants and hazardous constituents contained in the untreated waste stream and which has identified those toxic pollutants and hazardous constituents in the untreated waste stream to the appropriate permitting authority.

(4) The Administrator (or the State, in the case of a State with an authorized program), after notice and opportunity for comment, may modify the requirements of paragraph (1) for any surface impoundment if the owner or operator demonstrates that such surface impoundment is located, designed and operated so as to assure that there will be no migration of any hazardous constitutent[2] into ground water or surface water at any future time. The Administrator or the State shall take into account locational criteria established under section 6924(*o*)(7) of this title.

(5) The owner or operator of any surface impoundment potentially subject to paragraph (1) who has reason to believe that on the basis of paragraph (2), (3), or (4) such surface impoundment is not required to comply with the requirements of paragraph (1), shall apply to the Administrator (or the State, in the case of a State with an authorized program) not later than twenty-four months after November 8, 1984, for a determination of the applicability of paragraph (1) (in the case of paragraph (2) or (3)) or for a modification of the requirements of paragraph (1) (in the case of paragraph (4)), with respect to such surface impoundment. Such owner or operator shall provide, with such application, evidence pertinent to such decision, including:

(A) an application for a final determination regarding the issuance of a permit under subsection (c) of this section for such facility, if not previously submitted;

(B) evidence as to compliance with all applicable ground water monitoring requirements and the information and analysis from such monitoring;

(C) all reasonably ascertainable evidence as to whether such surface impoundment is leaking; and

(D) in the case of applications under paragraph (2) or (3), a certification by a registered professional engineer with academic training and experience in ground water hydrology that—

(i) under paragraph (2), the liner of such surface impoundment is designed, constructed, and operated in accordance with applicable requirements, such surface impoundment is more than one-quarter mile from an underground source of drinking water and there is no evidence such liner is leaking; or

(ii) under paragraph (3), based on analysis of those toxic pollutants and hazardous constituents that are likely to be present in the untreated waste stream, such impoundment satisfies the conditions of paragraph (3).

In the case of any surface impoundment for which the owner or operator fails to apply under this paragraph within the time provided by this paragraph or paragraph (6), such surface impoundment shall comply with paragraph (1) notwithstanding paragraph (2), (3), or (4). Within twelve months after receipt of such application and evidence and not later than thirty-six months after November 8, 1984, and after notice and opportunity to comment, the Administrator (or, if appropriate, the State) shall advise such owner or operator on the applicability of paragraph (1) to such surface impoundment or as to whether and how the requirements of paragraph (1) shall be modified and applied to such surface impoundment.

(6)(A) In any case in which a surface impoundment becomes subject to paragraph (1) after November 8, 1984, due to the promulgation of additional listings or characteristics for the identification of hazardous waste under section 6921 of this title, the period for compliance in paragraph (1) shall be four years after the date of such promulgation, the period for demonstrations under paragraph (4) and for submission of evidence under paragraph (5) shall be not later than twenty-four months after the date of such promulgation, and the period for the Administrator (or if appropriate, the State) to advise such owners or operators under paragraph (5) shall be not later than thirty-six months after the date of promulgation.

(B) In any case in which a surface impoundment is initially determined to be excluded from the requirements of paragraph (1) but due to a change in condition (including the existence of a leak) no longer satisfies the provisions of paragraph (2), (3), or (4) and therefore becomes subject to paragraph (1), the period for compliance in paragraph (1) shall be two years after the date of discovery of such change of condition, or in the case of a surface impoundment excluded under paragraph (3) three years after such date of discovery.

(7)(A) The Administrator shall study and report to the Congress on the number, range of size, construction, likelihood of hazardous constituents migrating into ground water, and potential threat to human health and the environment of existing surface impoundments excluded by paragraph (3) from the requirements of paragraph (1). Such report shall address the need, feasibility, and estimated costs of subjecting such existing surface impoundments to the requirements of paragraph (1).

(B) In the case of any existing surface impoundment or class of surface impoundments from which the Administrator (or the State, in the case of a State with an authorized program) determines hazardous constituents are likely to migrate into ground water, the Administrator (or if appropriate, the State) is authorized to impose such requirements as may be necessary to protect human health and the environment, including the requirements of section 6924(*o*) of this title which would apply to such impoundments if they were new.

(C) In the case of any surface impoundment excluded by paragraph (3) from the requirements of paragraph (1) which is subsequently determined to be leaking, the Administrator (or, if appropriate, the State) shall require compliance with paragraph (1), unless the Administrator (or, if appropriate, the State) determines that such compliance is not necessary to protect human health and the environment.

(8) In the case of any surface impoundment in which the liners and leak detection system have been installed pursuant to the requirements of paragraph (1) and in good faith compliance with section 6924(*o*) of this title and the Administrator's regulations and guidance documents governing liners and leak detection systems, no liner or leak detection system which is different from that which was so installed pursuant to paragraph (1) shall be required for such unit by the Administrator when issuing the first permit under this section to such facility. Nothing in this paragraph shall preclude the Administrator from requiring installation of a new liner when the Administrator has reason to believe that any liner installed pursuant to the requirements of this subsection is leaking.

(9) In the case of any surface impoundment which has been excluded by paragraph (2) on the basis of a liner meeting the definition under paragraph (12)(A)(ii), at the closure of such impoundment the Administrator shall require the owner or operator of such impoundment to remove or decontaminate all waste residues, all contaminated liner material, and contaminated soil to the extent practicable. If all contaminated soil is not removed or decontaminated, the owner or operator of such impoundment shall be required to comply with appropriate post-closure requirements, including but not limited to ground water monitoring and corrective action.

(10) Any incremental cost attributable to the requirements of this subsection or section 6924(*o*) of this title shall not be considered by the Administrator (or the State, in the case of a State with an authorized program under section 1342 of title 33)—

(A) in establishing effluent limitations and standards under section 1311, 1314, 1316, 1317, or 1342 of title 33 based on effluent limitations guidelines and standards promulgated any time before twelve months after November 8, 1984; or

(B) in establishing any other effluent limitations to carry out the provisions of section 1311, 1317, or 1342 of title 33 on or before October 1, 1986.

(11)(A) If the Administrator allows a hazardous waste which is prohibited from one or more methods of land disposal under subsection (d), (e) or (g) of section 6924 of this title (or under regulations promulgated by the Administrator under such subsections) to be placed in a surface impoundment (which is operating pursuant to interim status) for storage or treatment, such impoundment shall meet the requirements that are applicable to new surface impoundments under section 6924(*o*)(1) of this title, unless such impoundment meets the requirements of paragraph (2) or (4).

(B) In the case of any hazardous waste which is prohibited from one or more methods of land disposal under subsection (d), (e), or (g) of section 6924 of this title (or under regulations promulgated by the Administrator under such subsection) the placement or maintenance of such hazardous waste in a surface impoundment for treatment is prohibited as of the effective date of such prohibition unless the treatment residues which are hazardous are, at a minimum, removed for subsequent management within one year of the entry of the waste into the surface impoundment.

(12)(A) For the purposes of paragraph (2)(A) of this subsection, the term "liner" means—

(i) a liner designed, constructed, installed, and operated to prevent hazardous waste from passing into the liner at any time during the active life of the facility; or

(ii) a liner designed, constructed, installed, and operated to prevent hazardous waste from migrating beyond the liner to adjacent subsurface soil, ground water, or surface water at any time during the active life of the facility.

(B) For the purposes of this subsection, the term "aggressive biological treatment facility" means a system of surface impoundments in which the initial impoundment of the secondary treatment segment of the facility utilizes intense mechanical aeration to enhance biological activity to degrade waste water pollutants and

(i) the hydraulic retention time in such initial impoundment is no longer than 5 days under normal operating conditions, on an annual average basis;

(ii) the hydraulic retention time in such initial impoundment is no longer than thirty days under normal operating conditions, on an annual average basis: *Provided,* That the sludge in such impoundment does not constitute a hazardous waste as identified by the extraction procedure toxicity characteristic in effect on November 8, 1984; or

(iii) such system utilizes activated sludge treatment in the first portion of secondary treatment.

(C) For the purposes of this subsection, the term "underground source or [3] drinking water" has the same meaning as provided in regulations under the Safe Drinking Water Act (title XIV of the Public Health Service Act) [42 U.S.C. 300f et seq.].

(13) The Administrator may modify the requirements of paragraph (1) in the case of a surface impoundment for which the owner or operator, prior to October 1, 1984, has entered into, and is in compliance with, a consent order, decree, or agreement with the Administrator or a State with an authorized program mandating corrective action with respect to such surface impoundment that provides a degree of protection of human health and the environment which is at a minimum equivalent to that provided by paragraph (1).

(Pub.L. 89–272, title II, § 3005, as added Oct. 21, 1976, Pub.L. 94–580, § 2, 90 Stat. 2808, and amended Nov. 8, 1978, Pub.L. 95–609, § 7(h), 92 Stat. 3082; Oct. 21, 1980, Pub.L. 96–482, §§ 10, 11, 94 Stat. 2338; Nov. 8, 1984, Pub.L. 98–616, title II, §§ 211, 212, 213(a), (c), 214(a), 215, 224(b), 243(c), 98 Stat. 3240–3243, 3253, 3261.)

1 So in original.

2 So in original. Probably should be constituent.

3 So in original. Probably should be "of".

Cross References

Federally permitted release defined as including releases in compliance with legally enforceable final permit issued pursuant to this section, see section 9601 of this title.

Code of Federal Regulations

Federal waste permit program, see 40 CFR 270.1 et seq.
Requirements, see 40 CFR 122.1 et seq., 123.1 et seq., 264.1 et seq., 265.1 et seq., 267.1 et seq.
Underground injection control program, see 40 CFR 144.1 et seq., 145.1 et seq.

§ 6926. Authorized State hazardous waste programs

(a) Federal guidelines

Not later than eighteen months after October 21, 1976, the Administrator, after consultation with State authorities, shall promulgate guidelines to assist States in the Development of State hazardous waste programs.

(b) Authorization of State program

Any State which seeks to administer and enforce a hazardous waste program pursuant to this subchapter may develop and, after notice and opportunity for public hearing, submit to the Administrator an application, in such form as he shall require, for authorization of such program. Within ninety days following submission of an application under this subsection, the Administrator shall issue a notice as to whether or not he expects such program to be authorized, and within ninety days following such notice (and after opportunity for public hearing) he shall publish his findings as to whether or not the conditions listed in items (1), (2), and (3) below have been met. Such State is authorized to carry out such program in lieu of the Federal program under this subchapter in such State and to issue and enforce permits for the storage, treatment, or disposal of hazardous waste (and to enforce permits deemed to have been issued under section 6935(d)(1) of this title) unless, within ninety days following submission of the application the Administrator notifies such State that such program may not be authorized and, within ninety days following such notice and after opportunity for public hearing, he finds that (1) such State program is not equivalent to the Federal program under this subchapter, (2) such program is not consistent with the Federal or State programs applicable in other States, or (3) such program does not provide adequate enforcement of compliance with the requirements of this subchapter. In authorizing a State program, the Administrator may base his findings on the Federal program in effect one year prior to submission of a State's application or in effect on January 26, 1983, whichever is later.

(c) Interim authorization

(1) Any State which has in existence a hazardous waste program pursuant to State law before the date ninety days after the date of promulgation of regulations under sections 6922, 6923, 6924, and 6925 of this title, may submit to the Administrator evidence of such existing program and may request a temporary authorization to carry out such program under this subchapter. The Administrator shall, if the evidence submitted shows the existing State program to be substantially equivalent to the Federal program under this subchapter, grant an interim authorization to the State to carry out such program in lieu of the Federal program pursuant to this subchapter for a period ending no later than January 31, 1986.

(2) The Administrator shall, by rule, establish a date for the expiration of interim authorization under this subsection.

(3) Pending interim or final authorization of a State program for any State which reflects the amendments made by the Hazardous and Solid Waste Amendments of 1984, the State may enter into an agreement with the Administrator under which the State may assist in the administration of the requirements and prohibitions which take effect pursuant to such Amendments.

(4) In the case of a State permit program for any State which is authorized under subsection (b) of this section or under this subsection, until such program is amended to reflect the amendments made by the Hazardous and Solid Waste Amendments of 1984 and such program amendments receive interim or final authorization, the Administrator shall have the authority in such State to issue or deny permits or those portions of permits affected by the requirements and prohibitions established by the Hazardous and Solid Waste Amendments of 1984. The Administrator shall coordinate with States the procedures for issuing such permits.

(d) Effect of State permit

Any action taken by a State under a hazardous waste program authorized under this section shall have the same force and effect as action taken by the Administrator under this subchapter.

(e) Withdrawal of authorization

Whenever the Administrator determines after public hearing that a State is not administering and enforcing a program authorized under this section in accordance with requirements of this section, he shall so notify the State and, if appropriate corrective action is not taken within a reasonable time, not to exceed ninety days, the Administrator shall withdraw authorization of such program and establish a Federal program pursuant to this subchapter. The Administrator shall not withdraw authorization of any such program unless he shall first have notified the State, and made public, in writing, the reasons for such withdrawal.

(f) Availability of information

No State program may be authorized by the Administrator under this section unless—

(1) such program provides for the public availability of information obtained by the State regarding facilities and sites for the treatment, storage, and disposal of hazardous waste; and

(2) such information is available to the public in substantially the same manner, and to the same degree, as would be the case if the Administrator was carrying out the provisions of this subchapter in such State.

(g) Amendments made by 1984 act

(1) Any requirement or prohibition which is applicable to the generation, transportation, treatment, storage, or disposal of hazardous waste and which is imposed under this subchapter pursuant to the amendments made by the Hazardous and Solid Waste Amendments of 1984 shall take effect in each State having an interim or finally authorized State program on the same date as such requirement takes effect in other States. The administrator shall carry out such requirement directly in each such State unless the State program is finally authorized (or is granted interim authorization as provided in paragraph (2)) with respect to such requirement.

(2) Any State which, before November 8, 1984, has an existing hazardous waste program which has been granted interim or final authorization under this section may submit to the Administrator evidence that such existing program contains (or has been amended to include) any requirement which is substantially equivalent to a requirement referred to in paragraph (1) and may request interim authorization to carry out that requirement under this subchapter. The Administrator shall, if the evidence submitted shows the State requirement to be substantially equivalent to the requirement referred to in paragraph (1), grant an interim authorization to the State to carry out such requirement in lieu of direct administration in the State by the Administrator of such requirement.

(h) State programs for used oil

In the case of used oil which is not listed or identified under this subtitle as a hazardous waste but which is regulated under section 6935 of this title, the provisions of this section regarding State programs shall apply in the same manner and to the same extent as such provisions apply to hazardous waste identified or listed under this subtitle.

(Pub.L. 89–272, title II, § 3006, as added Oct. 21, 1976, Pub.L. 94–580, § 2, 90 Stat. 2809, and amended Nov. 8, 1978, Pub.L. 95–609, § 7(i), 92 Stat. 3082; Nov. 8, 1984, Pub.L. 98–616, title II, §§ 225, 226(a), 227, 228, 241(b)(2), 98 Stat. 3254, 3255, 3260; Oct. 17, 1986, Pub.L. 99–499, Title II, § 205(j), 100 Stat. 1703.)

Cross References

Transfer of liability becomes effective after owner or operator of hazardous waste disposal facility notifies Administrator of Environmental Protection Agency and State where it has authorized program under this section, see section 9607 of this title.

Code of Federal Regulations

State program requirements, see 40 CFR 123.1 et seq.
State program requirements, see 40 CFR 123.1 et seq., 271.1 et seq.

§ 6927. Inspections

(a) Access entry

For purposes of developing or assisting in the development of any regulation or enforcing the provisions of this chapter, any person who generates, stores, treats, transports, disposes of, or otherwise handles or has handled hazardous wastes shall, upon request of any officer, employee or representative of the Environmental Protection Agency, duly designated by the Administrator, or upon request of any duly designated officer, employee or representative of a State having an authorized hazardous waste program, furnish information relating to such wastes and permit such person at all reasonable times to have access to, and to copy all records relating to such wastes. For the purposes of developing or assisting in the development of any regulation or enforcing the provisions of this chapter, such officers, employees or representatives are authorized—

(1) to enter at reasonable times any establishment or other place where hazardous wastes are or have been generated, stored, treated, disposed of, or transported from;

(2) to inspect and obtain samples from any person of any such wastes and samples of any containers or labeling for such wastes.

Each such inspection shall be commenced and completed with reasonable promptness. If the officer, employee or representative obtains any samples, prior to leaving the premises, he shall give to the owner, operator, or agent in charge a receipt describing the sample obtained and if requested a portion of each such sample equal in volume or weight to the portion retained. If any analysis is made of such samples, a copy of the results of such analysis shall be furnished promptly to the owner, operator, or agent in charge.

(b) Availability to public

(1) Any records, reports, or information (including records, reports, or information obtained by representatives of the Environmental Protection Agency) obtained from any person under this section (including records, reports, or information obtained by representatives of the Environmental Protection Agency) shall be available to the public, except that upon a showing satisfactory to the Administrator (or the State, as the case may be) by any person that records, reports, or information, or particular part thereof, to which the Administrator (or the State, as the case may be) or any officer, employee or representative thereof has access under this section if made public, would divulge information entitled to protection under section 1905 of Title 18, such information or particular portion thereof shall be considered confidential in accordance with the purposes of that section, except that such record, report, document, or information may be disclosed to other officers, employees, or authorized representatives of the United States concerned with carrying out this chapter, or when relevant in any proceeding under this chapter.

(2) Any person not subject to the provisions of section 1905 of Title 18 who knowingly and willfully divulges or discloses any information entitled to protection under this subsection shall, upon conviction, be subject to a fine of not more than $5,000 or to imprisonment not to exceed one year, or both.

(3) In submitting data under this chapter, a person required to provide such data may—

(A) designate the data which such person believes is entitled to protection under this subsection, and

(B) submit such designated data separately from other data submitted under this chapter.

A designation under this paragraph shall be made in writing and in such manner as the Administrator may prescribe.

(4) Notwithstanding any limitation contained in this section or any other provision of law, all information reported to, or otherwise obtained by, the Administrator (or any representative of the Administrator) under this chapter shall be made available, upon written request of any duly authorized committee of the Congress, to such committee.

(c) Federal facility inspections

Beginning twelve months after November 8, 1984, the Administrator shall, or in the case of a State with an authorized hazardous waste program the State may, undertake on an annual basis a thorough inspection of each facility for the treatment, storage, or disposal of hazardous waste which is owned or operated by a Federal agency to enforce its compliance with this subchapter and the regulations promulgated thereunder. The records of such inspections shall be available to the public as provided in subsection (b) of this section.

(d) State-operated facilities

The Administrator shall annually undertake a through inspection of every facility for the treatment, storage, or disposal of hazardous waste which is operated by a State or local government for which a permit is required under section 6925 of this title. The records of such inspection shall be available to the public as provided in subsection (b) of this section.

(e) Mandatory inspections

(1) The Administrator (or the State in the case of a State having an authorized hazardous waste program under this subchapter) shall commence a program to thoroughly inspect every facility for the treatment, storage, or disposal of hazardous waste for which a permit is required under section 6925 of this title no less often than every two years as to its compliance with this subchapter (and the regulations promulgated under this subchapter). Such inspections shall commence not later than twelve months after November 8, 1984. The Administrator shall, after notice and opportunity for public comment, promulgate regulations governing the minimum frequency and manner of such inspections, including the manner in which records of such inspections shall be maintained and the manner in which reports of such inspections shall be filed. The Administrator may distinguish between classes and categories of facilities commensurate with the risks posed by each class or category.

(2) Not later than six months after November 8, 1984, the Administrator shall submit to the Congress a report on the potential for inspections of hazardous waste treatment, storage, or disposal facilities by nongovernmental inspectors as a supplement to inspections conducted by officers, employees, or representatives of the Environmental Protection Agency or States having authorized hazardous waste programs or operating under a cooperative agreement with the Administrator. Such report shall be prepared in cooperation with the States, insurance companies offering environmental impairment insurance, independent companies providing inspection services, and other such groups as appropriate. Such report shall contain recommendations on provisions and requirements for a program of private inspections to supplement governmental inspections.

(Pub.L. 89–272, title II, § 3007, as added Oct. 21, 1976, Pub.L. 94–580, § 2, 90 Stat. 2810, and amended Nov. 8, 1978, Pub.L. 95–609, § 7(j), 92 Stat. 3082; Oct. 21, 1980, Pub.L. 96–482, § 12, 94 Stat. 2339; Nov. 8, 1984, Pub.L. 98–616, title II, §§ 229–231, title V, § 502(a), 98 Stat. 3255, 3256, 3276.)

Cross References

Guidelines for using the imminent hazard, enforcement, and emergency response authorities to include powers authorized by this section, see section 9606 of this title.

Code of Federal Regulations

Definitions, additional requirements, see 40 CFR 122.1 et seq.
Hazardous waste management generally, see 40 CFR 260.1 et seq. to 271.1 et seq.
Hazardous waste treatment facilities, standards for owners and operators, see 40 CFR 264.1 et seq., 265.1 et seq.
Public information, see 40 CFR 2.1 et seq.
State program requirements, see 40 CFR 123.1 et seq.

§ 6928. Federal enforcement

(a) Compliance orders

(1) Except as provided in paragraph (2), whenever on the basis of any information the Administrator determines that any person has violated or is in violation of any requirement of this subchapter, the Administrator may issue an order assessing a civil penalty for any past or current violation, requiring compliance immediately or within a specified time period, or both, or the Administrator may commence a civil action in the United States district court in the district in which the violation occurred for appropriate relief, including a temporary or permanent injunction.

(2) In the case of a violation of any requirement of this subchapter where such violation occurs in a State which is authorized to carry out a hazardous waste program under section 6926 of this title, the Administrator shall give notice to the State in which such violation has occurred prior to issuing an order or commencing a civil action under this section.

(3) Any order issued pursuant to this subsection may include a suspension or revocation of any permit issued by the Administrator or a State under this subchapter and shall state with reasonable specificity the nature of the violation. Any penalty assessed in the order shall not exceed $25,000 per day of noncompliance for each violation of a requirement of this subchapter. In assessing such a penalty, the Administrator shall take into account the seriousness of the violation and any good faith efforts to comply with applicable requirements.

(b) Public hearing

Any order issued under this section shall become final unless, no later than thirty days after the order is served, the person or persons named therein request a public hearing. Upon such request the Administrator shall promptly conduct a public hearing. In connection with any proceeding under this section the Administrator may issue subpenas for the attendance and testimony of witnesses and the production of relevant papers, books, and documents, and may promulgate rules for discovery procedures.

(c) Violation of compliance orders

If a violator fails to take corrective action within the time specified in a compliance order, the Administrator may assess a civil penalty of not more than $25,000 for each day of continued noncompliance with the order and the Administrator may suspend or revoke any permit issued to the violator (whether issued by the Administrator or the State).

(d) Criminal penalties

Any person who—

(1) knowingly transports or causes to be transported any hazardous waste identified or listed under this subchapter to a facility which does not have a permit under this subchapter or pursuant to title I of the Marine Protection, Research, and Sanctuaries Act (86 Stat. 1052) [33 U.S.C.A. § 1411 et seq.],

(2) knowingly treats, stores, or disposes of any hazardous waste identified or listed under this subchapter—

(A) without a permit under this subchapter or pursuant to title I of the Marine Protection, Research, and Sanctuaries Act (86 Stat. 1052) [33 U.S.C.A § 1411 et seq.]; or

(B) in knowing violation of any material condition or requirement of such permit;

(C) in knowing violation of any material condition or requirement of any applicable interim status regulations or standards;

(3) knowingly omits material information or makes any false material statement or representation in any application, label, manifest, record, report, permit, or other document filed, maintained, or used for purposes of compliance with regulations promulgated by the Administrator (or by a State in the case of an authorized State program) under this subchapter;

(4) knowingly generates, stores, treats, transports, disposes of, exports, or otherwise handles any hazardous waste or any used oil not identified or listed as a hazardous waste under this subchapter (whether such activity took place before or takes place after the date of the enactment of this paragraph) and who knowingly destroys, alters, conceals, or fails to file any record, application, manifest, report, or other document required to be maintained or filed for purposes of compliance with regulations promulgated by the Administrator (or by a State in the case of an authorized State program) under this subchapter;

(5) knowingly transports without a manifest, or causes to be transported without a manifest, any hazardous waste or any used oil not identified or listed as a hazardous waste under this subchapter required by regulations promulgated under this subchapter (or by a State in the case of a State program authorized under this subchapter) to be accompanied by a manifest;

(6) knowingly exports a hazardous waste identified or listed under this subchapter (A) without the consent of the receiving country or, (B) where there exists an international agreement between the United States and the government of the receiving country establishing notice, export, and enforcement procedures for the transportation, treatment, storage, and disposal of hazardous wastes, in a manner which is not in conformance with such agreement; or

(7) knowingly stores, treats, transports, or causes to be transported, disposes of, or otherwise handles any used oil not identified or listed as a hazardous waste under this subchapter—

(A) in knowing violation of any material condition or requirement of a permit under this subchapter; or

(B) in knowing violation of any material condition or requirement of any applicable regulations or standards under this chapter;

shall, upon conviction, be subject to a fine of not more than $50,000 for each day of violation, or imprisonment not to exceed two years (five years in the case of a violation of paragraph (1) or (2)), or both. If the conviction is for a violation committed after a first conviction of such person under this paragraph, the maximum punishment under the respective paragraph shall be doubled with respect to both fine and imprisonment.

(e) Knowing endangerment

Any person who knowingly transports, treats, stores, disposes of, or exports any hazardous waste identified or listed under this subchapter or used oil not identified or listed as a hazardous waste under this subchapter in violation of paragraph (1), (2), (3), (4), (5), (6), or (7) of subsection (d) of this section who knows at that time that he thereby places another person in imminent danger of death or serious bodily injury, shall, upon conviction, be subject to a fine of not more than $250,000 or imprisonment for not more than fifteen years, or both. A defendant that is an organization shall, upon conviction of violating this subsection, be subject to a fine of not more than $1,000,000.

(f) Special rules

For the purposes of subsection (e) of this section—

(1) A person's state of mind is knowing with respect to—

(A) his conduct, if he is aware of the nature of his conduct;

(B) an existing circumstance, if he is aware or believes that the circumstance exists; or

(C) a result of his conduct, if he is aware or believes that his conduct is substantially certain to cause danger of death or serious bodily injury.

(2) In determining whether a defendant who is a natural person knew that his conduct placed another person in imminent danger of death or serious bodily injury—

(A) the person is responsible only for actual awareness or actual belief that he possessed; and

(B) knowledge possessed by a person other than the defendant but not by the defendant himself may not be attributed to the defendant;

Provided, That in proving the defendant's possession of actual knowledge, circumstantial evidence may be used, including evidence that the defendant took affirmative steps to shield himself from relevant information.

(3) It is an affirmative defense to a prosecution that the conduct charged was consented to by the person endangered and that the danger and conduct charged were reasonably foreseeable hazards of—

(A) an occupation, a business, or a profession; or

(B) medical treatment or medical or scientific experimentation conducted by professionally approved methods and such other person had been made aware of the risks involved prior to giving consent.

The defendant may establish an affirmative defense under this subsection by a preponderance of the evidence.

(4) All general defenses, affirmative defenses, and bars to prosecution that may apply with respect to other Federal criminal offenses may apply under subsection (e) of this section and shall be determined by the courts of the United States according to the principles of common law as they may be interpreted in the light of reason and experience. Concepts of justification and excuse applicable under this section may be developed in the light of reason and experience.

(5) The term "organization" means a legal entity, other than a government, established or organized for any purpose, and such term includes a corporation, company, association, firm, partnership, joint stock company, foundation, institution, trust, society, union, or any other association of persons.

(6) The term "serious bodily injury" means—

(A) bodily injury which involves a substantial risk of death;

(B) unconsciousness;

(C) extreme physical pain;

(D) protracted and obvious disfigurement; or

(E) protracted loss or impairment of the function of a bodily member, organ, or mental faculty.

(g) Civil penalty

Any person who violates any requirement of this subchapter shall be liable to the United States for a civil penalty in an amount not to exceed $25,000 for each such violation. Each day of such violation shall, for purposes of this subsection, constitute a separate violation.

(h) Interim status corrective action

(1) Whenever on the basis of any information the Administrator determines that there is or has been a release of hazardous waste into the environment from a facility authorized to operate under section 6925(e) of this title, the Administrator may issue an order requiring corrective action or such other response measure as he deems necessary to protect human health or the environment or the Administrator may commence a civil action in the United States district court in the district in which the facility is located for appropriate relief, including a temporary or permanent injunction.

(2) Any order issued under this subsection may include a suspension or revocation of authorization to operate under section 6925(e) of this title, shall state with reasonable specificity the nature of the required corrective action or other response measure, and shall specify a time for compliance. If any person named in an order fails to comply with the order, the Administrator may assess, and such person shall be liable to the United States for, a civil penalty in an amount not to exceed $25,000 for each day of noncompliance with the order.

(Pub.L. 89–272, title II, § 3008, as added Oct. 21, 1976, Pub.L. 94–580, § 2, 90 Stat. 2811, and amended Nov. 8, 1978, Pub.L. 95–609, § 7(k), 92 Stat. 3082; Oct. 21, 1980, Pub.L. 96–482, § 13, 94 Stat. 2339; Nov. 8, 1984, Pub.L. 98–616, title II, §§ 232, 233, 245(c), title IV, § 403(d)(1)–(3), 98 Stat. 3256, 3257, 3264, 3272; Oct. 17, 1986, Pub.L. 99–499, Title II, § 205(i), 100 Stat. 1703.)

Cross References

Guidelines for using the imminent hazard, enforcement, and emergency response authorities to include powers authorized by this section, see section 9606 of this title.

Code of Federal Regulations

Debarment and suspension, see 40 CFR, 32.100 et seq.
Permits, rules concerning revocation and suspension of, see 40 CFR 22.01 et seq.

§ 6929. Retention of State authority

Upon the effective date of regulations under this subchapter no State or political subdivision may impose any requirements less stringent than those authorized under this subchapter respecting the same matter as governed by such regulations, except that if application of a regulation with respect to any matter under this subchapter is postponed or enjoined by the action of any court, no State or political subdivision shall be prohibited from acting with respect to the same aspect of such matter until such time as such regulation takes effect. Nothing in this chapter shall be construed to prohibit any State or political subdivision thereof from imposing any requirements, including those for site selection, which are more stringent than those imposed by such regulations. Nothing in this chapter (or in any regulation adopted under this chapter) shall be construed to prohibit any State from requiring that the State be provided with a copy of each manifest used in connection with hazardous waste which is generated within that State or transported to a treatment, storage, or disposal facility within that State.

(Pub.L. 89–272, title II, § 3009, as added Oct. 21, 1976, Pub.L. 94–580, § 2, 90 Stat. 2812, and amended Oct. 21, 1980, Pub.L. 96–482, § 14, 94 Stat. 2342; Nov. 8, 1984, Pub.L. 98–616, title II, § 213(b), 98 Stat. 3242.)

United States Supreme Court

Preemption, validity of state control prohibiting importation of solid or liquid waste, see City of Philadelphia v. New Jersey, 1978, 98 S.Ct. 2531, 437 U.S. 617, 57 L.Ed.2d 475.

§ 6930. Effective date

(a) Preliminary notification

Not later than ninety days after promulgation of regulations under section 6921 of this title identifying by its characteristics or listing any substance as hazardous waste subject to this subchapter, any person generating or transporting such substance or owning or operating a facility for treatment, storage, or disposal of such substance shall file with the Administrator (or with States having authorized hazardous waste permit programs under section 6926 of this title) a notification stating the location and general description of such activity and the identified or listed hazardous wastes handled by such person. Not later than fifteen months after November 8, 1984—

(1) the owner or operator of any facility which produces a fuel (A) from any hazardous waste identified or listed under section 6921 of this title, (B) from such hazardous waste identified or listed under section 6921 of this title and any other material, (C) from used oil, or (D) from used oil and any other material;

(2) the owner or operator of any facility (other than a single- or two-family residence) which burns for purposes of energy recovery any fuel produced as provided in paragraph (1) or any fuel which otherwise contains used oil or any hazardous waste identified or listed under section 6921 of this title; and

(3) any person who distributes or markets any fuel which is produced as provided in paragraph (1) or any fuel which otherwise contains used oil or any hazardous waste identified or listed under section 6921 of this title

shall file with the Administrator (and with the State in the case of a State with an authorized hazardous waste program) a notification stating the location and general description of the facility, together with a description of the identified or listed hazardous waste involved and, in the case of a facility referred to in paragraph (1) or (2), a description of the production or energy recovery activity carried out at the facility and such other information as the Administrator deems necessary. For purposes of the preceding sentence, the term "hazardous waste listed under section 6921 of this title" also includes any commercial chemical product which is listed under section 6921 of this title and which, in lieu of its original intended use, is (i) produced for use as (or as a component of) a fuel, (ii) distributed for use as a fuel, or (iii) burned as a fuel. Notification shall not be required under the second sentence of this subsection in the case of facilities (such as residential boilers) where the Administrator determines that such notification is not necessary in order for the Administrator to obtain sufficient information respecting current practices of facilities using hazardous waste for energy recovery. Nothing in this subsection shall be construed to affect or impair the provisions of section 6921(b)(3) of this title. Nothing in this subsection shall affect regulatory determinations under section 6935 of this title. In revising any regulation under section 6921 of this title identifying additional characteristics of hazardous waste or listing any additional substance as hazardous waste subject to this subchapter, the Administrator may require any person referred to in the preceding provisions to file with the Administrator (or with States having authorized hazardous waste permit programs under section 6926 of this title) the notification described in the preceding provisions. Not more than one such notification shall be required to be filed with respect to the same substance. No identified or listed hazardous waste subject to this subchapter may be transported, treated, stored, or disposed of unless notification has been given as required under this subsection.

(b) Effective date of regulation

The regulations under this subchapter respecting requirements applicable to the generation, transportation, treatment, storage, or disposal of hazardous waste (including requirements respecting permits for such treatment, storage, or disposal) shall take effect on the date six months after the date of promulgation thereof (or six months after the date of revision in the case of any regulation which is revised after the date required for promulgation thereof). At the time a regulation is promulgated, the Administrator may provide for a shorter period prior to the effective date, or an immediate effective date for:

(1) a regulation with which the Administrator finds the regulated community does not need six months to come into compliance;

(2) a regulation which responds to an emergency situation; or

(3) other good cause found and published with the regulation.

(Pub.L. 89–272, title II, § 3010, as added Oct. 21, 1976, Pub.L. 94–580, § 2, 90 Stat. 2812, and amended Oct. 21, 1980, Pub.L. 96–482, § 15, 94 Stat. 2342; Nov. 8, 1984, Pub.L. 98–616, title II, §§ 204(a), 234, 98 Stat. 3235, 3258.)

Code of Federal Regulations

Hazardous waste management, see 40 CFR 260.1 et seq.

§ 6931. Authorization of assistance to States

(a) Authorization of appropriations

There is authorized to be appropriated $25,000,000 for each of the fiscal years 1978 and 1979 [1] $20,000,000 for fiscal year 1980, $35,000,000 for fiscal year 1981, $40,000,000 for the fiscal year 1982, $55,000,000 for the fiscal year 1985, $60,000,000 for the fiscal year 1986, $60,000,000 for the fiscal year 1987, and $60,000,000 for the fiscal year 1988 to be used to make grants to the States for purposes of assisting the States in the development and implementation of authorized State hazardous waste programs.

(b) Allocation

Amounts authorized to be appropriated under subsection (a) of this section shall be allocated among the States on the basis of regulations promulgated by the Administrator, after consultation with the States, which take into account, the extent to which hazardous waste is generated, transported, treated, stored, and disposed of within such State, the extent of exposure of human beings and the environment within such State to such waste, and such other factors as the Administrator deems appropriate.

(c) Activities included

State hazardous waste programs for which grants may be made under subsection (a) of this section may include (but shall not be limited to) planning for hazardous waste treatment, storage and disposal facilities, and the development and execution of programs to protect health and the environment from inactive facilities which may contain hazardous waste.

(Pub.L. 89–272, title II, § 3011, as added Oct. 21, 1976, Pub.L. 94–580, § 2, 90 Stat. 2812, and amended Oct. 21, 1980, Pub.L. 96–482, §§ 16, 31(b), 94 Stat. 2342, 2352; Nov. 8, 1984, Pub.L. 98–616, § 2(b), 98 Stat. 3222.)

[1] So in original. A comma is probably needed.

Code of Federal Regulations

State and local assistance, see 40 CFR 35.001 et seq.

§ 6932. Transferred

§ 6933. Hazardous waste site inventory

(a) State inventory programs

Each State shall, as expeditiously as practicable, undertake a continuing program to compile, publish, and submit to the Administrator an inventory describing the location of each site within such State at which hazardous waste has at any time been stored or disposed of. Such inventory shall contain—

(1) a description of the location of the sites at which any such storage or disposal has taken place before the date on which permits are required under section 6925 of this title for such storage or disposal;

(2) such information relating to the amount, nature, and toxicity of the hazardous waste at each such site as may be practicable to obtain and as may be necessary to determine the extent of any health hazard which may be associated with such site;

(3) the name and address, or corporate headquarters of, the owner of each such site, determined as of the date of preparation of the inventory;

(4) an identification of the types or techniques of waste treatment or disposal which have been used at each such site; and

(5) information concerning the current status of the site, including information respecting whether or not hazardous waste is currently being treated or disposed of at such site (and if not, the date on which such activity ceased) and information respecting the nature of any other activity currently carried out at such site.

For purposes of assisting the States in compiling information under this section, the Administrator shall make available to each State undertaking a program under this section such information as is available to him concerning the items specified in paragraphs (1) through (5) with respect to the sites within such State, including such information as the Administrator is able to obtain from other agencies or departments of the United States and from surveys and studies carried out by any committee or subcommittee of the Congress. Any State may exercise the authority of section 6927 of this title for purposes of this section in the same manner and to the same extent as provided in such section in the case of States having an authorized hazardous waste program, and any State may by order require any person to submit such information as may be necessary to compile the data referred to in paragraphs (1) through (5).

(b) Environmental Protection Agency program

If the Administrator determines that any State program under subsection (a) of this section is not adequately providing information respecting the sites in such State referred to in subsection (a) of this section, the Administrator shall notify the State. If within ninety days following such notification, the State program has not been revised or amended in such manner as will adequately provide such information, the Administrator shall carry out the inventory program in such State. In any such case—

(1) the Administrator shall have the authorities provided with respect to State programs under subsection (a) of this section;

(2) the funds allocated under subsection (c) of this section for grants to States under this section may be used by the Administrator for carrying out such program in such State; and

(3) no further expenditure may be made for grants to such State under this section until such time as the Administrator determines that such State is carrying out, or will carry out, an inventory program which meets the requirements of this section.

(c) Grants

(1) Upon receipt of an application submitted by any State to carry out a program under this section, the Administrator may make grants to the States for purposes of carrying out such a program. Grants under this section shall be allocated among the several States by the Administrator based upon such regulations as he prescribes to carry out the purposes of this section. The Administrator may make grants to any State which has conducted an inventory program which effectively carried out the purposes of this section before October 21, 1980, to reimburse such State for all, or any portion of, the costs incurred by such State in conducting such program.

(2) There are authorized to be appropriated to carry out this section $25,000,000 for each of the fiscal years 1985 through 1988.

(d) No impediment to immediate remedial action

Nothing in this section shall be construed to provide that the Administrator or any State should, pending completion of the inventory required under this section, postpone undertaking any enforcement or remedial action with respect to any site at which hazardous waste has been treated, stored, or disposed of.

(Pub.L. 89–272, Title II, § 3012, as added Oct. 21, 1980, Pub.L. 96–482, § 17(a), 94 Stat. 2342, and amended Nov. 8, 1984, Pub.L. 98–616, § 2(c), 98 Stat. 3222.)

§ 6934. Monitoring, analysis, and testing

(a) Authority of Administrator

If the Administrator determines, upon receipt of any information, that—

(1) the presence of any hazardous waste at a facility or site at which hazardous waste is, or has been, stored, treated, or disposed of, or

(2) the release of any such waste from such facility or site

may present a substantial hazard to human health or the environment, he may issue an order requiring the owner or operator of such facility or site to conduct such monitoring, testing, analysis, and reporting with respect to such facility or site as the

Administrator deems reasonable to ascertain the nature and extent of such hazard.

(b) Previous owners and operators

In the case of any facility or site not in operation at the time a determination is made under subsection (a) of this section with respect to the facility or site, if the Administrator finds that the owner of such facility or site could not reasonably be expected to have actual knowledge of the presence of hazardous waste at such facility or site and of its potential for release, he may issue an order requiring the most recent previous owner or operator of such facility or site who could reasonably be expected to have such actual knowledge to carry out the actions referred to in subsection (a) of this section.

(c) Proposal

An order under subsection (a) or (b) of this section shall require the person to whom such order is issued to submit to the Administrator within 30 days from the issuance of such order a proposal for carrying out the required monitoring, testing, analysis, and reporting. The Administrator may, after providing such person with an opportunity to confer with the Administrator respecting such proposal, require such person to carry out such monitoring, testing, analysis, and reporting in accordance with such proposal, and such modifications in such proposal as the Administrator deems reasonable to ascertain the nature and extent of the hazard.

(d) Monitoring, etc., carried out by Administrator

(1) If the Administrator determines that no owner or operator referred to in subsection (a) or (b) of this section is able to conduct monitoring, testing, analysis, or reporting satisfactory to the Administrator, if the Administrator deems any such action carried out by an owner or operator to be unsatisfactory, or if the Administrator cannot initially determine that there is an owner or operator referred to in subsection (a) or (b) of this section who is able to conduct such monitoring, testing, analysis, or reporting, he may—

(A) conduct monitoring, testing, or analysis (or any combination thereof) which he deems reasonable to ascertain the nature and extent of the hazard associated with the site concerned, or

(B) authorize a State or local authority or other person to carry out any such action,

and require, by order, the owner or operator referred to in subsection (a) or (b) of this section to reimburse the Administrator or other authority or person for the costs of such activity.

(2) No order may be issued under this subsection requiring reimbursement of the costs of any action carried out by the Administrator which confirms the results of an order issued under subsection (a) or (b) of this section.

(3) For purposes of carrying out this subsection, the Administrator or any authority or other person authorized under paragraph (1), may exercise the authorities set forth in section 6927 of this title.

(e) Enforcement

The Administrator may commence a civil action against any person who fails or refuses to comply with any order issued under this section. Such action shall be brought in the United States district court in which the defendant is located, resides, or is doing business. Such court shall have jurisdiction to require compliance with such order and to assess a civil penalty of not to exceed $5,000 for each day during which such failure or refusal occurs.

(Pub.L. 89–272, Title II, § 3013, as added Oct. 21, 1980, Pub.L. 96–482, § 17(a), 94 Stat. 2344.)

Cross References

Guidelines for using the imminent hazard, enforcement, and emergency response authorities to include powers authorized by this section, see section 9606 of this title.

§ 6935. Restrictions on recycled oil

(a) In general

Not later than one year after October 15, 1980, the Administrator shall promulgate regulations establishing such performance standards and other requirements as may be necessary to protect the public health and the environment from hazards associated with recycled oil. In developing such regulations, the Administrator shall conduct an analysis of the economic impact of the regulations on the oil recycling industry. The Administrator shall ensure that such regulations do not discourage the recovery or recycling of used oil, consistent with the protection of human health and the environment.

(b) Identification or listing of used oil as hazardous waste

Not later than twelve months after November 8, 1984, the Administrator shall propose whether to list or identify used automobile and truck crankcase oil as hazardous waste under section 6921 of this title. Not later than twenty-four months after November 8, 1984, the Administrator shall make a final determination whether to list or identify used automobile and truck crankcase oil and other used oil as hazardous wastes under section 6921 of this title.

(c) Used oil which is recycled

(1) With respect to generators and transporters of used oil identified or listed as a hazardous waste

under section 6921 of this title, the standards promulgated under section 6921(d), 6922, and 6923 of this title shall not apply to such used oil if such used oil is recycled.

(2)(A) In the case of used oil which is exempt under paragraph (1), not later than twenty-four months after November 8, 1984, the Administrator shall promulgate such standards under this subsection regarding the generation and transportation of used oil which is recycled as may be necessary to protect human health and the environment. In promulgating such regulations with respect to generators, the Administrator shall take into account the effect of such regulations on environmentally acceptable types of used oil recycling and the effect of such regulations on small quantity generators and generators which are small businesses (as defined by the Administrator).

(B) The regulations promulgated under this subsection shall provide that no generator of used oil which is exempt under paragraph (1) from the standards promulgated under section 6921(d), 6922, and 6923 of this title shall be subject to any manifest requirement or any associated recordkeeping and reporting requirement with respect to such used oil if such generator—

(i) either—

(I) enters into an agreement or other arrangement (including an agreement or arrangement with an independent transporter or with an agent of the recycler) for delivery of such used oil to a recycling facility which has a permit under section 6925(c) of this title (or for which a valid permit is deemed to be in effect under subsection (d) of this section), or

(II) recycles such used oil at one or more facilities of the generator which has such a permit under section 6925 of this title (or for which a valid permit is deemed to have been issued under subsection (d) of this section);

(ii) such used oil is not mixed by the generator with other types of hazardous wastes; and

(iii) the generator maintains such records relating to such used oil, including records of agreements or other arrangements for delivery of such used oil to any recycling facility referred to in clause (i)(I), as the Administrator deems necessary to protect human health and the environment.

(3) The regulations under this subsection regarding the transportation of used oil which is exempt from the standards promulgated under section 6921(d), 6922, and 6923 of this title under paragraph (1) shall require the transporters of such used oil to deliver such used oil to a facility which has a valid permit under section 6925 of this title or which is deemed to have a valid permit under subsection (d) of this section. The Administrator shall also establish other standards for such transporters as may be necessary to protect human health and the environment.

(d) Permits

(1) The owner or operator of a facility which recycles used oil which is exempt under subsection (c)(1) of this section, shall be deemed to have a permit under this subsection for all such treatment or recycling (and any associated tank or container storage) if such owner and operator comply with standards promulgated by the Administrator under section 6924 of this title; except that the Administrator may require such owners and operators to obtain an individual permit under section 6925(c) of this title if he determines that an individual permit is necessary to protect human health and the environment.

(2) Notwithstanding any other provision of law, any generator who recycles used oil which is exempt under subsection (c)(1) of this section shall not be required to obtain a permit under section 6925(c) of this title with respect to such used oil until the Administrator has promulgated standards under section 6924 of this title regarding the recycling of such used oil.

(Pub.L. 89–272, title II, § 3014, formerly § 3012, as added Oct. 15, 1980, Pub.L. 96–463, § 7(a), 94 Stat. 2057, renumbered and amended Nov. 8, 1984, Pub.L. 98–616, title II, §§ 241(a), 242, title V, § 502(g)(1), 98 Stat. 3258, 3260, 3277.)

§ 6936. Expansion during interim status

(a) Waste piles

The owner or operator of a waste pile qualifying for the authorization to operate under section 6925(e) of this title shall be subject to the same requirements for liners and leachate collection systems or equivalent protection provided in regulations promulgated by the Administrator under section 6924 of this title before October 1, 1982, or revised under section 6924(*o*) of this title (relating to minimum technological requirements), for new facilities receiving individual permits under subsection (c) of section 6925 of this title, with respect to each new unit, replacement of an existing unit, or lateral expansion of an existing unit that is within the waste management area identified in the permit application submitted under section 6925 of this title, and with respect to waste received beginning six months after November 8, 1984.

(b) Landfills and surface impoundments

(1) The owner or operator of a landfill or surface impoundment qualifying for the authorization to operate under section 6925(e) of this title shall be subject to the requirements of section 6924(*o*)of this title (relating to minimum technological requirements), with respect to each new unit, replacement of an existing unit, or lateral expansion of an existing unit that is within the waste management area identified in the permit application submitted under this section, and with respect to waste received beginning 6 months after November 8, 1984.

(2) The owner or operator of each unit referred to in paragraph (1) shall notify the Administrator (or the State, if appropriate) at least sixty days prior to receiving waste. The Administrator (or the State) shall require the filing, within six months of receipt of such notice, of an application for a final determination regarding the issuance of a permit for each facility submitting such notice.

(3) In the case of any unit in which the liner and leachate collection system has been installed pursuant to the requirements of this section and in good faith compliance with the Administrator's regulations and guidance documents governing liners and leachate collection systems, no liner or leachate collection system which is different from that which was so installed pursuant to this section shall be required for such unit by the Administrator when issuing the first permit under section 6925 of this title to such facility, except that the Administrator shall not be precluded from requiring installation of a new liner when the Administrator has reason to believe that any liner installed pursuant to the requirements of this section is leaking. The Administrator may, under section 6924 of this title, amend the requirements for liners and leachate collection systems required under this section as may be necessary to provide additional protection for human health and the environment.

(Pub.L. 89–272, title II, § 3015, as added Nov. 8, 1984, Pub.L. 98–616, title II, § 243(a), 98 Stat. 3260.)

§ 6937. Inventory of Federal agency hazardous waste facilities

(a) Program requirement; submission; availability; contents

Each Federal agency shall undertake a continuing program to compile, publish, and submit to the Administrator (and to the State in the case of sites in States having an authorized hazardous waste program) an inventory of each site which the Federal agency owns or operates or has owned or operated at which hazardous waste is stored, treated, or disposed of or has been disposed of at any time. The inventory shall be submitted every two years beginning January 31, 1986. Such inventory shall be available to the public as provided in section 6927(b) of this title. Information previously submitted by a Federal agency under section 9603 of this title or under section 6925 or 6930 of this title, or under this section need not be resubmitted except that the agency shall update any previous submission to reflect the latest available data and information. The inventory shall include each of the following:

(1) A description of the location of each site at which any such treatment, storage, or disposal has taken place before the date on which permits are required under section 6925 of this title for such storage, treatment, or disposal, and where hazardous waste has been disposed, a description of hydrogeology of the site and the location of withdrawal wells and surface water within one mile of the site.

(2) Such information relating to the amount, nature, and toxicity of the hazardous waste in each site as may be necessary to determine the extent of any health hazard which may be associated with any site.

(3) Information on the known nature and extent of environmental contamination at each site, including a description of the monitoring data obtained.

(4) Information concerning the current status of the site, including information respecting whether or not hazardous waste is currently being treated, stored, or disposed of at such site (and if not, the date on which such activity ceased) and information respecting the nature of any other activity currently carried out at such site.

(5) A list of sites at which hazardous waste has been disposed and environmental monitoring data has not been obtained, and the reasons for the lack of monitoring data at each site.

(6) A description of response actions undertaken or contemplated at contaminated sites.

(7) An identification of the types of techniques of waste treatment, storage, or disposal which have been used at each site.

(8) The name and address and responsible Federal agency for each site, determined as of the date of preparation of the inventory.

(b) Environmental Protection Agency program

If the Administrator determines that any Federal agency under subsection (a) of this section is not adequately providing information respecting the sites referred to in subsection (a) of this section, the Administrator shall notify the chief official of such agency. If within ninety days following such notification, the Federal agency has not undertaken a program to adequately provide such information, the Administrator shall carry out the inventory program for such agency.

(Pub.L. 89–272, title II, § 3016, as added Nov. 8, 1984, Pub.L. 98–616, title II, § 244, 98 Stat. 3261.)

§ 6938. Export of hazardous wastes

(a) In general

Beginning twenty-four months after November 8, 1984, no person shall export any hazardous waste identified or listed under this subchapter unless

(1)(A) such person has provided the notification required in subsection (c) of this section,

(B) the government of the receiving country has consented to accept such hazardous waste,

(C) a copy of the receiving country's written consent is attached to the manifest accompanying each waste shipment, and

(D) the shipment conforms with the terms of the consent of the government of the receiving country required pursuant to subsection (e) of this section or

(2) the United States and the government of the receiving country have entered into an agreement as provided for in subsection (f) of this section and the shipment conforms with the terms of such agreement.

(b) Regulations

Not later than twelve months after November 8, 1984, the Administrator shall promulgate the regulations necessary to implement this section. Such regulations shall become effective one hundred and eighty days after promulgation.

(c) Notification

Any person who intends to export a hazardous waste identified or listed under this subchapter beginning twelve months after November 8, 1984, shall, before such hazardous waste is scheduled to leave the United States, provide notification to the Administrator. Such notification shall contain the following information:

(1) the name and address of the exporter;

(2) the types and estimated quantities of hazardous waste to be exported;

(3) the estimated frequency or rate at which such waste is to be exported; and the period of time over which such waste is to be exported;

(4) the ports of entry;

(5) a description of the manner in which such hazardous waste will be transported to and treated, stored, or disposed in the receiving country; and

(6) the name and address of the ultimate treatment, storage or disposal facility.

(d) Procedures for requesting consent of the receiving country

Within thirty days of the Administrator's receipt of a complete notification under this section, the Secretary of State, acting on behalf of the Administrator, shall—

(1) forward a copy of the notification to the government of the receiving country;

(2) Advise the government that United States law prohibits the export of hazardous waste unless the receiving country consents to accept the hazardous waste;

(3) request the government to provide the Secretary with a written consent or objection to the terms of the notification; and

(4) forward to the government of the receiving country a description of the Federal regulations which would apply to the treatment, storage, and disposal of the hazardous waste in the United States.

(e) Conveyance of written consent to exporter

Within thirty days of receipt by the Secretary of State of the receiving country's written consent or objection (or any subsequent communication withdrawing a prior consent or objection), the Administrator shall forward such a consent, objection, or other communication to the exporter.

(f) International agreements

Where there exists an international agreement between the United States and the government of the receiving country establishing notice, export, and enforcement procedures for the transportation, treatment, storage, and disposal of hazardous wastes, only the requirements of subsections (a)(2) and (g) of this section shall apply.

(g) Reports

After November 8, 1984, any person who exports any hazardous waste identified or listed under section 6921 of this title shall file with the Administrator no later than March 1 of each year, a report summarizing the types, quantities, frequency, and ultimate destination of all such hazardous waste exported during the previous calendar year.

(h) Other standards

Nothing in this section shall preclude the Administrator from establishing other standards for the export of hazardous wastes under section 6922 or 6923 of this title.

(Pub.L. 89–272, title II, § 3017, as added Nov. 8, 1984, Pub.L. 98–616, title II, § 245(a), 98 Stat. 3262.)

§ 6939. Domestic sewage

(a) Report

The Administrator shall, not later than 15 months after November 8, 1984, submit a report to the Congress concerning those substances identified or listed under section 6921 of this title which are not regulated under this subchapter by reason of the exclusion for mixtures of domestic sewage and other wastes that pass through a sewer system to a publicly owned treatment works. Such report shall include the types, size and number of generators which dispose of such substances in this manner, the types and quantities disposed of in this manner, and the identification of significant generators, wastes, and waste constituents not regulated under existing Federal law or regulated in a manner sufficient to protect human health and the environment.

(b) Revisions of regulations

Within eighteen months after submitting the report specified in subsection (a) of this section, the Administrator shall revise existing regulations and promulgate such additional regulations pursuant to this subchapter (or any other authority of the Administrator, including section 1317 of title 33) as are necessary to assure that substances identified or listed under section 6921 of this title which pass through a sewer system to a publicly owned treatment works are adequately controlled to protect human health and the environment.

(c) Report on wastewater lagoon

The Administrator shall, within thirty-six months after November 8, 1984, submit a report to Congress concerning wastewater lagoons at publicly owned treatment works and their effect on groundwater quality. Such report shall include—

(1) the number and size of such lagoons;

(2) the types and quantities of waste contained in such lagoons;

(3) the extent to which such waste has been or may be released from such lagoons and contaminate ground water; and

(4) available alternatives for preventing or controlling such releases.

The Administrator may utilize the authority of sections 6927 and 6934 of this title for the purpose of completing such report.

(d) Application of sections 6927 and 6930

The provisions of sections 6927 and 6930 of this title shall apply to solid or dissolved materials in domestic sewage to the same extent and in the same manner as such provisions apply to hazardous waste.

(Pub.L. 89–272, title II, § 3018, as added Nov. 8, 1984, Pub.L. 98–616, title II, § 246(a), 98 Stat. 3264.)

§ 6939a. Exposure information and health assessments

(a) Exposure information

Beginning on the date nine months after November 8, 1984, each application for a final determination regarding a permit under section 6925(c) of this title for a landfill or surface impoundment shall be accompanied by information reasonably ascertainable by the owner or operator on the potential for the public to be exposed to hazardous wastes or hazardous constituents through releases related to the unit. At a minimum, such information must address:

(1) reasonably foreseeable potential releases from both normal operations and accidents at the unit, including releases associated with transportation to or from the unit;

(2) the potential pathways of human exposure to hazardous wastes or constituents resulting from the releases described under paragraph (1); and

(3) the potential magnitude and nature of the human exposure resulting from such releases.

The owner or operator of a landfill or surface impoundment for which an application for such a final determination under section 6925(c) of this title has been submitted prior to November 8, 1984, shall submit the information required by this subsection to the Administrator (or the State, in the case of a State with an authorized program) no later than the date nine months after November 8, 1984.

(b) Health assessments

(1) The Administrator (or the State, in the case of a State with an authorized program) shall make the information required by subsection (a) of this section, together with other relevant information, available to the Agency for Toxic Substances and Disease Registry established by section 9604(i) of this title.

(2) Whenever in the judgment of the Administrator, or the State (in the case of a State with an authorized program), a landfill or a surface impoundment poses a substantial potential risk to human health, due to the existence of releases of hazardous constituents, the magnitude of contamination with hazardous constituents which may be the result of a release, or the magnitude of the population exposed to such release or contamination, the Administrator or the State (with the concurrence of the Administrator) may request the

Administrator of the Agency for Toxic Substances and Disease Registry to conduct a health assessment in connection with such facility and take other appropriate action with respect to such risks as authorized by section 9604(b) and (i) of this title. If funds are provided in connection with such request the Administrator of such Agency shall conduct such health assessment.

(c) Members of the public

Any member of the public may submit evidence of releases of or exposure to hazardous constituents from such a facility, or as to the risks or health effects associated with such releases or exposure, to the Administrator of the Agency for Toxic Substances and Disease Registry, the Administrator, or the State (in the case of a State with an authorized program).

(d) Priority

In determining the order in which to conduct health assessments under this subsection, the Administrator of the Agency for Toxic Substances and Disease Registry shall give priority to those facilities or sites at which there is documented evidence of release of hazardous constituents, at which the potential risk to human health appears highest, and for which in the judgment of the Administrator of such Agency existing health assessment data is inadequate to assess the potential risk to human health as provided in subsection (f) of this section.

(e) Periodic reports

The Administrator of such Agency shall issue periodic reports which include the results of all the assessments carried out under this section. Such assessments or other activities shall be reported after appropriate peer review.

(f) Definition

For the purposes of this section, the term "health assessments" shall include preliminary assessments of the potential risk to human health posed by individual sites and facilities subject to this section, based on such factors as the nature and extent of contamination, the existence of potential for pathways of human exposure (including ground or surface water contamination, air emissions, and food chain contamination), the size and potential susceptibility of the community within the likely pathways of exposure, the comparison of expected human exposure levels to the short-term and long-term health effects associated with identified contaminants and any available recommended exposure or tolerance limits for such contaminants, and the comparison of existing morbidity and mortality data on diseases that may be associated with the observed levels of exposure. The assessment shall include an evaluation of the risks to the potentially affected population from all sources of such contaminants, including known point or nonpoint sources other than the site or facility in question. A purpose of such preliminary assessments shall be to help determine whether full-scale health or epidemiological studies and medical evaluations of exposed populations shall be undertaken.

(g) Cost recovery

In any case in which a health assessment performed under this section discloses the exposure of a population to the release of a hazardous substance, the costs of such health assessment may be recovered as a cost of response under section 9607 of this title from persons causing or contributing to such release of such hazardous substance or, in the case of multiple releases contributing to such exposure, to all such release.

(Pub.L. 89–272, title II, § 3019, as added Nov. 8, 1984, Pub.L. 98–616, title II, § 247(a), 98 Stat. 3265.)

§ 6939b. Interim control of hazardous waste injection

(a) Underground source of drinking water

No hazardous waste may be disposed of by underground injection—

(1) into a formation which contains (within one-quarter mile of the well used for such underground injection) an underground source of drinking water; or

(2) above such a formation.

The prohibitions established under this section shall take effect 6 months after November 8, 1984, except in the case of any State in which identical or more stringent prohibitions are in effect before such date under the Safe Drinking Water Act [42 U.S.C. 300f et seq.].

(b) Actions under Comprehensive Environmental Response, Compensation and Liability Act

Subsection (a) of this section shall not apply to the injection of contaminated ground water into the aquifer from which it was withdrawn, if—

(1) such injection is—

(A) a response action taken under section 104 [42 U.S.C. 9604] or 106 [42 U.S.C. 9606] of the Comprehensive Environmental Response, Compensation and Liability Act of 1980 [42 U.S.C. 9601 et seq.], or

(B) part of corrective action required under this chapter

intended to clean up such contamination;

(2) such contaminated ground water is treated to substantially reduce hazardous constituents prior to such injection; and

(3) such response action or corrective action will, upon completion, be sufficient to protect human health and the environment.

(c) Enforcement

In addition to enforcement under the provisions of this chapter, the prohibitions established under paragraphs (1) and (2) of subsection (a) of this section shall be enforceable under the Safe Drinking Water Act [42 U.S.C. 300f et seq.] in any State—

(1) which has adopted identical or more stringent prohibitions under part C of the Safe Drinking Water Act [42 U.S.C. 300h et seq.] and which has assumed primary enforcement responsibility under that Act [42 U.S.C. 300f et seq.] for enforcement of such prohibitions; or

(2) in which the Administrator has adopted identical or more stringent prohibitions under the Safe Drinking Water Act [42 U.S.C. 300f et seq.] and is exercising primary enforcement responsibility under that Act [42 U.S.C. 300f et seq.] for enforcement of such prohibitions.

(d) Definitions

The terms "primary enforcement responsibility", "underground source of drinking water", "formation" and "well" have the same meanings as provided in regulations of the Administrator under the Safe Drinking Water Act [42 U.S.C. 300f et seq.]. The term "Safe Drinking Water Act" means title XIV of the Public Health Service Act [42 U.S.C. 300f et seq.].

(Pub.L. 89–272, Title II, § 3020, formerly § 7010, as added Nov. 8, 1984, Pub.L. 98–616, Title IV, § 405(a), 98 Stat. 3273, and renumbered and amended June 19, 1986, Pub.L. 99–339, Title II, § 201(c), 100 Stat. 654.)

SUBCHAPTER IV—STATE OR REGIONAL SOLID WASTE PLANS

§ 6941. Objectives of subchapter

The objectives of this subchapter are to assist in developing and encouraging methods for the disposal of solid waste which are environmentally sound and which maximize the utilization of valuable resources including energy and materials which are recoverable from solid waste and to encourage resource conservation. Such objectives are to be accomplished through Federal technical and financial assistance to States or regional authorities for comprehensive planning pursuant to Federal guidelines designed to foster cooperation among Federal, State, and local governments and private industry. In developing such comprehensive plans, it is the intention of this chapter that in determining the size of the waste-to-energy facility, adequate provision shall be given to the present and reasonably anticipated future needs, including those needs created by thorough implementation of section 6962(h) of this title, of the recycling and resource recovery interest within the area encompassed by the planning process.

(Pub.L. 89–272, title II, § 4001, as added Oct. 21, 1976, Pub.L. 94–580, § 2, 90 Stat. 2813, and amended Oct. 21, 1980, Pub.L. 96–482, § 32(b), 94 Stat. 2353; Nov. 8, 1984, Pub.L. 98–616, title III, § 301(a), title V, § 501(f)(1), 98 Stat. 3267, 3276.)

§ 6941a. Energy and materials conservation and recovery; Congressional findings

The Congress finds that—

(1) significant savings could be realized by conserving materials in order to reduce the volume or quantity of material which ultimately becomes waste;

(2) solid waste contains valuable energy and material resources which can be recovered and used thereby conserving increasingly scarce and expensive fossil fuels and virgin materials;

(3) the recovery of energy and materials from municipal waste, and the conservation of energy and materials contributing to such waste streams, can have the effect of reducing the volume of the municipal waste stream and the burden of disposing of increasing volumes of solid waste;

(4) the technology to conserve resources exists and is commercially feasible to apply;

(5) the technology to recover energy and materials from solid waste is of demonstrated commercial feasibility; and

(6) various communities throughout the nation have different needs and different potentials for conserving resources and for utilizing techniques for the recovery of energy and materials from waste, and Federal assistance in planning and implementing such energy and materials conservation and recovery programs should be available to all such communities on an equitable basis in relation to their needs and potential.

(Oct. 21, 1980, Pub.L. 96–482, § 32(a), 94 Stat. 2353.)

§ 6942. Federal guidelines for plans

(a) Guidelines for identification of regions

For purposes of encouraging and facilitating the development of regional planning for solid waste management, the Administrator, within one hundred and eighty days after October 21, 1976, and after consultation with appropriate Federal, State, and local authorities, shall by regulation publish guidelines for the identification of those areas which have common solid waste management problems and are appropriate units for planning regional solid waste management services. Such guidelines shall consider—

(1) the size and location of areas which should be included,

(2) the volume of solid waste which should be included, and

(3) the available means of coordinating regional planning with other related regional planning and for coordination of such regional planning into the State plan.

(b) Guidelines for State plans

Not later than eighteen months after October 21, 1976, and after notice and hearing, the Administrator shall, after consultation with appropriate Federal, State, and local authorities, promulgate regulations containing guidelines to assist in the development and implementation of State solid waste management plans (hereinafter in this chapter referred to as "State plans"). The guidelines shall contain methods for achieving the objectives specified in section 6941 of this title. Such guidelines shall be reviewed from time to time, but not less frequently than every three years, and revised as may be appropriate.

(c) Considerations for State plan guidelines

The guidelines promulgated under subsection (b) of this section shall consider—

(1) the varying regional, geologic, hydrologic, climatic, and other circumstances under which different solid waste practices are required in order to insure the reasonable protection of the quality of the ground and surface waters from leachate contamination, the reasonable protection of the quality of the surface waters from surface runoff contamination, and the reasonable protection of ambient air quality;

(2) characteristics and conditions of collection, storage, processing, and disposal operating methods, techniques and practices, and location of facilities where such operating methods, techniques, and practices are conducted, taking into account the nature of the material to be disposed;

(3) methods for closing or upgrading open dumps for purposes of eliminating potential health hazards;

(4) population density, distribution, and projected growth;

(5) geographic, geologic, climatic, and hydrologic characteristics;

(6) the type and location of transportation;

(7) the profile of industries;

(8) the constituents and generation rates of waste;

(9) the political, economic, organizational, financial, and management problems affecting comprehensive solid waste management;

(10) types of resource recovery facilities and resource conservation systems which are appropriate; and

(11) available new and additional markets for recovered material and energy and energy resources recovered from solid waste as well as methods for conserving such materials and energy.

(Pub.L. 89–272, title II, § 4002, as added Oct. 21, 1976, Pub.L. 94–580, § 2, 90 Stat. 2813, and amended Oct. 21, 1980, Pub.L. 96–482, § 32(c), 94 Stat. 2353.)

Code of Federal Regulations

Guidelines, see 40 CFR 256.01 et seq.

§ 6943. Requirements for approval of plans

(a) Minimum requirements

In order to be approved under section 6947 of this title, each State plan must comply with the following minimum requirements—

(1) The plan shall identify (in accordance with section 6946(b) of this title) (A) the responsibilities of State, local, and regional authorities in the implementation of the State plan, (B) the distribution of Federal funds to the authorities responsible for development and implementation of the State plan, and (C) the means for coordinating regional planning and implementation under the State plan.

(2) The plan shall, in accordance with sections 6944(b) and 6945(a) of this title, prohibit the establishment of new open dumps within the State, and contain requirements that all solid waste (including solid waste originating in other States, but not including hazardous waste) shall be (A) utilized for resource recovery or (B) disposed of in sanitary landfills (within the meaning of section 6944(a) of this title) or otherwise disposed of in an environmentally sound manner.

(3) The plan shall provide for the closing or upgrading of all existing open dumps within the State pursuant to the requirements of section 6945 of this title.

(4) The plan shall provide for the establishment of such State regulatory powers as may be necessary to implement the plan.

(5) The plan shall provide that no State or local government within the State shall be prohibited under State or local law from negotiating and entering into long-term contracts for the supply of solid waste to resource recovery facilities, from entering into long-term contracts for the operation of such facilities, or from securing long-term markets for material and energy recovered from such facilities or for conserving materials or energy by reducing the volume of waste.

(6) The plan shall provide for such resource conservation or recovery and for the disposal of solid waste in sanitary landfills or any combination of practices so as may be necessary to use or dispose of such waste in a manner that is environmentally sound.

(b) Discretionary plan provisions relating to recycled oil

Any State plan submitted under this subchapter may include, at the option of the State, provisions to carry out each of the following:

(1) Encouragement, to the maximum extent feasible and consistent with the protection of the public health and the environment, of the use of recycled oil in all appropriate areas of State and local government.

(2) Encouragement of persons contracting with the State to use recycled oil to the maximum extent feasible, consistent with protection of the public health and the environment.

(3) Informing the public of the uses of recycled oil.

(4) Establishment and implementation of a program (including any necessary licensing of persons and including the use, where appropriate, of manifests) to assure that used oil is collected, transported, treated, stored, reused, and disposed of, in a manner which does not present a hazard to the public health or the environment.

Any plan submitted under this chapter before October 15, 1980, may be amended, at the option of the State, at any time after such date to include any provision referred to in this subsection.

(c) Energy and materials conservation and recovery feasibility planning and assistance

(1) A State which has a plan approved under this subchapter or which has submitted a plan for such approval shall be eligible for assistance under section 6948(a)(3) of this title if the Administrator determines that under such plan the State will—

(A) analyze and determine the economic and technical feasibility of facilities and programs to conserve resources which contribute to the waste stream or to recover energy and materials from municipal waste;

(B) analyze the legal, institutional, and economic impediments to the development of systems and facilities for conservation of energy or materials which contribute to the waste stream or for the recovery of energy and materials from municipal waste and make recommendations to appropriate governmental authorities for overcoming such impediments;

(C) assist municipalities within the State in developing plans, programs, and projects to conserve resources or recover energy and materials from municipal waste; and

(D) coordinate the resource conservation and recovery planning under subparagraph (C).

(2) The analysis referred to in paragraph (1)(A) shall include—

(A) the evaluation of, and establishment of priorities among, market opportunities for industrial and commercial users of all types (including public utilities and industrial parks) to utilize energy and materials recovered from municipal waste;

(B) comparisons of the relative costs of energy recovered from municipal waste in relation to the costs of energy derived from fossil fuels and other sources;

(C) studies of the transportation and storage problems and other problems associated with the development of energy and materials recovery technology, including curbside source separation;

(D) the evaluation and establishment of priorities among ways of conserving energy or materials which contribute to the waste stream;

(E) comparison of the relative total costs between conserving resources and disposing of or recovering such waste; and

(F) studies of impediments to resource conservation or recovery, including business practices, transportation requirements, or storage difficulties.

Such studies and analyses shall also include studies of other sources of solid waste from which energy and materials may be recovered or minimized.

(d) Size of waste-to-energy facilities

Notwithstanding any of the above requirements, it is the intention of this chapter and the planning process developed pursuant to this chapter that in determining the size of the waste-to-energy facility, adequate provision shall be given to the present and reasonably anticipated future needs of the recycling and resource recovery interest within the area encompassed by the planning process.

(Pub.L. 89–272, title II, § 4003, as added Oct. 21, 1976, Pub.L. 94–580, § 2, 90 Stat. 2814, and amended Oct. 15, 1980, Pub.L. 96–463, § 5(a), (b), 94 Stat. 2056; Oct. 21, 1980, Pub.L. 96–482, §§ 18, 32(d), 94 Stat. 2345, 2353; Nov. 8, 1984, Pub.L. 98–616, title III, § 301(b), title V, § 502(h), 98 Stat. 3267, 3277.)

§ 6944. Criteria for sanitary landfills; sanitary landfills required for all disposal

(a) Criteria for sanitary landfills

Not later than one year after October 21, 1976, after consultation with the States, and after notice and public hearings, the Administrator shall promulgate regulations containing criteria for determining which facilities shall be classified as sanitary landfills and which shall be classified as open dumps within the meaning of this chapter. At a minimum, such criteria shall provide that a facility may be classified as a sanitary landfill and not an open dump only if there is no reasonable probability of adverse effects on health or the environment from disposal of solid waste at such facility. Such regulations may provide for the classification of the types of sanitary landfills.

(b) Disposal required to be in sanitary landfills, etc.

For purposes of complying with section 6943(2) of this title each State plan shall prohibit the establishment of open dumps and contain a requirement that disposal of all solid waste within the State shall be in compliance with such section 6943(2) of this title.

(c) Effective date

The prohibition contained in subsection (b) of this section shall take effect on the date six months after the date of promulgation of regulations under subsection (a) of this section.

(Pub.L. 89–272, title II, § 4004, as added Oct. 21, 1976, Pub.L. 94–580, § 2, 90 Stat. 2815, and amended Nov. 8, 1984, Pub.L. 98–616, Title III, § 302(b), 98 Stat. 3268.)

Code of Federal Regulations

Solid waste disposal facilities and practices, criteria for classification of, see 40 CFR 257.1 et seq.

§ 6945. Upgrading of open dumps

(a) Closing or upgrading of existing open dumps

Upon promulgation of criteria under section 6907(a)(3) of this title, any solid waste management practice or disposal of solid waste or hazardous waste which constitutes the open dumping of solid waste or hazardous waste is prohibited, except in the case of any practice or disposal of solid waste under a timetable or schedule for compliance established under this section. The prohibition contained in the preceding sentence shall be enforceable under section 6972 of this title against persons engaged in the act of open dumping. For purposes of complying with section 6943(a)(2) and 6943(a)(3) of this title, each State plan shall contain a requirement that all existing disposal facilities or sites for solid waste in such State which are open dumps listed in the inventory under subsection (b) of this section shall comply with such measures as may be promulgated by the Administrator to eliminate health hazards and minimize potential health hazards. Each such plan shall establish, for any entity which demonstrates that it has considered other public or private alternatives for solid waste management to comply with the prohibition on open dumping and is unable to utilize such alternatives to so comply, a timetable or schedule for compliance for such practice or disposal of solid waste which specifies a schedule of remedial measures, including an enforceable sequence of actions or operations, leading to compliance with the prohibition on open dumping of solid waste within a reasonable time (not to exceed 5 years from the date of publication of criteria under section 6907(a)(3) of this title).

(b) Inventory

To assist the States in complying with section 6943(a)(3) of this title, not later than one year after promulgation of regulations under section 6944 of this title, the Administrator, with the cooperation of the Bureau of the Census shall publish an inventory of all disposal facilities or sites in the United States which are open dumps within the meaning of this chapter.

(c) Control of hazardous disposal

(1)(A) Not later than 36 months after November 8, 1984, each State shall adopt and implement a permit program or other system of prior approval and conditions to assure that each solid waste management facility within such State which may receive hazardous household waste or hazardous waste due to the provision of section 6921(d) of this title for small quantity generators (otherwise not subject to the requirement for a permit under section 6925 of this title) will comply with the applicable criteria promulgated under section 6944(a) and 6907(a)(3) of this title.

(B) Not later than eighteen months after the promulgation of revised criteria under section 6944(a) of this title (as required by section 6949a(c) of this title), each State shall adopt and implement a permit program or other system or [1] prior approval and conditions, to assure that each solid waste management facility within such State which may receive hazardous household waste or hazardous waste due to the provision of section 6921(d) of this title for small quantity generators (otherwise not subject to the requirement for a permit under section 6925 of this title) will comply with the criteria revised under section 6944(a) of this title.

(C) The Administrator shall determine whether each State has developed an adequate program under this paragraph. The Administrator may make such a determination in conjunction with approval, disapproval or partial approval of a State plan under section 6947 of this title.

(2)(A) In any State that the Administrator determines has not adopted an adequate program for such facilities under paragraph (1)(B) by the date provided in such paragraph, the Administrator may use the authorities available under sections 6927 and 6928 of this title to enforce the prohibition contained in subsection (a) of this section with respect of such facilities.

(B) For purposes of this paragraph, the term "requirement of this subchapter" in section 6928 of this title shall be deemed to include criteria promulgated by the Administrator under sections 6907(a)(3) and 6944(a) of this title, and the term "hazardous wastes" in section 6927 of this title shall be deemed to include solid waste at facilities that may handle hazardous household wastes or hazardous wastes from small quantity generators.

(Pub.L. 89–272, title II, § 4005, as added Oct. 21, 1976, Pub.L. 94–580, § 2, 90 Stat. 2815, and amended Oct. 21, 1980, Pub.L. 96–482, § 19(a), (b), 94 Stat. 2345; Nov. 8, 1984, Pub.L. 98–616, title III, § 302(c), title IV, § 403(c), title V, § 502(c), 98 Stat. 3268, 3272, 3276.)

[1] So in original. Probably should be "of".

§ 6946. Procedure for development and implementation of State plan

(a) Identification of regions

Within one hundred and eighty days after publication of guidelines under section 6942(a) of this title (relating to identification of regions), the Governor of each State, after consultation with local elected officials, shall promulgate regulations based on such guidelines identifying the boundaries of each area within the State which, as a result of urban concentrations, geographic conditions, markets, and other factors, is appropriate for carrying out regional solid waste management. Such regulations may be modified from time to time (identifying additional or different regions) pursuant to such guidelines.

(b) Identification of State and local agencies and responsibilities

(1) Within one hundred and eighty days after the Governor promulgates regulations under subsection (a) of this section, for purposes of facilitating the development and implementation of a State plan which will meet the minimum requirements of section 6943 of this title, the State, together with appropriate elected officials of general purpose units of local government, shall jointly (A) identify an agency to develop the State plan and identify one or more agencies to implement such plan, and (B) identify which solid waste management activities will, under such State plan, be planned for and carried out by the State and which such management activities will, under such State plan, be planned for and carried out by a regional or local authority or a combination of regional or local and State authorities. If a multi-functional regional agency authorized by State law to conduct solid waste planning and management (the members of which are appointed by the Governor) is in existence on October 21, 1976, the Governor shall identify such authority for purposes of carrying out within such region clause (A) of this paragraph. Where feasible, designation of the agency for the affected area designated under section 1288 of Title 33 shall be considered. A State agency identified under this paragraph shall be established or designated by the Governor of such State. Local or regional agencies identified under this paragraph shall be composed of individuals at least a majority of whom are elected local officials.

(2) If planning and implementation agencies are not identified and designated or established as required under paragraph (1) for any affected area, the governor shall, before the date two hundred and seventy days after promulgation of regulations under subsection (a) of this section, establish or designate a State agency to develop and implement the State plan for such area.

(c) Interstate regions

(1) In the case of any region which, pursuant to the guidelines published by the Administrator under section 6942(a) of this title (relating to identification of regions), would be located in two or more States, the Governors of the respective States, after consultation with local elected officials, shall consult, cooperate, and enter into agreements identifying the boundaries of such region pursuant to subsection (a) of this section.

(2) Within one hundred and eighty days after an interstate region is identified by agreement under paragraph (1), appropriate elected officials of general purpose units of local government within such region shall jointly establish or designate an agency to develop a plan for such region. If no such agency is established or designated within such period by such officials, the Governors of the respective States may, by agreement, establish or designate for such purpose a single representative organization including elected officials of general purpose units of local government within such region.

(3) Implementation of interstate regional solid waste management plans shall be conducted by units of local government for any portion of a region within their jurisdiction, or by multijurisdictional agencies or authorities designated in accordance with State law, including those designated by agreement by such units of local government for such purpose. If no such unit, agency, or authority is so designated, the respective Governors shall designate or establish a single interstate agency to implement such plan.

(4) For purposes of this subchapter, so much of an interstate regional plan as is carried out within a particular State shall be deemed part of the State plan for such State.

(Pub.L. 89–272, title II, § 4006, as added Oct. 21, 1976, Pub.L. 94–580, § 2, 90 Stat. 2816, and amended Oct. 21, 1980, Pub.L. 96–482, § 19(b), 94 Stat. 2345.)

Code of Federal Regulations

Regions and agencies for solid waste management, identification of, see 40 CFR 255.1 et seq.

United States Supreme Court

State regulation or control, nonhazardous solid waste, see City of Philadelphia v. New Jersey, 1978, 98 S.Ct. 2531, 437 U.S. 617, 57 L.Ed.2d 475.

§ 6947. Approval of State plan; Federal assistance

(a) Plan approval

The Administrator shall, within six months after a State plan has been submitted for approval, approve or disapprove the plan. The Administrator shall approve a plan if he determines that—

(1) it meets the requirements of paragraphs (1), (2), (3), and (5) of section 6943 of this title; and

(2) it contains provision for revision of such plan, after notice and public hearing, whenever the Administrator, by regulation, determines—

(A) that revised regulations respecting minimum requirements have been promulgated under paragraphs (1), (2), (3), and (5) of section 6943 of this title with which the State plan is not in compliance;

(B) that information has become available which demonstrates the inadequacy of the plan to effectuate the purposes of this subchapter; or

(C) that such revision is otherwise necessary.

The Administrator shall review approved plans from time to time and if he determines that revision or corrections are necessary to bring such plan into compliance with the minimum requirements promulgated under section 6943 of this title (including new or revised requirements), he shall, after notice and opportunity for public hearing, withdraw his approval of such plan. Such withdrawal of approval shall cease to be effective upon the Administrator's determination that such complies with such minimum requirements.

(b) Eligibility of States for Federal financial assistance

(1) The Administrator shall approve a State application for financial assistance under this subchapter, and make grants to such State, if such State and local and regional authorities within such State have complied with the requirements of section 6946 of this title within the period required under such section and if such State has a State plan which has been approved by the Administrator under this subchapter.

(2) The Administrator shall approve a State application for financial assistance under this subchapter, and make grants to such State, for fiscal years 1978 and 1979 if the Administrator determines that the State plan continues to be eligible for approval under subsection (a) of this section and is being implemented by the State.

(3) Upon withdrawal of approval of a State plan under subsection (a) of this section, the Administrator shall withhold Federal financial and technical assistance under this subchapter (other than such technical assistance as may be necessary to assist in obtaining the reinstatement of approval) until such time as such approval is reinstated.

(c) Existing activities

Nothing in this subchapter shall be construed to prevent or affect any activities respecting solid waste planning or management which are carried out by State, regional, or local authorities unless such activities are inconsistent with a State plan approved by the Administrator under this subchapter.

(Pub.L. 89–272, title II, § 4007, as added Oct. 21, 1976, Pub.L. 94–580, § 2, 90 Stat. 2817, and amended Nov. 8, 1978, Pub.L. 95–609, § 7(*l*), 92 Stat. 3082.)

§ 6948. Federal assistance

(a) Authorization of Federal financial assistance

(1) There are authorized to be appropriated $30,000,000 for fiscal year 1978, $40,000,000 for fiscal year 1979, $20,000,000 for fiscal year 1980, $15,000,000 for fiscal year 1981, $20,000,000 for the fiscal year 1982, and $10,000,000 for each of the fiscal years 1985 through 1988 for purposes of financial assistance to States and local, regional, and interstate authorities for the development and implementation of plans approved by the Administrator under this subchapter (other than the provisions of such plans referred to in section 6943(b) of

this title, relating to feasibility planning for municipal waste energy and materials conservation and recovery).

(2)(A) The Administrator is authorized to provide financial assistance to States, counties, municipalities, and intermunicipal agencies and State and local public solid waste management authorities for implementation of programs to provide solid waste management, resource recovery, and resource conservation services and hazardous waste management. Such assistance shall include assistance for facility planning and feasibility studies; expert consultation; surveys and analyses of market needs; marketing of recovered resources; technology assessments; legal expenses; construction feasibility studies; source separation projects; and fiscal or economic investigations or studies; but such assistance shall not include any other element of construction, or any acquisition of land or interest in land, or any subsidy for the price of recovered resources. Agencies assisted under this subsection shall consider existing solid waste management and hazardous waste management services and facilities as well as facilities proposed for construction.

(B) An applicant for financial assistance under this paragraph must agree to comply with respect to the project or program assisted with the applicable requirements of section 6945 of this title and subchapter III of this chapter and apply applicable solid waste management practices, methods, and levels of control consistent with any guidelines published pursuant to section 6907 of this title. Assistance under this paragraph shall be available only for programs certified by the State to be consistent with any applicable State or areawide solid waste management plan or program. Applicants for technical and financial assistance under this section shall not preclude or foreclose consideration of programs for the recovery of recyclable materials through source separation or other resource recovery techniques.

(C) There are authorized to be appropriated $15,000,000 for each of the fiscal years 1978 and 1979 for purposes of this section. There are authorized to be appropriated $10,000,000 for fiscal year 1980, $10,000,000 for fiscal year 1981, $10,000,000 for fiscal year 1982, and $10,000,000 for each of the fiscal years 1985 through 1988 for purposes of this paragraph.

(D) There are authorized—

(i) to be made available $15,000,000 out of funds appropriated for fiscal year 1985, and

(ii) to be appropriated for each of the fiscal years 1986 though[1] 1988, $20,000,000

for grants to States (and where appropriate to regional, local, and interstate agencies) to implement programs requiring compliance by solid waste management facilities with the criteria promulgated under section 6944(a) of this title and section 6907(a)(3) of this title and with the provisions of section 6945 of this title. To the extent practicable, such programs shall require such compliance not later than thirty-six months after November 8, 1984.

(3)(A) There is authorized to be appropriated for the fiscal year beginning October 1, 1981, and for each fiscal year thereafter before October 1, 1986, $4,000,000 for purposes of making grants to States to carry out section 6943(b) of this title. No amount may be appropriated for such purposes for the fiscal year beginning on October 1, 1986, or for any fiscal year thereafter.

(B) Assistance provided by the Administrator under this paragraph shall be used only for the purposes specified in section 6943(b) of this title. Such assistance may not be used for purposes of land acquisition, final facility design, equipment purchase, construction, startup or operation activities.

(C) Where appropriate, any State receiving assistance under this paragraph may make all or any part of such assistance available to municipalities within the State to carry out the activities specified in section 6943(b)(1)(A) and (B) of this title.

(b) State allotment

The sums appropriated in any fiscal year under subsection (a)(1) of this section shall be allotted by the Administrator among all States, in the ratio that the population in each State bears to the population in all of the States, except that no State shall receive less than one-half of 1 per centum of the sums so allotted in any fiscal year. No State shall receive any grant under this section during any fiscal year when its expenditures of non-Federal funds for other than non-recurrent expenditures for solid waste management control programs will be less than its expenditures were for such programs during fiscal year 1975, except that such funds may be reduced by an amount equal to their proportionate share of any general reduction of State spending ordered by the Governor or legislature of such State. No State shall receive any grant for solid waste management programs unless the Administrator is satisfied that such grant will be so used as to supplement and, to the extent practicable, increase the level of State, local, regional, or other non-Federal funds that would in the absence of such grant be made available for the maintenance of such programs.

(c) Distribution of Federal financial assistance within the State

The Federal assistance allotted to the States under subsection (b) of this section shall be allocated by the State receiving such funds to State, local, regional, and interstate authorities carrying out planning and implementation of the State plan. Such allocation shall be based upon the responsibilities of the respective parties as determined pursuant to section 6946(b) of this title.

(d) Technical assistance

(1) The Administrator may provide technical assistance to State and local governments for purposes of developing and implementing State plans. Technical assistance respecting resource recovery and conservation may be provided through resource recovery and conservation panels, established in the Environmental Protection Agency under subchapter II of this chapter, to assist the State and local governments with respect to particular resource recovery and conservation projects under consideration and to evaluate their effect on the State plan.

(2) In carrying out this subsection, the Administrator may, upon request, provide technical assistance to States to assist in the removal or modification of legal, institutional, economic, and other impediments to the recycling of used oil. Such impediments may include laws, regulations, and policies, including State procurement policies, which are not favorable to the recycling of used oil.

(3) In carrying out this subsection, the Administrator is authorized to provide technical assistance to States, municipalities, regional authorities, and intermunicipal agencies upon request, to assist in the removal or modification of legal, institutional, and economic impediments which have the effect of impeding the development of systems and facilities to recover energy and materials from municipal waste or to conserve energy or materials which contribute to the waste stream. Such impediments may include—

(A) laws, regulations, and policies, including State and local procurement policies, which are not favorable to resource conservation and recovery policies, systems, and facilities;

(B) impediments to the financing of facilities to conserve or recover energy and materials from municipal waste through the exercise of State and local authority to issue revenue bonds and the use of State and local credit assistance; and

(C) impediments to institutional arrangements necessary to undertake projects for the conservation or recovery of energy and materials from municipal waste, including the creation of special districts, authorities, or corporations where necessary having the power to secure the supply of waste of a project, to conserve resources, to implement the project, and to undertake related activities.

(e) Special communities

(1) The Administrator, in cooperation with State and local officials, shall identify local governments within the United States (A) having a solid waste disposal facility (i) which is owned by the unit of local government, (ii) for which an order has been issued by the State to cease receiving solid waste for treatment, storage, or disposal, and (iii) which is subject to a State-approved end-use recreation plan, and (B) which are located over an aquifer which is the source of drinking water for any person or public water system and which has serious environmental problems resulting from the disposal of such solid waste, including possible methane migration.

(2) There is authorized to be appropriated to the Administrator $2,500,000 for the fiscal year 1980 and $1,500,000 for each of the fiscal years 1981 and 1982 to make grants to be used for containment and stabilization of solid waste located at the disposal sites referred to in paragraph (1). Not more than one community in any State shall be eligible for grants under this paragraph and not more than one project in any State shall be eligible for such grants. No unit of local government shall be eligible for grants under this paragraph with respect to any site which exceeds 65 acres in size.

(f) Assistance to States for discretionary program for recycled oil

(1) The Administrator may make grants to States, which have a State plan approved under section 6947 of this title, or which have submitted a State plan for approval under such section, if such plan includes the discretionary provisions described in section 6943(b) of this title. Grants under this subsection shall be for purposes of assisting the State in carrying out such discretionary provisions. No grant under this subsection may be used for construction or for the acquisition of land or equipment.

(2) Grants under this subsection shall be allotted among the States in the same manner as provided in the first sentence of subsection (b) of this section.

(3) No grant may be made under this subsection unless an application therefor is submitted to, and approved by, the Administrator. The application shall be in such form, be submitted in such manner, and contain such information as the Administrator may require.

(4) For purposes of making grants under this subsection, there are authorized to be appropriated $5,000,000 for fiscal year 1982, $5,000,000 for fiscal year 1983, and $5,000,000 for each of the fiscal years 1985 through 1988.

(g) Assistance to municipalities for energy and materials conservation and recovery planning activities

(1) The Administrator is authorized to make grants to municipalities, regional authorities, and intermunicipal agencies to carry out activities described in subparagraphs (A) and (B) of section 6943(b)(1) of this title. Such grants may be made only pursuant to an application submitted to the Administrator by the municipality which application has been approved by the State and determined by the State to be consistent with any State plan approved or submitted under this subchapter or any other appropriate planning carried out by the State.

(2) There is authorized to be appropriated for the fiscal year beginning October 1, 1981, and for each fiscal year thereafter before October 1, 1986, $8,000,000 for purposes of making grants to municipalities under this subsection. No amount may be appropriated for such purposes for the fiscal year beginning on October 1, 1986, or for any fiscal year thereafter.

(3) Assistance provided by the Administrator under this subsection shall be used only for the purposes specified in paragraph (1). Such assistance may not be used for purposes of land acquisition, final facility design, equipment purchase, construction, startup or operation activities.

(Pub.L. 89–272, title II, § 4008, as added Oct. 21, 1976, Pub.L. 94–580, § 2, 90 Stat. 2818, and amended Oct. 15, 1980, Pub.L. 96–463, §§ 5(b), 6, 94 Stat. 2057; Oct. 21, 1980, Pub.L. 96–482, §§ 20, 31(c), (d), 32(e), (f), 94 Stat. 2345, 2352, 2354, 2355; Nov. 8, 1984, Pub.L. 98–616, § 2(d)–(g), (k), title V, § 502(d), (e), 98 Stat. 3222, 3223, 3276.)

1 So in original. Probably should be through.

Library References

United States ⚷82(3).
C.J.S. United States § 122.

§ 6949. Rural communities assistance

(a) In general

The Administrator shall make grants to States to provide assistance to municipalities with a population of five thousand or less, or counties with a population of ten thousand or less or less than twenty persons per square mile and not within a metropolitan area, for solid waste management facilities (including equipment) necessary to meet the requirements of section 6945 of this title or restrictions on open burning or other requirements arising under the Clean Air Act [42 U.S.C. 7401 et seq.] or the Federal Water Pollution Control Act [33 U.S.C. 1251 et seq.]. Such assistance shall only be available—

(1) to any municipality or county which could not feasibly be included in a solid waste management system or facility serving an urbanized, multijurisdictional area because of its distance from such systems;

(2) where existing or planned solid waste management services or facilities are unavailable or insufficient to comply with the requirements of section 6945 of this title; and

(3) for systems which are certified by the State to be consistent with any plans or programs established under any State or areawide planning process.

(b) Allotment

The Administrator shall allot the sums appropriated to carry out this section in any fiscal year among the States in accordance with regulations promulgated by him on the basis of the average of the ratio which the population of rural areas of each State bears to the total population of rural areas of all the States, the ratio which the population of counties in each State having less than twenty persons per square mile bears to the total population of such counties in all the States, and the ratio which the population of such low-density counties in each State having 33 per centum or more of all families with incomes not in excess of 125 per centum of the poverty level bears to the total population of such counties in all the States.

(c) Limit

The amount of any grant under this section shall not exceed 75 per centum of the costs of the project. No assistance under this section shall be available for the acquisition of land or interests in land.

(d) Authorization of appropriations

There are authorized to be appropriated $25,000,000 for each of the fiscal years 1978 and 1979 to carry out this section. There are authorized to be appropriated $10,000,000 for the fiscal year 1980 and $15,000,000 for each of the fiscal years 1981 and 1982 to carry out this section.

(Pub.L. 89–272, title II, § 4009, as added Oct. 21, 1976, Pub.L. 94–580, § 2, 90 Stat. 2819, and amended Pub.L. 96–482, § 31(e), Oct. 21, 1980, 94 Stat. 2353.)

Code of Federal Regulations

State and local assistance, see 40 CFR 35.001 et seq.

Library References

United States ⚷82(3).
C.J.S. United States § 122.

§ 6949a. Adequacy of certain guidelines and criteria

(a) Study

The Administrator shall conduct a study of the extent to which the guidelines and criteria under this chapter (other than guidelines and criteria for facilities to which subchapter III of this chapter applies) which are applicable to solid waste management and disposal facilities, including, but not limited to landfills and surface impoundments, are adequate to protect human health and the environment from ground water contamination. Such study shall include a detailed assessment of the degree to which the criteria under section 6907(a) of this title and the criteria under section 6944 of this title regarding monitoring, prevention of contamination, and remedial action are adequate to protect ground water and shall also include recommendation with respect to any additional enforcement authorities which the Administrator, in consultation with the Attorney General, deems necessary for such purposes.

(b) Report

Not later than thirty-six months after November 8, 1984, the Administrator shall submit a report to the Congress setting forth the results of the study required under this section, together with any recommendations made by the Administrator on the basis of such study.

(c) Revisions of guidelines and criteria

Not later than March 31, 1988, the Administrator shall promulgate revisions of the criteria promulgated under paragraph (1) of section 6944(a) of this title and under section 6907(a)(3) of this title for facilities that may receive hazardous household wastes or hazardous wastes from small quantity generators under section 6921(d) of this title. The criteria shall be those necessary to protect human health and the environment and may take into account the practicable capability of such facilities. At a minimum such revisions for facilities potentially receiving such wastes should require ground water monitoring as necessary to detect contamination, establish criteria for the acceptable location of new or existing facilities, and provide for corrective action as appropriate.

(Pub.L. 89–272, title II, § 4010, as added Nov. 8, 1984, Pub.L. 98–616, title III, § 302(a)(1), 98 Stat. 3267.)

SUBCHAPTER V—DUTIES OF THE SECRETARY OF COMMERCE IN RESOURCE AND RECOVERY

§ 6951. Functions

The Secretary of Commerce shall encourage greater commercialization of proven resource recovery technology by providing—

(1) accurate specifications for recovered materials;

(2) stimulation of development of markets for recovered materials;

(3) promotion of proven technology; and

(4) a forum for the exchange of technical and economic data relating to resource recovery facilities.

(Pub.L. 89–272, title II, § 5001, as added Oct. 21, 1976, Pub.L. 94–580, § 2, 90 Stat. 2820.)

§ 6952. Development of specifications for secondary materials

The Secretary of Commerce, acting through the National Bureau of Standards, and in conjunction with national standards-setting organizations in resource recovery, shall, after public hearings, and not later than two years after September 1, 1979, publish guidelines for the development of specifications for the classification of materials recovered from waste which were destined for disposal. The specifications shall pertain to the physical and chemical properties and characteristics of such materials with regard to their use in replacing virgin materials in various industrial, commercial, and governmental uses. In establishing such guidelines the Secretary shall also, to the extent feasible, provide such information as may be necessary to assist Federal agencies with procurement of items containing recovered materials. The Secretary shall continue to cooperate with national standards-setting organizations, as may be necessary, to encourage the publication, promulgation and updating of standards for recovered materials and for the use of recovered materials in various industrial, commercial, and governmental uses.

(Pub.L. 89–272, title II, § 5002, as added Oct. 21, 1976, Pub.L. 94–580, § 2, 90 Stat. 2820, and amended Oct. 21, 1980, Pub.L. 96–482, § 21(a), 94 Stat. 2346.)

§ 6953. Development of markets for recovered materials

The Secretary of Commerce shall within two years after September 1, 1979, take such actions as may be necessary to—

(1) identify the geographical location of existing or potential markets for recovered materials;

(2) identify the economic and technical barriers to the use of recovered materials; and

(3) encourage the development of new uses for recovered materials.

(Pub.L. 89–272, title II, § 5003, as added Oct. 21, 1976, Pub.L. 94–580, § 2, 90 Stat. 2821, and amended Oct. 21, 1980, Pub.L. 96–482, § 21(b), 94 Stat. 2346.)

§ 6954. Technology promotion

The Secretary of Commerce is authorized to evaluate the commercial feasibility of resource recovery facilities and to publish the results of such evaluation, and to develop a data base for purposes of assisting persons in choosing such a system.

(Pub.L. 89–272, title II, § 5004, as added Oct. 21, 1976, Pub.L. 94–580, § 2, 90 Stat. 2821.)

§ 6955. Marketing policies, establishment; nondiscrimination requirement

In establishing any policies which may affect the development of new markets for recovered materials and in making any determination concerning whether or not to impose monitoring or other controls on any marketing or transfer of recovered materials, the Secretary of Commerce may consider whether to establish the same or similar policies or impose the same or similar monitoring or other controls on virgin materials.

(Pub.L. 89–272, Title II, § 5005, as added Oct. 21, 1980, Pub.L. 96–482, § 21(c)(1), 94 Stat. 2346.)

§ 6956. Authorization of appropriations

There are authorized to be appropriated to the Secretary of Commerce $5,000,000 for each of fiscal years 1980, 1981, and 1982 and $1,500,000 for each of the fiscal years 1985 through 1988 to carry out the purposes of this subchapter.

(Pub.L. 89–272, Title II, § 5006, as added Oct. 21, 1980, Pub.L. 96–482, § 31(f)(1), 94 Stat. 2353, and amended Nov. 8, 1984, Pub.L. 98–616, § 2(h), 98 Stat. 3223.)

SUBCHAPTER VI—FEDERAL RESPONSIBILITIES

§ 6961. Application of Federal, State, and local law to Federal facilities

Each department, agency, and instrumentality of the executive, legislative, and judicial branches of the Federal Government (1) having jurisdiction over any solid waste management facility or disposal site, or (2) engaged in any activity resulting, or which may result, in the disposal or management of solid waste or hazardous waste shall be subject to, and comply with, all Federal, State, interstate, and local requirements, both substantive and procedural (including any requirement for permits or reporting or any provisions for injunctive relief and such sanctions as may be imposed by a court to enforce such relief), respecting control and abatement of solid waste or hazardous waste disposal in the same manner, and to the same extent, as any person is subject to such requirements, including the payment of reasonable service charges. Neither the United States, nor any agent, employee, or officer thereof, shall be immune or exempt from any process or sanction of any State or Federal Court with respect to the enforcement of any such injunctive relief. The President may exempt any solid waste management facility of any department, agency, or instrumentality in the executive branch from compliance with such a requirement if he determines it to be in the paramount interest of the United States to do so. No such exemption shall be granted due to lack of appropriation unless the President shall have specifically requested such appropriation as a part of the budgetary process and the Congress shall have failed to make available such requested appropriation. Any exemption shall be for a period not in excess of one year, but additional exemptions may be granted for periods not to exceed one year upon the President's making a new determination. The President shall report each January to the Congress all exemptions from the requirements of this section granted during the preceding calendar year, together with his reason for granting each such exemption.

(Pub.L. 89–272, title II, § 6001, as added Oct. 21, 1976, Pub.L. 94–580, § 2, 90 Stat. 2821, and amended Nov. 8, 1978, Pub.L. 95–609, § 7(m), 92 Stat. 3082.)

Code of Federal Regulations

Federal facilities and Native American Reservations, inclusion of, see 40 CFR 255.33 et seq.

§ 6962. Federal procurement

(a) Application of section

Except as provided in subsection (b) of this section, a procuring agency shall comply with the requirements set forth in this section and any regulations issued under this section, with respect to any purchase or acquisition of a procurement item where the purchase price of the item exceeds $10,000 or where the quantity of such items or of functionally equivalent items purchased or acquired in the course of the preceding fiscal year was $10,000 or more.

(b) Procurement subject to other law

Any procurement, by any procuring agency, which is subject to regulations of the Administrator under section 6964 of this title (as promulgated before October 21, 1976, under comparable provisions of prior law) shall not be subject to the requirements of this section to the extent that such requirements are inconsistent with such regulations.

(c) Requirements

(1) After the date specified in applicable guidelines prepared pursuant to subsection (e) of this section, each procuring agency which procures any

items designated in such guidelines shall procure such items composed of the highest percentage of recovered materials practicable (and in the case of paper, the highest percentage of the postconsumer recovered materials referred to in subsection (h)(1) of this section practicable), consistent with maintaining a satisfactory level of competition, considering such guidelines. The decision not to procure such items shall be based on a determination that such procurement items—

(A) are not reasonably available within a reasonable period of time;

(B) fail to meet the performance standards set forth in the applicable specifications or fail to meet the reasonable performance standards of the procuring agencies; or

(C) are only available at an unreasonable price. Any determination under subparagraph (B) shall be made on the basis of the guidelines of the Bureau of Standards in any case in which such material is covered by such guidelines.

(2) Agencies that generate heat, mechanical, or electrical energy from fossil fuel in systems that have the technical capability of using energy or fuels derived from solid waste as a primary or supplementary fuel shall use such capability to the maximum extent practicable.

(3) After the date specified in any applicable guidelines prepared pursuant to subsection (e) of this section, contracting officers shall require that vendors:

(A) certify that the percentage of recovered materials to be used in the performance of the contract will be at least the amount required by applicable specifications or other contractual requirements, and

(B) estimate the percentage of the total material utilized for the performance of the contract which is recovered materials.

(d) Specifications

All Federal agencies that have the responsibility for drafting or reviewing specifications for procurement items procured by Federal agencies shall—

(1) as expeditiously as possible but in any event no later than eighteen months after November 8, 1984, eliminate from such specifications—

(A) any exclusion of recovered materials and

(B) any requirement that items be manufactured from virgin materials; and

(2) within one year after the date of publication of applicable guidelines under subsection (e) of this section, or as otherwise specified in such guidelines, assure that such specifications require the use of recovered materials to the maximum extent possible without jeopardizing the intended end use of the item.

(e) Guidelines

The Administrator, after consultation with the Administrator of General Services, the Secretary of Commerce (acting through the Bureau of Standards), and the Public Printer, shall prepare, and from time to time revise, guidelines for the use of procuring agencies in complying with the requirements of this section. Such guidelines shall—

(1) designate those items which are or can be produced with recovered materials and whose procurement by procuring agencies will carry out the objectives of this section, and in the case of paper, provide for maximizing the use of post consumer recovered materials referred to in subsection (h)(1) of this section;

(2) set forth recommended practices with respect to the procurement of recovered materials and items containing such materials and with respect to certification by vendors of the percentage of recovered materials used,

and shall provide information as to the availability, relative price, and performance of such materials and items and where appropriate shall recommend the level of recovered material to be contained in the procured product. The Administrator shall prepare final guidelines for paper within one hundred and eighty days after November 8, 1984, and for three additional product categories (including tires) by October 1, 1985. In making the designation under paragraph (1), the Administrator shall consider, but is not limited in his considerations, to—

(A) the availability of such items;

(B) the impact of the procurement of such items by procuring agencies on the volume of solid waste which must be treated, stored or disposed of;

(C) the economic and technological feasibility of producing and using such items; and

(D) other uses for such recovered materials.

(f) Procurement of services

A procuring agency shall, to the maximum extent practicable, manage or arrange for the procurement of solid waste management services in a manner which maximizes energy and resource recovery.

(g) Executive Office

The Office of Procurement Policy in the Executive Office of the President, in cooperation with the Administrator, shall implement the requirements of this section. It shall be the responsibility of the Office of Procurement Policy to coordinate this policy with other policies for Federal procurement, in such a way as to maximize the use of recovered resources, and to, every two years beginning in 1984, report to the Congress on actions taken by Federal agencies and the progress made in the implementation of this section, including agency compliance with subsection (d) of this section.

(h) Definitions

As used in this section, in the case of paper products, the term "recovered materials" includes—

(1) postconsumer materials such as—

(A) paper, paperboard, and fibrous wastes from retail stores, office buildings, homes, and so forth, after they have passed through their end-usage as a consumer item, including: used corrugated boxes; old newspapers; old magazines; mixed waste paper; tabulating cards; and used cordage; and

(B) all paper, paperboard, and fibrous wastes that enter and are collected from municipal solid waste, and

(2) manufacturing, forest residues, and other wastes such as—

(A) dry paper and paperboard waste generated after completion of the papermaking process (that is, those manufacturing operations up to and including the cutting and trimming of the paper machine reel into smaller rolls or rough sheets) including: envelope cuttings, bindery trimmings, and other paper and paperboard waste, resulting from printing, cutting, forming, and other converting operations; bag, box, and carton manufacturing wastes; and butt rolls, mill wrappers, and rejected unused stock; and

(B) finished paper and paperboard from obsolete inventories of paper and paperboard manufacturers, merchants, wholesalers, dealers, printers, converters, or others;

(C) fibrous byproducts of harvesting, manufacturing, extractive, or wood-cutting processes, flax, straw, linters, bagasse, slash, and other forest residues;

(D) wastes generated by the conversion of goods made from fibrous material (that is, waste rope from cordage manufacture, textile mill waste, and cuttings); and

(E) fibers recovered from waste water which otherwise would enter the waste stream.

(i) Procurement program

(1) Within one year after the date of publication of applicable guidelines under subsection (e) of this section, each procuring agency shall develop an affirmative procurement program which will assure that items composed of recovered materials will be purchased to the maximum extent practicable and which is consistent with applicable provisions of Federal procurement law.

(2) Each affirmative procurement program required under this subsection shall, at a minimum, contain—

(A) a recovered materials preference program;

(B) an agency promotion program to promote the preference program adopted under subparagraph (A);

(C) a program for requiring estimates of the total percentage of recovered material utilized in the performance of a contract; certification of minimum recovered material content actually utilized, where appropriate; and reasonable verification procedures for estimates and certifications; and

(D) annual review and monitoring of the effectiveness of an agency's affirmative procurement program.

In the case of paper, the recovered materials preference program required under subparagraph (A) shall provide for the maximum use of the post consumer recovered materials referred to in subsection (h)(1) of this section.

(3) In developing the preference program, the following options shall be considered for adoption:

(A) Case-by-Case Policy Development: Subject to the limitations of subsection (c)(1)(A) through (C) of this section, a policy of awarding contracts to the vendor offering an item composed of the highest percentage of recovered materials practicable (and in the case of paper, the highest percentage of the post consumer recovered materials referred to in subsection (h)(1) of this section). Subject to such limitations, agencies may make an award to a vendor offering items with less than the maximum recovered materials content.

(B) Minimum Content Standards: Minimum recovered materials content specifications which are set in such a way as to assure that the recovered materials content (and in the case of paper, the content of post consumer materials referred to in subsection (h)(1) of this section) required is the maximum available without jeopardizing the intended end use of the item, or violating the limitations of subsection (c)(1)(A) through (C) of this section.

Procuring agencies shall adopt one of the options set forth in subparagraphs (A) and (B) or a substantially equivalent alternative, for inclusion in the affirmative procurement program.

(Pub.L. 89–272, title II, § 6002, as added Oct. 21, 1976, Pub.L. 94–580, § 2, 90 Stat. 2822, and amended Nov. 8, 1978, Pub.L. 95–609, § 7(n), 92 Stat. 3082; Oct. 21, 1980, Pub.L. 96–482, § 22, 94 Stat. 2346; Dec. 21, 1982, Pub.L. 97–375, title I, § 102, 96 Stat. 1819; Nov. 8, 1984, Pub.L. 98–616, title V, § 501(a)–(e), 98 Stat. 3274–3276.)

Code of Federal Regulations

Cement and fly ash concrete, see 40 CFR 249.01 et seq.

§ 6963. Cooperation with Environmental Protection Agency

(a) General rule

All Federal agencies shall assist the Administrator in carrying out his functions under this chapter and shall promptly make available all requested information concerning past or present Agency waste management practices and past or present Agency owned, leased, or operated solid or hazardous waste facilities. This information shall be provided in such format as may be determined by the Administrator.

(b) Information relating to energy and materials conservation and recovery

The Administrator shall collect, maintain, and disseminate information concerning the market potential of energy and materials recovered from solid waste, including materials obtained through source separation, and information concerning the savings potential of conserving resources contributing to the waste stream. The Administrator shall identify the regions in which the increased substitution of such energy for energy derived from fossil fuels and other sources is most likely to be feasible, and provide information on the technical and economic aspects of developing integrated resource conservation or recovery systems which provide for the recovery of source-separated materials to be recycled or the conservation of resources. The Administrator shall utilize the authorities of subsection (a) of this section in carrying out this subsection.

(Pub.L. 89–272, title II, § 6003, as added Oct. 21, 1976, Pub.L. 94–580, § 2, 90 Stat. 2823, and amended Oct. 21, 1980, Pub.L. 96–482, § 32(g), 94 Stat. 2355.)

§ 6964. Applicability of solid waste disposal guidelines to Executive agencies

(a) Compliance

(1) If—

(A) an Executive agency (as defined in section 105 of Title 5) or any unit of the legislative branch of the Federal Government has jurisdiction over any real property or facility the operation or administration of which involves such agency in solid waste management activities, or

(B) such an agency enters into a contract with any person for the operation by such person of any Federal property or facility, and the performance of such contract involves such person in solid waste management activities,

then such agency shall insure compliance with the guidelines recommended under section 6907 of this title and the purposes of this chapter in the operation or administration of such property or facility, or the performance of such contract, as the case may be.

(2) Each Executive agency or any unit of the legislative branch of the Federal Government which conducts any activity—

(A) which generates solid waste, and

(B) which, if conducted by a person other than such agency, would require a permit or license from such agency in order to dispose of such solid waste,

shall insure compliance with such guidelines and the purposes of this chapter in conducting such activity.

(3) Each Executive agency which permits the use of Federal property for purposes of disposal of solid waste shall insure compliance with such guidelines and the purposes of this chapter in the disposal of such waste.

(4) The President or the Committee on House Administration of the House of Representatives and the Committee on Rules and Administration of the Senate with regard to any unit of the legislative branch of the Federal Government shall prescribe regulations to carry out this subsection.

(b) Licenses and permits

Each Executive agency which issues any license or permit for disposal of solid waste shall, prior to the issuance of such license or permit, consult with the Administrator to insure compliance with guidelines recommended under section 6907 of this title and the purposes of this chapter.

(Pub.L. 89–272, title II, § 6004, as added Oct. 21, 1976, Pub.L. 94–580, § 2, 90 Stat. 2823, and amended Nov. 8, 1978, Pub.L. 95–609, § 7(*o*), 92 Stat. 3083; Oct. 21, 1980, Pub.L. 96–482, § 23, 94 Stat. 2347.)

Code of Federal Regulations

Solid waste management guidelines and procedures, see 40 CFR 244.100 et seq., 245.100 et seq., 246.100 et seq.

SUBCHAPTER VII—MISCELLANEOUS PROVISIONS

§ 6971. Employee protection

(a) General

No person shall fire, or in any other way discriminate against, or cause to be fired or discriminated against, any employee or any authorized representative of employees by reason of the fact that such employee or representative has filed, instituted, or caused to be filed or instituted any proceeding under this chapter or under any applicable implementation plan, or has testified or is about to testify in any proceeding resulting from the administration or enforcement of the provisions of this chapter or of any applicable implementation plan.

(b) Remedy

Any employee or a representative of employees who believes that he has been fired or otherwise discriminated against by any person in violation of subsection (a) of this section may, within thirty days after such alleged violation occurs, apply to the Secretary of Labor for a review of such firing or alleged discrimination. A copy of the application shall be sent to such person who shall be the respondent. Upon receipt of such application, the Secretary of Labor shall cause such investigation to be made as he deems appropriate. Such investigation shall provide an opportunity for a public hearing at the request of any party to such review to enable the parties to present information relating to such alleged violation. The parties shall be given written notice of the time and place of the hearing at least five days prior to the hearing. Any such hearing shall be of record and shall be subject to section 554 of title 5. Upon receiving the report of such investigation, the Secretary of Labor shall make findings of fact. If he finds that such violation did occur, he shall issue a decision, incorporating an order therein and his findings, requiring the party committing such violation to take such affirmative action to abate the violation as the Secretary of Labor deems appropriate, including, but not limited to, the rehiring or reinstatement of the employee or representative of employees to his former position with compensation. If he finds that there was no such violation, he shall issue an order denying the application. Such order issued by the Secretary of Labor under this subparagraph shall be subject to judicial review in the same manner as orders and decisions of the Administrator or subject to judicial review under this chapter.

(c) Costs

Whenever an order is issued under this section to abate such violation, at the request of the applicant, a sum equal to the aggregate amount of all costs and expenses (including the attorney's fees) as determined by the Secretary of Labor, to have been reasonably incurred by the applicant for, or in connection with, the institution and prosecution of such proceedings, shall be assessed against the person committing such violation.

(d) Exception

This section shall have no application to any employee who, acting without direction from his employer (or his agent) deliberately violates any requirement of this chapter.

(e) Employment shifts and loss

The Administrator shall conduct continuing evaluations of potential loss or shifts of employment which may result from the administration or enforcement of the provisions of this chapter and applicable implementation plans, including, where appropriate, investigating threatened plant closures or reductions in employment allegedly resulting from such administration or enforcement. Any employee who is discharged, or laid off, threatened with discharge or layoff, or otherwise discriminated against by any person because of the alleged results of such administration or enforcement, or any representative of such employee, may request the Administrator to conduct a full investigation of the matter. The Administrator shall thereupon investigate the matter and, at the request of any party, shall hold public hearings on not less than five days' notice, and shall at such hearings require the parties, including the employer involved, to present information relating to the actual or potential effect of such administration or enforcement on employment and on any alleged discharge, layoff, or other discrimination and the detailed reasons or justification therefor. Any such hearing shall be of record and shall be subject to section 554 of title 5. Upon receiving the report of such investigation, the Administrator shall make findings of fact as to the effect of such administration or enforcement on employment and on the alleged discharge, layoff, or discrimination and shall make such recommendations as he deems appropriate. Such report, findings, and recommendations shall be available to the public. Nothing in this subsection shall be construed to require or authorize the Administrator or any State to modify or withdraw any standard, limitation, or any other requirement of this chapter or any applicable implementation plan.

(f) Occupational safety and health

In order to assist the Secretary of Labor and the Director of the National Institute for Occupational Safety and Health in carrying out their duties under the Occupational Safety and Health Act of 1970 [29 U.S.C. 651 et seq.], the Administrator shall—

(1) provide the following information, as such information becomes available, to the Secretary and the Director:

(A) the identity of any hazardous waste generation, treatment, storage, disposal facility or site where cleanup is planned or underway;

(B) information identifying the hazards to which persons working at a hazardous waste generation, treatment, storage, disposal facility or site or otherwise handling hazardous waste may be exposed, the nature and extent of the exposure, and methods to protect workers from such hazards; and

(C) incidents of worker injury or harm at a hazardous waste generation, treatment, storage or disposal facility or site; and

(2) notify the Secretary and the Director of the Administrator's receipt of notifications under section 6930 or reports under sections 6922, 6923, and 6924 of this title and make such notifications and reports available to the Secretary and the Director.

(Pub.L. 89–272, title II, § 7001, as added Oct. 21, 1976, Pub.L. 94–580, § 2, 90 Stat. 2824, and amended Oct. 21, 1980, Pub.L. 96–482, § 24, 94 Stat. 2347.)

Code of Federal Regulations

Discrimination complaints, procedure, see 29 CFR 24.1 et seq.

§ 6972. Citizens' suits

(a) In general

Except as provided in subsection (b) or (c) of this section, any person may commence a civil action on his own behalf—

(1)(A) against any person (including (a) the United States, and (b) any other governmental instrumentality or agency, to the extent permitted by the eleventh amendment to the Constitution) who is alleged to be in violation of any permit, standard, regulation, condition, requirement, prohibition, or order which has become effective pursuant to this chapter; or

(B) against any person, including the United States, and any other governmental instrumentality or agency, to the extent permitted by the eleventh amendment to the Constitution, and including any past or present generator, past or present transporter, or past or present owner or operator of a treatment, storage, or disposal facility, who has contributed or who is contributing to the past or present handling, storage, treatment, transportation, or disposal of any solid or hazardous waste which may present an imminent and substantial endangerment to health or the environment; or

(2) against the Administrator where there is alleged a failure of the Administrator to perform any act or duty under this chapter which is not discretionary with the Administrator.

Any action under paragraph (a)(1) of this subsection shall be brought in the district court for the district in which the alleged violation occurred or the alleged endangerment may occur. Any action brought under paragraph (a)(2) of this subsection may be brought in the district court for the district in which the alleged violation occurred or in the District Court of the District of Columbia. The district court shall have jurisdiction, without regard to the amount in controversy or the citizenship of the parties, to enforce the permit, standard, regulation, condition, requirement, prohibition, or order, referred to in paragraph (1)(A), to restrain any person who has contributed or who is contributing to the past or present handling, storage, treatment, transportation, or disposal of any solid or hazardous waste referred to in paragraph (1)(B), to order such person to take such other action as may be necessary, or both, or to order the Administrator to perform the act or duty referred to in paragraph (2), as the case may be, and to apply any appropriate civil penalties under section 6928(a) and (g) of this title.

(b) Actions prohibited

(1) No action may be commenced under subsection (a)(1)(A) of this section—

(A) prior to 60 days after the plaintiff has given notice of the violation to—

(i) the Administrator;

(ii) the State in which the alleged violation occurs; and

(iii) to any alleged violator of such permit, standard, regulation, condition, requirement, prohibition, or order,

except that such action may be brought immediately after such notification in the case of an action under this section respecting a violation of subchapter III of this chapter; or

(B) if the Administrator or State has commenced and is diligently prosecuting a civil or criminal action in a court of the United States or a State to require compliance with such permit, standard, regulation, condition, requirement, prohibition, or order.

In any action under subsection (a)(1)(A) of this section in a court of the United States, any person may intervene as a matter of right.

(2)(A) No action may be commenced under subsection (a)(1)(B) of this section prior to ninety days after the plaintiff has given notice of the endangerment to—

(i) the Administrator;

(ii) the State in which the alleged endangerment may occur;

(iii) any person alleged to have contributed or to be contributing to the past or present handling, storage, treatment, transportation, or disposal of any solid or hazardous waste referred to in subsection (a)(1)(B) of this section,

except that such action may be brought immediately after such notification in the case of an action under this section respecting a violation of subchapter III of this chapter.

(B) No action may be commenced under subsection (a)(1)(B) of this section if the Administrator, in order to restrain or abate acts or conditions which may have contributed or are contributing to the activities which may present the alleged endangerment—

(i) has commenced and is diligently prosecuting an action under section 6973 of this title or under section 106 of the Comprehensive Environmental Response, Compensation and Liability Act of 1980 [42 U.S.C. 9606];

(ii) is actually engaging in a removal action under section 104 of the Comprehensive Environmental Response, Compensation and Liability Act of 1980 [42 U.S.C. 9604];

(iii) has incurred costs to initiate a Remedial Investigation and Feasibility Study under section 104 of the Comprehensive Environmental Response, Compensation and Liability Act of 1980 [42 U.S.C. 9604] and is diligently proceeding with a remedial action under that Act [42 U.S.C. 9601 et seq.]; or

(iv) has obtained a court order (including a consent decree) or issued an administrative order under section 106 of the Comprehensive Environmental Response, Compensation and Liability Act of 980 [1] [42 U.S.C. 9606] or section 6973 of this title pursuant to which a responsible party is diligently conducting a removal action, Remedial Investigation and Feasibility Study (RIFS), or proceeding with a remedial action.

In the case of an administrative order referred to in clause (iv), actions under subsection (a)(1)(B) of this section are prohibited only as to the scope and duration of the administrative order referred to in clause (iv).

(C) No action may be commenced under subsection (a)(1)(B) of this section if the State, in order to restrain or abate acts or conditions which may have contributed or are contributing to the activities which may present the alleged endangerment—

(i) has commenced and is diligently prosecuting an action under subsection (a)(1)(B) of this section;

(ii) is actually engaging in a removal action under section 104 of the Comprehensive Environmental Response, Compensation and Liability Act of 1980 [42 U.S.C. 9604]; or

(iii) has incurred costs to initiate a Remedial Investigation and Feasibility Study under section 104 of the Comprehensive Environmental Response, Compensation and Liability Act of 1980 [42 U.S.C. 9604] and is diligently proceeding with a remedial action under that Act [42 U.S.C. 9601 et seq.].

(D) No action may be commenced under subsection (a)(1)(B) of this section by any person (other than a State or local government) with respect to the siting of a hazardous waste treatment, storage, or a disposal facility, nor to restrain or enjoin the issuance of a permit for such facility.

(E) In any action under subsection (a)(1)(B) of this section in a court of the United States, any person may intervene as a matter of right when the applicant claims an interest relating to the subject of the action and he is so situated that the disposition of the action may, as a practical matter, impair or impede his ability to protect that interest, unless the Administrator or the State shows that the applicant's interest is adequately represented by existing parties.

(F) Whenever any action is brought under subsection (a)(1)(B) of this section in a court of the United States, the plaintiff shall serve a copy of the complaint on the Attorney General of the United States and with the Administrator.

(c) Notice

No action may be commenced under paragraph (a)(2) of this section prior to sixty days after the plaintiff has given notice to the Administrator that he will commence such action, except that such action may be brought immediately after such notification in the case of an action under this section respecting a violation of subchapter III of this chapter. Notice under this subsection shall be given in such manner as the Administrator shall prescribe by regulation. Any action respecting a violation under this chapter may be brought under this section only in the judicial district in which such alleged violation occurs.

(d) Intervention

In any action under this section the Administrator, if not a party, may intervene as a matter of right.

(e) Costs

The court, in issuing any final order in any action brought pursuant to this section or section 6976 of this title, may award costs of litigation (including reasonable attorney and expert witness fees) to the prevailing or substantially prevailing party, whenever the court determines such an award is appropriate. The court may, if a temporary restraining order or preliminary injunction is sought, require the filing of a bond or equivalent security in accordance with the Federal Rules of Civil Procedure.

(f) Other rights preserved

Nothing in this section shall restrict any right which any person (or class of persons) may have under any statute or common law to seek enforcement of any standard or requirement relating to the management of solid waste or hazardous waste, or to seek any other relief (including relief against the Administrator or a State agency).

(g) Transporters

A transporter shall not be deemed to have contributed or to be contributing to the handling, storage, treatment, or disposal, referred to in subsection (a)(1)(B) of this section taking place after such solid waste or hazardous waste has left the possession or control of such transporter, if the transportation of such waste was under a sole contractual arrangement arising from a published tariff and acceptance for carriage by common carrier by rail and such transporter has exercised due care in the past or present handling, storage, treatment, transportation and disposal of such waste.

(Pub.L. 89–272, title II, § 7002, as added Oct. 21, 1976, Pub.L. 94–580, § 2, 90 Stat. 2825, and amended Nov. 8, 1978, Pub.L. 95–609, § 7(p), 92 Stat. 3083; as amended Nov. 8, 1984, Pub.L. 98–616, title IV, § 401, 98 Stat. 3268.)

1 So in original. Probably should be 1980.

Code of Federal Regulations

Citizen suits, prior notice of, see 40 CFR 254.1 et seq.

Library References

Health and Environment ⚡25.15(4).
C.J.S. Health and Environment § 83 et seq.

§ 6973. Imminent hazard

(a) Authority of Administrator

Notwithstanding any other provision of this chapter, upon receipt of evidence that the past or present handling, storage, treatment, transportation or disposal of any solid waste or hazardous waste may present an imminent and substantial endangerment to health or the environment, the Administrator may bring suit on behalf of the United States in the appropriate district court against any person (including any past or present generator, past or present transporter, or past or present owner or operator of a treatment, storage, or disposal facility) who has contributed or who is contributing to such handling, storage, treatment, transportation or disposal to restrain such person from such handling, storage, treatment, transportation, or disposal, to order such person to take such other action as may be necessary, or both. A transporter shall not be deemed to have contributed or to be contributing to such handling, storage, treatment, or disposal taking place after such solid waste or hazardous waste has left the possession or control of such transporter if the transportation of such waste was under a sole contractural[1] arrangement arising from a published tariff and acceptance for carriage by common carrier by rail and such transporter has exercised due care in the past or present handling, storage, treatment, transportation and disposal of such waste. The Administrator shall provide notice to the affected State of any such suit. The Administrator may also, after notice to the affected State, take other action under this section including, but not limited to, issuing such orders as may be necessary to protect public health and the environment.

(b) Violations

Any person who willfully violates, or fails or refuses to comply with, any order of the Administrator under subsection (a) of this section may, in an action brought in the appropriate United States district court to enforce such order, be fined not more than $5,000 for each day in which such violation occurs or such failure to comply continues.

(c) Immediate notice

Upon receipt of information that there is hazardous waste at any site which has presented an imminent and substantial endangerment to human health or the environment, the Administrator shall provide immediate notice to the appropriate local government agencies. In addition, the Administrator shall require notice of such endangerment to be promptly posted at the site where the waste is located.

(d) Public participation in settlements

Whenever the United States or the Administrator proposes to covenant not to sue or to forbear from suit or to settle any claim arising under this section, notice, and opportunity for a public meeting in the affected area, and a reasonable opportunity to comment on the proposed settlement prior to its final entry shall be afforded to the public. The decision of the United States or the Administrator to enter into or not to enter into such Consent Decree, covenant or agreement shall not constitute a final agency action subject to judicial review under this chapter or subchapter II of chapter 5 of Title 5.

(Pub.L. 89–272, title II, § 7003, as added Oct. 21, 1976, Pub.L. 94–580, § 2, 90 Stat. 2826, and amended Nov. 8, 1978, Pub.L. 95–609 § 7(q), 92 Stat. 3083; Oct. 21, 1980, Pub.L. 96–482, § 25, 94 Stat. 2348; Nov. 8, 1984, Pub.L. 98–616, title IV, §§ 402, 403(a), 404, 98 Stat. 3271, 3273.)

1 So in original. Probably should be contractual.

Cross References

Guidelines for using the imminent hazard, enforcement, and emergency response authorities to include powers authorized by this section, see section 9606 of this title.

§ 6974. Petition for regulations; public participation

(a) Petition

Any person may petition the Administrator for the promulgation, amendment, or repeal of any regulation under this chapter. Within a reasonable time following receipt of such petition, the Administrator shall take action with respect to such petition and shall publish notice of such action in the Federal Register, together with the reasons therefor.

(b) Public participation

(1) Public participation in the development, revision, implementation, and enforcement of any regulation, guideline, information, or program under this chapter shall be provided for, encouraged, and assisted by the Administrator and the States. The Administrator, in cooperation with the States, shall develop and publish minimum guidelines for public participation in such processes.

(2) Before the issuing of a permit to any person with any respect to any facility for the treatment, storage, or disposal of hazardous wastes under section 6925 of this title, the Administrator shall—

(A) cause to be published in major local newspapers of general circulation and broadcast over local radio stations notice of the agency's intention to issue such permit, and

(B) transmit in writing notice of the agency's intention to issue such permit to each unit of local government having jurisdiction over the area in which such facility is proposed to be located and to each State agency having any authority under State law with respect to the construction or operation of such facility.

If within 45 days the Administrator receives written notice of opposition to the agency's intention to issue such permit and a request for a hearing, or if the Administrator determines on his own initiative, he shall hold an informal public hearing (including an opportunity for presentation of written and oral views) on whether he should issue a permit for the proposed facility. Whenever possible the Administrator shall schedule such hearing at a location convenient to the nearest population center to such proposed facility and give notice in the aforementioned manner of the date, time, and subject matter of such hearing. No State program which provides for the issuance of permits referred to in this paragraph may be authorized by the Administrator under section 6926 of this title unless such program provides for the notice and hearing required by the paragraph.

(Pub.L. 89–272, title II, § 7004, as added Oct. 21, 1976, Pub.L. 94–580, § 2, 90 Stat. 2826, and amended Oct. 21, 1980, Pub.L. 96–482, § 26, 94 Stat. 2348.)

Code of Federal Regulations

Hazardous waste management, see 40 CFR 260.1 et seq.
Hazardous waste management generally, see 40 CFR 260.1 et seq. to 271.1 et seq.
National Pollutant Discharge Elimination System, see 40 CFR 122.1 et seq., 125.1 et seq.
Public participation, see 40 CFR 25.1 et seq.
State programs, see 40 CFR 123.1 et seq.
Underground Injection Control Program, see 40 CFR 146.1 et seq.

§ 6975. Separability of provisions

If any provision of this chapter, or the application of any provision of this chapter to any person or circumstance, is held invalid, the application of such provision to other persons or circumstances, and the remainder of this chapter, shall not be affected thereby.

(Pub.L. 89–272, title II, § 7005, as added Oct. 21, 1976, Pub.L. 94–580, § 2, 90 Stat. 2827.)

§ 6976. Judicial review

(a) Review of final regulations and certain petitions

Any judicial review of final regulations promulgated pursuant to this chapter and the Administrator's denial of any petition for the promulgation, amendment, or repeal of any regulation under this chapter shall be in accordance with sections 701 through 706 of Title 5, except that—

(1) a petition for review of action of the Administrator in promulgating any regulation, or requirement under this chapter or denying any petition for the promulgation, amendment or repeal of any regulation under this chapter may be filed only in the United States Court of Appeals for the District of Columbia, and such petition shall be filed within ninety days from the date of such promulgation or denial, or after such date if such petition for review is based solely on grounds arising after such ninetieth day; action of the Administrator with respect to which review could have been obtained under this subsection shall not be subject to judicial review in civil or criminal proceedings for enforcement; and

(2) in any judicial proceeding brought under this section in which review is sought of a determination under this chapter required to be made on the record after notice and opportunity for hearing, if a party seeking review under this chapter applies to the court for leave to adduce additional evidence, and shows to the satisfaction of the court that the information is material and that there were reasonable grounds for the fail-

ure to adduce such evidence in the proceeding before the Administrator, the court may order such additional evidence (and evidence in rebuttal thereof) to be taken before the Administrator, and to be adduced upon the hearing in such manner and upon such terms and conditions as the court may deem proper; the Administrator may modify his findings as to the facts, or make new findings, by reason of the additional evidence so taken, and he shall file with the court such modified or new findings and his recommendation, if any, for the modification or setting aside of his original order, with the return of such additional evidence.

(b) Review of certain actions under sections 6925 and 6926 of this title

Review of the Administrator's action (1) in issuing, denying, modifying, or revoking any permit under section 6925 of this title (or in modifying or revoking any permit which is deemed to have been issued under section 6935(d)(1) of this title), or (2) in granting, denying, or withdrawing authorization or interim authorization under section 6926 of this title, may be had by any interested person in the Circuit Court of Appeals of the United States for the Federal judicial district in which such person resides or transacts such business upon application by such person. Any such application shall be made within ninety days from the date of such issuance, denial, modification, revocation, grant, or withdrawal, or after such date only if such application is based solely on grounds which arose after such ninetieth day. Action of the Administrator with respect to which review could have been obtained under this subsection shall not be subject to judicial review in civil or criminal proceedings for enforcement. Such review shall be in accordance with sections 701 through 706 of Title 5.

(Pub.L. 89–272, title II, § 7006, as added Oct. 21, 1976, Pub.L. 94–580, § 2, 90 Stat. 2827, and amended Oct. 21, 1980, Pub.L. 96–482, § 27, 94 Stat. 2349; Nov. 8, 1984, Pub.L. 98–616, Title II, § 241(b)(1), Title IV, § 403(d)(5), 98 Stat. 3259, 3273.)

United States Supreme Court

Supreme Court review, obtaining views of state supreme court on issue of preemption of state statute by this Chapter, see City of Philadelphia v. New Jersey 1977, 97 S.Ct. 987, 430 U.S. 141, 51 L.Ed.2d 224.

§ 6977. Grants or contracts for training projects

(a) General authority

The Administrator is authorized to make grants to, and contracts with any eligible organization. For purposes of this section the term "eligible organization" means a State or interstate agency, a municipality, educational institution, and any other organization which is capable of effectively carrying out a project which may be funded by grant under subsection (b) of this section.

(b) Purposes

(1) Subject to the provisions of paragraph (2), grants or contracts may be made to pay all or a part of the costs, as may be determined by the Administrator, of any project operated or to be operated by an eligible organization, which is designed—

(A) to develop, expand, or carry out a program (which may combine training, education, and employment) for training persons for occupations involving the management, supervision, design, operation, or maintenance of solid waste management and resource recovery equipment and facilities; or

(B) to train instructors and supervisory personnel to train or supervise persons in occupations involving the design, operation, and maintenance of solid waste management and resource recovery equipment and facilities.

(2) A grant or contract authorized by paragraph (1) of this subsection may be made only upon application to the Administrator at such time or times and containing such information as he may prescribe, except that no such application shall be approved unless it provides for the same procedures and reports (and access to such reports and to other records) as required by section 3254a(b)(4) and (5) of this title (as in effect before October 21, 1976) with respect to applications made under such section (as in effect before October 21, 1976).

(c) Study

The Administrator shall make a complete investigation and study to determine—

(1) the need for additional trained State and local personnel to carry out plans assisted under this chapter and other solid waste and resource recovery programs;

(2) means of using existing training programs to train such personnel; and

(3) the extent and nature of obstacles to employment and occupational advancement in the solid waste management and resource recovery field which may limit either available manpower or the advancement of personnel in such field.

He shall report the results of such investigation and study, including his recommendations to the President and the Congress.

(Pub.L. 89–272, title II, § 7007, as added Oct. 21, 1976, Pub.L. 94–580, § 2, 90 Stat. 2827, and amended Nov. 8, 1978, Pub.L. 95–609, § 7(r), 92 Stat. 3083.)

Code of Federal Regulations

Grants and manpower forecasting, see 40 CFR 45.100 et seq.

Library References

United States ⚷82(3).
C.J.S. United States § 122.

§ 6978. Payments

(a) General rule

Payments of grants under this chapter may be made (after necessary adjustment on account of previously made underpayments or overpayments) in advance or by way of reimbursement, and in such installments and on such conditions as the Administrator may determine.

(b) Prohibition

No grant may be made under this chapter to any private profitmaking organization.

(Pub.L. 89–272, title II, § 7008, as added Oct. 21, 1976, Pub.L. 94–580, § 2, 90 Stat. 2828.)

§ 6979. Labor standards

No grant for a project of construction under this chapter shall be made unless the Administrator finds that the application contains or is supported by reasonable assurance that all laborers and mechanics employed by contractors or subcontractors on projects of the type covered by the Davis-Bacon Act, as amended (40 U.S.C. 276a—276a-5), will be paid wages at rates not less than those prevailing on similar work in the locality as determined by the Secretary of Labor in accordance with that Act; and the Secretary of Labor shall have with respect to the labor standards specified in this section the authority and functions set forth in Reorganization Plan Numbered 14 of 1950 (15 F.R. 3176) and section 276c of Title 40.

(Pub.L. 89–272, title II, § 7009, as added Oct. 21, 1976, Pub.L. 94–580, § 2, 90 Stat. 2828, and amended Oct. 21, 1980, Pub.L. 96–482, § 28, 94 Stat. 2349.)

Code of Federal Regulations

Interpretation of fringe benefits provisions, see 29 CFR 5.20 et seq.
Wage rate predetermination, see 29 CFR 1.1 et seq.

Library References

Labor Relations ⚷1129, 1132.
C.J.S. Labor Relations §§ 1039 et seq., 1042.

§ 6979a. Transferred

Section, Pub.L. 89–272, Title II, § 7010, as added Pub.L. 98–616, Title IV, § 405(a), Nov. 8, 1984, 98 Stat. 3273, was renumbered section 3020 of Pub.L. 89–272 by Pub.L. 99–339, Title II, § 201(c)(2), June 19, 1986, 100 Stat. 654, and transferred to section 6939b of this title.

§ 6979b. Law enforcement authority

The Attorney General of the United States shall, at the request of the Administrator and on the basis of a showing of need, deputize qualified employees of the Environmental Protection Agency to serve as special deputy United States marshals in criminal investigations with respect to violations of the criminal provisions of this chapter.

(Pub.L. 89–272, title II, § 7010, formerly § 7012, as added Nov. 8, 1984, Pub.L. 98–616, title IV, § 403(b)(1), 98 Stat. 3272, and renumbered June 19, 1986, Pub.L. 99–339, Title II, § 201(c)(1), 100 Stat. 654.)

SUBCHAPTER VIII—RESEARCH, DEVELOPMENT, DEMONSTRATION, AND INFORMATION

§ 6981. Research, demonstrations, training and other activities

(a) General authority

The Administrator, alone or after consultation with the Secretary of Energy, shall conduct, and encourage, cooperate with, and render financial and other assistance to appropriate public (whether Federal, State, interstate, or local) authorities, agencies, and institutions, private agencies and institutions, and individuals in the conduct of, and promote the coordination of, research, investigations, experiments, training, demonstrations, surveys, public education programs, and studies relating to—

(1) any adverse health and welfare effects of the release into the environment of material present in solid waste, and methods to eliminate such effects;

(2) the operation and financing of solid waste management programs;

(3) the planning, implementation, and operation of resource recovery and resource conservation systems and hazardous waste management systems, including the marketing of recovered resources;

(4) the production of usable forms of recovered resources, including fuel, from solid waste;

(5) the reduction of the amount of such waste and unsalvageable waste materials;

(6) the development and application of new and improved methods of collecting and disposing of solid waste and processing and recovering materials and energy from solid wastes;

(7) the identification of solid waste components and potential materials and energy recoverable from such waste components;

(8) small scale and low technology solid waste management systems, including but not limited to, resource recovery source separation systems;

(9) methods to improve the performance characteristics of resources recovered from solid waste and the relationship of such performance characteristics to available and potentially available markets for such resources;

(10) improvements in land disposal practices for solid waste (including sludge) which may reduce the adverse environmental effects of such disposal and other aspects of solid waste disposal on land, including means for reducing the harmful environmental effects of earlier and existing landfills, means for restoring areas damaged by such earlier or existing landfills, means for rendering landfills safe for purposes of construction and other uses, and techniques of recovering materials and energy from landfills;

(11) methods for the sound disposal of, or recovery of resources, including energy, from, sludge (including sludge from pollution control and treatment facilities, coal slurry pipelines, and other sources);

(12) methods of hazardous waste management, including methods of rendering such waste environmentally safe; and

(13) any adverse effects on air quality (particularly with regard to the emission of heavy metals) which result from solid waste which is burned (either alone or in conjunction with other substances) for purposes of treatment, disposal or energy recovery.

(b) Management program

(1)(A) In carrying out his functions pursuant to this chapter, and any other Federal legislation respecting solid waste or discarded material research, development, and demonstrations, the Administrator shall establish a management program or system to insure the coordination of all such activities and to facilitate and accelerate the process of development of sound new technology (or other discoveries) from the research phase, through development, and into the demonstration phase.

(B) The Administrator shall (i) assist, on the basis of any research projects which are developed with assistance under this chapter or without Federal assistance, the construction of pilot plant facilities for the purpose of investigating or testing the technological feasibility of any promising new fuel, energy, or resource recovery or resource conservation method or technology; and (ii) demonstrate each such method and technology that appears justified by an evaluation at such pilot plant stage or at a pilot plant stage developed without Federal assistance. Each such demonstration shall incorporate new or innovative technical advances or shall apply such advances to different circumstances and conditions, for the purpose of evaluating design concepts or to test the performance, efficiency, and economic feasibility of a particular method or technology under actual operating conditions. Each such demonstration shall be so planned and designed that, if successful, it can be expanded or utilized directly as a full-scale operational fuel, energy, or resource recovery or resource conservation facility.

(2) Any energy-related research, development, or demonstration project for the conversion including bioconversion, of solid waste carried out by the Environmental Protection Agency or by the Secretary of Energy pursuant to this chapter or any other Act shall be administered in accordance with the May 7, 1976, Interagency Agreement between the Environmental Protection Agency and the Secretary of Energy on the Development of Energy from Solid Wastes and specifically, that in accordance with this agreement, (A) for those energy-related projects of mutual interest, planning will be conducted jointly by the Environmental Protection Agency and the Secretary of Energy, following which project responsibility will be assigned to one agency; (B) energy-related portions of projects for recovery of synthetic fuels or other forms of energy from solid waste shall be the responsibility of the Secretary of Energy; (C) the Environmental Protection Agency shall retain responsibility for the environmental, economic, and institutional aspects of solid waste projects and for assurance that such projects are consistent with any applicable suggested guidelines published pursuant to section 6907 of this title, and any applicable State or regional solid waste management plan; and (D) any activities undertaken under provisions of sections 6982 and 6983 of this title as related to energy; as related to energy or synthetic fuels recovery from waste; or as related to energy conservation shall be accomplished through coordination and consultation with the Secretary of Energy.

(c) Authorities

(1) In carrying out subsection (a) of this section respecting solid waste research, studies, development, and demonstration, except as otherwise specifically provided in section 6984(d) of this title, the Administrator may make grants to or enter into contracts (including contracts for construction) with, public agencies and authorities or private persons.

(2) Contracts for research, development, or demonstrations or for both (including contracts for construction) shall be made in accordance with and subject to the limitations provided with respect to research contracts of the military departments in section 2353 of title 10, except that the determina-

tion, approval, and certification required thereby shall be made by the Administrator.

(3) Any invention made or conceived in the course of, or under, any contract under this chapter shall be subject to section 9 of the Federal Nonnuclear Energy Research and Development Act of 1974 [42 U.S.C. 5908] to the same extent and in the same manner as inventions made or conceived in the course of contracts under such Act [42 U.S.C. 5901 et seq.], except that in applying such section, the Environmental Protection Agency shall be substituted for the Secretary of Energy and the words "solid waste" shall be substituted for the word "energy" where appropriate.

(4) For carrying out the purpose of this chapter the Administrator may detail personnel of the Environmental Protection Agency to agencies eligible for assistance under this section.

(Pub.L. 89–272, title II, § 8001, as added Oct. 21, 1976, Pub.L. 94–580, § 2, 90 Stat. 2829, and amended Aug. 4, 1977, Pub.L. 95–91, Title III, § 301, Title VII, §§ 703, 707, 91 Stat. 577, 606, 607; Nov. 8, 1978, Pub.L. 95–609, § 7(s), 92 Stat. 3083.)

Cross References

Precedence of patent rights in inventions made with federal assistance over inventions within this section, see section 210 of Title 35, Patents.

Code of Federal Regulations.

Grants, see 40 CFR 40.100 et seq., 45.100 et seq.

§ 6982. Special studies; plans for research, development, and demonstrations

(a) Glass and plastic

The Administrator shall undertake a study and publish a report on resource recovery from glass and plastic waste, including a scientific, technological, and economic investigation of potential solutions to implement such recovery.

(b) Composition of waste stream

The Administrator shall undertake a systematic study of the composition of the solid waste stream and of anticipated future changes in the composition of such stream and shall publish a report containing the results of such study and quantitatively evaluating the potential utility of such components.

(c) Priorities study

For purposes of determining priorities for research on recovery of materials and energy from solid waste and developing materials and energy recovery research, development, and demonstration strategies, the Administrator shall review, and make a study of, the various existing and promising techniques of energy recovery from solid waste (including, but not limited to, waterwall furnace incinerators, dry shredded fuel systems, pyrolysis, densified refuse-derived fuel systems, anerobic digestion, and fuel and feedstock preparation systems). In carrying out such study the Administrator shall investigate with respect to each such technique—

(1) the degree of public need for the potential results of such research, development, or demonstration,

(2) the potential for research, development, and demonstration without Federal action, including the degree of restraint on such potential posed by the risks involved, and

(3) the magnitude of effort and period of time necessary to develop the technology to the point where Federal assistance can be ended.

(d) Small-scale and low technology study

The Administrator shall undertake a comprehensive study and analysis of, and publish a report on, systems of small-scale and low technology solid waste management, including household resource recovery and resource recovery systems which have special application to multiple dwelling units and high density housing and office complexes. Such study and analysis shall include an investigation of the degree to which such systems could contribute to energy conservation.

(e) Front-end source separation

The Administrator shall undertake research and studies concerning the compatibility of front-end source separation systems with high technology resource recovery systems and shall publish a report containing the results of such research and studies.

(f) Mining waste

The Administrator, in consultation with the Secretary of the Interior, shall conduct a detailed and comprehensive study on the adverse effects of solid wastes from active and abandoned surface and underground mines on the environment, including, but not limited to, the effects of such wastes on humans, water, air, health, welfare, and natural resources, and on the adequacy of means and measures currently employed by the mining industry, Government agencies, and others to dispose of and utilize such solid wastes and to prevent or substantially mitigate such adverse effects. Such study shall include an analysis of—

(1) the sources and volume of discarded material generated per year from mining;

(2) present disposal practices;

(3) potential dangers to human health and the environment from surface runoff of leachate and air pollution by dust;

(4) alternatives to current disposal methods;

(5) the cost of those alternatives in terms of the impact on mine product costs; and

(6) potential for use of discarded material as a secondary source of the mine product.

In furtherance of this study, the Administrator shall, as he deems appropriate, review studies and other actions of other Federal agencies concerning such wastes with a view toward avoiding duplication of effort and the need to expedite such study. Not later than thirty-six months after October 21, 1980, the Administrator shall publish a report of such study and shall include appropriate findings and recommendations for Federal and non-Federal actions concerning such effects. Such report shall be submitted to the Committee on Environment and Public Works of the United States Senate and the Committee on Energy and Commerce of the United States House of Representatives.

(g) Sludge

The Administrator shall undertake a comprehensive study and publish a report on sludge. Such study shall include an analysis of—

(1) what types of solid waste (including but not limited to sewage and pollution treatment residues and other residues from industrial operations such as extraction of oil from shale, liquefaction and gasification of coal and coal slurry pipeline operations) shall be classified as sludge;

(2) the effects of air and water pollution legislation on the creation of large volumes of sludge;

(3) the amounts of sludge originating in each State and in each industry producing sludge;

(4) methods of disposal of such sludge, including the cost, efficiency, and effectiveness of such methods;

(5) alternative methods for the use of sludge, including agricultural applications of sludge and energy recovery from sludge; and

(6) methods to reclaim areas which have been used for the disposal of sludge or which have been damaged by sludge.

(h) Tires

The Administrator shall undertake a study and publish a report respecting discarded motor vehicle tires which shall include an analysis of the problems involved in the collection, recovery of resources including energy, and use of such tires.

(i) Resource recovery facilities

The Administrator shall conduct research and report on the economics of, and impediments, to the effective functioning of resource recovery facilities.

(j) Resource Conservation Committee

(1) The Administrator shall serve as Chairman of a Committee composed of himself, the Secretary of Commerce, the Secretary of Labor, the Chairman of the Council on Environmental Quality, the Secretary of Treasury, the Secretary of the Interior, the Secretary of Energy, the Chairman of the Counsel of Economic Advisors, and a representative of the Office of Management and Budget, which shall conduct a full and complete investigation and study of all aspects of the economic, social, and environmental consequences of resource conservation with respect to—

(A) the appropriateness of recommended incentives and disincentives to foster resource conservation;

(B) the effect of existing public policies (including subsidies and economic incentives and disincentives, percentage depletion allowances, capital gains treatment and other tax incentives and disincentives) upon resource conservation, and the likely effect of the modification or elimination of such incentives and disincentives upon resource conservation;

(C) the appropriateness and feasibility of restricting the manufacture or use of categories of consumer products as a resource conservation strategy;

(D) the appropriateness and feasibility of employing as a resource conservation strategy the imposition of solid waste management charges on consumer products, which charges would reflect the costs of solid waste management services, litter pickup, the value of recoverable components of such product, final disposal, and any social value associated with the nonrecycling or uncontrolled disposal of such product; and

(E) the need for further research, development, and demonstration in the area of resource conservation.

(2) The study required in paragraph (1)(D) may include pilot scale projects, and shall consider and evaluate alternative strategies with respect to—

(A) the product categories on which such charges would be imposed;

(B) the appropriate state in the production of such consumer product at which to levy such charge;

(C) appropriate criteria for establishing such charges for each consumer product category;

(D) methods for the adjustment of such charges to reflect actions such as recycling which would reduce the overall quantities of solid waste requiring disposal; and

(E) procedures for amending, modifying, or revising such charges to reflect changing conditions.

(3) The design for the study required in paragraph (1) of this subsection shall include timetables for the completion of the study. A preliminary report putting forth the study design shall be sent to the President and the Congress within six months following October 21, 1976, and followup reports shall be sent six months thereafter. Each recommendation resulting from the study shall include at least two alternatives to the proposed recommendation.

(4) The results of such investigation and study, including recommendations, shall be reported to the President and the Congress not later than two years after October 21, 1976.

(5) There are authorized to be appropriated not to exceed $2,000,000 to carry out this subsection.

(k) Airport landfills

The Administrator shall undertake a comprehensive study and analysis of and publish a report on systems to alleviate the hazards to aviation from birds congregating and feeding on landfills in the vicinity of airports.

(*l*) Completion of research and studies

The Administrator shall complete the research and studies, and submit the reports, required under subsections (b), (c), (d), (e), (f), (g), and (k) of this section not later than October 1, 1978. The Administrator shall complete the research and studies, and submit the reports, required under subsections (a), (h), and (i) of this section not later than October 1, 1979. Upon completion, each study specified in subsections (a) through (k) of this section, the Administrator shall prepare a plan for research, development, and demonstration respecting the findings of the study and shall submit any legislative recommendations resulting from such study to appropriate committees of Congress.

(m) Drilling fluids, produced waters, and other wastes associated with the exploration, development, or production of crude oil or natural gas or geothermal energy

(1) The Administrator shall conduct a detailed and comprehensive study and submit a report on the adverse effects, if any, of drilling fluids, produced waters, and other wastes associated with the exploration, development, or production of crude oil or natural gas or geothermal energy on human health and the environment, including, but not limited to, the effects of such wastes on humans, water, air, health, welfare, and natural resources and on the adequacy of means and measures currently employed by the oil and gas and geothermal drilling and production industry, Government agencies, and others to dispose of and utilize such wastes and to prevent or substantially mitigate such adverse effects. Such study shall include an analysis of—

(A) the sources and volume of discarded material generated per year from such wastes;

(B) present disposal practices;

(C) potential danger to human health and the environment from the surface runoff or leachate;

(D) documented cases which prove or have caused danger to human health and the environment from surface runoff or leachate;

(E) alternatives to current disposal methods;

(F) the cost of such alternatives; and

(G) the impact of those alternatives on the exploration for, and development and production of, crude oil and natural gas or geothermal energy.

In furtherance of this study, the Administrator shall, as he deems appropriate, review studies and other actions of other Federal agencies concerning such wastes with a view toward avoiding duplication of effort and the need to expedite such study. The Administrator shall publish a report of such study and shall include appropriate findings and recommendations for Federal and non-Federal actions concerning such effects.

(2) The Administrator shall complete the research and study and submit the report required under paragraph (1) not later than twenty-four months from October 21, 1980. Upon completion of the study, the Administrator shall prepare a summary of the findings of the study, a plan for research, development, and demonstration respecting the findings of the study, and shall submit the findings and the study, along with any recommendations resulting from such study, to the Committee on Environment and Public Works of the United States Senate and the Committee on Energy and Commerce of the United States House of Representatives.

(3) There are authorized to be appropriated not to exceed $1,000,000 to carry out the provisions of this subsection.

(n) Materials generated from the combustion of coal and other fossil fuels

The Administrator shall conduct a detailed and comprehensive study and submit a report on the adverse effects on human health and the environment, if any, of the disposal and utilization of fly ash waste, bottom ash waste, slag waste, flue gas emission control waste, and other byproduct materials generated primarily from the combustion of coal or other fossil fuels. Such study shall include an analysis of—

(1) the source and volumes of such material generated per year;

(2) present disposal and utilization practices;

(3) potential danger, if any, to human health and the environment from the disposal and reuse of such materials;

(4) documented cases in which danger to human health or the environment from surface runoff or leachate has been proved;

(5) alternatives to current disposal methods;

(6) the costs of such alternatives;

(7) the impact of those alternatives on the use of coal and other natural resources; and

(8) the current and potential utilization of such materials.

In furtherance of this study, the Administrator shall, as he deems appropriate, review studies and other actions of other Federal and State agencies concerning such material and invite participation by other concerned parties, including industry and other Federal and State agencies, with a view toward avoiding duplication of effort. The Administrator shall publish a report on such study, which shall include appropriate findings, not later than twenty-four months after October 21, 1980. Such study and findings shall be submitted to the Committee on Environment and Public Works of the United States Senate and the Committee on Energy and Commerce of the United States House of Representatives.

(*o*) Cement kiln dust waste

The Administrator shall conduct a detailed and comprehensive study of the adverse effects on human health and the environment, if any, of the disposal of cement kiln dust waste. Such study shall include an analysis of—

(1) the source and volumes of such materials generated per year;

(2) present disposal practices;

(3) potential danger, if any, to human health and the environment from the disposal of such materials;

(4) documented cases in which danger to human health or the environment has been proved;

(5) alternatives to current disposal methods;

(6) the costs of such alternatives;

(7) the impact of those alternatives on the use of natural resources; and

(8) the current and potential utilization of such materials.

In furtherance of this study, the Administrator shall, as he deems appropriate, review studies and other actions of other Federal and State agencies concerning such waste or materials and invite participation by other concerned parties, including industry and other Federal and State agencies, with a view toward avoiding duplication of effort. The Administrator shall publish a report of such study, which shall include appropriate findings, not later than thirty-six months after October 21, 1980. Such report shall be submitted to the Committee on Environment and Public Works of the United States Senate and the Committee on Energy and Commerce of the United States House of Representatives.

(p) Materials generated from the extraction, beneficiation, and processing of ores and minerals, including phosphate rock and overburden from uranium mining

The Administrator shall conduct a detailed and comprehensive study on the adverse effects on human health and the environment, if any, of the disposal and utilization of solid waste from the extraction, beneficiation, and processing of ores and minerals, including phosphate rock and overburden from uranium mining. Such study shall be conducted in conjunction with the study of mining wastes required by subsection (f) of this section and shall include an analysis of—

(1) the source and volumes of such materials generated per year;

(2) present disposal and utilization practices;

(3) potential danger, if any, to human health and the environment from the disposal and reuse of such materials;

(4) documented cases in which danger to human health or the environment has been proved;

(5) alternatives to current disposal methods;

(6) the costs of such alternatives;

(7) the impact of those alternatives on the use of phosphate rock and uranium ore, and other natural resources; and

(8) the current and potential utilization of such materials.

In furtherance of this study, the Administrator shall, as he deems appropriate, review studies and other actions of other Federal and State agencies concerning such waste or materials and invite participation by other concerned parties, including industry and other Federal and State agencies, with a view toward avoiding duplication of effort. The Administrator shall publish a report of such study, which shall include appropriate findings, in conjunction with the publication of the report of the study of mining wastes required to be conducted under subsection (f) of this section. Such report and findings shall be submitted to the Committee on Environment and Public Works of the United States Senate and the Committee on Energy and Commerce of the United States House of Representatives.

(q) Authorization of appropriations

There are authorized to be appropriated not to exceed $8,000,000 for the fiscal years 1978 and 1979 to carry out this section other than subsection (j) of this section.

(r) Minimization of hazardous waste

The Administrator shall compile, and not later than October 1, 1986, submit to the Congress, a report on the feasibility and desirability of establishing standards of performance or of taking other additional actions under this chapter to require the generators of hazardous waste to reduce the volume or quantity and toxicity of the hazardous waste they generate, and of establishing with respect to hazardous wastes required management practices or other requirements to assure such wastes are managed in ways that minimize present and future risks to human health and the environment. Such report shall include any recommendations for legislative changes which the Administrator determines are feasible and desirable to implement the national policy established by section 6902 of this title.

(s) Extending the useful life of sanitary landfills

The Administrator shall conduct detailed, comprehensive studies of methods to extend the useful life of sanitary landfills and to better use sites in which filled or closed landfills are located. Such studies shall address—

(1) methods to reduce the volume of materials before placement in landfills;

(2) more efficient systems for depositing waste in landfills;

(3) methods to enhance the rate of decomposition of solid waste in landfills, in a safe and environmentally acceptable manner;

(4) methane production from closed landfill units;

(5) innovative uses of closed landfill sites, including use for energy production such as solar or wind energy and use for metals recovery;

(6) potential for use of sewage treatment sludge in reclaiming landfilled areas; and

(7) methods to coordinate use of a landfill owned by one municipality by nearby municipalities, and to establish equitable rates for such use, taking into account the need to provide future landfill capacity to replace that so used.

The Administrator is authorized to conduct demonstrations in the areas of study provided in this subsection. The Administrator shall periodically report on the results of such studies, with the first such report not later than October 1, 1986. In carrying out this subsection, the Administrator need not duplicate other studies which have been completed and may rely upon information which has previously been compiled.

(Pub.L. 89–272, title II, § 8002, as added Oct. 21, 1976, Pub.L. 94–580, § 2, 90 Stat. 2831, and amended Nov. 8, 1978, Pub.L. 95–609, § 7(t), 92 Stat. 3083; H.Res. 549, Mar. 25, 1980; Oct. 21, 1980, Pub.L. 96–482, § 29, 94 Stat. 2349; Nov. 8, 1984, Pub.L. 98–616, title II, § 224(c), title VII, § 702, 98 Stat. 3253, 3289.)

§ 6983. Coordination, collection, and dissemination of information

(a) Information

The Administrator shall develop, collect, evaluate, and coordinate information on—

(1) methods and costs of the collection of solid waste;

(2) solid waste management practices, including data on the different management methods and the cost, operation, and maintenance of such methods;

(3) the amounts and percentages of resources (including energy) that can be recovered from solid waste by use of various solid waste management practices and various technologies;

(4) methods available to reduce the amount of solid waste that is generated;

(5) existing and developing technologies for the recovery of energy or materials from solid waste and the costs, reliability, and risks associated with such technologies;

(6) hazardous solid waste, including incidents of damage resulting from the disposal of hazardous solid wastes; inherently and potentially hazardous solid wastes; methods of neutralizing or properly disposing of hazardous solid wastes; facilities that properly dispose of hazardous wastes;

(7) methods of financing resource recovery facilities or, sanitary landfills, or hazardous solid waste treatment facilities, whichever is appropriate for the entity developing such facility or landfill (taking into account the amount of solid waste reasonably expected to be available to such entity);

(8) the availability of markets for the purchase of resources, either materials or energy, recovered from solid waste; and

(9) research and development projects respecting solid waste management.

(b) Library

(1) The Administrator shall establish and maintain a central reference library for (A) the materials collected pursuant to subsection (a) of this section and (B) the actual performance and cost effectiveness records and other data and information with respect to—

(i) the various methods of energy and resource recovery from solid waste,

(ii) the various systems and means of resource conservation,

(iii) the various systems and technologies for collection, transport, storage, treatment, and final disposition of solid waste, and

(iv) other aspects of solid waste and hazardous solid waste management.

Such central reference library shall also contain, but not be limited to, the model codes and model accounting systems developed under this section, the information collected under subsection (d) of this section, and, subject to any applicable requirements of confidentiality, information respecting any aspect of solid waste provided by officers and employees of the Environmental Protection Agency which has been acquired by them in the conduct of their functions under this chapter and which may be of value to Federal, State, and local authorities and other persons.

(2) Information in the central reference library shall, to the extent practicable, be collated, analyzed, verified, and published and shall be made available to State and local governments and other persons at reasonable times and subject to such reasonable charges as may be necessary to defray expenses of making such information available.

(c) Model accounting system

In order to assist State and local governments in determining the cost and revenues associated with the collection and disposal of solid waste and with resource recovery operations, the Administrator shall develop and publish a recommended model cost and revenue accounting system applicable to the solid waste management functions of State and local governments. Such system shall be in accordance with generally accepted accounting principles. The Administrator shall periodically, but not less frequently than once every five years, review such accounting system and revise it as necessary.

(d) Model codes

The Administrator is authorized, in cooperation with appropriate State and local agencies, to recommend model codes, ordinances, and statutes, providing for sound solid waste management.

(e) Information programs

(1) The Administrator shall implement a program for the rapid dissemination of information on solid waste management, hazardous waste management, resource conservation, and methods of resource recovery from solid waste, including the results of any relevant research, investigations, experiments, surveys, studies, or other information which may be useful in the implementation of new or improved solid waste management practices and methods and information on any other technical, managerial, financial, or market aspect of resource conservation and recovery facilities.

(2) The Administrator shall develop and implement educational programs to promote citizen understanding of the need for environmentally sound solid waste management practices.

(f) Coordination

In collecting and disseminating information under this section, the Administrator shall coordinate his actions and cooperate to the maximum extent possible with State and local authorities.

(g) Special restriction

Upon request, the full range of alternative technologies, programs or processes deemed feasible to meet the resource recovery or resource conservation needs of a jurisdiction shall be described in such a manner as to provide a sufficient evaluative basis from which the jurisdiction can make its decisions, but no officer or employee of the Environmental Protection Agency shall, in an official capacity, lobby for or otherwise represent an agency position in favor of resource recovery or resource conservation, as a policy alternative for adoption into ordinances, codes, regulations, or law by any State or political subdivision thereof.

(Pub.L. 89–272, title II, § 8003, as added Oct. 21, 1976, Pub.L. 94–580, § 2, 90 Stat. 2834, and amended Nov. 8, 1978, Pub.L. 95–609, § 7(u), 92 Stat. 3083.)

§ 6984. Full-scale demonstration facilities

(a) Authority

The Administrator may enter into contracts with public agencies or authorities or private persons for the construction and operation of a full-scale demonstration facility under this chapter, or provide financial assistance in the form of grants to a full-scale demonstration facility under this chapter only if the Administrator finds that—

(1) such facility or proposed facility will demonstrate at full scale a new or significantly improved technology or process, a practical and significant improvement in solid waste management practice, or the technological feasibility and cost effectiveness of an existing, but unproven technology, process, or practice, and will not duplicate any other Federal, State, local, or commercial facility which has been constructed or with respect to which construction has begun (determined as of the date action is taken by the Administrator under this chapter),

(2) such contract or assistance meets the requirements of section 6981 of this title and meets other applicable requirements of this chapter,

(3) such facility will be able to comply with the guidelines published under section 6907 of this title and with other laws and regulations for the protection of health and the environment,

(4) in the case of a contract for construction or operation, such facility is not likely to be constructed or operated by State, local, or private persons or in the case of an application for financial assistance, such facility is not likely to receive adequate financial assistance from other sources, and

(5) any Federal interest in, or assistance to, such facility will be disposed of or terminated, with appropriate compensation, within such period of time as may be necessary to carry out the basic objectives of this chapter.

(b) Time limitation

No obligation may be made by the Administrator for financial assistance under this subchapter for any full-scale demonstration facility after the date ten years after October 21, 1976. No expenditure of funds for any such full-scale demonstration facility under this subchapter may be made by the Administrator after the date fourteen years after October 21, 1976.

(c) Cost sharing

(1) Wherever practicable, in constructing, operating, or providing financial assistance under this subchapter to a full-scale demonstration facility, the Administrator shall endeavor to enter into agreements and make other arrangements for maximum practicable cost sharing with other Federal, State, and local agencies, private persons, or any combination thereof.

(2) The Administrator shall enter into arrangements, wherever practicable and desirable, to provide monitoring of full-scale solid waste facilities (whether or not constructed or operated under this chapter) for purposes of obtaining information concerning the performance, and other aspects, of such facilities. Where the Administrator provides only monitoring and evaluation instruments or personnel (or both) or funds for such instruments or personnel and provides no other financial assistance to a facility, notwithstanding section 6981(c)(3) of this title, title to any invention made or conceived of in the course of developing, constructing, or operating such facility shall not be required to vest in the United States and patents respecting such invention shall not be required to be issued to the United States.

(d) Prohibition

After October 21, 1976, the Administrator shall not construct or operate any full-scale facility (except by contract with public agencies or authorities or private persons).

(Pub.L. 89–272, title II, § 8004, as added Oct. 21, 1976, Pub.L. 94–580, § 2, 90 Stat. 2836, and amended Nov. 8, 1978, Pub.L. 95–609, § 7(v), 92 Stat. 3084; Nov. 8, 1984, Pub.L. 98–616, title V, § 502(f), 98 Stat. 3276.)

Cross References

Consultation with Environmental Protection Agency to insure compliance with this section relating to municipal waste reprocessing demonstration facilities, see section 5920 of this title.

Code of Federal Regulations

Grants, see 40 CFR 40.100 et seq.

§ 6985. Special study and demonstration projects on recovery of useful energy and materials

(a) Studies

The Administrator shall conduct studies and develop recommendations for administrative or legislative action on—

(1) means of recovering materials and energy from solid waste, recommended uses of such materials and energy for national or international welfare, including identification of potential markets for such recovered resources, the impact of distribution of such resources on existing markets, and potentials for energy conservation through resource conservation and resource recovery;

(2) actions to reduce waste generation which have been taken voluntarily or in response to governmental action, and those which practically could be taken in the future, and the economic, social, and environmental consequences of such actions;

(3) methods of collection, separation, and containerization which will encourage efficient utilization of facilities and contribute to more effec-

tive programs of reduction, reuse, or disposal of wastes;

(4) the use of Federal procurement to develop market demand for recovered resources;

(5) recommended incentives (including Federal grants, loans, and other assistance) and disincentives to accelerate the reclamation or recycling of materials from solid wastes, with special emphasis on motor vehicle hulks;

(6) the effect of existing public policies, including subsidies and economic incentives and disincentives, percentage depletion allowances, capital gains treatment and other tax incentives and disincentives, upon the recycling and reuse of materials, and the likely effect of the modification or elimination of such incentives and disincentives upon the reuse, recycling and conservation of such materials;

(7) the necessity and method of imposing disposal or other charges on packaging, containers, vehicles, and other manufactured goods, which charges would reflect the cost of final disposal, the value of recoverable components of the item, and any social costs associated with nonrecycling or uncontrolled disposal of such items;

(8) the legal constraints and institutional barriers to the acquisition of land needed for solid waste management, including land for facilities and disposal sites;

(9) in consultation with the Secretary of Agriculture, agricultural waste management problems and practices, the extent of reuse and recovery of resources in such wastes, the prospects for improvement, Federal, State, and local regulations governing such practices, and the economic, social, and environmental consequences of such practices; and

(10) in consultation with the Secretary of the Interior, mining waste management problems, and practices, including an assessment of existing authorities, technologies, and economics, and the environmental and public health consequences of such practices.

(b) Demonstration

The Administrator is also authorized to carry out demonstration projects to test and demonstrate methods and techniques developed pursuant to subsection (a) of this section.

(c) Application of other sections

Section 6981(b) and (c) of this title shall be applicable to investigations, studies, and projects carried out under this section.

(Pub.L. 89–272, title II, § 8005, as added Oct. 21, 1976, Pub.L. 94–580, § 2, 90 Stat. 2837.)

Code of Federal Regulations

Grants, see 40 CFR 40.100 et seq.

§ 6986. Grants for resource recovery systems and improved solid waste disposal facilities

(a) Authority

The Administrator is authorized to make grants pursuant to this section to any State, municipal, or interstate or intermunicipal agency for the demonstration of resource recovery systems or for the construction of new or improved solid waste disposal facilities.

(b) Conditions

(1) Any grant under this section for the demonstration of a resource recovery system may be made only if it (A) is consistent with any plans which meet the requirements of subchapter IV of this chapter; (B) is consistent with the guidelines recommended pursuant to section 6907 of this title; (C) is designed to provide area-wide resource recovery systems consistent with the purposes of this chapter, as determined by the Administrator, pursuant to regulations promulgated under subsection (d) of this section; and (D) provides an equitable system for distributing the costs associated with construction, operation, and maintenance of any resource recovery system among the users of such system.

(2) The Federal share for any project to which paragraph (1) applies shall not be more than 75 percent.

(c) Limitations

(1) A grant under this section for the construction of a new or improved solid waste disposal facility may be made only if—

(A) a State or interstate plan for solid waste disposal has been adopted which applies to the area involved, and the facility to be constructed (i) is consistent with such plan, (ii) is included in a comprehensive plan for the area involved which is satisfactory to the Administrator for the purposes of this chapter, and (iii) is consistent with the guidelines recommended under section 6907 of this title, and

(B) the project advances the state of the art by applying new and improved techniques in reducing the environmental impact of solid waste disposal, in achieving recovery of energy or resources, or in recycling useful materials.

(2) The Federal share for any project to which paragraph (1) applies shall be not more than 50 percent in the case of a project serving an area which includes only one municipality, and not more than 75 percent in any other case.

(d) Regulations

(1) The Administrator shall promulgate regulations establishing a procedure for awarding grants under this section which—

(A) provides that projects will be carried out in communities of varying sizes, under such conditions as will assist in solving the community waste problems of urban-industrial centers, metropolitan regions, and rural areas, under representative geographic and environmental conditions; and

(B) provides deadlines for submission of, and action on, grant requests.

(2) In taking action on applications for grants under this section, consideration shall be given by the Administrator (A) to the public benefits to be derived by the construction and the propriety of Federal aid in making such grant; (B) to the extent applicable, to the economic and commercial viability of the project (including contractual arrangements with the private sector to market any resources recovered); (C) to the potential of such project for general application to community solid waste disposal problems; and (D) to the use by the applicant of comprehensive regional or metropolitan area planning.

(e) Additional limitations

A grant under this section—

(1) may be made only in the amount of the Federal share of (A) the estimated total design and construction costs, plus (B) in the case of a grant to which subsection (b)(1) of this section applies, the first-year operation and maintenance costs;

(2) may not be provided for land acquisition or (except as otherwise provided in paragraph (1)(B)) for operating or maintenance costs;

(3) may not be made until the applicant has made provision satisfactory to the Administrator for proper and efficient operation and maintenance of the project (subject to paragraph (1)(B)); and

(4) may be made subject to such conditions and requirements, in addition to those provided in this section, as the Administrator may require to properly carry out his functions pursuant to this chapter.

For purposes of paragraph (1), the non-Federal share may be in any form, including, but not limited to, lands or interests therein needed for the project or personal property or services, the value of which shall be determined by the Administrator.

(f) Single State

(1) Not more than 15 percent of the total of funds authorized to be appropriated for any fiscal year to carry out this section shall be granted under this section for projects in any one State.

(2) The Administrator shall prescribe by regulation the manner in which this subsection shall apply to a grant under this section for a project in an area which includes all or part of more than one State.

(Pub.L. 89–272, title II, § 8006, as added Oct. 21, 1976, Pub.L. 94–580, § 2, 90 Stat. 2838.)

Code of Federal Regulations

Grants, see 40 CFR 40.100 et seq.

Library References

United States ⚖82(3).
C.J.S. United States § 122.

§ 6987. Authorization of appropriations

There are authorized to be appropriated not to exceed $35,000,000 for the fiscal year 1978 to carry out the purposes of this subchapter (except for section 6982 of this title).

(Pub.L. 89–272, title II, § 8007, as added Oct. 21, 1976, Pub.L. 94–580, § 2, 90 Stat. 2839.)

Library References

United States ⚖82(3).
C.J.S. United States § 122.

SUBCHAPTER IX—REGULATION OF UNDERGROUND STORAGE TANKS

§ 6991. Definitions and exemptions

For the purposes of this subchapter—

(1) The term "underground storage tank" means any one or combination of tanks (including underground pipes connected thereto) which is used to contain an accumulation of regulated substances, and the volume of which (including the volume of the underground pipes connected thereto) is 10 per centum or more beneath the surface of the ground. Such term does not include any—

(A) farm or residential tank of 1,100 gallons or less capacity used for storing motor fuel for noncommercial purposes,

(B) tank used for storing heating oil for consumptive use on the premises where stored,

(C) septic tank,

(D) pipeline facility (including gathering lines) regulated under—

(i) the Natural Gas Pipeline Safety Act of 1968 (49 U.S.C.App. 1671, et seq.) [49 U.S.C. 1671 et seq.], (**ii**) the Hazardous Liquid Pipeline Safety Act of 1979 (49 U.S.C.App. 2001, et seq.) [49 U.S.C. 2001 et seq.], or

(**iii**) which is an intrastate pipeline facility regulated under State laws comparable to the provisions of law referred to in clause (i) or (ii) of this subparagraph,

(**E**) surface impoundment, pit, pond, or lagoon,

(**F**) storm water or waste water collection system,

(**G**) flow-through process tank,

(**H**) liquid trap or associated gathering lines directly related to oil or gas production and gathering operations, or

(**I**) storage tank situated in an underground area (such as a basement, cellar, mineworking, drift, shaft, or tunnel) if the storage tank is situated upon or above the surface of the floor.

The term "underground storage tank" shall not include any pipes connected to any tank which is described in subparagraphs (A) through (I).

(**2**) The term "regulated substance" means—

(**A**) any substance defined in section 9601(14) of this title (but not including any substance regulated as a hazardous waste under subchapter III of this chapter), and

(**B**) petroleum.

(**3**) The term "owner" means—

(**A**) in the case of an underground storage tank in use on November 8, 1984, or brought into use after that date, any person who owns an underground storage tank used for the storage, use, or dispensing of regulated substances, and

(**B**) in the case of any underground storage tank in use before November 8, 1984, but no longer in use on November 8, 1984, any person who owned such tank immediately before the discontinuation of its use.

(**4**) The term "operator" means any person in control of, or having responsibility for, the daily operation of the underground storage tank.

(**5**) The term "release" means any spilling, leaking, emitting, discharging, escaping, leaching, or disposing from an underground storage tank into ground water, surface water or subsurface soils.

(**6**) The term "person" has the same meaning as provided in section 6903(15) of this title, except that such term includes a consortium, a joint venture, and a commercial entity, and the United States Government.

(**7**) The term "nonoperational storage tank" means any underground storage tank in which regulated substances will not be deposited or from which regulated substances will not be dispensed after November 8, 1984.

(**8**) The term "petroleum" means petroleum, including crude oil or any fraction thereof which is liquid at standard conditions of temperature and pressure (60 degrees Fahrenheit and 14.7 pounds per square inch absolute).

(Pub.L. 89–272, title II, § 9001, as added Nov. 8, 1984, Pub.L. 98–616, title VI, § 601(a), 98 Stat. 3277, and amended Oct. 17, 1986, Pub.L. 99–499, Title II, § 205(a), 100 Stat. 1696.)

Library References

Health and Environment ⚷25.5(3).
C.J.S. Health and Environment § 91 et seq.

§ 6991a. Notification

(a) Underground storage tanks

(**1**) Within 18 months after November 8, 1984, each owner of an underground storage tank shall notify the State or local agency or department designated pursuant to subsection (b)(1) of this section of the existence of such tank, specifying the age, size, type, location, and uses of such tank.

(**2**)(**A**) For each underground storage tank taken out of operation after January 1, 1974, the owner of such tank shall, within eighteen months after November 8, 1984, notify the State or local agency, or department designated pursuant to subsection (b)(1) of this section of the existence of such tanks (unless the owner knows the tank subsequently was removed from the ground). The owner of a tank taken out of operation on or before January 1, 1974, shall not be required to notify the State or local agency under this subsection.

(**B**) Notice under subparagraph (A) shall specify, to the extent known to the owner—

(**i**) the date the tank was taken out of operation,

(**ii**) the age of the tank on the date taken out of operation,

(**iii**) the size, type and location of the tank, and

(**iv**) the type and quantity of substances left stored in such tank on the date taken out of operation.

(**3**) Any owner which brings into use an underground storage tank after the initial notification period specified under paragraph (1), shall notify the designated State or local agency or department within thirty days of the existence of such tank, specifying the age, size, type, location and uses of such tank.

(4) Paragraphs (1) through (3) of this subsection shall not apply to tanks for which notice was given pursuant to section 9603(c) of this title.

(5) Beginning thirty days after the Administrator prescribes the form of notice pursuant to subsection (b)(2) of this section and for eighteen months thereafter, any person who deposits regulated substances in an underground storage tank shall reasonably notify the owner or operator of such tank of the owner's notification requirements pursuant to this subsection.

(6) Beginning thirty days after the Administrator issues new tank performance standards pursuant to section 6991b(c) of this title, any person who sells a tank intended to be used as an underground storage tank shall notify the purchaser of such tank of the owner's notification requirements pursuant to this subsection.

(b) Agency designation

(1) Within one hundred and eighty days after November 8, 1984, the Governors of each State shall designate the appropriate State agency or department or local agencies or departments to receive the notifications under subsection (a)(1), (2), or (3) of this section.

(2) Within twelve months after November 8, 1984, the Administrator, in consultation with State and local officials designated pursuant to subsection (b)(1) of this section, and after notice and opportunity for public comment, shall prescribe the form of the notice and the information to be included in the notifications under subsection (a)(1), (2), or (3) of this section. In prescribing the form of such notice, the Administrator shall take into account the effect on small businesses and other owners and operators.

(c) State inventories

Each State shall make 2 separate inventories of all underground storage tanks in such State containing regulated substances. One inventory shall be made with respect to petroleum and one with respect to other regulated substances. In making such inventories, the State shall utilize and aggregate the data in the notification forms submitted pursuant to subsections (a) and (b) of this section. Each State shall submit such aggregated data to the Administrator not later than 270 days after October 17, 1986.

(Pub.L. 89–272, title II, § 9002, as added Nov. 8, 1984, Pub.L. 98–616, title VI, § 601(a), 98 Stat. 3278, and amended Oct. 17, 1986, Pub.L. 99–499, Title II, § 205(b), 100 Stat. 1696.)

§ 6991b. Release, detection, prevention, and correction regulations

(a) Regulations

The Administrator, after notice and opportunity for public comment, and at least three months before the effective dates specified in subsection (f) of this section, shall promulgate release detection, prevention, and correction regulations applicable to all owners and operators of underground storage tanks, as may be necessary to protect human health and the environment.

(b) Distinction in regulations

In promulgating regulations under this section, the Administrator may distinguish between types, classes, and ages of underground storage tanks. In making such distinctions, the Administrator may take into consideration factors, including, but not limited to: location of the tanks, soil and climate conditions, uses of the tanks, history of maintenance, age of the tanks, current industry recommended practices, national consensus codes, hydrogeology, water table, size of the tanks, quantity of regulated substances periodically deposited in or dispensed from the tank, the technical capability of the owners and operators, and the compatibility of the regulated substance and the materials of which the tank is fabricated.

(c) Requirements

The regulations promulgated pursuant to this section shall include, but need not be limited to, the following requirements respecting all underground storage tanks—

(1) requirements for maintaining a leak detection system, an inventory control system together with tank testing, or a comparable system or method designed to identify releases in a manner consistent with the protection of human health and the environment;

(2) requirements for maintaining records of any monitoring or leak detection system or inventory control system or tank testing or comparable system;

(3) requirements for reporting of releases and corrective action taken in response to a release from an underground storage tank;

(4) requirements for taking corrective action in response to a release from an underground storage tank;

(5) requirements for the closure of tanks to prevent future releases of regulated substances into the environment; and

(6) requirements for maintaining evidence of financial responsibility for taking corrective ac-

tion and compensating third parties for bodily injury and property damage caused by sudden and nonsudden accidental releases arising from operating an underground storage tank.

(d) Financial responsibility

(1) Financial responsibility required by this subsection may be established in accordance with regulations promulgated by the Administrator by any one, or any combination, of the following: insurance, guarantee, surety bond, letter of credit, qualification as a self-insurer or any other method satisfactory to the Administrator. In promulgating requirements under this subsection, the Administrator is authorized to specify policy or other contractual terms, conditions, or defenses which are necessary or are unacceptable in establishing such evidence of financial responsibility in order to effectuate the purposes of this chapter.

(2) In any case where the owner or operator is in bankruptcy, reorganization, or arrangement pursuant to the Federal Bankruptcy Code or where with reasonable diligence jurisdiction in any State court of the Federal Courts cannot be obtained over an owner or operator likely to be solvent at the time of judgment, any claim arising from conduct for which evidence of financial responsibility must be provided under this subsection may be asserted directly against the guarantor providing such evidence of financial responsibility. In the case of any action pursuant to this paragraph such guarantor shall be entitled to invoke all rights and defenses which would have been available to the owner or operator if any action had been brought against the owner or operator by the claimant and which would have been available to the guarantor if an action had been brought against the guarantor by the owner or operator.

(3) The total liability of any guarantor shall be limited to the aggregate amount which the guarantor has provided as evidence of financial responsibility to the owner or operator under this section. Nothing in this subsection shall be construed to limit any other State or Federal statutory, contractual or common law liability of a guarantor to its owner or operator including, but not limited to, the liability of such guarantor for bad faith either in negotiating or in failing to negotiate the settlement of any claim. Nothing in this subsection shall be construed to diminish the liability of any person under section 9607 or 9611 of this title or other applicable law.

(4) For the purpose of this subsection, the term "guarantor" means any person, other than the owner or operator, who provides evidence of financial responsibility for an owner or operator under this subsection.

(5)(A) The Administrator, in promulgating financial responsibility regulations under this section, may establish an amount of coverage for particular classes or categories of underground storage tanks containing petroleum which shall satisfy such regulations and which shall not be less than $1,000,000 for each occurrence with an appropriate aggregate requirement.

(B) The Administrator may set amounts lower than the amounts required by subparagraph (A) of this paragraph for underground storage tanks containing petroleum which are at facilities not engaged in petroleum production, refining, or marketing and which are not used to handle substantial quantities of petroleum.

(C) In establishing classes and categories for purposes of this paragraph, the Administrator may consider the following factors:

(i) The size, type, location, storage, and handling capacity of underground storage tanks in the class or category and the volume of petroleum handled by such tanks.

(ii) The likelihood of release and the potential extent of damage from any release from underground storage tanks in the class or category.

(iii) The economic impact of the limits on the owners and operators of each such class or category, particularly relating to the small business segment of the petroleum marketing industry.

(iv) The availability of methods of financial responsibility in amounts greater than the amount established by this paragraph.

(v) Such other factors as the Administrator deems pertinent.

(D) The Administrator may suspend enforcement of the financial responsibility requirements for a particular class or category of underground storage tanks or in a particular State, if the Administrator makes a determination that methods of financial responsibility satisfying the requirements of this subsection are not generally available for underground storage tanks in that class or category, and—

(i) steps are being taken to form a risk retention group for such class of tanks; or

(ii) such State is taking steps to establish a fund pursuant to section 6991c of this title to be submitted as evidence of financial responsibility.

A suspension by the Administrator pursuant to this paragraph shall extend for a period not to exceed 180 days. A determination to suspend may be made with respect to the same class or category or for the same State at the end of such period, but only if substantial progress has been made in establishing a risk retention group, or the owners or operators in the class or category demonstrate, and the Administrator finds, that the formation of such a group is not possible and that the State is unable or unwilling to establish such a fund pursuant to clause (ii).

(e) New tank performance standards

The Administrator shall, not later than three months prior to the effective date specified in subsection (f) of this section, issue performance standards for underground storage tanks brought into use on or after the effective date of such standards. The performance standards for new underground storage tanks shall include, but need not be limited to, design, construction, installation, release detection, and compatibility standards.

(f) Effective dates

(1) Regulations issued pursuant to subsection (c) and (d) of this section, and standards issued pursuant to subsection (e) of this section, for underground storage tanks containing regulated substances defined in section 6991(2)(B) of this title (petroleum, including crude oil or any fraction thereof which is liquid at standard conditions of temperature and pressure) shall be effective not later than thirty months after November 8, 1984.

(2) Standards issued pursuant to subsection (e) of this section (entitled "New Tank Performance Standards") for underground storage tanks containing regulated substances defined in section 6991(2)(A) of this title shall be effective not later than thirty-six months after November 8, 1984.

(3) Regulations issued pursuant to subsection (c) of this section (entitled "Requirements") and standards issued pursuant to subsection (d) of this section (entitled "Financial Responsibility") for underground storage tanks containing regulated substances defined in section 6991(2)(A) of this title shall be effective not later than forty-eight months after November 8, 1984.

(g) Interim prohibition

(1) Until the effective date of the standards promulgated by the Administrator under subsection (e) of this section and after one hundred and eighty days after November 8, 1984, no person may install an underground storage tank for the purpose of storing regulated substances unless such tank (whether of single or double wall construction)—

(A) will prevent releases due to corrosion or structural failure for the operational life of the tank;

(B) is cathodically protected against corrosion, constructed of noncorrosive material, steel clad with a noncorrosive material, or designed in a manner to prevent the release or threatened release of any stored substance; and

(C) the material used in the construction or lining of the tank is compatible with the substance to be stored.

(2) Notwithstanding paragraph (1), if soil tests conducted in accordance with ASTM Standard G57–78, or another standard approved by the Administrator, show that soil resistivity in an installation location is 12,000 ohm/cm or more (unless a more stringent standard is prescribed by the Administrator by rule), a storage tank without corrosion protection may be installed in that location during the period referred to in paragraph (1).

(h) EPA Response Program for Petroleum

(1) Before regulations

Before the effective date of regulations under subsection (c) of this section, the Administrator (or a State pursuant to paragraph (7)) is authorized to—

(A) require the owner or operator of an underground storage tank to undertake corrective action with respect to any release of petroleum when the Administrator (or the State) determines that such corrective action will be done properly and promptly by the owner or operator of the underground storage tank from which the release occurs; or

(B) undertake corrective action with respect to any release of petroleum into the environment from an underground storage tank if such action is necessary, in the judgment of the Administrator (or the State), to protect human health and the environment.

The corrective action undertaken or required under this paragraph shall be such as may be necessary to protect human health and the environment. The Administrator shall use funds in the Leaking Underground Storage Tank Trust Fund for payment of costs incurred for corrective action under subparagraph (B), enforcement action under subparagraph (A), and cost recovery under paragraph (6) of this subsection. Subject to the priority requirements of paragraph (3), the Administrator (or the State) shall give priority in undertaking such actions under subparagraph (B) to cases where the Administrator (or the State) cannot identify a solvent owner or operator of the tank who will undertake action properly.

(2) After regulations

Following the effective date of regulations under subsection (c) of this section, all actions or orders of the Administrator (or a State pursuant to paragraph (7)) described in paragraph (1) of this subsection shall be in conformity with such regulations. Following such effective date, the Administrator (or the State) may undertake corrective action with respect to any release of petroleum into the environment from an underground storage tank only if such action is necessary, in the judgment of the Administrator (or the State), to protect human health and the environment and one or more of the following situations exists:

(A) No person can be found, within 90 days or such shorter period as may be necessary to protect human health and the environment, who is—

(i) an owner or operator of the tank concerned,

(ii) subject to such corrective action regulations, and

(iii) capable of carrying out such corrective action properly.

(B) A situation exists which requires prompt action by the Administrator (or the State) under this paragraph to protect human health and the environment.

(C) Corrective action costs at a facility exceed the amount of coverage required by the Administrator pursuant to the provisions of subsections (c) and (d)(5) of this section and, considering the class or category of underground storage tank from which the release occurred, expenditures from the Leaking Underground Storage Tank Trust Fund are necessary to assure an effective corrective action.

(D) The owner or operator of the tank has failed or refused to comply with an order of the Administrator under this subsection or section 6991e of this title or with the order of a State under this subsection to comply with the corrective action regulations.

(3) Priority of corrective actions

The Administrator (or a State pursuant to paragraph (7)) shall give priority in undertaking corrective actions under this subsection, and in issuing orders requiring owners or operators to undertake such actions, to releases of petroleum from underground storage tanks which pose the greatest threat to human health and the environment.

(4) Corrective action orders

The Administrator is authorized to issue orders to the owner or operator of an underground storage tank to carry out subparagraph (A) of paragraph (1) or to carry out regulations issued under subsection (c)(4) of this section. A State acting pursuant to paragraph (7) of this subsection is authorized to carry out subparagraph (A) of paragraph (1) only until the State's program is approved by the Administrator under section 6991c of this title. Such orders shall be issued and enforced in the same manner and subject to the same requirements as orders under section 6991e of this title.

(5) Allowable corrective actions

The corrective actions undertaken by the Administrator (or a State pursuant to paragraph (7)) under paragraph (1) or (2) may include temporary or permanent relocation of residents and alternative household water supplies. In connection with the performance of any corrective action under paragraph (1) or (2), the Administrator may undertake an exposure assessment as defined in paragraph (10) of this subsection or provide for such an assessment in a cooperative agreement with a State pursuant to paragraph (7) of this subsection. The costs of any such assessment may be treated as corrective action for purposes of paragraph (6), relating to cost recovery.

(6) Recovery of costs

(A) In general

Whenever costs have been incurred by the Administrator, or by a State pursuant to paragraph (7), for undertaking corrective action or enforcement action with respect to the release of petroleum from an underground storage tank, the owner or operator of such tank shall be liable to the Administrator or the State for such costs. The liability under this paragraph shall be construed to be the standard of liability which obtains under section 311 of the Federal Water Pollution Control Act.

(B) Recovery

In determining the equities for seeking the recovery of costs under subparagraph (A), the Administrator (or a State pursuant to paragraph (7) of this subsection) may consider the amount of financial responsibility required to be maintained under subsections (c) and (d)(5) of this section and the factors considered in establishing such amount under subsection (d)(5) of this section.

(C) Effect on liability

(i) No transfers of liability

No indemnification, hold harmless, or similar agreement or conveyance shall be effective to transfer from the owner or operator of any underground storage tank or from any person who may be liable for a release or threat of release under this subsection, to any other person the liability imposed under this subsection. Nothing in this subsection shall bar any agreement to insure, hold harmless, or indemnify a party to such agreement for any liability under this section.

(ii) No bar to cause of action

Nothing in this subsection, including the provisions of clause (i) of this subparagraph, shall bar a cause of action that an owner or operator or any other person subject to liability under this section, or a guarantor, has or would have, by reason of subrogation or otherwise against any person.

(D) Facility

For purposes of this paragraph, the term "facility" means, with respect to any owner or operator, all underground storage tanks used for the storage of petroleum which are owned or operated by such owner or operator and located on a single parcel of property (or on any contiguous or adjacent property).

(7) State authorities

(A) General

A State may exercise the authorities in paragraphs (1) and (2) of this subsection, subject to the terms and conditions of paragraphs (3), (5), (9), (10), and (11), and including the authorities of paragraphs (4), (6), and (8) of this subsection if—

(i) the Administrator determines that the State has the capabilities to carry out effective corrective actions and enforcement activities; and

(ii) the Administrator enters into a cooperative agreement with the State setting out the actions to be undertaken by the State.

The Administrator may provide funds from the Leaking Underground Storage Tank Trust Fund for the reasonable costs of the State's actions under the cooperative agreement.

(B) Cost share

Following the effective date of the regulations under subsection (c) of this section, the State shall pay 10 per centum of the cost of corrective actions undertaken either by the Administrator or by the State under a cooperative agreement, except that the Administrator may take corrective action at a facility where immediate action is necessary to respond to an imminent and substantial endangerment to human health or the environment if the State fails to pay the cost share.

(8) Emergency procurement powers

Notwithstanding any other provision of law, the Administrator may authorize the use of such emergency procurement powers as he deems necessary.

(9) Definition of owner

As used in this subsection, the term "owner" does not include any person who, without participating in the management of an underground storage tank and otherwise not engaged in petroleum production, refining, and marketing, holds indicia of ownership primarily to protect the owner's security interest in the tank.

(10) Definition of exposure assessment

As used in this subsection, the term "exposure assessment" means an assessment to determine the extent of exposure of, or potential for exposure of, individuals to petroleum from a release from an underground storage tank based on such factors as the nature and extent of contamination and the existence of or potential for pathways of human exposure (including ground or surface water contamination, air emissions, and food chain contamination), the size of the community within the likely pathways of exposure, and the comparison of expected human exposure levels to the short-term and long-term health effects associated with identified contaminants and any available recommended exposure or tolerance limits for such contaminants. Such assessment shall not delay corrective action to abate immediate hazards or reduce exposure.

(11) Facilities without financial responsibility

At any facility where the owner or operator has failed to maintain evidence of financial responsibility in amounts at least equal to the amounts established by subsection (d)(5)(A) of this section (or a lesser amount if such amount is applicable to such facility as a result of subsection (d)(5)(B) of this section) for whatever reason the Administrator shall expend no monies from the Leaking Underground Storage Tank Trust Fund to clean up releases at such facility pursuant to the provisions of paragraph (1) or (2) of this subsection. At such facilities the Administrator shall use the authorities provided in subparagraph (A) of paragraph (1) and paragraph (4) of this subsection and section 6991e of this title to order corrective action to clean up such releases. States acting pursuant to paragraph (7) of this subsection shall use the authorities provided in subparagraph (A) of paragraph (1) and paragraph (4) of this subsection to order corrective action to clean up such releases. Notwithstanding the provisions of this paragraph, the Administrator may use monies from the fund to take the corrective actions authorized by paragraph (5) of this subsection to protect human health at such facilities and shall seek full recovery of the costs of all such actions pursuant to the provisions of paragraph (6)(A) of this subsection and without consideration of the factors in paragraph (6)(B) of this subsection. Nothing in this paragraph shall prevent the Administrator (or a State pursuant to paragraph (7) of this subsection) from taking corrective action at a facility where there is no solvent owner or operator or where immediate action is necessary to respond to an imminent and substantial endangerment of human health or the environment.

(Pub.L. 89–272, title II, § 9003, as added Nov. 8, 1984, Pub.L. 98–616, title VI, § 601(a), 98 Stat. 3279, and amended Oct. 17, 1986, Pub.L. 99–499, Title II, § 205(c), (d), 100 Stat. 1697, 1698.)

§ 6991c. Approval of State programs

(a) Elements of State programs

Beginning 30 months after November 8, 1984, any State may,[1] submit an underground storage tank release detection, prevention, and correction program for review and approval by the Administrator. The program may cover tanks used to store regulated substances referred to in section 6991(2)(A) or (B) of this title or both. A State program may be approved by the Administrator under this section only if the State demonstrates that the State program includes the following requirements and standards and provides for adequate enforcement of compliance with such requirements and standards—

(1) requirements for maintaining a leak detection system, an inventory control system together with tank testing, or a comparable system or method designed to identify releases in a manner consistent with the protection of human health and the environment;

(2) requirements for maintaining records of any monitoring or leak detection system or inventory control system or tank testing system;

(3) requirements for reporting of any releases and corrective action taken in response to a release from an underground storage tank;

(4) requirements for taking corrective action in response to a release from an underground storage tank;

(5) requirements for the closure of tanks to prevent future releases of regulated substances into the environment;

(6) requirements for maintaining evidence of financial responsibility for taking corrective action and compensating third parties for bodily injury and property damage caused by sudden and nonsudden accidental releases arising from operating an underground storage tank;

(7) standards of performance for new underground storage tanks; and

(8) requirements—

(A) for notifying the appropriate State agency or department (or local agency or department) designated according to section 6991a(b)(1) of this title of the existence of any operational or non-operational underground storage tank; and

(B) for providing the information required on the form issued pursuant to section 6991a(b)(2) of this title.

(b) Federal standards

(1) A State program submitted under this section may be approved only if the requirements under paragraphs (1) through (7) of subsection (a) of this section are no less stringent than the corresponding requirements standards promulgated by the Administrator pursuant to section 6991b(a) of this title.

(2)(A) A State program may be approved without regard to whether or not the requirements referred to in paragraphs (1), (2), (3), and (5) of subsection (a) of this section are less stringent than the corresponding standards under section 6991b(a) of this title during the one-year period commencing on the date of promulgation of regulations under section 6991b(a) of this title if State regulatory action but no State legislative action is required in order to adopt a State program.

(B) If such State legislative action is required, the State program may be approved without regard to whether or not the requirements referred to in paragraphs (1), (2), (3), and (5) of subsection (a) of this section are less stringent than the corresponding standards under section 6991b(a) of this title during the two-year period commencing on the date of promulgation of regulations under section 6991b(a) of this title (and during an additional one-year period after such legislative action if regulations are required to be promulgated by the State pursuant to such legislative action).

(c) Financial responsibility

(1) Corrective action and compensation programs administered by State or local agencies or departments may be submitted for approval under subsection (a)(6) of this section as evidence of financial responsibility.

(2) Financial responsibility required by this subsection may be established in accordance with regulations promulgated by the Administrator by any one, or any combination, of the following: insurance, guarantee, surety bond, letter of credit, qualification as a self-insurer or any other method satisfactory to the Administrator. In promulgating requirements under this subsection, the Administrator is authorized to specify policy or other contractual terms including the amount of coverage required for various classes and categories of underground storage tanks pursuant to section 6991b(d)(5) of this title, conditions, or defenses which are necessary or are unacceptable in establishing such evidence of financial responsibility in order to effectuate the purposes of this subchapter.

(3) In any case where the owner or operator is in bankruptcy, reorganization, or arrangement pursuant to the Federal Bankruptcy Code or where with reasonable diligence jurisdiction in any State court of the Federal courts cannot be obtained over an owner or operator likely to be solvent at the time of judgment, any claim arising from conduct for which evidence of financial responsibility must be provided under this subsection may be asserted directly against the guarantor providing such evidence of financial responsibility. In the case of any action pursuant to this paragraph such guarantor shall be entitled to invoke all rights and defenses which would have been available to the owner or operator if any action had been brought against the owner or operator by the claimant and which would have been available to the guarantor if an action had been brought against the guarantor by the owner or operator.

(4) The total liability of any guarantor shall be limited to the aggregate amount which the guarantor has provided as evidence of financial responsibility to the owner or operator under this section. Nothing in this subsection shall be construed to limit any other State or Federal statutory, contractual or common law liability of a guarantor to its owner or operator including, but not limited to, the liability of such guarantor for bad faith either in negotiating or in failing to negotiate the settlement of any claim. Nothing in this subsection shall be construed to diminish the liability of any person under section 9607 or 9611 of this title or other applicable law.

(5) For the purpose of this subsection, the term "guarantor" means any person, other than the owner or operator, who provides evidence of financial responsibility for an owner or operator under this subsection.

(d) EPA determination

(1) Within one hundred and eighty days of the date of receipt of a proposed State program, the Administrator shall, after notice and opportunity for public comment, make a determination whether the State's program complies with the provisions of this section and provides for adequate enforcement of compliance with the requirements and standards adopted pursuant to this section.

(2) If the Administrator determines that a State program complies with the provisions of this section and provides for adequate enforcement of compliance with the requirements and standards adopted pursuant to this section, he shall approve the State program in lieu of the Federal program and the State shall have primary enforcement responsibility with respect to requirements of its program.

(e) Withdrawal of authorization

Whenever the Administrator determines after public hearing that a State is not administering and enforcing a program authorized under this subchapter in accordance with the provisions of this section, he shall so notify the State. If appropriate action is not taken within a reasonable time, not to exceed one hundred and twenty days after such notification, the Administrator shall withdraw approval of such program and reestablish the Federal program pursuant to this subchapter.

(Pub.L. 89–272, title II, § 9004, as added Nov. 8, 1984, Pub.L. 98–616, title VI, § 601(a), 98 Stat. 3282, and amended Oct. 17, 1986, Pub.L. 99–499, Title II, § 205(e), 100 Stat. 1702.)

[1] So in original.

§ 6991d. Inspections, monitoring, testing and corrective action

(a) Furnishing information

For the purposes of developing or assisting in the development of any regulation, conducting any study taking any corrective action, or enforcing the provisions of this subchapter, any owner or operator of an underground storage tank (or any tank subject to study under section 6991h of this title that is used for storing regulated substances) shall, upon request of any officer, employee or representative of the Environmental Protection Agency, duly designated by the Administrator, or upon request of any duly designated officer, employee, or representative of a State acting pursuant to subsection (h)(7) of section 6991b of this title or with an approved program, furnish information relating to such tanks, their associated equipment, their contents, conduct monitoring or testing, permit such officer at all reasonable times to have access to, and to copy all records relating to such tanks and permit such officer to have access for corrective action. For the purposes of developing or assisting in the development of any regulation, conducting any study, taking corrective action, or enforcing the provisions of this subchapter, such officers, employees, or representatives are authorized—

(1) to enter at reasonable times any establishment or other place where an underground storage tank is located;

(2) to inspect and obtain samples from any person of any regulated substances contained in such tank;

(3) to conduct monitoring or testing of the tanks, associated equipment, contents, or surrounding soils, air, surface water or ground water; and

(4) to take corrective action.

Each such inspection shall be commenced and completed with reasonable promptness.

(b) Confidentiality

(1) Any records, reports, or information obtained from any persons under this section shall be available to the public, except that upon a showing satisfactory to the Administrator (or the State, as the case may be) by any person that records, reports, or information, or a particular part thereof, to which the Administrator (or the State, as the case may be) or any officer, employee, or representative thereof has access under this section if made public, would divulge information entitled to protection under section 1905 of Title 18, such information or particular portion thereof shall be considered confidential in accordance with the purposes of that section, except that such record, report, document, or information may be disclosed to other officers, employees, or authorized representatives of the United States concerned with carrying out this chapter, or when relevent [1] in any proceeding under this chapter.

(2) Any person not subject to the provisions of section 1905 of Title 18 who knowingly and willfully divulges or discloses any information entitled to protection under this subsection shall, upon conviction, be subject to a fine of not more than $5,000 or to imprisonment not to exceed one year, or both.

(3) In submitting data under this subchapter, a person required to provide such data may—

(A) designate the data which such person believes is entitled to protection under this subsection, and

(B) submit such designated data separately from other data submitted under this subchapter.

A designation under this paragraph shall be made in writing and in such manner as the Administrator may prescribe.

(4) Notwithstanding any limitation contained in this section or any other provision of law, all information reported to, or otherwise obtained, by the Administrator (or any representative of the Administrator) under this chapter shall be made available, upon written request of any duly authorized committee of the Congress, to such committee (including records, reports, or information obtained by representatives of the Environmental Protection Agency).

(Pub.L. 89–272, title II, § 9005, as added Nov. 8, 1984, Pub.L. 98–616, title VI, § 601(a), 98 Stat. 3284, and amended Oct. 17, 1986, Pub.L. 99–499, Title II, § 205(f), 100 Stat. 1702.)

[1] So in original. Probably should be relevant.

§ 6991e. Federal enforcement

(a) Compliance orders

(1) Except as provided in paragraph (2), whenever on the basis of any information, the Administrator determines that any person is in violation of any requirement of this subchapter, the Administrator may issue an order requiring compliance within a reasonable specified time period or the Administrator may commence a civil action in the United States district court in which the violation occurred for appropriate relief, including a temporary or permanent injunction.

(2) In the case of a violation of any requirement of this subchapter where such violation occurs in a State with a program approved under section 6991c of this title the Administrator shall give notice to the State in which such violation has occurred prior to issuing an order or commencing a civil action under this section.

(3) If a violator fails to comply with an order under this subsection within the time specified in the order, he shall be liable for a civil penalty of not more than $25,000 for each day of continued noncompliance.

(b) Procedure

Any order issued under this section shall become final unless, no later than thirty days after the order is served, the person or persons named therein request a public hearing. Upon such request the Administrator shall promptly conduct a public hearing. In connection with any proceeding under this section the Administrator may issue subpoenas for the attendance and testimony of witnesses and the production of relevant papers, books, and documents, and may promulgate rules for discovery procedures.

(c) Contents of order

Any order issued under this section shall state with reasonable specificity the nature of the violation, specify a reasonable time for compliance, and assess a penalty, if any, which the Administrator determines is reasonable taking into account the seriousness of the violation and any good faith efforts to comply with the applicable requirements.

(d) Civil penalties

(1) Any owner who knowingly fails to notify or submits false information pursuant to section 6991a(a) of this title shall be subject to a civil penalty not to exceed $10,000 for each tank for which notification is not given or false information is submitted.

(2) Any owner or operator of an underground storage tank who fails to comply with—

(A) any requirement or standard promulgated by the Administrator under section 6991b of this title;

(B) any requirement or standard of a State program approved pursuant to section 6991c of this title; or

(C) the provisions of section 6991b(g) of this title (entitled "Interim Prohibition")

shall be subject to a civil penalty not to exceed $10,000 for each tank for each day of violation.

(Pub.L. 89–272, title II, § 9006, as added Nov. 8, 1984, Pub.L. 98–616, title VI, § 601(a), 98 Stat. 3286.)

§ 6991f. Federal facilities

(a) Application of subchapter

Each department, agency, and instrumentality of the executive, legislative, and judicial branches of the Federal Government having jurisdiction over any underground storage tank shall be subject to and comply with all Federal, State, interstate, and local requirements, applicable to such tank, both substantive and procedural, in the same manner, and to the same extent, as any other person is subject to such requirements, including payment of reasonable service charges. Neither the United States, nor any agent, employee, or officer thereof, shall be immune or exempt from any process or sanction of any State or Federal court with respect to the enforcement of any such injunctive relief.

(b) Presidential exemption

The President may exempt any underground storage tanks of any department, agency, or instrumentality in the executive branch from compliance with such a requirement if he determines it to be in the paramount interest of the United States to do so. No such exemption shall be granted due to lack of appropriation unless the President shall have specifically requested such appropriation as a part of the budgetary process and the Congress shall have failed to make available such requested appropriations. Any exemption shall be for a period not in excess of one year, but additional exemptions may be granted for periods not to exceed one year upon the President's making a new determination. The President shall report each January to the Congress all exemptions from the requirements of this section granted during the preceding calendar year, together with his reason for granting each such exemption.

(Pub.L. 89–272, title II, § 9007, as added Nov. 8, 1984, Pub.L. 98–616, title VI, § 601(a), 98 Stat. 3286.)

§ 6991g. State authority

Nothing in this subchapter shall preclude or deny any right of any State or political subdivision thereof to adopt or enforce any regulation, requirement, or standard of performance respecting underground storage tanks that is more stringent than a regulation, requirement, or standard of performance in effect under this subchapter or to impose any additional liability with respect to the release of regulated substances within such State or political subdivision.

(Pub.L. 89–272, title II, § 9008, as added Nov. 8, 1984, Pub.L. 98–616, title VI, § 601(a), 98 Stat. 3286, and amended Oct. 17, 1986, Pub.L. 99–499, Title II, § 205(g), 100 Stat. 1702.)

§ 6991h. Study of underground storage tanks

(a) Petroleum tanks

Not later than twelve months after November 8, 1984, the Administrator shall complete a study of underground storage tanks used for the storage of regulated substances defined in section 6991(2)(B) of this title.

(b) Other tanks

Not later than thirty-six months after November 8, 1984, the Administrator shall complete a study of all other underground storage tanks.

(c) Elements of studies

The studies under subsections (a) and (b) of this section shall include an assessment of the ages, types (including methods of manufacture, coatings, protection systems, the compatibility of the construction materials and the installation methods) and locations (including the climate of the locations) of such tanks; soil conditions, water tables, and the hydrogeology of tank locations; the relationship between the foregoing factors and the likelihood of releases from underground storage tanks; the effectiveness and costs of inventory systems, tank testing, and leak detection systems; and such other factors as the Administrator deems appropriate.

(d) Farm and heating oil tanks

Not later than thirty-six months after November 8, 1984, the Administrator shall conduct a study regarding the tanks referred to in section 6991(1)(A) and (B) of this title. Such study shall include estimates of the number and location of such tanks and an analysis of the extent to which there may be releases or threatened releases from such tanks into the environment.

(e) Reports

Upon completion of the studies authorized by this section, the Administrator shall submit reports to the President and to the Congress containing the results of the studies and recommendations respecting whether or not such tanks should be subject to the preceding provisions of this subchapter.

(f) Reimbursement

(1) If any owner or operator (excepting an agency, department, or instrumentality of the United States Government, a State or a political subdivision thereof) shall incur costs, including the loss of business opportunity, due to the closure or interruption of operation of an underground storage tank solely for the purpose of conducting studies authorized by this section, the Administrator shall provide such person fair and equitable reimbursement for such costs.

(2) All claims for reimbursement shall be filed with the Administrator not later than ninety days after the closure or interruption which gives rise to the claim.

(3) Reimbursements made under this section shall be from funds appropriated by the Congress pursuant to the authorization contained in section 6916(g) of this title.

(4) For purposes of judicial review, a determination by the Administrator under this subsection shall be considered final agency action.

(Pub.L. 89–272, title II, § 9009, as added Nov. 8, 1984, Pub.L. 98–616, title VI, § 601(a), 98 Stat. 3287.)

§ 6991i. Authorization of appropriations

For authorization of appropriations to carry out this subchapter, see section 6916(g) of this title.

(Pub.L. 89–272, title II, § 9010, as added Nov. 8, 1984, Pub.L. 98–616, title VI, § 601(a), 98 Stat. 3287.)

AIR POLLUTION PREVENTION AND CONTROL

(42 U.S.C.A. §§ 7401 to 7642)

CHAPTER 85—AIR POLLUTION PREVENTION AND CONTROL

SUBCHAPTER I—PROGRAMS AND ACTIVITIES

PART A—AIR QUALITY AND EMISSION LIMITATIONS

Former Sections

The Clean Air Act, now AIR POLLUTION PREVENTION AND CONTROL, 42 U.S.C.A. § 7401 et seq., set out in the following pages, was formerly classified to Chapter 15B—AIR POLLUTION CONTROL, 42 U.S.C.A. § 1857 et seq. The researcher may wish to see the table of the latter set out in title 42, United States Code Annotated, preceding § 1857 for reference purposes.

SUBCHAPTER I—PROGRAMS AND ACTIVITIES

PART A—AIR QUALITY AND EMISSION LIMITATIONS

Cross References

Action under this chapter not to be deemed major federal action within meaning of National Environmental Policy Act of 1969, see section 793 of Title 15, Commerce and Trade.

Applicable environmental requirements defined to include standard, limitation or requirement established by this chapter for purposes of Powerplant and Industrial Fuel Use Act of 1978, see section 8302 of this title.

Authority of Administrator under this chapter not affected by provisions of Atomic Energy Act of 1954 applicable to byproduct material, see section 2022 of this title.

Availability to Science Advisory Board of proposed environmental criteria document, standard, limitation or regulation under this chapter, see section 4365 of this title.

Certification of compliance with procedures for determination of environmental impact of proposed urban mass transportation projects, see section 1604 of Title 49, Transportation.

Coal leases to contain provisions requiring compliance with this chapter, see section 201 of Title 30, Mineral Lands and Mining.

Congressional finding under Solid Waste Disposal Act that greater amounts of solid waste have been created as result of this chapter, see section 6901 of this title.

Consideration of standards under this chapter in establishing noise emission standards for products distributed in commerce, see section 4905 of this title.

Construction of Coastal Zone Management Act of 1972 with existing requirements of water and air pollution programs, see section 1456 of Title 16, Conservation.

Construction of highways to be consistent with plans for implementation of ambient air quality standards, see section 109 of Title 23, Highways.

Construction of Surface Mining Control and Reclamation Act of 1977 as not superseding, amending, modifying or repealing this chapter, see section 1292 of Title 30, Mineral Lands and Mining.

Consumer Product Safety Commission to have no authority to regulate risk of injury if risk could be eliminated by actions taken under this chapter, see section 2080 of Title 15, Commerce and Trade.

Control of environmental impacts of surface coal mining, see section 1251 et seq. of Title 30, Mineral Lands and Mining.

Coordination of regulatory and inspection activities under Surface Mining Control and Reclamation Act of 1977 and this chapter, see section 1303 of Title 30.

Deepwater port to be considered new source for purposes of this chapter, see section 1502 of Title 33, Navigation and Navigable Waters.

Demonstrations of energy-related pollution control technologies to fulfill provisions of this chapter, see section 4363a of this title.

Federal Energy Administrator defined for purposes of this chapter, see section 798 of Title 15, Commerce and Trade.

Guarantee of loans for developing new underground coal mines, necessity of having contract for sale or resale of coal with person certified as able to burn such coal in compliance with this chapter, see section 6211 of this title.

Income tax deduction for amortization of pollution control facilities, see section 169 of Title 26, Internal Revenue Code.

Integration of Solid Waste Disposal Act with this chapter, see section 6905 of this title.

License for ownership, construction and operation of deepwater ports, conformance of port with this chapter as condition for issuance, see section 1503 of Title 33, Navigation and Navigable Waters.

Loans to assist powerplant acquisitions of air pollution control equipment, see section 8402 of this title.

Monitoring of emissions from new and existing electric powerplants required to use coal or other alternate fuels, see section 8455 of this title.

Permit for increased use of petroleum by existing powerplants, necessity of certification that powerplant cannot comply with requirements of this chapter, see section 8375 of this title.

Policy of Congress to promote substitution of methane-fueled vehicles in areas where substitution would facilitate plans under this chapter, see section 3801 of Title 15, Commerce and Trade.

Regulations for leasing of Outer Continental Shelf to include provisions for compliance with national ambient air quality standards, see section 1334 of Title 43, Public Lands.

Restriction on use of funds under Department of Energy Organization Act to pay penalties under this chapter, see section 7273 of this title.
Rural communities assistance for solid waste management facilities necessary to meet requirements under this chapter, see section 6949 of this title.
Solid waste management guidelines to describe levels of performance that provide for protection of ambient air quality, see section 6907 of this title.
State or local toxic substance requirements preempted by federal requirements unless requirement is adopted under this chapter, see section 2617 of Title 15, Commerce and Trade.
Testing of advanced automobile propulsion systems to determine whether vehicle complies with requirements of this chapter, see section 2706 of Title 15.

West's Federal Forms

Enforcement and review of administrative decisions and orders, see § 851 et seq.
Jurisdiction and venue of district courts, see § 1003 et seq.
Preliminary injunctions and temporary restraining orders, see § 5271 et seq.

West's Federal Practice Manual

Environmental Law, see § 4381 et seq.

Code of Federal Regulations

Air pollution from motor vehicles, control, see 40 CFR 85.401 et seq.
New motor vehicles, certification and testing, see 40 CFR 86.078–3 et seq.
Air programs, generally, see 40 CFR 50.1 et seq.
Aircraft, control of air pollution, see 40 CFR 87.1 et seq.
Environmental Protection Agency—
Ambient air quality surveillance, see 40 CFR 50.1 et seq.
Emission standards for hazardous pollutants, see 40 CFR 61.01 et seq.
State penalty programs, standards for approval, see 40 CFR 67.1 et seq.
Fuels, regulation of, see 40 CFR 80.1 et seq.
Hazardous pollutants, emission standards for, see 40 CFR 61.01 et seq.
Implementation plans, generally, see 40 CFR 51.1 et seq.
New stationary sources, standards, see 40 CFR 60.1 et seq.
Primary nonferrous smelter orders, see 40 CFR 57.101 et seq.
Public information, see 40 CFR 2.100 et seq.
State and local assistance, see 40 CFR 35.001 et seq.

United States Supreme Court

State plan for achieving federal ambient air quality standards, approval of variances, see Train v. Natural Resources Defense Council, Inc., 1975, 95 S.Ct. 1470, 421 U.S. 60, 43 L.Ed.2d 731.

WESTLAW Electronic Research

See WESTLAW guide following the Explanation pages of this pamphlet.

§ 7401. Congressional findings and declaration of purpose

(a) The Congress finds—

(1) that the predominant part of the Nation's population is located in its rapidly expanding metropolitan and other urban areas, which generally cross the boundary lines of local jurisdictions and often extend into two or more States;

(2) that the growth in the amount and complexity of air pollution brought about by urbanization, industrial development, and the increasing use of motor vehicles, has resulted in mounting dangers to the public health and welfare, including injury to agricultural crops and livestock, damage to and the deterioration of property, and hazards to air and ground transportation;

(3) that the prevention and control of air pollution at its source is the primary responsibility of States and local governments; and

(4) that Federal financial assistance and leadership is essential for the development of cooperative Federal, State, regional, and local programs to prevent and control air pollution.

(b) The purposes of this subchapter are—

(1) to protect and enhance the quality of the Nation's air resources so as to promote the public health and welfare and the productive capacity of its population;

(2) to initiate and accelerate a national research and development program to achieve the prevention and control of air pollution;

(3) to provide technical and financial assistance to State and local governments in connection with the development and execution of their air pollution prevention and control programs; and

(4) to encourage and assist the development and operation of regional air pollution control programs.

(July 14, 1955, ch. 360, title I, § 101, formerly § 1, as added Dec. 17, 1963, Pub.L. 88–206, § 1, 77 Stat. 392, and amended and renumbered Oct. 20, 1965, Pub.L. 89–272, title I, § 101(2), (3), 79 Stat. 992; Nov. 21, 1967, Pub.L. 90–148, § 2, 81 Stat. 485.)

Cross References

Dioxins from resource recovery facilities. Solid Waste Disposal Act as not preempting or affecting authorities under this chapter to regulate emissions of polychlorinated dibenzo-p-dioxins, see section 6905 of this title.

West's Federal Practice Manual

Environmental law, see § 4381 et seq.

Code of Federal Regulations

Air planning, designation of areas for, see 40 CFR 81.1 et seq.
Air quality conformity, see 23 CFR 770.1 et seq.
Hazardous pollutants, emission standards for, see 40 CFR 61.01 et seq.
Implementation plans, approval and promulgation of, see 40 CFR 52.01 et seq.
Implementation plans, requirements concerning, see 40 CFR 51.1 et seq.
New stationary sources, performance standards, see 40 CFR 60.1 et seq.
State plans, see 40 CFR 62.01 et seq.

Library References

Health and Environment ⟹25.6(1) et seq., 28.
C.J.S. Health and Environment § 91 et seq.

§ 7402. Cooperative activities

(a) Interstate cooperation; uniform State laws; State compacts

The Administrator shall encourage cooperative activities by the States and local governments for the prevention and control of air pollution; encourage the enactment of improved and, so far as practicable in the light of varying conditions and needs, uniform State and local laws relating to the prevention and control of air pollution; and encourage the making of agreements and compacts between States for the prevention and control of air pollution.

(b) Federal cooperation

The Administrator shall cooperate with and encourage cooperative activities by all Federal departments and agencies having functions relating to the prevention and control of air pollution, so as to assure the utilization in the Federal air pollution control program of all appropriate and available facilities and resources within the Federal Government.

(c) Consent of Congress to compacts

The consent of the Congress is hereby given to two or more States to negotiate and enter into agreements or compacts, not in conflict with any law or treaty of the United States, for (1) cooperative effort and mutual assistance for the prevention and control of air pollution and the enforcement of their respective laws relating thereto, and (2) the establishment of such agencies, joint or otherwise, as they may deem desirable for making effective such agreements or compacts. No such agreement or compact shall be binding or obligatory upon any State a party thereto unless and until it has been approved by Congress. It is the intent of Congress that no agreement or compact entered into between States after November 21, 1967, which relates to the control and abatement of air pollution in an air quality control region, shall provide for participation by a State which is not included (in whole or in part) in such air quality control region.

(July 14, 1955, ch. 360, title I, § 102, formerly § 2, as added Dec. 17, 1963, Pub.L. 88–206, § 1, 77 Stat. 393, renumbered Oct. 20, 1965, Pub.L. 89–272, title I, § 101(3), 79 Stat. 992, and amended Nov. 21, 1967, Pub.L. 90–148, § 2, 81 Stat. 485; Dec. 31, 1970, Pub.L. 91–604, § 15(c)(2), 84 Stat. 1713.)

Library References

States ⟹4.19, 6.
C.J.S. States §§ 28, 31 et seq.

§ 7403. Research, investigation, training, and other activities

(a) Research and development program for prevention and control of air pollution

The Administrator shall establish a national research and development program for the prevention and control of air pollution and as part of such program shall—

(1) conduct, and promote the coordination and acceleration of, research, investigations, experiments, demonstrations, surveys, and studies relating to the causes, effects, extent, prevention, and control of air pollution;

(2) encourage, cooperate with, and render technical services and provide financial assistance to air pollution control agencies and other appropriate public or private agencies, institutions, and organizations, and individuals in the conduct of such activities;

(3) conduct investigations and research and make surveys concerning any specific problem of air pollution in cooperation with any air pollution control agency with a view to recommending a solution of such problem, if he is requested to do so by such agency or if, in his judgment, such problem may affect any community or communities in a State other than that in which the source of the matter causing or contributing to the pollution is located;

(4) establish technical advisory committees composed of recognized experts in various aspects of air pollution to assist in the examination and evaluation of research progress and proposals and to avoid duplication of research, and

(5) conduct and promote coordination and acceleration of training for individuals relating to the causes, effects, extent, prevention, and control of air pollution.

(b) Authorized activities of Administrator in establishing research and development program

In carrying out the provisions of the preceding subsection the Administrator is authorized to—

(1) collect and make available, through publications and other appropriate means, the results of and other information, including appropriate recommendations by him in connection therewith, pertaining to such research and other activities;

(2) cooperate with other Federal departments and agencies, with air pollution control agencies, with other public and private agencies, institutions, and organizations, and with any industries involved, in the preparation and conduct of such research and other activities;

(3) make grants to air pollution control agencies, to other public or nonprofit private agencies, institutions, and organizations, and to individuals, for purposes stated in subsection (a)(1) of this section;

(4) contract with public or private agencies, institutions, and organizations, and with individuals, without regard to section 529 of title 31 and section 5 of title 41;

(5) establish and maintain research fellowships, in the Environmental Protection Agency and at public or nonprofit private educational institutions or research organizations;

(6) collect and disseminate, in cooperation with other Federal departments and agencies, and with other public or private agencies, institutions, and organizations having related responsibilities, basic data on chemical, physical, and biological effects of varying air quality and other information pertaining to air pollution and the prevention and control thereof; and

(7) develop effective and practical processes, methods, and prototype devices for the prevention or control of air pollution.

In carrying out the provisions of subsection (a) of this section, the Administrator shall provide training for, and make training grants to, personnel of air pollution control agencies and other persons with suitable qualifications and make grants to such agencies, to other public or nonprofit private agencies, institutions, and organizations for the purposes stated in subsection (a)(5) of this section. Reasonable fees may be charged for such training provided to persons other than personnel of air pollution control agencies but such training shall be provided to such personnel of air pollution control agencies without charge.

(c) Results of other scientific studies

In carrying out the provisions of subsection (a) of this section the Administrator shall conduct research on, and survey the results of other scientific studies on, the harmful effects on the health or welfare of persons by the various known air pollutants.

(d) Construction of facilities

The Administrator is authorized to construct such facilities and staff and equip them as he determines to be necessary to carry out his functions under this chapter.

(e) Potential air pollution problems; conferences; findings and recommendations of Administrator

If in the judgment of the Administrator, an air pollution problem of substantial significance may result from discharge or discharges into the atmosphere, he may call a conference concerning this potential air pollution problem to be held in or near one or more of the places where such discharge or discharges are occurring or will occur. All interested persons shall be given an opportunity to be heard at such conference, either orally or in writing, and shall be permitted to appear in person or by representative in accordance with procedures prescribed by the Administrator. If the Administrator finds, on the basis of the evidence presented at such conference, that the discharge or discharges if permitted to take place or continue are likely to cause or contribute to air pollution subject to abatement under section 7415 of this title, he shall send such findings, together with recommendations concerning the measures which he finds reasonable and suitable to prevent such pollution, to the person or persons whose actions will result in the discharge or discharges involved; to air pollution agencies of the State or States and of the municipality or municipalities where such discharge or discharges will originate; and to the interstate air pollution control agency, if any, in the jurisdictional area of which any such municipality is located. Such findings and recommendations shall be advisory only, but shall be admitted together with the record of the conference, as part of the proceedings under subsections (b), (c), (d), (e), and (f) of section 7415 of this title.

(f) Accelerated research programs

(1) In carrying out research pursuant to this chapter, the Administrator shall give special emphasis to research on the short- and long-term effects of air pollutants on public health and welfare. In the furtherance of such research, he shall conduct an accelerated research program—

(A) to improve knowledge of the contribution of air pollutants to the occurrence of adverse effects on health, including, but not limited to, behavioral, physiological, toxicological, and biochemical effects; and

(B) to improve knowledge of the short- and long-term effects of air pollutants on welfare.

(2) In carrying out the provisions of this subsection the Administrator may—

(A) conduct epidemiological studies of the effects of air pollutants on mortality and morbidity;

(B) conduct clinical and laboratory studies on the immunologic, biochemical, physiological, and the toxicological effects including carcinogenic, teratogenic, and mutagenic effects of air pollutants;

(C) utilize, on a reimbursable basis, the facilities of existing Federal scientific laboratories and research centers;

(D) utilize the authority contained in paragraphs (1) through (4) of subsection (b) of this section; and

(E) consult with other appropriate Federal agencies to assure that research or studies conducted pursuant to this subsection will be coordinated with research and studies of such other Federal agencies.

(3) In entering into contracts under this subsection, the Administrator is authorized to contract for a term not to exceed 10 years in duration. For the purposes of this paragraph, there are authorized to be appropriated $15,000,000. Such amounts as are appropriated shall remain available until expended and shall be in addition to any other appropriations under this chapter.

(July 14, 1955, ch. 360, title I, § 103, formerly § 3, as added Dec. 17, 1963, Pub.L. 88–206, § 1, 77 Stat. 394, and amended and renumbered Oct. 20, 1965, Pub.L. 89–272, title I, §§ 101(3), 103, 79 Stat. 992, 996; Nov. 21, 1967, Pub.L. 90–148, § 2, 81 Stat. 486; Dec. 31, 1970, Pub.L. 91–604, §§ 2(a), 4(2), 15(a)(2), (c)(2), 84 Stat. 1676, 1689, 1710, 1713; Aug. 7, 1977, Pub.L. 95–95, title I, § 101(a), (b), 91 Stat. 686, 687.)

Library References

Health and Environment ⚷25.6(1) et seq., 28.
C.J.S. Health and Environment § 91 et seq.

§ 7404. Research relating to fuels and vehicles

(a) Research programs; grants; contracts; pilot and demonstration plants; byproducts research

The Administrator shall give special emphasis to research and development into new and improved methods, having industry-wide application, for the prevention and control of air pollution resulting from the combustion of fuels. In furtherance of such research and development he shall—

(1) conduct and accelerate research programs directed toward development of improved, low-cost techniques for—

(A) control of combustion byproducts of fuels,

(B) removal of potential air pollutants from fuels prior to combustion,

(C) control of emissions from the evaporation of fuels,

(D) improving the efficiency of fuels combustion so as to decrease atmospheric emissions, and

(E) producing synthetic or new fuels which, when used, result in decreased atmospheric emissions.

(2) provide for Federal grants to public or nonprofit agencies, institutions, and organizations and to individuals, and contracts with public or private agencies, institutions, or persons, for payment of (A) part of the cost of acquiring, constructing, or otherwise securing for research and development purposes, new or improved devices or methods having industrywide application of preventing or controlling discharges into the air of various types of pollutants; (B) part of the cost of programs to develop low emission alternatives to the present internal combustion engine; (C) the cost to purchase vehicles and vehicle engines, or portions thereof, for research, development, and testing purposes; and (D) carrying out the other provisions of this section, without regard to section 3324(a) and (b) of title 31 and section 5 of title 41: *Provided,* That research or demonstration contracts awarded pursuant to this subsection (including contracts for construction) may be made in accordance with, and subject to the limitations provided with respect to research contracts of the military departments in, section 2353 of title 10, except that the determination, approval, and certification required thereby shall be made by the Secretary: *Provided further,* That no grant may be made under this paragraph in excess of $1,500,000;

(3) determine, by laboratory and pilot plant testing, the results of air pollution research and studies in order to develop new or improved processes and plant designs to the point where they can be demonstrated on a large and practical scale;

(4) construct, operate, and maintain, or assist in meeting the cost of the construction, operation, and maintenance of new or improved demonstration plants or processes which have promise of accomplishing the purposes of this chapter;

(5) study new or improved methods for the recovery and marketing of commercially valuable byproducts resulting from the removal of pollutants.

(b) Powers of Administrator in establishing research and development programs

In carrying out the provisions of this section, the Administrator may—

(1) conduct and accelerate research and development of low-cost instrumentation techniques to facilitate determination of quantity and quality of air pollutant emissions, including, but not limited to, automotive emissions;

(2) utilize, on a reimbursable basis, the facilities of existing Federal scientific laboratories;

(3) establish and operate necessary facilities and test sites at which to carry on the research, testing, development, and programming necessary to effectuate the purposes of this section;

(4) acquire secret processes, technical data, inventions, patent applications, patents, licenses, and an interest in lands, plants, and facilities, and other property or rights by purchase, license, lease, or donation; and

(5) cause on-site inspections to be made of promising domestic and foreign projects, and cooperate and participate in their development in instances in which the purposes of the chapter will be served thereby.

(c) Authorization of appropriations

For the purposes of this section there are authorized to be appropriated $75,000,000 for the fiscal year ending June 30, 1971, $125,000,000 for the fiscal year ending June 30, 1972, $150,000,000 for the fiscal year ending June 30, 1973, and $150,000,000 for the fiscal year ending June 30, 1974, and $150,000,000 for the fiscal year ending June 30, 1975. Amounts appropriated pursuant to this subsection shall remain available until expended.

(July 14, 1955, ch. 360, title I, § 104, as added Nov. 21, 1967, Pub.L. 90–148, § 2, 81 Stat. 487, and amended Dec. 5, 1969, Pub.L. 91–137, 83 Stat. 283; Dec. 31, 1970, Pub.L. 91–604, §§ 2(b), (c), 13(a), 15(c)(2), 84 Stat. 1676, 1677, 1709, 1713; Apr. 9, 1973, Pub.L. 93–15, § 1(a), 87 Stat. 11; June 22, 1974, Pub.L. 93–319, § 13(a), 88 Stat. 265; Sept. 13, 1982, Pub.L. 97–258, § 4(b), 96 Stat. 1067.)

Library References

Health and Environment ⇐25.6(1) et seq., 28.
C.J.S. Health and Environment § 91 et seq.

§ 7405. Grants for support of air pollution planning and control programs

(a) Amounts; limitations; assurances of plan development capability

(1)(A) The Administrator may make grants to air pollution control agencies in an amount up to two-thirds of the cost of planning, developing, establishing, or improving, and up to one-half of the cost of maintaining, programs for the prevention and control of air pollution or implementation of national primary and secondary ambient air quality standards.

(B) Subject to subparagraph (C), the Administrator may make grants to air pollution control agencies within the meaning of paragraph (1), (2), or (4) of section 7602(b) of this title in an amount up to three-fourths of the cost of planning, developing, establishing, or improving, and up to three-fifths of the cost of maintaining, any program for the prevention and control of air pollution or implementation of national primary and secondary ambient air quality standards in an area that includes two or more municipalities, whether in the same or different States.

(C) With respect to any air quality control region or portion thereof for which there is an applicable implementation plan under section 7410 of this title, grants under subparagraph (B) may be made only to air pollution control agencies which have substantial responsibilities for carrying out such applicable implementation plan.

(2) Before approving any grant under this subsection to any air pollution control agency within the meaning of sections 7602(b)(2) and 7602(b)(4) of this title, the Administrator shall receive assurances that such agency provides for adequate representation of appropriate State, interstate, local, and (when appropriate) international, interests in the air quality control region.

(3) Before approving any planning grant under this subsection to any air pollution control agency within the meaning of sections 7602(b)(2) and 7602(b)(4) of this title, the Administrator shall receive assurances that such agency has the capability of developing a comprehensive air quality plan for the air quality control region, which plan shall include (when appropriate) a recommended system of alerts to avert and reduce the risk of situations in which there may be imminent and serious danger to the public health or welfare from air pollutants and the various aspects relevant to the establishment of air quality standards for such air quality control region, including the concentration of industries, other commercial establishments, population and naturally occurring factors which shall affect such standards.

(b) Terms and conditions; regulations; factors for consideration; maintenance of effort; waiver of maintenance of effort requirement; consultation requirement

From the sums available for the purposes of subsection (a) of this section for any fiscal year, the Administrator shall from time to time make grants to air pollution control agencies upon such terms and conditions as the Administrator may find necessary to carry out the purpose of this section. In establishing regulations for the granting of such funds the Administrator shall, so far as practicable, give due consideration to (1) the population, (2) the extent of the actual or potential air pollution problem, and (3) the financial need of the respective agencies. No agency shall receive any grant under this section during any fiscal year when its expenditures of non-Federal funds for other than nonrecurrent expenditures for air pollution control programs will be less than its expenditures were for such programs during the preceding fiscal year, unless the Administrator, after notice and opportunity for public hearing, determines that a reduction in expenditures is attributable to a nonselective reduction in expenditures in the programs of all executive branch agencies of the applicable unit of Government; and no agency shall receive any grant under this section with respect to the maintenance of a program for the prevention and control of air pollution unless the Administrator is satisfied that such grant will be so used to supplement and, to the extent practicable, increase the level of State, local, or other non-Federal funds that would in the absence of such grant be made available for the maintenance of such program, and will in no event supplant such State, local, or other non-Federal funds. No grant shall be made under this section until the Administrator has consulted with the appropriate official as designated by the Governor or Governors of the State or States affected.

(c) State expenditure limitations

Not more than 10 per centum of the total of funds appropriated or allocated for the purposes of subsection (a) of this section shall be granted for air pollution control programs in any one State. In the case of a grant for a program in an area crossing State boundaries, the Administrator shall determine the portion of such grant that is chargeable to the percentage limitation under this subsection for each State into which such area extends. In fiscal year 1978 and subsequent fiscal years, subject to the provisions of subsection (b) of this section, no State shall receive less than one-half of 1 per centum of the annual appropriation for grants under this section for grants to agencies within such State.

(d) Reduction of payments; availability of reduced amounts; reduced amount as deemed paid to agency for purpose of determining amount of grant

The Administrator, with the concurrence of any recipient of a grant under this section, may reduce the payments to such recipient by the amount of the pay, allowances, traveling expenses, and any other costs in connection with the detail of any officer or employee to the recipient under section 7601 of this title, when such detail is for the convenience of, and at the request of, such recipient and for the purpose of carrying out the provisions of this chapter. The amount by which such payments have been reduced shall be available for payment of such costs by the Administrator, but shall, for the purpose of determining the amount of any grant to a recipient under subsection (a) of this section, be deemed to have been paid to such agency.

(e) Notice and opportunity for hearing when affected by adverse action

No application by a State for a grant under this section may be disapproved by the Administrator without prior notice and opportunity for a public hearing in the affected State, and no commitment or obligation of any funds under any such grant may be revoked or reduced without prior notice and opportunity for a public hearing in the affected State (or in one of the affected States if more than one State is affected).

(July 14, 1955, ch. 360, title I, § 105, formerly § 4, as added Dec. 17, 1963, Pub.L. 88–206, § 1, 77 Stat. 395, renumbered § 104 and amended Oct. 20, 1965, Pub.L. 89–272, title I, § 101(2)–(4), 79 Stat. 992; Oct. 15, 1966, Pub.L. 89–675, § 3, 80 Stat. 954, and renumbered § 105 and amended Nov. 21, 1967, Pub.L. 90–148, § 2, 81 Stat. 489; Dec. 31, 1970, Pub.L. 91–604, §§ 3(a), (b)(1), 15(c)(2), 84 Stat. 1677, 1713; Aug. 7, 1977, Pub.L. 95–95, title I, § 102, title III, § 305(b), 91 Stat. 687, 776.)

Code of Federal Regulations

State and local assistance, see 40 CFR 35.001 et seq.

Library References

Health and Environment ⚷25.6(1) et seq., 28.
United States ⚷82(2).
C.J.S. Health and Environment § 91 et seq.
C.J.S. United States § 122.

§ 7406. Interstate air quality agencies; program cost limitations

For the purpose of developing implementation plans for any interstate air quality control region designated pursuant to section 7407 of this title, the Administrator is authorized to pay, for two years, up to 100 per centum of the air quality planning program costs of any agency designated by the Governors of the affected States, which agency shall be capable of recommending to the Governors plans for implementation of national primary and secondary ambient air quality standards and shall include representation from the States and appropriate political subdivisions within the air quality control region. After the initial two-year period the Administrator is authorized to make grants to such agency in an amount up to three-fourths of the air quality planning program costs of any agency.

(July 14, 1955, ch. 360, title I, § 106, as added Nov. 21, 1967, Pub.L. 90–148, § 2, 81 Stat. 490, and amended Dec. 31, 1970, Pub.L. 91–604, § 3(c), 84 Stat. 1677.)

Library References

Health and Environment ⚷25.6(1) et seq., 28.
C.J.S. Health and Environment § 91 et seq.

§ 7407. Air quality control regions

(a) Responsibility of each State for air quality; submission of implementation plan

Each State shall have the primary responsibility for assuring air quality within the entire geographic area comprising such State by submitting an implementation plan for such State which will specify the manner in which national primary and secondary ambient air quality standards will be achieved and maintained within each air quality control region in such State.

(b) Designated regions

For purposes of developing and carrying out implementation plans under section 7410 of this title—

(1) an air quality control region designated under this section before December 31, 1970, or a region designated after such date under subsection (c) of this section, shall be an air quality control region; and

(2) the portion of such State which is not part of any such designated region shall be an air quality control region, but such portion may be subdivided by the State into two or more air quality control regions with the approval of the Administrator.

(c) Authority of Administrator to designate regions; notification of Governors of affected States

The Administrator shall, within 90 days after December 31, 1970, after consultation with appropriate State and local authorities, designate as an air quality control region any interstate area or major intrastate area which he deems necessary or appropriate for the attainment and maintenance of ambient air quality standards. The Administrator shall immediately notify the Governors of the affected States of any designation made under this subsection.

(d) List of noncomplying regions

(1) For the purpose of transportation control planning, part D of this subchapter (relating to nonattainment), part C of this subchapter (relating to prevention of significant deterioration of air quality), and for other purposes, each State, within one hundred and twenty days after August 7, 1977, shall submit to the Administrator a list, together with a summary of the available information, identifying those air quality control regions, or portions thereof, established pursuant to this section in such State which on August 7, 1977—

(A) do not meet a national primary ambient air quality standard for any air pollutant other than sulfur dioxide or particulate matter;

(B) do not meet, or in the judgment of the State may not in the time period required by an applicable implementation plan attain or maintain, any national primary ambient air quality standard for sulfur dioxide or particulate matter;

(C) do not meet a national secondary ambient air quality standard;

(D) cannot be classified under subparagraph (B) or (C) of this paragraph on the basis of available information, for ambient air quality levels for sulfur oxides or particulate matter; or

(E) have ambient air quality levels better than any national primary or secondary air quality standard other than for sulfur dioxide or particulate matter, or for which there is not sufficient data to be classified under subparagraph (A) or (C) of this paragraph.

(2) Not later than sixty days after submittal of the list under paragraph (1) of this subsection the Administrator shall promulgate each such list with such modifications as he deems necessary. Whenever the Administrator proposes to modify a list submitted by a State, he shall notify the State and request all available data relating to such region or portion, and provide such State with an opportunity to demonstrate why any proposed modification is inappropriate.

(4)[1] Any region or portion thereof which is not classified under subparagraph (B) or (C) of paragraph (1) of this subsection for sulfur dioxide or particulate matter within one hundred and eighty days after August 7, 1977, shall be deemed to be a region classified under subparagraph (D) of paragraph (1) of this subsection.

(5) A State may from time to time review, and as appropriate revise and resubmit, the list required under this subsection. The Administrator shall consider and promulgate such revised list in accordance with this subsection.

(e) Redesignation of air quality control regions

(1) Except as otherwise provided in paragraph (2), the Governor of each State is authorized, with the approval of the Administrator, to redesignate from time to time the air quality control regions within such State for purposes of efficient and effective air quality management. Upon such redesignation, the list under subsection (d) of this section shall be modified accordingly.

(2) In the case of an air quality control region in a State, or part of such region, which the Administrator finds may significantly affect air pollution concentrations in another State, the Governor of the State in which such region, or part of a region, is located may redesignate from time to time the boundaries of so much of such air quality control region as is located within such State only with the approval of the Administrator and with the consent of all Governors of all States which the Administrator determines may be significantly affected.

(3) No compliance date extension granted under section 7413(d)(5) of this title (relating to coal conversion) shall cease to be effective by reason of the regional limitation provided in section 7413(d)(5) of this title if the violation of such limitation is due solely to a redesignation of a region under this subsection.

(July 14, 1955, ch. 360, title I, § 107, as added Dec. 31, 1970, Pub.L. 91–604, § 4(a), 84 Stat. 1678, and amended Aug. 7, 1977, Pub.L. 95–95, title I, § 103, 91 Stat. 687.)

[1] So in original. Subsec. (d) enacted without a par. (3).

Library References

Health and Environment ⚷25.6(1) et seq., 28.
C.J.S. Health and Environment § 91 et seq.

§ 7408. Air quality criteria and control techniques

(a) Air pollutant list; publication and revision by Administrator; issuance of air quality criteria for air pollutants

(1) For the purpose of establishing national primary and secondary ambient air quality standards, the Administrator shall within 30 days after December 31, 1970, publish, and shall from time to time thereafter revise, a list which includes each air pollutant—

(A) emissions of which, in his judgment, cause or contribute to air pollution which may reasonably be anticipated to endanger public health or welfare;

(B) the presence of which in the ambient air results from numerous or diverse mobile or stationary sources; and

(C) for which air quality criteria had not been issued before December 31, 1970 but for which he plans to issue air quality criteria under this section.

(2) The Administrator shall issue air quality criteria for an air pollutant within 12 months after he has included such pollutant in a list under paragraph (1). Air quality criteria for an air pollutant shall accurately reflect the latest scientific knowledge useful in indicating the kind and extent of all identifiable effects on public health or welfare which may be expected from the presence of such pollutant in the ambient air, in varying quantities. The criteria for an air pollutant, to the extent practicable, shall include information on—

(A) those variable factors (including atmospheric conditions) which of themselves or in combination with other factors may alter the effects on public health or welfare of such air pollutant;

(B) the types of air pollutants which, when present in the atmosphere, may interact with such pollutant to produce an adverse effect on public health or welfare; and

(C) any known or anticipated adverse effects on welfare.

(b) Issuance by Administrator of information on air pollution control techniques; standing consulting committees for air pollutants; establishment; membership

(1) Simultaneously with the issuance of criteria under subsection (a) of this section, the Administrator shall, after consultation with appropriate advisory committees and Federal departments and agencies, issue to the States and appropriate air pollution control agencies information on air pollution control techniques, which information shall include data relating to the cost of installation and operation, energy requirements, emission reduction benefits, and environmental impact of the emission control technology. Such information shall include such data as are available on available technology and alternative methods of prevention and control of air pollution. Such information shall also include data on alternative fuels, processes, and operating methods which will result in elimination or significant reduction of emissions.

(2) In order to assist in the development of information on pollution control techniques, the Administrator may establish a standing consulting committee for each air pollutant included in a list published pursuant to subsection (a)(1) of this section, which shall be comprised of technically qualified individuals representative of State and local governments, industry, and the academic community. Each such committee shall submit, as appropriate, to the Administrator information related to that required by paragraph (1).

(c) Review, modification, and reissuance of criteria or information

The Administrator shall from time to time review, and, as appropriate, modify, and reissue any criteria or information on control techniques issued pursuant to this section. Not later than six months after August 7, 1977, the Administrator shall revise and reissue criteria relating to concentrations of NO_2 over such period (not more than three hours) as he deems appropriate. Such criteria shall include a discussion of nitric and nitrous acids, nitrites, nitrates, nitrosamines, and other carcinogenic and potentially carcinogenic derivatives of oxides of nitrogen.

(d) Publication in Federal Register; availability of copies for general public

The issuance of air quality criteria and information on air pollution control techniques shall be announced in the Federal Register and copies shall be made available to the general public.

(e) Transportation planning and guidelines

The Administrator shall, after consultation with the Secretary of Transportation and the Secretary of Housing and Urban Development and State and local officials and within 180 days after August 7, 1977, and from time to time thereafter, publish guidelines on the basic program elements for the planning process assisted under section 7505 of this title. Such guidelines shall include information on—

(1) methods to identify and evaluate alternative planning and control activities;

(2) methods of reviewing plans on a regular basis as conditions change or new information is presented;

(3) identification of funds and other resources necessary to implement the plan, including interagency agreements on providing such funds and resources;

(4) methods to assure participation by the public in all phases of the planning process; and

(5) such other methods as the Administrator determines necessary to carry out a continuous planning process.

(f) Information regarding processes, procedures, and methods to reduce or control pollutants in transportation; reduction of mobile source related pollutants; reduction of impact on public health

(1) The Administrator shall publish and make available to appropriate Federal agencies, States, and air pollution control agencies, including agencies assisted under section 7505 of this title within 6 months after August 7, 1977, for clauses (i), (ii), (iii), and (iv) of subparagraph (A) and within one year after August 7, 1977, for the balance of this subsection (and from time to time thereafter),

(A) information, prepared, as appropriate, in cooperation with the Secretary of Transportation, regarding processes, procedures, and methods to reduce or control each such pollutant, including but not limited to—

(i) motor vehicle emission inspection and maintenance programs;

(ii) programs to control vapor emissions from fuel transfer and storage operations and operations using solvents;

(iii) programs for improved public transit;

(iv) programs to establish exclusive bus and carpool lanes and areawide carpool programs;

(v) programs to limit portions of road surfaces or certain sections of the metropolitan areas to the use of common carriers, both as to time and place;

(vi) programs for long-range transit improvements involving new transportation policies and transportation facilities or major changes in existing facilities;

(vii) programs to control on-street parking;

(viii) programs to construct new parking facilities and operate existing parking facilities for the purpose of park and ride lots and fringe parking;

(ix) programs to limit portions of road surfaces or certain sections of the metropolitan area to the use of nonmotorized vehicles or pedestrian use, both as to time and place;

(x) provisions for employer participation in programs to encourage carpooling, vanpooling, mass transit, bicycling, and walking;

(xi) programs for secure bicycle storage facilities and other facilities, including bicycle lanes, for the convenience and protection of bicyclists, in both public and private areas;

(xii) programs of staggered hours of work;

(xiii) programs to institute road user charges, tolls, or differential rates to discourage single occupancy automobile trips;

(xiv) programs to control extended idling of vehicles;

(xv) programs to reduce emissions by improvements in traffic flow;

(xvi) programs for the conversion of fleet vehicles to cleaner engines or fuels, or to otherwise control fleet vehicle operations;

(xvii) programs for retrofit of emission devices or controls on vehicles and engines, other than light duty vehicles, not subject to regulations under section 7521 of this title; and

(xviii) programs to reduce motor vehicle emissions which are caused by extreme cold start conditions;

(B) information on additional methods or strategies that will contribute to the reduction of mobile source related pollutants during periods in which any primary ambient air quality standard will be exceeded and during episodes for which an air pollution alert, warning, or emergency has been declared;

(C) information on other measures which may be employed to reduce the impact on public health or protect the health of sensitive or susceptible individuals or groups; and

(D) information on the extent to which any process, procedure, or method to reduce or control such air pollutant may cause an increase in the emissions or formation of any other pollutant.

(2) In publishing such information the Administrator shall also include an assessment of—

(A) the relative effectiveness of such processes, procedures, and methods;

(B) the potential effect of such processes, procedures, and methods on transportation systems and the provision of transportation services; and

(C) the environmental, energy, and economic impact of such processes, procedures, and methods.

(July 14, 1955, ch. 360, title I, § 108, as added Dec. 31, 1970, Pub.L. 91–604, § 4(a), 84 Stat. 1678, and amended Aug. 7, 1977, Pub.L. 95–95, title I, §§ 104, 105, title IV, § 401(a), 91 Stat. 689, 790.)

Library References

Health and Environment ⚖25.6(1) et seq., 28.
C.J.S. Health and Environment § 91 et seq.

§ 7409. National primary and secondary ambient air quality standards

(a) Promulgation

(1) The Administrator—

(A) within 30 days after December 31, 1970, shall publish proposed regulations prescribing a national primary ambient air quality standard and a national secondary ambient air quality standard for each air pollutant for which air quality criteria have been issued prior to such date; and

(B) after a reasonable time for interested persons to submit written comments thereon (but no later than 90 days after the initial publication of such proposed standards) shall by regulation promulgate such proposed national primary and secondary ambient air quality standards with such modifications as he deems appropriate.

(2) With respect to any air pollutant for which air quality criteria are issued after December 31, 1970, the Administrator shall publish, simultaneously with the issuance of such criteria and information, proposed national primary and secondary ambient air quality standards for any such pollutant. The procedure provided for in paragraph (1)(B) of this subsection shall apply to the promulgation of such standards.

(b) Protection of public health and welfare

(1) National primary ambient air quality standards, prescribed under subsection (a) of this section shall be ambient air quality standards the attainment and maintenance of which in the judgment of the Administrator, based on such criteria and allowing an adequate margin of safety, are requisite to protect the public health. Such primary standards may be revised in the same manner as promulgated.

(2) Any national secondary ambient air quality standard prescribed under subsection (a) of this section shall specify a level of air quality the attainment and maintenance of which in the judgment of the Administrator, based on such criteria, is requisite to protect the public welfare from any known or anticipated adverse effects associated with the presence of such air pollutant in the ambient air. Such secondary standards may be revised in the same manner as promulgated.

(c) National primary ambient air quality standard for nitrogen dioxide

The Administrator shall, not later than one year after August 7, 1977, promulgate a national primary ambient air quality standard for NO_2 concentrations over a period of not more than 3 hours unless, based on the criteria issued under section 7408(c) of this title, he finds that there is no significant evidence that such a standard for such a period is requisite to protect public health.

(d) Review and revision of criteria and standards; independent scientific review committee; appointment; advisory functions

(1) Not later than December 31, 1980, and at five-year intervals thereafter, the Administrator shall complete a thorough review of the criteria published under section 7408 of this title and the national ambient air quality standards promulgated under this section and shall make such revisions in such criteria and standards and promulgate such new standards as may be appropriate in accordance with section 7408 of this title and subsection (b) of this section. The Administrator may review and revise criteria or promulgate new standards earlier or more frequently than required under this paragraph.

(2)(A) The Administrator shall appoint an independent scientific review committee composed of seven members including at least one member of the National Academy of Sciences, one physician, and one person representing State air pollution control agencies.

(B) Not later than January 1, 1980, and at five-year intervals thereafter, the committee referred to in subparagraph (A) shall complete a review of the criteria published under section 7408 of this title and the national primary and secondary ambient air quality standards promulgated under this section and shall recommend to the Administrator any new national ambient air quality standards and revisions of existing criteria and standards as may be appropriate under section 7408 of this title and subsection (b) of this section.

(C) Such committee shall also (i) advise the Administrator of areas in which additional knowledge is required to appraise the adequacy and basis of existing, new, or revised national ambient air quality standards, (ii) describe the research efforts necessary to provide the required information, (iii) advise the Administrator on the relative contribution to air pollution concentrations of natural as well as anthropogenic activity, and (iv) advise the Administrator of any adverse public health, welfare, social, economic, or energy effects which may result from various strategies for attainment and maintenance of such national ambient air quality standards.

(July 14, 1955, ch. 360, title I, § 109, as added Dec. 31, 1970, Pub.L. 91–604, § 4(a), 84 Stat. 1679, and amended Aug. 7, 1977, Pub.L. 95–95, title I, § 106, 91 Stat. 691.)

Code of Federal Regulations

Air programs, generally, see 40 CFR 50.1 et seq.

Library References

Health and Environment ⚷25.6(1) et seq., 28.
C.J.S. Health and Environment § 91 et seq.

§ 7410. State implementation plans for national primary and secondary ambient air quality standards

(a) Adoption of plan by State; submission to Administrator; content of plan; revision; new sources; indirect source review program; supplemental or intermittent control systems

(1) Each State shall, after reasonable notice and public hearings, adopt and submit to the Administrator, within nine months after the promulgation of a national primary ambient air quality standard (or any revision thereof) under section 7409 of this title for any air pollutant, a plan which provides for implementation, maintenance, and enforcement of such primary standard in each air quality control region (or portion thereof) within such State. In addition, such State shall adopt and submit to the Administrator (either as a part of a plan submitted under the preceding sentence or separately) within nine months after the promulgation of a national ambient air quality secondary standard (or revision thereof), a plan which provides for implementation, maintenance, and enforcement of such secondary standard in each air quality control region (or portion thereof) within such State. Unless a separate public hearing is provided, each State shall consider its plan implementing such secondary standard at the hearing required by the first sentence of this paragraph.

(2) The Administrator shall, within four months after the date required for submission of a plan under paragraph (1), approve or disapprove such plan, or any portion thereof. The Administrator shall approve such plan, or any portion thereof, if he determines that it was adopted after reasonable notice and hearing and that—

(A) except as may be provided in subparagraph (I)(i) in the case of a plan implementing a national primary ambient air quality standard, it provides for the attainment of such primary standard as expeditiously as practicable but (subject to subsection (e) of this section) in no case later than three years from the date of approval of such plan (or any revision thereof to take account of a revised primary standard); and (ii) in the case of a plan implementing a national secondary ambient air quality standard, it specifies a reasonable time at which such secondary standard will be attained;

(B) it includes emission limitations, schedules, and timetables for compliance with such limitations, and such other measures as may be necessary to insure attainment and maintenance of such primary or secondary standard, including, but not limited to, transportation controls, air quality maintenance plans, and preconstruction review of direct sources of air pollution as provided in subparagraph (D);

(C) it includes provision for establishment and operation of appropriate devices, methods, systems, and procedures necessary to (i) monitor, compile, and analyze data on ambient air quality and, (ii) upon request, make such data available to the Administrator;

(D) it includes a program to provide for the enforcement of emission limitations and regulation of the modification, construction, and operation of any stationary source, including a permit program as required in parts C and D of this subchapter and a permit or equivalent program for any major emitting facility, within such region as necessary to assure (i) that national ambient air quality standards are achieved and maintained, and (ii) a procedure, meeting the requirements of paragraph (4), for review (prior to construction or modification) of the location of new sources to which a standard of performance will apply;

(E) it contains adequate provisions (i) prohibiting any stationary source within the State from emitting any air pollutant in amounts which will (I) prevent attainment or maintenance by any other State of any such national primary or secondary ambient air quality standard, or (II) interfere with measures required to be included in the applicable implementation plan for any other State under part C of this subchapter to prevent significant deterioration of air quality or to protect visibility, and (ii) insuring compliance with the requirements of section 7426 of this title, relating to interstate pollution abatement;

(F) it provides (i) necessary assurances that the State will have adequate personnel, funding, and authority to carry out such implementation plan, (ii) requirements for installation of equipment by owners or operators of stationary sources to monitor emissions from such sources, (iii) for periodic reports on the nature and amounts of such emissions; (iv) that such reports shall be correlated by the State agency with any emission limitations or standards established pursuant to this chapter, which reports shall be available at reasonable times for public inspection; (v) for authority comparable to that in section 7603 of this title, and adequate contingency plans to implement such authority; and (vi) requirements that the State comply with the requirements respecting State boards under section 7428 of this title;

(G) it provides, to the extent necessary and practicable, for periodic inspection and testing of motor vehicles to enforce compliance with applicable emission standards;

(H) it provides for revision, after public hearings, of such plan (i) from time to time as may be necessary to take account of revisions of such national primary or secondary ambient air quality standard or the availability of improved or more expeditious methods of achieving such primary or secondary standard; or (ii) except as provided in paragraph (3)(C), whenever the Administrator finds on the basis of information available to him that the plan is substantially inadequate to achieve the national ambient air quality primary or secondary standard which it implements or to otherwise comply with any additional requirements established under the Clean Air Act Amendments of 1977;

(I) it provides that after June 30, 1979, no major stationary source shall be constructed or modified in any nonattainment area (as defined in section 7501(2) of this title) to which such plan applies, if the emissions from such facility will cause or contribute to concentrations of any pollutant for which a national ambient air quality standard is exceeded in such area, unless, as of the time of application for a permit for such construction or modification, such plan meets the requirements of part D of this subchapter (relating to nonattainment areas);

(J) it meets the requirements of section 7421 of this title (relating to consultation), section 7427 of this title (relating to public notification), part C of this subchapter (relating to prevention of significant deterioration of air quality and visibility protection); and

(K) it requires the owner or operator of each major stationary source to pay to the permitting authority as a condition of any permit required under this chapter a fee sufficient to cover—

(i) the reasonable costs of reviewing and acting upon any application for such a permit, and

(ii) if the owner or operator receives a permit for such source, whether before or after August 7, 1977, the reasonable costs (incurred after such date) of implementing and enforcing the terms and conditions of any such permit (not including any court costs or other costs associated with any enforcement action).

(3)(A) The Administrator shall approve any revision of an implementation plan applicable to an air quality control region if he determines that it meets the requirements of paragraph (2) and has been adopted by the State after reasonable notice and public hearings.

(B) As soon as practicable, the Administrator shall, consistent with the purposes of this chapter and the Energy Supply and Environmental Coordination Act of 1974 [15 U.S.C. 791 et seq.], review each State's applicable implementation plans and report to the State on whether such plans can be revised in relation to fuel burning stationary sources (or persons supplying fuel to such sources) without interfering with the attainment and maintenance of any national ambient air quality standard within the period permitted in this section. If the Administrator determines that any such plan can be revised, he shall notify the State that a plan revision may be submitted by the State. Any plan revision which is submitted by the State shall, after public notice and opportunity for public hearing, be approved by the Administrator if the revision relates only to fuel burning stationary sources (or persons supplying fuel to such sources), and the plan as revised complies with paragraph (2) of this subsection. The Administrator shall approve or disapprove any revision no later than three months after its submission.

(C) Neither the State, in the case of a plan (or portion thereof) approved under this subsection, nor the Administrator, in the case of a plan (or portion thereof) promulgated under subsection (c) of this section, shall be required to revise an applicable implementation plan because one or more exemptions under section 7418 of this title (relating to Federal facilities), enforcement orders under section 7413(d) of this title, suspensions under subsection (f) or (g) of this section (relating to temporary energy or economic authority), orders under section 7419 of this title (relating to primary nonferrous smelters), or extensions of compliance in decrees entered under section 7413(e) of this title (relating to iron- and steel-producing operations) have been granted, if such plan would have met the requirements of this section if no such exemptions, orders, or extensions had been granted.

(D) Any applicable implementation plan for which an attainment date later than December 31, 1982, is provided pursuant to section 7502(a)(2) of this title shall be revised by July 1, 1979, to include the comprehensive measures and requirements referred to in subsection (c)(5)(B) of this section.

(4) The procedure referred to in paragraph (2)(D) for review, prior to construction or modification, of the location of new sources shall (A) provide for adequate authority to prevent the construction or modification of any new source to which a standard of performance under section 7411 of this title will apply at any location which the State determines will prevent the attainment or maintenance within any air quality control region (or portion thereof) within such State of a national ambient air quality primary or secondary standard, and (B) require that prior to commencing construction or modification of any such source, the owner or operator thereof shall submit to such State such information as may be necessary to permit the State to make a determination under clause (A).

(5)(A)(i) Any State may include in a State implementation plan, but the Administrator may not require as a condition of approval of such plan under this section, any indirect source review program. The Administrator may approve and enforce, as part of an applicable implementation plan, an indirect source review program which the State chooses to adopt and submit as part of its plan.

(ii) Except as provided in subparagraph (B), no plan promulgated by the Administrator shall include any indirect source review program for any air quality control region, or portion thereof.

(iii) Any State may revise an applicable implementation plan approved under this subsection to suspend or revoke any such program included in such plan, provided that such plan meets the requirements of this section.

(B) The Administrator shall have the authority to promulgate, implement and enforce regulations under subsection (c) of this section respecting indirect source review programs which apply only to federally assisted highways, airports, and other major federally assisted indirect sources and federally owned or operated indirect sources.

(C) For purposes of this paragraph, the term "indirect source" means a facility, building, structure, installation, real property, road, or highway which attracts, or may attract, mobile sources of pollution. Such term includes parking lots, parking garages, and other facilities subject to any measure for management of parking supply (within the meaning of subsection (c)(2)(D)(ii) of this section), including regulation of existing off-street parking but such term does not include new or existing on-street parking. Direct emissions sources or facilities at, within, or associated with, any indirect source shall not be deemed indirect sources for the purpose of this paragraph.

(D) For purposes of this paragraph the term "indirect source review program" means the facility-by-facility review of indirect sources of air pollution, including such measures as are necessary to assure, or assist in assuring, that a new or modified indirect source will not attract mobile sources of air pollution, the emissions from which would cause or contribute to air pollution concentrations—

(i) exceeding any national primary ambient air quality standard for a mobile source-related air pollutant after the primary standard attainment date, or

(ii) preventing maintenance of any such standard after such date.

(E) For purposes of this paragraph and paragraph (2)(B), the term "transportation control measure" does not include any measure which is an "indirect source review program".

(6) No State plan shall be treated as meeting the requirements of this section unless such plan provides that in the case of any source which uses a supplemental, or intermittent control system for purposes of meeting the requirements of an order under section 7413(d) of this title or section 7419 of this title (relating to primary nonferrous smelter orders), the owner or operator of such source may not temporarily reduce the pay of any employee by reason of the use of such supplemental or intermittent or other dispersion dependent control system.

(b) Extension of period for submission of plans

The Administrator may, wherever he determines necessary, extend the period for submission of any plan or portion thereof which implements a national secondary ambient air quality standard for a period not to exceed 18 months from the date otherwise required for submission of such plan.

(c) Preparation and publication by Administrator of proposed regulations setting forth implementation plan; transportation regulations study and report; parking surcharge; suspension authority; plan implementation

(1) The Administrator shall, after consideration of any State hearing record, promptly prepare and publish proposed regulations setting forth an implementation plan, or portion thereof, for a State if—

(A) the State fails to submit an implementation plan which meets the requirements of this section,

(B) the plan, or any portion thereof, submitted for such State is determined by the Administrator not to be in accordance with the requirements of this section, or

(C) the State fails, within 60 days after notification by the Administrator or such longer period as he may prescribe, to revise an implementation plan as required pursuant to a provision of its plan referred to in subsection (a)(2)(H) of this section.

If such State held no public hearing associated with respect to such plan (or revision thereof), the Administrator shall provide opportunity for such hearing within such State on any proposed regulation. The Administrator shall, within six months after the date required for submission of such plan (or revision thereof), promulgate any such regulations unless, prior to such promulgation, such State has adopted and submitted a plan (or revision) which the Administrator determines to be in accordance with the requirements of this section. Notwithstanding the preceding sentence, any portion of a plan relating to any measure described in the first sentence of section 7421 of this title (relating to consultation) or the consultation process required under such section 7421 of this title shall not be required to be promulgated before the date eight months after such date required for submission.

(2)(A) The Administrator shall conduct a study and shall submit a report to the Committee on Interstate and Foreign Commerce of the United States House of Representatives and the Committee on Environment and Public Works of the United States Senate not later than three months after June 22, 1974, on the necessity of parking surcharge, management of parking supply, and preferential bus/carpool lane regulations as part of the applicable implementation plans required under this section to achieve and maintain national primary ambient air quality standards. The study shall include an assessment of the economic impact of such regulations, consideration of alternative means of reducing total vehicle miles traveled, and an assessment of the impact of such regulations on other Federal and State programs dealing with energy or transportation. In the course of such study, the Administrator shall consult with other Federal officials including, but not limited to, the Secretary of Transportation, the Secretary of Energy, and the Chairman of the Council on Environmental Quality.

(B) No parking surcharge regulation may be required by the Administrator under paragraph (1) of this subsection as a part of an applicable implementation plan. All parking surcharge regulations previously required by the Administrator shall be void upon June 22, 1974. This subparagraph shall not prevent the Administrator from approving parking surcharges if they are adopted and submitted by a State as part of an applicable implementation plan. The Administrator may not condition approval of any implementation plan submitted by a State on such plan's including a parking surcharge regulation.

(C) The Administrator is authorized to suspend until January 1, 1975, the effective date or applicability of any regulations for the management of parking supply or any requirement that such regulations be a part of an applicable implementation plan approved or promulgated under this section. The exercise of the authority under this subparagraph shall not prevent the Administrator from approving such regulations if they are adopted and submitted by a State as part of an applicable implementation plan. If the Administrator exercises the authority under this subparagraph, regulations requiring a review or analysis of the impact of proposed parking facilities before construction which take effect on or after January 1, 1975, shall not apply to parking facilities on which construction has been initiated before January 1, 1975.

(D) For purposes of this paragraph—

(i) The term "parking surcharge regulation" means a regulation imposing or requiring the imposition of any tax, surcharge, fee, or other charge on parking spaces, or any other area used for the temporary storage of motor vehicles.

(ii) The term "management of parking supply" shall include any requirement providing that any new facility containing a given number of parking spaces shall receive a permit or other prior approval, issuance of which is to be conditioned on air quality considerations.

(iii) The term "preferential bus/carpool lane" shall include any requirement for the setting aside of one or more lanes of a street or highway on a permanent or temporary basis for the exclusive use of buses or carpools, or both.

(E) No standard, plan, or requirement, relating to management of parking supply or preferential bus/carpool lanes shall be promulgated after June 22, 1974, by the Administrator pursuant to this section, unless such promulgation has been subjected to at least one public hearing which has been held in the area affected and for which reasonable notice has been given in such area. If substantial changes are made following public hearings, one or more additional hearings shall be held in such area after such notice.

(3) Upon application of the chief executive officer of any general purpose unit of local government, if the Administrator determines that such unit has adequate authority under State or local law, the Administrator may delegate to such unit the authority to implement and enforce within the jurisdiction of such unit any part of a plan promulgated under this subsection. Nothing in this paragraph shall prevent the Administrator from implementing or enforcing any applicable provision of a plan promulgated under this subsection.

(4) In the case of any applicable implementation plan containing measures requiring—

(A) retrofits on other than commercially owned in-use vehicles,

(B) gas rationing which the Administrator finds would have seriously disruptive and widespread economic or social effects, or

(C) the reduction of the supply of on-street parking spaces,

the Governor of the State may, after notice and opportunity for public hearing, temporarily suspend such measures notwithstanding the requirements of this section until January 1, 1979, or the date on which a plan revision under subsection (a)(2)(I) of this section is submitted, whichever is earlier. No such suspension shall be granted unless the State agrees to prepare, adopt, and submit such plan revision as determined by the Administrator.

(5)(A) Any measure in an applicable implementation plan which requires a toll or other charge for the use of a bridge located entirely within one city shall be eliminated from such plan by the Administrator upon application by the Governor of the State, which application shall include a certification by the Governor that he will revise such plan in accordance with subparagraph (B).

(B) In the case of any applicable implementation plan with respect to which a measure has been eliminated under subparagraph (A), such plan shall, not later than one year after August 7, 1977, be revised to include comprehensive measures (including the written evidence required by part D of this subchapter), to:

(i) establish, expand, or improve public transportation measures to meet basic transportation needs, as expeditiously as is practicable; and

(ii) implement transportation control measures necessary to attain and maintain national ambient air quality standards,

and such revised plan shall, for the purpose of implementing such comprehensive public transportation measures, include requirements to use (insofar as is necessary) Federal grants, State or local funds, or any combination of such grants and funds as may be consistent with the terms of the legislation providing such grants and funds. Such measures shall, as a substitute for the tolls or charges eliminated under subparagraph (A), provide for emissions reductions equivalent to the reductions which may reasonably be expected to be achieved through the use of the tolls or charges eliminated.

(C) Any revision of an implementation plan for purposes of meeting the requirements of subparagraph (B) shall be submitted in coordination with any plan revision required under part D of this subchapter.

(d) Applicable implementation plan

For purposes of this chapter, an applicable implementation plan is the implementation plan, or most recent revision thereof, which has been approved under subsection (a) of this section or promulgated under subsection (c) of this section and which implements the requirements of this section.

(e) Extension of time period for attainment of national primary ambient air quality standard in implementation plan; procedure; approval of extension by Administrator

(1) Upon application of a Governor of a State at the time of submission of any plan implementing a national ambient air quality primary standard, the Administrator may (subject to paragraph (2)) extend the three-year period referred to in subsection (a)(2)(A)(i) of this section for not more than two years for an air quality control region if after review of such plan the Administrator determines that—

(A) one or more emission sources (or classes of moving sources) are unable to comply with the requirements of such plan which implement such primary standard because the necessary technology or other alternatives are not available or will not be available soon enough to permit compliance within such three-year period, and

(B) the State has considered and applied as a part of its plan reasonably available alternative means of attaining such primary standard and has justifiably concluded that attainment of such primary standard within the three years cannot be achieved.

(2) The Administrator may grant an extension under paragraph (1) only if he determines that the State plan provides for—

(A) application of the requirements of the plan which implement such primary standard to all emission sources in such region other than the sources (or classes) described in paragraph (1)(A) within the three-year period, and

(B) such interim measures of control of the sources (or classes) described in paragraph (1)(A)

as the Administrator determines to be reasonable under the circumstances.

(f) National or regional energy emergencies; determination by President

(1) Upon application by the owner or operator of a fuel burning stationary source, and after notice and opportunity for public hearing, the Governor of the State in which such source is located may petition the President to determine that a national or regional energy emergency exists of such severity that—

(A) a temporary suspension of any part of the applicable implementation plan may be necessary, and

(B) other means of responding to the energy emergency may be inadequate.

Such determination shall not be delegable by the President to any other person. If the President determines that a national or regional energy emergency of such severity exists, a temporary emergency suspension of any part of an applicable implementation plan adopted by the State may be issued by the Governor of any State covered by the President's determination under the condition specified in paragraph (2) and may take effect immediately.

(2) A temporary emergency suspension under this subsection shall be issued to a source only if the Governor of such State finds that—

(A) there exists in the vicinity of such source a temporary energy emergency involving high levels of unemployment or loss of necessary energy supplies for residential dwellings; and

(B) such unemployment or loss can be totally or partially alleviated by such emergency suspension.

Not more than one such suspension may be issued for any source on the basis of the same set of circumstances or on the basis of the same emergency.

(3) A temporary emergency suspension issued by a Governor under this subsection shall remain in effect for a maximum of four months or such lesser period as may be specified in a disapproval order of the Administrator, if any. The Administrator may disapprove such suspension if he determines that it does not meet the requirements of paragraph (2).

(4) This subsection shall not apply in the case of a plan provision or requirement promulgated by the Administrator under subsection (c) of this section, but in any such case the President may grant a temporary emergency suspension for a four month period of any such provision or requirement if he makes the determinations and findings specified in paragraphs (1) and (2).

(5) The Governor may include in any temporary emergency suspension issued under this subsection a provision delaying for a period identical to the period of such suspension any compliance schedule (or increment of progress) to which such source is subject under section 1857c–10 of this title, as in effect before August 7, 1977, or section 7413(d) of this title, upon a finding that such source is unable to comply with such schedule (or increment) solely because of the conditions on the basis of which a suspension was issued under this subsection.

(g) Governor's authority to issue temporary emergency suspensions

(1) In the case of any State which has adopted and submitted to the Administrator a proposed plan revision which the State determines—

(A) meets the requirements of this section, and

(B) is necessary (i) to prevent the closing for one year or more of any source of air pollution, and (ii) to prevent substantial increases in unemployment which would result from such closing, and

which the Administrator has not approved or disapproved under this section within the required four month period, the Governor may issue a temporary emergency suspension of the part of the applicable implementation plan for such State which is proposed to be revised with respect to such source. The determination under subparagraph (B) may not be made with respect to a source which would close without regard to whether or not the proposed plan revision is approved.

(2) A temporary emergency suspension issued by a Governor under this subsection shall remain in effect for a maximum of four months or such lesser period as may be specified in a disapproval order of the Administrator. The Administrator may disapprove such suspension if he determines that it does not meet the requirements of this subsection.

(3) The Governor may include in any temporary emergency suspension issued under this subsection a provision delaying for a period identical to the period of such suspension any compliance schedule (or increment of progress) to which such source is subject under section 1857c–10 of this title as in effect before August 7, 1977, or under section 7413(d) of this title upon a finding that such source is unable to comply with such schedule (or increment) solely because of the conditions on the basis of which a suspension was issued under this subsection.

(h) Annual publication of comprehensive document for each State setting forth requirements of applicable implementation plan

(1) Not later than one year after August 7, 1977, and annually thereafter, the Administrator shall assemble and publish a comprehensive document for each State setting forth all requirements of the applicable implementation plan for such State and shall publish notice in the Federal Register of the availability of such documents. Each such document shall be revised as frequently as practicable but not less often than annually.

(2) The Administrator may promulgate such regulations as may be reasonably necessary to carry out the purpose of this subsection.

(i) Modification of requirements prohibited

Except for a primary nonferrous smelter order under section 7419 of this title, a suspension under subsection (f) or (g) of this section (relating to emergency suspensions), an exemption under section 7418 of this title (relating to certain Federal facilities), an order under section 7413(d) of this title (relating to compliance orders), a plan promulgation under subsection (c) of this section, or a plan revision under subsection (a)(3) of this section; no order, suspension, plan revision, or other action modifying any requirement of an applicable implementation plan may be taken with respect to any stationary source by the State or by the Administrator.

(j) Technological systems of continuous emission reduction on new or modified stationary sources; compliance with performance standards

As a condition for issuance of any permit required under this subchapter, the owner or operator of each new or modified stationary source which is required to obtain such a permit must show to the satisfaction of the permitting authority that the technological system of continuous emission reduction which is to be used will enable such source to comply with the standards of performance which are to apply to such source and that the construction or modification and operation of such source will be in compliance with all other requirements of this chapter.

(July 14, 1955, ch. 369, title I, § 110, as added Dec. 31, 1970, Pub.L. 91–604, § 4(a), 84 Stat. 1680, and amended June 22, 1974, Pub.L. 93–319, § 4, 88 Stat. 256; S.Res. 4, Feb. 4, 1977; Aug. 4, 1977, Pub.L. 95–91, title III, § 301(a), title VII, § 703, 91 Stat. 577, 606; Aug. 7, 1977, Pub.L. 95–95, title I, §§ 107, 108, 91 Stat. 691, 693; Nov. 16, 1977, Pub.L. 95–190, § 14(a)(1)–(6), 91 Stat. 1399; July 17, 1981, Pub.L. 97–23, § 3, 95 Stat. 142.)

Cross References

Documentation includable in petition to President to exercise authorities pursuant to section 7425 of this title with respect to major fuel burning stationary source to support finding of significant local or regional economic disruption or unemployment, see section 6215 of this title.

Federally permitted release defined to include emissions into air subject to permit or control regulation under state implementation plan submitted in accordance with this section for purposes of Comprehensive Environmental Response, Compensation, and Liability Act of 1980, see section 9601 of this title.

Permit authorizing increased uses of petroleum by existing powerplants, necessity of certification that powerplant cannot comply with requirements of implementation plan, see section 8375 of this title.

Suspension of emission limitations or other requirements of applicable implementation plans required by emergency prohibition on use of natural gas or petroleum to be issued in accordance with subsec. (f) of this section, see section 8374 of this title.

Code of Federal Regulations

Environmental Protection Agency,
- Ambient air quality surveillance, see 40 CFR 58.1 et seq.
- Emission standards for hazardous pollutants, see 40 CFR 61.01 et seq.
- Implementation plans, requirements concerning, see 40 CFR 51.1 et seq.
- National primary and secondary ambient air quality standards, see 40 CFR 50.1 et seq.
- New stationary sources, performance standards for, see 40 CFR 60.1 et seq.
- Primary nonferrous smelter orders, see 40 CFR 57.101 et seq.

Library References

Health and Environment ⇐25.6(1) et seq., 28.
States ⇐4.19.
C.J.S. Health and Environment § 91 et seq.
C.J.S. States § 28.

United States Supreme Court

Approval of plan, economic and technological feasibility, see Union Elec. Co. v. Environmental Protection Agency, 1976, 96 S.Ct. 2518, 427 U.S. 246, 49 L.Ed.2d 474.

Extension of time for revision of plan, see Train v. Natural Resources Defense Council, Inc., 1975, 95 S.Ct. 1470, 421 U.S. 60, 43 L.Ed.2d 731.

§ 7411. Standards of performance for new stationary sources

(a) Definitions

For purposes of this section:

(1) The term "standard of performance" means—

(A) with respect to any air pollutant emitted from a category of fossil fuel fired stationary sources to which subsection (b) of this section applies, a standard—

(i) establishing allowable emission limitations for such category of sources, and

(ii) requiring the achievement of a percentage reduction in the emissions from such category of sources from the emissions which would have resulted from the use of fuels which are not subject to treatment prior to combustion,

(B) with respect to any air pollutant emitted from a category of stationary sources (other than fossil fuel fired sources) to which subsection (b) of this section applies, a standard such as that referred to in subparagraph (A)(i); and

(C) with respect to any air pollutant emitted from a particular source to which subsection (d) of this section applies, a standard which the State (or the Administrator under the conditions specified in subsection (d)(2) of this section) determines is applicable to that source and which reflects the degree of emission reduction achievable through the application of the best system of continuous emission reduction which (taking into consideration the cost of achieving such emission reduction, and any nonair quality health and environmental impact and energy requirements) the Administrator determines has been adequately demonstrated for that category of sources.

For the purpose of subparagraphs (A)(i) and (ii) and (B), a standard of performance shall reflect the degree of emission limitation and the percentage reduction achievable through application of the best technological system of continuous emission reduction which (taking into consideration the cost of achieving such emission reduction, any nonair quality health and environmental impact and energy requirements) the Administrator determines has been adequately demonstrated. For the purpose of subparagraph (1)(A)(ii), any cleaning of the fuel or reduction in the pollution characteristics of the fuel after extraction and prior to combustion may be credited, as determined under regulations promulgated by the Administrator, to a source which burns such fuel.

(2) The term "new source" means any stationary source, the construction or modification of which is commenced after the publication of regulations (or, if earlier, proposed regulations) prescribing a standard of performance under this section which will be applicable to such source.

(3) The term "stationary source" means any building, structure, facility, or installation which emits or may emit any air pollutant.

(4) The term "modification" means any physical change in, or change in the method of operation of, a stationary source which increases the amount of any air pollutant emitted by such source or which results in the emission of any air pollutant not previously emitted.

(5) The term "owner or operator" means any person who owns, leases, operates, controls, or supervises a stationary source.

(6) The term "existing source" means any stationary source other than a new source.

(7) The term "technological system of continuous emission reduction" means—

(A) a technological process for production or operation by any source which is inherently low-polluting or nonpolluting, or

(B) a technological system for continuous reduction of the pollution generated by a source before such pollution is emitted into the ambient air, including precombustion cleaning or treatment of fuels.

(8) A conversion to coal (A) by reason of an order under section 2(a) of the Energy Supply and Environmental Coordination Act of 1974 [15 U.S.C. 792(a)] or any amendment thereto, or any subsequent enactment which supersedes such Act [15 U.S.C. 791 et seq.], or (B) which qualifies under section 7413(d)(5)(A)(ii) of this title, shall not be deemed to be a modification for purposes of paragraphs (2) and (4) of this subsection.

(b) List of categories of stationary sources; standards of performance; information on pollution control techniques; sources owned or operated by United States; particular systems; revised standards

(1)(A) The Administrator shall, within 90 days after December 31, 1970, publish (and from time to time thereafter shall revise) a list of categories of stationary sources. He shall include a category of sources in such list if in his judgment it causes, or contributes significantly to, air pollution which may reasonably be anticipated to endanger public health or welfare.

(B) Within 120 days after the inclusion of a category of stationary sources in a list under subparagraph (A), the Administrator shall publish proposed regulations, establishing Federal standards of performance for new sources within such category. The Administrator shall afford interested persons an opportunity for written comment on such proposed regulations. After considering such comments, he shall promulgate, within 90 days after such publication, such standards with such modifications as he deems appropriate. The Administrator shall, at least every four years, review and, if appropriate, revise such standards following the procedure required by this subsection for promulgation of such standards. Standards of performance or revisions thereof shall become effective upon promulgation.

(2) The Administrator may distinguish among classes, types, and sizes within categories of new sources for the purpose of establishing such standards.

(3) The Administrator shall, from time to time, issue information on pollution control techniques for categories of new sources and air pollutants subject to the provisions of this section.

(4) The provisions of this section shall apply to any new source owned or operated by the United States.

(5) Except as otherwise authorized under subsection (h) of this section, nothing in this section shall be construed to require, or to authorize the Administrator to require, any new or modified source to install and operate any particular technological system of continuous emission reduction to comply with any new source standard of performance.

(6) The revised standards of performance required by enactment of subsection (a)(1)(A)(i) and (ii) of this section shall be promulgated not later than one year after August 7, 1977. Any new or modified fossil fuel fired stationary source which commences construction prior to the date of publication of the proposed revised standards shall not be required to comply with such revised standards.

(c) State implementation and enforcement of standards of performance

(1) Each State may develop and submit to the Administrator a procedure for implementing and enforcing standards of performance for new sources located in such State. If the Administrator finds the State procedure is adequate, he shall delegate to such State any authority he has under this chapter to implement and enforce such standards.

(2) Nothing in this subsection shall prohibit the Administrator from enforcing any applicable standard of performance under this section.

(d) Standards of performance for existing sources; remaining useful life of source

(1) The Administrator shall prescribe regulations which shall establish a procedure similar to that provided by section 7410 of this title under which each State shall submit to the Administrator a plan which (A) establishes standards of performance for any existing source for any air pollutant (i) for which air quality criteria have not been issued or which is not included on a list published under section 7408(a) or 7412(b)(1)(A) of this title but (ii) to which a standard of performance under this section would apply if such existing source were a new source, and (B) provides for the implementation and enforcement of such standards of performance. Regulations of the Administrator under this paragraph shall permit the State in applying a standard of performance to any particular source under a plan submitted under this paragraph to take into consideration, among other factors, the remaining useful life of the existing source to which such standard applies.

(2) The Administrator shall have the same authority—

(A) to prescribe a plan for a State in cases where the State fails to submit a satisfactory plan as he would have under section 7410(c) of this title in the case of failure to submit an implementation plan, and

(B) to enforce the provisions of such plan in cases where the State fails to enforce them as he would have under sections 7413 and 7414 of this title with respect to an implementation plan.

In promulgating a standard of performance under a plan prescribed under this paragraph, the Administrator shall take into consideration, among other factors, remaining useful lives of the sources in the category of sources to which such standard applies.

(e) Prohibited acts

After the effective date of standards of performance promulgated under this section, it shall be unlawful for any owner or operator of any new source to operate such source in violation of any standard of performance applicable to such source.

(f) New source standards of performance

(1) Not later than one year after August 7, 1977, the Administrator shall promulgate regulations listing under subsection (b)(1)(A) of this section the categories of major stationary sources which are not on August 7, 1977, included on the list required under subsection (b)(1)(A) of this section. The Administrator shall promulgate regulations establishing standards of performance for the percentage of such categories of sources set forth in the following table before the expiration of the corresponding period set forth in such table:

Percentage of source categories required to be listed for which standards must be established:	Period by which standards must be promulgated after date list is required to be promulgated:
25	2 years.
75	3 years.
100	4 years.

(2) In determining priorities for promulgating standards for categories of major stationary sources for the purpose of paragraph (1), the Administrator shall consider—

(A) the quantity of air pollutant emissions which each such category will emit, or will be designed to emit;

(B) the extent to which each such pollutant may reasonably be anticipated to endanger public health or welfare; and

(C) the mobility and competitive nature of each such category of sources and the consequent need for nationally applicable new source standards of performance.

(3) Before promulgating any regulations under this subsection or listing any category of major stationary sources as required under this subsection, the Administrator shall consult with appropriate representatives of the Governors and of State air pollution control agencies.

(g) Revision of regulations

(1) Upon application by the Governor of a State showing that the Administrator has failed to specify in regulations under subsection (f)(1) of this section any category of major stationary sources required to be specified under such regulations, the Administrator shall revise such regulations to specify any such category.

(2) Upon application of the Governor of a State, showing that any category of stationary sources which is not included in the list under subsection (b)(1)(A) of this section contributes significantly to air pollution which may reasonably be anticipated to endanger public health or welfare (notwithstanding that such category is not a category of major stationary sources), the Administrator shall revise such regulations to specify such category of stationary sources.

(3) Upon application of the Governor of a State showing that the Administrator has failed to apply properly the criteria required to be considered under subsection (f)(2) of this section, the Administrator shall revise the list under subsection (b)(1)(A) of this section to apply properly such criteria.

(4) Upon application of the Governor of a State showing that—

(A) a new, innovative, or improved technology or process which achieves greater continuous emission reduction has been adequately demonstrated for any category of stationary sources, and

(B) as a result of such technology or process, the new source standard of performance in effect under this section for such category no longer reflects the greatest degree of emission limitation achievable through application of the best technological system of continuous emission reduction which (taking into consideration the cost of achieving such emission reduction, and any non-air quality health and environmental impact and energy requirements) has been adequately demonstrated,

the Administrator shall revise such standard of performance for such category accordingly.

(5) Upon application by the Governor of a State showing that the Administrator has failed to list any air pollutant which causes, or contributes to, air pollution which may reasonably be anticipated to result in an increase in mortality or an increase in serious irreversible, or incapacitating reversible, illness as a hazardous air pollutant under section 7412 of this title the Administrator shall revise the list of hazardous air pollutants under such section to include such pollutant.

(6) Upon application by the Governor of a State showing that any category of stationary sources of a hazardous air pollutant listed under section 7412 of this title is not subject to emission standards under such section, the Administrator shall propose and promulgate such emission standards applicable to such category of sources.

(7) Unless later deadlines for action of the Administrator are otherwise prescribed under this section or section 7412 of this title, the Administrator shall, not later than three months following the date of receipt of any application by a Governor of a State, either—

(A) find that such application does not contain the requisite showing and deny such application, or

(B) grant such application and take the action required under this subsection.

(8) Before taking any action required by subsection (f) of this section or by this subsection, the Administrator shall provide notice and opportunity for public hearing.

(h) Design, equipment, work practice, or operational standard; alternative emission limitation

(1) For purposes of this section, if in the judgment of the Administrator, it is not feasible to prescribe or enforce a standard of performance, he may instead promulgate a design, equipment, work practice, or operational standard, or combination thereof, which reflects the best technological system of continuous emission reduction which (taking into consideration the cost of achieving such emission reduction, and any non-air quality health and environmental impact and energy requirements) the Administrator determines has been adequately demonstrated. In the event the Administrator promulgates a design or equipment standard under this subsection, he shall include as part of such standard such requirements as will assure the proper opera-

tion and maintenance of any such element of design or equipment.

(2) For the purpose of this subsection, the phrase "not feasible to prescribe or enforce a standard of performance" means any situation in which the Administrator determines that (A) a pollutant or pollutants cannot be emitted through a conveyance designed and constructed to emit or capture such pollutant, or that any requirement for, or use of, such a conveyance would be inconsistent with any Federal, State, or local law, or (B) the application of measurement methodology to a particular class of sources is not practicable due to technological or economic limitations.

(3) If after notice and opportunity for public hearing, any person establishes to the satisfaction of the Administrator that an alternative means of emission limitation will achieve a reduction in emissions of any air pollutant at least equivalent to the reduction in emissions of such air pollutant achieved under the requirements of paragraph (1), the Administrator shall permit the use of such alternative by the source for purposes of compliance with this section with respect to such pollutant.

(4) Any standard promulgated under paragraph (1) shall be promulgated in terms of standard of performance whenever it becomes feasible to promulgate and enforce such standard in such terms.

(5) Any design, equipment, work practice, or operational standard, or any combination thereof, described in this subsection shall be treated as a standard of performance for purposes of the provisions of this chapter (other than the provisions of subsection (a) of this section and this subsection).

(i) Country elevators

Any regulations promulgated by the Administrator under this section applicable to grain elevators shall not apply to country elevators (as defined by the Administrator) which have a storage capacity of less than two million five hundred thousand bushels.

(j) Innovative technological systems of continuous emission reduction

(1)(A) Any person proposing to own or operate a new source may request the Administrator for one or more waivers from the requirements of this section for such source or any portion thereof with respect to any air pollutant to encourage the use of an innovative technological system or systems of continuous emission reduction. The Administrator may, with the consent of the Governor of the State in which the source is to be located, grant a waiver under this paragraph, if the Administrator determines after notice and opportunity for public hearing, that—

(i) the proposed system or systems have not been adequately demonstrated,

(ii) the proposed system or systems will operate effectively and there is a substantial likelihood that such system or systems will achieve greater continuous emission reduction than that required to be achieved under the standards of performance which would otherwise apply, or achieve at least an equivalent reduction at lower cost in terms of energy, economic, or nonair quality environmental impact,

(iii) the owner or operator of the proposed source has demonstrated to the satisfaction of the Administrator that the proposed system will not cause or contribute to an unreasonable risk to public health, welfare, or safety in its operation, function, or malfunction, and

(iv) the granting of such waiver is consistent with the requirements of subparagraph (C).

In making any determination under clause (ii), the Administrator shall take into account any previous failure of such system or systems to operate effectively or to meet any requirement of the new source performance standards. In determining whether an unreasonable risk exists under clause (iii), the Administrator shall consider, among other factors, whether and to what extent the use of the proposed technological system will cause, increase, reduce, or eliminate emissions of any unregulated pollutants; available methods for reducing or eliminating any risk to public health, welfare, or safety which may be associated with the use of such system; and the availability of other technological systems which may be used to conform to standards under this section without causing or contributing to such unreasonable risk. The Administrator may conduct such tests and may require the owner or operator of the proposed source to conduct such tests and provide such information as is necessary to carry out clause (iii) of this subparagraph. Such requirements shall include a requirement for prompt reporting of the emission of any unregulated pollutant from a system if such pollutant was not emitted, or was emitted in significantly lesser amounts without use of such system.

(B) A waiver under this paragraph shall be granted on such terms and conditions as the Administrator determines to be necessary to assure—

(i) emissions from the source will not prevent attainment and maintenance of any national ambient air quality standards, and

(ii) proper functioning of the technological system or systems authorized.

Any such term or condition shall be treated as a standard of performance for the purposes of subsection (e) of this section and section 7413 of this title.

(C) The number of waivers granted under this paragraph with respect to a proposed technological system of continuous emission reduction shall not exceed such number as the Administrator finds necessary to ascertain whether or not such system will achieve the conditions specified in clauses (ii) and (iii) of subparagraph (A).

(D) A waiver under this paragraph shall extend to the sooner of—

(i) the date determined by the Administrator, after consultation with the owner or operator of the source, taking into consideration the design, installation, and capital cost of the technological system or systems being used, or

(ii) the date on which the Administrator determines that such system has failed to—

(I) achieve at least an equivalent continuous emission reduction to that required to be achieved under the standards of performance which would otherwise apply, or

(II) comply with the condition specified in paragraph (1)(A)(iii),

and that such failure cannot be corrected.

(E) In carrying out subparagraph (D)(i), the Administrator shall not permit any waiver for a source or portion thereof to extend beyond the date—

(i) seven years after the date on which any waiver is granted to such source or portion thereof, or

(ii) four years after the date on which such source or portion thereof commences operation,

whichever is earlier.

(F) No waiver under this subsection shall apply to any portion of a source other than the portion on which the innovative technological system or systems of continuous emission reduction is used.

(2)(A) If a waiver under paragraph (1) is terminated under clause (ii) of paragraph (1)(D), the Administrator shall grant an extension of the requirements of this section for such source for such minimum period as may be necessary to comply with the applicable standard of performance under this section. Such period shall not extend beyond the date three years from the time such waiver is terminated.

(B) An extension granted under this paragraph shall set forth emission limits and a compliance schedule containing increments of progress which require compliance with the applicable standards of performance as expeditiously as practicable and include such measures as are necessary and practicable in the interim to minimize emissions. Such schedule shall be treated as a standard of performance for purposes of subsection (e) of this section and section 7413 of this title.

(July 14, 1955, ch. 360, title I, § 111, as added Dec. 31, 1970, Pub.L. 91–604, § 4(a), 84 Stat. 1683, and amended Nov. 18, 1971, Pub.L. 92–157, title III, § 302(f), 85 Stat. 464; Aug. 7, 1977, Pub.L. 95–95, title I, § 109(a)–(d)(1), (e), (f), title IV, § 401(b), 91 Stat. 697–703, 791; Nov. 16, 1977, Pub.L. 95–190, § 14(a)(7)–(9), 91 Stat. 1399; Nov. 9, 1978, Pub.L. 95–623, § 13(a), 92 Stat. 3457.)

Cross References

Federally permitted release defined to include emissions into air subject to permit or control regulation under this section for purposes of Comprehensive Environmental Response, Compensation, and Liability Act of 1980, see section 9601 of this title.

Library References

Health and Environment ⚷25.6(1) et seq., 28.
C.J.S. Health and Environment § 91 et seq.

§ 7412. National emission standards for hazardous air pollutants

(a) Definitions

For purposes of this section—

(1) The term "hazardous air pollutant" means an air pollutant to which no ambient air quality standard is applicable and which in the judgment of the Administrator causes, or contributes to, air pollution which may reasonably be anticipated to result in an increase in mortality or an increase in serious irreversible, or incapacitating reversible, illness.

(2) The term "new source" means a stationary source the construction or modification of which is commenced after the Administrator proposes regulations under this section establishing an emission standard which will be applicable to such source.

(3) The terms "stationary source", "modification", "owner or operator" and "existing source" shall have the same meaning as such terms have under section 7411(a) of this title.

(b) List of hazardous air pollutants; emission standards; pollution control techniques

(1)(A) The Administrator shall, within 90 days after December 31, 1970, publish (and shall from time to time thereafter revise) a list which includes each hazardous air pollutant for which he intends to establish an emission standard under this section.

(B) Within 180 days after the inclusion of any air pollutant in such list, the Administrator shall publish proposed regulations establishing emission standards for such pollutant together with a notice of a public hearing within thirty days. Not later than 180 days after such publication, the Administrator shall prescribe an emission standard for such pollutant, unless he finds, on the basis of information presented at such hearings, that such pollutant clearly is not a hazardous air pollutant. The Administrator shall establish any such standard at the level which in his judgment provides an ample margin of safety to protect the public health from such hazardous air pollutant.

(C) Any emission standard established pursuant to this section shall become effective upon promulgation.

(2) The Administrator shall, from time to time, issue information on pollution control techniques for air pollutant subject to the provisions of this section.

(c) Prohibited acts; exemption

(1) After the effective date of any emission standard under this section—

(A) no person may construct any new source or modify any existing source which in the Administrator's judgment, will emit an air pollutant to which such standard applies unless the Administrator finds that such source if properly operated will not cause emissions in violation of such standard, and

(B) no air pollutant to which such standard applies may be emitted from any stationary source in violation of such standard, except that in the case of an existing source—

(i) such standard shall not apply until 90 days after its effective date, and

(ii) the Administrator may grant a waiver permitting such source a period of up to two years after the effective date of a standard to comply with the standard, if he finds that such period is necessary for the installation of controls and that steps will be taken during the period of the waiver to assure that the health of persons will be protected from imminent endangerment.

(2) The President may exempt any stationary source from compliance with paragraph (1) for a period of not more than two years if he finds that the technology to implement such standards is not available and the operation of such source is required for reasons of national security. An exemption under this paragraph may be extended for one or more additional periods, each period not to exceed two years. The President shall make a report to Congress with respect to each exemption (or extension thereof) made under this paragraph.

(d) State implementation and enforcement

(1) Each State may develop and submit to the Administrator a procedure for implementing and enforcing emission standards for hazardous air pollutants for stationary sources located in such State. If the Administrator finds the State procedure is adequate, he shall delegate to such State any authority he has under this chapter to implement and enforce such standards.

(2) Nothing in this subsection shall prohibit the Administrator from enforcing any applicable emission standard under this section.

(e) Design, equipment, work practice, and operational standards

(1) For purposes of this section, if in the judgment of the Administrator, it is not feasible to prescribe or enforce an emission standard for control of a hazardous air pollutant or pollutants, he may instead promulgate a design, equipment, work practice, or operational standard, or combination thereof, which in his judgment is adequate to protect the public health from such pollutant or pollutants with an ample margin of safety. In the event the Administrator promulgates a design or equipment standard under this subsection, he shall include as part of such standard such requirements as will assure the proper operation and maintenance of any such element of design or equipment.

(2) For the purpose of this subsection, the phrase "not feasible to prescribe or enforce an emission standard" means any situation in which the Administrator determines that (A) a hazardous pollutant or pollutants cannot be emitted through a conveyance designed and constructed to emit or capture such pollutant, or that any requirement for, or use of, such a conveyance would be inconsistent with any Federal, State, or local law, or (B) the application of measurement methodology to a particular class of sources is not practicable due to technological or economic limitations.

(3) If after notice and opportunity for public hearing, any person establishes to the satisfaction of the Administrator that an alternative means of emission limitation will achieve a reduction in emissions of any air pollutant at least equivalent to the reduction in emissions of such air pollutant achieved under the requirements of paragraph (1), the Administrator shall permit the use of such alternative by the source for purposes of compliance with this section with respect to such pollutant.

(4) Any standard promulgated under paragraph (1) shall be promulgated in terms of an emission standard whenever it becomes feasible to promulgate and enforce such standard in such terms.

(5) Any design, equipment, work practice, or operational standard, or any combination thereof, de-

scribed in this subsection shall be treated as an emission standard for purposes of the provisions of this chapter (other than the provisions of this subsection).

(July 14, 1955, ch. 360, title I, § 112, as added Dec. 31, 1970, Pub.L. 91–604, § 4(a), 84 Stat. 1685, and amended Aug. 7, 1977, Pub.L. 95–95, title I, §§ 109(d)(2), 110, title IV, § 401(c), 91 Stat. 701, 703, 791; Nov. 9, 1978, Pub.L. 95–623, § 13(b), 92 Stat. 3458.)

Cross References

Federally permitted release defined to include emissions into air subject to permit or control regulation under this section for purposes of Comprehensive Environmental Response, Compensation, and Liability Act of 1980, see section 9601 of this title.

Code of Federal Regulations

Emission standards for hazardous pollutants, see 40 CFR 61.01 et seq.

New stationary sources, standards of performance for, see 40 CFR 60.1 et seq.

Library References

Health and Environment ⚷25.6(1) et seq., 28.

C.J.S. Health and Environment § 91 et seq.

§ 7413. Federal enforcement procedures

(a) Finding of violation; notice; compliance order; civil action; State failure to enforce plan; construction or modification of major stationary sources

(1) Whenever, on the basis of any information available to him, the Administrator finds that any person is in violation of any requirement of an applicable implementation plan, the Administrator shall notify the person in violation of the plan and the State in which the plan applies of such finding. If such violation extends beyond the 30th day after the date of the Administrator's notification, the Administrator may issue an order requiring such person to comply with the requirements of such plan or he may bring a civil action in accordance with subsection (b) of this section.

(2) Whenever, on the basis of information available to him, the Administrator finds that violations of an applicable implementation plan are so widespread that such violations appear to result from a failure of the State in which the plan applies to enforce the plan effectively, he shall so notify the State. If the Administrator finds such failure extends beyond the 30th day after such notice, he shall give public notice of such finding. During the period beginning with such public notice and ending when such State satisfies the Administrator that it will enforce such plan (hereafter referred to in this section as "period of federally assumed enforcement"), the Administrator may enforce any requirement of such plan with respect to any person—

(A) by issuing an order to comply with such requirement, or

(B) by bringing a civil action under subsection (b) of this section.

(3) Whenever, on the basis of any information available to him, the Administrator finds that any person is in violation of section 7411(e) of this title (relating to new source performance standards), section 7412(c) of this title (relating to standards for hazardous emissions), or section 1857c–10(g) of this title (relating to energy-related authorities) is in violation of any requirement of section 7414 of this title (relating to inspections, etc.), he may issue an order requiring such person to comply with such section or requirement, or he may bring a civil action in accordance with subsection (b) of this section.

(4) An order issued under this subsection (other than an order relating to a violation of section 7412 of this title) shall not take effect until the person to whom it is issued has had an opportunity to confer with the Administrator concerning the alleged violation. A copy of any order issued under this subsection shall be sent to the State air pollution control agency of any State in which the violation occurs. Any order issued under this subsection shall state with reasonable specificity the nature of the violation, specify a time for compliance which the Administrator determines is reasonable, taking into account the seriousness of the violation and any good faith efforts to comply with applicable requirements. In any case in which an order under this subsection (or notice to a violator under paragraph (1)) is issued to a corporation, a copy of such order (or notice) shall be issued to appropriate corporate officers.

(5) Whenever, on the basis of information available to him, the Administrator finds that a State is not acting in compliance with any requirement of the regulation referred to in section 129(a)(1) of the Clean Air Act Amendments of 1977 (relating to certain interpretative regulations) or any plan provisions required under section 7410(a)(2)(I) of this title and part D of this subchapter, he may issue an order prohibiting the construction or modification of any major stationary source in any area to which such provisions apply or he may bring a civil action under subsection (b)(5) of this section.

(b) Violations by owners or operators of major stationary sources

The Administrator shall, in the case of any person which is the owner or operator of a major stationary source, and may, in the case of any other person, commence a civil action for a permanent or temporary injunction, or to assess and recover a civil penalty of not more than $25,000 per day of violation, or both, whenever such person—

(1) violates or fails or refuses to comply with any order issued under subsection (a) of this section; or

(2) violates any requirement of an applicable implementation plan (A) during any period of Federally assumed enforcement, or (B) more than 30 days after having been notified by the Administrator under subsection (a)(1) of this section of a finding that such person is violating such requirement; or

(3) violates section 7411(e), section 7412(c), section 1857c–10(g) of this title (as in effect before August 7, 1977), subsection (d)(5) of this section (relating to coal conversion), section 7624 of this title (relating to cost of certain vapor recovery), section 7419 of this title (relating to smelter orders), or any regulation under part B of subchapter (relating to ozone); or

(4) fails or refuses to comply with any requirement of section 7414 of this title or subsection (d) of this section; or

(5) attempts to construct or modify a major stationary source in any area with respect to which a finding under subsection (a)(5) of this section has been made.

The Administrator may commence a civil action for recovery of any noncompliance penalty under section 7420 of this title or for recovery of any nonpayment penalty for which any person is liable under section 7420 of this title or for both. Any action under this subsection may be brought in the district court of the United States for the district in which the violation occurred or in which the defendant resides or has his principal place of business, and such court shall have jurisdiction to restrain such violation, to require compliance, to assess such civil penalty and to collect any noncompliance penalty (and nonpayment penalty) owed under section 7420 of this title. In determining the amount of any civil penalty to be assessed under this subsection, the court shall take into consideration (in addition to other factors) the size of the business, the economic impact of the penalty on the business, and the seriousness of the violation. Notice of the commencement of such action shall be given to the appropriate State air pollution control agency. In the case of any action brought by the Administrator under this subsection, the court may award costs of litigation (including reasonable attorney and expert witness fees) to the party or parties against whom such action was brought in any case where the court finds that such action was unreasonable.

(c) Penalties

(1) Any person who knowingly—

(A) violates any requirement of an applicable implementation plan (i) during any period of Federally assumed enforcement, or (ii) more than 30 days after having been notified by the Administrator under subsection (a)(1) of this section that such person is violating such requirement, or

(B) violates or fails or refuses to comply with any order under section 7419 of this title or under subsection (a) or (d) of this section, or

(C) violates section 7411(e), section 7412(c) of this title, or

(D) violates any requirement of section 1857c–10(g) of this title (as in effect before August 7, 1977), subsection (b)(7) or (d)(5) of section 7420 of this title (relating to noncompliance penalties), or any requirement of part B of this subchapter (relating to ozone)[1]

shall be punished by a fine of not more than $25,000 per day of violation, or by imprisonment for not more than one year, or by both. If the conviction is for a violation committed after the first conviction of such person under this paragraph, punishment shall be by a fine of not more than $50,000 per day of violation, or by imprisonment for not more than two years, or by both.

(2) Any person who knowingly makes any false statement, representation, or certification in any application, record, report, plan, or other document filed or required to be maintained under this chapter or who falsifies, tampers with, or knowingly renders inaccurate any monitoring device or method required to be maintained under this chapter, shall upon conviction, be punished by a fine of not more than $10,000, or by imprisonment for not more than six months, or by both.

(3) For the purpose of this subsection, the term "person" includes, in addition to the entities referred to in section 7602(e) of this title, any responsible corporate officer.

(d) Final compliance orders

(1) A State (or, after thirty days notice to the State, the Administrator) may issue to any stationary source which is unable to comply with any requirement of an applicable implementation plan an order which specifies a date for final compliance with such requirement later than the date for attainment of any national ambient air quality standard specified in such plan if—

(A) such order is issued after notice to the public (and, as appropriate, to the Administrator) containing the content of the proposed order and opportunity for public hearing;

(B) the order contains a schedule and timetable for compliance;

(C) the order requires compliance with applicable interim requirements as provided in paragraph (5)(B) (relating to sources converting to coal), and paragraph (6) and (7) (relating to all sources receiving such orders) and requires the emission monitoring and reporting by the source authorized to be required under sections 7410(a)(2)(F) and 7414(a)(1) of this title;

(D) the order provides for final compliance with the requirement of the applicable implementation plan as expeditiously as practicable, but (except as provided in paragraph (4) or (5)) in no event later than July 1, 1979, or three years after the date for final compliance with such requirement specified in such plan, whichever is later; and

(E) in the case of a major stationary source, the order notifies the source that, unless exempted under section 7420(a)(2)(B) or (C), it will be required to pay a noncompliance penalty effective July 1, 1979, as provided under section 7420 of this title or by such later date as is set forth in the order in accordance with section 7420(b)(3) or (g) of this title in the event such source fails to achieve final compliance by July 1, 1979.

(2) In the case of any major stationary source, no such order issued by the State shall take effect until the Administrator determines that such order has been issued in accordance with the requirements of this chapter. The Administrator shall determine, not later than 90 days after receipt of notice of the issuance of an order under this subsection with respect to any major stationary source, whether or not any State order under this subsection is in accordance with the requirements of this chapter. In the case of any source other than a major stationary source, such order issued by the State shall cease to be effective upon a determination by the Administrator that it was not issued in accordance with the requirements of this chapter. If the Administrator so objects, he shall simultaneously proceed to issue an enforcement order in accordance with subsection (a) of this section or an order under this subsection. Nothing in this section shall be construed as limiting the authority of a State or political subdivision to adopt and enforce a more stringent emission limitation or more expeditious schedule or timetable for compliance than that contained in an order by the Administrator.

(3) If any source not in compliance with any requirement of an applicable implementation plan gives written notification to the State (or the Administrator) that such source intends to comply by means of replacement of the facility, a complete change in production process, or a termination of operation, the State (or the Administrator) may issue an order under paragraph (1) of this subsection permitting the source to operate until July 1, 1979, without any interim schedule of compliance: *Provided*, That as a condition of the issuance of any such order, the owner or operator of such source shall post a bond or other surety in an amount equal to the cost of actual compliance by such facility and any economic value which may accrue to the owner or operator of such source by reason of the failure to comply. If a source for which the bond or other surety required by this paragraph has been posted fails to replace the facility, change the production process, or terminate the operations as specified in the order by the required date, the owner or operator shall immediately forfeit on the bond or other surety and the State (or the Administrator) shall have no discretion to modify the order under this paragraph or to compromise the bond or other surety.

(4) An order under paragraph (1) of this subsection may be issued to an existing stationary source if—

(A) the source will expeditiously use new means of emission limitation which the Administrator determines is likely to be adequately demonstrated (within the meaning of section 7411(a)(1)) of this title upon expiration of the order,

(B) such new means of emission limitation is not likely to be used by such source unless an order is granted under this subsection.[2]

(C) such new means of emission limitation is determined by the Administrator to have a substantial likelihood of—

(i) achieving greater continuous emission reduction than the means of emission limitation which, but for such order, would be required; or

(ii) achieving an equivalent continuous reduction at lower cost in terms of energy, economic, or nonair quality environmental impact; and

(D) compliance by the source with the requirement of the applicable implementation plan would be impracticable prior to, or during, the installation of such new means.

Such an order shall provide for final compliance with the requirement in the applicable implementation plan as expeditiously as practicable, but in no event later than five years after the date on which the source would otherwise be required to be in full compliance with the requirement.

(5)(A) In the case of a major stationary source which is burning petroleum products or natural gas, or both and which—

(i) is prohibited from doing so under an order pursuant to the provisions of section 792(a) of title 15, or any amendment thereto, or any subsequent enactment which supersedes such provisions, or

(ii) within one year after August 7, 1977, gives notice of intent to convert to coal as its primary energy source because of actual or anticipated curtailment of natural gas supplies under any curtailment plan or schedule approved by the Federal Power Commission (or, in the case of intrastate natural gas supplies, approved by the appropriate State regulatory commission),

and which thereby would no longer be in compliance with any requirement under an applicable implementation plan, an order may be issued by the Administrator under paragraph (1) of this subsection for such source which specifies a date for final compliance with such requirement as expeditiously as practicable, but not later than December 31, 1980. The Administrator may issue an additional order under paragraph (1) of this subsection for such source providing an additional period for such source to come into compliance with the requirement in the applicable implementation plan, which shall be as expeditiously as practicable, but in no event later than five years after the date required for compliance under the preceding sentence.

(B) In issuing an order pursuant to subparagraph (A), the Administrator shall prescribe (and may from time to time modify) emission limitations, requirements respecting pollution characteristics of coal, or other enforceable measures for control of emissions for each source to which such an order applies. Such limitations, requirements, and measures shall be those which the Administrator determines must be complied with by the source in order to assure (throughout the period before the date for final compliance established in the order) that the burning of coal by such source will not result in emissions which cause or contribute to concentrations of any air pollutant in excess of any national primary ambient air quality standard for such pollutant.

(C) The Administrator may, by regulation, establish priorities under which manufacturers of continuous emission reduction systems necessary to carry out this paragraph shall provide such systems to users thereof, if he finds, after consultation with the States, that priorities must be imposed in order to assure that such systems are first provided to sources subject to orders under this paragraph in air quality control regions in which national primary ambient air quality standards have not been achieved. No regulation under this subparagraph may impair the obligation of any contract entered into before August 7, 1977.

(D) No order issued to a source under this paragraph with respect to an air pollutant shall be effective if the national primary ambient air quality standard with respect to such pollutant is being exceeded at any time in the air quality control region in which such source is located. The preceding sentence shall not apply to a source if, upon submission by any person of evidence satisfactory to the Administrator, the Administrator determines (after notice and public hearing)—

(i) that emissions of such air pollutant from such source will affect only infrequently the air quality concentrations of such pollutant in each portion of the region where such standard is being exceeded at any time;

(ii) that emissions of such air pollutant from such source will have only insignificant effect on the air quality concentrations of such pollutant in each portion of the region where such standard is being exceeded at any time; and

(iii) with reasonable statistical assurance that emissions of such air pollutant from such source will not cause or contribute to air quality concentrations of such pollutant in excess of the national primary ambient air quality standard for such pollutant.

(6) An order issued to a source under this subsection shall set forth compliance schedules containing increments of progress which require compliance with the requirement postponed as expeditiously as practicable.

(7) A source to which an order is issued under paragraph (1), (3), (4), or (5) of this subsection shall use the best practicable system or systems of emission reduction (as determined by the Administrator taking into account the requirement with which the source must ultimately comply) for the period during which such order is in effect and shall comply with such interim requirements as the Administrator determines are reasonable and practicable. Such interim requirements shall include—

(A) such measures as the Administrator determines are necessary to avoid an imminent and substantial endangerment to health of persons, and

(B) a requirement that the source comply with the requirements of the applicable implementation plan during any such period insofar as such source is able to do so (as determined by the Administrator).

(8) Any order under paragraph (1) of this subsection shall be terminated if the Administrator determines on the record, after notice and hearing, that the inability of the source to comply no longer exists. If the owner or operator of the source to which the order is issued demonstrates that prompt termination of such order would result in undue hardship, the termination shall become effective at the earliest practicable date on which such undue hardship would not result, but in no event later than the date required under this subsection.

(9) If the Administrator determines that a source to which an order is issued under this subsection is in violation of any requirement of this subsection, he shall—

(A) enforce such requirement under subsections (a), (b), or (c) of this section,

(B) (after notice and opportunity for public hearing) revoke such order and enforce compliance with the requirement with respect to which such order was granted,

(C) give notice of noncompliance and commence action under section 7420 of this title, or

(D) take any appropriate combination of such actions.

(10) During the period of the order in effect under this subsection and where the owner or operator is in compliance with the terms of such order, no Federal enforcement action pursuant to this section and no action under section 7604 of this title shall be pursued against such owner or operator based upon noncompliance during the period the order is in effect with the requirement for the source covered by such order.

(11) For the purposes of sections 7410, 7604, and 7607 of this title, any order issued by the State and in effect pursuant to this subsection shall become part of the applicable implementation plan.

(12) Any enforcement order issued under subsection (a) of this section or any consent decree in an enforcement action which is in effect on August 7, 1977, shall remain in effect to the extent that such order or consent decree is (A) not inconsistent with the requirements of this subsection and section 7419 of this title or (B) the administrative orders on consent issued by the Administrator on November 5, 1975 and February 26, 1976 and requiring compliance with sulfur dioxide emission limitations or standards at least as stringent as those promulgated under section 7411 of this title. Any such enforcement order issued under subsection (a) of this section or consent decree which provides for an extension beyond July 1, 1979, except such administrative orders on consent, is void unless modified under this subsection within one year after August 7, 1977, to comply with the requirements of this subsection.

(e) Steel industry compliance extension

(1) The Administrator may, in his discretion, in the case of any person which is the owner or operator of a stationary source in an iron- and steel-producing operation not in compliance with the emission limitation requirements of an applicable implementation plan, consent to entry of a Federal judicial decree, or to the modification of an existing Federal judicial decree, with such person establishing a schedule for compliance for such source extending beyond December 31, 1982, but ending not later than December 31, 1985, on the following conditions:

(A) the Administrator finds, on the basis of information submitted by the applicant and other information available to him, that such extension of compliance is necessary to allow such person to make capital investments in its iron- and steel-producing operations to improve their efficiency and productivity;

(B) the Administrator finds, on the basis of information submitted by the applicant and other information available to him, that an amount equal to the funds the expenditure of which would have been required to comply by December 31, 1982, with those requirements of an applicable implementation plan for which such extensions of compliance are granted and whose expenditure for such purposes are being deferred until after December 31, 1982, pursuant to such extensions will be invested prior to two years from July 17, 1981, in additional capital investments in the iron- and steel-producing operations owned or operated by such person, and located in communities which already contain iron- and steel-producing operations, to improve their efficiency and productivity;

(C) the Administrator and such person consent to entry of Federal judicial decree(s) establishing a phased program of compliance to bring each stationary source at all of such person's iron- and steel-producing operations into compliance with the emission limitation requirements of applicable implementation plans (or, with respect to existing stationary sources located in any nonattainment area for which no implementation plan has been approved as meeting the requirements of part D and subject to implementation plan(s) which do not require compliance with emission limitations which represent at least reasonably available control technology, compliance with emission limitations which represent reasonably available control technology) as expeditiously as practicable but no later than December 31, 1982, or, in the case of sources for which extensions of compliance have been granted, no later than December 31, 1985; such decree(s) shall also contain, at a minimum, (i) requirements for interim controls (which may include operation and maintenance procedures); (ii) increments of compliance sufficient to assure compliance by the final compliance deadlines; (iii) requirement(s) that the amount referred to in subparagraph (B) above, is to be invested in projects representing additional capital investments in the iron- and steel-producing operations owned or operated by such person for the purposes specified in such subparagraph and shall contain schedule(s) specifying when each such project (or specified alternative project) is to be commenced and completed, as well as increments of progress toward completion; (iv) stipulated monetary penalties covering completion of the air pollution control projects required by the decree, the projects referred to under (iii) above, and such other items as appropriate; (v) monitoring requirements; (vi) reporting requirements (including provision for periodic reports to be filed with the court); and (vii) provisions for preventing increases of emissions from each stationary source;

(D) the Administrator finds, on the basis of information submitted by the applicant and other information available to him, that such person will have sufficient funds to comply with all applicable requirements by the times set forth in the judicial decree(s) entered into pursuant to subparagraph (C) of this subsection;

(E) the Administrator finds, on the basis of information submitted by the applicant and other information available to him, that the applicant is in compliance with existing Federal judicial decrees (if any) entered under this section applicable to its iron- and steel-producing operations or that any violations of such decrees are de minimus in nature; and

(F) the Administrator finds, on the basis of information submitted by the applicant and other information available to him, that any extension of compliance granted pursuant to this subsection will not result in degradation of air quality during the term of the extension.

(2) For the purpose of this subsection, "iron- and steel-producing operations" include production facilities for iron and steel, as well as associated processing, coke making and sintering facilities. For the purpose of this subsection, "phased program of compliance" means a program assuring, to the extent possible, that capital expenditures for achieving compliance at all sources owned or operated by such person in iron- and steel-producing operations must be made during the second and each succeeding year of the period covered by the decree(s) in an amount such that at the end of each such year the cumulative expenditures under the decree(s) will be at least equal to the amount which would have been spent if the total expenditures to be made under the decree(s) were made in equal increments during each year of the decree(s). For the purpose of this subsection, "additional capital investments in iron- and steel-producing operations" means investments which the Administrator finds would not be made during the same time period if extension(s) of time for compliance with clean air requirements were not granted under this subsection. The decree entered into pursuant to subparagraph (C) of paragraph (1) of this subsection shall specify the projects which represent additional capital investment in iron- and steel-producing operations, but may also contain specified alternative projects. The decree may also be modified to substitute equivalent projects for those specified. The owner or operator of iron- and steel-producing operations seeking an extension of compliance under this subsection has the burden of satisfying the Administrator with regard to the findings required in paragraphs (A), (B), (D), (E), and (F). A person which is subject to a judicial decree entered or modified pursuant to this subsection shall not be assessed a noncompliance penalty under section 7420 of this title for any source with an extension of compliance under such decree for the period of time covered by the decree only if such source remains in compliance with all provisions and requirements of such decree.

(3) Any records, reports, or information obtained by the Administrator under this subsection shall be available to the public, except that upon a showing satisfactory to the Administrator by any person that records, reports, or information, or particular part thereof (other than emission data) to which the Administrator has access under this section if made public, is likely to cause substantial harm to the person's competitive position, the Administrator shall consider such record, report, or information or particular portion thereof confidential in accordance with the purposes of section 1905 of Title 18, except that such record, report, or information may be disclosed to other officers, employees, or authorized representatives of the United States concerned with carrying out this chapter or when relevant in any proceeding under this chapter. Any regulations promulgated under section 7414 of this title apply with equal force to this subsection subject, however, to any changes that the Administrator shall determine are necessary. This paragraph does not constitute authority to withhold records, reports, or information from the Congress.

(4) Nothing in this subsection shall preclude or deny the right of any State or political subdivision to enforce any air pollution requirements in any State judicial or administrative forum.

(5) The provisions of this subsection shall be self-executing, and no implementing regulations shall be required.

(6) Upon receipt of an application for an extension of time under this subsection with respect to any stationary source the Administrator shall promptly—

(i) publish notice of such receipt in the Federal Register;

(ii) notify the Governor of the State in which the stationary source is located; and

(iii) notify the chief elected official of the political subdivision in which the source is located.

(7)(A) The Administrator shall publish in the Federal Register notice of any finding made, or other action taken, by him in connection with the entry of any consent decree or modification of an existing consent decree pursuant to this subsection or in connection with the Administrator's failure or refusal to consent to such a decree.

(B)(i) Except as provided in clause (ii), any finding or other action of the Administrator under this subsection with respect to any stationary source, and any failure or refusal of the Administrator to make any such finding or to take any such action under this subsection, shall be reviewable only by a court in which a civil action under this section is brought against the owner or operator of such stationary source.

(ii) Where, before July 17, 1981, a civil action was brought under this chapter against the owner or operator of such stationary source, any finding or other action of the Administrator under this subsection with respect to such stationary source, and any failure or refusal of the Administrator to make any such finding or to take any such action under this subsection, shall be reviewable only by the court in which the civil action was brought.

(8) The provisions of section 7604(b)(1)(B) of this title shall be applicable to this subsection.

(9) For a source which receives an extension under this subsection, air pollution requirements specified in Federal judicial decrees entered into or modified under this subsection that involves such source may not be modified to extend beyond December 31, 1985.

(July 14, 1955, ch. 360, title I, § 113, as added Dec. 31, 1970, Pub.L. 91–604, § 4(a), 84 Stat. 1686, and amended Nov. 18, 1971, Pub.L. 92–157, title III, § 302(b), (c), 85 Stat. 464; June 22, 1974, Pub.L. 93–319, § 6(a)(1)–(3), 88 Stat. 259; Aug. 7, 1977, Pub.L. 95–95, title I, §§ 111, 112(a), 91 Stat. 704, 705; Nov. 16, 1977, Pub.L. 95–190, § 14(a)(10)–(21), (b)(1), 91 Stat. 1400, 1404; July 17, 1981, Pub.L. 97–23, § 2, 95 Stat. 139.)

1 So in original. Probably should have a comma inserted here.

2 So in original. Probably the period should be a comma.

Cross References

Guidelines for using imminent hazard, enforcement, and emergency response authorities to include assignment of responsibility for coordinating response actions with imminent hazard and emergency powers authorized by this section, see section 9606 of this title.

Federal Practice and Procedure

Requirements for issuance of declaratory judgment in matters involving public law, see Wright, Miller & Kane: Civil 2d § 2763.

Code of Federal Regulations

Delayed compliance orders, see 40 CFR 65.01 et seq.

Library References

Health and Environment ⚷25.6(1) et seq., 28, 37.
C.J.S. Health and Environment §§ 48 et seq., 91 et seq.

United States Supreme Court

Certiorari to supreme court, appeals concerning Administrator's authority to compel implement—and enforcement actions by states, see Environmental Protection Agency v. Brown, 1977, 97 S.Ct. 1635, 431 U.S. 99, 52 L.Ed.2d 166.

§ 7414. Recordkeeping, inspections, monitoring, and entry

(a) Authority of Administrator or authorized representative

For the purpose (i) of developing or assisting in the development of any implementation plan under section 7410 or section 7411(d) of this title, any standard of performance under section 7411 of this title, or any emission standard under section 7412 of this title, (ii) of determining whether any person is in violation of any such standard or any requirement of such a plan, or (iii) carrying out any provision of this chapter (except a provision of subchapter II of this chapter with respect to a manufacturer of new motor vehicles or new motor vehicle engines)—

(1) the Administrator may require any person who owns or operates any emission source or who is subject to any requirement of this chapter (other than a manufacturer subject to the provisions of section 7525(c) or 7542 of this title) with respect to a provision of subchapter II of this chapter to (A) establish and maintain such records, (B) make such reports, (C) install, use, and maintain such monitoring equipment or methods, (D) sample such emissions (in accordance with such methods, at such locations, at such intervals, and in such manner as the Administrator shall prescribe), and (E) provide such other information as he may reasonably require; and

(2) the Administrator or his authorized representative, upon presentation of his credentials—

(A) shall have a right of entry to, upon, or through any premises of such person or in which any records required to be maintained under paragraph (1) of this section are located, and

(B) may at reasonable times have access to and copy any records, inspect any monitoring equipment or method required under paragraph (1), and sample any emissions which such person is required to sample under paragraph (1).

(b) State enforcement

(1) Each State may develop and submit to the Administrator a procedure for carrying out this section in such State. If the Administrator finds the State procedure is adequate, he may delegate to such State any authority he has to carry out this section.

(2) Nothing in this subsection shall prohibit the Administrator from carrying out this section in a State.

(c) Availability of records, reports, and information to public; disclosure of trade secrets

Any records, reports or information obtained under subsection (a) of this section shall be available to the public, except that upon a showing satisfactory to the Administrator by any person that records, reports, or information, or particular part thereof (other than emission data), to which the Administrator has access under this section if made public, would divulge methods or processes entitled to protection as trade secrets of such person, the Administrator shall consider such record, report, or information or particular portion thereof confidential in accordance with the purposes of section 1905 of title 18, except that such record, report, or information may be disclosed to other officers, employees, or authorized representatives of the United States concerned with carrying out this chapter or when relevant in any proceeding under this chapter.

(d) Notice of proposed entry, inspection, or monitoring

(1) In the case of any emission standard or limitation or other requirement which is adopted by a State, as part of an applicable implementation plan or as part of an order under section 7413(d) of this title, before carrying out an entry, inspection, or monitoring under paragraph (2) of subsection (a) of this section with respect to such standard, limitation, or other requirement, the Administrator (or his representatives) shall provide the State air pollution control agency with reasonable prior notice of such action, indicating the purpose of such action. No State agency which receives notice under this paragraph of an action proposed to be taken may use the information contained in the notice to inform the person whose property is proposed to be affected of the proposed action. If the Administrator has reasonable basis for believing that a State agency is so using or will so use such information, notice to the agency under this paragraph is not required until such time as the Administrator determines the agency will no longer so use information contained in a notice under this paragraph. Nothing in this section shall be construed to require notification to any State agency of any action taken by the Administrator with respect to any standard, limitation, or other requirement which is not part of an applicable implementation plan or which was promulgated by the Administrator under section 7410(c) of this title.

(2) Nothing in paragraph (1) shall be construed to provide that any failure of the Administrator to comply with the requirements of such paragraph shall be a defense in any enforcement action brought by the Administrator or shall make inadmissible as evidence in any such action any information or material obtained notwithstanding such failure to comply with such requirements.

(July 14, 1955, ch. 360, title I, § 114, as added Dec. 31, 1970, Pub.L. 91–604, § 4(a), 84 Stat. 1687, and amended June 22, 1974, Pub.L. 93–319, § 6(a)(4), 88 Stat. 259; Aug. 7, 1977, Pub.L. 95–95, title I, §§ 109(d)(3), 113, title III, § 305(d), 91 Stat. 701, 709, 776; Nov. 16, 1977, Pub.L. 95–190, § 14(a)(22), (23), 91 Stat. 1400.)

Cross References

Guidelines for using imminent hazard, enforcement and emergency response authorities to include assignment of responsibility for coordinating response actions with imminent hazard and emergency powers authorized by this section, see section 9606 of this title.

Federal Practice and Procedure

Holding back of trade secrets, see Wright & Graham: Evidence § 5437.

Code of Federal Regulations

Emission standards for hazardous pollutants, see 40 CFR 61.01 et seq.
Implementation plans, requirements regarding, see 40 CFR 51.1 et seq.
New stationary sources, standards of performance for, see 40 CFR 60.1 et seq.
Primary nonferrous smelter orders, see 40 CFR 57.101 et seq.
Public information, see 40 CFR 2.100 et seq.

Library References

Health and Environment ⚷25.6(6).
Records ⚷30.
C.J.S. Health and Environment § 91 et seq.
C.J.S. Records § 34 et seq.

United States Supreme Court

State trade secret law, not protecting chemical company from federal aerial monitoring, see Dow Chemical Co. v. U.S., 1986, 106 S.Ct. 1819, 90 L.Ed.2d 226.

§ 7415. International air pollution

(a) Endangerment of public health or welfare in foreign countries from pollution emitted in United States

Whenever the Administrator, upon receipt of reports, surveys or studies from any duly constituted international agency has reason to believe that any air pollutant or pollutants emitted in the United States cause or contribute to air pollution which may reasonably be anticipated to endanger public health or welfare in a foreign country or whenever the Secretary of State requests him to do so with respect to such pollution which the Secretary of State alleges is of such a nature, the Administrator shall give formal notification thereof to the Governor of the State in which such emissions originate.

(b) Prevention or elimination of endangerment

The notice of the Administrator shall be deemed to be a finding under section 7410(a)(2)(H)(ii) of this title which requires a plan revision with respect to so much of the applicable implementation plan as is inadequate to prevent or eliminate the endangerment referred to in subsection (a) of this section. Any foreign country so affected by such emission of pollutant or pollutants shall be invited to appear at any public hearing associated with any revision of the appropriate portion of the applicable implementation plan.

(c) Reciprocity

This section shall apply only to a foreign country which the Administrator determines has given the United States essentially the same rights with respect to the prevention or control of air pollution occurring in that country as is given that country by this section.

(d) Recommendations

Recommendations issued following any abatement conference conducted prior to August 7, 1977, shall remain in effect with respect to any pollutant for which no national ambient air quality standard has been established under section 7409 of this title unless the Administrator, after consultation with all agencies which were party to the conference, rescinds any such recommendation on grounds of obsolescence.

(July 14, 1955, ch. 360, title I, § 115, formerly § 5, as added Dec. 17, 1963, Pub.L. 88–206, § 1, 77 Stat. 396, renumbered § 105 and amended Oct. 20, 1965, Pub.L. 89–272, title I, §§ 101(2), (3), 102, 79 Stat. 992, 995, renumbered § 108 and amended Nov. 21, 1967, Pub.L. 90–148, § 2, 81 Stat. 491, renumbered § 115 and amended Dec. 31, 1970, Pub.L. 91–604, §§ 4(a), (b)(2)–(10), 15(c)(2), 84 Stat. 1678, 1688, 1689, 1713; Aug. 7, 1977, Pub.L. 95–95, title I, § 114, 91 Stat. 710.)

Library References

Health and Environment ⚩25.6(1).
C.J.S. Health and Environment § 91 et seq.

§ 7416. Retention of State authority

Except as otherwise provided in sections 1857c–10(c), (e), and (f) (as in effect before August 7, 1977), 7543, 7545(c)(4), and 7573 of this title (preempting certain State regulation of moving sources) nothing in this chapter shall preclude or deny the right of any State or political subdivision thereof to adopt or enforce (1) any standard or limitation respecting emissions of air pollutants or (2) any requirement respecting control or abatement of air pollution; except that if an emission standard or limitation is in effect under an applicable implementation plan or under section 7411 or section 7412 of this title, such State or political subdivision may not adopt or enforce any emission standard or limitation which is less stringent than the standard or limitation under such plan or section.

(July 14, 1955, ch. 360, title I, § 116, formerly § 109, as added Nov. 21, 1967, Pub.L. 90–148, § 2, 81 Stat. 497, renumbered and amended Dec. 31, 1970, Pub.L. 91–604, § 4(a), (c), 84 Stat. 1678, 1689; June 22, 1974, Pub.L. 93–319, § 6(b), 88 Stat. 259; Nov. 16, 1977, Pub.L. 95–190, § 14(a)(24), 91 Stat. 1400.)

Code of Federal Regulations

Hazardous pollutants, emission standards for, see 40 CFR 61.01 et seq.
New stationary sources, performance standards, see 40 CFR 60.1 et seq.

Library References

States ⚩4.19.
C.J.S. States § 28.

§ 7417. Advisory committees

(a) Establishment; membership

In order to obtain assistance in the development and implementation of the purposes of this chapter including air quality criteria, recommended control techniques, standards, research and development, and to encourage the continued efforts on the part of industry to improve air quality and to develop economically feasible methods for the control and abatement of air pollution, the Administrator shall from time to time establish advisory committees. Committee members shall include, but not be limited to, persons who are knowledgeable concerning air quality from the standpoint of health, welfare, economics or technology.

(b) Compensation

The members of any other advisory committees appointed pursuant to this chapter who are not officers or employees of the United States while attending conferences or meetings or while otherwise serving at the request of the Administrator, shall be entitled to receive compensation at a rate to be fixed by the Administrator, but not exceeding $100 per diem, including traveltime, and while away from their homes or regular places of business they may be allowed travel expenses, including per diem in lieu of subsistence, as authorized by section 5703 of title 5 for persons in the Government service employed intermittently.

(c) Consultations by Administrator

Prior to—

(1) issuing criteria for an air pollutant under section 7408(a)(2) of this title,

(2) publishing any list under section 7411(b)(1)(A) or section 7412(b)(1)(A) of this title,

(3) publishing any standard under section 7411 or section 7412 of this title, or

(4) publishing any regulation under section 7521(a) of this title,

the Administrator shall, to the maximum extent practicable within the time provided, consult with appropriate advisory committees, independence experts, and Federal departments and agencies.

(July 14, 1955, ch. 360, title I, § 117, formerly § 6, as added Dec. 17, 1963, Pub.L. 88–206, § 1, 77 Stat. 399, renumbered § 106, Oct. 20, 1965, Pub.L. 89–272, title I, § 101(3), 79 Stat. 992, renumbered § 110 and amended Nov. 21, 1967, Pub.L. 90–148, § 2, 81 Stat. 498, renumbered § 117 and amended Dec. 31, 1970, Pub.L. 91–604, §§ 4(a), (d), 15(c)(2), 84 Stat. 1678, 1689, 1713; Aug. 7, 1977, Pub.L. 95–95, title I, § 115, 91 Stat. 711; Nov. 9, 1978, Pub.L. 95–623, § 13(c), 92 Stat. 3458.)

Library References

Health and Environment ⚷25.6(1) et seq., 28.
C.J.S. Health and Environment § 91 et seq.

§ 7418. Control of pollution from Federal facilities

(a) Compliance with requirements, administrative authority, process, and sanctions respecting control and abatement of air pollution

Each department, agency, and instrumentality of the executive, legislative, and judicial branches of the Federal Government (1) having jurisdiction over any property or facility, or (2) engaged in any activity resulting, or which may result, in the discharge of air pollutants, and each officer, agent, or employee thereof, shall be subject to, and comply with, all Federal, State, interstate, and local requirements, administrative authority, and process and sanctions respecting the control and abatement of air pollution in the same manner, and to the same extent as any nongovernmental entity. The preceding sentence shall apply (A) to any requirement whether substantive or procedural (including any recordkeeping or reporting requirement, any requirement respecting permits and any other requirement whatsoever), (B) to the exercise of any Federal, State, or local administrative authority, and (C) to any process and sanction, whether enforced in Federal, State, or local courts or in any other manner. This subsection shall apply notwithstanding any immunity of such agencies, officers, agents, or employees under any law or rule of law. No officer, agent, or employee of the United States shall be personally liable for any civil penalty for which he is not otherwise liable.

(b) Exemption

The President may exempt any emission source of any department, agency, or instrumentality in the executive branch from compliance with such a requirement if he determines it to be in the paramount interest of the United States to do so, except that no exemption may be granted from section 7411 of this title, and an exemption from section 7412 of this title may be granted only in accordance with section 7412(c) of this title. No such exemption shall be granted due to lack of appropriation unless the President shall have specifically requested such appropriation as a part of the budgetary process and the Congress shall have failed to make available such requested appropriation. Any exemption shall be for a period not in excess of one year, but additional exemptions may be granted for periods of not to exceed one year upon the President's making a new determination. In addition to any such exemption of a particular emission source, the President may, if he determines it to be in the paramount interest of the United States to do so, issue regulations exempting from compliance with the requirements of this section any weaponry, equipment, aircraft, vehicles, or other classes or categories of property which are owned or operated by the Armed Forces of the United States (including the Coast Guard) or by the National Guard of any State and which are uniquely military in nature. The President shall reconsider the need for such regulations at three-year intervals. The President shall report each January to the Congress all exemptions from the requirements of this section granted during the preceding calendar year, together with his reason for granting each such exemption.

(July 14, 1955, ch. 360, title I, § 118, formerly § 7, as added Dec. 17, 1963, Pub.L. 88–206, § 1, 77 Stat. 399, renumbered § 107, Oct. 20, 1965, Pub.L. 89–272, title I, § 101(3), 79 Stat. 992, renumbered § 111 and amended Nov. 21, 1967, Pub.L. 90–148, § 2, 81 Stat. 499, and renumbered § 118 and amended Dec. 31, 1970, Pub.L. 91–604, §§ 4(a), 5, 84 Stat. 1678, 1689; Aug. 7, 1977, Pub.L. 95–95, title I, § 116, 91 Stat. 711.)

Library References

Health and Environment ⚷25.6(5).
C.J.S. Health and Environment § 91 et seq.

§ 7419. Primary nonferrous smelter orders

(a) Issuance; hearing; enforcement orders; statement of grounds for application; findings

(1) Upon application by the owner or operator of a primary nonferrous smelter, a primary nonferrous

smelter order under subsection (b) of this section may be issued—

(A) by the Administrator, after thirty days' notice to the State, or

(B) by the State in which such source is located, but no such order issued by the State shall take effect until the Administrator determines that such order has been issued in accordance with the requirements of this chapter.

Not later than ninety days after submission by the State to the Administrator of notice of the issuance of a primary nonferrous smelter order under this section, the Administrator shall determine whether or not such order has been issued by the State in accordance with the requirements of this chapter. If the Administrator determines that such order has not been issued in accordance with such requirements, he shall conduct a hearing respecting the reasonably available control technology for primary nonferrous smelters.

(2)(A) An order issued under this section to a primary nonferrous smelter shall be referred to as a "primary nonferrous smelter order". No primary nonferrous smelter may receive both an enforcement order under section 7413(d) of this title and a primary nonferrous smelter order under this section.

(B) Before any hearing conducted under this section, in the case of an application made by the owner or operator of a primary nonferrous smelter for a second order under this section, the applicant shall furnish the Administrator (or the State as the case may be) with a statement of the grounds on which such application is based (including all supporting documents and information). The statement of the grounds for the proposed order shall be provided by the Administrator or the State in any case in which such State or Administrator is acting on its own initiative. Such statement (including such documents and information) shall be made available to the public for a thirty-day period before such hearing and shall be considered as part of such hearing. No primary nonferrous smelter order may be granted unless the applicant establishes that he meets the conditions required for the issuance of such order (or the Administrator or State establishes the meeting of such conditions when acting on their own initiative).

(C) Any decision with respect to the issuance of a primary nonferrous smelter order shall be accompanied by a concise statement of the findings and of the basis of such findings.

(3) For the purposes of sections 7410, 7604, and 7607 of this title, any order issued by the State and in effect pursuant to this subsection shall become part of the applicable implementation plan.

(b) Prerequisites to issuance of orders

A primary nonferrous smelter order under this section may be issued to a primary nonferrous smelter if—

(1) such smelter is in existence on August 7, 1977;

(2) the requirement of the applicable implementation plan with respect to which the order is issued is an emission limitation or standard for sulfur oxides which is necessary and intended to be itself sufficient to enable attainment and maintenance of national primary and secondary ambient air quality standards for sulfur oxides; and

(3) such smelter is unable to comply with such requirement by the applicable date for compliance because no means of emission limitation applicable to such smelter which will enable it to achieve compliance with such requirement has been adequately demonstrated to be reasonably available (as determined by the Administrator, taking into account the cost of compliance, non-air quality health and environmental impact, and energy consideration).

(c) Second orders

(1) A second order issued to a smelter under this section shall set forth compliance schedules containing increments of progress which require compliance with the requirement postponed as expeditiously as practicable. The increments of progress shall be limited to requiring compliance with subsection (d) of this section and, in the case of a second order, to procuring, installing, and operating the necessary means of emission limitation as expeditiously as practicable after the Administrator determines such means have been adequately demonstrated to be reasonably available within the meaning of subsection (b)(3) of this section.

(2) Not in excess of two primary nonferrous smelter orders may be issued under this section to any primary nonferrous smelter. The first such order issued to a smelter shall not result in the postponement of the requirement with respect to which such order is issued beyond January 1, 1983. The second such order shall not result in the postponement of such requirement beyond January 1, 1988.

(d) Interim measures; continuous emission reduction technology

(1)(A) Each primary nonferrous smelter to which an order is issued under this section shall be required to use such interim measures for the period during which such order is in effect as may be necessary in the judgment of the Administrator to assure attainment and maintenance of the national primary and secondary ambient air quality standards during such period, taking into account the aggregate effect on air quality of such order together with all variances, extensions, waivers, enforcement orders, delayed compliance orders and primary nonferrous smelter orders previously issued under this chapter.

(B) Such interim requirements shall include—

(i) a requirement that the source to which the order applies comply with such reporting requirements and conduct such monitoring as the Administrator determines may be necessary, and

(ii) such measures as the Administrator determines are necessary to avoid an imminent and substantial endangerment to health of persons.

(C) Such interim measures shall also, except as provided in paragraph (2), include continuous emission reduction technology. The Administrator shall condition the use of any such interim measures upon the agreement of the owner or operator of the smelter—

(i) to comply with such conditions as the Administrator determines are necessary to maximize the reliability and enforceability of such interim measures, as applied to the smelter, in attaining and maintaining the national ambient air quality standards to which the order relates, and

(ii) to commit reasonable resources to research and development of appropriate emission control technology.

(2) The requirement of paragraph (1) for the use of continuous emission reduction technology may be waived with respect to a particular smelter by the State or the Administrator, after notice and a hearing on the record, and upon a showing by the owner or operator of the smelter that such requirement would be so costly as to necessitate permanent or prolonged temporary cessation of operations of the smelter. Upon application for such waiver, the Administrator shall be notified and shall, within ninety days, hold a hearing on the record in accordance with section 554 of title 5. At such hearing the Administrator shall require the smelter involved to present information relating to any alleged cessation of operations and the detailed reasons or justifications therefor. On the basis of such hearing the Administrator shall make findings of fact as to the effect of such requirement and on the alleged cessation of operations and shall make such recommendations as he deems appropriate. Such report, findings, and recommendations shall be available to the public, and shall be taken into account by the State or the Administrator in making the decision whether or not to grant such waiver.

(3) In order to obtain information for purposes of a waiver under paragraph (2), the Administrator may, on his own motion, conduct an investigation and use the authority of section 7621 of this title.

(4) In the case of any smelter which on August 7, 1977, uses continuous emission reduction technology and supplemental controls and which receives an initial primary nonferrous smelter order under this section, no additional continuous emission reduction technology shall be required as a condition of such order unless the Administrator determines, at any time, after notice and public hearing, that such additional continuous emission reduction technology is adequately demonstrated to be reasonably available for the primary nonferrous smelter industry.

(e) Termination of orders

At any time during which an order under this section applies, the Administrator may enter upon a public hearing respecting the availability of technology. Any order under this section shall be terminated if the Administrator determines on the record, after notice and public hearing, that the conditions upon which the order was based no longer exist. If the owner or operator of the smelter to which the order is issued demonstrates that prompt termination of such order would result in undue hardship, the termination shall become effective at the earliest practicable date on which such undue hardship would not result, but in no event later than the date required under subsection (c) of this section.

(f) Violation of requirements

If the Administrator determines that a smelter to which an order is issued under this section is in violation of any requirement of subsection (c) or (d) of this section, he shall—

(1) enforce such requirement under section 7413 of this title,

(2) (after notice and opportunity for public hearing) revoke such order and enforce compliance with the requirement with respect to which such order was granted,

(3) give notice of noncompliance and commence action under section 7420 of this title, or

(4) take any appropriate combination of such actions.

(July 14, 1955, ch. 360, title I, § 119, as added Aug. 7, 1977, Pub.L. 95–95, title I, § 117(b), 91 Stat. 712, and amended Nov. 16, 1977, Pub.L. 95–190, § 14(a)(25)–(27), 91 Stat. 1401.)

Code of Federal Regulations

Primary nonferrous smelter orders, see 40 CFR 57.101 et seq.

Library References

Health and Environment ⚷25.6(5).
C.J.S. Health and Environment § 91 et seq.

§ 7420. Noncompliance penalty

(a) Assessment and collection

(1)(A) Not later than 6 months after August 7, 1977, and after notice and opportunity for a public hearing, the Administrator shall promulgate regulations requiring the assessment and collection of a noncompliance penalty against persons referred to in paragraph (2)(A).

(B)(i) Each State may develop and submit to the Administrator a plan for carrying out this section in such State. If the Administrator finds that the State plan meets the requirements of this section, he may delegate to such State any authority he has to carry out this section.

(ii) Notwithstanding a delegation to a State under clause (i), the Administrator may carry out this section in such State under the circumstances described in subsection (b)(2)(B) of this section.

(2)(A) Except as provided in subparagraph (B) or (C) of this paragraph, the State or the Administrator shall assess and collect a noncompliance penalty against every person who owns or operates—

(i) a major stationary source (other than a primary nonferrous smelter which has received a primary nonferrous smelter order under section 7419 of this title), which is not in compliance with any emission limitation, emission standard or compliance schedule under any applicable implementation plan (whether or not such source is subject to a Federal or State consent decree), or

(ii) a stationary source which is not in compliance with an emission limitation, emission standard, standard of performance, or other requirement established under section 7411 or 7412 of this title, or

(iii) any source referred to in clause (i) or (ii) (for which an extension, order, or suspension referred to in subparagraph (B), or Federal or State consent decree is in effect), or a primary nonferrous smelter which has received a primary nonferrous smelter order under section 7419 of this title which is not in compliance with any interim emission control requirement or schedule of compliance under such extension, order, suspension, or consent decree.

For purposes of subsection (d)(2) of this section, in the case of a penalty assessed with respect to a source referred to in clause (iii) of this subparagraph, the costs referred to in such subsection (d)(2) shall be the economic value of noncompliance with the interim emission control requirement or the remaining steps in the schedule of compliance referred to in such clause.

(B) Notwithstanding the requirements of subparagraph (A)(i) and (ii), the owner or operator of any source shall be exempted from the duty to pay a noncompliance penalty under such requirements with respect to that source if, in accordance with the procedures in subsection (b)(5) of this section, the owner or operator demonstrates that the failure of such source to comply with any such requirement is due solely to—

(i) a conversion by such source from the burning of petroleum products or natural gas, or both, as the permanent primary energy source to the burning of coal pursuant to an order under section 7413(d)(5) of this title or section 1857c–10 of this title (as in effect before August 7, 1977);

(ii) in the case of a coal-burning source granted an extension under the second sentence of section 1857c–10(c)(1) of this title (as in effect before August 7, 1977), a prohibition from using petroleum products or natural gas or both, by reason of an order under the provisions of section 792(a) and (b) of title 15 or under any legislation which amends or supersedes such provisions;

(iii) the use of innovative technology sanctioned by an enforcement order under section 7413(d)(4) of this title;

(iv) an inability to comply with any such requirement, for which inability the source has received an order under section 7413(d) of this title (or an order under section 7413 of this title issued before August 7, 1977) which has the effect of permitting a delay or violation of any requirement of this chapter (including a requirement of an applicable implementation plan) which inability results from reasons entirely beyond the control of the owner or operator of such source or of any entity controlling, controlled by, or under common control with the owner or operator of such source; or

(v) the conditions by reason of which a temporary emergency suspension is authorized under section 7410(f) or (g) of this title.

An exemption under this subparagraph shall cease to be effective if the source fails to comply with the interim emission control requirements or schedules of compliance (including increments of progress) under any such extension, order, or suspension.

(C) The Administrator may, after notice and opportunity for public hearing, exempt any source from the requirements of this section with respect to a particular instance of noncompliance if he finds that such instance of noncompliance is de minimis in nature and in duration.

(b) Regulations

Regulations under subsection (a) of this section shall—

(1) permit the assessment and collection of such penalty by the State if the State has a delegation of authority in effect under subsection (a)(1)(B)(i) of this section;

(2) provide for the assessment and collection of such penalty by the Administrator, if—

(A) the State does not have a delegation of authority in effect under subsection (a)(1)(B)(i) of this section, or

(B) the State has such a delegation in effect but fails with respect to any particular person or source to assess or collect the penalty in accordance with the requirements of this section;

(3) require the States, or in the event the States fail to do so, the Administrator, to give a brief but reasonably specific notice of noncompliance under this section to each person referred to in subsection (a)(2)(A) of this section with respect to each source owned or operated by such person which is not in compliance as provided in such subsection, not later than July 1, 1979, or thirty days after the discovery of such noncompliance, whichever is later;

(4) require each person to whom notice is given under paragraph (3) to—

(A) calculate the amount of the penalty owed (determined in accordance with subsection (d)(2) of this section) and the schedule of payments (determined in accordance with subsection (d)(3) of this section) for each such source and, within forty-five days after the issuance of such notice or after the denial of a petition under subparagraph (B), to submit that calculation and proposed schedule, together with the information necessary for an independent verification thereof, to the State and to the Administrator, or

(B) submit a petition, within forty-five days after the issuance of such notice, challenging such notice of noncompliance or alleging entitlement to an exemption under subsection (a)(2)(B) of this section with respect to a particular source;

(5) require the Administrator to provide a hearing on the record (within the meaning of subchapter II of chapter 5 of title 5) and to make a decision on such petition (including findings of fact and conclusions of law) not later than ninety days after the receipt of any petition under paragraph (4)(B), unless the State agrees to provide a hearing which is substantially similar to such a hearing on the record and to make a decision on such petition (including such findings and conclusions) within such ninety-day period;

(6)(A) authorize the Administrator on his own initiative to review the decision of the State under paragraph (5) and disapprove it if it is not in accordance with the requirements of this section, and (B) require the Administrator to do so not later than sixty days after receipt of a petition under this subparagraph, notice, and public hearing and a showing by such petitioner that the State decision under paragraph (5) is not in accordance with the requirements of this section;

(7) require payment, in accordance with subsection (d) of this section, of the penalty by each person to whom notice of noncompliance is given under paragraph (3) with respect to each noncomplying source for which such notice is given unless there has been a final determination granting a petition under paragraph (4)(B) with respect to such source;

(8) authorize the State or the Administrator to adjust (and from time to time to readjust) the amount of the penalty assessment calculated or the payment schedule proposed by such owner or operator under paragraph (4), if the Administrator finds after notice and opportunity for a hearing on the record that the penalty or schedule does not meet the requirements of this section; and

(9) require a final adjustment of the penalty within 180 days after such source comes into compliance in accordance with subsection (d)(4) of this section.

In any case in which the State establishes a noncompliance penalty under this section, the State shall provide notice thereof to the Administrator. A noncompliance penalty established by a State under this section shall apply unless the Administrator, within ninety days after the date of receipt of notice of the State penalty assessment under this section, objects in writing to the amount of the penalty as less than would be required to comply with guidelines established by the Administrator. If the Administrator objects, he shall immediately establish a substitute noncompliance penalty applicable to such source.

(c) Contract to assist in determining amount of penalty assessment or payment schedule

If the owner or operator of any stationary source to whom a notice is issued under subsection (b)(3) of this section—

(1) does not submit a timely petition under subsection (b)(4)(B) of this section, or

(2) submits a petition under subsection (b)(4)(B) of this section which is denied, and fails to submit a calculation of the penalty assessment, a schedule for payment, and the information necessary for independent verification thereof, the State (or the Administrator, as the case may be) may enter into a contract with any person who has no financial interest in the owner or operator of the source (or in any person controlling, controlled by or under common control with such source) to assist in determining the amount of the penalty assessment or payment schedule with respect to such source. The cost of carrying out such contract may be added to the penalty to be assessed against the owner or operator of such source.

(d) Payment

(1) All penalties assessed by the Administrator under this section shall be paid to the United States Treasury. All penalties assessed by the State under this section shall be paid to such State.

(2) The amount of the penalty which shall be assessed and collected with respect to any source under this section shall be equal to—

(A) the amount determined in accordance with regulations promulgated by the Administrator under subsection (a) of this section, which is no less than the economic value which a delay in compliance beyond July 1, 1979, may have for the owner of such source, including the quarterly equivalent of the capital costs of compliance and debt service over a normal amortization period, not to exceed ten years, operation and maintenance costs foregone as a result of noncompliance, and any additional economic value which such a delay may have for the owner or operator of such source, minus

(B) the amount of any expenditure made by the owner or operator of that source during any such quarter for the purpose of bringing that source into, and maintaining compliance with, such requirement, to the extent that such expenditures have not been taken into account in the calculation of the penalty under subparagraph (A).

To the extent that any expenditure under subparagraph (B) made during any quarter is not subtracted for such quarter from the costs under subparagraph (A), such expenditure may be subtracted for any subsequent quarter from such costs. In no event shall the amount paid be less than the quarterly payment minus the amount attributed to actual cost of construction.

(3)(A) The assessed penalty required under this section shall be paid in quarterly installments for the period of covered noncompliance. All quarterly payments (determined without regard to any adjustment or any subtraction under paragraph (2)(B)) after the first payment shall be equal.

(B) The first payment shall be due on the date six months after the date of issuance of the notice of noncompliance under subsection (b)(3) of this section with respect to any source or on January 1, 1980, whichever is later. Such first payment shall be in the amount of the quarterly installment for the upcoming quarter, plus the amount owed for any preceding period within the period of covered noncompliance for such source.

(C) For the purpose of this section, the term "period of covered noncompliance" means the period which begins—

(i) two years after August 7, 1977, in the case of a source for which notice of noncompliance under subsection (b)(3) of this section is issued on or before the date two years after August 7, 1977, or

(ii) on the date of issuance of the notice of noncompliance under subsection (b)(3) of this section, in the case of a source for which such notice is issued after July 1, 1979,

and ending on the date on which such source comes into (or for the purpose of establishing the schedule of payments, is estimated to come into) compliance with such requirement.

(4) Upon making a determination that a source with respect to which a penalty has been paid under this section is in compliance and is maintaining compliance with the applicable requirement, the State (or the Administrator as the case may be) shall review the actual expenditures made by the owner or operator of such source for the purpose of attaining and maintaining compliance, and shall within 180 days after such source comes into compliance—

(A) provide reimbursement with interest (to be paid by the State or Secretary of the Treasury, as the case may be) at appropriate prevailing rates (as determined by the Secretary of the Treasury) for any overpayment by such person, or

(B) assess and collect an additional payment with interest at appropriate prevailing rates (as determined by the Secretary of the Treasury) for any underpayment by such person.

(5) Any person who fails to pay the amount of any penalty with respect to any source under this section on a timely basis shall be required to pay in addition a quarterly nonpayment penalty for each quarter during which such failure to pay persists. Such nonpayment penalty shall be in an amount equal to 20 percent of the aggregate amount of such person's penalties and nonpayment penalties with respect to such source which are unpaid as of the beginning of such quarter.

(e) Judicial review

Any action pursuant to this section, including any objection of the Administrator under the last sentence of subsection (b) of this section, shall be considered a final action for purposes of judicial review of any penalty under section 7607 of this title.

(f) Other orders, payments, sanctions, or requirements

Any orders, payments, sanctions, or other requirements under this section shall be in addition to any other permits, orders, payments, sanctions, or other requirements established under this chapter, and shall in no way affect any civil or criminal enforcement proceedings brought under any provision of this chapter or State or local law.

(g) More stringent emission limitations or other requirements

In the case of any emission limitation or other requirement approved or promulgated by the Administrator under this chapter after August 7, 1977, which is more stringent than the emission limitation or requirement for the source in effect prior to such approval or promulgation, if any, or where there was no emission limitation or requirement approved or promulgated before August 7, 1977, the date for imposition of the non-compliance penalty under this section, shall be either July 1, 1979, or the date on which the source is required to be in full compliance with such emission limitation or requirement, whichever is later, but in no event later than three years after the approval or promulgation of such emission limitation or requirement.

(July 14, 1955, ch. 360, title I, § 120, as added Aug. 7, 1977, Pub.L. 95–95, title I, § 118, 91 Stat. 714, and amended Nov. 16, 1977, Pub.L. 95–190, § 14(a)(28)–(38), 91 Stat. 1401.)

Code of Federal Regulations

Environmental Protection Agency,
 Non-compliance penalty, proceedings for assessment of, see 40 CFR 66.1 et seq.
 Standards for approval of state non-compliance penalty programs, see 40 CFR 67.1 et seq.

Library References

Health and Environment ⚷25.6(9).
C.J.S. Health and Environment § 104 et seq.

§ 7421. Consultation

In carrying out the requirements of this chapter requiring applicable implementation plans to contain—

(1) any transportation controls, air quality maintenance plan requirements or preconstruction review of direct sources of air pollution, or

(2) any measure referred to—

(A) in part D (pertaining to nonattainment requirements), or

(B) in part C (pertaining to prevention of significant deterioration),

and in carrying out the requirements of section 7413(d) of this title (relating to certain enforcement orders), the State shall provide a satisfactory process of consultation with general purpose local governments, designated organizations of elected officials of local governments and any Federal land manager having authority over Federal land to which the State plan applies, effective with respect to any such requirement which is adopted more than one year after August 7, 1977, as part of such plan. Such process shall be in accordance with regulations promulgated by the Administrator to assure adequate consultation. Such regulations shall be promulgated after notice and opportunity for public hearing and not later than 6 months after August 7, 1977. Only a general purpose unit of local government, regional agency, or council of governments adversely affected by action of the Administrator approving any portion of a plan referred to in this subsection[1] may petition for judicial review of such action on the basis of a violation of the requirements of this section.

(July 14, 1955, ch. 360, title I, § 121, as added Aug. 7, 1977, Pub.L. 95–95, title I, § 119, 91 Stat. 719.)

[1] So in original. Probably should be "section".

Code of Federal Regulations

Implementation plans, requirements, see 40 CFR 51.1 et seq.

§ 7422. Listing of certain unregulated pollutants

(a) Radioactive pollutants, cadmium, arsenic, and polycyclic organic matter

Not later than one year after August 7, 1977 (two years for radioactive pollutants) and after notice and opportunity for public hearing, the Administrator shall review all available relevant information and determine whether or not emissions of radioactive pollutants (including source material, special nuclear material, and byproduct material), cadmium, arsenic and polycyclic organic matter into the ambient air will cause, or contribute to, air pollution which may reasonably be anticipated to endanger public health. If the Administrator makes an affirmative determination with respect to any such substance, he shall simultaneously with such determination include such substance in the list published under section 7408(a)(1) or 7412(b)(1)(A) of this title (in the case of a substance which, in the judgment of the Administrator, causes, or contributes to, air pollution which may reasonably be anticipated to result in an increase in mortality or an increase in serious irreversible, or incapacitating reversible, illness), or shall include each category of stationary sources emitting such substance in significant amounts in the list published under section 7411(b)(1)(A) of this title, or take any combination of such actions.

(b) Revision authority

Nothing in subsection (a) of this section shall be construed to affect the authority of the Administrator to revise any list referred to in subsection (a) of this section with respect to any substance (whether or not enumerated in subsection (a) of this section).

(c) Consultation with Nuclear Regulatory Commission; interagency agreement; notice and hearing

(1) Before listing any source material, special nuclear, or byproduct material (or component or derivative thereof) as provided in subsection (a) of this section, the Administrator shall consult with the Nuclear Regulatory Commission.

(2) Not later than six months after listing any such material (or component or derivative thereof) the Administrator and the Nuclear Regulatory Commission shall enter into an interagency agreement with respect to those sources or facilities which are under the jurisdiction of the Commission. This agreement shall, to the maximum extent practicable consistent with this chapter, minimize duplication of effort and conserve administrative resources in the establishment, implementation, and enforcement of emission limitations, standards of performance, and other requirements and authorities (substantive and procedural) under this chapter respecting the emission of such material (or component or derivative thereof) from such sources or facilities.

(3) In case of any standard or emission limitation promulgated by the Administrator, under this chapter or by any State (or the Administrator) under any applicable implementation plan under this chapter, if the Nuclear Regulatory Commission determines, after notice and opportunity for public hearing that the application of such standard or limitation to a source or facility within the jurisdiction of the Commission would endanger public health or safety, such standard or limitation shall not apply to such facilities or sources unless the President determines otherwise within ninety days from the date of such finding.

(July 14, 1955, ch. 360, title I, § 122, as added Aug. 7, 1977, Pub.L. 95–95, title I, § 120(a), 91 Stat. 720.)

Library References

Health and Environment ⚡25.6(5).
C.J.S. Health and Environment § 91 et seq.

§ 7423. Stack heights

(a) Heights in excess of good engineering practice; other dispersion techniques

The degree of emission limitation required for control of any air pollutant under an applicable implementation plan under this subchapter shall not be affected in any manner by—

(1) so much of the stack height of any source as exceeds good engineering practice (as determined under regulations promulgated by the Administrator), or

(2) any other dispersion technique.

The preceding sentence shall not apply with respect to stack heights in existence before December 31, 1970, or dispersion techniques implemented before such date. In establishing an emission limitation for coal-fired steam electric generating units which are subject to the provisions of section 7418 of this title and which commenced operation before July 1, 1957, the effect of the entire stack height of stacks for which a construction contract was awarded before February 8, 1974, may be taken into account.

(b) Dispersion technique

For the purpose of this section, the term "dispersion technique" includes any intermittent or supplemental control of air pollutants varying with atmospheric conditions.

(c) Regulations; good engineering practice

Not later than six months after August 7, 1977, the Administrator, shall after notice and opportunity for public hearing, promulgate regulations to carry out this section. For purposes of this section, good engineering practice means, with respect to stack heights, the height necessary to insure that emissions from the stack do not result in excessive concentrations of any air pollutant in the immediate vicinity of the source as a result of atmospheric downwash, eddies and wakes which may be created by the source itself, nearby structures or nearby terrain obstacles (as determined by the Administrator). For purposes of this section such height shall not exceed two and a half times the height of such source unless the owner or operator of the source demonstrates, after notice and opportunity for public hearing, to the satisfaction of the Administrator, that a greater height is necessary as provided under the preceding sentence. In no event may the Administrator prohibit any increase in any stack height or restrict in any manner the stack height of any source.

(July 14, 1955, ch. 360, title I, § 123, as added Aug. 7, 1977, Pub.L. 95–95, title I, § 121, 91 Stat. 721.)

Code of Federal Regulations

Implementation plans, requirements concerning, see 40 CFR 51.1 et seq.

Library References

Health and Environment ⚡25.6(5).
C.J.S. Health and Environment § 91 et seq.

§ 7424. Assurance of adequacy of State plans

(a) State review of implementation plans which relate to major fuel burning sources

As expeditiously as practicable but not later than one year after August 7, 1977, each State shall review the provisions of its implementation plan which relate to major fuel burning sources and shall determine—

(1) the extent to which compliance with requirements of such plan is dependent upon the use by major fuel burning stationary sources of petroleum products or natural gas,

(2) the extent to which such plan may reasonably be anticipated to be inadequate to meet the requirements of this chapter in such State on a reliable and long-term basis by reason of its dependence upon the use of such fuels, and

(3) the extent to which compliance with the requirements of such plan is dependent upon use of coal or coal derivatives which is not locally or regionally available.

Each State shall submit the results of its review and its determination under this paragraph to the Administrator promptly upon completion thereof.

(b) Plan revision

(1) Not later than eighteen months after August 7, 1977, the Administrator shall review the submissions of the States under subsection (a) of this section and shall require each State to revise its plan if, in the judgment of the Administrator, such plan revision is necessary to assure that such plan will be adequate to assure compliance with the requirements of this chapter in such State on a reliable and long-term basis, taking into account the actual or potential prohibitions on use of petroleum products or natural gas, or both, under any other authority of law.

(2) Before requiring a plan revision under this subsection, with respect to any State the Administrator shall take into account the report of the review conducted by such State under paragraph (1) and shall consult with the Governor of the State respecting such required revision.

(July 14, 1955, ch. 360, title I, § 124, as added Aug. 7, 1977, Pub.L. 95–95, title I, § 122, 91 Stat. 722.)

Library References

Health and Environment ⚷25.6(2).
C.J.S. Health and Environment § 125 et seq.

§ 7425. Measures to prevent economic disruption or unemployment

(a) Determination that action is necessary

After notice and opportunity for a public hearing—

(1) the Governor of any State in which a major fuel burning stationary source referred to in this subsection (or class or category thereof) is located,

(2) the Administrator, or

(3) the President (or his designee),

may determine that action under subsection (b) of this section is necessary to prevent or minimize significant local or regional economic disruption or unemployment which would otherwise result from use by such source (or class or category) of—

(A) coal or coal derivatives other than locally or regionally available coal,

(B) petroleum products,

(C) natural gas, or

(D) any combination of fuels referred to in subparagraphs (A) through (C),

to comply with the requirements of a State implementation plan.

(b) Use of locally or regionally available coal or coal derivatives to comply with implementation plan requirements

Upon a determination under subsection (a) of this section—

(1) such Governor, with the written consent of the President or his designee,

(2) the President's designee with the written consent of such Governor, or

(3) the President

may by rule or order prohibit any such major fuel burning stationary source (or class or category thereof) from using fuels other than locally or regionally available coal or coal derivatives to comply with implementation plan requirements. In taking any action under this subsection, the Governor, the President, or the President's designee as the case may be, shall take into account, the final cost to the consumer of such an action.

(c) Contracts; schedules

The Governor, in the case of action under subsection (b)(1) of this section, or the Administrator, in the case of an action under subsection (b)(2) or (3) of this section shall, by rule or order, require each source to which such action applies to—

(1) enter into long-term contracts of at least ten years in duration (except as the President or his designee may otherwise permit or require by rule or order for good cause) for supplies of regionally available coal or coal derivatives,

(2) enter into contracts to acquire any additional means of emission limitation which the Administrator or the State determines may be necessary

to comply with the requirements of this chapter while using such coal or coal derivatives as fuel, and

(3) comply with such schedules (including increments of progress), timetables and other requirements as may be necessary to assure compliance with the requirements of this chapter.

Requirements under this subsection shall be established simultaneously with, and as a condition of, any action under subsection (b) of this section.

(d) Existing or new major fuel burning stationary sources

This section applies only to existing or new major fuel burning stationary sources—

(1) which have the design capacity to produce 250,000,000 Btu's per hour (or its equivalent), as determined by the Administrator, and

(2) which are not in compliance with the requirements of an applicable implementation plan or which are prohibited from burning oil or natural gas, or both, under any other authority of law.

(e) Actions not to be deemed modifications of major fuel burning stationary sources

Except as may otherwise be provided by rule by the State or the Administrator for good cause, any action required to be taken by a major fuel burning stationary source under this section shall not be deemed to constitute a modification for purposes of section 7411(a)(2) and (4) of this title.

(f) Treatment of prohibitions, rules, or orders as requirements or parts of plans under other provisions

For purposes of sections 7413 and 7420 of this title a prohibition under subsection (b) of this section, and a corresponding rule or order under subsection (c) of this section, shall be treated as a requirement of section 7413 of this title. For purposes of any plan (or portion thereof) promulgated under section 7410(c) of this title, any rule or order under subsection (c) of this section corresponding to a prohibition under subsection (b) of this section, shall be treated as a part of such plan. For purposes of section 7413 of this title, a prohibition under subsection (b) of this section, applicable to any source, and a corresponding rule or order under subsection (c) of this section, shall be treated as part of the applicable implementation plan for the State in which subject source is located.

(g) Delegation of Presidential authority

The President may delegate his authority under this section to an officer or employee of the United States designated by him on a case-by-case basis or in any other manner he deems suitable.

(h) Locally or regionally available coal or coal derivatives

For the purpose of this section the term "locally or regionally available coal or coal derivatives" means coal or coal derivatives which is, or can in the judgment of the State or the Administrator feasibly be, mined or produced in the local or regional area (as determined by the Administrator) in which the major fuel burning stationary source is located.

(July 14, 1955, ch. 360, title I, § 125, as added Aug. 7, 1977, Pub.L. 95–95, title I, § 122, 91 Stat. 722.)

Cross References

Petition to President to exercise his authorities pursuant to this section with respect to major fuel burning stationary source, see section 6215 of this title.

Library References

Health and Environment ⚷25.6(2).
C.J.S. Health and Environment § 125 et seq.

§ 7426. Interstate pollution abatement

(a) Written notice to all nearby States

Each applicable implementation plan shall—

(1) require each major proposed new (or modified) source—

(A) subject to part C of this subchapter (relating to significant deterioration of air quality) or

(B) which may significantly contribute to levels of air pollution in excess of the national ambient air quality standards in any air quality control region outside the State in which such source intends to locate (or make such modification),

to provide written notice to all nearby States the air pollution levels of which may be affected by such source at least sixty days prior to the date on which commencement of construction is to be permitted by the State providing notice, and

(2) identify all major existing stationary sources which may have the impact described in paragraph (1) with respect to new or modified sources and provide notice to all nearby States of the identity of such sources not later than three months after August 7, 1977.

(b) Petition for finding that major sources emit or would emit prohibited air pollutants

Any State or political subdivision may petition the Administrator for a finding that any major source emits or would emit any air pollutant in violation of the prohibition of section 7410(a)(2)(E)(i) of this title. Within 60 days after receipt of any petition under this subsection and after public hearing, the Administrator shall make such a finding or deny the petition.

(c) Violations; allowable continued operation

Notwithstanding any permit which may have been granted by the State in which the source is located (or intends to locate), it shall be a violation of the applicable implementation plan in such State—

(1) for any major proposed new (or modified) source with respect to which a finding has been made under subsection (b) of this section to be constructed or to operate in violation of the prohibition of section 7410(a)(2)(E)(i) of this title, or

(2) for any major existing source to operate more than three months after such finding has been made with respect to it.

The Administrator may permit the continued operation of a source referred to in paragraph (2) beyond the expiration of such three-month period if such source complies with such emission limitations and compliance schedules (containing increments of progress) as may be provided by the Administrator to bring about compliance with the requirements contained in section 7410(a)(2)(E)(i) of this title as expeditiously as practicable, but in no case later than three years after the date of such finding. Nothing in the preceding sentence shall be construed to preclude any such source from being eligible for an enforcement order under section 7413(d) of this title after the expiration of such period during which the Administrator has permitted continuous operation.

(July 14, 1955, ch. 360, title I, § 126, as added Aug. 7, 1977, Pub.L. 95–95, title I, § 123, 91 Stat. 724, and amended Nov. 16, 1977, Pub.L. 95–190, § 14(a)(39), 91 Stat. 1401.)

Library References

Health and Environment ⚷25.6(2).
C.J.S. Health and Environment § 125 et seq.

§ 7427. Public notification

(a) Warning signs; television, radio, or press notices or information

Each State plan shall contain measures which will be effective to notify the public during any calendar[1] on a regular basis of instances or areas in which any national primary ambient air quality standard is exceeded or was exceeded during any portion of the preceding calendar year to advise the public of the health hazards associated with such pollution, and to enhance public awareness of the measures which can be taken to prevent such standards from being exceeded and the ways in which the public can participate in regulatory and other efforts to improve air quality. Such measures may include the posting of warning signs on interstate highway access points to metropolitan areas or television, radio, or press notices or information.

(b) Grants

The Administrator is authorized to make grants to States to assist in carrying out the requirements of subsection (a) of this section.

(July 14, 1955, ch. 360, title I, § 127, as added Aug. 7, 1977, Pub.L. 95–95, title I, § 124, 91 Stat. 725.)

[1] So in original. Probably should read "calendar year".

Library References

Health and Environment ⚷25.6(2).
United States ⚷82(2).
C.J.S. Health and Environment § 125 et seq.
C.J.S. United States § 122.

§ 7428. State boards

(a)[1] Not later than the date one year after August 7, 1977, each applicable implementation plan shall contain requirements that—

(1) any board or body which approves permits or enforcement orders under this chapter shall have at least a majority of members who represent the public interest and do not derive any significant portion of their income from persons subject to permits or enforcement orders under this chapter, and

(2) any potential conflicts of interest by members of such board or body or the head of an executive agency with similar powers be adequately disclosed.

A State may adopt any requirements respecting conflicts of interest for such boards or bodies or heads of executive agencies, or any other entities which are more stringent than the requirements of paragraph (1) and (2), and the Administrator shall approve any such more stringent requirements submitted as part of an implementation plan.

(July 14, 1955, ch. 360, title I, § 128, as added Aug. 7, 1977, Pub.L. 95–95, title I, § 125, 91 Stat. 725.)

[1] So in original. Section enacted without subsec. (b).

Part B—Ozone Protection

§ 7450. Congressional declaration of purpose

The purposes of this part are (1) to provide for a better understanding of the effects of human actions on the stratosphere, especially the ozone in the stratosphere, (2) to provide for a better understanding of the effects of changes in the stratosphere, especially the ozone in the stratosphere on the public health and welfare, (3) to provide information on the progress of regulation of activities which may reasonably be anticipated to affect the ozone in the stratosphere in such a way as to cause or contribute to endangerment of the public health or welfare, and (4) to provide information on the need for additional legislation in this area, if any.

(July 14, 1955, ch. 360, title I, § 150, as added Aug. 7, 1977, Pub.L. 95–95, title I, § 126, Aug. 7, 1977, 91 Stat. 726.)

Library References

Health and Environment ⇔25.6(1), 28.
C.J.S. Health and Environment § 91 et seq.

§ 7451. Congressional findings

(a)[1] The Congress finds, on the basis of presently available information, that—

(1) halocarbon compounds introduced into the environment potentially threaten to reduce the concentration of ozone in the stratosphere;

(2) ozone reduction will lead to increased incidence of solar ultraviolet radiation at the surface of the Earth;

(3) increased incidence of solar ultraviolet radiation is likely to cause increased rates of disease in humans (including increased rates of skin cancer), threaten food crops, and otherwise damage the natural environment;

(4) other substances, practices, processes, and activities may affect the ozone in the stratosphere, and should be investigated to give early warning of any potential problem and to develop the basis for possible future regulatory action; and

(5) there is some authority under existing law, to regulate certain substances, practices, processes, and activities which may affect the ozone in the stratosphere.

(July 14, 1955, ch. 360, title I, § 151, as added Aug. 7, 1977, Pub.L. 95–95, title I, § 126, 91 Stat. 726.)

1 So in original. Section enacted without a subsec. (b).

§ 7452. Definitions

For the purposes of this part—

(1) the term "halocarbon" means the chemical compounds $CFCl_3$ and CF_2Cl_2 and such other halogenated compounds as the Administrator determines may reasonably be anticipated to contribute to reductions in the concentration of ozone in the stratosphere;

(2) the term "stratosphere" means that part of the atmosphere above the tropopause.

(July 14, 1955, ch. 360, title I, § 152, as added Aug. 7, 1977, Pub.L. 95–95, title I, § 126, 91 Stat. 726.)

§ 7453. Studies by Environmental Protection Agency

(a) Study of cumulative effect of all substances, practices, processes, and activities on the stratosphere

The Administrator shall conduct a study of the cumulative effect of all substances, practices, processes, and activities which may affect the stratosphere, especially ozone in the stratosphere. The study shall include an analysis of the independent effects on the stratosphere especially such ozone in the stratosphere of—

(1) the release into the ambient air of halocarbons,

(2) the release into the ambient air of other sources of chlorine,

(3) the uses of bromine compounds, and

(4) emissions of aircraft and aircraft propulsion systems employed by operational and experimental aircraft.

The study shall also include such physical, chemical, atmospheric, biomedical, or other research and monitoring as may be necessary to ascertain (A) any direct or indirect effects upon the public health and welfare of changes in the stratosphere, especially ozone in the stratosphere, and (B) the probable causes of changes in the stratosphere, especially the ozone in the stratosphere.

(b) Research

The Administrator shall undertake research on—

(1) methods to recover and recycle substances which directly or indirectly affect the stratosphere, especially ozone in the stratosphere,

(2) methods of preventing the escape of such substances,

(3) safe substitutes for such substances, and

(4) other methods to regulate substances, practices, processes, and activities which may reasonably be anticipated to affect the stratosphere, especially ozone in the stratosphere.

(c) Cooperation and assistance in studies and research

(1) The studies and research conducted under this section may be undertaken with such cooperation and assistance from universities and private industry as may be available. Each department, agency, and instrumentality of the United States having the capability to do so is authorized and encouraged to provide assistance to the Administrator in carrying out the requirements of this section, including (notwithstanding any other provision of law) any services which such department, agency, or instrumentality may have the capability to render or obtain by contract with third parties.

(2) The Administrator shall encourage the cooperation and assistance of other nations in carrying out the studies and research under this section. The Administrator is authorized to cooperate with and support similar research efforts of other nations.

(d) Study by National Academy of Sciences

(1) The Administrator shall undertake to contract with the National Academy of Sciences to study the state of knowledge and the adequacy of research efforts to understand (A) the effects of all substances, practices, processes, and activities which may affect the stratosphere, especially ozone in the stratosphere; (B) the health and welfare effects of modifications of the stratosphere, especially ozone in the stratosphere; and (C) methods of control of such substances, practices, processes, and activities including alternatives, costs, feasibility, and timing. The Academy shall make a report of its findings by January 1, 1978.

(2) The Administrator shall make available to the Academy such information in the Administrator's possession as is needed for the purposes of the study provided for in this subsection.

(e) Study by Secretary of Labor

The Secretary of Labor shall study and transmit a report to the Administrator and the Congress not later than six months after August 7, 1977, with respect to the losses and gains to industry and employment which could result from the elimination of the use of halocarbons in aerosol containers and for other purposes. Such report shall include recommended means of alleviating unemployment or other undesirable economic impact, if any, resulting therefrom.

(f) Coordination in carrying out research and studies; Coordinating Committee

(1) The Administrator shall establish and act as Chairman of a Coordinating Committee for the purpose of insuring coordination of the efforts of other Federal agencies carrying out research and studies related to or supportive of the research provided for in subsections (a) and (b) of this section and section 7454 of this title.

(2) Members of the Coordinating Committee shall include the appropriate official responsible for the relevant research efforts of each of the following agencies:

(A) the National Oceanic and Atmospheric Administration,

(B) the National Aeronautics and Space Administration,

(C) the Federal Aviation Administration,

(D) the Department of Agriculture,

(E) the National Cancer Institute,

(F) the National Institute of Environmental Health Sciences,

(G) the National Science Foundation, and the appropriate officials responsible for the relevant research efforts of such other agencies carrying out related efforts as the Chairman shall designate. A representative of the Department of State shall sit on the Coordinating Committee to encourage and facilitate international coordination.

(3) The Coordinating Committee shall review and comment on plans for, and the execution and results of, pertinent research and studies. For this purpose, the agencies named in or designated under paragraph (2) of this subsection shall make appropriate and timely reports to the Coordinating Committee on plans for and the execution and results of such research and studies.

(4) The Chairman may request a report from any Federal Agency for the purpose of determining if that agency should sit on the Coordinating Committee.

(g) Reports to Congressional committees

Not later than January 1, 1978, and biennially thereafter, the Administrator shall report to the appropriate committees of the House and the Senate, the results of the studies and research conducted under this section and the results of related research and studies conducted by other Federal agencies.

(July 14, 1955, ch. 360, title I, § 153, as added Aug. 7, 1977, Pub.L. 95–95, title I, § 126, 91 Stat. 726.)

§ 7454. Research and monitoring by other agencies

(a) National Oceanic and Atmospheric Administration

The Administrator of the National Oceanic and Atmospheric Administration shall establish a continuing program of research and monitoring of the stratosphere for the purpose of early detection of changes in the stratosphere and climatic effects of such changes. Such Administrator shall on or before January 1, 1978, and biennially thereafter, transmit such report to the Administrator and the Congress on the findings of such research and monitoring. Such report shall contain any appropriate recommendations for legislation or regulation (or both).

(b) National Aeronautics and Space Administration

The National Aeronautics and Space Administration shall, pursuant to its authority under title IV of the National Aeronautics and Space Act of 1958 [42 U.S.C. 2481 et seq.] continue programs of research, technology, and monitoring of the stratosphere for the purpose of understanding the physics and chemistry of the stratosphere and for the early detection of potentially harmful changes in the ozone in the stratosphere. Such Administration shall transmit reports by January 1, 1978, and biennially thereafter to the Administrator and the Congress on the results of the programs authorized in this subsection, together with any appropriate recommendations for legislation or regulation (or both).

(c) National Science Foundation

The Director of the National Science Foundation shall encourage and support ongoing stratospheric research programs and continuing research programs that will increase scientific knowledge of the effects of changes in the ozone layer in the stratosphere upon living organisms and ecosystems. Such Director shall transmit reports by January 1, 1978, and biennially thereafter to the Administrator and the Congress on the results of such programs, together with any appropriate recommendations for legislation or regulation (or both).

(d) Department of Agriculture

The Secretary of Agriculture shall encourage and support continuing research programs that will increase scientific knowledge of the effects of changes in the ozone in the stratosphere upon animals, crops, and other plant life. Such Secretary shall transmit reports by January 1, 1978, and biennially thereafter to the Administrator and the Congress on the results of such programs together with any appropriate recommendations for legislation or regulation (or both).

(e) Department of Health and Human Services

The Secretary of Health and Human Services shall encourage and support continuing research programs that will increase scientific knowledge of the effects of changes in the ozone in the stratosphere upon human health. Such Secretary shall transmit reports by January 1, 1978, and biennially thereafter, to the Administrator and the Congress on the results of such programs, together with any appropriate recommendations for legislation or regulation (or both).

(f) Cooperation and assistance

In carrying out subsections (a) through (e) of this section, the agencies involved (1) shall enlist and encourage cooperation and assistance from other Federal agencies, universities, and private industry, and (2) shall solicit the views of the Administrator with regard to plans for the research involved so that any such research will, if regulatory action by the Administrator is indicated, provide the preliminary information base for such action.

(July 14, 1955, ch. 360, title I, § 154, as added Aug. 7, 1977, Pub.L. 95–95, title I, § 126, 91 Stat. 728, and amended Oct. 17, 1979, Pub.L. 96–88, title V, § 509(b), 93 Stat. 695.)

§ 7455. Progress of regulation

The Administrator shall provide an interim report to the Congress by January 1, 1978, shall provide a final report within two years after August 7, 1977, and shall provide follow-up reports annually thereafter on the actions taken by the Environmental Protection Agency and all other Federal agencies to regulate sources of halocarbon emissions, the results of such regulations in protecting the ozone layer, and the need for additional regulatory action, if any. The reports under this section shall also include recommendations for the control of substances, practices, processes, and activities other than those involving halocarbons, which are found to affect the ozone in the stratosphere and which may cause or contribute to harmful effects on public health or welfare.

(July 14, 1955, ch. 360, title I, § 155, as added Aug. 7, 1977, Pub.L. 95–95, title I, § 126, 91 Stat. 729.)

§ 7456. International cooperation

The President shall undertake to enter into international agreements to foster cooperative research which complements studies and research authorized by this part, and to develop standards and regulations which protect the stratosphere consistent with regulations applicable within the United States. For these purposes the President through the Secretary of State and the Assistant Secretary of State for Oceans and International Environmental and Scientific Affairs, shall negotiate multilateral treaties, conventions, resolutions, or other agreements, and formulate, present, or support proposals at the United Nations and other appropriate international forums and shall report to the Congress periodically on efforts to arrive at such agreements.

(July 14, 1955, ch. 360, title I, § 156, as added Aug. 7, 1977, Pub.L. 95–95, title I, § 126, 91 Stat. 729.)

§ 7457. Regulations

(a) Endangerment of public health or welfare prior to submission of final report

If at any time prior to the submission of the final report referred to in section 7455 of this title in the Administrator's judgment, any substance, practice, process, or activity may reasonably be anticipated to affect the stratosphere, especially ozone in the stratosphere, and such effect may reasonably be anticipated to endanger public health or welfare, the Administrator shall promptly promulgate regulations respecting the control of such substance, practice, process, or activity, and shall simultaneously submit notice of the promulgation of such regulations to the Congress.

(b) Proposed regulations; final form of regulations; revision

Upon submission of the final report referred to in section 7455 of this title, and after consideration of the research and study under sections 7453 and 7454 of this title and, consultation with appropriate Federal agencies and scientific entities, the Administrator shall propose regulations for the control of any substance, practice, process, or activity (or any combination thereof) which in his judgment may reasonably be anticipated to affect the stratosphere, especially ozone in the stratosphere, if such effect in the stratosphere may reasonably be anticipated to endanger public health or welfare. Such regulations shall take into account the feasibility and the costs of achieving such control. Such regulations may exempt medical use products for which the Administrator determines there is no suitable substitute. Not later than three months after proposal of such regulations the Administrator shall promulgate such regulations in final form. From time to time, and under the same procedures, the Administrator may revise any of the regulations submitted under this subsection.

(July 14, 1955, ch. 360, title I, § 157, as added Aug. 7, 1977, Pub.L. 95–95, title I, § 126, 91 Stat. 729.)

§ 7458. Other provisions unaffected

Nothing in this part shall be construed to alter or affect the authority of the Administrator under section 7603 of this title (relating to emergency powers), under section 7571 of this title (relating to aircraft emission standards), or under any other provision of this chapter or to affect the authority of any other department, agency, or instrumentality of the United States under any other provision of law to promulgate or enforce any requirement respecting the control of any substance, practice, process, or activity for purposes of protecting the stratosphere or ozone in the stratosphere. In the case of any proposed rule respecting ozone in the stratosphere which has been published under the Toxic Substances Control Act [15 U.S.C. 2601 et seq.] prior to August 7, 1977, notwithstanding section 9(b) of such Act [15 U.S.C. 2608(b)], nothing in this part shall be construed to prohibit or restrict the Administrator from taking any action under the Toxic Substances Control Act respecting the promulgation or enforcement of such rule.

(July 14, 1955, ch. 360, title I, § 158, as added Aug. 7, 1977, Pub.L. 95–95, title I, § 126, 91 Stat. 730.)

§ 7459. State authority

(a) Efforts of States or political subdivisions to protect the stratosphere

Nothing in this part shall preclude or deny any State or political subdivision thereof from adopting or enforcing any requirement respecting the control of any substance, practice, process, or activity for purposes of protecting the stratosphere or ozone in the stratosphere except as otherwise provided in subsection (b) of this section.

(b) Identical requirements of State and Federal regulations

If a regulation of any substance, practice, process, or activity is in effect under this part in order to prevent or abate any risk to the stratosphere, or ozone in the stratosphere, no State or political subdivision thereof may adopt or attempt to enforce any requirement respecting the control of any such substance, practice, process, or activity to prevent or abate such risk, unless the requirement of the State or political subdivision is identical to the requirement of such regulation. The preceding sentence shall not apply with respect to any law or regulation of any State or political subdivision controlling the use of halocarbons as propellants in aerosol spray containers.

(July 14, 1955, ch. 360, title I, § 159, as added Aug. 7, 1977, Pub.L. 95–95, title I, § 126, 91 Stat. 730.)

Library References

States ⚷4.10.
C.J.S. States § 24.

PART C—PREVENTION OF SIGNIFICANT DETERIORATION OF AIR QUALITY

Cross References

Class I or class II redesignation of New River Gorge National River for purposes of this part, see section 460m–24 of Title 16, Conservation.

Federally permitted release defined to include emissions into air subject to permit or control regulation under this part for purposes of Comprehensive Environmental Response, Compensation, and Liability Act of 1980, see section 9601 of this title.

Subpart I—Clean Air

§ 7470. Congressional declaration of purpose

The purposes of this part are as follows:

(1) to protect public health and welfare from any actual or potential adverse effect which in the Administrator's judgment may reasonably be anticipate[1] to occur from air pollution or from exposures to pollutants in other media, which pollutants originate as emissions to the ambient air)[2],

notwithstanding attainment and maintenance of all national ambient air quality standards;

(2) to preserve, protect, and enhance the air quality in national parks, national wilderness areas, national monuments, national seashores, and other areas of special national or regional natural, recreational, scenic, or historic value;

(3) to insure that economic growth will occur in a manner consistent with the preservation of existing clean air resources;

(4) to assure that emissions from any source in any State will not interfere with any portion of the applicable implementation plan to prevent significant deterioration of air quality for any other State; and

(5) to assure that any decision to permit increased air pollution in any area to which this section applies is made only after careful evaluation of all the consequences of such a decision and after adequate procedural opportunities for informed public participation in the decisionmaking process.

(July 14, 1955, ch. 360, title I, § 160, as added Aug. 7, 1977, Pub.L. 95–95, title I, § 127(a), 91 Stat. 731.)

1 So in original. Probably should read "anticipated".

2 So in original. Section was enacted without an opening parenthesis.

Code of Federal Regulations

Emission standards for hazardous pollutants, see 40 CFR 61.01 et seq.
Implementation plans, requirements concerning, see 40 CFR 51.1 et seq.
New stationary sources, performance standards for, see 40 CFR 60.1 et seq.

Library References

Health and Environment ⚷25.6(1) et seq.
C.J.S. Health and Environment § 91 et seq.

§ 7471. Plan requirements

In accordance with the policy of section 7401(b)(1) of this title, each applicable implementation plan shall contain emission limitations and such other measures as may be necessary, as determined under regulations promulgated under this part, to prevent significant deterioration of air quality in each region (or portion thereof) identified pursuant to section 7407(d)(1)(D) or (E) of this title.

(July 14, 1955, ch. 360, title I, § 161, as added Aug. 7, 1977, Pub.L. 95–95, title I, § 127(a), 91 Stat. 731.)

§ 7472. Initial classifications

(a) Areas designated as class I

Upon the enactment of this part, all—

(1) international parks,

(2) national wilderness areas which exceed 5,000 acres in size,

(3) national memorial parks which exceed 5,000 acres in size, and

(4) national parks which exceed six thousand acres in size,

and which are in existence on August 7, 1977, shall be class I areas and may not be redesignated. All areas which were redesignated as class I under regulations promulgated before August 7, 1977, shall be class I areas which may be redesignated as provided in this part.

(b) Areas designated as class II

All areas in such State identified pursuant to section 7407(d)(1)(D) or (E) of this title which are not established as class I under subsection (a) of this section shall be class II areas unless redesignated under section 7474 of this title.

(July 14, 1955, ch. 360, title I, § 162, as added Aug. 7, 1977, Pub.L. 95–95, title I, § 127(a), 91 Stat. 731, and amended Nov. 16, 1977, Pub.L. 95–190, § 14(a)(40), 91 Stat. 1401.)

§ 7473. Increments and ceilings

(a) Sulfur oxide and particulate matter; requirement that maximum allowable increases and maximum allowable concentrations not be exceeded

In the case of sulfur oxide and particulate matter, each applicable implementation plan shall contain measures assuring that maximum allowable increases over baseline concentrations of, and maximum allowable concentrations of, such pollutant shall not be exceeded. In the case of any maximum allowable increase (except an allowable increase specified under section 7475(d)(2)(C)(iv) of this title) for a pollutant based on concentrations permitted under national ambient air quality standards for any period other than an annual period, such regulations shall permit such maximum allowable increase to be exceeded during one such period per year.

(b) Maximum allowable increases in concentrations over baseline concentrations

(1) For any class I area, the maximum allowable increase in concentrations of sulfur dioxide and particulate matter over the baseline concentration of such pollutants shall not exceed the following amounts:

Pollutant	Maximum allowable increase (in micrograms per cubic meter)
Particulate matter:	
Annual geometric mean	5
Twenty-four-hour maximum	10

Pollutant	Maximum allowable increase (in micrograms per cubic meter)
Sulfur dioxide:	
Annual arithmetic mean	2
Twenty-four-hour maximum	5
Three-hour maximum	25

(2) For any class II area, the maximum allowable increase in concentrations of sulfur dioxide and particulate matter over the baseline concentration of such pollutants shall not exceed the following amounts:

Pollutant	Maximum allowable increase (in micrograms per cubic meter)
Particulate matter:	
Annual geometric mean	19
Twenty-four-hour maximum	37
Sulfur dioxide:	
Annual arithmetic mean	20
Twenty-four-hour maximum	91
Three-hour maximum	512

(3) For any class III area, the maximum allowable increase in concentrations of sulfur dioxide and particulate matter over the baseline concentration of such pollutants shall not exceed the following amounts:

Pollutant	Maximum allowable increase (in micrograms per cubic meter)
Particulate matter:	
Annual geometric mean	37
Twenty-four-hour maximum	75
Sulfur dioxide:	
Annual arithmetic mean	40
Twenty-four-hour maximum	182
Three-hour maximum	700

(4) The maximum allowable concentration of any air pollutant in any area to which this part applies shall not exceed a concentration for such pollutant for each period of exposure equal to—

(A) the concentration permitted under the national secondary ambient air quality standard, or

(B) the concentration permitted under the national primary ambient air quality standard,

whichever concentration is lowest for such pollutant for such period of exposure.

(c) Orders or rules for determining compliance with maximum allowable increases in ambient concentrations of air pollutants

(1) In the case of any State which has a plan approved by the Administrator for purposes of carrying out this part, the Governor of such State may, after notice and opportunity for public hearing, issue orders or promulgate rules providing that for purposes of determining compliance with the maximum allowable increases in ambient concentrations of an air pollutant, the following concentrations of such pollutant shall not be taken into account:

(A) concentrations of such pollutant attributable to the increase in emissions from stationary sources which have converted from the use of petroleum products, or natural gas, or both, by reason of an order which is in effect under the provisions of sections 792(a) and (b) of title 15 (or any subsequent legislation which supersedes such provisions) over the emissions from such sources before the effective date of such order[1].

(B) the concentrations of such pollutant attributable to the increase in emissions from stationary sources which have converted from using natural gas by reason of a natural gas curtailment pursuant to a natural gas curtailment plan in effect pursuant to the Federal Power Act [16 U.S.C. 791a et seq.] over the emissions from such sources before the effective date of such plan,

(C) concentrations of particulate matter attributable to the increase in emissions from construction or other temporary emission-related activities, and

(D) the increase in concentrations attributable to new sources outside the United States over the concentrations attributable to existing sources which are included in the baseline concentration determined in accordance with section 7479(4) of this title.

(2) No action taken with respect to a source under paragraph (1)(A) or (1)(B) shall apply more than five years after the effective date of the order referred to in paragraph (1)(A) or the plan referred to in paragraph (1)(B), whichever is applicable. If both such order and plan are applicable, no such action shall apply more than five years after the later of such effective dates.

(3) No action under this subsection shall take effect unless the Governor submits the order or rule providing for such exclusion to the Administrator and the Administrator determines that such order or rule is in compliance with the provisions of this subsection.

(July 14, 1955, ch. 360, title I, § 163, as added Aug. 7, 1977, Pub.L. 95–95, title I, § 127(a), 91 Stat. 732, and amended Nov. 16, 1977, Pub.L. 95–190, § 14(a)(41), 91 Stat. 1401.)

[1] So in original. The period should be a comma.

Library References

Health and Environment ⟹25.6(4), 28.
C.J.S. Health and Environment §§ 91 et seq., 95 et seq.

§ 7474. Area redesignation

(a) Authority of States to redesignate areas

Except as otherwise provided under subsection (c) of this section, a State may redesignate such areas as it deems appropriate as class I areas. The following areas may be redesignated only as class I or II:

(1) an area which exceeds ten thousand acres in size and is a national monument, a national primitive area, a national preserve, a national recreation area, a national wild and scenic river, a national wildlife refuge, a national lakeshore or seashore, and

(2) a national park or national wilderness area established after August 7, 1977, which exceeds ten thousand acres in size.

Any area (other than an area referred to in paragraph (1) or (2) or an area established as class I under the first sentence of section 7472(a) of this title) may be redesignated by the State as class III if—

(A) such redesignation has been specifically approved by the Governor of the State, after consultation with the appropriate Committees of the legislature if it is in session or with the leadership of the legislature if it is not in session (unless State law provides that such redesignation must be specifically approved by State legislation) and if general purpose units of local government representing a majority of the residents of the area so redesignated enact legislation (including for such units of local government resolutions where appropriate) concurring in the State's redesignation;

(B) such redesignation will not cause, or contribute to, concentrations of any air pollutant which exceed any maximum allowable increase or maximum allowable concentration permitted under the classification of any other area; and

(C) such redesignation otherwise meets the requirements of this part.

Subparagraph (A) of this paragraph shall not apply to area redesignations by Indian tribes.

(b) Notice and hearing; notice to Federal land manager; written comments and recommendations; regulations; disapproval of redesignation

(1)(A) Prior to redesignation of any area under this part, notice shall be afforded and public hearings shall be conducted in areas proposed to be redesignated and in areas which may be affected by the proposed redesignation. Prior to any such public hearing a satisfactory description and analysis of the health, environmental, economic, social, and energy effects of the proposed redesignation shall be prepared and made available for public inspection and prior to any such redesignation, the description and analysis of such effects shall be reviewed and examined by the redesignating authorities.

(B) Prior to the issuance of notice under subparagraph (A) respecting the redesignation of any area under this subsection, if such area includes any Federal lands, the State shall provide written notice to the appropriate Federal land manager and afford adequate opportunity (but not in excess of 60 days) to confer with the State respecting the intended notice of redesignation and to submit written comments and recommendations with respect to such intended notice of redesignation. In redesignating any area under this section with respect to which any Federal land manager has submitted written comments and recommendations, the State shall publish a list of any inconsistency between such redesignation and such recommendations and an explanation of such inconsistency (together with the reasons for making such redesignation against the recommendation of the Federal land manager).

(C) The Administrator shall promulgate regulations not later than six months after August 7, 1977, to assure, insofar as practicable, that prior to any public hearing on redesignation of any area, there shall be available for public inspection any specific plans for any new or modified major emitting facility which may be permitted to be constructed and operated only if the area in question is designated or redesignated as class III.

(2) The Administrator may disapprove the redesignation of any area only if he finds, after notice and opportunity for public hearing, that such redesignation does not meet the procedural requirements of this section or is inconsistent with the requirements of section 7472(a) of this title or of subsection (a) of this section. If any such disapproval occurs, the classification of the area shall be that which was in effect prior to the redesignation which was disapproved.

(c) Indian reservations

Lands within the exterior boundaries of reservations of federally recognized Indian tribes may be redesignated only by the appropriate Indian governing body. Such Indian governing body shall be subject in all respect to the provisions of subsection (e) of this section.

(d) Review of national monuments, primitive areas, and national preserves

The Federal Land Manager shall review all national monuments, primitive areas, and national preserves, and shall recommend any appropriate areas for redesignation as class I where air quality related values are important attributes of the area. The Federal Land Manager shall report such recommendations, within[1] supporting analysis, to the Congress and the affected States within one year after August 7, 1977. The Federal Land Manager shall consult with the appropriate States before making such recommendations.

(e) Resolution of disputes between State and Indian Tribes

If any State affected by the redesignation of an area by an Indian tribe or any Indian tribe affected by the redesignation of an area by a State disagrees with such redesignation of any area, or if a permit is proposed to be issued for any new major emitting facility proposed for construction in any State which the Governor of an affected State or governing body of an affected Indian tribe determines will cause or contribute to a cumulative change in air quality in excess of that allowed in this part within the affected State or tribal reservation, the Governor or Indian ruling body may request the Administrator to enter into negotiations with the parties involved to resolve such dispute. If requested by any State or Indian tribe involved, the Administrator shall make a recommendation to resolve the dispute and protect the air quality related values of the lands involved. If the parties involved do not reach agreement, the Administrator shall resolve the dispute and his determination, or the results of agreements reached through other means, shall become part of the applicable plan and shall be enforceable as part of such plan. In resolving such disputes relating to area redesignation, the Administrator shall consider the extent to which the lands involved are of sufficient size to allow effective air quality management or have air quality related values of such an area.

(July 14, 1955, ch. 360, title I, § 164, as added Aug. 7, 1977, Pub.L. 95–95, title I, § 127(a), 91 Stat. 733, and amended Nov. 16, 1977, Pub.L. 95–190, § 14(a)(42), (43), 91 Stat. 1402.)

[1] So in original. Probably should be "with".

Library References

Health and Environment ⇐25.6(4).
C.J.S. Health and Environment § 95 et seq.

§ 7475. Preconstruction requirements

(a) Major emitting facilities on which construction is commenced

No major emitting facility on which construction is commenced after August 7, 1977, may be constructed in any area to which this part applies unless—

(1) a permit has been issued for such proposed facility in accordance with this part setting forth emission limitations for such facility which conform to the requirements of this part;

(2) the proposed permit has been subject to a review in accordance with this section, the required analysis has been conducted in accordance with regulations promulgated by the Administrator, and a public hearing has been held with opportunity for interested persons including representatives of the Administrator to appear and submit written or oral presentations on the air quality impact of such source, alternatives thereto, control technology requirements, and other appropriate considerations;

(3) the owner or operator of such facility demonstrates, as required pursuant to section 7410(j) of this title, that emissions from construction or operation of such facility will not cause, or contribute to, air pollution in excess of any (A) maximum allowable increase or maximum allowable concentration for any pollutant in any area to which this part applies more than one time per year, (B) national ambient air quality standard in any air quality control region, or (C) any other applicable emission standard or standard of performance under this chapter;

(4) the proposed facility is subject to the best available control technology for each pollutant subject to regulation under this chapter emitted from, or which results from, such facility;

(5) the provisions of subsection (d) of this section with respect to protection of class I areas have been complied with for such facility;

(6) there has been an analysis of any air quality impacts projected for the area as a result of growth associated with such facility;

(7) the person who owns or operates, or proposes to own or operate, a major emitting facility for which a permit is required under this part agrees to conduct such monitoring as may be necessary to determine the effect which emissions from any such facility may have, or is having, on air quality in any area which may be affected by emissions from such source; and

(8) in the case of a source which proposes to construct in a class III area, emissions from which would cause or contribute to exceeding the maximum allowable increments applicable in a class II area and where no standard under section 7411 of this title has been promulgated subsequent to August 7, 1977, for such source category, the Administrator has approved the determination of best available technology as set forth in the permit.

(b) Exception

The demonstration pertaining to maximum allowable increases required under subsection (a)(3) of this section shall not apply to maximum allowable increases for class II areas in the case of an expansion or modification of a major emitting facility which is in existence on August 7, 1977, whose allowable emissions of air pollutants, after compliance with subsection (a)(4) of this section, will be less than fifty tons per year and for which the owner or operator of such facility demonstrates that emissions of particulate matter and sulfur oxides will not cause or contribute to ambient air quality levels in excess of the national secondary ambient air quality standard for either of such pollutants.

(c) Permit applications

Any completed permit application under section 7410 of this title for a major emitting facility in any area to which this part applies shall be granted or denied not later than one year after the date of filing of such completed application.

(d) Action taken on permit applications; notice; adverse impact on air quality related values; variance; emission limitations

(1) Each State shall transmit to the Administrator a copy of each permit application relating to a major emitting facility received by such State and provide notice to the Administrator of every action related to the consideration of such permit.

(2)(A) The Administrator shall provide notice of the permit application to the Federal Land Manager and the Federal official charged with direct responsibility for management of any lands within a class I area which may be affected by emissions from the proposed facility.

(B) The Federal Land Manager and the Federal official charged with direct responsibility for management of such lands shall have an affirmative responsibility to protect the air quality related values (including visibility) of any such lands within a class I area and to consider, in consultation with the Administrator, whether a proposed major emitting facility will have an adverse impact on such values.

(C)(i) In any case where the Federal official charged with direct responsibility for management of any lands within a class I area or the Federal Land Manager of such lands, or the Administrator, or the Governor of an adjacent State containing such a class I area files a notice alleging that emissions from a proposed major emitting facility may cause or contribute to a change in the air quality in such area and identifying the potential adverse impact of such change, a permit shall not be issued unless the owner or operator of such facility demonstrates that emissions of particulate matter and sulfur dioxide will not cause or contribute to concentrations which exceed the maximum allowable increases for a class I area.

(ii) In any case where the Federal Land Manager demonstrates to the satisfaction of the State that the emissions from such facility will have an adverse impact on the air quality-related values (including visibility) of such lands, notwithstanding the fact that the change in air quality resulting from emissions from such facility will not cause or contribute to concentrations which exceed the maximum allowable increases for a class I area, a permit shall not be issued.

(iii) In any case where the owner or operator of such facility demonstrates to the satisfaction of the Federal Land Manager, and the Federal Land Manager so certifies, that the emissions from such facility will have no adverse impact on the air quality-related values of such lands (including visibility), notwithstanding the fact that the change in air quality resulting from emissions from such facility will cause or contribute to concentrations which exceed the maximum allowable increases for class I areas, the State may issue a permit.

(iv) In the case of a permit issued pursuant to clause (iii), such facility shall comply with such emission limitations under such permit as may be necessary to assure that emissions of sulfur oxides and particulates from such facility will not cause or contribute to concentrations of such pollutant which exceed the following maximum allowable increases over the baseline concentration for such pollutants:

	Maximum allowable increase (in micrograms per cubic meter)
Particulate matter:	
Annual geometric mean	19
Twenty-four-hour maximum	37
Sulfur dioxide:	
Annual arithmetic mean	20
Twenty-four-hour maximum	91
Three-hour maximum	325

(D)(i) In any case where the owner or operator of a proposed major emitting facility who has been denied a certification under subparagraph (C)(iii) demonstrates to the satisfaction of the Governor, after notice and public hearing, and the Governor finds, that the facility cannot be constructed by reason of any maximum allowable increase for sulfur dioxide for periods of twenty-four hours or less applicable to any class I area and, in the case of Federal mandatory class I areas, that a variance under this clause will not adversely affect the air quality related values of the area (including visibility), the Governor, after consideration of the Federal Land Manager's recommendation (if any) and subject to his concurrence, may grant a variance from such maximum allowable increase. If such variance is granted, a permit may be issued to such source pursuant to the requirements of this subparagraph.

(ii) In any case in which the Governor recommends a variance under this subparagraph in which the Federal Land Manager does not concur, the recommendations of the Governor and the Federal Land Manager shall be transmitted to the President. The President may approve the Governor's recommendation if he finds that such variance is in the national interest. No Presidential finding shall be reviewable in any court. The variance shall take effect if the President approves the Governor's recommendations. The President shall approve or disapprove such recommendation within ninety days after his receipt of the recommendations of the Governor and the Federal Land Manager.

(iii) In the case of a permit issued pursuant to this subparagraph, such facility shall comply with such emission limitations under such permit as may be necessary to assure that emissions of sulfur oxides from such facility will not (during any day on which the otherwise applicable maximum allowable increases are exceeded) cause or contribute to concentrations which exceed the following maximum allowable increases for such areas over the baseline concentration for such pollutant and to assure that such emissions will not cause or contribute to concentrations which exceed the otherwise applicable maximum allowable increases for periods of exposure of 24 hours or less on more than 18 days during any annual period:

MAXIMUM ALLOWABLE INCREASE

[In micrograms per cubic meter]

Period of exposure	Low terrain areas	High terrain areas
24-hr maximum	36	62
3-hr maximum	130	221

(iv) For purposes of clause (iii), the term "high terrain area" means with respect to any facility, any area having an elevation of 900 feet or more above the base of the stack of such facility, and the term "low terrain area" means any area other than a high terrain area.

(e) Analysis; continuous air quality monitoring data; regulations; model adjustments

(1) The review provided for in subsection (a) of this section shall be preceded by an analysis in accordance with regulations of the Administrator, promulgated under this subsection, which may be conducted by the State (or any general purpose unit of local government) or by the major emitting facility applying for such permit, of the ambient air quality at the proposed site and in areas which may be affected by emissions from such facility for each pollutant subject to regulation under this chapter which will be emitted from such facility.

(2) Effective one year after August 7, 1977, the analysis required by this subsection shall include continuous air quality monitoring data gathered for purposes of determining whether emissions from such facility will exceed the maximum allowable increases or the maximum allowable concentration permitted under this part. Such data shall be gathered over a period of one calendar year preceding the date of application for a permit under this part unless the State, in accordance with regulations promulgated by the Administrator, determines that a complete and adequate analysis for such purposes may be accomplished in a shorter period. The results of such analysis shall be available at the time of the public hearing on the application for such permit.

(3) The Administrator shall within six months after August 7, 1977, promulgate regulations respecting the analysis required under this subsection which regulations—

(A) shall not require the use of any automatic or uniform buffer zone or zones,

(B) shall require an analysis of the ambient air quality, climate and meteorology, terrain, soils and vegetation, and visibility at the site of the proposed major emitting facility and in the area potentially affected by the emissions from such facility for each pollutant regulated under this chapter which will be emitted from, or which results from the construction or operation of, such facility, the size and nature of the proposed facility, the degree of continuous emission reduction which could be achieved by such facility, and such other factors as may be relevant in determining the effect of emissions from a proposed facility on any air quality control region,

(C) shall require the results of such analysis shall be available at the time of the public hearing on the application for such permit, and

(D) shall specify with reasonable particularity each air quality model or models to be used under specified sets of conditions for purposes of this part.

Any model or models designated under such regulations may be adjusted upon a determination, after notice and opportunity for public hearing, by the Administrator that such adjustment is necessary to take into account unique terrain or meteorological characteristics of an area potentially affected by emissions from a source applying for a permit required under this part.

(July 14, 1955, ch. 360, title I, § 165, as added Aug. 7, 1977, Pub.L. 95–95, title I, § 127(a), 91 Stat. 735, and amended Nov. 16, 1977, Pub.L. 95–190, § 14(a)(44)–(51), 91 Stat. 1402.)

Library References

Health and Environment ⚬═25.6(5).
C.J.S. Health and Environment § 91 et seq.

§ 7476. Other pollutants

(a) Hydrocarbons, carbon monoxide, petrochemical oxidants, and nitrogen oxides

In the case of the pollutants hydrocarbons, carbon monoxide, photochemical oxidants, and nitrogen oxides, the Administrator shall conduct a study and not later than two years after August 7, 1977, promulgate regulations to prevent the significant deterioration of air quality which would result from the emissions of such pollutants. In the case of pollutants for which national ambient air quality standards are promulgated after August 7, 1977, he shall promulgate such regulations not more than 2 years after the date of promulgation of such standards.

(b) Effective date of regulations

Regulations referred to in subsection (a) of this section shall become effective one year after the date of promulgation. Within 21 months after such date of promulgation such plan revision shall be submitted to the Administrator who shall approve or disapprove the plan within 25 months after such date or promulgation in the same manner as required under section 7410 of this title.

(c) Contents of regulations

Such regulations shall provide specific numerical measures against which permit applications may be evaluated, a framework for stimulating improved control technology, protection of air quality values, and fulfill the goals and purposes set forth in section 7401 and section 7470 of this title.

(d) Specific measures to fulfill goals and purposes

The regulations of the Administrator under subsection (a) of this section shall provide specific measures at least as effective as the increments established in section 7473 of this title to fulfill such goals and purposes, and may contain air quality increments, emission density requirements, or other measures.

(e) Area classification plan not required

With respect to any air pollutant for which a national ambient air quality standard is established other than sulfur oxides or particulate matter, an area classification plan shall not be required under this section if the implementation plan adopted by the State and submitted for the Administrator's approval or promulgated by the Administrator under section 7410(c) of this title contains other provisions which when considered as a whole, the Administrator finds will carry out the purposes in section 7470 of this title at least as effectively as an area classification plan for such pollutant. Such other provisions referred to in the preceding sentence need not require the establishment of maximum allowable increases with respect to such pollutant for any area to which this section applies.

(July 14, 1955, ch. 360, title I, § 166, as added Aug. 7, 1977, Pub.L. 95–95, title I, § 127(a), 91 Stat. 739.)

Library References

Health and Environment ⚬═25.6(3).
C.J.S. Health and Environment § 92.

§ 7477. Enforcement

The Administrator shall, and a State may, take such measures, including issuance of an order, or seeking injunctive relief, as necessary to prevent the construction of a major emitting facility which does not conform to the requirements of this part, or which is proposed to be constructed in any area included in the list promulgated pursuant to paragraph (1)(D) or (E) of subsection (d) of section 7407 of this title and which is not subject to an implementation plan which meets the requirements of this part.

(July 14, 1955, ch. 360, title I, § 167, as added Aug. 7, 1977, Pub.L. 95–95, title I, § 127(a), 91 Stat. 740.)

Library References

Health and Environment ⚬═25.6(9).
C.J.S. Health and Environment § 104 et seq.

§ 7478. Period before plan approval

(a) Existing regulations to remain in effect

Until such time as an applicable implementation plan is in effect for any area, which plan meets the requirements of this part to prevent significant deterioration of air quality with respect to any air pollutant, applicable regulations under this chapter prior to August 7, 1977, shall remain in effect to prevent significant deterioration of air quality in any such area for any such pollutant except as otherwise provided in subsection (b) of this section.

(b) Regulations deemed amended; construction commenced after June 1, 1975

If any regulation in effect prior to August 7, 1977, to prevent significant deterioration of air quality would be inconsistent with the requirements of section 7472(a), section 7473(b) or section 7474(a) of this title, then such regulations shall be deemed amended so as to conform with such requirements.

In the case of a facility on which construction was commenced (in accordance with the definition of "commenced" in section 7479(2) of this title) after June 1, 1975, and prior to August 7, 1977, the review and permitting of such facility shall be in accordance with the regulations for the prevention of significant deterioration in effect prior to August 7, 1977.

(July 14, 1955, ch. 360, title I, § 168, as added Aug. 7, 1977, Pub.L. 95–95, title I, § 127(a), 91 Stat. 740, and amended Nov. 16, 1977, Pub.L. 95–190, § 14(a)(52), 91 Stat. 1402.)

Library References

Health and Environment ⚿25.6(4).
C.J.S. Health and Environment § 95 et seq.

§ 7479. Definitions

For purposes of this part—

(1) The term "major emitting facility" means any of the following stationary sources of air pollutants which emit, or have the potential to emit, one hundred tons per year or more of any air pollutant from the following types of stationary sources: fossil-fuel fired steam electric plants of more than two hundred and fifty million British thermal units per hour heat input, coal cleaning plants (thermal dryers), kraft pulp mills, Portland Cement plants, primary zinc smelters, iron and steel mill plants, primary aluminum ore reduction plants, primary copper smelters, municipal incinerators capable of charging more than two hundred and fifty tons of refuse per day, hydrofluoric, sulfuric, and nitric acid plants, petroleum refineries, lime plants, phosphate rock processing plants, coke oven batteries, sulfur recovery plants, carbon black plants (furnace process), primary lead smelters, fuel conversion plants, sintering plants, secondary metal production facilities, chemical process plants, fossil-fuel boilers of more than two hundred and fifty million British thermal units per hour heat input, petroleum storage and transfer facilities with a capacity exceeding three hundred thousand barrels, taconite ore processing facilities, glass fiber processing plants, charcoal production facilities. Such term also includes any other source with the potential to emit two hundred and fifty tons per year or more of any air pollutant. This term shall not include new or modified facilities which are nonprofit health or education institutions which have been exempted by the State.

(2)(A) The term "commenced" as applied to construction of a major emitting facility means that the owner or operator has obtained all necessary preconstruction approvals or permits required by Federal, State, or local air pollution emissions and air quality laws or regulations and either has (i) begun, or caused to begin, a continuous program of physical on-site construction of the facility or (ii) entered into binding agreements or contractual obligations, which cannot be canceled or modified without substantial loss to the owner or operator, to undertake a program of construction of the facility to be completed within a reasonable time.

(B) The term "necessary preconstruction approvals or permits" means those permits or approvals, required by the permitting authority as a precondition to undertaking any activity under clauses (i) or (ii) of subparagraph (A) of this paragraph.

(C) The term "construction" when used in connection with any source or facility, includes the modification (as defined in section 7411(a) of this title) of any source or facility.

(3) The term "best available control technology" means an emission limitation based on the maximum degree of reduction of each pollutant subject to regulation under this chapter emitted from or which results from any major emitting facility, which the permitting authority, on a case-by-case basis, taking into account energy, environmental, and economic impacts and other costs, determines is achievable for such facility through application of production processes and available methods, systems, and techniques, including fuel cleaning or treatment or innovative fuel combustion techniques for control of each such pollutant. In no event shall application of "best available control technology" result in emissions of any pollutants which will exceed the emissions allowed by any applicable standard established pursuant to section 7411 or 7412 of this title.

(4) The term "baseline concentration" means, with respect to a pollutant, the ambient concentration levels which exist at the time of the first application for a permit in an area subject to this part, based on air quality data available in the Environmental Protection Agency or a State air pollution control agency and on such monitoring data as the permit applicant is required to submit. Such ambient concentration levels shall take into account all projected emissions in, or which may affect, such area from any major emitting facility on which construction commenced prior to January 6, 1975, but which has not begun operation by the date of the baseline air quality concentration determination. Emissions of sulfur oxides and particulate matter from any major emitting facility on which construction commenced after January 6, 1975, shall not be included in the baseline and shall be counted against the maximum allowable increases in pollutant concentrations established under this part.

(July 14, 1955, ch. 360, title I, § 169, as added Aug. 7, 1977, Pub.L. 95–95, title I, § 127(a), 91 Stat. 740, and amended Nov. 16, 1977, Pub.L. 95–190, § 14(a)(54), 91 Stat. 1402.)

Library References

Health and Environment ⇨25.6(1) et seq.
C.J.S. Health and Environment § 91 et seq.

Subpart II—Visibility Protection

§ 7491. Visibility protection for Federal class I areas

(a) Impairment of visibility; list of areas; study and report

(1) Congress hereby declares as a national goal the prevention of any future, and the remedying of any existing, impairment of visibility in mandatory class I Federal areas which impairment results from manmade air pollution.

(2) Not later than six months after August 7, 1977, the Secretary of the Interior in consultation with other Federal land managers shall review all mandatory class I Federal areas and identify those where visibility is an important value of the area. From time to time the Secretary of the Interior may revise such identifications. Not later than one year after August 7, 1977, the Administrator shall, after consultation with the Secretary of the Interior, promulgate a list of mandatory class I Federal areas in which he determines visibility is an important value.

(3) Not later than eighteen months after August 7, 1977, the Administrator shall complete a study and report to Congress on available methods for implementing the national goal set forth in paragraph (1). Such report shall include recommendations for—

(A) methods for identifying, characterizing, determining, quantifying, and measuring visibility impairment in Federal areas referred to in paragraph (1), and

(B) modeling techniques (or other methods) for determining the extent to which manmade air pollution may reasonably be anticipated to cause or contribute to such impairment, and

(C) methods for preventing and remedying such manmade air pollution and resulting visibility impairment.

Such report shall also identify the classes or categories of sources and the types of air pollutants which, alone or in conjunction with other sources or pollutants, may reasonably be anticipated to cause or contribute significantly to impairment of visibility.

(4) Not later than twenty-four months after August 7, 1977, and after notice and public hearing, the Administrator shall promulgate regulations to assure (A) reasonable progress toward meeting the national goal specified in paragraph (1), and (B) compliance with the requirements of this section.

(b) Regulations

Regulations under subsection (a)(4) of this section shall—

(1) provide guidelines to the States, taking into account the recommendations under subsection (a)(3) of this section on appropriate techniques and methods for implementing this section (as provided in subparagraphs (A) through (C) of such subsection (a)(3)), and

(2) require each applicable implementation plan for a State in which any area listed by the Administrator under subsection (a)(2) of this section is located (or for a State the emissions from which may reasonably be anticipated to cause or contribute to any impairment of visibility in any such area) to contain such emission limits, schedules of compliance and other measures as may be necessary to make reasonable progress toward meeting the national goal specified in subsection (a) of this section, including—

(A) except as otherwise provided pursuant to subsection (c) of this section, a requirement that each major stationary source which is in existence on August 7, 1977, but which has not been in operation for more than fifteen years as of such date, and which, as determined by the State (or the Administrator in the case of a plan promulgated under section 7410(c) of this title) emits any air pollutant which may reasonably be anticipated to cause or contribute to any impairment of visibility in any such area, shall procure, install, and operate, as expeditiously as practicable (and maintain thereafter) the best available retrofit technology, as determined by the State (or the Administrator in the case of a plan promulgated under section 7410(c) of this title) for controlling emissions from such source for the purpose of eliminating or reducing any such impairment, and

(B) a long-term (ten to fifteen years) strategy for making reasonable progress toward meeting the national goal specified in subsection (a) of this section.

In the case of a fossil-fuel fired generating powerplant having a total generating capacity in excess of 750 megawatts, the emission limitations required under this paragraph shall be determined pursuant to guidelines, promulgated by the Administrator under paragraph (1).

(c) Exemptions

(1) The Administrator may, by rule, after notice and opportunity for public hearing, exempt any major stationary source from the requirement of subsection (b)(2)(A) of this section, upon his determination that such source does not or will not, by itself or in combination with other sources, emit any air pollutant which may reasonably be anticipated to cause or contribute to a significant impairment of visibility in any mandatory class I Federal area.

(2) Paragraph (1) of this subsection shall not be applicable to any fossil-fuel fired powerplant with total design capacity of 750 megawatts or more, unless the owner or operator of any such plant demonstrates to the satisfaction of the Administrator that such powerplant is located at such distance from all areas listed by the Administrator under subsection (a)(2) of this section that such powerplant does not or will not, by itself or in combination with other sources, emit any air pollutant which may reasonably be anticipated to cause or contribute to significant impairment of visibility in any such area.

(3) An exemption under this subsection shall be effective only upon concurrence by the appropriate Federal land manager or managers with the Administrator's determination under this subsection.

(d) Consultations with appropriate Federal land managers

Before holding the public hearing on the proposed revision of an applicable implementation plan to meet the requirements of this section, the State (or the Administrator, in the case of a plan promulgated under section 7410(c) of this title) shall consult in person with the appropriate Federal land manager or managers and shall include a summary of the conclusions and recommendations of the Federal land managers in the notice to the public.

(e) Buffer zones

In promulgating regulations under this section, the Administrator shall not require the use of any automatic or uniform buffer zone or zones.

(f) Nondiscretionary duty

For purposes of section 7604(a)(2) of this title, the meeting of the national goal specified in subsection (a)(1) of this section by any specific date or dates shall not be considered a "nondiscretionary duty" of the Administrator.

(g) Definitions

For the purpose of this section—

(1) in determining reasonable progress there shall be taken into consideration the costs of compliance, the time necessary for compliance, and the energy and nonair quality environmental impacts of compliance, and the remaining useful life of any existing source subject to such requirements;

(2) in determining best available retrofit technology the State (or the Administrator in determining emission limitations which reflect such technology) shall take into consideration the costs of compliance, the energy and nonair quality environmental impacts of compliance, any existing pollution control technology in use at the source, the remaining useful life of the source, and the degree of improvement in visibility which may reasonably be anticipated to result from the use of such technology;

(3) the term "manmade air pollution" means air pollution which results directly or indirectly from human activities;

(4) the term "as expeditiously as practicable" means as expeditiously as practicable but in no event later than five years after the date of approval of a plan revision under this section (or the date of promulgation of such a plan revision in the case of action by the Administrator under section 7410(c) of this title for purposes of this section);

(5) the term "mandatory class I Federal areas" means Federal areas which may not be designated as other than class I under this part;

(6) the terms "visibility impairment" and "impairment of visibility" shall include reduction in visual range and atmospheric discoloration; and

(7) the term "major stationary source" means the following types of stationary sources with the potential to emit 250 tons or more of any pollutant: fossil-fuel fired steam electric plants of more than 250 million British thermal units per hour heat input, coal cleaning plants (thermal dryers), kraft pulp mills, Portland Cement plants, primary zinc smelters, iron and steel mill plants, primary aluminum ore reduction plants, primary copper smelters, municipal incenerators [1] capable of charging more than 250 tons of refuse per day, hydrofluoric, sulfuric, and nitric acid plants, petroleum refineries, lime plants, phosphate rock processing plants, coke oven batteries, sulfur recovery plants, carbon black plants (furnace process), primary lead smelters, fuel conversion plants, sintering plants, secondary metal production facilities, chemical process plants, fossil-fuel boilers of more than 250 million British thermal units per hour heat input, petroleum storage and transfer facilities with a capacity exceeding

300,000 barrels, taconite ore processing facilities, glass fiber processing plants, charcoal production facilities.

(July 14, 1955, ch. 360, title I, § 169A, as added Aug. 7, 1977, Pub.L. 95–95, title I, § 128, 91 Stat. 742.)

[1] So in original. Probably should be "incinerators".

Code of Federal Regulations

Emission standards for hazardous pollutants, see 40 CFR 61.01 et seq.
New stationary sources, performance standards for, see 40 CFR 60.1 et seq.

Library References

Health and Environment ⚷25.6(3).
C.J.S. Health and Environment § 92.

PART D—PLAN REQUIREMENTS FOR NONATTAINMENT AREAS

Cross References

Federally permitted release defined to include emissions into air subject to permit or control regulation under this part for purposes of Comprehensive Environmental Response, Compensation, and Liability Act of 1980, see section 9601 of this title.

§ 7501. Definitions

For the purpose of this part and section 7410(a)(2)(I) of this title—

(1) The term "reasonable further progress" means annual incremental reductions in emissions of the applicable air pollutant (including substantial reductions in the early years following approval or promulgation of plan provisions under this part and section 7410(a)(2)(I) of this title and regular reductions thereafter) which are sufficient in the judgment of the Administrator, to provide for attainment of the applicable national ambient air quality standard by the date required in section 7502(a) of this title.

(2) The term "nonattainment area" means, for any air pollutant an area which is shown by monitored data or which is calculated by air quality modeling (or other methods determined by the Administrator to be reliable) to exceed any national ambient air quality standard for such pollutant. Such term includes any area identified under subparagraphs (A) through (C) of section 7407(d)(1) of this title.

(3) The term "lowest achievable emission rate" means for any source, that rate of emissions which reflects—

(A) the most stringent emission limitation which is contained in the implementation plan of any State for such class or category of source, unless the owner or operator of the proposed source demonstrates that such limitations are not achievable, or

(B) the most stringent emission limitation which is achieved in practice by such class or category of source, whichever is more stringent.

In no event shall the application of this term permit a proposed new or modified source to emit any pollutant in excess of the amount allowable under applicable new source standards of performance.

(4) The terms "modifications" and "modified" mean the same as the term "modification" as used in section 7411(a)(4) of this title.

(July 14, 1955, ch. 360, title I, § 171, as added Aug. 7, 1977, Pub.L. 95–95, title I, § 129(b), 91 Stat. 746.)

Code of Federal Regulations

Air pollution from motor vehicles, control of, see 40 CFR 86.078–3 et seq.
Air programs, see 40 CFR 81.1 et seq.
Implementation plans, requirements for preparation, adoption and submittal of, see 40 CFR 51.1 et seq.

Library References

Health and Environment ⚷25.6(4).
C.J.S. Health and Environment § 95 et seq.

§ 7502. Nonattainment plan provisions

(a) Expeditious attainment of national ambient air quality standards

(1) The provisions of an applicable implementation plan for a State relating to attainment and maintenance of national ambient air quality standards in any nonattainment area which are required by section 7410(a)(2)(I) of this title as a precondition for the construction or modification of any major stationary source in any such area on or after July 1, 1979, shall provide for attainment of each such national ambient air quality standard in each such area as expeditiously as practicable, but, in the case of national primary ambient air quality standards, not later than December 31, 1982.

(2) In the case of the national primary ambient air quality standard for photochemical oxidants or carbon monoxide (or both) if the State demonstrates to[1] the satisfaction of the Administrator (on or before the time required for submission of such plan) that such attainment is not possible in an area with respect to either or both of such pollutants within the period prior to December 31, 1982, despite the implementation of all reasonably available measures, such provisions shall provide for the attainment of the national primary standard for the pollutant (or pollutants) with respect to which such

demonstration is made, as expeditiously as practicable but not later than December 31, 1987.

(b) Requisite provisions of plan

The plan provisions required by subsection (a) of this section shall—

(1) be adopted by the State (or promulgated by the Administrator under section 7410(c) of this title) after reasonable notice and public hearing;

(2) provide for the implementation of all reasonably available control measures as expeditiously as practicable;

(3) require, in the interim, reasonable further progress (as defined in section 7501(1) of this title) including such reduction in emissions from existing sources in the area as may be obtained through the adoption, at a minimum, of reasonably available control technology;

(4) include a comprehensive, accurate, current inventory of actual emissions from all sources (as provided by rule of the Administrator) of each such pollutant for each such area which is revised and resubmitted as frequently as may be necessary to assure that the requirements of paragraph (3) are met and to assess the need for additional reductions to assure attainment of each standard by the date required under subsection (a) of this section;

(5) expressly identify and quantify the emissions, if any, of any such pollutant which will be allowed to result from the construction and operation of major new or modified stationary sources for each such area;

(6) require permits for the construction and operation of new or modified major stationary sources in accordance with section 7503 of this title (relating to permit requirements);

(7) identify and commit the financial and manpower resources necessary to carry out the plan provisions required by this subsection;

(8) contain emission limitations, schedules of compliance and such other measures as may be necessary to meet the requirements of this section;

(9) evidence public, local government, and State legislative involvement and consultation in accordance with section 7504 of this title (relating to planning procedures) and include (A) an identification and analysis of the air quality, health, welfare, economic, energy, and social effects of the plan provisions required by this subsection and of the alternatives considered by the State, and (B) a summary of the public comment on such analysis;

(10) include written evidence that the State, the general purpose local government or governments, or a regional agency designated by general purpose local governments for such purpose, have adopted by statute, regulation, ordinance, or other legally enforceable document, the necessary requirements and schedules and timetables for compliance, and are committed to implement and enforce the appropriate elements of the plan;

(11) in the case of plans which make a demonstration pursuant to paragraph (2) of subsection (a) of this section—

(A) establish a program which requires, prior to issuance of any permit for construction or modification of a major emitting facility, an analysis of alternative sites, sizes, production processes, and environmental control techniques for such proposed source which demonstrates that benefits of the proposed source significantly outweigh the environmental and social costs imposed as a result of its location, construction, or modification;

(B) establish a specific schedule for implementation of a vehicle emission control inspection and maintenance program; and

(C) identify other measures necessary to provide for attainment of the applicable national ambient air quality standard not later than December 31, 1987.

(c) Attainment of applicable standard not later than July 1, 1987

In the case of a State plan revision required under the Clean Air Act Amendments of 1977 to be submitted before July 1, 1982, by reason of a demonstration under subsection (a)(2) of this section, effective on such date such plan shall contain enforceable measures to assure attainment of the applicable standard not later than December 31, 1987.

(July 14, 1955, ch. 360, title I, § 172, as added Aug. 7, 1977, Pub.L. 95–95, title I, § 129(b), 91 Stat. 746, and amended Nov. 16, 1977, Pub.L. 95–190, § 14(a)(55), (56), 91 Stat. 1402.)

[1] So in original.

Code of Federal Regulations

Emission regulations, see 40 CFR 86.078–3 et seq.
Implementation plans, requirements for preparation, adoption and submittal of, see 40 CFR 51.1 et seq.
New stationary sources, performance standards for, see 40 CFR 60.1 et seq.

Library References

Health and Environment ⚷25.6(4).
C.J.S. Health and Environment § 95 et seq.

§ 7503. Permit requirements

The permit program required by section 7502(b)(6) of this title shall provide that permits to construct and operate may be issued if—

(1) the permitting agency determines that—

(A) by the time the source is to commence operation, total allowable emissions from existing sources in the region, from new or modified sources which are not major emitting facilities, and from the proposed source will be sufficiently less than total emissions from existing sources allowed under the applicable implementation plan prior to the application for such permit to construct or modify so as to represent (when considered together with the plan provisions required under section 7502 of this title) reasonable further progress (as defined in section 7501 of this title); or

(B) that emissions of such pollutant resulting from the proposed new or modified major stationary source will not cause or contribute to emissions levels which exceed the allowance permitted for such pollutant for such area from new or modified major stationary sources under section 7502(b) of this title;

(2) the proposed source is required to comply with the lowest achievable emission rate;

(3) the owner or operator of the proposed new or modified source has demonstrated that all major stationary sources owned or operated by such person (or by any entity controlling, controlled by, or under common control with such person) in such State are subject to emission limitations and are in compliance, or on a schedule for compliance, with all applicable emission limitations and standards under this chapter; and

(4) the applicable implementation plan is being carried out for the nonattainment area in which the proposed source is to be constructed or modified in accordance with the requirements of this part.

Any emission reductions required as a precondition of the issuance of a permit under paragraph (1)(A) shall be legally binding before such permit may be issued.

(July 14, 1955, ch. 360, title I, § 173, as added Aug. 7, 1977, Pub.L. 95–95, title I, § 129(b), 91 Stat. 748, and amended Nov. 16, 1977, Pub.L. 95–190, § 14(a)(57), (58), 91 Stat. 1403.)

Code of Federal Regulations

Implementation plans, requirements for preparation, adoption and submittal of, see 40 CFR 51.1 et seq.

§ 7504. Planning procedures

(a) Preparation of implementation plan by designated organization

Within six months after August 7, 1977, for each region in which the national primary ambient air quality standard for carbon monoxide or photochemical oxidants will not be attained by July 1, 1979, the State and elected officials of affected local governments shall jointly determine which elements of a revised implementation plan will be planned for and implemented or enforced by the State and which such elements will be planned for and implemented or enforced by local governments or regional agencies, or any combination of local governments, regional agencies, or the State. Where possible within the time required under this subsection, the implementation plan required by this part shall be prepared by an organization of elected officials of local governments designated by agreement of the local governments in an affected area, and certified by the State for this purpose. Where such an organization has not been designated by agreement within six months after August 7, 1977, the Governor (or, in the case of an interstate area, Governors), after consultation with elected officials of local governments, and in accordance with the determination under the first sentence of this subparagraph, shall designate an organization of elected officials of local governments in the affected area or a State agency to prepare such plan. Where feasible, such organization shall be the metropolitan planning organization designated to conduct the continuing, cooperative and comprehensive transportation planning process for the area under section 134 of title 23, or the organization responsible for the air quality maintenance planning process under regulations implementing this section, or the organization with both responsibilities.

(b) Coordination of plan preparation

The preparation of implementation plan provisions under this part shall be coordinated with the continuing, cooperative, and comprehensive transportation planning process required under section 134 of title 23 and the air quality maintenance planning process required under section 7410 of this title, and such planning processes shall take into account the requirements of this part.

(July 14, 1955, ch. 360, title I, § 174, as added Aug. 7, 1977, Pub.L. 95–95, title I, § 129(b), 91 Stat. 748.)

Code of Federal Regulations

Implementation plans, requirements for preparation, adoption and submittal of, see 40 CFR 51.1 et seq.

Planning assistance and standards, see 23 CFR 450.100 et seq., 49 CFR 613.100 et seq.

§ 7505. Environmental Protection Agency grants

(a) Plan revision development costs

The Administrator shall make grants to any organization of local elected officials with transportation or air quality maintenance planning responsibilities recognized by the State under section 7504(a) of this title for payment of the reasonable costs of developing a plan revision under this part.

(b) Uses of grant funds

The amount granted to any organization under subsection (a) of this section shall be 100 percent of any additional costs of developing a plan revision under this part for the first two fiscal years following receipt of the grant under this paragraph, and shall supplement any funds available under Federal law to such organization for transportation or air quality maintenance planning. Grants under this section shall not be used for construction.

(July 14, 1955, ch. 360, title I, § 175, as added Aug. 7, 1977, Pub.L. 95–95, title I, § 129(b), 91 Stat. 749.)

Code of Federal Regulations

Implementation plans, requirements for preparation, adoption and submittal of, see 40 CFR 51.1 et seq.

Library References

Health and Environment ⟹25.6(1).
United States ⟹82(2).
C.J.S. Health and Environment § 91 et seq.
C.J.S. United States § 122.

§ 7506. Limitations on certain Federal assistance

(a) Approval of projects or award of grants

The Administrator shall not approve any projects or award any grants authorized by this chapter and the Secretary of Transportation shall not approve any projects or award any grants under title 23, other than for safety, mass transit, or transportation improvement projects related to air quality improvement or maintenance, in any air quality control region—

(1) in which any national primary ambient air quality standard has not been attained,

(2) where transportation control measures are necessary for the attainment of such standard, and

(3) where the Administrator finds after July 1, 1979, that the Governor has not submitted an implementation plan which considers each of the elements required by section 7502 of this title or that reasonable efforts toward submitting such an implementation plan are not being made (or, after July 1, 1982, in the case of an implementation plan revision required under section 7502 of this title to be submitted before July 1, 1982).

(b) Implementation of approved or promulgated plans

In any area in which the State or, as the case may be, the general purpose local government or governments or any regional agency designated by such general purpose local governments for such purpose, is not implementing any requirement of an approved or promulgated plan under section 7410 of this title, including any requirement for a revised implementation plan under this part, the Administrator shall not make any grants under this chapter.

(c) Activities not conforming to approved or promulgated plans

No department, agency, or instrumentality of the Federal Government shall (1) engage in, (2) support in any way or provide financial assistance for, (3) license or permit, or (4) approve, any activity which does not conform to a plan after it has been approved or promulgated under section 7410 of this title. No metropolitan planning organization designated under section 134 of title 23, shall give its approval to any project, program, or plan which does not conform to a plan approved or promulgated under section 7410 of this title. The assurance of conformity to such a plan shall be an affirmative responsibility of the head of such department, agency, or instrumentality.

(d) Priority of achieving and maintaining national primary ambient air quality standards

Each department, agency, or instrumentality of the Federal Government having authority to conduct or support any program with air- quality related transportation consequences shall give priority in the exercise of such authority, consistent with statutory requirements for allocation among States or other jurisdictions, to the implementation of those portions of plans prepared under this section to achieve and maintain the national primary ambient air quality standard. This paragraph extends to, but is not limited to, authority exercised under the Urban Mass Transportation Act [49 U.S.C. 1601 et seq.], title 23, and the Housing and Urban Development Act.

(July 14, 1955, ch. 360, title I, § 176, as added Aug. 7, 1977, Pub.L. 95–95, title I, § 129(b), 91 Stat. 749, and amended Nov. 16, 1977, Pub.L. 95–190, § 14(a)(59), 91 Stat. 1403.)

Code of Federal Regulations

Air quality conformity and priority procedures, see 23 CFR 770.1 et seq.
Implementation plans, requirements for preparation, adoption and submittal of, see 40 CFR 51.1 et seq.
Planning assistance and standards, see 23 CFR 450.100 et seq., 49 CFR 613.100 et seq.

§ 7507. New motor vehicle emission standards in nonattainment areas

Notwithstanding section 7543(a) of this title, any State which has plan provisions approved under this part may adopt and enforce for any model year standards relating to control of emissions from new motor vehicles or new motor vehicle engines and take such other actions as are referred to in section 7543(a) of this title respecting such vehicles if—

(1) such standards are identical to the California standards for which a waiver has been granted for such model year, and

(2) California and such State adopt such standards at least two years before commencement of such model year (as determined by regulations of the Administrator).

(July 14, 1955, ch. 360, title I, § 177, as added Aug. 7, 1977, Pub.L. 95–95, title I, § 129(b), 91 Stat. 750.)

Code of Federal Regulations

Implementation plans, requirements for preparation, adoption and submittal of, see 40 CFR 51.1 et seq.

§ 7508. Guidance documents

The Administrator shall issue guidance documents under section 7408 of this title for purposes of assisting States in implementing requirements of this part respecting the lowest achievable emission rate. Such a document shall be published not later than nine months after August 7, 1977, and shall be revised at least every two years thereafter.

(July 14, 1955, ch. 360, title I, § 178, as added Aug. 7, 1977, Pub.L. 95–95, title I, § 129(b), 91 Stat. 750.)

Code of Federal Regulations

Implementation plans, requirements for preparation, adoption and submittal of, see 40 CFR 51.1 et seq.

SUBCHAPTER II—EMISSION STANDARDS FOR MOVING SOURCES

Part A—Motor Vehicle Emission and Fuel Standards

§ 7521. Emission standards for new motor vehicles or new motor vehicle engines

(a) Authority of Administrator to prescribe by regulation

Except as otherwise provided in subsection (b) of this section—

(1) The Administrator shall by regulation prescribe (and from time to time revise) in accordance with the provisions of this section, standards applicable to the emission of any air pollutant from any class or classes of new motor vehicles or new motor vehicle engines, which in his judgment cause, or contribute to, air pollution which may reasonably be anticipated to endanger public health or welfare. Such standards shall be applicable to such vehicles and engines for their useful life (as determined under subsection (d) of this section, relating to useful life of vehicles for purposes of certification), whether such vehicles and engines are designed as complete systems or incorporate devices to prevent or control such pollution.

(2) Any regulation prescribed under paragraph (1) of this subsection (and any revision thereof) shall take effect after such period as the Administrator finds necessary to permit the development and application of the requisite technology, giving appropriate consideration to the cost of compliance within such period.

(3)(A)(i) The Administrator shall prescribe regulations under paragraph (1) of this subsection applicable to emissions of carbon monoxide, hydrocarbons, and oxides of nitrogen from classes or categories of heavy-duty vehicles or engines manufactured during and after model year 1979. Such regulations applicable to such pollutants from such classes or categories of vehicles or engines manufactured during model years 1979 through 1982 shall contain standards which reflect the greatest degree of emission reduction achievable through the application of technology which the Administrator determines will be available for the model year to which such standards apply, giving appropriate consideration to the cost of applying such technology within the period of time available to manufacturers and to noise, energy, and safety factors associated with the application of such technology.

(ii) Unless a different standard is temporarily promulgated as provided in subparagraph (B) or unless the standard is changed as provided in subparagraph (E), regulations under paragraph (1) of this subsection applicable to emissions from vehicles or engines manufactured during and after model year—

(I) 1983, in the case of hydrocarbons and carbon monoxide, shall contain standards which require a reduction of at least 90 per cent, and

(II) 1985, in the case of oxides of nitrogen, shall contain standards which require a reduction of at least 75 per cent,

from the average of the actually measured emissions from heavy-duty gasoline-fueled vehicles or engines, or any class or category thereof, manufactured during the baseline model year.

(iii) The Administrator shall prescribe regulations under paragraph (1) of this subsection applicable to emissions of particulate matter from classes or categories of vehicles manufactured during and after model year 1981 (or during any earlier model year, if practicable). Such regulations shall contain standards which reflect the greatest degree of emission reduction achievable through the application of technology which the

Administrator determines will be available for the model year to which such standards apply, giving appropriate consideration to the cost of applying such technology within the period of time available to manufacturers and to noise, energy, and safety factors associated with the application of such technology. Such standards shall be promulgated and shall take effect as expeditiously as practicable taking into account the period necessary for compliance.

(iv) In establishing classes or categories of vehicles or engines for purposes of regulations under this paragraph, the Administrator may base such classes or categories on gross vehicle weight, horsepower, or such other factors as may be appropriate.

(v) For the purpose of this paragraph, the term "baseline model year" means, with respect to any pollutant emitted from any vehicle or engine, or class or category thereof, the model year immediately preceding the model year in which Federal standards applicable to such vehicle or engine, or class or category thereof, first applied with respect to such pollutant.

(B) During the period of June 1 through December 31, 1978, in the case of hydrocarbons and carbon monoxide, or during the period of June 1 through December 31, 1980, in the case of oxides of nitrogen, and during each period of June 1 through December 31 of each third year thereafter, the Administrator may, after notice and opportunity for a public hearing promulgate regulations revising any standard prescribed as provided in subparagraph (A)(ii) for any class or category of heavy-duty vehicles or engines. Such standard shall apply only for the period of three model years beginning four model years after the model year in which such revised standard is promulgated. In revising any standard under this subparagraph for any such three model year period, the Administrator shall determine the maximum degree of emission reduction which can be achieved by means reasonably expected to be available for production of such period and shall prescribe a revised emission standard in accordance with such determination. Such revised standard shall require a reduction of emissions from any standard which applies in the previous model year.

(C) Action revising any standard for any period may be taken by the Administrator under subparagraph (B) only if he finds—

(i) that compliance with the emission standards otherwise applicable for such model year cannot be achieved by technology, processes, operating methods, or other alternatives reasonably expected to be available for production for such model year without increasing cost or decreasing fuel economy to an excessive and unreasonable degree; and

(ii) the National Academy of Sciences has not, pursuant to its study and investigation under subsection (c) of this section, issued a report substantially contrary to the findings of the Administrator under clause (i).

(D) A report shall be made to the Congress with respect to any standard revised under subparagraph (B) which shall contain—

(i) a summary of the health effects found, or believed to be associated with, the pollutant covered by such standard,

(ii) an analysis of the cost-effectiveness of other strategies for attaining and maintaining national ambient air quality standards and carrying out regulations under part C of subchapter I of this chapter (relating to significant deterioration) in relation to the cost-effectiveness for such purposes of standards which, but for such revision, would apply.[1]

(iii) a summary of the research and development efforts and progress being made by each manufacturer for purposes of meeting the standards promulgated as provided in subparagraph (A)(ii) or, if applicable, subparagraph (E), and

(iv) specific findings as to the relative costs of compliance, and relative fuel economy, which may be expected to result from the application for any model year of such revised standard and the application for such model year of the standard, which, but for such revision, would apply.

(E)(i) The Administrator shall conduct a continuing pollutant-specific study concerning the effects of each air pollutant emitted from heavy-duty vehicles or engines and from other sources of mobile source related pollutants on the public health and welfare. The results of such study shall be published in the Federal Register and reported to the Congress not later than June 1, 1978, in the case of hydrocarbons and carbon monoxide, and June 1, 1980, in the case of oxides of nitrogen, and before June 1 of each third year thereafter.

(ii) On the basis of such study and such other information as is available to him (including the studies under section 7548 of this title), the Administrator may, after notice and opportunity for a public hearing, promulgate regulations under paragraph (1) of this subsection changing any standard prescribed in subparagraph (A)(ii) (or revised under subparagraph (B) or previously changed under this subparagraph). No such changed standard shall apply for any model year before the model year four years after the model year during which regulations containing such changed standard are promulgated.

(F) For purposes of this paragraph, motorcycles and motorcycle engines shall be treated in the same manner as heavy-duty vehicles and engines (except as otherwise permitted under section 7525(f)(1) of this title) unless the Administrator promulgates a rule reclassifying motorcycles as light-duty vehicles within the meaning of this section or unless the Administrator promulgates regulations under subsection (a) of this section applying standards applicable to the emission of air pollutants from motorcycles as a separate class or category. In any case in which such standards are promulgated for such emissions from motorcycles as a separate class or category, the Administrator, in promulgating such standards, shall consider the need to achieve equivalency of emission reductions between motorcycles and other motor vehicles to the maximum extent practicable.

(4)(A) Effective with respect to vehicles and engines manufactured after model year 1978, no emission control device, system, or element of design shall be used in a new motor vehicle or new motor vehicle engine for purposes of complying with standards prescribed under this subsection if such device, system, or element of design will cause or contribute to an unreasonable risk to public health, welfare, or safety in its operation or function.

(B) In determining whether an unreasonable risk exists under subparagraph (A), the Administrator shall consider, among other factors, (i) whether and to what extent the use of any device, system, or element of design causes, increases, reduces, or eliminates emissions of any unregulated pollutants; (ii) available methods for reducing or eliminating any risk to public health, welfare, or safety which may be associated with the use of such device, system, or element of design, and (iii) the availability of other devices, systems, or elements of design which may be used to conform to standards prescribed under this subsection without causing or contributing to such unreasonable risk. The Administrator shall include in the consideration required by this paragraph all relevant information developed pursuant to section 7548 of this title.

(5)(A) If the Administrator promulgates final regulations which define the degree of control required and the test procedures by which compliance could be determined for gasoline vapor recovery of uncontrolled emissions from the fueling of motor vehicles, the Administrator shall, after consultation with the Secretary of Transportation with respect to motor vehicle safety, prescribe, by regulation, fill pipe standards for new motor vehicles in order to insure effective connection between such fill pipe and any vapor recovery system which the Administrator determines may be required to comply with such vapor recovery regulations. In promulgating such standards the Administrator shall take into consideration limits on fill pipe diameter, minimum design criteria for nozzle retainer lips, limits on the location of the unleaded fuel restrictors, a minimum access zone surrounding a fill pipe, a minimum pipe or nozzle insertion angle, and such other factors as he deems pertinent.

(B) Regulations prescribing standards under subparagraph (A) shall not become effective until the introduction of the model year for which it would be feasible to implement such standards, taking into consideration the restraints of an adequate leadtime for design and production.

(C) Nothing in subparagraph (A) shall (i) prevent the Administrator from specifying different nozzle and fill neck sizes for gasoline with additives and gasoline without additives or (ii) permit the Administrator to require a specific location, configuration, modeling, or styling of the motor vehicle body with respect to the fuel tank fill neck or fill nozzle clearance envelope.

(D) For the purpose of this paragraph, the term "fill pipe" shall include the fuel tank fill pipe, fill neck, fill inlet, and closure.

(6) The Administrator shall determine the feasibility and desirability of requiring new motor vehicles to utilize onboard hydrocarbon control technology which would avoid the necessity of gasoline vapor recovery of uncontrolled emissions emanating from the fueling of motor vehicles. The Administrator shall compare the costs and effectiveness of such technology to that of implementing and maintaining vapor recovery systems (taking into consideration such factors as fuel economy, economic costs of such technology, administrative burdens, and equitable distribution of costs). If the Administrator finds that it is feasible and desirable to employ such technology, he shall, after consultation with the Secretary of Transportation with respect to motor vehicle safety, prescribe, by regulation, standards requiring the use of onboard hydrocarbon technology which shall not become effective until the introduction to the model year for which it would be feasible to implement such standards, taking into consideration compliance costs and the restraints of an adequate lead time for design and production.

(b) Emissions of carbon monoxide, hydrocarbons, and oxides of nitrogen; annual report to Congress; waiver of emission standards; research objectives

(1)(A) The regulations under subsection (a) of this section applicable to emissions of carbon monoxide and hydrocarbons from light-duty vehicles and engines manufactured during model years 1977 through 1979 shall contain standards which provide that such emissions from such vehicles and engines may not exceed 1.5 grams per vehicle mile of hydrocarbons and 15.0 grams per vehicle mile of carbon monoxide. The regulations under subsection (a) of this section applicable to emissions of carbon monoxide from light-duty vehicles and engines manufactured during the model year 1980 shall contain standards which provide that such emissions may not exceed 7.0 grams per vehicle mile. The regulations under subsection (a) of this section applicable to emissions of hydrocarbons from light-duty vehicles and engines manufactured during or after model year 1980 shall contain standards which require a reduction of at least 90 percent from emissions of such pollutant allowable under the standards under this section applicable to light-duty vehicles and engines manufactured in model year 1970. Unless waived as provided in paragraph (5), regulations under subsection (a) of this section applicable to emissions of carbon monoxide from light-duty vehicles and engines manufactured during or after the model year 1981 shall contain standards which require a reduction of at least 90 percent from emissions of such pollutant allowable under the standards under this section applicable to light-duty vehicles and engines manufactured in model year 1970.

(B) The regulations under subsection (a) of this section applicable to emissions of oxides of nitrogen from light-duty vehicles and engines manufactured during model years 1977 through 1980 shall contain standards which provide that such emissions from such vehicles and engines may not exceed 2.0 grams per vehicle mile. The regulations under subsection (a) of this section applicable to emissions of oxides of nitrogen from light-duty vehicles and engines manufactured during the model year 1981 and thereafter shall contain standards which provide that such emissions from such vehicles and engines may not exceed 1.0 gram per vehicle mile. The Administrator shall prescribe standards in lieu of those required by the preceding sentence, which provide that emissions of oxides of nitrogen may not exceed 2.0 grams per vehicle mile for any light-duty vehicle manufactured during model years 1981 and 1982 by any manufacturer whose production, by corporate identity, for calendar year 1976 was less than three hundred thousand light-duty motor vehicles worldwide if the Administrator determines that—

(i) the ability of such manufacturer to meet emission standards in the 1975 and subsequent model years was, and is, primarily dependent upon technology developed by other manufacturers and purchased from such manufacturers; and

(ii) such manufacturer lacks the financial resources and technological ability to develop such technology.

(C) Effective with respect to vehicles and engines manufactured after model year 1978 (or in the case of heavy-duty vehicles or engines, such later model year as the Administrator determines is the earliest feasible model year), the test procedure promulgated under paragraph (2) for measurement of evaporative emissions of hydrocarbons shall require that such emissions be measured from the vehicle or engine as a whole. Regulations to carry out this subparagraph shall be promulgated not later than two hundred and seventy days after August 7, 1977.

(2) Emission standards under paragraph (1), and measurement techniques on which such standards are based (if not promulgated prior to December 31, 1970), shall be prescribed by regulation within 180 days after such date.

(3) For purposes of this part—

(A)(i) The term "model year" with reference to any specific calendar year means the manufacturer's annual production period (as determined by the Administrator) which includes January 1 of such calendar year. If the manufacturer has no annual production period, the term "model year" shall mean the calendar year.

(ii) For the purpose of assuring that vehicles and engines manufactured before the beginning of a model year were not manufactured for purposes of circumventing the effective date of a standard required to be prescribed by subsection (b) of this section, the Administrator may prescribe regulations defining "model year" otherwise than as provided in clause (i).

(B) The term "light duty vehicles and engines" means new light duty motor vehicles and new light duty motor vehicle engines, as determined under regulations of the Administrator.

(C) The term "heavy duty vehicle" means a truck, bus, or other vehicle manufactured primarily for use on the public streets, roads, and highways (not including any vehicle operated exclusively on a rail or rails) which has a gross vehicle weight (as determined under regulations promulgated by the Administrator) in excess of six thousand pounds. Such term includes any such vehicle which has special features enabling off-street or off-highway operation and use.

(4) On July 1 of 1971, and of each year thereafter, the Administrator shall report to the Congress with respect to the development of systems necessary to implement the emission standards established pursuant to this section. Such reports shall include information regarding the continuing effects of such air pollutants subject to standards under this section on the public health and welfare, the extent and progress of efforts being made to develop the necessary systems, the costs associated with development and application of such systems, and following such hearings as he may deem advisable, any recommendations for additional congressional action necessary to achieve the purposes of this chapter. In gathering information for the purposes of this paragraph and in connection with any hearing, the provisions of section 7607(a) of this title (relating to subpenas) shall apply.

(5)(A) At any time after August 31, 1978, any manufacturer may file an application requesting the waiver for model years 1981 and 1982 of the effective date of the emission standard required by paragraph (1)(A) for carbon monoxide applicable to any model (as determined by the Administration) of light-duty motor vehicles and engines manufactured in such model years. The Administrator shall make his determination with respect to any such application within sixty days after such application is filed with respect to such model. If he determines, in accordance with the provisions of this paragraph, that such waiver should be granted, he shall simultaneously with such determination prescribe by regulation emission standards which shall apply (in lieu of the standards required to be prescribed by paragraph (1)(A) of this subsection) to emissions of carbon monoxide from such model of vehicles or engines manufactured during model years 1981 and 1982.

(B) Any standards prescribed under this paragraph shall not permit emissions of carbon monoxide from vehicles and engines to which such waiver applies to exceed 7.0 grams per vehicle per mile.

(C) Within sixty days after receipt of the application for any such waiver and after public hearing, the Administrator shall issue a decision granting or refusing such waiver. The Administrator may grant such waiver if he finds that protection of the public health does not require attainment of such 90 percent reduction for carbon monoxide for the model years to which such waiver applies in the case of such vehicles and engines and if he determines that—

(i) such waiver is essential to the public interest or the public health and welfare of the United States;

(ii) all good faith efforts have been made to meet the standards established by this subsection;

(iii) the applicant has established that effective control technology, processes, operating methods, or other alternatives are not available or have not been available with respect to the model in question for a sufficient period of time to achieve compliance prior to the effective date of such standards, taking into consideration costs, driveability, and fuel economy; and

(iv) studies and investigations of the National Academy of Sciences conducted pursuant to subsection (c) of this section and other information available to him has not indicated that technology, processes, or other alternatives are available (within the meaning of clause (iii)) to meet such standards.

(6)(A) Upon the petition of any manufacturer, the Administrator, after notice and opportunity for public hearing, may waive the standard required under subparagraph (B) of paragraph (1) to not exceed 1.5 grams of oxides of nitrogen per vehicle mile for any class or category of light-duty vehicles or engines manufactured by such manufacturer during any period of up to four model years beginning after the model year 1980 if the manufacturer demonstrates that such waiver is necessary to permit the use of an innovative power train technology, or innovative emission control device or system, in such class or category of vehicles or engines and that such technology or system was not utilized by more than 1 percent of the light-duty vehicles sold in the United States in the 1975 model year. Such waiver may be granted only if the Administrator determines—

(i) that such waiver would not endanger public health,

(ii) that there is a substantial likelihood that the vehicles or engines will be able to comply with the applicable standard under this section at the expiration of the waiver, and

(iii) that the technology or system has a potential for long-term air quality benefit and has the potential to meet or exceed the average fuel economy standard applicable under the Energy Policy and Conservation Act [42 U.S.C. 6201 et seq.] upon the expiration of the waiver.

No waiver under this subparagraph granted to any manufacturer shall apply to more than 5 percent of such manufacturer's production or more than fifty thousand vehicles or engines, whichever is greater.

(B) Upon the petition of any manufacturer, the Administrator, after notice and opportunity for public hearing, may waive the standard required under subparagraph (B) of paragraph (1) to not to exceed 1.5 grams of oxides of nitrogen per vehicle mile for any class or category of light-duty vehicles and engines manufactured by such manufacturer during the four model year period beginning with the model year 1981 if the manufacturer can show that such waiver is necessary to permit the use of diesel engine technology in such class or category of vehicles or engines. Such waiver may be granted if the Administrator determines—

(i) that such waiver will not endanger public health,

(ii) that such waiver will result in significant fuel savings at least equal to the fuel economy standard applicable in each year under the Energy Policy and Conservation Act [42 U.S.C. 6201 et seq.], and

(iii) that the technology has a potential for long-term air quality benefit and has the potential to meet or exceed the average fuel economy standard applicable under the Energy Policy and Conservation Act [42 U.S.C. 6201 et seq.] at the expiration of the waiver.

(7) The Congress hereby declares and establishes as a research objective, the development of propulsion systems and emission control technology to achieve standards which represent a reduction of at least 90 per centum from the average emissions of oxides of nitrogen actually measured from light duty motor vehicles manufactured in model year 1971 not subject to any Federal or State emission standard for oxides of nitrogen. The Administrator shall, by regulations promulgated within one hundred and eighty days after August 7, 1977, require each manufacturer whose sales represent at least 0.5 per centum of light duty motor vehicle sales in the United States, to build and, on a regular basis, demonstrate the operation of light duty motor vehicles that meet this research objective, in addition to any other applicable standards or requirements for other pollutants under this chapter. Such demonstration vehicles shall be submitted to the Administrator no later than model year 1979 and in each model year thereafter. Such demonstration shall, in accordance with applicable regulations, to the greatest extent possible, (A) be designed to encourage the development of new powerplant and emission control technologies that are fuel efficient, (B) assure that the demonstration vehicles are or could reasonably be expected to be within the productive capability of the manufacturers, and (C) assure the utilization of optimum engine, fuel, and emission control systems.

(c) Feasibility study and investigation by National Academy of Sciences; reports to Administrator and Congress; availability of information

(1) The Administrator shall undertake to enter into appropriate arrangements with the National Academy of Sciences to conduct a comprehensive study and investigation of the technological feasibility of meeting the emissions standards required to be prescribed by the Administrator by subsection (b) of this section.

(2) Of the funds authorized to be appropriated to the Administrator by this chapter, such amounts as are required shall be available to carry out the study and investigation authorized by paragraph (1) of this subsection.

(3) In entering into any arrangement with the National Academy of Sciences for conducting the study and investigation authorized by paragraph (1) of this subsection, the Administrator shall request the National Academy of Sciences to submit semiannual reports on the progress of its study and investigation to the Administrator and the Congress, beginning not later than July 1, 1971, and continuing until such study and investigation is completed.

(4) The Administrator shall furnish to such Academy at its request any information which the Academy deems necessary for the purpose of conducting the investigation and study authorized by paragraph (1) of this subsection. For the purpose of furnishing such information, the Administrator may use any authority he has under this chapter (A) to obtain information from any person, and (B) to require such person to conduct such tests, keep such records, and make such reports respecting research or other activities conducted by such person as may be reasonably necessary to carry out this subsection.

(d) Useful life of vehicles

The Administrator shall prescribe regulations under which the useful life of vehicles and engines shall be determined for purposes of subsection (a)(1) of this section and section 7541 of this title. Such regulations shall provide that useful life shall—

(1) in the case of light duty vehicles and light duty vehicle engines, be a period of use of five years or of fifty thousand miles (or the equivalent), whichever first occurs;

(2) in the case of any other motor vehicle or motor vehicle engine (other than motorcycles or motorcycle engines), be a period of use set forth in paragraph (1) unless the Administrator determines that a period of use of greater duration or mileage is appropriate; and

(3) in the case of any motorcycle or motorcycle engine, be a period of use the Administrator shall determine.

(e) New power sources or propulsion systems

In the event a new power source or propulsion system for new motor vehicles or new motor vehicle engines is submitted for certification pursuant to section 7525(a) of this title, the Administrator may postpone certification until he has prescribed standards for any air pollutants emitted by such vehicle or engine which in his judgment cause, or contribute to, air pollution which may reasonably be anticipated to endanger the public health or welfare but for which standards have not been prescribed under subsection (a) of this section.

(f) High altitude regulations

(1) The high altitude regulation in effect with respect to model year 1977 motor vehicles shall not apply to the manufacture, distribution, or sale of 1978 and later model year motor vehicles. Any future regulation affecting the sale or distribution of motor vehicles or engines manufactured before the model year 1984 in high altitude areas of the country shall take effect no earlier than model year 1981.

(2) Any such future regulation applicable to high altitude vehicles or engines shall not require a percentage of reduction in the emissions of such vehicles which is greater than the required percentage of reduction in emissions from motor vehicles as set forth in subsection (b) of this section. This percentage reduction shall be determined by comparing any proposed high altitude emission standards to high altitude emissions from vehicles manufactured during model year 1970. In no event shall regulations applicable to high altitude vehicles manufactured before the model year 1984 establish a numerical standard which is more stringent than that applicable to vehicles certified under non-high altitude conditions.

(3) Section 7607(d) of this title shall apply to any high altitude regulation referred to in paragraph (2) and before promulgating any such regulation, the Administrator shall consider and make a finding with respect to—

(A) the economic impact upon consumers, individual high altitude dealers, and the automobile industry of any such regulation, including the economic impact which was experienced as a result of the regulation imposed during model year 1977 with respect to high altitude certification requirements;

(B) the present and future availability of emission control technology capable of meeting the applicable vehicle and engine emission requirements without reducing model availability; and

(C) the likelihood that the adoption of such a high altitude regulation will result in any significant improvement in air quality in any area to which it shall apply.

(July 14, 1955, ch. 360, title II, § 202, as added Oct. 20, 1965, Pub.L. 89–272, title I, § 101(8), 79 Stat. 992, and amended Nov. 21, 1967, Pub.L. 90–148, § 2, 81 Stat. 499; Dec. 31, 1970, Pub.L. 91–604, § 6(a), 84 Stat. 1690; June 22, 1974, Pub.L. 93–319, § 5, 88 Stat. 258; Aug. 7, 1977, Pub.L. 95–95, title II, §§ 201, 202(b), 213(b), 214(a), 215–217, 224(a), (b), (g), title IV, § 401(d), 91 Stat. 751–753, 758–761, 765, 767, 769, 791; Nov. 16, 1977, Pub.L. 95–190, § 14(a)(60)–(65), (b)(5), 91 Stat. 1403, 1405.)

1 So in original. Probably should be a comma.

Cross References

Emissions standards under this section as category of federal standards for purposes of average fuel economy standards, see section 2002 of Title 15, Commerce and Trade.

Low-emission motor vehicle defined for purposes of exemption from safety standards, see section 1410 of Title 15.

Code of Federal Regulations

Air pollution from motor vehicles, control of, see 40 CFR 85.401 et seq.

Control of air pollution from new motor vehicles, certification and test procedures, see 40 CFR 86.078–3 et seq.

Library References

Health and Environment ⚷25.6(6).
C.J.S. Health and Environment § 91 et seq.

§ 7522. Prohibited acts

(a) Enumerated prohibitions

The following acts and the causing thereof are prohibited—

(1) in the case of a manufacturer of new motor vehicles or new motor vehicle engines for distribution in commerce, the sale, or the offering for sale, or the introduction, or delivery for introduction, into commerce, or (in the case of any person, except as provided by regulation of the Administrator), the importation into the United States, of any new motor vehicle or new motor vehicle engine, manufactured after the effective date of regulations under this part which are applicable to such vehicle or engine unless such vehicle or engine is covered by a certificate of conformity issued (and in effect) under regulations prescribed under this part (except as provided in subsection (b) of this section);

(2) for any person to fail or refuse to permit access to or copying of records or to fail to make reports or provide information, required under section 7542 of this title or for any person to fail or refuse to permit entry, testing, or inspection authorized under section 7525(c) of this title;

(3)(A) for any person to remove or render inoperative any device or element of design installed on or in a motor vehicle or motor vehicle engine in compliance with regulations under this subchapter prior to its sale and delivery to the ultimate purchaser, or for any manufacturer or dealer knowingly to remove or render inoperative any such device or element of design after such sale and delivery to the ultimate purchaser; or

(B) for any person engaged in the business of repairing, servicing, selling, leasing, or trading motor vehicles or motor vehicle engines, or who operates a fleet of motor vehicles, knowingly to remove or render inoperative any device or element of design installed on or in a motor vehicle or motor vehicle engine in compliance with regulations under this subchapter following its sale and delivery to the ultimate purchaser; or

(4) for any manufacturer of a new motor vehicle or new motor vehicle engine subject to standards prescribed under section 7521 of this title—

(A) to sell or lease any such vehicle or engine unless such manufacturer has complied with the requirements of section 7541(a) and (b) of this title with respect to such vehicle or engine, and unless a label or tag is affixed to such vehicle or engine in accordance with section 7541(c)(3) of this title,

(B) to fail or refuse to comply with the requirements of section 7541(c) or (e) of this title,

(C) except as provided in subsection (c)(3) of section 7541 of this title, to provide directly or indirectly in any communication to the ultimate purchaser or any subsequent purchaser that the coverage of any warranty under this chapter is conditioned upon use of any part, component, or system manufactured by such manufacturer or any person acting for such manufacturer or under his control, or conditioned upon service performed by any such person, or

(D) to fail or refuse to comply with the terms and conditions of the warranty under section 7541(a) or (b) of this title with respect to any vehicle.

No action with respect to any element of design referred to in paragraph (3) (including any adjustment or alteration of such element) shall be treated as a prohibited Act[1] under such paragraph (3) if such action is in accordance with section 7549 of this title. Nothing in paragraph (3) shall be construed to require the use of manufacturer parts in maintaining or repairing any motor vehicle or motor vehicle engine. For the purposes of the preceding sentence, the term "manufacturer parts" means, with respect to a motor vehicle engine, parts produced or sold by the manufacturer of the motor vehicle or motor vehicle engine.

(b) Exemptions; refusal to admit vehicle or engine into United States; vehicles or engines intended for export

(1) The Administrator may exempt any new motor vehicle or new motor vehicle engine, from subsection (a) of this section, upon such terms and conditions as he may find necessary for the purpose of research, investigations, studies, demonstrations, or training, or for reasons of national security.

(2) A new motor vehicle or new motor vehicle engine offered for importation or imported by any person in violation of subsection (a) of this section shall be refused admission into the United States, but the Secretary of the Treasury and the Administrator may, by joint regulation, provide for deferring final determination as to admission and authorizing the delivery of such a motor vehicle or engine offered for import to the owner or consignee thereof upon such terms and conditions (including the furnishing of a bond) as may appear to them appropriate to insure that any such motor vehicle or engine will be brought into conformity with the standards, requirements, and limitations applicable to it under this part. The Secretary of the Treasury shall, if a motor vehicle or engine is finally refused admission under this paragraph, cause disposition thereof in accordance with the customs laws unless it is exported, under regulations prescribed by such Secretary, within ninety days of the date of notice of such refusal or such additional time as may be permitted pursuant to such regulations, except that disposition in accordance with the customs laws may not be made in such manner as may result, directly or indirectly, in the sale, to the ultimate consumer, of a new motor vehicle or new motor vehicle engine that fails to comply with applicable standards of the Administrator under this part.

(3) A new motor vehicle or new motor vehicle engine intended solely for export, and so labeled or tagged on the outside of the container and on the vehicle or engine itself, shall be subject to the provisions of subsection (a) of this section, except that if the country which is to receive such vehicle or engine has emission standards which differ from the standards prescribed under section 7521 of this title, then such vehicle or engine shall comply with the standards of such country which is to receive such vehicle or engine.

(c) Exemption to permit modification of emission control device or system

Upon application therefor, the Administrator may exempt from subsection (a)(3) of this section any vehicles (or class thereof) manufactured before the 1974 model year from subsection (a)(3) of this section[2] for the purpose of permitting modifications to the emission control device or system of such vehicle in order to use fuels other than those specified in certification testing under section 7525(a)(1) of this title, if the Administrator, on the basis of information submitted by the applicant, finds that such modification will not result in such vehicle or engine not complying with standards under section 7521 of this title applicable to such vehicle or engine. Any such exemption shall identify (1) the vehicle or vehicles so exempted, (2) the specific nature of the modification, and (3) the person or class of persons to whom the exemption shall apply.

(July 14, 1955, ch. 360, title II, § 203, as added Oct. 20, 1965, Pub.L. 89–272, title I, § 101(8), 79 Stat. 993, and amended Nov. 21, 1967, Pub.L. 90–148, § 2, 81 Stat. 499; Dec. 31, 1970, Pub.L. 91–604, §§ 7(a), 11(a)(2)(A), 15(c)(2), 84 Stat. 1693, 1705, 1713; Aug. 7, 1977, Pub.L. 95–95, title II, §§ 206, 211(a), 218(a), (d), 219(a), (b), 91 Stat. 755, 757, 761, 762; Nov. 16, 1977, Pub.L. 95–190, § 14(a)(66)–(68), 91 Stat. 1403.)

[1] So in original. Probably should be "act".
[2] So in original.

Code of Federal Regulations

Air pollution from motor vehicles, control of, see 40 CFR 85.401 et seq.

Library References

Health and Environment ⇔25.6(6), 37, 38.
C.J.S. Health and Environment, §§ 48 et seq., 91 et seq.

§ 7523. Actions to restrain violations

(a) Jurisdiction

The district courts of the United States shall have jurisdiction to restrain violations of section 7522(a) of this title.

(b) Actions brought by or in name of United States; subpenas

Actions to restrain such violations shall be brought by and in the name of the United States. In any such action, subpenas for witnesses who are required to attend a district court in any district may run into any other district.

(July 14, 1955, ch. 360, title II, § 204, as added Oct. 20, 1965, Pub.L. 89–272, title I, § 101(8), 79 Stat. 994, and amended Nov. 21, 1967, Pub.L. 90–148, § 2, 81 Stat. 500; Dec. 31, 1970, Pub.L. 91–604, § 7(b), 84 Stat. 1694; Aug. 7, 1977, Pub.L. 95–95, title II, § 218(b), 91 Stat. 761.)

Library References

Federal Courts ⇔192.
C.J.S. Federal Courts § 30 et seq.

§ 7524. Penalties

Any person who violates paragraph (1), (2), or (4) of section 7522(a) of this title or any manufacturer, dealer, or other person who violates paragraph (3)(A) of section 7522(a) of this title shall be subject to a civil penalty of not more than $10,000. Any person who violates paragraph (3)(B) of such section 7522(a) shall be subject to a civil penalty of not more than $2,500. Any such violation with respect to paragraph (1), (3), or (4) of section 7522(a) of this title shall constitute a separate offense with respect to each motor vehicle or motor vehicle engine.

(July 14, 1955, ch. 360, title I, § 205, as added Oct. 20, 1965, Pub.L. 89–272, title I, § 101(8), 79 Stat. 994, and amended Nov. 21, 1967, Pub.L. 90–148, § 2, 81 Stat. 500; Dec. 31, 1970, Pub.L. 91–604, § 7(c), 84 Stat. 1694; Aug. 7, 1977, Pub.L. 95–95, title II, § 219(c), 91 Stat. 762.)

Code of Federal Regulations

Control of air pollution from new motor vehicles, certification and test procedures, see 40 CFR 86.078–3 et seq.

Library References

Health and Environment ⇔38.
C.J.S. Health and Environment § 49 et seq.

§ 7525. Motor vehicle and motor vehicle engine compliance testing and certification

(a) Testing and issuance of certificate of conformity

(1) The Administrator shall test, or require to be tested in such manner as he deems appropriate, any new motor vehicle or new motor vehicle engine submitted by a manufacturer to determine whether such vehicle or engine conforms with the regulations prescribed under section 7521 of this title. If such vehicle or engine conforms to such regulations, the Administrator shall issue a certificate of conformity upon such terms, and for such period (not in excess of one year), as he may prescribe. In the case of any manufacturer of vehicles or vehicle engines whose projected sales in the United States for any model year (as determined by the Administrator) will not exceed three hundred, the regulations prescribed by the Administrator concerning testing by the manufacturer for purposes of determining compliance with regulations under section 7521 of this title for the useful life of the vehicle or engine shall not require operation of any vehicle or engine manufactured during such model year for more than five thousand miles or one hundred and sixty hours, respectively, but the Administrator shall apply such adjustment factors as he deems appropriate to assure that each such vehicle or engine will comply during its useful life (as determined under section 7521(d) of this title) with the regulations prescribed under section 7521 of this title.

(2) The Administrator shall test any emission control system incorporated in a motor vehicle or motor vehicle engine submitted to him by any person, in order to determine whether such system enables such vehicle or engine to conform to the standards required to be prescribed under section 7521(b) of this title. If the Administrator finds on the basis of such tests that such vehicle or engine conforms to such standards, the Administrator shall issue a verification of compliance with emission standards for such system when incorporated in vehicles of a class of which the tested vehicle is representative. He shall inform manufacturers and the National Academy of Sciences, and make available to the public, the results of such tests. Tests under this paragraph shall be conducted under such terms and conditions (including requirements for preliminary testing by qualified independent laboratories) as the Administrator may prescribe by regulations.

(3)(A) A certificate of conformity may be issued under this section only if the Administrator determines that the manufacturer (or in the case of a vehicle or engine for import, any person) has established to the satisfaction of the Administrator that any emission control device, system, or element of design installed on, or incorporated in, such vehicle or engine conforms to applicable requirements of section 7521(a)(4) of this title.

(B) The Administrator may conduct such tests and may require the manufacturer (or any such person) to conduct such tests and provide such information as is necessary to carry out subparagraph (A) of this paragraph. Such requirements shall include a requirement for prompt reporting of the emission of any unregulated pollutant from a system, device, or element of design if such pollutant was not emitted, or was emitted in significantly lesser amounts, from the vehicle or engine without use of the system, device, or element of design.

(b) Testing procedures; hearing; judicial review; additional evidence

(1) In order to determine whether new motor vehicles or new motor vehicle engines being manufactured by a manufacturer do in fact conform with the regulations with respect to which the certificate of conformity was issued, the Administrator is authorized to test such vehicles or engines. Such tests may be conducted by the Administrator directly or, in accordance with conditions specified by the Administrator, by the manufacturer.

(2)(A)(i) If, based on tests conducted under paragraph (1) on a sample of new vehicles or engines covered by a certificate of conformity, the Administrator determines that all or part of the vehicles or engines so covered do not conform with the regulations with respect to which the certificate of conformity was issued and with the requirements of section 7521(a)(4) of this title, he may suspend or revoke such certificate in whole or in part, and shall so notify the manufacturer. Such suspension or revocation shall apply in the case of any new motor vehicles or new motor vehicle engines manufactured after the date of such notification (or manufactured before such date if still in the hands of the manufacturer), and shall apply until such time as the Administrator finds that vehicles and engines manufactured by the manufacturer do conform to such regulations and requirements. If, during any period of suspension or revocation, the Administrator finds that a vehicle or engine actually conforms to such regulations and requirements, he shall issue a certificate of conformity applicable to such vehicle or engine.

(ii) If, based on tests conducted under paragraph (1) on any new vehicle or engine, the Administrator determines that such vehicle or engine does not conform with such regulations and requirements, he may suspend or revoke such certificate insofar as it applies to such vehicle or engine until such time as he finds such vehicle or engine actually so conforms with such regulations and requirements, and he shall so notify the manufacturer.

(B)(i) At the request of any manufacturer the Administrator shall grant such manufacturer a hearing as to whether the tests have been properly conducted or any sampling methods have been properly applied, and make a determination on the record with respect to any suspension or revocation under subparagraph (A); but suspension or revocation under subparagraph (A) shall not be stayed by reason of such hearing.

(ii) In any case of actual controversy as to the validity of any determination under clause (i), the manufacturer may at any time prior to the 60th day after such determination is made file a petition with the United States court of appeals for the circuit wherein such manufacturer resides or has his principal place of business for a judicial review of such determination. A copy of the petition shall be forthwith transmitted by the clerk of the court to the Administrator or other officer designated by him for that purpose. The Administrator thereupon shall file in the court the record of the proceedings on which the Administrator based his determination, as provided in section 2112 of title 28.

(iii) If the petitioner applies to the court for leave to adduce additional evidence, and shows to the satisfaction of the court that such additional evidence is material and that there were reasonable grounds for the failure to adduce such evidence in the proceeding before the Administrator, the court may order such additional evidence (and evidence in rebuttal thereof) to be taken before the Administrator, in such manner and upon such terms and conditions as the court may deem proper. The Administrator may modify his findings as to the facts, or make new findings, by reason of the additional evidence so taken and he shall file such modified or new findings, and his recommendation, if any, for the modification or setting aside of his original determination, with the return of such additional evidence.

(iv) Upon the filing of the petition referred to in clause (ii), the court shall have jurisdiction to review the order in accordance with chapter 7 of title 5 and to grant appropriate relief as provided in such chapter.

(c) Inspection

For purposes of enforcement of this section, officers or employees duly designated by the Administrator, upon presenting appropriate credentials to the manufacturer or person in charge, are authorized (1) to enter, at reasonable times, any plant or other establishment of such manufacturer, for the purpose of conducting tests of vehicles or engines in the hands of the manufacturer, or (2) to inspect, at reasonable times, records, files, papers, processes, controls, and facilities used by such manufacturer in conducting tests under regulations of the Administrator. Each such inspection shall be commenced and completed with reasonable promptness.

(d) Rules and regulations

The Administrator shall by regulation establish methods and procedures for making tests under this section.

(e) Publication of test results

The Administrator shall announce in the Federal Register and make available to the public the results of his tests of any motor vehicle or motor vehicle engine submitted by a manufacturer under subsection (a) of this section as promptly as possible after December 31, 1970, and at the beginning of each model year which begins thereafter. Such results shall be described in such nontechnical manner as will reasonably disclose to prospective ultimate purchasers of new motor vehicles and new motor vehicle engines the comparative performance of the vehicles and engines tested in meeting the standards prescribed under section 7521 of this title.

(f) High altitude regulations

(1) All light duty vehicles and engines manufactured during or after model year 1984 shall comply with the requirements of section 7521 of this title regardless of the altitude at which they are sold.

(2) By October 1, 1978, the Administrator shall report to the Congress on the economic impact and technological feasibility of the requirements found in subparagraph (1) of this subsection. The report is also to evaluate the technological feasibility and the health consequences of separate proportional emission standards for light duty vehicles and engines in high altitude areas that would reflect a comparable percentage of reduction in emissions to that achieved by light duty vehicles and engines in low altitude areas.

(g) Nonconformance penalty

(1) In the case of any class or category of heavy-duty vehicles or engines to which a standard promulgated under section 7521(a) of this title applies, except as provided in paragraph (2), a certificate of conformity shall be issued under subsection (a) of this section and shall not be suspended or revoked under subsection (b) of this section for such vehicles or engines manufactured by a manufacturer notwithstanding the failure of such vehicles or engines to meet such standard if such manufacturer pays a nonconformance penalty as provided under regulations promulgated by the Administrator after notice and opportunity for public hearing. In the case of motorcycles to which such a standard applies, such a certificate may be issued notwithstanding such failure if the manufacturer pays such a penalty.

(2) No certificate of conformity may be issued under paragraph (1) with respect to any class or category of vehicle or engine if the degree by which the manufacturer fails to meet any standard promulgated under section 7521(a) of this title with respect to such class or category exceeds the percentage determined under regulations promulgated by the Administrator to be practicable. Such regulations shall require such testing of vehicles or engines being produced as may be necessary to determine the percentage of the classes or categories of vehicles or engines which are not in compliance with the regulations with respect to which a certificate of conformity was issued and shall be promulgated not later than one year after August 7, 1977.

(3) The regulations promulgated under paragraph (1) shall, not later than one year after August 7, 1977, provide for nonconformance penalties in amounts determined under a formula established by the Administrator. Such penalties under such formula—

(A) may vary from pollutant-to-pollutant;

(B) may vary by class or category or vehicle or engine;

(C) shall take into account the extent to which actual emissions of any air pollutant exceed allowable emissions under the standards promulgated under section 7521 of this title;

(D) shall be increased periodically in order to create incentives for the development of production vehicles or engines which achieve the required degree of emission reduction; and

(E) shall remove any competitive disadvantage to manufacturers whose engines or vehicles achieve the required degree of emission reduction (including any such disadvantage arising from the application of paragraph (4)).

(4) In any case in which a certificate of conformity has been issued under this subsection, any warranty required under section 7541(b)(2) of this title and any action under section 7541(c) of this title shall be required to be effective only for the emission levels which the Administrator determines that such certificate was issued and not for the emission levels required under the applicable standard.

(5) The authorities of section 7542(a) of this title shall apply, subject to the conditions of section 7542(b) of this title, for purposes of this subsection.

(July 14, 1955, ch. 360, title II, § 206, as added Dec. 31, 1970, Pub.L. 91–604, § 8(a), 84 Stat. 1694, and amended Aug. 7, 1977, Pub.L. 95–95, title II, §§ 213(a), 214(b), (c), 220, 224(e), 91 Stat. 758–760, 762, 768; Nov. 16, 1977, Pub.L. 95–190, § 14(a)(69), 91 Stat. 1403.)

Cross References

Determination of fuel economy for purposes of gas guzzler tax, see section 4064 of Title 26, Internal Revenue Code.

Fuel economy defined for purposes of Automobile Propulsion Research and Development Act of 1978, see section 2702 of Title 15, Commerce and Trade.

Testing and calculation procedures for measurement of average fuel economy, see section 2003 of Title 15.

Code of Federal Regulations

Control of air pollution from new motor vehicles, certification and test procedures, see 40 CFR 86.078–3 et seq.

Library References

Health and Environment ⚷25.6(6).
C.J.S. Health and Environment § 91 et seq.

§ 7541. Compliance by vehicles and engines in actual use

(a) Warranty; certification; payment of replacement costs of parts, devices, or components designed for emission control

(1) Effective with respect to vehicles and engines manufactured in model years beginning more than 60 days after December 31, 1970, the manufacturer of each new motor vehicle and new motor vehicle engine shall warrant to the ultimate purchaser and each subsequent purchaser that such vehicle or engine is (A) designed, built, and equipped so as to conform at the time of sale with applicable regulations under section 7521 of this title, and (B) free from defects in materials and workmanship which cause such vehicle or engine to fail to conform with applicable regulations for its useful life (as determined under section 7521(d) of this title).

(2) In the case of a motor vehicle part or motor vehicle engine part, the manufacturer or rebuilder of such part may certify that use of such part will not result in a failure of the vehicle or engine to comply with emission standards promulgated under section 7521 of this title. Such certification shall be made only under such regulations as may be promulgated by the Administrator to carry out the purposes of subsection (b) of this section. The Administrator shall promulgate such regulations no later than two years following August 7, 1977.

(3) The cost of any part, device, or component of any light-duty vehicle that is designed for emission control and which in the instructions issued pursuant to subsection (c)(3) of this section is scheduled for replacement during the useful life of the vehicle in order to maintain compliance with regulations under section 7521 of this title, the failure of which shall not interfere with the normal performance of the vehicle, and the expected retail price of which, including installation costs, is greater than 2 percent of the suggested retail price of such vehicle, shall be borne or reimbursed at the time of replacement by the vehicle manufacturer and such replacement shall be provided without cost to the ultimate purchaser, subsequent purchaser, or dealer. The term "designed for emission control" as used in the preceding sentence means a catalytic converter, thermal reactor, or other component installed on or in a vehicle for the sole or primary purpose of reducing vehicle emissions (not including those vehicle components which were in general use prior to model year 1968 and the primary function of which is not related to emission control).

(b) Testing methods and procedures

If the Administrator determines that (i) there are available testing methods and procedures to ascertain whether, when in actual use throughout its useful life (as determined under section 7521(d) of this title), each vehicle and engine to which regulations under section 7521 of this title apply complies with the emission standards of such regulations, (ii) such methods and procedures are in accordance with good engineering practices, and (iii) such methods and procedures are reasonably capable of being correlated with tests conducted under section 7525(a)(1) of this title, then—

(1) he shall establish such methods and procedures by regulation, and

(2) at such time as he determines that inspection facilities or equipment are available for purposes of carrying out testing methods and procedures established under paragraph (1), he shall prescribe regulations which shall require manufacturers to warrant the emission control device or system of each new motor vehicle or new motor vehicle engine to which a regulation under section 7521 of this title applies and which is manufactured in a model year beginning after the Administrator first prescribes warranty regulations under this paragraph (2). The warranty under such regulations shall run to the ultimate purchaser and each subsequent purchaser and shall provide that if—

(A) the vehicle or engine is maintained and operated in accordance with instructions under subsection (c)(3) of this section,

(B) it fails to conform at any time during its useful life (as determined under section 7521(d) of this title) to the regulations prescribed under section 7521 of this title, and

(C) such nonconformity results in the ultimate purchaser (or any subsequent purchaser) of such vehicle or engine having to bear any penalty or other sanction (including the denial of the right to use such vehicle or engine) under State or Federal law, then such manufacturer shall remedy such nonconformity under such warranty with the cost thereof to be borne by the manufacturer. No such warranty shall be invalid on the basis of any part used in the maintenance or repair of a vehicle or engine if such part was certified as provided under subsection (a)(2) of this section.

For purposes of the warranty under this subsection, for the period after twenty-four months or twenty-four thousand miles (whichever first occurs) the term "emission control device or system" means a catalytic converter, thermal reactor, or other component installed on or in a vehicle for the sole or primary purpose of reducing vehicle emissions. Such term shall not include those vehicle components which were in general use prior to model year 1968.

(c) Nonconforming vehicles; plan for remedying nonconformity; instructions for maintenance and use; label or tag

Effective with respect to vehicles and engines manufactured during model years beginning more than 60 days after December 31, 1970—

(1) If the Administrator determines that a substantial number of any class or category of vehicles or engines, although properly maintained and used, do not conform to the regulations prescribed under section 7521 of this title, when in actual use throughout their useful life (as determined under section 7521(d) of this title), he shall immediately notify the manufacturer thereof of such nonconformity, and he shall require the manufacturer to submit a plan for remedying the nonconformity of the vehicles or engines with respect to which such notification is given. The plan shall provide that the nonconformity of any such vehicles or engines which are properly used and maintained will be remedied at the expense of the manufacturer. If the manufacturer disagrees with such determination of nonconformity and so advises the Administrator, the Administrator shall afford the manufacturer and other interested persons an opportunity to present their views and evidence in support thereof at a public hearing. Unless, as a result of such hearing the Administrator withdraws such determination of nonconformity, he shall, within 60 days after the completion of such hearing, order the manufacturer to provide prompt notification of such nonconformity in accordance with paragraph (2).

(2) Any notification required by paragraph (1) with respect to any class or category of vehicles or engines shall be given to dealers, ultimate purchasers, and subsequent purchasers (if known) in such manner and containing such information as the Administrator may by regulations require.

(3)(A) The manufacturer shall furnish with each new motor vehicle or motor vehicle engine written instructions for the proper maintenance and use of the vehicle or engine by the ultimate purchaser and such instructions shall correspond to regulations which the Administrator shall promulgate. The manufacturer shall provide in boldface type on the first page of the written maintenance instructions notice that maintenance, replacement, or repair of the emission control devices and systems may be performed by any automotive repair establishment or individual using any automotive part which has been certified as provided in subsection (a)(2) of this section.

(B) The instruction under subparagraph (A) of this paragraph shall not include any condition on the ultimate purchaser's using, in connection with such vehicle or engine, any component or service (other than a component or service provided without charge under the terms of the purchase agreement) which is identified by brand, trade, or corporate name; or directly or indirectly distinguishing between service performed by the franchised dealers of such manufacturer or any other service establishments with which such manufacturer has a commercial relationship, and service performed by independent automotive repair facilities with which such manufacturer has no commercial relationship; except that the prohibition of this subsection may be waived by the Administrator if—

(i) the manufacturer satisfies the Administrator that the vehicle or engine will function properly only if the component or service so identified is used in connection with such vehicle or engine, and

(ii) the Administrator finds that such a waiver is in the public interest.

(C) In addition, the manufacturer shall indicate by means of a label or tag permanently affixed to such vehicle or engine that such vehicle or engine is covered by a certificate of conformity issued for the purpose of assuring achievement of emissions standards prescribed under section 7521 of this title. Such label or tag shall contain such other information relating to control of motor vehicle emissions as the Administrator shall prescribe by regulation.

(d) Dealer costs borne by manufacturer

Any cost obligation of any dealer incurred as a result of any requirement imposed by subsection (a), (b), or (c) of this section shall be borne by the manufacturer. The transfer of any such cost obligation from a manufacturer to any dealer through franchise or other agreement is prohibited.

(e) Cost statement

If a manufacturer includes in any advertisement a statement respecting the cost or value of emission control devices or systems, such manufacturer shall set forth in such statement the cost or value attributed to such devices or systems by the Secretary of Labor (through the Bureau of Labor Statistics). The Secretary of Labor, and his representatives, shall have the same access for this purpose to the books, documents, papers, and records of a manufacturer as the Comptroller General has to those of a recipient of assistance for purposes of section 7611 of this title.

(f) Inspection after sale to ultimate purchaser

Any inspection of a motor vehicle or a motor vehicle engine for purposes of subsection (c)(1) of this section, after its sale to the ultimate purchaser, shall be made only if the owner of such vehicle or engine voluntarily permits such inspection to be made, except as may be provided by any State or local inspection program.

(g) Replacement and maintenance costs borne by owner

For the purposes of this section, the owner of any motor vehicle or motor vehicle engine warranted under this section is responsible in the proper maintenance of such vehicle or engine to replace and to maintain, at his expense at any service establishment or facility of his choosing, such items as spark plugs, points, condensers, and any other part, item, or device related to emission control (but not designed for emission control under the terms of the last three sentences of subsection (a)(1)[1] of this section), unless such part, item, or device is covered by any warranty not mandated by this chapter.

(h) Dealer certification

(1) Upon the sale of each new light-duty motor vehicle by a dealer, the dealer shall furnish to the purchaser a certificate that such motor vehicle conforms to the applicable regulations under section 7521 of this title, including notice of the purchaser's rights under paragraph (2).

(2) If at any time during the period for which the warranty applies under subsection (b) of this section, a motor vehicle fails to conform to the applicable regulations under section 7521 of this title as determined under subsection (b) of this section such nonconformity shall be remedied by the manufacturer at the cost of the manufacturer pursuant to such warranty as provided in subsection (b)(2) of this section (without regard to subparagraph (C) thereof).

(3) Nothing in section 7543(a) of this title shall be construed to prohibit a State from testing, or requiring testing of, a motor vehicle after the date of sale of such vehicle to the ultimate purchaser (except that no new motor vehicle manufacturer or dealer may be required to conduct testing under this paragraph).

(July 14, 1955, ch. 360, title II, § 207, as added Dec. 31, 1970, Pub.L. 91–604, § 8(a), 84 Stat. 1696, and amended Aug. 7, 1977, Pub.L. 95–95, title II, §§ 205, 208–210, 212, 91 Stat. 754–756, 758; Nov. 16, 1977, Pub.L. 95–190, § 14(a)(70)–(72), 91 Stat. 1403.)

[1] So in original. Probably should be "(a)(3)".

Code of Federal Regulations

Air pollution from motor vehicles, control of, see 40 CFR 85.401 et seq.
Control of air pollution from new motor vehicles, certification and test procedures, see 40 CFR 86.078–3 et seq.

Library References

Health and Environment ⇐25.6(6).
C.J.S. Health and Environment § 91 et seq.

§ 7542. Records and reports

(a) Manufacturer's responsibility

Every manufacturer shall establish and maintain such records, make such reports, and provide such information, as the Administrator may reasonably require to enable him to determine whether such manufacturer has acted or is acting in compliance with this part and regulations thereunder and shall, upon request of an officer or employee duly designated by the Administrator, permit such officer or employee at reasonable times, to have access to and copy such records.

(b) Availability to public; trade secrets

Any records, reports or information obtained under subsection (a) of this section shall be available to the public, except that upon a showing satisfactory to the Administrator by any person that records, reports, or information, or particular part thereof (other than emission data), to which the Administrator has access under this section if made public, would divulge methods or processes entitled to protection as trade secrets of such person, the Administrator shall consider such record, report, or information or particular portion thereof confidential in accordance with the purposes of section 1905 of title 18, except that such record, report, or information may be disclosed to other officers, employees, or authorized representatives of the United States concerned with carrying out this chapter or when relevant in any proceeding under this chapter. Nothing in this section shall authorize the withholding of information by the Administrator or any officer or employee under his control, from the duly authorized committees of the Congress.

(July 14, 1955, ch. 360, title II, § 208, formerly § 207, as added Oct. 20, 1965, Pub.L. 89–272, title I, § 101(8), 79 Stat. 994, amended Nov. 21, 1967, Pub.L. 90–148, § 2, 81 Stat. 501, renumbered and amended Dec. 31, 1970, Pub.L. 91–604, §§ 8(a), 10(a), 11(a)(2)(A), 15(c)(2), 84 Stat. 1694, 1700, 1705, 1713.)

Code of Federal Regulations

Air pollution from motor vehicles, control of, see 40 CFR 85.401 et seq.
Control of air pollution from new motor vehicles, certification and test procedures, see 40 CFR 86.078–3 et seq.
Public information, see 40 CFR 2.100 et seq.

Library References

Records ⚟30.
C.J.S. Records § 34 et seq.

§ 7543. State standards

(a) Prohibition

No State or any political subdivision thereof shall adopt or attempt to enforce any standard relating to the control of emissions from new motor vehicles or new motor vehicle engines subject to this part. No State shall require certification, inspection, or any other approval relating to the control of emissions from any new motor vehicle or new motor vehicle engine as condition precedent to the initial retail sale, titling (if any), or registration of such motor vehicle, motor vehicle engine, or equipment.

(b) Waiver

(1) The Administrator shall, after notice and opportunity for public hearing, waive application of this section to any State which has adopted standards (other than crankcase emission standards) for the control of emissions from new motor vehicles or new motor vehicle engines prior to March 30, 1966, if the State determines that the State standards will be, in the aggregate, at least as protective of public health and welfare as applicable Federal standards. No such waiver shall be granted if the Administrator finds that—

(A) the determination of the State is arbitrary and capricious,

(B) such State does not need such State standards to meet compelling and extraordinary conditions, or

(C) such State standards and accompanying enforcement procedures are not consistent with section 7521(a) of this title.

(2) If each State standard is at least as stringent as the comparable applicable Federal standard, such State standard shall be deemed to be at least as protective of health and welfare as such Federal standards for purposes of paragraph (1).

(3) In the case of any new motor vehicle or new motor vehicle engine to which State standards apply pursuant to a waiver granted under paragraph (1), compliance with such State standards shall be treated as compliance with applicable Federal standards for purposes of this subchapter.

(c) Certification of vehicle parts or engine parts

Whenever a regulation with respect to any motor vehicle part or motor vehicle engine part is in effect under section 7541(a)(2) of this title, no State or political subdivision thereof shall adopt or attempt to enforce any standard or any requirement of certification, inspection, or approval which relates to motor vehicle emissions and is applicable to the same aspect of such part. The preceding sentence shall not apply in the case of a State with respect to which a waiver is in effect under subsection (b) of this section.

(d) Control, regulation, or restrictions on registered or licensed motor vehicles

Nothing in this part shall preclude or deny to any State or political subdivision thereof the right otherwise to control, regulate, or restrict the use, operation, or movement of registered or licensed motor vehicles.

(July 14, 1955, ch. 360, title II, § 209, formerly § 208, as added Nov. 21, 1967, Pub.L. 90–148, § 2, 81 Stat. 501, renumbered and amended Dec. 31, 1970, Pub.L. 91–604, §§ 8(a), 11(a)(2)(A), 15(c)(2), 84 Stat. 1694, 1705, 1713; Aug. 7, 1977, Pub.L. 95–95, title II, §§ 207, 221, 91 Stat. 755, 762.)

Cross References

Emission standards applicable by reason of this section as category of federal standards for purposes of average fuel economy standards, see section 2002 of Title 15, Commerce and Trade.

Library References

Health and Environment ⚟25.6(2).
C.J.S. Health and Environment § 125 et seq.

§ 7544. State grants

The Administrator is authorized to make grants to appropriate State agencies in an amount up to two-thirds of the cost of developing and maintaining effective vehicle emission devices and systems inspection and emission testing and control programs, except that—

(1) no such grant shall be made for any part of any State vehicle inspection program which does not directly relate to the cost of the air pollution control aspects of such a program;

(2) no such grant shall be made unless the Secretary of Transportation has certified to the Administrator that such program is consistent with any highway safety program developed pursuant to section 402 of title 23; and

(3) no such grant shall be made unless the program includes provisions designed to insure that emission control devices and systems on vehicles in actual use have not been discontinued or rendered inoperative.

Grants may be made under this section by way of reimbursement in any case in which amounts have been expended by the State before the date on which any such grant was made.

(July 14, 1955, ch. 360, title II, § 210, formerly § 209, as added Nov. 21, 1967, Pub.L. 90–148, § 2, 81 Stat. 502, and renumbered and amended Dec. 31, 1970, Pub.L. 91–604, §§ 8(a), 10(b), 84 Stat. 1694, 1700; Aug. 7, 1977, Pub.L. 95–95, title II, § 204, 91 Stat. 754.)

Library References

United States ⚷82(2).
C.J.S. United States § 122.

§ 7545. Regulation of fuels

(a) Authority of Administrator to regulate

The Administrator may by regulation designate any fuel or fuel additive and, after such date or dates as may be prescribed by him, no manufacturer or processor of any such fuel or additive may sell, offer for sale, or introduce into commerce such fuel or additive unless the Administrator has registered such fuel or additive in accordance with subsection (b) of this section.

(b) Registration requirement

(1) For the purpose of registration of fuels and fuel additives, the Administrator shall require—

(A) the manufacturer of any fuel to notify him as to the commercial identifying name and manufacturer of any additive contained in such fuel; the range of concentration of any additive in the fuel; and the purpose-in-use of any such additive; and

(B) the manufacturer of any additive to notify him as to the chemical composition of such additive.

(2) For the purpose of registration of fuels and fuel additives, the Administrator may also require the manufacturer of any fuel or fuel additive—

(A) to conduct tests to determine potential public health effects of such fuel or additive (including, but not limited to, carcinogenic, teratogenic, or mutagenic effects), and

(B) to furnish the description of any analytical technique that can be used to detect and measure any additive in such fuel, the recommended range of concentration of such additive, and the recommended purpose-in-use of such additive, and such other information as is reasonable and necessary to determine the emissions resulting from the use of the fuel or additive contained in such fuel, the effect of such fuel or additive on the emission control performance of any vehicle or vehicle engine, or the extent to which such emissions affect the public health or welfare.

Tests under subparagraph (A) shall be conducted in conformity with test procedures and protocols established by the Administrator. The result of such tests shall not be considered confidential.

(3) Upon compliance with the provision of this subsection, including assurances that the Administrator will receive changes in the information required, the Administrator shall register such fuel or fuel additive.

(c) Offending fuels and fuel additives; control; prohibition

(1) The Administrator may, from time to time on the basis of information obtained under subsection (b) of this section or other information available to him, by regulation, control or prohibit the manufacture, introduction into commerce, offering for sale, or sale of any fuel or fuel additive for use in a motor vehicle or motor vehicle engine (A) if in the judgment of the Administrator any emission product of such fuel or fuel additive causes, or contributes, to air pollution which may reasonably be anticipated to endanger the public health or welfare, or (B) if emission products of such fuel or fuel additive will impair to a significant degree the performance of any emission control device or system which is in general use, or which the Administrator finds has been developed to a point where in a reasonable time it would be in general use were such regulation to be promulgated.

(2)(A) No fuel, class of fuels, or fuel additive may be controlled or prohibited by the Administrator pursuant to clause (A) of paragraph (1) except after consideration of all relevant medical and scientific evidence available to him, including consideration of other technologically or economically feasible means of achieving emission standards under section 7521 of this title.

(B) No fuel or fuel additive may be controlled or prohibited by the Administrator pursuant to clause (B) of paragraph (1) except after consideration of available scientific and economic data, including a cost benefit analysis comparing emission control devices or systems which are or will be in general use and require the proposed control or prohibition with emission control devices or systems which are or will be in general use and do not require the proposed control or prohibition. On request of a manufacturer of motor vehicles, motor vehicle engines, fuels, or fuel additives submitted within 10 days of notice of proposed rulemaking, the Administrator shall hold a public hearing and publish findings with respect to any matter he is required to consider under this subparagraph. Such findings shall be published at the time of promulgation of final regulations.

(C) No fuel or fuel additive may be prohibited by the Administrator under paragraph (1) unless he finds, and publishes such finding, that in his judgment such prohibition will not cause the use of any other fuel or fuel additive which will produce emissions which will endanger the public health or welfare to the same or greater degree than the use of the fuel or fuel additive proposed to be prohibited.

(3)(A) For the purpose of obtaining evidence and data to carry out paragraph (2), the Administrator may require the manufacturer of any motor vehicle or motor vehicle engine to furnish any information which has been developed concerning the emissions from motor vehicles resulting from the use of any fuel or fuel additive, or the effect of such use on the performance of any emission control device or system.

(B) In obtaining information under subparagraph (A), section 7607(a) of this title (relating to subpenas) shall be applicable.

(4)(A) Except as otherwise provided in subparagraph (B) or (C), no State (or political subdivision thereof) may prescribe or attempt to enforce, for purposes of motor vehicle emission control, any control or prohibition respecting use of a fuel or fuel additive in a motor vehicle or motor vehicle engine—

(i) if the Administrator has found that no control or prohibition under paragraph (1) is necessary and has published his finding in the Federal Register, or

(ii) if the Administrator has prescribed under paragraph (1) a control or prohibition applicable to such fuel or fuel additive, unless State prohibition or control is identical to the prohibition or control prescribed by the Administrator.

(B) Any State for which application of section 7543(a) of this title has at any time been waived under section 7543(b) of this title may at any time prescribe and enforce, for the purpose of motor vehicle emission control, a control or prohibition respecting any fuel or fuel additive.

(C) A State may prescribe and enforce, for purposes of motor vehicle emission control, a control or prohibition respecting the use of a fuel or fuel additive in a motor vehicle or motor vehicle engine if an applicable implementation plan for such State under section 7410 of this title so provides. The Administrator may approve such provision in an implementation plan, or promulgate an implementation plan containing such a provision, only if he finds that the State control or prohibition is necessary to achieve the national primary or secondary ambient air quality standard which the plan implements.

(d) Penalty

Any person who violates subsection (a) or (f) of this section or the regulations prescribed under subsection (c) of this section or who fails to furnish any information required by the Administrator under subsection (b) of this section shall forfeit and pay to the United States a civil penalty of $10,000 for each and every day of the continuance of such violation, which shall accrue to the United States and be recovered in a civil suit in the name of the United States, brought in the district where such person has his principal office or in any district in which he does business. The Administrator may, upon application therefor, remit or mitigate any forfeiture provided for in this subsection and he shall have authority to determine the facts upon all such applications.

(e) Testing of fuels and fuel additives

(1) Not later than one year after August 7, 1977, and after notice and opportunity for a public hearing, the Administrator shall promulgate regulations which implement the authority under subsection (b)(2)(A) and (B) of this section with respect to each fuel or fuel additive which is registered on the date of promulgation of such regulations and with respect to each fuel or fuel additive for which an application for registration is filed thereafter.

(2) Regulations under subsection (b) of this section to carry out this subsection shall require that the requisite information be provided to the Administrator by each such manufacturer—

(A) prior to registration, in the case of any fuel or fuel additive which is not registered on the date of promulgation of such regulations; or

(B) not later than three years after the date of promulgation of such regulations, in the case of any fuel or fuel additive which is registered on such date.

(3) In promulgating such regulations, the Administrator may—

(A) exempt any small business (as defined in such regulations) from or defer or modify the requirements of, such regulations with respect to any such small business;

(B) provide for cost-sharing with respect to the testing of any fuel or fuel additive which is manufactured or processed by two or more persons or otherwise provide for shared responsibility to meet the requirements of this section without duplication; or

(C) exempt any person from such regulations with respect to a particular fuel or fuel additive upon a finding that any additional testing of such fuel or fuel additive would be duplicative of adequate existing testing.

(f) New fuels and fuel additives

(1) Effective upon March 31, 1977, it shall be unlawful for any manufacturer of any fuel or fuel additive to first introduce into commerce, or to increase the concentration in use of, any fuel or fuel additive for general use in light duty motor vehicles manufactured after model year 1974 which is not substantially similar to any fuel or fuel additive utilized in the certification of any model year 1975, or subsequent model year, vehicle or engine under section 7525 of this title.

(2) Effective November 30, 1977, it shall be unlawful for any manufacturer of any fuel to introduce into commerce any gasoline which contains a concentration of manganese in excess of .0625 grams per gallon of fuel, except as otherwise provided pursuant to a waiver under paragraph (4).

(3) Any manufacturer of any fuel or fuel additive which prior to March 31, 1977, and after January 1, 1974, first introduced into commerce or increased the concentration in use of a fuel or fuel additive that would otherwise have been prohibited under paragraph (1) if introduced on or after March 31, 1977 shall, not later than September 15, 1978, cease to distribute such fuel or fuel additive in commerce. During the period beginning 180 days after August 7, 1977, and before September 15, 1978, the Administrator shall prohibit, or restrict the concentration of any fuel additive which he determines will cause or contribute to the failure of an emission control device or system (over the useful life of any vehicle in which such device or system is used) to achieve compliance by the vehicle with the emission standards with respect to which it has been certified under section 7525 of this title.

(4) The Administrator, upon application of any manufacturer of any fuel or fuel additive, may waive the prohibitions established under paragraph (1) or (3) of this subsection or the limitation specified in paragraph (2) of this subsection, if he determines that the applicant has established that such fuel or fuel additive or a specified concentration thereof, and the emission products of such fuel or additive or specified concentration thereof, will not cause or contribute to a failure of any emission control device or system (over the useful life of any vehicle in which such device or system is used) to achieve compliance by the vehicle with the emission standards with respect to which it has been certified pursuant to section 7525 of this title. If the Administrator has not acted to grant or deny an application under this paragraph within one hundred and eighty days of receipt of such application, the waiver authorized by this paragraph shall be treated as granted.

(5) No action of the Administrator under this section may be stayed by any court pending judicial review of such action.

(g) Small refineries

(1) For the purposes of this subsection:

(A) The terms "gasoline" and "refinery" have the meaning provided under regulations of the Administrator promulgated under this section.

(B) The term "small refinery" means a refinery or a portion of refinery producing gasoline—

(i) the gasoline producing capacity of which was in operation or under construction at any time during the one-year period immediately preceding October 1, 1976, and

(ii) which has a crude oil or bona fide feed stock capacity (as determined by the Administrator) of 50,000 barrels per day or less, and

(iii) which is owned or controlled by a refiner with a total combined crude oil or bona fide feed stock capacity (as determined by the Administrator) of 137,500 barrels per day or less.

(2) No regulations of the Administrator under this section (or any amendment or revision thereof) respecting the control or prohibition of lead additives in gasoline shall require a small refinery prior to October 1, 1982, to reduce the average lead content per gallon of gasoline refined at such refinery below the applicable amount specified in the table below:

If the average gasoline production of the small refinery for the immediately preceding calendar year (or, in the case of refineries under construction, half the designed crude oil capacity) was (in barrels per day):	The applicable amount is (in grams per gallon)
5,000 or under	2.65.
5,001 to 10,000	2.15.
10,001 to 15,000	1.65.
15,001 to 20,000	1.30.
20,001 to 25,000	.80.
25,001 or over	as prescribed by the Administrator, but not greater than 0.80.

The Administrator may promulgate such regulations as he deems appropriate with respect to the reduction of the average lead content of gasoline refined by small refineries on and after October 1, 1982, taking into account the experience under the preceding provisions of this paragraph.

(3) Effective on August 7, 1977, the regulations of the Administrator under this section respecting fuel additives (40 CFR part 80) shall be deemed amended to comply with the requirement contained in paragraph (2).

(4) Nothing in this section shall be construed to preempt the right of any State to take action as permitted by subsection (c)(4) of this section.

(July 14, 1955, ch. 360, title II, § 211, formerly § 210, as added Nov. 21, 1967, Pub.L. 90–148, § 2, 81 Stat. 502, and renumbered and amended Dec. 31, 1970, Pub.L. 91–604, §§ 8(a), 9(a), 84 Stat. 1694, 1698; Nov. 18, 1971, Pub.L. 92–157, title III, § 302(d), (e), 85 Stat. 464; Aug. 7, 1977, Pub.L. 95–95, title II, §§ 222, 223, title IV, § 401(e), 91 Stat. 762, 764, 791; Nov. 16, 1977, Pub.L. 95–190, § 14(a)(73), (74), 91 Stat. 1403, 1404.)

Code of Federal Regulations

Control of air pollution from motor vehicles, generally, see 40 CFR 85.401 et seq.
Fuels and fuel additives, registration and regulation of, see 40 CFR 79.1 et seq., 80.1 et seq.
Jurisdiction and venue in district courts, matters pertaining to, see § 1000 et seq.
Suspension and revocation of permits, rules governing, see 40 CFR 22.07 et seq.

Library References

Health and Environment ⚯20, 25.6(1).
C.J.S. Health and Environment §§ 2 et seq., 91 et seq.

§ 7546. Low-emission vehicles

(a) Definitions

For the purpose of this section—

(1) The term "Board" means the Low-Emission Vehicle Certification Board.

(2) The term "Federal Government" includes the legislative, executive, and judicial branches of the Government of the United States, and the government of the District of Columbia.

(3) The term "motor vehicle" means any self-propelled vehicle designed for use in the United States on the highways, other than a vehicle designed or used for military field training, combat, or tactical purposes.

(4) The term "low-emission vehicle" means any motor vehicle which—

(A) emits any air pollutant in amounts significantly below new motor vehicle standards applicable under section 7521 of this title at the time of procurement to that type of vehicle; and

(B) with respect to all other air pollutants meets the new motor vehicle standards applicable under section 7521 of this title at the time of procurement to that type of vehicle.

(5) The term "retail price" means (A) the maximum statutory price applicable to any class or model of motor vehicle; or (B) in any case where there is no applicable maximum statutory price, the most recent procurement price paid for any class or model of motor vehicle.

(b) Low-Emission Vehicle Certification Board

(1) There is established a Low-Emission Vehicle Certification Board to be composed of the Administrator or his designee, the Secretary of Transportation or his designee, the Chairman of the Council on Environmental Quality or his designee, the Director of the National Highway Traffic Safety Administration in the Department of Transportation, the Administrator of General Services, and two members appointed by the President. The President shall designate one member of the Board as Chairman.

(2) Any member of the Board not employed by the United States may receive compensation at the rate of $125 for each day such member is engaged upon work of the Board. Each member of the Board shall be reimbursed for travel expenses, including per diem in lieu of subsistence as authorized by section 5703 of title 5 for persons in the Government service employed intermittently.

(3)(A) The Chairman, with the concurrence of the members of the Board, may employ and fix the compensation of such additional personnel as may be necessary to carry out the functions of the Board, but no individual so appointed shall receive compensation in excess of the rate authorized for GS–18 by section 5332 of title 5.

(B) The Chairman may fix the time and place of such meetings as may be required, but a meeting of the Board shall be called whenever a majority of its members so request.

(C) The Board is granted all other powers necessary for meeting its responsibilities under this section.

(c) Determination of qualifying vehicles

The Administrator shall determine which models or classes of motor vehicles qualify as low-emission vehicles in accordance with the provisions of this section.

(d) Certification

(1) The Board shall certify any class or model of motor vehicles—

(A) for which a certification application has been filed in accordance with paragraph (3) of this subsection;

(B) which is a low-emission vehicle as determined by the Administrator; and

(C) which it determines is suitable for use as a substitute for a class or model of vehicles at that time in use by agencies of the Federal Government.

The Board shall specify with particularity the class or model of vehicles for which the class or model of vehicles described in the application is a suitable substitute. In making the determination under this subsection the Board shall consider the following criteria:

(i) the safety of the vehicle;

(ii) its performance characteristics;

(iii) its reliability potential;

(iv) its serviceability;

(v) its fuel availability;

(vi) its noise level; and

(vii) its maintenance costs as compared with the class or model of motor vehicle for which it may be a suitable substitute.

(2) Certification under this section shall be effective for a period of one year from the date of issuance.

(3)(A) Any party seeking to have a class or model of vehicle certified under this section shall file a certification application in accordance with regulations prescribed by the Board.

(B) The Board shall publish a notice of each application received in the Federal Register.

(C) The Administrator and the Board shall make determinations for the purpose of this section in accordance with procedures prescribed by regulation by the Administrator and the Board, respectively.

(D) The Administrator and the Board shall conduct whatever investigation is necessary, including actual inspection of the vehicle at a place designated in regulations prescribed under subparagraph (A).

(E) The Board shall receive and evaluate written comments and documents from interested parties in support of, or in opposition to, certification of the class or model of vehicle under consideration.

(F) Within 90 days after the receipt of a properly filed certification application, the Administrator shall determine whether such class or model of vehicle is a low-emission vehicle, and within 180 days of such determination, the Board shall reach a decision by majority vote as to whether such class or model of vehicle, having been determined to be a low-emission vehicle, is a suitable substitute for any class or classes of vehicles presently being purchased by the Federal Government for use by its agencies.

(G) Immediately upon making any determination or decision under subparagraph (F), the Administrator and the Board shall each publish in the Federal Register notice of such determination or decision, including reasons therefor and in the case of the Board any dissenting views.

(e) Acquisition by Federal Government in lieu of other vehicles; procurement costs; contract provisions

(1) Certified low-emission vehicles shall be acquired by purchase or lease by the Federal Government for use by the Federal Government in lieu of other vehicles if the Administrator of General Services determines that such certified vehicles have procurement costs which are no more than 150 per centum of the retail price of the least expensive class or model of motor vehicle for which they are certified substitutes.

(2) In order to encourage development of inherently low-polluting propulsion technology, the Board may, at its discretion, raise the premium set forth in paragraph (1) of this subsection to 200 per centum of the retail price of any class or model of motor vehicle for which a certified low-emission vehicle is a certified substitute, if the Board determines that the certified low-emission vehicle is powered by an inherently low-polluting propulsion system.

(3) Data relied upon by the Board and the Administrator in determining that a vehicle is a certified low-emission vehicle shall be incorporated in any contract for the procurement of such vehicle.

(f) Priority for purchase by procuring agency

The procuring agency shall be required to purchase available certified low-emission vehicles which are eligible for purchase to the extent they are available before purchasing any other vehicles for which any low-emission vehicle is a certified substitute. In making purchasing selections between competing eligible certified low-emission vehicles, the procuring agency shall give priority to (1) any class or model which does not require extensive periodic maintenance to retain its low-polluting qualities or which does not require the use of fuels which are more expensive than those of the classes or models of vehicles for which it is a certified substitute; and (2) passenger vehicles other than buses.

(g) Waiver of statutory price limitations

For the purpose of procuring certified low-emission vehicles any statutory price limitations shall be waived.

(h) Testing of emissions from certified low-emission vehicles purchased by Federal Government; procedure; recertification

The Administrator shall, from time to time as the Board deems appropriate, test the emissions from certified low-emission vehicles purchased by the Federal Government. If at any time he finds that the emission rates exceed the rates on which certification under this section was based, the Administrator shall notify the Board. Thereupon the Board shall give the supplier of such vehicles written notice of this finding, issue public notice of it, and give the supplier an opportunity to make necessary repairs, adjustments, or replacements. If no such repairs, adjustments, or replacements are made within a period to be set by the Board, the Board may order the supplier to show cause why the vehicle involved should be eligible for recertification.

(i) Authorization of appropriations

There are authorized to be appropriated for paying additional amounts for motor vehicles pursuant to, and for carrying out the provisions of, this section, $5,000,000 for the fiscal year ending June 30, 1971, and $25,000,000 for each of the four succeeding fiscal years.

(j) Promulgation by Board of implementing procedures

The Board shall promulgate the procedures required to implement this section within one hundred and eighty days after December 31, 1970.

(July 14, 1955, ch. 360, title II, § 212, as added Dec. 31, 1970, Pub.L. 91–604, § 10(c), 84 Stat. 1700, and amended Dec. 31, 1970, Pub.L. 91–605, § 202(a), 84 Stat. 1739; Apr. 9, 1973, Pub.L. 93–15, § 1(b), 87 Stat. 11; June 22, 1974, Pub.L. 93–319, § 13(b), 88 Stat. 265.)

Library References

Health and Environment ⟹25.6(6).
C.J.S. Health and Environment § 91 et seq.

§ 7547. Fuel economy improvement from new motor vehicles

(a)[1]**(1)** The Administrator and the Secretary of Transportation shall conduct a joint study, and shall report to the Committee on Interstate and Foreign Commerce of the United States House of Representatives and the Committees on Public Works and Commerce of the United States Senate within one hundred and twenty days following June 22, 1974, concerning the practicability of establishing a fuel economy improvement standard of 20 per centum for new motor vehicles manufactured during and after model year 1980. Such study and report shall include, but not be limited to, the technological problems of meeting any such standard, including the leadtime involved; the test procedures required to determine compliance; the economic costs associated with such standard, including any beneficial economic impact; the various means of enforcing such standard; the effect on consumption of natural resources, including energy consumed; and the impact of applicable safety and emission standards. In the course of performing such study, the Administrator and the Secretary of Transportation shall utilize the research previously performed in the Department of Transportation, and the Administrator and the Secretary shall consult with the Federal Energy Administrator, the Chairman of the Council on Environmental Quality, and the Secretary of the Treasury. The Office of Management and Budget may review such report before its submission to such committees of the Congress, but such Office may not revise the report or delay its submission beyond the date prescribed for its submission, and may submit to Congress its comments respecting such report. In connection with such study, the Administrator may utilize the authority provided in section 7607(a) of this title to obtain necessary information.

(2) For the purpose of this section, the term "fuel economy improvement standard" means a requirement of a percentage increase in the number of miles of transportation provided by a manufacturer's entire annual production of new motor vehicles per unit of fuel consumed, as determined for each manufacturer in accordance with test procedures established by the Administrator pursuant to this chapter. Such term shall not include any requirement for any design standard or any other requirement specifying or otherwise limiting the manufacturer's discretion in deciding how to comply with the fuel economy improvement standard by any lawful means.[1]

(July 14, 1955, ch. 360, title II, § 213, as added June 22, 1974, Pub.L. 93–319, § 10, 88 Stat. 261.)

[1] So in original. No subsec. (b) has been enacted.

§ 7548. Study of particulate emissions from motor vehicles

(a) Study and analysis

(1) The Administrator shall conduct a study concerning the effects on health and welfare of particulate emissions from motor vehicles or motor vehicle engines to which section 7521 of this title applies. Such study shall characterize and quantify such emissions and analyze the relationship of such emissions to various fuels and fuel additives.

(2) The study shall also include an analysis of particulate emissions from mobile sources which are not related to engine emissions (including, but not limited to tire debris, and asbestos from brake lining).

(b) Report to Congress

The Administrator shall report to the Congress the findings and results of the study conducted under subsection (a) of this section not later than two years after August 7, 1977. Such report shall also include recommendations for standards or methods to regulate particulate emissions described in paragraph (2) of subsection (a) of this section.

(July 14, 1955, ch. 360, title II, § 214, as added Aug. 7, 1977, Pub.L. 95–95, title II, § 224(d), 91 Stat. 767.)

§ 7549. High altitude performance adjustments

(a) Instruction of manufacturer

(1) Any action taken with respect to any element of design installed on or in a motor vehicle or motor vehicle engine in compliance with regulations under this subchapter (including any alteration or adjustment of such element), shall be treated as not in violation of section 7522(a) of this title if such action is performed in accordance with high altitude adjustment instructions provided by the manufacturer under subsection (b) of this section and approved by the Administrator.

(2) If the Administrator finds that adjustments or modifications made pursuant to instructions of the manufacturer under paragraph (1) will not insure emission control performance with respect to each standard under section 7521 of this title at least equivalent to that which would result if no such adjustments or modifications were made, he shall disapprove such instructions. Such finding shall be based upon minimum engineering evaluations consistent with good engineering practice.

(b) Regulations

(1) Instructions respecting each class or category of vehicles or engines to which this subchapter applies providing for such vehicle and engine adjustments and modifications as may be necessary to insure emission control performance at different altitudes shall be submitted by the manufacturer to the Administrator pursuant to regulations promulgated by the Administrator.

(2) Any knowing violation by a manufacturer of requirements of the Administrator under paragraph (1) shall be treated as a violation by such manufacturer of section 7522(a)(3) of this title for purposes of the penalties contained in section 7524 of this title.

(3) Such instructions shall provide, in addition to other adjustments, for adjustments for vehicles moving from high altitude areas to low altitude areas after the initial registration of such vehicles.

(c) Manufacturer parts

No instructions under this section respecting adjustments or modifications may require the use of any manufacturer parts (as defined in section 7522(a) of this title) unless the manufacturer demonstrates to the satisfaction of the Administrator that the use of such manufacturer parts is necessary to insure emission control performance.

(d) State inspection and maintenance programs

Before January 1, 1981 the authority provided by this section shall be available in any high altitude State (as determined under regulations of the Administrator under regulations promulgated before August 7, 1977) but after December 31, 1980, such authority shall be available only in any such State in which an inspection and maintenance program for the testing of motor vehicle emissions has been instituted for the portions of the State where any national ambient air quality standard for auto-related pollutants has not been attained.

(July 14, 1955, ch. 360, title II, § 215, as added Aug. 7, 1977, Pub.L. 95–95, title II, § 211(b), 91 Stat. 757, and amended Nov. 16, 1977, Pub.L. 95–190, § 14(a)(75), 91 Stat. 1404.)

§ 7550. Definitions

As used in this part—

(1) The term "manufacturer" as used in sections 7521, 7522, 7525, 7541, and 7542 of this title means any person engaged in the manufacturing or assembling of new motor vehicles or new motor vehicle engines, or importing such vehicles or engines for resale, or who acts for and is under the control of any such person in connection with the distribution of new motor vehicles or new motor vehicle engines, but shall not include any dealer with respect to new motor vehicles or new motor vehicle engines received by him in commerce.

(2) The term "motor vehicle" means any self-propelled vehicle designed for transporting persons or property on a street or highway.

(3) Except with respect to vehicles or engines imported or offered for importation, the term "new motor vehicle" means a motor vehicle the equitable or legal title to which has never been transferred to an ultimate purchaser; and the term "new motor vehicle engine" means an engine in a new motor vehicle or a motor vehicle engine the equitable or legal title to which has never been transferred to the ultimate purchaser; and with respect to imported vehicles or engines, such terms mean a motor vehicle and engine, respectively, manufactured after the effective date of a regulation issued under section 7521 of this title which is applicable to such vehicle or engine (or which would be applicable to such vehicle or engine had it been manufactured for importation into the United States).

(4) The term "dealer" means any person who is engaged in the sale or the distribution of new motor vehicles or new motor vehicle engines to the ultimate purchaser.

(5) The term "ultimate purchaser" means, with respect to any new motor vehicle or new motor vehicle engine, the first person who in good faith purchases such new motor vehicle or new engine for purposes other than resale.

(6) The term "commerce" means (A) commerce between any place in any State and any place outside thereof; and (B) commerce wholly within the District of Columbia.

(July 14, 1955, ch. 360, title II, § 216, formerly § 208, as added Oct. 20, 1965, Pub.L. 89–272, title I, § 101(8), 79 Stat. 994, renumbered § 212, and amended Nov. 21, 1967, Pub.L. 90–148, § 2, 81 Stat. 503, renumbered § 213, and amended Dec. 31, 1970, Pub.L. 91–604, §§ 8(a), 10(d), 11(a)(2)(A), 84 Stat. 1694, 1703, 1705, renumbered § 214, June 22, 1974, Pub.L. 93–319, § 10, 88 Stat. 261, renumbered § 216, Aug. 7, 1977, Pub.L. 95–95, Title II, § 224(d), 91 Stat. 767.)

Code of Federal Regulations

Control of air pollution from motor vehicles, generally, see 40 CFR 85.401 et seq.
Control of air pollution from new motor vehicles, certification and test procedures, see 40 CFR 86.078–3 et seq.
Suspension or revocation of permits, rules governing, see 40 CFR 22.01 et seq.

§ 7551. Study and report on fuel consumption

Following each motor vehicle model year, the Administrator of the Environmental Protection Agency shall report to the Congress respecting the motor vehicle fuel consumption associated with the standards applicable for the immediately preceding model year.

(Aug. 7, 1977, Pub.L. 95–95, title II, § 203, 91 Stat. 754; Dec. 21, 1982, Pub.L. 97–375, Title I, § 106(a), 96 Stat. 1820.)

Part B—Aircraft Emission Standards

§ 7571. Establishment of standards

(a) Study; proposed standards; hearings; issuance of regulations

(1) Within 90 days after December 31, 1970, the Administrator shall commence a study and investigation of emissions of air pollutants from aircraft in order to determine—

(A) the extent to which such emissions affect air quality in air quality control regions throughout the United States, and

(B) the technological feasibility of controlling such emissions.

(2) The Administrator shall, from time to time, issue proposed emission standards applicable to the emission of any air pollutant from any class or classes of aircraft engines which in his judgment causes, or contributes to, air pollution which may reasonably be anticipated to endanger public health or welfare.

(3) The Administrator shall hold public hearings with respect to such proposed standards. Such hearings shall, to the extent practicable, be held in air quality control regions which are most seriously affected by aircraft emissions. Within 90 days after the issuance of such proposed regulations, he shall issue such regulations with such modifications as he deems appropriate. Such regulations may be revised from time to time.

(b) Effective date of regulations

Any regulation prescribed under this section (and any revision thereof) shall take effect after such period as the Administrator finds necessary (after consultation with the Secretary of Transportation) to permit the development and application of the requisite technology, giving appropriate consideration to the cost of compliance within such period.

(c) Regulations which create hazards to aircraft safety

Any regulations in effect under this section on August 7, 1977, or proposed or promulgated thereafter, or amendments thereto, with respect to aircraft shall not apply if disapproved by the President, after notice and opportunity for public hearing, on the basis of a finding by the Secretary of Transportation that any such regulation would create a hazard to aircraft safety. Any such finding shall include a reasonably specific statement of the basis upon which the finding was made.

(July 14, 1955, ch. 360, title II, § 231, as added Dec. 31, 1970, Pub.L. 91–604, § 11(a)(1), 84 Stat. 1703, and amended Aug. 7, 1977, Pub.L. 95–95, title II, § 225, title IV, § 401(f), 91 Stat. 769, 791.)

Cross References

Aviation fuel standards, establishment, implementation and enforcement, see section 1421 of Title 49, Transportation.

Code of Federal Regulations

Air pollution from aircrafts, control of, see 40 CFR 87.1 et seq.

Library References

Health and Environment ⇔20, 25.6(6).
C.J.S. Health and Environment §§ 2 et seq., 91 et seq.

§ 7572. Enforcement of standards

(a) Regulations to insure compliance with standards

The Secretary of Transportation, after consultation with the Administrator, shall prescribe regulations to insure compliance with all standards prescribed under section 7571 of this title by the Administrator. The regulations of the Secretary of Transportation shall include provisions making such standards applicable in the issuance, amendment, modification, suspension, or revocation of any certificate authorized by the Federal Aviation Act [49 U.S.C. 1301 et seq.] or the Department of Transportation Act [49 U.S.C. 1651 et seq.]. Such Secretary shall insure that all necessary inspections are accomplished, and,[1] may execute any power or duty vested in him by any other provision of law in the execution of all powers and duties vested in him under this section.

(b) Notice and appeal rights

In any action to amend, modify, suspend, or revoke a certificate in which violation of an emission standard prescribed under section 7571 of this title or of a regulation prescribed under subsection (a) of this section is at issue, the certificate holder shall have the same notice and appeal rights as are prescribed for such holders in the Federal Aviation Act of 1958 [49 U.S.C. 1301 et seq.] or the Department of Transportation Act [49 U.S.C. 1651 et seq.], except that in any appeal to the National Transportation Safety Board, the Board may amend, modify, or revoke the order of the Secretary of Transportation only if it finds no violation of such standard or regulation and that such amendment, modification, or revocation is consistent with safety in air transportation.

(July 14, 1955, ch. 360, title II, § 232, as added Dec. 31, 1970, Pub.L. 91–604, § 11(a)(1), 84 Stat. 1704.)

1 So in original. The comma probably should not have appeared.

Library References

Health and Environment ⚷25.6(6).
C.J.S. Health and Environment § 91 et seq.

§ 7573. State standards and controls

No State or political subdivision thereof may adopt or attempt to enforce any standard respecting emissions of any air pollutant from any aircraft or engine thereof unless such standard is identical to a standard applicable to such aircraft under this part.

(July 14, 1955, ch. 360, title II, § 233, as added Dec. 31, 1970, Pub.L. 91–604, § 11(a)(1), 84 Stat. 1704.)

Library References

States ⚷4.11.
C.J.S. States § 24.

§ 7574. Definitions

Terms used in this part (other than Administrator) shall have the same meaning as such terms have under section 1301 of title 49.

(July 14, 1955, ch. 360, title II, § 234, as added Dec. 31, 1970, Pub.L. 91–604, § 11(a)(1), 84 Stat. 1705.)

SUBCHAPTER III—GENERAL PROVISIONS

§ 7601. Administration

(a) Regulations; delegation of powers and duties; regional officers and employees

(1) The Administrator is authorized to prescribe such regulations as are necessary to carry out his functions under this chapter. The Administrator may delegate to any officer or employee of the Environmental Protection Agency such of his powers and duties under this chapter, except the making of regulations, as he may deem necessary or expedient.

(2) Not later than one year after August 7, 1977, the Administrator shall promulgate regulations establishing general applicable procedures and policies for regional officers and employees (including the Regional Administrator) to follow in carrying out a delegation under paragraph (1), if any. Such regulations shall be designed—

(A) to assure fairness and uniformity in the criteria, procedures, and policies applied by the various regions in implementing and enforcing the chapter;

(B) to assure at least an adequate quality audit of each State's performance and adherence to the requirements of this chapter in implementing and enforcing the chapter, particularly in the review of new sources and in enforcement of the chapter; and

(C) to provide a mechanism for identifying and standardizing inconsistent or varying criteria, procedures, and policies being employed by such officers and employees in implementing and enforcing the chapter.

(b) Detail of Environmental Protection Agency personnel to air pollution control agencies

Upon the request of an air pollution control agency, personnel of the Environmental Protection Agency may be detailed to such agency for the purpose of carrying out the provisions of this chapter.

(c) Payments under grants; installments; advances or reimbursements

Payments under grants made under this chapter may be made in installments, and in advance or by way of reimbursement, as may be determined by the Administrator.

(July 14, 1955, ch. 360, title III, § 301, formerly § 8, as added Dec. 17, 1963, Pub.L. 88–206, § 1, 77 Stat. 400, renumbered Oct. 20, 1965, Pub.L. 89–272, title I, § 101(4), 79 Stat. 992, and amended Nov. 21, 1967, Pub.L. 90–148, § 2, 81 Stat. 504; Dec. 31, 1970, Pub.L. 91–604, §§ 3(b)(2), 15(c)(2), 84 Stat. 1677, 1713; Aug. 7, 1977, Pub.L. 95–95, title III, § 305(e), 91 Stat. 776.)

Code of Federal Regulations

Environmental Protection Agency,
- Aircrafts, control of air pollution from, see 40 CFR 87.1 et seq.
- Air pollution from motor vehicles, control of, see 40 CFR 85.401 et seq.
- Air quality standards, see 40 CFR 50.1 et seq.
- Ambient air quality surveillance, see 40 CFR 58.1 et seq.
- Compliance orders, see 40 CFR 65.01 et seq.
- Energy related authority, see 40 CFR 55.01 et seq.
- Fuels,
  - Registration of, see 40 CFR 79.1 et seq.
  - Regulation of, see 40 CFR 80.1 et seq.
- Hazardous air pollutants, emission standards, see 40 CFR 61.01 et seq.
- Implementation plans, requirements concerning, see 40 CFR 51.1 et seq.
- Information, requests for, see 40 CFR 2.100 et seq.
- New stationary sources, performance standards, see 40 CFR 60.1 et seq.
- Nonferrous smelter orders, see 40 CFR 57.101 et seq.
- Regional consistency, see 40 CFR 56.1 et seq.

Library References

Health and Environment ⚷20.
C.J.S. Health and Environment § 2 et seq.

§ 7602. Definitions

When used in this chapter—

(a) The term "Administrator" means the Administrator of the Environmental Protection Agency.

(b) The term "air pollution control agency" means any of the following:

(1) A single State agency designated by the Governor of that State as the official State air pollution control agency for purposes of this chapter;

(2) An agency established by two or more States and having substantial powers or duties pertaining to the prevention and control of air pollution;

(3) A city, county, or other local government health authority, or, in the case of any city, county, or other local government in which there is an agency other than the health authority charged with responsibility for enforcing ordinances or laws relating to the prevention and control of air pollution, such other agency; or

(4) An agency of two or more municipalities located in the same State or in different States and having substantial powers or duties pertaining to the prevention and control of air pollution.

(c) The term "interstate air pollution control agency" means—

(1) an air pollution control agency established by two or more States, or

(2) an air pollution control agency of two or more municipalities located in different States.

(d) The term "State" means a State, the District of Columbia, the Commonwealth of Puerto Rico, the Virgin Islands, Guam, and American Samoa and includes the Commonwealth of the Northern Mariana Islands.

(e) The term "person" includes an individual, corporation, partnership, association, State, municipality, political subdivision of a State, and any agency, department, or instrumentality of the United States and any officer, agent, or employee thereof.

(f) The term "municipality" means a city, town, borough, county, parish, district, or other public body created by or pursuant to State law.

(g) The term "air pollutant" means any air pollution agent or combination of such agents, including any physical, chemical, biological, radioactive (including source material, special nuclear material, and byproduct material) substance or matter which is emitted into or otherwise enters the ambient air.

(h) All language referring to effects on welfare includes, but is not limited to, effects on soils, water, crops, vegetation, manmade materials, animals, wildlife, weather, visibility, and climate, damage to and deterioration of property, and hazards to transportation, as well as effects on economic values and on personal comfort and well-being.

(i) The term "Federal land manager" means, with respect to any lands in the United States, the Secretary of the department with authority over such lands.

(j) Except as otherwise expressly provided, the terms "major stationary source" and "major emitting facility" mean any stationary facility or source of air pollutants which directly emits, or has the potential to emit, one hundred tons per year or more of any air pollutant (including any major emitting facility or source of fugitive emissions of any such pollutant, as determined by rule by the Administrator).

(k) The terms "emission limitation" and "emission standard" mean a requirement established by the State or the Administrator which limits the quantity, rate, or concentration of emissions of air pollutants on a continuous basis, including any requirement relating to the operation or maintenance of a source to assure continuous emission reduction.

(*l*) The term "standard of performance" means a requirement of continuous emission reduction, including any requirement relating to the operation or maintenance of a source to assure continuous emission reduction.

(m) The term "means of emission limitation" means a system of continuous emission reduction (including the use of specific technology or fuels with specified pollution characteristics).

(n) The term "primary standard attainment date" means the date specified in the applicable implementation plan for the attainment of a national primary ambient air quality standard for any air pollutant.

(*o*) The term "delayed compliance order" means an order issued by the State or by the Administrator to an existing stationary source, postponing the date required under an applicable implementation plan for compliance by such source with any requirement of such plan.

(p) The term "schedule and timetable of compliance" means a schedule of required measures including an enforceable sequence of actions or operations leading to compliance with an emission limitation, other limitation, prohibition, or standard.

(July 14, 1955, ch. 360, title III, § 302, formerly § 9, as added Dec. 17, 1963, Pub.L. 88–206, § 1, 77 Stat. 400, renumbered Oct. 20, 1965, Pub.L. 89–272, title I, § 101(4), 79 Stat. 992, and amended Nov. 21, 1967, Pub.L. 90–148, § 2, 81 Stat. 504; Dec. 31, 1970, Pub.L. 91–604, § 15(a)(1), (c)(1), 84 Stat. 1710, 1713; Aug. 7, 1977, Pub.L. 95–95, title II, § 218(c), title III, § 301, 91 Stat. 761, 769; Nov. 16, 1977, Pub.L. 95–190, § 14(a)(76), 91 Stat. 1404.)

Cross References

Air pollution control agency to have same meaning given such term by subsec. (b) of this section for purposes of Powerplant and Industrial Fuel Use Act of 1978, see section 8302 of this title.

State certifying authority to mean air pollution control agency as defined in subsec. (b) of this section for purposes of amortization of pollution control facilities, see section 169 of Title 26, Internal Revenue Code.

Federal Practice and Procedure

Review of administrative decisions in courts of appeals, see Wright, Miller, Cooper & Gressman: Jurisdiction § 3941.

Code of Federal Regulations

Fuels, regulation of, see 40 CFR 80.1 et seq.

§ 7603. Emergency powers

(a) Suits in United States district court; emergency orders; consultation

Notwithstanding any other provision of this chapter, the Administrator, upon receipt of evidence that a pollution source or combination of sources (including moving sources) is presenting an imminent and substantial endangerment to the health of persons, and that appropriate State or local authorities have not acted to abate such sources, may bring suit on behalf of the United States in the appropriate United States district court to immediately restrain any person causing or contributing to the alleged pollution to stop the emission of air pollutants causing or contributing to such pollution or to take such other action as may be necessary. If it is not practicable to assure prompt protection of the health of persons solely by commencement of such a civil action, the Administrator may issue such orders as may be necessary to protect the health of persons who are, or may be, affected by such pollution source (or sources). Prior to taking any action under this section, the Administrator shall consult with the State and local authorities in order to confirm the correctness of the information on which the action proposed to be taken is based and to ascertain the action which such authorities are, or will be, taking. Such order shall be effective for a period of not more than twenty-four hours unless the Administrator brings an action under the first sentence of this subsection before the expiration of such period. Whenever the Administrator brings such an action within such period, such order shall be effective for a period of forty-eight hours or such longer period as may be authorized by the court pending litigation or thereafter.

(b) Willful violation or failure or refusal to comply with orders

Any person who willfully violates, or fails or refuses to comply with, any order issued by the Administrator under subsection (a) of this section may, in an action brought in the appropriate United States district court to enforce such order, be fined not more than $5,000 for each day during which such violation occurs or failure to comply continues.

(July 14, 1955, ch. 360, title III, § 303, as added Dec. 31, 1970, Pub.L. 91–604, § 12(a), 84 Stat. 1705, and amended Aug. 7, 1977, Pub.L. 95–95, title III, § 302(a), 91 Stat. 770.)

Cross References

Guidelines for using imminent hazard, enforcement, and emergency response authorities to include assignment of responsibility for coordinating response actions with imminent hazard and emergency powers authorized by this section, see section 9606 of this title.

§ 7604. Citizen suits

(a) Authority to bring civil action; jurisdiction

Except as provided in subsection (b) of this section, any person may commence a civil action on his own behalf—

(1) against any person (including (i) the United States, and (ii) any other governmental instrumentality or agency to the extent permitted by the Eleventh Amendment to the Constitution) who is alleged to be in violation of (A) an emission standard or limitation under this chapter or (B) an order issued by the Administrator or a State with respect to such a standard or limitation,

(2) against the Administrator where there is alleged a failure of the Administrator to perform any act or duty under this chapter which is not discretionary with the Administrator, or

(3) against any person who proposes to construct or constructs any new or modified major emitting facility without a permit required under part C of subchapter I of this chapter (relating to significant deterioration of air quality) or part D of subchapter I of this chapter (relating to nonattainment) or who is alleged to be in violation of any condition of such permit.

The district courts shall have jurisdiction, without regard to the amount in controversy or the citizenship of the parties, to enforce such an emission standard or limitation, or such an order, or to order the Administrator to perform such act or duty, as the case may be.

(b) Notice

No action may be commenced—

(1) under subsection (a)(1) of this section—

(A) prior to 60 days after the plaintiff has given notice of the violation (i) to the Administrator, (ii) to the State in which the violation occurs, and (iii) to any alleged violator of the standard, limitation, or order, or

(B) if the Administrator or State has commenced and is diligently prosecuting a civil action in a court of the United States or a State to require compliance with the standard, limitation, or order, but in any such action in a court of the United States any person may intervene as a matter of right.

(2) under subsection (a)(2) of this section prior to 60 days after the plaintiff has given notice of such action to the Administrator,

except that such action may be brought immediately after such notification in the case of an action under this section respecting a violation of section 7412(c)(1)(B) of this title or an order issued by the Administrator pursuant to section 7413(a) of this title. Notice under this subsection shall be given in such manner as the Administrator shall prescribe by regulation.

(c) Venue; intervention by Administrator

(1) Any action respecting a violation by a stationary source of an emission standard or limitation or an order respecting such standard or limitation may be brought only in the judicial district in which such source is located.

(2) In such action under this section, the Administrator, if not a party, may intervene as a matter of right.

(d) Award of costs; security

The court, in issuing any final order in any action brought pursuant to subsection (a) of this section, may award costs of litigation (including reasonable attorney and expert witness fees) to any party, whenever the court determines such award is appropriate. The court may, if a temporary restraining order or preliminary injunction is sought, require the filing of a bond or equivalent security in accordance with the Federal Rules of Civil Procedure.

(e) Nonrestriction of other rights

Nothing in this section shall restrict any right which any person (or class of persons) may have under any statute or common law to seek enforcement of any emission standard or limitation or to seek any other relief (including relief against the Administrator or a State agency). Nothing in this section or in any other law of the United States shall be construed to prohibit, exclude, or restrict any State, local, or interstate authority from—

(1) bringing any enforcement action or obtaining any judicial remedy or sanction in any State or local court, or

(2) bringing any administrative enforcement action or obtaining any administrative remedy or sanction in any State or local administrative agency, department or instrumentality,

against the United States, any department, agency, or instrumentality thereof, or any officer, agent, or employee thereof under State or local law respecting control and abatement of air pollution. For provisions requiring compliance by the United States, departments, agencies, instrumentalities, officers, agents, and employees in the same manner as nongovernmental entities, see section 7418 of this title.

(f) Definition

For purposes of this section, the term "emission standard or limitation under this chapter" means—

(1) a schedule or timetable of compliance, emission limitation, standard of performance or emission standard,

(2) a control or prohibition respecting a motor vehicle fuel or fuel additive, or

(3) any condition or requirement of a permit under part C of subchapter I of this chapter (relating to significant deterioration of air quality) or part D of subchapter I of this chapter (relating to nonattainment), any condition or requirement of section 7413(d) of this title (relating to certain enforcement orders), section 7419 of this title (relating to primary nonferrous smelter orders), any condition or requirement under an applicable implementation plan relating to transportation control measures, air quality maintenance plans, vehicle inspection and maintenance programs or vapor recovery requirements, section 7545 (e) and (f) of this title (relating to fuels and fuel additives), section 7491 of this title (relating to visibility protection), any condition or requirement under part B of subchapter I of this chapter (relating to ozone protection), or any requirement under section 7411 or 7412 of this title (without regard to whether such requirement is expressed as an emission standard or otherwise).[1]

which is in effect under this chapter (including a requirement applicable by reason of section 7418 of this title) or under an applicable implementation plan.

(July 14, 1955, ch. 360, title III, § 304, as added Dec. 31, 1970, Pub.L. 91–604, § 12(a), 84 Stat. 1706, and amended Aug. 7, 1977, Pub.L. 95–95, title III, § 303(a)–(c), 91 Stat. 771, 772; Nov. 16, 1977, Pub.L. 95–190, § 14(a)(77), (78), 91 Stat. 1404.)

[1] So in original. Probably should be a comma.

Federal Practice and Procedure

Allowability of suit by any person, see Wright, Miller & Cooper: Jurisdiction § 3531.
Attorney's fees, see Wright, Miller & Kane: Civil 2d § 2675.
Jurisdictional amount in controversy, see Wright, Miller & Cooper: Jurisdiction § 3701 et seq.
Venue in district courts, see Wright, Miller & Cooper: Jurisdiction § 3825.

Library References

Health and Environment ⟹25.6(1), 28.
C.J.S. Health and Environment § 91 et seq.

United States Supreme Court

Attorney fees, superior quality of counsel's performance, see Pennsylvania v. Delaware Valley Citizens' Council for Clean Air, 1986, 106 S.Ct. 3088, 92 L.Ed.2d 439.

§ 7605. Representation in litigation

(a) Attorney General; attorneys appointed by Administrator

The Administrator shall request the Attorney General to appear and represent him in any civil action instituted under this chapter to which the Administrator is a party. Unless the Attorney General notifies the Administrator that he will appear in such action, within a reasonable time, attorneys appointed by the Administrator shall appear and represent him.

(b) Memorandum of understanding regarding legal representation

In the event the Attorney General agrees to appear and represent the Administrator in any such action, such representation shall be conducted in accordance with, and shall include participation by, attorneys appointed by the Administrator to the extent authorized by, the memorandum of understanding between the Department of Justice and the Environmental Protection Agency, dated June 13, 1977, respecting representation of the agency by the department in civil litigation.

(July 14, 1955, ch. 360, title III, § 305, as added Dec. 31, 1970, Pub.L. 91–604, § 12(a), 84 Stat. 1707, and amended Aug. 7, 1977, Pub.L. 95–95, title III, § 304(a), 91 Stat. 772.)

Library References

Attorney General ⟹7.
C.J.S. Attorney General § 8 et seq.

§ 7606. Federal procurement

(a) Contracts with violators prohibited

No Federal agency may enter into any contract with any person who is convicted of any offense under section 7413(c)(1) of this title for the procurement of goods, materials, and services to perform such contract at any facility at which the violation which gave rise to such conviction occurred if such facility is owned, leased, or supervised by such person. The prohibition in the preceding sentence shall continue until the Administrator certifies that the condition giving rise to such a conviction has been corrected.

(b) Notification procedures

The Administrator shall establish procedures to provide all Federal agencies with the notification necessary for the purposes of subsection (a) of this section.

(c) Federal agency contracts

In order to implement the purposes and policy of this chapter to protect and enhance the quality of the Nation's air, the President shall, not more than 180 days after December 31, 1970, cause to be issued an order (1) requiring each Federal agency authorized to enter into contracts and each Federal agency which is empowered to extend Federal assistance by way of grant, loan, or contract to effectuate the purpose and policy of this chapter in such contracting or assistance activities, and (2) setting forth procedures, sanctions, penalties, and such other provisions, as the President determines necessary to carry out such requirement.

(d) Exemptions; notification to Congress

The President may exempt any contract, loan, or grant from all or part of the provisions of this section where he determines such exemption is necessary in the paramount interest of the United States and he shall notify the Congress of such exemption.

(e) Annual report to Congress

The President shall annually report to the Congress on measures taken toward implementing the purpose and intent of this section, including but not limited to the progress and problems associated with implementation of this section.

(July 14, 1955, ch. 360, title III, § 306, as added Dec. 31, 1970, Pub.L. 91–604, § 12(a), 84 Stat. 1707.)

Library References

United States ⚷68.
C.J.S. United States § 90.

§ 7607. Administrative proceedings and judicial review

(a) Administrative subpenas; confidentiality; witnesses

(1) In connection with any determination under section 7410(f) or section 7521(b)(5) of this title, or for purposes of obtaining information under section 7521(b)(4) or 7545(c)(3) of this title, the Administrator may issue subpenas for the attendance and testimony of witnesses and the production of relevant papers, books, and documents, and he may administer oaths. Except for emission data, upon a showing satisfactory to the Administrator by such owner or operator that such papers, books, documents, or information or particular part thereof, if made public, would divulge trade secrets or secret processes of such owner or operator, the Administrator shall consider such record, report, or information or particular portion thereof confidential in accordance with the purposes of section 1905 of title 18, except that such paper, book, document, or information may be disclosed to other officers, employees, or authorized representatives of the United States concerned with carrying out this chapter, to persons carrying out the National Academy of Sciences' study and investigation provided for in section 7521(c) of this title, or when relevant in any proceeding under this chapter. Witnesses summoned shall be paid the same fees and mileage that are paid witnesses in the courts of the United States. In case of contumacy or refusal to obey a subpena served upon any person under this subparagraph, the district court of the United States for any district in which such person is found or resides or transacts business, upon application by the United States and after notice to such person, shall have jurisdiction to issue an order requiring such person to appear and give testimony before the Administrator to appear and produce papers, books, and documents before the Administrator, or both, and any failure to obey such order of the court may be punished by such court as a contempt thereof.[1]

(b) Judicial review

(1) A petition for review of action of the Administrator in promulgating any national primary or secondary ambient air quality standard, any emission standard or requirement under section 7412 of this title, any standard of performance or requirement under section 7411 of this title, any standard under section 7521 of this title (other than a standard required to be prescribed under section 7521(b)(1) of this title), any determination under section 7521(b)(5) of this title, any control or prohibition under section 7545 of this title, any standard under section 7571 of this title, any rule issued under section 7413, 7419, or under section 7420 of this title, or any other nationally applicable regulations promulgated, or final action taken, by the Administrator under this chapter may be filed only in the United States Court of Appeals for the District of Columbia. A petition for review of the Administrator's action in approving or promulgating any implementation plan under section 7410 of this title or section 7411(d) of this title, any order under section 7411(j) of this title, under section 7412(c) of this title, under section 7413(d) of this title, under section 7419 of this title, or under section 7420 of this title, or his action under section 1857c–10(c)(2)(A), (B), or (C) of this title (as in effect before August 7, 1977) or under regulations thereunder, or any other final action of the Administrator under this chapter (including any denial or disapproval by the Administrator under subchapter I of this chapter) which is locally or regionally applicable may be filed only in the United States Court of Appeals for the appropriate circuit. Notwithstanding the preceding sentence a petition for review of any action referred to in such sentence may be filed only in the United States Court of Appeals for the District of Columbia if such action is based on a determination of nationwide scope or effect and if in taking such action the Administrator finds and publishes that such action is based on such a determination. Any petition for review under this subsection shall be filed within sixty days from the date notice of such promulgation, approval, or action appears in the Federal Register, except that if such petition is based solely on grounds arising after such sixtieth day, then any petition for review under this subsection shall be filed within sixty days after such grounds arise.

(2) Action of the Administrator with respect to which review could have been obtained under paragraph (1) shall not be subject to judicial review in civil or criminal proceedings for enforcement.

(c) Additional evidence

In any judicial proceeding in which review is sought of a determination under this chapter required to be made on the record after notice and opportunity for hearing, if any party applies to the court for leave to adduce additional evidence, and shows to the satisfaction of the court that such additional evidence is material and that there were reasonable grounds for the failure to adduce such evidence in the proceeding before the Administrator, the court may order such additional evidence (and evidence in rebuttal thereof) to be taken before the Administrator, in such manner and upon such terms and conditions as to[2] the court may deem proper. The Administrator may modify his findings as to the facts, or make new findings, by reason of the additional evidence so taken and he shall file such modified or new findings, and his recommendation, if any, for the modification or setting aside of his original determination, with the return of such additional evidence.

(d) Rulemaking

(1) This subsection applies to—

(A) the promulgation or revision of any national ambient air quality standard under section 7409 of this title,

(B) the promulgation or revision of an implementation plan by the Administrator under section 7410(c) of this title,

(C) the promulgation or revision of any standard of performance under section 7411 of this title or emission standard under section 7412 of this title,

(D) the promulgation or revision of any regulation pertaining to any fuel or fuel additive under section 7545 of this title,

(E) the promulgation or revision of any aircraft emission standard under section 7571 of this title,

(F) promulgation or revision of regulations pertaining to orders for coal conversion under section 7413(d)(5) of this title (but not including orders granting or denying any such orders),

(G) promulgation or revision of regulations pertaining to primary nonferrous smelter orders under section 7419 of this title (but not including the granting or denying of any such order),

(H) promulgation or revision of regulations under part B of subchapter I of this chapter (relating to stratosphere and ozone protection),

(I) promulgation or revision of regulations under part C of subchapter I of this chapter (relating to prevention of significant deterioration of air quality and protection of visibility),

(J) promulgation or revision of regulations under section 7521 of this title and test procedures for new motor vehicles or engines under section 7525 of this title and the revision of a standard under section 7521(a)(3) of this title,

(K) promulgation or revision of regulations for noncompliance penalties under section 7420 of this title,

(L) promulgation or revision of any regulations promulgated under section 7541 of this title (relating to warranties and compliance by vehicles in actual use),

(M) action of the Administrator under section 7426 of this title (relating to interstate pollution abatement), and

(N) such other actions as the Administrator may determine.

The provisions of section 553 through 557 and section 706 of title 5 shall not, except as expressly provided in this subsection, apply to actions to which this subsection applies. This subsection shall not apply in the case of any rule or circumstance referred to in subparagraphs (A) or (B) of subsection 553(b) of title 5.

(2) Not later than the date of proposal of any action to which this subsection applies, the Administrator shall establish a rulemaking docket for such action (hereinafter in this subsection referred to as a "rule"). Whenever a rule applies only within a particular State, a second (identical) docket shall be simultaneously established in the appropriate regional office of the Environmental Protection Agency.

(3) In the case of any rule to which this subsection applies, notice of proposed rulemaking shall be published in the Federal Register, as provided under section 553(b) of title 5, shall be accompanied by a statement of its basis and purpose and shall specify the period available for public comment (hereinafter referred to as the "comment period"). The notice of proposed rulemaking shall also state the docket number, the location or locations of the docket, and the times it will be open to public inspection. The statement of basis and purpose shall include a summary of—

(A) the factual data on which the proposed rule is based;

(B) the methodology used in obtaining the data and in analyzing the data; and

(C) the major legal interpretations and policy considerations underlying the proposed rule.

The statement shall also set forth or summarize and provide a reference to any pertinent findings, recommendations, and comments by the Scientific Review Committee established under section 7409(d) of this title and the National Academy of Sciences, and, if the proposal differs in any important respect from any of these recommendations, an explanation of the reasons for such differences. All data, information, and documents referred to in this paragraph on which the proposed rule relies shall be included in the docket on the date of publication of the proposed rule.

(4)(A) The rulemaking docket required under paragraph (2) shall be open for inspection by the public at reasonable times specified in the notice of proposed rulemaking. Any person may copy documents contained in the docket. The Administrator shall provide copying facilities which may be used at the expense of the person seeking copies, but the Administrator may waive or reduce such expenses in such instances as the public interest requires. Any person may request copies by mail if the person pays the expenses, including personnel costs to do the copying.

(B)(i) Promptly upon receipt by the agency, all written comments and documentary information on the proposed rule received from any person for inclusion in the docket during the comment period shall be placed in the docket. The transcript of public hearings, if any, on the proposed rule shall also be included in the docket promptly upon receipt from the person who transcribed such hearings. All documents which become available after the proposed rule has been published and which the Administrator determines are of central relevance to the rulemaking shall be placed in the docket as soon as possible after their availability.

(ii) The drafts of proposed rules submitted by the Administrator to the Office of Management and Budget for any interagency review process prior to proposal of any such rule, all documents accompanying such drafts, and all written comments thereon by other agencies and all written responses to such written comments by the Administrator shall be placed in the docket no later than the date of proposal of the rule. The drafts of the final rule submitted for such review process prior to promulgation and all such written comments thereon, all documents accompanying such drafts, and written responses thereto shall be placed in the docket no later than the date of promulgation.

(5) In promulgating a rule to which this subsection applies (i) the Administrator shall allow any person to submit written comments, data, or documentary information; (ii) the Administrator shall give interested persons an opportunity for the oral presentation of data, views, or arguments, in addition to an opportunity to make written submissions; (iii) a transcript shall be kept of any oral presentation; and (iv) the Administrator shall keep the record of such proceeding open for thirty days after completion of the proceeding to provide an opportunity for submission of rebuttal and supplementary information.

(6)(A) The promulgated rule shall be accompanied by (i) a statement of basis and purpose like that referred to in paragraph (3) with respect to a proposed rule and (ii) an explanation of the reasons for any major changes in the promulgated rule from the proposed rule.

(B) The promulgated rule shall also be accompanied by a response to each of the significant comments, criticisms, and new data submitted in written or oral presentations during the comment period.

(C) The promulgated rule may not be based (in part or whole) on any information or data which has not been placed in the docket as of the date of such promulgation.

(7)(A) The record for judicial review shall consist exclusively of the material referred to in paragraph (3), clause (i) of paragraph (4)(B), and subparagraphs (A) and (B) of paragraph (6).

(B) Only an objection to a rule or procedure which was raised with reasonable specificity during the period for public comment (including any public hearing) may be raised during judicial review. If the person raising an objection can demonstrate to the Administrator that it was impracticable to raise such objection within such time or if the grounds for such objection arose after the period for public comment (but within the time specified for judicial review) and if such objection is of central relevance to the outcome of the rule, the Administrator shall convene a proceeding for reconsideration of the rule and provide the same procedural rights as would have been afforded had the information been available at the time the rule was proposed. If the Administrator refuses to convene such a proceeding, such person may seek review of such refusal in the United States court of appeals for the appropriate circuit (as provided in subsection (b) of this section). Such reconsideration shall not postpone the effectiveness of the rule. The effectiveness of the rule may be stayed during such reconsideration, however, by the Administrator or the court for a period not to exceed three months.

(8) The sole forum for challenging procedural determinations made by the Administrator under this subsection shall be in the United States court of appeals for the appropriate circuit (as provided in subsection (b) of this section) at the time of the substantive review of the rule. No interlocutory appeals shall be permitted with respect to such procedural determinations. In reviewing alleged procedural errors, the court may invalidate the rule only if the errors were so serious and related to matters of such central relevance to the rule that there is a substantial likelihood that the rule would have been significantly changed if such errors had not been made.

(9) In the case of review of any action of the Administrator to which this subsection applies, the court may reverse any such action found to be—

(A) arbitrary, capricious, an abuse of discretion, or otherwise not in accordance with law;

(B) contrary to constitutional right, power, privilege, or immunity;

(C) in excess of statutory jurisdiction, authority, or limitations, or short of statutory right; or

(D) without observance of procedure required by law, if (i) such failure to observe such procedure is arbitrary or capricious, (ii) the requirement of paragraph (7)(B) has been met, and (iii) the condition of the last sentence of paragraph (8) is met.

(10) Each statutory deadline for promulgation of rules to which this subsection applies which requires promulgation less than six months after date of proposal may be extended to not more than six months after date of proposal by the Administrator upon a determination that such extension is necessary to afford the public, and the agency, adequate opportunity to carry out the purposes of this subsection.

(11) The requirements of this subsection shall take effect with respect to any rule the proposal of which occurs after ninety days after August 7, 1977.

(e) Other methods of judicial review not authorized

Nothing in this chapter shall be construed to authorize judicial review of regulations or orders of the Administrator under this chapter, except as provided in this section.

(f) Costs

In any judicial proceeding under this section, the court may award costs of litigation (including reasonable attorney and expert witness fees) whenever it determines that such award is appropriate.

(g) Stay, injunction, or similar relief in proceedings relating to noncompliance penalties

In any action respecting the promulgation of regulations under section 7420 of this title or the administration or enforcement of section 7420 of this title no court shall grant any stay, injunctive, or similar relief before final judgment by such court in such action.

(July 14, 1955, ch. 360, title III, § 307, as added Dec. 31, 1970, Pub.L. 91–604, § 12(a), 84 Stat. 1707, and amended Nov. 18, 1971, Pub.L. 92–157, title III, § 302(a), 85 Stat. 464; June 22, 1974, Pub.L. 93–319, § 6(c), 88 Stat. 259; Aug. 7, 1977, Pub.L. 95–95, title III, §§ 303(d), 305(a), (c), (f)–(h), 91 Stat. 772, 776, 777; Nov. 16, 1977, Pub.L. 95–190, § 14(a)(79), (80), 91 Stat. 1404.)

[1] So in original. Subsec. (a) enacted without a par. (2).

[2] So in original. The word "to" probably should not appear.

Federal Practice and Procedure

Holding back of trade secrets, see Wright & Graham: Evidence § 5437.

Code of Federal Regulations

Public information, see 40 CFR 2.100 et seq.

Library References

Health and Environment ⚷25.6(1), 28.
C.J.S. Health and Environment § 91 et seq.

United States Supreme Court

Attorney fees, appropriateness of award by federal court in absence of success on merits, see Ruckelshaus v. Sierra Club, 1983, 103 S.Ct. 3274, 462 U.S. 680, 77 L.Ed.2d 938.

§ 7608. Mandatory licensing

Whenever the Attorney General determines, upon application of the Administrator—

(1) that—

(A) in the implementation of the requirements of section 7411, 7412, or 7521 of this title, a right under any United States letters patent, which is being used or intended for public or commercial use and not otherwise reasonably available, is necessary to enable any person required to comply with such limitation to so comply, and

(B) there are no reasonable alternative methods to accomplish such purpose, and

(2) that the unavailability of such right may result in a substantial lessening of competition or tendency to create a monopoly in any line of commerce in any section of the country,

the Attorney General may so certify to a district court of the United States, which may issue an order requiring the person who owns such patent to license it on such reasonable terms and conditions as the court, after hearing, may determine. Such certification may be made to the district court for the district in which the person owning the patent resides, does business, or is found.

(July 14, 1955, ch. 360, title III, § 308, as added Dec. 31, 1970, Pub.L. 91–604, § 12(a), 84 Stat. 1708.)

Library References

Health and Environment ⚷25.6(1).
C.J.S. Health and Environment § 91 et seq.

§ 7609. Policy review

(a) Environmental impact

The Administrator shall review and comment in writing on the environmental impact of any matter relating to duties and responsibilities granted pursuant to this chapter or other provisions of the authority of the Administrator, contained in any (1) legislation proposed by any Federal department or agency, (2) newly authorized Federal projects for construction and any major Federal agency action (other than a project for construction) to which section 4332(2)(C) of this title applies, and (3) proposed regulations published by any department or agency of the Federal Government. Such written comment shall be made public at the conclusion of any such review.

(b) Unsatisfactory legislation, action, or regulation

In the event the Administrator determines that any such legislation, action, or regulation is unsatisfactory from the standpoint of public health or welfare or environmental quality, he shall publish his determination and the matter shall be referred to the Council on Environmental Quality.

(July 14, 1955, ch. 360, title III, § 309, as added Dec. 31, 1970, Pub.L. 91–604, § 12(a), 84 Stat. 1709.)

Code of Federal Regulations

Council on Environmental Quality,
- Agency compliance, see 40 CFR 1507.1 et seq.
- Agency decisions, see 40 CFR 1505.1 et seq.
- Commenting, see 40 CFR 1503.1 et seq.
- Environmental quality, see 14 CFR 1216.100 et seq.
- Impact statements, see 40 CFR 1502.1 et seq.
- National Science Foundation, compliance with NEPA, see 45 CFR 640.1 et seq.
- NEPA,
  - Agency planning, see 40 CFR 1501.1 et seq.
  - Purpose, policy and mandate, see 40 CFR 1500.1 et seq.
- Other NEPA requirements, see 40 CFR 1506.1 et seq.
- Predecision referrals to Council, see 40 CFR 1504.1 et seq.
- Terminology, see 40 CFR 1508.1 et seq.

Library References

Health and Environment ⚷25.6(1).
C.J.S. Health and Environment § 91 et seq.

§ 7610. Other authority

(a) Authority and responsibilities under other laws not affected

Except as provided in subsection (b) of this section, this chapter shall not be construed as superseding or limiting the authorities and responsibilities, under any other provision of law, of the Administrator or any other Federal officer, department, or agency.

(b) Nonduplication of appropriations

No appropriation shall be authorized or made under section 241, 243, or 246 of this title for any fiscal year after the fiscal year ending June 30, 1964, for any purpose for which appropriations may be made under authority of this chapter.

(July 14, 1955, ch. 360, title III, § 310, formerly § 10, as added Dec. 17, 1963, Pub.L. 88–206, § 1, 77 Stat. 401, renumbered § 303, Oct. 20, 1965, Pub.L. 89–272, title I, § 101(4), 79 Stat. 992, amended Nov. 21, 1967, Pub.L. 90–148, § 2, 81 Stat. 505, and renumbered § 310, and amended Dec. 31, 1970, Pub.L. 91–604, §§ 12(a), 15(c)(2), 84 Stat. 1705, 1713.)

Library References

United States ⚷85.
C.J.S. United States § 123.

§ 7611. Records and audit

(a) Recipients of assistance to keep prescribed records

Each recipient of assistance under this chapter shall keep such records as the Administrator shall prescribe, including records which fully disclose the amount and disposition by such recipient of the proceeds of such assistance, the total cost of the project or undertaking in connection with which such assistance is given or used, and the amount of that portion of the cost of the project or undertaking supplied by other sources, and such other records as will facilitate an effective audit.

(b) Audits

The Administrator and the Comptroller General of the United States, or any of their duly authorized representatives, shall have access for the purpose of audit and examinations to any books, documents, papers, and records of the recipients that are pertinent to the grants received under this chapter.

(July 14, 1955, ch. 360, title III, § 311, formerly § 11, as added Dec. 17, 1963, Pub.L. 88–206, § 1, 77 Stat. 401, renumbered § 304, Oct. 20, 1965, Pub.L. 89–272, title I, § 101(4), 79 Stat. 992, amended Nov. 21, 1967, Pub.L. 90–148, § 2, 81 Stat. 505, and renumbered § 311, and amended Dec. 31, 1970, Pub.L. 91–604, §§ 12(a), 15(c)(2), 84 Stat. 1705, 1713.)

Library References

Health and Environment ⚷25.6(2).
C.J.S. Health and Environment § 125 et seq.

§ 7612. Cost studies

(a) Detailed cost estimate; comprehensive cost and economic impact studies; annual reevaluation

In order to provide the basis for evaluating programs authorized by this chapter and the development of new programs and to furnish the Congress with the information necessary for authorization of appropriations by fiscal years beginning after June

30, 1969, the Administrator, in cooperation with State, interstate, and local air pollution control agencies, shall make a detailed estimate of the cost of carrying out the provisions of this chapter; a comprehensive study of the cost of program implementation by affected units of government; and a comprehensive study of the economic impact of air quality standards on the Nation's industries, communities, and other contributing sources of pollution, including an analysis of the national requirements for and the cost of controlling emissions to attain such standard of air quality as may be established pursuant to this chapter or applicable State law. The Administrator shall submit such detailed estimate and the results of such comprehensive study of cost for the five-year period beginning July 1, 1969, and the results of such other studies, to the Congress not later than January 10, 1969, and shall submit a reevaluation of such estimate and studies annually thereafter.

(b), (c) Omitted

(July 14, 1955, c. 360, Title III, § 312, formerly § 305, as added Nov. 21, 1967, Pub.L. 90–148, § 2, 81 Stat. 505, and renumbered and amended Dec. 31, 1970, Pub.L. 91–604, §§ 12(a), 15(c)(2), 84 Stat. 1705, 1713; Aug. 7, 1977, Pub.L. 95–95, Title II, § 224(c), 91 Stat. 767.)

§ 7613. Additional reports to Congress

Not later than six months after November 21, 1967, and not later than January 10 of each calendar year beginning after such date, the Administrator shall report to the Congress on measures taken toward implementing the purpose and intent of this chapter including, but not limited to, (1) the progress and problems associated with control of automotive exhaust emissions and the research efforts related thereto; (2) the development of air quality criteria and recommended emission control requirements; (3) the status of enforcement actions taken pursuant to this chapter; (4) the status of State ambient air standards setting, including such plans for implementation and enforcement as have been developed; (5) the extent of development and expansion of air pollution monitoring systems; (6) progress and problems related to development of new and improved control techniques; (7) the development of quantitative and qualitative instrumentation to monitor emissions and air quality; (8) standards set or under consideration pursuant to subchapter II of this chapter; (9) the status of State, interstate, and local pollution control programs established pursuant to and assisted by this chapter; (10) the reports and recommendations made by the President's Air Quality Advisory Board; and (11)(A) the status of plan provisions developed by States as required under section 7410(a)(2)(F)(v) of this title, and an accounting of States failing to develop suitable plans; (B) the number of annual incidents of air pollution reaching or exceeding levels determined to present an imminent and substantial endangerment to health (within the meaning of section 7603 of this title) by location, date, pollution source, and the duration of the emergency; (C) measures taken pursuant to section 7410(a)(2)(F)(v) of this title, and an evaluation of their effectiveness in reducing pollution; and (D) an accounting of those instances in which an air pollution alert, warning, or emergency is declared as required under regulations of the Administrator and in which no action is taken by either the Administrator, State, or local officials, together with an explanation for the failure to take action.

(July 14, 1955, ch. 360, title III, § 313, formerly § 306, as added Nov. 21, 1967, Pub.L. 90–148, § 2, 81 Stat. 506, and renumbered and amended Dec. 31, 1970, Pub.L. 91–604, §§ 12(a), 15(c)(2), 84 Stat. 1705, 1713; Aug. 7, 1977, Pub.L. 95–95, title III, § 302(b), 91 Stat. 771.)

Code of Federal Regulations

Air quality surveillance, see 40 CFR 58.1 et seq.

Library References

Health and Environment ⚬25.6(4).
C.J.S. Health and Environment § 95 et seq.

§ 7614. Labor standards

The Administrator shall take such action as may be necessary to insure that all laborers and mechanics employed by contractors or subcontractors on projects assisted under this chapter shall be paid wages at rates not less than those prevailing for the same type of work on similar construction in the locality as determined by the Secretary of Labor, in accordance with the Act of March 3, 1931, as amended, known as the Davis-Bacon Act (46 Stat. 1494; 40 U.S.C. 276a—276a–5). The Secretary of Labor shall have, with respect to the labor standards specified in this subsection, the authority and functions set forth in Reorganization Plan Numbered 14 of 1950 (15 F.R. 3176; 64 Stat. 1267) and section 276c of title 40.

(July 14, 1955, ch. 360, title III, § 314, formerly § 307, as added Nov. 21, 1967, Pub.L. 90–148, § 2, 81 Stat. 506, and renumbered and amended Dec. 31, 1970, Pub.L. 91–604, §§ 12(a), 15(c)(2), 84 Stat. 1705, 1713.)

Library References

Labor Relations ⚬1129.
C.J.S. Labor Relations § 1039 et seq.

§ 7615. Separability of provisions

If any provision of this chapter, or the application of any provision of this chapter to any person or circumstance, is held invalid, the application of such provision to other persons or circumstances, and the remainder of this chapter shall not be affected thereby.

(July 14, 1955, ch. 360, title III, § 315, formerly § 12, as added Dec. 17, 1963, Pub.L. 88–206, § 1, 77 Stat. 401, renumbered § 305, Oct. 20, 1965, Pub.L. 89–272, title I, § 101(4), 79 Stat. 992, amended and renumbered § 308, Nov. 21, 1967, Pub.L. 90–148, § 2, 81 Stat. 506, and renumbered § 315, Dec. 31, 1970, Pub.L. 91–604, § 12(a), 84 Stat. 1705.)

Library References

Statutes ⚷64(2).
C.J.S. Statutes § 96 et seq.

§ 7616. Sewage treatment grants

(a) Construction

No grant which the Administrator is authorized to make to any applicant for construction of sewage treatment works in any area in any State may be withheld, conditioned, or restricted by the Administrator on the basis of any requirement of this chapter except as provided in subsection (b) of this section.

(b) Withholding, conditioning, or restriction of construction grants

The Administrator may withhold, condition, or restrict the making of any grant for construction referred to in subsection (a) of this section only if he determines that—

(1) such treatment works will not comply with applicable standards under section 7411 or 7412 of this title,

(2) the State does not have in effect, or is not carrying out, a State implementation plan approved by the Administrator which expressly quantifies and provides for the increase in emissions of each air pollutant (from stationary and mobile sources in any area to which either part C or part D of subchapter I of this chapter applies for such pollutant) which increase may reasonably be anticipated to result directly or indirectly from the new sewage treatment capacity which would be created by such construction.

(3) the construction of such treatment works would create new sewage treatment capacity which—

(A) may reasonably be anticipated to cause or contribute to, directly or indirectly, an increase in emissions of any air pollutant in excess of the increase provided for under the provisions referred to in paragraph (2) for any such area, or

(B) would otherwise not be in conformity with the applicable implementation plan, or

(4) such increase in emissions would interfere with, or be inconsistent with, the applicable implementation plan for any other State.

In the case of construction of a treatment works which would result, directly or indirectly, in an increase in emissions of any air pollutant from stationary and mobile sources in an area to which part D of subchapter I of this chapter applies, the quantification of emissions referred to in paragraph (2) shall include the emissions of any such pollutant resulting directly or indirectly from areawide and nonmajor stationary source growth (mobile and stationary) for each such area.

(c) National Environmental Policy Act

Nothing in this section shall be construed to amend or alter any provision of the National Environmental Policy Act [42 U.S.C. 4321 et seq.] or to affect any determination as to whether or not the requirements of such Act have been met in the case of the construction of any sewage treatment works.

(July 14, 1955, ch. 360, title III, § 316, as added Aug. 7, 1977, Pub.L. 95–95, title III, § 306, 91 Stat. 777.)

Library References

Health and Environment ⚷25.7(7).
United States ⚷82(2).
C.J.S. Health and Environment § 108 et seq.
C.J.S. United States § 122.

§ 7617. Economic impact assessment

(a) Notice of proposed rulemaking; substantial revisions

This section applies to action of the Administrator in promulgating or revising—

(1) any new source standard of performance under section 7411 of this title,

(2) any regulation under section 7411(d) of this title,

(3) any regulation under part B of subchapter I of this chapter (relating to ozone and stratosphere protection),

(4) any regulation under part C of subchapter I of this chapter (relating to prevention of significant deterioration of air quality),

(5) any regulation establishing emission standards under section 7521 of this title and any other regulation promulgated under that section,

(6) any regulation controlling or prohibiting any fuel or fuel additive under section 7545(c) of this title, and

(7) any aircraft emission standard under section 7571 of this title.

Nothing in this section shall apply to any standard or regulation described in paragraphs (1) through (7) of this subsection unless the notice of proposed rulemaking in connection with such standard or regulation is published in the Federal Register after the date ninety days after August 7, 1977. In the case of revisions of such standards or regulations, this section shall apply only to revisions which the Administrator determines to be substantial revisions.

(b) Preparation of assessment by Administrator

Before publication of notice of proposed rulemaking with respect to any standard or regulation to which this section applies, the Administrator shall prepare an economic impact assessment respecting such standard or regulation. Such assessment shall be included in the docket required under section 7607(d)(2) of this title and shall be available to the public as provided in section 7607(d)(4) of this title. Notice of proposed rulemaking shall include notice of such availability together with an explanation of the extent and manner in which the Administrator has considered the analysis contained in such economic impact assessment in proposing the action. The Administrator shall also provide such an explanation in his notice of promulgation of any regulation or standard referred to in subsection (a) of this section. Each such explanation shall be part of the statements of basis and purpose required under sections 7607(d)(3) and 7607(d)(6) of this title.

(c) Analysis

Subject to subsection (d) of this section, the assessment required under this section with respect to any standard or regulation shall contain an analysis of—

(1) the costs of compliance with any such standard or regulation, including extent to which the costs of compliance will vary depending on (A) the effective date of the standard or regulation, and (B) the development of less expensive, more efficient means or methods of compliance with the standard or regulation;

(2) the potential inflationary or recessionary effects of the standard or regulation;

(3) the effects on competition of the standard or regulation with respect to small business;

(4) the effects of the standard or regulation on consumer costs; and

(5) the effects of the standard or regulation on energy use.

Nothing in this section shall be construed to provide that the analysis of the factors specified in this subsection affects or alters the factors which the Administrator is required to consider in taking any action referred to in subsection (a) of this section.

(d) Extensiveness of assessment

The assessment required under this section shall be as extensive as practicable, in the judgment of the Administrator taking into account the time and resources available to the Environmental Protection Agency and other duties and authorities which the Administrator is required to carry out under this chapter.

(e) Limitations on construction of section

Nothing in this section shall be construed—

(1) to alter the basis on which a standard or regulation is promulgated under this chapter;

(2) to preclude the Administrator from carrying out his responsibility under this chapter to protect public health and welfare; or

(3) to authorize or require any judicial review of any such standard or regulation, or any stay or injunction of the proposal, promulgation, or effectiveness of such standard or regulation on the basis of failure to comply with this section.

(f) Citizen suits

The requirements imposed on the Administrator under this section shall be treated as nondiscretionary duties for purposes of section 7604(a)(2) of this title, relating to citizen suits. The sole method for enforcement of the Administrator's duty under this section shall be by bringing a citizen suit under such section 7604(a)(2) for a court order to compel the Administrator to perform such duty. Violation of any such order shall subject the Administrator to penalties for contempt of court.

(g) Costs

In the case of any provision of this chapter in which costs are expressly required to be taken into account, the adequacy or inadequacy of any assessment required under this section may be taken into consideration, but shall not be treated for purposes of judicial review of any such provision as conclusive with respect to compliance or noncompliance with the requirement of such provision to take cost into account.

(July 14, 1955, ch. 360, title III, § 317, as added Aug. 7, 1977, Pub.L. 95–95, title III, § 307, 91 Stat. 778, and amended Nov. 9, 1978, Pub.L. 95–623, § 13(d), 92 Stat. 3458.)

§ 7618. Financial disclosure; conflicts of interest

(a) Statement; filing; availability to public

Each person who—

(1) has any known financial interest in (A) any person subject to this chapter, or (B) any person who applies for or receives any grant, contract, or

other form of financial assistance pursuant to this chapter, and

(2) is (A) an officer or employee of the Environmental Protection Agency who performs any function of[1] duty under this chapter, (B) a member of the National Commission on Air Quality appointed as a member of the public, or (C) a member of the scientific review committee under section 7409(d) of this title

shall, beginning six months after August 7, 1977, annually file with the Administrator a written statement concerning all such interests held by such officer, employee, or member during the preceding calendar year. Such statement shall be available to the public.

(b) Known financial interest; monitoring and enforcement of requirement; annual report to Congress

The Administrator shall—

(1) act within ninety days after August 7, 1977—

(A) to define the term "known financial interest" for purposes of subsection (a) of this section;

(B) to establish the methods by which the requirement to file written statements specified in subsection (a) of this section will be monitored and enforced, including appropriate provisions for the filing by such officers, employees and members of such statements and the review by the Administrator (or the Commission in the case of members of the Commission) of such statements; and

(2) report to the Congress on June 1 of each calendar year with respect to such statements to the Administrator and the actions taken in regard thereto during the preceding calendar year.

(c) Conflict of interest

After the date one year after August 7, 1977, no person who—

(1) is employed by, serves as attorney for, acts as a consultant for, or holds any other official or contractual relationship to—

(A) the owner or operator of any major stationary source or any stationary source which is subject to a standard of performance or emission standard under section 7411 or 7412 of this title,

(B) any manufacturer of any class or category of mobile sources if such mobile sources are subject to regulation under this chapter,

(C) any trade or business association of which such owner or operator referred to in subparagraph (A) or such manufacturer referred to in subparagraph (B) is a member[2] or

(D) any organization (whether or not nonprofit) which is a party to litigation, or engaged in political, educational, or informational activities, relating to air quality, or

(2) owns, or has any financial interest in, any stock, bonds, or other financial interest which ownership or interest may be inconsistent with a position as an officer or employee of the Environmental Protection Agency, as determined under regulations of the Administrator,

may concurrently serve as such an officer or employee of the Environmental Protection Agency.

(d) Exemptions; particular ownerships or financial interests

The Administrator shall promulgate rules for purposes of subsections (b) and (c) of this section which—

(1) identify specific offices or positions within such agency which are of a nonregulatory or nonpolicymaking nature and provide that officers or employees occupying such positions shall be exempt from the requirements of this section, and

(2) identify the ownership or financial interests which may be inconsistent with particular regulatory or policymaking offices or positions within the Environmental Protection Agency.

(e) Penalty

Any officer or employee of the Environmental Protection Agency or member of the National Commission on Air Quality or of the scientific review committee under section 7409(d) of this title who is subject to, and knowingly violates, this section or any regulation issued thereunder, shall be fined not more than $2,500 or imprisoned not more than one year, or both.

(f) Disclosure or conflict of interest under other Federal statutes; generally applicable requirements

Nothing in this section shall be construed to affect or impair any other Federal statutory requirements respecting disclosure or conflict of interest applicable to the Environmental Protection Agency. Subsections (c) and (d) of this section shall not apply after the effective date of any such requirements respecting conflicts of interest which are generally applicable to departments, agencies, and instrumentalities of the United States.

(July 14, 1955, ch. 360, title III, § 318, as added Aug. 7, 1977, Pub.L. 95–95, title III, § 308, 91 Stat. 780.)

1 So in original. Probably should be "or".

2 So in original. Probably should be followed by a comma.

§ 7619. Air quality monitoring

Not later than one year after August 7, 1977, and after notice and opportunity for public hearing, the Administrator shall promulgate regulations establishing an air quality monitoring system throughout the United States which—

(1) utilizes uniform air quality monitoring criteria and methodology and measures such air quality according to a uniform air quality index,

(2) provides for air quality monitoring stations in major urban areas and other appropriate areas throughout the United States to provide monitoring such as will supplement (but not duplicate) air quality monitoring carried out by the States required under any applicable implementation plan,

(3) provides for daily analysis and reporting of air quality based upon such uniform air quality index, and

(4) provides for recordkeeping with respect to such monitoring data and for periodic analysis and reporting to the general public by the Administrator with respect to air quality based upon such data.

The operation of such air quality monitoring system may be carried out by the Administrator or by such other departments, agencies, or entities of the Federal Government (including the National Weather Service) as the President may deem appropriate. Any air quality monitoring system required under any applicable implementation plan under section 7410 of this title shall, as soon as practicable following promulgation of regulations under this section, utilize the standard criteria and methodology, and measure air quality according to the standard index, established under such regulations.

(July 14, 1955, ch. 360, title III, § 319, as added Aug. 7, 1977, Pub.L. 95–95, title III, § 309, 91 Stat. 781.)

Code of Federal Regulations

Air programs, generally, see 40 CFR 50.1 et seq.
Implementation plans, requirements concerning, see 40 CFR 51.1 et seq.
New stationary sources, performance standards, see 40 CFR 60.1 et seq.
Surveillance of ambient air quality, see 40 CFR 58.1 et seq.

Library References

Health and Environment ⚷25.6(1).
C.J.S. Health and Environment § 91 et seq.

§ 7620. Standardized air quality modeling

(a) Conferences

Not later than six months after August 7, 1977, and at least every three years thereafter, the Administrator shall conduct a conference on air quality modeling. In conducting such conference, special attention shall be given to appropriate modeling necessary for carrying out part C of subchapter I of this chapter (relating to prevention of significant deterioration of air quality).

(b) Conferees

The conference conducted under this section shall provide for participation by the National Academy of Sciences, representatives of State and local air pollution control agencies, and appropriate Federal agencies, including the National Science Foundation;[1] the National Oceanic and Atmospheric Administration, and the National Bureau of Standards.

(c) Comments; transcripts

Interested persons shall be permitted to submit written comments and a verbatim transcript of the conference proceedings shall be maintained.

(d) Promulgation and revision of regulations relating to air quality modeling

The comments submitted and the transcript maintained pursuant to subsection (c) of this section shall be included in the docket required to be established for purposes of promulgating or revising any regulation relating to air quality modeling under part C of subchapter I of this chapter.

(July 14, 1955, ch. 360, title III, § 320, as added Aug. 7, 1977, Pub.L. 95–95, title III, § 310, 91 Stat. 782.)

[1] So in original. Probably should be a comma.

§ 7621. Employment effects

(a) Continuous evaluation of potential loss or shifts of employment

The Administrator shall conduct continuing evaluations of potential loss or shifts of employment which may result from the administration or enforcement of the provision of this chapter and applicable implementation plans, including where appropriate, investigating threatened plant closures or reductions in employment allegedly resulting from such administration or enforcement.

(b) Request for investigation; hearings; record; report

Any employee, or any representative of such employee, who is discharged or laid off, threatened with discharge or layoff, or whose employment is otherwise adversely affected or threatened to be adversely affected because of the alleged results of any requirement imposed or proposed to be imposed under this chapter, including any requirement applicable to Federal facilities and any requirement imposed by a State or political subdivision thereof, may request the Administrator to conduct a full investigation of the matter. Any such request shall be reduced to writing, shall set forth with reasonable particularity the grounds for the request, and shall be signed by the employee, or representative of such employee, making the request. The Administrator shall thereupon investigate the matter and, at the request of any party, shall hold public hearings on not less than five days' notice. At such hearings, the Administrator shall require the parties, including the employer involved, to present information relating to the actual or potential effect of such requirements on employment and the detailed reasons or justification therefor. If the Administrator determines that there are no reasonable grounds for conducting a public hearing he shall notify (in writing) the party requesting such hearing of such a determination and the reasons therefor. If the Administrator does convene such a hearing, the hearing shall be on the record. Upon receiving the report of such investigation, the Administrator shall make findings of fact as to the effect of such requirements on employment and on the alleged actual or potential discharge, layoff, or other adverse effect on employment, and shall make such recommendations as he deems appropriate. Such report, findings, and recommendations shall be available to the public.

(c) Subpenas; confidential information; witnesses; penalty

In connection with any investigation or public hearing conducted under subsection (b) of this section or as authorized in section 7419 of this title (relating to primary nonferrous smelter orders), the Administrator may issue subpenas for the attendance and testimony of witnesses and the production of relevant papers, books and documents, and he may administer oaths. Except for emission data, upon a showing satisfactory to the Administrator by such owner or operator that such papers, books, documents, or information or particular part thereof, if made public, would divulge trade secrets or secret processes of such owner, or operator, the Administrator shall consider such record, report, or information or particular portion thereof confidential in accordance with the purposes of section 1905 of title 18, except that such paper, book, document, or information may be disclosed to other officers, employees, or authorized representatives of the United States concerned with carrying out this chapter, or when relevant in any proceeding under this chapter. Witnesses summoned shall be paid the same fees and mileage that are paid witnesses in the courts of the United States. In cases of contumacy or refusal to obey a subpena served upon any person under this subparagraph, the district court of the United States for any district in which such person is found or resides or transacts business, upon application by the United States and after notice to such person, shall have jurisdiction to issue an order requiring such person to appear and give testimony before the Administrator, to appear and produce papers, books, and documents before the Administrator, or both, and any failure to obey such order of the court may be punished by such court as a contempt thereof.

(d) Limitations on construction of section

Nothing in this section shall be construed to require or authorize the Administrator, the States, or political subdivisions thereof, to modify or withdraw any requirement imposed or proposed to be imposed under this chapter.

(July 14, 1955, ch. 360, title III, § 321, as added Aug. 7, 1977, Pub.L. 95–95, title III, § 311, 91 Stat. 782.)

§ 7622. Employee protection

(a) Discharge or discrimination prohibited

No employer may discharge any employee or otherwise discriminate against any employee with respect to his compensation, terms, conditions, or privileges of employment because the employee (or any person acting pursuant to a request of the employee)—

(1) commenced, caused to be commenced, or is about to commence or cause to be commenced a proceeding under this chapter or a proceeding for the administration or enforcement of any requirement imposed under this chapter or under any applicable implementation plan,

(2) testified or is about to testify in any such proceeding, or

(3) assisted or participated or is about to assist or participate in any manner in such a proceeding or in any other action to carry out the purposes of this chapter.

(b) Complaint charging unlawful discharge or discrimination; investigation; order

(1) Any employee who believes that he has been discharged or otherwise discriminated against by any person in violation of subsection (a) of this section may, within thirty days after such violation occurs, file (or have any person file on his behalf) a complaint with the Secretary of Labor (hereinafter in this subsection referred to as the "Secretary") alleging such discharge or discrimination. Upon receipt of such a complaint, the Secretary shall notify the person named in the complaint of the filing of the complaint.

(2)(A) Upon receipt of a complaint filed under paragraph (1), the Secretary shall conduct an investigation of the violation alleged in the complaint. Within thirty days of the receipt of such complaint, the Secretary shall complete such investigation and shall notify in writing the complainant (and any person acting in his behalf) and the person alleged to have committed such violation of the results of the investigation conducted pursuant to this subparagraph. Within ninety days of the receipt of such complaint the Secretary shall, unless the proceeding on the complaint is terminated by the Secretary on the basis of a settlement entered into by the Secretary and the person alleged to have committed such violation, issue an order either providing the relief prescribed by subparagraph (B) or denying the complaint. An order of the Secretary shall be made on the record after notice and opportunity for public hearing. The Secretary may not enter into a settlement terminating a proceeding on a complaint without the participation and consent of the complainant.

(B) If, in response to a complaint filed under paragraph (1), the Secretary determines that a violation of subsection (a) of this section has occurred, the Secretary shall order the person who committed such violation to (i) take affirmative action to abate the violation, and (ii) reinstate the complainant to his former position together with the compensation (including back pay), terms, conditions, and privileges of his employment, and the Secretary may order such person to provide compensatory damages to the complainant. If an order is issued under this paragraph, the Secretary, at the request of the complainant, shall assess against the person against whom the order is issued a sum equal to the aggregate amount of all costs and expenses (including attorneys' and expert witness fees) reasonably incurred, as determined by the Secretary, by the complainant for, or in connection with, the bringing of the complaint upon which the order was issued.

(c) Review

(1) Any person adversely affected or aggrieved by an order issued under subsection (b) of this section may obtain review of the order in the United States court of appeals for the circuit in which the violation, with respect to which the order was issued, allegedly occurred. The petition for review must be filed within sixty days from the issuance of the Secretary's order. Review shall conform to chapter 7 of title 5. The commencement of proceedings under this subparagraph shall not, unless ordered by the court, operate as a stay of the Secretary's order.

(2) An order of the Secretary with respect to which review could have been obtained under paragraph (1) shall not be subject to judicial review in any criminal or other civil proceeding.

(d) Enforcement of order by Secretary

Whenever a person has failed to comply with an order issued under subsection (b)(2) of this section, the Secretary may file a civil action in the United States district court for the district in which the violation was found to occur to enforce such order. In actions brought under this subsection, the district courts shall have jurisdiction to grant all appropriate relief including, but not limited to, injunctive relief, compensatory, and exemplary damages.

(e) Enforcement of order by person on whose behalf order was issued

(1) Any person on whose behalf an order was issued under paragraph (2) of subsection (b) of this section may commence a civil action against the person to whom such order was issued to require compliance with such order. The appropriate United States district court shall have jurisdiction, without regard to the amount in controversy or the citizenship of the parties, to enforce such order.

(2) The court, in issuing any final order under this subsection, may award costs of litigation (including reasonable attorney and expert witness fees) to any party whenever the court determines such award is appropriate.

(f) Mandamus

Any nondiscretionary duty imposed by this section shall be enforceable in a mandamus proceeding brought under section 1361 of title 28.

(g) Deliberate violation by employee

Subsection (a) of this section shall not apply with respect to any employee who, acting without direction from his employer (or the employer's agent), deliberately causes a violation of any requirement of this chapter.

(July 14, 1955, ch. 360, title III, § 322, as added Aug. 7, 1977, Pub.L. 95–95, title III, § 312, 91 Stat. 783.)

Code of Federal Regulations

Discrimination complaints, procedures, see 29 CFR 24.1 et seq.

§ 7623. Repealed. Pub. L. 96–300, § 1(c), July 2, 1980, 94 Stat. 831.

§ 7624. Cost of vapor recovery equipment

(a) Costs to be borne by owner of retail outlet

The regulations under this chapter applicable to vapor recovery with respect to mobile source fuels at retail outlets of such fuels shall provide that the cost of procurement and installation of such vapor recovery shall be borne by the owner of such outlet (as determined under such regulations). Except as provided in subsection (b) of this section, such regulations shall provide that no lease of a retail outlet by the owner thereof which is entered into or renewed after August 7, 1977, may provide for a payment by the lessee of the cost of procurement and installation of vapor recovery equipment. Such regulations shall also provide that the cost of procurement and installation of vapor recovery equipment may be recovered by the owner of such outlet by means of price increases in the cost of any product sold by such owner, notwithstanding any provision of law.

(b) Payment by lessee

The regulations of the Administrator referred to in subsection (a) of this section shall permit a lease of a retail outlet to provide for payment by the lessee of the cost of procurement and installation of vapor recovery equipment over a reasonable period (as determined in accordance with such regulations), if the owner of such outlet does not sell, trade in, or otherwise dispense any product at wholesale or retail at such outlet.

(July 14, 1955, ch. 360, title III, § 323 formerly § 324, as added Aug. 7, 1977, Pub.L. 95–95, title III, § 314(a), 91 Stat. 788, amended Nov. 16, 1977, Pub.L. 95–190, § 14(a)(82), 91 Stat. 1404, and renumbered and amended July 2, 1980, Pub.L. 96–300, § 1(b), (c), 94 Stat. 831.)

§ 7625. Vapor recovery for small business marketers of petroleum products

(a) Marketers of gasoline

The regulations under this chapter applicable to vapor recovery from fueling of motor vehicles at retail outlets of gasoline shall not apply to any outlet owned by an independent small business marketer of gasoline having monthly sales of less than 50,000 gallons. In the case of any other outlet owned by an independent small business marketer, such regulations shall provide, with respect to independent small business marketers of gasoline, for a three-year phase-in period for the installation of such vapor recovery equipment at such outlets under which such marketers shall have—

(1) 33 percent of such outlets in compliance at the end of the first year during which such regulations apply to such marketers,

(2) 66 percent at the end of such second year, and

(3) 100 percent at the end of the third year.

(b) State requirements

Nothing in subsection (a) of this section shall be construed to prohibit any State from adopting or enforcing, with respect to independent small business marketers of gasoline having monthly sales of less than 50,000 gallons, any vapor recovery requirements for mobile source fuels at retail outlets. Any vapor recovery requirement which is adopted by a State and submitted to the Administrator as part of its implementation plan may be approved and enforced by the Administrator as part of the applicable implementation plan for that State.

(c) Refiners

For purposes of this section, an independent small business marketer of gasoline is a person engaged in the marketing of gasoline who would be required to pay for procurement and installation of vapor recovery equipment under section 7624 of this title or under regulations of the Administrator, unless such person—

(1)(A) is a refiner, or

(B) controls, is controlled by, or is under common control with, a refiner,

(C) is otherwise directly or indirectly affiliated (as determined under the regulations of the Administrator) with a refiner or with a person who controls, is controlled by, or is under a common control with a refiner (unless the sole affiliation referred to herein is by means of a supply contract or an agreement or contract to use a trademark, trade name, service mark, or other identifying symbol or name owned by such refiner or any such person), or

(2) receives less than 50 percent of his annual income from refining or marketing of gasoline.

For the purpose of this section, the term "refiner" shall not include any refiner whose total refinery capacity (including the refinery capacity of any person who controls, is controlled by, or is under common control with, such refiner) does not exceed 65,000 barrels per day. For purposes of this section, "control" of a corporation means ownership of more than 50 percent of its stock.

(July 14, 1955, ch. 360, title III, § 324, formerly § 325, as added Aug. 7, 1977, Pub.L. 95–95, title III, § 314(b), 91 Stat. 789, and renumbered July 2, 1980, Pub.L. 96–300, § 1(c), 94 Stat. 831.)

§ 7625–1. Exemptions for certain territories

(a)(1) Upon petition by the governor of Guam, American Samoa, or the Commonwealth of the Northern Mariana Islands, the Administrator is authorized to exempt any person or source or class of persons or sources in such territory from any requirement under this chapter other than section 7412 of this title or any requirement under section 7410 of this title or part D of subchapter I of this chapter necessary to attain or maintain a national primary ambient air quality standard. Such exemption may be granted if the Administrator finds that compliance with such requirement is not feasible or is unreasonable due to unique geographical, meteorological, or economic factors of such territory, or such other local factors as the Administrator deems significant. Any such petition shall be considered in accordance with section 7607(d) of this title and any exemption under this subsection shall be considered final action by the Administrator for the purposes of section 7607(b) of this title.

(2) The Administrator shall promptly notify the Committees on Energy and Commerce and on Interior and Insular Affairs of the House of Representatives and the Committees on Environment and Public Works and on Energy and Natural Resources of the Senate upon receipt of any petition under this subsection and of the approval or rejection of such petition and the basis for such action.

(b) Notwithstanding any other provision of this chapter, any fossil fuel fired steam electric power plant operating within Guam as of December 8, 1983 is hereby exempted from:

(1) any requirement of the new source performance standards relating to sulfur dioxide promulgated under section 7411 of this title as of December 8, 1983; and

(2) any regulation relating to sulfur dioxide standards or limitations contained in a State implementation plan approved under section 7410 of this title as of December 8, 1983: *Provided,* That such exemption shall expire eighteen months after December 8, 1983, unless the Administrator determines that such plant is making all emissions reductions practicable to prevent exceedances of the national ambient air quality standards for sulfur dioxide.

(July 14, 1955, ch. 360, title III, § 325, as added Dec. 8, 1983, Pub.L. 98–213, § 11, 97 Stat. 1461.)

§ 7625a. Statutory construction

The parenthetical cross references in any provision of this chapter to other provisions of the chapter, or other provisions of law, where the words "relating to" or "pertaining to" are used, are made only for convenience, and shall be given no legal effect.

(July 14, 1955, ch. 360, title III, § 325, formerly § 326, as added Nov. 16, 1977, Pub.L. 95–190, § 14(a)(84), 91 Stat. 1404, and renumbered July 2, 1980, Pub.L. 96–300, § 1(c), 94 Stat. 831.)

§ 7626. Authorization of appropriations

(a) There are authorized to be appropriated to carry out this chapter (other than provisions for which amounts are authorized under subsection (b) of this section), $200,000,000 for the fiscal year 1978 and for each of the three fiscal years beginning thereafter.

(b)(1) There are authorized to be appropriated to carry out section 7505 of this title beginning in fiscal year 1978, $75,000,000 to be available until expended.

(2) There are authorized to be appropriated for use in carrying out section 7623 of this title (relating to National Commission on Air Quality), not to exceed $10,000,000 beginning in fiscal year 1978. For the study authorized under section 7623 of this title there shall be made available by contract to the National Commission on Air Quality from the appropriation to the Environmental Protection Agency for fiscal year 1977 the sum of $1,000,000.

(3) There are authorized to be appropriated to carry out section 7427 of this title (relating to grants for public notification) $4,000,000 for the fiscal year 1978 and each of the three succeeding fiscal years.

(4) For purposes of section 7403(a)(5) of this title, there are authorized to be appropriated $7,500,000 for the fiscal year 1978 and each of the three fiscal years beginning after August 7, 1977.

(5) For the purpose of carrying out the provisions of part B of subchapter I of this chapter relating to studies and reports, there are authorized to be appropriated—

(A) to the National Aeronautics and Space Administration, the National Science Foundation, and the Department of State, such sums as may be necessary for the fiscal year ending September 30, 1977, and the fiscal year ending September 30, 1978;

(B) to the Environmental Protection Agency, $157,000,000 for fiscal year 1978; and

(C) to all other agencies such sums as may be necessary.

(6) There are authorized to be appropriated for carrying out research, development and demonstration under sections 7403 and 7404 of this title $120,000,000 for fiscal year 1978.

(July 14, 1955, ch. 360, title III, § 326, formerly § 325, as added Aug. 7, 1977, Pub.L. 95–95, title III, § 315, 91 Stat. 790, renumbered § 327 and amended Nov. 16, 1977, Pub.L. 95–190, § 14(a)(83), 91 Stat. 1404, renumbered § 326, July 2, 1980, Pub.L. 96–300, § 1(c), 94 Stat. 831.)

Library References

United States ⟹85.
C.J.S. United States § 123.

SUBCHAPTER IV—NOISE POLLUTION

§ 7641. Noise abatement

(a) Office of Noise Abatement and Control

The Administrator shall establish within the Environmental Protection Agency an Office of Noise Abatement and Control, and shall carry out through such Office a full and complete investigation and study of noise and its effect on the public health and welfare in order to (1) identify and classify causes and sources of noise, and (2) determine—

(A) effects at various levels;

(B) projected growth of noise levels in urban areas through the year 2000;

(C) the psychological and physiological effect on humans;

(D) effects of sporadic extreme noise (such as jet noise near airports) as compared with constant noise;

(E) effect on wildlife and property (including values);

(F) effect of sonic booms on property (including values); and

(G) such other matters as may be of interest in the public welfare.

(b) Investigation techniques; report and recommendations

In conducting such investigation, the Administrator shall hold public hearings, conduct research, experiments, demonstrations, and studies. The Administrator shall report the results of such investigation and study, together with his recommendations for legislation or other action, to the President and the Congress not later than one year after December 31, 1970.

(c) Abatement of noise from Federal activities

In any case where any Federal department or agency is carrying out or sponsoring any activity resulting in noise which the Administrator determines amounts to a public nuisance or is otherwise objectionable, such department or agency shall consult with the Administrator to determine possible means of abating such noise.

(July 14, 1955, ch. 360, title IV, § 402, as added Dec. 31, 1970, Pub.L. 91–604, § 14, 84 Stat. 1709.)

Library References

Health and Environment ⚿25.8.
C.J.S. Health and Environment § 61 et seq.

§ 7642. Authorization of appropriations

There is authorized to be appropriated such amount, not to exceed $30,000,000, as may be necessary for the purposes of this subchapter.

(July 14, 1955, ch. 360, title IV, § 403, as added Dec. 31, 1970, Pub.L. 91–604, § 14, 84 Stat. 1710.)

COMPREHENSIVE ENVIRONMENTAL RESPONSE, COMPENSATION AND LIABILITY

(42 U.S.C.A. §§ 9601 to 9675)

CHAPTER 103—COMPREHENSIVE ENVIRONMENTAL RESPONSE, COMPENSATION, AND LIABILITY

SUBCHAPTER I—HAZARDOUS SUBSTANCES RELEASES, LIABILITY, COMPENSATION

SUBCHAPTER IV—POLLUTION INSURANCE

West's Federal Forms

Administrative agency decisions and orders, enforcement and review, see § 851 et seq.
Administrative subpoenas, enforcement, see § 6004 et seq.
Depositions and discovery, see §§ 3271 et seq., 3681 et seq.
Intervention, motion for leave, see § 3111 et seq.
Jurisdiction and venue in district courts, see § 1003 et seq.
Production of documents, motions and orders pertaining to, see § 3551 et seq.
Sentence and fine, see § 7531 et seq.
Subpoenas, see § 3981 et seq.

WESTLAW Electronic Research

See WESTLAW guide following the Explanation pages of this pamphlet.

SUBCHAPTER I—HAZARDOUS SUBSTANCES RELEASES, LIABILITY, COMPENSATION

§ 9601. Definitions

For purpose of this subchapter—

(1) The term "act of God" means an unanticipated grave natural disaster or other natural phenomenon of an exceptional, inevitable, and irresistible character, the effects of which could not have been prevented or avoided by the exercise of due care or foresight.

(2) The term "Administrator" means the Administrator of the United States Environmental Protection Agency.

(3) The term "barrel" means forty-two United States gallons at sixty degrees Fahrenheit.

(4) The term "claim" means a demand in writing for a sum certain.

(5) The term "claimant" means any person who presents a claim for compensation under this chapter.

(6) The term "damages" means damages for injury or loss of natural resources as set forth in section 9607(a) or 9611(b) of this title.

(7) The term "drinking water supply" means any raw or finished water source that is or may be used by a public water system (as defined in the Safe Drinking Water Act [42 U.S.C. 300f et seq.]) or as drinking water by one or more individuals.

(8) The term "environment" means (A) the navigable waters, the waters of the contiguous zone, and the ocean waters for which the natural resources are under the exclusive management authority of the United States under the Magnuson Fishery Conservation and Management Act [16 U.S.C. 1801 et seq.], and (B) any other surface water, ground water, drinking water supply, land surface or subsurface strata, or ambient air within the United States or under the jurisdiction of the United States.

(9) The term "facility" means (A) any building, structure, installation, equipment, pipe or pipeline (including any pipe into a sewer or publicly owned treatment works), well, pit, pond, lagoon, impoundment, ditch, landfill, storage container, motor vehicle, rolling stock, or aircraft, or (B) any site or area where a hazardous substance has been deposited, stored, disposed of, or placed, or otherwise come to be located; but does not include any consumer product in consumer use or any vessel.

(10) The term "federally permitted release" means (A) discharges in compliance with a permit under section 1342 of Title 33, (B) discharges resulting from circumstances identified and reviewed and made part of the public record with respect to a permit issued or modified under section 1342 of Title 33 and subject to a condition of such permit, (C) continuous or anticipated intermittent discharges from a point source, identified in a permit or permit application under section 1342 of Title 33, which are caused by events occurring within the scope of relevant operating or treatment systems, (D) discharges in compliance with a legally enforceable permit under section 1344 of Title 33, (E) releases in compliance with a legally enforceable final permit issued pursuant to section 3005(a) through (d) of the Solid Waste Disposal Act [42 U.S.C. 6925(a) to (d)] from a hazardous waste treatment, storage, or disposal facility when such permit specifically

identifies the hazardous substances and makes such substances subject to a standard of practice, control procedure or bioassay limitation or condition, or other control on the hazardous substances in such releases, (F) any release in compliance with a legally enforceable permit issued under section 1412 of Title 33 of[1] section 1413 of Title 33, (G) any injection of fluids authorized under Federal underground injection control programs or State programs submitted for Federal approval (and not disapproved by the Administrator of the Environmental Protection Agency) pursuant to part C of the Safe Drinking Water Act [42 U.S.C. 300h et seq.], (H) any emission into the air subject to a permit or control regulation under section 111 [42 U.S.C. 7411], section 112 [42 U.S.C. 7412], Title I part C [42 U.S.C. 7470 et seq.], Title I part D [42 U.S.C. 7501 et seq.], or State implementation plans submitted in accordance with section 110 of the Clean Air Act [42 U.S.C. 7410] (and not disapproved by the administrator of the Environmental Protection Agency), including any schedule or waiver granted, promulgated, or approved under these sections, (I) any injection of fluids or other materials authorized under applicable State law (i) for the purpose of stimulating or treating wells for the production of crude oil, natural gas, or water, (ii) for the purpose of secondary, tertiary, or other enhanced recovery of crude oil or natural gas, or (iii) which are brought to the surface in conjunction with the production of crude oil or natural gas and which are reinjected, (J) the introduction of any pollutant into a publicly owned treatment works when such pollutant is specified in and in compliance with applicable pretreatment standards of section 1317(b) or (c) of Title 33 and enforceable requirements in a pretreatment program submitted by a State or municipality for Federal approval under section 1342 of Title 33, and (K) any release of source, special nuclear, or byproduct material, as those terms are defined in the Atomic Energy Act of 1954 [42 U.S.C. 2011 et seq.], in compliance with a legally enforceable license, permit, regulation, or order issued pursuant to the Atomic Energy Act of 1954.

(11) The term "Fund" or "Trust Fund" means the Hazardous Substance Superfund established by section 9507 of Title 26.

(12) The term "ground water" means water in a saturated zone or stratum beneath the surface of land or water.

(13) The term "guarantor" means any person, other than the owner or operator, who provides evidence of financial responsibility for an owner or operator under this chapter.

(14) The term "hazardous substance" means (A) any substance designated pursuant to section 1321(b)(2)(A) of Title 33, (B) any element, compound, mixture, solution, or substance designated pursuant to section 9602 of this title, (C) any hazardous waste having the characteristics identified under or listed pursuant to section 3001 of the Solid Waste Disposal Act [42 U.S.C. 6921] (but not including any waste the regulation of which under the Solid Waste Disposal Act [42 U.S.C. 6901 et seq.] has been suspended by Act of Congress), (D) any toxic pollutant listed under section 1317(a) of Title 33, (E) any hazardous air pollutant listed under section 112 of the Clean Air Act [42 U.S.C. 7412], and (F) any imminently hazardous chemical substance or mixture with respect to which the Administrator has taken action pursuant to section 2606 of Title 15. The term does not include petroleum, including crude oil or any fraction thereof which is not otherwise specifically listed or designated as a hazardous substance under subparagraphs (A) through (F) of this paragraph, and the term does not include natural gas, natural gas liquids, liquefied natural gas, or synthetic gas usable for fuel (or mixtures of natural gas and such synthetic gas).

(15) The term "navigable waters" or "navigable waters of the United States" means the waters of the United States, including the territorial seas.

(16) The term "natural resources" means land, fish, wildlife, biota, air, water, ground water, drinking water supplies, and other such resources belonging to, managed by, held in trust by, appertaining to, or otherwise controlled by the United States (including the resources of the fishery conservation zone established by the Magnuson Fishery Conservation and Management Act [16 U.S.C. 1801 et seq.]) any State or local government, any foreign government, any Indian tribe, or, if such resources are subject to a trust restriction on alienation, any member of an Indian tribe.

(17) The term "offshore facility" means any facility of any kind located in, on, or under, any of the navigable waters of the United States, and any facility of any kind which is subject to the jurisdiction of the United States and is located in, on, or under any other waters, other than a vessel or a public vessel.

(18) The term "onshore facility" means any facility (including, but not limited to, motor vehicles and rolling stock) of any kind located in, on, or under, any land or nonnavigable waters within the United States.

(19) The term "otherwise subject to the jurisdiction of the United States" means subject to the jurisdiction of the United States by virtue of United States citizenship, United States vessel documentation or numbering, or as provided by international agreement to which the United States is a party.

(20)(A) The term "owner or operator" means (i) in the case of a vessel, any person owning, operating, or chartering by demise, such vessel, (ii) in the case of an onshore facility or an offshore facility, any person owning or operating such facility, and (iii) in the case of any facility, title or control of which was conveyed due to bankruptcy, foreclosure, tax delinquency, abandonment, or similar means to a unit of State or local government, any person who owned, operated or otherwise controlled activities at such facility immediately beforehand. Such term does not include a person, who, without participating in the management of a vessel or facility, holds indicia of ownership primarily to protect his security interest in the vessel or facility.

(B) In the case of a hazardous substance which has been accepted for transportation by a common or contract carrier and except as provided in section 9607(a)(3) or (4) of this title, (i) the term "owner or operator" shall mean such common carrier or other bona fide for hire carrier acting as an independent contractor during such transportation, (ii) the shipper of such hazardous substance shall not be considered to have caused or contributed to any release during such transportation which resulted solely from circumstances or conditions beyond his control.

(C) In the case of a hazardous substance which has been delivered by a common or contract carrier to a disposal or treatment facility and except as provided in section 9607(a)(3) or (4) of this title (i) the term "owner or operator" shall not include such common or contract carrier, and (ii) such common or contract carrier shall not be considered to have caused or contributed to any release at such disposal or treatment facility resulting from circumstances or conditions beyond its control.

(D) The term "owner or operator" does not include a unit of State or local government which acquired ownership or control involuntarily through bankruptcy, tax delinquency, abandonment, or other circumstances in which the government involuntarily acquires title by virtue of its function as sovereign. The exclusion provided under this paragraph shall not apply to any State or local government which has caused or contributed to the release or threatened release of a hazardous substance from the facility, and such a State or local government shall be subject to the provisions of this chapter in the same manner and to the same extent, both procedurally and substantively, as any nongovernmental entity, including liability under section 9607 of this title.

(21) The term "person" means an individual, firm, corporation, association, partnership, consortium, joint venture, commercial entity, United States Government, State, municipality, commission, political subdivision of a State, or any interstate body.

(22) The term "release" means any spilling, leaking, pumping, pouring, emitting, emptying, discharging, injecting, escaping, leaching, dumping, or disposing into the environment (including the abandonment or discarding of barrels, containers, and other closed receptacles containing any hazardous substance or pollutant or contaminant), but excludes (A) any release which results in exposure to persons solely within a workplace, with respect to a claim which such persons may assert against the employer of such persons, (B) emissions from the engine exhaust of a motor vehicle, rolling stock, aircraft, vessel, or pipeline pumping station engine, (C) release of source, byproduct, or special nuclear material from a nuclear incident, as those terms are defined in the Atomic Energy Act of 1954 [42 U.S.C. 2011 et seq.], if such release is subject to requirements with respect to financial protection established by the Nuclear Regulatory Commission under section 170 of such Act [42 U.S.C. 2210], or, for the purposes of section 9604 of this title or any other response action, any release of source byproduct, or special nuclear material from any processing site designated under section 7912(a)(1) or 7942(a) of this title, and (D) the normal application of fertilizer.

(23) The term "remove" or "removal" means the cleanup or removal of released hazardous substances from the environment, such actions as may be necessary[2] taken in the event of the threat of release of hazardous substances into the environment, such actions as may be necessary to monitor, assess, and evaluate the release or threat or release of hazardous substances, the disposal of removed material, or the taking of such other actions as may be necessary to prevent, minimize, or mitigate damage to the public health or welfare or to the environment, which may otherwise result from a release or threat of release. The term includes, in addition, without being limited to, security fencing or other measures to limit access, provision of alternative water supplies, temporary evacuation and housing of threatened individuals not otherwise provided for, action taken under section 9604(b) of this title, and any emergency assistance which may be provided under the Disaster Relief Act of 1974 [42 U.S.C. 5121 et seq.].

(24) The term "remedy" or "remedial action" means those actions consistent with permanent remedy taken instead of or in addition to removal actions in the event of a release or threatened release of a hazardous substance into the environment, to prevent or minimize the release of hazardous substances so that they do not migrate to cause substantial danger to present or future public health or welfare or the environment. The term includes, but is not limited to, such actions at the location of the release as storage, confinement, perimeter protection using dikes, trenches, or ditches, clay cover, neutralization, cleanup of released hazardous substances or contaminated materials, recycling or reuse, diversion, destruction, segregation of reactive wastes, dredging or excavations, repair or replacement of leaking containers, collection of leachate and runoff, onsite treatment or incineration, provision of alternative water supplies, and any monitoring reasonably required to assure that such actions protect the public health and welfare and the environment. The term includes the costs of permanent relocation of residents and businesses and community facilities where the President determines that, alone or in combination with other measures, such relocation is more cost-effective than and environmentally preferable to the transportation, storage, treatment, destruction, or secure disposition offsite of hazardous substances, or may otherwise be necessary to protect the public health or welfare; the term includes offsite transport and offsite storage, treatment, destruction, or secure disposition of hazardous substances and associated contaminated materials.

(25) The term "respond" or "response" means remove, removal, remedy, and remedial action, all such terms (including the terms "removal" and "remedial action") include enforcement activities related thereto.

(26) The term "transport" or "transportation" means the movement of a hazardous substance by any mode, including pipeline (as defined in the Pipeline Safety Act), and in the case of a hazardous substance which has been accepted for transportation by a common or contract carrier, the term "transport" or "transportation" shall include any stoppage in transit which is temporary, incidental to the transportation movement, and at the ordinary operating convenience of a common or contract carrier, and any such stoppage shall be considered as a continuity of movement and not as the storage of a hazardous substance.

(27) The terms "United States" and "State" include the several States of the Unites States, the District of Columbia, the Commonwealth of Puerto Rico, Guam, American Samoa, the United States Virgin Islands, the Commonwealth of the Northern Marianas, and any other territory or possession over which the United States has jurisdiction.

(28) The term "vessel" means every description of watercraft or other artificial contrivance used, or capable of being used, as a means of transportation on water.

(29) The terms "disposal", "hazardous waste", and "treatment" shall have the meaning provided in section 1004 of the Solid Waste Disposal Act [42 U.S.C. 6903].

(30) The terms "territorial sea" and "contiguous zone" shall have the meaning provided in section 1362 of Title 33.

(31) The term "national contingency plan" means the national contingency plan published under section 1321(c) of Title 33 or revised pursuant to section 9605 of this title.

(32) The term "liable" or "liability" under this subchapter shall be construed to be the standard of liability which obtains under section 1321 of Title 33.

(33) The term "pollutant or contaminant" shall include, but not be limited to, any element, substance, compound, or mixture, including disease-causing agents, which after release into the environment and upon exposure, ingestion, inhalation, or assimilation into any organism, either directly from the environment or indirectly by ingestion through food chains, will or may reasonably be anticipated to cause death, disease, behavioral abnormalities, cancer, genetic mutation, physiological malfunctions (including malfunctions in reproduction) or physical deformations, in such organisms or their offspring; except that the term "pollutant or contaminant" shall not include petroleum, including crude oil or any fraction thereof which is not otherwise specifically listed or designated as a hazardous substance under subparagraphs (A) through (F) of paragraph (14) and shall not include natural gas, liquefied natural gas, or synthetic gas of pipeline quality (or mixtures of natural gas and such synthetic gas).

(34) The term "alternative water supplies" includes, but is not limited to, drinking water and household water supplies.

(35)(A) The term "contractual relationship", for the purpose of section 9607(b)(3) of this title includes, but is not limited to, land contracts, deeds or other instruments transferring title or possession, unless the real property on which the facility concerned is located was acquired by the defendant after the disposal or placement of the hazardous substance on, in, or at the facility, and one or more of the circumstances described in clause (i), (ii), or (iii) is also established by the defendant by a preponderance of the evidence:

(i) At the time the defendant acquired the facility the defendant did not know and had no reason to know that any hazardous substance which is the subject of the release or threatened release was disposed of on, in, or at the facility.

(ii) The defendant is a government entity which acquired the facility by escheat, or through any other involuntary transfer or acquisition, or through the exercise of eminent domain authority by purchase or condemnation.

(iii) The defendant acquired the facility by inheritance or bequest.

In addition to establishing the foregoing, the defendant must establish that he has satisfied the requirements of section 9607(b)(3)(a) and (b) of this title.

(B) To establish that the defendant had no reason to know, as provided in clause (i) of subparagraph (A) of this paragraph, the defendant must have undertaken, at the time of acquisition, all appropriate inquiry into the previous ownership and uses of the property consistent with good commercial or customary practice in an effort to minimize liability. For purposes of the preceding sentence the court shall take into account any specialized knowledge or experience on the part of the defendant, the relationship of the purchase price to the value of the property if uncontaminated, commonly known or reasonably ascertainable information about the property, the obviousness of the presence or likely presence of contamination at the property, and the ability to detect such contamination by appropriate inspection.

(C) Nothing in this paragraph or in section 9607(b)(3) of this title shall diminish the liability of any previous owner or operator of such facility who would otherwise be liable under this chapter. Notwithstanding this paragraph, if the defendant obtained actual knowledge of the release or threatened release of a hazardous substance at such facility when the defendant owned the real property and then subsequently transferred ownership of the property to another person without disclosing such knowledge, such defendant shall be treated as liable under section 9607(a)(1) of this title and no defense under section 9607(b)(3) of this title shall be available to such defendant.

(D) Nothing in this paragraph shall affect the liability under this chapter of a defendant who, by any act or omission, caused or contributed to the release or threatened release of a hazardous substance which is the subject of the action relating to the facility.

(36) The term "Indian tribe" means any Indian tribe, band, nation, or other organized group or community, including any Alaska Native village but not including any Alaska Native regional or village corporation, which is recognized as eligible for the special programs and services provided by the United States to Indians because of their status as Indians.

(37)(A) The term "service station dealer" means any person—

(i) who owns or operates a motor vehicle service station, filling station, garage, or similar retail establishment engaged in the business of selling, repairing, or servicing motor vehicles, where a significant percentage of the gross revenue of the establishment is derived from the fueling, repairing, or servicing of motor vehicles, and

(ii) who accepts for collection, accumulation, and delivery to an oil recycling facility, recycled oil that (I) has been removed from the engine of a light duty motor vehicle or household appliances by the owner of such vehicle or appliances, and (II) is presented, by such owner, to such person for collection, accumulation, and delivery to an oil recycling facility.

(B) For purposes of section 9614(c) of this title the term "service station dealer" shall, notwithstanding the provisions of subparagraph (A), include any government agency that establishes a facility solely for the purpose of accepting recycled oil that satisfies the criteria set forth in subclauses (I) and (II) of subparagraph (A)(ii), and, with respect to recycled oil that satisfies the criteria set forth in subclauses (I) and (II), owners or operators of refuse collection services who are compelled by State law to collect, accumulate, and deliver such oil to an oil recycling facility.

(C) The President shall promulgate regulations regarding the determination of what constitutes a significant percentage of the gross revenues of an establishment for purposes of this paragraph.

(38) The term "incineration vessel" means any vessel which carries hazardous substances for the purpose of incineration of such substances, so long as such substances or residues of such substances are on board.

(Dec. 11, 1980, Pub.L. 96–510, Title I, § 101, 94 Stat. 2767; Dec. 22, 1980, Pub.L. 96–561, Title II, § 238(b), 94 Stat. 3300; as amended Oct. 17, 1986, Pub.L. 99–499, Title I, §§ 101, 114(b), 127(a), Title V, § 517(c)(2), 100 Stat. 1615, 1652, 1692, 1774.)

1 So in original. Probably should be "or".

2 So in original. Probably should be "necessarily".

Cross References

Storage and disposal of nondefense materials on Department of Defense installations, definition of materials to include materials referred to in par. (14) of this section, see section 2692 of Title 10, Armed Forces.

Code of Federal Regulations

Assistance agreements, procurement under, see 40 CFR 33.001 et seq.

§ 9602. Designation of additional hazardous substances and establishment of reportable released quantities; regulations

(a) The Administrator shall promulgate and revise as may be appropriate, regulations designating as hazardous substances, in addition to those referred to in section 9601(14) of this title, such elements, compounds, mixtures, solutions, and substances which, when released into the environment may present substantial danger to the public health or welfare or the environment, and shall promulgate regulations establishing that quantity of any hazardous substance the release of which shall be reported pursuant to section 9603 of this title. The Administrator may determine that one single quantity shall be the reportable quantity for any hazardous substance, regardless of the medium into which the hazardous substance is released. For all hazardous substances for which proposed regulations establishing reportable quantities were published in the Federal Register under this subsection on or before March 1, 1986, the Administrator shall promulgate under this subsection final regulations establishing reportable quantities not later than December 31, 1986. For all hazardous substances for which proposed regulations establishing reportable quantities were not published in the Federal Register under this subsection on or before March 1, 1986, the Administrator shall publish under this subsection proposed regulations establishing reportable quantities not later than December 31, 1986, and promulgate final regulations under this subsection establishing reportable quantities not later than April 30, 1988.

(b) Unless and until superseded by regulations establishing a reportable quantity under subsection (a) of this section for any hazardous substance as defined in section 9601(14) of this title, (1) a quantity of one pound, or (2) for those hazardous substances for which reportable quantities have been established pursuant to section 1321(b)(4) of Title 33, such reportable quantity, shall be deemed that quantity, the release of which requires notification pursuant to section 9603(a) or (b) of this title.

(Dec. 11, 1980, Pub.L. 96–510, Title I, § 102, 94 Stat. 2772, as amended Oct. 17, 1986, Pub.L. 99–499, Title I, § 102, 100 Stat. 1617.)

Cross References

Storage and disposal of nondefense materials on Department of Defense installations, definition of materials to include materials designated under this section, see § 2692 of Title 10, Armed Forces.

Library References

Health and Environment ⚷25.5(1), 25.6, 25.7.

C.J.S. Health and Environment §§ 61 et seq., 91 et seq., 106 et seq.

§ 9603. Notification requirements respecting released substances

(a) Notice to National Response Center upon release from vessel or offshore or onshore facility by person in charge; conveyance of notice by Center

Any person in charge of a vessel or an offshore or an onshore facility shall, as soon as he has knowledge of any release (other than a federally permitted release) of a hazardous substance from such vessel or facility in quantities equal to or greater than those determined pursuant to section 9602 of this title, immediately notify the National Response Center established under the Clean Water Act [33 U.S.C. 1251 et seq.] of such release. The National Response Center shall convey the notification expeditiously to all appropriate Government agencies, including the Governor of any affected State.

(b) Penalties for failure to notify; use of notice or information pursuant to notice in criminal case

Any person—

(1) in charge of a vessel from which a hazardous substance is released, other than a federally permitted release, into or upon the navigable waters of the United States, adjoining shorelines, or into or upon the waters of the contiguous zone, or

(2) in charge of a vessel from which a hazardous substance is released, other than a federally permitted release, which may affect natural resources belonging to, appertaining to, or under the exclusive management authority of the United States (including resources under the Magnuson Fishery Conservation and Management Act [16 U.S.C. 1801 et seq.]), and who is otherwise subject to the jurisdiction of the United States at the time of the release, or

(3) in charge of a facility from which a hazardous substance is released, other than a federally permitted release,

in a quantity equal to or greater than that determined pursuant to section 9602 of this title who fails to notify immediately the appropriate agency of the United States Government as soon as he has knowledge of such release or who submits in such a notification any information which he knows to be false or misleading shall, upon conviction, be fined in accordance with the applicable provisions of Title 18 or imprisoned for not more than 3 years (or not more than 5 years in the case of a second or subsequent conviction), or both. Notification received pursuant to this subsection or information obtained by the exploitation of such notification shall not be used against any such person in any criminal case, except a prosecution for perjury or for giving a false statement.

(c) Notice to Administrator of EPA of existence of storage, etc., facility by owner or operator; exceptions; time, manner, and form of notice; penalties for failure to notify; use of notice or information pursuant to notice in criminal case

Within one hundred and eighty days after December 11, 1980, any person who owns or operates or who at the time of disposal owned or operated, or who accepted hazardous substances for transport and selected, a facility at which hazardous substances (as defined in section 9601(14)(C) of this title) are or have been stored, treated, or disposed of shall, unless such facility has a permit issued under, or has been accorded interim status under, subtitle C of the Solid Waste Disposal Act [42 U.S.C. 6921 et seq.], notify the Administrator of the Environmental Protection Agency of the existence of such facility, specifying the amount and type of any hazardous substance to be found there, and any known, suspected, or likely releases of such substances from such facility. The Administrator may prescribe in greater detail the manner and form of the notice and the information included. The Administrator shall notify the affected State agency, or any department designated by the Governor to receive such notice, of the existence of such facility. Any person who knowingly fails to notify the Administrator of the existence of any such facility shall, upon conviction, be fined not more than $10,000, or imprisoned for not more than one year, or both. In addition, any such person who knowingly fails to provide the notice required by this subsection shall not be entitled to any limitation of liability or to any defenses to liability set out in section 9607 of this title: *Provided however*, That notification under this subsection is not required for any facility which would be reportable hereunder solely as a result of any stoppage in transit which is temporary, incidental to the transportation movement, or at the ordinary operating convenience of a common or contract carrier, and such stoppage shall be considered as a continuity of movement and not as the storage of a hazardous substance. Notification received pursuant to this subsection or information obtained by the exploitation of such notification shall not be used against any such person in any criminal case, except a prosecution for perjury or for giving a false statement.

(d) Recordkeeping requirements; promulgation of rules and regulations by Administrator of EPA; penalties for violations; waiver of retention requirements

(1) The Administrator of the Environmental Protection Agency is authorized to promulgate rules and regulations specifying, with respect to—

(A) the location, title, or condition of a facility, and

(B) the identity, characteristics, quantity, origin, or condition (including containerization and previous treatment) of any hazardous substances contained or deposited in a facility;

the records which shall be retained by any person required to provide the notification of a facility set out in subsection (c) of this section. Such specification shall be in accordance with the provisions of this subsection.

(2) Beginning with December 11, 1980, for fifty years thereafter or for fifty years after the date of establishment of a record (whichever is later), or at any such earlier time as a waiver if obtained under paragraph (3) of this subsection, it shall be unlawful for any such person knowingly to destroy, mutilate, erase, dispose of, conceal, or otherwise render unavailable or unreadable or falsify any records identified in paragraph (1) of this subsection. Any person who violates this paragraph shall, upon conviction, be fined in accordance with the applicable provisions of Title 18 or imprisoned for not more than 3 years (or not more than 5 years in the case of a second or subsequent conviction), or both.

(3) At any time prior to the date which occurs fifty years after December 11, 1980, any person identified under paragraph (1) of this subsection may apply to the Administrator of the Environmental Protection Agency for a waiver of the provisions of the first sentence of paragraph (2) of this subsection. The Administrator is authorized to grant such waiver if, in his discretion, such waiver would not unreasonably interfere with the attainment of the purposes and provisions of this chapter. The Administrator shall promulgate rules and regulations regarding such a waiver so as to inform parties of the proper application procedure and conditions for approval of such a waiver.

(4) Notwithstanding the provisions of this subsection, the Administrator of the Environmental Protection Agency may in his discretion require any such person to retain any record identified pursuant to paragraph (1) of this subsection for such a time period in excess of the period specified in paragraph (2) of this subsection as the Administrator determines to be necessary to protect the public health or welfare.

(e) Applicability to registered pesticide product

This section shall not apply to the application of a pesticide product registered under the Federal Insecticide, Fungicide, and Rodenticide Act [7 U.S.C. 136 et seq.] or to the handling and storage of such a pesticide product by an agricultural producer.

(f) Exemptions from notice and penalty provisions for substances reported under other Federal law or is in continuous release, etc.

No notification shall be required under subsection (a) or (b) of this section for any release of a hazardous substance—

(1) which is required to be reported (or specifically exempted from a requirement for reporting) under subtitle C of the Solid Waste Disposal Act [42 U.S.C. 6921 et seq.] or regulations thereunder and which has been reported to the National Response Center, or

(2) which is a continuous release, stable in quantity and rate, and is—

(A) from a facility for which notification has been given under subsection (c) of this section, or

(B) a release of which notification has been given under subsections (a) and (b) of this section for a period sufficient to establish the continuity, quantity, and regularity of such release:

Provided, That notification in accordance with subsections (a) and (b) of this paragraph shall be given for releases subject to this paragraph annually, or at such time as there is any statistically significant increase in the quantity of any hazardous substance or constituent thereof released, above that previously reported or occurring.

(Dec. 11, 1980, Pub.L. 96–510, Title I, § 103, 94 Stat. 2772; Dec. 22, 1980, Pub.L. 96–561, Title II, § 238(b), 94 Stat. 3300; as amended Oct. 17, 1986, Pub.L. 99–499, Title I, §§ 103, 109(a)(1), (2), 100 Stat. 1617, 1632, 1633.)

Library References

Health and Environment ⇐25.5(10), 25.6(3), (9), 25.7(3), (24).
C.J.S. Health and Environment §§ 92, 103 et seq., 106, 113 et seq.

§ 9604. Response authorities

(a) Removal and other remedial action by President; applicability of national contingency plan; response by potentially responsible parties; public health threats; limitations on response: exception

(1) Whenever (A) any hazardous substance is released or there is a substantial threat of such a release into the environment, or (B) there is a release or substantial threat of release into the environment of any pollutant or contaminant which may present an imminent and substantial danger to the public health or welfare, the President is authorized to act, consistent with the national contingency plan, to remove or arrange for the removal of, and provide for remedial action relating to such hazardous substance, pollutant, or contaminant at any time (including its removal from any contaminated natural resource), or take any other response measure consistent with the national contingency plan which the President deems necessary to protect the public health or welfare or the environment. When the President determines that such action will be done properly and promptly by the owner or operator of the facility or vessel or by any other responsible party, the President may allow such person to carry out the action, conduct the remedial investigation, or conduct the feasibility study in accordance with section 9622 of this title. No remedial investigation or feasibility study (RI/FS) shall be authorized except on a determination by the President that the party is qualified to conduct the RI/FS and only if the President contracts with or arranges for a qualified person to assist the President in overseeing and reviewing the conduct of such RI/FS and if the responsible party agrees to reimburse the Fund for any cost incurred by the President under, or in connection with, the oversight contract or arrangement. In no event shall a potentially responsible party be subject to a lesser standard of liability, receive preferential treatment, or in any other way, whether direct or indirect, benefit from any such arrangements as a response action contractor, or as a person hired or retained by such a response action contractor, with respect to the release or facility in question. The President shall give primary attention to those releases which the President deems may present a public health threat.

(2) Removal action

Any removal action undertaken by the President under this subsection (or by any other person referred to in section 9622 of this title) should, to the extent the President deems practicable, contribute to the efficient performance of any long term remedial action with respect to the release or threatened release concerned.

(3) Limitations on response

The President shall not provide for a removal or remedial action under this section in response to a release or threat of release—

(A) of a naturally occurring substance in its unaltered form, or altered solely through naturally occurring processes or phenomena, from a location where it is naturally found;

(B) from products which are part of the structure of, and result in exposure within, residential buildings or business or community structures; or

(C) into public or private drinking water supplies due to deterioration of the system through ordinary use.

(4) Exception to limitations

Notwithstanding paragraph (3) of this subsection, to the extent authorized by this section, the President may respond to any release or threat of release if in the President's discretion, it constitutes a public health or environmental emergency and no other person with the authority and capability to respond to the emergency will do so in a timely manner.

(b) Investigations, monitoring, etc., by President

(1) Information; studies and investigations

Whenever the President is authorized to act pursuant to subsection (a) of this section, or whenever the President has reason to believe that a release has occurred or is about to occur, or that illness, disease, or complaints thereof may be attributable to exposure to a hazardous substance, pollutant, or contaminant and that a release may have occurred or be occurring, he may undertake such investigations, monitoring, surveys, testing, and other information gathering as he may deem necessary or appropriate to identify the existence and extent of the release or threat thereof, the source and nature of the hazardous substances, pollutants or contaminants involved, and the extent of danger to the public health or welfare or to the environment. In addition, the President may undertake such planning, legal, fiscal, economic, engineering, architectural, and other studies or investigations as he may deem necessary or appropriate to plan and direct response actions, to recover the costs thereof, and to enforce the provisions of this chapter.

(2) Coordination of investigations

The President shall promptly notify the appropriate Federal and State natural resource trustees of potential damages to natural resources resulting from releases under investigation pursuant to this section and shall seek to coordinate the assessments, investigations, and planning under this section with such Federal and State trustees.

(c) Criteria for continuance of obligations from Fund over specified amount for response actions; consultation by President with affected States; contracts or cooperative agreements by States with President prior to remedial actions; cost-sharing agreements; selection by President of remedial actions; State credits: granting of credit, expenses before listing or agreement, response actions between 1978 and 1980, State expenses after December 11, 1980, in excess of 10 percent of costs, item-by-item approval, use of credits; operation and maintenance; limitation on source of funds for O&M; recontracting; siting

(1) Unless (A) the President finds that (i) continued response actions are immediately required to prevent, limit, or mitigate an emergency, (ii) there is an immediate risk to public health or welfare or the environment, and (iii) such assistance will not otherwise be provided on a timely basis, or (B) the President has determined the appropriate remedial actions pursuant to paragraph (2) of this subsection and the State or States in which the source of the release is located have complied with the requirements of paragraph (3) of this subsection, or (C) continued response action is otherwise appropriate and consistent with the remedial action to be taken [1] obligations from the Fund, other than those authorized by subsection (b) of this section, shall not continue after $2,000,000 has been obligated for response actions or 12 months has elapsed from the date of initial response to a release or threatened release of hazardous substances.

(2) The President shall consult with the affected State or States before determining any appropriate remedial action to be taken pursuant to the authority granted under subsection (a) of this section.

(3) The President shall not provide any remedial actions pursuant to this section unless the State in which the release occurs first enters into a contract or cooperative agreement with the President providing assurances deemed adequate by the President that (A) the State will assure all future maintenance of the removal and remedial actions provided for the expected life of such actions as determined by the President; (B) the State will assure the availability of a hazardous waste disposal facility acceptable to the President and in compliance with the requirements of subtitle C of the Solid Waste Disposal Act [42 U.S.C.A. § 6921 et seq.] for any necessary offsite storage, destruction, treatment, or secure disposition of the hazardous substances; and (C) the State will pay or assure payment of (i) 10 per centum of the costs of the remedial action, including all future maintenance, or (ii) 50 percent (or such greater amount as the President may determine appropriate, taking into account the degree of responsibility of the State or political subdivision for the release) of any sums expended in response to a release at a facility, that was operated by the State or a political subdivision thereof, either directly or through a contractual relationship or otherwise, at the time of any disposal of hazardous substances therein. For the purpose of clause (ii) of this subparagraph, the term "facility" does not include navigable waters or the beds underlying those waters. The President shall grant the State a credit against the share of the costs for which it is responsible under this paragraph for any documented direct out-of-pocket non-Federal funds expended or obligated by the State or a political subdivision thereof after January 1, 1978, and before December 11, 1980, for cost-eligible response actions and claims

for damages compensable under section 9611 of this title relating to the specific release in question: *Provided, however,* That in no event shall the amount of the credit granted exceed the total response costs relating to the release. In the case of remedial action to be taken on land or water held by an Indian tribe, held by the United States in trust for Indians, held by a member of an Indian tribe (if such land or water is subject to a trust restriction on alienation), or otherwise within the borders of an Indian reservation, the requirements of this paragraph for assurances regarding future maintenance and cost-sharing shall not apply, and the President shall provide the assurance required by this paragraph regarding the availability of a hazardous waste disposal facility.

(4) Selection of remedial action

The President shall select remedial actions to carry out this section in accordance with section 9621 of this title (relating to cleanup standards).

(5) State credits

(A) Granting of credit

The President shall grant a State a credit against the share of the costs, for which it is responsible under paragraph (3) with respect to a facility listed on the National Priorities List under the National Contingency Plan, for amounts expended by a State for remedial action at such facility pursuant to a contract or cooperative agreement with the President. The credit under this paragraph shall be limited to those State expenses which the President determines to be reasonable, documented, direct out-of-pocket expenditures of non-Federal funds.

(B) Expenses before listing or agreement

The credit under this paragraph shall include expenses for remedial action at a facility incurred before the listing of the facility on the National Priorities List or before a contract or cooperative agreement is entered into under subsection (d) of this section for the facility if—

(i) after such expenses are incurred the facility is listed on such list and a contract or cooperative agreement is entered into for the facility, and

(ii) the President determines that such expenses would have been credited to the State under subparagraph (A) had the expenditures been made after listing of the facility on such list and after the date on which such contract or cooperative agreement is entered into.

(C) Response actions between 1978 and 1980

The credit under this paragraph shall include funds expended or obligated by the State or a political subdivision thereof after January 1, 1978, and before December 11, 1980, for cost-eligible response actions and claims for damages compensable under section 9611 of this title.

(D) State expenses after December 11, 1980, in excess of 10 percent of costs

The credit under this paragraph shall include 90 percent of State expenses incurred at a facility owned, but not operated, by such State or by a political subdivision thereof. Such credit applies only to expenses incurred pursuant to a contract or cooperative agreement under subsection (d) of this section and only to expenses incurred after December 11, 1980, but before the date of the enactment of this paragraph [October 17, 1986].

(E) Item-by-item approval

In the case of expenditures made after October 17, 1986, the President may require prior approval of each item of expenditure as a condition of granting a credit under this paragraph.

(F) Use of credits

Credits granted under this paragraph for funds expended with respect to a facility may be used by the State to reduce all or part of the share of costs otherwise required to be paid by the State under paragraph (3) in connection with remedial actions at such facility. If the amount of funds for which credit is allowed under this paragraph exceeds such share of costs for such facility, the State may use the amount of such excess to reduce all or part of the share of such costs at other facilities in that State. A credit shall not entitle the State to any direct payment.

(6) Operation and maintenance

For the purposes of paragraph (3) of this subsection, in the case of ground or surface water contamination, completed remedial action includes the completion of treatment or other measures, whether taken onsite or offsite, necessary to restore ground and surface water quality to a level that assures protection of human health and the environment. With respect to such measures, the operation of such measures for a period of up to 10 years after the construction or installation and commencement of operation shall be considered remedial action. Activities required to maintain the effectiveness of such measures following such period or the completion of remedial action, whichever is earlier, shall be considered operation or maintenance.

(7) **Limitation on source of funds for O&M**

During any period after the availability of funds received by the Hazardous Substance Superfund established under subchapter A of chapter 98 of title 26 from tax revenues or appropriations from general revenues, the Federal share of the payment of the cost of operation or maintenance pursuant to paragraph (3)(C)(i) or paragraph (6) of this subsection (relating to operation and maintenance) shall be from funds received by the Hazardous Substance Superfund from amounts recovered on behalf of such fund under this chapter.

(8) **Recontracting**

The President is authorized to undertake or continue whatever interim remedial actions the President determines to be appropriate to reduce risks to public health or the environment where the performance of a complete remedial action requires recontracting because of the discovery of sources, types, or quantities of hazardous substances not known at the time of entry into the original contract. The total cost of interim actions undertaken at a facility pursuant to this paragraph shall not exceed $2,000,000.

(9) **Siting**

Effective 3 years after October 17, 1986, the President shall not provide any remedial actions pursuant to this section unless the State in which the release occurs first enters into a contract or cooperative agreement with the President providing assurances deemed adequate by the President that the State will assure the availability of hazardous waste treatment or disposal facilities which—

(A) have adequate capacity for the destruction, treatment, or secure disposition of all hazardous wastes that are reasonably expected to be generated within the State during the 20-year period following the date of such contract or cooperative agreement and to be disposed of, treated, or destroyed,

(B) are within the State or outside the State in accordance with an interstate agreement or regional agreement or authority,

(C) are acceptable to the President, and

(D) are in compliance with the requirements of subtitle C of the Solid Waste Disposal Act [42 U.S.C. 6921 et seq.]

(d) Contracts or cooperative agreements by President with States or political subdivisions or Indian tribes; State applications, terms and conditions; reimbursements; cost-sharing provisions; enforcement requirements and procedures

(1) **Cooperative agreements**

(A) **State applications**

A State or political subdivision thereof or Indian tribe may apply to the President to carry out actions authorized in this section. If the President determines that the State or political subdivision or Indian tribe has the capability to carry out any or all of such actions in accordance with the criteria and priorities established pursuant to section 9605(a)(8) of this title and to carry out related enforcement actions, the President may enter into a contract or cooperative agreement with the State or political subdivision or Indian tribe to carry out such actions. The President shall make a determination regarding such an application within 90 days after the President receives the application.

(B) **Terms and conditions**

A contract or cooperative agreement under this paragraph shall be subject to such terms and conditions as the President may prescribe. The contract or cooperative agreement may cover a specific facility or specific facilities.

(C) **Reimbursements**

Any State which expended funds during the period beginning September 30, 1985, and ending on October 17, 1986, for response actions at any site included on the National Priorities List and subject to a cooperative agreement under this chapter shall be reimbursed for the share of costs of such actions for which the Federal Government is responsible under this chapter.

(2) If the President enters into a cost-sharing agreement pursuant to subsection (c) of this section or a contract or cooperative agreement pursuant to this subsection, and the State or political subdivision thereof fails to comply with any requirements of the contract, the President may, after providing sixty days notice, seek in the appropriate Federal district court to enforce the contract or to recover any funds advanced or any costs incurred because of the breach of the contract by the State or political subdivision.

(3) Where a State or a political subdivision thereof is acting in behalf of the President, the President is authorized to provide technical and legal assistance in the administration and enforcement of any contract or subcontract in connection with response actions assisted under this subchapter, and to inter-

vene in any civil action involving the enforcement of such contract or subcontract.

(4) Where two or more noncontiguous facilities are reasonably related on the basis of geography, or on the basis of the threat, or potential threat to the public health or welfare or the environment, the President may, in his discretion, treat these related facilities as one for purposes of this section.

(e) Information gathering and access; action authorized, access to information, entry, inspection and samples; authority and samples, compliance orders; issuance and compliance, other authority, confidentiality of information; basis for withholding

(1) Action authorized

Any officer, employee, or representative of the President, duly designated by the President, is authorized to take action under paragraph (2), (3), or (4) (or any combination thereof) at a vessel, facility, establishment, place, property, or location or, in the case of paragraph (3) or (4), at any vessel, facility, establishment, place, property, or location which is adjacent to the vessel, facility, establishment, place, property, or location referred to in such paragraph (3) or (4). Any duly designated officer, employee, or representative of a State or political subdivision under a contract or cooperative agreement under subsection (d)(1) of this section is also authorized to take such action. The authority of paragraphs (3) and (4) may be exercised only if there is a reasonable basis to believe there may be a release or threat of release of a hazardous substance or pollutant or contaminant. The authority of this subsection may be exercised only for the purposes of determining the need for response, or choosing or taking any response action under this subchapter, or otherwise enforcing the provisions of this subchapter.

(2) Access to information

Any officer, employee, or representative described in paragraph (1) may require any person who has or may have information relevant to any of the following to furnish, upon reasonable notice, information or documents relating to such matter:

(A) The identification, nature, and quantity of materials which have been or are generated, treated, stored, or disposed of at a vessel or facility or transported to a vessel or facility.

(B) The nature or extent of a release or threatened release of a hazardous substance or pollutant or contaminant at or from a vessel or facility.

(C) Information relating to the ability of a person to pay for or to perform a cleanup.

In addition, upon reasonable notice, such person either (i) shall grant any such officer, employee, or representative access at all reasonable times to any vessel, facility, establishment, place, property, or location to inspect and copy all documents or records relating to such matters or (ii) shall copy and furnish to the officer, employee, or representative all such documents or records, at the option and expense of such person.

(3) Entry

Any officer, employee, or representative described in paragraph (1) is authorized to enter at reasonable times any of the following:

(A) Any vessel, facility, establishment, or other place or property where any hazardous substance or pollutant or contaminant may be or has been generated, stored, treated, disposed of, or transported from.

(B) Any vessel, facility, establishment, or other place or property from which or to which a hazardous substance or pollutant or contaminant has been or may have been released.

(C) Any vessel, facility, establishment, or other place or property where such release is or may be threatened.

(D) Any vessel, facility, establishment, or other place or property where entry is needed to determine the need for response or the appropriate response or to effectuate a response action under this subchapter.

(4) Inspection and samples

(A) Authority

Any officer, employee or representative described in paragraph (1) is authorized to inspect and obtain samples from any vessel, facility, establishment, or other place or property referred to in paragraph (3) or from any location of any suspected hazardous substance or pollutant or contaminant. Any such officer, employee, or representative is authorized to inspect and obtain samples of any containers or labeling for suspected hazardous substances or pollutants or contaminants. Each such inspection shall be completed with reasonable promptness.

(B) Samples

If the officer, employee, or representative obtains any samples, before leaving the premises he shall give to the owner, operator, tenant, or other person in charge of the place from which the samples were obtained a receipt describing the sample obtained and, if requested, a portion of each such sample. A copy of the results of any analysis made of such samples shall be furnished promptly to the owner, operator, tenant, or other person in charge, if such person can be located.

(5) Compliance orders

(A) Issuance

If consent is not granted regarding any request made by an officer, employee, or representative under paragraph (2), (3), or (4), the President may issue an order directing compliance with the request. The order may be issued after such notice and opportunity for consultation as is reasonably appropriate under the circumstances.

(B) Compliance

The President may ask the Attorney General to commence a civil action to compel compliance with a request or order referred to in subparagraph (A). Where there is a reasonable basis to believe there may be a release or threat of a release of a hazardous substance or pollutant or contaminant, the court shall take the following actions:

(i) In the case of interference with entry or inspection, the court shall enjoin such interference or direct compliance with orders to prohibit interference with entry or inspection unless under the circumstances of the case the demand for entry or inspection is arbitrary and capricious, an abuse of discretion, or otherwise not in accordance with law.

(ii) In the case of information or document requests or orders, the court shall enjoin interference with such information or document requests or orders or direct compliance with the requests or orders to provide such information or documents unless under the circumstances of the case the demand for information or documents is arbitrary and capricious, an abuse of discretion, or otherwise not in accordance with law.

The court may assess a civil penalty not to exceed $25,000 for each day of noncompliance against any person who unreasonably fails to comply with the provisions of paragraph (2), (3), or (4) or an order issued pursuant to subparagraph (A) of this paragraph.

(6) Other authority

Nothing in this subsection shall preclude the President from securing access or obtaining information in any other lawful manner.

(7) Confidentiality of information

(A) Any records, reports, or information obtained from any person under this section (including records, reports, or information obtained by representatives of the President) shall be available to the public, except that upon a showing satisfactory to the President (or the State, as the case may be) by any person that records, reports, or information, or particular part thereof (other than health or safety effects data), to which the President (or the State, as the case may be) or any officer, employee, or representative has access under this section if made public would divulge information entitled to protection under section 1905 of Title 18, such information or particular portion thereof shall be considered confidential in accordance with the purposes of that section, except that such record, report, document or information may be disclosed to other officers, employees, or authorized representatives of the United States concerned with carrying out this chapter, or when relevant in any proceeding under this chapter.

(B) Any person not subject to the provisions of section 1905 of Title 18 who knowingly and willfully divulges or discloses any information entitled to protection under this subsection shall, upon conviction, be subject to a fine of not more than $5,000 or to imprisonment not to exceed one year, or both.

(C) In submitting data under this chapter, a person required to provide such data may (i) designate the data which such person believes is entitled to protection under this subsection and (ii) submit such designated data separately from other data submitted under this chapter. A designation under this paragraph shall be made in writing and in such manner as the President may prescribe by regulation.

(D) Notwithstanding any limitation contained in this section or any other provision of law, all information reported to or otherwise obtained by the President (or any representative of the President) under this chapter shall be made available, upon written request of any duly authorized committee of the Congress, to such committee.

(E) No person required to provide information under this chapter may claim that the information is entitled to protection under this paragraph unless such person shows each of the following:

(i) Such person has not disclosed the information to any other person, other than a member of a local emergency planning committee established under title III of the Amendments and Reauthorization Act of 1986 [42 U.S.C.A. § 11001 et seq.], an officer or employee of the United States or a State or local government, an employee of such person, or a person who is bound by a confidentiality agreement, and such person has taken reasonable measures to protect the confidentiality of such information and intends to continue to take such measures.

(ii) The information is not required to be disclosed, or otherwise made available, to the public under any other Federal or State law.

(iii) Disclosure of the information is likely to cause substantial harm to the competitive position of such person.

(iv) The specific chemical identity, if sought to be protected, is not readily discoverable through reverse engineering.

(F) The following information with respect to any hazardous substance at the facility or vessel shall not be entitled to protection under this paragraph:

(i) The trade name, common name, or generic class or category of the hazardous substance.

(ii) The physical properties of the substance, including its boiling point, melting point, flash point, specific gravity, vapor density, solubility in water, and vapor pressure at 20 degrees Celsius.

(iii) The hazards to health and the environment posed by the substance, including physical hazards (such as explosion) and potential acute and chronic health hazards.

(iv) The potential routes of human exposure to the substance at the facility, establishment, place, or property being investigated, entered, or inspected under this subsection.

(v) The location of disposal of any waste stream.

(vi) Any monitoring data or analysis of monitoring data pertaining to disposal activities.

(vii) Any hydrogeologic or geologic data.

(viii) Any groundwater monitoring data.

(f) Contracts for response action; compliance with Federal health and safety standards

In awarding contracts to any person engaged in response actions, the President or the State, in any case where it is awarding contracts pursuant to a contract entered into under subsection (d) of this section, shall require compliance with Federal health and safety standards established under section 9651(f) of this title by contractors and subcontractors as a condition of such contracts.

(g) Rates for wages and labor standards applicable to covered work

(1) All laborers and mechanics employed by contractors or subcontractors in the performance of construction, repair, or alteration work funded in whole or in part under this section shall be paid wages at rates not less than those prevailing on projects of a character similar in the locality as determined by the Secretary of Labor in accordance with the Davis-Bacon Act [40 U.S.C. 276a et seq.]. The President shall not approve any such funding without first obtaining adequate assurance that required labor standards will be maintained upon the construction work.

(2) The Secretary of Labor shall have, with respect to the labor standards specified in paragraph (1), the authority and functions set forth in Reorganization Plan Numbered 14 of 1950 (15 F.R. 3176; 64 Stat. 1267) and section 276c of Title 40.

(h) Emergency procurement powers; exercise by President

Notwithstanding any other provision of law, subject to the provisions of section 9611 of this title, the President may authorize the use of such emergency procurement powers as he deems necessary to effect the purpose of this chapter. Upon determination that such procedures are necessary, the President shall promulgate regulations prescribing the circumstances under which such authority shall be used and the procedures governing the use of such authority.

(i) Agency for Toxic Substances and Disease Registry; establishment, functions, etc.

(1) There is hereby established within the Public Health Service an agency, to be known as the Agency for Toxic Substances and Disease Registry, which shall report directly to the Surgeon General of the United States. The Administrator of said Agency shall, with the cooperation of the Administrator of the Environmental Protection Agency, the Commissioner of the Food and Drug Administration, the Directors of the National Institute of Medicine, National Institute of Environmental Health Sciences, National Institute of Occupational Safety and Health, Centers for Disease Control, the Administrator of the Occupational Safety and Health Administration, the Administrator of the Social Security Administration, the Secretary of Transportation, and appropriate State and local health officials, effectuate and implement the health related authorities of this chapter. In addition, said Administrator shall—

(A) in cooperation with the States, establish and maintain a national registry of serious diseases and illnesses and a national registry of persons exposed to toxic substances;

(B) establish and maintain inventory of literature, research, and studies on the health effects of toxic substances;

(C) in cooperation with the States, and other agencies of the Federal Government, establish and maintain a complete listing of areas closed to the public or otherwise restricted in use because of toxic substance contamination;

(D) in cases of public health emergencies caused or believed to be caused by exposure to toxic substances, provide medical care and testing to exposed individuals, including but not limited to tissue sampling, chromosomal testing where appropriate, epidemiological studies, or any other assistance appropriate under the circumstances; and

(E) either independently or as part of other health status survey, conduct periodic survey and screening programs to determine relationships between exposure to toxic substances and illness. In cases of public health emergencies, exposed persons shall be eligible for admission to hospitals and other facilities and services operated or provided by the Public Health Service.

(2)(A) Within 6 months after October 17, 1986, the Administrator of the Agency for Toxic Substances and Disease Registry (ATSDR) and the Administrator of the Environmental Protection Agency (EPA) shall prepare a list, in order of priority, of at least 100 hazardous substances which are most commonly found at facilities on the National Priorities List and which, in their sole discretion, they determine are posing the most significant potential threat to human health due to their known or suspected toxicity to humans and the potential for human exposure to such substances at facilities on the National Priorities List or at facilities to which a response to a release or a threatened release under this section is under consideration.

(B) Within 24 months after October 17, 1986, the Administrator of ATSDR and the Administrator of EPA shall revise the list prepared under subparagraph (A). Such revision shall include, in order of priority, the addition of 100 or more such hazardous substances. In each of the 3 consecutive 12-month periods that follow, the Administrator of ATSDR and the Administrator of EPA shall revise, in the same manner as provided in the 2 preceding sentences, such list to include not fewer than 25 additional hazardous substances per revision. The Administrator of ATSDR and the Administrator of EPA shall not less often than once every year thereafter revise such list to include additional hazardous substances in accordance with the criteria in subparagraph (A).

(3) Based on all available information, including information maintained under paragraph (1)(B) and data developed and collected on the health effects of hazardous substances under this paragraph, the Administrator of ATSDR shall prepare toxicological profiles of each of the substances listed pursuant to paragraph (2). The toxicological profiles shall be prepared in accordance with guidelines developed by the Administrator of ATSDR and the Administrator of EPA. Such profiles shall include, but not be limited to each of the following:

(A) An examination, summary, and interpretation of available toxicological information and epidemiologic evaluations on a hazardous substance in order to ascertain the levels of significant human exposure for the substance and the associated acute, subacute, and chronic health effects.

(B) A determination of whether adequate information on the health effects of each substance is available or in the process of development to determine levels of exposure which present a significant risk to human health of acute, subacute, and chronic health effects.

(C) Where appropriate, an identification of toxicological testing needed to identify the types or levels of exposure that may present significant risk of adverse health effects in humans.

Any toxicological profile or revision thereof shall reflect the Administrator of ATSDR's assessment of all relevant toxicological testing which has been peer reviewed. The profiles required to be prepared under this paragraph for those hazardous substances listed under subparagraph (A) of paragraph (2) shall be completed, at a rate of no fewer than 25 per year, within 4 years after October 17, 1986. A profile required on a substance listed pursuant to subparagraph (B) of paragraph (2) shall be completed within 3 years after addition to the list. The profiles prepared under this paragraph shall be of those substances highest on the list of priorities under paragraph (2) for which profiles have not previously been prepared. Profiles required under this paragraph shall be revised and republished as necessary, but no less often than once every 3 years. Such profiles shall be provided to the States and made available to other interested parties.

(4) The Administrator of the ATSDR shall provide consultations upon request on health issues relating to exposure to hazardous or toxic substances, on the basis of available information, to the Administrator of EPA, State officials, and local officials. Such consultations to individuals may be provided by States under cooperative agreements established under this chapter.

(5)(A) For each hazardous substance listed pursuant to paragraph (2), the Administrator of ATSDR (in consultation with the Administrator of EPA and other agencies and programs of the Public Health Service) shall assess whether adequate information on the health effects of such substance is available. For any such substance for which adequate information is not available (or under development), the Administrator of ATSDR, in cooperation with the Director of the National Toxicology Program, shall assure the initiation of a program of research designed to determine the health effects (and techniques for development of methods to determine such health effects) of such substance. Where feasible, such program shall seek to develop methods to determine the health effects of such substance in combination with other substances with which it is commonly found. Before assuring the initiation of such program, the Administrator of ATSDR shall consider recommendations of the Interagency Testing Committee established under section 4(e) of the Toxic Substances Control Act [15 U.S.C.A. 2603(e)] on the types of research that should be done. Such program shall include, to the extent necessary to supplement existing information, but shall not be limited to—

(i) laboratory and other studies to determine short, intermediate, and long-term health effects;

(ii) laboratory and other studies to determine organ-specific, site-specific, and system-specific acute and chronic toxicity;

(iii) laboratory and other studies to determine the manner in which such substances are metabolized or to otherwise develop an understanding of the biokinetics of such substances; and

(iv) where there is a possibility of obtaining human data, the collection of such information.

(B) In assessing the need to perform laboratory and other studies, as required by subparagraph (A), the Administrator of ATSDR shall consider—

(i) the availability and quality of existing test data concerning the substance on the suspected health effect in question;

(ii) the extent to which testing already in progress will, in a timely fashion, provide data that will be adequate to support the preparation of toxicological profiles as required by paragraph (3); and

(iii) such other scientific and technical factors as the Administrator of ATSDR may determine are necessary for the effective implementation of this subsection.

(C) In the development and implementation of any research program under this paragraph, the Administrator of ATSDR and the Administrator of EPA shall coordinate such research program implemented under this paragraph with the National Toxicology Program and with programs of toxicological testing established under the Toxic Substances Control Act [15 U.S.C.A. 2601 et seq.] and the Federal Insecticide, Fungicide and Rodenticide Act [7 U.S.C.A. 136 et seq.]. The purpose of such coordination shall be to avoid duplication of effort and to assure that the hazardous substances listed pursuant to this subsection are tested thoroughly at the earliest practicable date. Where appropriate, consistent with such purpose, a research program under this paragraph may be carried out using such programs of toxicological testing.

(D) It is the sense of the Congress that the costs of research programs under this paragraph be borne by the manufacturers and processors of the hazardous substance in question, as required in programs of toxicological testing under the Toxic Substances Control Act. Within 1 year after October 17, 1986, the Administrator of EPA shall promulgate regulations which provide, where appropriate, for payment of such costs by manufacturers and processors under the Toxic Substances Control Act, and registrants under the Federal Insecticide, Fungicide, and Rodenticide Act, and recovery of such costs from responsible parties under this chapter.

(6)(A) The Administrator of ATSDR shall perform a health assessment for each facility on the National Priorities List established under section 9605 of this title. Such health assessment shall be completed not later than December 10, 1988, for each facility proposed for inclusion on such list prior to the date of the enactment of the Superfund Amendments and Reauthorization Act of 1986 or not later than one year after the date of proposal for inclusion on such list for each facility proposed for inclusion on such list after October 17, 1986.

(B) The Administrator of ATSDR may perform health assessments for releases or facilities where individual persons or licensed physicians provide information that individuals have been exposed to a hazardous substance, for which the probable source of such exposure is a release. In addition to other methods (formal or informal) of providing such information, such individual persons or licensed physicians may submit a petition to the Administrator of ATSDR providing such information and requesting a health assessment. If such a petition is submitted and the Administrator of ATSDR does not initiate a health assessment, the Administrator of ATSDR shall provide a written explanation of why a health assessment is not appropriate.

(C) In determining the priority in which to conduct health assessments under this subsection, the Administrator of ATSDR, in consultation with the Administrator of EPA, shall give priority to those facilities at which there is documented evidence of the release of hazardous substances, at which the potential risk to human health appears highest, and for which in the judgment of the Administrator of ATSDR existing health assessment data are inadequate to assess the potential risk to human health as provided in subparagraph (F). In determining the priorities for conducting health assessments under this subsection, the Administrator of ATSDR shall consider the National Priorities List schedules and the needs of the Environmental Protection Agency and other Federal agencies pursuant to schedules for remedial investigation and feasibility studies.

(D) Where a health assessment is done at a site on the National Priorities List, the Administrator of ATSDR shall complete such assessment promptly and, to the maximum extent practicable, before the completion of the remedial investigation and feasibility study at the facility concerned.

(E) Any State or political subdivision carrying out a health assessment for a facility shall report the results of the assessment to the Administrator of ATSDR and the Administrator of EPA and shall include recommendations with respect to further activities which need to be carried out under this section. The Administrator of ATSDR shall state such recommendation in any report on the results of any assessment carried out directly by the Administrator of ATSDR for such facility and shall issue periodic reports which include the results of all the assessments carried out under this subsection.

(F) For the purposes of this subsection and section 9611(c)(4) of this title the term "health assessments" shall include preliminary assessments of the potential risk to human health posed by individual sites and facilities, based on such factors as the nature and extent of contamination, the existence of potential pathways of human exposure (including ground or surface water contamination, air emissions, and food chain contamination), the size and potential susceptibility of the community within the likely pathways of exposure, the comparison of expected human exposure levels to the short-term and long-term health effects associated with identified hazardous substances and any available recommended exposure or tolerance limits for such hazardous substances, and the comparison of existing morbidity and mortality data on diseases that may be associated with the observed levels of exposure. The Administrator of ATSDR shall use appropriate data, risk assessments, risk evaluations and studies available from the Administrator of EPA.

(G) The purpose of health assessments under this subsection shall be to assist in determining whether actions under paragraph (11) of this subsection should be taken to reduce human exposure to hazardous substances from a facility and whether additional information on human exposure and associated health risks is needed and should be acquired by conducting epidemiological studies under paragraph (7), establishing a registry under paragraph (8), establishing a health surveillance program under paragraph (9), or through other means. In using the results of health assessments for determining additional actions to be taken under this section, the Administrator of ATSDR may consider additional information on the risks to the potentially affected population from all sources of such hazardous substances including known point or nonpoint sources other than those from the facility in question.

(H) At the completion of each health assessment, the Administrator of ATSDR shall provide the Administrator of EPA and each affected State with the results of such assessment, together with any recommendations for further actions under this subsection or otherwise under this chapter. In addition, if the health assessment indicates that the release or threatened release concerned may pose a serious threat to human health or the environment, the Administrator of ATSDR shall so notify the Administrator of EPA who shall promptly evaluate such release or threatened release in accordance with the hazard ranking system referred to in section 9605(a)(8)(A) of this title to determine whether the site shall be placed on the National Priorities List or, if the site is already on the list, the Administrator of ATSDR may recommend to the Administrator of EPA that the site be accorded a higher priority.

(7)(A) Whenever in the judgment of the Administrator of ATSDR it is appropriate on the basis of the results of a health assessment, the Administrator of ATSDR shall conduct a pilot study of health effects for selected groups of exposed individuals in order to determine the desirability of conducting full scale epidemiological or other health studies of the entire exposed population.

(B) Whenever in the judgment of the Administrator of ATSDR it is appropriate on the basis of the results of such pilot study or other study or health assessment, the Administrator of ATSDR shall conduct such full scale epidemiological or other health studies as may be necessary to determine the health effects on the population exposed to hazardous substances from a release or threatened release. If a significant excess of disease in a population is identified, the letter of transmittal of such study shall include an assessment of other risk factors, other than a release, that may, in the judgment of the peer review group, be associated with such disease, if such risk factors were not taken into account in the design or conduct of the study.

(8) In any case in which the results of a health assessment indicate a potential significant risk to human health, the Administrator of ATSDR shall consider whether the establishment of a registry of exposed persons would contribute to accomplishing the purposes of this subsection, taking into account circumstances bearing on the usefulness of such a registry, including the seriousness or unique character of identified diseases or the likelihood of population migration from the affected area.

(9) Where the Administrator of ATSDR has determined that there is a significant increased risk of adverse health effects in humans from exposure to hazardous substances based on the results of a health assessment conducted under paragraph (6), an epidemiologic study conducted under paragraph (7), or an exposure registry that has been established under paragraph (8), and the Administrator of ATSDR has determined that such exposure is the result of a release from a facility, the Administrator of ATSDR shall initiate a health surveillance program for such population. This program shall include but not be limited to—

(A) periodic medical testing where appropriate of population subgroups to screen for diseases for which the population or subgroup is at significant increased risk; and

(B) a mechanism to refer for treatment those individuals within such population who are screened positive for such diseases.

(10) Two years after October 17, 1986, and every 2 years thereafter, the Administrator of ATSDR shall prepare and submit to the Administrator of EPA and to the Congress a report on the results of the activities of ATSDR regarding—

(A) health assessments and pilot health effects studies conducted;

(B) epidemiologic studies conducted;

(C) hazardous substances which have been listed under paragraph (2), toxicological profiles which have been developed, and toxicologic testing which has been conducted or which is being conducted under this subsection;

(D) registries established under paragraph (8); and

(E) an overall assessment, based on the results of activities conducted by the Administrator of ATSDR, of the linkage between human exposure to individual or combinations of hazardous substances due to releases from facilities covered by this chapter or the Solid Waste Disposal Act [42 U.S.C.A. 6901 et seq.] and any increased incidence or prevalence of adverse health effects in humans.

(11) If a health assessment or other study carried out under this subsection contains a finding that the exposure concerned presents a significant risk to human health, the President shall take such steps as may be necessary to reduce such exposure and eliminate or substantially mitigate the significant risk to human health. Such steps may include the use of any authority under this chapter, including, but not limited to—

(A) provision of alternative water supplies, and

(B) permanent or temporary relocation of individuals.

In any case in which information is insufficient, in the judgment of the Administrator of ATSDR or the President to determine a significant human exposure level with respect to a hazardous substance, the President may take such steps as may be necessary to reduce the exposure of any person to such hazardous substance to such level as the President deems necessary to protect human health.

(12) In any case which is the subject of a petition, a health assessment or study, or a research program under this subsection, nothing in this subsection shall be construed to delay or otherwise affect or impair the authority of the President, the Administrator of ATSDR, or the Administrator of EPA to exercise any authority vested in the President, the Administrator of ATSDR or the Administrator of EPA under any other provision of law (including, but not limited to, the imminent hazard authority of section 7003 of the Solid Waste Disposal Act) [42 U.S.C.A. 6973] or the response and abatement authorities of this chapter.

(13) All studies and results of research conducted under this subsection (other than health assessments) shall be reported or adopted only after appropriate peer review. Such peer review shall be completed, to the maximum extent practicable, within a period of 60 days. In the case of research conducted under the National Toxicology Program, such peer review may be conducted by the Board of Scientific Counselors. In the case of other research, such peer review shall be conducted by panels consisting of no less than three nor more than seven members, who shall be disinterested scientific experts selected for such purpose by the Administrator of ATSDR or the Administrator of EPA, as appropriate, on the basis of their reputation for scientific objectivity and the lack of institutional ties with any person involved in the conduct of the study or research under review. Support services for such panels shall be provided by the Agency for Toxic Substances and Disease Registry, or by the Environmental Protection Agency, as appropriate.

(14) In the implementation of this subsection and other health-related authorities of this chapter, the Administrator of ATSDR shall assemble, develop as necessary, and distribute to the States, and upon request to medical colleges, physicians, and other health professionals, appropriate educational materials (including short courses) on the medical surveillance, screening, and methods of diagnosis and treatment of injury or disease related to exposure to hazardous substances (giving priority to those listed in paragraph (2)), through such means as the Administrator of ATSDR deems appropriate.

(15) The activities of the Administrator of ATSDR described in this subsection and section 9611(c)(4) of this title shall be carried out by the Administrator of ATSDR, either directly or through cooperative agreements with States (or political subdivisions thereof) which the Administrator of ATSDR determines are capable of carrying out such activities. Such activities shall include provision of consultations on health information, the conduct of health assessments, including those required under section 3019(b) of the Solid Waste Disposal Act [42 U.S.C.A. 6939a(b), health studies, registries, and health surveillance.

(16) The President shall provide adequate personnel for ATSDR, which shall not be fewer than 100 employees. For purposes of determining the number of employees under this subsection, an employee employed by ATSDR on a part-time career employment basis shall be counted as a fraction which is determined by dividing 40 hours into the average number of hours of such employee's regularly scheduled workweek.

(17) In accordance with section 9620 of this title (relating to Federal facilities), the Administrator of ATSDR shall have the same authorities under this section with respect to facilities owned or operated by a department, agency, or instrumentality of the United States as the Administrator of ATSDR has with respect to any nongovernmental entity.

(18) If the Administrator of ATSDR determines that it is appropriate for purposes of this section to treat a pollutant or contaminant as a hazardous substance, such pollutant or contaminant shall be treated as a hazardous substance for such purpose.

(j) Acquisition of property

(1) Authority

The President is authorized to acquire, by purchase, lease, condemnation, donation, or otherwise, any real property or any interest in real property that the President in his discretion determines is needed to conduct a remedial action under this chapter. There shall be no cause of action to compel the President to acquire any interest in real property under this chapter.

(2) State assurance

—The President may use the authority of paragraph (1) for a remedial action only if, before an interest in real estate is acquired under this subsection, the State in which the interest to be acquired is located assures the President, through a contract or cooperative agreement or otherwise, that the State will accept transfer of the interest following completion of the remedial action.

(3) Exemption

—No Federal, State, or local government agency shall be liable under this chapter solely as a result of acquiring an interest in real estate under this subsection.

(Dec. 11, 1980, Pub.L. 96–510, Title I, § 104, 94 Stat. 2774, as amended Oct. 17, 1986, Pub.L. 99–499, Title I, §§ 104, 110, Title II, § 207(b), 100 Stat. 1617, 1642, 1705.)

[1] So in original. Probably should be followed by a comma.

Cross References

Solid Waste Disposal Act, action prohibited under if State is engaging in a removal action or is proceeding with a remedial action under this section, see section 6972(b) of this title.

Library References

Health and Environment ⚷25.6, 25.7.
C.J.S. Health and Environment §§ 91 et seq., 106 et seq.

§ 9605. National contingency plan; preparation, contents, etc.

(a) Revision and republication

Within one hundred and eighty days after December 11, 1980, the President shall, after notice and opportunity for public comments, revise and republish the national contingency plan for the removal of oil and hazardous substances, originally prepared and published pursuant to section 1321 of Title 33, to reflect and effectuate the responsibilities and powers created by this chapter, in addition to those matters specified in section 1321(c)(2) of Title 33. Such revision shall include a section of the plan to be known as the national hazardous substance response plan which shall establish procedures and standards for responding to releases of hazardous substances, pollutants, and contaminants, which shall include at a minimum:

(1) methods for discovering and investigating facilities at which hazardous substances have been disposed of or otherwise come to be located;

(2) methods for evaluating, including analyses of relative cost, and remedying any releases or threats of releases from facilities which pose substantial danger to the public health or the environment;

(3) methods and criteria for determining the appropriate extent of removal, remedy, and other measures authorized by this chapter;

(4) appropriate roles and responsibilities for the Federal, State, and local governments and for interstate and nongovernmental entities in effectuating the plan;

(5) provision for identification, procurement, maintenance, and storage of response equipment and supplies;

(6) a method for and assignment of responsibility for reporting the existence of such facilities which may be located on federally owned or controlled properties and any releases of hazardous substances from such facilities;

(7) means of assuring that remedial action measures are cost-effective over the period of potential exposure to the hazardous substances or contaminated materials;

(8)(A) criteria for determining priorities among releases or threatened releases throughout the United States for the purpose of taking remedial action and, to the extent practicable taking into account the potential urgency of such action, for the purpose of taking removal action. Criteria and priorities under this paragraph shall be based upon relative risk or danger to public health or welfare or the environment, in the judgment of the President, taking into account to the extent possible the population at risk, the hazard potential of the hazardous substances at such facilities, the potential for contamination of drinking water supplies, the potential for direct human contact, the potential for destruction of sensitive ecosystems, the damage to natural resources which may affect the human food chain and which is associated with any release or threatened release, the contamination or potential contamination of the ambient air which is associated with the release or threatened release, State preparedness to assume State costs and responsibilities, and other appropriate factors;

(B) based upon the criteria set forth in subparagraph (A) of this paragraph, the President shall list as part of the plan national priorities among the known releases or threatened releases throughout the United States and shall revise the list no less often than annually. Within one year after December 11, 1980, and annually thereafter, each State shall establish and submit for consideration by the President priorities for remedial action among known releases and potential releases in that State based upon the criteria set forth in subparagraph (A) of this paragraph. In assembling or revising the national list, the President shall consider any priorities established by the States. To the extent practicable, the highest priority facilities shall be designated individually and shall be referred to as the "top priority among known response targets", and, to the extent practicable, shall include among the one hundred highest priority facilities one such facility from each State which shall be the facility designated by the State as presenting the greatest danger to public health or welfare or the environment among the known facilities in such State. A State shall be allowed to designate its highest priority facility only once. Other priority facilities or incidents may be listed singly or grouped for response priority purposes;

(9) specified roles for private organizations and entities in preparation for response and in responding to releases of hazardous substances, including identification of appropriate qualifications and capacity therefor and including consideration of minority firms in accordance with subsection (f) of this section; and

(10) standards and testing procedures by which alternative or innovative treatment technologies can be determined to be appropriate for utilization in response actions authorized by this chapter.

The plan shall specify procedures, techniques, materials, equipment, and methods to be employed in identifying, removing, or remedying releases of hazardous substances comparable to those required under section 1321(c)(2)(F) and (G) and (j)(1) of Title 33. Following publication of the revised national contingency plan, the response to and actions to minimize damage from hazardous substances releases shall, to the greatest extent possible, be in accordance with the provisions of the plan. The President may, from time to time, revise and republish the national contingency plan.

(b) Revision of plan

Not later than 18 months after October 17, 1986, the President shall revise the National Contingency Plan to reflect the requirements of such amendments. The portion of such Plan known as "the National Hazardous Substance Response Plan" shall be revised to provide procedures and standards for remedial actions undertaken pursuant to this chapter which are consistent with amendments made by the Superfund Amendments and Reauthorization Act of 1986 relating to the selection of remedial action.

(c) Hazard ranking system

(1) Revision

Not later than 18 months after October 17, 1986, and after publication of notice and opportunity for submission of comments in accordance with section 553 of Title 5, the President shall by rule promulgate amendments to the hazard ranking system in effect on September 1, 1984. Such amendments shall assure, to the maximum extent feasible, that the hazard ranking system accurately assesses the relative degree of risk to human health and the environment posed by sites and facilities subject to review. The President shall establish an effective date for the amended hazard ranking system which is not later than 24 months after October 17, 1986. Such amended hazard ranking system shall be applied to any site or facility to be newly listed on the National Priorities List after the effective date established by the President. Until such effective date of the regulations, the hazard ranking system in effect on September 1, 1984, shall continue in full force and effect.

(2) Health assessment of water contamination risks

In carrying out this subsection, the President shall ensure that the human health risks associated with the contamination or potential contamination (either directly or as a result of the runoff of any hazardous substance or pollutant or contaminant from sites or facilities) of surface water are appropriately assessed where such surface water is, or can be, used for recreation or potable water consumption. In making the assessment required pursuant to the preceding sentence, the President shall take into account the potential migration of any hazardous substance or pollutant or contaminant through such surface water to downstream sources of drinking water.

(3) Reevaluation not required

The President shall not be required to reevaluate, after October 17, 1986, the hazard ranking of any facility which was evaluated in accordance with the criteria under this section before the effective date of the amendments to the hazard ranking system under this subsection and which was assigned a national priority under the National Contingency Plan.

(4) New information

Nothing in paragraph (3) shall preclude the President from taking new information into account in undertaking response actions under this chapter.

(d) Petition for assessment of release

Any person who is, or may be, affected by a release or threatened release of a hazardous substance or pollutant or contaminant, may petition the President to conduct a preliminary assessment of the hazards to public health and the environment which are associated with such release or threatened release. If the President has not previously conducted a preliminary assessment of such release, the President shall, within 12 months after the receipt of any such petition, complete such assessment or provide an explanation of why the assessment is not appropriate. If the preliminary assessment indicates that the release or threatened release concerned may pose a threat to human health or the environment, the President shall promptly evaluate such release or threatened release in accordance with the hazard ranking system referred to in paragraph (8)(A) of subsection (a) of this section to determine the national priority of such release or threatened release.

(e) Releases from earlier sites

Whenever there has been, after January 1, 1985, a significant release of hazardous substances or pollutants or contaminants from a site which is listed by the President as a "Site Cleaned Up To Date" on the National Priorities List (revised edition, December 1984) the site shall be restored to the National Priorities List, without application of the hazard ranking system.

(f) Minority contractors

In awarding contracts under this chapter, the President shall consider the availability of qualified minority firms. The President shall describe, as part of any annual report submitted to the Congress under this chapter, the participation of minority firms in contracts carried out under this chapter. Such report shall contain a brief description of the contracts which have been awarded to minority firms under this chapter and of the efforts made by the President to encourage the participation of such firms in programs carried out under this chapter.

(g) Special study wastes

(1) Application

This subsection applies to facilities—

(A) which as of October 17, 1986, were not included on, or proposed for inclusion on, the National Priorities List; and

(B) at which special study wastes described in paragraph (2), (3)(A)(ii) or (3)(A)(iii) of section 6921(b) of this title are present in significant quantities, including any such facility from which there has been a release of a special study waste.

(2) Considerations in adding facilities to NPL

Pending revision of the hazard ranking system under subsection (c) of this section, the President shall consider each of the following factors in adding facilities covered by this section to the National Priorities List:

(A) The extent to which hazard ranking system score for the facility is affected by the presence of any special study waste at, or any release from, such facility.

(B) Available information as to the quantity, toxicity, and concentration of hazardous substances that are constituents of any special study waste at, or released from such facility, the extent of or potential for release of such hazardous constituents, the exposure or potential exposure to human population and the environment, and the degree of hazard to human health or the environment posed by the release of such hazardous constituents at such facility. This subparagraph refers only to available information on actual concentrations of hazardous substances and not on the total quantity of special study waste at such facility.

(3) Savings provisions

Nothing in this subsection shall be construed to limit the authority of the President to remove any facility which as of October 17, 1986 is included on the National Priorities List from such list, or not to list any facility which as of such date is proposed for inclusion on such list.

(4) Information gathering and analysis

Nothing in this chapter shall be construed to preclude the expenditure of monies from the Fund for gathering and analysis of information which will enable the President to consider the specific factors required by paragraph (2).

(Dec. 11, 1980, Pub.L. 96–510, Title I, § 105, 94 Stat. 2779, as amended Oct. 17, 1986, Pub.L. 99–499, Title I, § 105, 100 Stat. 1625.)

Code of Federal Regulations

Oil and hazardous substances pollution contingency plan, see 40 CFR 300.1 et seq.

Library References

Health and Environment ⚬25.6, 25.7.
C.J.S. Health and Environment §§ 91 et seq., 106 et seq.

§ 9606. Abatement actions

(a) Maintenance, jurisdiction, etc.

In addition to any other action taken by a State or local government, when the President determines that there may be an imminent and substantial endangerment to the public health or welfare or the environment because of an actual or threatened release of a hazardous substance from a facility, he may require the Attorney General of the United States to secure such relief as may be necessary to abate such danger or threat, and the district court of the United States in the district in which the threat occurs shall have jurisdiction to grant such relief as the public interest and the equities of the case may require. The President may also, after notice to the affected State, take other action under this section including, but not limited to, issuing such orders as may be necessary to protect public health and welfare and the environment.

(b) Fines; reimbursement

(1) Any person who, without sufficient cause, willfully violates, or fails or refuses to comply with, any order of the President under subsection (a) of this section may, in an action brought in the appropriate United States district court to enforce such order, be fined not more than $25,000 for each day in which such violation occurs or such failure to comply continues.

(2)(A) Any person who receives and complies with the terms of any order issued under subsection (a) of this section may, within 60 days after completion of the required action, petition the President for reimbursement from the Fund for the reasonable costs of such action, plus interest. Any interest payable under this paragraph shall accrue on the amounts expended from the date of expenditure at the same rate as specified for interest on investments of the Hazardous Substance Superfund established under subchapter A of chapter 98 of Title 26.

(B) If the President refuses to grant all or part of a petition made under this paragraph, the petitioner may within 30 days of receipt of such refusal file an action against the President in the appropriate United States district court seeking reimbursement from the Fund.

(C) Except as provided in subparagraph (D), to obtain reimbursement, the petitioner shall establish by a preponderance of the evidence that it is not liable for response costs under section 9607(a) of this title and that costs for which it seeks reimbursement are reasonable in light of the action required by the relevant order.

(D) A petitioner who is liable for response costs under section 9607(a) of this title may also recover its reasonable costs of response to the extent that it can demonstrate, on the administrative record, that the President's decision in selecting the response action ordered was arbitrary and capricious or was otherwise not in accordance with law. Reimbursement awarded under this subparagraph shall include all reasonable response costs incurred by the petitioner pursuant to the portions of the order found to be arbitrary and capricious or otherwise not in accordance with law.

(E) Reimbursement awarded by a court under subparagraph (C) or (D) may include appropriate costs, fees, and other expenses in accordance with subsections (a) and (d) of section 2412 of Title 28.

(c) Guidelines for using imminent hazard, enforcement, and emergency response authorities; promulgation by Administrator of EPA, scope, etc.

Within one hundred and eighty days after December 11, 1980, the Administrator of the Environmental Protection Agency shall, after consultation with the Attorney General, establish and publish guidelines for using the imminent hazard, enforcement, and emergency response authorities of this section and other existing statutes administered by the Administrator of the Environmental Protection Agency to effectuate the responsibilities and powers created by this chapter. Such guidelines shall to the extent practicable be consistent with the national hazardous substance response plan, and shall include, at a minimum, the assignment of responsibility for coordinating response actions with the issuance of administrative orders, enforcement of standards and permits, the gathering of information, and other imminent hazard and emergency powers authorized by (1) sections 1321(c)(2), 1318, 1319, and 1364(a) of Title 33, (2) sections 6927, 6928, 6934, and 6973 of this title, (3) sections 300j–4 and 300i of this title, (4) sections 7413, 7414, and 7603 of this title, and (5) section 2606 of Title 15.

(Dec. 11, 1980, Pub.L. 96–510, Title I, § 106, 94 Stat. 2780, as amended Oct. 17, 1986, Pub.L. 99–499, Title I, §§ 106, 109(b), 100 Stat. 1628, 1633.)

Cross References

Solid Waste Disposal Act, actions prohibited under if Administrator of EPA is diligently prosecuting an action under this section, see section 6972(b) of this title.

Library References

Health and Environment ⟹25.5(10), 25.6(3), (9), 25.7(3), (24).
C.J.S. Health and Environment §§ 92, 103 et seq., 106, 113 et seq.

§ 9607. Liability

(a) Covered persons; scope; recoverable costs and damages; interest rate; "comparable maturity" date

Notwithstanding any other provision or rule of law, and subject only to the defenses set forth in subsection (b) of this section—

(1) the owner and operator of a vessel or a facility,

(2) any person who at the time of disposal of any hazardous substance owned or operated any facility at which such hazardous substances were disposed of,

(3) any person who by contract, agreement, or otherwise arranged for disposal or treatment, or arranged with a transporter for transport for disposal or treatment, of hazardous substances owned or possessed by such person, by any other party or entity, at any facility or incineration vessel owned or operated by another party or entity and containing such hazardous substances, and

(4) any person who accepts or accepted any hazardous substances for transport to disposal or treatment facilities, incineration vessels or sites selected by such person, from which there is a release, or a threatened release which causes the incurrence of response costs, of a hazardous substance, shall be liable for—

(A) all costs of removal or remedial action incurred by the United States Government or a State or an Indian tribe not inconsistent with the national contingency plan;

(B) any other necessary costs of response incurred by any other person consistent with the national contingency plan;

(C) damages for injury to, destruction of, or loss of natural resources, including the reasonable costs of assessing such injury, destruction, or loss resulting from such a release; and

(D) the costs of any health assessment or health effects study carried out under section 9604(i) of this title.

The amounts recoverable in an action under this section shall include interest on the amounts recoverable under subparagraphs (A) through (D). Such interest shall accrue from the later of (i) the date payment of a specified amount is demanded in writing, or (ii) the date of the expenditure concerned. The rate of interest on the outstanding unpaid balance of the amounts recoverable under this section shall be the same rate as is specified for interest on investments of the Hazardous Substance Superfund established under subchapter A of chapter 98 of Title 26. For purposes of applying such amendments to interest under this subsection, the term "comparable maturity" shall be determined with reference to the date on which interest accruing under this subsection commences.

(b) Defenses

There shall be no liability under subsection (a) of this section for a person otherwise liable who can establish by a preponderance of the evidence that the release or threat of release of a hazardous substance and the damages resulting therefrom were caused solely by—

(1) an act of God;

(2) an act of war;

(3) an act or omission of a third party other than an employee or agent of the defendant, or than one whose act or omission occurs in connection with a contractual relationship, existing directly or indirectly, with the defendant (except where the sole contractual arrangement arises from a published tariff and acceptance for carriage by a common carrier by rail), if the defendant establishes by a preponderance of the evidence that (a) he exercised due care with respect to the hazardous substance concerned, taking into consideration the characteristics of such hazardous substance, in light of all relevant facts and circumstances, and (b) he took precautions against foreseeable acts or omissions of any such third party and the consequences that could foreseeably result from such acts or omissions; or

(4) any combination of the foregoing paragraphs.

(c) Determination of amounts

(1) Except as provided in paragraph (2) of this subsection, the liability under this section of an owner or operator or other responsible person for each release of a hazardous substance or incident involving release of a hazardous substance shall not exceed—

(A) for any vessel, other than an incineration vessel, which carries any hazardous substance as cargo or residue, $300 per gross ton, or $5,000,000, whichever is greater;

(B) for any other vessel, other than an incineration vessel, $300 per gross ton, or $500,000, whichever is greater;

(C) for any motor vehicle, aircraft, pipeline (as defined in the Hazardous Liquid Pipeline Safety Act of 1979 [49 U.S.C. 2001 et seq.]), or rolling stock, $50,000,000 or such lesser amount as the President shall establish by regulation, but in no event less than $5,000,000 (or, for releases of hazardous substances as defined in section 9601(14)(A) of this title into the navigable waters, $8,000,000). Such regulations shall take into account the size, type, location, storage, and handling capacity and other matters relating to the likelihood of release in each such class and to the economic impact of such limits on each such class; or

(D) for any incineration vessel or any facility other than those specified in subparagraph (C) of this paragraph, the total of all costs of response plus $50,000,000 for any damages under this subchapter.

(2) Notwithstanding the limitations in paragraph (1) of this subsection, the liability of an owner or operator or other responsible person under this section shall be the full and total costs of response and damages, if (A)(i) the release or threat of release of a hazardous substance was the result of willful misconduct or willful negligence within the privity or knowledge of such person, or (ii) the primary cause of the release was a violation (within the privity or knowledge of such person) of applicable safety, construction, or operating standards or regulations; or (B) such person fails or refuses to provide all reasonable cooperation and assistance requested by a responsible public official in connection with response activities under the national contingency plan with respect to regulated carriers subject to the provisions of title 49 or vessels subject to the provisions of title 33 or 46, subparagraph (A)(ii) of this paragraph shall be deemed to refer to Federal standards or regulations.

(3) If any person who is liable for a release or threat of release of a hazardous substance fails without sufficient cause to properly provide removal or remedial action upon order of the President pursuant to section 9604 or 9606 of this title, such person may be liable to the United States for punitive damages in an amount at least equal to, and not more than three times, the amount of any costs incurred by the Fund as a result of such failure to take proper action. The President is authorized to commence a civil action against any such person to recover the punitive damages, which shall be in addition to any costs recovered from such person pursuant to section 9612(c) of this title. Any moneys received by the United States pursuant to this subsection shall be deposited in the Fund.

(d) Rendering care or advice

(1) In general

Except as provided in paragraph (2), no person shall be liable under this subchapter for costs or damages as a result of actions taken or omitted in the course of rendering care, assistance, or advice in accordance with the National Contingency Plan ("NCP") or at the direction of an on scene coordinator appointed under such plan, with respect to an incident creating a danger to public health or welfare or the environment as a result of any releases of a hazardous substance or the threat thereof. This paragraph shall not preclude liability for costs or damages as the result of negligence on the part of such person.

(2) State and local governments

No State or local government shall be liable under this subchapter for costs or damages as a result of actions taken in response to an emergency created by the release or threatened release of a hazardous substance generated by or from a facility owned by another person. This paragraph shall not preclude liability for costs or damages as a result of gross negligence or intentional misconduct by the State or local government. For the purpose of the preceding sentence, reckless, willful, or wanton misconduct shall constitute gross negligence.

(3) Savings provision

This subsection shall not alter the liability of any person covered by the provisions of paragraph (1), (2), (3), or (4) of subsection (a) of this section with respect to the release or threatened release concerned.

(e) Indemnification, hold harmless, etc., agreements or conveyances; subrogation rights

(1) No indemnification, hold harmless, or similar agreement or conveyance shall be effective to transfer from the owner or operator of any vessel or facility or from any person who may be liable for a release or threat of release under this section, to any other person the liability imposed under this section. Nothing in this subsection shall bar any agreement to insure, hold harmless, or indemnify a party to such agreement for any liability under this section.

(2) Nothing in this subchapter, including the provisions of paragraph (1) of this subsection, shall bar a cause of action that an owner or operator or any other person subject to liability under this section, or a guarantor, has or would have, by reason of subrogation or otherwise against any person.

(f) Actions involving natural resources; maintenance, scope, etc.

(1) Natural resources liability; use of recovered funds; measure of damages; double recovery

In the case of an injury to, destruction of, or loss of natural resources under subparagraph (C) of subsection (a) of this section liability shall be to the United States Government and to any State for natural resources within the State or belonging to, managed by, controlled by, or appertaining to such State: *Provided, however,* That no liability to the United States or State shall be imposed under subparagraph (C) of subsection (a) of this section, where the party sought to be charged has demonstrated that the damages to natural resources complained of were specifically identified as an irreversible and irretrievable commitment of natural resources in an environmental impact statement, or other comparable environment analysis, and the decision to grant a permit or license authorizes such commitment of natural resources, and the facility or project was otherwise operating within the terms of its permit or license. The President, or the authorized representative of any State, shall act on behalf of the public as trustee of such natural resources to recover for such damages. Sums recovered by the United States Government as trustee under this subsection shall be retained by the trustee, without further appropriation, for use only to restore, replace, or acquire the equivalent of such natural resources. Sums recovered by a State as trustee under this subsection shall be available for use only to restore, replace, or acquire the equivalent of such natural resources by the State. The measure of damages in any action under subparagraph (C) of subsection (a) of this section shall not be limited by the sums which can be used to restore or replace such resources. There shall be no double recovery under this chapter for natural resource damages, including the costs of damage assessment or restoration, rehabilitation, or acquisition for the same release and natural resource. There shall be no recovery under the authority of subparagraph (C) of subsection (a) of this section where such damages and the release of a hazardous substance from which such damages resulted have occurred wholly before December 11, 1980.

(2) Designation of Federal and State officials

(A) Federal

The President shall designate in the National Contingency Plan published under section 9605 of this chapter the Federal officials who shall act on behalf of the public as trustees for natural resources under this chapter and section 1321 of Title 33. Such officials shall assess damages for injury to, destruction of, or loss of natural resources for purposes of this chapter and such section 1321 of Title 33 for those resources under their trusteeship and may, upon request of and reimbursement from a State and at the Federal officials' discretion, assess damages for those natural resources under the State's trusteeship.

(B) State

The Governor of each State shall designate State officials who may act on behalf of the public as trustees for natural resources under this chapter and section 1321 of Title 33 and shall notify the President of such designations. Such State officials shall assess damages to natural resources for the purposes of this chapter and such section 1321 of Title 33 for those natural resources under their trusteeship.

(C) Rebuttable presumption

Any determination or assessment of damages to natural resources for the purposes of this chapter and section 1321 of Title 33 made by a Federal or State trustee in accordance with the regulations promulgated under section 9651 of this title shall have the force and effect of a rebuttable presumption on behalf of the trustee in any administrative or judicial proceeding under this chapter or section 1321 of Title 33.

(g) Federal agencies

For provisions relating to Federal agencies, see section 9620 of this title.

(h) Owner or operator of vessel

The owner or operator of a vessel shall be liable in accordance with this section, under maritime tort law, and as provided under section 9614 of this title notwithstanding any provision of the Act of March 3, 1851 (46 U.S.C. 183ff) or the absence of any physical damage to the proprietary interest of the claimant.

(i) Application of registered pesticide product

No person (including the United States or any State or Indian tribe) may recover under the authority of this section for any response costs or damages resulting from the application of a pesticide product registered under the Federal Insecticide, Fungicide, and Rodenticide Act [7 U.S.C.A. § 136 et seq.]. Nothing in this paragraph shall affect or modify in any way the obligations or liability of any person under any other provision of State or Federal law, including common law, for damages, injury, or loss resulting from a release of any hazardous substance or for removal or remedial action or the costs of removal or remedial action of such hazardous substance.

(j) Obligations or liability pursuant to federally permitted release

Recovery by any person (including the United States or any State or Indian tribe) for response costs or damages resulting from a federally permitted release shall be pursuant to existing law in lieu of this section. Nothing in this paragraph shall affect or modify in any way the obligations or liability of any person under any other provision of State or Federal law, including common law, for damages, injury, or loss resulting from a release of any hazardous substance or for removal or remedial action or the costs of removal or remedial action of such hazardous substance. In addition, costs of response incurred by the Federal Government in connection with a discharge specified in section 9601(10)(B) or (C) of this title shall be recoverable in an action brought under section 1319(b) of Title 33.

(k) Transfer to, and assumption by, Post-Closure Liability Fund of liability of owner or operator of hazardous waste disposal facility in receipt of permit under applicable solid waste disposal law; time, criteria applicable, procedures, etc.; monitoring costs; reports

(1) The liability established by this section or any other law for the owner or operator of a hazardous waste disposal facility which has received a permit under subtitle C of the Solid Waste Disposal Act [42 U.S.C. 6921 et seq.], shall be transferred to and assumed by the Post-closure Liability Fund established by section 9641 of this title when—

(A) such facility and the owner and operator thereof has complied with the requirements of subtitle C of the Solid Waste Disposal Act [42 U.S.C. 6921 et seq.] and regulations issued thereunder, which may affect the performance of such facility after closure; and

(B) such facility has been closed in accordance with such regulations and the conditions of such permit, and such facility and the surrounding area have been monitored as required by such regulations and permit conditions for a period not to exceed five years after closure to demonstrate that there is no substantial likelihood that any migration offsite or release from confinement of any hazardous substance or other risk to public health or welfare will occur.

(2) Such transfer of liability shall be effective ninety days after the owner or operator of such facility notifies the Administrator of the Environmental Protection Agency (and the State where it has an authorized program under section 3006(b) of the Solid Waste Disposal Act [42 U.S.C. 6926(b)]) that the conditions imposed by this subsection have been satisfied. If within such ninety-day period the Administrator of the Environmental Protection Agency or such State determines that any such facility has not complied with all the conditions imposed by this subsection or that insufficient information has been provided to demonstrate such compliance, the Administrator or such State shall so notify the owner and operator of such facility and the administrator of the Fund established by section 9641 of this title, and the owner and operator of such facility shall continue to be liable with respect to such facility under this section and other law until such time as the Administrator and such State determines that such facility has complied with all conditions imposed by this subsection. A determination by the Administrator or such State that a facility has not complied with all conditions imposed by this subsection or that insufficient information has been supplied to demonstrate compliance, shall be a final administrative action for purposes of judicial review. A request for additional information shall state in specific terms the data required.

(3) In addition to the assumption of liability of owners and operators under paragraph (1) of this subsection, the Post-closure Liability Fund established by section 9641 of this title may be used to pay costs of monitoring and care and maintenance of a site incurred by other persons after the period of monitoring required by regulations under subtitle C of the Solid Waste Disposal Act [42 U.S.C. 6921 et seq.] for hazardous waste disposal facilities meeting the conditions of paragraph (1) of this subsection.

(4)(A) Not later than one year after December 11, 1980, the Secretary of the Treasury shall conduct a study and shall submit a report thereon to the Congress on the feasibility of establishing or qualifying an optional system of private insurance for postclosure financial responsibility for hazardous waste disposal facilities to which this subsection applies. Such study shall include a specification of adequate and realistic minimum standards to assure that any such privately placed insurance will carry out the purposes of this subsection in a reliable, enforceable, and practical manner. Such a study shall include an examination of the public and private incentives, programs, and actions necessary to make privately placed insurance a practical and effective option to the financing system for the Post-closure Liability Fund provided in subchapter II of this chapter.

(B) Not later than eighteen months after December 11, 1980, and after a public hearing, the President shall by rule determine whether or not it is feasible to establish or qualify an optional system of private insurance for postclosure financial responsibility for hazardous waste disposal facilities to which this subsection applies. If the President determines the establishment or qualification of such a system would be infeasible, he shall promptly publish an explanation of the reasons for such a determination. If the President determines the establishment or qualification of such a system would be feasible, he shall promptly publish notice of such determination. Not later than six months after an affirmative determination under the preceding sentence and after a public hearing, the President shall by rule promulgate adequate and realistic minimum standards which must be met by any such privately placed insurance, taking into account the purposes of this chapter and this subsection. Such rules shall also specify reasonably expeditious procedures by which privately placed insurance plans can qualify as meeting such minimum standards.

(C) In the event any privately placed insurance plan qualifies under subparagraph (B), any person enrolled in, and complying with the terms of, such plan shall be excluded from the provisions of paragraphs (1), (2), and (3) of this subsection and exempt from the requirements to pay any tax or fee to the Post-closure Liability Fund under subchapter II of this chapter.

(D) The President may issue such rules and take such other actions as are necessary to effectuate the purposes of this paragraph.

(5) Suspension of liability transfer

Notwithstanding paragraphs (1), (2), (3), and (4) of this subsection and subsection (j) of section 9611 of this title, no liability shall be transferred to or assumed by the Post-Closure Liability Trust Fund established by section 9641 of this title prior to completion of the study required under paragraph (6) of this subsection, transmission of a report of such study to both Houses of Congress, and authorization of such a transfer or assumption by Act of Congress following receipt of such study and report.

(6) Study of options for Post-closure program

(A) Study

The Comptroller General shall conduct a study of options for a program for the management of the liabilities associated with hazardous waste treatment, storage, and disposal sites after their closure which complements the policies set forth in the Hazardous and Solid Waste Amendments of 1984 [42 U.S.C. 6901 note] and assures the protection of human health and the environment.

(B) Program elements

The program referred to in subparagraph (A) shall be designed to assure each of the following:

(i) Incentives are created and maintained for the safe management and disposal of hazardous wastes so as to assure protection of human health and the environment.

(ii) Members of the public will have reasonable confidence that hazardous wastes will be managed and disposed of safely and that resources will be available to address any problems that may arise and to cover costs of long-term monitoring, care, and maintenance of such sites.

(iii) Persons who are or seek to become owners and operators of hazardous waste disposal facilities will be able to manage their potential future liabilities and to attract the investment capital necessary to build, operate, and close such facilities in a manner which assures protection of human health and the environment.

(C) Assessments

The study under this paragraph shall include assessments of treatment, storage, and disposal facilities which have been or are likely to be issued a permit under section 3005 of the Solid Waste Disposal Act [42 U.S.C. 6925] and the likelihood of future insolvency on the part of owners and operators of such facilities. Separate assessments shall be made for different classes of facilities and for different classes of land disposal facilities and shall include but not be limited to—

(i) the current and future financial capabilities of facility owners and operators;

(ii) the current and future costs associated with facilities, including the costs of routine monitoring and maintenance, compliance monitoring, corrective action, natural resource damages, and liability for damages to third parties; and

(iii) the availability of mechanisms by which owners and operators of such facilities can assure that current and future costs, including post-closure costs, will be financed.

(D) Procedures

In carrying out the responsibilities of this paragraph, the Comptroller General shall consult with the Administrator, the Secretary of Commerce, the Secretary of the Treasury, and the heads of other appropriate Federal agencies.

(E) Consideration of options

In conducting the study under this paragraph, the Comptroller General shall consider various mechanisms and combinations of mechanisms to complement the policies set forth in the Hazardous and Solid Waste Amendments of 1984 [42 U.S.C. 6901 note] to serve the purposes set forth in subparagraph (B) and to assure that the current and future costs associated with hazardous waste facilities, including post-closure costs, will be adequately financed and, to the greatest extent possible, borne by the owners and operators of such facilities. Mechanisms to be considered include, but are not limited to—

(i) revisions to closure, post-closure, and financial responsibility requirements under subtitles C and I of the Solid Waste Disposal Act [42 U.S.C. 6921 et seq. and § 6991 et seq.];

(ii) voluntary risk pooling by owners and operators;

(iii) legislation to require risk pooling by owners and operators;

(iv) modification of the Post-Closure Liability Trust Fund previously established by section 9641 of this title, and the conditions for transfer of liability under this subsection, including limiting the transfer of some or all liability under this subsection only in the case of insolvency of owners and operators;

(v) private insurance;

(vi) insurance provided by the Federal Government;

(vii) coinsurance, reinsurance, or pooled-risk insurance, whether provided by the private sector or provided or assisted by the Federal Government; and

(viii) creation of a new program to be administered by a new or existing Federal agency or by a federally chartered corporation.

(F) Recommendations

The Comptroller General shall consider options for funding any program under this section and shall, to the extent necessary, make recommendations to the appropriate committees of Congress for additional authority to implement such program.

(*l*) Federal lien

(1) In general

All costs and damages for which a person is liable to the United States under subsection (a) of this section (other than the owner or operator of a vessel under paragraph (1) of subsection (a) of this section) shall constitute a lien in favor of the United States upon all real property and rights to such property which—

(A) belong to such person; and

(B) are subject to or affected by a removal or remedial action.

(2) Duration

The lien imposed by this subsection shall arise at the later of the following:

(A) The time costs are first incurred by the United States with respect to a response action under this chapter.

(B) The time that the person referred to in paragraph (1) is provided (by certified or registered mail) written notice of potential liability.

Such lien shall continue until the liability for the costs (or a judgment against the person arising out of such liability) is satisfied or becomes unenforceable through operation of the statute of limitations provided in section 9613 of this title.

(3) Notice and validity

The lien imposed by this subsection shall be subject to the rights of any purchaser, holder of a security interest, or judgment lien creditor whose interest is perfected under applicable State law before notice of the lien has been filed in the appropriate office within the State (or county or other governmental subdivision), as designated by State law, in which the real property subject to the lien is located. Any such purchaser, holder of a security interest, or judgment lien creditor shall be afforded the same protections against the lien imposed by this subsection as are afforded under State law against a judgment lien which arises out of an unsecured obligation and which arises as of the time of the filing of the notice of the lien imposed by this subsection. If the State has not by law designated one office for the receipt of such notices of liens, the notice shall be filed in the office of the clerk of the United States district court for the district in which the real property is located. For purposes of this subsection, the terms "purchaser" and "security interest" shall have the definitions provided under section 6323(h) of Title 26.

(4) Action in rem

The costs constituting the lien may be recovered in an action in rem in the United States district court for the district in which the removal or remedial action is occurring or has occurred. Nothing in this subsection shall affect the right of the United States to bring an action against any person to recover all costs and damages for which such person is liable under subsection (a) of this section.

(m) Maritime lien

All costs and damages for which the owner or operator of a vessel is liable under subsection (a)(1) of this section with respect to a release or threatened release from such vessel shall constitute a maritime lien in favor of the United States on such vessel. Such costs may be recovered in an action in rem in the district court of the United States for the district in which the vessel may be found. Nothing in this subsection shall affect the right of the United States to bring an action against the owner or operator of such vessel in any court of competent jurisdiction to recover such costs.

(Dec. 11, 1980, Pub.L. 96–510, Title I, § 107, 94 Stat. 2781, as amended Oct. 17, 1986, Pub.L. 99–499, Title I, §§ 107(a)–(d)(2), (e), (f), 127(b), (e), Title II, §§ 201, 207(c), 100 Stat. 1628–1630, 1692, 1693, 1705, 1706.)

Cross References

Solid Waste Disposal Act, financial responsibility provisions under as not diminishing liabilities of persons under this section, see sections 6924(t)(3), 6991b(d)(3), and 6991c(c)(4) of this title.

Library References

Health and Environment ⚷25.7(23).
C.J.S. Health and Environment § 113 et seq.

§ 9608. Financial responsibility

(a) Establishment and maintenance by owner or operator of vessel; amount; failure to obtain certification of compliance

(1) The owner or operator of each vessel (except a nonself-propelled barge that does not carry hazardous substances as cargo) over three hundred gross tons that uses any port or place in the United States or the navigable waters or any offshore facility, shall establish and maintain, in accordance with regulations promulgated by the President, evidence of financial responsibility of $300 per gross ton (or for a vessel carrying hazardous substances as cargo, or $5,000,000, whichever is greater to cover the liability prescribed under paragraph (1) of section 9607 of this title). Financial responsibility may be established by any one, or any combination, of the following: insurance, guarantee, surety bond, or qualification as a self-insurer. Any bond filed shall be issued by a bonding company authorized to do business in the United States. In cases where an owner or operator owns, operates, or charters more than one vessel subject to this subsection, evidence of financial responsibility need be established only to meet the maximum liability applicable to the largest of such vessels.

(2) The Secretary of the Treasury shall withhold or revoke the clearance required by section 91 of Title 46 of any vessel subject to this subsection that does not have certification furnished by the President that the financial responsibility provisions of paragraph (1) of this subsection have been complied with.

(3) The Secretary of Transportation, in accordance with regulations issued by him, shall (A) deny entry to any port or place in the United States or navigable waters to, and (B) detain at the port or place in the United States from which it is about to depart for any other port or place in the United States, any vessel subject to this subsection that, upon request, does not produce certification furnished by the President that the financial responsibility provisions of paragraph (1) of this subsection have been complied with.

(4) In addition to the financial responsibility provisions of paragraph (1) of this subsection, the President shall require additional evidence of financial responsibility for incineration vessels in such amounts, and to cover such liabilities recognized by law, as the President deems appropriate, taking into account the potential risks posed by incineration and transport for incineration, and any other factors deemed relevant.

(b) Establishment and maintenance by owner or operator of production, etc., facilities; amount; adjustment; consolidated form of responsibility; coverage of motor carriers

(1) Beginning not earlier than five years after December 11, 1980, the President shall promulgate requirements (for facilities in addition to those under subtitle C of the Solid Waste Disposal Act [42 U.S.C. 6921 et seq.] and other Federal law) that classes of facilities establish and maintain evidence of financial responsibility consistent with the degree and duration of risk associated with the production, transportation, treatment, storage, or disposal of

hazardous substances. Not later than three years after December 11, 1980, the President shall identify those classes for which requirements will be first developed and publish notice of such identification in the Federal Register. Priority in the development of such requirements shall be accorded to those classes of facilities, owners, and operators which the President determines present the highest level of risk of injury.

(2) The level of financial responsibility shall be initially established, and, when necessary, adjusted to protect against the level of risk which the President in his discretion believes is appropriate based on the payment experience of the Fund, commercial insurers, courts settlements and judgments, and voluntary claims satisfaction. To the maximum extent practicable, the President shall cooperate with and seek the advice of the commercial insurance industry in developing financial responsibility requirements. Financial responsibility may be established by any one, or any combination, of the following: insurance, guarantee, surety bond, letter of credit, or qualification as a self-insurer. In promulgating requirements under this section, the President is authorized to specify policy or other contractual terms, conditions, or defenses which are necessary, or which are unacceptable, in establishing such evidence of financial responsibility in order to effectuate the purposes of this chapter.

(3) Regulations promulgated under this subsection shall incrementally impose financial responsibility requirements as quickly as can reasonably be achieved but in no event more than 4 years after the date of promulgation. Where possible, the level of financial responsibility which the President believes appropriate as a final requirement shall be achieved through incremental, annual increases in the requirements.

(4) Where a facility is owned or operated by more than one person, evidence of financial responsibility covering the facility may be established and maintained by one of the owners or operators, or, in consolidated form, by or on behalf of two or more owners or operators. When evidence of financial responsibility is established in a consolidated form, the proportional share of each participant shall be shown. The evidence shall be accompanied by a statement authorizing the applicant to act for and in behalf of each participant in submitting and maintaining the evidence of financial responsibility.

(5) The requirements for evidence of financial responsibility for motor carriers covered by this chapter shall be determined under section 30 of the Motor Carrier Act of 1980, Public Law 96–296.

(c) Direct action

(1) Releases from vessels

In the case of a release or threatened release from a vessel, any claim authorized by section 9607 or 9611 of this title may be asserted directly against any guarantor providing evidence of financial responsibility for such vessel under subsection (a) of this section. In defending such a claim, the guarantor may invoke all rights and defenses which would be available to the owner or operator under this subchapter. The guarantor may also invoke the defense that the incident was caused by the willful misconduct of the owner or operator, but the guarantor may not invoke any other defense that the guarantor might have been entitled to invoke in a proceeding brought by the owner or operator against him.

(2) Releases from facilities

In the case of a release or threatened release from a facility, any claim authorized by section 9607 or 9611 of this title may be asserted directly against any guarantor providing evidence of financial responsibility for such facility under subsection (b) of this section, if the person liable under section 9607 of this title is in bankruptcy, reorganization, or arrangement pursuant to the Federal Bankruptcy Code, or if, with reasonable diligence, jurisdiction in the Federal courts cannot be obtained over a person liable under section 9607 of this title who is likely to be solvent at the time of judgment. In the case of any action pursuant to this paragraph, the guarantor shall be entitled to invoke all rights and defenses which would have been available to the person liable under section 9607 of this title if any action had been brought against such person by the claimant and all rights and defenses which would have been available to the guarantor if an action had been brought against the guarantor by such person.

(d) Limitation of guarantor liability

(1) Total liability

The total liability of any guarantor in a direct action suit brought under this section shall be limited to the aggregate amount of the monetary limits of the policy of insurance, guarantee, surety bond, letter of credit, or similar instrument obtained from the guarantor by the person subject to liability under section 9607 of this title for the purpose of satisfying the requirement for evidence of financial responsibility.

(2) Other liability

Nothing in this subsection shall be construed to limit any other State or Federal statutory, contractual, or common law liability of a guarantor, including, but not limited to, the liability of such guarantor for bad faith either in negotiating or in failing to negotiate the settlement of any claim. Nothing in this subsection shall be construed, interpreted, or applied to diminish the liability of any person under section 9607 of this title or other applicable law.

(Dec. 11, 1980, Pub.L. 96–510, Title I, § 108, 94 Stat. 2785, as amended Oct. 17, 1986, Pub.L. 99–499, Title I, §§ 108, 127(c), 100 Stat. 1631, 1692.)

Library References

Health and Environment ⚷25.7(3).
C.J.S. Health and Environment § 106.

§ 9609. Civil penalties and awards

(a) Class I administrative penalty

(1) Violations

A civil penalty of not more than $25,000 per violation may be assessed by the President in the case of any of the following—

(A) A violation of the requirements of section 9603(a) or (b) of this title (relating to notice).

(B) A violation of the requirements of section 9603(d)(2) of this title (relating to destruction of records, etc.).

(C) A violation of the requirements of section 9608 of this title (relating to financial responsibility, etc.), the regulations issued under section 9608 of this title, or with any denial or detention order under section 9608 of this title.

(D) A violation of an order under section 9622(d)(3) of this title (relating to settlement agreements for action under section 9604(b) of this title).

(E) Any failure or refusal referred to in section 9622(*l*) of this title (relating to violations of administrative orders, consent decrees, or agreements under section 9620 of this title).

(2) Notice and hearings

No civil penalty may be assessed under this subsection unless the person accused of the violation is given notice and opportunity for a hearing with respect to the violation.

(3) Determining amount

In determining the amount of any penalty assessed pursuant to this subsection, the President shall take into account the nature, circumstances, extent and gravity of the violation or violations and, with respect to the violator, ability to pay, any prior history of such violations, the degree of culpability, economic benefit or savings (if any) resulting from the violation, and such other matters as justice may require.

(4) Review

Any person against whom a civil penalty is assessed under this subsection may obtain review thereof in the appropriate district court of the United States by filing a notice of appeal in such court within 30 days from the date of such order and by simultaneously sending a copy of such notice by certified mail to the President. The President shall promptly file in such court a certified copy of the record upon which such violation was found or such penalty imposed. If any person fails to pay an assessment of a civil penalty after it has become a final and unappealable order or after the appropriate court has entered final judgment in favor of the United States, the President may request the Attorney General of the United States to institute a civil action in an appropriate district court of the United States to collect the penalty, and such court shall have jurisdiction to hear and decide any such action. In hearing such action, the court shall have authority to review the violation and the assessment of the civil penalty on the record.

(5) Subpoenas

The President may issue subpoenas for the attendance and testimony of witnesses and the production of relevant papers, books, or documents in connection with hearings under this subsection. In case of contumacy or refusal to obey a subpoena issued pursuant to this paragraph and served upon any person, the district court of the United States for any district in which such person is found, resides, or transacts business, upon application by the United States and after notice to such person, shall have jurisdiction to issue an order requiring such person to appear and give testimony before the administrative law judge or to appear and produce documents before the administrative law judge, or both, and any failure to obey such order of the court may be punished by such court as a contempt thereof.

(b) Class II administrative penalty

A civil penalty of not more than $25,000 per day for each day during which the violation continues may be assessed by the President in the case of any of the following—

(1) A violation of the notice requirements of section 9603(a) or (b) of this title.

(2) A violation of section 9603(d)(2) of this title (relating to destruction of records, etc.).

(3) A violation of the requirements of section 9608 of this title (relating to financial responsibility, etc.), the regulations issued under section 9608 of this title, or with any denial or detention order under section 9608 of this title.

(4) A violation of an order under section 9622(d)(3) of this title (relating to settlement agreements for action under section 9604(b) of this title).

(5) Any failure or refusal referred to in section 9622(*l*) of this title (relating to violations of administrative orders, consent decrees, or agreements under section 9620 of this title).

In the case of a second or subsequent violation the amount of such penalty may be not more than $75,000 for each day during which the violation continues. Any civil penalty under this subsection shall be assessed and collected in the same manner, and subject to the same provisions, as in the case of civil penalties assessed and collected after notice and opportunity for hearing on the record in accordance with section 554 of Title 5. In any proceeding for the assessment of a civil penalty under this subsection the President may issue subpoenas for the attendance and testimony of witnesses and the production of relevant papers, books, and documents and may promulgate rules for discovery procedures. Any person who requested a hearing with respect to a civil penalty under this subsection and who is aggrieved by an order assessing the civil penalty may file a petition for judicial review of such order with the United States Court of Appeals for the District of Columbia Circuit or for any other circuit in which such person resides or transacts business. Such a petition may only be filed within the 30-day period beginning on the date the order making such assessment was issued.

(c) Judicial assessment

The President may bring an action in the United States district court for the appropriate district to assess and collect a penalty of not more than $25,000 per day for each day during which the violation (or failure or refusal) continues in the case of any of the following—

(1) A violation of the notice requirements of section 9603(a) or (b) of this title.

(2) A violation of section 9603(d)(2) of this title (relating to destruction of records, etc.).

(3) A violation of the requirements of section 9608 of this title (relating to financial responsibility, etc.), the regulations issued under section 9608 of this title, or with any denial or detention order under section 9608 of this title.

(4) A violation of an order under section 9622(d)(3) of this title (relating to settlement agreements for action under section 9604(b) of this title).

(5) Any failure or refusal referred to in section 9622(*l*) of this title (relating to violations of administrative orders, consent decrees, or agreements under section 9620 of this title).

In the case of a second or subsequent violation (or failure or refusal), the amount of such penalty may be not more than $75,000 for each day during which the violation (or failure or refusal) continues. For additional provisions providing for judicial assessment of civil penalties for failure to comply with a request or order under section 9604(e) of this title (relating to information gathering and access authorities), see section 9604(e) of this title.

(d) Awards

The President may pay an award of up to $10,000 to any individual who provides information leading to the arrest and conviction of any person for a violation subject to a criminal penalty under this chapter, including any violation of section 9603 of this title and any other violation referred to in this section. The President shall, by regulation, prescribe criteria for such an award and may pay any award under this subsection from the Fund, as provided in section 9611 of this title.

(e) Procurement procedures

Notwithstanding any other provision of law, any executive agency may use competitive procedures or procedures other than competitive procedures to procure the services of experts for use in preparing or prosecuting a civil or criminal action under this chapter, whether or not the expert is expected to testify at trial. The executive agency need not provide any written justification for the use of procedures other than competitive procedures when procuring such expert services under this chapter and need not furnish for publication in the Commerce Business Daily or otherwise any notice of solicitation or synopsis with respect to such procurement.

(f) Savings clause

Action taken by the President pursuant to this section shall not affect or limit the President's authority to enforce any provisions of this chapter.

(Dec. 11, 1980, Pub.L. 96–510, Title I, § 109, 94 Stat. 2787, as amended Oct. 17, 1986, Pub.L. 99–499, Title I, § 109(c), 100 Stat. 1633.)

Library References

Health and Environment ⚯25.7(24).
C.J.S. Health and Environment § 113 et seq.

§ 9610. Employee protection

(a) Activities of employee subject to protection

No person shall fire or in any other way discriminate against, or cause to be fired or discriminated against, any employee or any authorized representative of employees by reason of the fact that such employee or representative has provided information to a State or to the Federal Government, filed, instituted, or caused to be filed or instituted any proceeding under this chapter, or has testified or is about to testify in any proceeding resulting from the administration or enforcement of the provisions of this chapter.

(b) Administrative grievance procedure in cases of alleged violations

Any employee or a representative of employees who believes that he has been fired or otherwise discriminated against by any person in violation of subsection (a) of this section may, within thirty days after such alleged violation occurs, apply to the Secretary of Labor for a review of such firing or alleged discrimination. A copy of the application shall be sent to such person, who shall be the respondent. Upon receipt of such application, the Secretary of Labor shall cause such investigation to be made as he deems appropriate. Such investigation shall provide an opportunity for a public hearing at the request of any party to such review to enable the parties to present information relating to such alleged violation. The parties shall be given written notice of the time and place of the hearing at least five days prior to the hearing. Any such hearing shall be of record and shall be subject to section 554 of Title 5. Upon receiving the report of such investigation, the Secretary of Labor shall make findings of fact. If he finds that such violation did occur, he shall issue a decision, incorporating an order therein and his findings, requiring the party committing such violation to take such affirmative action to abate the violation as the Secretary of Labor deems appropriate, including, but not limited to, the rehiring or reinstatement of the employee or representative of employees to his former position with compensation. If he finds that there was no such violation, he shall issue an order denying the application. Such order issued by the Secretary of Labor under this subparagraph shall be subject to judicial review in the same manner as orders and decisions are subject to judicial review under this chapter.

(c) Assessment of costs and expenses against violator subsequent to issuance of order of abatement

Whenever an order is issued under this section to abate such violation, at the request of the applicant a sum equal to the aggregate amount of all costs and expenses (including the attorney's fees) determined by the Secretary of Labor to have been reasonably incurred by the applicant for, or in connection with, the institution and prosecution of such proceedings, shall be assessed against the person committing such violation.

(d) Defenses

This section shall have no application to any employee who acting without discretion from his employer (or his agent) deliberately violates any requirement of this chapter.

(e) Presidential evaluations of potential loss of shifts of employment resulting from administration or enforcement of provisions; investigations; procedures applicable, etc.

The President shall conduct continuing evaluations of potential loss of shifts of employment which may result from the administration or enforcement of the provisions of this chapter, including, where appropriate, investigating threatened plant closures or reductions in employment allegedly resulting from such administration or enforcement. Any employee who is discharged, or laid off, threatened with discharge or layoff, or otherwise discriminated against by any person because of the alleged results of such administration or enforcement, or any representative of such employee, may request the President to conduct a full investigation of the matter and, at the request of any party, shall hold public hearings, require the parties, including the employer involved, to present information relating to the actual or potential effect of such administration or enforcement on employment and any alleged discharge, layoff, or other discrimination, and the detailed reasons or justification therefore. Any such hearing shall be of record and shall be subject to section 554 of Title 5. Upon receiving the report of such investigation, the President shall make findings of fact as to the effect of such administration or enforcement on employment and on the alleged discharge, layoff, or discrimination and shall make such recommendations as he deems appropriate. Such report, findings, and recommendations shall be available to the public. Nothing in this subsection shall be construed to require or authorize the President or any State to modify or withdraw any action, standard, limitation, or any other requirement of this chapter.

(Dec. 11, 1980, Pub.L. 96–510, Title I, § 110, 94 Stat. 2787.)

Library References

Health and Environment ⚩25.6(3), 25.7(3).
C.J.S. Health and Environment §§ 92, 106.

§ 9611. Use of Fund

(a) In general

For the purposes specified in this section there is authorized to be appropriated from the Hazardous Substance Superfund established under subchapter A of chapter 98 of Title 26 not more than $8,500,000,000 for the 5-year period beginning on October 17, 1986, and such sums shall remain available until expended. The preceding sentence constitutes a specific authorization for the funds appropriated under title II of Public Law 99–160 (relating to payment to the Hazardous Substances Trust Fund).

(1) Payment of governmental response costs incurred pursuant to section 9604 of this title, including costs incurred pursuant to the Intervention on the High Seas Act [33 U.S.C.A. § 1471 et seq.].

(2) Payment of any claim for necessary response costs incurred by any other person as a result of carrying out the national contingency plan established under section 1321(c) of Title 33 and amended by section 9605 of this title: *Provided, however,* That such costs must be approved under said plan and certified by the responsible Federal official.

(3) Payment of any claim authorized by subsection (b) of this section and finally decided pursuant to section 9612 of this title, including those costs set out in subsection 9612(c)(3) of this title.

(4) Payment of costs specified under subsection (c) of this section.

(5) Grants for technical assistance

The cost of grants under section 9617(e) of this title (relating to public participation grants for technical assistance).

(6) Lead contaminated soil

Payment of not to exceed $15,000,000 for the costs of a pilot program for removal, decontamination, or other action with respect to lead-contaminated soil in one to three different metropolitan areas.

The President shall not pay for any administrative costs or expenses out of the Fund unless such costs and expenses are reasonably necessary for and incidental to the implementation of this subchapter.

(b) Additional authorized purposes

(1) In general

Claims asserted and compensable but unsatisfied under provisions of section 1321 of Title 33, which are modified by section 304 of this Act may be asserted against the Fund under this subchapter; and other claims resulting from a release or threat of release of a hazardous substance from a vessel or a facility may be asserted against the Fund under this subchapter for injury to, or destruction or loss of, natural resources, including cost for damage assessment: *Provided, however,* That any such claim may be asserted only by the President, as trustee, for natural resources over which the United States has sovereign rights, or natural resources within the territory or the fishery conservation zone of the United States to the extent they are managed or protected by the United States, or by any State for natural resources within the boundary of that State belonging to, managed by, controlled by, or appertaining to the State, or by any Indian tribe or by the United States acting on behalf of any Indian tribe for natural resources belonging to, managed by, controlled by, or appertaining to such tribe, or held in trust for the benefit of such tribe, or belonging to a member of such tribe if such resources are subject to a trust restriction on alienation.

(2) Limitation on payment of natural resource claims

(A) General requirements

No natural resource claim may be paid from the Fund unless the President determines that the claimant has exhausted all administrative and judicial remedies to recover the amount of such claim from persons who may be liable under section 9607 of this title.

(B) Definition

As used in this paragraph, the term "natural resource claim" means any claim for injury to, or destruction or loss of, natural resources. The term does not include any claim for the costs of natural resource damage assessment.

(c) Peripheral matters and limitations

Uses of the Fund under subsection (a) of this section include—

(1) The costs of assessing both short-term and long-term injury to, destruction of, or loss of any natural resources resulting from a release of a hazardous substance.

(2) The costs of Federal or State or Indian tribe efforts in the restoration, rehabilitation, or replacement or acquiring the equivalent of any natural resources injured, destroyed, or lost as a result of a release of a hazardous substance.

(3) Subject to such amounts as are provided in appropriation Acts, the costs of a program to identify, investigate, and take enforcement and abatement action against releases of hazardous substances.

(4) Any costs incurred in accordance with subsection (m) of this section (relating to ATSDR) and section 9604(i) of this title including the costs of epidemiologic and laboratory studies, health assessments, preparation of toxicologic profiles, development and maintenance of a registry of persons exposed to hazardous substances to allow long-term health effect studies, and diagnostic services not otherwise available to determine whether persons in populations exposed to hazardous substances in connection with a release or a suspected release are suffering from long-latency diseases.

(5) Subject to such amounts as are provided in appropriation Acts, the costs of providing equipment and similar overhead, related to the purposes of this chapter and section 1321 of Title 33, and needed to supplement equipment and services available through contractors or other non-Federal entities, and of establishing and maintaining damage assessment capability, for any Federal agency involved in strike forces, emergency task forces, or other response teams under the national contingency plan.

(6) Subject to such amounts as are provided in appropriation Acts, the costs of a program to protect the health and safety of employees involved in response to hazardous substance releases. Such program shall be developed jointly by the Environmental Protection Agency, the Occupational Safety and Health Administration, and the National Institute for Occupational Safety and Health and shall include, but not be limited to, measures for identifying and assessing hazards to which persons engaged in removal, remedy, or other response to hazardous substances may be exposed, methods to protect workers from such hazards, and necessary regulatory and enforcement measures to assure adequate protection of such employees.

(7) Evaluation costs under petition provisions of section 9605(d)

Costs incurred by the President in evaluating facilities pursuant to petitions under section 9605(d) of this title (relating to petitions for assessment of release).

(8) Contract costs under section 9604(a)(1)

The costs of contracts or arrangements entered into under section 9604(a)(1) of this title to oversee and review the conduct of remedial investigations and feasibility studies undertaken by persons other than the President and the costs of appropriate Federal and State oversight of remedial activities at National Priorities List sites resulting from consent orders or settlement agreements.

(9) Acquisition costs under section 9604(j)

The costs incurred by the President in acquiring real estate or interests in real estate under section 9604(j) of this title (relating to acquisition of property).

(10) Research, development, and demonstration costs under section 9660

The cost of carrying out section 9660a of this title (relating to research, development, and demonstration), except that the amounts available for such purposes shall not exceed the amounts specified in subsection (n) of this section.

(11) Local government reimbursement

Reimbursements to local governments under section 9623 of this title, except that during the 5-fiscal-year period beginning October 1, 1986, not more than 0.1 percent of the total amount appropriated from the Fund may be used for such reimbursements.

(12) Worker training and education grants

The costs of grants under section 9660a of this title for training and education of workers to the extent that such costs do not exceed $10,000,000 for each of the fiscal years 1987, 1988, 1989, 1990, and 1991.

(13) Awards under section 9609

The costs of any awards granted under section 9609(d) of this title.

(14) Lead poisoning study

The cost of carrying out the study under subsection (f) of section 118 of the Superfund Amendments and Reauthorization Act of 1986 [42 U.S.C. 6981 note] (relating to lead poisoning in children).

(d) Additional limitations

(1) No money in the Fund may be used under subsection (c)(1) and (2) of this section, nor for the payment of any claim under subsection (b) of this section, where the injury, destruction, or loss of natural resources and the release of a hazardous substance from which such damages resulted have occurred wholly before December 11, 1980.

(2) No money in the Fund may be used for the payment of any claim under subsection (b) of this section where such expenses are associated with injury or loss resulting from long-term exposure to ambient concentrations of air pollutants from multiple or diffuse sources.

(e) Funding requirements respecting moneys in Fund; limitation on certain claims; Fund use outside Federal property boundaries

(1) Claims against or presented to the Fund shall not be valid or paid in excess of the total money in the Fund at any one time. Such claims become valid only when additional money is collected, appropriated, or otherwise added to the Fund. Should the total claims outstanding at any time exceed the current balance of the Fund, the President shall pay such claims, to the extent authorized under this section, in full in the order in which they were finally determined.

(2) In any fiscal year, 85 percent of the money credited to the Fund under subchapter II of this chapter shall be available only for the purposes specified in paragraphs (1), (2), and (4) of subsection (a) of this section. No money in the Fund may be used for the payment of any claim under subsection (a)(3) or subsection (b) of this section in any fiscal year for which the President determines that all of the Fund is needed for response to threats to public health from releases or threatened releases of hazardous substances.

(3) No money in the Fund shall be available for remedial action, other than actions specified in subsection (c) of this section, with respect to federally owned facilities; except that money in the Fund shall be available for the provision of alternative water supplies (including the reimbursement of costs incurred by a municipality) in any case involving groundwater contamination outside the boundaries of a federally owned facility in which the federally owned facility is not the only potentially responsible party.

(4) Paragraphs (1) and (4) of subsection (a) of this section shall in the aggregate be subject to such amounts as are provided in appropriation Acts.

(f) Obligation of moneys by Federal officials; obligation of moneys or settlement of claims by State officials or Indian tribe

The President is authorized to promulgate regulations designating one or more Federal officials who may obligate money in the Fund in accordance with this section or portions thereof. The President is also authorized to delegate authority to obligate money in the Fund or to settle claims to officials of a State or Indian tribe operating under a contract or cooperative agreement with the Federal Government pursuant to section 9604(d) of this title.

(g) Notice to potential injured parties by owner and operator of vessel or facility causing release of substance; rules and regulations

The President shall provide for the promulgation of rules and regulations with respect to the notice to be provided to potential injured parties by an owner and operator of any vessel, or facility from which a hazardous substance has been released. Such rules and regulations shall consider the scope and form of the notice which would be appropriate to carry out the purposes of this subchapter. Upon promulgation of such rules and regulations, the owner and operator of any vessel or facility from which a hazardous substance has been released shall provide notice in accordance with such rules and regulations. With respect to releases from public vessels, the President shall provide such notification as is appropriate to potential injured parties. Until the promulgation of such rules and regulations, the owner and operator of any vessel or facility from which a hazardous substance has been released shall provide reasonable notice to potential injured parties by publication in local newspapers serving the affected area.

(h) Repealed. Pub.L. 99–499, Title I, § 111(c)(2), Oct. 17, 1986, 100 Stat. 1643

(i) Restoration, etc., of natural resources

Except in a situation requiring action to avoid an irreversible loss of natural resources or to prevent or reduce any continuing danger to natural resources or similar need for emergency action, funds may not be used under this chapter for the restoration, rehabilitation, or replacement or acquisition of the equivalent of any natural resources until a plan for the use of such funds for such purposes has been developed and adopted by affected Federal agencies and the Governor or Governors of any State and by the governing body of an Indian tribe having sustained damage to natural resources belonging to, managed by, controlled by, or appertaining to such tribe, or held in trust for the benefit of such tribe, or belonging to a member of such tribe if such resources are subject to a trust restriction on alienation, having sustained damage to natural resources within its borders, belonging to, managed by or appertaining to such State, after adequate public notice and opportunity for hearing and consideration of all public comment.

(j) Use of Post-closure Liability Fund

The President shall use the money in the Post-closure Liability Fund for any of the purposes specified in subsection (a) of this section with respect to a hazardous waste disposal facility for which liability has transferred to such fund under section 9607(k) of this title, and, in addition, for payment of any claim or appropriate request for costs of response, damages, or other compensation for injury or loss under section 9607 of this title or any other State or Federal law, resulting from a release of a hazardous substance from such a facility.

(k) Inspector General

In each fiscal year, the Inspector General of each department, agency, or instrumentality of the United States which is carrying out any authority of this chapter shall conduct an annual audit of all payments, obligations, reimbursements, or other uses of the Fund in the prior fiscal year, to assure that the Fund is being properly administered and that claims are being appropriately and expeditiously considered. The audit shall include an examination of a sample of agreements with States (in accordance with the provisions of the Single Audit Act) carrying out response actions under this subchapter and an examination of remedial investigations and feasibility studies prepared for remedial actions. The Inspector General shall submit to the Congress an annual report regarding the audit report required under this subsection. The report shall contain such recommendations as the Inspector General deems appropriate. Each department, agency, or instrumentality of the United States shall cooperate with its inspector general in carrying out this subsection.

(*l*) Foreign claimants

To the extent that the provisions of this chapter permit, a foreign claimant may assert a claim to the same extent that a United States claimant may assert a claim if—

(1) the release of a hazardous substance occurred (A) in the navigable waters or (B) in or on the territorial sea or adjacent shoreline of a foreign country of which the claimant is a resident;

(2) the claimant is not otherwise compensated for his loss;

(3) the hazardous substance was released from a facility or from a vessel located adjacent to or within the navigable waters or was discharged in connection with activities conducted under the Outer Continental Shelf Lands Act, as amended (43 U.S.C. 1331 et seq.) or the Deepwater Port Act of 1974, as amended (33 U.S.C. 1501 et seq.); and

(4) recovery is authorized by a treaty or an executive agreement between the United States and foreign country involved, or if the Secretary of State, in consultation with the Attorney General and other appropriate officials, certifies that such country provides a comparable remedy for United States claimants.

(m) Agency for Toxic Substances and Disease Registry

There shall be directly available to the Agency for Toxic Substances and Disease Registry to be used for the purpose of carrying out activities described in subsection (c)(4) of this section and section 9604(i) of this title not less than $50,000,000 per fiscal year for each of fiscal years 1987 and 1988, not less than $55,000,000 for fiscal year 1989, and not less than $60,000,000 per fiscal year for each of fiscal years 1990 and 1991. Any funds so made available which are not obligated by the end of the fiscal year in which made available shall be returned to the Fund.

(n) Limitations on research, development, and demonstration program

(1) Section 9660(b)

For each of the fiscal years 1987, 1988, 1989, 1990, and 1991, not more than $20,000,000 of the amounts available in the Fund may be used for the purposes of carrying out the applied research, development, and demonstration program for alternative or innovative technologies and training program authorized under section 9660(b) of this title (relating to research, development, and demonstration) other than basic research. Such amounts shall remain available until expended.

(2) Section 9660(a)

From the amounts available in the Fund, not more than the following amounts may be used for the purposes of section 9660(a) of this title (relating to hazardous substance research, demonstration, and training activities):

(A) For the fiscal year 1987, $3,000,000.

(B) For the fiscal year 1988, $10,000,000.

(C) For the fiscal year 1989, $20,000,000.

(D) For the fiscal year 1990, $30,000,000.

(E) For the fiscal year 1991, $35,000,000.

No more than 10 percent of such amounts shall be used for training under section 9660(a) of this title in any fiscal year.

(3) Section 9660(d)

For each of the fiscal years 1987, 1988, 1989, 1990, and 1991, not more than $5,000,000 of the amounts available in the Fund may be used for the purposes of section 311(d) (relating to university hazardous substance research centers).

(*o*) Notification procedures for limitations on certain payments

Not later than 90 days after October 17, 1986, the President shall develop and implement procedures to adequately notify, as soon as practicable after a site is included on the National Priorities List, concerned local and State officials and other concerned persons of the limitations, set forth in subsection (a)(2) of this section, on the payment of claims for necessary response costs incurred with respect to such site.

(p) General revenue share of Superfund

(1) In general

The following sums are authorized to be appropriated, out of any money in the Treasury not otherwise appropriated, to the Hazardous Substance Superfund:

(A) For fiscal year 1987, $212,500,000.

(B) For fiscal year 1988, $212,500,000.

(C) For fiscal year 1989, $212,500,000.

(D) For fiscal year 1990, $212,500,000.

(E) For fiscal year 1991, $212,500,000.

In addition there is authorized to be appropriated to the Hazardous Substance Superfund for each fiscal year an amount equal to so much of the aggregate amount authorized to be appropriated under this subsection (and paragraph (2) of section 9631(b) of this title) as has not been appropriated before the beginning of the fiscal year involved.

(2) **Computation**

The amounts authorized to be appropriated under paragraph (1) of this subsection in a given fiscal year shall be available only to the extent that such amount exceeds the amount determined by the Secretary under section 9507(b)(2) of Title 26 for the prior fiscal year.

(Dec. 11, 1980, Pub.L. 96–510, Title I, § 111, 94 Stat. 2788, as amended Oct. 17, 1986, Pub.L. 99–499, Title I, § 111, Title II, § 207(d), 100 Stat. 1642, 1706.)

Cross References

Solid Waste Disposal Act, financial responsibility provisions under as not diminishing liabilities of persons under this section, see sections 6924(t)(3), 6991b(d)(3), and 6991c(c)(4) of this title.

Library References

Health and Environment ⚷25.6(3), 25.7(3).
C.J.S. Health and Environment §§ 92, 106.

§ 9612. Claims procedure

(a) Claims against the Fund for response costs

No claim may be asserted against the Fund pursuant to section 9611(a) of this title unless such claim is presented in the first instance to the owner, operator, or guarantor of the vessel or facility from which a hazardous substance has been released, if known to the claimant, and to any other person known to the claimant who may be liable under section 9607 of this title. In any case where the claim has not been satisfied within 60 days of presentation in accordance with this subsection, the claimant may present the claim to the Fund for payment. No claim against the Fund may be approved or certified during the pendency of an action by the claimant in court to recover costs which are the subject of the claim.

(b) Forms and procedures applicable

(1) **Prescribing forms and procedures**

The President shall prescribe appropriate forms and procedures for claims filed hereunder, which shall include a provision requiring the claimant to make a sworn verification of the claim to the best of his knowledge. Any person who knowingly gives or causes to be given any false information as a part of any such claim shall, upon conviction, be fined in accordance with the applicable provisions of Title 18 of the United States Code or imprisoned for not more than 3 years (or not more than 5 years in the case of a second or subsequent conviction), or both.

(2) **Payment or request for hearing**

The President may, if satisfied that the information developed during the processing of the claim warrants it, make and pay an award of the claim, except that no claim may be awarded to the extent that a judicial judgment has been made on the costs that are the subject of the claim. If the President declines to pay all or part of the claim, the claimant may, within 30 days after receiving notice of the President's decision, request an administrative hearing.

(3) **Burden of proof**

In any proceeding under this subsection, the claimant shall bear the burden of proving his claim.

(4) **Decisions**

All administrative decisions made hereunder shall be in writing, with notification to all appropriate parties, and shall be rendered within 90 days of submission of a claim to an administrative law judge, unless all the parties to the claim agree in writing to an extension or unless the President, in his discretion, extends the time limit for a period not to exceed sixty days.

(5) **Finality and appeal**

All administrative decisions hereunder shall be final, and any party to the proceeding may appeal a decision within 30 days of notification of the award or decision. Any such appeal shall be made to the Federal district court for the district where the release or threat of release took place. In any such appeal, the decision shall be considered binding and conclusive, and shall not be overturned except for arbitrary or capricious abuse of discretion.

(6) **Payment**

Within 20 days after the expiration of the appeal period for any administrative decision concerning an award, or within 20 days after the final judicial determination of any appeal taken pursuant to this subsection, the President shall pay any such award from the Fund. The President shall determine the method, terms, and time of payment.

(c) Subrogation rights; actions maintainable

(1) Payment of any claim by the Fund under this section shall be subject to the United States Government acquiring by subrogation the rights of the claimant to recover those costs of removal or damages for which it has compensated the claimant from the person responsible or liable for such release.

(2) Any person, including the Fund, who pays compensation pursuant to this chapter to any claim-

ant for damages or costs resulting from a release of a hazardous substance shall be subrogated to all rights, claims, and causes of action for such damages and costs of removal that the claimant has under this chapter or any other law.

(3) Upon request of the President, the Attorney General shall commence an action on behalf of the Fund to recover any compensation paid by the Fund to any claimant pursuant to this subchapter, and, without regard to any limitation of liability, all interest, administrative and adjudicative costs, and attorney's fees incurred by the Fund by reason of the claim. Such an action may be commenced against any owner, operator, or guarantor, or against any other person who is liable, pursuant to any law, to the compensated claimant or to the Fund, for the damages or costs for which compensation was paid.

(d) Statute of limitations

(1) Claims for recovery of costs

No claim may be presented under this section for recovery of the costs referred to in section 9607(a) of this title after the date 6 years after the date of completion of all response action.

(2) Claims for recovery of damages

No claim may be presented under this section for recovery of the damages referred to in section 9607(a) of this title unless the claim is presented within 3 years after the later of the following:

(A) The date of the discovery of the loss and its connection with the release in question.

(B) The date on which final regulations are promulgated under section 9651(c) of this title.

(3) Minors and incompetents

The time limitations contained herein shall not begin to run—

(A) against a minor until the earlier of the date when such minor reaches 18 years of age or the date on which a legal representative is duly appointed for the minor, or

(B) against an incompetent person until the earlier of the date on which such person's incompetency ends or the date on which a legal representative is duly appointed for such incompetent person.

(e) Other statutory or common law claims not waived, etc.

Regardless of any State statutory or common law to the contrary, no person who asserts a claim against the Fund pursuant to this subchapter shall be deemed or held to have waived any other claim not covered or assertable against the Fund under this subchapter arising from the same incident, transaction, or set of circumstances, nor to have split a cause of action. Further, no person asserting a claim against the Fund pursuant to this subchapter shall as a result of any determination of a question of fact or law made in connection with that claim be deemed or held to be collaterally estopped from raising such question in connection with any other claim not covered or assertable against the Fund under this subchapter arising from the same incident, transaction, or set of circumstances.

(f) Double recovery prohibited

Where the President has paid out of the Fund for any response costs or any costs specified under section 9611(c)(1) or (2) of this title, no other claim may be paid out of the Fund for the same costs.

(Dec. 11, 1980, Pub.L. 96–510, Title I, § 112, 94 Stat. 2792, as amended Oct. 17, 1986, Pub.L. 99–499, Title I, §§ 109(a)(3), 112, 100 Stat. 1633, 1646.)

Library References

Health and Environment ⚷25.6(3), 25.7(3).
C.J.S. Health and Environment §§ 92, 106.

§ 9613. Civil proceedings

(a) Review of regulations in Circuit Court of Appeals of the United States for the District of Columbia

Review of any regulation promulgated under this chapter may be had upon application by any interested person only in the Circuit Court of Appeals of the United States for the District of Columbia. Any such application shall be made within ninety days from the date of promulgation of such regulations. Any matter with respect to which review could have been obtained under this subsection shall not be subject to judicial review in any civil or criminal proceeding for enforcement or to obtain damages or recovery of response costs.

(b) Jurisdiction; venue

Except as provided in subsections (a) and (h) of this section, the United States district courts shall have exclusive original jurisdiction over all controversies arising under this chapter, without regard to the citizenship of the parties or the amount in controversy. Venue shall lie in any district in which the release or damages occurred, or in which the defendant resides, may be found, or has his principal office. For the purposes of this section, the Fund shall reside in the District of Columbia.

(c) Controversies or other matters resulting from tax collection or tax regulation review

The provisions of subsections (a) and (b) of this section shall not apply to any controversy or other matter resulting from the assessment of collection of any tax, as provided by subchapter II of this chapter, or to the review of any regulation promulgated under Title 26.

(d) Litigation commenced prior to December 11, 1980

No provision of this chapter shall be deemed or held to moot any litigation concerning any release of any hazardous substance, or any damages associated therewith, commenced prior to December 11, 1980.

(e) Nationwide service of process

In any action by the United States under this chapter, process may be served in any district where the defendant is found, resides, transacts business, or has appointed an agent for the service of process.

(f) Contribution

(1) Contribution

Any person may seek contribution from any other person who is liable or potentially liable under section 9607(a) of this title, during or following any civil action under section 9606 of this title or under section 9607(a) of this title. Such claims shall be brought in accordance with this section and the Federal Rules of Civil Procedure, and shall be governed by Federal law. In resolving contribution claims, the court may allocate response costs among liable parties using such equitable factors as the court determines are appropriate. Nothing in this subsection shall diminish the right of any person to bring an action for contribution in the absence of a civil action under section 9606 or section 9607 of this title.

(2) Settlement

A person who has resolved its liability to the United States or a State in an administrative or judicially approved settlement shall not be liable for claims for contribution regarding matters addressed in the settlement. Such settlement does not discharge any of the other potentially liable persons unless its terms so provide, but it reduces the potential liability of the others by the amount of the settlement.

(3) Persons not party to settlement

(A) If the United States or a State has obtained less than complete relief from a person who has resolved its liability to the United States or the State in an administrative or judicially approved settlement, the United States or the State may bring an action against any person who has not so resolved its liability.

(B) A person who has resolved its liability to the United States or a State for some or all of a response action or for some or all of the costs of such action in an administrative or judicially approved settlement may seek contribution from any person who is not party to a settlement referred to in paragraph (2).

(C) In any action under this paragraph, the rights of any person who has resolved its liability to the United States or a State shall be subordinate to the rights of the United States or the State. Any contribution action brought under this paragraph shall be governed by Federal law.

(g) Period in which action may be brought

(1) Actions for natural resources damages

Except as provided in paragraphs (3) and (4), no action may be commenced for damages (as defined in section 9601(6)) of this title, unless that action is commenced within 3 years after the later of the following:

(A) The date of the discovery of the loss and its connection with the release in question.

(B) The date on which regulations are promulgated under section 9651(c) of this title.

With respect to any facility listed on the National Priorities list (NPL), any Federal facility identified under section 9620 of this title (relating to Federal facilities), or any vessel or facility at which a remedial action under this chapter is otherwise scheduled, an action for damages under this chapter must be commenced within 3 years after the completion of the remedial action (excluding operation and maintenance activities) in lieu of the dates referred to in subparagraph (A) or (B). In no event may an action for damages under this chapter with respect to such a vessel or facility be commenced (i) prior to 60 days after the Federal or State natural resource trustee provides to the President and the potentially responsible party a notice of intent to file suit, or (ii) before selection of the remedial action if the President is diligently proceeding with a remedial investigation and feasibility study under section 9604(b) of this title or section 9620 of this title (relating to Federal facilities). The limitation in the preceding sentence on commencing an action before giving notice or before selection of the remedial action does not apply to actions filed on or before October 17, 1986.

(2) Actions for recovery of costs

An initial action for recovery of the costs referred to in section 9607 of this title must be commenced—

(A) for a removal action, within 3 years after completion of the removal action, except that such cost recovery action must be brought within 6 years after a determination to grant a waiver under section 9604(c)(1)(C) of this title for continued response action; and

$2 million/site

(B) for a remedial action, within 6 years after initiation of physical on-site construction of the remedial action, except that, if the remedial action is initiated within 3 years after the completion of the removal action, costs incurred in the removal action may be recovered in the cost recovery action brought under this subparagraph.

In any such action described in this subsection, the court shall enter a declaratory judgment on liability for response costs or damages that will be binding on any subsequent action or actions to recover further response costs or damages. A subsequent action or actions under section 9607 of this title for further response costs at the vessel or facility may be maintained at any time during the response action, but must be commenced no later than 3 years after the date of completion of all response action. Except as otherwise provided in this paragraph, an action may be commenced under section 9607 of this title for recovery of costs at any time after such costs have been incurred.

(3) Contribution

No action for contribution for any response costs or damages may be commenced more than 3 years after—

(A) the date of judgment in any action under this chapter for recovery of such costs or damages, or

(B) the date of an administrative order under section 9622(g) of this title (relating to de minimis settlements) or 9622(h) of this title (relating to cost recovery settlements) or entry of a judicially approved settlement with respect to such costs or damages.

(4) Subrogation

No action based on rights subrogated pursuant to this section by reason of payment of a claim may be commenced under this subchapter more than 3 years after the date of payment of such claim.

(5) Actions to recover indemnification payments

Notwithstanding any other provision of this subsection, where a payment pursuant to an indemnification agreement with a response action contractor is made under section 9619 of this title, an action under section 9607 of this title for recovery of such indemnification payment from a potentially responsible party may be brought at any time before the expiration of 3 years from the date on which such payment is made.

(6) Minors and incompetents

The time limitations contained herein shall not begin to run—

(A) against a minor until the earlier of the date when such minor reaches 18 years of age or the date on which a legal representative is duly appointed for such minor, or

(B) against an incompetent person until the earlier of the date on which such incompetent's incompetency ends or the date on which a legal representative is duly appointed for such incompetent.

(h) Timing of review

No Federal court shall have jurisdiction under Federal law other than under section 1332 of Title 28 (relating to diversity of citizenship jurisdiction) or under State law which is applicable or relevant and appropriate under section 9621 of this title (relating to cleanup standards) to review any challenges to removal or remedial action selected under section 9604 of this title, or to review any order issued under section 9606(a) of this title, in any action except one of the following:

(1) An action under section 9607 of this title to recover response costs or damages or for contribution.

(2) An action to enforce an order issued under section 9606(a) of this title or to recover a penalty for violation of such order.

(3) An action for reimbursement under section 9606(b)(2) of this title.

(4) An action under section 9659 of this title (relating to citizens suits) alleging that the removal or remedial action taken under section 9604 of this title or secured under section 9606 of this title was in violation of any requirement of this chapter. Such an action may not be brought with regard to a removal where a remedial action is to be undertaken at the site.

(5) An action under section 9606 of this title in which the United States has moved to compel a remedial action.

(i) Intervention

In any action commenced under this chapter or under the Solid Waste Disposal Act [42 USC 6901 et seq.] in a court of the United States, any person may intervene as a matter of right when such person claims an interest relating to the subject of the action and is so situated that the disposition of the action may, as a practical matter, impair or impede the person's ability to protect that interest, unless the President or the State shows that the person's interest is adequately represented by existing parties.

(j) Judicial review

(1) Limitation

In any judicial action under this chapter, judicial review of any issues concerning the adequacy of any response action taken or ordered by the President shall be limited to the administrative record. Otherwise applicable principles of administrative law shall govern whether any supplemental materials may be considered by the court.

(2) Standard

In considering objections raised in any judicial action under this chapter, the court shall uphold the President's decision in selecting the response action unless the objecting party can demonstrate, on the administrative record, that the decision was arbitrary and capricious or otherwise not in accordance with law.

(3) Remedy

If the court finds that the selection of the response action was arbitrary and capricious or otherwise not in accordance with law, the court shall award (A) only the response costs or damages that are not inconsistent with the national contingency plan, and (B) such other relief as is consistent with the National Contingency Plan.

(4) Procedural errors

In reviewing alleged procedural errors, the court may disallow costs or damages only if the errors were so serious and related to matters of such central relevance to the action that the action would have been significantly changed had such errors not been made.

(k) Administrative record and participation procedures

(1) Administrative record

The President shall establish an administrative record upon which the President shall base the selection of a response action. The administrative record shall be available to the public at or near the facility at issue. The President also may place duplicates of the administrative record at any other location.

(2) Participation procedures

(A) Removal action

The President shall promulgate regulations in accordance with chapter 5 of Title 5 of the United States Code establishing procedures for the appropriate participation of interested persons in the development of the administrative record on which the President will base the selection of removal actions and on which judicial review of removal actions will be based.

(B) Remedial action

The President shall provide for the participation of interested persons, including potentially responsible parties, in the development of the administrative record on which the President will base the selection of remedial actions and on which judicial review of remedial actions will be based. The procedures developed under this subparagraph shall include, at a minimum, each of the following:

(i) Notice to potentially affected persons and the public, which shall be accompanied by a brief analysis of the plan and alternative plans that were considered.

(ii) A reasonable opportunity to comment and provide information regarding the plan.

(iii) An opportunity for a public meeting in the affected area, in accordance with section 9617(a)(2) of this title (relating to public participation).

(iv) A response to each of the significant comments, criticisms, and new data submitted in written or oral presentations.

(v) A statement of the basis and purpose of the selected action.

For purposes of this subparagraph, the administrative record shall include all items developed and received under this subparagraph and all items described in the second sentence of section 9617(d) of this title. The President shall promulgate regulations in accordance with chapter 5 of Title 5 of the United States Code to carry out the requirements of this subparagraph.

(C) Interim record

Until such regulations under subparagraphs (A) and (B) are promulgated, the administrative record shall consist of all items developed and received pursuant to current procedures for selection of the response action, including procedures for the participation of interested parties and the public. The development of an administrative record and the selection of response action under this chapter shall not include an adjudicatory hearing.

(D) Potentially responsible parties

The President shall make reasonable efforts to identify and notify potentially responsible parties as early as possible before selection of a response action. Nothing in this paragraph shall be construed to be a defense to liability.

(l) Notice of actions

Whenever any action is brought under this chapter in a court of the United States by a plaintiff other than the United States, the plaintiff shall provide a copy of the complaint to the Attorney General of the United States and to the Administrator of the Environmental Protection Agency.

(Dec. 11, 1980, Pub.L. 96–510, Title I, § 113, 94 Stat. 2795, as amended Oct. 17, 1986, Pub.L. 99–499, Title I, § 113, 100 Stat. 1647.)

Library References

Health and Environment ⚖25.6(3), 25.7(3).
C.J.S. Health and Environment §§ 92, 106.

§ 9614. Relationship to other law

(a) Additional State liability or requirements with respect to release of substances within State

Nothing in this chapter shall be construed or interpreted as preempting any State from imposing any additional liability or requirements with respect to the release of hazardous substances within such State.

(b) Recovery under other State or Federal law of compensation for removal costs or damages, or payment of claims

Any person who receives compensation for removal costs or damages or claims pursuant to this chapter shall be precluded from recovering compensation for the same removal costs or damages or claims pursuant to any other State or Federal law. Any person who receives compensation for removal costs or damages or claims pursuant to any other Federal or State law shall be precluded from receiving compensation for the same removal costs or damages or claims as provided in this chapter.

(c) Recycled oil

(1) Service station dealers, etc.

No person (including the United States or any State) may recover, under the authority of subsection (a)(3) or (a)(4) of section 9607 of this title, from a service station dealer for any response costs or damages resulting from a release or threatened release of recycled oil, or use the authority of section 9606 of this title against a service station dealer other than a person described in subsection (a)(1) or (a)(2) of section 9607 of this title, if such recycled oil—

(A) is not mixed with any other hazardous substance, and

(B) is stored, treated, transported, or otherwise managed in compliance with regulations or standards promulgated pursuant to section 301 of the Solid Waste Disposal Act [42 USC 6935] and other applicable authorities.

Nothing in this paragraph shall affect or modify in any way the obligations or liability of any person under any other provision of State or Federal law, including common law, for damages, injury, or loss resulting from a release or threatened release of any hazardous substance or for removal or remedial action or the costs of removal or remedial action.

(2) Presumption

Solely for the purposes of this subsection, a service station dealer may presume that a small quantity of used oil is not mixed with other hazardous substances if it—

(A) has been removed from the engine of a light duty motor vehicle or household appliances by the owner of such vehicle or appliances, and

(B) is presented, by such owner, to the dealer for collection, accumulation, and delivery to an oil recycling facility.

(3) Definition

For purposes of this subsection, the terms "used oil" and "recycled oil" have the same meanings as set forth in sections 1004(36) and 1004(37) of the Solid Waste Disposal Act [42 U.S.C. 6903(36) and (37)] and regulations promulgated pursuant to that Act [42 U.S.C. 6901 et seq.].

(4) Effective date

The effective date of paragraphs (1) and (2) of this subsection shall be the effective date of regulations or standards promulgated under section 3014 of the Solid Waste Disposal Act that include, among other provisions, a requirement to conduct corrective action to respond to any releases of recycled oil under subtitle C of subtitle I of such Act [42 U.S.C. 6921 et seq. or 6991 et seq.].

(d) Financial responsibility of owner or operator of vessel or facility under State or local law, rule, or regulation

Except as provided in this subchapter, no owner or operator of a vessel or facility who establishes and maintains evidence of financial responsibility in accordance with this subchapter shall be required under any State or local law, rule, or regulation to establish or maintain any other evidence of financial responsibility in connection with liability for the release of a hazardous substance from such vessel or facility. Evidence of compliance with the financial responsibility requirements of this subchapter shall be accepted by a State in lieu of any other requirement of financial responsibility imposed by such State in connection with liability for the release of a hazardous substance from such vessel or facility.

(Dec. 11, 1980, Pub.L. 96–510, Title I, § 114, 94 Stat. 2795, as amended Oct. 17, 1986, Pub.L. 99–499, Title I, § 114(a), 100 Stat. 1652.)

Library References

Health and Environment ⚬25.6(3), 25.7(3).
C.J.S. Health and Environment §§ 92, 106.

United States Supreme Court

Intention of Congress to prohibit state funds that cover Superfund-eligible expenses, see Exxon Corp. v. Hunt, 1986, 106 S.Ct. 1103, 89 L.Ed.2d 364.

§ 9615. Presidential delegation and assignment of duties or powers and promulgation of regulations

The President is authorized to delegate and assign any duties or powers imposed upon or assigned to him and to promulgate any regulations necessary to carry out the provisions of this subchapter.

(Dec. 11, 1980, Pub.L. 96–510, Title I, § 115, 94 Stat. 2796.)

Library References

Health and Environment ⚬25.6(3), 25.7(3).
C.J.S. Health and Environment §§ 92, 106.

§ 9616. Schedules

(a) Assessment and listing of facilities

It shall be a goal of this chapter that, to the maximum extent practicable—

(1) not later than January 1, 1988, the President shall complete preliminary assessments of all facilities that are contained (as of October 17, 1986) on the Comprehensive Environmental Response, Compensation, and Liability Information System (CERCLIS) including in each assessment a statement as to whether a site inspection is necessary and by whom it should be carried out; and

(2) not later than January 1, 1989, the President shall assure the completion of site inspections at all facilities for which the President has stated a site inspection is necessary pursuant to paragraph (1).

(b) Evaluation

Within 4 years after October 17, 1986, each facility listed (as of October 17, 1986) in the CERCLIS shall be evaluated if the President determines that such evaluation is warranted on the basis of a site inspection or preliminary assessment. The evaluation shall be in accordance with the criteria established in section 9605 of this title under the National Contingency Plan for determining priorities among release for inclusion on the National Priorities List. In the case of a facility listed in the CERCLIS after October 17, 1986, the facility shall be evaluated within 4 years after the date of such listing if the President determines that such evaluation is warranted on the basis of a site inspection or preliminary assessment.

(c) Explanations

If any of the goals established by subsection (a) or (b) of this section are not achieved, the President shall publish an explanation of why such action could not be completed by the specified date.

(d) Commencement of RI/FS

The President shall assure that remedial investigations and feasibility studies (RI/FS) are commenced for facilities listed on the National Priorities List, in addition to those commenced prior to October 17, 1986, in accordance with the following schedule:

(1) not fewer than 275 by the date 36 months after October 17, 1986, and

(2) if the requirement of paragraph (1) is not met, not fewer than an additional 175 by the date 4 years after October 17, 1986, an additional 200 by the date 5 years after October 17, 1986, and a total of 650 by the date 5 years after October 17, 1986.

(e) Commencement of remedial action

The President shall assure that substantial and continuous physical on-site remedial action commences at facilities on the National Priorities List, in addition to those facilities on which remedial action has commenced prior to the date of October 17, 1986, at a rate not fewer than:

(1) 175 facilities during the first 36-month period after October 17, 1986; and

(2) 200 additional facilities during the following 24 months after such 36-month period.

(Pub.L. 96–510, Title I, § 116, as added Oct. 17, 1986, Pub.L. 99–499, Title I, § 116, 100 Stat. 1653.)

§ 9617. Public participation

(a) Proposed plan

Before adoption of any plan for remedial action to be undertaken by the President, by a State, or by any other person, under section 9604, 9606, 9620, or 9622 of this title, the President or State, as appropriate, shall take both of the following actions:

(1) Publish a notice and brief analysis of the proposed plan and make such plan available to the public.

(2) Provide a reasonable opportunity for submission of written and oral comments and an opportunity for a public meeting at or near the

facility at issue regarding the proposed plan and regarding any proposed findings under section 9621(d)(4) of this title (relating to cleanup standards). The President or the State shall keep a transcript of the meeting and make such transcript available to the public.

The notice and analysis published under paragraph (1) shall include sufficient information as may be necessary to provide a reasonable explanation of the proposed plan and alternative proposals considered.

(b) Final plan

Notice of the final remedial action plan adopted shall be published and the plan shall be made available to the public before commencement of any remedial action. Such final plan shall be accompanied by a discussion of any significant changes (and the reasons for such changes) in the proposed plan and a response to each of the significant comments, criticisms, and new data submitted in written or oral presentations under subsection (a) of this section.

(c) Explanation of differences

After adoption of a final remedial action plan—

(1) if any remedial action is taken,

(2) if any enforcement action under section 9606 of this title is taken, or

(3) if any settlement or consent decree under section 9606 or section 9622 of this title is entered into,

and if action, settlement, or decree differs in any significant respects from the final plan, the President or the State shall publish an explanation of the significant differences and the reasons such changes were made.

(d) Publication

For the purposes of this section, publication shall include, at a minimum, publication in a major local newspaper of general circulation. In addition, each item developed, received, published, or made available to the public under this section shall be available for public inspection and copying at or near the facility at issue.

(e) Grants for technical assistance

(1) Authority

Subject to such amounts as are provided in appropriations Acts and in accordance with rules promulgated by the President, the President may make grants available to any group of individuals which may be affected by a release or threatened release at any facility which is listed on the National Priorities List under the National Contingency Plan. Such grants may be used to obtain technical assistance in interpreting information with regard to the nature of the hazard, remedial investigation and feasibility study, record of decision, remedial design, selection and construction of remedial action, operation and maintenance, or removal action at such facility.

(2) Amount

The amount of any grant under this subsection may not exceed $50,000 for a single grant recipient. The President may waive the $50,000 limitation in any case where such waiver is necessary to carry out the purposes of this subsection. Each grant recipient shall be required, as a condition of the grant, to contribute at least 20 percent of the total of costs of the technical assistance for which such grant is made. The President may waive the 20 percent contribution requirement if the grant recipient demonstrates financial need and such waiver is necessary to facilitate public participation in the selection of remedial action at the facility. Not more than one grant may be made under this subsection with respect to a single facility, but the grant may be renewed to facilitate public participation at all stages of remedial action.

(Pub.L. 96–510, Title I, § 117, as added Oct. 17, 1986, Pub.L. 99–499, Title I, § 117, 100 Stat. 1654.)

§ 9618. High priority for drinking water supplies

For purposes of taking action under section 9604 or 9606 of this title and listing facilities on the National Priorities List, the President shall give a high priority to facilities where the release of hazardous substances or pollutants or contaminants has resulted in the closing of drinking water wells or has contaminated a principal drinking water supply.

(Pub.L. 96–510, Title I, § 118, as added Oct. 17, 1986, Pub.L. 99–499, Title I, § 118, 100 Stat. 1655.)

Library References

Health and Environment ⚡25.7(3).
Waters and Water Courses ⚡196.
C.J.S. Health and Environment § 106.
C.J.S. Waters §§ 232 et seq.

§ 9619. Response action contractors

(a) Liability of response action contractors

(1) Response action contractors

A person who is a response action contractor with respect to any release or threatened release of a hazardous substance or pollutant or contaminant from a vessel or facility shall not be liable under this subchapter or under any other Federal law to any person for injuries, costs, damages, expenses, or other liability (including but not limited to claims for indemnification or contribution and claims by third parties for death, personal injury, illness or loss of or damage to property or economic loss) which results from such release or threatened release.

(2) Negligence, etc.

Paragraph (1) shall not apply in the case of a release that is caused by conduct of the response action contractor which is negligent, grossly negligent, or which constitutes intentional misconduct.

(3) Effect on warranties; employer liability

Nothing in this subsection shall affect the liability of any person under any warranty under Federal, State, or common law. Nothing in this subsection shall affect the liability of an employer who is a response action contractor to any employee of such employer under any provision of law, including any provision of any law relating to worker's compensation.

(4) Governmental employees

A state employee or an employee of a political subdivision who provides services relating to response action while acting within the scope of his authority as a governmental employee shall have the same exemption from liability (subject to the other provisions of this section) as is provided to the response action contractor under this section.

(b) Savings provisions

(1) Liability of other persons

The defense provided by section 9607(b)(3) of this title shall not be available to any potentially responsible party with respect to any costs or damages caused by any act or omission of a response action contractor. Except as provided in subsection (a)(4) of this section and the preceding sentence, nothing in this section shall affect the liability under this chapter or under any other Federal or State law of any person, other than a response action contractor.

(2) Burden of plaintiff

Nothing in this section shall affect the plaintiff's burden of establishing liability under this subchapter.

(c) Indemnification

(1) In general

The President may agree to hold harmless and indemnify any response action contractor meeting the requirements of this subsection against any liability (including the expenses of litigation or settlement) for negligence arising out of the contractor's performance in carrying out response action activities under this subchapter, unless such liability was caused by conduct of the contractor which was grossly negligent or which constituted intentional misconduct.

(2) Applicability

This subsection shall apply only with respect to a response action carried out under written agreement with—

(A) the President;

(B) any Federal agency;

(C) a State or political subdivision which has entered into a contract or cooperative agreement in accordance with section 9604(d)(1) of this title; or

(D) any potentially responsible party carrying out any agreement under section 9622 of this title (relating to settlements) or section 9606 of this title (relating to abatement).

(3) Source of funding

This subsection shall not be subject to section 1301 or 1341 of Title 31 or section 11 of Title 41 or to section 9662 of this title. For purposes of section 9611 of this title, amounts expended pursuant to this subsection for indemnification of any response action contractor (except with respect to federally owned or operated facilities) shall be considered governmental response costs incurred pursuant to section 9604 of this title. If sufficient funds are unavailable in the Hazardous Substance Superfund established under subchapter A of chapter 98 of Title 26 to make payments pursuant to such indemnification or if the Fund is repealed, there are authorized to be appropriated such amounts as may be necessary to make such payments.

(4) Requirements

An indemnification agreement may be provided under this subsection only if the President determines that each of the following requirements are met:

(A) The liability covered by the indemnification agreement exceeds or is not covered by insurance available, at a fair and reasonable price, to the contractor at the time the contractor enters into the contract to provide response action, and adequate insurance to cover such liability is not generally available at the time the response action contract is entered into.

(B) The response action contractor has made diligent efforts to obtain insurance coverage from non-Federal sources to cover such liability.

(C) In the case of a response action contract covering more than one facility, the response action contractor agrees to continue to make such diligent efforts each time the contractor begins work under the contract at a new facility.

(5) **Limitations**

(A) **Liability covered**

Indemnification under this subsection shall apply only to response action contractor liability which results from a release of any hazardous substance or pollutant or contaminant if such release arises out of response action activities.

(B) **Deductibles and limits**

An indemnification agreement under this subsection shall include deductibles and shall place limits on the amount of indemnification to be made available.

(C) **Contracts with potentially responsible parties**

(i) **Decision to indemnify**

In deciding whether to enter into an indemnification agreement with a response action contractor carrying out a written contract or agreement with any potentially responsible party, the President shall determine an amount which the potentially responsible party is able to indemnify the contractor. The President may enter into such an indemnification agreement only if the President determines that such amount of indemnification is inadequate to cover any reasonable potential liability of the contractor arising out of the contractor's negligence in performing the contract or agreement with such party. The President shall make the determinations in the preceding sentences (with respect to the amount and the adequacy of the amount) taking into account the total net assets and resources of potentially responsible parties with respect to the facility at the time of such determinations.

(ii) **Conditions**

The President may pay a claim under an indemnification agreement referred to in clause (i) for the amount determined under clause (i) only if the contractor has exhausted all administrative, judicial, and common law claims for indemnification against all potentially responsible parties participating in the clean-up of the facility with respect to the liability of the contractor arising out of the contractor's negligence in performing the contract or agreement with such party. Such indemnification agreement shall require such contractor to pay any deductible established under subparagraph (B) before the contractor may recover any amount from the potentially responsible party or under the indemnification agreement.

(D) **RCRA facilities**

No owner or operator of a facility regulated under the Solid Waste Disposal Act [42 U.S.C. 6901 et seq.] may be indemnified under this subsection with respect to such facility.

(E) **Persons retained or hired**

A person retained or hired by a person described in subsection (e)(2)(B) of this section shall be eligible for indemnification under this subsection only if the President specifically approves of the retaining or hiring of such person.

(6) **Cost recovery**

For purposes of section 9607 of this title, amounts expended pursuant to this subsection for indemnification of any person who is a response action contractor with respect to any release or threatened release shall be considered a cost of response incurred by the United States Government with respect to such release.

(7) **Regulations**

The President shall promulgate regulations for carrying out the provisions of this subsection. Before promulgation of the regulations, the President shall develop guidelines to carry out this section. Development of such guidelines shall include reasonable opportunity for public comment.

(8) **Study**

The Comptroller General shall conduct a study in the fiscal year ending September 30, 1989, on the application of this subsection, including whether indemnification agreements under this subsection are being used, the number of claims that have been filed under such agreements, and the need for this subsection. The Comptroller General shall report the findings of the study to Congress no later than September 30, 1989.

(d) **Exception**

The exemption provided under subsection (a) of this section and the authority of the President to offer indemnification under subsection (c) of this section shall not apply to any person covered by the provisions of paragraph (1), (2), (3), or (4) of section 9607(a) of this title with respect to the release or threatened release concerned if such person would be covered by such provisions even if such person had not carried out any actions referred to in subsection (e) of this section.

(e) Definitions

For purposes of this section—

(1) Response action contract

The term "response action contract" means any written contract or agreement entered into by a response action contractor (as defined in paragraph (2)(A) of this subsection) with—

(A) the President;

(B) any Federal agency;

(C) a State or political subdivision which has entered into a contract or cooperative agreement in accordance with section 9604(d)(1) of this title; or

(D) any potentially responsible party carrying out an agreement under section 9606 or 9622 of this title;

to provide any remedial action under this chapter at a facility listed on the National Priorities List, or any removal under this chapter, with respect to any release or threatened release of a hazardous substance or pollutant or contaminant from the facility or to provide any evaluation, planning, engineering, surveying and mapping, design, construction, equipment, or any ancillary services thereto for such facility.

(2) Response action contractor

The term "response action contractor" means—

(A) any—

(i) person who enters into a response action contract with respect to any release or threatened release of a hazardous substance or pollutant or contaminant from a facility and is carrying out such contract; and

(ii) person, public or nonprofit private entity, conducting a field demonstration pursuant to section 11021(b) of this title; and

(B) any person who is retained or hired by a person described in subparagraph (A) to provide any services relating to a response action.

(3) Insurance

The term "insurance" means liability insurance which is fair and reasonably priced, as determined by the President, and which is made available at the time the contractor enters into the response action contract to provide response action.

(f) Competition

Response action contractors and subcontractors for program management, construction management, architectural and engineering, surveying and mapping, and related services shall be selected in accordance with title IX of the Federal Property and Administrative Services Act of 1949 [40 U.S.C. 541 et seq.]. The Federal selection procedures shall apply to appropriate contracts negotiated by all Federal governmental agencies involved in carrying out this chapter. Such procedures shall be followed by response action contractors and subcontractors.

(Pub.L. 96–510, Title I, § 119, as added Oct. 17, 1986, Pub.L. 99–499, Title I, § 119, 100 Stat. 1662.)

Library References

Health and Environment ⚿18, 25.7(23).
C.J.S. Health and Environment §§ 54 et seq., 113 et seq.

§ 9620. Federal facilities

(a) Application of chapter to Federal Government

(1) In general

Each department, agency, and instrumentality of the United States (including the executive, legislative, and judicial branches of government) shall be subject to, and comply with, this chapter in the same manner and to the same extent, both procedurally and substantively, as any nongovernmental entity, including liability under section 9607 of this title. Nothing in this section shall be construed to affect the liability of any person or entity under sections 9606 and 9607 of this title.

(2) Application or requirements to Federal facilities

All guidelines, rules, regulations, and criteria which are applicable to preliminary assessments carried out under this chapter for facilities at which hazardous substances are located, applicable to evaluations of such facilities under the National Contingency Plan, applicable to inclusion on the National Priorities List, or applicable to remedial actions at such facilities shall also be applicable to facilities which are owned or operated by a department, agency, or instrumentality of the United States in the same manner and to the extent as such guidelines, rules, regulations, and criteria are applicable to other facilities. No department, agency, or instrumentality of the United States may adopt or utilize any such guidelines, rules, regulations, or criteria which are inconsistent with the guidelines, rules, regulations, and criteria established by the Administrator under this chapter.

(3) Exceptions

This subsection shall not apply to the extent otherwise provided in this section with respect to applicable time periods. This subsection shall also not apply to any requirements relating to bonding, insurance, or financial responsibility. Nothing in this chapter shall be construed to require a State to comply with section 9604(c)(3) of this title in the case of a facility which is owned or operated by any department, agency, or instrumentality of the United States.

(4) State laws

State laws concerning removal and remedial action, including State laws regarding enforcement, shall apply to removal and remedial action at facilities owned or operated by a department, agency, or instrumentality of the United States when such facilities are not included on the National Priorities List. The preceding sentence shall not apply to the extent a State law would apply any standard or requirement to such facilities which is more stringent than the standards and requirements applicable to facilities which are not owned or operated by any such department, agency, or instrumentality.

(b) Notice

Each department, agency, and instrumentality of the United States shall add to the inventory of Federal agency hazardous waste facilities required to be submitted under section 3016 of the Solid Waste Disposal Act [42 USC 6937] (in addition to the information required under section 3016(a)(3) of such Act) [42 USC 6937(a)(3)] information on contamination from each facility owned or operated by the department, agency, or instrumentality if such contamination affects contiguous or adjacent property owned by the department, agency, or instrumentality or by any other person, including a description of the monitoring data obtained.

(c) Federal Agency Hazardous Waste Compliance Docket

The Administrator shall establish a special Federal Agency Hazardous Waste Compliance Docket (hereinafter in this section referred to as the "docket") which shall contain each of the following:

(1) All information submitted under section 3016 of the Solid Waste Disposal Act [42 USC 6937] and subsection (b) of this section regarding any Federal facility and notice of each subsequent action taken under this chapter with respect to the facility.

(2) Information submitted by each department, agency, or instrumentality of the United States under section 3005 or 3010 of such Act [42 USC 6925 or 6930].

(3) Information submitted by the department, agency, or instrumentality under section 9603 of this title.

The docket shall be available for public inspection at reasonable times. Six months after establishment of the docket and every 6 months thereafter, the Administrator shall publish in the Federal Register a list of the Federal facilities which have been included in the docket during the immediately preceding 6-month period. Such publication shall also indicate where in the appropriate regional office of the Environmental Protection Agency additional information may be obtained with respect to any facility on the docket. The Administrator shall establish a program to provide information to the public with respect to facilities which are included in the docket under this subsection.

(d) Assessment and evaluation

Not later than 18 months after October 17, 1986, the Administrator shall take steps to assure that a preliminary assessment is conducted for each facility on the docket. Following such preliminary assessment, the Administrator shall, where appropriate—

(1) evaluate such facilities in accordance with the criteria established in accordance with section 9605 of this title under the National Contingency Plan for determining priorities among releases; and

(2) include such facilities on the National Priorities List maintained under such plan if the facility meets such criteria.

Such criteria shall be applied in the same manner as the criteria are applied to facilities which are owned or operated by other persons. Evaluation and listing under this subsection shall be completed not later than 30 months after October 17, 1986. Upon the receipt of a petition from the Governor of any State, the Administrator shall make such an evaluation of any facility included in the docket.

(e) Required action by department

(1) RI/FS

Not later than 6 months after the inclusion of any facility on the National Priorities List, the department, agency, or instrumentality which owns or operates such facility shall, in consultation with the Administrator and appropriate State authorities, commence a remedial investigation and feasibility study for such facility. In the case of any facility which is listed on such list before October 17, 1986, the department, agency, or instrumentality which owns or operates such facility shall, in consultation with the Administrator and appropriate State authorities, commence such an investigation and study for such facility within one year after October 17, 1986. The Administrator and appropriate State authorities shall publish a timetable and deadlines for expeditious completion of such investigation and study.

(2) Commencement of remedial action; interagency agreement

The Administrator shall review the results of each investigation and study conducted as provided in paragraph (1). Within 180 days thereafter, the head of the department, agency, or instrumentality concerned shall enter into an interagency agreement with the Administrator for the expeditious completion by such department, agency, or instrumentality of all necessary remedial action at such facility. Substantial continuous physical onsite remedial action shall be commenced at each facility not later than 15 months after completion of the investigation and study. All such interagency agreements, including review of alternative remedial action plans and selection of remedial action, shall comply with the public participation requirements of section 9617 of this title.

(3) Completion of remedial actions

Remedial actions at facilities subject to interagency agreements under this section shall be completed as expeditiously as practicable. Each agency shall include in its annual budget submissions to the Congress a review of alternative agency funding which could be used to provide for the costs of remedial action. The budget submission shall also include a statement of the hazard posed by the facility to human health, welfare, and the environment and identify the specific consequences of failure to begin and complete remedial action.

(4) Contents of agreement

Each interagency agreement under this subsection shall include, but shall not be limited to, each of the following:

(A) A review of alternative remedial actions and selection of a remedial action by the head of the relevant department, agency, or instrumentality and the Administrator or, if unable to reach agreement on selection of a remedial action, selection by the Administrator.

(B) A schedule for the completion of each such remedial action.

(C) Arrangements for long-term operation and maintenance of the facility.

(5) Annual report

Each department; agency, or instrumentality responsible for compliance with this section shall furnish an annual report to the Congress concerning its progress in implementing the requirements of this section. Such reports shall include, but shall not be limited to, each of the following items:

(A) A report on the progress in reaching interagency agreements under this section.

(B) The specific cost estimates and budgetary proposals involved in each interagency agreement.

(C) A brief summary of the public comments regarding each proposed interagency agreement.

(D) A description of the instances in which no agreement was reached.

(E) A report on progress in conducting investigations and studies under paragraph (1).

(F) A report on progress in conducting remedial actions.

(G) A report on progress in conducting remedial action at facilities which are not listed on the National Priorities List.

With respect to instances in which no agreement was reached within the required time period, the department, agency, or instrumentality filing the report under this paragraph shall include in such report an explanation of the reasons why no agreement was reached. The annual report required by this paragraph shall also contain a detailed description on a State-by-State basis of the status of each facility subject to this section, including a description of the hazard presented by each facility, plans and schedules for initiating and completing response action, enforcement status (where appropriate), and an explanation of any postponements or failure to complete response action. Such reports shall also be submitted to the affected States.

(6) Settlements with other parties

If the Administrator, in consultation with the head of the relevant department, agency, or instrumentality of the United States, determines that remedial investigations and feasibility studies or remedial action will be done properly at the Federal facility by another potentially responsible party within the deadlines provided in paragraphs (1), (2), and (3) of this subsection, the Administrator may enter into an agreement with such party under section 9622 of this title (relating to settlements). Following approval by the Attorney General of any such agreement relating to a remedial action, the agreement shall be entered in the appropriate United States district court as a consent decree under section 9606 of this title.

(f) State and local participation

The Administrator and each department, agency, or instrumentality responsible for compliance with this section shall afford to relevant State and local officials the opportunity to participate in the planning and selection of the remedial action, including but not limited to the review of all applicable data as it becomes available and the development of studies, reports, and action plans. In the case of State officials, the opportunity to participate shall be provided in accordance with section 9621 of this title.

(g) Transfer of authorities

Except for authorities which are delegated by the Administrator to an officer or employee of the Environmental Protection Agency, no authority vested in the Administrator under this section may be transferred, by executive order of the President or otherwise, to any other officer or employee of the United States or to any other person.

(h) Property transferred by Federal agencies

(1) Notice

After the last day of the 6-month period beginning on the effective date of regulations under paragraph (2) of this subsection, whenever any department, agency, or instrumentality of the United States enters into any contract for the sale or other transfer of real property which is owned by the United States and on which any hazardous substance was stored for one year or more, known to have been released, or disposed of, the head of such department, agency, or instrumentality shall include in such contract notice of the type and quantity of such hazardous substance and notice of the time at which such storage, release, or disposal took place, to the extent such information is available on the basis of a complete search of agency files.

(2) Form of notice; regulations

Notice under this subsection shall be provided in such form and manner as may be provided in regulations promulgated by the Administrator. As promptly as practicable after October 17, 1986, but not later than 18 months after October 17, 1986, and after consultation with the Administrator of the General Services Administration, the Administrator shall promulgate regulations regarding the notice required to be provided under this subsection.

(3) Contents of certain deeds

After the last day of the 6-month period beginning on the effective date of regulations under paragraph (2) of this subsection, in the case of any real property owned by the United States on which any hazardous substance was stored for one year or more, known to have been released, or disposed of, each deed entered into for the transfer of such property by the United States to any other person or entity shall contain—

(A) to the extent such information is available on the basis of a complete search of agency files—

(i) a notice of the type and quantity of such hazardous substances,

(ii) notice of the time at which such storage, release, or disposal took place, and

(iii) a description of the remedial action taken, if any, and

(B) a covenant warranting that—

(i) all remedial action necessary to protect human health and the environment with respect to any such substance remaining on the property has been taken before the date of such transfer, and

(ii) any additional remedial action found to be necessary after the date of such transfer shall be conducted by the United States.

The requirements of subparagraph (B) shall not apply in any case in which the person or entity to whom the property is transferred is a potentially responsible party with respect to such real property.

(i) Obligations under Solid Waste Disposal Act

Nothing in this section shall affect or impair the obligation of any department, agency, or instrumentality of the United States to comply with any requirement of the Solid Waste Disposal Act [42 U.S.C. 6901 et seq.] (including corrective action requirements).

(j) National security

(1) Site specific Presidential orders

The President may issue such orders regarding response actions at any specified site or facility of the Department of Energy or the Department of Defense as may be necessary to protect the national security interests of the United States at that site or facility. Such orders may include, where necessary to protect such interests, an exemption from any requirement contained in this subchapter or under title III of the Superfund Amendments and Reauthorization Act of 1986 [42 U.S.C. 11021 et seq.] with respect to the site or facility concerned. The President shall notify the Congress within 30 days of the issuance of an order under this paragraph providing for any such exemption. Such notification shall include a statement of the reasons for the granting of the exemption. An exemption under this paragraph shall be for a specified period which may not exceed one year. Additional exemptions may be granted, each upon the President's issuance of a new order under this paragraph for the site or facility concerned. Each such additional exemption shall be for a specified period which may not exceed one year. It is the intention of the Congress that whenever an exemption is issued under this paragraph the response action shall proceed as expeditiously as practicable. The Congress shall be notified periodically of the progress of any response action with respect to which an exemption has been issued under this paragraph. No exemption shall be granted under this paragraph due to lack of appropriation unless the President shall have specifically requested such appropriation as a part of the budgetary process and the Congress shall have failed to make available such requested appropriation.

(2) Classified information

Notwithstanding any other provision of law, all requirements of the Atomic Energy Act [42 U.S.C. 2011 et seq.] and all Executive orders concerning the handling of restricted data and national security information, including "need to know" requirements, shall be applicable to any grant of access to classified information under the provisions of this chapter or under title III of the Superfund Amendments and Reauthorization Act of 1986 [42 U.S.C. 11021 et seq.]

(Pub.L. 96–510, Title I, § 120, as added Oct. 17, 1986, Pub.L. 99–499, Title I, § 120(a), 100 Stat. 1666.)

Library References

Health and Environment ⚬25.5(5.5).
C.J.S. Health and Environment § 91 et seq.

§ 9621. Cleanup standards

(a) Selection of remedial action

The President shall select appropriate remedial actions determined to be necessary to be carried out under section 9604 or secured under section 9606 of this title which are in accordance with this section and, to the extent practicable, the national contingency plan, and which provide for cost-effective response. In evaluating the cost effectiveness of proposed alternative remedial actions, the President shall take into account the total short- and long-term costs of such actions, including the costs of operation and maintenance for the entire period during which such activities will be required.

(b) General rules

(1) Remedial actions in which treatment which permanently and significantly reduces the volume, toxicity or mobility of the hazardous substances, pollutants, and contaminants is a principal element, are to be preferred over remedial actions not involving such treatment. The offsite transport and disposal of hazardous substances or contaminated materials without such treatment should be the least favored alternative remedial action where practicable treatment technologies are available. The President shall conduct an assessment of permanent solutions and alternative treatment technologies or resource recovery technologies that, in whole or in part, will result in a permanent and significant decrease in the toxicity, mobility, or volume of the hazardous substance, pollutant, or contaminant. In making such assessment, the President shall specifically address the long-term effectiveness of various alternatives. In assessing alternative remedial actions, the President shall, at a minimum, take into account:

(A) the long-term uncertainties associated with land disposal;

(B) the goals, objectives, and requirements of the Solid Waste Disposal Act [42 U.S.C. 6901 et seq.];

(C) the persistence, toxicity, mobility, and propensity to bioaccumulate of such hazardous substances and their constituents;

(D) short- and long-term potential for adverse health effects from human exposure;

(E) long-term maintenance costs;

(F) the potential for future remedial action costs if the alternative remedial action in question were to fail; and

(G) the potential threat to human health and the environment associated with excavation, transportation, and redisposal, or containment.

The President shall select a remedial action that is protective of human health and the environment, that is cost effective, and that utilizes permanent solutions and alternative treatment technologies or resource recovery technologies to the maximum extent practicable. If the President selects a remedial action not appropriate for a preference under this subsection, the President shall publish an explanation as to why a remedial action involving such reductions was not selected.

(2) The President may select an alternative remedial action meeting the objectives of this subsection whether or not such action has been achieved in practice at any other facility or site that has similar characteristics. In making such a selection, the President may take into account the degree of support for such remedial action by parties interested in such site.

(c) Review

If the President selects a remedial action that results in any hazardous substances, pollutants, or contaminants remaining at the site, the President shall review such remedial action no less often than each 5 years after the initiation of such remedial action to assure that human health and the environment are being protected by the remedial action being implemented. In addition, if upon such review it is the judgment of the President that action is appropriate at such site in accordance with section 9604 or 9606 of this title, the President shall take or require such action. The President shall report to the Congress a list of facilities for which such review is required, the results of all such reviews, and any actions taken as a result of such reviews.

(d) Degree of cleanup

(1) Remedial actions selected under this section or otherwise required or agreed to by the President under this chapter shall attain a degree of cleanup of hazardous substances, pollutants, and contaminants released into the environment and of control of further release at a minimum which assures protection of human health and the environment. Such remedial actions shall be relevant and appropriate under the circumstances presented by the release or threatened release of such substance, pollutant, or contaminant.

(2)(A) With respect to any hazardous substance, pollutant or contaminant that will remain onsite, if—

(i) any standard, requirement, criteria, or limitation under any Federal environmental law, including, but not limited to, the Toxic Substances Control Act [15 U.S.C. § 2601 et seq.], the Safe Drinking Water Act [42 U.S.C. 300f et seq.], the Clear Air Act [42 U.S.C. 7401 et seq.], the Clean Water Act [33 U.S.C. 1251 et seq.], the Marine Protection, Research and Sanctuaries Act [33 U.S.C. 1401 et seq.], or the Solid Waste Disposal Act [42 U.S.C. 6901 et seq.]; or

(ii) any promulgated standard, requirement, criteria, or limitation under a State environmental or facility siting law that is more stringent than any Federal standard, requirement, criteria, or limitation, including each such State standard, requirement, criteria, or limitation contained in a program approved, authorized or delegated by the Administrator under a statute cited in subparagraph (A), and that has been identified to the President by the State in a timely manner,

is legally applicable to the hazardous substance or pollutant or contaminant concerned or is relevant and appropriate under the circumstances of the release or threatened release of such hazardous substance or pollutant or contaminant, the remedial action selected under section 9604 of this title or secured under section 9606 of this title shall require, at the completion of the remedial action, a level or standard of control for such hazardous substance or pollutant or contaminant which at least attains such legally applicable or relevant and appropriate standard, requirement, criteria, or limitation. Such remedial action shall require a level or standard of control which at least attains Maximum Contaminant Level Goals established under the Safe Drinking Water Act [42 U.S.C. 300f et seq.] and water quality criteria established under section 304 or 303 of the Clean Water Act [33 U.S.C. 1314 or 1313], where such goals or criteria are relevant and appropriate under the circumstances of the release or threatened release.

(B)(i) In determining whether or not any water quality criteria under the Clean Water Act [33 U.S.C. 1251 et seq.] is relevant and appropriate under the circumstances of the release or threatened release, the President shall consider the designated or potential use of the surface or groundwater, the environmental media affected, the purposes for which such criteria were developed, and the latest information available.

(ii) For the purposes of this section, a process for establishing alternate concentration limits to those otherwise applicable for hazardous constituents in groundwater under subparagraph (A) may not be used to establish applicable standards under this paragraph if the process assumes a point of human exposure beyond the boundary of the facility, as defined at the conclusion of the remedial investigation and feasibility study, except where—

(I) there are known and projected points of entry of such groundwater into surface water; and

(II) on the basis of measurements or projections, there is or will be no statistically significant increase of such constituents from such groundwater in such surface water at the point of entry or at any point where there is reason to believe accumulation of constituents may occur downstream; and

(III) the remedial action includes enforceable measures that will preclude human exposure to the contaminated groundwater at any point between the facility boundary and all known and projected points of entry of such groundwater into surface water,

then the assumed point of human exposure may be at such known and projected points of entry.

(C)(i) Clause (ii) of this subparagraph shall be applicable only in cases where, due to the President's selection, in compliance with subsection (b)(1) of this section, of a proposed remedial action which does not permanently and significantly reduce the volume, toxicity, or mobility of hazardous substances, pollutants, or contaminants, the proposed disposition of waste generated by or associated with the remedial action selected by the President is land disposal in a State referred to in clause (ii).

(ii) Except as provided in clauses (iii) and (iv), a State standard, requirement, criteria, or limitation (including any State siting standard or requirement) which could effectively result in the statewide prohibition of land disposal of hazardous substances, pollutants, or contaminants shall not apply.

(iii) Any State standard, requirement, criteria, or limitation referred to in clause (ii) shall apply where each of the following conditions is met:

(I) The State standard, requirement, criteria, or limitation is of general applicability and was adopted by formal means.

(II) The State standard, requirement, criteria, or limitation was adopted on the basis of hydrologic, geologic, or other relevant considerations and was not adopted for the purpose of precluding onsite remedial actions or other land disposal for reasons unrelated to protection of human health and the environment.

(III) The State arranges for, and assures payment of the incremental costs of utilizing, a facility for disposition of the hazardous substances, pollutants, or contaminants concerned.

(iv) Where the remedial action selected by the President does not conform to a State standard and the State has initiated a law suit against the Environmental Protection Agency prior to May 1, 1986, to seek to have the remedial action conform to such standard, the President shall conform the remedial action to the State standard. The State shall assure the availability of an offsite facility for such remedial action.

(3) In the case of any removal or remedial action involving the transfer of any hazardous substance or pollutant or contaminant offsite, such hazardous substance or pollutant or contaminant shall only be transferred to a facility which is operating in compliance with section 3004 and 3005 of the Solid Waste Disposal Act [42 U.S.C. 6924 and 6925] (or, where applicable, in compliance with the Toxic Substances Control Act [15 U.S.C. 2601 et seq.] or other applicable Federal law) and all applicable State requirements. Such substance or pollutant or contaminant may be transferred to a land disposal facility only if the President determines that both of the following requirements are met:

(A) The unit to which the hazardous substance or pollutant or contaminant is transferred is not releasing any hazardous waste, or constituent thereof, into the groundwater or surface water or soil.

(B) All such releases from other units at the facility are being controlled by a corrective action program approved by the Administrator under subtitle C of the Solid Waste Disposal Act [42 U.S.C. 6921 et seq.].

The President shall notify the owner or operator of such facility of determinations under this paragraph.

(4) The President may select a remedial action meeting the requirements of paragraph (1) that does not attain a level or standard of control at least equivalent to a legally applicable or relevant and appropriate standard, requirement, criteria, or limitation as required by paragraph (2) (including subparagraph (B) thereof), if the President finds that—

(A) the remedial action selected is only part of a total remedial action that will attain such level or standard of control when completed;

(B) compliance with such requirement at that facility will result in greater risk to human health and the environment than alternative options;

(C) compliance with such requirements is technically impracticable from an engineering perspective;

(D) the remedial action selected will attain a standard of performance that is equivalent to that required under the otherwise applicable standard, requirement, criteria, or limitation, through use of another method or approach;

(E) with respect to a State standard, requirement, criteria, or limitation, the State has not consistently applied (or demonstrated the intention to consistently apply) the standard, requirement, criteria, or limitation in similar circumstances at other remedial actions within the State; or

(F) in the case of a remedial action to be undertaken solely under section 9604 of this title using the Fund, selection of a remedial action that attains such level or standard of control will not provide a balance between the need for protection of public health and welfare and the environment at the facility under consideration, and the availability of amounts from the Fund to respond to other sites which present or may present a threat to public health or welfare or the environment, taking into consideration the relative immediacy of such threats.

The President shall publish such findings, together with an explanation and appropriate documentation.

(e) Permits and enforcement

(1) No Federal, State, or local permit shall be required for the portion of any removal or remedial action conducted entirely onsite, where such remedial action is selected and carried out in compliance with this section.

(2) A State may enforce any Federal or State standard, requirement, criteria, or limitation to which the remedial action is required to conform under this chapter in the United States district court for the district in which the facility is located. Any consent decree shall require the parties to attempt expeditiously to resolve disagreements concerning implementation of the remedial action informally with the appropriate Federal and State agencies. Where the parties agree, the consent decree may provide for administrative enforcement. Each consent decree shall also contain stipulated penalties for violations of the decree in an amount not to exceed $25,000 per day, which may be enforced by either the President or the State. Such stipulated penalties shall not be construed to impair or affect the authority of the court to order compliance with the specific terms of any such decree.

(f) State involvement

(1) The President shall promulgate regulations providing for substantial and meaningful involvement by each State in initiation, development, and selection of remedial actions to be undertaken in that State. The regulations, at a minimum, shall include each of the following:

(A) State involvement in decisions whether to perform a preliminary assessment and site inspection.

(B) Allocation of responsibility for hazard ranking system scoring.

(C) State concurrence in deleting sites from the National Priorities List.

(D) State participation in the long-term planning process for all remedial sites within the State.

(E) A reasonable opportunity for States to review and comment on each of the following:

(i) The remedial investigation and feasibility study and all data and technical documents leading to its issuance.

(ii) The planned remedial action identified in the remedial investigation and feasibility study.

(iii) The engineering design following selection of the final remedial action.

(iv) Other technical data and reports relating to implementation of the remedy.

(v) Any proposed finding or decision by the President to exercise the authority of subsection (d)(4) of this section.

(F) Notice to the State of negotiations with potentially responsible parties regarding the scope of any response action at a facility in the State and an opportunity to participate in such negotiations and, subject to paragraph (2), be a party to any settlement.

(G) Notice to the State and an opportunity to comment on the President's proposed plan for remedial action as well as on alternative plans under consideration. The President's proposed decision regarding the selection of remedial action shall be accompanied by a response to the comments submitted by the State, including an explanation regarding any decision under subsection (d)(4) of this section on compliance with promulgated State standards. A copy of such response shall also be provided to the State.

(H) Prompt notice and explanation of each proposed action to the State in which the facility is located.

Prior to the promulgation of such regulations, the President shall provide notice to the State of negotiations with potentially responsible parties regarding the scope of any response action at a facility in the State, and such State may participate in such negotiations and, subject to paragraph (2), any settlements.

(2)(A) This paragraph shall apply to remedial actions secured under section 9606 of this title. At least 30 days prior to the entering of any consent decree, if the President proposes to select a remedial action that does not attain a legally applicable or relevant and appropriate standard, requirement, criteria, or limitation, under the authority of subsection (d)(4) of this section, the President shall provide an opportunity for the State to concur or not concur in such selection. If the State concurs, the State may become a signatory to the consent decree.

(B) If the State does not concur in such selection, and the State desires to have the remedial action conform to such standard, requirement, criteria, or limitation, the State shall intervene in the action under section 9606 of this title before entry of the consent decree, to seek to have the remedial action so conform. Such intervention shall be a matter of right. The remedial action shall conform to such standard, requirement, criteria, or limitation if the State establishes, on the administrative record, that the finding of the President was not supported by substantial evidence. If the court determines that the remedial action shall conform to such standard, requirement, criteria, or limitation, the remedial action shall be so modified and the State may become a signatory to the decree. If the court determines that the remedial action need not conform to such standard, requirement, criteria, or limitation, and the State pays or assures the payment of the additional costs attributable to meeting such standard, requirement, criteria, or limitation, the remedial action shall be so modified and the State shall become a signatory to the decree.

(C) The President may conclude settlement negotiations with potentially responsible parties without State concurrence.

(3)(A) This paragraph shall apply to remedial actions at facilities owned or operated by a department, agency, or instrumentality of the United States. At least 30 days prior to the publication of the President's final remedial action plan, if the President proposes to select a remedial action that does not attain a legally applicable or relevant and appropriate standard, requirement, criteria, or limitation, under the authority of subsection (d)(4) of this section, the President shall provide an opportunity for the State to concur or not concur in such selection. If the State concurs, or does not act within 30 days, the remedial action may proceed.

(B) If the State does not concur in such selection as provided in subparagraph (A), and desires to have the remedial action conform to such standard, requirement, criteria, or limitation, the State may maintain an action as follows:

(i) If the President has notified the State of selection of such a remedial action, the State may bring an action within 30 days of such notification for the sole purpose of determining whether the finding of the President is supported by substantial evidence. Such action shall be brought in the United States district court for the district in which the facility is located.

(ii) If the State establishes, on the administrative record, that the President's finding is not supported by substantial evidence, the remedial action shall be modified to conform to such standard, requirement, criteria, or limitation.

(iii) If the State fails to establish that the President's finding was not supported by substantial evidence and if the State pays, within 60 days of judgment, the additional costs attributable to meeting such standard, requirement, criteria, or limitation, the remedial action shall be selected to meet such standard, requirement, criteria, or limitation. If the State fails to pay within 60 days, the remedial action selected by the President shall proceed through completion.

(C) Nothing in this section precludes, and the court shall not enjoin, the Federal agency from taking any remedial action unrelated to or not inconsistent with such standard, requirement, criteria, or limitation.

(Pub.L. 96–510, Title I, § 121, as added Oct. 17, 1986, Pub.L. 99–499, Title I, § 121(a), Oct. 17, 1986, 100 Stat. 1672.)

Library References

Health and Environment ⚷25.5(5.5), 25.7(23).
C.J.S. Health and Environment §§ 91 et seq., 113 et seq.

§ 9622. Settlements

(a) Authority to enter into agreements

The President, in his discretion, may enter into an agreement with any person (including the owner or operator of the facility from which a release or substantial threat of release emanates, or any other potentially responsible person), to perform any response action (including any action described in section 9604(b) of this title) if the President determines that such action will be done properly by such person. Whenever practicable and in the public interest, as determined by the President, the President shall act to facilitate agreements under this section that are in the public interest and consistent with the National Contingency Plan in order to expedite effective remedial actions and minimize litigation. If the President decides not to use the procedures in this section, the President shall notify in writing potentially responsible parties at the facility of such decision and the reasons why use of the procedures is inappropriate. A decision of the President to use or not to use the procedures in this section is not subject to judicial review.

(b) Agreements with potentially responsible parties

(1) Mixed funding

An agreement under this section may provide that the President will reimburse the parties to the agreement from the Fund, with interest, for certain costs of actions under the agreement that the parties have agreed to perform but which the President has agreed to finance. In any case in which the President provides such reimbursement, the President shall make all reasonable efforts to recover the amount of such reimbursement under section 9607 of this title or under other relevant authorities.

(2) Reviewability

The President's decisions regarding the availability of fund financing under this subsection shall not be subject to judicial review under subsection (d) of this section.

(3) Retention of funds

If, as part of any agreement, the President will be carrying out any action and the parties will be paying amounts to the President, the President may, notwithstanding any other provision of law, retain and use such amounts for purposes of carrying out the agreement.

(4) Future obligation of fund

In the case of a completed remedial action pursuant to an agreement described in paragraph (1), the Fund shall be subject to an obligation for subsequent remedial actions at the same facility but only to the extent that such subsequent actions are necessary by reason of the failure of the original remedial action. Such obligation shall be in a proportion equal to, but not exceeding, the proportion contributed by the Fund for the original remedial action. The Fund's obligation for such future remedial action may be met through Fund expenditures or through payment, following settlement or enforcement action, by parties who were not signatories to the original agreement.

(c) Effect of agreement

(1) Liability

Whenever the President has entered into an agreement under this section, the liability to the United States under this chapter of each party to the agreement, including any future liability to the United States, arising from the release or threatened release that is the subject of the agreement shall be limited as provided in the agreement pursuant to a covenant not to sue in accordance with subsection (f) of this section. A covenant not to sue may provide that future liability to the United States of a settling potentially responsible party under the agreement may be limited to the same proportion as that established in the original settlement agreement. Nothing in this section shall limit or otherwise affect the authority of any court to review in the consent decree process under subsection (d) of this section any covenant not to sue contained in an agreement under this section. In determining the extent to which the liability of parties to an agreement shall be limited pursuant to a covenant not to sue, the President shall be guided by the principle that a more complete covenant not to sue shall be provided for a more permanent remedy undertaken by such parties.

(2) Actions against other persons

If an agreement has been entered into under this section, the President may take any action under section 9606 of this title against any person who is not a party to the agreement, once the period for submitting a proposal under subsection (e)(2)(B) of this section has expired. Nothing in this section shall be construed to affect either of the following:

(A) The liability of any person under section 9606 or 9607 of this title with respect to any costs or damages which are not included in the agreement.

(B) The authority of the President to maintain an action under this chapter against any person who is not a party to the agreement.

(d) Enforcement

(1) Cleanup agreements

(A) Consent decree

Whenever the President enters into an agreement under this section with any potentially responsible party with respect to remedial action under section 9606 of this title, following approval of the agreement by the Attorney General, except as otherwise provided in the case of certain administrative settlements referred to in subsection (g) of this section, the agreement shall be entered in the appropriate United States district court as a consent decree. The President need not make any finding regarding an imminent and substantial endangerment to the public health or the environment in connection with any such agreement or consent decree.

(B) Effect

The entry of any consent decree under this subsection shall not be construed to be an acknowledgment by the parties that the release or threatened release concerned constitutes an imminent and substantial endangerment to the public health or welfare or the environment. Except as otherwise provided in the Federal Rules of Evidence, the participation by any party in the process under this section shall not be considered an admission of liability for any purpose, and the fact of such participation shall not be admissible in any judicial or administrative proceeding, including a subsequent proceeding under this section.

(C) Structure

The President may fashion a consent decree so that the entering of such decree and compliance with such decree or with any determination or agreement made pursuant to this section shall not be considered an admission of liability for any purpose.

(2) Public participation

(A) Filing of proposed judgment

At least 30 days before a final judgment is entered under paragraph (1), the proposed judgment shall be filed with the court.

(B) Opportunity for comment

The Attorney General shall provide an opportunity to persons who are not named as parties to the action to comment on the proposed judgment before its entry by the court as a final judgment. The Attorney General shall consider, and file with the court, any written comments, views, or allegations relating to the proposed judgment. The Attorney General may withdraw or withhold its consent to the proposed judgment if the comments, views, and allegations concerning the judgment disclose facts or considerations which indicate that the proposed judgment is inappropriate, improper, or inadequate.

(3) 9604(b) agreements

Whenever the President enters into an agreement under this section with any potentially responsible party with respect to action under section 9604(b) of this title, the President shall issue an order or enter into a decree setting forth the obligations of such party. The United States district court for the district in which the release or threatened release occurs may enforce such order or decree.

(e) Special notice procedures

(1) Notice

Whenever the President determines that a period of negotiation under this subsection would facilitate an agreement with potentially responsible parties for taking response action (including any action described in section 9604(b) of this title) and would expedite remedial action, the President shall so notify all such parties and shall provide them with information concerning each of the following:

(A) The names and addresses of potentially responsible parties (including owners and operators and other persons referred to in section 9607(a) of this title), to the extent such information is available.

(B) To the extent such information is available, the volume and nature of substances contributed by each potentially responsible party identified at the facility.

(C) A ranking by volume of the substances at the facility, to the extent such information is available.

The President shall make the information referred to in this paragraph available in advance of notice under this paragraph upon the request of a potentially responsible party in accordance with procedures provided by the President. The provisions of subsection (e) of section 9604 of this title regarding protection of confidential information apply to information provided under this paragraph. Disclosure of information generated by the President under this section to persons other than the Congress, or any duly authorized Committee thereof, is subject to other privileges or protections provided by law, including (but not limited to) those applicable to attorney work product. Nothing contained in this paragraph or in other provisions of this chapter shall be construed, interpreted, or applied to diminish the required disclosure of information under other provisions of this or other Federal or State laws.

(2) Negotiation

(A) Moratorium

Except as provided in this subsection, the President may not commence action under section 9604(a) of this title or take any action under section 9606 of this title for 120 days after providing notice and information under this subsection with respect to such action. Except as provided in this subsection, the President may not commence a remedial investigation and feasibility study under section 9604(b) of this title for 90 days after providing notice and information under this subsection with respect to such action. The President may commence any additional studies or investigations authorized under section 9604(b) of this title, including remedial design, during the negotiation period.

(B) Proposals

Persons receiving notice and information under paragraph (1) of this subsection with respect to action under section 9606 of this title shall have 60 days from the date of receipt of such notice to make a proposal to the President for undertaking or financing the action under section 9606 of this title. Persons receiving notice and information under paragraph (1) of this subsection with respect to action under section 9604(b) of this title shall have 60 days from the date of receipt of such notice to make a proposal to the President for undertaking or financing the action under section 9604(b) of this title.

(C) Additional parties

If an additional potentially responsible party is identified during the negotiation period or after an agreement has been entered into under this subsection concerning a release or threatened release, the President may bring the additional party into the negotiation or enter into a separate agreement with such party.

(3) Preliminary allocation of responsibility

(A) In general

The President shall develop guidelines for preparing nonbinding preliminary allocations of responsibility. In developing these guidelines the President may include such factors as the President considers relevant, such as: volume, toxicity, mobility, strength of evidence, ability to pay, litigative risks, public interest considerations, precedential value, and inequities and aggravating factors. When it would expedite settlements under this section and remedial action, the President may, after completion of the remedial investigation and feasibility study, provide a nonbinding preliminary allocation of responsibility which allocates percentages of the total cost of response among potentially responsible parties at the facility.

(B) Collection of information

To collect information necessary or appropriate for performing the allocation under subparagraph (A) or for otherwise implementing this section, the President may by subpoena require the attendance and testimony of witnesses and the production of reports, papers, documents, answers to questions, and other information that the President deems necessary. Witnesses shall be paid the same fees and mileage that are paid witnesses in the courts of the United States. In the event of contumacy or failure or refusal of any person to obey any such subpoena, any district court of the United States in which venue is proper shall have jurisdiction to order any such person to comply with such subpoena. Any failure to obey such an order of the court is punishable by the court as a contempt thereof.

(C) Effect

The nonbinding preliminary allocation of responsibility shall not be admissible as evidence in any proceeding, and no court shall have jurisdiction to review the nonbinding preliminary allocation of responsibility. The nonbinding preliminary allocation of responsibility shall not constitute an apportionment or other statement on the divisibility of harm or causation.

(D) Costs

The costs incurred by the President in producing the nonbinding preliminary allocation of responsibility shall be reimbursed by the potentially responsible parties whose offer is accepted by the President. Where an offer under this section is not accepted, such costs shall be considered costs of response.

(E) Decision to reject offer

Where the President, in his discretion, has provided a nonbinding preliminary allocation of responsibility and the potentially responsible parties have made a substantial offer providing for response to the President which he rejects, the reasons for the rejection shall be provided in a written explanation. The President's decision to reject such an offer shall not be subject to judicial review.

(4) Failure to propose

If the President determines that a good faith proposal for undertaking or financing action under section 9606 of this title has not been submitted within 60 days of the provision of notice pursuant to this subsection, the President may thereafter commence action under section 9604(a) of this title or take an action against any person under section 9606 of this title. If the President determines that a good faith proposal for undertaking or financing action under section 9604(b) of this title has not been submitted within 60 days after the provision of notice pursuant to this subsection, the President may thereafter commence action under section 9604(b) of this title.

(5) Significant threats

Nothing in this subsection shall limit the President's authority to undertake response or enforcement action regarding a significant threat to public health or the environment within the negotiation period established by this subsection.

(6) Inconsistent response action

When either the President, or a potentially responsible party pursuant to an administrative order or consent decree under this chapter, has initiated a remedial investigation and feasibility study for a particular facility under this chapter, no potentially responsible party may undertake any remedial action at the facility unless such remedial action has been authorized by the President.

(f) Covenant not to sue

(1) Discretionary covenants

The President may, in his discretion, provide any person with a covenant not to sue concerning any liability to the United States under this chapter, including future liability, resulting from a release or threatened release of a hazardous substance addressed by a remedial action, whether that action is onsite or offsite, if each of the following conditions is met:

(A) The covenant not to sue is in the public interest.

(B) The covenant not to sue would expedite response action consistent with the National Contingency Plan under section 9605 of this title.

(C) The person is in full compliance with a consent decree under section 9606 of this title (including a consent decree entered into in accordance with this section) for response to the release or threatened release concerned.

(D) The response action has been approved by the President.

(2) Special covenants not to sue

In the case of any person to whom the President is authorized under paragraph (1) of this subsection to provide a covenant not to sue, for the portion of remedial action—

(A) which involves the transport and secure disposition offsite of hazardous substances in a facility meeting the requirements of sections 6924(c), (d), (e), (f), (g), (m), (*o*), (p), (u), and (v) of 6925(c) of this title, where the President has rejected a proposed remedial action that is consistent with the National Contingency Plan that does not include such offsite disposition and has thereafter required offsite disposition; or

(B) which involves the treatment of hazardous substances so as to destroy, eliminate, or permanently immobilize the hazardous constituents of such substances, such that, in the judgment of the President, the substances no longer present any current or currently foreseeable future significant risk to public health, welfare or the environment, no byproduct of the treatment or destruction process presents any significant hazard to public health, welfare or the environment, and all byproducts are themselves treated, destroyed, or contained in a manner which assures that such byproducts do not present any current or currently foreseeable future significant risk to public health, welfare or the environment,

the president shall provide such person with a covenant not to sue with respect to future liability to the United States under this chapter for a future release or threatened release of hazardous substances from such facility, and a person provided such covenant not to sue shall not be liable to the United States under section 9606 or 9607 of this title with respect to such release or threatened release at a future time.

(3) Requirement that remedial action be completed

A covenant not to sue concerning future liability to the United States shall not take effect until the President certifies that remedial action has been completed in accordance with the requirements of this chapter at the facility that is the subject of such covenant.

(4) Factors

In assessing the appropriateness of a covenant not to sue under paragraph (1) and any condition to be included in a covenant not to sue under paragraph (1) or (2), the President shall consider whether the covenant or condition is in the public interest on the basis of such factors as the following:

(A) The effectiveness and reliability of the remedy, in light of the other alternative remedies considered for the facility concerned.

(B) The nature of the risks remaining at the facility.

(C) The extent to which performance standards are included in the order or decree.

(D) The extent to which the response action provides a complete remedy for the facility, including a reduction in the hazardous nature of the substances at the facility.

(E) The extent to which the technology used in the response action is demonstrated to be effective.

(F) Whether the Fund or other sources of funding would be available for any additional remedial actions that might eventually be necessary at the facility.

(G) Whether the remedial action will be carried out, in whole or in significant part, by the responsible parties themselves.

(5) Satisfactory performance

Any covenant not to sue under this subsection shall be subject to the satisfactory performance by such party of its obligations under the agreement concerned.

(6) Additional condition for future liability

(A) Except for the portion of the remedial action which is subject to a covenant not to sue under paragraph (2) or under subsection (g) of this section (relating to de minimis settlements), a covenant not to sue a person concerning future liability to the United States shall include an exception to the covenant that allows the President to sue such person concerning future liability resulting from the release or threatened release that is the subject of the covenant where such liability arises out of conditions which are unknown at the time the President certifies under paragraph (3) that remedial action has been completed at the facility concerned.

(B) In extraordinary circumstances, the President may determine, after assessment of relevant factors such as those referred to in paragraph (4) and volume, toxicity, mobility, strength of evidence, ability to pay, litigative risks, public interest considerations, precedential value, and inequities and aggravating factors, not to include the exception referred to in subparagraph (A) if other terms, conditions, or requirements of the agreement containing the covenant not to sue are sufficient to provide all reasonable assurances that public health and the environment will be protected from any future releases at or from the facility.

(C) The President is authorized to include any provisions allowing future enforcement action under section 9606 or 9607 of this title that in the discretion of the President are necessary and appropriate to assure protection of public health, welfare, and the environment.

(g) De minimis settlements

(1) Expedited final settlement

Whenever practicable and in the public interest, as determined by the President, the President shall as promptly as possible reach a final settlement with a potentially responsible party in an administrative or civil action under section 9606 or 9607 of this title if such settlement involves only a minor portion of the response costs at the facility concerned and, in the judgment of the President, the conditions in either of the following subparagraph (A) or (B) are met:

(A) Both of the following are minimal in comparison to other hazardous substances at the facility:

(i) The amount of the hazardous substances contributed by that party to the facility.

(ii) The toxic or other hazardous effects of the substances contributed by that party to the facility.

(B) The potentially responsible party—

(i) is the owner of the real property on or in which the facility is located;

(ii) did not conduct or permit the generation, transportation, storage, treatment, or disposal of any hazardous substance at the facility; and

(iii) did not contribute to the release or threat of release of a hazardous substance at the facility through any action or omission.

This subparagraph (B) does not apply if the potentially responsible party purchased the real property with actual or constructive knowledge that the property was used for the generation, transportation, storage, treatment, or disposal of any hazardous substance.

(2) Covenant not to sue

The President may provide a covenant not to sue with respect to the facility concerned to any party who has entered into a settlement under this subsection unless such a covenant would be inconsistent with the public interest as determined under subsection (f) of this section.

(3) Expedited agreement

The President shall reach any such settlement or grant any such covenant not to sue as soon as possible after the President has available the information necessary to reach such a settlement or grant such a covenant.

(4) Consent decree or administrative order

A settlement under this subsection shall be entered as a consent decree or embodied in an administrative order setting forth the terms of the settlement. In the case of any facility where the total response costs exceed $500,000 (excluding interest), if the settlement is embodied as an administrative order, the order may be issued only with the prior written approval of the Attorney General. If the Attorney General or his designee has not approved or disapproved the order within 30 days of this referral, the order shall be deemed to be approved unless the Attorney General and the Administrator have agreed to extend the time. The district court for the district in which the release or threatened release occurs may enforce any such administrative order.

(5) Effect of agreement

A party who has resolved its liability to the United States under this subsection shall not be liable for claims for contribution regarding matters addressed in the settlement. Such settlement does not discharge any of the other potentially responsible parties unless its terms so provide, but it reduces the potential liability of the others by the amount of the settlement.

(6) Settlements with other potentially responsible parties

Nothing in this subsection shall be construed to affect the authority of the President to reach settlements with other potentially responsible parties under this chapter.

(h) Cost recovery settlement authority

(1) Authority to settle

The head of any department or agency with authority to undertake a response action under this chapter pursuant to the national contingency plan may consider, compromise, and settle a claim under section 9607 of this title for costs incurred by the United States Government if the claim has not been referred to the Department of Justice for further action. In the case of any facility where the total response costs exceed $500,000 (excluding interest), any claim referred to in the preceding sentence may be compromised and settled only with the prior written approval of the Attorney General.

(2) Use of arbitration

Arbitration in accordance with regulations promulgated under this subsection may be used as a method of settling claims of the United States where the total response costs for the facility concerned do not exceed $500,000 (excluding interest). After consultation with the Attorney General, the department or agency head may establish and publish regulations for the use of arbitration or settlement under this subsection.

(3) Recovery of claims

If any person fails to pay a claim that has been settled under this subsection, the department or agency head shall request the Attorney General to bring a civil action in an appropriate district court to recover the amount of such claim, plus costs, attorneys' fees, and interest from the date of the settlement. In such an action, the terms of the settlement shall not be subject to review.

(4) Claims for contribution

A person who has resolved its liability to the United States under this subsection shall not be liable for claims for contribution regarding matters addressed in the settlement. Such settlement shall not discharge any of the other potentially liable persons unless its terms so provide, but it reduces the potential liability of the others by the amount of the settlement.

(i) Settlement procedures

(1) Publication in Federal Register

At least 30 days before any settlement (including any settlement arrived at through arbitration) may become final under subsection (h) of this section, or under subsection (g) of this section in the case of a settlement embodied in an administrative order, the head of the department or agency which has jurisdiction over the proposed settlement shall publish in the Federal Register notice of the proposed settlement. The notice shall identify the facility concerned and the parties to the proposed settlement.

(2) Comment period

For a 30-day period beginning on the date of publication of notice under paragraph (1) of a proposed settlement, the head of the department or agency which has jurisdiction over the proposed settlement shall provide an opportunity for persons who are not parties to the proposed settlement to file written comments relating to the proposed settlement.

(3) Consideration of comments

The head of the department or agency shall consider any comments filed under paragraph (2) in determining whether or not to consent to the proposed settlement and may withdraw or withhold consent to the proposed settlement if such comments disclose facts or considerations which indicate the proposed settlement is inappropriate, improper, or inadequate.

(j) Natural resources

(1) Notification of trustee

Where a release or threatened release of any hazardous substance that is the subject of negotiations under this section may have resulted in damages to natural resources under the trusteeship of the United States, the President shall notify the Federal natural resource trustee of the negotiations and shall encourage the participation of such trustee in the negotiations.

(2) Covenant not to sue

An agreement under this section may contain a covenant not to sue under section 9607(a)(4)(C) of this title for damages to natural resources under the trusteeship of the United States resulting from the release or threatened release of hazardous substances that is the subject of the agreement, but only if the Federal natural resource trustee has agreed in writing to such covenant. The Federal natural resource trustee may agree to such covenant if the potentially responsible party agrees to undertake appropriate actions necessary to protect and restore the natural resources damaged by such release or threatened release of hazardous substances.

(k) Section not applicable to vessels

The provisions of this section shall not apply to releases from a vessel.

(*l*) Civil penalties

A potentially responsible party which is a party to an administrative order or consent decree entered pursuant to an agreement under this section or section 9620 of this title (relating to Federal facilities) or which is a party to an agreement under section 9620 of this title and which fails or refuses to comply with any term or condition of the order, decree or agreement shall be subject to a civil penalty in accordance with section 9609 of this title.

(m) Applicability of general principles of law

In the case of consent decrees and other settlements under this section (including covenants not to sue), no provision of this chapter shall be construed to preclude or otherwise affect the applicability of general principles of law regarding the setting aside or modification of consent decrees or other settlements.

(Pub.L. 96–510, Title I, § 122, as added Oct. 17, 1986, Pub.L. 99–499, Title I, § 122(a), 100 Stat. 1678.)

Library References

Health and Environment ⚷25.5(5.5), 25.7(23).
C.J.S. Health and Environment §§ 91 et seq., 113 et seq.

§ 9623. Reimbursement to local governments

(a) Application

Any general purpose unit of local government for a political subdivision which is affected by a release or threatened release at any facility may apply to the President for reimbursement under this section.

(b) Reimbursement

(1) Temporary emergency measures

The President is authorized to reimburse local community authorities for expenses incurred (before or after October 17, 1986) in carrying out temporary emergency measures necessary to prevent or mitigate injury to human health or the environment associated with the release or threatened release of any hazardous substance or pollutant or contaminant. Such measures may include, where appropriate, security fencing to limit access, response to fires and explosions, and other measures which require immediate response at the local level.

(2) Local funds not supplanted

Reimbursement under this section shall not supplant local funds normally provided for response.

(c) Amount

The amount of any reimbursement to any local authority under subsection (b)(1) of this section may not exceed $25,000 for a single response. The reimbursement under this section with respect to a single facility shall be limited to the units of local government having jurisdiction over the political subdivision in which the facility is located.

(d) Procedure

Reimbursements authorized pursuant to this section shall be in accordance with rules promulgated by the Administrator within one year after October 17, 1986.

(Pub.L. 96–510, Title I, § 123, as added Oct. 17, 1986, Pub.L. 99–499, Title I, § 123(a), 100 Stat. 1688.)

§ 9624. Methane recovery

(a) In general

In the case of a facility at which equipment for the recovery or processing (including recirculation of condensate) of methane has been installed, for purposes of this chapter:

(1) The owner or operator of such equipment shall not be considered an "owner or operator", as defined in section 9601(20) of this title, with respect to such facility.

(2) The owner or operator of such equipment shall not be considered to have arranged for disposal or treatment of any hazardous substance at such facility pursuant to section 9607 of this title.

(3) The owner or operator of such equipment shall not be subject to any action under section 9606 of this title with respect to such facility.

(b) Exceptions

Subsection (a) of this section does not apply with respect to a release or threatened release of a hazardous substance from a facility described in subsection (a) of this section if either of the following circumstances exist:

(1) The release or threatened release was primarily caused by activities of the owner or operator of the equipment described in subsection (a) of this section.

(2) The owner or operator of such equipment would be covered by paragraph (1), (2), (3), or (4) of subsection (a) of section 9607 of this title with respect to such release or threatened release if he were not the owner or operator of such equipment.

In the case of any release or threatened release referred to in paragraph (1), the owner or operator of the equipment described in subsection (a) shall be liable under this chapter only for costs or damages primarily caused by the activities of such owner or operator.

(Pub.L. 96–510, Title I, § 124, as added Oct. 17, 1986, Pub.L. 99–499, Title I, § 124(a), 100 Stat. 1688.)

§ 9625. Section 6921(b)(3)(A)(i) waste

(a) Revision of hazard ranking system

This section shall apply only to facilities which are not included or proposed for inclusion on the National Priorities List and which contain substantial volumes of waste described in section 6921(b)(3)(A)(i) of this title. As expeditiously as practicable, the President shall revise the hazard ranking system in effect under the National Contingency Plan with respect to such facilities in a manner which assures appropriate consideration of each of the following site-specific characteristics of such facilities:

(1) The quantity, toxicity, and concentrations of hazardous constituents which are present in such waste and a comparison thereof with other wastes.

(2) The extent of, and potential for, release of such hazardous constituents into the environment.

(3) The degree of risk to human health and the environment posed by such constituents.

(b) Inclusion prohibited

Until the hazard ranking system is revised as required by this section, the President may not include on the National Priorities List any facility which contains substantial volumes of waste described in section 6921(b)(3)(A)(i) of this title on the basis of an evaluation made principally on the volume of such waste and not on the concentrations of the hazardous constituents of such waste. Nothing in this section shall be construed to affect the President's authority to include any such facility on the National Priorities List based on the presence of other substances at such facility or to exercise any other authority of this chapter with respect to such other substances.

(Pub.L. 96–510, Title I, § 125, as added Oct. 17, 1986, Pub.L. 99–499, Title I, § 125, 100 Stat. 1689.)

§ 9626. Indian tribes

(a) Treatment generally

The governing body of an Indian tribe shall be afforded substantially the same treatment as a State with respect to the provisions of section 9603(a) of this title (regarding notification of releases), section 9604(c)(2) of this title (regarding consultation on remedial actions), section 9604(e) of this title (regarding access to information), section 9604(i) of this title (regarding health authorities) and section 9605 of this title (regarding roles and responsibilities under the national contingency plan and submittal of priorities for remedial action, but not including the provision regarding the inclusion of at least one facility per State on the National Priorities List).

(b) Community relocation

Should the President determine that proper remedial action is the permanent relocation of tribal members away from a contaminated site because it is cost effective and necessary to protect their health and welfare, such finding must be concurred in by the affected tribal government before relocation shall occur. The President, in cooperation with the Secretary of the Interior, shall also assure that all benefits of the relocation program are provided to the affected tribe and that alternative land of equivalent value is available and satisfactory to the tribe. Any lands acquired for relocation of tribal members shall be held in trust by the United States for the benefit of the tribe.

(c) Study

The President shall conduct a survey, in consultation with the Indian tribes, to determine the extent of hazardous waste sites on Indian lands. Such survey shall be included within a report which shall make recommendations on the program needs of tribes under this chapter, with particular emphasis on how tribal participation in the administration of such programs can be maximized. Such report shall be submitted to Congress along with the President's budget request for fiscal year 1988.

(d) Limitation

Notwithstanding any other provision of this chapter, no action under this chapter by an Indian tribe shall be barred until the later of the following:

(1) The applicable period of limitations has expired.

(2) 2 years after the United States, in its capacity as trustee for the tribe, gives written notice to the governing body of the tribe that it will not present a claim or commence an action on behalf of the tribe or fails to present a claim or commence an action within the time limitations specified in this chapter.

(Pub.L. 96–510, Title I, § 126, as added Oct. 17, 1986, Pub.L. 99–499, Title II, § 207(e), 100 Stat. 1706.)

SUBCHAPTER II—HAZARDOUS SUBSTANCE RESPONSE REVENUE

PART A—HAZARDOUS SUBSTANCE RESPONSE TRUST FUND

§§ 9631 to 9633. Repealed. Pub.L. 99–499, Title V, § 517(c)(1), Oct. 17, 1986, 100 Stat. 1774

PART B—POST-CLOSURE LIABILITY TRUST FUND

§ 9641. Repealed. Pub.L. 99–499, Title V, § 514(b), Oct. 17, 1986, 100 Stat. 1767

SUBCHAPTER III—MISCELLANEOUS PROVISIONS

§ 9651. Reports and studies

(a) Implementation experiences; identification and disposal of waste

(1) The President shall submit to the Congress, within four years after December 11, 1980, a comprehensive report on experience with the implementation of this chapter including, but not limited to—

(A) the extent to which the chapter and Fund are effective in enabling Government to respond to and mitigate the effects of releases of hazardous substances;

(B) a summary of past receipts and disbursements from the Fund;

(C) a projection of any future funding needs remaining after the expiration of authority to collect taxes, and of the threat to public health, welfare, and the environment posed by the projected releases which create any such needs;

(D) the record and experience of the Fund in recovering Fund disbursements from liable parties;

(E) the record of State participation in the system of response, liability, and compensation established by this chapter;

(F) the impact of the taxes imposed by subchapter II of this chapter on the Nation's balance of trade with other countries;

(G) an assessment of the feasibility and desirability of a schedule of taxes which would take into account one or more of the following: the likelihood of a release of a hazardous substance, the degree of hazard and risk of harm to public health, welfare, and the environment resulting from any such release, incentives to proper handling, recycling, incineration, and neutralization of hazardous wastes, and disincentives to improper or illegal handling or disposal of hazardous materials, administrative and reporting burdens on Government and industry, and the extent to which the tax burden falls on the substances and parties which create the problems addressed by this chapter. In preparing the report, the President shall consult with appropriate Federal, State, and local agencies, affected industries and claimants, and such other interested parties as he may find useful. Based upon the analyses and consultation required by this subsection, the President shall also include in the report any recommendations for legislative changes he may deem necessary for the better effectuation of the purposes of this chapter, including but not limited to recommendations concerning authorization levels, taxes, State participation, liability and liability limits, and financial responsibility provisions for the Response Trust Fund and the Post-closure Liability Trust Fund;

(H) an exemption from or an increase in the substances or the amount of taxes imposed by section 4661 of Title 26 for copper, lead, and zinc oxide, and for feedstocks when used in the manufacture and production of fertilizers, based upon the expenditure experience of the Response Trust Fund;

(I) the economic impact of taxing coal-derived substances and recycled metals.

(2) The Administrator of the Environmental Protection Agency (in consultation with the Secretary of the Treasury) shall submit to the Congress (i) within four years after December 11, 1980, a report identifying additional wastes designated by rule as hazardous after the effective date of this chapter and pursuant to section 3001 of the Solid Waste Disposal Act [42 U.S.C. 6921] and recommendations on appropriate tax rates for such wastes for the Post-closure Liability Trust Fund. The report shall, in addition, recommend a tax rate, considering the quantity and potential danger to human health and the environment posed by the disposal of any wastes which the Administrator, pursuant to subsection 3001(b)(2)(B) and subsection 3001(b)(3)(A) of the Solid Waste Disposal Act of 1980 [42 U.S.C. 6921(b)(2)(B) and 6921(b)(3)(A)], has determined should be subject to regulation under subtitle C of such Act [42 U.S.C. 6921 et seq.], (ii) within three years after December 11, 1980, a report on the necessity for and the adequacy of the revenue raised, in relation to estimated future requirements, of the Post-closure Liability Trust Fund.

(b) Private insurance protection

The President shall conduct a study to determine (1) whether adequate private insurance protection is available on reasonable terms and conditions to the owners and operators of vessels and facilities subject to liability under section 9607 of this title, and (2) whether the market for such insurance is sufficiently competitive to assure purchasers of features such as a reasonable range of deductibles, coinsurance provisions, and exclusions. The President shall submit the results of his study, together with his recommendations, within two years of December 11, 1980, and shall submit an interim report on his study within one year of December 11, 1980.

(c) Regulations respecting assessment of damages to natural resources

(1) The President, acting through Federal officials designated by the National Contingency Plan published under section 9605 of this title, shall study and, not later than two years after December 11, 1980, shall promulgate regulations for the assessment of damages for injury to, destruction of, or loss of natural resources resulting from a release of oil or a hazardous substance for the purposes of this chapter and section 1321(f)(4) and (5) of Title 33. Notwithstanding the failure of the President to promulgate the regulations required under this subsection on the required date, the President shall promulgate such regulations not later than 6 months after October 17, 1986.

(2) Such regulations shall specify (A) standard procedures for simplified assessments requiring minimal field observation, including establishing measures of damages based on units of discharge or release or units of affected area, and (B) alternative protocols for conducting assessments in individual cases to determine the type and extent of short-

and long-term injury, destruction, or loss. Such regulations shall identify the best available procedures to determine such damages, including both direct and indirect injury, destruction, or loss and shall take into consideration factors including, but not limited to, replacement value, use value, and ability of the ecosystem or resource to recover.

(3) Such regulations shall be reviewed and revised as appropriate every two years.

(d) Issues, alternatives, and policy considerations involving selection of locations for waste treatment, storage, and disposal facilities

The Administrator of the Environmental Protection Agency shall, in consultation with other Federal agencies and appropriate representatives of State and local governments and nongovernmental agencies, conduct a study and report to the Congress within two years of December 11, 1980, on the issues, alternatives, and policy considerations involved in the selection of locations for hazardous waste treatment, storage, and disposal facilities. This study shall include—

(A) an assessment of current and projected treatment, storage, and disposal capacity needs and shortfalls for hazardous waste by management category on a State-by-State basis;

(B) an evaluation of the appropriateness of a regional approach to siting and designing hazardous waste management facilities and the identification of hazardous waste management regions, interstate or intrastate, or both, with similar hazardous waste management needs;

(C) solicitation and analysis of proposals for the construction and operation of hazardous waste management facilities by nongovernmental entities, except that no proposal solicited under terms of this subsection shall be analyzed if it involves cost to the United States Government or fails to comply with the requirements of subtitle C of the Solid Waste Disposal Act [42 U.S.C. 6921 et seq.] and other applicable provisions of law;

(D) recommendations on the appropriate balance between public and private sector involvement in the siting, design, and operation of new hazardous waste management facilities;

(E) documentation of the major reasons for public opposition to new hazardous waste management facilities; and

(F) an evaluation of the various options for overcoming obstacles to siting new facilities, including needed legislation for implementing the most suitable option or options.

(e) Adequacy of existing common law and statutory remedies

(1) In order to determine the adequacy of existing common law and statutory remedies in providing legal redress for harm to man and the environment caused by the release of hazardous substances into the environment, there shall be submitted to the Congress a study within twelve months of December 11, 1980.

(2) This study shall be conducted with the assistance of the American Bar Association, the American Law Institute, the Association of American Trial Lawyers, and the National Association of State Attorneys General with the President of each entity selecting three members from each organization to conduct the study. The study chairman and one reporter shall be elected from among the twelve members of the study group.

(3) As part of their review of the adequacy of existing common law and statutory remedies, the study group shall evaluate the following:

(A) the nature, adequacy, and availability of existing remedies under present law in compensating for harm to man from the release of hazardous substances;

(B) the nature of barriers to recovery (particularly with respect to burdens of going forward and of proof and relevancy) and the role such barriers play in the legal system;

(C) the scope of the evidentiary burdens placed on the plaintiff in proving harm from the release of hazardous substances, particularly in light of the scientific uncertainty over causation with respect to—

(i) carcinogens, mutagens, and teratogens, and

(ii) the human health effects of exposure to low doses of hazardous substances over long periods of time;

(D) the nature and adequacy of existing remedies under present law in providing compensation for damages to natural resources from the release of hazardous substances;

(E) the scope of liability under existing law and the consequences, particularly with respect to obtaining insurance, of any changes in such liability;

(F) barriers to recovery posed by existing statutes of limitations.

(4) The report shall be submitted to the Congress with appropriate recommendations. Such recommendations shall explicitly address—

(A) the need for revisions in existing statutory or common law, and

(B) whether such revisions should take the form of Federal statutes or the development of a model code which is recommended for adoption by the States.

(5) The Fund shall pay administrative expenses incurred for the study. No expenses shall be available to pay compensation, except expenses on a per diem basis for the one reporter, but in no case shall the total expenses of the study exceed $300,000.

(f) Modification of national contingency plan

The President, acting through the Administrator of the Environmental Protection Agency, the Secretary of Transportation, the Administrator of the Occupational Safety and Health Administration, and the Director of the National Institute for Occupational Safety and Health shall study and, not later than two years after December 11, 1980, shall modify the national contingency plan to provide for the protection of the health and safety of employees involved in response actions.

(g) Insurability study

(1) Study by Comptroller General

The Comptroller General of the United States, in consultation with the persons described in paragraph (2), shall undertake a study to determine the insurability, and effects on the standard of care, of the liability of each of the following:

(A) Persons who generate hazardous substances: liability for costs and damages under this chapter.

(B) Persons who own or operate facilities: liability for costs and damages under this chapter.

(C) Persons liable for injury to persons or property caused by the release of hazardous substances into the environment.

(2) Consultation

In conducting the study under this subsection, the Comptroller General shall consult with the following:

(A) Representatives of the Administrator.

(B) Representatives of persons described in subparagraphs (A) through (C) of the preceding paragraph.

(C) Representatives (i) of groups or organizations comprised generally of persons adversely affected by releases or threatened releases of hazardous substances and (ii) of groups organized for protecting the interests of consumers.

(D) Representatives of property and casualty insurers.

(E) Representatives of reinsurers.

(F) Persons responsible for the regulation of insurance at the State level.

(3) Items evaluated

The study under this section shall include, among other matters, an evaluation of the following:

(A) Current economic conditions in, and the future outlook for, the commercial market for insurance and reinsurance.

(B) Current trends in statutory and common law remedies.

(C) The impact of possible changes in traditional standards of liability, proof, evidence, and damages on existing statutory and common law remedies.

(D) The effect of the standard of liability and extent of the persons upon whom it is imposed under this chapter on the protection of human health and the environment and on the availability, underwriting, and pricing of insurance coverage.

(E) Current trends, if any, in the judicial interpretation and construction of applicable insurance contracts, together with the degree to which amendments in the language of such contracts and the description of the risks assumed, could affect such trends.

(F) The frequency and severity of a representative sample of claims closed during the calendar year immediately preceding Oct. 17, 1986.

(G) Impediments to the acquisition of insurance or other means of obtaining liability coverage other than those referred to in the preceding subparagraphs.

(H) The effects of the standards of liability and financial responsibility requirements imposed pursuant to this chapter on the cost of, and incentives for, developing and demonstrating alternative and innovative treatment technologies, as well as waste generation minimization.

(4) Submission

The Comptroller General shall submit a report on the results of the study to Congress with appropriate recommendations within 12 months after October 17, 1986.

(h) Report and oversight requirements

(1) Annual report by EPA

On January 1 of each year the Administrator of the Environmental Protection Agency shall submit an annual report to Congress of such Agency on the progress achieved in implementing this chapter during the preceding fiscal year. In addition such report shall specifically include each of the following:

(A) A detailed description of each feasibility study carried out at a facility under title I of this chapter.

(B) The status and estimated date of completion of each such study.

(C) Notice of each such study which will not meet a previously published schedule for completion and the new estimated date for completion.

(D) An evaluation of newly developed feasible and achievable permanent treatment technologies.

(E) Progress made in reducing the number of facilities subject to review under section 9621(c) of this title.

(F) A report on the status of all remedial and enforcement actions undertaken during the prior fiscal year, including a comparison to remedial and enforcement actions undertaken in prior fiscal years.

(G) An estimate of the amount of resources, including the number of work years or personnel, which would be necessary for each department, agency, or instrumentality which is carrying out any activities of this chapter to complete the implementation of all duties vested in the department, agency, or instrumentality under this chapter.

(2) Review by Inspector General

Consistent with the authorities of the Inspector General Act of 1978 [5 U.S.C. App. 3, 1 et seq.] the Inspector General of the Environmental Protection Agency shall review any report submitted under paragraph (1) related to EPA's activities for reasonableness and accuracy and submit to Congress, as a part of such report a report on the results of such review.

(3) Congressional oversight

After receiving the reports under paragraphs (1) and (2) of this subsection in any calendar year, the appropriate authorizing committees of Congress shall conduct oversight hearings to ensure that this chapter is being implemented according to the purposes of this chapter and congressional intent in enacting this chapter.

(Dec. 11, 1980, Pub.L. 96–510, Title III, § 301, 94 Stat. 2805, as amended Oct. 17, 1986, Pub.L. 99–499, Title I, § 107(d)(3), Title II, §§ 208, 212, 100 Stat. 1630, 1707, 1726.)

Library References

Health and Environment ⚖25.5.

C.J.S. Health and Environment § 61 et seq.

§ 9652. Effective dates; savings provisions

(a) Unless otherwise provided, all provisions of this chapter shall be effective on December 11, 1980.

(b) Any regulation issued pursuant to any provisions of section 1321 of Title 33 which is repealed or superseded by this chapter and which is in effect on the date immediately preceding the effective date of this chapter shall be deemed to be a regulation issued pursuant to the authority of this chapter and shall remain in full force and effect unless or until superseded by new regulations issued thereunder.

(c) Any regulation—

(1) respecting financial responsibility,

(2) issued pursuant to any provision of law repealed or superseded by this chapter, and

(3) in effect on the date immediately preceding the effective date of this chapter shall be deemed to be a regulation issued pursuant to the authority of this chapter and shall remain in full force and effect unless or until superseded by new regulations issued thereunder.

(d) Nothing in this chapter shall affect or modify in any way the obligations or liabilities of any person under other Federal or State law, including common law, with respect to releases of hazardous substances or other pollutants or contaminants. The provisions of this chapter shall not be considered, interpreted, or construed in any way as reflecting a determination, in part or whole, of policy regarding the inapplicability of strict liability, or strict liability doctrines, to activities relating to hazardous substances, pollutants, or contaminants or other such activities.

(Dec. 11, 1980, Pub.L. 96–510, Title III, § 302, 94 Stat. 2808.)

§ 9653. Repealed. Pub.L. 99–499, Title V, § 511(b), Oct. 17, 1986, 100 Stat. 1761

§ 9654. Applicability of Federal water pollution control funding, etc., provisions

(a) Omitted.

(b) One-half of the unobligated balance remaining before December 11, 1980, under subsection (k) of section 1321 of Title 33 and all sums appropriated under section 1364(b) of Title 33 shall be transferred to the Fund established under subchapter II of this chapter.

(c) In any case in which any provision of section 1321 of Title 33 is determined to be in conflict with any provisions of this chapter, the provisions of this chapter shall apply.

(Dec. 11, 1980, Pub.L. 96–510, Title III, § 304, 94 Stat. 2809.)

§ 9655. Legislative veto of rule or regulation

(a) Transmission to Congress upon promulgation or repromulgation of rule or regulation; disapproval procedures

Notwithstanding any other provision of law, simultaneously with promulgation or repromulgation of any rule or regulation under authority of subchapter I of this chapter, the head of the department, agency, or instrumentality promulgating such rule or regulation shall transmit a copy thereof to the Secretary of the Senate and the Clerk of the House of Representatives. Except as provided in subsection (b) of this section, the rule or regulation shall not become effective, if—

(1) within ninety calendar days of continuous session of Congress after the date of promulgation, both Houses of Congress adopt a concurrent resolution, the matter after the resolving clause of which is as follows: "That Congress disapproves the rule or regulation promulgated by the ________ dealing with the matter of ________, which rule or regulation was transmitted to Congress on ________.", the blank spaces therein being appropriately filled; or

(2) within sixty calendar days of continuous session of Congress after the date of promulgation, one House of Congress adopts such a concurrent resolution and transmits such resolution to the other House, and such resolution is not disapproved by such other House within thirty calendar days of continuous session of Congress after such transmittal.

(b) Approval; effective dates

If, at the end of sixty calendar days of continuous session of Congress after the date of promulgation of a rule or regulation, no committee of either House of Congress has reported or been discharged from further consideration of a concurrent resolution disapproving the rule or regulation and neither House has adopted such a resolution, the rule or regulation may go into effect immediately. If, within such sixty calendar days, such a committee has reported or been discharged from further consideration of such a resolution, or either House has adopted such a resolution, the rule or regulation may go into effect not sooner than ninety calendar days of continuous session of Congress after such rule is prescribed unless disapproved as provided in subsection (a) of this section.

(c) Sessions of Congress as applicable

For purposes of subsections (a) and (b) of this section—

(1) continuity of session is broken only by an adjournment of Congress sine die; and

(2) the days on which either House is not in session because of an adjournment of more than three days to a day certain are excluded in the computation of thirty, sixty, and ninety calendar days of continuous session of Congress.

(d) Congressional inaction on, or rejection of, resolution of disapproval

Congressional inaction on, or rejection of, a resolution of disapproval shall not be deemed an expression of approval of such rule or regulation.

(Dec. 11, 1980, Pub.L. 96–510, Title III, § 305, 94 Stat. 2809.)

Library References

Health and Environment ⟹25.5(1).
C.J.S. Health and Environment § 61 et seq.

§ 9656. Transportation of hazardous substances; listing as hazardous material; liability for release

(a) Each hazardous substance which is listed or designated as provided in section 9601(14) of this title shall, within 30 days after October 17, 1986, or at the time of such listing or designation, whichever is later, be listed and regulated as a hazardous material under the Hazardous Materials Transportation Act [49 U.S.C. 1801 et seq.].

(b) A common or contract carrier shall be liable under other law in lieu of section 9607 of this title for damages or remedial action resulting from the release of a hazardous substance during the course of transportation which commenced prior to the effective date of the listing and regulation of such substance as a hazardous material under the Hazardous Materials Transportation Act [49 U.S.C. 1801 et seq.], or for substances listed pursuant to subsection (a) of this section, prior to the effective date of such listing: *Provided, however,* That this subsection shall not apply where such a carrier can demonstrate that he did not have actual knowledge of the identity or nature of the substance released.

(Dec. 11, 1980, Pub.L. 96–510, Title III, § 306(a), (b), 94 Stat. 2810, as amended Oct. 17, 1986, Pub.L. 99–499, Title II, § 202, 100 Stat. 1695.)

§ 9657. Separability of provisions; contribution

If any provision of this chapter, or the application of any provision of this chapter to any person or circumstance, is held invalid, the application of such provision to other persons or circumstances and the remainder of this chapter shall not be affected thereby. If an administrative settlement under section 9622 of this title has the effect of limiting any person's right to obtain contribution from any party to such settlement, and if the effect of such limitation would constitute a taking without just compensation in violation of the fifth amendment of the Constitution of the United States, such person shall not be entitled, under other laws of the United States, to recover compensation from the United States for such taking, but in any such case, such limitation on the right to obtain contribution shall be treated as having no force and effect.

(Dec. 11, 1980, Pub.L. 96–510, Title III, § 308, 94 Stat. 2811, as amended Oct. 7, 1986, Pub.L. 99–499, Title I, § 122(b), 100 Stat. 1688.)

Library References

Statutes ⚷64.
C.J.S. Statutes § 92.

§ 9658. Actions under State law for damages from exposure to hazardous substances

(a) State statutes of limitations for hazardous substance cases

(1) Exception to state statutes

In the case of any action brought under State law for personal injury, or property damages, which are caused or contributed to by exposure to any hazardous substance, or pollutant or contaminant, released into the environment from a facility, if the applicable limitations period for such action (as specified in the State statute of limitations or under common law) provides a commencement date which is earlier than the federally required commencement date, such period shall commence at the federally required commencement date in lieu of the date specified in such State statute.

(2) State law generally applicable

Except as provided in paragraph (1), the statute of limitations established under State law shall apply in all actions brought under State law for personal injury, or property damages, which are caused or contributed to by exposure to any hazardous substance, or pollutant or contaminant, released into the environment from a facility.

(3) Actions under section 9607

Nothing in this section shall apply with respect to any cause of action brought under section 9607 of this chapter.

(b) Definitions

As used in this section—

(1) Subchapter I terms

The terms used in this section shall have the same meaning as when used in subchapter I of this chapter.

(2) Applicable limitations period

The term "applicable limitations period" means the period specified in a statute of limitations during which a civil action referred to in subsection (a)(1) of this section may be brought.

(3) Commencement date

The term "commencement date" means the date specified in a statute of limitations as the beginning of the applicable limitations period.

(4) Federally required commencement date

(A) In general

Except as provided in subparagraph (B), the term "federally required commencement date" means the date the plaintiff knew (or reasonably should have known) that the personal injury or property damages referred to in subsection (a)(1) of this section were caused or contributed to by the hazardous substance or pollutant or contaminant concerned.

(B) Special rules

In the case of a minor or incompetent plaintiff, the term "federally required commencement date" means the later of the date referred to in subparagraph (A) or the following:

(i) In the case of a minor, the date on which the minor reaches the age of majority, as determined by State law, or has a legal representative appointed.

(ii) In the case of an incompetent individual, the date on which such individual becomes competent or has had a legal representative appointed.

(Pub.L. 96–510, Title III, § 309, as added Oct. 17, 1986, Pub.L. 99–499, Title II, § 203(a), 100 Stat. 1695.)

Library References

Health and Environment ⚷25.5(5.5), 38.
C.J.S. Health and Environment §§ 49 et seq., 91 et seq.

§ 9659. Citizens suits

(a) Authority to bring civil actions

Except as provided in subsections (d) and (e) of this section and in section 9613(h) of this title (relating to timing of judicial review), any person may commence a civil action on his own behalf—

(1) against any person (including the United States and any other governmental instrumentality or agency, to the extent permitted by the eleventh amendment to the Constitution) who is alleged to be in violation of any standard, regulation, condition, requirement, or order which has become effective pursuant to this chapter (including any provision of an agreement under section 9620 of this title, relating to Federal facilities); or

(2) against the President or any other officer of the United States (including the Administrator of the Environmental Protection Agency and the Administrator of the ATSDR) where there is alleged a failure of the President or of such other officer to perform any act or duty under this chapter, including an act or duty under section 9620 of this title (relating to Federal facilities), which is not discretionary with the President or such other officer.

Paragraph (2) shall not apply to any act or duty under the provisions of section 9660 of this title (relating to research, development, and demonstration).

(b) Venue

(1) Actions under subsection (a)(1)

Any action under subsection (a)(1) of this section shall be brought in the district court for the district in which the alleged violation occurred.

(2) Actions under subsection (a)(2)

Any action brought under subsection (a)(2) of this section may be brought in the United States District Court for the District of Columbia.

(c) Relief

The district court shall have jurisdiction in actions brought under subsection (a)(1) of this section to enforce the standard, regulation, condition, requirement, or order concerned (including any provision of an agreement under section 9620 of this title), to order such action as may be necessary to correct the violation, and to impose any civil penalty provided for the violation. The district court shall have jurisdiction in actions brought under subsection (a)(2) of this section to order the President or other officer to perform the act or duty concerned.

(d) Rules applicable to subsection (a)(1) actions

(1) Notice

No action may be commenced under subsection (a)(1) of this section before 60 days after the plaintiff has given notice of the violation to each of the following:

(A) The President.

(B) The State in which the alleged violation occurs.

(C) Any alleged violator of the standard, regulation, condition, requirement, or order concerned (including any provision of an agreement under section 9620 of this title).

Notice under this paragraph shall be given in such manner as the President shall prescribe by regulation.

(2) Diligent prosecution

No action may be commenced under paragraph (1) of subsection (a) of this section if the President has commenced and is diligently prosecuting an action under this chapter, or under the Solid Waste Disposal Act [42 U.S.C. 6901 et seq.] to require compliance with the standard, regulation, condition, requirement, or order concerned (including any provision of an agreement under section 9620 of this title).

(e) Rules applicable to subsection (a)(2) actions

No action may be commenced under paragraph (2) of subsection (a) of this section before the 60th day following the date on which the plaintiff gives notice to the Administrator or other department, agency, or instrumentality that the plaintiff will commence such action. Notice under this subsection shall be given in such manner as the President shall prescribe by regulation.

(f) Costs

The court, in issuing any final order in any action brought pursuant to this section, may award costs of litigation (including reasonable attorney and expert witness fees) to the prevailing or the substantially prevailing party whenever the court determines such an award is appropriate. The court may, if a temporary restraining order or preliminary injunction is sought, require the filing of a bond or equivalent security in accordance with the Federal Rules of Civil Procedure.

(g) Intervention

In any action under this section, the United States or the State, or both, if not a party may intervene as a matter of right. For other provisions regarding intervention, see section 9613 of this title.

(h) Other rights

This chapter does not affect or otherwise impair the rights of any person under Federal, State, or common law, except with respect to the timing of review as provided in section 9613(h) of this Title or as otherwise provided in section 9658 of this title (relating to actions under State law).

(i) Definitions

The terms used in this section shall have the same meanings as when used in subchapter I of this chapter.

(Pub.L. 96–510, Title III, § 310, as added Oct. 17, 1986, Pub.L. 99–499, Title II, § 206, 100 Stat. 1703.)

Library References

Health and Environment ⟹38.
C.J.S. Health and Environment § 49 et seq.

§ 9660. Research, development, and demonstration

(a) Hazardous substance research and training

(1) Authorities of secretary

The Secretary of Health and Human Services (hereinafter in this subsection referred to as the Secretary), in consultation with the Administrator, shall establish and support a basic research and training program (through grants, cooperative agreements, and contracts) consisting of the following:

(A) Basic research (including epidemiologic and ecologic studies) which may include each of the following:

(i) Advanced techniques for the detection, assessment, and evaluation of the effects on human health of hazardous substances.

(ii) Methods to assess the risks to human health presented by hazardous substances.

(iii) Methods and technologies to detect hazardous substances in the environment and basic biological, chemical, and physical methods to reduce the amount and toxicity of hazardous substances.

(B) Training, which may include each of the following:

(i) Short courses and continuing education for State and local health and environment agency personnel and other personnel engaged in the handling of hazardous substances, in the management of facilities at which hazardous substances are located, and in the evaluation of the hazards to human health presented by such facilities.

(ii) Graduate or advanced training in environmental and occupational health and safety and in the public health and engineering aspects of hazardous waste control.

(iii) Graduate training in the geosciences, including hydrogeology, geological engineering, geophysics, geochemistry, and related fields necessary to meet professional personnel needs in the public and private sectors and to effectuate the purposes of this chapter.

(2) Director of NIEHS

The Director of the National Institute for Environmental Health Sciences shall cooperate fully with the relevant Federal agencies referred to in subparagraph (A) of paragraph (5) in carrying out the purposes of this section.

(3) Recipients of grants, etc.

A grant, cooperative agreement, or contract may be made or entered into under paragraph (1) with an accredited institution of higher education. The institution may carry out the research or training under the grant, cooperative agreement, or contract through contracts, including contracts with any of the following:

(A) Generators of hazardous wastes.

(B) Persons involved in the detection, assessment, evaluation, and treatment of hazardous substances.

(C) Owners and operators of facilities at which hazardous substances are located.

(D) State and local governments.

(4) Procedures

In making grants and entering into cooperative agreements and contracts under this subsection, the Secretary shall act through the Director of the National Institute for Environmental Health Sciences. In considering the allocation of funds for training purposes, the Director shall ensure that at least one grant, cooperative agreement, or contract shall be awarded for training described in each of clauses (i), (ii), and (iii) of paragraph (1)(B). Where applicable, the Director may choose to operate training activities in cooperation with the Director of the National Institute for Occupational Safety and Health. The procedures applicable to grants and contracts under title IV of the Public Health Service Act [42 U.S.C. 281 et seq.] shall be followed under this subsection.

(5) Advisory council

To assist in the implementation of this subsection and to aid in the coordination of research and demonstration and training activities funded from the Fund under this section, the Secretary shall appoint an advisory council (hereinafter in this subsection referred to as the "Advisory Council") which shall consist of representatives of the following:

(A) The relevant Federal agencies.

(B) The chemical industry.

(C) The toxic waste management industry.

(D) Institutions of higher education.

(E) State and local health and environmental agencies.

(F) The general public.

(6) Planning

Within nine months after October 17, 1986, the Secretary, acting through the Director of the National Institute for Environmental Health Sciences, shall issue a plan for the implementation of paragraph (1). The plan shall include priorities for actions under paragraph (1) and include research and training relevant to scientific and technological issues resulting from site specific hazardous substance response experience. The Secretary shall, to the maximum extent practicable, take appropriate steps to coordinate program activities under this plan with the activities of other Federal agencies in order to avoid duplication of effort. The plan shall be consistent with the need for the development of new technologies for meeting the goals of response actions in accordance with the provisions of this chapter. The Advisory Council shall be provided an opportunity to review and comment on the plan and priorities and assist appropriate coordination among the relevant Federal agencies referred to in subparagraph (A) of paragraph (5).

(b) Alternative or innovative treatment technology research and demonstration program

(1) Establishment

The Administrator is authorized and directed to carry out a program of research, evaluation, testing, development, and demonstration of alternative or innovative treatment technologies (hereinafter in this subsection referred to as the "program") which may be utilized in response actions to achieve more permanent protection of human health and welfare and the environment.

(2) Administration

The program shall be administered by the Administrator, acting through an office of technology demonstration and shall be coordinated with programs carried out by the Office of Solid Waste and Emergency Response and the Office of Research and Development.

(3) Contracts and grants

In carrying out the program, the Administrator is authorized to enter into contracts and cooperative agreements with, and make grants to, persons, public entities, and nonprofit private entities which are exempt from tax under section 501(c)(3) of Title 26. The Administrator shall, to the maximum extent possible, enter into appropriate cost sharing arrangements under this subsection.

(4) Use of sites

In carrying out the program, the Administrator may arrange for the use of sites at which a response may be undertaken under section 9604 of this title for the purposes of carrying out research, testing, evaluation, development, and demonstration projects. Each such project shall be carried out under such terms and conditions as the Administrator shall require to assure the protection of human health and the environment and to assure adequate control by the Administrator of the research, testing, evaluation, development, and demonstration activities at the site.

(5) Demonstration assistance

(A) Program components

The demonstration assistance program shall include the following:

(i) The publication of a solicitation and the evaluation of applications for demonstration projects utilizing alternative or innovative technologies.

(ii) The selection of sites which are suitable for the testing and evaluation of innovative technologies.

(iii) The development of detailed plans for innovative technology demonstration projects.

(iv) The supervision of such demonstration projects and the providing of quality assurance for data obtained.

(v) The evaluation of the results of alternative innovative technology demonstration projects and the determination of whether or not the technologies used are effective and feasible.

(B) Solicitation

Within 90 days after October 17, 1986, and no less often than once every 12 months thereafter, the Administrator shall publish a solicitation for innovative or alternative technologies at a stage of development suitable for full-scale demonstrations at sites at which a response action may be undertaken under section 9604 of this title. The purpose of any such project shall be to demonstrate the use of an alternative or innovative treatment technology with respect to hazardous substances or pollutants or contaminants which are located at the site or which are to be removed from the site. The solicitation notice shall prescribe information to be included in the application, including technical and economic data derived from the applicant's own research and development efforts, and other information sufficient to permit the Administrator to assess the technology's potential and the types of remedial action to which it may be applicable.

(C) Applications

Any person and any public or private nonprofit entity may submit an application to the Administrator in response to the solicitation. The application shall contain a proposed demonstration plan setting forth how and when the project is to be carried out and such other information as the Administrator may require.

(D) Project selection

In selecting technologies to be demonstrated, the Administrator shall fully review the applications submitted and shall consider at least the criteria specified in paragraph (7). The Administrator shall select or refuse to select a project for demonstration under this subsection within 90 days of receiving the completed application for such project. In the case of a refusal to select the project, the Administrator shall notify the applicant within such 90-day period of the reasons for his refusal.

(E) Site selection

The Administrator shall propose 10 sites at which a response may be undertaken under section 9604 of this title to be the location of any demonstration project under this subsection within 60 days after the close of the public comment period. After an opportunity for notice and public comment, the Administrator shall select such sites and projects. In selecting any such site, the Administrator shall take into account the applicant's technical data and preferences either for onsite operation or for utilizing the site as a source of hazardous substances or pollutants or contaminants to be treated offsite.

(F) Demonstration plan

Within 60 days after the selection of the site under this paragraph to be the location of a demonstration project, the Administrator shall establish a final demonstration plan for the project, based upon the demonstration plan contained in the application for the project. Such plan shall clearly set forth how and when the demonstration project will be carried out.

(G) Supervision and testing

Each demonstration project under this subsection shall be performed by the applicant, or by a person satisfactory to the applicant, under the supervision of the Administrator. The Administrator shall enter into a written agreement with each applicant granting the Administrator the responsibility and authority for testing procedures, quality control, monitoring, and other measurements necessary to determine and evaluate the results of the demonstration project. The Administrator may pay the costs of testing, monitoring, quality control, and other measurements required by the Administrator to determine and evaluate the results of the demonstration project, and the limitations established by subparagraph (J) shall not apply to such costs.

(H) Project completion

Each demonstration project under this subsection shall be completed within such time as is established in the demonstration plan.

(I) Extensions

The Administrator may extend any deadline established under this paragraph by mutual agreement with the applicant concerned.

(J) Funding restrictions

The Administrator shall not provide any Federal assistance for any part of a full-scale field demonstration project under this subsection to any applicant unless such applicant can demonstrate that it cannot obtain appropriate private financing on reasonable terms and conditions sufficient to carry out such demonstration project without such Federal assistance. The total Federal funds for any full-scale field demonstration project under this subsection shall not exceed 50 percent of the total cost of such project estimated at the time of the award of such assistance. The Administrator shall not expend more than $10,000,000 for assistance under the program in any fiscal year and shall not expend more than $3,000,000 for any single project.

(6) Field demonstrations

In carrying out the program, the Administrator shall initiate or cause to be initiated at least 10 field demonstration projects of alternative or innovative treatment technologies at sites at which a response may be undertaken under section 9604 of this title, in fiscal year 1987 and each of the succeeding three fiscal years. If the Administrator determines that 10 field demonstration projects under this subsection cannot be initiated consistent with the criteria set forth in paragraph (7) in any of such fiscal years, the Administrator shall transmit to the appropriate committees of Congress a report explaining the reasons for his inability to conduct such demonstration projects.

(7) Criteria

In selecting technologies to be demonstrated under this subsection, the Administrator shall, consistent with the protection of human health and the environment, consider each of the following criteria:

(A) The potential for contributing to solutions to those waste problems which pose the greatest threat to human health, which cannot be adequately controlled under present technologies, or which otherwise pose significant management difficulties.

(B) The availability of technologies which have been sufficiently developed for field demonstration and which are likely to be cost-effective and reliable.

(C) The availability and suitability of sites for demonstrating such technologies, taking into account the physical, biological, chemical, and geological characteristics of the sites, the extent and type of contamination found at the site, and the capability to conduct demonstration projects in such a manner as to assure the protection of human health and the environment.

(D) The likelihood that the data to be generated from the demonstration project at the site will be applicable to other sites.

(8) Technology transfer

In carrying out the program, the Administrator shall conduct a technology transfer program including the development, collection, evaluation, coordination, and dissemination of information relating to the utilization of alternative or innovative treatment technologies for response actions. The Administrator shall establish and maintain a central reference library for such information. The information maintained by the Administrator shall be made available to the public, subject to the provisions of section 552 of Title 5 and section 1905 of Title 18, and to other Government agencies in a manner that will facilitate its dissemination; except, that upon a showing satisfactory to the Administrator by any person that any information or portion thereof obtained under this subsection by the Administrator directly or indirectly from such person, would, if made public, divulge—

(A) trade secrets; or

(B) other proprietary information of such person,

the Administrator shall not disclose such information and disclosure thereof shall be punishable under section 1905 of Title 18. This subsection is not authority to withhold information from Congress or any committee of Congress upon the request of the chairman of such committee.

(9) Training

The Administrator is authorized and directed to carry out, through the Office of Technology Demonstration, a program of training and an evaluation of training needs for each of the following:

(A) Training in the procedures for the handling and removal of hazardous substances for employees who handle hazardous substances.

(B) Training in the management of facilities at which hazardous substances are located and in the evaluation of the hazards to human health presented by such facilities for State and local health and environment agency personnel.

(10) Definition

For purposes of this subsection, the term "alternative or innovative treatment technologies" means those technologies, including proprietary or patented methods, which permanently alter the composition of hazardous waste through chemical, biological, or physical means so as to significantly reduce the toxicity, mobility, or volume (or any combination thereof) of the hazardous waste or contaminated materials being treated. The term also includes technologies that characterize or assess the extent of contamination, the chemical and physical character of the contaminants, and the stresses imposed by the contaminants on complex ecosystems at sites.

(c) Hazardous substance research

The Administrator may conduct and support, through grants, cooperative agreements, and contracts, research with respect to the detection, assessment, and evaluation of the effects on and risks to human health of hazardous substances and detection of hazardous substances in the environment. The Administrator shall coordinate such research with the Secretary of Health and Human Services, acting through the advisory council established under this section, in order to avoid duplication of effort.

(d) University hazardous substance research centers

(1) Grant program

The Administrator shall make grants to institutions of higher learning to establish and operate not fewer than 5 hazardous substance research centers in the United States. In carrying out the program under this subsection, the Administrator should seek to have established and operated 10 hazardous substance research centers in the United States.

(2) Responsibilities of centers

The responsibilities of each hazardous substance research center established under this subsection shall include, but not be limited to, the conduct of research and training relating to the manufacture, use, transportation, disposal, and management of hazardous substances and publication and dissemination of the results of such research.

(3) Applications

Any institution of higher learning interested in receiving a grant under this subsection shall submit to the Administrator an application in such form and containing such information as the Administrator may require by regulation.

(4) Selection criteria

The Administrator shall select recipients of grants under this subsection on the basis of the following criteria:

(A) The hazardous substance research center shall be located in a State which is representative of the needs of the region in which such State is located for improved hazardous waste management.

(B) The grant recipient shall be located in an area which has experienced problems with hazardous substance management.

(C) There is available to the grant recipient for carrying out this subsection demonstrated research resources.

(D) The capability of the grant recipient to provide leadership in making national and regional contributions to the solution of both long-range and immediate hazardous substance management problems.

(E) The grant recipient shall make a commitment to support ongoing hazardous substance research programs with budgeted institutional funds of at least $100,000 per year.

(F) The grant recipient shall have a interdisciplinary staff with demonstrated expertise in hazardous substance management and research.

(G) The grant recipient shall have a demonstrated ability to disseminate results of hazardous substance research and educational programs through an interdisciplinary continuing education program.

(H) The projects which the grant recipient proposes to carry out under the grant are necessary and appropriate.

(5) Maintenance of effort

No grant may be made under this subsection in any fiscal year unless the recipient of such grant enters into such agreements with the Administrator as the Administrator may require to ensure that such recipient will maintain its aggregate expenditures from all other sources for establishing and operating a regional hazardous substance research center and related research activities at or above the average level of such expenditures in its 2 fiscal years preceding October 17, 1986.

(6) Federal share

The Federal share of a grant under this subsection shall not exceed 80 percent of the costs of establishing and operating the regional hazardous substance research center and related research activities carried out by the grant recipient.

(7) Limitation on use of funds

No funds made available to carry out this subsection shall be used for acquisition of real property (including buildings) or construction of any building.

(8) Administration through the Office of the Administrator

Administrative responsibility for carrying out this subsection shall be in the Office of the Administrator.

(9) Equitable distribution of funds

The Administrator shall allocate funds made available to carry out this subsection equitably among the regions of the United States.

(10) Technology transfer activities

Not less than five percent of the funds made available to carry out this subsection for any fiscal year shall be available to carry out technology transfer activities.

(e) Report to Congress

At the time of the submission of the annual budget request to Congress, the Administrator shall submit to the appropriate committees of the House of Representatives and the Senate and to the advisory council established under subsection (a) of this section, a report on the progress of the research, development, and demonstration program authorized by subsection (b) of this section, including an evaluation of each demonstration project completed in the preceding fiscal year, findings with respect to the efficacy of such demonstrated technologies in achieving permanent and significant reductions in risk from hazardous wastes, the costs of such demonstration projects, and the potential applicability of, and projected costs for, such technologies at other hazardous substance sites.

(f) Saving provision

Nothing in this section shall be construed to affect the provisions of the Solid Waste Disposal Act [42 U.S.C. 6901 et seq.].

(g) Small business participation

The Administrator shall ensure, to the maximum extent practicable, an adequate opportunity for small business participation in the program established by subsection (b) of this section.

(Pub.L. 96–510, Title III, § 311, as added Oct. 17, 1986, Pub.L. 99–499, Title II, § 209(b), 100 Stat. 1708.)

Library References

Health and Environment ⇐25.5(5.5).
C.J.S. Health and Environment § 91 et seq.

§ 9660a. Grant program

(1) Grant purposes

Grants for the training and education of workers who are or may be engaged in activities related to hazardous waste removal or containment or emergency response may be made under this subsection.

(2) Administration

Grants under this subsection shall be administered by the National Institute of Environmental Health Sciences.

(3) Grant recipients

Grants shall be awarded to nonprofit organizations which demonstrate experience in implementing and operating worker health and safety training and education programs and demonstrate the ability to reach and involve in training programs target populations of workers who are or will be engaged in hazardous waste removal or containment or emergency response operations.

(Oct. 17, 1986, Pub.L. 99–499, Title I, § 126(g), 100 Stat. 1692.)

§ 9661. Love Canal property acquisition

(a) Acquisition of property in emergency declaration area

The Administrator of the Environmental Protection Agency (hereinafter referred to as the "Administrator") may make grants not to exceed $2,500,000 to the State of New York (or to any duly constituted public agency or authority thereof) for purposes of acquisition of private property in the Love Canal Emergency Declaration Area. Such acquisition shall include (but shall not be limited to) all private property within the Emergency Declaration Area, including non-owner occupied residential properties, commercial, industrial, public, religious, non-profit, and vacant properties.

(b) Procedures for acquisition

No property shall be acquired pursuant to this section unless the property owner voluntarily agrees to such acquisition. Compensation for any property acquired pursuant to this section shall be based upon the fair market value of the property as it existed prior to the emergency declaration. Valuation procedures for property acquired with funds provided under this section shall be in accordance with those set forth in the agreement entered into between the New York State Disaster Preparedness Commission and the Love Canal Revitalization Agency on October 9, 1980.

(c) State ownership

The Administrator shall not provide any funds under this section for the acquisition of any properties pursuant to this section unless a public agency or authority of the State of New York first enters into a cooperative agreement with the Administrator providing assurances deemed adequate by the Administrator that the State or an agency created under the laws of the State shall take title to the properties to be so acquired.

(d) Maintenance of property

The Administrator shall enter into a cooperative agreement with an appropriate public agency or authority of the State of New York under which the Administrator shall maintain or arrange for the maintenance of all properties within the Emergency Declaration Area that have been acquired by any public agency or authority of the State. Ninety (90) percent of the costs of such maintenance shall be paid by the Administrator. The remaining portion of such costs shall be paid by the State (unless a credit is available under section 9604(c) of this title). The Administrator is authorized, in his discretion, to provide technical assistance to any public agency or authority of the State of New York in order to implement the recommendations of the habitability and land-use study in order to put the land within the Emergency Declaration Area to its best use.

(e) Habitability and land use study

The Administrator shall conduct or cause to be conducted a habitability and land-use study. The study shall—

(1) assess the risks associated with inhabiting of the Love Canal Emergency Declaration Area;

(2) compare the level of hazardous waste contamination in that Area to that present in other comparable communities; and

(3) assess the potential uses of the land within the Emergency Declaration Area, including but

not limited to residential, industrial, commercial and recreational, and the risks associated with such potential uses.

The Administrator shall publish the findings of such study and shall work with the State of New York to develop recommendations based upon the results of such study.

(f) Funding

For purposes of section 9611 [and 9631(c) of this chapter], the expenditures authorized by this section shall be treated as a cost specified in section 9611(c) of this title.

(g) Response

The provisions of this section shall not affect the implementation of other response actions within the Emergency Declaration Area that the Administrator has determined (before October 17, 1986) to be necessary to protect the public health or welfare or the environment.

(h) Definitions

For purposes of this section:

(1) Emergency declaration area

The terms "Emergency Declaration Area" and "Love Canal Emergency Declaration Area" mean the Emergency Declaration Area as defined in section 950, paragraph (2) of the General Municipal Law of the State of New York, Chapter 259, Laws of 1980 [McKinney N.Y. General Municipal Law, § 950, par. 2] as in effect on October 17, 1986.

(2) Private property

As used in subsection (a) of this section the term "private property" means all property which is not owned by a department, agency, or instrumentality of—

(A) the United States, or

(B) the State of New York (or any public agency or authority thereof).

(Pub.L. 96–510, Title III, § 312, as added Oct. 17, 1986, Pub.L. 99–499, Title II, § 213(b), 100 Stat. 1727.)

Library References

United States ⚷59, 60.
C.J.S. United States §§ 81 et seq., 83 et seq.

§ 9662. Limitation on contract and borrowing authority

Any authority provided by this chapter, including any amendment made by this chapter, to enter into contracts to obligate the United States or to incur indebtedness for the repayment of which the United States is liable shall be effective only to such extent or in such amounts as are provided in appropriation Acts.

(Oct. 17, 1986, Pub.L. 99–499, § 3, 100 Stat. 1614.)

Library References

Health and Environment ⚷25.7(23).
C.J.S. Health and Environment § 113 et seq.

SUBCHAPTER IV—POLLUTION INSURANCE

§ 9671. Definitions

As used in this title—

(1) Insurance

The term "insurance" means primary insurance, excess insurance, reinsurance, surplus lines insurance, and any other arrangement for shifting and distributing risk which is determined to be insurance under applicable State or Federal law.

(2) Pollution liability

The term "pollution liability" means liability for injuries arising from the release of hazardous substances or pollutants or contaminants.

(3) Risk retention group

The term "risk retention group" means any corporation or other limited liability association taxable as a corporation, or as an insurance company, formed under the laws of any State—

(A) whose primary activity consists of assuming and spreading all, or any portion, of the pollution liability of its group members;

(B) which is organized for the primary purpose or conducting the activity described under subparagraph (A);

(C) which is chartered or licensed as an insurance company and authorized to engage in the business of insurance under the laws of any State; and

(D) which does not exclude any person from membership in the group solely to provide for members of such a group a competitive advantage over such a person.

(4) Purchasing group

The term "purchasing group" means any group of persons which has as one of its purposes the purchase of pollution liability insurance on a group basis.

(5) State

The term "State" means any State of the United States, the District of Columbia, the Commonwealth of Puerto Rico, Guam, American Samoa, the Virgin Islands, the Commonwealth of the Northern Marianas, and any other territory or possession over which the United States has jurisdiction.

(Pub.L. 96–510, Title IV, § 401, as added Oct. 17, 1986, Pub.L. 99–499, Title II, § 210(a), formerly § 210, 100 Stat. 1716, as renumbered Oct. 27, 1986, Pub.L. 99–563, § 11(c)(1), 100 Stat. 3177.)

Library References

Health and Environment ⚬25.6(1), 25.7(1).
Insurance ⚬124.1.
C.J.S. Health and Environment §§ 91 et seq., 106 et seq.
C.J.S. Insurance § 224.

§ 9672. State laws; scope of subchapter

(a) State laws

Nothing in this subchapter shall be construed to affect either the tort law or the law governing the interpretation of insurance contracts of any State. The definitions of pollution liability and pollution liability insurance under any State law shall not be applied for the purposes of this subchapter, including recognition or qualification of risk retention groups or purchasing groups.

(b) Scope of title

The authority to offer or to provide insurance under this subchapter shall be limited to coverage of pollution liability risks and this subchapter does not authorize a risk retention group or purchasing group to provide coverage of any other line of insurance.

(Pub.L. 96–510, Title IV, § 402, as added Oct. 17, 1986, Pub.L. 99–499, Title II, § 210(a), formerly § 210, 100 Stat. 1716, as renumbered Oct. 27, 1986, Pub.L. 99–563, § 11(c)(1), 100 Stat. 3177.)

Library References

Health and Environment ⚬25.6(1), 25.7(1).
Insurance ⚬124.1.
C.J.S. Health and Environment §§ 91 et seq., 106 et seq.
C.J.S. Insurance § 224.

§ 9673. Risk retention groups

(a) Exemption

Except as provided in this section, a risk retention group shall be exempt from the following:

(1) A State law, rule, or order which makes unlawful, or regulates, directly or indirectly, the operation of a risk retention group.

(2) A State law, rule, or order which requires or permits a risk retention group to participate in any insurance insolvency guaranty association to which an insurer licensed in the State is required to belong.

(3) A State law, rule, or order which requires any insurance policy issued to a risk retention group or any member of the group to be countersigned by an insurance agent or broker residing in the State.

(4) A State law, rule, or order which otherwise discriminates against a risk retention group or any of its members.

(b) Exceptions

(1) State laws generally applicable

Nothing in subsection (a) of this section shall be construed to affect the applicability of State laws generally applicable to persons or corporations. The State in which a risk retention group is chartered may regulate the formation and operation of the group.

(2) State regulations not subject to exemption

Subsection (a) of this section shall not apply to any State law which requires a risk retention group to do any of the following:

(A) Comply with the unfair claim settlement practices law of the State.

(B) Pay, on a nondiscriminatory basis, applicable premium and other taxes which are levied on admitted insurers and surplus line insurers, brokers, or policyholders under the laws of the State.

(C) Participate, on a nondiscriminatory basis, in any mechanism established or authorized under the law of the State for the equitable apportionment among insurers of pollution liability insurance losses and expenses incurred on policies written through such mechanism.

(D) Submit to the appropriate authority reports and other information required of licensed insurers under the laws of a State relating solely to pollution liability insurance losses and expenses.

(E) Register with and designate the State insurance commissioner as its agent solely for the purpose of receiving service of legal documents or process.

(F) Furnish, upon request, such commissioner a copy of any financial report submitted by the risk retention group to the commissioner of the chartering or licensing jurisdiction.

(G) Submit to an examination by the State insurance commissioner in any State in which the group is doing business to determine the group's financial condition, if—

(i) the commissioner has reason to believe the risk retention group is in a financially impaired condition; and

(ii) the commissioner of the jurisdiction in which the group is chartered has not begun or has refused to initiate an examination of the group.

(H) Comply with a lawful order issued in a delinquency proceeding commenced by the State insurance commissioner if the commissioner of the jurisdiction in which the group is chartered has failed to initiate such a proceeding after notice of a finding of financial impairment under subparagraph (G).

(c) Application of exemptions

The exemptions specified in subsection (a) of this section apply to—

(1) pollution liability insurance coverage provided by a risk retention group for—

(A) such group; or

(B) any person who is a member of such group;

(2) the sale of pollution liability insurance coverage for a risk retention group; and

(3) the provision of insurance related services or management services for a risk retention group or any member of such a group.

(d) Agents or brokers

A State may require that a person acting, or offering to act, as an agent or broker for a risk retention group obtain a license from that State, except that a State may not impose any qualification or requirement which discriminates against a nonresident agent or broker.

(Pub.L. 96–510, Title IV, § 403, as added Oct. 17, 1986, Pub.L. 99–499, Title II, § 210(a), formerly § 210, 100 Stat. 1717, as renumbered Oct. 27, 1986, Pub.L. 99–563, § 11(c)(1), 100 Stat. 3177.)

Library References

Health and Environment ⚷25.6(1), 25.7(1).
Insurance ⚷124.1.
C.J.S. Health and Environment §§ 91 et seq., 106 et seq.
C.J.S. Insurance § 224.

§ 9674. Purchasing groups

(a) Exemption

Except as provided in this section, a purchasing group is exempt from the following:

(1) A State law, rule, or order which prohibits the establishment of a purchasing group.

(2) A State law, rule, or order which makes it unlawful for an insurer to provide or offer to provide insurance on a basis providing, to a purchasing group or its member, advantages, based on their loss and expense experience, not afforded to other persons with respect to rates, policy forms, coverages, or other matters.

(3) A State law, rule, or order which prohibits a purchasing group or its members from purchasing insurance on the group basis described in paragraph (2) of this subsection.

(4) A State law, rule, or order which prohibits a purchasing group from obtaining insurance on a group basis because the group has not been in existence for a minimum period of time or because any member has not belonged to the group for a minimum period of time.

(5) A State law, rule, or order which requires that a purchasing group must have a minimum number of members, common ownership or affiliation, or a certain legal form.

(6) A State law, rule, or order which requires that a certain percentage of a purchasing group must obtain insurance on a group basis.

(7) A State law, rule, or order which requires that any insurance policy issued to a purchasing group or any members of the group be countersigned by an insurance agent or broker residing in that State.

(8) A State law, rule, or order which otherwise discriminate [1] against a purchasing group or any of its members.

(b) Application of exemptions

The exemptions specified in subsection (a) of this section apply to the following:

(1) Pollution liability insurance, and comprehensive general liability insurance which includes this coverage, provided to—

(A) a purchasing group; or

(B) any person who is a member of a purchasing group.

(2) The sale of any one of the following to a purchasing group or a member of the group:

(A) Pollution liability insurance and comprehensive general liability coverage.

(B) Insurance related services.

(C) Management services.

(c) Agents or brokers

A State may require that a person acting, or offering to act, as an agent or broker for a purchasing group obtain a license from that State, except that a State may not impose any qualification or requirement which discriminates against a nonresident agent or broker.

(Pub.L. 96–510, Title IV, § 404, as added Oct. 17, 1986, Pub.L. 99–499, Title II, § 210(a), formerly § 210, 100 Stat. 1718, as renumbered Oct. 27, 1986, Pub.L. 99–563, § 11(c)(1), 100 Stat. 3177.)

[1] So in original. Probably should be "discriminates".

Library References

Health and Environment ⚷25.6(1), 25.7(1).
Insurance ⚷124.1.
C.J.S. Health and Environment §§ 91 et seq., 106 et seq.
C.J.S. Insurance § 224.

§ 9675. Applicability of securities laws

(a) Ownership interests

The ownership interests of members of a risk retention group shall be considered to be—

(1) exempted securities for purposes of section 5 of the Securities Act of 1933 [15 U.S.C. 77e] and for purposes of section 12 of the Securities Exchange Act of 1934 [15 U.S.C. 78*l*]; and

(2) securities for purposes of the provisions of section 17 of the Securities Act of 1933 [15 U.S.C. 77q] and the provisions of section 10 of the Securities Exchange Act of 1934 [15 U.S.C. 78j].

(b) Investment Company Act

A risk retention group shall not be considered to be an investment company for purposes of the Investment Company Act of 1940 (15 U.S.C. 80a–1 et seq.).

(c) Blue sky law

The ownership interests of members in a risk retention group shall not be considered securities for purposes of any State blue sky law.

(Pub.L. 96–510, Title IV, § 405, as added Oct. 17, 1986, Pub.L. 99–499, Title II, § 210(a), formerly § 210, 100 Stat. 1719, as renumbered Oct. 27, 1986, Pub.L. 99–563, § 11(c)(1), 100 Stat. 3177.)

APPENDIX A

OCCUPATIONAL SAFETY AND HEALTH ACT

(Selections From 29 U.S.C.A. § 651 et seq.)

CHAPTER 15

OCCUPATIONAL SAFETY AND HEALTH

Table of Contents

§ 651. Congressional statement of findings and declaration of purpose and policy

(a)[1] The Congress finds that personal injuries and illnesses arising out of work situations impose a substantial burden upon, and are a hindrance to, interstate commerce in terms of lost production, wage loss, medical expenses, and disability compensation payments.

(b) The Congress declares it to be its purpose and policy, through the exercise of its powers to regulate commerce among the several States and with foreign nations and to provide for the general welfare, to assure so far as possible every working man and woman in the

1. Section was enacted without subsec. (a) designation, which has been supplied editorially.

Nation safe and healthful working conditions and to preserve our human resources—

(1) by encouraging employers and employees in their efforts to reduce the number of occupational safety and health hazards at their places of employment, and to stimulate employers and employees to institute new and to perfect existing programs for providing safe and healthful working conditions;

(2) by providing that employers and employees have separate but dependent responsibilities and rights with respect to achieving safe and healthful working conditions;

(3) by authorizing the Secretary of Labor to set mandatory occupational safety and health standards applicable to businesses affecting interstate commerce, and by creating an Occupational Safety and Health Review Commission for carrying out adjudicatory functions under this chapter;

(4) by building upon advances already made through employer and employee initiative for providing safe and healthful working conditions;

(5) by providing for research in the field of occupational safety and health, including the psychological factors involved, and by developing innovative methods, techniques, and approaches for dealing with occupational safety and health problems;

(6) by exploring ways to discover latent diseases, establishing causal connections between diseases and work in environmental conditions, and conducting other research relating to health problems, in recognition of the fact that occupational health standards present problems often different from those involved in occupational safety;

(7) by providing medical criteria which will assure insofar as practicable that no employee will suffer diminished health, functional capacity, or life expectancy as a result of his work experience;

(8) by providing for training programs to increase the number and competence of personnel engaged in the field of occupational safety and health;

(9) by providing for the development and promulgation of occupational safety and health standards;

(10) by providing an effective enforcement program which shall include a prohibition against giving advance notice of any inspection and sanctions for any individual violating this prohibition;

(11) by encouraging the States to assume the fullest responsibility for the administration and enforcement of their occupational safety and health laws by providing grants to the States to assist in identifying their needs and responsibilities in the area of occupational safety and health, to develop plans in accordance with the

provisions of this chapter, to improve the administration and enforcement of State occupational safety and health laws, and to conduct experimental and demonstration projects in connection therewith;

(12) by providing for appropriate reporting procedures with respect to occupational safety and health which procedures will help achieve the objectives of this chapter and accurately describe the nature of the occupational safety and health problems;

(13) by encouraging joint labor-management efforts to reduce injuries and disease arising out of employment.

Pub.L. 91–596, § 2, Dec. 29, 1970, 84 Stat. 1590.

§ 652. Definitions

For the purposes of this chapter—

(1) The term "Secretary" mean [1] the Secretary of Labor.

(2) The term "Commission" means the Occupational Safety and Health Review Commission established under this chapter.

(3) The term "commerce" means trade, traffic, commerce, transportation, or communication among the several States, or between a State and any place outside thereof, or within the District of Columbia, or a possession of the United States (other than the Trust Territory of the Pacific Islands), or between points in the same State but through a point outside thereof.

(4) The term "person" means one or more individuals, partnerships, associations, corporations, business trusts, legal representatives, or any organized group of persons.

(5) The term "employer" means a person engaged in a business affecting commerce who has employees, but does not include the United States or any State or political subdivision of a State.

(6) The term "employee" means an employee of an employer who is employed in a business of his employer which affects commerce.

(7) The term "State" includes a State of the United States, the District of Columbia, Puerto Rico, the Virgin Islands, American Samoa, Guam, and the Trust Territory of the Pacific Islands.

(8) The term "occupational safety and health standard" means a standard which requires conditions, or the adoption or use of one or more practices, means, methods, operations, or processes, reasonably necessary or appropriate to provide safe or healthful employment and places of employment.

(9) The term "national consensus standard" means any occupational safety and health standard or modification thereof which (1) has been adopted and promulgated by a nationally recognized

1. So in original. Probably should be "means".

standards-producing organization under procedures whereby it can be determined by the Secretary that persons interested and affected by the scope or provisions of the standard have reached substantial agreement on its adoption, (2) was formulated in a manner which afforded an opportunity for diverse views to be considered and (3) has been designated as such a standard by the Secretary, after consultation with other appropriate Federal agencies.

(10) The term "established Federal standard" means any operative occupational safety and health standard established by any agency of the United States and presently in effect, or contained in any Act of Congress in force on December 29, 1970.

(11) The term "Committee" means the National Advisory Committee on Occupational Safety and Health established under this chapter.

(12) The term "Director" means the Director of the National Institute for Occupational Safety and Health.

(13) The term "Institute" means the National Institute for Occupational Safety and Health established under this chapter.

(14) The term "Workmen's Compensation Commission" means the National Commission on State Workmen's Compensation Laws established under this chapter.

Pub.L. 91–596, § 3, Dec. 29, 1970, 84 Stat. 1591.

§ 654. Duties of employers and employees

(a) Each employer—

(1) shall furnish to each of his employees employment and a place of employment which are free from recognized hazards that are causing or are likely to cause death or serious physical harm to his employees;

(2) shall comply with occupational safety and health standards promulgated under this chapter.

(b) Each employee shall comply with occupational safety and health standards and all rules, regulations, and orders issued pursuant to this chapter which are applicable to his own actions and conduct.

Pub.L. 91–596, § 5, Dec. 29, 1970, 84 Stat. 1593.

§ 655. Standards

PROMULGATION BY SECRETARY OF NATIONAL CONSENSUS STANDARDS AND ESTABLISHED FEDERAL STANDARDS; TIME FOR PROMULGATION; CONFLICTING STANDARDS

(a) Without regard to chapter 5 of Title 5 or to the other subsections of this section, the Secretary shall, as soon as practicable during the period beginning with the effective date of this chapter and ending two years after such date, by rule promulgate as an occupational safety or health standard any national consensus standard, and any established Federal standard, unless he determines that the promulgation of such a standard would not result in improved safety or health for specifically designated employees. In the event of conflict among any such standards, the Secretary shall promulgate the standard which assures the greatest protection of the safety or health of the affected employees.

PROCEDURE FOR PROMULGATION, MODIFICATION, OR REVOCATION OF STANDARDS

(b) The Secretary may by rule promulgate, modify, or revoke any occupational safety or health standard in the following manner:

(1) Whenever the Secretary, upon the basis of information submitted to him in writing by an interested person, a representative of any organization of employers or employees, a nationally recognized standards-producing organization, the Secretary of Health and Human Services, the National Institute for Occupational Safety and Health, or a State or political subdivision, or on the basis of information developed by the Secretary or otherwise available to him, determines that a rule should be promulgated in order to serve the objectives of this chapter, the Secretary may request the recommendations of an advisory committee appointed under section 656 of this title. The Secretary shall provide such an advisory committee with any proposals of his own or of the Secretary of Health and Human Services, together with all pertinent factual information developed by the Secretary or the Secretary of Health and Human Services, or otherwise available, including the results of research, demonstrations, and experiments. An advisory committee shall submit to the Secretary its recommendations regarding the rule to be promulgated within ninety days from the date of its appointment or within such longer or shorter period as may be prescribed by the Secretary, but in no event for a period which is longer than two hundred and seventy days.

(2) The Secretary shall publish a proposed rule promulgating, modifying, or revoking an occupational safety or health standard in the Federal Register and shall afford interested persons a period of thirty days after publication to submit written data or comments. Where an advisory committee is appointed and the Secretary determines that a rule should be issued, he shall publish the proposed rule within sixty days after the submission of the advisory committee's recommendations or the expiration of the period prescribed by the Secretary for such submission.

(3) On or before the last day of the period provided for the submission of written data or comments under paragraph (2), any interested person may file with the Secretary written objections to the proposed rule, stating the grounds therefor and requesting a public hearing on such objections. Within thirty days after the last day for filing such objections, the Secretary shall publish in the

Federal Register a notice specifying the occupational safety or health standard to which objections have been filed and a hearing requested, and specifying a time and place for such hearing.

(4) Within sixty days after the expiration of the period provided for the submission of written data or comments under paragraph (2), or within sixty days after the completion of any hearing held under paragraph (3), the Secretary shall issue a rule promulgating, modifying, or revoking an occupational safety or health standard or make a determination that a rule should not be issued. Such a rule may contain a provision delaying its effective date for such period (not in excess of ninety days) as the Secretary determines may be necessary to insure that affected employers and employees will be informed of the existence of the standard and of its terms and that employers affected are given an opportunity to familiarize themselves and their employees with the existence of the requirements of the standard.

(5) The Secretary, in promulgating standards dealing with toxic materials or harmful physical agents under this subsection, shall set the standard which most adequately assures, to the extent feasible, on the basis of the best available evidence, that no employee will suffer material impairment of health or functional capacity even if such employee has regular exposure to the hazard dealt with by such standard for the period of his working life. Development of standards under this subsection shall be based upon research, demonstrations, experiments, and such other information as may be appropriate. In addition to the attainment of the highest degree of health and safety protection for the employee, other considerations shall be the latest available scientific data in the field, the feasibility of the standards, and experience gained under this and other health and safety laws. Whenever practicable, the standard promulgated shall be expressed in terms of objective criteria and of the performance desired.

(6)(A) Any employer may apply to the Secretary for a temporary order granting a variance from a standard or any provision thereof promulgated under this section. Such temporary order shall be granted only if the employer files an application which meets the requirements of clause (B) and establishes that (i) he is unable to comply with a standard by its effective date because of unavailability of professional or technical personnel or of materials and equipment needed to come into compliance with the standard or because necessary construction or alteration of facilities cannot be completed by the effective date, (ii) he is taking all available steps to safeguard his employees against the hazards covered by the standard, and (iii) he has an effective program for coming into compliance with the standard as quickly as practicable. Any temporary order issued under this paragraph shall prescribe the practices, means, methods, operations, and processes which the employer must adopt and use while the order is in effect and state in detail his program for coming into compliance with the standard. Such a temporary order may be granted only after notice to employees and an opportunity for a hearing: *Provided,* That the Secretary may issue one interim order to be effective until a decision is made on the basis of the hearing. No temporary order may be in effect for longer than the period needed by the employer to achieve compliance with the standard or one year, whichever is shorter, except that such an order may be renewed not more than twice (I) so long as the requirements of this paragraph are met and (II) if an application for renewal is filed at least 90 days prior to the expiration date of the order. No interim renewal of an order may remain in effect for longer than 180 days.

(B) An application for a temporary order under this paragraph (6) shall contain:

(i) a specification of the standard or portion thereof from which the employer seeks a variance,

(ii) a representation by the employer, supported by representations from qualified persons having firsthand knowledge of the facts represented, that he is unable to comply with the standard or portion thereof and a detailed statement of the reasons therefor,

(iii) a statement of the steps he has taken and will take (with specific dates) to protect employees against the hazard covered by the standard,

(iv) a statement of when he expects to be able to comply with the standard and what steps he has taken and what steps he will take (with dates specified) to come into compliance with the standard, and

(v) a certification that he has informed his employees of the application by giving a copy thereof to their authorized representative, posting a statement giving a summary of the application and specifying where a copy may be examined at the place or places where notices to employees are normally posted, and by other appropriate means.

A description of how employees have been informed shall be contained in the certification. The information to employees shall also inform them of their right to petition the Secretary for a hearing.

(C) The Secretary is authorized to grant a variance from any standard or portion thereof whenever he determines, or the Secretary of Health and Human Services certifies, that such variance is necessary to permit an employer to participate in an experiment approved by him or the Secretary of Health and Human Services designed to demonstrate or validate new and improved techniques to safeguard the health or safety of workers.

(7) Any standard promulgated under this subsection shall prescribe the use of labels or other appropriate forms of warning as are necessary to insure that employees are apprised of all hazards to which they are exposed, relevant symptoms and appropriate emergency treatment, and proper conditions and precautions of safe use or exposure. Where appropriate, such standard shall also prescribe suitable protective equipment and control or technological procedures to be used in connection with such hazards and shall provide for monitoring or measuring employee exposure at such locations and intervals, and in such manner as may be necessary for the protection of employees. In addition, where appropriate, any such standard shall prescribe the type and frequency of medical examinations or other tests which shall be made available, by the employer or at his cost, to employees exposed to such hazards in order to most effectively determine whether the health of such employees is adversely affected by such exposure. In the event such medical examinations are in the nature of research, as determined by the Secretary of Health and Human Services, such examinations may be furnished at the expense of the Secretary of Health and Human Services. The results of such examinations or tests shall be furnished only to the Secretary or the Secretary of Health and Human Services, and, at the request of the employee, to his physician. The Secretary, in consultation with the Secretary of Health and Human Services, may by rule promulgated pursuant to section 553 of Title 5, make appropriate modifications in the foregoing requirements relating to the use of labels or other forms of warning, monitoring or measuring, and medical examinations, as may be warranted by experience, information, or medical or technological developments acquired subsequent to the promulgation of the relevant standard.

(8) Whenever a rule promulgated by the Secretary differs substantially from an existing national consensus standard, the Secretary shall, at the same time, publish in the Federal Register a statement of the reasons why the rule as adopted will better effectuate the purposes of this chapter than the national consensus standard.

EMERGENCY TEMPORARY STANDARDS

(c)(1) The Secretary shall provide, without regard to the requirements of chapter 5 of Title 5, for an emergency temporary standard to take immediate effect upon publication in the Federal Register if he determines (A) that employees are exposed to grave danger from exposure to substances or agents determined to be toxic or physically harmful or from new hazards, and (B) that such emergency standard is necessary to protect employees from such danger.

(2) Such standard shall be effective until superseded by a standard promulgated in accordance with the procedures prescribed in paragraph (3) of this subsection.

(3) Upon publication of such standard in the Federal Register the Secretary shall commence a proceeding in accordance with subsection (b) of this section, and the standard as published shall also serve as a proposed rule for the proceeding. The Secretary shall promulgate a standard under this paragraph no later than six months after publication of the emergency standard as provided in paragraph (2) of this subsection.

VARIANCES FROM STANDARDS; PROCEDURE

(d) Any affected employer may apply to the Secretary for a rule or order for a variance from a standard promulgated under this section. Affected employees shall be given notice of each such application and an opportunity to participate in a hearing. The Secretary shall issue such rule or order if he determines on the record, after opportunity for an inspection where appropriate and a hearing, that the proponent of the variance has demonstrated by a preponderance of the evidence that the conditions, practices, means, methods, operations, or processes used or proposed to be used by an employer will provide employment and places of employment to his employees which are as safe and healthful as those which would prevail if he complies with the standard. The rule or order so issued shall prescribe the conditions the employer must maintain, and the practices, means, methods, operations, and processes which he must adopt and utilize to the extent they differ from the standard in question. Such a rule or order may be modified or revoked upon application by an employer, employees, or by the Secretary on his own motion, in the manner prescribed for its issuance under this subsection at any time after six months from its issuance.

STATEMENT OF REASONS FOR SECRETARY'S DETERMINATIONS; PUBLICATION IN FEDERAL REGISTER

(e) Whenever the Secretary promulgates any standard, makes any rule, order, or decision, grants any exemption or extension of time, or compromises, mitigates, or settles any penalty assessed under this chapter, he shall include a statement of the reasons for such action, which shall be published in the Federal Register.

JUDICIAL REVIEW

(f) Any person who may be adversely affected by a standard issued under this section may at any time prior to the sixtieth day after such standard is promulgated file a petition challenging the validity of such standard with the United States court of appeals for the circuit wherein such person resides or has his principal place of business, for a judicial review of such standard. A copy of the petition shall be forthwith transmitted by the clerk of the court to the Secretary. The filing of such petition shall not, unless otherwise ordered by the court, operate as a stay of the standard. The determinations of the Secretary shall be conclusive if supported by substantial evidence in the record considered as a whole.

PRIORITY FOR ESTABLISHMENT OF STANDARDS

(g) In determining the priority for establishing standards under this section, the Secretary shall give due regard to the urgency of the need for mandatory safety and health standards for particular industries, trades, crafts, occupations, businesses, workplaces or work environments. The Secretary shall also give due regard to the recommendations of the Secretary of Health and Human Services regarding the need for mandatory standards in determining the priority for establishing such standards.

Pub.L. 91–596, § 6, Dec. 29, 1970, 84 Stat. 1593; Pub.L. 96–88, Title V, § 509(b), Oct. 17, 1979, 93 Stat. 695.

APPENDIX B

CODE OF FEDERAL REGULATIONS

TITLE 40—PROTECTION OF ENVIRONMENT

CHAPTER V

COUNCIL ON ENVIRONMENTAL QUALITY

Revised as of June 1, 1987

Table of Contents

Part 1500

Purpose, Policy, and Mandate

AUTHORITY: NEPA, the Environmental Quality Improvement Act of 1970, as amended (42 U.S.C. 4371 *et seq.*), sec. 309 of the Clean Air Act, as amended (42 U.S.C. 7609) and E.O. 11514, Mar. 5, 1970, as amended by E.O. 11991, May 24, 1977).

SOURCE: 43 FR 55990, Nov. 28, 1978, unless otherwise noted.

§ 1500.1 Purpose

(a) The National Environmental Policy Act (NEPA) is our basic national charter for protection of the environment. It establishes policy, sets goals (section 101), and provides means (section 102) for carrying out the policy. Section 102(2) contains "action-forcing" provisions to make sure that federal agencies act according to the letter and spirit of the Act. The regulations that follow implement section 102(2). Their purpose is to tell federal agencies what they must do to comply with the procedures and achieve the goals of the Act. The President, the federal agencies, and the courts share responsibility for enforcing the Act so as to achieve the substantive requirements of section 101.

(b) NEPA procedures must insure that environmental information is available to public officials and citizens before decisions are made and before actions are taken. The information must be of high quality. Accurate scientific analysis, expert agency comments, and public scrutiny are essential to implementing NEPA. Most important, NEPA documents must concentrate on the issues that are truly significant to the action in question, rather than amassing needless detail.

(c) Ultimately, of course, it is not better documents but better decisions that count. NEPA's purpose is not to generate paperwork—even excellent paperwork—but to foster excellent action. The NEPA process is intended to help public officials make decisions that are based on understanding of environmental consequences, and take actions that protect, restore, and enhance the environment. These regulations provide the direction to achieve this purpose.

§ 1500.2 Policy

Federal agencies shall to the fullest extent possible:

(a) Interpret and administer the policies, regulations, and public laws of the United States in accordance with the policies set forth in the Act and in these regulations.

(b) Implement procedures to make the NEPA process more useful to decisionmakers and the public; to reduce paperwork and the accumulation of extraneous background data; and to emphasize real environmental issues and alternatives. Environmental impact statements shall be concise, clear, and to the point, and shall be supported by evidence that agencies have made the necessary environmental analyses.

(c) Integrate the requirements of NEPA with other planning and environmental review procedures required by law or by agency practice so that all such procedures run concurrently rather than consecutively.

(d) Encourage and facilitate public involvement in decisions which affect the quality of the human environment.

(e) Use the NEPA process to identify and assess the reasonable alternatives to proposed actions that will avoid or minimize adverse effects of these actions upon the quality of the human environment.

(f) Use all practicable means, consistent with the requirements of the Act and other essential considerations of national policy, to restore and enhance the quality of the human environment and avoid or minimize any possible adverse effects of their actions upon the quality of the human environment.

§ 1500.3 Mandate

Parts 1500 through 1508 of this title provide regulations applicable to and binding on all Federal agencies for implementing the procedural provisions of the National Environmental Policy Act of 1969, as amended (Pub.L. 91–190, 42 U.S.C. 4321 et seq.) (NEPA or the Act) except where compliance would be inconsistent with other statutory requirements. These regulations are issued pursuant to NEPA, the Environmental Quality Improvement Act of 1970, as amended (42 U.S.C. 4371 et seq.) section 309 of the Clean Air Act, as amended (42 U.S.C. 7609) and Executive Order 11514, Protection and Enhancement of Environmental Quality (March 5, 1970, as amended by Executive Order 11991, May 24, 1977). These regulations, unlike the predecessor guidelines, are not confined to sec. 102(2)(C) (environmental impact statements). The regulations apply to the whole of section 102(2). The provisions of the Act and of these regulations must be read together as a whole in order to comply with the spirit and letter of the law. It is the Council's intention that judicial review of agency compliance with these regulations not occur before an agency has filed the final environmental impact statement, or has made a final finding of no significant impact (when such a finding will result in action affecting the environment), or takes action that will result in irreparable injury. Furthermore, it is the Council's intention that any trivial violation of these regulations not give rise to any independent cause of action.

§ 1500.4 Reducing paperwork

Agencies shall reduce excessive paperwork by:

(a) Reducing the length of environmental impact statements (§ 1502.2(c)), by means such as setting appropriate page limits (§§ 1501.7(b)(1) and 1502.7).

(b) Preparing analytic rather than encyclopedic environmental impact statements (§ 1502.2(a)).

(c) Discussing only briefly issues other than significant ones (§ 1502.2(b)).

(d) Writing environmental impact statements in plain language (§ 1502.8).

(e) Following a clear format for environmental impact statements (§ 1502.10).

(f) Emphasizing the portions of the environmental impact statement that are useful to decisionmakers and the public (§§ 1502.14 and 1502.15) and reducing emphasis on background material (§ 1502.16).

(g) Using the scoping process, not only to identify significant environmental issues deserving of study, but also to deemphasize insignificant issues, narrowing the scope of the environmental impact statement process accordingly (§ 1501.7).

(h) Summarizing the environmental impact statement (§ 1502.12) and circulating the summary instead of the entire environmental impact statement if the latter is unusually long (§ 1502.19).

(i) Using program, policy, or plan environmental impact statements and tiering from statements of broad scope to those of narrower scope, to eliminate repetitive discussions of the same issues (§§ 1502.4 and 1502.20).

(j) Incorporating by reference (§ 1502.21).

(k) Integrating NEPA requirements with other environmental review and consultation requirements (§ 1502.25).

(*l*) Requiring comments to be as specific as possible (§ 1503.3).

(m) Attaching and circulating only changes to the draft environmental impact statement, rather than rewriting and circulating the entire statement when changes are minor (§ 1503.4(c)).

(n) Eliminating duplication with State and local procedures, by providing for joint preparation (§ 1506.2), and with other Federal procedures, by providing that an agency may adopt appropriate environmental documents prepared by another agency (§ 1506.3).

(*o*) Combining environmental documents with other documents (§ 1506.4).

(p) Using categorical exclusions to define categories of actions which do not individually or cumulatively have a significant effect on the human environment and which are therefore exempt from requirements to prepare an environmental impact statement (§ 1508.4).

(q) Using a finding of no significant impact when an action not otherwise excluded will not have a significant effect on the human environment and is therefore exempt from requirements to prepare an environmental impact statement (§ 1508.13).

[43 FR 55990, Nov. 29, 1978; 44 FR 873, Jan. 3, 1979]

§ 1500.5 Reducing delay

Agencies shall reduce delay by:

(a) Integrating the NEPA process into early planning (§ 1501.-2).

(b) Emphasizing interagency cooperation before the environmental impact statement is prepared, rather then submission of adversary comments on a completed document (§ 1501.6).

(c) Insuring the swift and fair resolution of lead agency disputes (§ 1501.5).

(d) Using the scoping process for an early identification of what are and what are not the real issues (§ 1501.7).

(e) Establishing appropriate time limits for the environmental impact statement process (§§ 1501.7(b)(2) and 1501.8).

(f) Preparing environmental impact statements early in the process (§ 1502.5).

(g) Integrating NEPA requirements with other environmental review and consultation requirements (§ 1502.25).

(h) Eliminating duplication with State and local procedures by providing for joint preparation (§ 1506.2) and with other Federal procedures by providing that an agency may adopt appropriate environmental documents prepared by another agency (§ 1506.3).

(i) Combining environmental documents with other documents (§ 1506.4).

(j) Using accelerated procedures for proposals for legislation (§ 1506.8).

(k) Using categorical exclusions to define categories of actions which do not individually or cumulatively have a significant effect on the human environment (§ 1508.4) and which are therefore exempt from requirements to prepare an environmental impact statement.

(*l*) Using a finding of no significant impact when an action not otherwise excluded will not have a significant effect on the human environment (§ 1508.13) and is therefore exempt from requirements to prepare an environmental impact statement.

§ 1500.6 Agency authority

Each agency shall interpret the provisions of the Act as a supplement to its existing authority and as a mandate to view traditional policies and missions in the light of the Act's national environmental objectives. Agencies shall review their policies, procedures, and regulations accordingly and revise them as necessary to insure full compliance with the purposes and provisions of the Act. The phrase "to the fullest extent possible" in section 102 means that each agency of the Federal Government shall comply with that section unless existing law applicable to the agency's operations expressly prohibits or makes compliance impossible.

Part 1501

NEPA and Agency Planning

AUTHORITY: NEPA, the Environmental Quality Improvement Act of 1970, as amended (42 U.S.C. 4371 *et seq.*), sec. 309 of the Clean Air Act, as amended (42 U.S.C. 7609), and E.O. 11514 (Mar. 5, 1970, as amended by E.O. 11991, May 24, 1977).

SOURCE: 43 FR 55992, Nov. 29, 1978, unless otherwise noted.

§ 1501.1 Purpose

The purposes of this part include:

(a) Integrating the NEPA process into early planning to insure appropriate consideration of NEPA's policies and to eliminate delay.

(b) Emphasizing cooperative consultation among agencies before the environmental impact statement is prepared rather than submission of adversary comments on a completed document.

(c) Providing for the swift and fair resolution of lead agency disputes.

(d) Identifying at an early stage the significant environmental issues deserving of study and deemphasizing insignificant issues, narrowing the scope of the environmental impact statement accordingly.

(e) Providing a mechanism for putting appropriate time limits on the environmental impact statement process.

§ 1501.2 Apply NEPA early in the process

Agencies shall integrate the NEPA process with other planning at the earliest possible time to insure that planning and decisions reflect environmental values, to avoid delays later in the process, and to head off potential conflicts. Each agency shall:

(a) Comply with the mandate of section 102(2)(A) to "utilize a systematic, interdisciplinary approach which will insure the integrated use of the natural and social sciences and the environmental design arts in planning and in decisionmaking which may have an impact on man's environment," as specified by § 1507.2.

(b) Identify environmental effects and values in adequate detail so they can be compared to economic and technical analyses. Environmental documents and appropriate analyses shall be circulated and reviewed at the same time as other planning documents.

(c) Study, develop, and describe appropriate alternatives to recommended courses of action in any proposal which involves unresolved conflicts concerning alternative uses of available resources as provided by section 102(2)(E) of the Act.

(d) Provide for cases where actions are planned by private applicants or other non-Federal entities before Federal involvement so that:

(1) Policies or designated staff are available to advise potential applicants of studies or other information foreseeably required for later Federal action.

(2) The Federal agency consults early with appropriate State and local agencies and Indian tribes and with interested private persons and organizations when its own involvement is reasonably foreseeable.

(3) The Federal agency commences its NEPA process at the earliest possible time.

§ 1501.3 When to prepare an environmental assessment

(a) Agencies shall prepare an environmental assessment (§ 1508.9) when necessary under the procedures adopted by individual agencies to supplement these regulations as described in § 1507.3. An assessment is not necessary if the agency has decided to prepare an environmental impact statement.

(b) Agencies may prepare an environmental assessment on any action at any time in order to assist agency planning and decisionmaking.

§ 1501.4 Whether to prepare an environmental impact statement

In determining whether to prepare an environmental impact statement the Federal agency shall:

(a) Determine under its procedures supplementing these regulations (described in § 1507.3) whether the proposal is one which:

(1) Normally requires an environmental impact statement, or

(2) Normally does not require either an environmental impact statement or an environmental assessment (categorical exclusion).

(b) If the proposed action is not covered by paragraph (a) of this section, prepare an environmental assessment (§ 1508.9). The agency shall involve environmental agencies, applicants, and the public, to the extent practicable, in preparing assessments required by § 1508.9(a)(1).

(c) Based on the environmental assessment make its determination whether to prepare an environmental impact statement.

(d) Commence the scoping process (§ 1501.7), if the agency will prepare an environmental impact statement.

(e) Prepare a finding of no significant impact (§ 1508.13), if the agency determines on the basis of the environmental assessment not to prepare a statement.

(1) The agency shall make the finding of no significant impact available to the affected public as specified in § 1506.6.

(2) In certain limited circumstances, which the agency may cover in its procedures under § 1507.3, the agency shall make the finding of no significant impact available for public review (including State and areawide clearinghouses) for 30 days before the agency makes its final determination whether to prepare an environmental impact statement and before the action may begin. The circumstances are:

(i) The proposed action is, or is closely similar to, one which normally requires the preparation of an environmental impact statement under the procedures adopted by the agency pursuant to § 1507.3, or

(ii) The nature of the proposed action is one without precedent.

§ 1501.5 Lead agencies

(a) A lead agency shall supervise the preparation of an environmental impact statement if more than one Federal agency either:

(1) Proposes or is involved in the same action; or

(2) Is involved in a group of actions directly related to each other because of their functional interdependence or geographical proximity.

(b) Federal, State, or local agencies, including at least one Federal agency, may act as joint lead agencies to prepare an environmental impact statement (§ 1506.2).

(c) If an action falls within the provisions of paragraph (a) of this section the potential lead agencies shall determine by letter or memorandum which agency shall be the lead agency and which shall be cooperating agencies. The agencies shall resolve the lead agency question so as not to cause delay. If there is disagreement among the agencies, the following factors (which are listed in order of descending importance) shall determine lead agency designation:

(1) Magnitude of agency's involvement.

(2) Project approval/disapproval authority.

(3) Expertise concerning the action's environmental effects.

(4) Duration of agency's involvement.

(5) Sequence of agency's involvement.

(d) Any Federal agency, or any State or local agency or private person substantially affected by the absence of lead agency designation, may make a written request to the potential lead agencies that a lead agency be designated.

(e) If Federal agencies are unable to agree on which agency will be the lead agency or if the procedure described in paragraph (c) of this section has not resulted within 45 days in a lead agency designation, any of the agencies or persons concerned may file a request with the Council asking it to determine which Federal agency shall be the lead agency.

A copy of the request shall be transmitted to each potential lead agency. The request shall consist of:

(1) A precise description of the nature and extent of the proposed action.

(2) A detailed statement of why each potential lead agency should or should not be the lead agency under the criteria specified in paragraph (c) of this section.

(f) A response may be filed by any potential lead agency concerned within 20 days after a request is filed with the Council. The Council shall determine as soon as possible but not later than 20 days after receiving the request and all responses to it which Federal agency shall be the lead agency and which other Federal agencies shall be cooperating agencies.

[43 FR 55992, Nov. 29, 1978; 44 FR 873, Jan. 3, 1979]

§ 1501.6 Cooperating agencies

The purpose of this section is to emphasize agency cooperation early in the NEPA process. Upon request of the lead agency, any other Federal agency which has jurisdiction by law shall be a cooperating agency. In addition any other Federal agency which has special expertise with respect to any environmental issue, which should be addressed in the statement may be a cooperating agency upon request of the lead agency. An agency may request the lead agency to designate it a cooperating agency.

(a) The lead agency shall:

(1) Request the participation of each cooperating agency in the NEPA process at the earliest possible time.

(2) Use the environmental analysis and proposals of cooperating agencies with jurisdiction by law or special expertise, to the

maximum extent possible consistent with its responsibility as lead agency.

(3) Meet with a cooperating agency at the latter's request.

(b) Each cooperating agency shall:

(1) Participate in the NEPA process at the earliest possible time.

(2) Participate in the scoping process (described below in § 1501.7).

(3) Assume on request of the lead agency responsibility for developing information and preparing environmental analyses including portions of the environmental impact statement concerning which the cooperating agency has special expertise.

(4) Make available staff support at the lead agency's request to enhance the latter's interdisciplinary capability.

(5) Normally use its own funds. The lead agency shall, to the extent available funds permit, fund those major activities or analyses it requests from cooperating agencies. Potential lead agencies shall include such funding requirements in their budget requests.

(c) A cooperating agency may in response to a lead agency's request for assistance in preparing the environmental impact statement (described in paragraph (b)(3), (4) or (5) of this section) reply that other program commitments preclude any involvement or the degree of involvement requested in the action that is the subject of the environmental impact statement. A copy of this reply shall be submitted to the Council.

§ 1501.7 Scoping

There shall be an early and open process for determining the scope of issues to be addressed and for identifying the significant issues related to a proposed action. This process shall be termed scoping. As soon as practicable after its decision to prepare an environmental impact statement and before the scoping process the lead agency shall publish a notice of intent (§ 1508.22) in the FEDERAL REGISTER except as provided in § 1507.3(e).

(a) As part of the scoping process the lead agency shall:

(1) Invite the participation of affected Federal, State, and local agencies, any affected Indian tribe, the proponent of the action, and other interested persons (including those who might not be in accord with the action on environmental grounds), unless there is a limited exception under § 1507.3(c). An agency may give notice in accordance with § 1506.6.

(2) Determine the scope (§ 1508.25) and the significant issues to be analyzed in depth in the environmental impact statement.

(3) Identify and eliminate from detailed study the issues which are not significant or which have been covered by prior environ-

mental review (§ 1506.3), narrowing the discussion of these issues in the statement to a brief presentation of why they will not have a significant effect on the human environment or providing a reference to their coverage elsewhere.

(4) Allocate assignments for preparation of the environmental impact statement among the lead and cooperating agencies, with the lead agency retaining responsibility for the statement.

(5) Indicate any public environmental assessments and other environmental impact statements which are being or will be prepared that are related to but are not part of the scope of the impact statement under consideration.

(6) Identify other environmental review and consultation requirements so the lead and cooperating agencies may prepare other required analyses and studies concurrently with, and integrated with, the environmental impact statement as provided in § 1502.-25.

(7) Indicate the relationship between the timing of the preparation of environmental analyses and the agency's tentative planning and decisionmaking schedule.

(b) As part of the scoping process the lead agency may:

(1) Set page limits on environmental documents (§ 1502.7).

(2) Set time limits (§ 1501.8).

(3) Adopt procedures under § 1507.3 to combine its environmental assessment process with its scoping process.

(4) Hold an early scoping meeting or meetings which may be integrated with any other early planning meeting the agency has. Such a scoping meeting will often be appropriate when the impacts of a particular action are confined to specific sites.

(c) An agency shall revise the determinations made under paragraphs (a) and (b) of this section if substantial changes are made later in the proposed action, or if significant new circumstances or information arise which bear on the proposal or its impacts.

§ 1501.8 Time limits

Although the Council has decided that prescribed universal time limits for the entire NEPA process are too inflexible, Federal agencies are encouraged to set time limits appropriate to individual actions (consistent with the time intervals required by § 1506.10). When multiple agencies are involved the reference to agency below means lead agency.

(a) The agency shall set time limits if an applicant for the proposed action requests them: *Provided,* That the limits are consistent with the purposes of NEPA and other essential considerations of national policy.

(b) The agency may:

(1) Consider the following factors in determining time limits:

(i) Potential for environmental harm.

(ii) Size of the proposed action.

(iii) State of the art of analytic techniques.

(iv) Degree of public need for the proposed action, including the consequences of delay.

(v) Number of persons and agencies affected.

(vi) Degree to which relevant information is known and if not known the time required for obtaining it.

(vii) Degree to which the action is controversial.

(viii) Other time limits imposed on the agency by law, regulations, or executive order.

(2) Set overall time limits or limits for each constituent part of the NEPA process, which may include:

(i) Decision on whether to prepare an environmental impact statement (if not already decided).

(ii) Determination of the scope of the environmental impact statement.

(iii) Preparation of the draft environmental impact statement.

(iv) Review of any comments on the draft environmental impact statement from the public and agencies.

(v) Preparation of the final environmental impact statement.

(vi) Review of any comments on the final environmental impact statement.

(vii) Decision on the action based in part on the environmental impact statement.

(3) Designate a person (such as the project manager or a person in the agency's office with NEPA responsibilities) to expedite the NEPA process.

(c) State or local agencies or members of the public may request a Federal Agency to set time limits.

Part 1502

Environmental Impact Statement

Sec.

AUTHORITY: NEPA, the Environmental Quality Improvement Act of 1970, as amended (42 U.S.C. 4371 *et seq.*), sec. 309 of the Clean Air Act, as amended (42 U.S.C. 7609), and E.O. 11514 (Mar. 5, 1970, as amended by E.O. 11991, May 24, 1977).

SOURCE: 43 FR 55994, Nov. 29, 1978, unless otherwise noted.

§ 1502.1 Purpose

The primary purpose of an environmental impact statement is to serve as an action-forcing device to insure that the policies and goals defined in the Act are infused into the ongoing programs and actions of the Federal Government. It shall provide full and fair discussion of significant environmental impacts and shall inform decisionmakers and the public of the reasonable alternatives which would avoid or minimize adverse impacts or enhance the quality of the human environment. Agencies shall focus on significant environmental issues and alternatives and shall reduce paperwork and the accumulation of extraneous background data. Statements shall be concise, clear, and to the point, and shall be supported by evidence that the agency has made the necessary environmental analyses. An environmental impact statement is more than a disclosure document. It shall be used by Federal officials in conjunction with other relevant material to plan actions and make decisions.

§ 1502.2 Implementation

To achieve the purposes set forth in § 1502.1 agencies shall prepare environmental impact statements in the following manner:

(a) Environmental impact statements shall be analytic rather than encyclopedic.

(b) Impacts shall be discussed in proportion to their significance. There shall be only brief discussion of other than significant issues. As in a finding of no significant impact, there should be only enough discussion to show why more study is not warranted.

(c) Environmental impact statements shall be kept concise and shall be no longer than absolutely necessary to comply with NEPA and with these regulations. Length should vary first with potential environmental problems and then with project size.

(d) Environmental impact statements shall state how alternatives considered in it and decisions based on it will or will not achieve the requirements of sections 101 and 102(1) of the Act and other environmental laws and policies.

(e) The range of alternatives discussed in environmental impact statements shall encompass those to be considered by the ultimate agency decisionmaker.

(f) Agencies shall not commit resources prejudicing selection of alternatives before making a final decision (§ 1506.1).

(g) Environmental impact statements shall serve as the means of assessing the environmental impact of proposed agency actions, rather than justifying decisions already made.

§ 1502.3 Statutory requirements for statements.

As required by sec. 102(2)(C) of NEPA environmental impact statements (§ 1508.11) are to be included in every recommendation or report.

On proposals (§ 1508.23).

For legislation and (§ 1508.17).

Other major Federal actions (§ 1508.18).

Significantly (§ 1508.27).

Affecting (§§ 1508.3, 1508.8).

The quality of the human environment (§ 1508.14).

§ 1502.4 Major Federal actions requiring the preparation of environmental impact statements

(a) Agencies shall make sure the proposal which is the subject of an environmental impact statement is properly defined. Agencies shall use the criteria for scope (§ 1508.25) to determine which proposal(s) shall be the subject of a particular statement. Proposals or parts of proposals which are related to each other closely enough to be, in effect, a single course of action shall be evaluated in a single impact statement.

(b) Environmental impact statements may be prepared, and are sometimes required, for broad Federal actions such as the adoption of new agency programs or regulations (§ 1508.18). Agencies shall prepare statements on broad actions so that they are relevant to policy and are timed to coincide with meaningful points in agency planning and decisionmaking.

(c) When preparing statements on broad actions (including proposals by more than one agency), agencies may find it useful to evaluate the proposal(s) in one of the following ways:

(1) Geographically, including actions occurring in the same general location, such as body of water, region, or metropolitan area.

(2) Generically, including actions which have relevant similarities, such as common timing, impacts, alternatives, methods of implementation, media, or subject matter.

(3) By stage of technological development including federal or federally assisted research, development or demonstration programs for new technologies which, if applied, could significantly affect the quality of the human environment. Statements shall be prepared on such programs and shall be available before the program has reached a stage of investment or commitment to implementation likely to determine subsequent development or restrict later alternatives.

(d) Agencies shall as appropriate employ scoping (§ 1501.7), tiering (§ 1502.20), and other methods listed in §§ 1500.4 and 1500.5 to relate broad and narrow actions and to avoid duplication and delay.

§ 1502.5 Timing

An agency shall commence preparation of an environmental impact statement as close as possible to the time the agency is developing or is presented with a proposal (§ 1508.23) so that preparation can be completed in time for the final statement to be included in any recommendation or report on the proposal. The statement shall be prepared early enough so that it can serve practically as an important contribution to the decisionmaking process and will not be used to rationalize or justify decisions already made (§§ 1500.2(c), 1501.2, and 1502.2). For instance:

(a) For projects directly undertaken by Federal agencies the environmental impact statement shall be prepared at the feasibility analysis (go-no go) stage and may be supplemented at a later stage if necessary.

(b) For applications to the agency appropriate environmental assessments or statements shall be commenced no later than immediately after the application is received. Federal agencies are encouraged to begin preparation of such assessments or statements earlier, preferably jointly with applicable State or local agencies.

(c) For adjudication, the final environmental impact statement shall normally precede the final staff recommendation and that portion of the public hearing related to the impact study. In appropriate circumstances the statement may follow preliminary hearings designed to gather information for use in the statements.

(d) For informal rulemaking the draft environmental impact statement shall normally accompany the proposed rule.

§ 1502.6 Interdisciplinary preparation

Environmental impact statements shall be prepared using an interdisciplinary approach which will insure the integrated use of the natural and social sciences and the environmental design arts (section 102(2)(A) of the Act). The disciplines of the preparers shall be appropriate to the scope and issues identified in the scoping process (§ 1501.7).

§ 1502.7 Page limits

The text of final environmental impact statements (e.g., paragraphs (d) through (g) of § 1502.10) shall normally be less than 150 pages and for proposals of unusual scope or complexity shall normally be less than 300 pages.

§ 1502.8 Writing

Environmental impact statements shall be written in plain language and may use appropriate graphics so that decisionmakers and the public can readily understand them. Agencies should employ writers of clear prose or editors to write, review, or edit statements, which will be based upon the analysis and supporting data from the natural and social sciences and the environmental design arts.

§ 1502.9 Draft, final, and supplemental statements

Except for proposals for legislation as provided in § 1506.8 environmental impact statements shall be prepared in two stages and may be supplemented.

(a) Draft environmental impact statements shall be prepared in accordance with the scope decided upon in the scoping process. The lead agency shall work with the cooperating agencies and shall obtain comments as required in Part 1503 of this chapter. The draft statement must fulfill and satisfy to the fullest extent possible the requirements established for final statements in section 102(2)(C) of the Act. If a draft statement is so inadequate as to preclude meaningful analysis, the agency shall prepare and circulate a revised draft of the appropriate portion. The agency shall make every effort to disclose and discuss at appropriate points in the draft statement all major points of view on the environmental impacts of the alternatives including the proposed action.

(b) Final environmental impact statements shall respond to comments as required in Part 1503 of this chapter. The agency shall discuss at appropriate points in the final statement any responsible opposing view which was not adequately discussed in the draft statement and shall indicate the agency's response to the issues raised.

(c) Agencies:

(1) Shall prepare supplements to either draft or final environmental impact statements if:

(i) The agency makes substantial changes in the proposed action that are relevant to environmental concerns; or

(ii) There are significant new circumstances or information relevant to environmental concerns and bearing on the proposed action or its impacts.

(2) May also prepare supplements when the agency determines that the purposes of the Act will be furthered by doing so.

(3) Shall adopt procedures for introducing a supplement into its formal administrative record, if such a record exists.

(4) Shall prepare, circulate, and file a supplement to a statement in the same fashion (exclusive of scoping) as a draft and final statement unless alternative procedures are approved by the Council.

§ 1502.10 Recommended format

Agencies shall use a format for environmental impact statements which will encourage good analysis and clear presentation of the alternatives including the proposed action. The following standard format for environmental impact statements should be followed unless the agency determines that there is a compelling reason to do otherwise:

(a) Cover sheet.

(b) Summary.

(c) Table of contents.

(d) Purpose of and need for action.

(e) Alternatives including proposed action (sections 102(2)(C)(iii) and 102(2)(E) of the Act).

(f) Affected environment.

(g) Environmental consequences (especially sections 102(2)(C)(i), (ii), (iv), and (v) of the Act).

(h) List of preparers.

(i) List of Agencies, Organizations, and persons to whom copies of the statement are sent.

(j) Index.

(k) Appendices (if any).

If a different format is used, it shall include paragraphs (a), (b), (c), (h), (i), and (j), of this section and shall include the substance of paragraphs (d), (e), (f), (g), and (k) of this section, as further described in §§ 1502.11 through 1502.18, in any appropriate format.

§ 1502.11 Cover sheet

The cover sheet shall not exceed one page. It shall include:

(a) A list of the responsible agencies including the lead agency and any cooperating agencies.

(b) The title of the proposed action that is the subject of the statement (and if appropriate the titles of related cooperating agency actions), together with the State(s) and county(ies) (or other jurisdiction if applicable) where the action is located.

(c) The name, address, and telephone number of the person at the agency who can supply further information.

(d) A designation of the statement as a draft, final, or draft or final supplement.

(e) A one paragraph abstract of the statement.

(f) The date by which comments must be received (computed in cooperation with EPA under § 1506.10).

The information required by this section may be entered on Standard Form 424 (in items 4, 6, 7, 10, and 18).

§ 1502.12 Summary

Each environmental impact statement shall contain a summary which adequately and accurately summarizes the statement. The summary shall stress the major conclusions, areas of controversy (including issues raised by agencies and the public), and the issues to be resolved (including the choice among alternatives). The summary will normally not exceed 15 pages.

§ 1502.13 Purpose and need

The statement shall briefly specify the underlying purpose and need to which the agency is responding in proposing the alternatives including the proposed action.

§ 1502.14 Alternatives including the proposed action

This section is the heart of the environmental impact statement. Based on the information and analysis presented in the sections on the Affected Environment (§ 1502.15) and the Environmental Consequences (§ 1502.16), it should present the environmental impacts of the proposal and the alternatives in comparative form, thus sharply defining the issues and providing a clear basis for choice among options by the decisionmaker and the public. In this section agencies shall:

(a) Rigorously explore and objectively evaluate all reasonable alternatives, and for alternatives which were eliminated from detailed study, briefly discuss the reasons for their having been eliminated.

(b) Devote substantial treatment to each alternative considered in detail including the proposed action so that reviewers may evaluate their comparative merits.

(c) Include reasonable alternatives not within the jurisdiction of the lead agency.

(d) Include the alternative of no action.

(e) Identify the agency's preferred alternative or alternatives, if one or more exists, in the draft statement and identify such alternative in the final statement unless another law prohibits the expression of such a preference.

(f) Include appropriate mitigation measures not already included in the proposed action or alternatives.

§ 1502.15 Affected environment

The environmental impact statement shall succinctly describe the environment of the area(s) to be affected or created by the alternatives under consideration. The descriptions shall be no longer than is necessary to understand the effects of the alternatives. Data and analyses in a statement shall be commensurate with the importance of the impact, with less important material summarized, consolidated, or simply referenced. Agencies shall avoid useless bulk in statements and shall concentrate effort and attention on important issues. Verbose descriptions of the affected environment are themselves no measure of the adequacy of an environmental impact statement.

§ 1502.16 Environmental consequences

This section forms the scientific and analytic basis for the comparisons under § 1502.14. It shall consolidate the discussions of those elements required by sections 102(2)(C)(i), (ii), (iv), and (v) of NEPA which are within the scope of the statement and as much of section 102(2)(C)(iii) as is necessary to support the comparisons. The discussion will include the environmental impacts of the alternatives including the proposed action, any adverse environmental effects which cannot be avoided should the proposal be implemented, the relationship between short-term uses of man's environment and the maintenance and enhancement of long-term productivity, and any irreversible or irretrievable commitments of resources which would be involved in the proposal should it be implemented. This section should not duplicate discussions in § 1502.14. It shall include discussions of:

(a) Direct effects and their significance (§ 1508.8).

(b) Indirect effects and their significance (§ 1508.8).

(c) Possible conflicts between the proposed action and the objectives of Federal, regional, State, and local (and in the case of a reservation, Indian tribe) land use plans, policies and controls for the area concerned. (See § 1506.2(d).)

(d) The environmental effects of alternatives including the proposed action. The comparisons under § 1502.14 will be based on this discussion.

(e) Energy requirements and conservation potential of various alternatives and mitigation measures.

(f) Natural or depletable resource requirements and conservation potential of various alternatives and mitigation measures.

(g) Urban quality, historic and cultural resources, and the design of the built environment, including the reuse and conservation potential of various alternatives and mitigation measures.

(h) Means to mitigate adverse environmental impacts (if not fully covered under § 1502.14(f)).

[43 FR 55994, Nov. 29, 1978; 44 FR 873, Jan. 3, 1979]

§ 1502.17 List of preparers

The environmental impact statement shall list the names, together with their qualifications (expertise, experience, professional disciplines), of the persons who were primarily responsible for preparing the environmental impact statement or significant background papers, including basic components of the statement (§§ 1502.6 and 1502.8). Where possible the persons who are responsible for a particular analysis, including analyses in background papers, shall be identified. Normally the list will not exceed two pages.

§ 1502.18 Appendix

If an agency prepares an appendix to an environmental impact statement the appendix shall:

(a) Consist of material prepared in connection with an environmental impact statement (as distinct from material which is not so prepared and which is incorporated by reference (§ 1502.21)).

(b) Normally consist of material which substantiates any analysis fundamental to the impact statement.

(c) Normally be analytic and relevant to the decision to be made.

(d) Be circulated with the environmental impact statement or be readily available on request.

§ 1502.19 Circulation of the environmental impact statement

Agencies shall circulate the entire draft and final environmental impact statements except for certain appendices as provided in

§ 1502.18(d) and unchanged statements as provided in § 1503.4(c). However, if the statement is unusually long, the agency may circulate the summary instead, except that the entire statement shall be furnished to:

(a) Any Federal agency which has jurisdiction by law or special expertise with respect to any environmental impact involved and any appropriate Federal, State or local agency authorized to develop and enforce environmental standards.

(b) The applicant, if any.

(c) Any person, organization, or agency requesting the entire environmental impact statement.

(d) In the case of a final environmental impact statement any person, organization, or agency which submitted substantive comments on the draft.

If the agency circulates the summary and thereafter receives a timely request for the entire statement and for additional time to comment, the time for that requestor only shall be extended by at least 15 days beyond the minimum period.

§ 1502.20 Tiering

Agencies are encouraged to tier their environmental impact statements to eliminate repetitive discussions of the same issues and to focus on the actual issues ripe for decision at each level of environmental review (§ 1508.28). Whenever a broad environmental impact statement has been prepared (such as a program or policy statement) and a subsequent statement or environmental assessment is then prepared on an action included within the entire program or policy (such as a site specific action) the subsequent statement or environmental assessment need only summarize the issues discussed in the broader statement and incorporate discussions from the broader statement by reference and shall concentrate on the issues specific to the subsequent action. The subsequent document shall state where the earlier document is available. Tiering may also be appropriate for different stages of actions. (Section 1508.28).

§ 1502.21 Incorporation by reference

Agencies shall incorporate material into an environmental impact statement by reference when the effect will be to cut down on bulk without impeding agency and public review of the action. The incorporated material shall be cited in the statement and its content briefly described. No material may be incorporated by reference unless it is reasonably available for inspection by potentially interested persons within the time allowed for comment. Material based on proprietary data which is itself not available for review and comment shall not be incorporated by reference.

§ 1502.22 Incomplete or unavailable information

When an agency is evaluating reasonably foreseeable significant adverse effects on the human environment in an environmental impact statement and there is incomplete or unavailable information, the agency shall always make clear that such information is lacking.

(a) If the incomplete information relevant to reasonably foreseeable significant adverse impacts is essential to a reasoned choice among alternatives and the overall costs of obtaining it are not exorbitant, the agency shall include the information in the environmental impact statement.

(b) If the information relevant to reasonably foreseeable significant adverse impacts cannot be obtained because the overall costs of obtaining it are exorbitant or the means to obtain it are not known, the agency shall include within the environmental impact statement: (1) A statement that such information is incomplete or unavailable; (2) a statement of the relevance of the incomplete or unavailable information to evaluating reasonably foreseeable significant adverse impacts on the human environment; (3) a summary of existing credible scientific evidence which is relevant to evaluating the reasonably foreseeable significant adverse impacts on the human environment, and (4) the agency's evaluation of such impacts based upon theoretical approaches or research methods generally accepted in the scientific community. For the purposes of this section, "reasonably foreseeable" includes impacts which have catastrophic consequences, even if their probability of occurrence is low, provided that the analysis of the impacts is supported by credible scientific evidence, is not based on pure conjecture, and is within the rule of reason.

(c) The amended regulation will be applicable to all environmental impact statements for which a Notice of Intent (40 CFR 1508.22) is published in the Federal Register on or after May 27, 1986. For environmental impact statements in progress, agencies may choose to comply with the requirements of either the original or amended regulation.

[51 FR 15625, Apr. 25, 1986]

§ 1502.23 Cost-benefit analysis

If a cost-benefit analysis relevant to the choice among environmentally different alternatives is being considered for the proposed action, it shall be incorporated by reference or appended to the statement as an aid in evaluating the environmental consequences. To assess the adequacy of compliance with section 102(2)(B) of the Act the statement shall, when a cost-benefit analysis is prepared, discuss the relationship between that analysis and any analyses of unquantified environmental impacts, values, and amenities. For purposes of complying with the Act, the weighing of the merits and drawbacks of the various alternatives need not be displayed in a monetary cost-benefit analysis and should not be when there are important qualitative considerations. In any event, an environmental impact statement should at least indicate those considerations, including factors not related to environmental quality, which are likely to be relevant and important to a decision.

§1502.24 Methodology and scientific accuracy

Agencies shall insure the professional integrity, including scientific integrity, of the discussions and analyses in environmental impact statements. They shall identify any methodologies used and shall make explicit reference by footnote to the scientific and other sources relied upon for conclusions in the statement. An agency may place discussion of methodology in an appendix.

§ 1502.25 Environmental review and consultation requirements

(a) To the fullest extent possible, agencies shall prepare draft environmental impact statements concurrently with and integrated with environmental impact analyses and related surveys and studies required by the Fish and Wildlife Coordination Act (16 U.S.C. 661 et seq.), the National Historic Preservation Act of 1966 (16 U.S.C. 470 et seq.), the Endangered Species Act of 1973 (16 U.S.C. 1531 et seq.), and other environmental review laws and executive orders.

(b) The draft environmental impact statement shall list all Federal permits, licenses, and other entitlements which must be obtained in implementing the proposal. If it is uncertain whether a Federal permit, license, or other entitlement is necessary, the draft environmental impact statement shall so indicate.

Part 1503

Commenting

Sec.

AUTHORITY: NEPA, the Environmental Quality Improvement Act of 1970, as amended (42 U.S.C. 4371 *et seq.*), sec. 309 of the Clean Air Act, as amended (42 U.S.C. 7609), and E.O. 11514 (Mar. 5, 1970, as amended by E.O. 11991, May 24, 1977).

SOURCE: 43 FR 55997, Nov. 29, 1978, unless otherwise noted.

§ 1503.1 Inviting comments

(a) After preparing a draft environmental impact statement and before preparing a final environmental impact statement the agency shall:

(1) Obtain the comments of any Federal agency which has jurisdiction by law or special expertise with respect to any environmental impact involved or which is authorized to develop and enforce environmental standards.

(2) Request the comments of:

(i) Appropriate State and local agencies which are authorized to develop and enforce environmental standards;

(ii) Indian tribes, when the effects may be on a reservation; and

(iii) Any agency which has requested that it receive statements on actions of the kind proposed.

Office of Management and Budget Circular A–95 (Revised), through its system of clearinghouses, provides a means of securing the views of State and local environmental agencies. The clearinghouses may be used, by mutual agreement of the lead agency and the clearinghouse, for securing State and local reviews of the draft environmental impact statements.

(3) Request comments from the applicant, if any.

(4) Request comments from the public, affirmatively soliciting comments from those persons or organizations who may be interested or affected.

(b) An agency may request comments on a final environmental impact statement before the decision is finally made. In any case other agencies or persons may make comments before the final decision unless a different time is provided under § 1506.10.

§ 1503.2 Duty to comment

Federal agencies with jurisdiction by law or special expertise with respect to any environmental impact involved and agencies which are authorized to develop and enforce environmental standards shall comment on statements within their jurisdiction, expertise, or authority. Agencies shall comment within the time period specified for comment in § 1506.10. A Federal agency may reply that it has no comment. If a cooperating agency is satisfied that its views are adequately reflected in the environmental impact statement, it should reply that it has no comment.

§ 1503.3 Specificity of comments

(a) Comments on an environmental impact statement or on a proposed action shall be as specific as possible and may address either the adequacy of the statement or the merits of the alternatives discussed or both.

(b) When a commenting agency criticizes a lead agency's predictive methodology, the commenting agency should describe the alternative methodology which it prefers and why.

(c) A cooperating agency shall specify in its comments whether it needs additional information to fulfill other applicable environmental reviews or consultation requirements and what information it needs. In particular, it shall specify any additional information it needs to comment adequately on the draft statement's analysis of significant site-specific effects associated with the granting or approving by that cooperating agency of necessary Federal permits, licenses, or entitlements.

(d) When a cooperating agency with jurisdiction by law objects to or expresses reservations about the proposal on grounds of environmental impacts, the agency expressing the objection or reservation shall specify the mitigation measures it considers necessary to allow the agency to grant or approve applicable permit, license, or related requirements or concurrences.

§ 1503.4 Response to comments

(a) An agency preparing a final environmental impact statement shall assess and consider comments both individually and collectively, and shall respond by one or more of the means listed below, stating its response in the final statement. Possible responses are to:

(1) Modify alternatives including the proposed action.

(2) Develop and evaluate alternatives not previously given serious consideration by the agency.

(3) Supplement, improve, or modify its analyses.

(4) Make factual corrections.

(5) Explain why the comments do not warrant further agency response, citing the sources, authorities, or reasons which support the agency's position and, if appropriate, indicate those circumstances which would trigger agency reappraisal or further response.

(b) All substantive comments received on the draft statement (or summaries thereof where the response has been exceptionally voluminous), should be attached to the final statement whether or not the comment is thought to merit individual discussion by the agency in the text of the statement.

(c) If changes in response to comments are minor and are confined to the responses described in paragraphs (a)(4) and (5) of this section, agencies may write them on errata sheets and attach them to the statement instead of rewriting the draft statement. In such cases only the comments, the responses, and the changes and not the final statement need be circulated (§ 1502.19). The entire document with a new cover sheet shall be filed as the final statement (§ 1506.9).

Part 1504

Predecision Referrals to the Council of Proposed Federal Actions Determined to be Environmentally Unsatisfactory

AUTHORITY: NEPA, the Environmental Quality Improvement Act of 1970, as amended (42 U.S.C. 4371 *et seq.*), sec. 309 of the Clean Air Act, as amended (42 U.S.C. 7609), and E.O. 11514 (Mar. 5, 1970, as amended by E.O. 11991, May 24, 1977).

SOURCE: 43 FR 55998, Nov. 29, 1978, unless otherwise noted.

§ 1504.1 Purpose

(a) This part establishes procedures for referring to the Council Federal interagency disagreements concerning proposed major Federal actions that might cause unsatisfactory environmental effects. It provides means for early resolution of such disagreements.

(b) Under section 309 of the Clean Air Act (42 U.S.C. 7609), the Administrator of the Environmental Protection Agency is directed to review and comment publicly on the environmental impacts of Federal activities, including actions for which environmental impact statements are prepared. If after this review the Administrator determines that the matter is "unsatisfactory from the standpoint of public health or welfare or environmental quality," section 309 directs that the matter be referred to the Council (hereafter "environmental referrals").

(c) Under section 102(2)(C) of the Act other Federal agencies may make similar reviews of environmental impact statements, including judgments on the acceptability of anticipated environmental impacts. These reviews must be made available to the President, the Council and the public.

§ 1504.2 Criteria for referral

Environmental referrals should be made to the Council only after concerted, timely (as early as possible in the process), but unsuccessful attempts to resolve differences with the lead agency. In determining what environmental objections to the matter are appropriate to refer to the Council, an agency should weigh potential adverse environmental impacts, considering:

(a) Possible violation of national environmental standards or policies.

(b) Severity.

(c) Geographical scope.

(d) Duration.

(e) Importance as precedents.

(f) Availability of environmentally preferable alternatives.

§ 1504.3 Procedure for referrals and response

(a) A Federal agency making the referral to the Council shall:

(1) Advise the lead agency at the earliest possible time that it intends to refer a matter to the Council unless a satisfactory agreement is reached.

(2) Include such advice in the referring agency's comments on the draft environmental impact statement, except when the statement does not contain adequate information to permit an assessment of the matter's environmental acceptability.

(3) Identify any essential information that is lacking and request that it be made available at the earliest possible time.

(4) Send copies of such advice to the Council.

(b) The referring agency shall deliver its referral to the Council not later than twenty-five (25) days after the final environmental impact statement has been made available to the Environmental Protection Agency, commenting agencies, and the public. Except when an extension of this period has been granted by the lead agency, the Council will not accept a referral after that date.

(c) The referral shall consist of:

(1) A copy of the letter signed by the head of the referring agency and delivered to the lead agency informing the lead agency of the referral and the reasons for it, and requesting that no action be taken to implement the matter until the Council acts upon the referral. The letter shall include a copy of the statement referred to in (c)(2) of this section.

(2) A statement supported by factual evidence leading to the conclusion that the matter is unsatisfactory from the standpoint of public health or welfare or environmental quality. The statement shall:

(i) Identify any material facts in controversy and incorporate (by reference if appropriate) agreed upon facts,

(ii) Identify any existing environmental requirements or policies which would be violated by the matter,

(iii) Present the reasons why the referring agency believes the matter is environmentally unsatisfactory,

(iv) Contain a finding by the agency whether the issue raised is of national importance because of the threat to national environmental resources or policies or for some other reason,

(v) Review the steps taken by the referring agency to bring its concerns to the attention of the lead agency at the earliest possible time, and

(vi) Give the referring agency's recommendations as to what mitigation alternative, further study, or other course of action (including abandonment of the matter) are necessary to remedy the situation.

(d) Not later than twenty-five (25) days after the referral to the Council the lead agency may deliver a response to the Council, and the referring agency. If the lead agency requests more time and gives assurance that the matter will not go forward in the interim, the Council may grant an extension. The response shall:

(1) Address fully the issues raised in the referral.

(2) Be supported by evidence.

(3) Give the lead agency's response to the referring agency's recommendations.

(e) Interested persons (including the applicant) may deliver their views in writing to the Council. Views in support of the referral should be delivered not later than the referral. Views in support of the response shall be delivered not later than the response.

(f) Not later than twenty-five (25) days after receipt of both the referral and any response or upon being informed that there will be no response (unless the lead agency agrees to a longer time), the Council may take one or more of the following actions:

(1) Conclude that the process of referral and response has successfully resolved the problem.

(2) Initiate discussions with the agencies with the objective of mediation with referring and lead agencies.

(3) Hold public meetings or hearings to obtain additional views and information.

(4) Determine that the issue is not one of national importance and request the referring and lead agencies to pursue their decision process.

(5) Determine that the issue should be further negotiated by the referring and lead agencies and is not appropriate for Council consideration until one or more heads of agencies report to the Council that the agencies' disagreements are irreconcilable.

(6) Publish its findings and recommendations (including where appropriate a finding that the submitted evidence does not support the position of an agency).

(7) When appropriate, submit the referral and the response together with the Council's recommendation to the President for action.

(g) The Council shall take no longer than 60 days to complete the actions specified in paragraph (f)(2), (3), or (5) of this section.

(h) When the referral involves an action required by statute to be determined on the record after opportunity for agency hearing, the referral shall be conducted in a manner consistent with 5 U.S.C. 557(d) (Administrative Procedure Act).

[43 FR 55998, Nov. 29, 1978; 44 FR 873, Jan. 3, 1979]

Part 1505

NEPA and Agency Decisionmaking

AUTHORITY: NEPA, the Environmental Quality Improvement Act of 1970, as amended (42 U.S.C. 4371 *et seq.*), sec. 309 of the Clean Air Act, as amended (42 U.S.C. 7609), and E.O. 11514 (Mar. 5, 1970, as amended by E.O. 11991, May 24, 1977).

SOURCE: 43 FR 55999, Nov. 29, 1978, unless otherwise noted.

§ 1505.1 Agency decisionmaking procedures

Agencies shall adopt procedures (§ 1507.3) to ensure that decisions are made in accordance with the policies and purposes of the Act. Such procedures shall include but not be limited to:

(a) Implementing procedures under section 102(2) to achieve the requirements of sections 101 and 102(1).

(b) Designating the major decision points for the agency's principal programs likely to have a significant effect on the human environment and assuring that the NEPA process corresponds with them.

(c) Requiring that relevant environmental documents, comments, and responses be part of the record in formal rulemaking or adjudicatory proceedings.

(d) Requiring that relevant environmental documents, comments, and responses accompany the proposal through existing agency review processes so that agency officials use the statement in making decisions.

(e) Requiring that the alternatives considered by the decisionmaker are encompassed by the range of alternatives discussed in the relevant environmental documents and that the decisionmaker consider the alternatives described in the environmental impact statement. If another decision document accompanies the relevant environmental documents to the decisionmaker, agencies are encouraged to make available to the public before the decision is made any part of that document that relates to the comparison of alternatives.

§ 1505.2 Record of decision in cases requiring environmental impact statements

At the time of its decision (§ 1506.10) or, if appropriate, its recommendation to Congress, each agency shall prepare a concise public record of decision. The record, which may be integrated into any other record prepared by the agency, including that required by OMB Circular A–95 (Revised), part I, sections 6(c) and (d), and part II, section 5(b)(4), shall:

(a) State what the decision was.

(b) Identify all alternatives considered by the agency in reaching its decision, specifying the alternative or alternatives which were considered to be environmentally preferable. An agency may discuss preferences among alternatives based on relevant factors including economic and technical considerations and agency statutory missions. An agency shall identify and discuss all such factors including any essential considerations of national policy which were balanced by the agency in making its decision and state how those considerations entered into its decision.

(c) State whether all practicable means to avoid or minimize environmental harm from the alternative selected have been adopted, and if not, why they were not. A monitoring and enforcement program shall be adopted and summarized where applicable for any mitigation.

§ 1505.3 Implementing the decision

Agencies may provide for monitoring to assure that their decisions are carried out and should do so in important cases. Mitigation (§ 1505.2(c)) and other conditions established in the environmental impact statement or during its review and committed as part of the decision shall be implemented by the lead agency or other appropriate consenting agency. The lead agency shall:

(a) Include appropriate conditions in grants, permits or other approvals.

(b) Condition funding of actions on mitigation.

(c) Upon request, inform cooperating or commenting agencies on progress in carrying out mitigation measures which they have proposed and which were adopted by the agency making the decision.

(d) Upon request, make available to the public the results of relevant monitoring.

Part 1506

Other Requirements of NEPA

Sec.

AUTHORITY: NEPA, the Environmental Quality Improvement Act of 1970, as amended (42 U.S.C. 4371 *et seq.*), sec. 309 of the Clean Air Act, as amended (42 U.S.C. 7609), and E.O. 11514 (Mar. 5, 1970, as amended by E.O. 11991, May 24, 1977).

SOURCE: 43 FR 56000, Nov. 29, 1978, unless otherwise noted.

§ 1506.1 Limitations on actions during NEPA process

(a) Until an agency issues a record of decision as provided in § 1505.2 (except as provided in paragraph (c) of this section), no action concerning the proposal shall be taken which would:

(1) Have an adverse environmental impact; or

(2) Limit the choice of reasonable alternatives.

(b) If any agency is considering an application from a non-Federal entity, and is aware that the applicant is about to take an action within the agency's jurisdiction that would meet either of the criteria in paragraph (a) of this section, then the agency shall promptly notify the applicant that the agency will take appropriate action to insure that the objectives and procedures of NEPA are achieved.

(c) While work on a required program environmental impact statement is in progress and the action is not covered by an existing program statement, agencies shall not undertake in the interim any major Federal action covered by the program which may significantly affect the quality of the human environment unless such action:

(1) Is justified independently of the program;

(2) Is itself accompanied by an adequate environmental impact statement; and

(3) Will not prejudice the ultimate decision on the program. Interim action prejudices the ultimate decision on the program

when it tends to determine subsequent development or limit alternatives.

(d) This section does not preclude development by applicants of plans or designs or performance of other work necessary to support an application for Federal, State or local permits or assistance. Nothing in this section shall preclude Rural Electrification Administration approval of minimal expenditures not affecting the environment (*e.g.* long leadtime equipment and purchase options) made by non-governmental entities seeking loan guarantees from the Administration.

§ 1506.2 Elimination of duplication with State and local procedures

(a) Agencies authorized by law to cooperate with State agencies of statewide jurisdiction pursuant to section 102(2)(D) of the Act may do so.

(b) Agencies shall cooperate with State and local agencies to the fullest extent possible to reduce duplication between NEPA and State and local requirements, unless the agencies are specifically barred from doing so by some other law. Except for cases covered by paragraph (a) of this section, such cooperation shall to the fullest extent possible include:

(1) Joint planning processes.

(2) Joint environmental research and studies.

(3) Joint public hearings (except where otherwise provided by statute.

(4) Joint environmental assessments.

(c) Agencies shall cooperate with State and local agencies to the fullest extent possible to reduce duplication between NEPA and comparable State and local requirements, unless the agencies are specifically barred from doing so by some other law. Except for cases covered by paragraph (a) of this section, such cooperation shall to the fullest extent possible include joint environmental impact statements. In such cases one or more Federal agencies and one or more State or local agencies shall be joint lead agencies. Where State laws or local ordinances have environmental impact statement requirements in addition to but not in conflict with those in NEPA, Federal agencies shall cooperate in fulfilling these requirements as well as those of Federal laws so that one document will comply with all applicable laws.

(d) To better integrate environmental impact statements into State or local planning processes, statements shall discuss any inconsistency of a proposed action with any approved State or local plan and laws (whether or not federally sanctioned). Where an inconsistency exists, the statement should describe the extent to which the agency would reconcile its proposed action with the plan or law.

§ 1506.3 Adoption

(a) An agency may adopt a Federal draft or final environmental impact statement or portion thereof provided that the statement or portion thereof meets the standards for an adequate statement under these regulations.

(b) If the actions covered by the original environmental impact statement and the proposed action are substantially the same, the agency adopting another agency's statement is not required to recirculate it except as a final statement. Otherwise the adopting agency shall treat the statement as a draft and recirculate it (except as provided in paragraph (c) of this section).

(c) A cooperating agency may adopt without recirculating the environmental impact statement of a lead agency when, after an independent review of the statement, the cooperating agency concludes that its comments and suggestions have been satisfied.

(d) When an agency adopts a statement which is not final within the agency that prepared it, or when the action it assesses is the subject of a referral under Part 1504, or when the statement's adequacy is the subject of a judicial action which is not final, the agency shall so specify.

§ 1506.4 Combining documents

Any environmental document in compliance with NEPA may be combined with any other agency document to reduce duplication and paperwork.

§ 1506.5 Agency responsibility

(a) *Information.* If an agency requires an applicant to submit environmental information for possible use by the agency in preparing an environmental impact statement, then the agency should assist the applicant by outlining the types of information required. The agency shall independently evaluate the information submitted and shall be responsible for its accuracy. If the agency chooses to use the information submitted by the applicant in the environmental impact statement, either directly or by reference, then the names of the persons responsible for the independent evaluation shall be included in the list of preparers (§ 1502.17). It is the intent of this paragraph that acceptable work not be redone, but that it be verified by the agency.

(b) *Environmental assessments.* If an agency permits an applicant to prepare an environmental assessment, the agency, besides fulfilling the requirements of paragraph (a) of this section, shall make its own evaluation of the environmental issues and take responsibility for the scope and content of the environmental assessment.

(c) *Environmental impact statements.* Except as provided in §§ 1506.2 and 1506.3 any environmental impact statement prepared pursuant to the requirements of NEPA shall be prepared directly by or by a contractor selected by the lead agency or where appropriate under § 1501.6(b), a cooperating agency. It is the intent of these regulations that the contractor be chosen solely by the lead agency, or by the lead agency in cooperation with cooperating agencies, or where appropriate by a cooperating agency to avoid any conflict of interest. Contractors shall execute a disclosure statement prepared by the lead agency, or where appropriate the cooperating agency, specifying that they have no financial or other interest in the outcome of the project. If the document is prepared by contract, the responsible Federal official shall furnish guidance and participate in the preparation and shall independently evaluate the statement prior to its approval and take responsibility for its scope and contents. Nothing in this section is intended to prohibit any agency from requesting any person to submit information to it or prohibit any person from submitting information to any agency.

§ 1506.6 Public involvement

Agencies shall:

(a) Make diligent efforts to involve the public in preparing and implementing their NEPA procedures.

(b) Provide public notice of NEPA-related hearings, public meetings, and the availability of environmental documents so as to inform those persons and agencies who may be interested or affected.

(1) In all cases the agency shall mail notice to those who have requested it on an individual action.

(2) In the case of an action with effects of national concern notice shall include publication in the FEDERAL REGISTER and notice by mail to national organizations reasonably expected to be interested in the matter and may include listing in the *102 Monitor.* An agency engaged in rulemaking may provide notice by mail to national organizations who have requested that notice regularly be provided. Agencies shall maintain a list of such organizations.

(3) In the case of an action with effects primarily of local concern the notice may include:

(i) Notice to State and areawide clearinghouses pursuant to OMB Circular A–95 (Revised).

(ii) Notice to Indian tribes when effects may occur on reservations.

(iii) Following the affected State's public notice procedures for comparable actions.

(iv) Publication in local newspapers (in papers of general circulation rather than legal papers).

(v) Notice through other local media.

(vi) Notice to potentially interested community organizations including small business associations.

(vii) Publication in newsletters that may be expected to reach potentially interested persons.

(viii) Direct mailing to owners and occupants of nearby or affected property.

(ix) Posting of notice on and off site in the area where the action is to be located.

(c) Hold or sponsor public hearings or public meetings whenever appropriate or in accordance with statutory requirements applicable to the agency. Criteria shall include whether there is:

(1) Substantial environmental controversy concerning the proposed action or substantial interest in holding the hearing.

(2) A request for a hearing by another agency with jurisdiction over the action supported by reasons why a hearing will be helpful. If a draft environmental impact statement is to be considered at a public hearing, the agency should make the statement available to the public at least 15 days in advance (unless the purpose of the hearing is to provide information for the draft environmental impact statement).

(d) Solicit appropriate information from the public.

(e) Explain in its procedures where interested persons can get information or status reports on environmental impact statements and other elements of the NEPA process.

(f) Make environmental impact statements, the comments received, and any underlying documents available to the public pursuant to the provisions of the Freedom of Information Act (5 U.S.C. 552), without regard to the exclusion for interagency memoranda where such memoranda transmit comments of Federal agencies on the environmental impact of the proposed action. Materials to be made available to the public shall be provided to the public without charge to the extent practicable, or at a fee which is not more than the actual costs of reproducing copies required to be sent to other Federal agencies, including the Council.

§ 1506.7 Further guidance

The Council may provide further guidance concerning NEPA and its procedures including:

(a) A handbook which the Council may supplement from time to time, which shall in plain language provide guidance and instructions concerning the application of NEPA and these regulations.

(b) Publication of the Council's Memoranda to Heads of Agencies.

(c) In conjunction with the Environmental Protection Agency and the publication of the 102 Monitor, notice of:

(1) Research activities;

(2) Meetings and conferences related to NEPA; and

(3) Successful and innovative procedures used by agencies to implement NEPA.

§ 1506.8 Proposals for legislation

(a) The NEPA process for proposals for legislation (§ 1508.17) significantly affecting the quality of the human environment shall be integrated with the legislative process of the Congress. A legislative environmental impact statement is the detailed statement required by law to be included in a recommendation or report on a legislative proposal to Congress. A legislative environmental impact statement shall be considered part of the formal transmittal of a legislative proposal to Congress; however, it may be transmitted to Congress up to 30 days later in order to allow time for completion of an accurate statement which can serve as the basis for public and Congressional debate. The statement must be available in time for Congressional hearings and deliberations.

(b) Preparation of a legislative environmental impact statement shall conform to the requirements of these regulations except as follows:

(1) There need not be a scoping process.

(2) The legislative statement shall be prepared in the same manner as a draft statement, but shall be considered the "detailed statement" required by statute; *Provided,* That when any of the following conditions exist both the draft and final environmental impact statement on the legislative proposal shall be prepared and circulated as provided by §§ 1503.1 and 1506.10.

(i) A Congressional Committee with jurisdiction over the proposal has a rule requiring both draft and final environmental impact statements.

(ii) The proposal results from a study process required by statute (such as those required by the Wild and Scenic Rivers Act (16 U.S.C. 1271 et seq.) and the Wilderness Act (16 U.S.C. 1131 et seq.)).

(iii) Legislative approval is sought for Federal or federally assisted construction or other projects which the agency recommends be located at specific geographic locations. For proposals requiring an environmental impact statement for the acquisition of space by the General Services Administration, a draft statement shall accompany the Prospectus or the 11(b) Report of Building Project Surveys to the Congress, and a final statement shall be completed before site acquisition.

(iv) The agency decides to prepare draft and final statements.

(c) Comments on the legislative statement shall be given to the lead agency which shall forward them along with its own responses to the Congressional committees with jurisdiction.

§ 1506.9 Filing requirements

Environmental impact statements together with comments and responses shall be filed with the Environmental Protection Agency, attention Office of Federal Activities (A–104), 401 M Street SW., Washington, D.C. 20460. Statements shall be filed with EPA no earlier than they are also transmitted to commenting agencies and made available to the public. EPA shall deliver one copy of each statement to the Council, which shall satisfy the requirement of availability to the President. EPA may issue guidelines to agencies to implement its responsibilities under this section and § 1506.10.

§ 1506.10 Timing of agency action

(a) The Environmental Protection Agency shall publish a notice in the Federal Register each week of the environmental impact statements filed during the preceding week. The minimum time periods set forth in this section shall be calculated from the date of publication of this notice.

(b) No decision on the proposed action shall be made or recorded under § 1505.2 by a Federal agency until the later of the following dates:

(1) Ninety (90) days after publication of the notice described above in paragraph (a) of this section for a draft environmental impact statement.

(2) Thirty (30) days after publication of the notice described above in paragraph (a) of this section for a final environmental impact statement.

An exception to the rules on timing may be made in the case of an agency decision which is subject to a formal internal appeal. Some agencies have a formally established appeal process which allows other agencies or the public to take appeals on a decision and make their views known, after publication of the final environmental impact statement. In such cases, where a real opportunity exists to alter the decision, the decision may be made and recorded at the same time the environmental impact statement is published. This means that the period for appeal of the decision and the 30-day period prescribed in paragraph (b)(2) of this section may run concurrently. In such cases the environmental impact statement shall explain the timing and the public's right of appeal. An agency engaged in rulemaking under the Administrative Procedure Act or other statute for the purpose of protecting the public health or safety, may waive the time period in paragraph (b)(2) of this section and publish a decision on the final rule simultaneously with publication of the notice of the availability of the final environmental impact statement as described in paragraph (a) of this section.

(c) If the final environmental impact statement is filed within ninety (90) days after a draft environmental impact statement is filed with the Environmental Protection Agency, the minimum thirty (30) day period and the minimum ninety (90) day period may run concurrently. However, subject to paragraph (d) of this section agencies shall allow not less than 45 days for comments on draft statements.

(d) The lead agency may extend prescribed periods. The Environmental Protection Agency may upon a showing by the lead agency of compelling reasons of national policy reduce the prescribed periods and may upon a showing by any other Federal agency of compelling reasons of national policy also extend prescribed periods, but only after consultation with the lead agency. (Also see § 1507.3(d).) Failure to file timely comments shall not be a sufficient reason for extending a period. If the lead agency does not concur with the extension of time, EPA may not extend it for more than 30 days. When the Environmental Protection Agency reduces or extends any period of time it shall notify the Council.

[43 FR 56000, Nov. 29, 1978; 44 FR 874, Jan. 3, 1979]

§ 1506.11 Emergencies

Where emergency circumstances make it necessary to take an action with significant environmental impact without observing the provisions of these regulations, the Federal agency taking the action should consult with the Council about alternative arrangements. Agencies and the Council will limit such arrangements to actions necessary to control the immediate impacts of the emergency. Other actions remain subject to NEPA review.

§ 1506.12 Effective date

The effective date of these regulations is July 30, 1979, except that for agencies that administer programs that qualify under section 102(2)(D) of the Act or under sec. 104(h) of the Housing and Community Development Act of 1974 an additional four months shall be allowed for the State or local agencies to adopt their implementing procedures.

(a) These regulations shall apply to the fullest extent practicable to ongoing activities and environmental documents begun before the effective date. These regulations do not apply to an environmental impact statement or supplement if the draft statement was filed before the effective date of these regulations. No completed environmental documents need be redone by reasons of these regulations. Until these regulations are applicable, the Council's guidelines published in the FEDERAL REGISTER of August 1, 1973, shall continue to be applicable. In cases where these regulations are applicable the guidelines are superseded. However, nothing shall prevent an agency from proceeding under these regulations at an earlier time.

(b) NEPA shall continue to be applicable to actions begun before January 1, 1970, to the fullest extent possible.

Part 1507

Agency Compliance

AUTHORITY: NEPA, the Environmental Quality Improvement Act of 1970, as amended (42 U.S.C. 4371 *et seq.*), sec. 309 of the Clean Air Act, as amended (42 U.S.C. 7609), and E.O. 11514 (Mar. 5, 1970, as amended by E.O. 11991, May 24, 1977).

SOURCE: 43 FR 56002, Nov. 29, 1978, unless otherwise noted.

§ 1507.1 Compliance

All agencies of the Federal Government shall comply with these regulations. It is the intent of these regulations to allow each agency flexibility in adapting its implementing procedures authorized by § 1507.3 to the requirements of other applicable laws.

§ 1507.2 Agency capability to comply

Each agency shall be capable (in terms of personnel and other resources) of complying with the requirements enumerated below. Such compliance may include use of other's resources, but the using agency shall itself have sufficient capability to evaluate what others do for it. Agencies shall:

(a) Fulfill the requirements of section 102(2)(A) of the Act to utilize a systematic, interdisciplinary approach which will insure the integrated use of the natural and social sciences and the environmental design arts in planning and in decisionmaking which may have an impact on the human environment. Agencies shall designate a person to be responsible for overall review of agency NEPA compliance.

(b) Identify methods and procedures required by section 102(2)(B) to insure that presently unquantified environmental amenities and value may be given appropriate consideration.

(c) Prepare adequate environmental impact statements pursuant to section 102(2)(C) and comment on statements in the areas where the agency has jurisdiction by law or special expertise or is authorized to develop and enforce environmental standards.

(d) Study, develop, and describe alternatives to recommended courses of action in any proposal which involves unresolved conflicts concerning alternative uses of available resources. This requirement of section 102(2)(E) extends to all such proposals, not just the more limited scope of section 102(2)(C)(iii) where the discussion of alternatives is confined to impact statements.

(e) Comply with the requirements of section 102(2)(H) that the agency initiate and utilize ecological information in the planning and development of resource-oriented projects.

(f) Fulfill the requirements of sections 102(2)(F), 102(2)(G), and 102(2)(I), of the Act and of Executive Order 11514, Protection and Enhancement of Environmental Quality, Sec. 2.

§ 1507.3 Agency procedures

(a) Not later than eight months after publication of these regulations as finally adopted in the FEDERAL REGISTER, or five months after the establishment of an agency, whichever shall come later, each agency shall as necessary adopt procedures to supplement these regulations. When the agency is a department, major subunits are encouraged (with the consent of the department) to adopt their own procedures. Such procedures shall not paraphrase these regulations. They shall confine themselves to implementing procedures. Each agency shall consult with the Council while developing its procedures and before publishing them in the FEDERAL REGISTER for comment. Agencies with similar programs should consult with each other and the Council to coordinate their procedures, especially for programs requesting similar information from applicants. The procedures shall be adopted only after an opportunity for public review and after review by the Council for conformity with the Act and these regulations. The Council shall complete its review within 30 days. Once in effect they shall be filed with the Council and made readily available to the public. Agencies are encouraged to publish explanatory guidance for these regulations and their own procedures. Agencies shall continue to review their policies and procedures and in consultation with the Council to revise them as necessary to ensure full compliance with the purposes and provisions of the Act.

(b) Agency procedures shall comply with these regulations except where compliance would be inconsistent with statutory requirements and shall include:

(1) Those procedures required by §§ 1501.2(d), 1502.9(c)(3), 1505.1, 1506.6(e), and 1508.4.

(2) Specific criteria for and identification of those typical classes of action:

(i) Which normally do require environmental impact statements.

(ii) Which normally do not require either an environmental impact statement or an environmental assessment (categorical exclusions (§ 1508.4)).

(iii) Which normally require environmental assessments but not necessarily environmental impact statements.

(c) Agency procedures may include specific criteria for providing limited exceptions to the provisions of these regulations for classified proposals. They are proposed actions which are specifically authorized under criteria established by an Executive Order or statute to be kept secret in the interest of national defense or foreign policy and are in fact properly classified pursuant to such Executive Order or statute. Environmental assessments and environmental impact statements which address classified proposals may be safeguarded and restricted from public dissemination in accordance with agencies' own regulations applicable to classified information. These documents may be organized so that classified portions can be included as annexes, in order that the unclassified portions can be made available to the public.

(d) Agency procedures may provide for periods of time other than those presented in § 1506.10 when necessary to comply with other specific statutory requirements.

(e) Agency procedures may provide that where there is a lengthy period between the agency's decision to prepare an environmental impact statement and the time of actual preparation, the notice of intent required by § 1501.7 may be published at a reasonable time in advance of preparation of the draft statement.

Part 1508

Terminology and Index

Sec.

AUTHORITY: NEPA, the Environmental Quality Improvement Act of 1970, as amended (42 U.S.C. 4371 *et seq.*), sec. 309 of the Clear Air Act, as amended (42 U.S.C. 7609), and E.O. 11514 (Mar. 5, 1970, as amended by E.O. 11991, May 24, 1977).

SOURCE: 43 FR 56003, Nov. 29, 1978, unless otherwise noted.

§ 1508.1 Terminology

The terminology of this part shall be uniform throughout the Federal Government.

§ 1508.2 Act

"Act" means the National Environmental Policy Act, as amended (42 U.S.C. 4321, et seq.) which is also referred to as "NEPA."

§ 1508.3 Affecting

"Affecting" means will or may have an effect on.

§ 1508.4 Categorical exclusion

"Categorical exclusion" means a category of actions which do not individually or cumulatively have a significant effect on the human environment and which have been found to have no such effect in procedures adopted by a Federal agency in implementation of these regulations (§ 1507.3) and for which, therefore, neither an environmental assessment nor an environmental impact statement is required. An agency may decide in its procedures or otherwise, to prepare environmental assessments for the reasons stated in § 1508.9 even though it is not required to do so. Any procedures under this section shall provide for extraordinary circumstances in which a normally excluded action may have a significant environmental effect.

§ 1508.5 Cooperating agency

"Cooperating agency" means any Federal agency other than a lead agency which has jurisdiction by law or special expertise with respect to any environmental impact involved in a proposal (or a reasonable alternative) for legislation or other major Federal action significantly affecting the quality of the human environment. The selection and responsibilities of a cooperating agency are described in § 1501.6. A State or local agency of similar qualifications or, when the effects are on a reservation, an Indian Tribe, may by agreement with the lead agency become a cooperating agency.

§ 1508.6 Council

"Council" means the Council on Environmental Quality established by Title II of the Act.

§ 1508.7 Cumulative impact

"Cumulative impact" is the impact on the environment which results from the incremental impact of the action when added to other past, present, and reasonably foreseeable future actions regardless of what agency (Federal or non-Federal) or person undertakes such other actions. Cumulative impacts can result from individually minor but collectively significant actions taking place over a period of time.

§ 1508.8 Effects

"Effects" include:

(a) Direct effects, which are caused by the action and occur at the same time and place.

(b) Indirect effects, which are caused by the action and are later in time or farther removed in distance, but are still reasonably foreseeable. Indirect effects may include growth inducing effects and other effects related to induced changes in the pattern of land use, population density or growth rate, and related effects on air and water and other natural systems, including ecosystems.

Effects and impacts as used in these regulations are synonymous. Effects includes ecological (such as the effects on natural resources and on the components, structures, and functioning of affected ecosystems), aesthetic, historic, cultural, economic, social, or health, whether direct, indirect, or cumulative. Effects may also include those resulting from actions which may have both beneficial and detrimental effects, even if on balance the agency believes that the effect will be beneficial.

§ 1508.9 Environmental assessment

"Environmental assessment":

(a) Means a concise public document for which a Federal agency is responsible that serves to:

(1) Briefly provide sufficient evidence and analysis for determining whether to prepare an environmental impact statement or a finding of no significant impact.

(2) Aid an agency's compliance with the Act when no environmental impact statement is necessary.

(3) Facilitate preparation of a statement when one is necessary.

(b) Shall include brief discussions of the need for the proposal, of alternatives as required by section 102(2)(E), of the environmental impacts of the proposed action and alternatives, and a listing of agencies and persons consulted.

§ 1508.10 Environmental document

"Environmental document" includes the documents specified in § 1508.9 (environmental assessment), § 1508.11 (environmental impact statement), § 1508.13 (finding of no significant impact), and § 1508.22 (notice of intent).

§ 1508.11 Environmental impact statement

"Environmental impact statement" means a detailed written statement as required by section 102(2)(C) of the Act.

§ 1508.12 Federal agency

"Federal agency" means all agencies of the Federal Government. It does not mean the Congress, the Judiciary, or the President, including the performance of staff functions for the President in his Executive Office. It also includes for purposes of these regulations States and units of general local government and Indian tribes assuming NEPA responsibilities under section 104(h) of the Housing and Community Development Act of 1974.

§ 1508.13 Finding of no significant impact

"Finding of no significant impact" means a document by a Federal agency briefly presenting the reasons why an action, not otherwise excluded (§ 1508.4), will not have a significant effect on the human environment and for which an environmental impact statement therefore will not be prepared. It shall include the environmental assessment or a summary of it and shall note any other environmental documents related to it (§ 1501.7(a)(5)). If the assessment is included, the finding need not repeat any of the discussion in the assessment but may incorporate it by reference.

§ 1508.14 Human environment

"Human environment" shall be interpreted comprehensively to include the natural and physical environment and the relationship of people with that environment. (See the definition of "effects" (§ 1508.8).) This means that economic or social effects are not intended by themselves to require preparation of an environmental impact statement. When an environmental impact statement is prepared and economic or social and natural or physical environmental effects are interrelated, then the environmental impact statement will discuss all of these effects on the human environment.

§ 1508.15 Jurisdiction by law

"Jurisdiction by law" means agency authority to approve, veto, or finance all or part of the proposal.

§ 1508.16 Lead agency

"Lead agency" means the agency or agencies preparing or having taken primary responsibility for preparing the environmental impact statement.

§ 1508.17 Legislation

"Legislation" includes a bill or legislative proposal to Congress developed by or with the significant cooperation and support of a Federal agency, but does not include requests for appropriations. The test for significant cooperation is whether the proposal is in fact predominantly that of the agency rather than another source. Drafting does not by itself constitute significant cooperation. Proposals for legislation include requests for ratification of treaties. Only the agency which has primary responsibility for the subject matter involved will prepare a legislative environmental impact statement.

§ 1508.18 Major Federal action

"Major Federal action" includes actions with effects that may be major and which are potentially subject to Federal control and responsibility. Major reinforces but does not have a meaning independent of significantly (§ 1508.27). Actions include the circumstance where the responsible officials fail to act and that failure to act is reviewable by courts or administrative tribunals under the Administrative Procedure Act or other applicable law as agency action.

(a) Actions include new and continuing activities, including projects and programs entirely or partly financed, assisted, conducted, regulated, or approved by federal agencies; new or revised agency rules, regulations, plans, policies, or procedures; and legislative proposals (§§ 1506.8, 1508.17). Actions do not include funding assistance solely in the form of general revenue sharing funds, distributed under the State and Local Fiscal Assistance Act of 1972, 31 U.S.C. 1221 et seq., with no Federal agency control over the subsequent use of such funds. Actions do not include bringing judicial or administrative civil or criminal enforcement actions.

(b) Federal actions tend to fall within one of the following categories:

(1) Adoption of official policy, such as rules, regulations, and interpretations adopted pursuant to the Administrative Procedure Act, 5 U.S.C. 551 et seq.; treaties and international conventions or agreements; formal documents establishing an agency's policies which will result in or substantially alter agency programs.

(2) Adoption of formal plans, such as official documents prepared or approved by federal agencies which guide or prescribe alternative uses of federal resources, upon which future agency actions will be based.

(3) Adoption of programs, such as a group of concerted actions to implement a specific policy or plan; systematic and connected agency decisions allocating agency resources to implement a specific statutory program or executive directive.

(4) Approval of specific projects, such as construction or management activities located in a defined geographic area. Projects include actions approved by permit or other regulatory decision as well as federal and federally assisted activities.

§ 1508.19 Matter

"Matter" includes for purposes of Part 1504:

(a) With respect to the Environmental Protection Agency, any proposed legislation, project, action or regulation as those terms are used in section 309(a) of the Clean Air Act (42 U.S.C. 7609).

(b) With respect to all other agencies, any proposed major federal action to which section 102(2)(C) of NEPA applies.

§ 1508.20 Mitigation

"Mitigation" includes:

(a) Avoiding the impact altogether by not taking a certain action or parts of an action.

(b) Minimizing impacts by limiting the degree or magnitude of the action and its implementation.

(c) Rectifying the impact by repairing, rehabilitating, or restoring the affected environment.

(d) Reducing or eliminating the impact over time by preservation and maintenance operations during the life of the action.

(e) Compensating for the impact by replacing or providing substitute resources or environments.

§ 1508.21 NEPA process

"NEPA process" means all measures necessary for compliance with the requirements of section 2 and Title I of NEPA.

§ 1508.22 Notice of intent

"Notice of intent" means a notice that an environmental impact statement will be prepared and considered. The notice shall briefly:

(a) Describe the proposed action and possible alternatives.

(b) Describe the agency's proposed scoping process including whether, when, and where any scoping meeting will be held.

(c) State the name and address of a person within the agency who can answer questions about the proposed action and the environmental impact statement.

§ 1508.23 Proposal

"Proposal" exists at that stage in the development of an action when an agency subject to the Act has a goal and is actively preparing to make a decision on one or more alternative means of accomplishing that goal and the effects can be meaningfully evaluated. Preparation of an environmental impact statement on a proposal should be timed (§ 1502.5) so that the final statement may be completed in time for the statement to be included in any recommendation or report on the proposal. A proposal may exist in fact as well as by agency declaration that one exists.

§ 1508.24 Referring agency

"Referring agency" means the federal agency which has referred any matter to the Council after a determination that the matter is unsatisfactory from the standpoint of public health or welfare or environmental quality.

§ 1508.25 Scope

Scope consists of the range of actions, alternatives, and impacts to be considered in an environmental impact statement. The scope of an individual statement may depend on its relationships to other statements (§§ 1502.20 and 1508.28). To determine the scope of environmental impact statements, agencies shall consider 3 types of actions, 3 types of alternatives, and 3 types of impacts. They include:

(a) Actions (other than unconnected single actions) which may be:

(1) Connected actions, which means that they are closely related and therefore should be discussed in the same impact statement. Actions are connected if they:

(i) Automatically trigger other actions which may require environmental impact statements.

(ii) Cannot or will not proceed unless other actions are taken previously or simultaneously.

(iii) Are interdependent parts of a larger action and depend on the larger action for their justification.

(2) Cumulative actions, which when viewed with other proposed actions have cumulatively significant impacts and should therefore be discussed in the same impact statement.

(3) Similar actions, which when viewed with other reasonably foreseeable or proposed agency actions, have similarities that provide a basis for evaluating their environmental consequences together, such as common timing or geography. An agency may wish to analyze these actions in the same impact statement. It should do so when the best way to assess adequately the combined impacts of similar actions or reasonable alternatives to such actions is to treat them in a single impact statement.

(b) Alternatives, which include: (1) No action alternative.

(2) Other reasonable courses of actions.

(3) Mitigation measures (not in the proposed action).

(c) Impacts, which may be: (1) Direct; (2) indirect; (3) cumulative.

§ 1508.26 Special expertise

"Special expertise" means statutory responsibility, agency mission, or related program experience.

§ 1508.27 Significantly

"Significantly" as used in NEPA requires considerations of both context and intensity:

(a) *Context.* This means that the significance of an action must be analyzed in several contexts such as society as a whole (human, national), the affected region, the affected interests, and the locality. Significance varies with the setting of the proposed action. For instance, in the case of a site-specific action, significance would usually depend upon the effects in the locale rather than in the world as a whole. Both short- and long-term effects are relevant.

(b) *Intensity.* This refers to the severity of impact. Responsible officials must bear in mind that more than one agency may make decisions about partial aspects of a major action. The following should be considered in evaluating intensity:

(1) Impacts that may be both beneficial and adverse. A significant effect may exist even if the Federal agency believes that on balance the effect will be beneficial.

(2) The degree to which the proposed action affects public health or safety.

(3) Unique characteristics of the geographic area such as proximity to historic or cultural resources, park lands, prime farmlands, wetlands, wild and scenic rivers, or ecologically critical areas.

(4) The degree to which the effects on the quality of the human environment are likely to be highly controversial.

(5) The degree to which the possible effects on the human environment are highly uncertain or involve unique or unknown risks.

(6) The degree to which the action may establish a precedent for future actions with significant effects or represents a decision in principle about a future consideration.

(7) Whether the action is related to other actions with individually insignificant but cumulatively significant impacts. Significance exists if it is reasonable to anticipate a cumulatively significant impact on the environment. Significance cannot be avoided by terming an action temporary or by breaking it down into small component parts.

(8) The degree to which the action may adversely affect districts, sites, highways, structures, or objects listed in or eligible for listing in the National Register of Historic Places or may cause loss or destruction of significant scientific, cultural, or historical resources.

(9) The degree to which the action may adversely affect an endangered or threatened species or its habitat that has been determined to be critical under the Endangered Species Act of 1973.

(10) Whether the action threatens a violation of Federal, State, or local law or requirements imposed for the protection of the environment.

[43 FR 56003, Nov. 29, 1978; 44 FR 874, Jan. 3, 1979]

§ 1508.28 Tiering

"Tiering" refers to the coverage of general matters in broader environmental impact statements (such as national program or policy statements) with subsequent narrower statements or environmental analyses (such as regional or basinwide program statements or ultimately site-specific statements) incorporating by reference the general discussions and concentrating solely on the issues specific to the statement subsequently prepared. Tiering is appropriate when the sequence of statements or analyses is:

(a) From a program, plan, or policy environmental impact statement to a program, plan, or policy statement or analysis of lesser scope or to a site-specific statement or analysis.

(b) From an environmental impact statement on a specific action at an early stage (such as need and site selection) to a supplement (which is preferred) or a subsequent statement or analysis at a later stage (such as environmental mitigation). Tiering in such cases is appropriate when it helps the lead agency to focus on the issues which are ripe for decision and exclude from consideration issues already decided or not yet ripe.

Part 1515

Freedom of Information Act Procedures

AUTHORITY: 5 U.S.C. 552, as amended by Pub.L. 93–502.

SOURCE: 42 FR 65158, Dec. 30, 1977, unless otherwise noted.

PURPOSES

§ 1515.1 What are these procedures?

The Freedom of Information Act (5 U.S.C. 552, commonly known as FOIA) is a law which creates a procedure for any person to request official documents and other records from United States Government agencies. The law requires every Federal agency to make available to the public the material requested, unless the material falls under one of the limited exceptions stated in section 552(b)(5) of the Act, and the agency has good reason to refuse the request. These procedures explain how the Council on Environmental Quality—one of several offices in the Executive Office of the President—will carry out the Freedom of Information Act. They are written from the standpoint of a member of the public requesting material from the Council.

ORGANIZATION OF CEQ

§ 1515.2 What is the Council on Environmental Quality (CEQ)?

(a) The Council on Environmental Quality ("CEQ" or "the Council") was created by the National Environmental Policy Act of 1969, as amended (42 U.S.C. 4321–4347). The Council's authority is derived from that Act, the Environmental Quality Improvement Act of 1970, as amended (42 U.S.C. 4371–4374), Reorganization Plan No. 1 of 1977 (July 15, 1977), and Executive Order 11514, Protection and Enhancement of Environmental Quality, March 5, 1970, as amended by Executive Order 11991, May 24, 1977.

(b) The Council's primary responsibilities include the following:

(1) To review and evaluate the programs and activities of the Federal Government to determine how they are contributing to the attainment of the national environmental policy;

(2) To assist Federal agencies and departments in appraising the effectiveness of their existing and proposed facilities, programs, policies, and activities affecting environmental quality;

(3) To develop and recommend to the President policies to improve environmental quality to meet the conservation, social, economic, health, and other requirements and goals of the Nation;

(4) To advise and assist the President in achieving international cooperation for dealing with environmental problems;

(5) To assist in coordinating among Federal agencies and departments those programs which affect, protect, and improve environmental quality, including Federal compliance with the environmental impact statement process, and to seek resolution of significant environmental issues;

(6) To foster research relating to environmental quality and the impacts of new or changing technologies; and

(7) To analyze long and short term environmental problems and trends and assist in preparing an annual Environmental Quality Report to the President and the Congress.

(c) The Council maintains a "Quarterly Index" which lists its current policies and procedures, as required by section 552(a)(2) of the Freedom of Information Act. This index is updated and published in the Federal Register quarterly, starting in 1976. The Quarterly Index—and the specific items listed in the index—are available on request from the Freedom of Information Officer. You may also inspect or copy any of these materials at the Council's office during the hours stated below in § 1515.3(f).

§ 1515.3 How is CEQ organized?

(a) The Council is made up of three members appointed by the President and subject to approval by the Senate. One member is designated as chairman by the President. All three serve in a full-time capacity.

(b) The National Environmental Policy Act and the Environmental Quality Improvement Act give the Council the authority to hire any officers and staff that may be necessary to carry out responsibilities and functions specified in these two Acts. Also, the use of consultants and experts is permitted.

(c) In addition to the three members, the Council has program and legal staff.

(d) The Council has no field or regional offices.

(e) The Council has a public affairs office which is responsible for providing information to the general public, the Congress, and the press. If you are interested in general information about the Council or have questions about the Council's recent activities or policy positions, you should call this office at (202) 633–7005 or write to the "Public Affairs Office" of the Council at the address given in the next paragraph.

NOTE: The CEQ public affairs office can respond fully and promptly to most questions you may have; the Council suggests that the Freedom of Information Act procedures be used when you are seeking a specific document and have had difficulty obtaining it.

(f) The Council is located at 722 Jackson Place NW., Washington, D.C. 20006. Office hours are 9–5:30, Monday through Friday, except legal holidays. If you wish to meet with any of the staff, please write or phone ahead for an appointment. The main number is 202–633–7027.

PROCEDURES FOR REQUESTING RECORDS

§ 1515.5 How to make a Freedom of Information Act request

(a) The Chairman has appointed a Freedom of Information Officer who will be responsible for overseeing the Council's administration of the Freedom of Information Act and for receiving, routing, and overseeing the processing of all Freedom of Information requests. The Chairman has also appointed an Appeals Officer who is responsible for processing any appeals.

(b) *Requesting information from the Council.* (1) When you make a Freedom of Information Act request to the Council, the Freedom of Information Officer shall decide how to respond to—or "make an initial determination on"—your request within 10 working days from the date the Officer receives the request. The Freedom of Information Officer will then provide you with written notification of the determination.

(2) You can make a Freedom of Information Act request by writing a letter which states that you are making a Freedom of Information Act request. Address your letter to:

Freedom of Information Officer, Council on Environmental Quality, Executive Office of the President, 722 Jackson Place NW., Washington, D.C. 20006.

(3) In your request you should identify the desired record or reasonably describe it. The request should be as specific as possible so that the item can be readily found. You should not make blanket requests, such as requests for "the entire file of" or "all materials relating to" a specified subject.

(4) The Council will make a reasonable effort to assist you in defining the request to eliminate extraneous and unwanted materials and to keep search and copying fees to a minimum. If you have budgetary constraints and anticipate that your request might be costly you may wish to indicate the maximum fee you are prepared to pay for acquiring the information. (See § 1515.15(c) also.)

(5) The 10 day period for making a determination on a request will begin when the records requested are specified or reasonably identifiable.

(6) Despite its name, the Freedom of Information Act does not require a government agency to create or research information that you would like or that you may think the agency should have. The Act only requires that existing records be made available to the public.

(c) *Council's response to a request.* (1) Upon receipt of any request under the Act, the Freedom of Information Officer shall direct the request to the appropriate staff member at the Council, who will review the request and advise the Freedom of Information Officer as soon as possible.

(2) If it is appropriate to grant the request, the staff member will immediately collect the requested materials in order to accompany, wherever possible, the Freedom of Information Officer's letter notifying you of the decision.

(3) If your request is denied, in part or in full, the letter notifying you of the decision will be signed by the Freedom of Information Officer, and will include the names of any other individuals who participated in the decision. The letter will include the reasons for any denial and the procedure for filing an appeal.

(d) *Appeals.* (1) If you are not satisfied with the response you have received from the Freedom of Information Officer, you may ask the Council to reconsider the decision. You should explain what material you still wish to receive, and why you believe the Council should disclose this to you. This is called an "appeal." You must make your appeal within 45 days of the date on the letter which denied your request.

(2) You can make an appeal by writing a letter to:

FOIA Appeals Officer, Council on Environmental Quality, Executive Office of the President, 722 Jackson Place NW., Washington, D.C. 20006.

(3) Your letter should specify the records being requested and ask the Appeals Officer to review the determination made by the Freedom of Information Officer. The letter should explain the basis for the appeal.

(4) The Appeals Officer shall decide the appeal—or "make a final determination"—within 20 working days from the date the Officer receives the appeal. The Appeals Officer (or designee) will send you a letter informing you of the decision as soon as it is made. If the Appeals Officer denies your request, in part or in whole, the letter will also notify you of the provisions for judicial review and the names of any persons who participated in the final determination of the appeal.

(e) *Extending the Council's time to respond.* In unusual circumstances, the time limits for response to your request (paragraphs (b) and (d) of this section) may be extended by the Council for not more than 10 working days. Extensions may be granted by the Freedom of Information Officer in the case of initial requests and by the Appeals Officer in the case of any appeals. The extension period may be split between the initial request and the appeal but may not exceed 10 working days overall. Any extension will be made or confirmed to you in writing and will set forth the reasons for the extension and the date that the final determination is expected. The term "unusual circumstances" means:

(i) The need to search for and collect the requested records from * * * establishments that are separate from the office processing the request;

(ii) The need to search for, collect, and appropriately examine a voluminous amount of separate and distinct records which are demanded in a single request; or

(iii) The need for consultation, which shall be conducted with all practicable speed, with another agency having a substantial interest in the determination of the request or among two or more components of the agency having substantial subject-matter interest therein.

(5 U.S.C. 552(a)(6)(B))

AVAILABILITY OF INFORMATION

§ 1515.10 What information is available, and how can it be obtained?

(a) When a request for information has been approved, in whole or in part, you may make an appointment to inspect or copy the materials requested during regular business hours by writing or telephoning the Freedom of Information Officer at the address or phone number given in § 1515.3(f). You may be charged reasonable fees for copying materials, as explained by § 1515.15. The Council on Environmental Quality will permit copying of any available material but will reserve the right to limit the number of copies made with the Council's copying facilities.

(b) In general, all records of the Council are available to the public, as required by the Freedom of Information Act. The Council claims the right, where it is applicable, to withhold material under the provisions specified in the Freedom of Information Act as amended (5 U.S.C. 552(b)).

(c) The legislative history of the establishment of the Council states that the Congress intended the Council to be a confidential advisor to the President on matters of environmental policy. Therefore, members of the public should presume that communications between the Council and the President (and their staffs) are confidential and ordinarily will not be released; they will usually fall, at a minimum, within Exemption 5 of the Act. The Freedom of Information Officer shall review each request, however, to determine whether the record is exclusively factual or may have factual portions which may be reasonably segregated and made available to the requester. Furthermore, on the recommendation of the FOIA Officer or Appeals Officer, the Council will consider the release of an entire record, even if it comes within an exemption or contains policy advice, if its disclosure would not impair Executive policy-making processes or the Council's participation in decisionmaking.

COSTS

§ 1515.15 What fees may be charged, and how should they be paid?

(a) Following is the schedule of fees you may be charged for the search and reproduction of information available under the Freedom of Information Act, 5 U.S.C. 552, as amended.

(1) *Search for records.* Five dollars per hour when the search is conducted by a clerical employee. Eight dollars per hour when the search is conducted by a professional employee. There will be no charge for searches of less than one hour.

(2) *Duplication of records.* Records will be duplicated at a rate of $0.10 per page for copying of 10 pages or more. There will be no charge for duplicating 9 pages or less.

(3) *Other.* When no specific fee has been established for a service, or the request for a service does not fall under categories (1) and (2), the Administrative Officer is authorized to establish an appropriate fee based on "direct costs" as provided in the Freedom of Information Act. Examples of services covered by this provision include searches involving computer time or special travel, transportation, or communication costs.

(b) If the Council anticipates that the fees chargeable under this section will amount to more than $25, or the maximum amount specified in your request, you shall be promptly notified of the amount of the anticipated fee or the closest estimate of the amount. In such instances you will be advised of your option to consult with Council personnel in order to reformulate the request in a manner which will reduce the fees, yet still meet your needs. A reformulated request shall be considered a new request, thus beginning a new 10 working day period for processing.

(c) Fees must be paid in full prior to issuance of the requested copies. In the event you owe money for previous request, copies of records will not be provided for any subsequent request until the debt has been paid in full.

(d) Search costs are due and payable even if the record which was requested cannot be located after all reasonable efforts have been made, or if the FOI Officer determines that a record which has been requested is exempt under the Freedom of Information Act as amended and is to be withheld.

(e) Payment shall be in the form either of a personal check or bank draft drawn on a bank in the United States, or a postal money order. Checks shall be made payable to General Services Administration. You should mail or deliver any payment for services to the Administrative Office, Council on Environmental Quality, 722 Jackson Place NW., Washington, D.C. 20006.

(f) A receipt for fees paid will be given upon request. Refunds of fees paid for services actually rendered will not be made.

(g) The Council may waive all or part of any fee provided for in this section when the Freedom of Information Officer (or designee) deems it to be in either the Council's interest or in the general public's interest.

Part 1516

Privacy Act Implementation

Sec.

AUTHORITY: 5 U.S.C. 552a; Pub. L. 93–579.

SOURCE: 42 FR 32537, June 27, 1977, unless otherwise noted.

§ 1516.1 Purpose and scope

The purposes of these regulations are to:

(a) Establish a procedure by which an individual can determine if the Council on Environmental Quality (hereafter known as the Council) maintains a system of records which includes a record pertaining to the individual; and

(b) Establish a procedure by which an individual can gain access to a record pertaining to him or her for the purpose of review, amendment and/or correction.

§ 1516.2 Definitions

For the purpose of these regulations:

(a) The term "individual" means a citizen of the United States or an alien lawfully admitted for permanent residence;

(b) The term "maintain" means maintain, collect, use or disseminate;

(c) The term "record" means any item or collection or grouping of information about an individual that is maintained by the Council (including, but not limited to, his or her employment history, payroll information, and financial transactions), and that contains his or her name, or an identifying number, symbol, or other identifying particular assigned to the individual such as a social security number;

(d) The term "system of records" means a group of any records under the control of the Council from which information is retrieved by the name of the individual or by some identifying number, symbol, or other identifying particular assigned to the individual; and

(e) The term "routine use" means with respect to the disclosure of a record, the use of such record for a purpose which is compatible with the purpose for which it was collected.

§ 1516.3 Procedures for requests pertaining to individual records in a record system

An individual shall submit a written request to the Administrative Officer of the Council to determine if a system of records named by the individual contains a record pertaining to the individual. The individual shall submit a written request to the Administrative Officer of the Council which states the individual's desire to review his or her record. The Administrative Officer of the Council is available to answer questions regarding these regulations and to provide assistance in locating records in the Council's system of records.

[42 FR 32537, June 27, 1977; 42 FR 35960, July 13, 1977]

§ 1516.4 Times, places, and requirements for the identification of the individual making a request

An individual making a request to the Administrative Officer of the Council pursuant to § 1516.3 shall present the request at the Council's office, 722 Jackson Place, N.W., Washington, D.C. 20006, on any business day between the hours of 9 a.m. and 5 p.m. and should be prepared to identify himself by signature. Requests will also be accepted in writing if mailed to the Council's offices and signed by the requester.

§ 1516.5 Disclosure of requested information to the individual

Upon verification of identity, the Council shall disclose to the individual the information contained in the record which pertains to that individual.

(a) The individual may be accompanied for this purpose by a person of his choosing.

(b) Upon request of the individual to whom the record pertains, all information in the accounting of disclosures will be made available.

[42 FR 35960, July 13, 1977]

§ 1516.6 Request for correction or amendment to the record

The individual may submit a request to the Administrative Officer of the Council which states the individual's desire to correct or to amend his or her record. This request must be made in accordance with the procedures of § 1516.4 and shall describe in detail the change which is requested.

[42 FR 32537, June 27, 1977. Redesignated at 42 FR 35960, July 13, 1977]

§ 1516.7 Agency review of request for correction or amendment of the record

Within ten working days of the receipt of a request to correct or to amend a record, the Administrative Officer of the Council will acknowledge in writing such receipt and promptly either:

(a) Make any correction or amendment of any portion thereof which the individual believes is not accurate, relevant, timely, or complete; or

(b) Inform the individual of his or her refusal to correct or amend the record in accordance with the request, the reason for the refusal, and the procedure established by the Council for the individual to request a review of that refusal.

§ 1516.8 Appeal of an initial adverse agency determination on correction or amendment of the record

An individual may appeal refusal by the Administrative Officer of the Council to correct or to amend his or her record by submitting a request for a review of such refusal to the General Counsel, Council on Environmental Quality, 722 Jackson Place, N.W., Washington, D.C. 20006. The General Counsel shall, not later than thirty working days from the date on which the individual requests such a review, complete such review and make a final determination unless, for good cause shown, the General Counsel extends such thirty day period. If, after his or her review, the General Counsel also refuses to correct or to amend the record in accordance with the request, the individual may file with the Council a concise statement setting forth the reasons for his or her disagreement with the General Counsel's decision and may seek judicial relief under 5 U.S.C. 552a(g)(1)(A).

§ 1516.9 Disclosure of a record to a person other than the individual to whom the record pertains

The Council will not disclose a record to any individual other than to the individual to whom the record pertains without receiving the prior written consent of the individual to whom the record pertains, unless the disclosure either has been listed as a "routine use" in the Council's notices of its systems of records or falls within the special conditions of disclosure set forth in section 3 of the Privacy Act of 1974.

§ 1516.10 Fees

If an individual requests copies of his or her record, he or she shall be charged ten cents per page, excluding the cost of any search for the record, in advance of receipt of the pages.

Part 1517

Public Meeting Procedures of the Council on Environmental Quality

Sec.

AUTHORITY: 5 U.S.C. 552b(g); Pub. L. 94–409.

SOURCE: 42 FR 20818, Apr. 22, 1977, unless otherwise noted.

§ 1517.1 Policy and scope

Consistent with the policy that the public is entitled to the fullest information regarding the decisionmaking processes of the Federal Government, it is the purpose of this part to open the meetings of the Council on Environmental Quality to public observation while protecting the rights of individuals and the ability of the Council to carry out its primary responsibility of providing advice to the President. Actions taken by the Chairman acting as Director of the Office of Environmental Quality and Council actions involving advice to the President when such advice is not formulated collegially during a meeting are outside the scope of this part. In addition to conducting the meetings required by this part, it is the Council's policy to conduct, open to public observation, periodic meetings involving Council discussions of Council business, including where appropriate, matters outside the scope of this part. This part does not affect the procedures set forth in Part 1515 pursuant to which records of the Council are made available to the public for inspection and copying, except that the exemptions set forth in § 1517.4(a) shall govern in the case of any request made to copy or inspect the transcripts, recording or minutes described in § 1517.7.

[47 FR 6277, Feb. 11, 1982]

§ 1517.2 Definitions

For the purpose of this part:

(a) The term "Council" shall mean the Council on Environmental Quality established under Title II of the National Environmental Policy Act of 1969 (42 U.S.C. 4321–4347).

(b) The term "meeting" means the deliberations of at least two Council members where such deliberations determine or result in the joint conduct or disposition of official collegial Council business, but does not include deliberations to take actions to open or close a meeting under §§ 1517.4 and 1517.5 or to release or withhold information under §§ 1517.4 and 1517.7. "Meeting" shall not be construed to prevent Council members from considering individually Council business that is circulated to them sequentially in writing.

(c) "Director" means the Chairman of the Council on Environmental Quality acting as the head of the Office of Environmental Quality pursuant to the Environmental Quality Improvement Act of 1970, Pub. L. 91–224, 42 U.S.C. 4371–4374.

[44 FR 34946, June 18, 1979, as amended at 47 FR 6277, Feb. 11, 1982]

§ 1517.3 Open meeting requirement

(a) Every portion of every meeting of the Council is open to public observation subject to the exemptions provided in § 1517.4. Members of the Council may not jointly conduct or dispose of the business of the Council other than in accordance with this part.

(b) The Council will conduct open to public observation periodic meetings involving Council discussions of Council business including where appropriate matters outside the scope of this part. Such meetings will be noticed pursuant to § 1517.6.

(c) Members of the public may attend open meetings of the Council for the sole purpose of observation and may not participate in or photograph any meeting without prior permission of the Council. Members of the public who desire to participate in or photograph an open meeting of the Council may request permission to do so from the General Counsel of the Council before such meeting. Members of the public may record open meetings of the Council by means of any mechanical or electronic device unless the Council determines such recording would disrupt the orderly conduct of such meeting.

[44 FR 34946, June 18, 1979, as amended at 47 FR 6277, Feb. 11, 1982]

§ 1517.4 Exceptions

(a) A meeting or portion thereof may be closed to public observation, and information pertaining to such meeting or portion thereof may be withheld from the public, if the Council determines that such meeting or portion thereof or disclosure of such information is likely to:

(1) Disclose matters that are (i) specifically authorized under criteria established by an Executive order to be kept secret in the interest of national defense or foreign policy and (ii) in fact properly classified pursuant to that Executive order;

(2) Relate solely to the internal personnel rules and practices of the Council;

(3) Disclose matters specifically exempted from disclosure by statute (other than the Freedom of Information Act, 5 U.S.C. 552), provided that the statute: (i) Requires that the matters be withheld from the public in such a manner as to leave no discretion on the issue, or (ii) establishes particular criteria for withholding or refers to particular types of matters to be withheld;

(4) Disclose the trade secrets and commercial or financial information obtained from a person and privileged or confidential;

(5) Involve accusing any person of a crime, or formally censuring any person;

(6) Disclose information of a personal nature if disclosure would constitute a clearly unwarranted invasion of personal privacy;

(7) Disclose investigatory records compiled for law enforcement purposes, or information which if written would be contained in such records, but only to the extent that the production of those records or information would:

(i) Interfere with enforcement proceedings,

(ii) Deprive a person of a right to a fair trial or an impartial adjudication,

(iii) Constitute an unwarranted invasion of personal privacy,

(iv) Disclose the identity of a confidential source and, in the case of a record compiled by a criminal law enforcement authority in the course of a criminal investigation, or by an agency conducting a lawful national security intelligence investigation, confidential information furnished only by the confidential source,

(v) Disclose investigative techniques and procedures, or,

(vi) Endanger the life or physical safety of law enforcement personnel;

(8) Disclose information contained in or related to examination, operating, or condition reports prepared by, on behalf of, or for the use of an agency responsible for the regulation or supervision of financial institutions;

(9) Disclose information the premature disclosure of which would be likely to significantly frustrate implementation of a proposed action of the Council. This exception shall not apply in any instance where the Council has already disclosed to the public the content or nature of the proposed action, or where the Council is required by law to make such disclosure on its own initiative prior to taking final action on the proposal; or

(10) Specifically concern the issuance of a subpoena by the Council, or the participation of the Council in a civil action or proceeding, an action in a foreign court or international tribunal, or an arbitration, or the initiation, conduct, or disposition by the Council of a particular case of formal adjudication pursuant to the procedures in 5 U.S.C. 554 or otherwise involving a determination on the record after opportunity for a hearing.

(b) Before a meeting is closed to public observation the Council shall determine whether or not the public interest requires that the meeting be open. The Council may open a meeting to public observation which could be closed under paragraph (a) of this section, if the Council finds it to be in the public interest to do so.

§ 1517.5 Procedure for closing meetings

(a) A majority of the entire membership of the Council may vote to close to public observation a meeting or a portion or portions thereof, or to withhold information pertaining to such meeting. A separate vote of the members of the Council shall be taken with respect to each meeting of the Council, a portion or portions of which are proposed to be closed to the observation of the public or with respect to any information concerning such meetings or portion thereof. A single vote may be taken with respect to a series of meetings, a portion or portions of which are proposed to be closed to the public, or with respect to information concerning such series of meetings, so long as each meeting in such series involves the same particular matters and is scheduled to be held no more than thirty days after the initial meeting in such series. The vote of each member of the Council participating in a vote shall be recorded and no proxies shall be allowed.

(b) Whenever any person whose interest may be directly affected by a portion of a meeting requests that the Council close that portion to public observation for any of the reasons referred to in § 1517.4(a) the Council, upon request of any of the members of the Council, shall decide by recorded vote whether to close that portion of the meeting.

(c) For every meeting or portion thereof closed under this part, the General Counsel of the Council before such meeting is closed shall publicly certify that, in his or her opinion, the meeting may properly be closed to the public stating each relevant exemptive provision. The Council shall retain a copy of the General Counsel's certification, together with a statement from the presiding officer of the meeting setting forth the time and place of the meeting and listing the persons present.

(d) Within one day of any vote taken on a proposal to close a meeting, the Council shall make publicly available a record reflecting the vote of each member on the question. In addition, within one day of any vote which closes a portion or portions of a meeting to the public, the Council shall make publicly available a full written explanation of its closure action together with a list naming all persons expected to attend and identifying their affiliation, unless such disclosure would reveal the information that the meeting itself was closed to protect.

(e) Following any announcement that the Council intends to close a meeting or portion thereof, any person may make a request that the meeting or portion thereof be opened. Such request shall be made of the Chairman of the Council who shall ensure that the request is circulated to all members of the Council on the same business day on which it is received. The request shall set forth the reasons why the requestor believes the meeting should be open. The Council upon the request of any member or its General Counsel, shall vote on the request.

§ 1517.6 Notice of meetings

(a) Except as otherwise provided in this section, the Council shall make a public announcement at least one week before a meeting, to include the following:

(1) Time, place, and subject matter of the meeting;

(2) Whether the meeting is to be open or closed; and

(3) Name and telephone number of the official who will respond to requests for information about the meeting.

(b) A majority of the members of the Council may determine by recorded vote that the business of the Council requires a meeting to be called with less than one week's notice. At the earliest practicable time, the Council shall publicly announce the time, place and subject matter of the meeting, and whether or not it is to be open or closed to the public.

(c) If announcement of the subject matter of a closed meeting would reveal the information that the meeting itself was closed to protect, the subject matter shall not be announced.

(d) Following the public announcement required by paragraphs (a) or (b) of this section:

(1) A majority of the members of the Council may change the time or place of a meeting. At the earliest practicable time, the Council shall publicly announce the change.

(2) A majority of the entire membership of the Council may change the subject matter of a meeting, or the determination to open or close a meeting to the public, if it determines by a recorded vote that the change is required by the business of the Council and that no earlier announcement of the change was possible. At the earliest practicable time, the Council shall publicly announce the change, and the vote of each member upon the change.

(e) Individuals or organizations having a special interest in activities of the Council may request the Council to place them on a mailing list for receipt of information available under this section.

(f) Following public announcement of a meeting, the time or place of a meeting may be changed only if the change is announced publicly at the earliest practicable time. The subject matter of a meeting or the determination to open or close a meeting may be changed following public announcement of a meeting only if both of the following conditions are met:

(1) There must be a recorded vote of a majority of the Council that the business of the Council requires the change and that no earlier announcement of such change was possible; and

(2) There must be a public announcement of the change and of the individual Council members' votes at the earliest practicable time.

(g) Immediately following each public announcement required by this this section, the following information, as applicable, shall be submitted for publication in the FEDERAL REGISTER.

(1) Notice of the time, place, and subject matter of a meeting;

(2) Whether the meeting is open or closed;

(3) Any change in one of the preceding; and

(4) The name and telephone number of the official who will respond to requests for information about the meeting.

§ 1517.7 Records of closed meetings

(a) A record of each meeting or portion thereof which is closed to the public shall be made and retained for two years or for one year after the conclusion of any Council proceeding involved in the meeting whichever occurs later. The record of any portion of a meeting closed to the public shall be a verbatim transcript or electronic recording. In lieu of a transcript or recording, a comprehensive set of minutes may be produced if the closure decision was made pursuant to § 1517.4(a)(8) or (10).

(b) If minutes are produced, such minutes shall fully and clearly describe all matters discussed, provide a full and accurate summary of any actions taken and the reasons expressed therefor, and include a description of each of the views expressed on any item. The minutes shall also reflect the vote of each member of the Council on any roll call vote taken during the proceedings and identify all documents produced at the meeting.

(c) The following documents shall be retained by the Council as part of the transcript, recording, or minutes of the meeting:

(1) Certification by the General Counsel that the meeting may properly be closed; and

(2) Statement from the presiding officer of the meeting setting forth the date, time, and place of the meeting and listing the persons present.

(d) The Council shall make promptly available to the public at its offices at 722 Jackson Place, N.W., Washington, D.C. the transcript, electronic recording, or minutes maintained as a record of a closed meeting, except for such information as may be withheld under one of the provisions of § 1517.5. Copies of such transcript, minutes, or transcription of an electronic recording, disclosing the identity of each speaker, shall be furnished to any person at the actual cost of duplication or transcription.

(e) [Reserved]

(f) Requests to review or obtain copies of records other than transcripts, electronic recordings or minutes of a meeting will be processed under the Freedom of Information Act (5 U.S.C. 552) or, where applicable, the Privacy Act of 1974. (5 U.S.C. 552a). Nothing in these regulations authorizes the Council to withhold from any individual any record, including the transcripts or electronic recordings described in § 1517.8, to which the individual may have access under the Privacy Act of 1974 (5 U.S.C. 552a).

*

APPENDIX C

ADMINISTRATIVE PROCEDURE ACT

5 U.S.C., Chapter 5

§ 551. Definitions

For the purpose of this subchapter—

(1) "agency" means each authority of the Government of the United States, whether or not it is within or subject to review by another agency, but does not include—

(A) the Congress;

(B) the courts of the United States;

(C) the governments of the territories or possessions of the United States;

(D) the government of the District of Columbia, or except as to the requirements of section 552 of this title—

(E) agencies composed of representatives of the parties or of representatives of organizations of the parties to the disputes determined by them;

(F) courts martial and military commissions;

(G) military authority exercised in the field in time of war or in occupied territory; or

(H) functions conferred by sections 1738, 1739, 1743, and 1744 of title 12; chapter 2 of title 41; or sections 1622, 1884, 1891–1902, and former section 1641(b)(2), of title 50, appendix;

(2) "person" includes an individual, partnership, corporation, association, or public or private organization other than an agency;

(3) "party" includes a person or agency named or admitted as a party, or properly seeking and entitled as of right to be admitted as a party, in an agency proceeding, and a person or agency admitted by an agency as a party for limited purposes;

(4) "rule" means the whole or a part of an agency statement of general or particular applicability and future effect designed to implement, interpret, or prescribe law or policy or describing the organization, procedure, or practice requirements of an agency and includes the approval or prescription for the future of rates, wages, corporate or financial structures or reorganization thereof, prices, facilities, appli-

ances, services or allowances therefor or of valuations, costs, or accounting, or practices bearing on any of the foregoing;

(5) "rule making" means agency process for formulating, amending, or repealing a rule;

(6) "order" means the whole or a part of a final disposition, whether affirmative, negative, injunctive, or declaratory in form, of an agency in a matter other than rule making but including licensing;

(7) "adjudication" means agency process for the formulation of an order;

(8) "license" includes the whole or a part of an agency permit, certificate, approval, registration, charter, membership, statutory exemption or other form of permission;

(9) "licensing" includes agency process respecting the grant, renewal, denial, revocation, suspension, annulment, withdrawal, limitation, amendment, modification, or conditioning of a license;

(10) "sanction" includes the whole or a part of an agency—

(A) prohibition, requirement, limitation, or other condition affecting the freedom of a person;

(B) withholding of relief;

(C) imposition of penalty or fine;

(D) destruction, taking, seizure, or withholding of property;

(E) assessment of damages, reimbursement, restitution, compensation, costs, charges, or fees;

(F) requirement, revocation, or suspension of a license; or

(G) taking other compulsory or restrictive action;

(11) "relief" includes the whole or a part of an agency—

(A) grant of money, assistance, license, authority, exemption, exception, privilege, or remedy;

(B) recognition of a claim, right, immunity, privilege, exemption, or exception; or

(C) taking of other action on the application or petition of, and beneficial to, a person;

(12) "agency proceeding" means an agency process as defined by paragraphs (5), (7), and (9) of this section;

(13) "agency action" includes the whole or a part of an agency rule, order, license, sanction, relief, or the equivalent or denial thereof, or failure to act; and

(14) "ex parte communication" means an oral or written communication not on the public record with respect to which reasonable prior notice to all parties is not given, but it shall not include requests for status reports on any matter or proceeding covered by this subchapter.

§ 552. Public Information; Agency Rules, Opinions, Orders, Records, and Proceedings [Freedom of Information Act]

(a) Each agency shall make available to the public information as follows:

(1) Each agency shall separately state and currently publish in the Federal Register for the guidance of the public—

(A) descriptions of its central and field organization and the established places at which, the employees (and in the case of a uniformed service, the members) from whom, and the methods whereby, the public may obtain information, make submittals or requests, or obtain decisions;

(B) statements of the general course and method by which its functions are channeled and determined, including the nature and requirements of all formal and informal procedures available;

(C) rules of procedure, descriptions of forms available or the places at which forms may be obtained, and instructions as to the scope and contents of all papers, reports, or examinations;

(D) substantive rules of general applicability adopted as authorized by law, and statements of general policy or interpretations of general applicability formulated and adopted by the agency; and

(E) each amendment, revision, or repeal of the foregoing.

Except to the extent that a person has actual and timely notice of the terms thereof, a person may not in any manner be required to resort to, or be adversely affected by, a matter required to be published in the Federal Register and not so published. For the purpose of this paragraph, matter reasonably available to the class of persons affected thereby is deemed published in the Federal Register when incorporated by reference therein with the approval of the Director of the Federal Register.

(2) Each agency, in accordance with published rules, shall make available for public inspection and copying—

(A) final opinions, including concurring and dissenting opinions, as well as orders, made in the adjudication of cases;

(B) those statements of policy and interpretations which have been adopted by the agency and are not published in the Federal Register; and

(C) administrative staff manuals and instructions to staff that affect a member of the public;

unless the materials are promptly published and copies offered for sale. To the extent required to prevent a clearly unwarranted invasion of personal privacy, an agency may delete identifying details when it makes available or publishes an opinion, statement of policy, interpretation, or staff manual or instruction. However, in each case the justification for the deletion shall be explained fully in writing. Each agency shall also maintain and make available for public inspection and copying current indexes providing identifying information to the public as to any matter issued, adopted, or promulgated after July 4, 1967, and required by this paragraph to be made available or published. Each agency shall promptly publish, quarterly or more frequently, and distribute (by sale or otherwise) copies of each index or supplements thereto unless it determines by order published in the Federal Register that the publication would be unnecessary and impracticable, in which case the agency shall nonetheless provide copies of such index on request at a cost not to exceed the direct cost of duplication. A final order, opinion, statement of policy, interpretation, or staff manual or instruction that affects a member of the public may be relied on, used, or cited as precedent by an agency against a party other than an agency only if—

(i) it has been indexed and either made available or published as provided by this paragraph; or

(ii) the party has actual and timely notice of the terms thereof.

(3) Except with respect to the records made available under paragraphs (1) and (2) of this subsection, each agency, upon any request for records which (A) reasonably describes such records and (B) is made in accordance with published rules stating the time, place, fees (if any), and procedures to be followed, shall make the records promptly available to any person.

(4)(A) In order to carry out the provisions of this section, each agency shall promulgate regulations, pursuant to notice and receipt of public comment, specifying a uniform schedule of fees applicable to all constituent units of such agency. Such fees shall be limited to reasonable standard charges for document search and duplication and provide for recovery of only the direct costs of such search and duplication. Documents shall be furnished without charge or at a reduced charge where the agency determines that waiver or reduction of the fee is in the public interest because furnishing the information can be considered as primarily benefiting the general public.

(B) On complaint, the district court of the United States in the district in which the complainant resides, or has his principal place of business, or in which the agency records are situated, or in the District of Columbia, has jurisdiction to enjoin the agency from withholding agency records and to order the production of any agency records improperly withheld from the complainant. In such a case the court shall determine the matter de novo, and may examine the contents of such agency records in camera to determine whether such records or any part thereof shall be withheld under any of the exemptions set forth in subsection (b) of this section, and the burden is on the agency to sustain its action.

(C) Notwithstanding any other provision of law, the defendant shall serve an answer or otherwise plead to any complaint made under this subsection within thirty days after service upon the defendant of the pleading in which such complaint is made, unless the court otherwise directs for good cause shown.

(D) Except as to cases the court considers of greater importance, proceedings before the district court, as authorized by this subsection and appeals therefrom, take precedence on the docket over all cases and shall be assigned for hearing and trial or for argument at the earliest practicable date and expedited in every way.

(E) The court may assess against the United States reasonable attorney fees and other litigation costs reasonably incurred in any case under this section in which the complainant has substantially prevailed.

(F) Whenever the court orders the production of any agency record, improperly withheld from the complainant and assesses against the United States reasonable attorney fees and other litigation costs, and the court additionally issues a written finding that the circumstances surrounding the withholding raise questions whether agency personnel acted arbitrarily or capriciously with respect to the withholding, the Special Counsel shall promptly initiate a proceeding to determine whether disciplinary action is warranted against the officer or employee who was primarily responsible for the withholding. The Special Counsel, after investigation and consideration of the evidence submitted, shall submit its findings and recommendations to the administrative authority of the agency concerned and shall send copies of the findings and recommendations to the officer or employee or his representative. The administrative authority shall take the corrective action that the Special Counsel recommends.

(G) In the event of noncompliance with the order of the court, the district court may punish for contempt the responsible employee, and in the case of a uniformed service, the responsible member.

(5) Each agency having more than one member shall maintain and make available for public inspection a record of the final votes of each member in every agency proceeding.

(6)(A) Each agency, upon any request for records made under paragraph (1), (2), or (3) of this subsection, shall—

(i) determine within ten days (excepting Saturdays, Sundays and legal public holidays) after the receipt of any such request whether to comply with such request and shall immediately notify the person making such request of such determination and the reasons therefor, and of the right of such person to appeal to the head of the agency any adverse determination; and

(ii) make a determination with respect to any appeal within twenty days (excepting Saturdays, Sundays, and legal public holidays) after the receipt of such appeal. If on appeal the denial of the request for records is in whole or in part upheld, the agency shall notify the person making such request of the provisions for judicial review of that determination under paragraph (4) of this subsection.

(B) In unusual circumstances as specified in this subparagraph, the time limits prescribed in either clause (i) or clause (ii) of subparagraph (A) may be extended by written notice to the person making such request setting forth the reasons for such extension and the date on which a determination is expected to be dispatched. No such notice shall specify a date that would result in an extension for more than ten working days. As used in this subparagraph, "unusual circumstances" means, but only to the extent reasonably necessary to the proper processing of the particular request—

(i) the need to search for and collect the requested records from field facilities or other establishments that are separate from the office processing the request;

(ii) the need to search for, collect, and appropriately examine a voluminous amount of separate and distinct records which are demanded in a single request; or

(iii) the need for consultation, which shall be conducted with all practicable speed, with another agency having a substantial interest in the determination of the request or among two or more components of the agency having substantial subject-matter interest therein.

(C) Any person making a request to any agency for records under paragraph (1), (2), or (3) of this subsection shall be deemed to have exhausted his administrative remedies with respect to such request if the agency fails to comply with the applicable time limit provisions of this paragraph. If the Government can show exceptional circumstances exist and that the agency is exercising due diligence in responding to the request, the court may retain jurisdiction and allow the agency additional time to complete its review of the records. Upon any determination by an agency to comply with a request for records, the records shall be made promptly available to such person making such request. Any notification of denial of any request for records under this subsection shall set forth the names and titles or positions of each person responsible for the denial of such request.

(b) This section does not apply to matters that are—

(1)(A) specifically authorized under criteria established by an Executive order to be kept secret in the interest of national defense or foreign policy and (B) are in fact properly classified pursuant to such Executive order;

(2) related solely to the internal personnel rules and practices of an agency;

(3) specifically exempted from disclosure by statute (other than section 552b of this title), provided that such statute (A) requires that the matters be withheld from the public in such a manner as to leave no discretion on the issue, or (B) establishes particular criteria for withholding or refers to particular types of matters to be withheld;

(4) trade secrets and commercial or financial information obtained from a person and privileged or confidential;

(5) inter-agency or intra-agency memorandums or letters which would not be available by law to a party other than an agency in litigation with the agency;

(6) personnel and medical files and similar files the disclosure of which would constitute a clearly unwarranted invasion of personal privacy;

(7) investigatory records compiled for law enforcement purposes, but only to the extent that the production of such records would (A) interfere with enforcement proceedings, (B) deprive a person of a right to a fair trial or an impartial adjudication, (C) constitute an unwarranted invasion of personal privacy, (D) disclose the identity of a confidential source and, in the case of a record compiled by a criminal law enforcement authority in the course of a criminal investigation or by an agency conducting a lawful national security intelligence investigation, confidential information furnished only by the confidential source, (E) disclose investigative technique and procedures, or (F) endanger the life or physical safety of law enforcement personnel;

(8) contained in or related to examination, operating, or condition reports prepared by, on behalf of, or for the use of an agency responsible for the regulation or supervision of financial institutions; or

(9) geological and geophysical information and data, including maps, concerning wells.

Any reasonably segregable portion of a record shall be provided to any person requesting such record after deletion of the portions which are exempt under this subsection.

(c) This section does not authorize withholding of information or limit the availability of records to the public, except as specifically stated in this section. This section is not authority to withhold information from Congress.

(d) On or before March 1 of each calendar year, each agency shall submit a report covering the preceding calendar year to the Speaker of the House of Representatives and President of the Senate for referral to the appropriate committees of the Congress. The report shall include—

(1) the number of determinations made by such agency not to comply with requests for records made to such agency under subsection (a) and the reasons for each such determination;

(2) the number of appeals made by persons under subsection (a)(6), the result of such appeals, and the reason for the action upon each appeal that results in a denial of information;

(3) the names and titles or positions of each person responsible for the denial of records requested under this section, and the number of instances of participation for each;

(4) the results of each proceeding conducted pursuant to subsection (a)(4)(F), including a report of the disciplinary action taken against the officer or employee who was primarily responsible for improperly withholding records or an explanation of why disciplinary action was not taken;

(5) a copy of every rule made by such agency regarding this section;

(6) a copy of the fee schedule and the total amount of fees collected by the agency for making records available under this section; and

(7) such other information as indicates efforts to administer fully this section.

The Attorney General shall submit an annual report on or before March 1 of each calendar year which shall include for the prior calendar year a listing of the number of cases arising under this section, the exemption involved in each case, the disposition of such case, and the cost, fees, and penalties assessed under subsections (a)(4)(E), (F), and (G). Such report shall also include a description of the efforts undertaken by the Department of Justice to encourage agency compliance with this section.

(e) For purposes of this section, the term "agency" as defined in section 551(1) of this title includes any executive department, military department, Government corporation, Government controlled corporation, or other establishment in the executive branch of the Government (including the Executive Office of the President), or any independent regulatory agency.

[5 U.S.C.A. § 552a, The Privacy Protection Act, is omitted.]

§ 552b. Open Meetings [Government in the Sunshine Act]

(a) For purposes of this section—

(1) the term "agency" means any agency, as defined in section 552(e) of this title, headed by a collegial body composed of two or

more individual members, a majority of whom are appointed to such position by the President with the advice and consent of the Senate, and any subdivision thereof authorized to act on behalf of the agency;

(2) the term "meeting" means the deliberations of at least the number of individual agency members required to take action on behalf of the agency where such deliberations determine or result in the joint conduct or disposition of official agency business, but does not include deliberations required or permitted by subsection (d) or (e); and

(3) the term "member" means an individual who belongs to a collegial body heading an agency.

(b) Members shall not jointly conduct or dispose of agency business other than in accordance with this section. Except as provided in subsection (c), every portion of every meeting of an agency shall be open to public observation.

(c) Except in a case where the agency finds that the public interest requires otherwise, the second sentence of subsection (b) shall not apply to any portion of an agency meeting, and the requirements of subsections (d) and (e) shall not apply to any information pertaining to such meeting otherwise required by this section to be disclosed to the public, where the agency properly determines that such portion or portions of its meeting or the disclosure of such information is likely to—

(1) disclose matters that are (A) specifically authorized under criteria established by an Executive order to be kept secret in the interests of national defense or foreign policy and (B) in fact properly classified pursuant to such Executive order;

(2) relate solely to the internal personnel rules and practices of an agency;

(3) disclose matters specifically exempted from disclosure by statute (other than section 552 of this title), provided that such statute (A) requires that the matters be withheld from the public in such a manner as to leave no discretion on the issue, or (B) establishes particular criteria for withholding or refers to particular types of matters to be withheld;

(4) disclose trade secrets and commercial or financial information obtained from a person and privileged or confidential;

(5) involve accusing any person of a crime, or formally censuring any person;

(6) disclose information of a personal nature where disclosure would constitute a clearly unwarranted invasion of personal privacy;

(7) disclose investigatory records compiled for law enforcement purposes, or information which if written would be contained in such records, but only to the extent that the production of such records or information would (A) interfere with enforcement pro-

ceedings, (B) deprive a person of a right to a fair trial or an impartial adjudication, (C) constitute an unwarranted invasion of personal privacy, (D) disclose the identity of a confidential source and, in the case of a record compiled by a criminal law enforcement authority in the course of a criminal investigation, or by an agency conducting a lawful national security intelligence investigation, confidential information furnished only by the confidential source, (E) disclose investigative techniques and procedures, or (F) endanger the life or physical safety of law enforcement personnel;

(8) disclose information contained in or related to examination, operating, or condition reports prepared by, on behalf of, or for the use of an agency responsible for the regulation or supervision of financial institutions;

(9) disclose information the premature disclosure of which would—

(A) in the case of an agency which regulates currencies, securities, commodities, or financial institutions, be likely to (i) lead to significant financial speculation in currencies, securities, or commodities, or (ii) significantly endanger the stability of any financial institution; or

(B) in the case of any agency, be likely to significantly frustrate implementation of a proposed agency action,

except that subparagraph (B) shall not apply in any instance where the agency has already disclosed to the public the content or nature of its proposed action, or where the agency is required by law to make such disclosure on its own initiative prior to taking final agency action on such proposal; or

(10) specifically concern the agency's issuance of a subpoena, or the agency's participation in a civil action or proceeding, an action in a foreign court or international tribunal, or an arbitration, or the initiation, conduct, or disposition by the agency of a particular case of formal agency adjudication pursuant to the procedures in section 554 of this title or otherwise involving a determination on the record after opportunity for a hearing.

(d)(1) Action under subsection (c) shall be taken only when a majority of the entire membership of the agency (as defined in subsection (a)(1)) votes to take such action. A separate vote of the agency members shall be taken with respect to each agency meeting a portion or portions of which are proposed to be closed to the public pursuant to subsection (c), or with respect to any information which is proposed to be withheld under subsection (c). A single vote may be taken with respect to a series of meetings, a portion or portions of which are proposed to be closed to the public, or with respect to any information concerning such series of meetings, so long as each meeting in such series involves the same particular matters and is scheduled to be held no more than thirty days after the initial meeting in such series. The vote of each agency member participating in such vote shall be recorded and no proxies shall be allowed.

(2) Whenever any person whose interests may be directly affected by a portion of a meeting requests that the agency close such portion to the public for any of the reasons referred to in paragraph (5), (6), or (7) of subsection (c), the agency, upon request of any one of its members, shall vote by recorded vote whether to close such meeting.

(3) Within one day of any vote taken pursuant to paragraph (1) or (2), the agency shall make publicly available a written copy of such vote reflecting the vote of each member on the question. If a portion of a meeting is to be closed to the public, the agency shall, within one day of the vote taken pursuant to paragraph (1) or (2) of this subsection, make publicly available a full written explanation of its action closing the portion together with a list of all persons expected to attend the meeting and their affiliation.

(4) Any agency, a majority of whose meetings may properly be closed to the public pursuant to paragraph (4), (8), (9)(A), or (10) of subsection (c), or any combination thereof, may provide by regulation for the closing of such meetings or portions thereof in the event that a majority of the members of the agency votes by recorded vote at the beginning of such meeting, or portion thereof, to close the exempt portion or portions of the meeting, and a copy of such vote, reflecting the vote of each member on the question, is made available to the public. The provisions of paragraphs (1), (2), and (3) of this subsection and subsection (e) shall not apply to any portion of a meeting to which such regulations apply: *Provided,* That the agency shall, except to the extent that such information is exempt from disclosure under the provisions of subsection (c), provide the public with public announcement of the time, place, and subject matter of the meeting and of each portion thereof at the earliest practicable time.

(e)(1) In the case of each meeting, the agency shall make public announcement, at least one week before the meeting, of the time, place, and subject matter of the meeting, whether it is to be open or closed to the public, and the name and phone number of the official designated by the agency to respond to requests for information about the meeting. Such announcement shall be made unless a majority of the members of the agency determines by a recorded vote that agency business requires that such meeting be called at an earlier date, in which case the agency shall make public announcement of the time, place, and subject matter of such meeting, and whether open or closed to the public, at the earliest practicable time.

(2) The time or place of a meeting may be changed following the public announcement required by paragraph (1) only if the agency publicly announces such change at the earliest practicable

time. The subject matter of a meeting, or the determination of the agency to open or close a meeting, or portion of a meeting, to the public, may be changed following the public announcement required by this subsection only if (A) a majority of the entire membership of the agency determines by a recorded vote that agency business so requires and that no earlier announcement of the change was possible, and (B) the agency publicly announces such change and the vote of each member upon such change at the earliest practicable time.

(3) Immediately following each public announcement required by this subsection, notice of the time, place, and subject matter of a meeting, whether the meeting is open or closed, any change in one of the preceding, and the name and phone number of the official designated by the agency to respond to requests for information about the meeting, shall also be submitted for publication in the Federal Register.

(f)(1) For every meeting closed pursuant to paragraphs (1) through (10) of subsection (c), the General Counsel or chief legal officer of the agency shall publicly certify that, in his or her opinion, the meeting may be closed to the public and shall state each relevant exemptive provision. A copy of such certification, together with a statement from the presiding officer of the meeting setting forth the time and place of the meeting, and the persons present, shall be retained by the agency. The agency shall maintain a complete transcript or electronic recording adequate to record fully the proceedings of each meeting, or portion of a meeting, closed to the public, except that in the case of a meeting, or portion of a meeting, closed to the public pursuant to paragraph (8), (9)(A), or (10) of subsection (c), the agency shall maintain either such a transcript or recording, or a set of minutes. Such minutes shall fully and clearly describe all matters discussed and shall provide a full and accurate summary of any actions taken, and the reasons therefor, including a description of each of the views expressed on any item and the record of any rollcall vote (reflecting the vote of each member on the question). All documents considered in connection with any action shall be identified in such minutes.

(2) The agency shall make promptly available to the public, in a place easily accessible to the public, the transcript, electronic recording, or minutes (as required by paragraph (1)) of the discussion of any item on the agenda, or of any item of the testimony of any witness received at the meeting, except for such item or items of such discussion or testimony as the agency determines to contain information which may be withheld under subsection (c). Copies of such transcript, or minutes, or a transcription of such recording disclosing the identity of each speaker, shall be furnished to any person at the actual cost of duplication or transcription. The agency shall maintain a complete verbatim copy of the transcript, a

complete copy of the minutes, or a complete electronic recording of each meeting, or portion of a meeting, closed to the public, for a period of at least two years after such meeting, or until one year after the conclusion of any agency proceeding with respect to which the meeting or portion was held, whichever occurs later.

(g) Each agency subject to the requirements of this section shall, within 180 days after the date of enactment of this section, following consultation with the Office of the Chairman of the Administrative Conference of the United States and published notice in the Federal Register of at least thirty days and opportunity for written comment by any person, promulgate regulations to implement the requirements of subsections (b) through (f) of this section. Any person may bring a proceeding in the United States District Court for the District of Columbia to require an agency to promulgate such regulations if such agency has not promulgated such regulations within the time period specified herein. Subject to any limitations of time provided by law, any person may bring a proceeding in the United States Court of Appeals for the District of Columbia to set aside agency regulations issued pursuant to this subsection that are not in accord with the requirements of subsections (b) through (f) of this section and to require the promulgation of regulations that are in accord with such subsections.

(h)(1) The district courts of the United States shall have jurisdiction to enforce the requirements of subsections (b) through (f) of this section by declaratory judgment, injunctive relief, or other relief as may be appropriate. Such actions may be brought by any person against an agency prior to, or within sixty days after, the meeting out of which the violation of this section arises, except that if public announcement of such meeting is not initially provided by the agency in accordance with the requirements of this section, such action may be instituted pursuant to this section at any time prior to sixty days after any public announcement of such meeting. Such actions may be brought in the district court of the United States for the district in which the agency meeting is held or in which the agency in question has its headquarters, or in the District Court for the District of Columbia. In such actions a defendant shall serve his answer within thirty days after the service of the complaint. The burden is on the defendant to sustain his action. In deciding such cases the court may examine in camera any portion of the transcript, electronic recording, or minutes of a meeting closed to the public, and may take such additional evidence as it deems necessary. The court, having due regard for orderly administration and the public interest, as well as the interests of the parties, may grant such equitable relief as it deems appropriate, including granting an injunction against future violations of this section or ordering the agency to make available to the public such portion of the transcript, recording, or minutes of a meeting as is not authorized to be withheld under subsection (c) of this section.

(2) Any Federal court otherwise authorized by law to review agency action may, at the application of any person properly participating in the proceeding pursuant to other applicable law, inquire into violations by the agency of the requirements of this section and afford such relief as it deems appropriate. Nothing in this section authorizes any Federal court having jurisdiction solely on the basis of paragraph (1) to set aside, enjoin, or invalidate any agency action (other than an action to close a meeting or to withhold information under this section) taken or discussed at any agency meeting out of which the violation of this section arose.

(i) The court may assess against any party reasonable attorney fees and other litigation costs reasonably incurred by any other party who substantially prevails in any action brought in accordance with the provisions of subsection (g) or (h) of this section, except that costs may be assessed against the plaintiff only where the court finds that the suit was initiated by the plaintiff primarily for frivolous or dilatory purposes. In the case of assessment of costs against an agency, the costs may be assessed by the court against the United States.

(j) Each agency subject to the requirements of this section shall annually report to Congress regarding its compliance with such requirements, including a tabulation of the total number of agency meetings open to the public, the total number of meetings closed to the public, the reasons for closing such meetings, and a description of any litigation brought against the agency under this section, including any costs assessed against the agency in such litigation (whether or not paid by the agency).

(k) Nothing herein expands or limits the present rights of any person under section 552 of this title, except that the exemptions set forth in subsection (c) of this section shall govern in the case of any request made pursuant to section 552 to copy or inspect the transcripts, recordings, or minutes described in subsection (f) of this section. The requirements of chapter 33 of title 44, United States Code, shall not apply to the transcripts, recordings, and minutes described in subsection (f) of this section.

(*l*) This section does not constitute authority to withhold any information from Congress, and does not authorize the closing of any agency meeting or portion thereof required by any other provision of law to be open.

(m) Nothing in this section authorizes any agency to withhold from any individual any record, including transcripts, recording, or minutes required by this section, which is otherwise accessible to such individual under section 552a of this title.

§ 553. Rule Making

(a) This section applies, accordingly to the provisions thereof, except to the extent that there is involved—

(1) a military or foreign affairs function of the United States; or

(2) a matter relating to agency management or personnel or to public property, loans, grants, benefits, or contracts.

(b) General notice of proposed rule making shall be published in the Federal Register, unless persons subject thereto are named and either personally served or otherwise have actual notice thereof in accordance with law. The notice shall include—

(1) a statement of the time, place, and nature of public rule making proceedings;

(2) reference to the legal authority under which the rule is proposed; and

(3) either the terms or substance of the proposed rule or a description of the subjects and issues involved.

Except when notice or hearing is required by statute, this subsection does not apply—

(A) to interpretative rules, general statements of policy, or rules of agency organization, procedure, or practice; or

(B) when the agency for good cause finds (and incorporates the finding and a brief statement of reasons therefor in the rules issued) that notice and public procedure thereon are impracticable, unnecessary, or contrary to the public interest.

(c) After notice required by this section, the agency shall give interested persons an opportunity to participate in the rule making through submission of written data, views, or arguments with or without opportunity for oral presentation. After consideration of the relevant matter presented, the agency shall incorporate in the rules adopted a concise general statement of their basis and purpose. When rules are required by statute to be made on the record after opportunity for an agency hearing, sections 556 and 557 of this title apply instead of this subsection.

(d) The required publication or service of a substantive rule shall be made not less than 30 days before its effective date, except—

(1) a substantive rule which grants or recognizes an exemption or relieves a restriction;

(2) interpretative rules and statements of policy; or

(3) as otherwise provided by the agency for good cause found and published with the rule.

(e) Each agency shall give an interested person the right to petition for the issuance, amendment, or repeal of a rule.

§ 554. Adjudications

(a) This section applies, according to the provisions thereof, in every case of adjudication required by statute to be determined on the record after opportunity for an agency hearing, except to the extent that there is involved—

(1) a matter subject to a subsequent trial of the law and the facts de novo in a court;

(2) the selection or tenure of an employee, except an administrative law judge appointed under section 3105 of this title;

(3) proceedings in which decisions rest solely on inspections, tests, or elections;

(4) the conduct of military or foreign affairs functions;

(5) cases in which an agency is acting as an agent for a court; or

(6) the certification of worker representatives.

(b) Persons entitled to notice of an agency hearing shall be timely informed of—

(1) the time, place, and nature of the hearing;

(2) the legal authority and jurisdiction under which the hearing is to be held; and

(3) the matters of fact and law asserted.

When private persons are the moving parties, other parties to the proceeding shall give prompt notice of issues controverted in fact or law; and in other instances agencies may by rule require responsive pleading. In fixing the time and place for hearings, due regard shall be had for the convenience and necessity of the parties or their representatives.

(c) The agency shall give all interested parties opportunity for—

(1) the submission and consideration of facts, arguments, offers of settlement, or proposals of adjustment when time, the nature of the proceeding, and the public interest permit; and

(2) to the extent that the parties are unable so to determine a controversy by consent, hearing and decision on notice and in accordance with sections 556 and 557 of this title.

(d) The employee who presides at the reception of evidence pursuant to section 556 of this title shall make the recommended decision or initial decision required by section 557 of this title, unless he becomes unavailable to the agency. Except to the extent required for the disposition of ex parte matters as authorized by law, such an employee may not—

(1) consult a person or party on a fact in issue, unless on notice and opportunity for all parties to participate; or

(2) be responsible to or subject to the supervision or direction of an employee or agent engaged in the performance of investigative or prosecuting functions for an agency.

An employee or agent engaged in the performance of investigative or prosecuting functions for an agency in a case may not, in that or a factually related case, participate or advise in the decision, recommended decision, or agency review pursuant to section 557 of this title, except as witness or counsel in public proceedings. This subsection does not apply—

(A) in determining applications for initial licenses;

(B) to proceedings involving the validity or application of rates, facilities, or practices of public utilities or carriers; or

(C) to the agency or a member or members of the body comprising the agency.

(e) The agency, with like effect as in the case of other orders, and in its sound discretion, may issue a declaratory order to terminate a controversy or remove uncertainty.

§ 555. Ancillary Matters

(a) This section applies, according to the provisions thereof, except as otherwise provided by this subchapter.

(b) A person compelled to appear in person before an agency or representative thereof is entitled to be accompanied, represented, and advised by counsel or, if permitted by the agency, by other qualified representative. A party is entitled to appear in person or by or with counsel or other duly qualified representative in an agency proceeding. So far as the orderly conduct of public business permits, an interested person may appear before an agency or its responsible employees for the presentation, adjustment, or determination of an issue, request, or controversy in a proceeding, whether interlocutory, summary, or otherwise, or in connection with an agency function. With due regard for the convenience and necessity of the parties or their representatives and within a reasonable time, each agency shall proceed to conclude a matter presented to it. This subsection does not grant or deny a person who is not a lawyer the right to appear for or represent others before an agency or in an agency proceeding.

(c) Process, requirement of a report, inspection, or other investigative act or demand may not be issued, made, or enforced except as authorized by law. A person compelled to submit data or evidence is entitled to retain or, on payment of lawfully prescribed costs, procure a copy or transcript thereof, except that in a non-public investigatory proceeding the witness may for good cause be limited to inspection of the official transcript of his testimony.

(d) Agency subpoenas authorized by law shall be issued to a party on request and, when required by rules of procedure, on a statement or showing of general relevance and reasonable scope of the evidence sought. On contest, the court shall sustain the subpoena or similar process or demand to the extent that it is found to be in accordance with law. In a proceeding for enforcement, the court shall issue an order requiring the appearance of the witness or the production of the evidence or data within a reasonable time under penalty of punishment for contempt in cases of contumacious failure to comply.

(e) Prompt notice shall be given of the denial in whole or in part of a written application, petition, or other request of an interested person made in connection with any agency proceeding. Except in affirming a prior denial or when the denial is self-explanatory, the notice shall be accompanied by a brief statement of the grounds for denial.

§ 556. Hearings; Presiding Employees; Powers and Duties; Burden of Proof; Evidence; Record as Basis of Decision

(a) This section applies, according to the provisions thereof, to hearings required by section 553 or 554 of this title to be conducted in accordance with this section.

(b) There shall preside at the taking of evidence—

(1) the agency;

(2) one or more members of the body which comprises the agency; or

(3) one or more administrative law judges appointed under section 3105 of this title.

This subchapter does not supersede the conduct of specified classes of proceedings, in whole or in part, by or before boards or other employees specially provided for by or designated under statute. The functions of presiding employees and of employees participating in decisions in accordance with section 557 of this title shall be conducted in an impartial manner. A presiding or participating employee may at any time disqualify himself. On the filing in good faith of a timely and sufficient affidavit of personal bias or other disqualification of a presiding or participating employee, the agency shall determine the matters as a part of the record and decision in the case.

(c) Subject to published rules of the agency and within its powers, employees presiding at hearings may—

(1) administer oaths and affirmations;

(2) issue subpoenas authorized by law;

(3) rule on offers of proof and receive relevant evidence;

(4) take depositions or have depositions taken when the ends of justice would be served;

(5) regulate the course of the hearing;

(6) hold conferences for the settlement or simplification of the issues by consent of the parties;

(7) dispose of procedural requests or similar matters;

(8) make or recommend decisions in accordance with section 557 of this title; and

(9) take other action authorized by agency rule consistent with this subchapter.

(d) Except as otherwise provided by statute, the proponent of a rule or order has the burden of proof. Any oral or documentary evidence may be received, but the agency as a matter of policy shall provide for the exclusion of irrelevant, immaterial, or unduly repetitious evidence. A sanction may not be imposed or rule or order issued except on consideration of the whole record or those parts thereof cited by a party and supported by and in accordance with the reliable, probative, and substantial evidence. The agency may, to the extent consistent with the interests of justice and the policy of the underlying statutes administered by the agency, consider a violation of section 557(d) of this title sufficient grounds for a decision adverse to a party who has knowingly committed such violation or knowingly caused such violation to occur. A party is entitled to present his case or defense by oral or documentary evidence, to submit rebuttal evidence, and to conduct such cross-examination as may be required for a full and true disclosure of the facts. In rule making or determining claims for money or benefits or applications for initial licenses an agency may, when a party will not be prejudiced thereby, adopt procedures for the submission of all or part of the evidence in written form.

(e) The transcript of testimony and exhibits, together with all papers and requests filed in the proceeding, constitutes the exclusive record for decision in accordance with section 557 of this title and, on payment of lawfully prescribed costs, shall be made available to the parties. When an agency decision rests on official notice of a material fact not appearing in the evidence in the record, a party is entitled, on timely request, to an opportunity to show the contrary.

§ 557. Initial Decisions; Conclusiveness; Review by Agency; Submissions by Parties; Contents of Decisions; Record

(a) This section applies, according to the provisions thereof, when a hearing is required to be conducted in accordance with section 556 of this title.

(b) When the agency did not preside at the reception of the evidence, the presiding employee or, in cases not subject to section 554(d) of this title, an employee qualified to preside at hearings pursuant to section 556 of this title, shall initially decide the case unless the agency requires, either in specific cases or by general rule, the entire record to be certified to it for decision. When the presiding employee makes an initial decision, that decision then becomes the decision of the agency without further proceedings unless there is an appeal to, or review on motion of, the agency within time provided by rule. On appeal from or review of the initial decision, the agency has all the powers which it would have in making the initial decision except as it may limit the issues on notice or by rule. When the agency makes the decision without having presided at the reception of the evidence, the presiding employee or an employee qualified to preside at hearings pursuant to section 556 of this title shall first recommend a decision, except that in rule making or determining application for initial licenses—

(1) instead thereof the agency may issue a tentative decision or one of its responsible employees may recommend a decision; or

(2) this procedure may be omitted in a case in which the agency finds on the record that due and timely execution of its functions imperatively and unavoidably so requires.

(c) Before a recommended, initial, or tentative decision, or a decision on agency review of the decision of subordinate employees, the parties are entitled to a reasonable opportunity to submit for the consideration of the employees participating in the decisions—

(1) proposed finding and conclusions; or

(2) exceptions to the decisions or recommended decisions of subordinate employees or to tentative agency decisions; and

(3) supporting reasons for the exceptions or proposed findings or conclusions.

The record shall show the ruling on each finding, conclusion, or exception presented. All decisions, including initial, recommended, and tentative decisions, are a part of the record and shall include a statement of—

(A) findings and conclusions, and the reasons or basis therefor, on all the material issues of fact, law, or discretion presented on the record; and

(B) the appropriate rule, order, sanction, relief, or denial thereof.

(d)(1) In any agency proceeding which is subject to subsection (a) of this section, except to the extent required for the disposition of ex parte matters as authorized by law—

(A) no interested person outside the agency shall make or knowingly cause to be made to any member of the body comprising the agency, administrative law judge, or other employee who is or may reasonably be expected to be involved in the decisional process of the proceeding, an ex parte communication relevant to the merits of the proceeding;

(B) no member of the body comprising the agency, administrative law judge, or other employee who is or may reasonably be expected to be involved in the decisional process of the proceeding, shall make or knowingly cause to be made to any interested person outside the agency an ex parte communication relevant to the merits of the proceeding;

(C) a member of the body comprising the agency, administrative law judge, or other employee who is or may reasonably be expected to be involved in the decisional process of such proceeding who receives, or who makes or knowingly causes to be made, a communication prohibited by this subsection shall place on the public record of the proceeding:

(i) all such written communications;

(ii) memoranda stating the substance of all such oral communications; and

(iii) all written responses, and memoranda stating the substance of all oral responses, to the materials described in clauses (i) and (ii) of this subparagraph;

(D) upon receipt of a communication knowingly made or knowingly caused to be made by a party in violation of this subsection, the agency, administrative law judge, or other employee presiding at the hearing may, to the extent consistent with the interests of justice and the policy of the underlying statutes, require the party to show cause why his claim or interest in the proceeding should not be dismissed, denied, disregarded, or otherwise adversely affected on account of such violation; and

(E) the prohibitions of this subsection shall apply beginning at such time as the agency may designate, but in no case shall they begin to apply later than the time at which a proceeding is noticed for hearing unless the person responsible for the communication has knowledge that it will be noticed, in which case the prohibitions shall apply beginning at the time of his acquisition of such knowledge.

(2) This subsection does not constitute authority to withhold information from Congress.

§ 558. Imposition of Sanctions; Determination of Applications for Licenses; Suspension, Revocation, and Expiration of Licenses

(a) This section applies, according to the provisions thereof, to the exercise of a power or authority.

(b) A sanction may not be imposed or a substantive rule or order issued except with jurisdiction delegated to the agency and as authorized by law.

(c) When application is made for a license, required by law, the agency, with due regard for the rights and privileges of all the interested parties or adversely affected persons and within a reasonable time, shall set and complete proceedings required to be conducted in accordance with sections 556 and 557 of this title or other proceedings required by law and shall make its decision. Except in cases of willfulness or those in which public health, interest, or safety requires otherwise, the withdrawal, suspension, revocation, or annulment of a license is lawful only if, before the institution of agency proceedings therefor, the licensee has been given—

(1) notice by the agency in writing of the facts or conduct which may warrant the action; and

(2) opportunity to demonstrate or achieve compliance with all lawful requirements.

When the licensee has made timely and sufficient application for a renewal or a new license in accordance with agency rules, a license with reference to an activity of a continuing nature does not expire until the application has been finally determined by the agency.

§ 559. Effect on Other Laws; Effect of Subsequent Statute

This subchapter, chapter 7, and sections 1305, 3105, 3344, 4301(2)(E), 5372 and 7521 of this title, and the provisions of section 5335(a)(B) of this title that relate to administrative law judges, do not limit or repeal additional requirements imposed by statute or otherwise recognized by law. Except as otherwise required by law, requirements or privileges relating to evidence or procedure apply equally to agencies and persons. Each agency is granted the authority necessary to comply with the requirements of this subchapter through the issuance of rules or otherwise. Subsequent statute may not be held to supersede or modify this subchapter, chapter 7, sections 1305, 3105, 3344, 4301(2)(E), 5372 or 7521 of this title, or the provisions of section 5335(a)(B) of this title that relate to hearing examiners, except to the extent that it does so expressly.

CHAPTER 7

JUDICIAL REVIEW

§ 701. Application; Definitions

(a) This chapter applies, according to the provisions thereof, except to the extent that—

(1) statutes preclude judicial review; or

(2) agency action is committed to agency discretion by law.

(b) For the purpose of this chapter—

(1) "agency" means each authority of the Government of the United States, whether or not it is within or subject to review by another agency, but does not include—

(A) the Congress;

(B) the courts of the United States;

(C) the governments of the territories or possessions of the United States;

(D) the government of the District of Columbia;

(E) agencies composed of representatives of the parties or of representatives of organizations of the parties to the disputes determined by them;

(F) courts martial and military commissions;

(G) military authority exercised in the field in time of war or in occupied territory; or

(H) functions conferred by sections 1738, 1739, 1743, and 1744 of title 12; chapter 2 of title 41; or sections 1622, 1884, 1891–1902, and former section 1641(b)(2), of title 50, appendix; and

(2) "person", "rule", "order", "license", "sanction", "relief", and "agency action" have the meanings given them by section 551 of this title.

§ 702. Right of Review

A person suffering legal wrong because of agency action, or adversely affected or aggrieved by agency action within the meaning of a relevant statute, is entitled to judicial review thereof. An action in a court of the United States seeking relief other than money damages and stating a claim that an agency or an officer or employee thereof acted or failed to act in an official capacity or under color of legal authority shall not be dismissed nor relief therein be denied on the ground that it is against the United States or that the United States is an indispensable party. The United States may be named as a defendant in any such action, and a judgment or decree may be entered against the United States: *Provided,* That any mandatory or injunctive decree shall specify the Federal officer or officers (by name or by title), and their successors in office, personally responsible for compliance. Nothing herein (1) affects other limitations on judicial review or the power or duty of the court to dismiss any action or deny relief on any other appropriate legal or equitable ground; or (2) confers authority to grant relief if any other statute that grants consent to suit expressly or impliedly forbids the relief which is sought.

§ 703. Form and Venue of Proceeding

The form of proceeding for judicial review is the special statutory review proceeding relevant to the subject matter in a court specified by statute or, in the absence or inadequacy thereof, any applicable form of legal action, including actions for declaratory judgments or writs of prohibitory or mandatory injunction or habeas corpus, in a court of competent jurisdiction. If no special statutory review proceeding is applicable, the action for judicial review may be brought against the

United States, the agency by its official title, or the appropriate officer. Except to the extent that prior, adequate, and exclusive opportunity for judicial review is provided by law, agency action is subject to judicial review in civil or criminal proceedings for judicial enforcement.

§ 704. Actions Reviewable

Agency action made reviewable by statute and final agency action for which there is no adequate remedy in a court are subject to judicial review. A preliminary, procedural, or intermediate agency action or ruling not directly reviewable is subject to review on the review of the final agency action. Except as otherwise expressly required by statute, agency action otherwise final is final for the purposes of this section whether or not there has been presented or determined an application for a declaratory order, for any form of reconsideration, or, unless the agency otherwise requires by rule and provides that the action meanwhile is inoperative, for an appeal to superior agency authority.

§ 705. Relief Pending Review

When an agency finds that justice so requires, it may postpone the effective date of action taken by it, pending judicial review. On such conditions as may be required and to the extent necessary to prevent irreparable injury, the reviewing court, including the court to which a case may be taken on appeal from or on application for certiorari or other writ to a reviewing court, may issue all necessary and appropriate process to postpone the effective date of an agency action or to preserve status or rights pending conclusion of the review proceedings.

§ 706. Scope of Review

To the extent necessary to decision and when presented, the reviewing court shall decide all relevant questions of law, interpret constitutional and statutory provisions, and determine the meaning or applicability of the terms of an agency action. The reviewing court shall—

(1) compel agency action unlawfully withheld or unreasonably delayed; and

(2) hold unlawful and set aside agency action, findings, and conclusions found to be—

(A) arbitrary, capricious, an abuse of discretion, or otherwise not in accordance with law;

(B) contrary to constitutional right, power, privilege, or immunity;

(C) in excess of statutory jurisdiction, authority, or limitations, or short of statutory right;

(D) without observance of procedure required by law;

(E) unsupported by substantial evidence in a case subject to section 556 and 557 of this title or otherwise reviewed on the record of an agency hearing provided by statute; or

(F) unwarranted by the facts to the extent that the facts are subject to trial de novo by the reviewing court.

In making the foregoing determinations, the court shall review the whole record or those parts of it cited by a party, and due account shall be taken of the rule of prejudicial error.

---

§ 3105. Appointment of Administrative Law Judges

Each agency shall appoint as many administrative law judges as are necessary for proceedings required to be conducted in accordance with sections 556 and 557 of this title. Administrative law judges shall be assigned to cases in rotation so far as practicable, and may not perform duties inconsistent with their duties and responsibilities as administrative law judges.

§ 7521. Actions Against Administrative Law Judges

(a) An action may be taken against an administrative law judge appointed under section 3105 of this title by the agency in which the administrative law judge is employed only for good cause established and determined by the Merit Systems Protection Board on the record after opportunity for hearing before the Board.

(b) The actions covered by this section are—

(1) a removal;

(2) a suspension;

(3) a reduction in grade;

(4) a reduction in pay; and

(5) a furlough of 30 days or less;

but do not include—

(A) a suspension or removal under section 7532 of this title;

(B) a reduction-in-force action under section 3502 of this title; or

(C) any action initiated under section 1206 of this title.

§ 5372. Administrative Law Judges

Administrative law judges appointed under section 3105 of this title are entitled to pay prescribed by the Office of Personnel Management independently of agency recommendations or ratings and in accordance with subchapter III of this chapter and chapter 51 of this title.

§ 3344. Details; Administrative Law Judges

An agency as defined by section 551 of this title which occasionally or temporarily is insufficiently staffed with administrative law judges appointed under section 3105 of this title may use administrative law judges selected by the Office of Personnel Management from and with the consent of other agencies.

§ 1305. Administrative Law Judges

For the purpose of sections 3105, 3344, 4301(2)(D), and 5372 of this title and the provisions of section 5335(a)(B) of this title that relate to administrative law judges, the Office of Personnel Management may, and for the purpose of section 7521 of this title, the Merit Systems Protection Board may investigate, require reports by agencies, issue reports, including an annual report to Congress, prescribe regulations, appoint advisory committees as necessary, recommend legislation, subpoena witnesses and records, and pay witness fees as established for the courts of the United States.

†